SWING

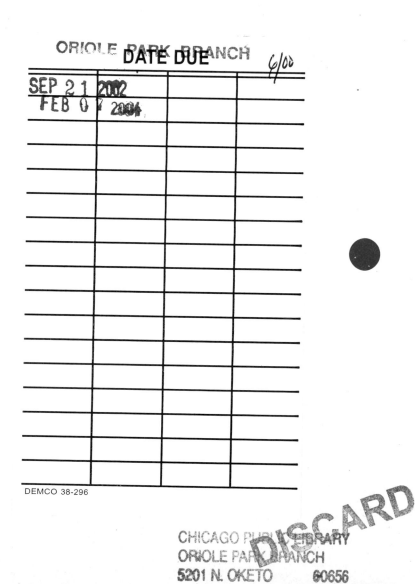

SWING

SCOTT YANOW

Miller Freeman Books   SAN FRANCISCO

Published by Miller Freeman Books
600 Harrison Street, San Francisco, CA 94107

un Miller Freeman
A United News & Media publication

Distributed to the book trade in the U.S. and Canada
by Publishers Group West
1700 Fourth Street, Berkeley, CA 94710

Distributed to the music trade in the U.S. and Canada
by Hal Leonard Publishing
P.O. Box 13819, Milwaukee, WI 53213

Cover design by Rich Leeds

Text design and composition by
Wilsted & Taylor Publishing Services

Front cover photo: Michael Ochs Archives
Back cover photos: The Wayne Knight Collection

Library of Congress Cataloging-in-Publication Data
Yanow, Scott
    Swing / Scott Yanow
        p. cm.
        Includes bibliographical references, discographies,
    and index.
        ISBN 0-87930-600-9 (alk. paper)
        1. Swing (Music)—History and criticism.   2. Jazz
    musicians.   3. Swing (Music)—Discography.   I. Title.
    ML3518.Y36 2000
    781.65′4—dc21   00-024401

Printed in the United States of America

00   01   02   03   04   05   5   4   3   2   1

CONTENTS

INTRODUCTION

●

Sixty years ago, the world was a much different place. Hundreds and hundreds of big bands performed music that was melodic and swinging. Couples touched while they danced. Talented songwriters and lyricists were in great demand, not only to write for Hollywood films and Broadway shows, but also to provide new material for a countless number of radio broadcasts. Although catchy novelties tended to outsell instrumentals, it was common for jazz originals to make the pop charts. Songs from movies actually became standards. Major clarinetists were matinee idols. It was not unusual for a popular Swing orchestra to play for six months at the same venue to large crowds. Most singers were considered less important than the songs they sang, and their "vocal refrain" was not always as significant as the hot trumpet solo that followed.

It was definitely a different world, although one should not idealize the Swing era. Unemployment was as high as 25 percent and, without unemployment compensation, welfare, social security, and credit cards, many people were literally starving on the streets. World War II was looming on the horizon, the Holocaust was under way, and Japan was terrorizing China. The average American wanted to let the rest of the world run itself, but most knew deep down that it was only a matter of time before the U.S. was drawn into the European and Asian conflicts. Racism was an institution and a fact of life, with the most famous black musicians having fewer rights than the lowest white derelict. Imagine what an average black band must have gone through playing one-nighters in the South, traveling in a broken-down bus!

And yet for some, it was a magical time. FDR was president, MGM was coming out with a movie a week (many of high quality), and it seemed as if every month an important new Swing band was being formed. Even the poorest person seemed able to afford a radio, which offered free entertainment and an opportunity to hear the major (and many of the minor) Swing bands. And it was relatively inexpensive to go out to a local dance hall and experience the rhythms of whichever orchestra was in town.

The Swing era (1935–46) was a special time when jazz and pop music overlapped, trombonists were always in demand, and it seemed that anyone who had strong organizational skills and a fresh idea for a new sound could (with a few lucky breaks) catch on and become a household name, at least to readers of *Downbeat* and *Metronome*.

A new book on Swing has been long overdue: one that would sum up the careers of the major bandleaders and sidemen, discuss their more significant reissue CDs, and put the music in its historic perspective. Rather than just stick to the Classic Swing period, this book also covers Swing music after the Swing era (from early rhythm and blues and ghost bands to mainstream jazz and the New Swing of the 1970s and '80s) and, most significantly, the current Retro Swing movement. Very little of substance has been written about the music of Retro Swing until now, since most articles have either dismissed the entire movement or focused on superficial elements such as fashion, lifestyles, and the novelty of young people at the end of the 20th century touching while they are dancing.

The most difficult aspect to writing this book was deciding where to draw the borders and what to include, particularly since there is plenty of music that straddles the boundaries between Swing and classic jazz, Swing and bebop and, these days, Swing and rockabilly. I decided not to cover Western Swing (the mixture of country music with Swing, best exemplified by Bob Wills's Texas Cowboys) or cool jazz of the 1950s (which owes a great debt to Swing), saving those areas for other books. Left out too are the great stride pianists (including James P. Johnson from the 1920s and such later players as Ralph Sutton, Dick Wellstood, and Judy Carmichael) who were not major parts of the Swing era (unlike Fats Waller), since they will be covered in a trad book, as will current New Orleans–oriented performers (including singer Banu Gibson) who often perform Swing. Also, sweet bands (such as Guy Lombardo, Russ Morgan, and Jan Garber),which had their own golden age during the Swing era, fall into a different area altogether. However, I do include some of the early R&B greats (such as Louis Jordan and Earl Bostic) whose music overlaps with Swing and who influenced the Retro Swing movement.

Some of the musicians covered will have additional aspects of their musical lives discussed in other books in this series, since their careers affected earlier or later styles such as Louis Armstrong (classic jazz, Swing, and Dixieland), Woody Herman (Swing, bebop, and modern jazz), and Stan Kenton, to cite three examples. Count Basie's life is divided in two, since he led a pair of separate orchestras that fit into two different time periods. Other giants (such as Benny Goodman, Artie Shaw, and Art Tatum) fit so securely into the Swing medium that everything they accomplished is of relevance to Swing.

A few words about the CD reviews: They are not exhaustive reviews of every single CD by every single Swing artist, but hopefully all significant releases are covered. Rather than list every possible overlapping sampler, I have provided readers with mentions of the main releases to acquire and a logical way to go about collecting them. In some cases a definitive sampler might be best, particularly if an artist only made a few essential recordings. In other situations, the Classics series (which reissues a musician's or singer's complete output from a particular period, although not the alternate takes) is the best way to start a collection, either because the artist only made a limited number of recordings (Teddy Hill) or because all of their records from the Swing era are well worth hearing (Cab Calloway).

In addition to the studio records that were available at the time, today's listeners can enjoy the surviving radio broadcasts and radio transcriptions. The most popular Swing big bands appeared regularly on the radio, often in 15-minute or half-hour broadcasts, and these performances differ from the conventional three-minute renditions that were released on 78 records. Radio transcriptions are a different matter altogether. During the Swing era and up until the early 1950s, most of the major labels did not want their releases to be played on the radio, believing that if the audience were able to hear a record for free on the air, they would not pay to buy the recording. This was definitely a different situation from the past 40 years, where radio is a primary vehicle for selling records! To fill in airtime between live performances and other shows, radio transcription services recorded most of the major big bands and combos for special performances that could be played on the radio, usually with the blessing of the labels. In some cases it was a matter of artists merely repeating their hits, but often many arrangements and selections were played that otherwise would not have been documented. And even the recreated hits sounded a little different from the original versions. These radio performances were not available commercially during the era, but began being released on records in piecemeal fashion in the 1950s and later on as collector's LPs. Nowadays the GHB/Jazzology family of companies has been coming out with many of the radio transcription dates, as has the Soundies label and some smaller companies.

I used a rating system for the CD reviews. Since this book mostly limits itself to important releases, relatively few of the CDs receive ratings lower than 5. Here are what the ratings mean:

*	*Limited edition box set—Most highly recommended for completists and veteran collectors, but make sure to get it while you can!*
10	*A gem that belongs in every serious jazz collection*
9	*Highly recommended*
8	*A very good release*
7	*An excellent acquisition*
6	*Good music but not quite essential*
5	*Decent but not one of this artist's more important works*
4	*So-so*
3	*A disappointing effort with just a few worthwhile moments*
2	*A weak release*
1	*Stinks!*

Although as the author of this book I am solely responsible for any errors that might have crept in, there are several people whom I would like to thank: Dorothy Cox and Matt Kelsey of Miller Freeman, for trusting me and believing in this important project; Brian Ashley, who got me started in the jazz writing business back in 1976 when he formed *Record Review*; the much-maligned but invaluable jazz publicists (including Ann Braithwaite, Lynda Bramble, Lori Hehr, and Terri Hinte) who make life much easier for jazz journalists; Chuck Cecil, whose syndicated radio show *The Swinging Years* introduced me (and millions others) to Swing music; and Louis Armstrong, who brought Swing and pure happiness to jazz. In addition, a special thanks to my wife Kathy and daughter Melody for their love and patience.

THE BEGINNINGS OF SWING—
THE 1920S

I n the 1969 edition of the *Random House Dictionary of the English Language,* the verb *Swing* is given 39 definitions, and the adjective has two others; however, it is the noun that concerns us here and two of the definitions fit. *Swing* is defined as: 1) a style of jazz, popular especially in the 1930s and often arranged for a large dance band, marked by a smoother beat and more flowing phrasing than Dixieland and having less complex harmonies and rhythms than modern jazz; and 2) the rhythmic element that excites dancers and listeners to move in time to jazz music.

In its own way, jazz swung from its earliest days in the 1890s when it was played by New Orleans brass bands, and it still swings today in most of its styles (except in some avant-garde jazz, where swing is an option, not a necessity). The Swing idiom is very difficult to define. At its best, it is music that makes you tap your toes and feel like swaying to the beat. It is characterized by a 4/4 walking bass (as opposed to classic jazz and Dixieland, which is often made up of two rather than four beats), solos that keep the melody in mind most of the time, and ensembles that are mostly arranged.

The earliest styles of jazz were characterized by musicians who improvised from the heart and rarely read music. Prior to 1920, very few jazz groups read music except in order to learn a particular song. In contrast, the commercial dance ensembles and military bands stuck exclusively to arrangements that were often a bit pompous and closer to classical music rhythmically than to jazz. However, the growing popularity of jazz as a dance music (starting with the Original Dixieland Jazz Band, which in 1917 caused a sensation with its first records) caused a gradual fusion of the two separate styles.

In the early 1920s, the music world faced a dilemma. Dancers wanted to hear orchestras perform the latest hits and play syncopated music that at least hinted at jazz. The problem was that, although three or four horns could jam together in ensembles, a larger group needed written music to keep the ensembles coherent. Ferde Grofe was a pioneer arranger with Art Hickman's Orchestra around 1918, but that band was not extensively documented or influential. A much more significant big band was led by Paul Whiteman, whose great popularity (starting in 1920) was partly due to his willingness to use arrangements that had the feel of jazz without the chance-taking, a safer version of the music played by blacks in smaller combos. His cornet soloist, Henry Busse, sounds quite dated today, but Busse's light and airy solos in the early 1920s were a perfect contrast to Whiteman's heavy orchestra, and they swung in their own fashion even though the solos were worked out in advance.

Fletcher Henderson started out as the black equivalent of Paul Whiteman, originally playing dance music that was at least five years behind the jazz played by musicians in more spontaneous groups. Don Redman's arrangements at first were closer to those used by Whiteman, but in 1924 that permanently changed. The arrival of Louis Armstrong, the first virtuoso soloist to be featured in a big band, forced the music to evolve quickly. As can be heard on some of his early recordings with Henderson, Armstrong's cornet solos were quite a contrast to Redman's stodgy charts. It was a bit of a shock to hear Satch swing hard in a brief outburst and then have the music decline in excitement as the ensemble went back to playing staccato phrases. Armstrong always stole the show, so Don Redman (to his credit) quickly learned from the cornetist about swinging, flowing legato phrases and building up the music to its climax.

By 1925, Don Redman's charts with Fletcher Henderson were pacesetters. Other dance bands began to swing more (including Whiteman's) and although the 1920s was not the big band era, there were several very impressive jazz-oriented orchestras active and recording by the second half of the decade, including those led by Bennie Moten (in Kansas City), Jean Goldkette, Ben Bernie, and Ben Pollack, plus McKinney's Cotton Pickers and Duke Ellington's Orchestra (which became a major force in 1927). The beginning of the Great Depression accelerated the trend as hot, happy-go-lucky small-group jazz went out of style (becoming a sad reminder of naïve and carefree days) and large dance orchestras started to dominate the music world.

THE EARLY SWING BANDS

ccording to legend, the Swing era began on August 21, 1935, when the Benny Goodman Orchestra practically caused a riot at Los Angeles's Palomar Ballroom. For the preceding five years, pop music had been dominated by soothing vocalists and large, unswinging orchestras such as those led by Guy Lombardo, Hal Kemp, and Eddy Duchin. The music was fine for backgrounds and romantic evenings, but excitement was purposely lacking, lest someone be reminded of the 1920s.

However, Swing itself had been around since Fletcher Henderson's Orchestra in 1924, and there were quite a few interesting big bands formed during the 1929–35 period. Duke Ellington's ensemble was at the top of the heap, and Paul Whiteman's Orchestra was still active. Among the more notable newcomers were Glen Gray's Casa Loma Orchestra, Luis Russell, Chick Webb, Cab Calloway, Claude Hopkins, the Dorsey Brothers, Jimmie Lunceford, and Earl Hines. In fact, the center of the Swing world during the period was Harlem, where Ellington, Webb, and Calloway were based.

Two of the major changes in the music world during 1929–31 were the replacement of the tuba by the string bass, and the banjo by the guitar. The development of the microphone made the quieter and more flexible guitar in greater demand, and orchestras found that they could swing harder (and keep the rhythm smoother) with a bass than with a tuba. The Swing bands of the period, with variations, usually consisted of two or three trumpets, two trombones, three reeds (a tenor and two altos, with at least one of the reeds doubling on clarinet), and a four-piece rhythm section composed of piano, rhythm guitar, bass, and drums. Mildred Bailey was the first female vocalist to be featured regularly with an orchestra (Paul Whiteman's in 1931), but male singers were more the norm, particularly if one of the musicians had a decent voice.

Although Duke Ellington was becoming well known as a composer and bandleader and his 1932 song proclaimed "It Don't Mean a Thing If It Ain't Got That Swing," quiet dance music was still the norm until the rise of Benny Goodman. Swing was essentially an underground movement until 1935.

AN OVERVIEW OF THE SWING ERA (1935–46)

Benny Goodman in 1934 was in the same position that Artie Shaw would be in in 1937 and Glenn Miller in 1938: well respected by his fellow musicians but completely unknown to the general public. After years as a studio musician, Goodman formed a big band in June 1934, and played regularly at Billy Rose's Music Hall for a few months. In November his group won an audition (by one vote) to become one of the three bands to appear regularly on NBC's *Let's Dance* radio show opposite Xavier Cugat's Latin ensemble and the sweet orchestra of Kel Murray. If BG had not gotten this job, chances are his orchestra would have broken up, and it would have been up to someone else to launch the Swing era.

The *Let's Dance* show ran its course, and had its final broadcast on May 25, 1935. Although Goodman had begun to record with his band for the Victor label, the orchestra's survival was quite uncertain. Since there was little work in New York, in mid-July it was decided that the clarinetist should take his orchestra cross-country. It was an erratic trip with some near-disasters, such as in Denver, where the band was forced by the management and complaining customers to play waltzes. Goodman and his musicians had their spirits lifted with a surprisingly successful one-night stand in Oakland but were afraid that that was merely a fluke. At the Palomar Ballroom in Hollywood, the clarinetist was therefore a bit gun-shy, mostly playing quiet dance music for the first couple sets. Finally, Goodman decided to throw caution to the wind and take a chance. He brought out the "killer-diller" numbers; the band romped; the teenagers went crazy; and history was made.

While the strong reaction surprised Benny Goodman, it signaled the beginning of the Swing era. Unknown to BG, the *Let's Dance* radio broadcasts had been very popular on the West Coast, and youngsters, unlike the older dancers in Denver who had never heard of him, were eagerly looking forward to his band's arrival. From that point on, success followed success. A three-week run at Chicago's Congress Hotel was extended to eight months. Press agents accurately crowned Goodman "the King of Swing," and the Swing era was under way.

Within a short period of time, many new Swing orchestras were formed. While it may seem strange to think of big bands being so plentiful during the Depression when money was so scarce, there was a great need for danceable bands. Dancing was inexpensive entertainment for millions and, with Swing becoming an important part of popular culture, the audience was huge and stayed that way until the mid-1940s.

Some bandleaders developed into celebrities who were written about not only in music publications but also in newspapers and general magazines. The bigger stars appeared in Hollywood films and became household names. Swing became the main soundtrack of the 1935–46 period.

It was fortunate that Swing came of age during a period when there was an unprecedented number of very talented songwriters. Composers such as Irving Berlin, George Gershwin (until his death in 1937), Jerome Kern, Hoagy Carmichael, Cole Porter, Harold Arlen, Richard Rodgers, Fats Waller, Harry Warren, and Duke Ellington, plus such lyricists as Johnny Mercer, Ira Gershwin, Al Dubin, Andy Razaf, Mitchell Parish, and Lorenz Hart came out with new standards on a regular basis, satisfying the Swing bands' constant need for new songs.

Not all of the Swing music of the era was played by big bands. Many big bandleaders enjoyed playing an occasional song with a smaller unit taken out of the orchestra. The trend started with the Benny Goodman Trio and Quartet and soon included Tommy Dorsey's Clambake Seven, Artie Shaw's Gramercy Five, Woody Herman's Chips and Woodchoppers, Bob Crosby's Bobcats, and Duke Ellington's small groups. On Swing Street (52nd Street in New York City), the emphasis was on combos playing in small clubs that were so close to each other that fans could hit several venues in a night. Imagine having Art Tatum playing across the street from Coleman Hawkins while Billie Holiday sang a block away! Trumpeters Wingy Manone and Louis Prima were popular attractions on the Street with their small groups, as was violinist Stuff Smith.

In time, big bands became bigger (often adding a third trombone and/or a fourth reed), and Benny Goodman faced stiffer competition. The clarinetist's fame reached a climax with his January 16, 1938, Carnegie Hall Concert (the first all-out jazz performance at the classical music temple), although he would remain a major name. After Count Basie's arrival in late 1936 from Kansas City, more Swing bands emulated his orchestra than Goodman's. Tommy Dorsey hit it big in 1937 with "Marie" and "Song of India." Artie Shaw was billed as the "King of the Clarinet" in 1938, and his band during 1938–39 was actually more popular than BG's. Glenn Miller became the biggest name of all in mid-1939, when his orchestra caught on. Gene Krupa and Jimmy Dorsey's bands became strong competitors in the early 1940s, and Harry James occupied the number-one spot during 1943–46.

Although Swing showed signs of running out of gas as early as 1939, it took two major disasters (World War II and the Musicians Union recording strike of 1942–44) along with competition from the New Orleans jazz revival, bebop, small R&B combos, and pop singers to eventually kill the big band era. But while it lasted, it was a glorious time for music!

THE TOP BIG BANDLEADERS

Nowadays, when nearly every big band is a part-time affair, orchestra leaders are usually arrangers who write most if not all of the charts. Their arrangements give each band its own musical personality, and the writing is often more significant than the individual players.

Things were different during the Swing era. Of the 52 big bands profiled in the next section, over half were led by brilliant musicians who would qualify for any top soloist list. Only 12 were arrangers who determined the direction of their bands (Les Brown, Benny Carter, Larry Clinton, Duke Ellington, Fletcher Henderson, Claude Hopkins, Stan Kenton, Jimmie Lunceford, Glenn Miller, Don Redman, Luis Russell, and Claude Thornhill) and just a few were important singers (most notably Louis Armstrong, Cab Calloway, and initially Woody Herman).

There were three main skills that a Swing era big bandleader needed in order to be successful:

1) He (one can say "he" in this section because so few early bandleaders were female) needed to be an attractive front man who acted as the symbol and figurehead of his band.

2) It was quite important to be an astute businessman, unless, as in the case of Bob Crosby, there was someone skilled in that area behind the scenes. A lack of business sense was what did Fletcher Henderson in, and resulted in some bandleaders (including Bunny Berigan and Jack Teagarden) having to file for bankruptcy.

3) It was also important for a bandleader to give his orchestra its own personality through his playing, singing, arranging, or showmanship. An original musical personality was always the key to a successful band. It made the difference between the Glenn Miller Orchestra of 1939 and the one he led in 1937. While it was not essential for a bandleader to be a virtuoso (Andy Kirk, Paul Whiteman, and Glenn Miller are good examples of part-time players), it was up to the leader (or the musical director) to set the musical atmosphere of the band and to contribute to its vision.

Bandleaders took many different approaches, depending on their personality. Glenn Miller and Tommy Dorsey could be real disciplinarians. Duke Ellington had a very lax attitude, because he knew that his sidemen were unique and irreplaceable. Benny Goodman, a spacey introvert, often gave the impression that he did not know where he was, but his musicianship and perfectionism led to his band's position among the best. Artie Shaw, an intellectual, knew everything that was going on. Charlie Barnet was constantly partying and ran a loose ship, but knew enough about business to be quite successful. Bunny Berigan was an alcoholic who never should have led his own big band. Will Bradley and Bob Crosby were miscast but still quite successful. Stan Kenton had a mission. Lionel Hampton just wanted to play.

With a few lucky breaks, it was possible for complete unknowns to become major celebrities within months. Fifty-two of the most important bandleaders and Swing orchestras are discussed in the next section.

The Classic Big Bandleaders

LOUIS ARMSTRONG
b. Aug. 4, 1901, New Orleans, LA, d. July 6, 1971, New York, NY

It would not be much of an exaggeration to say that Swing began with Louis Armstrong. The most important figure in the history of jazz, Louis Armstrong played in an exciting and explosive style in the mid-1920s that greatly influenced jazz to evolve from an ensemble-oriented music to one dominated by virtuosic soloists. While the Chicago jazzmen of the time (including Armstrong's idol, King Oliver) tended to play in ensembles and their counterparts in New York emphasized staccato outbursts (and thought that "playing hot" meant increasing their volume!), Armstrong's legato phrasing, his emphasis on placing notes in the most dramatic spots (making expert use of space and silence), and his ability to spontaneously build up improvisations changed jazz forever.

Louis Armstrong's main accomplishments were in three different areas. His improvisations as a cornetist (Satch permanently switched to trumpet during 1927) were years ahead of his contemporaries and became quite influential among virtually all jazz musicians to come up after him prior to the bebop era. Among the very first scat singers and an underrated interpreter of lyrics, Armstrong transferred his phrasing on the trumpet to his gravelly voice. He influenced Bing Crosby and through him all of popular music. And as a lovable personality, his remarkable popularity and worldwide fame earned him the nickname of "Ambassador Satch."

This biography emphasizes Armstrong's work before and during the Swing era; other periods of his life will be dealt with in more depth in other books in this series. Although during his lifetime he was believed to have been born on July 4, 1900 (which was a perfect date for this American hero), after his death writer Gary Giddins did some investigating and unearthed Louis's birth certificate, which shows that he was actually born on August 4, 1901.

Growing up in poverty in New Orleans, Armstrong loved music from an early age. He sang on the streets in a vocal group for pennies as a youth and enjoyed hearing the many brass bands that played at parades and social functions. On New Year's Eve 1912, he shot off a pistol in the air in celebration and was arrested and sent to live in a waifs' home as punishment since his mother (who had been deserted years earlier by Louis's father) was deemed unable to take care of him properly.

That incident ended up being one of the most significant of Louis Armstrong's life. At the waifs' home, he began seriously playing the cornet and, by the time he was released two years later, Armstrong was a promising young musician. Although he worked odd jobs as a teenager during the day in order to support himself, Louis had many opportunities to play with the local groups. He was inspired by Joe "King" Oliver (who at the time was considered the top cornetist in the city) and, when Oliver went up north in 1919, Armstrong took his place with trombonist Kid Ory's band. He also played on riverboats with the legendary pianist Fate Marable.

In 1922 King Oliver sent for his protégé to join his Creole Jazz Band at the Lincoln Gardens in Chicago. The Creole Jazz Band, a remarkable octet that also included clarinetist Johnny Dodds, trombonist Honore Dutrey, and Armstrong's future wife (his second of four) Lil Harden on piano, featured short solos but was mostly an ensemble band, a perfect example of a classic New Orleans jazz group. Even at this early stage, Louis was a stronger player than Oliver (as is hinted at in their recordings of 1923), although he was careful not to outshine his hero.

At Lil's urging (she was very ambitious for him), in 1924 Louis Armstrong reluctantly left King Oliver and accepted an offer to join Fletcher Henderson's Orchestra in New York. Although considered to be the pacesetting big band of the period (along with Paul Whiteman's Orchestra) and boasting strong musicianship, Henderson's orchestra of the pre-Armstrong era sounds quite dated today, often being bogged down in overly complex arrangements while lacking any major soloists. At his first rehearsal with the band, Armstrong was looked down upon by the other musicians due to his primitive clothes and informal manner. But as soon as he played, they knew he was a major talent. Louis's impact on the orchestra was almost

The 1948 Louis Armstrong All-Stars was composed of major Swing veterans: (left to right) drummer Cozy Cole, trombonist Jack Teagarden, Satch, the young bassist Arvell Shaw, clarinetist Barney Bigard, and pianist Earl Hines.

immediate (arranger Don Redman began to write much more swinging charts), and other New Yorkers began to listen closely to him and became influenced by his masterful playing.

After a year, Louis Armstrong returned to Chicago, where he played in big bands at night (including those of Erskine Tate and Carroll Dickerson) and started his highly influential Hot Five and Seven recordings. The Hot Five sides of 1925–27 (with Johnny Dodds, Kid Ory, his wife Lil Harden Armstrong on piano, and banjoist Johnny St. Cyr) find the trumpeter (who was already known as "Satchelmouth" and would soon become simply "Satchmo") stretching the boundaries of New Orleans jazz until it broke. His solos were so outstanding ("Cornet Chop Suey" in 1926 amazed fellow trumpeters) that it was clear he could no longer be confined strictly to leading ensembles and taking short breaks. The 1927 Hot Sevens (with John Thomas on trombone for Ory plus Pete Briggs on tuba and drummer Baby Dodds) were even more adventurous ("Potato Head Blues" is a classic), and in 1928 with the Savoy Ballroom Five, the music moved way beyond New Orleans jazz. By then the other horns were quite secondary, and Armstrong (who was a decade ahead of most of his contemporaries) was matched with the remarkable pianist Earl Hines, most notably on "West End Blues" (his personal favorite recording) and their time-defying duet "Weatherbird."

For Louis Armstrong, the big band era began in 1929. He had taken over the Carroll Dickerson Orchestra, and in May he took the band to New York. He started recording strictly in a big band format and emphasized current pop tunes rather than older jazz standards. Armstrong's mostly classic recordings of 1929–31 followed a pattern, with his orchestra playing the melody, Armstrong taking a vocal, and then Satch constructing a dramatic trumpet solo. Armstrong, who had already helped popularize such songs as "Heebies Jeebies," "Muskrat Ramble," "Big Butter and Egg Man," "Struttin' with Some Barbecue," "Basin Street Blues," and "St. James Infirmary," soon was helping to make famous Fats Waller's "Ain't Misbehavin'," "Black and Blue" (one of the first anti-racism protest songs), "When You're Smiling," "Rockin' Chair," "I'm Confessin' That I Love You," "Body and Soul," "Lazy River," "Star Dust," and his theme song, "Sleepy Time Down South."

Most of those songs were interpreted much differently by musicians and singers after Armstrong recorded them than they had been previously.

Satch used several different big bands during this time period, including the remains of the Dickerson band, the Luis Russell Orchestra, the Les Hite band (during his stay in Los Angeles in 1930), and an outfit run by trumpeter Zilmer Randolph. After a series of worthwhile but somewhat erratic recordings for Victor during 1932–33 (the backup band was underrehearsed), Louis Armstrong spent some time in Europe, only recording six numbers during a 29-month period. By the time he had returned to the U.S. (after having survived lip and manager problems) and was cutting his first recordings for the Decca label on October 3, 1935, the music world had changed quite a bit. The Swing era was under way, Benny Goodman was quickly becoming a household name, and Armstrong was thought of as a legend of the past, despite only being 34.

Louis Armstrong would be overshadowed to an extent by Benny Goodman and Glenn Miller during the next decade, but he always had steady work and remained a popular attraction. His memorable appearance in the 1936 film *Pennies from Heaven* with Bing Crosby resulted in other cameos in Hollywood movies, where he invariably stole the show with his natural comedy, mugging, and brilliant musical talents.

Armstrong recorded for Decca throughout the Swing era and, with just a few exceptions (including collaborations with the Mills Brothers), he used a big band. The orchestra (which was Luis Russell's old band) was chiefly utilized as a background for its leader, and few of its sidemen were ever featured very much. Satch's Decca recordings have often been underrated—being preceded by his classic Hot Fives and followed by his All-Star period—but they are generally pretty rewarding despite the eclectic material. Some of the songs are novelties or inferior remakes of earlier tunes, but many others are superior examples of Swing; all contain at least a few moments of Armstrong's magic.

Louis Armstrong kept his orchestra going into 1947 although it had ceased to be profitable; he could not bear the thought of putting his sidemen out of work. Over a three-year period, however, it became obvious to Armstrong and his manager Joe Glaser that it would make sense to lead a smaller band instead. Armstrong appeared at the Esquire All-American concert of 1944 (with a remarkable group that included not only his future sidemen Jack Teagarden, Barney Bigard, and Sid Catlett, but also Art Tatum and Coleman Hawkins), starred in the 1944 film *New Orleans* (a flawed movie that nevertheless contains a great deal of enjoyable music), guested on Eddie Condon's *Town Hall* radio series, and took over Edmond Hall's Sextet for a set at Carnegie Hall in early 1947. A *Town Hall* concert that year where he was joined by Teagarden and Bobby Hackett was so successful that within a short time the trumpeter finally disbanded his orchestra and formed the Louis Armstrong All-Stars, returning to his musical roots.

During the remaining 24 years of his life, Louis Armstrong would achieve a level of popularity and renown that was virtually unknown to any other jazz musician. His All-Stars (which in the early days featured Teagarden, Bigard, and Earl Hines and by the mid-1950s included trombonist Trummy Young and clarinetist Edmond Hall) toured virtually nonstop. Although some would criticize the general predictability of Armstrong's routines and repertoire in his live concerts (which did gradually change over time), the joy of his music never declined. With surprise hit records in 1955's "Mack the Knife," "Hello Dolly" in 1964, and "What a Wonderful World" (posthumously), frequent appearances on television and in movies, and an uncountable number of concert and club sets, Louis Armstrong was a household name up until his death at age 69 in 1971. In fact, decades after his passing, Satch is still the most famous and influential of all jazz musicians and singers.

●

8 *Portrait of the Artist as a Young Man / Apr. 6, 1923–Oct. 1934 / Columbia 57176*

This attractive four-CD set has many of the highlights from Louis Armstrong's first 11 years on record. The great trumpeter-singer is heard on three cuts with King Oliver's Creole Jazz Band in 1923, six numbers starring with Clarence Williams's Blue Five, four with the Fletcher Henderson Orchestra, 13 accompanying singers (ranging from Bessie Smith and country singer Jimmy Rodgers to the mildly annoying Lillie Delk Christian), one apiece with Erskine Tate's Vendome Orchestra and Johnny Dodds's Black Bottom Stompers, 23 Hot Five and Hot Seven recordings, and 28 selections with his own big bands. This is a fine introduction to listeners not familiar with Armstrong's early work (and the 78-page booklet has typically definitive liner notes by Dan Morgenstern), but all of the music is available elsewhere and most of the dates with singers could have been replaced by additional Hot Fives and Henderson recordings.

10 *Hot Fives, Vol. 1 / Nov. 12, 1925–June 23, 1926 / Columbia/Legacy 44049*

Louis Armstrong's Hot Five recordings were arguably the most significant jazz records of the 1920s. After decades of only putting out the recordings domestically in piecemeal fashion, Columbia finally reissued all of the important music complete and in chronological order in the late '80s/early '90s along with Satch's early big band titles. *Vol. 1* has the first 16 Hot Fives, which star Armstrong on cornet and vocals along with trombonist Kid Ory, clarinetist Johnny Dodds, pianist Lil Armstrong, and banjoist Johnny St. Cyr. Among the more notable selections on this CD are "Gut Bucket Blues" (Armstrong's first real talking on records), "Come Back Sweet Papa," "Heebies Jeebies" (which has a very influential scat vocal), the virtuosic "Cornet Chop Suey," and the earliest rendition of "Muskrat Ramble." As good as Dodds sounds, Armstrong was already way ahead of the other classic New Orleans jazz players at this early stage.

10 *Hot Fives and Sevens, Vol. 2 / June 28, 1926–May 13, 1927 / Columbia/Legacy 42253*

This set has eight of Louis Armstrong's Hot Five recordings and an equal number by his Hot Seven, which has the same personnel except that the unremarkable John Thomas is on trombone instead of Ory, and the quintet is augmented by Pete Briggs's tuba and drummer Baby Dodds. Of the former selections, "Jazz Lips" is full of hot breaks, "Skid-Dat-De-Dat" is quite impressionistic (and avant-garde for the time), and the happy "Big Butter and Egg Man" has May Alix joining Armstrong on vocals. If anything, the Hot Seven recordings were even better than the Hot Fives, with Johnny Dodds sometimes competing closely with the trumpeter for solo honors. Armstrong is brilliant on "Alligator Crawl," and the other numbers include classic renditions of "Willie the Weeper," "Wild Man Blues," and "Weary Blues."

10 *Hot Fives and Sevens, Vol. 3 / May 13, 1927–June 28, 1928 / Columbia/Legacy 44422*

The final three Hot Seven recordings (including the humorous "That's When I'll Come Back to You") are joined by the remaining nine selections by the Hot Five, plus the first four cuts by Louis Armstrong's Savoy Ballroom Five. On the Hot Fives, one can really hear Armstrong reaching far beyond his associates harmonically and especially rhythmically; plus his beautiful tone is difficult to resist! "Ory's Creole Trombone" (which was not released until the early 1940s) has some mishaps, but this rendition of "Struttin' with Some Barbecue" is perfect in every way, with the trumpeter's exciting improvisation having a beginning, a middle, and an end. On three songs, guitarist Lonnie Johnson makes the group a sextet with "Hotter Than That" living up to its name! The Savoy Ballroom Five is a completely different group which is sometimes also called the Hot Five (despite being six or seven pieces). Armstrong's 1928 unit includes trombonist Fred Robinson, Jimmy Strong on clarinet and tenor, and banjoist Mancy Cara, but the real co-stars are pianist Earl Hines and drummer Zutty Singleton. Their four numbers (which include "Fireworks" and Hines's "A Monday Date") hint at what was to come in *Vol. 4*.

10 *Louis Armstrong and Earl Hines, Vol. 4 / May 9, 1927–Dec. 12, 1928 / Columbia/Legacy 45142*

Louis Armstrong was as advanced a soloist in 1928 as he ever would be, sounding a decade ahead of most other players of the time, with the exception of pianist Earl Hines. This CD starts off with "Chicago Breakdown" in 1927, a big band title that was the first time that Satch and Hines appeared together on record. There are also two numbers ("Symphonic Raps" and "Savoyagers' Stomp") with Carroll Dickerson's Orchestra, but it is the 15 selections by Armstrong's Savoy Ballroom Five that are the most remarkable. The sextet (sometimes expanded to a septet with the addition of Don Redman on alto, clarinet, and providing arrangements) essentially has three giants (Satch, Hines, and drummer Zutty Singleton) and three backup players. "West End Blues," with its opening cadenza by the trumpeter, a memorable scat interlude, and a perfect solo, is a masterpiece, while the trumpet-piano duet "Weather Bird" finds the two masters challenging each other, playing with suspending time yet never losing the beat. Also included are such gems as "Sugar Foot Strut," the debut recording of "Basin Street Blues," "St. James Infirmary," "Beau Koo Jack," and "Tight Like This."

9 *Louis in New York, Vol. 5 / May 5, 1929–Nov. 26, 1929 / Columbia/Legacy 46148*

During the period covered by this CD, Louis Armstrong's recording career changed. Instead of being featured with small groups, he was now usually heard fronting an orchestra. This release begins with a jam session version of "Knockin' a Jug" that finds Satch recording for the first time with Jack Teagarden. In addition, there also three numbers in which he backs the vocals of Seger Ellis (who is nasal in the extreme) and two with Victoria Spivey. Much more significant are the big band tracks, particularly "I Can't Give You Anything but Love," the original version of "Mahogany Hall Stomp," "Ain't Misbehavin' " and "Black and Blue." In addition, this 1990 CD released for the first time two previously unissued versions of "After You've Gone," music that had gone unnoticed in the vaults for 60 years.

10 St. Louis Blues, Vol. 6 / Dec. 10, 1929–Oct. 9, 1930 / Columbia/Legacy 46996

Louis Armstrong's big band recordings of 1929–30 predated the Swing era by five or six years and really set a high standard. While Armstrong's backup bands (which on this CD include the Luis Russell Orchestra, the Mills Blue Rhythm Band, and Les Hite's Orchestra) are purely in a supportive role with only occasional solos, the leader's vocals and trumpet solos are of such a high caliber that one does not really mind. New alternate takes of "I Ain't Got Nobody," "Dallas Blues" and two of "St. Louis Blues" were unearthed in time for this CD's release. "I'm a Ding Dong Daddy from Dumas" has several miraculous moments, including Armstrong's vocal (which, after he sings "I dun forgot the words," becomes pure scat) and a trumpet solo that continuously builds. Other songs given definitive treatment include "Blue, Turning Grey over You," "Dinah," "Tiger Rag," "I'm Confessin' That I Love You" and "Body and Soul." A special bonus is a duet with pianist Buck Washington on "Dear Old Southland."

9 You're Driving Me Crazy, Vol. 7 / Oct. 16, 1930–Nov. 3, 1931 / Columbia/Legacy 48828

The final release in this essential seven-CD series of Louis Armstrong's early recordings as a leader features Satch's big band recordings of 1930–31: seven selections (and an alternate take) with Les Hite's New Cotton Club Orchestra and ten songs with an orchestra arranged by Zilner Randolph. Lionel Hampton (then known as a Los Angeles–based drummer) is with the former group and can be heard making his first (if brief) recorded appearances on vibes during "Memories of You" and "Shine." Armstrong has famous solos on "Sweethearts on Parade" and "Shine." While the

Zilner Randolph band sessions are not on the same level, there are some notable selections, particularly the trumpeter's first full-length version of his future theme song, "When It's Sleepy Time Down South," "Lazy River," and the humorous "I'll Be Glad When You're Dead, You Rascal You."

9 Complete RCA Victor Recordings / July 16, 1930– Aug. 1, 1956 / RCA 68682

Louis Armstrong recorded for the Victor label during 1932–33 (big band performances with an under-rehearsed and sometimes erratic orchestra), 1946–47 (the final dates by his orchestra, plus combo numbers that led to the formation of his All-Stars), 1956 (a couple of songs with the Hal Mooney Orchestra), and "Blue Yodel No. 9" in 1930 in which Louis's trumpet and Lil Armstrong's piano accompany country singer Jimmie Rodgers. All of the music is included on this four-CD set. The packaging is flawless, the extensive liner notes (by Dan Morgenstern) are perfect, and Louis Armstrong collectors will prefer this release to the many other RCA and Bluebird sets available, since it includes everything. Musically, the 1932–33 performances are not all that essential because, despite the presence of such players as Budd Johnson and Teddy Wilson, the band is quite streaky, and Armstrong sometimes sounds a bit sloppy. There are a few gems, however, most notably "That's My Home," "Hustlin' and Bustlin' for Baby," "There's a Cabin in the Pines" and two bizarre versions of "Laughin' Louie." The music on the second half of the release is on a higher level, particularly a couple of appearances with the 1946 Esquire All American Award Winners (Satch sounds fairly modern on "Snafu") and the combo recordings of "Do You Know What It Means to Miss New Orleans," "Ain't Misbehavin'," "Back O' Town Blues" and "Jack Armstrong Blues"; the latter has one of Armstrong's greatest solos of the 1940s.

6 Laughin' Louis / Dec. 8, 1932–Apr. 26, 1933 / Bluebird 9759

Not counting alternate takes, Louis Armstrong recorded 29 selections with big bands during 1932–33 before he took a recording hiatus and went to Europe. Twenty are on this single CD, and one will really not miss the other nine (particularly "Snowball"). The first two cuts have Armstrong backed by the Chick Webb Orchestra, while most of the remaining tracks are by an orchestra headed by Zilner Randolph and include Teddy Wilson over two years before he hooked up with Benny Goodman. Unfortunately the two big bands do not live up to their potential and are sometimes out of tune (such as during "High Society"), often sounding rushed and in need of more rehearsal time. Armstrong ranges from inspired (such as on "That's My Home," "I've Got the World on a String," the underrated classic "Hustlin' and Bustlin' for Baby" and "There's a Cabin in the Pines") to routine. Of particular interest is the odd comedy piece "Laughin' Louie" (the alternate take was mistakenly included here) and the two-part six-song "Medley of Armstrong Hits." But there are more significant Louis Armstrong recordings available, and the four-CD *Complete RCA Victor Recordings* has all of this material plus much more.

8 *1934–1936 / Oct. 1934–Feb. 4, 1936 / Classics 509*

Louis Armstrong's Swing era recordings have long been underrated and overlooked. One reason is that Decca (and later its owner MCA) never reissued all of the trumpeter's performances domestically in any coherent fashion (particularly his work after 1938), making it difficult to evaluate what Satch created during this time. Fortunately the European Classics label has completely covered Armstrong's 1934–42 period on six CDs (although it skipped over the occasional alternate takes). Its reissues of Satch's earlier 1925–33 recordings are just as complete, but less necessary now that Columbia and RCA have woken up to the importance of this music and have reissued it. This particular CD starts out with Louis Armstrong's only recording date of 1934, which was recorded in Paris with an 11-piece group that includes pianist Herman Chittison. The very jazz-oriented session features hot versions of "St. Louis Blues," "Tiger Rag," and "St. Louis Blues," the obscure "Will You, Won't You Be My Baby," a two-part rendition of "On the Sunny Side of the Street," and the atmospheric "Song of the Vipers," which has a rather eccentric vocal. Other than the last selection ("I'm Putting All My Eggs in One Basket"), the remainder of the CD is taken from Satch's first Decca sessions, in which he fronts the remains of the Luis Russell Orchestra. Unlike with his 1932–33 big band dates, these musicians are in tune and the arrangements are pretty smooth and swinging. Louis Armstrong is in particularly strong form on "I'm in the Mood for Love," a scat-filled "La Cucaracha," "I've Got My Fingers Crossed," "Red Sails in the Sunset," "On Treasure Island," and "Thanks a Million."

7 *1936–1937 / Feb. 4, 1936–Apr. 7, 1937 / Classics 512*

Nineteen thirty-six was the year Louis Armstrong appeared in the Bing Crosby film *Pennies from Heaven*. Among the 23 selections on this Classics CD are a medley of songs from the movie plus a version of "Pennies from Heaven" that matches Satch with Crosby and singer Frances Langford, backed by Jimmy Dorsey's Orchestra. Armstrong also recorded five selections on another date with JD, including "The Skeleton in the Closet" (his feature number in the film) and "Dippermouth Blues." Louis's regular band, the Luis Russell Orchestra, helps him out on nine numbers (including the remarkable "Swing That Music," which finds him hitting the same high note dozens of times over the last few choruses), a white band backs Armstrong on "Yes! Yes! My! My!" and there are a few unusual performances. Armstrong is heard on four charming if odd Hawaiian numbers with groups led by the ukulele player Andy Iona, and he interacts quite winningly with the Mills Brothers on "Carry Me Back to Old Virginny" and "Darling Nelly Gray." Overall this is fun music, much of which has not been reissued very often over the years.

7 *1937–1938 / June 29, 1937–May 13, 1938 / Classics 515*

Novelties mix in with unexpected classics on this CD. Louis Armstrong performs two numbers with the Mills Brothers ("In the Shade of the Old Apple Tree" and "The Old Folks at Home"), performs "Once in a While" and "On the Sunny Side of the Street" with an octet taken from the Luis Russell Orchestra (including trombonist J. C. Higginbotham), plays and sings three throwaway tunes plus his earliest version of "When the Saints Go Marching In" with a tentet, and otherwise performs with the full orchestra. Of the latter numbers, some are forgettable, but "I Double Dare You" is a practically unknown classic, "Jubilee" is pretty spectacular, and the remake of "Struttin' with Some Barbecue" is quite a bit different from the 1927 version.

6 *1938–1939 / May 18, 1938–Apr. 5, 1939 / Classics 523*

Like fellow Decca artist of the period Bing Crosby, Louis Armstrong had the opportunity to perform a wide variety of material during the Swing era, some of which worked better than others. His 12 numbers on this CD with his regular big band and a tentet contain some lesser remakes of earlier material, a few more recent tunes, and a classic in "Jeepers Creepers." Satch also performs three songs with the Mills Brothers (a combination that always worked quite well, as can be heard on a touching rendition of "The Song Is Ended"), sings four spirituals with the Decca Mixed Chorus, has a couple of strange "Elder Eatmore Sermons" talking records and performs two Hoagy Carmichael tunes ("Rockin' Chair" and "Lazybones") with the Casa Loma Orchestra.

5 *1939–1940 / Apr. 5, 1939–May 1, 1940 / Classics 615*
Despite being a big name during this era, Louis Armstrong was often given weak novelty material to record such as "Me and Brother Bill," "You're Just a No Account," "You've Got Me Voodoo'd," and "You Run Your Mouth, I'll Run My Business." This CD includes not only those songs but some lesser remakes of earlier classics (including "West End Blues," "Confessin'," "Our Monday Date," and "Sweethearts on Parade"), which do not reach the heights of the original versions. In fact, in contrast to those big band sides, the freshest selections on this CD are the four that Satch recorded with the Mills Brothers, particularly "W.P.A."

6 *1940–1942 / May 1, 1940–Apr. 17, 1942 / Classics 685*
Louis Armstrong was largely overshadowed during the Swing era, although he was still a famous soloist. The main reason is that his big band never really developed its own personality beyond its leader, mostly being confined to a supportive role, particularly on records. Of the ten orchestra numbers on this CD, only "When It's Sleepy Time Down South," "Coquette," and "Leap Frog" are memorable, and Armstrong is actually mostly absent on "Leap Frog." Certainly "Cut Off My Legs and Call Me Shorty" was not destined for immortality! In addition, surprisingly little happens on a pair of septet dates ("Hey Lawdy Mama" is a rare highlight). However, this CD does have the four songs from the last meeting on records by Armstrong and the great soprano-saxophonist Sidney Bechet (including "2:19 Blues" and "Down in Honky Tonk Town"), and it is fun to hear Satch and Bechet battle each other for supremacy.

4 *Highlights from His Decca Years / Oct. 10, 1924–Feb. 4, 1958 / GRP/Decca 2-638*

7 *Rhythm Saved the World / Oct. 3, 1935–Feb. 4, 1936 / GRP/Decca 602*

6 *Heart Full of Rhythm, Vol. 2 / Apr. 28, 1936–Jan. 15, 1938 / GRP/Decca*

7 *Pocketful of Dreams, Vol. 3 / Oct. 3, 1935–June 21, 1938 / GRP/Decca 649*

2 *The Composer / Nov. 21, 1935–Jan. 28, 1957 / MCA/ Decca 10121*
Unlike the Classics sets, the American reissues of Louis Armstrong's Decca years are pretty haphazard. *Highlights*, a two-CD set, has illogical programming: the songs are not really in chronological order and most sessions are not even close to being complete. The twofer begins with four numbers from the early days (with Armstrong heard as a sideman with Johnny Dodds, Lil's Hot Shots, and Fletcher Henderson), there are 13 titles (mostly with his big band) from 1935–45, and two selections from Satch's Symphony Hall Concert of 1947. The second disc has collaborations with the Mills Brothers, Ella Fitzgerald, Billie Holiday, Louis Jordan, and Bing Crosby, plus four songs with his later All-Stars, four with commercial orchestras and three taken from his *Musical Autobiography* project of 1956–57. Not a "greatest hits" introductory set or a gap filler, this release (despite some classic titles) was quite poorly planned. *Rhythm Saved the World* is a very similar CD to the Classics release *1934–1936*. In fact, the only difference is that the Paris session from 1934 is absent, replaced by a pair of alternate takes (for "Old Man Mose" and "Solitude") and an additional selection from the 1936 session ("Yes! Yes! My! My!"). Otherwise, the music is comprised of Louis Armstrong's 1935 recordings with the Luis Russell Orchestra. *Heart Full of Rhythm* has a sampling of Armstrong's big band dates of 1936–38. The 20 selections range from quite memorable ("Swing That Music," "The Skeleton in the Closet" and "Jubilee") to long-forgotten ("Somebody Stole My Break," "Public Melody Number One," and "Satchel Mouth Swing"), but the Classics equivalent (despite some fine liner notes here by Richard Sudhalter) is preferred. *Pocketful of Dreams* is a bit of surprise: It was as if Decca suddenly caught the completist fever for a moment, releasing four complete Armstrong big band sessions from 1938, including a quartet of alternate takes. Not all of the music is that significant, but it is enjoyable to hear two versions of "I Double Dare You," and a bonus is a recently discovered alternate version of 1935's "Got a Bran' New Suit." But more typical of Decca's many reissue programs is *The Composer*, a real misfire. Louis Armstrong was never a major composer, and "Someday You'll Be Sorry" was the only song of his to become a standard. The 13 numbers on this set include one tune mistakenly attrib-

uted to Louis but actually written by his wife Lil ("Struttin' with Some Barbecue"). The music (five selections with his Swing era big bands, three with his 1950s All-Stars, four from his *Musical Autobiography* series of remakes, and an orchestral version of "Someday" from 1953) is fine, but easily available elsewhere in more coherent form.

4 *Live in '43 / June 13, 1938–Dec. 7, 1943 / Jass 19*
Most of this CD features Louis Armstrong's otherwise unrecorded big band of 1943, taken from radio broadcasts. Joe Garland was its tenor soloist and main arranger, but Armstrong is the star throughout, taking vocals on every song but the closing theme and one vocal number apiece for Velma Middleton, Ann Baker, Jimmy Anderson, and Bea Booze. One can easily understand why the Armstrong big band's days were numbered (although it would hang on for nearly four more years): The sidemen (which include the young Dexter Gordon on tenor and sometimes pianist Gerry Wiggins and bassist Charles Mingus) have little to do but support the leader. The Mills Brothers are featured on "Paper Doll" and clarinetist Barney Bigard drops by for "Rose Room." Also, for no particular reason, the release begins with Armstrong's 1939 version of "Jeepers Creepers," which appeared in the soundtrack of the movie *Going Places*, plus the studio rendition of "The Song Is Ended" that Satch recorded with the Mills Brothers in 1938.

10 *Pops: 1940s Small Band Sides / Sept. 6, 1946–Oct. 16, 1947 / RCA/Bluebird 6378*
For those listeners who do not have the four-CD *Complete Victor Recordings of Louis Armstrong* or are mostly interested in his early All-Stars, this single disc is highly recommended. Prior to breaking up his big band in 1947, Armstrong appeared with small combos on a few special occasions, including the first five recording sessions that are featured here. Satch sings and plays four relaxed numbers with a septet that includes trombonist Vic Dickenson and clarinetist Barney Bigard and introduces "Do You Know What It Means to Miss New Orleans" during a reunion date with Kid Ory. On May 17, 1947 Louis Armstrong was presented at a Town Hall concert with an all-star group: Bobby Hackett, Jack Teagarden, clarinetist Peanuts Hucko, pianist Dick Cary, Bob Haggart, and Sid Catlett. The rave reviews given to Armstrong for his performance that night finally led to the end of his big band and the beginning of the All-Stars. The five numbers recorded for RCA from that concert are

here, including an untoppable version of "Ain't Misbehavin'," "Rockin' Chair" (teaming together the voices of Armstrong and Teagarden), and "Back O' Town Blues." A month later the same horn section (with baritonist Ernie Caceres, pianist Johnny Guarnieri, guitarist Al Casey, bassist Al Hall, and drummer Cozy Cole) recorded four numbers in the studios, including a remake of "Rockin' Chair" and the exciting "Jack Armstrong Blues," which, after a vocal and trumpet-trombone tradeoff by Jack T. and Armstrong, concludes with a perfectly constructed five-chorus trumpet solo. Also on this CD are the four songs from the first official recording date (Oct. 16, 1947) of the Louis Armstrong All-Stars (Armstrong, Teagarden, Bigard, Dick Cary, bassist Arvell Shaw, and Sid Catlett), including "A Song Was Born" and "Please Stop Playing Those Blues, Boy."

8 *Satchmo at Symphony Hall / Nov. 30, 1947 / GRP 661*
The success of the Louis Armstrong All-Stars was solidified by the success of his Symphony Hall concert. In fact, during the next few years and continuing throughout the remainder of his life, Armstrong would reach a level of popularity and fame that exceeded anything he had previously experienced. This single CD, which reissues 15 of the 18 numbers on the earlier two-LP set (dropping a bass feature, a Velma Middleton vocal, and unfortunately the comedy number "That's My Desire"), features the All-Stars when they were quite enthusiastic and the format was new. Jack Teagarden shows off his technique on "Lover," sings "Stars Fell on Alabama" and "Baby Won't You Please Come Home," and blends in quite well with Satch during the ensembles. Barney Bigard has "Tea for Two" as his feature, Sid Catlett is dominant on "Steak Face," Velma Middleton sings "Since I Fell for You," and Dick Cary and Arvell Shaw are fine in support. Louis Armstrong sounds happy to be freed of the big band, although he always did sound full of joy! Among the other highlights are "Black and Blue," "Royal Garden Blues," "Muskrat Ramble," and "On the Sunny Side of the Street."

9 *An American Icon / Apr. 27, 1946–July 23, 1968 / Hip-O 3-40138*
This intriguing and valuable sampler is different than most Louis Armstrong sets in that the emphasis is on his treatment of popular songs and ballads rather than Dixieland standards. There are some selections with his All-Stars (mostly in concert) but also many with studio orchestras

(usually led and arranged by Sy Oliver) and pairings with Billie Holiday ("You Can't Lose a Broken Heart"), Bing Crosby ("Gone Fishin' "), Ella Fitzgerald, and Duke Ellington. Covering his post-Swing years mostly in chronological order, this three-CD set shows just how strong and expressive a singer Louis Armstrong really was. Among the tunes included are "Pennies from Heaven," "La Vie en Rose," "Baby It's Cold Outside," "A Kiss to Build a Dream On," "C'est Si Bon," "Mack the Knife," "Blueberry Hill," an exquisite "Stars Fell on Alabama" (with Ella), "Hello Dolly," and the first version of "What a Wonderful World."

7 *Now You Has Jazz: Louis Armstrong at MGM / Aug. 28, 1942–July 26, 1965 / Rhino 72827*
Louis Armstrong was in many movies throughout his career, although usually just for a brief scene or two. This CD has the music that he recorded for 1951's *The Strip*, 1952's *Glory Alley*, 1956's *High Society*, and 1965's *When the Boys Meet the Girls*, plus an outtake from 1943's *Cabin in the Sky*. Not only is the music that was used in those films included (without the dialogue that often overshadowed it), but there are several alternate versions, plus performances that did not make it on screen. Jack Teagarden and Earl Hines make appearances, as does Bing Crosby in the famous score to *High Society* (which includes "I Love You Samantha," "High Society Calypso," and "Now You Has Jazz"). An interesting set that Rhino put out in 1997.

10 *Louis Armstrong Plays W. C. Handy / July 12, 1954– July 14, 1954 / Columbia/Legacy 64925*
Of all the recordings by Louis Armstrong's All-Stars, this is the most essential one. Armstrong's all-stars of 1954 (Trummy Young, Barney Bigard, pianist Billy Kyle, Arvell Shaw, drummer Barrett Deems, and singer Velma Middleton) were inspired by the fresh repertoire (which differed from what they played on a nightly basis), W. C. Handy himself was in the studio enjoying the sounds, and Satch was in one of his prime periods. The version of "St. Louis Blues" (which lasts nearly nine minutes) is a true classic, and other highlights are "Yellow Dog Blues," "Beale Street Blues," and "Ole Miss." One has to be careful because the first CD reissue of this material was quite flawed, with inferior alternate takes often substituted for the real thing, so be sure to get the 1997 CD. Three rehearsal takes, a humorous Louis Armstrong joke, and a brief interview with W. C. Handy are

tacked onto the end of the CD, but all of the original performances are fortunately here intact.

9 *The Complete Louis Armstrong & Duke Ellington Sessions / Apr. 3–4, 1961 / Roulette 7938442*
Other than a single song cut in 1946 ("Long Long Journey"), Louis Armstrong and Duke Ellington did not have a chance to record together at all until this delightful encounter. Although it would have been preferable to hear Armstrong play with the Duke Ellington Orchestra, what did occur is quite successful. Ellington sat in on piano with the trumpeter's All-Stars, which at the time included Trummy Young, Barney Bigard (Duke's former longtime clarinetist), bassist Mort Herbert, and drummer Danny Barcelona, for an all-Ellington program. Although Satch did not have any of these songs in his regular repertoire, he had no difficulty uplifting the material, including two newer tunes ("The Beautiful American" and "Azalea"). Such old favorites as "Cottontail," "Mood Indigo," "Drop Me Off at Harlem," and "I Got It Bad" sound quite fresh, and the mutual love shared by the two jazz giants can be felt throughout the music. One of Louis Armstrong's finest recordings of the 1960s.

LPS TO SEARCH FOR

Fortunately all of Louis Armstrong's studio recordings as a leader from the 1925–47 period are available on CD. Chief among the missing records of his later period is *Satch Plays Fats* (Columbia CL 708), a 1955 album that has the All-Stars adding their brand of joy to nine Fats Waller compositions, including "Honeysuckle Rose," "I'm Crazy 'Bout My Baby," and "Ain't Misbehavin'." It was reissued on CD in 1986 but, as with *Louis Armstrong Plays W. C. Handy,* the contents were fouled up, with the erasing of valuable edits and the substitution of alternate takes. Get the LP instead.

FILMS

Louis Armstrong was in 22 feature films throughout his career. Here are some of the best: 1936's *Pennies from Heaven* has him singing "Skeleton in the Closet" and, when accused of stealing chickens, he jumps out of a window! In *Going Places* (a 1938 movie with Dick Powell), Satch plays and sings "Jeepers Creepers" to a horse. 1946's *New Orleans* blows the opportunity to recreate the beginnings of jazz, but there is a lot of good music in it, and Armstrong is matched with Billie Holiday and Kid Ory. 1951's *The Strip* (a so-so Mickey Rooney movie) features the All-Stars with Jack

Teagarden. 1956's *High Society* does not have enough of Armstrong, but he does get to jam on "Now You Has Jazz" with Bing Crosby. 1959's *The Five Pennies* is a delight: the fictionalized life story of cornetist Red Nichols with Danny Kaye in the lead role and Armstrong (supposedly in the 1920s) battling Nichols on "Battle Hymn of the Republic." Satch is also in 1961's *Paris Blues* (Duke Ellington wrote the film score), plays a dramatic role in the 1966 Sammy Davis movie *A Man Called Adam,* and steals the show with his one vocal chorus on the title song in 1969's *Hello Dolly.*

CHARLIE BARNET

b. Oct. 26, 1913, New York, NY, d. Sept. 4, 1991, San Diego, CA

Charlie Barnet stood out among the Swing big bandleaders. Unlike his contemporaries, some of whom were perfectionists and had prickly personalities, Barnet always appeared to be one of the boys, a hell-raising party-lover whose main interest was playing jazz rather than running a commercially successful band, yet somehow he managed to do both. Born to a rich family, Barnet did not have to work for a living, so the lack of insecurity and money troubles were great assets. It allowed him to take chances with his music, including using black musicians during an era of strict segregation (as early as 1935), emulating the music of Duke Ellington and occasionally Count Basie instead of worrying about having pop hits, and essentially doing whatever he wanted throughout his life, including having a countless number of wives!

Barnet was best known for his enthusiastic tenor saxophone playing (his solo on "Cherokee" was famous during the early 1940s), but he could also sound a bit like Johnny Hodges on alto, and was one of the few musicians of the period (outside of Sidney Bechet) to play soprano sax. He was a household name by the time he was 26, although his prime period actually only lasted ten years.

At the end of the 1920s , when he was 16, Barnet became a professional musician over his family's objections; they wanted him to become a lawyer. He moved to New York in 1932 and started leading his own big bands on records in 1933, while he was still a teenager. However, it would take Barnet almost six years to find his own sound. His early recordings for Banner, ARC, Varsity, and Bluebird were quite erratic, sometimes including some strong jazz and other times being weighed down by dated arrangements and far too many indifferent vocalists (including himself). A 1936 recording of "Make-Believe Ballroom" was notable for featuring the Modernaires, a vocal group that a few years later would become associated with Glenn Miller.

Nineteen thirty-nine was the breakthrough year for Charlie Barnet. He had a powerful orchestra (key soloists were trumpeter Bobby Burnet and pioneering electric guitarist Bus Etri), "Cherokee" became a hit (and Barnet's theme song) midway through the year, and he had many other notable recordings during the 1939–42 period, including "The Duke's Idea," "The Count's Idea," "The Wrong Idea" (a hilarious satire of sweet bands), "Pompton Turnpike," "Southern Fried," "Redskin Rhumba" (a song built off of the closing vamp of "Cherokee"), and "Charleston Alley," plus many Ellington tunes. Although Barnet also recorded some ballads and vocal numbers, virtually all of his hits were swinging instrumentals.

Barnet switched to Decca in 1942, shortly before the recording strike. By 1944 he had a particularly strong outfit with such players as trumpeter-vocalist Peanuts Holland, pianist Dodo Marmarosa, guitarist Barney Kessel, the up-and-coming singer Kay Starr, and (on a few dates) guest trumpeter Roy Eldridge. "Skyliner," from 1944, became one of his biggest (and final) hits. Barnet continued leading his big band through the rest of the decade, recording for several other labels, and in 1947 featured the young trumpeter Clark Terry. Very open to newer sounds, Barnet's orchestra from 1948–49 was quite bebop oriented, and at one point in time he had a screaming trumpet section comprised of Maynard Ferguson, Doc Severinsen, Ray Wetzel, Rolf Ericson, and John Howell, recording several remarkable records for Capitol. However, that particular band was a flop commercially, and near the end of 1949, Barnet called it quits.

Only 36 at the time, Charlie Barnet would continue putting together groups for short tours and recordings (including for

Clef, Victor, Verve, Everest, Crown, and Vault) through 1966, but he no longer championed new music, mostly sticking to Swing standards and remakes of his earlier hits. He had made his mark on Swing and was content to enjoy life, retiring altogether 25 years before his death.

9 *Clap Hands Here Comes Charlie / Oct. 9, 1939–Aug. 14, 1941 / Bluebird 6273*

This is an excellent "greatest hits" sampler that gives one a strong overview of the Charlie Barnet Orchestra during the period when it became a major part of the Swing era. Although the 21 selections on this CD (put out in 1987, so possibly difficult to find today) are not in strict chronological order, they do hit most of the high points of Barnet's Bluebird years. His theme song "Cherokee" is here, as are "Pompton Turnpike," "Southern Fried," "Charleston Alley," "The Duke's Idea," "The Count's Idea," and "The Right Idea" (but regrettably not the riotous "The Wrong Idea"). In addition to Barnet on tenor, alto, and soprano, the main soloists include trumpeter Bobby Burnet, pianist Bill Miller, and the short-lived but advanced electric guitarist Bus Etri. Mary Ann McCall has two vocals and Lena Horne is featured on "You're My Thrill."

8 *The Transcription Performances 1941 / Jan. 27, 1941 / Hep 53*

All 25 selections on this CD from the Scottish Hep label were recorded by Charlie Barnet's Orchestra during one long radio transcription session for NBC's Thesaurus. None were originally available commercially. After a year and a half of major success, Barnet's band had become quite tight, yet it had a looseness about it that reflected its leader's easygoing but professional attitude. In addition to alternate versions of such familiar Barnet numbers as "Charleston Alley" and "Redskin Rhumba," many of the songs on this set were not otherwise recorded by Barnet, making the high-quality program of strong interest. Lena Horne sings "It's a Haunted Town," while ballad singer Bob Carroll happily appears just once. The arrangements are by Horace Henderson, Billy May, Barnet, Billy Moore, and Bud Estes, and the most important soloists, in addition to the leader (on tenor, alto, and soprano), are trumpeters Bobby Burnet and Bernie Privin, guitarist Bus Etri, and trombonist Spud Murphy; drummer Cliff Leeman is also a strong asset.

10 *Drop Me Off in Harlem / Apr. 30, 1942–June 16, 1946 / GRP/Decca 612*

During the period covered by this CD, Charlie Barnet's Orchestra was at the peak of its powers, cutting 44 selections for the Decca label. The 20 best are included here, such as the big hit "Skyliner," "The Moose," "The Great Lie," "Gulf Coast Blues," "West End Blues," and "Andy's Boogie." While Barnet's earlier band had few major names, the editions represented on this set include such sidemen as Peanuts Holland, Roy Eldridge, high-note trumpeter Al Killian, Dodo Marmarosa, clarinetist Buddy DeFranco, Barney Kessel, trombonist Lawrence Brown (visiting from Duke Ellington's band), and singers Kay Starr and Francis Wayne (on "That Old Black Magic"), plus the leader on his various saxophones.

7 *Those Swinging Years / Apr. 30, 1942–Dec. 6, 1945 / Hindsight 264*

The Hindsight label mostly specializes in rare radio transcriptions and broadcasts, but this CD is an exception. Although the liner notes are rather vague about the recording dates and unsure about some of the personnel (nothing is said about either on the outside of the CD), most of the 16 numbers seem to be studio recordings that were released by Decca. The music is excellent, the fiery trumpeter Roy Eldridge has a few appearances, and there are two spirited vocals apiece by Kay Starr and Peanuts Holland. Some of the high note trumpet work is taken by Al Killian, and Barnet has plenty of solo space on his three reeds. Highlights include "Yalta," "The Great Lie," "You Always Hurt the One You Love," "Gulf Coast Blues," and an uptempo "Drop Me Off in Harlem." Some of the performances are also available on the above Decca CD.

9 *The Capitol Big Band Sessions / Aug. 9, 1948–Dec. 4, 1950 / Capitol 21258*

Unlike some of the other Swing era bandleaders, Charlie Barnet never had any problem with his younger sidemen wanting to play and write bebop. His band sounded fairly modern by 1947 and was almost futuristic two years later.

This CD has all of Barnet's Capitol recordings, including "Redskin Rhumba" from 1948 (cut during a recording strike), four dance band numbers from 1950, and the 17 songs from 1949. One of the most modern big bands of that year, the last significant version of Barnet's Orchestra at one point in time had three screamers in the trumpet section (Maynard Ferguson, Doc Severinsen, and Ray Wetzel), plus the boppish soloist Rolf Ericson. Other sidemen heard from include trombonist Herbie Harper, altoist Vinnie Dean, tenor saxophonist Dick Hafer (who had a much cooler tone than Barnet), and pianist Claude Williamson (showcased on "Claude Reigns"). With arrangements by Manny Albam, Gil Fuller, Pete Rugolo, Dave Matthews, Johnny Richards, Tiny Kahn, and Paul Villepigue, the music was light years away from Barnet's "Cherokee" band. Among the more colorful selections are "Cu-Ba," two versions of "Charlie's Other Aunt," Matthews's "Portrait of Edward Kennedy Ellington," "Bebop Spoken Here" (which has vocals by Dave Lambert and Buddy Stewart), "Claude Reigns," and "Really?" This radical reworking of "All the Things You Are" (which features Maynard Ferguson) was originally withdrawn due to the protests of Jerome Kern's estate!

LPS TO SEARCH FOR

During 1977–82, RCA reissued every recording by the bandleader for the label on six double-LPs titled *The Com-* *plete Charlie Barnet Volumes I–VI* (Bluebird AXM2-5526, 5577, 5581, 5585, 5587, and 5590). While the first twofer (which covers the 1935–38 period) is quite erratic, with some hot Swing numbers (including "Growlin'," "Nagasaki," and "Devil's Holiday") overshadowed by too many dull vocals (including eight by Barnet) and dated arrangements, the other five sets are all well worth acquiring since RCA has not yet reissued the majority of its Charlie Barnet recordings on CD. Barnet did very few weak recordings during the 1939–42 period. Also of interest but in the rarity category are *Jazz Oasis* (Capitol 1403), which finds Barnet in 1960 in his only quartet date, and *Big Band 1967* (Creative World 1056), Barnet's final recording; altoist Willie Smith (who was also making his last recorded session) has a few fine solos.

FILMS

Charlie Barnet appeared in many band shorts and quite a few movies, although generally just for a song or two. He jams with Louis Armstrong, Tommy Dorsey, and Benny Goodman in the Danny Kaye film *A Song Is Born* (1946), is in the famous jam session scene with Art Tatum in *The Fabulous Dorseys* (1947) and pops up on the closing number of *Syncopation* (1942). Less known are his appearances in *Juke Box Jenny* (1942), *Music in Manhattan* (1944), *Jam Session* (1944), *Freddie Steps Out* (1946), *Idea Girl* (1946), and *The Big Beat* (1957).

COUNT BASIE PART 1
b. Aug. 21, 1904, Red Bank, NJ, d. Apr. 26, 1984, Hollywood, CA

It has been said of Count Basie that he was not merely a pianist or a bandleader but an institution. His two orchestras (the first of which is covered in this biography) set the standard for swinging big bands, epitomizing the word *Swing*. When his Kansas City group came to New York in late 1936, it was not long before the Basie band became a major influence on many other Swing orchestras, including those of Benny Goodman and (when it was formed a couple years later) Harry James.

Count Basie, who was originally a stride pianist influenced by Fats Waller, cut back his style to the bare essentials, playing simple rhythmic figures with his right hand and leaving lots of space with his left. His drummer, Jo Jones, shifted the time-keeping role from the usual bass drum to the cymbals, while bassist Walter Page and guitarist Freddie Green played four-to-the-bar and kept the rhythm steady and flowing. The result was a much lighter ensemble sound than had been common in most Swing bands, and it realigned the function of the rhythm section.

After a short period playing drums in a kids' band, Bill Basie switched to piano. He was encouraged by Fats Waller, who at the time was playing organ for silent movies. Years later Basie would follows Fats's lead and become one of the first jazz organists during infrequent occasions. Basie played locally in New Jersey and New York (including with June Clark and Elmer Snowden), and picked up several years of experience working with traveling revues in theaters. After two years with the Gonzelle White Show, he was left stranded when the show broke up in Kansas City in 1927. He soon gained a job accompanying silent pictures, enjoyed the local music scene, and decided to stay. A year later he joined Walter Page's Blue Devils, and then in 1929 became a member of Bennie Moten's Orchestra, the top Midwest territory big band of the decade. Although Moten was himself a pianist, he was so impressed with Basie that he ceded the piano spot to the younger player. Basie was featured on many of Moten's recordings from 1929 on, including a classic set in 1932 when the band featured trumpeter Hot Lips Page and tenor saxophonist Ben Webster.

Basie formed his own group in early 1934 in Little Rock, Arkansas but he soon rejoined Moten. When Bennie Moten died in 1935 from a botched tonsillectomy, the ensemble was taken over by Bennie's brother, Buster Moten. After a short time Basie again went out on his own, first with a trio, then as coleader of the Barons of Rhythm with altoist Buster Smith before completely taking over its leadership. Dubbed "Count" by a radio announcer around this time, Basie used several Moten alumni as the nucleus of his band, including Hot Lips Page (who was soon lured away), singer Jimmy Rushing, trombonists Dan Minor and Eddie Durham, baritonist Jack Washington, and bassist Walter Page. In addition, Basie's band soon featured a brilliant young tenor saxophonist, Lester Young, whose cool tone (a major contrast to Coleman Hawkins's harder sound, which was the dominant influence of the time) fit the swinging ensemble perfectly. Fellow tenor Herschel Evans (who was closer in tone to Hawkins) was an excellent contrast to Young, and the band also included (by 1936) trumpeter Buck Clayton (who was passing through Kansas City and discovered Basie's band), drummer Jo Jones, and guitarist-violinist Claude Williams.

The band's regular broadcast from the Reno Club on station W9XBY was heard one night by talent scout John Hammond in Chicago, who was so impressed that he immediately flew out to Kansas City and persuaded Basie to come East. Because Basie's band was only nine pieces at the time, he had to add some members to his orchestra (which up to that point had mostly played spontaneous head arrangements) in a hurry, and it took a few months for his big band to solidify. Their stay in Chicago at the Grand Terrace Ballroom did not work well (since the Count at the time had too many weak sight readers who could not play the music properly for specialty acts), and it took about a year in New York before Count Basie's Orchestra was considered one of the major Swing bands. By then John Hammond had gotten Basie to make some changes, including replacing Claude Williams with Freddie Green (Hammond was not fond of jazz violinists) and adding Earl Warren as lead alto.

By late 1937, Basie's Swing machine was impressing everyone, and its Decca recordings (which included his theme "One O'Clock Jump," "Jumpin' at the Woodside," blues numbers for Jimmy Rushing, and many riff-filled originals) were selling well. With the additions of trumpeter Harry "Sweets" Edison and trombonists Benny Morton and Dickie Wells, the group's solo strength was soon improved. Billie Holiday spent part of 1937–38 with the band (unfortunately she was signed to another label and made no commercial recordings with Basie during the era), but her successor, Helen Humes, made a better match with Jimmy Rushing. July 1938 to January 1939 was spent at the Famous Door in New York (where Basie's band really caught on), and then a six-month stay in Chicago was another success. A major loss was suffered when Herschel Evans suddenly died in February 1939. Luckily his replacement was Buddy Tate, who would be a fixture with the band for nine years.

Count Basie's Orchestra appeared at two of John Hammond's Spirituals to Swing concerts, in 1938 and 1939, and the following year Basie recorded as part of the Benny Goodman Sextet. There was brief talk at the time of both Goodman and Basie breaking up their orchestras and teaming up in an all-star small group with Buck Clayton, Lester Young, Charlie Christian, and the Basie rhythm section, but that never happened. Basie did record occasional combo sides (including the original versions of "Lester Leaps In" and "Dickie's Dream"), but most of his work in the 1940s was with his big band. Lester Young's decision to suddenly leave in 1941 was a major blow. He would return for a period from 1943–44, but otherwise his spot was taken by an impressive series of young tenors, including Don Byas, Illinois Jacquet, Lucky Thompson, and Paul Gonsalves. World War II led to several of Basie's stars being drafted (including Young, Jo Jones, Buck Clayton, and Walter Page), but his orchestra was able to survive any individual's departure. Other important players in Basie's band in the 1940s included trumpeters Emmett Berry, Joe Newman, Al Killian, and Clark Terry, altoist Tab Smith, and trombonist Vic Dickenson.

Count Basie's Orchestra was powerful enough at first to survive the end of the big band era and the rise of bebop. His big band had set the stage for bop (particularly in the playing of Lester Young and Basie's rhythm section), and its recordings of 1947–49 found bop being utilized in some arrangements, although the band's swinging style was virtually unchanged. But bad business deals and the difficulties of keeping a big band finally caused Count Basie to reluctantly break up his institution in August 1949. He would emerge a few months later leading a small group, and then a couple years later he began making an unlikely comeback as a big bandleader, one whose later success would dwarf that of his first band.

●

10 *The Complete Decca Recordings / Jan. 21, 1937–Feb. 4, 1939 / GRP/Decca 3-611*

8 *Rock-a-Bye Basie / Aug. 9, 1938–Mar. 7, 1940 / Vintage Jazz Classics 1033*

The Complete Decca Recordings, a three-CD set, is one of those reissues that every Swing fan has to own for their collections to be considered even semi-respectable. All 57 of the selections recorded by the Basie big band for Decca (plus six alternate takes) are here, including such Swing classics as "Honeysuckle Rose," "Boogie-Woogie," the original version of "One O'Clock Jump," "John's Idea," "Topsy," "Out the Window," "Sent for You Yesterday and Here You Come Today," "Every Tub," "Swingin' the Blues," "Blue and Sentimental," "Doggin' Around," the original "Jumpin' at the Woodside," "Shorty George," "You Can Depend on Me," and "Jive at Five." Few of the tracks are less than great, and one can hear such players as Lester Young, Herschel Evans, Buck Clayton, Harry "Sweets" Edison, and Dickie Wells, plus singer Jimmy Rushing in top form. The Count Basie band really made it big during its long engagement at the Famous Door. *Rock-a-Bye Basie* is taken from radio broadcasts during that period (August–October 1938 and June–July 1939 with two later cuts). Although the recording quality sometimes varies and a few numbers are incomplete, this is the best example of the early Basie band playing live onstage. The key musicians were all still in place and, in addition to their standbys, one gets to hear the band jam such otherwise unrecorded numbers as "Nagasaki," "King Porter Stomp," Eddie Durham's "Wo-Ta-Ta," "Yeah Man," and "Darktown Strutters Ball."

7 *The Essential Count Basie, Vol. 1 / Oct. 9, 1936–June 24, 1939 / Columbia 40608*

7 *The Essential Count Basie, Vol. 2 / Aug. 4, 1939–May 31, 1940 / Columbia 40835*

6 *The Essential Count Basie, Vol. 3 / Aug. 8, 1940 –Apr. 10, 1941 / Columbia 44150*

Unlike with Decca, Columbia has only reissued some of its very valuable Count Basie recordings as three samplers. The pair of ten-LP sets put out in the late 1970s by French Columbia are much preferred but impossible to find. There are many gems on these three CDs, including Lester Young's classic solo on *Vol. 1*'s "Lady Be Good" (the lone date from 1936), "Rock-a-Bye Basie," and "Taxi War Dance." *Vol. 2* has "Lester Leaps In," "Dickie's Dream," and "Tickle Toe," while the last volume includes Coleman Hawkins guesting quite successfully on "9:20 Special" and "Feedin' the Bean." But Count Basie's Columbia recordings in general remain some of the most important Swing music sessions to thus far be neglected by domestic labels.

9 *Old Manuscripts, Broadcast Transcriptions / July 1943–1945 / Music & Arts 884*

8 *Beaver Junction / May 27, 1944–Nov. 12, 1947 / Vintage Jazz Classics 1018*

The wartime Count Basie Orchestra is heard live on these enjoyable and very spirited performances. *Old Manuscripts* is of particular interest, because ten of the 25 songs (taken from radio broadcasts) are from the period when Lester Young had rejoined his former boss; Pres is explosive during a long solo on "Jumpin' at the Woodside." There are also many spots for Buddy Tate, Dickie Wells, and Harry "Sweets" Edison, a few solos by Lucky Thompson and Joe Newman, and vocals from Jimmy Rushing, Thelma Carpenter, Earle Warren, and Maxine Johnson. *Beaver Junction* draws its material from Basie's 1944 V-Disc sessions (although these are either alternate takes or previously unissued performances), and three Jubilee radio broadcasts, two from 1944 and the last one from 1947. Lester Young is on the V-Discs, and one of the 1944 Jubilee programs has Buddy Rich joyfully filling in for Jo Jones. Other stars include Rushing, Newman, Edison, Tate, Wells, and Illinois Jacquet.

9 *1947: Brand New Wagon / Jan. 3, 1947–Dec. 12, 1947 / Bluebird 2292*

Although far from complete, *Brand New Wagon* (which has 21 of the 40 selections recorded by Count Basie in 1947) has most of the high points of that busy year. Seven selections are performed with a small group that includes Emmett Berry and Paul Gonsalves (who is featured on "Sugar"). Among the big band titles, "Your Red Wagon," "One O'Clock Boogie," "South," and "Robbins' Nest" are highlights. *Shouting Blues* has 17 of the 19 big band selections that Count Basie's big band recorded in 1949 before it broke up. The orchestra was quite strong at the time, with such soloists as Harry Edison, Emmett Berry, and Clark Terry in the trumpet section, Dicky Wells, Paul Gonsalves, and Basie himself. Jimmy Rushing was still aboard, and the boppish arrangements by C. O. Price were quite up-to-date. But the shrinking market for big bands and bad luck in business led to the orchestra breaking up shortly after its August 5 session. This fine CD concludes with three of the four numbers cut on February 6, 1950, during Count Basie's first recording with his new small group, an octet including Edison, Wells, and both Georgie Auld and Gene Ammons on tenors. It is a pity, though, that three selections in all were bypassed, keeping this from being a "complete" collection.

LPS TO SEARCH FOR

The Count at the Chatterbox (Jazz Archives 16) is a set of live broadcasts featuring the Count Basie Orchestra right after they first arrived in New York, when Claude Williams was still the band's occasional violin specialist; it dates from January and February 1937. Well worth bidding on in auction lists are a couple of remarkable ten-LP sets: *The Complete Count Basie, Vol. 1–10, 1936–1941* (CBS 66101) and *The Complete Count Basie, Vol. 11–20, 1941–1951* (CBS 66102). Every one of Basie's Columbia recordings are here, with many alternate takes. Although one may not need four versions of "It's Square But It Rocks," five of "One-Two-Three-O'Lairy," or six of "Wild Bill's Boogie," the hits far outnumber the misses. The second box (which has Basie's big band sides of 1941–46) concludes with all of the music recorded during two extensive sessions by Basie's 1950 octet plus four big band titles (including "Little Pony") from 1951. *1942* (Tax 8025) has the Count's small group titles of July 24, 1942 (quartet romps plus some sextet numbers with Buck Clayton and Don Byas), and his July 27 big band session. *1944* (Hindsight 224) contains radio transcriptions featuring both Lester Young and Illinois Jacquet on tenors, singers Jimmy Rushing and Thelma Carpenter, and guest clarinetist Artie Shaw (on "Lady Be Good" and "Bird Calls"). Other worthwhile radio transcriptions from the period are featured on *1944* (Circle 60) and *More 1944* (Circle 130). *The Basie Special* (Everybody's 3004) has some of Basie's better radio performances (mostly from late 1944), and his V-Discs (dating from 1943–45) are reissued on *V-Discs* (Jazz Society 505) and *V-Discs, Vol. 2* (Jazz Society 506).

FILMS

Count Basie's Orchestra made two brief "Soundies" in 1941 (*Air Mail Special* and *Take Me Back, Baby*) and appeared in *Harlemania* (1938), *Policy Man* (1938), *Crazy House* (1943), *Hit Parade of 1943* (1943), *Reveille with Beverly* (1943, in which they play a classic version of "One O'Clock Jump"), *Stage Door Canteen* (1943, accompanying Ethel Waters on "Quicksand"), and *Top Man* (1943).

BUNNY BERIGAN
b. Nov. 2, 1908, Hilbert, WI, d. June 2, 1942, New York, NY

One of the greatest soloists in jazz history and arguably the top Swing trumpeter of 1935–38, Bunny Berigan was a brilliant player. He had a consistently warm tone, whether playing low notes or fairly high ones, his dramatic improvisations were full of chance-taking, and he had a very impressive technique in addition to being a strong sight reader. Berigan made his impact felt on nearly every session that he was on, and he was quite capable of playing Swing, Dixieland, and commercial music at a very high level.

Unfortunately Berigan was also an severe alcoholic, whose excessive drinking led to his life being greatly shortened. There have been many legendary tales of Bunny falling off the bandstand during performances (including on the radio, when he was supposed to be taking a solo with Tommy Dorsey). Although he was reasonably well-behaved when intoxicated (and still able to play quite well when he wasn't falling), his drinking eventually caught up with him.

Berigan began playing violin as a child before switching to trumpet. He worked with local bands, including the jazz group at the University of Wisconsin (although he did not attend college) and with territory bands. Bunny's big break occurred in 1930 when Hal Kemp hired him; he had been rejected in 1928 due to his weak tone, but soon discovered Louis Armstrong and completely changed his way of playing. After a European tour and some recordings, Berigan became part of the New York studio scene, working often with Fred Rich's Orchestra, spending a few months with Paul Whiteman (1932–33), and appearing on a countless number of recordings opposite such studio players as Benny Goodman, Tommy Dorsey, and Jimmy Dorsey. Even in the most commercial settings, Bunny's trumpet was a major asset, and his recordings with the Dorsey Brothers and the Boswell Sisters made it obvious that an exciting new trumpeter was on the scene.

In June 1935, with the rise of the big band era, Bunny Berigan was persuaded to leave the studios to work with Benny Goodman. Although with BG for only three months, Berigan was part of Goodman's initial success. He took famous solos on hit recordings of "King Porter Stomp" and "Sometimes I'm Happy," and traveled as part of the band as they went cross country from New York to Los Angeles in their dramatic rise to fame. However, the lure of the studio and its lucrative pay soon resulted in Berigan's returning to New York and continuing his freelance work on recordings and on radio. He occasionally led his own pickup bands, and in early 1937 thought seriously of putting together his own orchestra. But first Berigan accepted Tommy Dorsey's offer to join his band. During the six weeks that he was with TD, lightning struck again, and Berigan's choruses on Dorsey's records of "Marie" and "Song of India" pushed the trombonist's orchestra into the big time. In fact, those two solos with Dorsey became so famous that in later years they were orchestrated for TD's full trumpet section to play.

Now it was time for Bunny Berigan to enter the big band wars and see if he could have the same success that he had given to others. He formed an orchestra of his own after leaving Dorsey and soon had a recording contract with Victor and a big hit in "I Can't Get Started." With the young tenor saxophonist Georgie Auld as a top soloist and Buddy Rich on drums, Berigan had a promising new band. His drinking began to cause problems, however, and after a strong start in 1937, the band stalled the following year. Considered a minor-league outfit by then despite its leader's star appeal, the orchestra was often given inferior material to record by its label (it would be difficult to save such weak tunes as "An Old Straw Hat," " 'Round the Old Deserted Farm," and "Rinka Tinka Man!"), and opportunities were being missed. By 1939 (which ironically found the band recording better songs, including a set of Bix Beiderbecke tunes), Berigan's playing was starting to decline a bit, and his orchestra still had not come up with a second hit. The following year the trumpeter was forced to declare bankruptcy, and the three-year-old Bunny Berigan Orchestra came to an end.

Berigan went back to Tommy Dorsey's band, where he stayed six months, contributing a few solos (including on "I'm Nobody's Baby" and "East of the Sun") but sliding steadily downhill. His drinking accelerated, and Dorsey was forced to let him go. Berigan made two further attempts to lead his own big bands, but both his playing and his health steadily declined until he died from pneumonia and various drinking-related ailments when he was 33. Perhaps if there had been an Alcoholics Anonymous in the early 1940s, Bunny Berigan might have had a much longer life instead of becoming a quickly burnt-out legend.

●

7 *The ARC Years: 1931–36 / Feb. 21, 1931–Sep. 23, 1936 / IAJRC 1013*
During the period covered by this CD, Bunny Berigan appeared on an enormous amount of recordings, often playing commercial music with studio orchestras. Quite a few of the sessions include Berigan solos, including the 24 rarities on this disc; 19 are from 1931–32, and the remainder date from 1934 or 1936. Bunny is heard with orchestras led by Freddie Rich, Eddie Kirkeby, Bennie Kruger, and Smith Ballew, plus

the ARC House Orchestra and a few very anonymous groups. The dance music is easy to take and consistently uplifted by Berigan's contributions.

10 *The Pied Piper (1934–40) / Nov. 20, 1934–Aug. 3, 1940 / Bluebird 66615*
Although it is not a "complete" set of Bunny Berigan recordings, this single CD perfectly sums up the high-points of his career. Mostly in chronological order, the 22-song

program features Berigan on four songs with Benny Goodman (including "King Porter Stomp" and "Sometimes I'm Happy"), an obscure number apiece with Gene Gifford and Frankie Trumbauer, two cuts in an all-star quintet with Tommy Dorsey and Fats Waller (a classic "Honeysuckle Rose" and "Blues"), four songs with TD in 1937 (highlighted by the hits "Song of India" and "Marie"), eight numbers with his own orchestra (including "I Can't Get Started" and his exciting version of "The Prisoner's Song"), and "I've Found a New Baby" from a radio appearance with Dorsey in 1940. This is a perfect "greatest hits" package.

9 *Down by the Old Mill Stream / Oct. 22, 1936–1939 / Jazz Archives 3801112*

Containing some of Bunny Berigan's best radio appearances (mostly with his big band during 1938–39 but also three numbers with a radio orchestra in 1936), this CD features the trumpeter in peak form. His workout on "Down by the Old Mill Stream" shows off his entire range, and other highlights include "Dardanella," "Devil's Holiday," "Shanghai Shuffle," and "I'll Always Be in Love with You."

8 *Volume 1: Sing! Sing! Sing! / July 20, 1936 + June 27, 1938 / Jass 627*

7 *Volume 2, 1938: Devil's Holiday! / June 27, 1938 + Aug. 9, 1938 / Jass 638*

All of Bunny Berigan's radio transcriptions, formerly out on budget LPs, have been reissued in full on this pair of Jass CDs. The first 20 selections are from a marathon session in 1936, and actually predate the Bunny Berigan Orchestra. Berigan's ensemble does not have any names among the sidemen other than the clarinetist, who could possibly be Artie Shaw. The musicianship is excellent, the vocals by Peggy Lawson are easy to take, and there is plenty of Bunny's horn on such numbers as a pre-Benny Goodman "Sing, Sing, Sing," "I'm an Old Cowhand," "San Francisco," and "Dardanella." The final five selections of *Vol. 1* (part of another 20-song session) are from June 27, 1938, and feature Berigan's regular big band of the time with a vocal apiece

from Ruth Gaylor and Bernie Mackey ("Flat Foot Floogie"). The second CD has the remaining 15 numbers from the June 27 session, and 12 of the 16 titles cut on August 9. A third volume, which was supposed to complete this series, was never released. Berigan had faded just a little in 1938, although he is in generally good form throughout the performances. His band was not given that much strong material to record during the era, and Dick Wharton's five vocals are annoying, so a few of these tunes are throwaways, but the versions of "Shanghai Shuffle," "Devil's Holiday," "The Wearing of the Green," "Sunday," "I'll Always Be in Love with You," and "Sing You Sinners" are among the highlights. Georgie Auld, clarinetist Joe Dixon, and trombonist Ray Conniff have their spots, and Buddy Rich is on the later session.

LPS TO SEARCH FOR

The Great Soloists—Bunny Berigan (Biograph 10) has a cross-section of some of the trumpeter's better sideman appearances, including dates with the Boswell Sisters ("Everybody Loves My Baby"), the Dorsey Brothers, the Mound City Blue Blowers, Dick McDonough, and a few of his earlier small-group sessions. Bluebird, in a trio of double-LPs titled *The Complete Bunny Berigan Vols. I–III* (AXM2-5584, AXM2-5657, and 9953-1-RB), reissued all of the Berigan Orchestra's recordings of 1937–39. Classics has put out the same material on CD, but the LPs also have extensive liner notes. *Vols. 1* and *3* contain many strong moments, while *Vol. 2* has plenty of examples of the terrible turkeys that Berigan was persuaded to record, including "Piano Tuner Man," "Lovelight in the Starlight," "Moonshine over Kentucky," and "Never Felt Better, Never Had Less!" Also valuable but very difficult to find will be the Berigan releases of rarities put out by Bozy White's tiny Shoestring label.

FILMS

Bunny Berigan's only appearance on film was in 1936, playing "China Boy" and "Until Today" (a feature that also included a brief vocal) with Fred Rich's Orchestra.

WILL BRADLEY

d. July 12, 1912, Newton, NJ, d. July 15, 1989, Flemington, NJ

Trombonist Will Bradley's main joy was playing warm ballads, so it is ironic that he became best known for leading an orchestra that specialized in hot boogie-woogie numbers. Born Wilbur Schwichtenberg, Bradley grew up in Washington, New Jersey, moving to New York in 1928. After spending time playing with the bands of Milt Shaw and Red Nichols, Bradley became a busy studio musician, working for CBS. Other than a period playing with Ray Noble's American Band (1935–36), he kept busy in the studios and would have remained there were it not for the persuasive talents of MCA's Willard Alexander. Alexander convinced Bradley that he should be leading his own big band, using drummer and occasional singer Ray McKinley as the unofficial co-leader.

With future bandleader Freddy Slack on piano and the fine hot trumpeter Steve Lipkins, the Bradley band worked steadily but seemed destined to remain in the second rung of orchestras until McKinley and Slack began to wonder how it might sound to have boogie-woogie (which was beginning to become quite popular) played by a full big band. The result was Bradley's biggest hit, "Beat Me Daddy, Eight to the Bar." A jukebox favorite, that song was soon followed by "Rock-a-Bye the Boogie," "Scrub Me, Mama with a Boogie Beat," "I Boogied When I Should Have Woogied," "Boogie Woogie Conga," "Bounce Me Brother with a Solid Four," "Booglie Wooglie Piggy," and "Fry Me Cookie with a Can of Lard!" The Bradley Orchestra also played more straightforward tunes and had hits with "Down the Road a Piece" and the eccentric "Celery Stalks at Midnight," but it was always most famous for the boogie-woogie blues numbers.

By February 1942, Bradley was tired of the routine (boogie-woogie had largely run its course anyway) and he split with McKinley, who formed his own orchestra. Neither big band was around long (Bradley's lasted until July with the young Shelly Manne in McKinley's spot), and the trombonist went back to the studios. Other than emerging now and then (including cutting eight Dixieland titles in 1953), Will Bradley was happy to live the obscure but comfortable life of a studio musician.

●

9 *Hallelujah / Sept. 19, 1939–Mar. 15, 1940 / Hep 1061*
Subtitled *Vol. 1,* this CD has 24 of the first 30 selections cut by the Will Bradley Orchestra, skipping six indifferent vocal numbers. Among the better selections are "The Love Nest," "Memphis Blues," "I'm Comin' Virginia," "Celery Stalks at Midnight," "Strange Cargo," "Jimtown Blues," and "Rhumboogie." "Beat Me Daddy, Eight to the Bar" was still two months in the future when this CD ended, so the emphasis here is on solid Swing with occasional vocals by Ray McKinley and Carlotta Dale.

7 *Best of the Big Bands / Sept. 19, 1939–June 23, 1941 /*
Columbia 46151
Will Bradley recordings are a bit scarce on CD. This 1990 CD from Columbia unfortunately has breezy liner notes by Will Friedwald, but no personnel listing or mention of the recording dates. The Bradley band's main big sellers are here (including "Celery Stalks at Midnight," "Beat Me Daddy, Eight to the Bar," "Down the Road A-Piece," and "From the Land of the Sky-Blue Water") along with some

lesser-known vocal numbers, making this a worthwhile if not definitive acquisition which will do until a more logical release comes along.

LPS TO SEARCH FOR

The collectors' Ajax label released nine LPs that contain every recording put out under Will Bradley's name, not only seven albums of his big band titles from 1939–42 and orchestra dates from 1946 and 1947, but three small-group dates, including eight Dixieland selections with tenor saxophonist Bud Freeman and either Yank Lawson or Rex Stewart on trumpet/cornet in 1953 (on *Vol. 9*). The recording quality of these albums is not always the best, but they do give one an opportunity to hear everything. The Bandstand label came out with two LPs, *Rock-a-Bye the Boogie* (Bandstand 7112) and *Let's Dance* (Bandstand 7110), both of which contain 16 of Bradley's big band performances from the 1939–42 period. In addition, Bradley's radio transcriptions are heard on *Featuring Ray McKinley—1941* (Circle 88), a Swing (rather than boogie-woogie) oriented program that has pianist Freddie Slack often taking solo honors.

RANDY BROOKS

b. 1917, Sanford, ME, d. Mar. 21, 1967, Sanford, ME

Trumpeter Randy Brooks led a big band just when the Swing era was ending. He had a bit of success, but then was cut down by a stroke, which is why he is not remembered by many today.

Brooks started on the trumpet at age six, and five years later he was discovered by singer Rudy Vallee. Due to his age, Brooks was featured with Vallee's Connecticut Yankees as a type of child prodigy for two years. After finishing school, he played with the big bands of Hal Kemp, Claude Thornhill, Bob Allen, Art Jarrett (the Kemp ghost orchestra), and Les Brown (1944–45). When he started his own big band in 1945, Brooks was fairly successful, having hit records in "Tenderly" (a million-seller), "Harlem Nocturne," and "The Man with the Horn." The arrangements of the unrelated John Benson Brooks gave the big band its own personality as did Brooks's melancholy horn (best on ballads). The group in 1946 also featured for a short time the young Stan Getz on tenor. After breaking up the big band a couple of years later, Brooks married the glamorous bandleader Ina Ray Hutton and moved to the West Coast, where he probably would have worked in the studios. But a devastating stroke ended his promising career and, after years of being incapacitated, he died in a fire at his mother's home.

●

LPS TO SEARCH FOR

Long overdue to be rediscovered, Randy Brooks's 25 studio recordings for Decca would make a dandy CD, but no one has thought of it yet! Twelve of his best sides from 1946–47 were put out on the hard-to-find *Trumpet Moods* (Decca 8201), a definitive set that includes "Tenderly," "The Man with the Horn," "Harlem Nocturne," and a variety of superior instrumentals. The majority of Brooks's radio transcriptions are on *1944* (First Time Records 1511) and *1945–1947* (Circle 35).

LES BROWN

b. Mar. 14, 1912, Reinerton, PA

Of all the big bandleaders of the Swing era, Les Brown has led his orchestra the longest, over 60 years. Although never the most famous, colorful, or exciting band, the Les Brown Orchestra has always been quite reliable and consistent. The same could be said for the bandleader, who originally played clarinet and saxophones, but largely gave that up in the 1940s. Brown was a leader from the beginning of his career. While attending Duke University, in 1935 he formed his first big band, the Duke Blue Devils. That ensemble broke up after a year; Brown freelanced as both a player and an arranger, and then formed the Les Brown Orchestra in 1938. Influenced initially by Benny Goodman but developing its own sound over time, the Brown band worked steadily during the Swing era and had a huge hit in 1944 with "Sentimental Journey," which featured the singing of Doris Day. "Leap Frog" was its theme song, and in 1948 the release of "I've Got My Love to Keep Me Warm" (which was actually recorded in 1946 but not put out at the time) was one of the last big band Swing hits. By that time, trombonist Stumpy Brown (Les's brother), tenor saxophonist Ted Nash, and baritonist Butch Stone (known for his good-natured vocals) were fixtures with the orchestra.

Most of the Swing era big bands broke up during 1946–47, but Les Brown and His Band of Renown had a lucky break. He started working with Bob Hope on the radio, and the association lasted a half-century, keeping his orchestra in business. Although Brown recorded some fairly boppish arrangements in 1949, his band retained its original Swing sound through the decades. In the 1950s it was one of the finest big bands around, with Lucy Ann Polk and Jo Ann Greer being among the singers and including such strong soloists as tenorman Dave Pell, trombonist Ray Sims, and trumpeter Don Fagerquist. In

Les Brown led (and still leads!) one of the most consistent of all Swing bands. This photo, from August 1942, has among the sidemen trumpeter Billy Butterfield, trombonist Si Zentner, clarinetist Gus Bivona, and drummer Shelly Manne.

fact, the Dave Pell Octet (a major cool jazz group in the mid-1950s) was formed out of the personnel of the Brown big band. Although less active (other than its association with Bob Hope) in later years, Les Brown still gathered together his orchestra on a part-time basis in the 1990s for special appearances and concerts.

●

8 *Best of the Big Bands / Sep. 17, 1941–Mar. 14, 1961 / Columbia 45344*

The packaging is quite faulty on this poorly planned CD (why no personnel listings or recording dates?), but overall this is a fine "greatest hits" collection of Les Brown and His Band of Renown. The biggest sellers ("Leap Frog," "Sentimental Journey," "Bizet Has His Day," and "I've Got My Love to Keep Me Warm") are here, as are some of the better instrumentals. Overall this CD is the perfect place to begin exploring Les Brown's music, at least until a better collection comes along.

7 *Doris Day with Les Brown—Best of the Big Bands / Nov. 28, 1940–Sept. 14, 1946 / Columbia 46244*

6 *Les Brown and His Great Vocalists / May 22, 1941– Nov. 14, 1950 / Legacy/Columbia 66373*

Doris Day was Les Brown's vocalist during 1940–41 and 1945–46, and 16 of her better recordings with Brown are on the first CD, although not "Sentimental Journey." Unfortunately, once again there are no personnel listings or recording dates, but the music (highlighted by "Aren't You Glad You're You," "We'll Be Together Again," "There's Good Blues Tonight," and "It Could Happen to You") is consistently excellent and shows how strong a singer Doris Day could be. The second CD has 16 other vocal numbers, including three more by Day ("Sentimental Journey," "My Dreams Are Getting Better All the Time," and "Day by Day"). In addition, there are cuts featuring the vocalizing of Butch Stone ("A Good Man Is Hard to Find"), Betty Booney, Ralph Young, Gordon Drake, Jack Haskell, Eileen Wilson, Ray Kellogg, Stumpy Brown, Betty Taylor, and the underrated Lucy Ann Polk. The Brown Orchestra mostly plays a very supportive role on this fine collection.

6 *Les Brown and His Band of Renown / 1957 / Hindsight 252*

5 *22 Original Big Band Recordings / 1957 / Hindsight 408*

Both of these CDs are taken from a series of radio appearances that Les Brown made in 1957, with all of the performances being quite brief. With the exception of the lone instrumental "My Baby Just Cares for Me," the first set puts the focus completely on vocalists: Julie London, Jo Ann Greer, and June Christy, with one contribution ("Oh Baby") from Stumpy Brown. The vocalists are in good form with London's "September in the Rain," Greer's "Love Me or Leave Me," and Christy's portion overall (she performs seven numbers, including "Midnight Sun" and "I'll Take Romance") being highlights. Not recommended so much to Les Brown collectors as to fans of the three female singers, the band has little to do, and the renditions are generally quite brief. The best thing about *22 Original Big Band Recordings* is the singing of Jo Ann Greer, whose basic delivery and quietly swinging approach are quite appealing. The band swings nicely, but the lack of any stretching out (the longest song barely exceeds three minutes) by soloists is a disappointment.

6 *Digital Swing / Nov. 21, 1986 + Dec. 8, 1986 / Fantasy 9650*

To celebrate his 50th anniversary as a bandleader, Les Brown recorded for the first time in years in 1986. Two veterans of the early days are here (baritonist Butch Stone and bass trombonist Stumpy Brown), although neither has a single solo. With contributions from trumpeter Don Rader, trombonist Andy Martin, guitarist Mundell Lowe, pianist Eric Doney, and drummer Jack Sperling (who pushes the band) on a set dominated by standards (but no remakes of earlier hits), this is a solid swinging set. Nothing unusual occurs, but the music is pleasing.

LPS TO SEARCH FOR

The Early Years (Golden Era 15045) features Les Brown's first band, the Duke Blue Devils, during 1936–37. *The Uncollected Les Brown* (Hindsight 103) focuses on Brown's orchestra during 1944–46, when it was particularly strong; Doris Day has five vocals including an alternate version of "Sentimental Journey." *The Uncollected Les Brown Vol. 2* and *Vol. 3* (Hindsight 131 and 132) are both from 1949 and a bit unusual, because a few selections display the influence of bebop, including most notably "Boptized" and "Bopple Sauce." Among the soloists at the time were trumpeter Frank Beach, trombonist Ray Sims, clarinetist Abe Most, and tenor saxophonist Dave Pell. The boppish trend would soon disappear from Les Brown's band as the ensemble went back to its more conventional swinging ways.

FILMS

In addition to many band shorts, the Les Brown Orchestra appears in *Seven Days Leave* (1942) and *Rockabilly Baby* (1957).

WILLIE BRYANT

b. Aug. 30, 1908, New Orleans, LA, d. Feb. 9, 1964, Los Angeles, CA

Best-known throughout his career as a master of ceremonies and an occasional singer, Willie Bryant led a notable big band during 1934–38. Bryant, who grew up in Chicago, worked as a dancer and singer in shows (including with the Whitman Sisters) and vaudeville during 1926–33; at one point he shared a number ("Big Fat Ma and Skinny Pa") with Bessie Smith. Forming a big band in late 1934, Bryant recorded 22 selections for Victor and Bluebird during 1935–36, using such sidemen as pianist Teddy Wilson, drummer Cozy Cole, Benny Carter (on trumpet), and tenor saxophonist Ben Webster, among others. However, since those musicians were primarily guests for the recordings, Bryant's regular big band (which recorded four additional tunes in 1938) did not really catch on.

Willie Bryant himself was popular, and he worked for the remainder of his life as an actor (including appearing on Broadway opposite Ethel Waters in 1938's *Mamba's Daughter* and hosting a television series in 1949), an emcee (frequently at the Apollo), disc jockey, and singer. Bryant recorded eight additional songs for Apollo during 1945–49, including his composition "It's Over Because We're Through" and "Blues Around the Clock."

7 *Blues Around the Clock / Oct. 15, 1945–Sept. 30, 1949 / Delmark 685*

All eight of Willie Bryant's final recordings are on this CD, including "Blues Around the Country" and "Blues Around the Clock" (both of which are two-parts), and his original "It's Over Because We're Through," a song featuring the perfect title with which to end his career! Originally cut for the Apollo label, Bryant is heard with three different bands, including the Tab Smith Septet, a big band, and a combo featuring musicians from the Erskine Hawkins Orchestra. He was still in excellent voice, so it is a pity that Bryant did not record more. Also represented on this CD are Doc Pomus (who sings four numbers), Laurel Watson, Bob Range, and Ben Smith. Excellent music that could be considered late period Swing or early rhythm and blues.

LPS TO SEARCH FOR

All of Willie Bryant's big band recordings, except for his four-song date for Decca in 1938, are on the two-LP set *Willie Bryant and Jimmie Lunceford* (Bluebird AXM2-5502). Bryant's vocals are easy to take, and his big band (featuring arrangements by Edgar Battle, Alex Hill, Harry White, and Teddy Wilson) is full of impressive players, including such guests as Benny Carter, Teddy Wilson, and Ben Webster. Of the regular band members, trumpeters Taft Jordan and Edgar Battle and tenorman Johnny Russell are among the stars. The twofer concludes with ten numbers that Jimmie Lunceford cut for the Victor label: two in 1930 and eight (including "Swingin' Uptown" and "White Heat") from 1934.

BLANCHE CALLOWAY

b. 1902, Baltimore, MD, d. Dec. 16, 1978, Baltimore, MD

Blanche Calloway may only be a footnote in jazz history, but she was well known as a vocalist and personality before her younger brother Cab Calloway hit it big. A flamboyant and extroverted singer (Cab considered her an influence), Blanche started working in revues and shows in the early 1920s. She recorded a pair of blues in 1925 (in which she was backed by Louis Armstrong), and in 1931 worked with Andy Kirk's Orchestra in Philadelphia, recording three titles, including her trademark song, the ferocious "I Need Lovin'." What Blanche needed at the time was a big band, and she tried her best to steal Kirk's group away, but only succeeded in getting Kirk's trumpeters, Edgar "Puddinghead" Battle and Clarence Smith, to join her new orchestra, which soon also included tenor saxophonist Ben Webster, pianist Clyde Hart, and drummer Cozy Cole.

Blanche Calloway cut four record dates with her new band (including "Just a Crazy Song," "Make Me Know It," and "I Got What It Takes") in 1931 and one date apiece in 1934 and 1935 (highlighted by "You Ain't Livin' Right" and a remake of "I Need Lovin' "). But while Cab's star was rising, Blanche's was fading out. She broke up her big band in 1938 after declaring bankruptcy, performed in low-profile gigs as a solo singer, ran a successful cosmetic company, and in the 1960s worked as the director of a Florida radio station.

Blanche Calloway's 1931 sessions are available on two LPs. Andy Kirk's *All Out for Hicksville* (Hep 1007) has eight selections by Kirk's Clouds of Joy and the session that Calloway made with Kirk's band; she is heard on two versions of "There's Rhythm in the River" and three of "I Need Lovin'" (which are fascinating to hear back-to-back-to-back!). An album simply titled *Blanche Calloway* (Harlequin 2057) has the master takes of her four following sessions, including such numbers as "Just a Crazy Song," "It's Right Here for You," "Make Me Know It," and "Growlin' Dan."

CAB CALLOWAY

b. Dec. 25, 1907, Rochester, NY, d. Nov. 18, 1994, Hockessin, DE

The most famous black star of the 1930s (even better known for a time than Louis Armstrong and Duke Ellington), an influential performer, an underrated jazz vocalist, and the leader of a series of exciting big bands, Cab Calloway is still a household name today, even if mostly for "Minnie the Moocher." While the singers in many current Retro Swing bands do their best to emulate him, Calloway's magic is very difficult to duplicate, possibly because when he came up he was such a unique performer.

Born Cabell Calloway, Cab grew up in Baltimore and Chicago, sang locally with the Baltimore Melody Boys, attended Crane College, and then (inspired by his older sister Blanche's example) went into show business. He picked up experience working in some lower level shows as a singer and master of ceremonies. Calloway performed briefly with the Missourians in 1928, was in the Fats Waller revue "Hot Chocolates" (which also featured Louis Armstrong), and then took a group called the Alabamians to the Savoy in New York in October 1929. However, that band's musicianship was too primitive, and they did not last long. Calloway then renewed ties with the Missourians, a superior jazz band that was struggling and on the verge of breaking up. He took the group over, renamed it the Cab Calloway Orchestra, and made his recording debut on July 24, 1930, with "Gotta

The dynamic, colorful, and often outrageous Cab Calloway.

Darn Good Reason Now" and an exciting rendition of "St. Louis Blues." From that point on Calloway recorded regularly. After starting a residency at the Cotton Club in February 1931 and waxing "Minnie the Moocher" on March 3, he was on his way to stardom.

Calloway, whose singing could be considered a mixture of Louis Armstrong (in its phrasing and jazz feel), Al Jolson, opera singers, and his own zany personality, was a true original. More than just a singer, Calloway danced colorfully while his band wailed, his conducting with a baton was memorable, and he was always exciting to watch. His scat singing (which could be quite abstract), call-and-response with the audience (with plenty of "Hi-De-Ho's"), and his nutty but nonthreatening stage personality made him a sensation. He was a major attraction throughout the Swing era.

Cab Calloway was always careful to hire the best musicians, pay them top wages, and shield them as much as possible from racism (hiring a private train for road trips). Unlike Benny Goodman and some others, he knew that if his sidemen were top-notch players and potential stars, it made him look good, since he was the leader. Although his band was not always featured all that much on records in the early years, he knew how good they were, and they inspired him. Through the years Calloway's sidemen included trumpeters Doc Cheatham, Dizzy Gillespie, and Jonah Jones, tenor saxophonists Ben Webster, Chu Berry, Illinois Jacquet, Ike Quebec, and Sam "The Man" Taylor, pianist Bennie Payne, guitarist Danny Barker, bassist Milt Hinton, and drummer Cozy Cole, among many others.

Calloway was able to keep his orchestra together until April 1948, but times became tougher and he cut back to a sextet. Cab struggled on, leading combos into 1952 (Jonah Jones and Milt Hinton were with him until then), when he began a two-year run playing the role of "Sportin' Life" in George Gershwin's *Porgy & Bess,* which was only right because Gershwin had originally patterned the role after the singer! During the remainder of his life, Cab Calloway mostly performed as a solo act, sometimes putting together short-term big bands. He always remained a major name and never forgot to sing enthusiastic versions of "Minnie the Moocher" for his audience.

●

10 *Cab Calloway & The Missourians / June 3, 1929–Dec. 23, 1930 / JSP 328*

On this CD the British JSP label reissued all 14 selections recorded by the Missourians, along with the first ten numbers cut by the orchestra after Cab Calloway became its leader. The earlier instrumental sides are strong examples of pre-Swing music, hot performances by a nonet that may have lacked any big names but was full of spirit (as can be heard on such numbers as "Market Street Stomp," "400 Hop," "Swingin' Dem Cats," and "Stoppin' the Traffic"). The Calloway numbers (which are also included in the Classics CD *1930–1931*) show that, even in 1930, Cab was a dynamic performer. He really tears into "St. Louis Blues," "Happy Feet," and "Some of These Days," and his rendition of "St. James Infirmary" is timeless. Even with the duplication, this CD is well worth acquiring for the Missourians selections.

10 *1930–1931 / July 24, 1930–June 17, 1931 / Classics 516*

10 *1931–1932 / July 9, 1931–June 7, 1932 / Classics 526*

9 *1932 / June 7, 1932–Dec. 7, 1932 / Classics 537*

Despite the continual popularity of Cab Calloway, American labels have never reissued the bulk of his recordings, seemingly satisfied with putting out an occasional greatest hits collection. Listeners who want to fully explore Cab Calloway's music are well advised to acquire as many of his dozen CDs from the European Classics label as possible, for these sets contain all of his studio recordings from the 1930–1947 period—virtually his entire big band career. The few alternate takes that have surfaced are skipped over, but otherwise everything is here. The first volume covers Cab Calloway's first 11 months on records, and there are many gems, including the original version of "Minnie the Moocher," "St. Louis Blues," "Some of These Days," "St. James Infirmary," "Blues in My Heart," and "Six or Seven Times." The 23 selections on *1931–1932* are also quite colorful, with Cab sometimes going over the top in his emotional intensity. Among the numbers included are "Bugle Call Rag," "Somebody Stole My Gal," "Trickeration," "Kickin' the Gong Around," "Corinne Corinna," "Cabin in the Cotton," "Minnie the Moocher's Wedding Day," and "Dinah." It may have been the height of the Depression in 1932, with few records being made, but Cab Calloway was such a major star that he cut 32 selections that year. The *1932* CD has such exciting performances as "Old Yazoo," "Reefer Man," "Old Man of the Mountain," "You Gotta Ho-De-Ho," "I've Got the World on a String," "Dixie Doorway," "Beale Street Mama," and "The Man from Harlem." One particularly odd number, "Git Along," finds Calloway matched with the enthusiastic but insipid singer Chick Bullock and steel guitarist Roy Smeck, an experiment not repeated!

8 *1932–1934 / Dec. 7, 1932–Sept. 4, 1934 / Classics 544*

8 *1934–1937 / Sept. 4, 1934–Mar. 3, 1937 / Classics 554*

8 *1937–1938 / Mar. 3, 1937–Mar. 23, 1938 / Classics 568*

During 1930–32, Cab Calloway recorded for the Brunswick and Banner labels. In 1933 he signed with Victor and soon remade "Minnie the Moocher" and "Kickin' the Gong

Around," which only increased his fame. *1932–1934* has Cab singing "Doin' the New Low-Down" on a variety number with Don Redman's Orchestra and the Mills Brothers. Otherwise he is backed by his very capable band, which during the era featured trumpeter Lammar Wright, Eddie Barefield on clarinet, tenor saxophonist Walter Thomas, and pianist Bennie Payne. In addition to the newer versions of old hits, Cab is typically flamboyant on "The Lady with the Fan," "Harlem Camp Meeting," "Zaz Zuh Zaz," "I Learned About Love from Her," " 'Long About Midnight," "Margie," and the bizarre "Chinese Rhythm." *1934–1937* finds Calloway's Orchestra becoming stronger with the additions (by May 1936) of two new sidemen who added a great deal to the band's sound: tenor saxophonist Ben Webster (over three years before he joined Duke Ellington) and bassist Milt Hinton. Among the more memorable selections on this CD are "Keep That Hi-De-Hi in Your Soul," "Nagasaki," "I Love to Sing-A," "Copper Colored Gal," "The Hi-De-Ho Miracle Man," and "That Man Is Here Again." For the *1937–1938* CD, the orchestra was further strengthened by the additions of rhythm guitarist Danny Barker and tenor great Chu Berry (who replaced Ben Webster). Calloway is in typically exuberant form on such numbers as "She's Tall, She's Tan, She's Terrific," "Mama, I Wanna Make Rhythm," and "Hi-De-Ho Romeo," but this set also includes the atmospheric "Azure" and a few instrumentals such as "Queen Isabella," which is actually Berry's "Christopher Columbus!"

7 *1938–1939 / Mar. 23, 1938–Feb. 20, 1939 / Classics 576*

9 *1939–1940 / Mar. 28, 1939–Mar. 8, 1940 / Classics 595*

8 *1940 / Mar. 8, 1940–Aug. 28, 1940 / Classics 614*
Although it was not always obvious because of the leader's dominance, by 1938 he had one of the finest Swing orchestras around. Drummer Cozy Cole joined the band in 1939 and Chu Berry soloed on the majority of Calloway titles during the era. There is only one hit on *1938–1939*, "F. D. R. Jones," but Calloway infuses such numbers as "Hoy Hoy," "Mister Paganini, Swing for Minnie," and "Do You Wanna Jump, Children" with plenty of life. June Richmond has guest vocals on two numbers. In August 1939 trumpeter Dizzy Gillespie became a member of Cab Calloway's Orchestra, and with the lineup also including trumpeters Lammar Wright and Mario Bauza, trombonists Tyree Glenn and Quentin Jackson, altoist Hilton Jefferson, Chu Berry,

and a rhythm section comprised of Bennie Payne, Barker, Hinton, and Cole, Cab Calloway had the strongest band of his career. At this point in time, it was not unusual for Calloway to feature an instrumental or two on many of his sessions, and *1939–40* includes individual features for Cole ("Crescendo in Drums"), Hinton ("Pluckin' the Bass"), and Gillespie (the historically significant "Pickin' the Cabbage" which hints at bop). In addition, Calloway is typically zany on such numbers as "The Ghost of Smoky Joe," "The Jumpin' Jive," "Jiveformation Please," and "Chop, Chop Charlie Chan." On the *1940* CD there are many futuristic (if occasionally uncomfortable) trumpet solos by Gillespie (23 at the time) and plenty of solo space for Chu Berry. "Bye Bye Blues" is a highlight for both players, although Berry's most famous recording, an overly sentimental "Ghost of a Chance," is also on this CD. But lest anyone forget whose band this was, Calloway comes through on "Topsy Turvy," "Hi-De-Ho Serenade," "Fifteen Minute Intermission," "Papa's in Bed with His Britches On," and "Are You Hep to the Jive."

8 *1940–1941 / Aug. 28, 1940–July 24, 1941 / Classics 629*

8 *1941–1942 / July 24, 1941–July 27, 1942 / Classics 682*
Halfway through the *1940–1941* disc, trumpeter Jonah Jones became part of the Cab Calloway Orchestra, and his arrival was celebrated in the song "Jonah Joins the Cab." Dizzy Gillespie was still in the band, taking short solos on several tracks, including "Take the 'A' Train," while tenorman Chu Berry was Cab's musical director and favorite. This was a great orchestra, as heard on Benny Carter's arrangement of "Lonesome Nights," altoist Hilton Jefferson's feature on "Willow Weep for Me," and in Andy Gibson's arrangements in general. Calloway remade "St. James Infirmary" (which is heard twice on this CD) quite successfully and also sounds spirited on "A Chick Ain't Nothin' but a Bird," "Are You All Reet," "Hep Cat's Love Song," and "Geechy Joe." 1941 would bring some major changes to the Cab Calloway Orchestra. A spitball thrown at Calloway during a performance was blamed on Dizzy Gillespie, and a fight afterwards ended with Dizzy being fired; the real culprit (revealed years later) was Jonah Jones! A car accident in late October resulted in the death of tenor star Chu Berry. However, the strong Payne-Barker-Hinton-Cole rhythm section remained intact during the period covered in *1941–1942*, Jonah Jones

emerged as Calloway's main solo star, Buster Harding contributed many swinging arrangements to the orchestra (along with Andy Gibson), and the prosperous bandleader was able to occasionally use a vocal group (the Cabaliers), including most successfully on "Virginia, Georgia, and Caroline." Other notable selections include "Blues in the Night," "I Want to Rock," "I Get the Neck of the Chicken," and the third version of "Minnie the Moocher."

7 *1942–1947 / Feb. 2, 1942–Dec. 11, 1947 / Classics 996*
The final CD in this series covers a nearly-six-year period and has the last recordings by Cab Calloway's working band. There are a couple numbers from 1942 that were originally rejected but are fine ("What's Buzzin', Cousin?" and "Chant of the Jungle"), two V-disc selections from 1944, nine selections (including one V-disc) from 1945, just two songs from 1946, and ten tunes (one originally rejected) from 1947. The big band era was ending, and very soon Calloway would have to break up his orchestra and cut back to a sextet, but that does not take away from the general joy of his music. One can hear touches of bop in some of the later arrangements, but in general the style of the band was unchanged. "Dawn Time and "Afternoon Moon" are a bit frivolous, but such tunes as "A Blue Serge Suit with a Belt in the Back," "Don't Falter at the Altar," "Give Me Twenty Nickels for a Dollar," "Two Blocks Down, Turn to the Left," "The Calloway Boogie," "Everybody Eats When They Come to My

House," and the somewhat bizarre "The San Francisco Fan" are quite fun. Two songs from 1947 are by a septet called the Cab-Jivers, and there are many solos throughout the CD from trumpeter Jonah Jones and tenors Ike Quebec (1944–46) and Sam "The Man" Taylor (1947). Virtually all of these recordings were formerly quite obscure.

LPS TO SEARCH FOR

The Classics series makes all other "greatest hits" collections obsolete, including the two-LP 20-song *Hi De Ho Man* (Columbia 32593). *Jazz Off the Air, Vol. 4* (Spotlite 148), which features the Cab Calloway Orchestra performing live on the radio during 1943–46, has very few vocals, and emphasizes the soloists, particularly tenor saxophonist Ike Quebec and trumpeter Jonah Jones.

FILMS

Being a big star by 1931, Cab Calloway had feature numbers in many band shorts and quite a few full-length Hollywood films, including *The Big Broadcast* (1932), *International House* (1933), *The Singing Kid* (1936), *Manhattan Merry-Go-Round* (1937), the memorable *Stormy Weather* (1943), *Dixie Jamboree* (1944), and *Sensations of 1945* (1944). Later in life he had several acting roles, including in *St. Louis Blues* (1958), *The Cincinnati Kid* (1965), and *The Blues Brothers* (1980).

BENNY CARTER
b. Aug. 8, 1907, New York, NY

It would not be an exaggeration to say that the multitalented Benny Carter has had a rather impressive career. No other jazz musician has been at the top of his field longer, over 70 years. Although he never generated the most headlines (being very reliable, distinguished, consistent, and not at all controversial), Carter's consistent excellence has been remarkable. He was, along with Johnny Hodges, the top altoist of the Swing era and yet he was still in his prime in the mid-1990s. Carter's arranging (particularly for saxophones) has long been influential; his composing talents (which resulted in "When Lights Are Low," "Blues in My Heart," and "Cow Cow Boogie" among many others) have been underrated. He was a fine Swing trumpeter, and he has led several impressive orchestras, even if none ever caught on commercially.

Benny Carter, whose father was a guitarist and mother played organ and piano, began on the piano at an early age. He wanted to play trumpet, but he was impatient at not mastering the horn after a few hours, so he traded it in at a music store for a C-melody sax. In August 1924, Carter started working professionally, playing with June Clark's band on alto and then

Always reliable and professional, altoist Benny Carter writes out a part for a Capitol recording session in the mid-1940s.

gigging with Billy Paige's Broadway Syncopators, Lois Deppe's Serenaders, Earl Hines, and Horace Henderson's Collegians (1925–26). After short stints with Billy Fowler, James P. Johnson, and Fletcher Henderson, he was part of Charlie Johnson's Paradise Ten for a year, playing alongside Benny Waters and Jabbo Smith and making his recording debut in 1927.

Carter was with Fletcher Henderson off and on during 1928–31, contributing quite a few arrangements and gaining a strong reputation. After spending part of 1931 with Chick Webb, Carter became the musical director for McKinney's Cotton Pickers (1931–32), but the orchestra was declining during this period. Doubling by now on trumpet, he led his own orchestra during 1932–34. After playing and recording with Willie Bryant, Carter sailed in 1935 to Europe, where during the next three years he worked with Willie Lewis as staff arranger for Henry Hall's Orchestra, led bands of his own, and played all over the Continent where he was treated like royalty. In addition to his alto and trumpet, Carter recorded on clarinet, tenor, piano, and even a few unfortunate vocals.

Back in the U.S. by May 1938, Carter soon formed a swinging big band, which lasted until 1941. After spending time in New York heading a sextet, he moved to Los Angeles in 1943 and had another orchestra, off and on, to 1946. Carter, who contributed arrangements to many other big bands throughout the Swing era, began seriously working in the studios as a composer-arranger, starting with scoring the 1943 film *Stormy Weather*. He went on some tours with Jazz at the Philharmonic, recorded frequently both as a leader and as a sideman during the 1950s and, although learning from bebop and later styles, he retained his original sound and style. By the mid-1960s, Carter was not playing his horn much, because he was working full-time for the studios as a writer. A decade later he began to become more active as a player again and was soon back in prime form. Up until the present time (slowing down after he passed his 90th birthday), Benny Carter has remained one of the top altoists in jazz and continually busy as a writer.

●

9 *1929–1933 / Sept. 18, 1929–May 19, 1933 / Classics 522*

9 *1933–1936 / May 19, 1933–Apr. 1936 / Classics 530*

9 *1936 / June 1936–Oct. 19, 1936 / Classics 541*

9 *1937–1939 / Jan. 11, 1937–June 29, 1939 / Classics 552*

9 *1939–1940 / June 29, 1939–May 20, 1940 / Classics 579*
All of Benny Carter's recordings as a leader during the pre-swing years, his extended period in Europe, and shortly after his return to the U.S. are on these five CDs. *1929–1933* actually only has five numbers by Carter's bands (including "Six Bells Stampede") but includes his recordings with the all-star Chocolate Dandies (which is mostly comprised of top players from the Fletcher Henderson Orchestra of 1929–30) and the first 11 numbers from Spike Hughes's sessions of 1933. In addition to Carter, such players as Coleman Hawkins, Wayman Carver (taking some of his earliest flute solos), Fats Waller, Rex Stewart, Dickie Wells, and Henry "Red" Allen are prominent. *1933–1936* has the last date for both Spike Hughes and the Chocolate Dandies (this time including Chu Berry and Teddy Wilson), eight numbers by Benny Carter's Orchestra in 1934 (including "Symphony in Riffs," "Blue Lou," and "Everybody Shuffle"), plus Carter's first two London sessions in 1936. Heard on alto, trumpet, clarinet, and piano, Carter performs memorable versions of "When Day Is Done" and his "Just a Mood." *1936* finds him backing singer Elisabeth Welch on four numbers, recording with local bands in Copenhagen and Stockholm, and leading a big band, a quartet, and a quintet in London. These formerly very rare recordings include "Scandal in a Flat," "Accent on Swing," "Waltzing the Blues" (the first jazz waltz), "Bugle Call Rag," "Jingle Bells," and the earliest two recorded versions of "When Lights Are Low." *1937–1939* includes Benny Carter's last five European dates, recorded in London, Holland, and Paris. The first three sessions are at the head of big bands, so one hears not only Carter playing on alto, trumpet, clarinet, and tenor but also his arrangements of such numbers as "Nagasaki," "I'm in the Mood for Swing," "New Street Swing," "Skip It," and "Blues in My Heart." Carter also plays with an octet that includes Coleman Hawkins and pianist Freddy Johnson, and in another

one with Alix Combelle and Django Reinhardt. *1937–1939* concludes with Carter's first American date in five years, the debut of his new big band. *1939–1940* traces the development of the Benny Carter Orchestra, a band that also included in its early period trumpeter Joe Thomas, Vic Dickenson, Tyree Glenn, and Eddie Heywood. "When Lights Are Low," "Riff Romp," "Shufflebug Shuffle," and "O.K. for Baby" are among the better numbers, and there are four selections in which Coleman Hawkins is a guest.

8 *1940–1941 / May 25, 1940–Oct. 16, 1941 / Classics 631*

6 *All of Me / May 7, 1934–Mar. 1959 / Bluebird 3000*
The Benny Carter Orchestra was very much lost in the shuffle during the Swing era, working fairly regularly but never prospering. *1940–1941* has the last recordings by the big band, including a classic arrangement on "All of Me," "Cocktails for Two," "My Favorite Blues," and "Ill Wind." Trumpeter Sidney DeParis, Vic Dickenson, and pianist Sonny White are among the key players and Maxine Sullivan takes a couple vocals, but it was all for naught. *All of Me* has 12 of the 16 selections from the band's last dates, other tunes in which Carter guests with Mezz Mezzrow, Willie Bryant, Ethel Waters, Artie Shaw, and Lucky Thompson, plus four numbers from 1959 that were part of a project dealing with the music from the M Squad television series. This release is rather illogical!

8 *Cosmopolite: The Oscar Peterson Verve Sessions / Sept. 18, 1952–Nov. 12, 1954 / Verve 314 521 673*

7 *3, 4, 5—The Verve Small Group Sessions / Mar. 1955 / Verve 849 395*

9 *New Jazz Sounds: The Urbane Sessions / Sept. 18, 1952–Mar. 23, 1955 / Verve 314 531 637*
By the 1950s, Benny Carter had given up trying to lead a regular big band and he was doing quite well writing and playing in the studios. Fortunately he was also recording many jazz dates, including a series for Verve that in the above three releases has been totally reissued. On *Cosmopolite*, Carter's

alto is showcased on a variety of standards with pianist Oscar Peterson, either Barney Kessel or Herb Ellis on guitar, bassist Ray Brown, and Buddy Rich, J. C. Heard, or Bobby White on drums; four selections add the personable trombone of Bill Harris. *3, 4, 5* has Carter playing trios with Teddy Wilson and Jo Jones (that date was only out previously in Japan), in a quartet with pianist Don Abney, and finishing up his session with Peterson, Ellis, Brown, and Bobby White. The best one of the trio of Verve sets, *New Jazz Sounds,* is a two-CD set that features Carter backed by strings (the arrangements by Carter and Joe Glover are surprisingly stimulating) on the first disc. The second CD mostly finds him in a quintet with Roy Eldridge; there are four unusual selections in which Eldridge duets with drummer Alvin Stoller. In addition Carter jams two numbers in a septet with Dizzy Gillespie and Bill Harris and there is a leftover track from one of the Oscar Peterson dates. No matter what the setting, Benny Carter sounds swinging, tasteful, and creative.

7 *Jazz Giant / July 22, 1957–Apr. 21, 1958 / Original Jazz Classics 167*

6 *Swingin' the '20s / Nov. 2, 1958 / Original Jazz Classics 339*

10 *Further Definitions / Nov. 13, 1961–Mar. 4, 1966 / GRP/Impulse 229*

Jazz Giant teams Carter (on alto and trumpet) with Ben Webster and trombonist Frank Rosolino in an all-star septet, playing five Swing standards and a couple of his lesser-known originals. There are plenty of fine moments. *Swingin' the '20s* is a slight disappointment for, although it matches Carter with Earl Hines in a quartet, no sparks fly and the results (a dozen songs that are mostly from the 1920s) are tasteful and lightly swinging but lack any real excitement. *Further Definitions* is a different matter altogether. Benny Carter reunited with Coleman Hawkins and wrote for an octet also including altoist Phil Woods and tenor saxophonist Charlie Rouse. Their versions of "Honeysuckle Rose," "Crazy Rhythm," "Cotton Tail," and "Doozy" in particular are classic and Hawkins gets to come up with fresh variations on "Body and Soul." The CD reissue also includes the entire *Additions to Further Definitions* album, a follow-up in 1966 that has similar instrumentation but a completely different personnel, featuring Carter and Bud

Shank on altos with Teddy Edwards and either Buddy Collette or Bill Perkins on tenor. Although not up to the level of its predecessor, there are some good moments on this date (which includes "Fantastic, That's You," "If Dreams Come True," and a remake of "Doozy") and this would be Benny Carter's last small-group project until 1976.

8 *The King / Feb. 11, 1976 / Original Jazz Classics 883*

7 *Carter, Gillespie, Inc. / Apr. 27, 1976 / Original Jazz Classics 682*

7 *Wonderland / Nov. 1976 / Original Jazz Classics 967*

7 *'Live and Well in Japan! / Apr. 29, 1977 / Original Jazz Classics 736*

8 *Montreux '77 / July 13, 1977 / Original Jazz Classics 374*

Benny Carter's decision to resume playing alto on a full-time basis in the mid-1970s after a decade off the scene was a happy event. He recorded regularly for Pablo during 1976–77 (leading to these reissues in the Original Jazz Classics series) and occasionally afterwards. *The King* matches him with the Pablo All-Stars (including vibraphonist Milt Jackson, guitarist Joe Pass, and pianist Tommy Flanagan) on eight of his originals; best-known are "Easy Money" and "Blue Star." *Carter, Gillespie, Inc.* is a decent date but does not live up to its expectation considering the Carter–Dizzy Gillespie frontline; "Broadway" and "A Night in Tunisia" are best. *Wonderland* has the feel of a jam session as Carter joins tenorman Eddie "Lockjaw" Davis, Harry "Sweets" Edison, pianist Ray Bryant, Milt Hinton, and drummer Grady Tate; but, other than two standards, five of the songs are actually fairly obscure tunes by the altoist, so some planning certainly took place! *'Live and Well in Japan* really is a jam session as Carter leads an all-star ensemble (including Budd Johnson, trumpeters Cat Anderson and Joe Newman, trombonist Britt Woodman, and baritonist Cecil Payne) on three standards and a notable three-song Louis Armstrong tribute. The latter is highlighted by Newman's very close impression of Armstrong's voice on "When You're Smiling." *Montreux '77* is a superior showcase for Carter, backed by pianist Ray Bryant, bassist Niels Pedersen, and drummer Jimmie Smith on seven of Benny's favorite standards; he plays trumpet on "Body and Soul."

8 *Skyline Drive and Towards / Nov. 6, 1929–Sept. 15, 1982 / Phontastic 9305*

7 *A Gentleman and His Music / Aug. 1985 / Concord Jazz 285*

9 *Central City Sketches / 1987 / Music Masters*

7 *In the Mood for Swing / Nov. 9–12, 1987 / Music Masters 601244*

7 *Cookin' at Carlos / Oct. 5–9, 1988 / Music Masters 60230*

8 *Over the Rainbow / Oct. 18–19, 1988 / Music Masters 60196*

8 *My Man Benny/My Man Phil / Nov. 21–22, 1989 / Music Masters 5036*

6 *Live at Princeton / Nov. 11, 1990 / Music Masters 5059*
Before signing with Music Masters in 1987, Benny Carter spent a decade freelancing, recording with many labels. In 1982 Carter recorded a very good date for the Swedish Phontastic label (*Skyline Drive*) that includes Plas Johnson and Jerome Richardson on tenors, altoist Arne Domnerus, clarinetist Putte Wickman, trumpeter Jan Allen, and pianist Bengt Hallberg, plus a rhythm section; "Easy Money," "Stompin' at the Savoy," and "When Lights Are Low" are standouts. When this set was reissued on CD, eight vintage selections from 1929–39 were added, numbers that feature Carter with McKinney's Cotton Pickers, the Chocolate Dandies, Billie Holiday ("Sugar"), and his own band that remind one of the altoist's remarkable longevity. Benny Carter's lone album for Concord is an excellent one, an outing with an all-star septet that includes trumpeter Joe Wilder, tenor saxophonist Scott Hamilton, and pianist Gene Harris on four standards and two originals. The Music Masters label has been creative in featuring Carter on an extensive series of recordings. Carter utilized the American Jazz Orchestra in 1987 when he was 80 for *Central City Sketches,* a two-CD set. The all-star group (filled with top bop and Mainstream Swing players, all of whom were much younger than Carter) performs eight of the altoist's originals (including two versions of "Doozy"), his old theme, "Sleep," and a new six-part "Central City Sketches." Most of Benny Carter's Music Masters recordings were less ambitious but nearly as good. Carter plays 11 of his more obscure originals on *In the Mood for Swing,* welcoming guest Dizzy Gillespie to his quartet/quintet on three numbers. *Cookin' at Carlos* is a mostly standards quartet date with pianist Richard Wynads; Carter (at age 81) plays trumpet on "Time for The Blues." The Benny Carter All-Star Sax Ensemble (with Herb Geller on alto, Jimmy Heath and Frank Wess on tenors, and baritonist Joe Temperely in the octet) on *Over The Rainbow* finds Carter sharing the solo space with the veteran (but still much younger) players and contributing arrangements along with four of the eight selections (including "Easy Money"). Carter at age 82 battles altoist Phil Woods (then just 58) to a draw on *My Man Benny/My Man Phil,* taking two trumpet solos, contributing six of the ten songs (Woods brought in two tunes himself), and singing "My Man Phil." *All That Jazz* teams Carter with trumpeter Clark Terry and the Kenny Barron Trio but is weighed down slightly by Billy Hills' three vocals, which are ok but take away from the horn interplay.

8 *Harlem Renaissance / Feb. 7–9, 1992 / Music Masters 65080*

7 *Legends / June 16–17, 1992 / Music Masters 65087*

4 *Elegy in Blue / May 18–19, 1994 / Music Masters 65115*

7 *Songbook / June 26, 1995–Aug. 26, 1995 / Music Masters 65134*

6 *Songbook, Volume II / June 26, 1995–July 28, 1995 / Music Masters 65155*

7 *New York Nights / June 22–24, 1996 / Music Masters 65154*
At the age of 84, Benny Carter wrote two new extended works ("Tales of the Rising Sun Suite" and "Harlem Renaissance Suite") for a big band and the Rutgers University Orchestra (which includes a full string section). No problem! Although the apparently ageless Carter generously featured his sidemen, he still took solo honors on the two suites plus six older songs. *Legends* features Carter at 85 finding a rare elder musician to play with (87-year-old trumpeter Doc Cheatham, who is in fine form on three selections) and, in addition to some quartet numbers, Carter duets with Hank Jones on five of his originals. *Elegy in Blue* does not work so well, but that is because of 79-year-old Harry Edison, whose trumpet playing constantly falters, as opposed to Carter (then 87 himself), who is typically flawless. *Songbook* and *Songbook, Volume II* are interesting projects in which the focus is on Benny Carter the songwriter and even lyricist. The former date has Carter, cornetist Warren Vache, and pianist

Chris Neville's trio backing such singers as Dianne Reeves ("Only Trust Your Heart"), Carmen Bradford, Kenny Rankin, Joe Williams, Marlena Shaw, Jon Hendricks, Diana Krall, Billy Stritch, Shirley Horn, Bobby Short, Ruth Brown, Weslia Whitfield, Nancy Marano, and Peggy Lee on Carter's songs. The second volume (which has most of the same singers plus Lainie Kazan, Barbara Lea, and Carter himself on "When Hilma Smiles") generally concentrates on more obscure and recent material. Benny Carter's most recent recording to date, *New York Nights,* has the altoist (two months short of his 89th birthday) still playing in his prime, running through standards plus his "Easy Money" with Chris Neville's Trio. Yet another recommended Benny Carter CD!

LPS TO SEARCH FOR

1944 (Hindsight 218) features the Benny Carter Orchestra live in California with features for trombonist J. J. Johnson and guest clarinetist Barney Bigard, plus three for Carter on trumpet. Also from his mid-1940s big band are *In Hollywood 1944–46* (Jazz Society 502) and *Jazz off the Air, Vol. 3*

(Spotlite 147), which, particularly on the second record, have spots for many up-and-coming young modernists, including Johnson, trumpeter Miles Davis, and Dexter Gordon on tenor. Carter primarily leads specially assembled all-star big bands from 1946 on *The Deluxe Recordings* (Swingtime 1013), while *The Late Forties* (Official 3006) has Carter heading a big band behind a vocal group and jamming on other numbers with the likes of Buck Clayton, Vic Dickenson, and Ben Webster. *Summer Serenade* (Storyville 4047), from 1980, is an excellent quartet date with pianist Kenny Drew that alternates originals with standards. *The Benny Carter All-Stars* (Gazell 1004) has spots for cornetist Nat Adderley and (in one of his final recordings) vibraphonist Red Norvo on a jam session–flavored program.

FILMS

Benny Carter wrote the music for many films but actually appeared in relatively few. He plays trumpet with Fats Waller in *Stormy Weather* (1943) and is in one scene of *The Snows of Kilimanjaro* (1952). He is also seen throughout the one hour documentary *Symphony in Riffs* (Rhapsody Films).

CASA LOMA ORCHESTRA

Although the Fletcher Henderson Orchestra in 1924 could be considered the first Swing big band, the Casa Loma Orchestra in the early 1930s set the standard for Benny Goodman and the other orchestras that would follow. Their combination of hot stomps and vocal ballads, tightly arranged ensembles, and solo features in the early Depression years predated the Swing era and inspired Goodman and the Dorsey Brothers to form bands of their own.

The ensemble originally started out in the late 1920s as the Orange Blossoms, one of several units that Jean Goldkette ran in the Detroit area. Henry Biagini was its first leader, while Glen Gray (born June 7, 1906, in Roanoke, IL) was one of its saxophonists. In 1929 the group was scheduled to perform at a new Canadian nightclub called the Casa Loma, but the venue never opened. About this time Biagini was tossed out, and it was decided to name the reorganized orchestra (which would be run as the first co-op band) after the never-to-be club. In time Gray, who was elected president of the corporation because he was a skillful organizer and also an attractive frontman, became the Casa Loma Orchestra's official leader.

Gene Gifford's arrangements (which could be quite excitable, if a touch mechanical) gave the Casa Loma band its original personality. Such memorable and heated numbers as "China Girl," "San Sue Strut," "Casa Loma Stomp," "White Jazz," and "Black Jazz," plus the haunting "Smoke Rings," were among the orchestra's finest moments on record during 1930–32, before the word *Swing* was applied to the jazz style they were playing. Clarinetist Clarence Hutchenrider, trombonist Pee Wee Hunt (who contributed humorous vocals and would later make a name for himself in Dixieland), trumpeter Sonny Dunham, and saxophonist Kenny Sargent (who provided romantic ballad vocals) were among the band's key members. During 1933–34 the band initiated the "Camel Caravan" series of radio shows that in later years would add to Benny Goodman's fame.

Ironically, when the Swing era really got going in 1935, the Casa Loma Orchestra was greatly overshadowed by the competition it had inspired. The band worked steadily during the next ten years and even had some hits ("No Name Jive," Dunham's high-note feature on "Memories of You," and remakes of "Smoke Rings" and "Casa Loma Stomp"), but never reached the commercial heights of Benny Goodman, Tommy Dorsey, or Glenn Miller. Cornetists Red Nichols and Bobby Hackett, along with guitarist Herb Ellis, were with the Casa Loma Orchestra in the 1940s for short periods.

The band stopped recording after 1942 (although later radio transcriptions and live concerts have been released), and it struggled on until 1950. In 1956 Glen Gray revived the Casa Loma name and initiated a successful series of Swing recreation records for Capitol with studio bands, playing not only music associated with his orchestra but that of other big bands. He died of cancer on August 23, 1963, in Plymouth, Massachusetts, and the legacy of the Casa Loma Orchestra (which by then had been largely forgotten) as a pioneering Swing band died with him.

●

7 *Best of the Big Bands / Dec. 18, 1931–Dec. 24, 1934 / Columbia 45345*
There are few CDs featuring the Casa Loma Orchestra, so this sampler (which does not bother listing the personnel or dates) is probably the best bet at the moment. It includes such famous numbers as the first and best version of "Smoke Rings," "Black Jazz," "Casa Loma Stomp," and "Limehouse Blues" (which has some fine Sonny Dunham trumpet) along with some lesser items. A decent but not definitive look at the early Casa Loma Orchestra.

6 *The Continental / 1935 / Hindsight 261*
With far too many of the Casa Loma's earlier recordings out of print, this set of radio transcriptions helps to fill the gap a little. The emphasis is on Swing (only one Kenny Sargent vocal) and standards such as "Who's Sorry Now," "Ballin' the Jack," "Blue Room," and "Chinatown, My Chinatown"; this CD has none of the Casa Loma's hits. However, there is consistently fine playing, with solos from trumpeter Sonny Dunham, trombonists Pee Wee Hunt and Bill Rausch, Pat Davis on tenor, and clarinetist Clarence Hutchenrider.

LPS TO SEARCH FOR
Casa Loma Stomp (Hep 1010) has 14 of the big band's earliest recordings (from 1929–30), including "China Girl," "San Sue Strut," and the first "Casa Loma Stomp." *1929/*

1932 (Harrison N) and *Vol. 2 1930–1937* (Harrison T), with the exception of a few duplicates from the Hep album, adds to the orchestra's recorded legacy, which is richer than people might realize. *Glen Gray and the Original Casa Loma Orchestra's Greatest Hits* (Decca 75016) only has ten selections, but it does include the band's late '30s big sellers, including "No Name Jive," "Memories of You," "Casa Loma Stomp," and a later rendition of "Smoke Rings." *1939* (Circle 36) and *1940* (Circle 61) are a pair of LPs taken from radio transcriptions and in general are more commercial than most Casa Loma releases, with vocals on over half the selections; first-class dance band music rather than exciting jazz. *1939–40* (Hindsight 104) and *1943–1946, Vol. 2* (Hindsight 120) are also from transcriptions but are much stronger from a jazz standpoint. While *Vol. 1* has "No Name Jive," "Memories of You," and intriguing versions of three songs associated with Glenn Miller, *Vol. 2* is particularly valuable because the Casa Loma Orchestra was no longer recording by that time and the lineup was almost completely different from what it had been just before. Cornetist Red Nichols takes particularly memorable solos on "Don't Take Your Love from Me" and "Dancing on the Ceiling," cornetist Bobby Hackett pops up on five songs, and other soloists include pianist Lou Carter and guitarist Herb Ellis. As for Glen Gray's Swing recreation projects for Capitol (such as *Casa Loma in Hi-Fi* and *Sounds of the Great Bands*), those nostalgic and once popular recordings are long out of print.

BOB CHESTER
b. Mar. 20, 1908, Detroit, MI, d. Nov. 5, 1975

Bob Chester's Orchestra was the finest Swing band that no one has ever heard of. After Chester's first big band failed in 1939, Tommy Dorsey befriended him and convinced him to model a new orchestra after Glenn Miller's. TD's devious plot was to knock out Miller's big band so he would have less competition!

Chester was born to a rich family and he attended the University of Dayton. He worked as a tenor saxophonist with Paul Specht, Arnold Johnson, Ben Pollack, Russ Morgan, Irving Aaronson, and Ben Bernie and on the radio. Starting in 1935, he led a commercial big band that did not make much of an impression. In 1939 he followed Dorsey's advice and formed a group that essentially imitated Glenn Miller's. In fact, after Chester's engagement in one city preceded Miller's, one fan said to the latter, "Mr. Miller, your band sounds like Bob Chester's!"

However, that particular strategy did not work and Chester soon had his ensemble evolve into a strong Swing orchestra with its own sound. The big band recorded regularly for Bluebird during 1939–42. Although none of its sidemen became all that famous (other than trombonist Bill Harris, who was in an unrecorded 1943 edition), and it did not have any hits, it could swing as hard as most of its competitors and it had a fine singer in Dolores O'Neill (who was later succeeded by Betty Bradley). After the Swing era, Bob Chester (who led bands into the 1950s) faded away into complete obscurity; virtually every jazz encyclopedia does not even bother to list him. However, the Bob Chester Orchestra's Bluebird recordings (which have yet to be reissued on CD) remain unknown treasures for curious Swing collectors to discover.

●

LPS TO SEARCH FOR

RCA has taken little notice of its Bob Chester records, reissuing virtually nothing. However, *Easy Does It* (Golden Era 15003) and *Octave Jump* (Bandstand 7103) include 16 songs apiece with only one duplication. The Golden Era set is half studio recordings/half radio transcriptions, while Bandstand draws its music completely from the obscure studio sides. The Bandstand album (which has such numbers as "Octave Jump," "57th Street Drag," "Flingin' a Wing Ding,"

"Tanning Dr. Jekyll's Hyde," and "Beau Nite in Hotchkiss Corners") in particular shows what the Bob Chester Orchestra could do. Other Chester albums include *1940–41* (Circle 44) and *More 1940–41* (Circle 74), which are additional radio transcriptions and are in general more dance band and vocal-oriented, and the two-LP set *The Bob Chester Story* (Big Band International 2708), which has more radio performances, mostly from 1942.

BOB CROSBY
b. Aug. 23, 1913, Spokane, WA, d. Mar. 9, 1993, La Jolla, CA

Bob Crosby had a somewhat illogical life. Why would the younger brother of Bing Crosby become a singer (especially one with a limited voice) when there was no way that he could exceed the accomplishments of his sibling? What was even odder is that Bob Crosby ended up at the head of a Dixieland-oriented big band, and, because he was not a musician or an arranger, he is present on virtually none of his band's hits except as a spectator!

Although he attended Gonzaga College and planned to become a lawyer, Crosby was persuaded to try to make a go of it as a singer. He was with Anson Weeks's big band starting in 1932 and in 1934 sang with the Dorsey Brothers Orchestra, with whom he recorded. In 1935 the nucleus of the defunct Ben Pollack big band was looking for a leader. Trombonist Jack Teagarden seemed like the best choice, but Mr. T. had recently signed a five-year contract with Paul Whiteman. Bob Crosby, who was an attractive frontman who did not get in the way, was chosen while Gil Rodin (a nonsoloing saxophonist) took care of the business end.

At first the Bob Crosby Orchestra was a fairly conventional big band, featuring its leader's so-so vocals. But because there were so many talented and freewheeling soloists in the ensemble (including trumpeter Yank Lawson, clarinetist Matty Matlock, and tenor saxophonist Eddie Miller, plus guitarist-singer Nappy Lamare, bassist-arranger Bob Haggart, and drummer Ray Bauduc), in 1936 (when pianist Bob Zurke joined) the direction of the band changed. In the middle of the Swing era, the Bob Crosby Orchestra looked backward to the 1920s for inspiration while creating new music, and the result was a type of big band Dixieland that can be heard on such records as "Muskrat Ramble," "Come Back Sweet Papa," and "Sugar Foot Strut." In November 1937, Bob Crosby's Bobcats (a four-horn octet taken out of the big band) made their first recordings, and that unit was quite popular despite preceding the Dixieland revival by a couple of years. During Crosby's prime period (1937-40), his big band had such hits as Joe Sullivan's "Little Rock Getaway," Bob Haggart's "South Rampart Street Parade," and a song by the bassist originally called "I'm Free" but soon retitled "What's New?" while the Bobcats also made "March of the Bob Cats" (which was really just "Maryland, My Maryland") famous. Haggart and Bauduc collaborated on the bass-piano duet "Big Noise from Winnetka," and such soloists as trumpeter Billy Butterfield (who became a key player after Lawson joined Tommy Dorsey), clarinetist Irving Fazola, pianist Joe Sullivan (later replaced by Jess Stacy), and (in 1940) cornetist Muggsy Spanier were major assets.

Strangely enough, in 1941 Crosby's band changed course and became a much more routine Swing band. Crosby began to sing on some of the Bob Cats' sessions (which made them a bit pointless) and even the return of Yank Lawson did not rescue the band's sinking popularity. Crosby eventually lost interest and, with the hassles and shortages of the war years, he broke up the band in 1942. The remainder of Bob Crosby's life was anticlimactic although not uneventful. He served in the Marines during 1944-45, appeared in a lot of little-known films as an actor, had a radio series and a part-time orchestra, and in the 1950s hosted his own television show for a time. There were many Bobcat reunions and occasional recordings through the years, generally using some of his alumni. At these later concerts (which took place as late as the early 1990s), Bob Crosby would usually sing a song or two and then otherwise look on while his sidemen created the magic.

⬤

9 *South Rampart Street Parade / Apr. 13, 1936–Feb. 17, 1942 / GRP/Decca 615*

This excellent CD has 20 of the better selections by the Bob Crosby Orchestra during its prime years although nothing by Crosby's Bobcats. It gives one a fine overview of the band and includes such popular recordings as "Little Rock Getaway," "South Rampart Street Parade," "Big Noise from Winnetka," and the original version of "What's New?" ("I'm Free"). Most of the music is from the band's earlier Dixieland-oriented days, with just three numbers after 1939. An excellent introduction to Bob Crosby's happy music, and not a single vocal from the leader!

9 *1937–1938 / Feb. 8, 1937–Oct. 19, 1938 / ABC 838 477*

Part of a reissue series in which engineer Robert Parker successfully makes old recordings sound as if they were originally recorded in stereo, this CD (which contains 18 selections) only has four repeats from the *South Rampart Street Parade* Decca disc. Eleven of the numbers are actually by Bob Crosby's Bobcats (mostly Dixieland standards plus "March of the Bobcats," Eddie Miller's haunting "Slow Mood," and "The Big Crash from China") rather than the full orchestra. The Bobcats were quite a strong group at the time, consisting of Yank Lawson, trombonist Warren Smith, either Matty Matlock or Irving Fazola on clarinet, Eddie Miller, Bob Zurke, Nappy Lamare, Bob Haggart, and Ray Bauduc. Of the big band titles, Zurke's workout on "Honky Tonk Train" is a highlight.

4 *I Remember You / Sept. 1941–July 1942 / Vintage Jazz Classics 1046*

The Bob Crosby Orchestra was suffering an identity crisis at the time of the radio transcriptions included on this CD. There was still plenty of talent in the band, including Yank Lawson (who had just returned after a three year absence), Matty Matlock, Eddie Miller, pianist Jess Stacy, and Bob Haggart. However, the band was de-emphasizing the Dixieland spontaneity that had given it its distinctive personality. This disc has too many dull vocals by Crosby, David Street, Liz Tilton (who was not bad), Muriel Lane, and Gloria De Haven; in fact only seven of the 27 selections here are instrumentals. There are some good moments (particularly on "Sugar Foot Stomp" and "Russian Sailors' Dance") on what would be the last recordings by the Bob Crosby Orchestra before its breakup, but much less excitement than one would hope for.

5 *The Bob Crosby Orchestra / 1952–1957 / Hindsight 245*

The music on this set (which features Bob Crosby's Orchestra in 1952 and 1957) was originally recorded for Armed Forces Radio, to help the Marines on their recruitment drive. On the 16 selections, Bob Crosby has four good-natured and harmless vocals, Polly Bergen sings "Let's Fall in Love," and June Christy drops by for "Love Is Just Around the Corner" and "Willow Weep for Me." The other performances are instrumentals, with the 1952 band featuring trumpeter Charlie Teagarden, trombonist Jack Teagarden (showcased on "Lover"), Matty Matlock, and Eddie

Miller, while the 1957 band does not have the Teagardens but features trumpet solos from John Best and Dick Cathcart.

LPS TO SEARCH FOR

The Circle label documented Bob Crosby's early radio transcriptions on *1938* (Circle 1) and *More 1938* (Circle 34), alternating ballad vocals with instrumentals. The later Crosby band's transcriptions are heard on *1941–42* (Hindsight 192). With arrangements by Phil Moore, Bob Haggart, and Matty Matlock, and solos from Yank Lawson, Eddie Miller, Jess Stacy, and Matlock; this album has music superior to that of the Vintage Jazz Classics CD. *1952–53* (Hindsight 209) does not duplicate the Hindsight 245 CD and has plenty of strong moments from Charlie Teagarden, Jack Teagarden, Matlock, and Miller. And two albums recorded November 18, 1966, *Mardi Gras Parade* (Monmouth Evergreen 7026) and *Live at the Rainbow Grill* (Monmouth Evergreen 6815), feature the Crosby alumni (Lawson, trombonist Lou McGarity, Matlock, Miller, pianist Ralph Sutton, Haggart, and drummer Don Lamond) jamming happily on Dixieland standards.

FILMS

Bob Crosby and his Orchestra appear in *Let's Make Music* (1940), *Sir Hopkins* (1941), and *Presenting Lily Mars* (1943) and play "Big Noise From Winnetka" in *Reveille with Beverly* (1943). Of his acting roles, Crosby is most memorable as a corny bandleader-singer in *The Five Pennies* (1959).

DORSEY BROTHERS ORCHESTRA

They were sometimes called "the battling Dorseys" and the term certainly fit Tommy and Jimmy Dorsey. Although the brothers loved each other and greatly admired each other's musicianship, they just could not get along, particularly in their early days. Both were taught music by their father, Thomas F. Dorsey, and both were multi-instrumentalists, with Tommy playing not just trombone but also trumpet while Jimmy was equally talented on clarinet and alto sax in addition to enjoying playing occasional trumpet too. From the early 1920s on, they appeared together on many bandstands and recording dates. The technically skilled Dorseys freelanced in the studios starting in the mid- to late-1920s, keeping quite busy during the early Depression years.

The Dorsey Brothers Orchestra was originally a series of big bands strictly put together for recording dates. During 1928–33 their joint recordings ranged from mainstream jazz for the period to rather commercial music and their versatile dance band approach was influenced by Paul Whiteman. TD was best on ballads, while his jazz playing leaned towards Dixieland; JD was a virtuoso who could play complex lines with ease. The best dates tended to feature a hot trumpet solo from Bunny Berigan.

In 1934, the Dorseys decided to form a regularly working big band so as to escape the anonymity of the studios. With Charlie Spivak on first trumpet, Glenn Miller playing trombone in the ensembles (and more importantly contributing arrangements), vocals by Bob Crosby and Kay Weber, and fine support by drummer Ray McKinley, the big band (which recorded frequently) had potential. However, it had not yet developed a sound of its own when, in mid-1935, Tommy and Jimmy Dorsey fought over the tempo of "I'll Never Say 'Never Again' Again." Tommy left the bandstand in the middle of the performance and formed his own competing orchestra.

The brothers soon made up but realized that it was better to have separate groups. Both Tommy and Jimmy Dorsey had their share of successes during the Swing era and managed to keep their big bands together into 1953. Since they were both struggling by then, they decided to team up again. Jimmy and two of his sidemen (tenor saxophonist Buzzy Brauner and pianist Bob Carter) joined his brother's band, which was renamed the Dorsey Brothers Orchestra or alternately the Tommy Dorsey Orchestra featuring Jimmy Dorsey. The new band's repertoire was nostalgic and melodic and, other than occasional instrumentals (which often featured trumpeter Charlie Shavers), played primarily dance music. For a couple years the Dorseys did their best to bring back the big band era although with little success. Jackie Gleason sponsored them on their own television series, *Stage Show,* which ironically introduced Elvis Presley and Connie Francis.

The Dorsey Brothers Orchestra lasted until Nov. 26, 1956, when Tommy Dorsey choked to death in his sleep. Jimmy Dorsey took over the band, but he was ill himself with cancer and passed away the following June 12. Two ghost bands were carved out of the remains of their group. Lee Castle would run the Jimmy Dorsey band for over 30 years while Warren Covington was the first of several leaders of the posthumous Tommy Dorsey Orchestra.

8 *Mood Hollywood / Sept. 24, 1932–Oct. 17, 1933 / Hep 1005*

7 *Harlem Lullaby / Mar. 3, 1933–Oct. 17, 1933 / Hep 1006*

The first 11 performances on the *Mood Hollywood* disc feature Tommy and Jimmy Dorsey heading an octet that is most notable for starring the great trumpeter Bunny Berigan. Among the selections performed are TD's future theme song, "I'm Getting Sentimental Over You," which in this early version has a vocal by Jean Bowes. Also on the set is an orchestra date with vocals by Johnny Mercer, Mildred Bailey, and Jerry Cooper. Although the Dorsey Brothers get top billing on *Harlem Lullaby*, they are primarily in a supporting role, accompanying singers Bing Crosby (best on "Stay on the Right Side of the Road"), Mildred Bailey (including a touching "There's a Cabin in the Pines"), and Ethel Waters (who introduces "Stormy Weather"). Once again Bunny Berigan consistently steals solo honors.

5 *Best of the Big Bands / Sept. 14, 1932–June 4, 1934 / Columbia/Legacy 48908*

One would think from the generic title of this CD that the contents would at least be featuring the best of the Dorsey Brothers Orchestra from the period when it was a working band (1934–35). Instead the 16 titles are quite a hodgepodge, jumping around chronologically, duplicating some of the music released in more coherent form elsewhere by Hep, and containing only five numbers from the actual orchestra; the rest are from the Dorseys' studio groups of 1932–33. In general the music is worthwhile (although a few throwaways are included), with the highlights being "Someone Stole Gabriel's Horn," "Sing," "Old Man Harlem," a Bill Challis arrangement of "The Blue Room," and the initial version of "I'm Getting Sentimental Over You," but this is a bit of a mess.

THE WAYNE KNIGHT COLLECTION

Jimmy and Tommy Dorsey in a rare peaceful moment from their days (1934–35) as co-leaders of the Dorsey Brothers Orchestra.

6 *Swingin' in Hollywood / Dec. 18, 1941–July 20, 1944 / Rhino 75283*

7 *At the Casino Gardens 1946 / Feb. 10, 1945–July 1947 / Hep 59*

Tommy and Jimmy Dorsey share top billing on these two CDs although their separate orchestras are actually featured. In the 1940s many big bandleaders had roles (usually cameos) in Hollywood films; Tommy Dorsey was particularly prolific. *Swingin' in Hollywood* contains some of the musical highlights from TD's films (*Du Barry Was a Lady, Thrill of a Romance, Ship Ahoy, Broadway Rhythm,* and *Girl Crazy*) and two of Jimmy Dorsey's MGM movies (*I Dood It* and *Lost in a Harem*). Most of the 21 selections (just seven by Jimmy Dorsey) are fine but, amazingly enough, nowhere in the liner notes does it identify the soloists. Among the stars of the Tommy Dorsey tracks are trumpeter Ziggy Elman and drummer Buddy Rich, although the two pianists showcased on an extended version of "Well Git It" are not hinted at. Another fault is that the music is not programmed in any coherent order (why not by individual films?), making one wonder why Rhino went to all this trouble and then fouled up the packaging. Despite all of that, there are some musical gems included (along with occasional show biz numbers); highlights include "Well Git It," "Hawaiian War Chant," "One O'Clock Jump," "John Silver," and "Opus One." During the 1936–52 period, Tommy and Jimmy Dorsey rarely appeared together, but the Sept. 19 and 25, 1946, broadcasts that comprise the majority of *At the Casino Gardens* are major exceptions. The two orchestras appeared at Tommy's short-lived club near Los Angeles and alternated during their radio appearances, coming together on both occasions just during "Brotherly Jump" (a jam tune that they had recorded as a V-Disc). Both versions of that song are cut off by the radio announcer, but this release gives one an opportunity to compare the two bands near the end of the Swing era. In addition, there are a few unrelated numbers from other broadcasts to fill in this disc. Though there are several pop ballad vocals, this is primarily a jazz set.

Jimmy Dorsey's band on "Perdido" features early spots for baritonist Serge Chaloff and guitarist Herb Ellis, while trumpeter Charlie Shavers has several strong moments with TD.

7 *The Dorsey Brothers 1955 / June 3–4, 1955 / Jazz Unlimited 2026*

This CD gives one a good example of what the Dorsey Brothers Band sounded like during its later years. Swing standards (including a few remakes of hits), newer arrangements in the tradition, occasional pop vocals by Lynn Roberts, Bill Raymond, and Bruce Snyder, solo spots for Tommy Dorsey's warm trombone, Jimmy Dorsey on alto and clarinet, and trumpeter Charlie Shavers plus inventive backup work by drummer Louie Bellson combine to form an enjoyable and nostalgic show.

LPS TO SEARCH FOR

The Dorsey Brothers 1928, Volume One (The Old Masters 14) and *The Dorsey Brothers 1928–1930, Volume Two* (The Old Masters 15) contain most of the Dorsey Brothers' earliest recordings as leaders, superior dance band performances with touches of jazz. The second LP also has a solo feature apiece for Jimmy and Tommy plus their appearances with The Travelers.

JIMMY DORSEY
b. Feb. 29, 1904, Shenandoah, PA, d. June 12, 1957, New York, NY

A brilliant alto saxophonist and clarinetist who in the late 1920s was one of the top reed soloists in jazz, Jimmy Dorsey spent much of the Swing era as a famous but somewhat minor figure in his own orchestra. He always played well, but his big band did not really catch on until he began featuring the joint vocals of Helen O'Connell and Bob Eberly in the early '40s.

Dorsey was quite young when he started playing cornet and slide trumpet, performing with his father's band when he was seven and appearing with J. Carson McGee's King Trumpeters for a couple days in 1913. In 1915 he switched to alto sax and was a professional musician by the time he was a teenager. Jimmy often played with his younger brother, Tommy, in bands during the 1920s, including the Dorseys' Novelty Six (later renamed Dorseys' Wild Canaries) and with the Scranton Sirens. A studio musician beginning in 1925, Dorsey recorded with Red Nichols' Five Pennies, the California Ramblers, Jean Goldkette, Frankie Trumbauer (including "Singin' the Blues" with Bix Beiderbecke), and Paul Whiteman among many others during that decade. His recording work accelerated in the Depression, when he and Benny Goodman were often the main reed specialists for a countless number of commercial orchestras and dance bands. Jimmy co-led the Dorsey Brothers as an occasional recording group with his brother Tommy starting in 1928, and during 1934–35 they made a go of it as the Dorsey Brothers Orchestra, playing many engagements on the East Coast and recording frequently.

After the Dorseys split up in May 1935, Jimmy Dorsey took over the orchestra. His band worked regularly during the second half of the 1930s and had a few minor hits (including "Long John Silver" and "Parade of the Milk Bottle Caps").

Despite the presence of such sidemen as drummer Ray McKinley, pianist Freddie Slack, and trumpeter Shorty Sherock, during this era JD was definitely overshadowed by his brother. Bob Eberly was the band's vocalist as early as 1936 and Helen O'Connell joined in 1939, but it was not until early 1941 that they began to be combined on records. Often Eberly sang a ballad chorus, Dorsey followed with a brief instrumental section, and then O'Connell showed off her sensuous and somewhat excitable voice to conclude the song; sometimes O'Connell and Eberly switched places. The combination was first used for "Amapola" and "Yours" in 1941 (Toots Camarata did the arrangements) and, since "Amapola" was a hit, the winning routine was repeated several times during the next year, including on "In the Hush of the Night," "Time Was," "It Happened in Hawaii," "Any Bonds Today," "I Said No," "Not Mine," a filmed version of "Star Eyes," and most notably on best-selling records of "Green Eyes," "Tangerine," and "Brazil."

Jimmy Dorsey had one of the more popular big bands of the first half of the 1940s even though the leader's own playing often seemed to be used more as a prop than as a major force in the music. Dorsey never lost his ability to play, though, and occasionally he would cut loose to show people how good he still was. His band struggled through the postwar years, playing for smaller crowds than it had earlier. Dorsey mostly ignored the bebop innovations until 1949, when for a short time he had trumpeter Maynard Ferguson in his band. He felt more comfortable with Dixieland and that year often jammed with "the Original Dorseyland Jazz Band," a combo taken out of his orchestra that included trumpeter Charlie Teagarden and trombonist Cutty Cutshall. Dorsey kept his big band together until early 1953, when he finally broke it up to join his brother's orchestra. For three years, Jimmy and Tommy Dorsey buried their differences and co-led a nostalgia-oriented big band. At the time when Tommy suddenly died on November 26, 1956, Jimmy was already ailing from the cancer that would soon end his life. Ironically, he had just led his first record date in four years, 15 days before; one of the four songs, "So Rare," became a surprise hit. However, by the time the final eight numbers for the album were recorded, on June 17, 1957 (with Dick Stabile in JD's place), Jimmy Dorsey had passed away.

●

9 *Contrasts / July 7, 1936–Oct. 7, 1943 / GRP/Decca 626*
Jimmy Dorsey CDs are not all that common at this point, so fortunately this single disc does a fine job of summing up his band's Decca recordings. Helen O'Connell (heard solo on "All of Me" and "When the Sun Comes Out" and joining with Bob Eberly on their hit "Tangerine") is only a minor factor on this mostly-instrumental set, which emphasizes the jazz qualities of the Jimmy Dorsey Orchestra. "Parade of the Milk Bottle Caps," "I Got Rhythm," "Long John Silver," "Dusk in Upper Sandusky," JD's theme ("Contrasts"), and "King Porter Stomp" are among the more memorable selections.

8 *Dorseyland Jazz Band / 1950 / Jazz Crusade 3035*

7 *The Complete Standard Transcriptions / 1949 /*
Soundies 4111
During 1949–50 Jimmy Dorsey sometimes took a break from his big band to play Dixieland tunes on clarinet with his Original Dorseyland Jazz Band, a septet taken out of his orchestra. Although he generally just featured the group on a song or two on his radio appearances (they also recorded extensively in the studios), this disc is unusual for it has two

full-length radio broadcasts by the Dorseylanders. Dorsey shows that he had lost very little on the clarinet since the 1920s (he also plays alto on "Sweet Lorraine") and sounds quite happy interacting with trumpeter Charlie Teagarden, either Bud Hackman or Cutty Cutshall on trombone, and Frank Mayne or Buddy Bardach on tenor in this hot group; Pat O'Connor helps out with a couple of cheerful vocals.

The Soundies CD features Jimmy Dorsey in 1949 on 17 selections made as radio transcriptions. The music ranges from swinging jazz (including "Stop, Look, and Listen," "On The Alamo," "In A Little Spanish Town," and "Out Of Nowhere") to vocal features for Claire Hogan and Larry Noble; the soloists include Charlie Teagarden and trombonist Herb Winfield. This disc is valuable, because the later version of the Dorsey Orchestra made relatively few recordings. Concluding the CD is an interesting radio interview with JD from 1956 that was recorded less than a year before his death.

LPS TO SEARCH FOR

Many of Jimmy Dorsey's studio recordings have not yet appeared on CD. *The Early Years* (Bandstand 7104) helps fill the gap with obscurities from the 1936–41 period. Hindsight has put out five volumes of Dorsey's radio transcriptions: *1939–1940* (Hindsight 101); *1941–1944, Vol. 2* (Hindsight 153), which also includes three V-Discs; *1949–51, Vol. 3* (Hindsight 165); *1950, Vol. 4* (Hindsight 178); and *1950, Vol. 5* (Hindsight 203); the latter is a full album of performances by the Dorseyland band that does not duplicate the Jazz Crusade CD. Also valuable is the oddly titled *Uncle Dave's 78 rpm Nostalgia Party* (Sandy Hook 2046), which has JD's V-Discs, and *The Fabulous Jimmy Dorsey* (Fraternity 1008), which contains the final Jimmy Dorsey performances, including "So Rare."

FILMS

Jimmy Dorsey's Orchestra appeared in quite a few films, including *That Girl from Paris* (1936), *Lady Be Good* (1941), *The Fleet's In* (1942), *I Dood It* (1943), *Lost in a Harem* (an Abbott and Costello film from 1944), *Four Jills in a Jeep* (1944), *Hollywood Canteen* (1944), and *Music Man* (1948). Jimmy appeared with his brother Tommy in the erratic but interesting semifictional "biography" *The Fabulous Dorseys* (1947). In addition, the 1945 17-minute short *Catalina Interlude* is well worth searching for.

TOMMY DORSEY

b. Nov. 19, 1905, Shenandoah, PA, d. Nov. 26, 1956, Greenwich, CT

Tommy Dorsey had a very beautiful tone on trombone, best displayed on ballads. Throughout his 21 years of leading big bands, the ironically titled "Sentimental Gentleman of Swing" (who could be a mean drunk at times) always headed units that were quite musical. He was consistently a strong exponent of Swing (detesting bebop) and of putting on a show full of variety, influenced by the approach of Paul Whiteman in the 1920s.

Like his older brother, Jimmy, Tommy was taught trumpet by his father. Although he soon switched his main focus to trombone, TD was an effective trumpeter who in the 1920s featured a dirty tone that was a major contrast to his smooth sound on trombone. The only four selections that he recorded as a leader without his brother during 1928–29 were on trumpet. TD played with Jimmy early on as co-leaders of Dorsey's Novelty Six (later called the Wild Canaries) and the Scranton Sirens. Dorsey was with Jean Goldkette's Orchestra and Paul Whiteman (1927–28) but spent much of the 1925–33 period as a freelance studio musician, appearing on countless recordings. With Jimmy, he co-led a series of recording dates under the name of The Dorsey Brothers (starting in 1928). In 1934 the brothers sought to escape the anonymity of the studios and formed the Dorsey Brothers Orchestra. However, the Dorseys (despite their mutual love and respect) fought frequently at the slightest excuse and their 15 months together were quite stormy. In the summer of 1935, an argument on stage over the tempo of "I'll Never Say Never Again Again" led to TD's storming out of the building and permanently leaving the group. Soon he took over the Joe Haymes big band and the Tommy Dorsey Orchestra was born.

The unit was popular from the start, alternating Dixieland-flavored Swing stomps with pop ballads. "I'm Getting Sentimental Over You" became TD's theme song, Edythe Wright was his main singer, and, starting in late 1935, Dorsey recorded now and then with the Clambake Seven, a Dixieland group taken out of his orchestra. The breakthrough year was 1937. With Bunny Berigan contributing exciting trumpet solos during his six weeks in the band and Jack Leonard adding soothing vocals, the band had major hits on "Marie" and the instrumental "Song of India." So popular were these recordings that Tommy Dorsey's name was now mentioned in the same sentence with Benny Goodman, and he would be famous for the rest of his life.

During the next few years, such players as trumpeters Pee Wee Erwin and Yank Lawson, clarinetist Johnny Mince, and tenor saxophonist Bud Freeman, along with arranger Paul Weston, kept the music stimulating. In late 1939 Dorsey began to alter his sound with the times. Buddy Rich added excitement on drums, Sy Oliver defected from Jimmie Lunceford's band to give TD more updated Swing arrangements, and the young Frank Sinatra left Harry James to accept Dorsey's lucrative offer. Although Berigan's second stint with the band in 1940 was not too successful (his alcoholism by then was out of control), the additions of Jo Stafford, Connie Haynes, and the Pied Pipers gave Dorsey a vocal team that was the envy of all other dance bands. "I'll Never Smile Again" was a huge hit, as was the band workout "Opus One." By 1942, Dorsey was appearing frequently in Hollywood films and he was prosperous enough to add a string section to his orchestra. Notable sidemen of the 1942–45 period (in addition to Buddy Rich) included trumpeter Ziggy Elman and clarinetist Buddy De-Franco.

And then it all changed. The strings were gone by 1946, Swing was considered old hat, and Dorsey was no longer considered at the cutting edge of pop music. Charlie Shavers added a lot of fire to the trumpet section and Boomie Richman was a strong tenor soloist, but business was drastically falling off and many former dance halls and venues were closing. In frustration, Dorsey broke up his band at the end of 1946, but he could not stay away and was back at it by 1948, after appearing with brother Jimmy in the fictional but mostly entertaining Hollywood movie *The Fabulous Dorseys.* Musically, Dorsey's band did not decline (Louie Bellson was his drummer by 1948) but he was slipping behind the times and his orchestra was expensive to maintain. Since Jimmy Dorsey was also having difficulty keeping his group together, in 1953 the battling Dorseys decided to team up again. JD and a couple of his sidemen joined the Tommy Dorsey big band and the Dorsey Brothers Orchestra was reborn. For over three years the ensemble (which played the hits of both Dorsey bands plus dance music, pop vocals, and some Swing music) managed to do steady business due to the nostalgia of seeing the Swing era legends performing live. The Dorseys appeared regularly on their television series, *Stage Show,* and probably would have sailed fairly easily into the 1960s. But Tommy Dorsey, after eating a heavy meal and taking sleeping pills, choked to death in his sleep on November 26, 1956. A few months later Jimmy Dorsey was gone too. A Tommy Dorsey ghost orchestra (led by Warren Covington during its first few years) kept his music going for a couple more decades, but without the trombonist the magic was gone.

●

7 *Featuring the Clambake Seven / Nov. 14, 1935–Mar. 1936 / Jazz Archives 3801262*

8 *The Music Goes Round and Round / Dec. 9, 1935–Feb. 25, 1947 / Bluebird 3140*

8₅ *Having a Wonderful Time / Dec. 9, 1935–Mar. 2, 1946 / RCA 51643*

Although most of Tommy Dorsey's big band performances of 1935–38 are difficult to locate on CD (other than in the Classics series, which is in the early stage of reissuing Dorsey's recordings), ironically there are at least three CDs out that focus on his Clambake Seven. The Jazz Archives release has a dozen performances from an early version of the Clambake Seven, cut as radio transcriptions. The octet includes trumpeter Max Kaminsky (the star soloist), clarinetist Joe Dixon, and drummer Dave Tough in its personnel, with Edythe Wright taking some vocals. The material alternates between standards and novelties and is well worth picking up by Dixieland and Swing collectors alike. The disc concludes with four numbers (including "On Treasure Island") from a transcription date by Dorsey's big band. Even better is *The Music Goes Round and Round.* Dating from 1935–39, with four titles (including a previously unissued "Nothin' from Nothin' Leaves Nothin'") from 1946–47, there is solo space for the usual players (Dorsey on trombone, Sterling Bose, Max Kaminsky, Pee Wee Erwin, Yank Lawson, or

Charlie Shavers on trumpets, clarinetists Joe Dixon, Johnny Mince, and Buddy DeFranco, and, on a few dates, tenor saxophonist Bud Freeman), plus vocals by Edythe Wright, Sy Oliver, and Hannah Williams. Although some of the selections are novelties, there are also many strong Dixieland ensembles and worthwhile solos on every selection. The repertoire includes the title cut, "At the Codfish Ball," "The Lady Is a Tramp," "When the Midnight Choo-Choo Leaves for Alabam," two versions of "The Sheik of Araby," and "There's Good Blues Tonight." *Having a Wonderful Time* is an exact duplicate of an earlier 16-selection LP, even using the same liner notes. It contains some of the most enjoyable Clambake Seven recordings, and only three songs are repeats from *The Music Goes Round and Round.* All but three songs are from 1935–38, with Edythe Wright taking some of her most famous vocals, including "At the Codfish Ball" and "You Must Have Been a Beautiful Baby." Frank Sinatra has an appearance on 1940's "Head on My Pillow" (Bunny Berigan is in the background), while Sy Oliver in 1946 takes the vocal on "Don't Be a Baby, Baby."

6 *Radio Days / Nov. 30, 1936–Jan. 4, 1937 / Sounds Great 405*

Fairly typical radio performances by the early Tommy Dorsey Orchestra, this set of air checks is most valuable for the solos of Max Kaminsky and Bud Freeman. Edythe Wright and the Three Esquires take a few vocals, but the emphasis throughout is mostly on Dorsey's Swing band, which on the final six selections includes trumpeter Bunny Berigan.

9 *Yes, Indeed! / June 15, 1939–Sept. 20, 1945 / Bluebird 9987*

This fine sampler documents some of the high points of the Sy Oliver/Buddy Rich/Ziggy Elman period of Tommy Dorsey's Orchestra. With the exception of two vocals by Oliver "Yes Indeed" (which matches him with Jo Stafford, and "Swingin' on Nothin'") and "Well All Right," the set is comprised of instrumentals. Included are the two-part "Lonesome Road," "Easy Does It," the ironically titled "Quiet Please" (a feature for Rich's noisy drums), "Swing High," a classic reworking of "Swanee River," "Well, Git It!" (which has a famous trumpet tradeoff by Elman and Chuck Peterson), a remake-with-strings version of "Opus #1," and a guest appearance by Duke Ellington on piano for "The Minor Goes Muggin'."

* *The Song Is You / Feb. 1, 1940–July 2, 1942 / RCA 66353*

It would be difficult to improve upon this five-CD set for fans of early Frank Sinatra. All 110 studio selections and broadcast performances that Sinatra recorded with Tommy Dorsey are here, including the numbers that he performed with the Pied Pipers and Connie Haynes. Most of this material has been continually reissued through the years, but it is good to have it all in one box along with an attractive and very informative booklet. Among the more famous numbers on this perfectly-done reissue are "I'll Be Seeing You," "Polka Dots and Moonbeams," "Fools Rush In," "East of the Sun," "I'll Never Smile Again," "Stardust," "Without a Song," and "The Song Is You," among many others.

7 *Well, Git It! / Sept. 30, 1943–Jan. 4, 1946 / Jass 14*

This fine collector's CD has music from ten different radio broadcasts featuring the Tommy Dorsey Orchestra during the later years of the Swing era. Although there is a fair number of vocals (by Bonnie Lou Williams, Skip Nelson, the Sentimentalists, and Stuart Foster), it is the instrumentals that are of greatest interest. Drummers Gene Krupa and Buddy Rich (it is interesting to hear Krupa on Rich's feature "Not So Quiet, Please"), clarinetist Buddy DeFranco, pianist Jess Stacy (who was with TD for just a short period), Charlie Shavers, and the leader himself are the key soloists,

and the performances are generally more exciting than Dorsey's studio sessions of the period.

6 *The Post War Era / Jan. 31, 1946–June 13, 1950 / Bluebird 66156*

8 *The Complete Standard Transcriptions / 1950–Mar. 1952 / Soundies 4115*

The Bluebird set has 22 rarely reissued selections (four were not released at all until this 1993 CD) from the Tommy Dorsey Orchestra. There are some arrangements by Sy Oliver, Tommy Todd, Sid Cooper, and Charlie Shavers, but the majority of the charts are by Bill Finegan. Dorsey himself is barely on many of the songs (although he is showcased on "Trombonology") and the solo stars are mostly Charlie Shavers and Boomie Richman, with strong support from drummer Louis Bellson. One can hear the orchestra losing some of its enthusiasm by the 1949–50 recordings (their music had become quite predictable) but this CD mostly contains the cream of the era.

The four-CD *Standard Transcriptions* release draws its 91 selections from the final years of the TD Orchestra (before Jimmy Dorsey joined) and most of the music had never been out before. Although there are some vocal features for Johnny Amaroso, Jack Duffy, Frances Irvin, Bob London, and Marv Hudson, there are quite a few instrumentals and lots of solo space for the great Shavers (in consistently explosive form), Boomie Richman, and Dorsey.

LPS TO SEARCH FOR

Trumpets and Trombones (Broadway Intermission 112) features Tommy Dorsey with the 1928 Dorsey Brothers Orchestra (including several test pressings) and on some of his earlier and rarer sideman sessions. *Trumpets and Trombones Volume II* (Broadway Intermission 113) has soundtrack performances and other obscure material, both with the TD band during the Swing era and from the trombonist's earlier days. *The Complete Tommy Dorsey Vols. 1–8* (Bluebird AXM2-5521, 5549, 5560, 5564, 5573, 5578, 5582, and 5586), a set of twofers that unfortunately cut off on March 8, 1939, has all of Dorsey's recordings as a leader during his first four years with his orchestra. On CD, the Classics label has been gradually coming out with the same material.

FILMS

Tommy Dorsey was in quite a few Hollywood movies, including starring with brother Jimmy in *The Fabulous Dor-*

seys (1947), jamming with an all-star group in *A Song Is Born* (1948), and playing with his orchestra in *Las Vegas Nights* (1941), *Ship Ahoy* (1942), *Du Barry Was a Lady* (1943), *Girl* *Crazy* (1943), *Broadway Rhythm* (1944), *Thrill of a Romance* (1945), and *Disc Jockey* (1951).

DUKE ELLINGTON
b. Apr. 29, 1899, Washington, DC, d. May 24, 1974, New York, NY

Duke Ellington towers over the Swing era, yet he also stands completely apart from it. His achievements in four different areas are so enormous that there are few others who can even be compared to him. As a bandleader, Ellington led a unique orchestra during 1925–74, one that always ranked near the top and had its own sound. One of America's top composers, Duke wrote thousands of songs, hundreds of which became standards. Although he ranked with George Gershwin, Cole Porter, and the other major songwriters of the 1930s, Ellington also composed ambitious suites and music for many different situations, including (late in his career) three full-length sacred concerts, and he wrote all of this while running a big band and constantly traveling. As an arranger, Ellington did not break the rules so much as work without them. He wrote for his individual players rather than for a generic horn section, and he constantly rearranged even his best-known works, so they sounded different in each time period. Finally, as a pianist, Ellington was an excellent stride player in the 1920s in the style of James P. Johnson and Willie "the Lion" Smith but stayed continually modern. He became a percussive player who would influence Thelonious Monk, Roland Hanna, Randy Weston, and even Cecil Taylor, among others, in later years. In the 1960s, Ellington sounded as if he were in his thirties rather than his sixties, and his musical curiosity never became dulled with age.

Duke Ellington's life was taken up by music and filled with countless events. It was a whirlwind of performances, composing, and arranging (which often took place after the gig), traveling, constant recording, partying, and enormous productivity. Edward Kennedy Ellington's life began in Washington DC at the turn of the century. Nicknamed Duke early on by his friends due to his classy nature and charm, Ellington was originally interested in becoming an artist. However, he loved hearing the barrelhouse piano players of the time and, noticing the many women who flocked around the pianists, he switched to music. He started gigging around 1917, taking out a giant ad in the yellow pages, which resulted in a great deal of work (leading him to front several bands) even though he barely knew how to play piano at that point. Duke wrote his first composition, "Soda Fountain Rag," in 1917 and did his best to develop quickly as a pianist, slowing down James P. Johnson piano rolls so he could learn his songs and form his own style.

In 1922 Ellington and a few of his musical friends (drummer Sonny Greer, altoist Otto Hardwicke, and trumpeter Arthur Whetsol) went to New York, but after a short period as part of Wilbur Sweatman's show band, they were out of work and soon returned home. The following year Duke returned, and this time he was able to work with his friends as the Washingtonians under the leadership of banjoist Elmer Snowden. It was not long before an argument over money resulted in Snowden's being ousted, and the Washingtonians becoming Ellington's band. Soon he gained a job at the Hollywood Club (which was renamed the Kentucky Club) and for a couple months Sidney Bechet was with Ellington on soprano. Bubber Miley became Duke's cornet star and quickly developed into a brilliant plunger specialist largely responsible for Ellington's "jungle sound."

Duke Ellington recorded two songs in November 1924 ("Choo Choo" and "Rainy Nights") that were his debut (featuring Miley, Hardwicke, and trombonist Charlie Irvis), but the other recordings that he made during 1925–26 were mostly very primitive and largely unrecognizable. The band sounded underrehearsed and Miley was absent. However, the recording session of November 29, 1926, was the real birth of the Duke Ellington Orchestra, and it debuted his original theme song, "East St. Louis Toodle-oo." By then the band was 11 pieces and included both Miley and trombonist Tricky Sam Nanton. Soon the orchestra was recording gems such as "Black and Tan Fantasy" and "Creole Love Call" (which used Adelaide Hall's wordless voice as an instrument) and featuring Harry Carney (who would remain with Ellington for 48 years) on baritone. Later, in 1927, Duke's orchestra (with the assistance of manager Irving Mills) was hired by the Cotton Club, and the regular broadcasts from the club would soon result in the band being accurately billed as Duke Ellington's Famous Orchestra.

The experience of writing constantly for the Cotton Club shows during the next four years and the regular work served as a creative outlet for Ellington's talent to blossom. Thanks to Mills, Duke's band recorded for many labels simultaneously (sometimes under pseudonyms) and often he would alter the arrangements so that each performance of the same song sounded different and distinctive. In 1928 the big band gained strength as altoist Johnny Hodges and clarinetist Barney Bigard joined. Bubber Miley's unreliability due to his alcoholism resulted in Ellington's reluctantly letting him go in early 1929, but his replacement, Cootie Williams, soon surpassed him. In 1929 Ellington was in his first film (the short *Black and Tan*), and from the start he appeared distinguished and charming on screen, quite a change from the usual shuffling "no-account" stereotypes that blacks were forced to play. He would have cameos in a variety of films through the years, although no really meaty roles.

The Duke Ellington Orchestra stayed quite busy throughout the 1930s. After leaving the Cotton Club in 1931 (Cab Calloway took over as the house band), the road became Duke's home for the next 40 years; he toured Europe for the first time in 1933. The constant output from Duke (including such songs as "Mood Indigo," "Rockin' in Rhythm," "It Don't Mean a Thing If It Ain't Got That Swing," "Sophisticated Lady," "Drop Me Off at Harlem," "In a Sentimental Mood," "Caravan" [written with Juan Tizol], "Prelude to a Kiss," "Solitude," "Boy Meets Horn," and "I Let a Song Go Out of My Heart") were only a few of the standards that Ellington wrote during the era. He also was a pioneer at recording extended works, starting with a six-minute version of "Tiger Rag" in 1929 and including 1931's "Creole Rhapsody" and 1935's 12-minute "Reminiscing in Tempo." For sidemen, Ellington always preferred individualists over section players, and he loved writing around musicians' strengths and weaknesses. Rather than featuring just three soloists like most bands, Duke by 1935 had eight major players: Cootie Williams, Rex Stewart, Tricky Sam Nanton, Lawrence Brown, Barney Bigard, Johnny Hodges, Harry Carney, and the leader, plus Ivie Anderson on vocals. Recognized by many as a genius, Ellington was a household name before the Swing era even began.

After Benny Goodman caught on in 1935 and Swing bands popped up everywhere, the Ellington Orchestra had more competition, but Duke's inventive writing and his many major soloists resulted in his band continuing to grow in popularity. Between the big band recordings, the small group dates (ostensibly led by Duke's sidemen but featuring Ellington's writing and usually his piano), and the constant outflow of new material, years went by with very little time off. Many historians think of his 1940–42 orchestra as being Duke's greatest, due to the addition of his musical alter ego, composer-pianist Billy Strayhorn (a major writer who chose to spend his life under Ellington's shadow), Ben Webster (Duke's first important tenor soloist), and bassist Jimmy Blanton, whose hornlike playing revolutionized his instrument. Although Cootie Williams departed late in 1940, Ray Nance (who took his place for 20 years) proved to be a triple threat on cornet, violin, and vocals. And the early 1940s brought such songs from Ellington and Strayhorn as "Concerto for Cootie," "Cottontail," "Harlem Air Shaft," "All Too Soon," "Warm Valley," Strayhorn's "Take the 'A' Train" (which became Ellington's new and permanent theme), "Just A-Settin' and A-Rockin'," "I Got It Bad," "Jump for Joy," "Perdido," "Chelsea Bridge," " 'C' Jam Blues," and many others. In addition Duke's singer Herb Jeffries had a huge hit with a non-Ellington tune, "Flamingo."

There were also special projects in addition to the usual performances. In 1940 Duke Ellington and His Orchestra were involved in the short-lived but legendary show "Jump for Joy" in Los Angeles. In 1943 Ellington had his first Carnegie Hall concert, debuting his 50-minute suite "Black, Brown and Beige," which musically depicted the history of blacks in America. It received mixed reviews, and Duke would only perform excerpts in the future (including its spiritual theme, "Come Sunday"), but it was actually a masterpiece, as shown on the concert recording, which did not come out until the 1980s. His six Carnegie Hall concerts (which continued through 1948) introduced other major works, including the "Perfume Suite," "A Tonal Group," "The Liberian Suite," "The Tattooed Bride," and "Harlem."

After having had very stable personnel during 1929–42, there would be many changes during the next decade. Such new players as trumpeters Taft Jordan, Shorty Baker, and Cat Anderson (the greatest high-note player ever), Tyree Glenn (on trombone and vibes), tenor saxophonist Al Sears, clarinetist Jimmy Hamilton, and bassist Oscar Pettiford spent important periods with the band. "I'm Beginning to See the Light" and "Don't Get Around Much Anymore" were hits in the mid-'40s, but the second half of the decade found work opportunities beginning to slow down as the big band era ended. Ellington's song royalties and famous name kept the band together while most of the others broke up, but there were slow periods. Duke could not have been happy when Jimmy Forrest (who was with the orchestra briefly in 1949) took the closing theme from his "Happy Go Lucky Local," retitled it "Night Train," and had a huge hit without giving Duke any credit, but Ellington never complained.

The biggest blow to Duke's music was probably not the rise of bebop or R&B but the defection of three of his long-time sidemen in 1951: Johnny Hodges, Lawrence Brown, and Sonny Greer. Hodges decided to go out on his own and form a combo, taking the other two with him. Duke then conducted what was called the "Great James Robbery," luring Willie Smith, Juan Tizol (who had left Ellington years earlier), and Louie Bellson from Harry James's band (which was then working just part-time). Still, even after the recording of "Satin Doll" (Duke's last pop hit), the orchestra was in a commercial slump during 1953–54, although it remained quite capable of producing brilliant music. But then things changed. Johnny Hodges gave up his group in 1955 and rejoined Ellington. And at the 1956 Newport Jazz Festival, Paul Gonsalves's 27-chorus tenor solo on "Diminuendo and Crescendo in Blue" excited the crowd so much that it almost caused a riot, making worldwide headlines. Duke was back!

By then Ellington had at least 13 major soloists in his band (trumpeters Clark Terry, Ray Nance, Cat Anderson, and Willie Cook, trombonists Quentin Jackson, Buster Cooper, and Britt Woodman, his own piano, and a saxophone section that stayed together for over 15 years [Johnny Hodges, Russell Procope, Jimmy Hamilton, Paul Gonsalves, and Harry Carney]). Duke continued playing fresh versions of his older standards but also wrote many major works with Billy Strayhorn, including "Such Sweet Thunder," the soundtracks to *Anatomy of a Murder* and *Paris Blues*, "Suite Thursday," a delightful reworking of Tchaikovsky's "Nutcracker Suite," and Grieg's "Peer Gynt Suite," "Night Creature," "The Far East Suite," and the 1963 show *My People.* Ellington also made special recordings, including a date in which his big band and Count Basie's formed a giant all-star orchestra, a trio set with bassist Charles Mingus and drummer Max Roach, and meetings with Louis Armstrong, Coleman Hawkins, and John Coltrane.

Inevitably age began to take its toll, if not on Duke than on his sidemen. Billy Strayhorn passed away in 1967 and Jimmy Hamilton left the following year; after Ellington's 70th birthday celebration in 1969 (which was celebrated at the White House), other players departed. Among the new blood that helped Duke's band during its later years were Harold Ashby on tenor, altoist Norris Turney, and trumpeter Barry Lee Hall; organist Wild Bill Davis was also a member of the ensemble in 1969. And Duke was successful in a project close to his heart, writing the music for three sacred concerts. But the death of Johnny Hodges in 1970 and the departures of Cat Anderson and Lawrence Brown resulted in the Duke Ellington Orchestra being weaker in its last years than it had been earlier, with the leader taking over much of the solo space.

Still, Duke Ellington stayed quite busy until cancer struck him down in 1974. He passed away shortly after his 75th birthday. His music continues to be regularly explored and rediscovered. Ellington's 100th birthday was celebrated throughout the world in 1999 and, even 25 years after his death, a regular string of previously unheard recordings by Duke's band continues to come out. It points out the fact that Duke Ellington and his timeless music are still very much with us.

●

7 *The Birth of a Band / Nov. 1924–Dec. 1926 / Hot 'n' Sweet 5104*

* *The Centennial Edition / Jan. 10, 1927–Dec. 1, 1973 / RCA 09026-63386*

8 *Early Ellington (1927–1934) / Oct. 26, 1927–Jan. 10, 1934 / Bluebird 6852*

7 *Jungle Nights in Harlem (1927–1932) / Dec. 19, 1927–Jan. 9, 1932 / Bluebird 2499*

7 *Jubilee Stomp / Mar. 26, 1928–May 9, 1934 / Bluebird 66038*

The Birth of a Band CD has all of Ellington's earliest recordings, including his lone piano roll, "Jig Walk," the intriguing

"Choo Choo/Rainy Nights" session, and numbers in which Duke backs singers Alberta Prime, Joe Trent, Florence Bristol, Irving Mills, Alberta Jones, and even Sonny Greer. The band instrumentals from 1925 and early 1926 are disappointing and poorly recorded, but then magically, on November 26, 1926 (with "East St. Louis Toodle-oo" and "Birmingham Breakdown"), the Ellington genius emerges for the first time.

The Centennial Edition is a remarkable 24-CD box set that has every one of Duke's recordings for RCA Victor through the years. Included are his classic sides of 1927–34 (which are generally superior to his recordings for other labels during the era), the 1940–42 recordings of the Blanton/Webster band, many performances by his underrated mid-'40s band (1944–1946), a Seattle concert from 1952, his three sacred concerts (one of the albums was leased from Fantasy), *The Far East Suite, The Popular Duke Ellington* LP, a few piano solos, Duke's odd album with Arthur Fielder's Boston Pops Orchestra, the classic *And His Mother Called Him Bill* record, and Ellington's final recording, the music that resulted in *Eastbourne Performance*. All of the music is here, including alternate takes and some previously unreleased performances, and it forms quite a legacy by itself.

Those who missed the set or do not want to spend that much money can get some of the high points of Duke's early Victor recordings on the three Bluebird discs, which each cover the same time period; none attempts to be complete. *Early Ellington* has some of the best material, including "Black and Tan Fantasy," "Creole Love Call," "Black Beauty," "The Mooche," "Mood Indigo," "Rockin' in Rhythm," and "Solitude." *Jungle Nights in Harlem* has more obscurities and offbeat material, including the two-part "Night at the Cotton Club," "Bandanna Babies," "Harlemania," "Arabian Lover," "Jungle Nights in Harlem," and a six-song 15-minute medley. *Jubilee Stomp* is most notable for the title cut, "Limehouse Blues," "Bugle Call Rag," and a variety of atmospheric mood pieces.

10   *Early Ellington / Nov. 29, 1926–Jan. 20, 1931 / GRP / Decca 3-640*

9   *The Okeh Ellington / Mar. 22, 1927–Nov. 8, 1930 / Columbia 46177*

8   *The British Connexion / July 13, 1933–Oct. 17, 1958 / Jazz Unlimited 2069*

10   *The Duke's Men: Small Groups, Vol. 1 / Dec. 12, 1934– Jan. 19, 1938 / Columbia/Legacy 46995*

10   *The Duke's Men: Small Groups, Vol. 2 / Mar. 28, 1938– Mar. 20, 1939 / Columbia/Legacy 48835*

In addition to his work for Victor, Duke Ellington recorded for other labels during the same period that would later be owned by Decca and Columbia. All of his Brunswick and Vocalion recordings (purchased by Decca) are on the wonderful three-CD set *Early Ellington*, tracing his evolution from the first real Ellington session on November 29, 1926, through his initial extended composition, "Creole Rhapsody." The 67 performances (which include all of the alternate takes) constantly display Ellington's mastery of the three-minute 78 record, with every chorus counting and having its classic moments. Among the high points are the original version of "East St. Louis Toodle-oo," "Black and Tan Fantasy," "The Mooche," "Tiger Rag," "Doin' the New Lowdown" (with dancer-singer Bill "Bojangles" Robinson), "Wall Street Wail," "Double Check Stomp," "Mood Indigo," and "Rockin' in Rhythm." Perfectly done.

Unfortunately Columbia has yet to follow Decca's example, although it has released several attractive sets. *The Okeh Ellington,* a two-CD set with 50 selections, has all of the master takes of Duke's Columbia-owned recordings of 1927–30 but leaves off the valuable alternate takes. In general the music is almost at the same level as the Victor and Decca material. Among the many songs are "East St. Louis Toodle-oo," "Jubilee Stomp," "Black Beauty," "Hot and Bothered," "I Must Have That Man," "Saturday Night Function," "Double Check Stomp," "Ring Dem Bells," "Old Man Blues," and "Mood Indigo."

The British Connexion has a variety of Ellington music that was originally made available or heard in England. Six performances (four songs and two alternates) from a fine 1933 studio date are here, plus radio broadcasts from 1938–40 that were on the "America Dances" series beamed to Great Britain, giving alternate versions of such songs as "Jeep's Blues," "Harmony in Harlem," and "Cotton Tail." This CD concludes with Ellington playing "Take the 'A' Train" in 1958 with British sidemen in a trio.

Thus far Columbia has done a better job of reissuing Duke Ellington's small group dates from 1934–39 than it has his big band performances. The two small group releases (both two-CD sets) contain 45 and 43 selections, respectively, from sessions led by Rex Stewart, Barney Bigard,

Cootie Williams, and Johnny Hodges, plus one date by the Gotham Stompers. In addition to early (and often debut) versions) of such songs as "Caravan," "Stompy Jones," "Echoes of Harlem," "Jeep's Blues," "I Let a Song Go Out of My Heart," "Pyramid," "Prelude to a Kiss," and "The Jeep Is Jumpin'," the lesser-known stomps are generally quite rewarding and serve as superb examples of inventive small group Swing. It is a pity that the alternate takes have been bypassed, but otherwise this pair of twofers is beyond criticism.

7 *Cotton Club 1938—Volume 1 / Mar. 24, 1938–May 29, 1938 / Archives of Jazz 3801122*

7 *Cotton Club 1938—Volume 2 / Mar. 24, 1938–May 15, 1938 / Archives of Jazz 3801132*

7 *1939–40 / July 26, 1939 + Jan. 9, 1940 / Jazz Unlimited 2022*

10 *Fargo, ND, November 7, 1940 / Nov. 7, 1940 / Vintage Jazz Classics 1019/20*

8 *The Complete Standard Transcriptions / Jan. 15, 1941– Dec. 3, 1941 / Soundies 4107*

In addition to the enormous number of studio recordings that Duke Ellington made throughout his career, there were countless live sets that have been saved for posterity. The pair of *Cotton Club* air checks from the Europeans Archives of Jazz label gives listeners some fine examples of the 1938 Ellington Orchestra playing both Duke standards and such songs as (on *Volume 1*) "Dinah," "If Dreams Come True," and "Rose Room"; the second disc includes Rachmaninoff's "Prelude in 'C' Sharp Minor," "Three Blind Mice," and "On the Sunny Side of the Street." The recording quality is decent and the band sounds typically strong. *1939–40* has two broadcasts, including one with Jimmy Blanton, and such numbers as "Jazz Potpourri," "Old King Dooji," "Little Posey," and "Tootin' Through the Roof"; Ivie Anderson and Herb Jeffries take some vocals.

Fargo, ND, a two-CD set, features the Duke Ellington Orchestra on what would have been a long-forgotten concert most significant for being Ray Nance's first night with the band. But the excellent recording quality of this privately recorded performance (documented by Jack Towers on his portable disc cutter) and the consistently inspiring solos (including Ben Webster on "Stardust") make this a special release. It shows what the 1940 Ellington band sounded like

live playing their usual repertoire of the era. Also of strong interest is the two-CD Soundies release. Due to the ASCAP strike of the period, Ellington (and every other bandleader) had to scramble for material from non-ASCAP writers. The great majority of the 29 selections that he cut as standard radio transcriptions were composed by Billy Strayhorn, Mercer Ellington, or writers from outside of the band, so one hears a rather fresh and sometimes unusual repertoire performed by one of the finest of all of Duke's orchestras.

10 *The Blanton-Webster Band / Mar. 6, 1940–July 28, 1942 / Bluebird 5659*

8 *The Great Ellington Units / Nov. 2, 1940–Sept. 29, 1941 / Bluebird 6751*

8 *Solos, Duets and Trios / Feb. 9, 1932–Aug. 30, 1967 / Bluebird 2178*

9 *Black, Brown and Beige / Dec. 1, 1944–Sept. 3, 1946 / Bluebird 86641*

7 *Duke's Joint / Dec. 8, 1943–Oct. 15, 1945 / Buddha 7446599629*

All of the music on the four Bluebird sets is available as part of the mammoth *Centennial Edition.* The three-CD *Blanton-Webster Band* reissue has all of the master takes of the Duke Ellington's Big Band's recordings during a very productive period in its evolution. The 66 selections cover dozens of classics, including "Concerto for Cootie," "Cottontail," "Harlem Air Shaft," "All Too Soon," "In a Mellotone," "Take the 'A' Train," "I Got It Bad," "Rocks in My Bed," "Chelsea Bridge," "Perdido," "C Jam Blues," and many more. Essential music by one of the most significant big bands and jazz groups of all time. *The Great Ellington Units* has most (but not all) of the small-group dates led by Duke's sidemen (Johnny Hodges, Rex Stewart, and Barney Bigard) during the 1940–41 period, including the initial versions of "Day Dream," "Good Queen Bess," "Passion Flower," "Things Ain't What They Used to Be," and "C Jam Blues," renditions that preceded the more familiar orchestra versions. *Solos, Duets and Trios* has a variety of intimate performances by Ellington from a 35-year period. Duke is heard unaccompanied in 1932, 1941, and 1967, on a few numbers from a 1965 concert (including "House of Lords," in which Earl Hines joins him on second piano) and two trio cuts from 1945. Most significant are a pair of piano duets with Billy Strayhorn from 1946 ("Drawing Room Blues" and the exciting "Tonk") and Duke's four duets with Jimmy Blanton in 1940, which are augmented by five alternate takes. In the latter situation, Ellington generously features Blanton as the lead voice, an unprecedented showcase at the time for a jazz bassist.

Black, Brown and Beige has all of the Duke Ellington Orchestra's recordings (master takes only) from its 1944–46 period on Victor. Although not as renowned as its earlier performances, there are many gems to be heard, including "I Ain't Got Nothin' but the Blues," "I'm Beginning to See the Light," an exciting remake of "It Don't Mean a Thing," "Tonight I Shall Sleep," the "Perfume Suite," fresh renditions of standards, and the excerpts from "Black, Brown & Beige." *Duke's Joint* has music from three radio broadcasts (three songs from December 8, 1943, and the remainder from October 1 and 15, 1945), all of it previously unissued. There are vocals from Kay Davis, Joya Sherrill, and Ray Nance, and a rare one from Betty Roche, but it is the instrumentals (including "Three Cent Stomp," "Blues on the Double," and "Cotton Tail") that are of greatest interest.

- **10** *The Carnegie Hall Concerts (January 1943)* / Jan. 23–28, 1943 / Prestige 34004

- **8** *The Carnegie Hall Concerts (December 1944)* / Dec. 19, 1944 / Prestige 24073

- **8** *The Carnegie Hall Concerts (January 1946)* / Jan. 4, 1946 / Prestige 24074

- **9** *The Carnegie Hall Concerts (December 1947)* / Dec. 27, 1947 / Prestige 24075

- **8** *Carnegie Hall, November 13, 1948* / Nov. 13, 1948 / Vintage Jazz Classics 1024/25

Four of Duke Ellington's *Carnegie Hall Concerts* have been released fairly complete by Prestige on two-CD sets. The *January 1943* set (all from January 23 except for a few minutes substituted from a Boston concert of five days later to make up for a damaged section) is quite historic, highlighted by the full-length 50-minute version of "Black, Brown & Beige." In addition, there are superior interpretations of a variety of classic miniatures, including "Black and Tan Fantasy," "Jumpin' Punkins," "Portrait of Bojangles," "Johnny Come Lately," and "Cotton Tail." Except for the death of Jimmy Blanton and the departure of Ivie Anderson and Barney Bigard, the most famous edition of Ellington's orchestra was still intact for this famous concert.

The *December 1944* twofer debuts the "Perfume Suite," has a half-hour of excerpts from "Black, Brown & Beige," and includes such numbers as "Blutopia," "Midriff," "Trumpets No End," and "Frankie and Johnny" (featuring Tricky Sam Nanton). "Black, Brown & Beige" was down to just 19 minutes for the 1946 concert, but the band (featuring Al Sears, Cat Anderson, singer Al Hibbler, and the usual cast) sounds fine on such tunes as "Caravan," "Air Conditioned Jungle," "I'm Just a Lucky So and So," and the three-part "A Tonal Group." Second to the 1943 concert in quality among the Carnegie Hall appearances is the December 27, 1947, performance. In addition to the debut of the "Liberian Suite," highlights include "Triple Play," a Johnny Hodges medley, "On a Turquoise Cloud," "Cotton Tail," "Trumpets No End," and the nearly atonal "The Clothed Woman."

The two-CD 1948 Carnegie Hall concert (the sixth and final in the series) has a rare version of "Lush Life" (sung by the composer, Billy Strayhorn), the debut of "The Tattooed Bride," a revival of "Reminiscing in Tempo," and opportunities for Ben Webster (who was briefly back in the band) to be featured. Not everything works (including a slapdash hits medley and Al Hibbler's sappy vocal on "Trees"). But, since there are many other strong moments and this particular orchestra did not record (due to the 1948 recording strike), the 152 minutes of music are quite valuable.

- **8** *The Great Chicago Concerts* / Jan. 20, 1946 + Nov. 10, 1946 / Music Masters 65110

- **7** *Cornell University Concert* / Dec. 10, 1948 / Music Masters 65114

- **7** *Cornell University: Second Set* / Dec. 10, 1948 / Music Masters 65162

- **8** *Piano Duets—Great Times* / Sept. 13, 1950 – Nov. 1950 / Original Jazz Classics 108

- **7** *The 1952 Seattle Concert* / Mar. 28, 1952 / Bluebird 66531

- **7** *At Birdland 1952* / Nov. 20 + 24, 1952 / Jazz Unlimited 2036

The 1946 Duke Ellington Orchestra is featured during two performances on the two-CD *The Great Chicago Concerts*. Of particular interest is the three-part "Deep South Suite" (which concludes with "Happy-Go-Lucky Local," the basis for "Night Train"), a 12-minute excerpt from "Black, Brown & Beige," and four numbers on which guest Django

Reinhardt (who was touring with Duke during his only visit to the U.S.) is showcased with the rhythm section. The pair of discs that came from a concert at Cornell University (only a month after their last famous Carnegie Hall concert) once again finds Ben Webster as one of the stars with Ellington's orchestra. The material is similar, but of course the solos are different. The first set includes "The Tattooed Bride," "Reminiscing in Tempo," and the two-part "Symphomaniac," while the second disc has "Manhattan Murals," "How High the Moon," and a hits medley, among others.

Piano Duets—Great Times consists of some unusual performances. Ellington and Strayhorn are heard in a two-piano quartet that performs "Tonk," "Cottontail," and "Johnny Come Lately" among the eight intriguing numbers. In addition there are four cuts in which Oscar Pettiford (on cello) is the solo star, backed by Duke in a trio/quartet that sometimes includes Strayhorn on celeste. *The 1952 Seattle Concert* is more conventional, with two showcases for drummer Louie Bellson (including "Skin Deep"), a feature for trombonist Britt Woodman on "Sultry Serenade," and spots for Willie Smith, Juan Tizol, and Clark Terry ("Perdido"), plus one of the best versions ever of "Harlem." The Birdland concerts, taken from radio broadcasts, celebrate the 25th anniversary of Ellington's arrival at the Cotton Club. There are some brief verbal testimonials from celebrities, performances of Ellington favorites, "The Tattooed Bride," two versions of "Take the 'A' Train" (with Betty Roche), and a few short renditions of "Lullaby of Birdland." This music was released for the first time on this 1993 CD.

* *The Complete Capitol Recordings of Duke Ellington / Apr. 6, 1953–May 19, 1955 / Mosaic 5–160*

9 *Piano Reflections / Apr. 13, 1953–Dec. 3, 1953 / Capitol 92863*

8 *Happy Birthday Duke! / Apr. 29, 1953–Apr. 29, 1954 / Laserlight 15 965*

7 *In Hamilton / Feb. 8, 1954 / Radiex Music 1000*

9 *Ellington at Newport 1956 (Complete) / July 7–9, 1956 / Columbia/Legacy 64932*

9 *Such Sweet Thunder / Apr. 1957–May 1957 / Columbia/ Legacy 65568*

Although Duke Ellington received less publicity during 1953–55 than during probably any other period of his career and his band was struggling to keep its audience, Duke's music was still of high quality and there was no slump, at least not artistically. The five-CD limited-edition Mosaic box shows just how strong the big band still was, even with the absence of Johnny Hodges. With 11 major soloists, Duke's orchestra was still a mighty force. His Capitol recordings include a high-quality trio date (*Piano Reflections*), many recordings of non-Ellington standards (including completely reworked songs made famous by other bandleaders), a few attempts at hits ("Satin Doll" did much better than "Twelfth St. Rag Mambo!"), and even one of the earliest recordings of the electric piano (from 1955). The trio sessions (with bassist Wendell Marshall and drummer Butch Ballard) known as *Piano Reflections* are available as a single disc from Capitol, with 13 of the 15 songs being Ellington songs, some quite obscure. A superior showcase for his underrated piano.

By coincidence, Duke Ellington celebrated his birthday in both 1953 and 1954 by playing with his big band at McElroy's Ballroom in Portland, Oregon, and both concerts were recorded and saved. The three hours of music (released as a five-CD set and also available on five separate discs, although it could have fit onto three) contained on *Happy Birthday Duke!* shows that the Ellington Orchestra, even when playing standards for dancers during the era, was always capable of coming up with great moments. The two-CD *In Hamilton* has similar music, with four top trumpet soloists (Clark Terry, Willie Cook, Cat Anderson, and Ray Nance) often taking solo honors; highlights include "The Mooche," "How High the Moon," and Britt Woodman's feature on "Theme for Trambean."

After ending his association with Capitol and recording two albums for Bethlehem, Duke Ellington returned to Columbia. His 1956 Newport Jazz Festival concert was so successful that no one ever suggested again that Duke break up his big band and work full-time as a composer! While an album originally came out from the festival and some of the other cuts were released on an LP shared with Eddie Condon, the twofer *Ellington at Newport (Complete)* has the full story. The version of "Newport Jazz Festival Suite" on the original LP was actually recorded two days later in the studio, with crowd noises added. This twofer has both that version and the one that took place at the festival (which is slightly flawed) along with unissued tracks from both dates and the famous "Diminuendo in Blue and Crescendo in Blue." Even though Paul Gonsalves was slightly off mike during his famous 27-chorus solo on the latter, the excitement can certainly be felt as the crowd gets louder and louder, giving the band a large ovation while Gonsalves was still soloing. One of the great moments in jazz history.

Now that Duke Ellington was generating headlines again, he was free to start working on major projects in collaboration with Billy Strayhorn. One of their best was *Such Sweet Thunder,* a 12-part work in which each section is dedicated to one of William Shakespeare's characters. Britt Woodman, Cat Anderson (on "Madness in Great Ones"), Johnny Hodges, Paul Gonsalves, and Quentin Jackson are among the solo stars on these witty and fresh pieces. The CD reissue doubles the amount of music, with a dozen alternate takes, including one of the best-known pieces from the suite "The Star-Crossed Lovers."

7 *Studio Sessions; Chicago, 1956, Vol. 1 / Mar. 17, 1956– Dec. 16 1956 / Atlantic 83000*

7 *Dance Concerts; California, 1958, Vol. 2 / Mar. 4, 1958 / Atlantic 83001*

9 *Studio Sessions; New York, 1962, Vol. 3 / July 25, 1962– Sept. 13, 1962 / Atlantic 83002*

7 *Studio Sessions; New York, 1963, Vol. 4 / Apr. 17, 1963– July 18, 1963 / Atlantic 83003*

9 *The Suites; New York, 1968 & 1970, Vol. 5 / Nov. 6, 1968–June 15, 1970 / Atlantic 83004*

7 *Dance Dates; California 1958, Vol. 6 / Mar. 4–5, 1958 / Atlantic 91230*

7 *Studio Sessions; 1957 & 1962, Vol. 7 / Jan. 1957–June 6, 1962 / Atlantic 91231*

7 *Studio Sessions; 1957, 1965, 1966, 1967, Vol. 8 / Jan. 1957–July 11, 1967 / Atlantic 91232*

7 *Studio Sessions; New York, 1968, Vol. 9 / Nov. 23, 1968– Dec. 3, 1968 / Atlantic 91233*

8 *Studio Sessions; New York & Chicago 1965, 1966 and 1971, Vol. 10 / Mar. 4, 1965–May 6, 1971 / Atlantic 91234*

Duke Ellington recorded constantly from 1927 on, and, starting in the 1950s, he documented many of his band's rehearsals as he tried out new material, some of which he later abandoned. After his death, many labels were able to come out with previously unreleased material by the Ellington band. These ten CDs, originally released by the small Saja label and then picked up by Atlantic, should be of great interest to Ellington collectors for they often contain "new" compositions; and even on the better-known pieces, the solos are completely different solos from those heard previously. *Vol. 1* has performances from 1956, with the stars being Clark Terry, Ray Nance, Johnny Hodges, and Paul Gonsalves. *Vol. 2* consists of a dance concert from 1958, with only half of the music being Ellington and Strayhorn compositions. *Vol. 3,* one of the strongest in the series, is noteworthy for the inclusion of a Thelonious Monk song, "Monk's Dream" (not "Blue Monk" as listed), Paul Gonsalves' features on "Major" and "Minor," a few numbers that later appeared in Duke Ellington's sacred concerts, and "September 12th Blues," which serves as a "welcome back" for Cootie Williams, who had returned after a 21-year "vacation." *Vol. 4* has revivals of "Harmony in Harlem" and "Blue Rose," and lots of playing by Ray Nance (the only brassman on the dates). *Vol. 5* is comprised of two otherwise unrecorded suites: "Degas Suite" (written for an art film that was never made) and "The River," which was a ballet score. *Vol. 6* is a continuation of the dance date heard in *Vol. 2,* plus music from the following day, loosely played but with some exciting moments. *Vol. 7* has big band sessions from 1957 and 1962, experiments with a vocal group, plus an octet that on "Things Ain't What They Used to Be" reunites Ellington briefly with Sonny Greer. *Vol. 8* is from 1965–67, with one track from 1957. Cat Anderson, Johnny Hodges, and Paul Gonsalves star on many little-known Ellington compositions, and Louie Bellson sits in for a few numbers. *Vol. 9,* from late in Ellington's life, has remakes of standards plus a few completely unknown pieces ("Knuf," "Gigl," "Reva," "Ortseam," and "Elos") along with a some surprises. The final disc, *Vol. 10,* finds Ellington reworking three of his suites: "Black, Brown & Beige," "Harlem," and "Ad Lib on Nippon." The more serious Duke Ellington collectors will want all ten CDs in this intriguing series.

7 *Live at the 1957 Stratford Festival / July 1957 / Music & Arts 616*

5 *Black, Brown & Beige / Feb. 5–12, 1958 / Columbia/ Legacy 65566*

5 *Live at Newport 1958 / July 3, 1958 / Columbia/Legacy 53584*

8 *Jazz Party in Stereo / Feb. 19–25, 1959 / Mobile Fidelity 719*

8 *Anatomy of a Murder / May 29, 1959–June 2, 1959 / Columbia/Legacy 65569*

9 *Live at the Blue Note / Aug. 9, 1959 / Roulette 28637*
Duke Ellington's appearance at the prestigious Stratford Festival was fairly conventional although spirited as his orchestra performed features for Clark Terry, Jimmy Hamilton, Britt Woodman, Harry Carney ("Sophisticated Lady"), Cat Anderson, the cute "Pretty and the Wolf," and the "Harlem Suite." Ellington's *Black, Brown & Beige* album has always been a bit of a disappointment compared to the original version, for the excerpts are fairly unremarkable and Johnny Hodges is absent. Mahalia Jackson's two powerful appearances (on "Come Sunday" and the "23rd Psalm") largely save the day. The CD reissue has additional alternate takes to each of the movements, plus a couple of irrelevant instrumentals. A noble failure overall. Duke Ellington's appearance at the 1958 Newport Jazz Festival (reissued in full on a two-CD set) was very streaky due to scheduling problems, an excess of cameras, and live radio broadcasts that delayed some of the music. It was such a mess that the original LP of the same name actually consisted mostly of studio performances, with phony applause added! There are some good moments on this double-CD (which was nearly all previously unreleased), including a couple of appearances by Mahalia Jackson (heard on "Come Sunday" and "Keep Your Hand on the Plow") but the music is erratic. Best is a meeting between Gerry Mulligan and Harry Carney on "Prima Bara Dubla," which differs from the one previously included on the LP). Interesting but far from essential.

In contrast, *Jazz Party in Stereo,* although quite spontaneous in spots, works quite well. Dizzy Gillespie sits in with the band on "Upper Manhattan Medical Group" (his only recording with Ellington), Jimmy Rushing sings "Hello Little Girl," two intriguing selections feature nine symphonic percussionists, and Johnny Hodges and Paul Gonsalves star on the other numbers. Duke Ellington's first film score, *Anatomy of a Murder,* is considered a classic by some and so-so by others. The best-known selection is the title cut, which (with Peggy Lee's lyrics) would soon become "I'm Gonna Go Fishin'." This reissue is greatly augmented by alternate takes, and virtually all of the music that was recorded (but not always used) for the Jimmy Stewart film. The double-CD *Live at the Blue Note* features Duke Ellington stretching out on three full sets at his favorite Chicago nightclub. In addition to the usual older features, surprises include Billy

Strayhorn getting to sit in on "Take the 'A' Train," a few numbers from the *Anatomy of a Murder* soundtrack, piano duets by Ellington and Strayhorn on "Tonk" and "Drawing Room Blues," and an 11-minute rendition of "Mood Indigo."

10 *Three Suites / Mar. 3, 1960–Oct. 10, 1960 / Columbia 46825*

10 *Duke Ellington Meets Count Basie / July 6, 1961 / Columbia/Legacy 655471*

9 *Duke Ellington Meets Coleman Hawkins / Aug. 18, 1962 / Impulse 162*

9 *Money Jungle / Sept. 17, 1962 / Blue Note 85129*

10 *Duke Ellington & John Coltrane / Sept. 26, 1962 / Impulse 166*
All five of these early '60s releases are unique in their own way and contain essential performances. *Three Suites* has all of the music from three of the finest Ellington-Strayhorn works: Tchaikovsky's "The Nutcracker Suite," Grieg's "Peer Gynt Suites Nos. 1 & 2" (including "In the Hall of the Mountain King" and "Anitra's Dance") and "Suite Thursday" (a work dedicated to John Steinbeck). *Duke Ellington Meets Count Basie* (the CD reissue expands the original eight songs to 15) is a remarkably successful outing in which the Duke Ellington and Count Basie Orchestras are combined for such songs as "Corner Pocket," "Jumpin' at the Woodside," and "Wild Man." In addition to both Ellington and Basie on pianos, there are 15 major soloists, and Billy Strayhorn sits in on "Take the 'A' Train." "Segue in C" in particular is a classic.

Coleman Hawkins and Duke Ellington had crossed paths for 35 years by the time they finally met up in the recording studio in 1962. Hawkins is featured as part of an all-star octet with such Ellingtonians as Ray Nance, Lawrence Brown, Johnny Hodges, and Harry Carney. Highlights include "Mood Indigo," "Self Portrait of the Bean," and an exciting rendition of "The Jeep Is Jumpin'." *Money Jungle* is particularly unusual, for it matches Ellington in a trio with bassist Charles Mingus and drummer Max Roach. On such numbers as "Fleurette Africaine," "Caravan," "Wig Wise," and particularly "Money Jungle," Ellington sounds like the youngest and most modern player on the date! On this fascinating release, one can definitely hear the debt that Thelonious Monk and other later pianists owed Duke. Another example of Ellington's modern style can be heard in his meeting with John Coltrane. The co-leaders are joined by either 'Trane's rhythm section (bassist Jimmy Garrison and drummer Elvin Jones) or Duke's (bassist Aaron Bell and drummer Sam Woodyard) for five Ellington tunes, Billy Strayhorn's "My Little Brown Book," and Coltrane's "Big Nick." "Take the Coltrane" is memorable, but the classic of the date is a haunting and definitive version of "In a Sentimental Mood."

8 *Featuring Paul Gonsalves / May 1, 1962 / Original Jazz Classics 623*

7 *Afro-Bossa / Nov. 29, 1962–Jan. 5, 1963 / Discovery 71002*

7 *The Great London Concerts / Jan. 22, 1963 + Feb. 20, 1964 / Music Masters 65106*

7 *The Symphonic Ellington / Jan. 31, 1963–Feb. 21, 1963 / Discovery 71003*

9 *The Great Paris Concert / Feb. 1–23, 1963 / Atlantic 2-304*

6 *My People / Aug. 20–28, 1963 / Red Baron 52759*

7 *Harlem / Mar. 9, 1964 / Pablo 2308-245*

On May 1, 1962, Duke Ellington, for no particular reason, decided to showcase his longtime tenor saxophonist Paul Gonsalves as the only soloist on eight numbers, including "C Jam Blues," "Take the 'A' Train," "Jam with Sam," and "Paris Blues." Fortunately Gonsalves was in top form that day and inspired by this rare opportunity. This set was not released initially until 1984, when both Gonsalves and Ellington were long gone, but it still sounds fresh today. By 1962, the Duke Ellington Orchestra was involved in traveling the world. *Afro-Bossa* pays tribute to the many lands that the musicians were seeing, and the 11 new selections (along with the standard "Pyramid") are mostly concise gems. Best known among the pieces are "Purple Gazelle" and "Eighth Veil." *The Great London Concerts* has more typical material, mostly standards, with "Isfahan" and "Single Petal of a Rose" being the newest selections. In addition to a fine version of "Harlem," there are five numbers from the brief period when Cootie Williams (featured on "Caravan") and Ray Nance were both in the trumpet section; unfortunately they never trade off, a lost opportunity. In 1963 Ellington had the rare chance to combine his big band with a sym-

phony orchestra. Together they perform the three-movement "Night Creature," "Harlem Airshaft," "Non-Violent Integration," and "La Scala, She Too Pretty to Be Blue." In general the strings do not weigh the proceedings down and the collaboration works well.

One of his best live recordings from the 1960s, *The Great Paris Concert* (a double CD), shows how mighty the Duke Ellington Orchestra still was in 1963. Highlights include a rousing "Rockin' in Rhythm," Cootie Williams' feature on "Concerto for Cootie," "Jam with Sam," "Suite Thursday," "Harlem Suite," and some newer pieces. Ten soloists are heard from, including both Cootie Williams and Ray Nance. In 1963 Duke Ellington put together the *My People* show, using alumni and other close associates. The music is in the spirit of *Jump For Joy* (with its messages of equality and integration) and has some pieces taken from the "Black, Brown & Beige" suite, plus others that would reappear in Duke's first sacred concert. With vocals by Jimmy McPhail, Joya Sherrill, Jimmy Grissom, and Lil Greenwood, plus a band that includes Ray Nance, Bill Berry, Harold Ashby, Billy Strayhorn, and Louie Bellson, the results are interesting if not essential. Cootie Williams, Cat Anderson, Paul Gonsalves, and Johnny Hodges are the main soloists on *Harlem*, which, in addition to the title suite, includes "The Opener," "A Happy Reunion," "Blow by Blow," "The Prowling Cat," and various standards, all played enthusiastically during a Stockholm concert.

8 *New York Concert / May 20, 1964 / Music Masters 65122*

7 *In the Uncommon Market / 1966 / Pablo 2308-247*

6 *The Popular Duke Ellington / 1966 / RCA 68705*

7 *The Pianist / July 18, 1966–Jan. 7, 1970 / Original Jazz Classics 717*

10 *The Far East Suite—Special Mix / Dec. 19–21, 1966 / Bluebird 66551*

10 *And His Mother Called Him Bill / Aug. 28, 1967–Sept. 1, 1967 / Bluebird 6287*

Due to his constant activity with his big band, it was always easy to underrate Duke Ellington's skills as a pianist. *New York Concert* has four thoughtful, unaccompanied piano solos, trio features, a guest spot for Willie "The Lion" Smith (Duke's old idol) on "Carolina Shout," and a pair of Ellington-Strayhorn piano duets (including "Tonk"). Duke certainly does not sound 65! The Pablo label in the 1980s came out with several albums of previously unreleased material recorded by Norman Granz of Duke in the 1960s and early '70s. *In the Uncommon Market,* recorded at several concerts during a European tour, has mostly big band performances with an emphasis on little-known material (other than "Star-Crossed Lovers" and "In a Sentimental Mood"). A special bonus are three selections that Duke and his rhythm section performed specifically for Spanish painter Joan Miró. *The Popular Duke Ellington* is much more conventional, fairly routine versions by Ellington's orchestra of 11 warhorses, plus his blues "The Twitch." The results are well played but predictable. *The Pianist* once again puts the emphasis on Ellington's playing, and he sounds both modern and traditional in trios from 1966 and 1970, playing mostly spontaneous originals (other than the two versions of "The Shepherd").

The Far East Suite (which in the "Special Mix" edition adds four alternate takes and fixes the balance) was the last classic project that Duke Ellington and Billy Strayhorn worked on together. The nine songs pay tribute to the Asian countries the Ellington Orchestra visited, not by copying the native folk styles but by having the band's jazz music be open to the influences. "Isfahan" became a standard, and the lengthy "Ad Lib on Nippon," "Mount Harissa," and "Tourist Point of View" are memorable, but every one of the selections is haunting in its own way. After Strayhorn passed away in 1967, Duke Ellington and his big band recorded *And His Mother Called Him Bill,* an emotional and very inspired tribute that features 15 of Strayhorn's finest songs plus an alternate take; the original program was expanded from a dozen songs to 16 for this reissue. Among the numbers are "Blood Count" (Strayhorn's final composition), "Smada," "Rain Check," "Midriff," "Lotus Blossom," and "The Intimacy of the Blues."

| 7 | *1965–1972 / Mar. 31, 1965–Aug. 2, 1972 / Music Masters 5041* |

| 6 | *The Ellington Suites / Feb. 25, 1959–Dec. 5, 1972 / Original Jazz Classics 446* |

| 7 | *Berlin '65—Paris '67 / Feb. 3, 1965–Mar. 10, 1967 / Pablo 5304* |

| 7 | *The Intimacy of the Blues / Mar. 15, 1967–June 15, 1970 / Original Jazz Classics 624* |

| 7 | *Yale Concert / Jan. 26, 1968 / Original Jazz Classics 664* |

| 7 | *Latin American Suite / Oct. 1968 / Original Jazz Classics 469* |

| 6 | *The Intimate Ellington / Apr. 25, 1969–June 29, 1971 / Original Jazz Classics 730* |

| 6 | *Up in Duke's Workshop / Apr. 25, 1969–Dec. 1972 / Original Jazz Classics 633* |

Mercer Ellington oversaw the release of the music on the Music Masters CD in 1991, 15 selections covering a seven-year period and containing a few surprises. The latter includes Jimmy Hamilton's roaring tenor on "The Old Circus Train," Buster Cooper showing off his personality on "Trombone Buster," some songs that would be used in "The New Orleans Suite," three features for organist Wild Bill Davis, and other obscurities. *The Ellington Suites* has three of his lesser-known works: 1959's "The Queen's Suite" ("The Single Petal of a Rose" originated from this six-part work), 1971's "Goutelas Suite," and 1972's "The Uwis Suite." Decent but unremarkable music. The next CD has four songs from a Berlin concert in 1965 and six from a Paris date in '67. There are four features for Johnny Hodges, fine renditions of "Happy-Go-Lucky Local" and "Rockin' In Rhythm," and a surprise stride showcase for Ellington in "The Second Portrait of the Lion." *The Intimacy of the Blues* is split between a 1967 octet date (the six-part "Combo Suite" that includes the debut of Strayhorn's "The Intimacy of the Blues") and five numbers from 1970 that include some features for Wild Bill Davis.

After Billy Strayhorn's death, Duke Ellington (as if he realized that his own time would soon run out) wrote music even more prolifically than he had earlier. *Yale Concert,* other than "Warm Valley" and "Take the 'A' Train," consists of recently composed pieces, including "A Chromatic Love Affair," "The Little Purple Flower," and "Swamp Goo"; Russell Procope plays some New Orleans clarinet on the latter and there are some spots for Cootie, Carney, Gonsalves, and Cat. None of the seven songs on *Latin America Suite* would catch on, but the music overall certainly captures the atmosphere of the Latin and South American countries that the Ellington Orchestra had just visited. Gonsalves, Hodges, and Buster Cooper are heard from, but the main soloist throughout is the piano player. *The Intimate Ellington* and *Up in Duke's Workshop* are comprised of rehearsal performances, with Ellington trying out new songs and arrangements, some of which he would soon discard. Duke even takes a vocal on "Moon Maiden" from the former set, while Cootie Williams steals solo honors on "Love Is Just Around the Corner" on the latter CD. Neither release is essential but they both have their moments of interest.

10   *70th Birthday Concert* / Nov. 25–26, 1969 / Blue Note 32746

8   *The Afro-Eurasian Eclipse* / Feb. 11–17, 1971 / Original Jazz Classics 645

7   *Togo Brava Suite* / Oct. 22 + 24, 1971 / Blue Note 30082

7   *Live at the Whitney* / Apr. 10, 1972 / Impulse 173

8   *This One's for Blanton* / Dec. 5, 1972 / Original Jazz Classics 810

8   *Duke's Big Four* / Jan. 8, 1973 / Pablo 2310-703

5   *In Sweden 1973* / Oct. 25, 1973 / Caprice 21599

70th Birthday Concert is one of the final recordings that feature the Duke Ellington Orchestra at full strength. There are many inspiring moments on this two-CD set, including definitive renditions of "Rockin' in Rhythm" and "Take the 'A' Train" (with some great Cootie Williams), several Johnny Hodges features, "Perdido," the best hits medley that Ellington ever recorded (nine songs in 16 1/2 minutes), and an incredible high-note trumpet chorus by Cat Anderson on "Satin Doll." *The Afro-Eurasian Eclipse* is unusual, for it hints at rock on "Acth O'Clock Rock." Some of the other selections in this eight-piece suite look toward African folk music and surprisingly advanced areas of jazz. Harold Ashby, Paul Gonsalves, Harry Carney, Norris Turney, and drummer Rufus Jones (a major asset) are the main stars. The Ellington Orchestra was beginning to show its age by 1971, and Hodges, Cat Anderson, and Lawrence Brown were gone. However, there are some strong moments on *Togo Brava Suite*, including heroic Cootie Williams trumpet solos, Norris Turney's tribute to Hodges ("The Checkered Hat"), and spots for trombonist Booty Wood, Gonsalves, Ashby, and Duke, even if no one remembers the *Togo Brava Suite* today.

The next three CDs all put the focus on Duke Ellington's piano. At 73, Ellington's playing on the special concert released by Impulse (half of the songs add bassist Joe Benjamin and Rufus Jones) is a bit rusty in spots, and he jokingly stops his first composition ("Soda Fountain Rag") before it gets very far. Pity, for he never recorded it commercially. However, there are introspective and lyrical pieces that work quite well, and he is memorable on "A Mural from Two Perspectives," "New World A-Coming," and "Lotus Blossom." The audience is quite respectful and loving, inspiring Ellington to do his best. *This One's for Blanton* is a set of duets with bassist Ray Brown consisting of five standards (including "Pitter Panther Patter") and the four-part "Fragmented Suite for Piano and Bass." The results are often playful. *Duke's Big Four* finds Ellington being pushed by guitarist Joe Pass, Brown, and Louie Bellson in a quartet, and he comes up with rather modern and energetic solos on such numbers as "Cotton Tail," "Love You Madly," and "Everything But You."

Late in 1973, Duke Ellington made his final tour of Europe. He was 74 and starting to ail, and his band lacked most of his former stars (only Russell Procope, Harold Ashby, and the always reliable Harry Carney were still with him). But there were still moments. *In Sweden 1973* is noteworthy primarily for the beautiful singing on several songs (particularly "Serenade to Sweden") of the great Alice Babs. Otherwise there are OK run-throughs of ancient standards, some spots for trumpeters Rolf Ericson and Barry Lee Hall, a very interesting version of "St. Louis Blues" (featuring two trombonists and Duke), and an encore version of "Tiger Rag" that misses the mark.

LPS TO SEARCH FOR

Unlike RCA and MCA/Decca, the Columbia label has not reissued all of its early Duke Ellington recordings complete and in chronological order on CD. In the 1970s, French Columbia came out with a series of two-LP sets, *The Complete Duke Ellington Vols. 1–15* (CBS 67264, 68275, 88000, 88035, 88082, 88137, 88140, 88185, 88210, 88220, 88242, 88451, 88518, 88521, and 88522) that consist of all of Duke's valuable performances for the Columbia labels (both with his big band and with his sidemen's small groups) from the 1925–40 period, including the alternate takes. These twofers will be difficult to find but are worth the search, at least until the American label finally shows interest in its very valuable archives.

The Jimmy Blanton Years (Queen-Disc 007) has rare broadcast performances of the Ellington big band during 1940–41, when Blanton was its innovative bassist. In addition to big band selections (including "Ko Ko," "Cotton

Tail," "Jack the Bear," and "Chelsea Bridge"), Ellington and Blanton are heard on four songs as guests with the John Scott Trotter Orchestra (including "Jumpin' Punkins" and "Take the 'A' Train"). This music has thus far not been reissued on CD.

Strangely enough, Duke Ellington's second Carnegie Hall concert (from December 11, 1943) has only been released on *At Carnegie Hall* (Everest 327), a budget LP. No new works are heard but the music is consistently excellent in these remakes of Duke favorites. A superb six-LP set, *The Complete Duke Ellington 1947–1952* (CBS 66607), puts the focus on one of Ellington's most neglected periods. There are some novelties and forgettable vocals but also the "Controversial Suite," the "Liberian Suite," and many three-minute classics. These 76 performances, from a period when Duke was fighting to overcome competition from bebop, R&B ,and television, allows one to hear such players as Tyree Glenn (on trombone and vibes), trumpeter Al Killian, and tenor Jimmy Forrest during their brief periods with the band.

Masterpieces by Ellington (Columbia 4418), from 1950, for the first time found Ellington taking advantage of the LP to perform extensive versions of his older material ("Mood Indigo," "Sophisticated Lady," and "Solitude"), plus "The Tattooed Bride." *Ellington Uptown* (Columbia 40836), from 1951–52, is a classic, with Betty Roche's famous vocal on "Take the 'A' Train," extensive explorations of "The Mooche" and "Perdido" (the latter featuring a Gerald Wilson arrangement and Clark Terry's trumpet), "Harlem," Louie Bellson's showcase "Skin Deep," and the two-part "Controversial Suite." *Duke 56/62 Vols. 1–3* (CBS 88653, 88654, and 26306) are five albums (the first two volumes are double-LP sets) that contain often-fascinating alternate takes and unissued material from 1956–62.

Duke Ellington's Jazz Violin Session (Atlantic 1688) finds Duke and his rhythm section playing a supportive role for violinists Stephane Grappelli and Ray Nance, with Svend Asmussen on viola; some of the numbers add a three-piece horn section. The violinists interact joyfully on various Ellington and Strayhorn pieces, including "Take the 'A' Train," "Cotton Tail," and "String Along with Strings."

One of the most surprising successes of Duke Ellington's 1960s albums was *Mary Poppins* (Reprise 6141), an album in which his orchestra plays a dozen songs from the popular movie. On such tunes as "A Spoonful of Sugar," "Super-califragilisticexpialidocious" and "Chim Chim Cheree," the band sounds surprisingly inspired! The arrangements by Ellington and Strayhorn for what could have been a turkey are quite inventive. The excellent *Concert in the Virgin Islands* (Discovery 841) from 1965 includes the four-part "Virgin Islands Suite" and seven briefer pieces, including fine remakes of "Chelsea Bridge" and "Things Ain't What They Used to Be."

The five-LP box set called simply *Duke Ellington* (MF 204/5) has privately recorded studio and live material from the late 1950s through the early '70s (the exact recording dates are not given) that are probably not duplicated elsewhere, mostly fresh versions of standards, along with "La Plus Belle Africaine" and a ten-minute version of "Diminuendo and Crescendo in Blue." Usually when this box can be found, it is sold at a budget price; get it!

New Orleans Suite , from 1970, has Johnny Hodges's final recorded solo, tributes to Louis Armstrong (featuring Cootie Williams), Wellman Braud, Sidney Bechet, and Mahalia Jackson, and strong writing throughout. Duke Ellington's final album, *Eastbourne Performance* (RCA 1023), from December 1, 1973, was recorded 49 years after his debut. Ellington is mostly the main soloist and this is a fairly strong record despite most of Duke's veterans being gone. Highlights include "Creole Love Call," Harold Ashby on "I Can't Get Started," "Pitter Patter Panther," Money Johnson paying tribute to Louis Armstrong on "Basin Street Blues," and a spirited "Tiger Rag." It all ends with Ellington playing a heartfelt solo on "Meditation." Quite a career!

FILMS

Duke Ellington first appeared in 1929's *Black and Tan,* an interesting ten-minute short that has some spoken dialogue and a duet version of "Black and Tan Fantasy" with Arthur Whetsol. The 1930 *Amos & Andy* film is a waste except for an exciting full-length version of "Old Man Blues" by the Ellington band. *A Bundle Of Blues* (1933) is a short with Ivie Anderson singing "Stormy Weather." The Ellington Orchestra appears in 1934's *Murder at the Vanities* (playing "Ebony Rhapsody"), in back of harmonica player Larry Adler on "Sophisticated Lady" in *Many Happy Returns* (1934), and in a few spots in Mae West's *Belle of the Nineties* (1935). The 1935 short *Symphony in Black* is notable in depicting honestly the life of blacks (a rather radical concept for the time) and there is a blues chorus by a young Billie Holiday. The Ellington Orchestra recorded five Soundies in 1941: "Hot Chocolate" ("Cotton Tail"), "I Got It Bad," "Flamingo" (featuring Herb Jeffries), "Bli-Blip," and "Jam Session" (an exciting version of "C Jam Blues"). Their appearance in *Cabin in the Sky* (playing "Goin' Up") in 1942 is disappointingly brief. *Reveille with Beverly,* from 1943, features "Take the 'A' Train." A short film from 1943 has brief versions of four of Duke's hits, and Ellington interacts with one of George Pal's puppets in *Date with Duke,* playing parts of "The Perfume Suite." The 1949 short *Symphony in Swing* is highlighted by Tyree Glenn on "Frankie and Johnny." The 1950 *Salute to Duke Ellington* has "Violet Blue" sung by Kay Davis, and in 1952 Ellington and his band recorded seven songs as *Snader Telescriptions* to be inserted between television programs when there was extra time to fill. In the Jimmy Stewart film *Anatomy of a Murder,* Ellington makes a brief appearance in one scene as "Pie," with Stewart joining him for some four-handed piano. Duke and his band unfortunately do not appear in the other films for which he wrote soundtracks (1961's *Paris Blues,* 1966's *Assault on a Queen,* and 1970's *Change of Mind*), but Norman Granz did film *Duke Ellington at the Cote d'Azur* (1966) at a rehearsal; Ella Fitzgerald drops by for three songs. In addition, Duke Ellington appeared on television on an occasional basis during his last 20 years.

Of the available videos on Duke Ellington, *The Good Years of Jazz* (VAI 69301), a television special sponsored by Goodyear Tires, has a half-hour of music from 1962 (with solos by Ray Nance, Paul Gonsalves, Johnny Hodges, and others). *On the Road with Duke Ellington* (Direct Cinema Limited) is a remarkable hour-long documentary that features Ellington in 1967 talking about life, rehearsing his band, performing in several venues, preparing for his sacred concert, suffering from Billy Strayhorn's death, and talking to a joyous Louis Armstrong. What a pity that it is not ten hours long! *Memories of Duke* (A Vision 50187), although put together in 1980, is taken mostly from Ellington's 1968 tour of Mexico. Gonsalves, Hodges, Williams, and Procope are prominent, with the latter two being interviewed in 1978.

BENNY GOODMAN

b. May 30, 1909, Chicago, IL, d. June 13, 1986, New York, NY

Benny Goodman was the "King of Swing" and, unlike Paul Whiteman (who was crowned the "King of Jazz" in the 1920s at a time when his band's music barely qualified as jazz), BG deserved the title. He was the best clarinetist in jazz (only Artie Shaw and in later years Buddy DeFranco and Eddie Daniels deserved to be mentioned in the same sentence) and the leader of one of the great Swing orchestras. Goodman's success in 1935 did a great deal to launch the big band era.

Benny Goodman began playing clarinet when he was 11 and he developed very fast. A year later he won an amateur contest doing an imitation of Ted Lewis. Goodman had a lifelong love affair with the clarinet, practiced every day, and considered everything else secondary to his music. His absent-mindedness would drive people crazy in later years, as would his self-centeredness, but the result was that he was a brilliant player throughout his entire career.

Goodman joined the Musicians Union when he was 14 and soon started gigging in the Chicago area. In August 1925, the 16-year old joined Ben Pollack's Orchestra, where he was well featured from the start. A year later, in December 1926, he made his recording debut with Pollack. Goodman's sound, influenced in the early days by Jimmie Noone, was on its way to becoming distinctive, and his technique was very impressive from the start. In 1928 he had his first three opportunities to lead his own record dates, and one session found him leading a trio, seven years before the famous Benny Goodman Trio was formed. BG left Pollack's band in 1929, worked and recorded with Red Nichols' Five Pennies, led record sessions of his own (his early dates as a leader in the Depression were often commercial and are today little-known), and during 1929–33 was a very busy studio musician. His sight-reading abilities and skill at blending into ensembles (along with his professionalism) kept him greatly in demand for commercial record dates and for radio orchestras, even sometimes subbing on alto and baritone saxophones. Goodman did have occasional opportunities to record jazz during this period (including with the Charleston Chasers, the Joe Venuti–Eddie Lang All-Star Orchestra, and Irving Mills's Hotsy Totsy Gang). But as 1934 began, his name was unknown to the general public.

That year, Goodman put together his first big band, recording for Columbia and getting a break by winning an audition (by one vote) to be one of the three orchestras on the *Let's Dance* radio series. The show's main song soon became BG's lifelong theme, while "Goodbye" would become his closing theme later on. The regular series of broadcasts allowed him to put together a stable personnel of fine musicians, including trumpeter Pee Wee Erwin, altoist Toots Mondello, Arthur Rollini on tenor, and singer Helen Ward, plus it gave him a chance to commission arrangements from his favorite writer, Fletcher Henderson.

However, when the radio show ended in May 1935, the future of the Benny Goodman Orchestra was quite uncertain. The clarinetist had started recording regularly for Victor a month earlier, Gene Krupa was Goodman's new drummer, and trumpeter Bunny Berigan was persuaded to forego studio work to be part of the big band; his solos on BG's July 1, 1935, recordings of "King Porter Stomp" and "Sometimes I'm Happy" would become famous. In addition, pianist Teddy Wilson became a special attraction, teaming up with Goodman and Krupa as the Benny Goodman Trio (their first four recordings were on July 13, 1935). The trio's public appearances not only resulted in classic music but broke down racial boundaries. However, work for the Goodman Orchestra was not too steady and the clarinetist was rightfully worried.

Willard Alexander booked a cross-country tour for the Benny Goodman Orchestra to see if the big band had a future. It was an up-and-down trip, with some embarrassing episodes (such as when some club owners demanded that Goodman's band stick to waltzes and tangos), very small crowds, and difficulties. By the time the band made it to California, they were exhausted and somewhat discouraged. The musicians were well received in Oakland. And then the turning point took place, on August 21, 1935, at the Palomar Ballroom in Los Angeles. At first Goodman played it safe, performing relatively gentle dance music during the early set, and the crowd seemed polite but a bit bored. Finally realizing that it was now or never and that there was nothing much left to lose, Goodman had his band cut loose. The audience's reaction was explosive and the teenagers in the audience went crazy. This was just what they wanted. Unknown to BG, the *Let's Dance* radio show had been very popular on the West Coast, and, after five years of soothing ballads and commercial pop music, the new generation was hungry for the new music called *Swing*. Word of Goodman's surprise success reached the East Coast, and the big band era was officially launched.

Success followed success from this point on, with many new big bands being formed and following the Goodman model. After leaving California, BG had a long run at Chicago's Congress Hotel., He returned to New York in triumph and was a sensation at the Paramount Ballroom. By then Goodman was not only a household name but a major celebrity, an unusual role for an introverted clarinetist! "King Porter Stomp" and "Sometimes I'm Happy" were hits and, although Berigan soon went back to the studios, the momentum continued picking up. The 1935 Benny Goodman Orchestra was a well-oiled and solid unit, but it lacked any major soloists other than the leader. In 1936 (a year that included popular recordings of "Stompin' at the Savoy," "You Turned the Tables on Me," "Down South Camp Meeting," and "Bugle Call Rag"), Gene Krupa became more assertive in his playing, Jess Stacy proved to be a major asset on piano, Ziggy Elman became BG's hot trumpet soloist, and the Benny Goodman Quartet (with Lionel Hampton on vibes) was even more popular than the Trio. The year 1937 found Martha Tilton as the new vocalist (Helen Ward had left a year earlier to get married), Harry James became the trumpet star, and the recordings included "Sing, Sing, Sing," "Roll 'Em," "Avalon" (by the quartet), and "Sugar Foot Stomp."

The height of Benny Goodman's career was reached on January 16, 1938, at Carnegie Hall, when he performed the first full-length jazz concert at the classical music temple. Fortunately it was recorded, and it was released a dozen years later. Everything worked that night, including exciting versions of "Don't Be That Way" and "One O'Clock Jump," trio and quartet features, an interesting "history of jazz" medley, a jam session on "Honeysuckle Rose" with guests from the Count Basie and Duke Ellington bands, and a remarkable version of "Sing, Sing, Sing." During this last, Goodman spontaneously called out to Jess Stacy to take a solo, and the pianist's impressionistic improvisation virtually stole the show, even from the exciting Krupa. Benny Goodman was still just 28 at the time.

During the next seven years, Goodman would continue as one of the giants of the Swing era although there would be changes. A personality conflict resulted in Gene Krupa's departure a little over a month after the Carnegie Hall concert. Other big bandleaders (Artie Shaw in 1938 and Glenn Miller in 1939) surpassed BG's popularity, and in 1939 Harry James and Teddy Wilson left to form their own orchestras. That year Goodman added guitarist Charlie Christian to his small group (which became known as the Benny Goodman Sextet, although it sometimes was actually seven pieces), and the interplay between the clarinetist and the guitarist resulted in a great deal of musical magic. In 1940 the Benny Goodman Orchestra broke up for a few months as the leader battled sciatica, but it reformed later in the year, adding Cootie Williams to the trumpet section and Georgie Auld as tenor soloist. The Goodman Sextet, with Williams, Auld, Christian, and various pianists (including guest Count Basie and Johnny Guarnieri) was arguably his strongest-ever combo. Eddie Sauter's very adventurous charts for Goodman's big band during 1940–42 really challenged the clarinetist (although he rarely played any of those arrangements in later years) and Helen Forrest proved to be one of the finest singers with his band. In 1941 Christian was stricken with tuberculosis (he was never successfully replaced) and drummer Big Sid Catlett did not work out, but Goodman discovered Peggy Lee, and his new pianist-arranger was a brilliant teenager named Mel Powell.

With the onset of World War II, Goodman stayed busy, making movies in Hollywood and still appearing regularly on the radio. Although he broke up his big band, he formed new orchestras on several occasions. In 1944 Goodman sounded quite enthusiastic on a series of sextet sessions with vibraphonist Red Norvo, Teddy Wilson, and bassist Slam Stewart, and he had a fresh new big band during 1945–46. However, musical styles were starting to pass BG by. Younger musicians were playing bebop, times were getting harder for big bands, and, although Goodman would always be a major name, he was no longer close to being on the cutting edge, despite being in his prime; he was still only 36 in 1945. In 1947 he led a short-lived orchestra in Los Angeles. The following year he put together a bop-oriented septet that found him sharing the frontline with the brilliant young clarinetist Stan Hasselgard and tenor saxophonist Wardell Gray. BG was curious about bop at the time, although he never altered his style, having Hasselgard take the more modern solos. But the septet broke up after a few months; the only studio side, "Stealin' Apples," featured Gray and the great bop trumpeter Fats Navarro with Goodman. In 1949, as Capitol became one of several labels hoping to make a fad out of bop, Goodman recorded some modern big band arrangements (particularly by Chico O'Farrill) and alternated uneasily between bop and Swing. But in 1950 he gave up both the orchestra and any further interest in bebop.

For the remainder of BG's career, he stuck to the Swing music he loved, not bothering to advance with the times. Goodman put together big bands specifically for short tours (in 1952 he made his last real attempt to have a full-time orchestra but it was unsuccessful) and saved most of his best playing for small-group romps. There were many reunions with Gene Krupa, Teddy Wilson, and Lionel Hampton, some added publicity with the release of 1956's fictional movie *The Benny Goodman Story,* and a notable tour of the Soviet Union in 1962. Sidemen passing through Goodman's bands (mostly combos) included vibraphonist Terry Gibbs, trumpeters Buck Clayton, Ruby Braff, and Jack Sheldon, Paul Quinichette and Flip Phillips on tenors, trombonist Bill Harris, and pianist André Previn, among many others. In the 1960s and '70s Goodman even used pianist Herbie Hancock and guitarist George Benson in addition to his alumni. He slowed down during the '60s and was off records altogether during 1973–77. However, preparing for his 40th anniversary Carnegie Hall concert in 1978 was an incentive for BG to return with new records. After a few more years mostly off the scene, Benny Goodman returned one more time in the early 1980s, taking over the Loren Schoenberg big band, using Scott Hamilton and Warren Vaché in his group, and showing as late as his final appearances in 1986 (when he was nearing 75) that he was still the King of Swing.

●

8 *B.G. and Big Tea in NYC / Aug. 29, 1929–Oct. 1934 / GRP/Decca 609*

7 *1934 Bill Dodge All-Star Recordings / 1934 / Circle 111*

7 *1935—Let's Dance Broadcasts / Feb. 1935–May 1935 / Circle 50*

7 *Good to Go / June 6, 1935 / Buddha 7446599624*
The GRP/Decca CD features some of Benny Goodman better sideman appearances from his first period; all of the selections also feature Jack Teagarden's trombone and occa-

sional vocals. The clarinetist is heard on eight numbers with Red Nichols' Five Pennies (including "Indiana," "The Sheik of Araby," and "China Boy"), on a date by Irving Mills' Hotsy Totsy Gang that also includes a declining Bix Beiderbecke on cornet, four heated selections with the Joe Venuti–Eddie Lang All-Star Orchestra (including "Beale Street Blues" and "Farewell Blues"), and five decent numbers with bass saxophonist Adrian Rollini's Orchestra in 1934. But Goodman's enormous output of 1927–34 deserves much more extensive treatment on CD, for this disc just scratches the surface.

The two-CD Circle set from 1934 features Goodman leading a hot nonet under the anonymous name of Bill Dodge. Performed shortly before the *Let's Dance* broadcasts started, the set features not only Goodman but Bunny Berigan, Gene Krupa, and the great trombonist Jack Jenney; Red McKenzie also has a few vocals. The music on the following Circle CD is taken from the Benny Goodman Orchestra's legendary *Let's Dance* broadcasts. The BG big band sound was almost formed by then, featuring vocals by Helen Ward (who provided the insightful and informative liner notes) and the forgotten Ray Hendricks and solos from trumpeter Pee Wee Erwin, altoist Toots Mondello, and Art Rollini on tenor. However, Goodman is the star throughout. Among the selections are "Three Little Words," "I Got Rhythm," "Japanese Sandman," "I Know That You Know," and "King Porter Stomp."

On June 6, 1935, the little-known Benny Goodman Orchestra had a marathon session in which they recorded 50 (!) instrumentals as radio transcriptions. Despite the hype that surrounded the release of 25 of the cuts on the single-CD *Good to Go*, all of the music had come out before on three Sunbeam LPs. The BG Orchestra simply went through their book and ran through one number after another, not bothering with second takes. The results are quite consistent (the band was well rehearsed and tight), with solos from Goodman, Erwin, Mondello, and Rollini. A quiet Gene Krupa was on drums, while Frank Froeba was the pianist. It is a pity that Bunny Berigan was not with the band that day, for these solid performances could have benefited from his explosive trumpet. Easily enjoyable music, made right before Goodman had his major success.

10 *The Birth of Swing (1935–1936) / Apr. 4, 1935–Nov. 5, 1936 / Bluebird 61038*

10 *The Complete Small Group Recordings / July 13, 1935–Apr. 6, 1939 / RCA 68764*

7 *Sing, Sing, Sing / Apr. 4, 1935–Apr. 11, 1939 / Bluebird 5630*

7 *Vol. 1 Congress Hotel 1935-6 / Dec. 23, 1935–Jan. 13, 1936 / Circle 171*

7 *Vol. 2 Congress Hotel 1936 / Jan. 20, 1936 + Feb. 3, 1936 / Circle 172*

7 *Vol. 3 Congress Hotel 1936 / Feb. 10 + 17, 1936 / Circle 173*

A three-CD set, *The Birth of Swing* has all of the Benny Goodman Orchestra's Victor recordings during its first 19 months with the label, including a strong sampling of alternate takes. The 71 performances may not have been the very first Swing recordings, but they made Benny Goodman famous and launched the Swing era. Among the key players, in addition to the leader, are Bunny Berigan, Ziggy Elman, Jess Stacy, and Helen Ward. The many gems include "Japanese Sandman," "Always," "Blue Skies," "Sometimes I'm Happy," "King Porter Stomp," "Jingle Bells," "When Buddha Smiles," "Stompin' at the Savoy," "Goody Goody," "House Hop," "Swingtime in the Rockies," "You Turned the Tables on Me," "Down South Camp Meeting," "Bugle Call Rag," and "Jam Session," among many others. One can fully understand why Goodman loved this particular band because musically this ranks with his finest groups, a very solid, swinging orchestra.

Starting in mid-1935, Benny Goodman regularly rested his orchestra so he could stretch out with a trio also including Gene Krupa and Teddy Wilson; a year later Lionel Hampton joined up as a member of the Benny Goodman Quartet. Every studio recording by this band in the 1930s (including post-Krupa jams with Dave Tough, Buddy Schutz, or Hampton on drums and bassist John Kirby) is on *The Complete Small Group Recordings,* an exciting three-CD set. The 67 selections include 47 released performances and 20 alternate takes (two never out before). The classics include "After You've Gone," "Body and Soul," "China Boy," "All My Life" (with Helen Ward), "Nobody's Sweetheart," "Dinah," "Tiger Rag," "Stompin' at the Savoy," "Avalon," "Liza," "Bei Mir Bist Du Schon" (with Martha Tilton and Ziggy Elman), and "I Cried for You," among others. Essential music.

For listeners who just want one CD featuring the Benny Goodman big band, *Sing, Sing, Sing* will probably suffice. It covers BG's Victor period quite well, including the majority of his most influential selections, such as "King Porter Stomp," "Goody Goody," "Down South Camp Meeting," "Roll 'Em," and the original studio version of "Sing, Sing, Sing."

Goodman's six-month stint at Chicago's Congress Hotel (it was originally supposed to last only one month) consolidated his position as Swing's top bandleader. The three Circle CDs feature two or (in the case of Volume 1) three complete radio broadcasts taken from their weekly series. The band still lacked any major soloists other than its leader (the trumpet solos tended to be taken by Nate Kazebier) but the arrangements are swinging, Jess Stacy and Gene Krupa are aboard (if in quiet roles), and Helen Ward contributes plenty of pleasing vocals. There are no small-group numbers, but Goodman's consistently exciting playing and the historic nature of the broadcasts (which have decent sound quality despite their age) make the trio of CDs of strong interest to Swing collectors.

7 *The Harry James Years, Volume 1 / Jan. 14, 1937–Feb. 16, 1938 / Bluebird 66155*

7 *Wrappin' It Up: The Harry James Years, Volume 2 / Mar. 9, 1938–Mar. 4, 1939 / Bluebird 66549*

10 *On the Air (1937–1938) / Mar. 3, 1937–Sept. 20, 1938 / Columbia/Legacy 48836*

10 *Benny Goodman Carnegie Hall Jazz Concert / Jan. 16, 1938 / Columbia 65167*

Unlike the superbly done three-CD set *The Birth of Swing*, the two CDs released as *The Harry James Years* are merely samplers of Benny Goodman's 1937–39 recordings, important music that deserves to be reissued complete and in chronological order (as it had been on LP). To make matters worse for completists, each of the CDs has three or four previously unreleased takes (sometimes substituted for the superior versions), so this series was poorly planned. It is a pity, for the music is quite valuable. By 1937 the Benny Goodman Orchestra was different than it had been two years earlier, with Gene Krupa taking a much more assertive role and Harry James being featured on fiery trumpet solos. *Volume 1* includes "Peckin'," the studio recording of "Sing, Sing, Sing," "Roll 'Em," and two versions apiece of "Life Goes to a Party," "Don't Be That Way," and "One O'Clock Jump." *Volume 2* features the Goodman Orchestra after the departure of Krupa, with such songs as "The Blue Room," "Big John Special," "Wrappin' It Up," "Smoke House," and "Undecided" being among the better selections; both guest Lester Young and Bud Freeman make appearances.

Good as Benny Goodman's studio recordings were, his band was always more exciting live when they played before a large dancing audience. *On the Air* has 49 of the 1937–38 orchestra's best radio appearances, most of which were formerly put out as a double-LP called *Jazz Concert #2*; there

are 14 additional selections on this set. Alternating big band romps and trio/quartet features, this twofer has many stirring moments, including an extended version of "St. Louis Blues" featuring Harry James.

It was a fluke that Benny Goodman's historic Carnegie Hall concert was recorded, and that fact was quickly forgotten by the clarinetist, who kept the tapes in his closet for a dozen years! In 1950 he rediscovered them, and they became one of the major jazz releases of the period. Reissued as a two-CD set in 1999 with two additional selections ("Sometimes I'm Happy" and "When Dreams Come True") that were previously put out only by the collector's Sunbeam label, plus a fully restored version of the jam session "Honeysuckle Rose," this set is a treasure. Whether it be Krupa and Stacy on "Sing, Sing, Sing," the trio and quartet romps, "One O'Clock Jump," or "Don't Be That Way," this was a night to remember and one of the high points not only of Benny Goodman's career but of the Swing era itself. An essential acquisition for all serious music collections.

7 *Camel Caravan Broadcast 1939, Vol. I / Jan. 17–31, 1939 / Phontastic 8817*

7 *Camel Caravan Broadcast 1939, Vol. II / Feb. 21, 1939– Mar. 21, 1939 / Phontastic 8818*

7 *Camel Caravan Broadcast 1939, Vol. III / Mar. 28, 1939–Apr. 25, 1939 / Phontastic 8819*

6 *Best of the Big Bands / Aug. 16, 1939–Sept. 12, 1945 / Columbia 45338*

8 *Small Groups: 1941–1945 / Oct. 28, 1941–Feb. 4, 1945 / Columbia 44437*

8 *All the Cats Join In / Dec. 10, 1941–Aug. 7, 1946 / Columbia 44158*

7 *Featuring Helen Forrest / Mar. 1, 1940–June 4, 1941 / Columbia/Legacy 48902*

6 *Featuring Peggy Lee / Aug. 15, 1941–Dec. 10, 1941 / Columbia/Legacy 53422*

6 *Benny Goodman and His Great Vocalists / Dec. 18, 1933–Oct. 22, 1946 / Legacy/Columbia 66198*

The Benny Goodman Orchestra was in transition in 1939, switching half-way through the year from Victor to Columbia, trying to make up for the departure of Harry James, and welcoming Charlie Christian to BG's new sextet. Artie Shaw and soon Glenn Miller succeeded BG as the most popular bandleader of the era, but the clarinetist was far from forgotten. Most of the music on the three Phontastic discs (taken from Goodman's regular weekly series of *Camel Caravan Broadcasts*) was previously unreleased. There are some interesting guests on *Vol. 1*: Billie Holiday ("I Cried for You"), Leo Watson, Jack Teagarden, and Pete Johnson. Otherwise the focus is on the Goodman's Orchestra, his small groups (which still featured Hampton and Wilson), Martha Tilton, and Johnny Mercer, who sings now and then and acts as a good-humored if sometimes jivey emcee.

The Columbia label has yet to coherently reissue all of their Benny Goodman recordings (he was with the record company during 1939–46), although hopefully the Classics label (which is currently up to 1939) will do the job. In the meantime, there are several available CDs covering the period in incomplete form. *Best of the Big Bands* skips all over the place, does not bother with personnel or date listings, and has its moments but is far from essential; highlights include "Taking a Chance on Love," "Shake Down the Stars," "Air Mail Special," and Peggy Lee's hit "Why Don't You Do Right." *Small Groups* is much better since it features BG with his 1941–42 sextet (which includes trombonist Lou McGarity, Mel Powell, and occasionally Peggy Lee) and quartet, plus some numbers from his 1944–45 quintet (with Red Norvo, Teddy Wilson, and either Peggy Mann or Jane Harvey on vocals), plus an exciting quartet rendition of "The World Is Waiting for the Sunrise." *All the Cats Join In* has some of the more interesting Goodman big band selections from 1942 and 1945–46 (with one number from 1941). The modern Swing versions of "Six Flats Unfurnished," "Mission to Moscow," "Clarinade," "Rattle and Roll" (which has a tenor solo from the young Stan Getz), and "Oh Baby" are memorable.

Featuring Helen Forrest is a fairly coherent reissue, being comprised of 16 of the singer's best recordings with Goodman, including "The Man I Love," "I'm Always Chasing Rainbows," "This Is New," and "Oh! Look at Me Now." *Featuring Peggy Lee* has been supplanted by a more complete two-CD set (which is reviewed under Lee's name) but is a decent all-round set, letting one hear the singer evolve from being quite scared on the opening "Elmer's Tune" into a mature singer who sounds quite good on "I Got It Bad," "Let's Do It," and "Everything I Love." *Benny Goodman and His Great Vocalists* is a so-so sampler, going in chronological order and featuring the vocals of Billie Holiday (1933's

"Riffin' the Scotch"), Helen Ward, Martha Tilton, Louise Tobin, Mildred Bailey, Helen Forrest, Peggy Lee, Dick Haymes, Peggy Mann, Jane Harvey, Dottie Reid, Liza Morrow, Art Lund, and the forgotten Eve Young, on one or two songs apiece. Excellent music but just for very general collectors. But the way things look, we should not hold our breaths until Columbia finally reissues its valuable Benny Goodman recordings properly rather than on all of these samplers!

7 | *'Way Down Yonder* / Dec. 9, 1943–Jan. 1946 / Vintage Jazz Classics 1001

9 | *Slipped Disc, 1945–1946* / Feb. 4, 1945–Oct. 22, 1946 / Columbia 44292

7 | *Swing Sessions* / Oct. 17, 1945–Jan. 11, 1946 / Hindsight 254

* | *The Complete Capitol Small Group Recordings* / June 12, 1944–Dec. 14, 1955 / Mosaic 4-148

9 | *Undercurrent Blues* / Jan. 28, 1947–Oct. 15, 1949 / Capitol 32086

'Way Down Yonder, which contains V-Discs (some of which were never issued before), is particularly valuable for its inclusion of a few selections from Benny Goodman's barely documented 1943–44 band. Gene Krupa was temporarily back on drums and he can be heard pushing the band on "Dinah," a few versions of "Henderson Stomp," and "'Way Down Yonder in New Orleans." In addition, BG is heard with several of his small groups from the era, including a trio with Krupa and Jess Stacy and a quintet with Red Norvo and Teddy Wilson. *Slipped Disc* features mostly Goodman's 1945 sextet with Norvo, Wilson, Slam Stewart and occasionally singer Jane Harvey. The 17 selections include such hot tunes as the classic "Slipped Disc," "Rachel's Dream," "Tiger Rag," "Shine," and "Liza," plus three numbers by a different Goodman small group from the following year. *Swing Sessions,* all previously unreleased performances that were recorded for Armed Forces radio, has four numbers by Goodman's 1945 big band, a group that includes Mel Powell, the young Stan Getz on tenor, and singers Liza Morrow and Art Lund. However, the other nine tunes feature Goodman in a quintet with Norvo and Wilson, jamming happily on such standbys as "After You've Gone," "Lady Be Good," and "Rose Room."

The Mosaic box, a limited-edition four-CD set, has one

number from 1944 but otherwise dates from 1947–49 and 1954–55. Goodman was flirting with bop a bit during 1947–49, but very little of that can be heard in these Swing performances except on the 1948 version of "Stealin' Apples" with Fats Navarro and Wardell Gray. There are a few departures from the usual BG sound, including some tunes with the accordionist Ernie Felice, a guest appearance by Peggy Lee, the three "Hollywood Hucksters" numbers (including "Happy Blues," which has a very funny vocal duet by Goodman and Stan Kenton), and a couple of novelties. Red Norvo, Mel Powell, and Teddy Wilson are among the sidemen. The 1954–55 selections include meetings with trumpeters Charlie Shavers and Ruby Braff and a quintet set with Lionel Hampton. Although there are few surprises to be heard during these performances, Goodman sounds quite inspired and happy to be playing his usual Swing standards.

In contrast, nearly all of Benny Goodman's most boppish studio recordings are on *Undercurrent Blues,* a very interesting collection. With the exception of three numbers from 1947 (including a pair of Mary Lou Williams compositions) and 1948's "Stealin' Apples," the music all dates from 1949. With Chico O'Farrill contributing many of the arrangements and trumpeter Doug Mettome and Wardell Gray being well featured, Goodman (who had not changed his style at all) sounds a bit out-of-place in his own orchestra! Such numbers as "Undercurrent Blues," "Bop Hop," "Bedlam," and "Blue Lou" find the clarinetist looking ahead to a future that he would not participate in. By 1950, he had chosen to leave his bop experiment permanently behind and to stick to Swing.

9   *B.G. in Hi-Fi / Nov. 8–16, 1954 / Capitol 92864*

*   *Swing Swing Swing, Vols. 1–5 / Mar. 26, 1955–June 28, 1967 / Music Masters 65095*

*   *The King of Swing, Vols. 6–10 / 1954–June 29, 1967 / Music Masters 65130*

7   *The Benny Goodman Story / Dec. 7–14, 1955 / Capitol 33569*

*   *BG World-Wide / Dec. 14, 1956–Nov. 8, 1980 / TCB 4301*

8   *In Stockholm 1959 / Oct. 18, 1959 / Phontastic 8801*
After he gave up his bop experiment, Benny Goodman stuck permanently to Swing and was often grouped with nostalgia acts, although he continued to improvise creatively within

the genre. *B.G. in Hi-Fi* has the clarinetist jamming with a quintet that includes Charlie Shavers or Ruby Braff and Mel Powell for eight selections. The other numbers are with a 1954 big band, a pickup group that includes Braff, Powell, and tenorman Boomie Richman that was put together for just the occasion. Goodman sticks throughout to some of his favorite Swing standards, although he mostly avoids his earlier hits.

Late in life, Benny Goodman donated to the Yale University Music Library scores of unissued tapes of performances. After it was sorted through, music was released on 11 CDs (including a two-CD set) by the Music Masters label. In 1993 the music on Vols. 1–5 came out again as a six-CD set while Vols. 6–10 (five CDs) were reissued in 1996 as a second box. There is a great deal of enjoyable music in both of the boxes. *Swing Swing Swing* has a live octet CD with Ruby Braff, Paul Quinichette, and Teddy Wilson, a 1958 album with singers Jimmy Rushing and Ethel Ennis, music from *Basin Street East* in 1959 with Flip Phillips and Bill Harris, and many miscellaneous sessions from the 1955–67 era. *The King of Swing* features Goodman live in 1967 with Zoot Sims and Joe Newman, leading a 1966 sextet that includes Doc Cheatham and Herbie Hancock, playing more with his notable Flip Phillips/Bill Harris septet, quintet numbers with André Previn, a 1954 Basin Street live set with Charlie Shavers and Mel Powell, and a 1963 reunion with Teddy Wilson, Lionel Hampton, and Gene Krupa that does not duplicate their RCA sessions, plus much more. Timeless music that holds its own with Goodman's more familiar studio albums of the period.

The music on Capitol's *The Benny Goodman Story* does not contain the performances recorded for the 1955 movie (those were issued by Decca on an album of the same name) but does include 13 big band and six quintet selections, mostly of tunes featured in the film. Nothing too surprising occurs, but there are solos from Harry James (in a rare reunion with BG), Ruby Braff, Al Klink on tenor, Lionel Hampton, and Mel Powell, among others.

BG World-Wide combines four CDs that were originally issued as separate discs and were unissued before the 1990s. Goodman is heard leading a big band in Bangkok, Thailand, in 1956 and a 15-piece orchestra in Santiago, Chile, in 1961 that features Buck Clayton. He is also showcased with an all-star group (that includes Jack Sheldon, Bill Harris, Flip Phillips, and Red Norvo) during a very strong set from Basel, Switzerland, in 1959 and at the head of a quintet in

1980 Berlin; this last (one of Goodman's very few recordings from that era) is surprisingly inspired. This is a release well worth investing in. The Sheldon/Phillips/Harris band is also featured on *In Stockholm 1959,* a fun outing with a small big band that also includes altoist Jerry Dodgion, Red Norvo, pianist Russ Freeman, guitarist Jimmy Wyble, bassist Red Wooten, and drummer John Markham. Anita O'Day has a few decent vocals, some numbers showcase Goodman with the rhythm section, and each of the key musicians has his spots. This CD shows that there was plenty of musical life left in Benny Goodman, who was still just 50 at the time.

7 *Together Again / Feb. 13, 1963–Aug. 27, 1963 / Bluebird 6283*

7 *The King Swings / Dec. 8, 1973 / Starline 9007*

7 *Live! Benny: Let's Dance / Oct. 7, 1985 / Music Masters 20112*

In 1963, the original Benny Goodman Quartet had a reunion, and all four players proved to still be in their prime. For the recording, they performed ten songs that they had not previously documented in this format, including "Seven Come Eleven," "I've Found a New Baby," "Runnin' Wild," and an original blues called "Four Once More." The music would have been improved a bit if a bassist had been added (Krupa's bass drum work gets a bit ponderous), but there are a few moments where the performances catch fire and the old magic is rekindled. Otherwise, Goodman's studio recordings of the 1960s were often not all that interesting although he always had the potential to get inspired. *The King Swings,* from 1973, has fairly typical material played in Germany by a Goodman nonet that includes Slam Stewart, trumpeter John McLevy, trombonist George Masso, Al Klink, and vibraphonist Peter Appleyard. Best are "Avalon," Stewart on "Lady Be Good," and a Dixielandish "That's a Plenty."

Benny Goodman's final recording was actually the soundtrack for a PBS television special. He had performed at Carnegie Hall in 1978, dropped out of active playing again for a few years, and then was once again back on the scene, having fun leading what had been Loren Schoenberg's big band. Sticking mostly to Fletcher Henderson arrangements from the Swing era, Goodman plays such vintage material as "Don't Be That Way," "King Porter Stomp," and "Stealin'

Apples" with a big band that has such fine soloists as Randy Sandke, Ken Peplowski on tenor, Dick Hyman, and Louie Bellson. A fine ending to a remarkable career.

LPS TO SEARCH FOR

An enormous number of Benny Goodman LPs were issued during the 1960s, '70s, and '80s . In fact, the Sunbeam label was largely started specifically to release broadcasts and live appearances by Goodman's bands. Some, but far from all, of the Goodman recordings, radio air checks, and concert dates have since been reissued on CD by other record companies.

The two-LP *A Jazz Holiday* (MCA 4018) has some of Goodman's best late 1920s sessions as a sideman (with Adrian Rollini, Red Nichols, and the Joe Venuti–Eddie Lang All-Star Orchestra) plus eight of his earliest selections as a leader, including the satirical "Shirt Tail Stomp" and two numbers ("That's a Plenty" and "Clarinetitis") with a trio. Also, do not miss "Jungle Blues," which has Goodman's only recorded cornet solo. From the same period are *The Rare BG* (Sunbeam 112) and *The Whoopee Makers* (Sunbeam 114), primarily jazz-oriented recordings from 1928–29. Goodman's years as a studio musician (often taking short solos on otherwise commercial dance band tracks) are the main focus of *On the Side* (Sunbeam 107), *In a Melotone Manner* (Sunbeam 106, which includes his obscure 1931 dates as a leader), *Melotone Melodies* (Sunbeam 157), and *Ben Selvin Featuring Benny Goodman Vols. 1–3* (Sunbeam 108, 109, and 110). Quite valuable are three albums titled *The Early Years.* Volume 1 (Sunbeam 138) has BG's appearances with the 1931 Charleston Chasers and his own dates from 1933, which have vocals by Jack Teagarden and Billie Holiday (making her recording debut). Volume 2 (Sunbeam 139) includes three all-star sessions led by Goodman (two with Jack Teagarden and one with Coleman Hawkins and Mildred Bailey) and the first recordings by the clarinetist's regular big band (from August 16, 1934). Vol. 3 (Sunbeam 140) has four unusual numbers with Harry Rosenthal's Orchestra in 1934 and then a dozen studio numbers by the big band that Goodman used on the *Let's Dance* radio series during 1934–35, music that directly precedes Goodman's very successful Victor recordings.

Selections actually taken from the *Let's Dance* broadcasts can be heard on Volume 1 (Sunbeam 100) and Volume 2 (Sunbeam 104) and these do not duplicate the Circle CD taken from the same period.

All of the music from the marathon June 6, 1935, radio transcription session that has thus far been half reissued by Buddha was originally made available on three LPs, *Rhythm Makers Orchestra Vols. 1–3* (Sunbeam 101–103). During the mid- to late-1970s, all of Benny Goodman's recordings (including alternate takes) for the Victor label were reissued in a series of perfectly done two-LP sets. The music up until November 5, 1936 (which is all of the first two volumes plus three-fourths of Vol. 3) has been reissued on CD, but the other music has been only partly brought back. Get these twofers if you can: *The Complete Benny Goodman Vol. 1* (Bluebird AXM2-5505), *Vol. 2* (AXM2-5515), *Vol. 3* (AXM2-5532), *Vol. 4* (AXM2-5537), *Vol. 5* (AXM2-5557), *Vol. 6* (AXM2-5566), *Vol. 7* (AXM2-5567), *Vol. 8* (AXM2-5568). A ten-LP box set, *Benny Goodman at the Madhattan Room 1937–38* (Sunbeam 116–27), has a dozen full-length radio broadcasts by Goodman's orchestra from October 13–December 22, 1937, serving as a countdown to his Carnegie Hall concert; the giant box concludes with the two rarest numbers from that historic January 16, 1938, performance. There are plenty of hot solos from Harry James, forceful playing from Gene Krupa, and lots of excitement featured throughout this hard-to-find set. Other fine broadcasts from the same period (and not duplicating any of these other releases) can be found on the three LPs *Treasure Chest Vols. 1–3* (MGM 3788–3790).

Broadcasts from the period immediately after Gene Krupa departed can be heard on a pair of two-LP sets: *Swingtime—1938* (Sunbeam 152) and *Jerry Newhouse Presents Benny Goodman* (Phontastic 7625/26). The Giants of Jazz label came out with quite a few very valuable (and well-recorded) Goodman radio appearances from 1939 on. While the *Camel Caravan* broadcasts on *One O'Clock Jump* (Giants of Jazz 1036) and *Sing! Sing! Sing!* (Giants of Jazz 1039) have been put out on CD by Phontastic, the music on *Ciribiribin* (Giants of Jazz 1030), which is from January 3 and 10, 1939, *Swingin' Down the Lane* (Giants of Jazz 1033) from Feb. 7 and 14, 1939, and *Jumpin' at the Woodside* (Giants of Jazz 1042) have not. This last is from May 2 and 9, 1939, and is particularly intriguing because it finds Goodman experimenting with using electric guitarist George Rose, a few months before BG met Charlie Christian.

The five-LP set *The Legendary Benny Goodman* (Columbia 15536), although only containing only a chintzy 50 selections (the music could have fit on three albums), does contain many of the highlights from Goodman's 1939–42 and

1945–46 stints on Columbia plus four numbers from 1950–51. Other BG Columbia albums include *Presents Fletcher Henderson Arrangements* (Columbia 524) and the exciting *Presents Eddie Sauter Arrangements* (Columbia 523); the latter is highlighted by fairly radical versions of "Moonlight on the Ganges," "Love Walked In," "La Rosita," and "Superman." Big Sid Catlett's brief if unhappy period with the Benny Goodman Orchestra is documented on the two-LP *Roll 'Em* (Honeysuckle Rose 5004/5005), a set of live performances by the 1941 Goodman big band with the superb (if underappreciated) drummer. The 1945 big band is featured on a pair of excellent radio appearances on *Spotlighting Benny Goodman* (Giants of Jazz 1024).

Well worth searching for is the three-LP *An Album of Swing Classics,* a mid-1950s project that matches Goodman with Teddy Wilson, Ruby Braff, Paul Quinichette, and trombonist Urbie Green in a hard-swinging octet. *Happy Session* (Columbia 1324) has 1958 dates with either André Previn or Russ Freeman on piano and in settings ranging from a quintet to a big band. Most memorable are "You'd Be So Nice to Come Home To," a remake of "Clarinet à La King" and "Diga Diga Doo." The two-LP *Benny Goodman in Moscow* (RCA 6008) documents Goodman's historic if stormy visit to Russia in 1962. His big band and small groups were quite impressive, including such players as Joe Newman, trombonist Jimmy Knepper, altoist Phil Woods, Zoot Sims on tenor, pianists John Bunch and Teddy Wilson, and drummer Mel Lewis. It is a pity that Goodman's strange treatment of his sidemen resulted in dissension and the breakup of this orchestra shortly after their return to the U.S. because this was his strongest big band since the 1940s, and it is interesting hearing the clarinetist play on some of the more modern arrangements. This twofer is well worth searching for.

The 1972 double-LP *On Stage* (London 44182) has some hot Swing from Goodman, Zoot Sims, and vibraphonist Peter Appleyard. *Seven Come Eleven* (Columbia 38265) consists of rare performances from 1975, when Goodman was not all that active. The small-group dates include exciting matchups with George Benson on the title cut and "A Smooth One," a set with Joe Venuti, and small-group dates with Bucky Pizzarelli and pianists Hank Jones and John Bunch. The two-LP *Live at Carnegie Hall* (London 44182/83) has the highlights of Goodman's 40th anniversary Carnegie Hall Concert, which by all reports was a rather meandering and erratic affair. The twofer greatly benefits from the editing plus the contributions of band members Jack Sheldon and Warren Vache, Buddy Tate, and guitarist Cal Collins, plus guests Mary Lou Williams, Lionel Hampton, and Martha Tilton. It does not rise up to the classic level of the 1938 concert but it does have its strong moments.

FILMS

Benny Goodman first appeared in film in 1929 in an obscure musical short with Ben Pollack's Orchestra. His big band appeared early on in *Big Broadcast of 1937* (1936). *Hollywood Hotel* (1937) has his orchestra (with Harry James) playing "Sing, Sing, Sing" and the Benny Goodman Quartet really raging through an uptempo version of "I've Got a Heart Full

of Rhythm." BG is in the closing jam session number in *Syncopation* (1942), plays a few songs with his big band in *The Powers Girl* (1942) and *The Gang's All Here* (1943), and backs Peggy Lee on "Why Don't You Do Right" (in addition to playing "Bugle Call Rag") in 1943's *Stage Door Canteen*. While Goodman appeared in *Make Mine Music* (1945), he had two of his best acting roles in 1944's *Sweet and Low Down* (highlighted by a burning version of "The World Is Waiting for the Sunrise" with Jess Stacy) and the Danny Kaye movie *A Song Is Born* (1948), which includes "Stealin' Apples." Finally, there is the largely fictional but entertaining *Benny Goodman Story* (1955), which has Steve Allen acting as a very nice version of Benny Goodman while the unseen BG actually plays all of the clarinet solos.

LIONEL HAMPTON
b. Apr. 20, 1908, Louisville, KY

Lionel Hampton virtually introduced the vibraphone to jazz as an instrument. He played short spots on vibes behind Louis Armstrong on a pair of 1930 records ("Shine" and "Memories of You"), but it was when he joined the Benny Goodman Quartet six years later that the always-enthusiastic performer set the music world on fire.

Hampton grew up in Birmingham, Alabama, and Chicago. He started out as a drummer with Major N. Clark Smith's Chicago Defender Newsboys' Band. Hamp played in Chicago area groups and had a few lessons on xylophone from Jimmy Bertrand, a drummer of the period who occasionally doubled on xylophone (including on records). Hampton moved to Los Angeles in 1927, worked at first with the Spikes Brothers, and then played with Paul Howard's Quality Serenaders. Howard's band (with Hamp on drums) recorded in 1929–30 and was one of the hottest groups in California during the era. After leaving the Quality Serenaders, Hampton worked with the house band at Sebastian's Cotton Club, and it was with that unit (which was led by Les Hite) that he met up with Louis Armstrong. Satch noticed a set of vibes in the studio and suggested that Hampton play a few notes on them. Hamp, remembering his xylophone lessons, enthusiastically agreed.

Lionel Hampton continued with Les Hite for several years and then in 1934 formed his own orchestra. He appeared in the background of several movies and popped up in *Pennies from Heaven* in a nightclub scene with Louis Armstrong. In 1936 he was discovered by Benny Goodman and, after a few guest appearances, he became an important part of Goodman's organization, from November 1936 to July 1940. A colorful performer whose enthusiasm affected everyone (including the King of Swing), Hampton was part of BG's small groups, occasionally subbed on drums with his big band, and took a vocal now and then. Starting in 1937 he also started leading his own extensive series of all-star recording dates, which featured the who's who of the Swing era.

When Hampton finally left Goodman in the summer of 1940, it was on very good terms, and they would have many musical reunions through the years, a few of which were recorded. Hamp soon formed his own big band, and his third record date with his orchestra resulted in a very famous version of "Flying Home," featuring a classic tenor solo by Illinois Jacquet. So successful was that performance (and a 1944 remake recording called "Flying Home No. 2" that starred Arnett Cobb's tenor) that "Flying Home" would forever be closely identified with Hampton, Jacquet, and Cobb, all of whom used it as their theme song. The performance fit the style that Lionel Hampton was aiming for, extroverted excitement with honking tenors, screaming trumpets, basic chord changes, and one explosion after another. It also set the stage for rhythm and blues; in fact several saxophonists during the late 1940s/early '50s would base a large part of their repertoire on "Flying Home!"

An impressive variety of players passed through Hampton's Orchestra during the 1940s, including trumpeters Cat Anderson, Ernie Royal, Snooky Young, Kenny Dorham, Fats Navarro, and Benny Bailey, trombonist Fred Beckett, tenors Jacquet, Cobb, and Johnny Griffin, altoist Earl Bostic, guitarist Wes Montgomery, pianist Milt Buckner, bassist Charles Mingus, and singers Dinah Washington, Little Jimmy Scott, and Betty Carter, among others. Hampton had no difficulty adjusting to bebop, and his orchestra both preceded and embraced early rhythm and blues. Its shows were among the most exciting and exhibitionistic of the era. Hampton was always a very popular attraction, and throughout most of the 1950s he led big bands on and off, including one that went on a European tour in 1953 that included trumpeters Clifford Brown and Art Farmer, arranger-trumpeter Quincy Jones, altoist Gigi Gryce, pianist George Wallington, electric bass pioneer Monk Montgomery, and singer Annie Ross. In addition, Hampton performed on many small group recordings, including with Oscar Peterson, Buddy DeFranco and Art Tatum.

Through the decades, although Lionel Hampton was happy to add new material (he recorded a credible version of John Coltrane's "Giant Steps" in the 1980s), he never tired of playing his hits: "Flying Home," "Hamp's Boogie-Woogie," and "Hey Ba-Ba-Re-Bop." Few of his post-1960 big bands were all that notable, since his style did not change and the focus was generally on the leader. Hamp's series of records in the late 1970s for his Who's Who label with all-star groups did not reach the heights of his late 1930s classics, but, up until he had a serious stroke in the mid-1990s, Lionel Hampton's concerts were always full of hard-driving and joyful Swing. And even after the stroke, Hampton kept on performing (in greatly weakened condition) with young big bands. He loved the music too much to stop.

●

5 *Hot Mallets, Vol. 1 / Apr. 14, 1937–Sept. 11, 1939 / Bluebird 6458*

5 *The Jumpin' Jive, Vol. 2 / Feb. 8, 1937–Oct. 12, 1939 / Bluebird 2433*

5 *Tempo and Swing / Oct. 30, 1939–Aug. 21, 1940 / Bluebird 66039*

During 1937–41, Lionel Hampton led a consistently brilliant series of all-star small-group Swing sessions featuring sidemen from many different orchestras, including those of Benny Goodman, Duke Ellington, Cab Calloway, and Earl Hines, among others. In the late 1970s a six-LP set reissued all of the music in perfect fashion. In the CD era, RCA (in their Bluebird subsidiary) has come out with only these three samplers, which have incomplete sessions and sometimes split the same date between two different CDs! The music is excellent, of course, but the packaging and the lack of planning behind this series (blame it on the producers, Steve Backer, Orrin Keepnews, and Ed Michel) is quite unfortunate and is inexcusable for a large label. Get the *Lionel Hampton Classics* CDs (which do not include the alternate takes), search for the LP box set, or wait until RCA finally gets its act together. This trio of confusing CDs (worth getting if found at a budget price) only hints at what was recorded.

10 *Hamp! / May 26, 1942–Mar. 20, 1963 / GRP/Decca 652* This attractive two-CD set is a near-perfect sampling of Lionel Hampton's Decca recordings. Dating mostly from 1942–50 (with two selections from a 1963 date with trumpeter Charlie Teagarden), most of the main highlights of Lionel Hampton's 1940s sessions are here, including "Flying Home" (but surprisingly not "Flying Home #2"), "Hamp's Boogie Woogie," "Red Cross" (with guest Dizzy Gillespie), "Evil Gal Blues" (Dinah Washington's first hit), Hampton's famous solo on "Stardust" (possibly the high point of his career), "Blow Top Blues," "Hey! Ba-Ba-Re-Bop," "Red Top," "Mingus Fingers," "Midnight Sun," and "Rag Mop." Some of the numbers feature small groups out of the vibraphonist's orchestra, but most of the selections are by Lionel Hampton's Big Band. A definitive set.

9 *Midnight Sun / Jan. 29, 1946–Nov. 10, 1947 / GRP/ Decca 625* Eight of the 20 selections on this single CD are on the twofer *Hamp!* but those collectors who do not have that set will enjoy this excellent overview of Hampton's 1946–47 recordings. His big band was open to the influence of bop and more modern sounds (best heard on Charles Mingus's "Mingus Fingers") but really looked more towards extroverted rhythm and blues while holding on to its foundation in Swing. Many soloists are heard from, including trumpeters Jimmy Nottingham, Duke Garrette, Teddy Buckner, Kenny Dorham, and Leo "the Whistler" Shepperd, trombonists Booty Wood and Britt Woodman, the tenors of Arnett Cobb, Johnny Griffin, and Johnny Sparrow, and pianist Milt Buckner in addition to Hamp himself. Two-part extended renditions of "Rockin' in Rhythm" and "Airmail Special" are included along with such numbers as "Cobb's Idea," "Tempo's Birthday," "Jack the Fox Boogie," "Three Minutes on 52nd Street," and "Midnight Sun."

6 *Just Jazz All Stars / Aug. 4, 1947 / GNP/Crescendo 15*

5 *Lionel Hampton in Paris / Sept. 28, 1953 / Vogue 68214*

7 *You Better Know It / Oct. 26, 1964 / GRP/Impulse 140*
Lionel Hampton led big bands during the 1940s and on and off in the 1950s, but he also recorded a steady string of small-group sessions. The *Just Jazz All Stars* set was recorded at the same Pasadena Civic Auditorium concert that resulted in his famous "Stardust" solo (which was released on a Decca LP). The six selections on the GNP CD alternate blues and standards and find Hampton dominating a septet that also includes trumpeter Charlie Shavers, altoist Willie Smith, and tenor saxophonist Corky Corcoran. In 1953 Hampton took one of his finest big bands ever to France but strangely enough he forbade his sidemen from recording. The musicians (which included Clifford Brown and Quincy Jones) ignored Hampton, and the resulting furor ended up with the orchestra breaking up before it made any formal recordings. As shown on *Lionel Hampton in Paris,* the vibraphonist did not even follow his own advice, recording a jam session with a few of his sidemen (including trumpeter Walter Williams, trombonist James Cleveland, Clifford Scott on tenor, and electric bassist Monk Montgomery) and a few French players (tenorman Alix Combelle and pianist Claude Bolling). The resulting music (which includes such titles as "Real Crazy," "More Crazy," and "More and More Crazy") is swinging but overly loose and basic. Eleven years later, Hampton teamed up with an impressive sextet (trumpeter Clark Terry, tenor saxophonist Ben Webster, pianist Hank Jones, bassist Milt Hinton, and drummer Osie Johnson) to record some of his older standards and a few newer pieces (including Manny Albam's "Moon Over My Annie"). On a spontaneous "Swingle Jingle," Hampton switched to piano. The good feelings felt throughout the date (Clark Terry's presence is a strong asset) make the joyful set well worth picking up.

8 *Reunion at Newport 1967 / June 30, 1956–July 3, 1967 / Bluebird 66157*
At the 1967 Newport Jazz Festival, Lionel Hampton headed a particularly strong orchestra that was accurately titled his "All-Star Alumni Big Band." Trumpeters Wallace Davenport and Joe Newman (featured on "Meet Benny Bailey") and trombonist Al Grey get solo space, pianist Milt Buckner sits in on two numbers, and Illinois Jacquet rejoins his old boss on a memorable rendition of "Flying Home." Hampton sounds quite exuberant throughout. The final five numbers on the CD are from an unrelated 1956 session (half of the original album) in which Hampton's big band and quintet perform in Madrid, Spain, with a castanets player and (on two numbers) pianist Tete Monteliu. Recommended.

5 *Live at the Blue Note / June 11–13, 1991 / Telarc 83308*

3 *Just Jazz / June 11–13, 1991 / Telarc 83313*

2 *For the Love of Music / 1994–1995 / MoJazz 314530554*
It probably seemed like a good idea at the time, teaming Lionel Hampton in 1991 (when he was 82) with other veterans (trumpeters Clark Terry and Harry "Sweets" Edison, tenors James Moody and Buddy Tate, trombonist Al Grey, pianist Hank Jones, bassist Milt Hinton, and drummer Grady Tate) as the "Golden Men of Jazz." Their *Live at the Blue Note* set has its moments, even if Edison and Tate were clearly past their prime. Moody humorously sings and yodels on "Moody's Mood for Love" and Hampton sounds fine on "Lover," "Flyin' Home," and "Hamp's Boogie Woogie." However, the second *Just Jazz* release (from the same dates and with the same musicians) is very loose in spots (Clark Terry saves the day a couple times) and Hampton does his best to completely dominate the music, to the detriment of the band. Perhaps if these guys had rehearsed! In 1994 the MoJazz label made a big deal out of signing Hampton to a longtime contract even though he was already 85. As it turned out, *For the Love of Music* is their only Hampton release to date, and it is a case of dumping too much into one CD. The ancient vibraphonist is teamed with many players (the personnel and instrumentation change from song to song) and some songs work better than others. Best is a collaboration with Tito Puente on "Don't You Worry 'Bout a Thing." However, keyboardist Patrice Rushen sounds very much out-of-place on a funky "Flying Home," while saxophonist Grover Washington, Jr., seems to be only semi-conscious on "Another Part of Me." Other participants in-

clude Joshua Redman, Stevie Wonder, Chaka Khan (why?), Wallace Roney, R&B singer Johnny Kemp on a dumb "Jazz Me," and Dianne Reeves. On the whole, this CD demonstrates how more sometimes is less.

LPS TO SEARCH FOR

The Complete Lionel Hampton (RCA AXM6-5536) is a six-LP set that has all of the recordings led by Lionel Hampton prior to the debut of the Hampton Orchestra on record. There are many gems among the 95 selections (which includes all the alternate takes); in fact, every selection is well worth hearing. The list of all-stars is very impressive, including trumpeters Ziggy Elman, Cootie Williams, Jonah Jones, Harry James, Rex Stewart, Dizzy Gillespie, and Henry "Red" Allen, trombonists Lawrence Brown and J. C. Higginbotham, clarinetists Buster Bailey and Edmond Hall, altoists Johnny Hodges, Benny Carter, and Earl Bostic, tenors Herschel Evans, Chu Berry, Coleman Hawkins, Ben Webster, and Budd Johnson, baritonist Harry Carney, guitarists Charlie Christian, Al Casey, and Oscar Moore, pianists Jess Stacy, Billy Kyle, Clyde Hart, and Nat King Cole, bassists John Kirby and Milt Hinton, and drummers Gene Krupa, Cozy Cole, Sonny Greer, and Jo Jones, among many others. Also of interest is 1948 (Alamac 2419), a budget LP that has radio air checks from Hampton's otherwise unrecorded big band of 1948. Among the soloists are trumpeters Fats Navarro (heard on "Hot House"), Teddy Buckner, Bennie Bailey, and high-note specialist Leo "The Whistler" Shepherd, trombonists Britt Woodman and Al Grey, Johnny Sparrow on tenor, pianist Milt Buckner, bassist Charles Mingus, and (a decade before he was discovered) guitarist Wes Montgomery.

FILMS

Lionel Hampton plays himself in *A Song Is Born* (1948) and *The Benny Goodman Story* (1955).

ERSKINE HAWKINS
b. July 26, 1914, Birmingham, AL, d. Nov. 11, 1993, Willingboro, NJ

Erskine Hawkins led one of the great (and most underrated) big bands of the Swing era. Billed as "the 20th Century Gabriel," Hawkins had a dazzling technique and could hit high notes with apparent ease, but his somewhat bombastic solos tended to be criticized by overly serious jazz critics. Because he was generous with allocating solo space and often had trumpeter Dud Bascomb take jazz choruses (generally in the middle register), many of Bascomb's statements were initially mistakenly attributed to Hawkins!

Erskine Hawkins started out playing drums at seven, was on trombone for a couple years, and then permanently switched to trumpet as a teenager. Hawkins played with the 'Bama Street Collegians at the State Teachers College in Montgomery, Alabama, and was soon made its leader. In 1934 the band split from the college, relocated to New York, and became the Erskine Hawkins Orchestra. The trumpeter would never be a sideman again.

Hawkins's band always put the emphasis on swinging tempos that could excite black dancing audiences, particularly at the Savoy Ballroom, where it spent three years as the house orchestra. There were several main stars among the sidemen: trumpeter Dud Bascomb, Paul Bascomb and/or Julian Dash on tenors, pianist Avery Parrish, baritonist Haywood Henry, and (in the mid-1940s) altoist Bobby Smith. "After Hours" (featuring Parrish's bluish piano), the original version of "Tuxedo Junction" (which was cut a few months before the more famous Glenn Miller record), and 1945's "Tippin' In" were all major best-sellers. But beyond the hits, most Erskine Hawkins recordings (and he recorded extensively for Bluebird during 1938–42 and Victor during 1946–50) are quite rewarding.

Because of his band's popularity and basic approach, Hawkins was able to keep his orchestra going into the early 1950s, hinting at times at R&B and bebop, but not altering his group's sound much. In the '50s he was forced to eventually break up the big band, but Hawkins continued playing with a small group on a part-time basis into the 1980s, even having a recorded reunion of his orchestra in 1971.

"The 20th-Century Gabriel," trumpeter Erskine Hawkins had one of
the most swinging bands of the Swing era and beyond.

9 *The Original Tuxedo Junction / Sept. 12, 1938–Jan. 10, 1945 / Bluebird 9682*

This single CD perfectly sums up Erskine Hawkins' prime years. It starts off with his three big hits ("Tuxedo Junction," "After Hours," and "Tippin' In") and then progresses chronologically, mostly covering the 1938–42 period. In addition to the big sellers, the 21 selections include such spirited numbers as "Weary Blues," "Swing Out," "Gin Mill Special," "Cherry," and "Bear Mash Blues." It is obvious, listening to this introductory set, why dancers in Harlem just loved this solidly swinging big band.

9 *1936–1938 / July 20, 1936–Sept. 12, 1938 / Classics 653*

9 *1938–1939 / Sept. 12, 1938–Oct. 2, 1939 / Classics 667*

9 *1939–1940 / Oct. 2, 1939–Nov. 6, 1940 / Classics 678*

9 *1940–1941 / Nov. 6, 1940–Dec. 22, 1941 / Classics 701*

9 *1941–1945 / Dec. 22, 1941–Nov. 21, 1945 / Classics 868*

8 *1946–1947 / Apr. 24, 1946–Dec. 20, 1947 / Classics 1008*

Because the Erskine Hawkins Orchestra recorded very few duds or dull vocal ballads during its existence, listeners may not be totally satisfied with having just one CD of the band. The European Classics label, on these six CDs, has put out all of the recordings from the big band's first 11 years. Although Hawkins would record with his orchestra into 1952, plus three later albums and a few scattered titles, the essence is on these six discs. The band was strong from the start, never lost its power, and stuck to its swinging identity. And even in 1947, after Dud and Paul Bascomb had departed, the lineup of the orchestra could hold its own with practically any other band. Retro Swing groups would be well advised to dig into the legacy of Erskine Hawkins and revive more of these hot numbers.

comb, Julian Dash, Haywood Henry, and singer Jimmy Mitchelle all still sound surprisingly strong on this fairly rare LP, and even the ringers (such as Dud Bascomb, Jr., Ernie Hayes, and Earl Warren) blend in well on seven Swing era standards (including new versions of Hawkins's three big hits).

LPS TO SEARCH FOR

In 1971 Erskine Hawkins had a very successful reunion with many of his alumni that was recorded as *Live at Club Soul Sound* (Chess 9141). Hawkins, Dud Bascomb, Paul Bas-

FILMS

Other than the ten-minute short *Deviled Hams* (1937), it is quite possible that the Erskine Hawkins Orchestra never appeared on film at all.

FLETCHER HENDERSON
b. Dec. 1, 1897, Cuthbert, GA, d. Dec. 29, 1952, New York, NY

Although preceded by Paul Whiteman, Fletcher Henderson led the first swinging big band. During 1922–38, nearly every top young black musician was with Henderson at one time or another; the list of trumpeters alone includes Louis Armstrong, Joe Smith, Tommy Ladnier, Rex Stewart, Bobby Stark, Cootie Williams, Henry "Red" Allen, Roy Eldridge, and Emmett Berry. Strangely enough, Fletcher Henderson was actually fairly insignificant in his own group during the 1920s, since his piano playing was fairly basic and he did not arrange that much until the early 1930s. However, Henderson can be thought of as the father figure of Swing. His big band was the ancestor of all the other Swing orchestras and his arrangements for Benny Goodman (which were partly responsible for BG's success) helped set the standard for the Swing era.

Although he started playing piano when he was six, Henderson studied at Atlanta University College and earned a chemistry degree. He moved to New York in 1920, soon discovered that black chemists were not in great demand, and instead got a job demonstrating songs for the Pace-Handy Music Company. Henderson became involved with the Black Swan label (as their house pianist), started recording as early as 1921, and accompanied Ethel Waters (1921–22) on tour. Although never a virtuoso player on the level of James P. Johnson or the young Fats Waller, Henderson had a quiet and distinguished air about him and he looked like a bandleader. He recorded extensively in 1923 with his early orchestra, and by the end of the year (when his band started playing regularly in public) such musicians as tenor saxophonist Coleman Hawkins, drummer Kaiser Marshall, and altoist-clarinetist Don Redman were among his personnel. Redman was particularly significant, for he wrote the great majority of the arrangements for what at the time was a nonet (before it soon expanded). Even at this early stage, with their staccato phrasing, advanced harmonies, and futuristic atmosphere, Redman's charts put the Henderson group ahead of its rivals. And on July, 30, 1924, during the second half of their version of "Charley, My Boy" (featuring trombonist Charlie Green), the band for the first time on records was really swinging!

Swinging would become a much more common occurrence within a few months. Louis Armstrong, straight from Chicago and King Oliver's band, joined Henderson in October (as did clarinetist Buster Bailey), and his legato phrasing, use of space, and dramatic improvisations had a major effect not only on his fellow musicians with Henderson but on Redman's arranging style and on jazz in general. By the time Satch departed, in November 1925, the Fletcher Henderson Orchestra had no close competitors. Its prime years lasted through 1929 and its most significant recordings included "The Stampede" (which was highlighted by an influential Hawkins tenor chorus) and "King Porter Stomp" (versions in 1928, 1932, and 1933 that were actually hotter than Benny Goodman's hit recording of 1935). Such players as altoist Edgar Sampson (himself an important arranger-composer), bassist John Kirby, and trombonists Jimmy Harrison, Benny Morton, J. C. Higginbotham, and Dickie Wells would spend time with Henderson, and his younger brother Horace Henderson proved to be a talented arranger, too. After Don Redman departed, in 1928, to join McKinney's Cotton Pickers (a major loss), altoist Benny Carter became the band's main arranger. When Carter went out on his own in 1931, Henderson finally began to write more extensively. Among his charts were a remake of "Sugar Foot Stomp," "Honeysuckle Rose," "Down South Camp Meetin'," and "Wrappin' It Up."

Unfortunately Fletcher Henderson was not a strong businessman and he seemed to lose interest in his band during the Depression. Long based at the Roseland Ballroom, Henderson's orchestra began to miss opportunities and was soon overtaken by not only Duke Ellington but many other up-and-coming big bands. Coleman Hawkins departed in 1934 after 11 years (his replacement was briefly Lester Young and then Ben Webster) and, although still an all-star crew, the band broke up in 1935 just as the Swing era was really beginning. Henderson contributed arrangements to Benny Goodman for a year, and the clarinetist had much more commercial success with Henderson's charts than the pianist had ever enjoyed, recording (among others) "Japanese Sandman," "Blue Skies," "Sometimes I'm Happy," "King Porter Stomp," and "When Buddha Smiles" in 1935 alone. During 1936–38 Goodman would perform and document quite a few of Henderson's other arrangements, including "You Turned the Tables On Me," "Down South Camp Meeting," "St. Louis Blues," "Always," "Sugar Foot Stomp," "Minnie the Moocher's Wedding Day," "Make Believe," "The Blue Room," and "Wrappin' It Up."

With Swing becoming the thing, Henderson in early 1936 put together a new big band, one that initially had trumpeter Roy Eldridge and tenor saxophonist Chu Berry among its key soloists. Henderson's rendition of Berry's "Christopher Columbus" was a hit, and his theme song, "Stealin' Apples," was popular, but, as it turned out, Henderson's band never really caught on. His orchestra lasted until mid-1939, when he joined Goodman as a staff arranger and (for a short time) pianist with his sextet. Goodman always considered Henderson to be his favorite writer, and he would praise him and use his charts throughout his career. During the next decade, Henderson led several short-lived big bands, having a big band recording session apiece in 1941 and 1945 and a combo date in 1949. For a period in Chicago, the young Sun Ra (later an important avant-garde bandleader) was Henderson's pianist. During much of 1949, Henderson was back where he started, as an accompanist to Ethel Waters. In December 1950 he led a sextet at Café Society in New York, and a live recording from that engagement resulted. Just a few days after that performance, Henderson had a serious stroke, which forced him permanently out of action and resulted in his death two years later. Although never quite a household name to the Swing public, Fletcher Henderson's importance as a pioneering bandleader, a masterful talent scout, and a contributor to Benny Goodman's library cannot be overstated.

●

10 *A Study in Frustration / Aug. 9, 1923–May 28, 1938 / Columbia/Legacy 57596*

Formerly a four-LP set, this three-CD box really contains the very best of Fletcher Henderson's recordings, 64 selections in all. There are two early numbers, nine from the Louis Armstrong period, 26 from the glory years (1925–29), 19 from 1930–33, and eight from the 1936–38 band. Virtually every player mentioned in Henderson's biography is well featured, plus guest pianist Fats Waller. Just to point out a few of the more noteworthy selections, this essential box includes "Shanghai Shuffle," two versions of "Sugar Foot Stomp," "The Stampede," "Jackass Blues," "Henderson Stomp," "Tozo," "St. Louis Shuffle," "Hop Off," three classic renditions of "King Porter Stomp," "Oh Baby," "Raisin' the Roof," "Clarinet Marmalade," "Honeysuckle Rose," "Yeah Man," "Christopher Columbus," and "Stealin'

Apples." Swing started with this band and rarely sounded hotter.

5 *1921–1923 / June 1921–June 11, 1923 / Classics 794*

5 *1923 / June 25, 1923–Apr. 24, 1924 / Classics 697*

6 *1923–1924 / Nov. 30, 1923–Jan. 29, 1924 / Classics 683*

6 *1924 / Feb. 1924–May 6, 1924 / Classics 673*

6 *1924, Vol. 2 / May 21, 1924–Aug. 29, 1924 / Classics 657*

Even those Swing collectors who have *A Study in Frustration* will want to acquire a bunch of the Fletcher Henderson Classics CDs to get the entire story. These five discs cover Henderson's pre-Armstrong period, an era when his band was remarkably prolific. Many of the selections were formerly quite rare. On *1921–23,* Henderson is heard playing the only three unaccompanied piano solos that he ever recorded, heading studio groups and leading the early nucleus of what would be his orchestra. Coleman Hawkins joined Henderson in time to appear on the final few numbers on *1923*, but he would be a primitive player until Armstrong's arrival. On *1923–1924* and *1924*, Henderson's orchestra was still a bit stiff and played mostly first-class dance music of the period. The arrival of trombonist Charlie Green in June 1924 gave the band its first strong soloist, and his impact can be heard on "Charley, My Boy" from July 30. But this period can be subtitled "Waiting for Louis."

10   *Louis with Fletcher Henderson 1924–1925 / Oct. 7, 1924–Oct. 21, 1925 / Forte 38001/2/3*

3   *Fletcher Henderson and Louis Armstrong / Oct. 10, 1924–Oct. 21, 1925 / Timeless 1-003*

7   *1924, Vol. 3 / Sept. 8, 1924–Nov. 24, 1924 / Classics 647*

7   *1924–25 / Dec. 1924–Nov. 16, 1925 / Classics 633*

Louis Armstrong's year with Fletcher Henderson literally changed jazz forever. The Forte release is a three-CD set that has all 65 performances (including 22 alternate takes) that Satch cut with the big band, counting a date in which a quintet backs the vocal team of Coot Grant and Kid Wesley Wilson and two songs that combine Henderson's crew with that of Sam Lanin. One hears not only Armstrong's evolution from month to month (from "Manda" to "Carolina Stomp") but the gradual change of the Henderson orchestra from a dance band to a mighty jazz ensemble. The Timeless disc is an odd project in which only ten of the 24 selections are complete. The 14 excerpts (three are under a minute) concentrate on Louis's solos and occasionally splice in as an additional chorus or two from alternate takes. The project might have worked except that Timeless did not program the music in chronological order, making it all rather frivolous. The two Classics CDs contain all of the master takes (but no alternates) from Armstrong's dates with Henderson, plus the session before he joined (on *1924 Vol. 3*) and the first one after he left (*1924–25*). Since this is rather important music, search for the Forte release.

8   *1925–26 / Nov. 23, 1925–Apr. 14, 1926 / Classics 610*

9   *1926–27 / Apr. 14, 1926–Jan. 22, 1927 / Classics 597*

9   *1927 / Mar. 11, 1927–Oct. 24, 1927 / Classics 580*

9   *1927–31 / Nov. 4, 1927–Feb. 5, 1931 / Classics 572*

The Fletcher Henderson Orchestra was at the peak of its powers during 1925–32, although it did not record half as much as it should have during 1928–30. With Armstrong's departure, the big band had Joe Smith as its trumpet soloist and such fine players as trombonist Charlie Green, clarinetist Buster Bailey, and the rapidly maturing Coleman Hawkins on tenor; Hawkins even introduces "Dinah" on *1925–26* with a chorus on bass sax! *1926–1927* features trumpeter Tommy Ladnier as the most impressive soloist along with Hawkins and guest Fats Waller; highlights include "Stampede," "Jackass Blues," "Henderson Stomp," "The Chant," and "Snag It." On *1927*, Ladnier is assisted by the great trombonist Jimmy Harrison (catch his breaks on "Fidgety Feet"), Bailey, and Hawkins. Due to Henderson's mismanagement, some bad luck, and not taking care of business, his big band recorded only nine numbers in all of 1928, four in 1929, and just four more in 1930, so *1927–31* covers a fairly long period of time. Many top musicians played with the orchestra during this period, including trumpeters Rex Stewart and Bobby Stark, altoist Benny Carter (who wrote some of the arrangements), and the ever-present Coleman Hawkins and Buster Bailey. With such numbers as "King Porter Stomp" (the first time Jelly Roll Morton's song had been orchestrated for a big band), a boiling "Oh Baby," and "Raisin' the Roof" being among the obvious classics, it is a pity that Henderson's band was largely standing still commercially during the era, slipping behind its competition despite its strong music.

6   *Hocus Pocus / Apr. 27, 1927–Aug. 4, 1936 / Bluebird 9904*

7   *Tidal Wave / Apr. 1, 1931–Sept. 25, 1934 / GRP/Decca 643*

8   *1931 / Feb. 5, 1931–July 31, 1931 / Classics 555*

7   *1931–32 / July 31, 1931–Mar. 11, 1932 / Classics 546*

9   *1932–34 / Dec. 9, 1932–Sept. 12, 1934 / Classics 535*

By all rights, the Fletcher Henderson Orchestra should have been flourishing during 1931–34 since it had had quite a few years to establish its reputation and it boasted an all-star lineup. But instead it was struggling and would break up in early 1935. *Hocus Pocus* is a "best of" collection that has 21 of Henderson's 34 recordings for Victor-owned labels; two cuts from 1927, five from 1931–32, four from 1934, and nine dating from 1936. Whether it be "St. Louis Shuffle" in 1927, "Sugar Foot Stomp," "Roll On, Mississippi, Roll On," or "Sing, Sing, Sing" (slightly predating Benny Goodman's rendition), it is difficult to understand why Henderson's ensemble was not commercially successful, for it sure could swing. Three previously unreleased alternate takes have been included to this CD to really annoy completists! *Tidal Wave* also adds one new take (of "Memphis Blues"), but it reissues Henderson's five Decca-owned sessions complete. Eight songs are from 1931 (including a remake of "Sugar Foot Stomp," a tribute to Bix Beiderbecke on "Singin' the Blues," and the memorable "Radio Rhythm") and 13 from 1934, when the main soloists were Red Allen, Buster Bailey, and Ben Webster. The three Classics CDs (as usual) reissue everything but the alternate takes. On *1931* the solos of Stark, Stewart, trombonist Benny Morton, and Hawkins generally outshine the somewhat generic arrangements. *1931–32* has some commercial numbers (including the dreadful "Strangers" and "My Sweet Tooth Says I Wanna but My Wisdom Tooth Says No"), two songs in which the band backs the vocals of child star Rose Marie and some charts that sound as if they came from the Casa Loma Orchestra, but once again the individual solos tend to save the day. Surprisingly the music greatly improves on *1932–1934* despite the band's struggles. The first date (cut nine months after the session that closed *1931–32*) has classic versions of "New King Porter Stomp" (which has Bobby Stark's greatest solo) and "Honeysuckle Rose." The year 1933 yielded "Yeah Man," another version of "King Porter Stomp," "Queer Notions," and Coleman Hawkins's feature on "It's the Talk of the Town." Hawk left the band in 1934, but such soloists as Red Allen, Hilton Jefferson, and Ben Webster and charts such as "Limehouse Blues," "Big John's Special," and "Down South Camp Meeting" meant that Henderson's music did not decline despite the hard times.

8	*1934–37 / Sept. 25, 1934–Mar. 2, 1937 / Classics 527*
6	*1937–38 / Mar. 2, 1937–May 28, 1938 / Classics 519*
7	*Fletcher Henderson and His Orchestra, 1938 / July 11 + 13, 1938 / Jazz Unlimited 2053*

1934–1937 has the last date by the original Fletcher Henderson Orchestra (an ironically heated session that includes "Wild Party," "Rug Cutter's Swing," and "Hotter Than 'Ell"). With the exception of one cut from 1937, the remainder of this CD consists of Henderson's complete output of 1936. This particular band features trumpeter Roy Eldridge, tenorman Chu Berry, and the returning Buster Bailey. Fletcher and his brother Horace Henderson were responsible for most of the arrangements, and these include such swinging numbers as the hit "Christopher Columbus," "Blue Lou," "Stealin' Apples," "I'll Always Be in Love with You," "Riffin'," and "You Can Depend on Me." Unfortunately the big band's initial success did not last. *1937–1938* has the orchestra's last recordings. Eldridge had departed but trumpeter Emmett Berry, trombonist J. C. Higginbotham (present for the first seven numbers), and either Chu Berry, Ben Webster, or Franz Jackson on tenor are still heard from. Unfortunately Chuck Roberts takes vocals on 11 of the last 18 selections, and his singing does not help! However, "Back in Your Own Backyard," "Chris and His Gang," a remake of "Stealin' Apples," and "Moten Stomp" are quite worthwhile. The Jazz Unlimited CD has two radio broadcasts from the 1938 Fletcher Henderson Orchestra that were performed six weeks after their final recordings. Chuck Richards pops up again several times, but these performances (the only live dates to be documented of Henderson's big band of the 1930s) gives one a good idea how the group performed live. Emmett Berry, trombonist Ed Cuffee, and Franz Jackson are the solo stars.

LPS TO SEARCH FOR

Obviously Fletcher Henderson is well covered on CD. However, one may want to locate Fletcher *Henderson's Sextet—1950* (Alamac 2444), a budget LP that has Henderson's final performances. He sounds fine on December 20–21, 1950, with a sextet that includes trumpeter Dick Vance, clarinetist Eddie Barefield, and tenor saxophonist Lucky Thompson, less than two days before suffering his stroke. In 1957 Rex Stewart gathered quite an alumni group under the title of *The Fletcher Henderson All Stars. Big Reunion* (Hall of Fame 624) finds such players as Stewart, Berry, Higginbotham, Dickie Wells, Hawkins, Webster, and Bailey in a 17-piece band, wailing on "Sugar Foot Stomp," "Honeysuckle Rose," "Wrappin' It Up," and "King Porter Stomp," plus a few newer tunes.

Woody Herman jams with his orchestra in the early days of the original Herd. Chubby Jackson is on bass.

WOODY HERMAN

b. May 16, 1913, Milwaukee, WI, d. Oct. 29, 1987, Los Angeles, CA

Woody Herman was an important bandleader for over 50 years, and he did his best always to be contemporary and musically relevant, despising nostalgia. This biography concentrates on his first two bands.

Woodrow Herman was a performer as a child, singing in vaudeville. He began to play saxophone (soon settling on alto) when he was 11 and clarinet at 14, adding the instruments to his act. He worked with the territory bands of Myron Stewart and Joe Lichter (1928) while still quite young and picked up important experience playing regularly with Tom Gerun's group during 1929–34. After short stints with Harry Sosnick and Gus Arnheim, Herman joined the Isham Jones Orchestra in 1934, when he was still just 21. He made his recording debut with Jones in 1935 and was well featured as a singer and occasional clarinet, alto, and baritone soloist, particularly with Isham Jones's Juniors, a small group taken out of the big band. Through the years Herman (a decent player who was not a virtuoso on the level of Benny Goodman and Artie Shaw) would look toward Johnny Hodges in his alto work, while his clarinet playing hinted at Chicago-style Dixieland.

During the late summer of 1936, Isham Jones broke up his orchestra. Herman took advantage of the opportunity to form his own big band, using some of the Jones alumni as a nucleus. At the age of 23, the young bandleader had plenty of enthusiasm, which was a good thing because there would be 2½ years of struggle ahead. On most of the early Woody Herman records, Herman is featured as a crooning ballad vocalist, and his big band lacks any real personality of its own. However, on April 12, 1939, Herman recorded "Woodchoppers Ball" and the result was a major hit. Also recorded at the same date were "Dallas Blues," "Blues Downstairs," and "Blues Upstairs." Soon the safe dance band charts were replaced with other rousing blues-based numbers, and Herman's Orchestra became known as "The Band That Plays the Blues." Herman still sang, but now his singing was added for variety rather than being the main attraction. His orchestra at this point in time did not have any major soloists, although trumpeter Cappy Lewis and Joe Bishop (one of the first jazz flugelhornists) were fine players.

In 1942, Herman began to change direction. Dizzy Gillespie's chart "Down Under" made his band sound modern, and Dave Matthews's arrangements during the next couple of years were influenced by Duke Ellington. Guests such as tenors Ben Webster, Budd Johnson, and Georgie Auld, trumpeter Ray Nance, and altoist Johnny Hodges were heard on record dates. And, most importantly, Herman's older personnel began to be replaced by younger and more inventive players. Bassist Chubby Jackson, who joined Herman in 1943, helped recruit a variety of colorful modernists. Arranger-pianist Ralph Burns was an important new acquisition in 1944, as were arranger-trumpeter Neal Hefti, singer Frances Wayne, trumpeters Pete and Conte Candoli, guitarist Billy Bauer, drummer Dave Tough, and particularly trombonist Bill Harris and tenor saxophonist Flip Phillips. In fact, a comparison of the players with Herman in November 1943 with those who were in the band in December 1944 finds (not counting Herman and Jackson) only four of the other 16 musicians being the same.

The new band became known as Woody Herman's Herd and, years later, The First Herd. Phillips and Harris were both exciting soloists with sounds of their own, Pete Candoli contributed high-note trumpet blasts, there was a great deal of humor and drive in the music ("Your Father's Mustache" is nutty while "Apple Honey" is quite a rouser), and in 1945 the boppish trumpeter Sonny Berman, trumpeter-arranger Shorty Rogers, and vibraphonist Margaret Hyams (later replaced by Red Norvo) made the group even stronger. In fact, the Herd was the most exciting new band of 1944–45, playing music that fell between Swing and bop. So highly rated were they that Igor Stravinsky was moved to compose "Ebony Concerto" for the Herman Orchestra to debut, one of the first times that a major classical composer wrote a piece specifically for a jazz band.

Unfortunately after a two-year run the Herd (which was a commercial as well as an artistic success) was reluctantly disbanded by Herman at the end of 1946 because he needed time to spend with his ailing wife. Within a year Woody Herman was back with the Second Herd, the "Four Brothers" band that featured tenors Stan Getz, Zoot Sims, and later on Al Cohn. He would continue leading orchestras on and off until his death in 1987 (including the Third Herd in the early 1950s, an exciting new band during the first half of the 1960s, a rockish outfit in the 1970s, and the Young Thundering Herd during his final decade), but the First Herd (followed closely by the Second Herd) would be the most beloved of all of Woody Herman's big bands.

●

4 *1936–1937 / Feb. 3, 1936–Aug. 10, 1937 / Classics 1042*
1936–1937 starts out with a Woody Herman appearance with Isham Jones's Orchestra ("Stompin' at the Savoy") and six numbers with Jones's Juniors (an octet taken from the big band). Of Herman's four vocals, the best of the lot (and a future standard for him) is "Fan It." By November 1936 Herman was leading his own big band. At the beginning, Herman's orchestra band mostly featured his ballad vocalizing. In fact only one of the first 16 Herman orchestra selections (all included on this CD) is an instrumental ("Mr. Ghost Goes to Town"), and the leader's singing ranges from romantic and a bit dreary to swinging (in the case of "Doctor Jazz" and "It Happened Down in Dixieland"). Of mostly historic interest.

9 *Blues on Parade / Apr. 26, 1937–July 24, 1942 / GRP/ Decca 606*
Blues on Parade is a superior sampler that gives listeners most of the high points of Woody Herman's first big band.

The emphasis throughout the CD is on jazz that is often blues-based. The original version of "Woodchopper's Ball" is here, along with "Blue Prelude," "Blues Downstairs," "Chip's Blues" (one of two-small group numbers), Dizzy Gillespie's "Down Under," "Blues in the Night," and two versions of "Blues on Parade."

7 *Vol. 1: Live in 1944 / Aug. 2, 1944–Aug. 21, 1944 / Jass 621*

6 *Vol. 2: Live in 1945 / Feb. 18, 1945–Aug. 22, 1945 / Jass 625*
Vol. 1 features the early Woody Herman First Herd on a couple of radio broadcasts (one of which is actually a rehearsal) and during two engagements from the Hollywood Palladium. The Herd was fully formed at the time, with such players as pianist-arranger Ralph Burns, tenorman Flip Phillips, trombonist Bill Harris, and trumpeter Pete Candoli being among the key players. There are also eight vocals

by Herman and six from Frances Wayne on the 25 numbers. Since several of the songs were never recorded by the band commercially and there are some heated performances (although none of this group's better-known numbers), *Vol. 1* should be of great interest to collectors. The second CD is a little less interesting since the material is more common, but the versions of "Red Top," "Bijou," "Apple Honey," and two of Northwest Passage" have their strong moments, and this was a classic band.

10   *The Thundering Herds, 1945–1947 / Feb. 19, 1945–Dec. 27, 1947 / Columbia 44108*

4   *Best of the Big Bands / Feb. 26, 1945–Dec. 22, 1947 / Columbia 45340*

The Thundering Herds is the best single-CD sampling of Woody Herman's First Herd currently available. Fourteen of the 16 numbers are from 1945–46, including such popular jams as Herman's remake of "Woodchopper's Ball," "Apple Honey," "Northwest Passage," "Your Father's Moustache," and Bill Harris's workout on "Bijou." In addition, the set has two selections ("The Goof and I" and "Four Brothers") from the Second Herd. In contrast, *Best of the Big Bands* does not come close to living up to its name. Fortunately, of its 16 numbers, only four are repeats from *The Thundering Herds* but, other than "Caldonia," none of the additional material is too essential. As usual in this series, there are no recording dates or personnel included, just breezy and innocuous liner notes by Will Friedwald. Of lesser interest.

LPS TO SEARCH FOR

The Turning Point (Decca 79229) is an intriguing album, for it concentrates on the lesser-known November 1943–December 1944 period, when "The Band That Plays the Blues" evolved into the First Herd. Ben Webster, Allen Eager, Georgie Auld, Juan Tizol, and Johnny Hodges all make guest appearances, Dave Matthews's arrangements make Herman's band sound a bit like Duke Ellington's, and it is fascinating to hear the band changing from session to session. *The Thundering Herds* (Columbia C3L 25) is a perfectly done three-LP box that should have been duplicated on CD years ago. The First Herd is represented by 37 selections (including seven from the 1946 Woodchoppers), and there are also eight of the best songs by the Second Herd. Among the many gems are "Apple Honey," "Caldonia," "Northwest Passage," "The Good Earth," "Bijou," "Your Father's Mustache," "Fan It," "Let It Snow, Let It Snow, Let It Snow," the four-part "Summer Sequence," "I've Got News for You," and "Four Brothers."

FILMS

The Woody Herman Orchestra appears in *Wake Up and Dream* (1942), *Wintertime* (1943), *Sensations of 1945* (1944), *Earl Carroll Vanities* (1945), *Hit Parade of 1947* (1947), and briefly in *New Orleans* (1947).

TEDDY HILL
b. Dec. 7, 1909, Birmingham, AL, d. May 19, 1978, Cleveland, OH

Teddy Hill was a journeyman tenor saxophonist who for a few years in the mid-1930s led a promising big band that included quite a few notable players. Originally a drummer as a youth and then a trumpeter, Hill eventually switched to tenor. After touring with the Whitman Sisters show during 1926–27 and working with drummer George Howe's band, Hill was with the Luis Russell Orchestra during 1928–29, appearing on Russell's records in 1929 (and those of Henry "Red" Allen) but rarely soloing. After working a bit with James P. Johnson, Hill formed his own ensemble in 1932, which soon became known as Teddy Hill's NBC Orchestra. The 1935 edition of his group included trumpeters Roy Eldridge and Bill Coleman, tenor saxophonist Chu Berry, and trombonist Dicky Wells. During the next couple of years such trumpeters as Frankie Newton, Shad Collins, and Dizzy Gillespie (who was 20 in 1937) succeeded Eldridge and Coleman. Hill's big band worked regularly at the Savoy and toured Europe in 1937. He kept his orchestra together until 1940, at which time Hill became the longtime manager of Minton's Playhouse, a job that lasted until 1969. While at Minton's in the early days, Teddy Hill supervised the experimental after-hours sessions that helped lead to bebop, although by then he was no longer playing music.

9 *Dance with His NBC Orchestra / Feb. 26, 1935–May 17,*
1937 / Jazz Archives 157012

This generous CD has every recording by Teddy Hill's or-chestra, all 26 cuts. There is an excess of Bill Dillard vocals (nine) plus two by Beatrice Douglas and a few novelty num-bers. However, there are also a few near-classics and impor-tant early solos by Roy Eldridge, Dickie Wells, Chu Berry, and Dizzy Gillespie (who made his debut with "King Porter Stomp"). Among the better numbers are "Lookie, Lookie, Lookie Here Comes Cookie," "At the Rug Cutter's Ball," "Passionate," "A Study in Brown," and "China Boy."

EARL HINES

b. Dec. 28, 1903, Dusquesne, PA, d. Apr. 22, 1983, Oakland, CA

Earl Hines was one of the greatest jazz pianists of all time. In the 1920s , when nearly every fluent jazz pianist played a steady stride with his or her left hand (keeping a steady rhythm by "striding" back and forth between bass notes and chords), Hines had the world's trickiest left hand. He would play against time, sometimes just implying the rhythm and frequently playing out of tempo and suspending time but never losing the beat. His speedy right hand (which sometimes played octaves in a "trumpet style" so his notes would ring over his orchestra) was on the same level, and Hines was considered the first "mod-ern" jazz pianist. Of greatest relevance to the Swing era, for 19 years (1928–47) Hines led one of the finest big bands based outside of New York.

Inspired by his father, who played cornet with a local brass band, Earl Hines started out on cornet but also started study-ing piano when he was nine. He was discovered early on by singer Lois Deppe, who helped get him hired by Arthur Ride-out's orchestra. After Deppe formed his Pittsburgh Serenaders, Hines became his pianist, making his recording debut with Deppe in 1922. Hines played with the Harry Collins Orchestra in Pittsburgh and then moved to Chicago, where he spent a year working with Carroll Dickerson's orchestra and met up with Louis Armstrong. Hines and Armstrong clicked immedi-ately, both personally and musically. During 1925–29 they were the most advanced musicians in jazz. After having stints with Dickerson and Erskine Tate, Hines was with the Louis Armstrong Stompers in 1927, and Hines, Armstrong, and drummer Zutty Singleton briefly ran a club of their own.

The year 1928 was extremely productive for Earl Hines. He worked regularly with clarinetist Jimmie Noone's Apex Club Orchestra, recorded a dozen dazzling unaccompanied piano solos (including "A Monday Date" and "57 Varieties") and was featured on a series of records with Louis Armstrong's Savoy Ballroom Five (including "West End Blues" and their wondrous cornet-piano duet "Weather Bird Rag"). Later in the year (on his 25th birthday) Hines debuted at Chicago's Grand Terrace Café with his new big band.

The Grand Terrace Café would be the Hines Orchestra's home base for a dozen years. The pianist (who was given the nickname of "Fatha" by a radio announcer) always led first-class outfits that emphasized swinging. Hines's radio broadcasts made a strong impression, and he was the main early influence on Nat King Cole. Among his star sidemen were trumpeter-singer Walter Fuller (who sang on the earliest recording of Hines's "Rosetta"), clarinetist-altoist Omer Simeon, arranger Jimmy Mundy, trombonist Trummy Young, tenor saxophonist Budd Johnson, and, starting in 1940, singer Billy Eckstine. That year "Boogie Woogie on St. Louis Blues" was a big hit for Hines (who also wrote the standard "You Can Depend on Me"). Despite that, in 1940 Hines disbanded for a short time, but then reformed his orchestra with mostly new personnel but keeping Eckstine, Budd Johnson, and a few others. His most intriguing big band was unfortunately during the recording strike of 1943, when Hines featured trumpeter Dizzy Gillespie, Charlie Parker (on tenor), and singer Sarah Vaughan. By the time the strike had been settled, those three had departed to join Billy Eckstine's boppish big band, so one can only speculate how Hines's orchestra sounded during that period. Hines still had a worthwhile band during 1944–47 (tenor saxophonist Wardell Gray was a key soloist and singer Johnny Hartman was a discovery), but near the end of 1947, after for a short time utilizing a string section in his band, Earl Hines permanently broke up his orchestra.

The following year he began a three-year stint as a member of the Louis Armstrong All-Stars. However, it was difficult to rekindle the old magic with Satch, and Hines no longer had the temperament to be a sideman. In 1951 he went out on his own, starting out with a Swing combo in San Francisco and then switching to Dixieland for most of the decade with such sidemen as cornetist Muggsy Spanier, trombonist Jimmy Archey, and clarinetist Darnell Howard. Hines played well enough in this setting, but he often seemed to be on automatic pilot, since the Dixieland repertoire and routines did not challenge or inspire him. Other than occasional trio gigs and recordings, Hines was mostly stuck in trad jazz and was in danger of being forgotten altogether.

In 1964 critic Stanley Dance talked Earl Hines into playing a couple of concerts at the Little Theatre in New York. Performing in New York for the first time in many years and featured with a trio/quartet that sometimes included Budd Johnson, Hines was rediscovered at first by the New York critics and then by the jazz world. His career underwent a remarkable renaissance, which resulted in dozens of recordings (most either solos, trios, or quartets with Johnson), constant work, European tours, and a great deal of exciting music during his final 19 years.

●

10 *1928–1932 / Dec. 1928–June 28, 1932 / Classics 545*
The great Earl Hines is showcased on a dozen piano solos from 1928 ("Blues in Thirds," "Chicago High Life," "57 Varieties," and two versions of "A Monday Date" among them), plus one from 1929 ("Glad Rag Doll"). In addition, this CD has the first big band performances of the Earl Hines Orchestra, all from 1929 except for "Deep Forest" (Hines's theme song) from 1932. The 1929 ensemble falls between classic jazz and Swing on such numbers as "Everybody Loves My Baby" (which has one of three Hines vocals), "Beau Koo Jack," and "Chicago Rhythm."

9 *1932–1934 / July 14, 1932–Mar. 27, 1934 / Classics 514*

9 *1934–1937 / Sept. 12, 1934–Aug. 10, 1937 / Classics 528*

9 *1937–1939 / Aug. 10, 1937–Oct. 6, 1939 / Classics 538*
The Earl Hines Orchestra was one of the top Swing big band of the 1930s. The material on *1932–1934* is rarely reissued, which is a pity considering its high quality. During this period Hines's key musicians were Walter Fuller on trumpet and vocals, Omer Simeon on clarinet, alto, and baritone, trombonist Trummy Young (starting with the October 27, 1933, date), and arranger Jimmy Mundy, plus Hines himself. In addition to the big band numbers (which includes the initial version of "Rosetta") and a couple early vocals by Herb Jeffries, Hines takes "Love Me Tonight" and "Down Among the Sheltering Palms" as creative piano solos. *1934–1937,* which has solid arrangements by Mundy and Quinn Wilson, includes Hines's recordings for Decca (which have been reissued now and then) and some of the ones for Vocalion (put out by Epic). In addition to Fuller, Simeon, and Young, the band now included Darnell Howard on clarinet, alto, and violin. The arrangements really swing hard, including versions of "That's a Plenty," "Sweet Georgia Brown," "Copenhagen," "Rock and Rye," "Cavernism," and "Pianology." *1937–1939* has Hines's remaining output from 1937, seven rarely reissued titles from 1938 (with trumpeter-vocalist Ray Nance heard two years before he joined Duke Ellington), and some brilliant titles from 1939. Of the latter, Hines takes "The Father's Getaway" and "Reminiscing at Blue Note" as piano solos, and his big band (with Fuller, Simeon, and Budd Johnson on tenor) uplifts such tunes as "Indiana," "Father Steps Out," and "Piano Man."

8 *Piano Man / July 12, 1939–Mar. 19, 1942 / Bluebird 6750*

9 *1939–1940 / Oct. 6, 1939–Dec. 2, 1940 / Classics 567*

9 *1941 / Apr. 3, 1941–Nov. 17, 1941 / Classics 621*

9 *1942–1945 / Mar. 19, 1942–Jan. 12, 1945 / Classics 876*
Piano Man is a sampler of Earl Hines's 1939–42 recordings, with five piano solos, an appearance with soprano-saxophonist Sidney Bechet ("Blues in Thirds"), and 16 of Hines's better recordings with his big band. Of the latter, "Father Steps In," "Piano Man," the hit "Boogie Woogie on St. Louis Blues," "Jelly, Jelly" (which resulted in singer Billy Eckstine getting some initial fame), and "Second Balcony Jump" give listeners some fine examples of the power and versatility of the Earl Hines Orchestra. More serious Swing collectors will opt instead for the Classics releases. *1939–1940* has three of Hines's piano solos (including "Rosetta," which is the only track on the CD from 1939) and all of the Hines big band's 1940 performances, including "Boogie Woogie on St. Louis Blues," the pianist's "You Can Depend

on Me," and "Jelly, Jelly." *1941* includes Hines's four orchestra sessions from that year (highlights include "Windy City Jive," "The Father Jumps," and Eckstine's singing on "The Jitney Man") plus two typically inventive piano solos ("On the Sunny Side of the Street" and "My Melancholy Baby"). *1942–1945* starts off with Hines's one big band date (which includes "Second Balcony Jump" and "Stormy Monday Blues") before the ruinous recording strike made it impossible for his boppish orchestra of 1943 to be documented. Also on this diverse CD are four trio numbers (with guitarist Al Casey and bassist Oscar Pettiford) that formed a Fats Waller tribute date, six cuts with an all-star sextet that includes Ray Nance, altoist Johnny Hodges, tenor saxophonist Flip Phillips, Casey, Pettiford, and drummer Sid Catlett (Betty Roche takes three vocals), and the Hines big band's first session of 1945. By then his orchestra was playing primarily advanced Swing, with tenorman Wardell Gray being the top soloist among the sidemen.

7 *And the Duke's Men / May 16, 1944–May 14, 1947 / Delmark 470*

8 *1945–1947 / Sept. 1945–1947 / Classics 1041*
The Delmark CD has Earl Hines's six numbers with the all-star sextet in 1944 that are also included on Classics' *1942–1945*. However, the other two sessions (all three were originally cut for the Apollo label) are unrelated but complementary. Drummer Sonny Greer's "Rextet" has Greer leading an eight-piece group filled mostly with Ellingtonians and arranged by Brick Fleagle. In addition, the powerful high-note trumpeter Cat Anderson is featured in 1947 leading his short-lived big band, an ensemble with no real names but that swings well. Rarities galore are also on *1945–1947,* the last recordings by the Earl Hines Orchestra before its breakup other than a few numbers from December 1947. The performances (originally cut for the ARA, Jazz Selection, MGM, Sunrise, and Bravo labels) contain quite a few solos from Wardell Gray (during 1945–46). Sometimes the arrangements are a bit boppish and awkward, and there are a few vocals from the high-toned Lord Essex, Dorothy Parker, and Hines himself. On the plus side are the many instrumentals, a small-group number ("Sweet Honey Babe"), and Johnny Hartman's first four recorded vocals.

10 *Spontaneous Explorations / Mar. 7, 1964–Jan. 17, 1966 / Red Baron 57331*

10 *Blues in Thirds / Apr. 20, 1965 / Black Lion 760120*

10 *Four Jazz Giants / July 18–19, 1971 / Solo Art 111/112*
After spending the first 15 years (1948–63) of his post-big band era in obscurity as a member of the Louis Armstrong All-Stars and heading Dixieland groups in San Francisco, Earl Hines had his career reborn in 1964. He would record constantly during 1964–78, including many more than his share of classics. These will be covered in other books in this jazz series, but the three listed here are superb examples of the pianist's playing during his renaissance. *Spontaneous Explorations,* a two-CD set, has an outstanding solo performance that was made the same day as Hines's comeback concert at the Little Theatre, plus a superb trio set from 1966 that finds the veteran pianist holding his own with bassist Richard Davis and drummer Elvin Jones. The unaccompanied *Blues in Thirds* recital features Hines tearing into nine selections (plus two alternate takes), including "Blues in Thirds," "Tea for Two," and "Blues After Midnight." And *Four Jazz Giants* refers to Hines and the three giants to whom he pays tribute: W. C. Handy, Hoagy Carmichael, and Louis Armstrong. He recorded the 26 selections (originally three LPs that have been reissued as a double-CD) in two days; check out the pianist's 10 + minutes' exploration of "Star Dust." The Armstrong tribute (Satch had passed away less than two weeks before) is particularly touching.

LPS TO SEARCH FOR
Live at the New School (Chiaroscuro 157), from March 1973, a live solo set, has some miraculous playing by Earl Hines, particularly on "I've Got the World on a String," "Perdido," and a six-song "Fats Waller Medley."

FILMS
Earl Hines appears with the Louis Armstrong All-Stars in *The Strip* (1951), and the video *Earl Hines & Coleman Hawkins* (Rhapsody Films) features him in top form in 1965, although the camerawork is sometimes a bit annoying.

CLAUDE HOPKINS

b. Aug. 24, 1903, Alexandria, VA, d. Feb. 19, 1984, New York, NY

A brilliant stride pianist, Claude Hopkins led a promising big band in the early 1930s that never really lived up to its potential, breaking up altogether at the height of the Swing era. Hopkins grew up in Washington D. C., starting on the piano when he was seven. He studied to be a doctor but also played with orchestras in college (studying at Howard University and Washington Conservatory). He soon decided to become a professional musician, leading his own band in Atlantic City in the summer of 1924. After a stint with Wilbur Sweatham's group in 1925, Hopkins led the orchestra that accompanied Josephine Baker to Europe and worked with her for a time overseas.

Returning home in 1926, Hopkins led a few unrecorded groups during the next few years. He headed a new orchestra at the Savoy Ballroom in 1930 and was based at the Roseland Ballroom (replacing Fletcher Henderson) during 1931–34 and at the Cotton Club during 1935–36, having some early success. Jimmy Mundy provided arrangements and originals early on (most notably "Mush Mouth") and Hopkins wrote a tune that became a standard ("I Would Do Most Anything for You"). The Claude Hopkins Orchestra, which generally had a softer and quieter ensemble sound than most of the other big bands of the time, featured such soloists as trumpeter-vocalist Ovie Alston, trombonist Fernando Arbello, the Coleman Hawkins-inspired tenor saxophonist Bobby Sands, and Edmond Hall on clarinet and baritone, plus the leader. But the Hopkins band peaked early, making its most significant recordings during 1932–34. By the time the Swing era really got going, Hopkins's orchestra was largely lost in the shuffle, having not developed its own musical personality (beyond its leader's playing) and not catching on with a wider public. There were no recordings during March 1935–January 1937 (a crucial time period). Legendary trumpeter Jabbo Smith was on six titles on record dates in 1937 (unfortunately he was barely featured) and a few cuts were recorded in 1940, but later that year Hopkins broke up the orchestra.

Claude Hopkins led a different big band during 1941–42 (without leaving any recordings) and had a couple forgotten orchestras later in the decade (including one that had a three-year stay at the Club Zanzibar during 1944–47). He worked mostly in small groups from 1947 on, including as a sideman with Henry "Red" Allen, Herman Autrey, and clarinetist Sol Yaged, playing primarily Dixieland in obscurity. Hopkins led three Swing-oriented dates for Swingville during 1960–63 (all went out of print quickly at the time), spent 1967–69 with Wild Bill Davison's Jazz Giants, and gigged with Roy Eldridge in 1970. He was rediscovered to an extent in the late 1960s and recorded outstanding solo piano albums for Chiaroscuro and Sackville (both in 1972) in addition to appearing at some classic jazz festivals late in life, when he was rightfully considered a legend.

●

9 *1932–1934 / May 24, 1932–Jan. 1, 1934 / Classics 699*
The first of three Classics CDs that reissue all of the recordings by Claude Hopkins's orchestra is the one to get. The high-note vocalist Orlando Roberson was popular during the time, and he has seven vocals, but it is the other 16 tracks that find Hopkins's ensemble at its best. Jimmy Mundy's eccentric "Mush Mouth" is a highlight, as is "I Would Do Anything for You," "Three Little Words," "California Here I Come" (one of several features for the pianist), "Honeysuckle Rose," and "Washington Squabble." In addition to their Columbia and Brunswick recordings, this CD has radio transcriptions from 1932–33 that were previously available only on a Jazz Archives LP.

7 *1934–1935 / Jan. 11, 1934–Feb. 1, 1935 / Classics 716*

8 *The Transcription Performances 1935 / Oct. 1935–Nov. 1935 / Hep 1049*

6 *1937–1940 / Feb. 2, 1937–Mar. 4, 1940 / Classics 733*
The Claude Hopkins Orchestra in 1934 seemed to be on the brink of greater things. They were signed to the Decca label in September and would soon switch their home base from Roseland to the Cotton Club. Unfortunately both moves ended up badly. When Hopkins's records did not sell well, he was dropped by Decca, and the band made no commercial recordings for two years. In addition, the Cotton Club engagement was disappointing, and by 1937 the Hopkins orchestra was clearly on the decline. *1934–1935* unfortunately

has 14 vocals from Orlando Roberson ("Trees" is difficult to sit through) but the Hopkins Orchestra is generally in fine form, particularly on "Harlem Rhythm Dance," "Three Little Words," an exciting version of "King Porter Stomp," "In the Shade of the Old Apple Tree," and "Zozoi." Although off records for a long time after February 1, 1935, the Claude Hopkins Orchestra cut 28 selections as radio transcriptions in November 1935; 25 are on the Hep CD. The big band sounds as consistent as it ever did on these solidly swinging selections, and Roberson is happily absent! Trombonist Fred Norman's three Bert Williams-style talking vocals are amusing. *1937–1940* has Hopkins's six records of 1937 (five are features for the fine singer Beverly White, while trumpeter Jabbo Smith is barely heard from at all). It also contains eight selections led by Hopkins's former star trumpeter Ovie Austin (with his former boss sitting in on piano) and the six numbers cut in 1940 by Claude Hopkins's band, using a mostly different assortment of players (other than the loyal tenor Bobby Sands). It does seem strange that Hopkins's ensemble was not able to stay together longer during the big band era.

7 *Swing Time / Feb. 21, 1961 + May 22, 1963 / Prestige 24215*

Other than a couple of Dixieland records, Claude Hopkins hardly appeared on records at all during 1941–59. He made three albums for Swingville in 1960–63, and this single CD has the second and third ones reissued in full; the first has reappeared as part of a Buddy Tate CD. The point of the Swingville label (a subsidiary of Prestige) was to focus on surviving veterans of the Swing era who were still in their prime in the early 1960s. On his Swingville dates, surprisingly Hopkins barely strides at all and instead sounds inspired by Teddy Wilson while playing a subsidiary role. Trombonist Vic Dickenson and tenor saxophonist Budd Johnson are the stars of the *Swing Time* album, while trumpeter Bobby Johnson (formerly with Erskine Hawkins) is also in top form. The other Swingville set covered by this CD, *Let's Jam*, teams tenor saxophonist Buddy Tate (who plays some fine clarinet on "Late Evening") and the sorely underrated trumpeter Joe Thomas. They made for a fine team, but why didn't Claude Hopkins take a more assertive role on his own dates?

LPS TO SEARCH FOR

Late in life (1972) Claude Hopkins had opportunities to record a pair of unaccompanied piano solo albums, *Crazy Fingers* (Chiaroscuro 114) and *Soliloquy* (Sackville 3004), that find him not only in peak form but making one wonder why he did not record in that format much more extensively.

FILMS

Claude Hopkins's orchestra appears in the full-length film *Dance Team* (1931) and in the shorts *Barber Shop Blues* (1933) and *By Request* (1935).

INTERNATIONAL SWEETHEARTS OF RHYTHM

During the Swing era, there were quite a few all-female big bands, but most were merely novelties that were run by men and recruited women more for their looks than for their playing abilities. Ina Ray Hutton's Melodears was an exception, because that band (which recorded six selections in 1934, including "How About Tomorrow Night" and "Wild Party") could swing. Unfortunately that group lasted only a few years, and, by 1940, the attractive Hutton (who took vocals and conducted colorfully) was fronting an all-male outfit.

The International Sweethearts of Rhythm were on a different level altogether. Organized in 1939 at the Piney Woods County Life School in Mississippi, the 17-piece orchestra lasted until 1949 and could hold its own with any second-level male band. During an era (which would last at least into the 1980s) when musical women were expected to sing and perhaps play piano or violin (but certainly not a horn), the Sweethearts had such fine soloists as Viola Burnside on tenor and trumpeter Tiny Davis. Headed by singer Anna Mae Winburn (who also played saxophone), the group gained a certain amount of popularity on the East Coast and toured Europe in 1945.

Unfortunately the Sweethearts (whose arrangements were written primarily by Eddie Durham and Jesse Stone) recorded only five selections (two for Guild in 1945 and three for RCA in 1946), but a Rosetta LP in the 1980s (which includes four of those studio sides, all but "Tiny Boogie," which is available on a Bluebird sampler CD) adds to the Sweethearts's slim discography with the band's three appearances on the *Jubilee* radio series; two additional numbers are on the Hindsight three-CD box *Big Band Jazz—The Jubilee Sessions*.

The International Sweethearts of Rhythm broke up in 1949. Although Anna Mae Winburn put together later versions of the group through 1955, those bands did not gain much attention. None of the sidewomen in the original group had significant musical careers after leaving the Sweethearts. Generically if not musically, they were just too far ahead of their time.

●

LPS TO SEARCH FOR

International Sweethearts of Rhythm (Rosetta 1312) has nearly every existing recording by the big band: three radio appearances (all but two numbers) and four of their five stu-dio recordings. In addition, producer Rosetta Reitz wrote extensive and definitive liner notes as well as including quite a few photos of the musicians. Those women could swing!

HARRY JAMES
b. Mar. 15, 1916, Albany, GA, d. July 5, 1983, Las Vegas, NV

Harry James led the most popular Swing orchestra of 1943–46 and was the most famous trumpeter to emerge during the Swing era. At his best, he was a spectacular soloist and a strong jazz improviser. Although James was criticized for occasionally playing schmaltz with an exaggerated vibrato or resorting to virtuosic displays, he was consistently a brilliant player whose heart was in jazz.

After a stint on drums when he was seven, Harry James took trumpet lessons from his father, who conducted orchestras for circuses. Harry developed fast, and at 12 he was heading his own group for the Christy Brothers Circus. After playing with territory bands in Texas for several years (starting when he was 15), he joined Ben Pollack's orchestra in 1935, making his recording debut. In January 1937 James became a member of the Benny Goodman Orchestra, where he was part of a classic trumpet section that also featured Ziggy Elman and Chris Griffin. James was a hit from the start, taking exuberant solos on "St. Louis Blues," "Sing, Sing, Sing" (a song he soon became sick of), and his own "Life Goes to a Party," among others. His two years with Goodman groomed him for stardom.

However, when James put together his own big band in early 1939, two years of struggling lay ahead. He was unable to hold on to his first main vocalist (Frank Sinatra), who soon joined Tommy Dorsey. Although James was a big name and his recording of his theme song, "Ciribiribin" did well, his orchestra was just one of hundreds that were active in 1939. Things did change completely after he recorded "You Made Me Love You," a slow, sentimental ballad, on May 20, 1941, with strings. A major hit, that song quickly catapulted James's band to the top of the big band business. Within the next year, James had other big sellers in "I'll Get By" (with Dick Haymes on the vocal), the instrumental "Cherry," and three Helen Forrest features: "I Don't Want to Walk Without You," "I Cried for You," and "I Had the Craziest Dream." When Glenn Miller enlisted in the Army and broke up his band, James had no close competition for the attention of the American public.

The Musicians Union strike (which started in mid-1942) resulted in James's being off records for over two years. However, his popularity continued climbing during the era, helped by regular radio performances and appearances in many movies in which he invariably played a few songs. At the height of his fame, Harry James married the famous movie actress Betty Grable. When he returned to the recording studios in late 1944, James's band had additional hits in Duke Ellington's "I'm Beginning to See the Light" and the perfect end-of-the-war song, "It's Been a Long Long Time" (with singer Kitty Kallen). By then, James had two strong soloists in his orchestra who would remain with him for many years: tenor saxophonist Corky Corcoran (who joined James in 1941) and altoist Willie Smith (formerly with Jimmy Lunceford).

Harry James's career after 1945 was a bit anticlimactic. His series of hits stopped, and he actually broke up his big band altogether in December 1946, although he had a similar orchestra back on the road five months later. The string section was dropped in 1948, and James flirted with bebop a little (particularly on an extended 1947 recording of "Tuxedo Junction"). By 1950 he was back to playing strictly Swing again. Throughout the 1950s and '60s , James patterned his orchestra closely after one of his favorite big bands, Count Basie's; the arrangements of Ernie Wilkins and Neal Hefti helped a lot. Based in Las Vegas, Harry James and his orchestra often only played on a part-time basis, although he kept the big band (which at times had Louie Bellson or Buddy Rich on drums) going into the early 1980s. Forever associated with the Swing era, Harry James continually played his hits, added some similar swinging charts, tried to incorporate current pop tunes in his repertoire, and managed to survive as a legendary big bandleader up until his death; his last record was in 1979.

●

10 *1937–1939 / Dec. 1, 1937–Mar. 6, 1939 / Classics 903*
Harry James's early years as a bandleader are fully reissued on his first four CDs from the invaluable European Classics label. Actually, *1937–39* starts off with three four-song sessions that were cut while James was still a sideman with Benny Goodman. James would model his 1950s big band after Count Basie's, and his interest in Basie's music is obvious from the very start because his first two dates find him utilizing Count's sidemen. The eight selections include trombonist Eddie Durham, altoist Earl Warren, baritonist Jack Washington, tenor saxophonist Herschel Evans, bassist Walter Page, drummer Jo Jones, singer Helen Humes, and even Buck Clayton on ensemble trumpet; only pianist Jess Stacy and James himself are from Goodman's orchestra. Most notable are "Life Goes to a Party" and an early version of "One O'Clock Jump." James is also heard with BG sidemen (plus baritonist Harry Carney) on four numbers, and his February 1, 1939, session matches him with a trio featuring either Pete Johnson or Albert Ammons on boogie-woogie piano. The last six songs on *1937–1939* are the first from James's big band and include his initial version of his theme song, "Ciribiribin," and "Two O'Clock Jump."

8 *1939 / Apr. 6, 1939–Oct. 13, 1939 / Classics 936*

7 *1939–1940 / Nov. 8, 1939–Apr. 18, 1940 / Classics 970*

7 *1940–1941 / May 4, 1940–Jan. 22, 1941 / Classics 1014*
Although Harry James's band took a while to catch on (and lacked any big names other than the leader's), it was a reasonably impressive group in the early days. *1939* has good stomps in "Indiana," "King Porter Stomp," "Feet Dragging Blues," and a rare showcase for James with just his rhythm section on a classic rendition of "Sleepy Time Gal." Also on this CD are two spots for singer Connie Haines and Frank Sinatra's first eight vocals, including "All or Nothing at All."

The music on *1939–1940* was made during a difficult time for James, when his band was demoted by Columbia to its subsidiary label, Varsity. Sinatra soon defected to Tommy Dorsey's orchestra, but Dick Haymes proved to be an able replacement. Among the better selections on *1939–1940* are "Cross Country Jump," "Concerto for Trumpet," "Tuxedo Junction," "Alice Blue Gown," and James's workout on "Carnival of Venice." *1940–1941* finished up the Varsity period and (thanks to his band's increase in popularity) found them returning to Columbia. "Flight of the Bumble Bee," "Super Chief," "Exactly Like You," and "Music Makers" were recorded during this period, and James's quick rise to the top would finally start in May 1941.

8 *Bandstand Memories 1938 to 1948 / Apr. 2, 1938–Nov. 30, 1948 / Hindsight 503*

6 *The Radio Years 1940–41 / Mar. 19, 1940 + May 22, 1941 / Jazz Unlimited 2023*
Other than the vocals of Frank Sinatra (virtually all so-so ballads), Connie Haines, Helen Forrest, the forgotten Johnny McAfee, Dick Haymes, Kitty Kallen, and Buddy Di Vito plus two excellent ones by Helen Ward, *Bandstand Memories* (a three-CD set of previously unreleased radio performances) features the jazz side of the Harry James Orchestra. Of particular interest are the first seven numbers, which find James's then-obscure ensemble jamming at their best. This attractive box also has James and his band performing quite a few songs that they otherwise did not record. *The Radio Years* consists of a pair of radio broadcasts that show how James's band sounded on March 19, 1940, when it was struggling, and on May 22, 1941, when it had added a string section and was about ready to hit it big. In both cases James plays well, alternating swinging charts (such as "Tuxedo Junction," "Cherokee," and "Jeffrie's

Harry James in 1942 had the most popular big band in the world, one that included a full string section.

Blues") with ballad vocals from Dick Haymes, features for James's horn (including "Carnival of Venice"), and (on the later date) some Latin American numbers.

4 *Best of the Big Bands / Feb. 20, 1939–Nov. 13, 1946 / Columbia 45341*

6 *Harry James and His Great Vocalists / Jan. 5, 1938– Jan. 10, 1953 / Legacy/Columbia 66371*

9 *Snooty Fruity / Nov. 21, 1944–Feb. 15, 1955 / Columbia 45447*

More than 15 years after his death, Harry James is still a famous name. One would think the Columbia label, for whom James recorded prolifically during his most significant years (1939–55), would have reissued a large chunk of his jazz recordings, but no such luck. Instead Columbia is generally content to reissue the same music over and over again, leaving it to European labels to try to make up for the label's inexcusable neglect. *Best of the Big Bands* is typical of their treatment of the trumpet. Sixteen selections are reissued un-

der the generic title, there is no mention of personnel or recording dates, and hits ("I've Heard That Song Before," "I Had the Craziest Dream," "You Made Me Love You," "It's Been a Long Long Time," and "I'm Beginning to See the Light" among them) are mixed in with a few throwaways ("The Man with the Horn," Betty Grable singing "I Can't Begin to Tell You," "Carnival," and "The Devil Sat Down and Cried"), all of it somewhat randomly programmed. Several of the numbers are repeated on *Harry James and His Greatest Vocalists,* a slightly more logical, if far from definitive, package; the vocalists heard from are Dick Haymes, Helen Forrest, Helen Humes, Jimmy Saunders, Kitty Kallen, Betty Grable (again), Willie Smith, Buddy Di Vito, Marion Morgan, Art Lund, and even Rosemary Clooney in 1953. In most cases, these recordings hit the charts at the time. *Snooty Fruity* (which for some reason actually gives James's altoist Willie Smith top billing) is much better. A classic boppish version of "Tuxedo Junction" (which has one of James's finest solos) is here along with 17 other jazz-oriented selections, including several that were previously unreleased. It is only the tip of the iceberg, but at least this music was mostly fairly rare and shows how strong a jazz soloist Harry James could be.

6 *Jazz Masters 55 / 1959–Mar. 10, 1964 / Verve 314 529 902*

Harry James's MGM recordings of 1959–64 (which follow his OK Capitol records) are mostly unavailable on CD other than this sampler. James is heard with a septet on "I Surrender Dear" and otherwise with big bands playing arrangements by Ernie Wilkins, Bob Florence, Neal Hefti, Ralph Burns, and Thad Jones. In addition to the Swing songs (which sometimes have solos from altoist Willie Smith and Corky Corcoran on tenor), James augments his orchestra with the "Dixieland Five" (which includes tenor saxophonist Eddie Miller) on two numbers. A decent sampler that finds Harry James still playing quite well 15 years after the end of the Swing era.

LPS TO SEARCH FOR

Helping to partially fill in the gap left by Columbia's indifference, Hindsight came out with six albums' worth of Harry James radio appearances: *Vol. 1. 1943–1946* (HSR 102), *Vol. 2. 1943–1946* (HSR 123), *Vol. 3. 1948–1949* (HSR 135), *Vol. 4. 1943–1946* (HSR 141), *Vol. 5. 1943–1953* (HSR 142), and *Vol. 6. 1947–1949* (HSR 150). While Volumes 1, 2, and 4 feature the James Orchestra when it was at the height of its popularity, the other albums (particularly Volumes 3 and 6) show that the trumpeter was listening closely to bebop by 1947, letting the more modern style influence his group's music while still holding on to his Swing base. All six albums are recommended.

FILMS

Harry James was in many films, and not only because his wife was a famous movie star. Look for the trumpeter and his band in *Private Buckaroo* (1942), *Springtime in the Rockies* (1942), *Syncopation* (1942), *Best Foot Forward* (1943), *Bathing Beauty* (1944), *Two Girls and a Sailor* (1944), *Do You Love Me?* (1946), *If I'm Lucky* (1946), *Carnegie Hall* (1947), *I'll Get By* (1950), *The Benny Goodman Story* (1955), *The Opposite Sex* (1956), and *The Big Beat* (1957). In addition, he ghosted the rather prominent trumpet playing of Kirk Douglas in *Young Man with a Horn* (1949).

STAN KENTON

b. Dec. 15, 1911, Wichita, KS, d. Aug. 25, 1979, Los Angeles, CA

It was never Stan Kenton's goal to lead a Swing band that played for dancers. His ambitions were much loftier: to put together a jazz-based concert orchestra that would perform complex arrangements and elevate jazz to the level of "serious" music. Throughout the 39 years that he was a bandleader, Kenton headed a series of often-controversial groups, including the Innovations in Modern Music Orchestra of 1950–51 (which was 39 pieces, including a full string section), a more swinging outfit later in the decade, an early '60s unit that included four mellophoniums, the Neophonic Orchestra, and, in the years after 1962, young ensembles full of enthusiastic players who considered their tenure with Kenton to be the high point of their careers.

To stay within the confines of this book, we will stick to Stan Kenton's life and career prior to 1949. He grew up in California, started playing piano as a teenager, and performed locally with various territory bands. Kenton picked up experience working with Everett Hoagland during 1933–34, Russ Plummer, Hal Grayson, Gus Arnheim (1936), Vido Musso, and various theater groups. His early influence on piano (and one who could still be felt in his playing as late as the 1970s) was Earl Hines.

In 1940 Kenton put together a rehearsal band, which in the summer of 1941 gained a strong following playing at the Rendezvous Ballroom in Balboa Beach near Los Angeles. During the early period, Kenton did most of the writing for his band, including penning a theme song ("Artistry in Rhythm") that would be the unofficial name of his first group. He loved thick-toned tenors and screaming trumpets (the Jimmie Lunceford Orchestra was a favorite) and, although he admired the big bands of Count Basie and Duke Ellington, Kenton sought to go in another direction. During 1941–42 his orchestra made its recording debut, cutting nine songs for Decca, but none sold that well. Fortunately the Kenton band also cut an extensive series of radio transcriptions during this era, so one can see that his musical approach was quite original from the start. Hired to be the backup band for Bob Hope's radio shows, Kenton was unhappy in that subservient role and the association did not last long; in time Les Brown would happily fill the position.

The Kenton orchestra struggled for a couple years, but in late 1943 it began its 25-year association with Capitol by recording a hit, "Eager Beaver." Singer Anita O'Day (whose version of "And Her Tears Flowed Like Wine" with the band was popular) and tenor saxophonist Stan Getz were with Kenton for brief periods, but more lasting were the additions of arranger-composer Pete Rugolo (who wrote in a similar style to Kenton, building on Stan's ideas and taking over most of the arranging chores), altoist Art Pepper, tenor saxophonist Bob Cooper, trombonist Kai Winding, and such screaming trumpeters as Ray Wetzel and Al Porcino. June Christy's vocals (her recordings of "Tampico" and "Across the Alley from the Alamo" were famous) helped keep the band in business, allowing Kenton to perform more adventurous works, such as "Elegy for Alto," "Chorale for Brass, Piano and Bongo," "Concerto to End All Concertos," and Bob Graettinger's "Thermopolae." Much more accessible, Kenton's instrumental recordings of "Intermission Riff" and "The Peanut Vendor" were well known long after the Swing era ended. The recording strike of 1948 kept his band off records during its later period, and then Kenton, exhausted and feeling that this particular orchestra had run its course, took 1949 off altogether. He would return with more outlandish ideas and, until his death in 1979, would be one of the last of the big band "road warriors." His life was mostly spent traveling from one gig to another, living for music, and always fighting for his brand of "progressive jazz."

7 *Broadcast Transcriptions 1941–1945 / Aug. 1941–Dec. 1944 / Music & Arts 883*

This CD has two interesting sets of radio transcriptions. The first 13 selections were recorded before Stan Kenton's initial studio recordings, so they give listeners an early glimpse at how the band sounded near its beginning. Kenton did virtually all of the writing for this session (which includes "Reed Rapture," "Harlem Folk Dance," and "Etude for Saxophones") and there are short spots for trumpeter Chico Alvarez and Red Dorris on tenor. The remaining 17 numbers are from December 1944, the period when Anita O'Day was in the band (she has six vocals); Stan Getz can also be heard on two numbers. The most prominent soloists are trumpeter Buddy Childers and tenorman Emmett Carls, and the repertoire includes "Eager Beaver," "Tabby the Cat," and "And Her Tears Flowed Like Wine."

* *The Complete Capitol Studio Recordings of Stan Kenton 1943–47 / Nov. 19, 1943–Dec. 22, 1947 / Mosaic 7-163*

10 *Retrospective / Nov. 19, 1943–July 18, 1968 / Capitol 97350*

It would be quite difficult to improve upon these two sets. Mosaic's seven-CD limited-edition box has all 153 studio recordings that the Stan Kenton's Orchestra made during their first four years with the Capitol label. Prior to signing

with Capitol, it was not certain that Kenton would have an opportunity to achieve his musical goals or even continue leading a jazz orchestra. However, his second selection for Capitol, "Eager Beaver," was a hit, and for the next four years he was able to balance recording popular numbers and June Christy vocals with much more ambitious works. It is all on the Mosaic box, including "Artistry in Rhythm," "Tampico," "Southern Scandal," "Artistry Jumps," "Intermission Riff," "Come Back to Sorrento," "Artistry in Percussion," "Artistry in Bolero," "Concerto to End All Concertos," "Opus in Pastels," "Monotony," "Elegy for Alto," "The Peanut Vendor," "Thermopolae," "Interlude," and many more, including 18 previously unreleased performances. The Mosaic set will definitely disappear in time, as will certainly Capitol's four-CD *Retrospective,* which has 21 selections from the 1943-47 period, plus 51 other pieces from 1950-68. *Retrospective* hits most of the important highlights of Kenton's very productive career.

6 *In Hollywood / May 20, 1944–Dec. 6, 1944 / Mr. Music 7007*

9 *Tampico / May 4, 1945–Oct. 22, 1947 / Memoir 526*

In Hollywood has two radio broadcasts by the Stan Kenton Orchestra from 1944. Anita O'Day and Gene Howard take six vocals apiece, and there are only eight instrumentals, so in general these performances are more commercial than usual. Stan Getz pops up a few times on the two broadcasts, but fellow tenors Dave Matthews and Emmett Carls actually get as much solo space, as does trumpeter Buddy Childers. More essential is *Tampico,* which includes 25 of June Christy's vocals with Kenton. Christy had the image of being the sensual but nice girl next door, and her cheerful singing was a major asset to the band. All of her main numbers are on this delightful set, including "Tampico," "Shoo Fly Pie and Apple Pan Dowdy," "Easy Street," "Rika Jika Jack," "His Feet's Too Big for De Bed," "Across the Alley from the Alamo," and "He Was a Good Man As Good Men Go." Even Kenton fans who have these selections in scattered fashion on other releases may want to acquire this perfectly done English CD.

LPS TO SEARCH FOR

Radio transcriptions made available by Hindsight help fill in the early days of Stan Kenton's career: *1941* (Hindsight 118), *1941, Vol. 2* (Hindsight 124), *1943–44, Vol. 3* (Hindsight 136), *1944–45, Vol. 4* (Hindsight 147), and *1945–47, Vol. 5* (Hindsight 157). Although a few of the selections appeared on the Music & Arts release *Broadcast Transcriptions,* otherwise the music does not duplicate any of the above releases. Also, Creative World in the 1970s reissued many of Stan Kenton's studio sessions. *The Formative Years* (Creative World 1061), which has the nine Decca recordings of 1941–42 (including "Gambler's Blues," "Reed Rapture," and "Concerto for Doghouse") is historic, if quite brief at under 28 minutes.

FILMS

In addition to many band shorts, the Stan Kenton Orchestra appears in *Talk About a Lady* (1946).

ANDY KIRK
b. May 28, 1898, Newport, KY, d. Dec. 11, 1992, New York, NY

Andy Kirk was not much of a musician, playing bass saxophone, baritone, and tuba in the ensembles of his early bands before becoming just a front man, and he never wrote or arranged any music. But his Twelve Clouds of Joy was a major Kansas City-based orchestra of the 1930s and one of the first to catch on beyond its Missouri base.

Kirk grew up in Denver, played a bit of piano and alto sax before switching to his main axes, and worked in the early 1920s with George Morrison's band. In the mid-'20s he joined Terrence Holder's Dark Clouds of Joy in Dallas. A dispute over money led to Holder's departure in January 1929. Kirk was soon appointed leader (he looked the part) and his big band became based in Kansas City. They recorded during 1929–30, and at the time its most significant members were violinist Claude Williams and pianist-arranger Mary Lou Williams. The Andy Kirk Orchestra was off records altogether during 1931–35 (other than a recording date in 1931 under the leadership of Blanche Calloway) but worked steadily in Kansas City and the Midwest. In 1936 Kirk relocated to New York, and his orchestra during the next seven years recorded often for Decca. They had a major hit in "Until the Real Thing Comes Along," a feature for their high-note vocalist Pha Terrell. More important musically were the many Mary Lou Williams instrumental charts, including "Walkin' and Swingin'," "Corky," "A Mellow Bit of Rhythm," "Mary's Idea," and "Floyd's Guitar Blues" (which features an early if odd electric guitar solo by Floyd Smith). In addition to Williams (who was saluted on "The Lady Who Swings the Band"), the key soloist was the talented if short-lived tenorman Dick Wilson. Later players included trumpeter Harold "Shorty" Baker during 1940–41, Ken Kersey (who took over the piano spot after Williams left in 1942), trumpeters Howard McGhee (featured on 1942's "McGhee Special") and Fats Navarro, and in 1945–46 the tenors of Jimmy Forrest and Eddie "Lockjaw" Davis. By then, business was tailing off and Kirk was forced to break up his orchestra in 1948. He worked outside of music for the remainder of his career except for rare occasions when he fronted a band. There would be one "reunion" session for a Victor album in 1956 but, other than Ken Kersey, none of the musicians in that studio big band had actually been in Kirk's Orchestra! Andy Kirk lived to be 94.

10 *1929–1931 / Nov. 7, 1929–Mar. 2, 1931 / Classics 655*
All of the recordings by the early Andy Kirk Orchestra are on this single CD. The star soloists are altoist-baritonist John Williams, violinist Claude Williams, trumpeter Edgar "Puddinghead" Battle, and particularly pianist Mary Lou Williams. The music falls between hot 1920s jazz and early Swing and includes the numbers that Kirk's band made under Blanche Calloway's leadership in 1931.

9 *Mary's Idea / Mar. 2, 1936–Jan. 3, 1941 / GRP/Decca 622*
Most of the best Andy Kirk recordings from the 1936–41 period are on this definitive sampler. During the era, in addition to Mary Lou Williams (who wrote most of the arrangements and is heard at the head of a small group for two songs in 1940), the key soloist is tenor saxophonist Dick Williams. Among the highlights are "Walkin' and Swingin'," "Froggy Bottom," "The Lady Who Swings the Band," "Mess-a-Stomp," "What's Your Story, Morning Glory" (which has the only Pha Terrell vocal of the CD), "Mary's Idea," and "The Count." What is missing is their big hit "Until the Real Thing Comes Along," "Floyd's Guitar Blues," and "McGhee Special," but overall this is an excellent overview of Andy Kirk's Twelve Clouds of Joy.

9 *1936–1937 / Mar. 2, 1936–Feb. 15, 1937 / Classics 573*

6 *1937–1938 / Feb. 15, 1937–Feb. 8, 1938 / Classics 581*

6 *1938 / Sept. 8, 1938–Dec. 6, 1938 / Classics 598*

7 *1939–1940 / Mar. 16, 1939–June 25, 1940 / Classics 640*

8 *1940–1942 / July 8, 1940–July 29, 1942 / Classics 681*

7 *1943–1949 / Dec. 3, 1943–May 13, 1949 / Classics 1075*
For most listeners, *Mary's Idea* will be all they really need of Andy Kirk's Orchestra. It all depends on how much one enjoys the falsetto singing of Pha Terrell, whose recording

of "Until the Real Things Comes Along" was followed by many similar vocal features. These six Classics CDs have all of Andy Kirk's recordings from the 1936–49 period and the instrumental gems have mostly been reissued elsewhere. *1936–1937* starts off quite strong with such Mary Lou Williams arrangements of "Walkin' and Swingin'," "Moten Swing," "Lotta Sax Appeal," "Froggy Bottom," and "Corky." The hit is also included along with "The Lady Who Swings the Band" and "All the Jive Is Gone." *1937–1938* has 17 vocals (15 by Terrell) and just five instrumentals. The Kirk band was at the height of its popularity in 1938, recording 22 songs during a three-month period, all included on *1938* but with only three being instrumentals (including "Mary's Idea"). *1939–1940* includes "Floyd's Guitar Blues" (a feature for Floyd's Smith odd-sounding Hawaiian electric guitar), "Big Jim Blues," "Scratching in the Gravel," and a few vocals by the easy-to-take June Richmond in addition to more features for Terrell. During *1940–1942* Pha Terrell departed, Mary Lou Williams left (replaced in 1942 by Ken Kersey), Dick Wilson passed away, and trumpeter Howard McGhee joined Kirk. *1940–1942* is highlighted by "Little Miss," "The Count," "Twelfth Street Rag," "Ring Dem Bells," "Boogie Woogie Cocktail," and "McGhee Special."

The final recordings by the Andy Kirk Orchestra are on *1943–1949* and all of those selections are quite obscure. Howard McGhee is on the first three numbers, as is Fats Navarro who returns for four tunes in 1946; both of the trumpeters take brief boppish solos. "Hippy-Dippy" (only previously released in Japan) is a particularly interesting instrumental. Otherwise the vocals of the Jubalaires, Beverly White, Bea Booze, Billy Daniels, the Four Knights, and Joe Williams (whose recording debut is heard on two songs) dominate the 1946 selections. This CD concludes with two tracks from 1949 that find Kirk leading an unknown orchestra on a pair of R&Bish tracks.

GENE KRUPA
b. Jan. 15, 1909, Chicago, IL, d. Oct. 16, 1973, Yonkers, NY

One of the major names of the Swing era and the first drummer to become nationally famous, Gene Krupa was a flamboyant, gum-chewing performer who always seemed destined for stardom. He was not the best drummer of his time but the most exciting, making even the simplest drum breaks look difficult and colorful! He would still be remembered today if only for his playing on "Sing, Sing, Sing" with Benny Goodman, but Krupa had a lengthy and productive career.

After being classically trained on drums, in 1925 Krupa began freelancing in Chicago, including working with Al Gale, Joe Kayser, Leo Shukin, Thelma Terry, the Benson Orchestra of Chicago, and the Seattle Harmony Kings, among others. He made his recording debut in 1927 with the McKenzie-Condon Chicagoans where he was the first musician to record with a full drum set. After moving to New York in 1929, Krupa worked with Red Nichols, in the studios, and with such dance bands as Irving Aaronson's Commanders, Ross Columbo, and Mal Hallett. Krupa was still a relative unknown outside of musician circles in December 1934 when he became a member of the Benny Goodman Orchestra, but his anonymity would be gone permanently within a year.

With BG, Krupa rose to fame. He gave an exciting drive to Goodman's big band (particularly after 1936, when he started becoming much more assertive), was featured with the Benny Goodman Trio and Quartet, and became quite a crowd pleaser. Although one could argue that Chick Webb, Sid Catlett, Jo Jones, and Dave Tough were better drummers and that Krupa was never on the level of Buddy Rich, he was the most popular drummer of the era (perhaps of all time) and the first superstar to play drums; even Rich thought of him as a hero. After Benny Goodman's famous 1938 Carnegie Hall concert (which was highlighted by Krupa's playing on "Sing, Sing, Sing"), things came to a head

From 1937, Benny Goodman ("The King of Swing") poses with Gene Krupa, the world's most famous drummer.

between the two Swing giants (Goodman thought that Krupa was playing too loud and gaining too much applause) and the drummer soon departed to form his own big band.

As with Harry James, it took Krupa a couple years before his orchestra really caught on, although he was a famous attraction. His early group was known for "Drum Boogie" and it featured fine vocals by Irene Daye. During 1941–42, with Anita O'Day doing the singing and Roy Eldridge contributing explosive trumpet solos, Krupa had a memorable combination that resulted in quite a few hits, including "Let Me Off Uptown," "After You've Gone," "Rockin' Chair," "Thanks for the Boogie Ride," "That's What You Think," and "Massachusetts."

In May 1943, Gene Krupa was framed on a marijuana rap and was forced to give up his band. After being cleared, Krupa made a comeback, working for his old boss, Benny Goodman, during September–December 1943, joining Tommy Dorsey for seven months, and then forming a new big band. For a time Krupa added a string section to his orchestra, but that frivolity was gone by 1945. Krupa had success teaming up with tenor saxophonist Charlie Ventura and pianist Teddy Napoleon in a trio out of his band (most notably on their recording of "Dark Eyes"). He featured such soloists during the next few years as Ventura, trumpeters Red Rodney and Don Fagerquist, and altoist Charlie Kennedy, recording steadily, including "Leave Us Leap" (which featured the bop vocals of Dave Lambert and Buddy Stewart), "Opus No. 1" (with Anita O'Day temporarily back in the band), "Boogie Blues," and several Gerry Mulligan arrangements, most notably "Disc Jockey Jump." Krupa kept an open mind towards bop, although he always remained a Swing/Dixieland drummer at heart.

After reluctantly breaking up his big band in 1951, Gene Krupa worked primarily with trios and quartets in addition to touring with Jazz at the Philharmonic. *The Gene Krupa Story* (with Sal Mineo in the lead role), despite some good music, was a bit of a misfire (and in spots a self-parody of Hollywood jazz films), but the famous drummer did not really need the extra publicity anyway. In later years he taught at a drummer's school that he cofounded with Cozy Cole, cut back on his playing due to ill health, and remained semiactive (including participating in several reunions with the Benny Goodman Quartet and a final recording with Eddie Condon) up until his death.

●

9 *1935–1938 / Nov. 19, 1935–June 18, 1938 / Classics 754*

7 *1938 / July 19, 1938–Dec. 12, 1938 / Classics 767*

6 *1939 / Feb. 26, 1939–July 25, 1939 / Classics 799*

6 *1939–1940 / July 24, 1939–Feb. 12, 1940 / Classics 834*
Some of the best music on *1935–1938* comes from two sessions that Gene Krupa led while still a member of the Benny Goodman Orchestra. The 1935 date features Krupa with primarily BG's sidemen of the time (including Jess Stacy) plus bassist Israel Crosby, who is featured on "Blues of Israel." The four selections from 1936 have two Helen Ward vocals and a couple of explosive instrumentals ("I Hope Gabriel Likes My Music" and "Swing Is Here") that are jammed by Goodman himself, trumpeter Roy Eldridge, and tenor saxophonist Chu Berry. Otherwise this CD consists of the first 15 selections recorded by the new Gene Krupa Orchestra, with six vocals by Irene Daye, two from Helen Ward (including "Feelin' High and Happy"), and such instrumentals as "Prelude to a Stomp," "I Know That You Know," and "Wire Brush Stomp." Daye sings no less than 10 of the 22 numbers on *1938*, with only "Bolero at the Savoy" being memorable. In contrast, Leo Watson's four eccentric vocals (including "Nagasaki" and "Tutti Frutti") stick in one's memory. Of the soloists, tenors Vido Musso and his replacement Sam Donahue are the most impressive, with "Rhythm Jam" and Krupa's theme song, "Apurksody," being standouts. Daye also sings ten tunes on *1939* (highlighted by "The Lady's in Love with You" and a rare vocal version of "Moonlight Serenade"). Other than Donahue and Krupa, the big band still lacked any major soloists, even if the ensemble sounds fine on "The Madam Swings It," "Hodge Podge," and a variety of older folk songs. *1939–1940* continues in the same vein, with a few too many Irene Daye vocals (she is best on the catchy "Drummin' Man" and "Boog It") and a few worthy instrumentals (such as "Symphony in Riffs," "Three Little Words," and the two-part "Blue Rhythm Fantasy") but not many strong soloists other than trumpeter Shorty Sherock (who joined in time for the second half of

the program), Donahue, and Krupa. The Gene Krupa Orchestra was still searching for its own personality beyond its leader's playing.

4 *1940 / Feb. 19, 1940–June 3, 1940 / Classics 859*

3 *1940, Vol. 2 / Nov. 2, 1939–Sept. 3, 1940 / Classics 883*

2 *1940, Vol. 3 / Sept. 17, 1940–Nov. 28, 1940 / Classics 917*

6 *The Radio Years / 1940 / Jazz Unlimited 2021*
The Gene Krupa Orchestra recorded a great deal during 1940; one wishes that the big band had duplicated the feat during 1941–42, when it was a much more significant unit! Irene Daye was a fine pop/Swing vocalist, but unfortunately Howard Dulany (who joined early in the year) was a rather stiff and very dated ballad singer who was featured far too extensively. On *1940*, Dulany has seven vocals, Daye pops up six times, and there are only nine instrumentals. To make matters worse, two of Krupa's best soloists (trumpeter Shorty Sherock and trombonist Floyd O'Brien) departed during this period. The best recordings are "Manhattan Transfer," "Tiger Rag," and "No Name Jive," but overall this a is weak CD. *1940, Vol. 2* has two slightly earlier performances that were released for the first time on the CD. Otherwise there are only six instrumentals (including "The Sergeant Was Shy" and an originally rejected "St. Louis Blues") and 15 vocals, 12 by Dulany. *1940, Vol. 3* is more of the same, with only three forgettable nonvocal tracks. Shorty Sherock's return was not taken advantage of and only partly compensated for the departure of Sam Donahue. Much better is *The Radio Years,* a pair of radio broadcasts from just before Dulany joined the band. Although Irene Daye sings on every other song, the Krupa band gets to really stretch out on versions of "Bugle Call Rag," "Cherokee," "In the Mood," and a nearly six-minute rendition of "Pyramid." Trumpeters Sherock and Corky Cornelius, trombonist O'Brien, Donahue on tenor, and clarinetist Sam Musiker all get short spots, along with the drummer.

8 *Drum Boogie / Jan. 2, 1940 – Jan. 17, 1941 / Columbia/
Legacy 53425*

Rather than acquire the many Classics CDs, in the case of
the early Gene Krupa Orchestra, this CD will suffice. Although not reissued in chronological order, the reissue contains virtually all of the high points of Krupa's 1940 band,
including "Drum Boogie," "No Name Jive," "Rhumboogie," "Boog It," "Sweet Georgia Brown," and the two-part
"Blue Rhythm Fantasy." Irene Daye's best vocals are here
and Howard Dulany is completely absent!

7 *1941 / Jan. 17, 1941 – May 8, 1941 / Classics 960*

10 *Uptown / May 8, 1941 – May 9, 1949 / Columbia 45448*

The most famous version of the Gene Krupa Orchestra was
active during 1941-42. Anita O'Day replaced the departing
Irene Daye by the March 12, 1941, session, and trumpeter
Roy Eldridge joined up in time to be on the last four numbers on *1941*. The much-feared Howard Dulany lowers the
quality of nine numbers and shares "Green Eyes" with
O'Day, but *1941* also contains Daye's three final vocals (including the popular "Drum Boogie") and O'Day's first nine
with Krupa (including her big hit, "Let Me Off Uptown").
There is only one instrumental on the CD ("Siren Serenade"), but Anita O'Day's vocals are almost like solos anyway. *Uptown* is the definitive CD to acquire of the Gene
Krupa–Anita O'Day–Roy Eldridge collaborations. All but
the final four numbers (which date from 1949, when Eldridge rejoined Krupa's Orchestra) are from 1941-42.
Among the gems are "Green Eyes," "Let Me off Uptown,"
"After You've Gone," "Rockin' Chair," "Stop! The Red
Light's On," "The Walls Keep Talkin'," "Bolero at the Savoy," "Thanks for the Boogie Ride," and "That Drummer's
Band." This is the music that the Gene Krupa Orchestra will
always be most remembered for.

5 *Leave Us Leap / Jan. 11, 1945 – 1948 / Vintage Jazz
Classics 1047*

6 *Krupa and Rich / May 16, 1955 + Nov, 1, 1955 / Verve
314 521 643*

Leave Us Leap consists of radio broadcasts by the Gene
Krupa Orchestra (with and without a string section) from
1945, playing arrangements by Ed Finckel, featuring vocals

from Lillian Lane, Buddy Stewart, and the G-Noters, and
occasional solos from tenor saxophonist Charlie Ventura
and pianist Teddy Napoleon. The decent but varied CD
concludes with a version of "Disc Jockey Jump" from Krupa's big band of 1948. Gene Krupa and Buddy Rich had several "drum battles" during the 1950s, with Krupa's color
and personality trying its best to overcome Rich's pure virtuosity. *Krupa and Rich* actually finds the two drummers appearing together only on "Bernie's Tune," trading off during
a six-minute "battle." On two songs apiece, the drummers
are joined by a remarkable group that includes trumpeters
Dizzy Gillespie and Roy Eldridge, Flip Phillips and Illinois
Jacquet on tenors, plus the Oscar Peterson Trio. In addition,
there are two numbers from a Rich date with trumpeters
Thad Jones and Joe Newman, tenors Ben Webster and
Frank Wess, rhythm guitarist Freddie Green, pianist Oscar
Peterson, and bassist Ray Brown. Fine music despite the
lack of "battles."

LPS TO SEARCH FOR

Drummin' Man (Columbia C2L 29) is a boxed two-LP set
that has most of the Gene Krupa Orchestra's very best recordings of 1938–49 along with a colorful booklet. *Ace
Drummer Man* (Giants of Jazz 1006) has radio transcriptions, V-Discs, and live appearances by Krupa's big bands of
1945 and 1947, his famous trio of 1945 with Charlie Ventura
(including an alternate version of "Dark Eyes"), and his unknown trio of 1943, which included clarinetist Buddy DeFranco and pianist Dodo Marmarosa (jamming "Liza" and
"Hodge Podge"). *Transcribed* (IAJRC 10) contains transcriptions for the Capitol label that showcase Krupa's underrated big band of 1946; it features trumpeter Red Rodney, altoist Charlie Kennedy, both Ventura and Buddy Wise
on tenors, and Napoleon playing advanced Swing (including some Gerry Mulligan charts).

FILMS

The popular drummer and his big band, in addition to performing in a variety of shorts and Soundies, can be seen
playing "Drum Boogie" in *Ball of Fire* (1941) and making
appearances in *Some Like It Hot* (1939), *George White's
Scandals* (1945), *Beat the Band* (1947), *Glamour Girl* (1948),

and *Make Believe Ballroom* (1949). Krupa is in the closing jam session of *Syncopation* (1942), plays himself in *The Benny Goodman Story* (1955), and is portrayed in fictionalized fashion by Sal Mineo in *The Gene Krupa Story* (1959).

HARLAN LEONARD

b. July 2, 1905, Kansas City, MO, d. 1983, Los Angeles, CA

Harlan Leonard, who played alto, clarinet, and baritone, led a top-notch Kansas City Swing band that recorded four sessions (23 titles in all) during 1940. Leonard worked with George E. Lee's band in 1923 and then was a regular member of Bennie Moten's Orchestra during 1923–31, soloing on some of Moten's records. After going out on his own, he co-led the Kansas City Skyrockets with trombonist Thamon Hayes during 1931–34 and was its sole leader for the following three years. In 1938 Leonard put together a new big band (the Kansas City Rockets), which in 1940 went to New York for a short time, making its recordings in New York and Chicago. In its personnel at the time were the legendary but short-lived trombonist Fred Beckett (an acknowledged influence on the bebop innovator J.J. Johnson), tenor saxophonist Henry Bridges, and drummer Jesse Price. One of the orchestra's main arrangers was Tadd Dameron, who would be quite significant in the bop era a few years later. Leonard soon returned with his band to the Midwest, where they worked fairly steadily until 1943. The orchestra relocated to Los Angeles and then broke up in 1945. Harlan Leonard ended up retiring from music and getting a day job with the Internal Revenue Service.

●

10 *1940 / Jan. 11, 1940 – Nov. 13, 1940 / Classics 670*
All of Harlan Leonard's 23 recordings (although not the three alternate takes) are available on this single CD. Henry Bridges is the most impressive soloist, while Tadd Dameron contributed seven of the arrangements (including "Rock and Ride," "À La Bridges," and "Dameron Stomp"). Several of the mostly obscure numbers performed by the underrated Kansas City band are well deserving of being revived.

JIMMIE LUNCEFORD

b. June 6, 1902, Fulton, MS, d. July 13, 1947, Seaside, OR

The Jimmie Lunceford Orchestra was renowned for its showmanship, high musicianship, colorful stage shows, and tightness. Contemporary observers of the Swing era rated Lunceford at the top with the major bands, such as Ellington, Basie, and Goodman, but unfortunately many of its recordings often just hint at the orchestra's unique greatness.

Although Lunceford was well-trained on several instruments (reeds, trombone, and guitar), he rarely ever played with his big band (other than taking a 1940s flute feature on "Liza"), instead concentrating on fronting and directing his orchestra. He had studied music with Paul Whiteman's father (a well-respected music teacher in Denver) while in high school. Lunceford earned a music degree from Fisk University, played briefly in New York during college vacations, and was a music teacher in Memphis starting in 1926. He formed a local band comprised of his best students (as the Chickasaw Syncopators they recorded two titles in Dallas in 1927) and that was the nucleus of his orchestra when it became a professional ensemble in 1929. They recorded two songs in Memphis in 1930 and, after periods in Cleveland and Buffalo, the Jimmie Lunceford Orchestra relocated to New York in 1933.

By 1934, Lunceford's band was on its way to great popularity. Sy Oliver contributed catchy arrangements that gave the orchestra its own sound, many of the musicians turned out to be worthwhile singers (particularly as part of "glee club" choruses), Tommy Stevenson provided high-note trumpet blasts (which later influenced Stan Kenton), and among the key soloists were altoist Willie Smith, tenor saxophonist Joe Thomas, and (by 1937) trombonist Trummy Young. Not all of the Lunceford recordings are classics (Dan Grissom took far too many dull ballad vocals), but with such songs as "Swingin' Uptown," "Stomp It Off," "Rhythm Is Our Business," "Sleepy Time Gal" (which has a remarkable chorus by the sax section), "Four or Five Times," "Swanee River," "Organ Grinder's Swing," "For Dancers Only," "Margie" (with Trummy Young's famous vocal and trombone solo), and " 'Tain't What You Do," the Jimmie Lunceford Orchestra made its mark on the 1930s Swing scene.

In 1939 Sy Oliver was lured away by a lucrative offer from Tommy Dorsey. Despite that major loss, Lunceford (who soon added Snooky Young and Gerald Wilson to his trumpet section) still had a few prime years ahead. "Lunceford Special," "Hi Spook," "Yard Dog Mazurka" (the latter two by Wilson), "Blues in the Night" (which Lunceford introduced), and "Strictly Instrumental" were all quite popular. However, the war years found Jimmie Lunceford's orchestra declining. The low salaries that he paid his "family band" began to irk some of the key players who defected (including a very reluctant Willie Smith), and the group's string of hits stopped. Still, the Jimmie Lunceford Orchestra was working regularly in 1947 when its leader died of a heart attack at the age of 45 while signing autographs. Several people have speculated that Lunceford was actually poisoned by a racist restaurant owner who had been pressured into feeding the band. Joe Thomas and pianist Edwin Wilcox did their best to keep the orchestra together but gave up in 1949.

●

10 *Vol. 1, 1927–1934 / Dec. 13, 1927–Sept. 4, 1934 / Masters of Jazz 12*

10 *Vol. 2, 1934 / Sept. 5, 1934–Dec. 18, 1934 / Masters of Jazz 18*

7 *1930–1934 / June 6, 1930–Nov. 7, 1934 / Classics 501*
Like the Classics series, the Masters of Jazz label puts out complete sessions of an artist in chronological order. The difference between the two Jimmie Lunceford series is that the Masters company begins in *Vol. 1* with the two historic numbers from 1927 by the Chickasaw Syncopators and it also includes alternate takes (two on *Vol. 1* and three on *Vol. 2*), so it is actually more complete. Unfortunately this French label has thus far only come out with these two Jimmie Lunceford releases. *Vol. 1* has two numbers apiece recorded at sessions in Memphis in 1927 and 1930 (two instrumentals and a pair of "preaching" numbers for Moses Allen), a pair of songs from 1933 not released until the 1970s (including "Flaming Reeds and Screaming Brass"), and then quite a few examples of the 1934 band, including "White Heat," "Swingin' Uptown," "Rose Room," and three Ellington numbers: "Sophisticated Lady," "Mood Indigo," and "Black and Tan Fantasy." *1934* wraps up the orchestra's extensive output from their breakthrough year and has among its highlights "Dream of You," "Stomp It Off," "Solitude," and two versions of "Rhythm Is Our Business." Classics'

1930–1934 covers the same time period and is recommended only if the Masters of Jazz releases cannot be found.

8 *Stomp It Off / Sept. 4, 1934–May 29, 1935 / GRP/Decca 608*

9 *For Dancers Only / Sept. 23, 1935–June 15, 1937 / GRP/ Decca 645*
With the exception of five selections from May 29, 1935 (including a new take of "Four or Five Times" along with the miraculous version of "Sleepy Time Gal"), all of the music on *Stomp It Off* is included on the two Masters of Jazz CDs. However, this reissue is excellent at summing up Jimmie Lunceford's first year with the Decca label and the CD will be easier to find than the imports. The Ellington tunes and both versions of "Rhythm Is Our Business" are among the 21 cuts included in this "best of" collection. *For Dancers Only* covers a 21-month period that could be subtitled "The Sy Oliver Years," since Oliver wrote all but six of the 20 arrangements, takes hip vocals on many of the tracks, and also contributes some trumpet solos. Other key players of the period include Willie Smith and Joe Thomas, both of whom also sing. But it is the colorful charts (particularly Oliver's) that made the Lunceford Orchestra so distinctive during the era. Highlights include a reworking of "Swanee River," "My Blue Heaven," an exquisite "Organ Grinder's Swing," "The Merry Go Round Broke Down," and "For Dancers Only."

Known for their impeccable musicianship, colorful shows, and catchy arrangements, the Jimmie Lunceford Orchestra is pictured here in the mid-'40s.

6 *1934–1935 / Nov. 7, 1934–Sept. 30, 1935 / Classics 505*

7 *1935–1937 / Dec. 23, 1935–June 15, 1937 / Classics 510*

8 *1937–1939 / June 15, 1937–Jan. 3, 1939 / Classics 520*
Because of saxophonist Dan Grissom's occasional (and generally gruesome) vocals, not every Jimmie Lunceford recording is essential. Classics reissues everything anyway and, since most of the post-1937 recordings are not easily available elsewhere at this point, the later CDs in this series are valuable. *1934–1935* has "Solitude," "Rhythm Is Our Business," "Sleepy Time Gal," "Four or Five Times," and "Swanee River" among its highlights, although the two Decca discs already contain these and the other better selections from the period. *1935–1937* has "I'm Nuts About Screwy Music," "Organ Grinder's Swing," "Harlem Shout," "Slumming on Park Avenue," and "The Merry Go Round Breaks Down," while *1937–1939,* which wraps up

Jimmie Lunceford's period on Decca, includes such notable performances as "For Dancers Only," "Put on Your Old Grey Bonnet," trombonist Trummy Young's famous hit on "Margie," "By the River St. Marie," " 'Tain't What You Do," and "Cheatin' on Me."

8 *1939 / Jan. 31, 1939–Sept. 14, 1939 / Classics 532*

7 *1939–1940 / Dec. 14, 1939–June 19, 1940 / Classics 565*

7 *1940–1941 / July 9, 1940–Dec. 22, 1941 / Classics 622*
These three CDs feature the Jimmie Lunceford Orchestra at the height of its fame, thanks to its 1938–39 hit records of "Margie" and " 'Tain't What You Do." The band was now recording for CBS-owned labels (Vocalion and Okeh) and even the departure of Sy Oliver (who joined Tommy Dorsey) did not hurt its momentum for a time. "What Is This Thing Called Swing," "Ain't She Sweet," "Well All Right

Then," and "Belgium Stomp" are some of the high points of *1939*. *1939–1940* has "Wham," "Uptown Blues" (featuring Snooky Young and Willie Smith), "Lunceford Special," and "Swingin' on C," while *1940–1941* is most notable for "Battle Axe," the two-part "Blues in the Night," and Gerald Wilson's two arrangements ("Hi Spook" and "Yard Dog Mazurka").

6 *1941–1945 / Dec. 23, 1941–Aug. 9, 1945 / Classics 862*

7 *Margie / Apr. 25, 1946–May 1947 / Savoy 1209*

These two CDs nicely wrap up the recorded legacy of the Jimmie Lunceford Orchestra. The band was declining by 1942 ("Strictly Instrumental" was their only recent hit), and some of the veteran musicians (including Willie Smith and Trummy Young) would be departing the following year. *1941–1945,* in addition to two cuts from 1941 and seven songs from 1942, has two sessions apiece from 1944 ("Jeep Rhythm" is the strongest piece) and 1945. Lunceford's prime years were over, but the bandleader seemed to be regrouping during 1946–47. His Majestic recordings (reissued in full by Savoy) find Joe Thomas being the main star (as

tenor soloist and vocalist), trombonist Trummy Young popping back for one session (remaking "Margie"), and some promising new players (clarinetist Omer Simeon, trumpeter Joe Wilder, and trombonist Al Grey) helping out. It is interesting to hear the Jimmie Lunceford Orchestra this late in its existence, and one can speculate where it might have gone musically if it had survived, but the end was very near for its leader.

LPS TO SEARCH FOR

Jimmie Lunceford 1939-40 (CBS 66421) is a four-LP set that has all of the bandleader's recordings for CBS-owned labels, including nine alternate takes, one previously unreleased number, and the two songs that Lunceford cut in 1933. A perfect set put out by French CBS that has yet to be duplicated in this fashion on CD.

FILMS

Considering how visual Jimmie Lunceford's band was, it is frustrating how little footage has survived of the orchestra, just a ten-minute short in 1936 and one number in *Blues in the Night* (1941). In the latter film Snooky Young ghosts actor Jack Carson's trumpet.

JAY MCSHANN

b. Jan. 12, 1916, Muskogee, OK

A fine blues and Swing pianist who later in life developed into an excellent blues vocalist, Jay "Hootie" McShann led one of the last major big bands to emerge from Kansas City, following in the wake of Andy Kirk and Count Basie. Although not a particularly modern big band for 1940, McShann's outfit was most notable for featuring the great bop altoist Charlie Parker in his formative years.

Jay McShann (whose birthdate has sometimes been inaccurately given as 1909) began playing piano when he was 12, worked in Tulsa and Arkansas, went to Winfield College in Kansas, played in the Southwest, and then settled in Kansas City in the mid-1930s. McShann was part of the legendary Kansas City jazz scene, performing locally and often participating in the after-hours jam sessions. In 1937 he put together his own big band and worked regularly in Kansas City and the Midwest. Three years later he brought the orchestra to New York and briefly became well known nationally, particularly after he started recording for Decca in 1941. Unfortunately the record label wanted McShann to stick mostly to the blues, so the orchestra's Swing charts were largely undocumented. However, decades later a discovered set of small-group titles from 1939 (with Charlie Parker, bassist Gene Ramey, and drummer Gus Johnson, among others) finds McShann expertly playing Swing standards. In addition, in the 1980s the Charlie Parker CD *Early Bird* (Stash 542) showed how the big band really sounded on radio broadcasts. The Decca studio recordings yielded a hit in "Confessin' the Blues," with Walter Brown on the vocal. Charlie Parker can be heard in a few brief solos that caught the ears of other musicians of the period. The big band (which in its last year featured Paul Quinichette on tenor) lasted until 1944, when McShann was drafted.

After his discharge from the military later that year, the pianist led combos in Los Angeles and Kansas City that looked toward early rhythm and blues while retaining his roots in Swing and blues. Jimmy Witherspoon gained some fame for his work with McShann during this period. The pianist then spent over 20 years playing in Kansas City but was largely forgotten by the rest of the jazz world. He recorded an album in 1966 (for the first time singing on records) and was officially rediscovered in 1969. Since that time, Jay McShann has performed and recorded prolifically (sometimes teaming up with violinist Claude Williams), spreading the joy of Kansas City Swing and blues around the world.

9 *Blues from Kansas City / Apr. 30, 1941–Dec. 1, 1943 / GRP/Decca 614*

All 21 of Jay McShann's studio Decca recordings from 1941–43 are on this CD. McShann is heard leading his Kansas City Orchestra (which features a few short solos from altoist Charlie Parker and vocals by Walter Brown) on 11 cuts and playing the remaining ten in small groups ranging from a trio to a septet. "Confessin' the Blues" was a strong seller, and the other selections (which include four from 1943 after Parker had departed) are highlighted by "Swingmatism," "Vine Street Boogie," "The Jumpin' Blues," and "Sepian Bounce."

9 *Early Bird / Aug. 1940–Mar. 1944 / Stash 542*

Although Jay McShann led an excellent big band during 1937–44, it is today chiefly remembered for including Charlie "Bird" Parker as its occasional alto soloist. *Early Bird* (which was actually released under Parker's name) is a fascinating CD because it contains a great deal of rare and historic music. The earliest track, a poorly recorded "I Got Rhythm," finds Bird featured with McShann at a concert in August 1940. The seven selections that they recorded together at a radio station on November 30, 1940, were both McShann's and Parker's official debut on record (even though the music was not initially released until the 1970s), performing with a nonet from the big band. Parker is particularly brilliant on "Honeysuckle Rose," and McShann shows that his blues/Swing style was already fully formed. Released for the first time on this CD is a live radio broadcast from 1942 that shows how the McShann Orchestra really sounded outside of the studios. Although the speed sometimes varies a little, this air check for the first time features Parker really stretching out with McShann's orchestra ("I'm Forever Blowing Bubbles" is a highlight). In addition, Parker is heard jamming "Cherokee" at Monroe's Uptown House in 1942, and there are seven selections from a *Jubilee* radio broadcast that features McShann's orchestra in 1944,

when its personnel included altoist John Jackson and tenor saxophonist Paul Quinichette.

8 *The Man from Muskogee / June 4, 1972 / Sackville 2-3005*

9 *Paris All-Star Blues / June 13, 1989 / Music Masters 5052*

Jay McShann recorded many records after his official rediscovery in 1969. *The Man from Muskogee* teams him with fellow Kansas City veteran Claude Williams (heard on violin and guitar), bassist Don Thompson, and drummer Paul Gunther, happily jamming on a program dominated mostly by standards and blues. McShann takes four vocals, including "Hootie Blues." While most of the pianist's recordings in the years after the Swing era have been with small groups, *Paris All-Star Blues* (billed as "A Tribute to Charlie Parker") is quite a bit different. McShann heads a remarkable all-star group, performing tunes primarily from his Swing era repertoire (other than "Parker's Mood" and a couple of newer Ernie Wilkins songs). The 16-piece big band includes such musicians as Clark Terry and Terence Blanchard on trumpets, trombonist Al Grey, Benny Carter, and Phil Woods on altos, Jimmy Heath, Hal Singer, and James Moody on tenors, and singer Ernie Andrews. A gem that perfectly sums up Jay McShann's career, although he still had many performances and recordings (most notably for the Sackville label) to go.

LPS TO SEARCH FOR

The Band That Jumps The Blues! (Black Lion 30144) has music from 1947–49 that crosses the boundaries between Kansas City Swing and early R&B; among the sidemen on some selections are Jimmy Witherspoon, trumpeter Art Farmer, and Maxwell Davis on tenor. McShann's Piano (Capitol 2645) was Hootie's first recording in years. This 1966 date with a rhythm section has McShann's first vocals and typically swinging playing on 11 numbers, including "Vine Street Boogie," "Moten Swing," and "Dexter Blues."

No orchestra from the Swing era was more beloved (or better served
as a soundtrack for the time) than Glenn Miller's.

GLENN MILLER

b. Mar. 1, 1904, Clarinda, IA, d. Dec. 15, 1944, English Channel

The most famous and beloved of the big bands of the Swing era was Glenn Miller's. His orchestra had so many hits during 1939–42 that it essentially served as the soundtrack for a generation. Imagine the big band era without such songs as "Moonlight Serenade," "Sunrise Serenade," "Little Brown Jug," "In the Mood," "Stairway to the Stars," "Tuxedo Junction" (which was first recorded slightly earlier by Erskine Hawkins), "Pennsylvania 6–5000," "Chattanooga Choo Choo," "I Don't Know Why," "Elmer's Tune," "A String of Pearls," "Moonlight Cocktail," "American Patrol," "I've Got a Gal in Kalamazoo," "Serenade in Blue," "At Last," and "Jukebox Saturday Night!"

And yet in 1938 very few people knew who Glenn Miller was. Born Alton Glenn Miller, he had started out playing cornet and mandolin, switching to trombone in 1916. Miller was gigging professionally as early as 1921 (with Boyd Senter), but success was still 18 years in the future. After attending the University of Colorado, he worked with Max Fischer's band and then was with Ben Pollack (1926–28) as both a trombonist and an arranger, making his recording debut. Although Miller was originally Pollack's main trombone soloist, after Jack Teagarden joined the band, he was greatly overshadowed. At that point in time he probably realized that he was not going to become jazz's greatest trombonist and that his best bet for the future was to develop into a top arranger.

After leaving Pollack, Miller freelanced, played trombone with pit bands for shows, worked as a studio musician, and was part of the Dorsey Brothers Orchestra during 1934–35. He organized and arranged for Ray Noble's American Orchestra in

1935 and continued freelancing as an arranger until deciding to form his own big band in 1937. Unfortunately the start was premature, for Miller, in his own mind, had not developed the type of sound that he wanted yet. Despite the presence of some fine players, the first Glenn Miller Orchestra failed within a year.However, in early 1938 Miller was ready to try again. He decided that he wanted to form an all-round dance band rather than a jazz group, and he liked the idea of a clarinet doubling the melody an octave above the saxophones; that would become his trademark sound. A record contract with Bluebird started with three titles that September that hinted at the Glenn Miller sound. The third session, on April 4, 1939, resulted in "Moonlight Serenade" and the music world began to notice. When Miller appeared regularly at the Glen Island Casino during the summer of 1939, his orchestra was able to broadcast regularly on the radio, and within a short time they were a sensation. Tex Bencke and Marion Hutton provided good-natured vocals, Ray Eberle took care of the ballads (his singing is an acquired taste), and touches of jazz were provided by Beneke and either Clyde Hurley, Johnny Best, or (later on) Bobby Hackett on trumpets. With hit after hit being recorded and a whirlwind schedule of performances, broadcasts, and recordings, the Glenn Miller Orchestra by early 1940 was the most popular big band in the world; two years later there was still no sign of slowing down. It seemed as if every month there was at least another hit or two. Only Glenn Miller's decision to enlist in the Army Air Force at the end of the summer of 1942 (which meant the breakup of his band) halted his remarkable success.While in the Army, Major Glenn Miller successfully fought conservative bureaucrats and formed his greatest orchestra, the Army Air Force Band. The huge ensemble, which sometimes used strings, was quite strong from the jazz standpoint (with trumpeter Bobby Nichols, clarinetist Peanuts Hucko, pianist Mel Powell, and drummer Ray McKinley being among the major sidemen) and made "St. Louis Blues March" quite well-known. Throughout 1943 and '44, the orchestra performed at military functions, on broadcasts, and at goodwill concerts. Based in England by 1944, it was all set to begin playing on the Continent when Glenn Miller disappeared over the English Channel (probably shot down mistakenly by friendly fire) while on his way to France to set up some engagements.

The Glenn Miller Army Air Force Band stayed together for an additional year after its leader's death. With the end of World War II, there was still a demand for Glenn Miller's music, so a ghost band was formed, recreating the same hits over and over again. Among its leaders at different times during the next few decades were Tex Beneke, Ray McKinley, Buddy DeFranco, and Peanuts Hucko, but no one has been able to make this orchestra sound inventive and fresh. Jazz writers who later on criticized Glenn Miller's music for being predictable have generally missed the point. His goal was to play high-quality music, not just jazz. And one doubts that, had he lived, Glenn Miller would have been content to stick to endless remakes of his hits from the past! ●

---

7 *Best of the Big Bands / Apr. 25, 1935–May 23, 1938 / Columbia/Legacy 48831*

Considering that this CD reissues 16 of the 18 selections that Glenn Miller recorded for Columbia and Brunswick and that his first band was a flop, the generic title of the release makes even less sense than usual! It is a pity that two of the four selections from 1935 ("In A Little Spanish Town" and "Solo Hop") were left out of the CD and that, since four previously released alternate takes from a later date are included, the four master takes were not reissued, too. Twenty-two numbers would have easily fit on the CD. However, what is here is quite interesting. The first two selections have vocals by Smith Ballew and brief trumpet solos by Bunny Berigan. After recording six songs for Decca (which have not yet been reissued on CD), the first Glenn Miller Orchestra cut ten titles during 1937. A few of the numbers are solid jazz ("I Got Rhythm" and "Community Swing"),

while others have vocals by Kathleen Lane. What is missing is the distinctive Glenn Miller personality. After breaking up the band at the beginning of the year, Miller put together his second orchestra and struggled throughout 1938. This CD concludes with that group's first session, which resulted in two instrumentals (including "Dippermouth Blues") and two vocals; Ray Eberle makes his debut on "Don't Wake Up My Heart." But this was just the prelude.

* *The Complete Glenn Miller (1938–1942) / Sept. 27, 1938–July 16, 1942 / Bluebird 78636 10152*

10 *The Popular Recordings / Sept. 27, 1938–July 15, 1942 / Bluebird 9785*

After signing with the Victor label, the Glenn Miller Orchestra recorded four titles on September 27, 1938 (sounding like itself for the first time on "My Reverie"), four more on

February 6, 1939, and then four on its breakthrough session on April 4 that resulted in "Moonlight Serenade." By the summer (after "Little Brown Jug" hit), it was well on its way to the top. The 13-CD set *The Complete Glenn Miller* has everything that Miller recorded from that first Victor date until the last one in mid-1942, including the alternate takes (which are placed on the 13th disc). All of the hits and misses are here, packaged in an attractive and compact black box. True Glenn Miller fanatics will have to have that magnificent reissue.

There have been a seemingly infinite number of Glenn Miller samplers through the years. *The Popular Recordings,* a definitive three-CD set, is for casual listeners who want Miller's hits and his better jazz, ballads, and dance band records. It contains the essence of his timeless music.

6   *Volume One: Pennsylvania 6–5000 / Dec. 30, 1938– Oct. 7, 1940 / Vintage Jazz Classics 1014*

5   *Volume Two: Tuxedo Junction / July 20, 1939–Apr. 5, 1940 / Vintage Jazz Classics 1022*

6   *Volume Three: Little Brown Jug / June 20, 1939–Dec. 7, 1939 / Vintage Jazz Classics 1038*

10   *A Legendary Performer / May 17, 1939–Sept. 24, 1942 / Bluebird 0693*

Throughout his orchestra's four years, Glenn Miller appeared constantly on the radio, and many air checks have survived. *Volume One* of the three Vintage Jazz Classics sets is particularly interesting because, in addition to two regular performances from 1939–40, there is an early air check when no one knew who Miller was; most of those numbers were never recorded commercially by Miller. *Volume Two* has the usual Ray Eberle and Marion Hutton vocals, a bit of jazz, and a good mixture of dance music. *Volume Three* is a bit more jazz-oriented, with a few good trumpet solos from Clyde Hurley (who actually disliked Miller's music!). However, the live set to get first is *A Legendary Performer,* for in chronological order it has some of Miller's most significant radio performances. Starting shortly before the band made it (one can hear the announcer sounding bored with the unknown group), one can feel the years whizzing by as Glenn Miller has success after success. There is a New Year's Eve version of "In the Mood," Miller is awarded the first gold record in history for "Chattanooga Choo Choo" (which he

then performs), many of his hits are played in very different renditions, and the set concludes with the announcement of Miller's enlistment in the military. Harry James makes a surprise guest appearance in "Juke Box Saturday Night," and then Miller gives an emotional farewell to the audience before performing a final "Moonlight Serenade." In 70 minutes, this disc expertly tells the Glenn Miller story.

9   *Major Glenn Miller & the Army Air Force Band / Oct. 29, 1943–Apr. 22, 1944 / Bluebird 6360*

7   *The Glenn Miller V-Disc Sessions: Volume One / Oct. 29, 1943–May 13, 1944 / Mr. Music 7001*

8   *The Glenn Miller V-Disc Sessions: Volume Two / May 20, 1944–Nov. 17, 1945 / Mr. Music 7002*

Although Glenn Miller's Army Air Force Band did not make any commercially available records during its brief existence (1943–45), it performed regularly on the radio, cut some V-Discs, and made many special appearances. In recent times quite a few CDs have come out that feature Glenn Miller's greatest band. The Bluebird disc gives listeners the basics, including such numbers as "St. Louis Blues March," "Anvil Chorus," a hot "Everybody Loves My Baby," "There'll Be a Hot Time in the Town of Berlin," and "It Must Be Jelly." The two Mr. Music CDs have all 43 of Miller's V-Discs, and they show just how versatile Miller's band could be, playing advanced Swing, hot jams, mood pieces, and novelty vocals. The second volume is a little stronger in the jazz department and has five numbers cut nearly a year after Miller's plane disappeared; one can feel the slight influence of bop in spots.

9   *The Secret Broadcasts / Mar. 10, 1944–June 2, 1944 / RCA 75605-52500*

6   *The Lost Recordings / Oct. 30, 1944–Nov. 27, 1944 / RCA 09026-68320*

8   *Vol. One: American Patrol / Mar. 10, 1944–Apr. 21, 1944 / Avid 556*

8   *Vol. Two: Keep 'Em Flying / Mar. 10, 1944–May 19, 1944 / Avid 557*

7   *Vol. Three: All's Well Mademoiselle / Sept. 6, 1944–May 24, 1945 / Avid 558*

7 *Vol. Four: The Red Cavalry March / Jan. 22, 1945–June 4, 1945 / Avid 559*

7 *Vol. Five: The Complete Abbey Road Recordings / Sept. 16, 1944–Nov. 27, 1944 / Avid 560*

7 *Vol. Six: Blue Champagne / Nov. 27, 1943–May 20, 1944 / Avid 561*

RCA and the British Avid label have come out with quite a few recordings from the Glenn Miller Army Air Force Band in their series, some of which duplicate one another. *The Secret Broadcasts* is a three-CD set that was recorded while Miller's ensemble was in Great Britain and serves as a strong introduction to the greatly underrated orchestra. *The Lost Recordings* (which is two CDs) has the band's final recordings before Miller's disappearance. The six propaganda broadcasts (with a female announcer speaking in German and Miller doing his best phonetically to spread the message) contain plenty of fine music along with the talking. Of the Avids, *Vol. One* has 45 selections, 38 of which are on RCA's *The Secret Broadcasts*, while *Vol. Two* (also two CDs), which has 47 performances, duplicates the rest of the RCA set but also has 12 extra cuts. If one gets the pair of Avid twofers, they will have all of the RCA three-CD set plus 19 more performances! *Vol. Three* has all "new" music, including a program from November 17, 1944, large- and small-group selections from the next few weeks, a broadcast with the string section of the orchestra, and some cuts from May 1944 to 1945, when Ray McKinley was the band's new leader. *Vol. Four* is taken completely from the period after Miller's death. The music had not changed much and although a ghost band, the Army Air Force Band still swings hard and with spirit. *Vol. Five* is essentially a superior duplicate of RCA's *The Lost Recordings*. The two CDs contain not only all of the music on the RCA set but more dialogue between the announcer and Glenn Miller, four additional selections from an unrelated performance, and the opening and closing themes of the six broadcasts. Finally, *Vol. Six* has performances that are mostly earlier than the ones on the other Avid sets, including selections by the Miller orchestra before it left the U.S. Glenn Miller collectors should get either

RCA's *The Secret Broadcasts* or all six of the Avid releases (which total nine CDs).

5 *The Original Reunion of the Glenn Miller Band / Apr. 17, 1954 / GNP/Crescendo 76*

This historic live reunion of the Glenn Miller Orchestra (which occurred after the very successful release of *The Glenn Miller Story*) found producer Gene Norman gathering together as many of the surviving players as possible (including clarinetist-altoist Willie Schwartz, trumpeters Clyde Hurley, Johnny Best, Zeke Zarchey, and Billy May, trombonist Paul Tanner, and bassist Rolly Bundock), plus a few ringers (notably Eddie Miller on tenor). Their solos on the Miller warhorses do not necessarily follow the famous records, but Billy May's arrangements are quite close to the originals, other than a five-song "Miller Medley" and the theme song from *The Glenn Miller Story* ("Too Little Time"). No real surprises occur, but this must have been an emotional concert, even if Tex Beneke, Marion Hutton, and Ray Eberle are nowhere to be found.

LPS TO SEARCH FOR

The five-LP box *His Complete Recordings on Columbia Records—1928–1938* (Everest 4005/5) features Miller as a sideman with the Dorsey Brothers (as early as 1928), the Travelers, and Clark Randall's orchestra, plus all 18 of his Columbia selections as a leader. *The Glenn Miller Carnegie Hall Concert* (RCA 1506) is a spirited and happy set from October 6, 1939, a performance that really signaled the arrival of Miller at the top of the Swing world.

FILMS

The Glenn Miller Orchestra was prominently featured in two movies: *Sun Valley Serenade* (1941), which is highlighted by an extended version of "Chattanooga Choo Choo" with the amazing tap-dancing Nicholas Brothers, and *Orchestra Wives* (1942), which has "I've Got a Gal in Kalamazoo" as the major number. With Jimmy Stewart in the lead role, *The Glenn Miller Story* (1953) is one of the better Swing biography movies, even if "Little Brown Jug" was Miller's first (and not last) big hit!

LUCKY MILLINDER

b. Aug. 8, 1900, Anniston, AL, d. Sept. 28, 1966, New York, NY

As a singer and a front man, Lucky Millinder was comparatively minor. But his orchestra during 1940–52 consistently excited dancing audiences in Harlem and made some valuable recordings. Born Lucius Millinder, Lucky started his show biz career as a master of ceremonies in Chicago in the late 1920s. Millinder began leading big bands in 1931 and performed in Europe in 1933. However, none of his early orchestras recorded. Millinder fronted the Mills Blue Rhythm Band from 1934 until they disbanded in 1938. After heading a short-lived ensemble (originally under Bill Doggett's leadership), Millinder in September 1940 started leading his most important big band.

With Sister Rosetta Tharpe contributing passionate vocals and very fluent guitar solos, plus such sidemen as tenor saxophonist Stafford Simon, altoist Tab Smith, and (for a few months in 1942) trumpeter Dizzy Gillespie, Millinder had a powerful outfit that recorded for Decca (1941–47), Victor (1949), and King (1950–52). A hard-driving and fairly basic Swing band, the Millinder Orchestra (whose later sidemen included tenors Sam "The Man" Taylor, Eddie "Lockjaw" Davis, and Bull Moose Jackson) was able to stay together into 1952 by adapting to rhythm and blues. On records, Millinder himself was barely a factor after the mid-1940s, and, after his orchestra disbanded, he retired from music other than appearing at infrequent engagements. Lucky Millinder spent his later years working at a variety of jobs, including as a liquor salesman, a disc jockey, a publicist, and a fortune teller. But the best recordings of his spirited orchestra still sound quite good today.

9 *1941–1942 / June 27, 1941–July 29, 1942 / Classics 712*
During 1941–42, the Lucky Millinder Orchestra recorded 20 selections in five sessions, all of which are on this CD. Sister Rosetta Tharpe is the star on five rousing numbers ("Trouble in Mind," "Rock! Daniel," "Shout Sister, Shout," "Rock Me," and "That's All") that balance the sacred with the profane. Also quite notable are the hyper "Ride Red Ride" (which has Millinder's only vocal of the CD), "Apollo Jump," and two songs that feature trumpet solos from Dizzy Gillespie: "Mason Flyer" and the catchy "Little John Special" (which hints a bit at "Salt Peanuts"). Not every selection on this CD is on that level (particularly a couple of dated patriotic songs), but such players as altoist Tab Smith, clarinetist Buster Bailey, tenor saxophonist Stafford Simon, and pianist Bill Doggett all have their spots and show what a strong band the Lucky Millinder Orchestra could be.

6 *1943–1947 / Aug. 1943–Apr. 11, 1947 / Classics 1026*
Most of the material on this CD was formerly rare. The first four selections (V-Discs from 1943) feature Sister Rosetta Tharpe doing remakes of her hits; these would be her last recordings with Millinder, because she chose to return to religious music. Otherwise the focus is on the evolving Millinder Orchestra, which by 1946–47 had elements of both bop and early R&B in its music. Other than "Shipyard Social Function," all of the recordings on this CD have vocals, including two by Millinder, Wynonie Harris's first recordings, and contributions from such singers as Trevor Bacon, Judy Carol, Leon Ketchum, Annisteen Allen, and Paul Breckenridge, plus vocal groups called the Lucky Seven and the Lucky Four. Even with all the singing, there are plenty of solo spots for trumpeter Joe Guy, the tenors of Bull Moose Jackson and Sam "The Man" Taylor, and pianist Sir Charles Thompson.

LPS TO SEARCH FOR

1943–1944 (Kaydee 6) features the Lucky Millinder Orchestra performing on the radio during the war years. Sister Rosetta Tharpe, Tab Smith, trumpeter Joe Guy, and Sam "The Man" Taylor are the main stars of these *Jubilee* broadcasts.

FILMS

Lucky Millinder and Mamie Smith appear in *Paradise in Harlem* (1939), and the later Lucky Millinder Orchestra is in *Boarding House Blues* (1948).

MILLS BLUE RHYTHM BAND

The Mills Blue Rhythm Band existed for eight years (1930–38) without really developing its own distinctive personality. One problem was that it never really had a single musical vision, leader, or head arranger. It did leave behind a solid series of jazz recordings and was an excellent second-level band. The orchestra was originally known as the Blue Rhythm Band when it was run by drummer Willie Lynch. As the Coconut Grove Orchestra it backed Louis Armstrong on a few recordings. When manager-producer Irving Mills took over the big band in 1931, he renamed it after himself and used it as a relief band in the Cotton Club for Cab Calloway and Duke Ellington, two of his other clients. Pianist Edgar Hayes was the band's musical director and one of the key arrangers through 1936, while a variety of people fronted the orchestra (including Baron Lee and Billy Banks) before Lucky Millinder joined in 1933 as a permanent member.

Recording frequently during 1931–37, the Mills Blue Rhythm Band was at first largely a no-name outfit full of fine utility players. Altoist Charlie Holmes joined in 1931, and in 1934 trumpeter Henry "Red" Allen, trombonist J. C. Higginbotham, and clarinetist Buster Bailey greatly uplifted the orchestra's solo strength. Later members included altoist Tab Smith, pianist Billy Kyle, and trumpeters Harry "Sweets" Edison and Charlie Shavers. The Mills Blue Rhythm Band broke up in 1938.

●

7 *1931 / Jan. 21, 1931–July 30, 1931 / Classics 660*

7 *1931–1932 / July 30, 1931–Sept. 23, 1932 / Classics 676*
All of the Mills Blue Rhythm Band's recordings (other than a few alternate takes) have been reissued on five Classics CDs. In the early days, the arrangements of Harry White and Edgar Hayes were often more significant than the individual players. *1931* has cheerful if dated vocals by Dick Robertson, Charlie Lawman, George Morton, and Chick Bullock along with such numbers as "Blue Rhythm," "Red Devil," "Black and Tan Fantasy," and "Futuristic Jungleism." *1931–1932* finds Billy Banks taking over the vocalizing (which is a big improvement), and such instrumentals as "Savage Rhythm," "Snake Hips," "Heat Waves," "The Growl," and "Jazz Cocktail" disguise the fact that the ensemble lacked any highly original soloists. Solid Swing.

8 *1933–1934 / Mar. 1, 1933–Dec. 11, 1934 / Classics 686*

9 *1934–1936 / Dec. 19, 1934–May 20, 1936 / Classics 710*

8 *1936–1937 / May 20, 1936–July 1, 1937 / Classics 731*
The years 1933–36 represent the prime period for the Mills Blue Rhythm Band. The obscure trumpeter Ed Anderson developed into a fine soloist in 1933, the band was now emphasizing heated instrumentals (other than guest appearances by Adelaide Hall and an occasional dull vocal by Chuck Richards), and in 1934 J. C. Higginbotham, Henry "Red" Allen, Buster Bailey, and tenor saxophonist Joe Garland gave the orchestra solo strength that it had lacked before. *1933–1934* is highlighted by "Ridin' in Rhythm," "Harlem After Midnight," "The Stuff Is Here (and It's Mellow)," "The Growl," and "Dancing Dogs." *1934–1936* has "Back Beats," "Ride Red Ride," Garland's "There's Rhythm in Harlem" (which hints strongly at "In the Mood" several years before it was officially "composed"), "Harlem Heat," and "Truckin'"; these are only a few of the high points on this superior Swing CD. *1936–1937* starts out with 14 numbers by the same group (with Tab Smith and Billy Kyle making the orchestra even stronger). Together they perform such gems as "St. Louis Wiggle Rhythm," "Merry-Go-Round," "Big John's Special," and "Algiers Stomp." Notice how Tab Smith's "Barrelhouse" would a couple of years later become Harry Edison's "Jive at Five!" However, within a two-month period (December 1936–February 1937), the band underwent almost a 100 percent turnover, with only Smith and Kyle remaining. The final version of the Mills Blue Rhythm Band, which recorded 11 selections in 1937, was not a bad band (it did include the young trumpeters Charlie Shavers and Harry "Sweets" Edison), and the arrangements of Chappie Willet were fine. But overall the final edition of the orchestra was not quite on the same level as the Red Allen group.

OZZIE NELSON

b. Mar. 20, 1906, Ridgefield Park, NJ, d. June 3, 1975, Hollywood, CA

One might rightfully wonder what Ozzie Nelson (of *Ozzie and Harriet* and father of Ricky Nelson) is doing in this book, since he is best-known for his acting on the long-run family television sitcom. However, Nelson led a fine big band during the Swing era. Both of his parents were singers, and Ozzie learned to play banjo and saxophone, first performing in public when he was 14. After attending Rutgers University, Nelson became a professional bandleader and in 1930 fronted the first band to play at the Glen Island Casino, where Glenn Miller would become famous in 1939. Nelson (sticking to sax) rarely soloed with his orchestra and just took occasional vocals, as did his future wife, Harriet Hilliard, who joined the band in 1932. Ozzie Nelson was always aware of his limited musical abilities, as he showed in the novelty "I've Got Those Wave-a-Stick Blues." However, during the 1934–42 period, Nelson's orchestra recorded some hard-swinging instrumentals. Most impressive among his soloists were baritonist Charlie Bubeck and violinist Sid Brobaw.

In 1944 Ozzie and Harriet Nelson (who were married in 1935) began to star on the radio series *The Adventures of Ozzie and Harriet.* Very soon their big band became a forgotten bit of history.

●

LPS TO SEARCH FOR

There has thus far been no rush to reissue Ozzie Nelson's recordings on CD, but there were a few excellent LPs put out. Most of his best studio sides are on *Featuring Harriet Hilliard 1936–1941* (Bandstand 7119), including "Swamp Fire," "Streamline Strut," "Satan Takes a Holiday," and "The Sheik of Araby." Half of the 16 selections are instrumentals, and, among the vocals, one (talking about the wartime shortage of musicians) is actually titled "I'm Looking for a Guy Who Plays Alto and Baritone, Doubles on Clarinet and Wears a Size 37 Suit!" *1937* (Circle 27) has radio transcriptions but a few too many vocals by the leader. Better are *1940–42* (Hindsight 107) and *1937, Vol. 2* (Hindsight 189), which are primarily jazz-oriented and, in addition to baritonist Bubeck, are notable for the many strong trumpet solos by Bo Ashford.

RED NORVO

b. Mar. 31, 1908, Beardstown, IL, d. Apr. 6, 1999, Santa Monica, CA

Red Norvo introduced the xylophone to jazz as a solo instrument, and he was certainly the only xylophonist to lead a big band! Norvo, who would switch to vibraphone in 1943, had a long and productive career. Thanks to the advanced and inventive arrangements of Eddie Sauter and the singing of his wife, Mildred Bailey, he also had one of the more interesting big bands of the Swing era.

Born Kenneth Norville, he started on piano before switching to xylophone and marimba. By 1925, Norvo was touring with a marimba band called the Collegians. He worked in Chicago with the orchestras of Paul Ash and Ben Bernie, took a detour by attending the University of Missouri as a mining engineer, and then returned to music, working on radio and appearing in vaudeville as a tap dancer. After working with Victor Young, Norvo was featured with Paul Whiteman in the early 1930s, meeting and (in late 1933) marrying singer Mildred Bailey. Making his recording debut as a leader in 1933, Norvo was showcased on two numbers ("Knockin' on Wood" and "Hole in the Wall") while two others (Bix Beiderbecke's "In a Mist" and the eccentric "Dance of the Octopus") featured an atmospheric chamber group with Benny Goodman, on bass clarinet!

Norvo went out on his own in 1934, recording with all-star groups, leading a combo on 52nd Street, and in 1936 putting together a small big band. One would think that it would be very difficult for a xylophone to be heard over seven horns, but

SWING

106

Eddie Sauter's inventive voicings (which made expert use of dynamics, advanced harmonies, and space) made it possible. With Mildred Bailey contributing vocals, Norvo's band had a unique sound. During this era Norvo and Bailey were dubbed "Mr. and Mrs. Swing." By 1937-38 the Red Norvo Big Band had expanded to 14 pieces, and during the next few years the ensemble grew and shrunk in size several times before Norvo cut back to a small group after 1942. By then he had switched permanently to vibes and his marriage to Bailey was winding down (they would continue working together occasionally after their 1945 divorce). Norvo ended up the Swing era as a featured sideman with Benny Goodman (1944-45) and Woody Herman (1946).

Red Norvo had a flexible style, and on his recording session of June 6, 1945, he was able to fit in comfortably with not only Teddy Wilson but the bebop giants Dizzy Gillespie and Charlie Parker. He settled in California for a time in the late 1940s, leading a sextet, and then in 1949 emerged with a new trio featuring guitarist Tal Farlow and bassist Charles Mingus. The vibes-guitar-bass combination was quite appealing and Norvo's main outlet for the next few years (with guitarist Jimmy Raney and bassist Red Mitchell joining for a time). The vibraphonist led a variety of small groups during the next 25 years in addition to occasionally rejoining Benny Goodman. A serious ear operation in 1961 resulted in Norvo's not being all that active in the 1960s. But, after playing with the Newport All-Stars later in the decade, Red Norvo resumed a busy schedule until a stroke in the mid-1980s permanently knocked him out of action.

●

10 *Dance of the Octopus / Apr. 18, 1933–Mar. 16, 1936 / Hep 1044*

This is the Red Norvo CD to get. Included are all of his earliest sessions as a leader, which directly precede his forming a big band. Norvo's xylophone and marimba are showcased, with the backing of clarinetist Jimmy Dorsey, piano, and bass on "Knockin' on Wood" and "Hole in the Wall," a pair of 1933 performances that must have really impressed his fellow musicians. Bix Beiderbecke's "In a Mist" and the mysterious "Dance of the Octopus" match Norvo with Benny Goodman's bass clarinet, guitarist Dick McDonough, and bassist Artie Bernstein. In 1934 Norvo is heard heading an octet for four numbers that include such notables as Artie Shaw, Charlie Barnet, trombonist Jack Jenney, and Teddy Wilson; none were known to the general public at the time. He also jams four songs (including "Honeysuckle Rose") in 1935 with a nonet that includes Jenney, Wilson, Chu Berry, clarinetist Johnny Mince, Bunny Berigan, and Gene Krupa. The second half of this disc features Norvo's regularly working octet of early 1936 (one of the dates was originally issued under the fictional name of Ken Kenny). Not only are the ensembles unusual in having Norvo's xylophone instead of a piano, but arranger Eddie Sauter plays mellophone. A perfectly done reissue.

5 *Featuring Mildred Bailey / Aug. 26, 1936–Feb. 27, 1939 / Columbia/Legacy 53424*

7 *Live at the Blue Gardens / Jan. 4, 1942 / Music Masters 65090*

Featuring Mildred Bailey is a perfect example of why the European Classics label is necessary. Compilation producer Michael Brooks should be shot for the illogical and crummy programming. Rather than reissue Norvo's big band recordings in a logical fashion as a sampler, this CD jumps all over the place, mixing together familiar performances with two previously unissued numbers and two selections from a date actually led by Mildred Bailey; nothing is in chronological order, and the singer appears on only six of the 18 numbers, despite the CD's title. The music is quite worthwhile thanks to arranger Eddie Sauter and such soloists as Norvo, trumpeter Stew Pletcher, clarinetist Hank D'Amico, and tenorman Herbie Haymer but certainly deserves much better treatment. By 1942, Norvo was leading his last big band, a young outfit whose only "names" were trombonist Eddie Bert and guest singer Helen Ward. The Music Masters CD shows what the group (which recorded only two songs commercially and was of standard size) could do; Johnny Thompson's arrangements are a major asset.

7 *Volume One—The Legendary V-Disc Masters / Oct. 28, 1943–May 17, 1944 / Vintage Jazz Classics 1005*

8 *Red Norvo's Fabulous Jam Session / June 6, 1945 / Stash 2514*

In 1943 Red Norvo switched permanently to the vibes without losing his musical personality. *Volume One* has most of

Norvo's V-Discs of 1943–44, including a few alternate takes and a couple of brief breakdowns. On the first 17 cuts, Norvo jams with a septet also including trumpeter Dale Pierce, trombonist Dick Taylor, clarinetist Aaron Sachs, Flip Phillips on tenor, pianist Ralph Burns, bassist Clyde Lombardi, and drummer John Blowers; Helen Ward and Carol Bruce take vocals. Norvo, who sounds strong on such numbers as his "1-2-3-4 Jump," "Seven Come Eleven," "Flying Home," and "NBC Jump," would be joining Phillips and Burns in the Woody Herman Orchestra two years in the future. The final three numbers on this CD feature Norvo in a sextet with Sachs and a rhythm section. The Stash disc has all of the music that resulted from Norvo's famous session with trumpeter Dizzy Gillespie, altoist Charlie Parker, Flip Phillips, Teddy Wilson, bassist Slam Stewart, and Specs Powell or J. C. Heard on drums. The unusual grouping of Swing and bop all-stars performed only four numbers (two standards and two Norvo originals) but there are also five full-length alternate takes and three incomplete versions. Overall, however, the music is more significant in Charlie Parker's discography than in the vibraphonist's.

8 *Volume Two—The Norvo-Mingus-Farlow Trio / Oct. 28, 1943–1950 / Vintage Jazz Classics 1008*

7 *Move / May 3, 1950 –Apr. 13, 1951 / Savoy 0168*

8 *The Red Norvo Trios / Sept. 1953–Oct. 1955 / Prestige 24108*

The vibes-guitar-bass trio that Norvo put together in late 1949 with Tal Farlow and Charles Mingus was both unique and classic. *Volume Two* has three leftover selections from Norvo's V-Disc sessions (vocal numbers by Helen Ward on "I'll Be Around" and two versions of "Too Marvelous for Words") and then 30 mostly brief radio transcriptions of his 1949–50 trio. The interplay and telepathically quick reactions by the three musicians really made the Red Norvo Trio quite special. The rather chintzy *Move* has 12 of the 20 Red Norvo Trio recordings that they cut for Savoy during 1950–51, including "I'll Remember April," "Godchild," "Cheek to Cheek," and "Swedish Pastry." *The Red Norvo Trios* releases 19 of the 20 selections that were reissued 15 years earlier as a two-LP set, all that space would allow. The 78 1/2 minute set was recorded after Mingus had departed, so Red Mitchell is on bass. Farlow is on just four numbers, but his

replacement, Jimmy Raney, fits in perfectly. In fact, the Norvo-Raney-Mitchell retains and builds on the magic of the original trio.

9 *Just a Mood / Sept. 17, 1954–Jan. 18, 1957 / Bluebird 6278*

7 *The Forward Look / Dec. 31, 1957 / Reference 8*

Three separate four-song sessions comprise *Just a Mood,* and they show off the versatility of Red Norvo. He performs pieces with Swing-era all-stars (including Harry "Sweets" Edison and Ben Webster), a quartet of "blue" songs with a cool jazz group that includes flutist Buddy Collette, Farlow, and drummer Chico Hamilton, and four "rose" tunes in a septet with trumpeter Shorty Rogers, clarinetist Jimmy Giuffre, and pianist Pete Jolly. Everything works, particularly such numbers as "Just a Mood," "Blue Lou," and "Roses of Picardy." *The Forward Look* is an outing (first released in 1980) by Norvo's regular group of the late 1950s, a quintet with guitarist Jimmy Wyble and Jerry Dodgion on alto and flute that expertly mixed together aspects of Swing, bop, and cool jazz, just like its leader.

LPS TO SEARCH FOR

Quite a few sessions by the vibraphonist have not been reissued on CD yet. The three-LP box *Red Norvo* (Time-Life STL J14) has many of the highlights of Norvo's career along with a definitive 52-page book. Some of the scarcer Red Norvo big band titles of 1936–42 are on *Featuring Mildred Bailey* (Sounds of Swing 112). *Time in His Hands* (Xanadu 199) showcases Norvo on three small-group sessions in 1945, quintets with bassist Slam Stewart and pianist Johnny Guarnieri, plus a few obscure titles with some Ellington players and Charlie Ventura. *Norvo* (Pausa 9015) has his work for Capitol, including a date with the Hollywood Hucksters (an all-star group that includes Benny Goodman and Stan Kenton, who share the vocal on a hilarious "Happy Blues"). Other notables who make appearances include Benny Carter, Charlie Shavers, Jimmy Giuffre, Dexter Gordon, and Eddie Miller, plus a woodwind section and French horns on a unique rendition of "Twelfth Street Rag." *The Red Norvo Trio* (Savoy 2212), a two-LP set, has all of the Norvo-Farlow-Mingus Savoy recordings (including alternate takes). And near the end of his career Norvo recorded a 1979 quartet date with pianist Ross Tompkins (*Red & Ross*—Concord CJ-90) and an outing in 1983 with the Bucky Pizzarelli Trio (*Just Friends*—Stash 230).

The original Red Norvo–Tal Farlow–Charles Mingus Trio is seen in *Texas Carnival* (1951), while Norvo's late '50s group appears in *Screaming Mimi* (1957).

TONY PASTOR

b. Oct. 26, 1907, Middletown, CT, d. Oct. 31, 1969, Old Lyme, CT

A likable and jovial Italian singer and a decent tenor saxophonist, Tony Pastor led a big band for many years. Born Antonio Pestritto, Pastor started off playing C-melody saxophone in the 1920s before settling on tenor. He worked with John Cavallaro's band (1927), Irving Aaronson's Commanders, and Austin Wylie's group before heading his own orchestra (1931–34). Short stints with Smith Ballew, Joe Venuti, and Vincent Lopez preceded nearly four years spent as a featured soloist and vocalist with Artie Shaw's first two orchestras (1936–39). Pastor's Louis Armstrong–inspired singing was popular, and he shared the tenor solos with Georgie Auld on Shaw's 1938–39 records. When Artie Shaw (Pastor's friend since 1927) spontaneously departed for Mexico in 1939, Tony Pastor immediately formed his own big band. The orchestra was a solid Swing unit filled with excellent section players, although its most famous graduates were the Clooney Sisters (Rosemary and Betty Clooney, who were both teenagers when they joined in 1947). Alternating Swing tunes and ballads with plenty of good-humored novelties, the Tony Pastor Orchestra (with the leader's brother Stubby Pastor usually featured on trumpet) stayed together until 1959.

●

8 *Tony Pastor With the Clooney Sisters / June 5, 1947– Dec. 30, 1950 / Sony 30955*
Most of Tony Pastor's recordings with Rosemary and Betty Clooney (including some solo numbers for Rosemary) are on this CD, released in 2000. Pastor only takes a couple tenor solos but joins in happily in the vocalizing, often with the Clooney Sisters harmonizing behind him. His big band does not get to do much but the overall results are quite good-natured and listenable.

THE WAYNE KNIGHT COLLECTION

The always-exuberant Tony Pastor is joined by his most important discovery, the Clooney Sisters (Rosemary and Betty).

LPS TO SEARCH FOR

Tony Pastor recorded many titles for Bluebird (1940–42), Victor (1945) and Cosmo (1946), but good luck finding any of them on either CD or LP! The two-LP set *Horn Power* (Big Band Archives 2205) does not bother with personnel listings, dates, or even liner notes, but it does contain some excellent music from the 1940–57 period (mostly live recordings), with the emphasis on instrumentals. *1945–49* (First Time 1516) also focuses on the jazz side of Pastor's music (nine of the 14 numbers are instrumentals) and includes a few surprisingly boppish numbers from 1949 (including the Clooney Sisters' feature on "Euphoria" and "Biddy Bop").

BEN POLLACK

b. June 22, 1903, Chicago, IL, d. June 7, 1971, Palm Springs, CA

Ben Pollack had the distinction of having as his sidemen through the years such notables as Benny Goodman, Glenn Miller, Jack Teagarden, Bud Freeman, Yank Lawson, Eddie Miller, Harry James, and Muggsy Spanier, yet he never led a commercially successful orchestra. Pollack had a frequently exciting but ultimately frustrating career, failing to become a big name despite his strong ability as a talent scout.

As a drummer, Ben Pollack started working professionally in 1921, and the following year he landed an important job with the New Orleans Rhythm Kings, making his recording debut with that pacesetting ensemble. Pollack had short stints with obscure bands in Chicago, Los Angeles, and New York, and then in 1926 formed his own orchestra, which was soon featuring 17-year-old Benny Goodman, Glenn Miller on trombone, and cornetist Jimmy McPartland; BG and Miller made their first recordings with Pollack. By 1929 Jack Teagarden was the band's trombone soloist. By then, Pollack was mostly just conducting his band (Ray Bauduc was on drums) and doing his best to mix jazz tunes with more pop-oriented numbers. His sidemen were not always that happy with the repertoire or with the leader's occasional vocals; Pollack's voice was embarrassingly bad. Things became worse by 1934, when Pollack's main priority became to make his girlfriend, the limited vocalist Doris Robbins, famous. In December 1934, after he tried unsuccessfully to get Robbins some roles in Hollywood films while neglecting his band, the Ben Pollack Orchestra broke up. The sidemen (which by then included Yank Lawson and Eddie Miller) soon regrouped as the Bob Crosby Big Band.

In 1936, Ben Pollack put together a new orchestra and he discovered trumpeter Harry James in Texas. But after a half-year James accepted a much better offer to join Pollack's former sideman, Benny Goodman. Pollack continued on, using Muggsy Spanier, Clyde Hurley, and Andy Secrest as his trumpet soloists during the next few years. But his big bands (which featured no other major stars) struggled along as he watched Benny Goodman, Glenn Miller, Jack Teagarden, Bob Crosby, and Harry James all become household names. In 1942 (after he had discovered a teenage singer named Mel Torme), Pollack gave up. He headed a booking agency, briefly ran the Jewel record label, and eventually had a restaurant in Hollywood (and later Palm Springs), where his Dixieland combo (the Pick-a-Rib Boys) played. In 1971 the frustrated and obscure musician committed suicide.

7 *Ben Pollack and His Pick-a-Rib Boys / Apr. 25, 1950 – May 3, 1950 / Jazzology 224*

Ben Pollack's big band recordings have mostly not reappeared on CD yet. This disc features Pollack's Dixieland band of 1950, a fine sextet that has trumpeter Dick Cathcart, trombonist Moe Schneider, clarinetist Matty Matlock, pianist Ray Sherman, and bassist Walt Yoder joining the drummer-leader on a 20-song program dominated mostly by vintage standards. The performances (all under three minutes) were originally cut for World Transcriptions. The Pick-a-Rib Boys studio records plus his earlier and more significant work with his orchestras remain out of print.

LPS TO SEARCH FOR

Benny Goodman with Ben Pollack 1926–31 (Sunbeam 136) has some of the best recordings by Pollack's early big band, although the great majority of the selections on this collector's LP are actually alternate takes. Benny Goodman is on each selection and there are appearances by Glenn Miller, Jimmy McPartland, and Jack Teagarden (who sings "Beale Street Blues"). *Futuristic Rhythm* (Saville 154) has the master takes of all of Pollack's records of October 1928–November 1929, including "Buy, Buy for Baby," "Louise," "My Kinda Love," and "Keep Your Undershirt On." Some of the numbers on this British LP are more dance band–oriented than jazz, but there are some good moments from McPartland, Teagarden, and Goodman. *1933–1934* (VJM 43) has the complete output of Pollack's pre-Bob Crosby Orchestra. There are spots for Yank Lawson, Eddie Miller, and Matty Matlock, although the erratic material and arrangements (not to mention too many weak vocals) often keep the soloists from breaking loose; no wonder they were frustrated! *Ben Pollack Big Band* (Golden Era 15067) features Pollack's last orchestra, a swinging unit influenced by Benny Goodman and featuring fine trumpet solos from Andy Secrest.

DON REDMAN

b. July 29, 1900, Piedmont, WV, d. Nov. 30, 1964, New York, NY

Don Redman was a decent alto saxophonist, a pleasant if dated clarinetist, a singer who actually talked more than sang the lyrics, and the leader of an excellent orchestra throughout the 1930s. However, his main significance to music was that he was the first important big band arranger, practically originating the idea of utilizing trumpet, trombone, and saxophone sections.

Redman began playing trumpet when he was three, and by the time he was a teenager he could play practically any horn. His strong technical knowledge of each instrument's capabilities would always be a major asset. He studied music at Storer's College, Harper's Ferry, and conservatories in Chicago and Boston before joining Billy Paige's Broadway Syncopators, arriving in New York in early 1923. Redman soon met bandleader Fletcher Henderson, started appearing on his records, and in 1924 became an official member of the Henderson orchestra. He has the distinction on "My Papa Doesn't Two-Time" of taking the earliest scat vocal on records. Although for years it was assumed that Henderson was the main arranger, nearly all of the charts written for his big band through mid-1927 were created by Redman. From the start, his arrangements were somewhat futuristic and full of unusual ideas, if a bit stiff. But after Louis Armstrong joined Henderson later in 1924 and taught New Yorkers how to swing, Redman learned quickly and became one of the great jazz arrangers of all time. His work would be an inspiration to Duke Ellington.

In June 1927, Don Redman left Henderson to run McKinney's Cotton Pickers, and during the next four years, that orchestra would be one of jazz's main pacesetters. Redman (who also played and arranged in 1928 for some of Louis Armstrong's recordings with his Savoy Ballroom Five) during this period composed "Gee Baby, Ain't I Good to You" and "Cherry." In 1931 he left the Cotton Pickers (which soon quickly declined) and put together the Don Redman Orchestra. For the next nine years his band (whose theme song was Redman's memorable "Chant of the Weed") worked steadily with such key sidemen as trumpeter Sidney DeParis, Robert Carroll on tenor, and trombonist Quentin Jackson. In addition, Redman contributed arrangements to many other orchestras, including those of Paul Whiteman, Ben Pollack, and Isham Jones. But although Don Redman had helped set the stage for the Swing era, his own big band never really flourished or had any hit records.

After breaking up his orchestra in January 1940, Redman worked primarily as an arranger (including for Count Basie, Harry James and Jimmy Dorsey, contributing a hit version of "Deep Purple" for JD), briefly leading other ensembles. In 1946 his all-star big band (which included tenor saxophonist Don Byas and trumpeter Peanuts Holland) was the first American orchestra to tour Europe after World War II. The remainder of Don Redman's life was less significant; he worked as musical director for Pearl Bailey, led a few so-so record dates in 1958–59 (on which he played clarinet, soprano, and piano) and by the early 1960's was semi-retired from music. ●

9 *1931–1933 / Sept. 24, 1931–Feb. 2, 1933 / Classics 543*

5 *1933–1936 / Feb. 2, 1933–May 7, 1936 / Classics 553*

8 *1936–1939 / May 7, 1936–Mar. 23, 1939 / Classics 574*
Although Don Redman was a major force in making the Swing era possible, his own big band never made it big. Fortunately all of his orchestra's recordings have been reissued on these three CDs, plus a McKinney's Cotton Pickers CD on Classics that has his final two sessions with the big band. *1931–1933* features such soloists as trumpeters Henry "Red" Allen (on the first two dates) and Sidney DeParis, trombonists Claude Jones and Benny Morton, clarinetist Edward

Inge, and Robert Carroll on tenor in addition to Redman. Tap dancer Bill Robinson, Cab Calloway, and the Mills Brothers make appearances on a two-part version of "Doin' the New Lowdown." Other highlights include "Shakin' the African," "Chant of the Weed," "How'm I Doin'?," and "Nagasaki." The Redman Orchestra, after recording extensively in 1933, hardly made any records at all during 1934–35. *1933–1936* finds the band struggling a bit, weighed down by vocals on 22 of the 25 numbers (with eight by Harlan Lattimore and six from Chick Bullock). Most of the selections are a bit disappointing, and one gets as little as one would expect from such songs as "Mommy, I Don't Want to Go to

Bed," "Watching the Knife and Fork Spoon," "Puddin' Head Jones," and "Lazy Weather." *1936–1939* in contrast is much better, particularly "Bugle Call Rag," "Swingin' with the Fat Man," "Sweet Leilani," "Down Home Rag," and "Milenberg Joys." But one can understand why the Don Redman Orchestra did not make it into the top rung of Swing bands despite its leader's charm and writing talents: it did not have a unique personality or trademark sound.

5 *For Europeans Only / Sept. 15, 1946 / Steeple Chase 36020*

7 *Geneva 1946 / Oct. 27, 1946 / TCB 02112*

Don Redman led one of his finest orchestras in 1946 when he visited Europe, a big band that included trumpeter-singer Peanuts Holland, trombonist Quentin Jackson, Tyree Glenn doubling on trombone and vibes, pianist Billy Taylor, and the superb Don Byas on tenor. The tour was such a success that Byas and Holland both permanently stayed overseas. A version of the band early in 1946 had cut four obscure titles, but otherwise they went unrecorded. Years later Steeple Chase came out with *For Europeans Only,* a poorly recorded but interesting live concert that finds Byas in particular in top form. In 1999, *Geneva 1946* was released. It features the same band six weeks later on a much better-recorded radio broadcast. Only five of the dozen "new" selections are reruns from the other concert, and the solos are much different (and easier to hear). Most of the music is mainstream Swing and bebop is largely ignored. This tour was really the end of Don Redman's creative years in jazz and it concluded his important career with a major success.

ALVINO REY
b. 1911, Cleveland, OH

The first guitarist to lead a big band on a regular basis, Alvino Rey was quite unusual in that he played the electrified Hawaiian steel guitar (although he later claimed to dislike Hawaiian music!). Born Alvin McBurney and inspired by guitarists Eddie Lang and Andy Sanella, Rey (who also played acoustic rhythm guitar) was a sideman with Phil Spitalny, Russ Morgan, Freddie Martin, and Horace Heidt. In Horace Heidt's Orchestra, he was well featured along with the four King Sisters. Rey, who would marry Louise King, left Heidt along with the King Sisters in late 1938 and formed a radio band in Los Angeles. Broadcasting regularly on KHJ, the Alvino Rey Orchestra built up a big audience and was a hit when it finally appeared in public. By 1942, such arrangers as Neal Hefti, Ray Conniff, Johnny Mandel, and Billy May were writing for the ensemble, and Rey's band had developed into one of the better Swing orchestras around. Unfortunately, its studio recordings have not been reissued, and the 1942–44 recording ban prevented the later version of the big band from making any records, but radio transcriptions show how strong the Alvino Rey Orchestra was at its height. In 1944 the big band broke up when Alvino Rey entered the Navy. After being discharged in December 1945, he formed another orchestra (a huge one with 15 horns, including six trumpets) but it only lasted a year; his sidemen included Al Cohn, Zoot Sims, and/or Herbie Steward on tenors and Don Lamond or Dave Tough on drums. Alvino Rey eventually became a television and record producer, still playing on a part-time basis into the 1980s.

LP'S TO SEARCH FOR
Alvino Rey's RCA recordings of the 1940s, which apparently sold quite well, are not available on CD. However, Hindsight did put out two jazz-oriented LPs of radio transcriptions from the same year: *1946* (Hindsight 121) and *1946, Vol. 2* (Hindsight 167). Although the personnel is not always known from track to track, Sims, Cohn, or Steward are playing tenor on most of the selections (often soloing), Jo Ann Ryan takes a few pleasant vocals, Alvino Rey is in top form, and the arrangers include Billy May and Dean Kincaide.

FILMS
At the beginning of *Sing Your Worries Away* (1942), Alvino Rey's Orchestra and the King Sisters perform a colorful and memorable version of "Tiger Rag."

LUIS RUSSELL

b. Aug. 6, 1902, Careening Cay, Panama, d. Dec. 11, 1963, New York, NY

A good arranger and a supportive pianist who rarely soloed, Luis Russell led an orchestra that was at its prime during 1929–31. Early on he studied guitar, violin, organ, and piano in his native Panama. Russell accompanied silent films on piano and played locally. After winning $3,000 in a lottery in 1919, he moved to New Orleans with his mother and sister. Russell worked with Arnold Du Pas (1921–22) and Albert Nicholas in 1923; after Nicholas departed, he led the band for a year. Russell played with Doc Cook's Gingersnaps in Chicago and then became a member of King Oliver's Savannah Syncopators (1925–27), recording and touring with Oliver. He would use some of the members of Oliver's band in October 1927 as the nucleus for his new orchestra.

By 1929 the Luis Russell Orchestra (which played regularly in New York) featured four major soloists (trumpeter Henry "Red" Allen, trombonist J. C. Higginbotham, clarinetist Albert Nicholas, and altoist Charlie Holmes) plus two other fine players (trumpeter Bill Coleman and tenorman Teddy Hill), who ended up being frustrated by their lack of solo space. His big band was an important transition group, combining New Orleans-type solos with riff-filled ensembles. In addition, his rhythm section (which included guitarist Will Johnson, bassist Pops Foster, and drummer Paul Barbarin) was one of the finest of the period. Russell (who led his first sessions in 1926) recorded with this group during 1929–31 (including "Call of the Freaks," "Jersey Lightning," "Saratoga Shout," and "Louisiana Swing") and the band also backed up Louis Armstrong and was utilized on dates led by Red Allen and Jelly Roll Morton; Russell was absent on the latter.

After long periods playing at the Nest Club, the Saratoga Club, the Savoy, and Connie's Inn, the orchestra hit some hard times. A final session in 1934 (featuring cornetist Rex Stewart) preceded the group becoming the backup band for Louis Armstrong in 1935. For the next eight years, Russell was with Armstrong (surviving a major shakeup in 1940), working all the time but stuck in an anonymous background role with the band. He did lead another little-known orchestra during 1943–48, recording 24 titles during 1945–46 (most including the young Roy Haynes on drums). However, that band did not make much of an impression and Luis Russell largely retired from music in 1948, running a store, teaching piano and organ, occasionally playing classical music, and working as a chauffeur.

●

9 *1926–1929 / Mar. 10, 1926–Dec. 17, 1929 / Classics 588*

9 *1930–1931 / Jan. 24, 1930–Aug. 28, 1931 / Classics 606*

7 *1926–1934 / Mar. 10, 1926–Aug. 8, 1934 / Collectors Classics 7*

3 *1945–1946 / 1945–1946 / Classics 1066*

Luis Russell's prime recordings have been reissued on the first two Classics CDs. *1926–1929* has a couple of sessions from 1926 (with George Mitchell or Bob Shoffner on cornet, Kid Ory or Preston Jackson on trombone, Barney Bigard taking some of his finest tenor solos, and either Albert Nicholas or Darnell Howard on clarinet). After Russell officially became a bandleader, his first date was with his "Burning Eight" in early 1929, using a band similar to his upcoming orchestra except that Louis Metcalf was on trumpet and Nicholas was absent. The last three sessions in 1929 are among Russell's best, with such numbers as "Feelin' the Spirit," "Jersey Lightning," and "Broadway Rhythm" being among the finest big band Swing performances of the era. *1930–1931* is highlighted by "Saratoga Shout" (which has an impressive number of separate chord changes and themes), "Louisiana Swing," and "Panama." The last few numbers (from October 1930 on) are generally less interesting as the Russell band tried unsuccessfully to adjust its hot style to the early Depression dance band years. Both CDs are recommended. The Collectors Classics disc duplicates some of the same music (with two sessions from 1926 and one apiece from 1929, 1930, and 1931) but adds two alternate takes and concludes with the six selections cut by Luis Russell in his lone date from 1934, featuring some strong Rex Stewart cornet on "Ol' Man River."

1945–1946 reissues Russell's final recordings and these are all quite obscure. Unfortunately only three of the 22 numbers are instrumentals ("Boogie In The Basement," "1280 Jive," and "Luke The Spook") and, although his band sounds fine in ensembles, it is a no-name outfit other than drummer Roy Haynes. The so-so vocalist Lee Richardson dominates 13 of the selections, so the overall music is quite forgettable.

JAN SAVITT
b. Sept. 4, 1913, Petrograd, Russia, d. Oct. 4, 1948, Sacramento, CA

Jan Savitt's Top Hatters are best remembered for their one big hit, "720 in the Books" ("Quaker City Jazz" and "It's a Wonderful World" also did well), but it was actually a fine all-round jazz orchestra. Savitt, born in Russia and the son of a drummer in the Imperial Regimental Band of the Czar, was considered a brilliant young violinist by the time he was six. Moving to the United States with his family nine years later, Savitt studied at the Curtis Institute in Philadelphia and was the youngest musician to ever be a member of the Philadelphia Orchestra, working under Leopold Stokowski.

Savitt, however, enjoyed Swing and he chose to work regularly on the radio. He organized an orchestra for station KYW in 1937 and began performing in public with his big band the following year. Savitt's Top Hatters had a distinctive shuffle rhythm, was the first white orchestra to regularly feature a black singer (Bon Bon, whose real name was George Tunnel), and had a fine trumpet soloist in Johnny Austin during 1939–40. Savitt's band recorded regularly during 1937–42, adding a six-piece string section (including his own violin) in 1942. The orchestra was based in Los Angeles during its later years, breaking up after its leader's premature death, from a cerebral hemorrhage suffered while on his way to a gig in 1948, when he was just 35.

LPS TO SEARCH FOR

Jan Savitt recorded extensively for Variety (1937), Bluebird (1937–38), Decca (1939–41), and Victor (1941–42), although extremely little during his last six years. Almost nothing is currently available on CD. *The Top Hatters* (Decca 79243) has some of Savitt's prime records from 1939–41, including "That's a Plenty," "Vol Vistu Gaily Star," "720 in the Books,"

"It's a Wonderful World," and "It's Time to Jump and Shout." *1939* (Hindsight 213), a set of radio transcriptions, also includes a version of "720 in the Books" but also features a lot more obscure material. Hard to believe that Jan Savitt was only 25 at the time. His recordings are long overdue to be reissued on CD.

ARTIE SHAW
b. May 23, 1910, New York, NY

A giant of the Swing era and one of the finest jazz clarinetists of all time, Artie Shaw led more significant orchestras during the big band era than anyone else: five. An outspoken intellectual, Shaw seemed to spend much of his musical career running away from success but finding it at every turn despite himself!

Born Arthur Arshawsky, he started playing saxophone when he was 12 and developed remarkably fast. Soon he was playing with the New Haven High School band and leading the Bellevue Ramblers. Shaw was a strong enough musician at age 15 to go on the road. He played with a variety of obscure groups during the mid- to late-1920s (including those of Johnny Cavallaro, Joe Cantor, Merle Jacobs, Austin Wylie, and Irving Aaronson, with whom he made his recording debut), moved to New York in 1930, and freelanced locally (including with Paul Specht, Vincent Lopez, Roger Wolfe Kahn, and Red Nichols). After working as a studio musician for a couple of years, in 1934 Artie Shaw left music for the first time to live on a

During 1938–39 Artie Shaw had his most popular orchestra, helped by the definitive big band singer Helen Forrest.

farm and attempt to write a novel. Eventually running out of money, he returned to New York and the anonymous world of studio work.

Artie Shaw's big break came a year later. He was hired to lead a fill-in group for ten minutes at a major big band concert on April 8, 1936. Rather than putting together a loud orchestra, Shaw featured his clarinet on "Interlude in B Flat" with a string quartet and a rhythm section. His performance was the surprise hit of the concert (he had to play the piece a second time as an encore) and it led to calls for him to form a band of his own. Shaw took the radical step of putting together an ensemble consisting of four horns (including Tony Pastor on tenor and trumpeter Lee Castle), a string quartet, and a four-piece rhythm section. Although string sections had appeared before in dance music (most notably by Paul Whiteman), they were usually much larger and utilized for semi-classical works rather than as part of a Swing-oriented big band. Shaw tried his best and made some fine recordings, but his first major band lasted only a relatively brief time.

Disappointed by the commercial failure of his string group, a few months later the clarinetist formed a more conventional orchestra. It struggled for a year and then, at Shaw's first session for its new label, Bluebird (on July 24, 1938), he recorded "Begin the Beguine." The song was such a hit that almost overnight the Artie Shaw Orchestra was considered a sensation. Other high points of the year for Shaw included "Indian Love Call" (featuring Tony Pastor), "Any Old Time" (Billie Holiday's one recording during her brief and difficult time with the white orchestra), and such numbers as "Back Bay Shuffle," "Nightmare" (Shaw's theme song), "Nonstop Flight," and "Softly As in a Morning Sunrise." By 1939, with Helen Forrest as the group's regular vocalist, Georgie Auld soloing on tenor, and drummer Buddy Rich propelling the big band, for a few months (before the rise of Glenn Miller) the Artie Shaw Orchestra was considered the most popular in the world.

Unfortunately, being an adored celebrity did not suit Shaw's temperament. The pressure got to him, and in November

1939 he simply walked off the bandstand and fled to Mexico for two months, leaving his musicians to fend for themselves. Under Auld's leadership, the band fulfilled its engagements and recorded again but soon broke up.

Artie Shaw loved music too much to stay away for long. He put together a string orchestra for a record date on March 3, 1940, and lightning struck a second time when his very popular recording of "Frenesi" became a best-seller. Shaw, who was in Los Angeles to appear in the Fred Astaire movie *Second Chorus* (during which he debuted "Concerto for Clarinet"), soon put together his third orchestra, one that had a full string section and such soloists as trumpeter Billy Butterfield, trombonist Jack Jenney, Jerry Jerome on tenor, and pianist Johnny Guarnieri. The orchestra would become known as the "Stardust Band" due to an absolutely perfect version of that standard, featuring classic solos by Butterfield, Jenney, and Shaw. For the fun of it, the clarinetist also recorded with Butterfield and his rhythm section (with Guarnieri on harpsichord) as the Gramercy Five. The result: another major hit in "Summit Ridge Drive."

Eventually tiring of what could arguably be called his greatest orchestra, Shaw broke up the outfit in early 1941. After leading an intriguing interracial group (with Red Allen, J. C. Higginbotham, Benny Carter, Lena Horne, and strings) for a brief period, he organized his fourth big band, one containing some of his favorite alumni (most notably Georgie Auld and Johnny Guarnieri), strings, trombonist-arranger Ray Coniff, and trumpeter-singer Hot Lips Page. Shaw seemed to have fun with this orchestra, but in the spring of 1942 he broke it up when he joined the Navy.

While in the military he led a service band (unfortunately unrecorded) that toured the Pacific war theater. By late 1943 Shaw was seriously ill, and he was given a medical discharge in February 1944. He completely recovered within a few months, and a new big band was formed later in the year that featured trumpeter Roy Eldridge, pianist Dodo Marmarosa, guitarist Barney Kessel, and such numbers as "Little Jazz," "Lady Day," and a remarkable Ray Coniff arrangement of "Summertime." In addition, Shaw, Eldridge, and the rhythm section (no harpsichord this time) recorded as a new Gramercy Five.

Although Shaw recorded fairly frequently in 1946 (featuring Mel Torme and the Mel-Tones on some numbers, including a memorable "What Is This Thing Called Love?"), he was no longer leading a regular big band and was edging his way out of the music scene. Mostly inactive during 1947–48, Shaw toyed with the idea of becoming a classical clarinetist, and then in September 1949 he put together his last important big band, a bop-oriented ensemble that included trumpeter Don Fagerquist, altoist Herbie Steward, Al Cohn and Zoot Sims on tenors, and guitarist Jimmy Raney. Shaw had been open to the influence of bop as early as 1945 and had high hopes for this band, but it flopped commercially; the public wanted him to endlessly play "Begin the Beguine." The clarinetist made occasional recordings during the next few years and during 1953–54 led his last group, a final Gramercy Five, in which he was joined by a modern rhythm section (with pianist Hank Jones and either Tal Farlow or Joe Puma on guitar). In the recordings from that period, Artie Shaw showed that he was still a brilliant (and surprisingly modern) clarinetist. However, this musician, who formerly had run away from success, was now frustrated by a public indifferent to his newer music. In 1955 he made the rather surprising decision to permanently retire from music.

In the years since his musical retirement, Artie Shaw has written several books, sporadically fronted a big band (beginning in the mid-1980s) that recreates his orchestra's classic arrangements, and been continually eager to express his opinions on a wide variety of subjects. But having achieved near-perfection in his prime, he has never been tempted to play his clarinet again.

●

8 *The Best of the Big Bands / June 11, 1936–Oct. 30, 1936 / Columbia 46156*

7 *It Goes to Your Feet / Nov. 30,1936–May 13, 1937 / Columbia/Legacy 53423*

Artie Shaw's earliest recordings as a bandleader are on these two CDs. Although *The Best of the Big Bands* does not bother with such "frivolities" as personnel lists or dates, it does reissue Shaw's first four sessions (16 cuts in all) complete and in chronological order. During this period of time his band featured four horns, four strings, and a four-piece rhythm section. Its music was gentler than that offered by most of its competitors, and the ensemble sound was quite appealing. "The Japanese Sandman," "A Pretty Girl Is Like a Melody," "Sugar Foot Stomp," and "The Skeleton in the Closet" are the strongest instrumentals; Peg La Centra,

Tony Pastor, and Wes Vaughan provide vocals. *It Goes to Your Feet* has the last 15 selections from Shaw's first band (including "Sobbin' Blues," "Copenhagen," and "Streamline"), plus the first three cuts by his second orchestra, a more typical ten-horn, four-rhythm big band. That orchestra would record 33 more selections for Columbia-owned labels during 1937–38, but thus far they have not been reissued on CD.

9   *Begin the Beguine* / July 24, 1938–July 23, 1941 / Bluebird 6274

7   *Personal Best* / July 24, 1938–July 19, 1945 / Bluebird 61099

7   *22 Original Big Band Recordings* / 1938–1939 / Hindsight 401

7   *Radio Years, Vol. 1* / Nov. 25, 1938–Dec. 30, 1938 / Jazz Unlimited 2018

7   *Traffic Jam* / Dec. 14, 1938–May 30, 1939 / Natasha Imports 4013

Artie Shaw's Victor recordings would make a spectacular boxed set, but RCA has thus far only reissued his music on CD in piecemeal fashion. *Begin the Beguine* is a perfect introductory set to Artie Shaw, for it has the most famous recordings of his second and third bands, including "Nightmare" (his theme), Billie Holiday on "Any Old Time," "Traffic Jam," "Frenesi," "Summit Ridge Drive," "Star Dust," and the title cut, plus a couple of live numbers from 1939 (with Buddy Rich pushing the band on "Carioca"). Artie Shaw himself was asked to pick out his favorite recordings for *Personal Best*, and the only repeat from the other CD is "Any Old Time." Very much a sampler, the release has seven broadcast performances (including an earlier version of "Star Dust") and music from the second, third ("Concerto for Clarinet"), fourth, and fifth ("The Maid with the Flaccid Air") orchestras. *22 Original Big Band Recordings*, *Radio Years*, and *Traffic Jam* each feature Artie Shaw's 1938–39 big band on radio performances. Stars of the band during the era include Shaw, singer Helen Forrest, Georgie Auld on tenor, and (by 1939) drummer Rich. Unfortunately, no dates or personnel are given on *22 Original Big Band Recordings*, but the music (taken from many different performances) is excellent, with extended renditions of "Shine on Harvest Moon" (which is five minutes) and "If I Had You," plus a few songs not otherwise recorded by Shaw. *Radio Years* has two

complete broadcasts, with opening and closing themes and such hot tunes as "Sobbin Blues," "Copenhagen," and "Jungle Drums." *Traffic Jam* is more of the same from December 14, 1938, and February–May 1939. Highlights include "Non-Stop Flight," "Carioca," "Back Bay Shuffle," and "Copenhagen."

9   *The Complete Gramercy Five Sessions* / Sept. 3, 1940–Aug. 2, 1945 / Bluebird 7637

8   *Blues in the Night* / Sept. 2, 1941–July 26, 1945 / Bluebird 2432

The first two versions of Artie Shaw's Gramercy Five have all 15 of their performances reissued in their single Bluebird CD. The original group (with Billy Butterfield and Johnny Guarnieri on harpsichord) had a major hit in "Summit Ridge Drive" and surprisingly only cut eight songs (including "Special Delivery Stomp," "My Blue Heaven," and "Smoke Gets in Your Eyes"). The 1945 version was a bit more conventional but also quite strong, with Roy Eldridge, Dodo Marmarosa, and Barney Kessel heard as soloists. They cut only six songs plus an alternate take. Delightful music. *Blues in the Night* is a sampler of some of the better recordings from Shaw's fourth and fifth bands, putting the focus on the solo work of Hot Lips Page and Eldridge. Page is brilliant on "Blues in the Night" and the two-part "St. James Infirmary" (the second part is heard in two takes), while Eldridge shines on "Lady Day," "Little Jazz," Eddie Santer's reworking of "Summertime," and "The Man I Love." It is a pity that RCA has yet to release all of its Artie Shaw recordings on CD, so in the meantime these two discs will partly suffice.

5   *Mixed Bag* / Sept. 1945–Feb. 1954 / Music Masters 01612–65119

8   *1949* / 1949 / Music Masters 0234

Mixed Bag contains some of Artie Shaw's Musicraft recordings of 1945–46. There are four selections with his fourth big band (featuring trumpeter Roy Eldridge) and 14 numbers with a studio string orchestra that is often as close to middle-of-the-road mood music as it is to jazz; pleasant but not too substantial. Best are the selections that feature Mel Torme and the Mel-Tones (particularly "What Is This Thing Called Love?"). Wrapping up this CD is a number from 1954 by Shaw's Gramercy Five ("Sunny Side Up") that had not been included in his "last recordings" series. After spending 1947–48 out of music, Shaw came back in 1949 and formed a bebop orchestra. The group (Shaw's sixth and final big band) recorded only six songs in the studios for Decca (none reissued on CD), but the 1990 CD titled *1949* includes a full live set by the orchestra. With trumpeter Don Fagerquist, altoists Herbie Steward and Frank Socolow, Al Cohn (who gets a lot of solo space) and Zoot Sims on tenors, and guitarist Jimmy Raney, this ensemble definitely had potential. They perform updated versions of Swing standards and some originals with cool and restrained excitement that sometimes looks a bit towards West Coast jazz, too. Pity that this band did not last.

9 | *The Last Recordings / Feb. 1954–June 1954 / Music Masters 65071*

9 | *More Last Recordings / Feb. 1954–June 1954 / Music Masters 65101*

In 1954, Artie Shaw recorded fairly extensively for Verve with his new Gramercy Five, a group consisting of pianist Hank Jones, bassist Tommy Potter, drummer Irv Kluger, either Tal Farlow or Joe Puma on guitar, and sometimes vibraphonist Joe Roland. The pair of double-CDs released by Music Masters contain most of the music that this group recorded. Artie Shaw is heard throughout at the peak of his powers. *More Last Recordings* is particularly interesting, because the forward-thinking Shaw (who is quite boppish in spots) digs into many of his old hits (including "Begin the Beguine," "Stardust," "Summit Ridge Drive," and "Fren-

esi") and comes up with completely fresh solos, showing listeners that he really did choose to retire when he was right in his musical prime.

LPS TO SEARCH FOR

There is a lot of Artie Shaw on LP that has yet to be reissued. *The Complete Artie Shaw & The Rhythmakers Volume One* (Swingdom 7001/2), *Volume Two* (Swingdom 7003/4), and *Volumes Five Through Eight* (Swingdom 7005), six LPs in all, have all of Shaw's radio transcriptions from 1937–38. *The Complete Artie Shaw Vol. I* (Bluebird AXM2-5517), *Vol. II* (Bluebird AXM2-5533), *Vol. III* (Bluebird AXM2-5558), *Vol. IV* (Bluebird AXM2-5572), *Vol. V* (Bluebird AXM2-5576), *Vol. VI* (Bluebird AXM2-5579), and *Vol. VII* (Bluebird AXM2-5580) reissue on seven double-LPs every Shaw Victor recording (covering the years 1938–45), including alternate takes, music that deserves to be on CD. *Artie Shaw at the Hollywood Palladium* (Hep 19) has some rare radio broadcasts of the clarinetist's third and fourth bands, including the Gramercy Five on "Dr. Livingston I Presume." And the 1949 orchestra is heard live on *The Pied Piper* (First Heard 1005), an English LP that does not duplicate Music Masters' *1949*.

FILMS

Artie Shaw's orchestra is well featured in *Dancing Co-Ed* (1939). A transition string band with Billy Butterfield joins Shaw in *Second Chorus* (1940), most notably on "Concerto for Clarinet." Years later Shaw acted in the dramatic movie *Crash* (1978).

BOBBY SHERWOOD

b. May 30, 1914, Indianapolis, IN, d. Jan. 23, 1981, Auburn, MS

Bobby Sherwood was a multi-talented musician who played trumpet, and rhythm guitar, wrote arrangements, and even sang. He formed his Swing band rather late in the big band era and, although he had a quick hit in "The Elk's Parade," his orchestra never did prosper.

Sherwood was born to parents who were active in vaudeville, so he was familiar with show business from an early age. He began to play professionally in the late 1920s, and in 1933, when he was 19, he replaced the late Eddie Lang as Bing Crosby's guitar accompanist. After three years with Bing, Sherwood became a busy studio musician in Los Angeles during 1936–42, popping up on jazz records now and then, including playing guitar with Artie Shaw on the "Frenesi" session. In 1942 he was persuaded by Johnny Mercer to form a big band of his own and was immediately signed to Mercer's label, Capitol. Although Sherwood had planned to just have a studio group and stay in Los Angeles, "The Elk's Parade" was such a big hit that he had to form a real band and tour the country. Playing mostly trumpet in addition to writing the majority of the arrangements and taking some vocals, Sherwood worked hard for seven years without much success. Among his sidemen were tenors Stan Getz, Zoot Sims, Dave Pell, and Flip Phillips, baritonist Serge Chaloff, and trombonist Carl Fontana. After breaking up his orchestra in 1949, Bobby Sherwood worked as an actor and occasional musician on radio and television.

●

LPS TO SEARCH FOR

Few of Bobby Sherwood's recordings are available on CD. The best one of his LP's, the jazz-oriented *Out of Sherwood's Forest* (IAJRC 35), has a variety of rarities from 1942–47, but unfortunately "The Elk's Parade" and his other minor hit, "Sherwood's Forest," were purposely left off. His radio transcriptions were made available on *1944–1946* (Circle 28) and *More 1944–1946* (Circle 115), which alternate instrumentals with decent vocal numbers. Sherwood's 1945–47 band (with

Herbie Haymer on tenor) is heard on live broadcasts on *Politely* (Golden Era 15018). Sherwood's four numbers for Coral in 1954, in which he overdubbed all of the instrumental parts plus four vocals, have never been reissued.

FILMS

Bobby Sherwood's orchestra is in *Campus Sleuth* (1948), and he appears in the film *Pal Joey* (1957), as a bandleader!

FREDDY SLACK

b. Aug. 7, 1910, La Crosse, WI, d. Aug. 10, 1965, Hollywood, CA

A talented pianist who was a valuable part of two other major big bands, Freddie Slack (helped by singer Ella Mae Morse) had a best-seller in "Cow Cow Boogie" and led one of the more promising Swing orchestras to emerge in the early 1940s.

Slack originally played drums in high school and did not specialize on piano until he was 17. He freelanced around Chicago for a few years and then worked in Los Angeles with the bands of Henry Halsted, Earl Burtnett, Archie Rosate, and Lenny Hayton. After two years with Ben Pollack (1934–36), Slack became a member of the Jimmy Dorsey Orchestra (1936–39). A talented Swing pianist, Slack would become best known for his expertise at boogie-woogie. When Ray McKinley left Dorsey to join Will Bradley's band, Slack came along. During his period with Bradley, the pianist starred on "Beat Me Daddy, Eight to the Bar" and other big band boogie-woogie numbers that made the orchestra famous.

In 1941 Freddie Slack (who that year recorded four numbers backing Big Joe Turner) formed his own big band, which was based in Los Angeles. "Cow Cow Boogie," from 1942, put his orchestra on the map, and other popular numbers included "Strange Cargo," "Mister Five by Five," and "Blackout Boogie." During 1942–43 clarinetist Barney Bigard was in the band and Slack's orchestra recorded with such guests as future blues legend T-Bone Walker and Benny Carter. However, his big band faded out by 1947–48 and Slack (who actually preferred sweet music to boogie-woogie) struggled along out of the spotlight, playing in small Los Angeles clubs during his final 20 years; his last record was in 1955.

●

LPS TO SEARCH FOR

Behind the Eight-Beat (Pausa 9027) has a sampling of some of Freddie Slack's best recordings as a leader, including "Strange Cargo," "Southpaw Serenade," "Blackout Boogie," and "Cow Cow Boogie." In addition there are three numbers from 1945 in which Slack is showcased with a quartet.

FILMS

Freddie Slack performs "Cow Cow Boogie" both in *Reveille with Beverly* (1943) and in the television special (now available on video) *The Swingin' Singin' Years* (1960).

CLAUDE THORNHILL

b. Aug. 10, 1909, Terre Haute, IN, d. July 1, 1965, New York, NY

Pianist Claude Thornhill led one of the most unusual big bands of the 1940s, one that fell between Swing and sweet music and in its later period was a bit bebop-oriented while influencing 1950's West Coast jazz. Thornhill's orchestra often emphasized ballads and vocals (as a sweet band would), but it had an unique sound, with very little vibrato, lots of long floating tones, and unexpected colors.

Thornhill began playing piano when he was ten, and, after two years at the Cincinnati Conservatory and studying at the Curtis Institute in Philadelphia, he worked for a short period with the bands of Austin Wylie and Hal Kemp. After moving to New York in the early 1930s, Thornhill played with Don Voorhees, Freddy Martin, Paul Whiteman, and Benny Goodman (1934). He also had stints with Leo Reisman, Ray Noble's American Band, and André Kostelanetz. Thornhill helped singer Maxine Sullivan get her start (working as her musical director when she hit it big with "Loch Lomond") and then was active in the Hollywood studios as a pianist and arranger for a few years.

In 1940 Claude Thornhill formed his own orchestra and, in addition to his arrangements, Bill Borden did some important writing for the band. The instrumentation was conventional at first, but somehow the band sounded different, with all six reeds sometimes playing clarinets in unison. Thornhill was expert at adapting classical themes to a dance band style, as he showed on Brahms's "Hungarian Dance No. 5" and Schumann's "Traumerei." His theme song, "Snowfall," was particularly haunting, "Portrait of a Guinea Farm" gained some attention, and "Where or When" was a minor hit. Thornhill helped introduce the beautiful "Autumn Nocturne" and utilized Irving Fazola's clarinet in different ways as a lead voice. In 1942 Gil Evans began to write inventive charts for Thornhill (such as "Buster's Last Stand" and "There's a Small Hotel") and both a vocal group (the Snowflakes) and two French horns were added to the band. However, World War II intervened and Thornhill joined the Navy (playing for a time in Artie Shaw's service band) for three years.

After Thornhill was discharged in late 1945, he put together a new orchestra, using some of the same musicians from his earlier group; "A Sunday Kind of Love" (with Fran Warren on the vocal) was popular. By 1947, Thornhill's big band (which now included not only two French horns but a tuba) was particularly intriguing. Although the leader's tinkling piano style was virtually unchanged, his group had such modern soloists as altoist Lee Konitz and trumpeter Red Rodney (in addition to clarinetist Danny Polo and guitarist Barry Galbraith). Most importantly, Gil Evans was contributing many stimulating charts, including "Sorta Kinda," "Thrivin' on a Riff," "Anthropology," "Robbins' Nest," "Yardbird Suite," and "Donna Lee." In fact, the Claude Thornhill Orchestra during this era helped set the stage for the Cool Jazz of the 1950s, most notably Miles Davis's nonet.

Claude Thornhill kept his stimulating and atmospheric big band going into 1950, with recording dates on an occasional basis during the following decade, including a full set of Gerry Mulligan arrangements. In his last years he mostly led a small group and was in semi-retirement before dying from a heart attack at age 55.

●

9 *Snowfall / Sept. 20, 1940 – July 9, 1941 / Hep 1058*
The first 25 studio recordings of the Claude Thornhill Orchestra are on this single CD, tracing the progress of Thornhill's unusual band during its first year. The pianist-leader is mostly the main soloist, although there are spots for Irving Fazola's clarinet, trumpeter Rusty Dedrick, and Hammon Russum on tenor. With Thornhill and Bill Borden contributing the arrangements, there are decent vocals contributed by Dick Harding, Bob Jenney, Jane Essex, and Kay Doyle. However, it is the moody instrumentals that

stick in one's mind, including "Hungarian Dance No. 5," "Traumerei," "Portrait of a Guinea Farm," "Where or When," and "Snowfall."

7 *Best of the Big Bands / Mar. 10, 1941 – Dec. 17, 1947 / Columbia 46152*
Some of Claude Thornhill's better recordings are on this decent sampler. His 1941–42 band is represented by seven cuts, including "Snowfall," "Where or When," "Portrait of a Guinea Farm," and "Buster's Last Stand." Thornhill's

1946–47 orchestra is featured on the other nine selections, highlighted by "A Sunday Kind of Love" and Gil Evans's arrangements on "Robbin's Nest," "Yardbird Suite," and "Anthropology." The CD overall is not quite definitive (personnel and recording dates are missing), but it does have some of Thornhill's finest moments on records and serves as a strong introduction to his music.

8 *Transcription Performances / Sept. 25, 1947–Dec. 17, 1947 / Hep 60*

8 *The 1948 Transcription Performances / Apr. 1948–Oct. 1948 / Hep 17*

By 1947, Gil Evans was Claude Thornhill's most interesting arranger and the orchestra included such players as trumpeters Red Rodney and Ed Zandy, altoist Lee Konitz, clarinetist Danny Polo, and trombonist Tak Takvorian. The 1947 big band's radio transcriptions are on Hep 60, and these include alternate versions of "Robbins' Nest," "Polka Dots and Moonbeams," "Anthropology," "I Get the Blues When It Rains," "Sorta Kinda," "Donna Lee," and other memorable charts. Some of the same arrangements are in *The 1948 Transcription Performances* and the group is similar except that Brew Moore is on tenor during the last few numbers and Gerry Mulligan was now one of Thornhill's key writers. Fans of the Claude Thornhill Orchestra who are frustrated by the unavailability of some of his studio recordings will want to go out their way to acquire these two valuable CDs.

LPS TO SEARCH FOR

Tapestries (Affinity 1040), a British double-LP, has 32 of Claude Thornhill's best recordings, including 17 Gil Evans arrangements and quite a few numbers not on Columbia's so-called "Best of the Big Bands." *1941 & 1947* (Circle 19) and *1947* (Hindsight 108) add to the legacy of Thornhill's legacy by issuing radio transcriptions that do not duplicate the ones put out by Hep.

CHICK WEBB

b. Feb. 10, 1902, Baltimore, MD, d. June 16, 1939, Baltimore, MD

One of the top drummers of the Swing era, Chick Webb overcame serious physical problems to become a major big band-leader before passing away at the peak of his fame.

Named William Webb and nicknamed Chick, he was stricken early on by tuberculosis of the spine, which resulted in Webb's becoming a dwarf with a hunched back. Despite this, he began playing drums as a child and was a professional musician from an early age. After moving to New York in 1925, Webb led his own quintet at the Black Bottom Club for five months, and he would be a leader during nearly all of his career. The drummer played in all the main New York venues of the mid- to late-1920s, including the Paddock Club, Roseland, and the Cotton Club.

Starting in 1931, Chick Webb was a fixture at the Savoy Ballroom, and his band was soon the first to perform Edgar Sampson's "Stompin' at the Savoy." Webb began recording as a leader that year (with trombonist Jimmy Harrison and altoist Benny Carter among his sidemen) and quite regularly starting in late 1933. The Chick Webb Orchestra featured Taft Jordan and Bobby Stark on trumpets, trombonist Sandy Williams, tenor saxophonist Elmer Williams, and altoist Edgar Sampson, who, in addition to "Savoy," contributed to the band's repertoire such songs as "Don't Be That Way," "If Dreams Come True," and "Blue Lou." In addition, Wayman Carver (featured on four numbers with "Chick Webb and His Little Chicks") was one of jazz's first flute soloists (virtually the only one during the Swing era), and altoist Louis Jordan had his start with Webb. In 1935 the Chick Webb Orchestra added its most important new member, 18-year-old Ella Fitzgerald. Although not certain at first, the drummer soon saw her potential, and within a short time she was considered a major star, second in importance in the orchestra only to Webb himself.

Chick Webb's drumming was an inspiration to Gene Krupa, Buddy Rich, and (later on) Louie Bellson, although he soloed relatively little on records. Considered King of the Savoy by the mid-'30s , Webb "defeated" most of the other major Swing orchestras in "battle of the band" contests (including Benny Goodman and Count Basie, although he lost to Duke Elling-

This unique jam session featured drummer Chick Webb, clarinetist Artie Shaw, and pianist Duke Ellington, three rather major big bandleaders.

ton). Ella Fitzgerald's recording of "A-Tisket, A-Tasket" on May 2, 1938, was a major hit, and it is a measure of her popularity that 19 of the Chick Webb recordings from that year featured her singing.

Heart trouble started to plague Chick Webb in the summer of 1938 as well as pleurisy, and he spent a few short periods in the hospital before passing away the following year at the age of 37. His immortal last words were "I'm sorry but I gotta go." Ella Fitzgerald was designated to front Webb's big band, and the orchestra stayed together until she went solo in 1941.

10 *1929–1934 / June 14, 1929–Nov. 19, 1934 / Classics 502*

10 *1935–1938 / June 12, 1935–May 3, 1938 / Classics 517*

7 *Spinnin' the Webb / June 14, 1929–Feb. 17, 1939 / GRP/ Decca 635*

The two Classics CDs have every selection released under Chick Webb's name other than the ones featuring Ella Fitzgerald vocals (those are available in their Ella series) and the band's final two instrumentals. *1929–1934* contains two early tracks from 1929, a 1931 session that has one of the first versions of Benny Carter's "Blues in My Heart," and Webb's Savoy Orchestra's first 20 recordings. Of this last, the high-

lights include Taft Jordan's Louis Armstrong tribute on "On the Sunny Side of the Street" and the original versions of "When Dreams Come True," "Stompin' at the Savoy," "Don't Be That Way," and "Blue Lou." *1935–1938* continues at the same level, highlighted by the four numbers from Chick Webb's Little Chicks, plus "Go Harlem," "Clap Hands! Here Comes Charley," and "Liza." Typically for an American reissue program, *Spinnin' the Webb* is merely a sampler with 20 cuts (as compared to Classics' 25 apiece), although it does include the two later instrumentals ("Who Ya Hunchin'" and "In the Groove at the Grove") not included in the Classics sets.

PAUL WHITEMAN

b. Mar. 28, 1890, Denver, CO, d. Dec. 29, 1967, Doylestown, PA

Paul Whiteman led the most popular big band of the 1920s, one that had a million seller in "Whispering" back in 1920. Billed as the "King of Jazz," Whiteman could more accurately be called the "King of the Jazz Age." He put on a variety show, performing superior dance music, novelties, vocal features, semi-classical works, and occasional jazz numbers. A major influence on big bands, ironically Whiteman was a bit out-of-place during the Swing era, not quite certain how to handle the new music.

Paul Whiteman's father, Wilberforce Whiteman, was a top music teacher; one of his students would be Jimmie Lunceford. The younger Whiteman started playing violin when he was seven and was classically trained. He worked with the Denver Symphony Orchestra for a couple years starting in 1912 and, after moving to San Francisco in 1915, he became a member of the San Francisco Symphony Orchestra. After serving in the Navy during World War I, Whiteman formed his dance orchestra in 1919, playing in San Francisco and Los Angeles before working his way to New York. He was a hit from the start and his was the first big band to catch on. In addition to "Whispering," "The Japanese Sandman," "When Day Is Done," and "Hot Lips" (featuring his early star cornetist, Henry Busse) were quite popular. At a prestigious concert at Aeolian Hall (which he called "An Experiment in Modern Music"), Whiteman debuted "Rhapsody in Blue," with the composer, George Gershwin, on piano. Although the jazz content of his band was light in the early years, by late 1927 Whiteman had a particularly strong outfit, with cornetist Bix Beiderbecke, Frankie Trumbauer on C-melody sax, Jimmy Dorsey on clarinet and alto, and a vocal trio called the Rhythm Boys that consisted of Harry Barris, Al Rinker, and the unknown Bing Crosby. Bill Challis's arrangements best showed off the potential of the jazz orchestra while not discarding its dance band elements.

Whiteman always had a large ensemble and at its height it was 27 pieces, including six reed players, a full string section, two pianos, banjo, guitar, tuba, and string bass; that is not counting his many singers! After filming the rather erratic movie *The King of Jazz* (at the time the band included violinist Joe Venuti and guitarist Eddie Lang, although Bix Beiderbecke was gone), Whiteman was forced to cut costs a bit and drop down to a more manageable 18 pieces. He survived the Depression years due to his famous name. Mildred Bailey was one of his singers and Bunny Berigan spent a few months with Whiteman in 1933. One would think that with the rise of the big band era in 1935, Whiteman would have been leading the way. But, despite the presence of trombonist Jack Teagarden, trumpeter Charlie Teagarden, and longtime member Frankie Trumbauer, Whiteman's music remained an increasingly dated variety show, and he rarely took advantage of his orchestra's jazz strength, often preferring to present extended concert works like "Cuban Overture" and "An American in Paris." There were some intriguing experiments in 1938–39, with recordings by Whiteman's "Swing Wing" (featuring the Teagardens but with weak vocalists), the "Swinging Strings," his "Bouncing Brass," and a "Sax Soctette," but those records failed to sell well. Paul Whiteman's band was a regular on radio and he appeared in some films, but by the early '40s he was considered a legendary has-been. In 1945 Paul Whiteman recorded remakes of a couple of early 1920s arrangements ("San" and "Wang Wang Blues") and that served as a fitting close to his career, although he remained active on a part-time basis into the early 1960s.

Paul Whiteman's Swing era recordings are almost entirely unavailable, although his 1927–29 performances are constantly reissued due to the participation of Bix Beiderbecke. The Mr. Music CD has two complete radio broadcasts from 1938. Artie Shaw is a guest on one program (playing "I Surrender Dear" with Whiteman and "Flying Down to Floy Floy" with a quartet), while Bobby Hackett (with a Dixieland septet that includes clarinetist Pee Wee Russell and rhythm guitarist Eddie Condon) performs two numbers on the other broadcast. Otherwise, Joan Edwards has two vocals on each date, the Modernaires are heard from a couple of times, and trombonist Jack Teagarden (near the end of his five-year stint with Whiteman) gets a few solos. But the Paul Whiteman Orchestra itself did not display much of an original personality at this point. The Capitol set has what was really Whiteman's last act other than reunions. There are eight numbers from 1942, including "I've Found a New Baby," Billie Holiday guesting on "Trav'lin Light," two vocals by Martha Tilton, and a delightful version of "The Old Music Masters" with Jack Teagarden and Johnny Mercer. From 1945, the two interesting remakes of early 1920s arrangements of "San" and "Wang Wang Blues" (including some of the original musicians) are nostalgic and still pretty hot. The CD concludes with 1951 versions of "An American in Paris" and "Rhapsody in Blue" featuring pianist Roy Bargy and a studio orchestra.

LPS TO SEARCH FOR

The French Jazz Tribune double-LP *Jazz à La King* (RCA 42413) traces Paul Whiteman's career during 1920–36, from the early days of "Whispering" and "Hot Lips" to "Nobody's Sweetheart" and Mildred Bailey on "Rockin' Chair."

FILMS

Paul Whiteman's *King of Jazz* (1930) has its moments (including 90 seconds by the duo of Venuti and Lang and a feature for the Rhythm Boys) but a lot of very tiresome stretches. Whiteman's other film appearances include *Thanks a Million* (1935), *Strike Up the Band* (1940), *Atlantic City* (1944), *Rhapsody in Blue* (1945), and *The Fabulous Dorseys* (1947).

SIDEMEN, COMBO LEADERS, AND SINGERS OF THE SWING ERA

Trumpeters

Because there were literally thousands of talented musicians and singers active during the Swing era, the emphasis in this portion of the book is on the soloists, key vocalists, and leaders, those special performers who consistently made highly individual and personal statements that added to the legacy of Swing music.

For trumpeters of the Swing era, Louis Armstrong was everyone's main influence initially, particularly in phrasing and tone. The best trumpeters of the period were able to use Satch's style as a point of departure in developing an approach of their own. Bunny Berigan at times exceeded Armstrong's abilities, before alcoholism cut short Bunny's life. Harry James became famous for his virtuosic flights, flexibility, and warm tone. And Roy Eldridge moved beyond Armstrong in harmonic complexity, influencing the young Dizzy Gillespie.

By the early 1930s, big bands were in the process of expanding from using two trumpeters to utilizing three. Generally there would be a main soloist, a first trumpeter, who was responsible for the high notes in the ensembles (and did not get featured too often), and a third player, who was versatile, a good reader, and an occasional soloist. The range of the first trumpeter really started to expand during the Swing era, starting with Tommy Stevenson in the Jimmie Lunceford Orchestra and continuing with such superb high-note specialists as Snooky Young, Al Killian, Cat Anderson, and (by the late 1940s) Maynard Ferguson.

The talented trumpeters in this section range from Swing stylists to Dixielanders, lyrical players to high-note screamers.

HENRY "RED" ALLEN

b. Jan. 7, 1908, Algiers, LA, d. Apr. 17, 1967, New York, NY

Henry "Red" Allen was the last great New Orleans trumpeter of the early days to make an impact. His sound was fairly original, but it was his highly expressive and eccentric phrasing that made him most unique. Although thought of in later years as a Dixieland trumpeter, he recorded quite frequently as a leader during the Swing era, and in the mid-1940s he led a jump band that looked toward early rhythm and blues.

Allen's father (Henry Allen, Sr.) was a trumpeter and the leader of the New Orleans Brass Band. Red, who briefly played violin and alto horn, started out playing with his father's group in parades at a very young age, and he was always quite proud of his New Orleans heritage. He also worked with other brass ensembles (including the Excelsior Band), played on the riverboats, and spent a couple of months in 1927 working with King Oliver in St. Louis and New York, making his recording debut with Clarence Williams before returning home.

In 1929 Red Allen moved to New York, began recording as a leader (where he was for a time promoted as a competitor of Louis Armstrong's), and became a member of the Luis Russell Orchestra. He was Russell's star soloist for three years (1929–32) and then was one of the key players with Fletcher Henderson's big band (1933–34) and the Mills Blue Rhythm Band (1934–37). Throughout the 1930s, in addition to leading his own recording groups, Allen freelanced on many other artists' dates, including with Billie Holiday and Jelly Roll Morton. He spent most of 1937–40 back with Luis Russell, when the orchestra was being used mostly as a backup group for Louis Armstrong. Although Allen was generally well featured during the first set of their concerts (before Satch came onstage), he was largely invisible on Armstrong's records, just playing in the ensembles. However, after going out on his own in 1940, Allen worked primarily as a leader, heading a sextet throughout the 1940s that at times included J. C. Higginbotham, Dan Stovall, and Ken Kersey. His vocalizing (which was heard as early as 1929) was raspy and quite personal, adding humor and additional color to his performances. By the 1950s, Allen (who counted off tempos with a "Whamp, Whamp!") was playing primarily Dixieland and Swing standards at the Metropole (his home base during 1954–65) in his own unique fashion. He was one of the stars of the 1957 telecast *The Sound of Jazz*, toured Europe with trombonist Kid Ory in 1959, and in the 1960s mostly worked in New York with his quartet.

A couple years before his death, Red Allen, whose solos remained quite unpredictable to the end, was called by modernist Don Ellis "the most avant-garde trumpeter heard in New York today," quite a testament to his consistently adventurous yet traditional style.

●

9 *1929–1933 / July 16, 1929–Nov. 9, 1933 / Classics 540*

7 *1929–30 Vol. 2 / July 16, 1929–Dec. 17, 1930 / JSP 333*
Henry "Red" Allen debuted as a leader in 1929 in spectacular fashion with "It Should Be You," showing that a major new trumpet voice was ready to play. *1929–1933* (the first in a series of Classics CDs that reissue all of his Swing era recordings as a leader) has his first 23 selections. Two numbers ("Funny Feathers Blues" and "How Do They Do It That Way?") feature blues singer Victoria Spivey, and there are seven songs that Allen co-leads with Coleman Hawkins. In addition to "It Should Be You," the highlights include "Biff'ly Blues," "Pleasin' Paul," "Sugar Hill Function," and "I Wish I Could Shimmy Like My Sister Kate." The earliest sessions find Allen joined by the nucleus of the Luis Russell Orchestra, but the tunes with Hawkins utilize an all-star group. While JSP's *1929–30 Vol. 1* duplicates much of the music on the Classics CD, *1929–30 Vol. 2* is made up mostly of alternate takes from the early sessions (including two very different versions of "It Should Be You") plus four numbers with singer Addie Spivey and a few of the less common Luis Russell performances.

8 *1933–1935 / Nov. 9, 1933–July 19, 1935 / Classics 551*

8 *1935–1936 / Nov. 8, 1935–Aug. 31, 1936 / Classics 575*

6 *1936–1937 / Oct. 12, 1936–Apr. 29, 1937 / Classics 590*

8 *1937–1941 / June 19, 1937–July 22, 1941 / Classics 628*

Red Allen did not work in public as a leader during 1933–39 but he recorded quite frequently at the head of small groups, usually taking vocals and always contributing some colorful and unpredictable trumpet. He was not always given the best material to perform but was often able to turn indifferent tunes into gems. *1933–1935* has such numbers as "You're Gonna Lose Your Gal," "There's a House in Harlem for Sale," "Pardon My Southern Accent," "Rug Cutter Swing," "Rosetta," and "Truckin' " among the better numbers. The supporting cast includes Dicky Wells, Buster Bailey, and Chu Berry, among others. *1935–1936* frequently has J. C. Higginbotham and Tab Smith helping out. "On Treasure Island" and "Take Me Back to My Boots and Saddle" are given exciting treatments and also well worth hearing are "Lost," "On the Beach at Bali-Bali," and "Algiers Stomp." Tab Smith and Billy Kyle help Allen out on *1936–1937*, but much of the material is not all that strong, with "He Ain't Got Rhythm" and "This Year's Kisses" being exceptions. *1937–1941* has eight selections from 1937 and four heated New Orleans–style numbers from 1940, and then the set is wrapped up by seven songs (including the two-part "Sometimes I'm Happy" and Ken Kersey's feature on "K. K. Boogie") from 1941 by Allen's new band, an exciting sextet with J. C. Higginbotham and Edmond Hall.

6 *Henry "Red" Allen with Willie "The Lion" Smith / Feb. 24, 1952–Apr. 13, 1952 / Storyville 6049*

10 *World on a String / Mar. 21, 1957–Apr. 10, 1957 / Bluebird 2497*

By the early 1950s, Henry "Red" Allen was playing no-holds-barred (and frequently riotous) Dixieland on a nightly basis. His Storyville set with pianist Willie "The Lion" Smith (using a quintet that includes Buster Bailey, trombonist Big Chief Russell Moore, and drummer Arthur Trappier) is taken from the *Dr. Jazz* radio series and finds Allen in spirited form, even if the music is not too subtle. In contrast, *World on a String* is a classic. Joined by a rather impressive group (an octet that includes Higginbotham, Bailey, and Hawkins), Allen sounds very inspired and quite adventurous. His solo on "I've Got the World on a String" is quite modern, he romps on "Love Is Just Around the Corner" and "Algiers Bounce," and his sidemen (particularly Hawkins) are right with him. This is music that defies any strict categorization and is one of the highlights of Red Allen's career.

LPS TO SEARCH FOR

The Rhythmakers (IAJRC 4) matches Allen with clarinetist Pee Wee Russell in 1932 on some hot jams, including "Oh Peter" and "Who Stole the Lock on the Hen House Door." *The Very Great* (Rarities 14) features the studio recordings of Allen's bands of 1941, 1944, and 1946. The heated music (which falls between Swing, early R&B, and Dixieland) features Allen with Don Stovall and Higginbotham and is difficult not to enjoy.

FILMS

Red Allen leads an all-star group in *The Sound of Jazz* telecast (1957) for two numbers. The exciting performances of "Wild Man Blues" and "Rosetta" give one a good idea of how Allen must have sounded with his band at the Metropole.

CAT ANDERSON

b. Dec. 12, 1916, Greenville, SC, d. Apr. 29, 1981, Norwalk, CA

William Alonzo "Cat" Anderson was the greatest high-note trumpeter of all time. His stratospheric solos (which were usually in tune) over Duke Ellington's ensemble were high points (literally) of Duke's concerts. Cat was also handy with a mute and a decent Swing soloist.

An orphan by the time he was four, Anderson grew up at the Jenkins Orphanage, where he played in their famous band starting when he was seven. He was with the Carolina Cotton Pickers during 1932–37 (making his recording debut with them in 1937) and also played with other territory bands, including the Sunset Royals Orchestra. Anderson was briefly with Lucky Millinder in 1942 and joined Lionel Hampton for a few months. His stint with Erskine Hawkins was cut short when he outshone the leader; he gigged with Sabby Lewis in Boston, was back with Hampton during 1944, and then became a member of the Duke Ellington Orchestra. Cat is most famous for his association with Duke, which continued on and off for 27 years (including 1944–47, 1950–59, 1961–71). Check out his incredible chorus on the 1969 version of "Satin Doll" included on *Duke Ellington's* 70th *Birthday Concert* (Blue Note 32746). He also led his own big bands during 1947–49 and 1959–60, without much success. After leaving Ellington, Cat Anderson settled in Los Angeles, where he worked now and then with Bill Berry's big band and Louis Bellson's orchestra.

●

LPS TO SEARCH FOR

Cat Anderson recorded as a leader only on a rare basis, and the majority of his sessions were made in Europe. *Cat on a Hot Tin Horn* (Mercury 80008) features him with an all-star big band in 1958 that includes Jimmy Forrest on tenor, trombonist Jimmy Cleveland, and baritonist Sahib Shihab as soloists. *Cat Anderson & the Ellington All-Stars* (Swing 8412) showcases him in 1958 and 1964 with a sextet/septet that includes both players from Duke's band and some top French musicians, playing Swing and some effective Dixieland.

SHORTY BAKER
b. May 26, 1914, St. Louis, MI, d. Nov. 8, 1966, New York, NY

Harold "Shorty" Baker had a mellow tone and a fluent Swing style, making him a logical inheritor of the Arthur Whetsol position with Duke Ellington's orchestra. The lyrical trumpeter played early on with Fate Marable, Erskine Tate, and Eddie Johnson's Crackerjacks (1932–33), plus with some obscure groups. Baker spent the prime years of the Swing era with Don Redman's orchestra (1936–39), Teddy Wilson's short-lived big band (1939–40), and Andy Kirk (1940–42). While with Kirk, he married Mary Lou Williams and for a time co-led a sextet with her. Baker was a member of the Duke Ellington Orchestra during 1942–44 and 1946–52, with the middle years taken up by a stint in the military. He spent the 1952–57 period freelancing, most notably with Johnny Hodges' group (1954–55), and generally played with other mainstream Swing veterans. Baker was back with Ellington a third time during 1957–63; during each of his stints with Duke he was featured on quite a few records. After appearing regularly as a leader at the Metropole and the Embers in 1963–64, bad health forced Shorty Baker to retire.

●

7 *Shorty & Doc / Jan. 17, 1961 / Original Jazz Classics 839*
Shorty Baker led only two albums in his career; the first is an obscure effort for King from 1958. This CD matches him with fellow trumpeter Doc Cheatham in a quintet also including pianist Walter Bishop, Jr., bassist Wendell Marshall, and drummer J. C. Heard. Although Baker is Swing oriented and Cheatham hints more at Dixieland, they are quite compatible on the swinging straight-ahead set and their tradeoffs work quite well.

DUD BASCOMB
b. May 16, 1916, Birmingham, AL, d. Dec. 25, 1972, New York, NY

Wilbur "Dud" Bascomb took most of the medium-register trumpet solos with Erskine Hawkins's band, although Hawkins (a flamboyant high-note player) often received the credit! Bascomb began on trumpet while in grade school in Birmingham. After high school, he joined the Bama State Collegians in 1932. In 1934 the group moved to New York, where it became the

Erskine Hawkins Orchestra. Bascomb and his older brother, tenor saxophonist Paul Bascomb, were fixtures with the big band for many years, being featured on quite a few records, including "Tuxedo Junction." Dud stayed with Hawkins until he was persuaded by his sibling in 1944 to join his struggling combo. The group soon expanded to become a big band that lasted until 1947. Dud Bascomb spent a couple of short periods with Duke Ellington's orchestra but mostly led his own Swing-based groups in the 1950s and '60s in addition to working in the studios and with theater orchestras. Dizzy Gillespie long considered him to be an inspiration.

●

LPS TO SEARCH FOR

Dud Bascomb's only full-length album as a leader, *Tuxedo Junction* (Savoy 1161), has 15 concise selections by a nine- to ten-piece group from 1959–60 filled with Erskine Hawkins alumni. The melodic performances are brief (all but "Tuxedo Junction" are under three minutes) and were meant to be issued as singles. Surprisingly, only three of the tunes were released at all before this enjoyable 1986 LP came out.

BILLY BUTTERIELD

b. Jan. 14, 1917, Middletown, OH, d. Mar. 18, 1988, North Palm Beach, FL

One of the most respected trumpeters of the Swing era, Billy Butterfield had a beautiful tone, could play ballads very well, and yet could be as hot an improviser as any of his contemporaries. After some lessons on violin, bass, and trombone, Butterfield settled on trumpet. He studied medicine at Transylvania College but found playing in bands more to his liking. After working with Dick Raymond, Andy Anderson. and Austin Wylie, Butterfield became a member of Bob Crosby's Orchestra and Bobcats (1937–40). When Yank Lawson departed to join Tommy Dorsey in 1938, Butterfield became Crosby's main trumpet soloist, starring on the original version of "What's New." After leaving Crosby in June 1940, Butterfield appeared in the movie *Second Chorus* as part of Artie Shaw's band, gigged with Bob Strong, and then actually did become a member of Shaw's orchestra during September 1940 to February 1941. During that period, Butterfield soloed on Shaw's classic version of "Stardust" and was part of his popular Gramercy Five.

After Artie Shaw broke up his band, Butterfield played with Benny Goodman (1941–42) and Les Brown and then was a studio musician before spending time in the military (1943–45). During 1946–47 he led the Billy Butterfield Orchestra, a ballad-oriented group that put the emphasis on his pretty tone, along with the clarinet and alto playing of arranger Bill Stegmeyer. However, the band failed to catch on, and Butterfield soon returned to studio work, playing Dixieland at night (including working with Eddie Condon). He mostly freelanced, was used on many record dates due to his tone, spent a few short periods with Benny Goodman, and during 1968–73 joined Yank Lawson and Bob Haggart in the World's Greatest Jazz Band. Billy Butterfield was active in Dixieland circles up until his death.

●

LPS TO SEARCH FOR

Billy Butterfield's short-lived big band is heard on swinging radio transcriptions on *1946* (Hindsight 173). *With Ted Easton's Jazzband* (Circle 37), *Watch What Happens* (Jazzology 93), and *Just Friends* (Jazzology 117) are late-period (respectively 1975, 1977, and 1982) Dixieland dates. All are quite worthwhile, with *Watch What Happens* (which showcases Butterfield with a quartet on ballads and with a nonet on the stomps) being the one to get.

FILMS

In the Fred Astaire movie *Second Chorus* (1940), Billy Butterfield ghosts for Burgess Meredith (who plays a trumpeter). He also takes a solo with Artie Shaw on "Concerto for Clarinet."

BUCK CLAYTON

b. Nov. 12, 1911, Parsons, KS, d. Dec. 8, 1991, New York, NY

In the mid-1950s, writer Stanley Dance came up with the term *Mainstream* to describe the style of Buck Clayton and other Swing era veterans who played music that was more traditional than bop but more advanced than Dixieland. Clayton was a trumpeter and arranger who appealed to musicians in a wide variety of jazz styles, simply by always being himself. Although he gained fame early on for his middle-register style and the sound he displayed when using a cup mute, Clayton was a well-rounded player who could also hit high notes when it suited the music.

Wilbur "Buck" Clayton is best known for his association with Count Basie, but he had a productive career both before and long after his Basie years. He played piano when he was six, switching to trumpet as a teenager. After high school, Clayton moved to Los Angeles, where he worked with a variety of local bands. In 1934 he became leader of a 14-piece orchestra. Pianist Teddy Weatherford was in Los Angeles looking to find a band willing to take a job at the Canidrome Ballroom in Shanghai, China. Clayton's group was picked and he spent two years overseas. Upon his return to Los Angeles in 1936, Clayton led the 14 Gentlemen from Harlem for a few months. In the fall of 1936 he was hired to play with Willie Bryant's big band in New York. But while passing through Kansas City, Clayton met the musicians in Count Basie's orchestra and decided to join them instead, just in time for their first trip east. During the next seven years, Clayton would be the main trumpet soloist with Basie, appearing on many records (including dates with Billie Holiday and Teddy Wilson) and contributing both arrangements and compositions to the Basie book.

Buck only left the Basie band in November 1943 because he was drafted. Luckily he had opportunities to play with all-star service bands while in the military. After being discharged in 1946, he worked with Jazz at the Philharmonic, led his own combos, visited France during 1949–50, and then found himself in a bit of a musical dilemma. Because Swing was considered out of style, Clayton (while in the groups of Joe Bushkin and clarinetist Tony Parenti) hurriedly learned the Dixieland repertoire so he would be able to work more often. In the 1950s Clayton was quite busy in a variety of projects. He had a champion in producer John Hammond, and so Buck was featured on mainstream dates for the Vanguard label, often with other Basie alumni. For Columbia he led a series of legendary jam sessions that matched him with other compatible all-stars. Clayton was in *The Benny Goodman Story* (even though he was never a member of Goodman's big band), in 1958 appeared at a few concerts with Sidney Bechet, and often played Dixieland at night, including with Eddie Condon's groups.

The 1960s were more of the same for a time with European tours, collaborations in England with trumpeter Humphrey Lyttelton, and appearances at many festivals and concerts, including John Hammond's 30th anniversary Spirituals to Swing concert in 1967. Unfortunately Clayton developed serious problems with his lips and trumpet chops starting in 1968, and it soon forced his retirement from playing. Although he made a couple of attempts to come back, they were all unsuccessful. However, after some time out of the music scene altogether, Buck Clayton returned as an arranger, contributing charts to a record by the Dan Barrett–Howard Alden Quintet. In 1987 he formed the Buck Clayton Big Band, which allowed him to end his productive life on a high note.

●

7 *The Classic Swing of Buck Clayton / 1946 / Original Jazz Classics 1709*

8 *Buck Clayton in Paris / Oct. 10, 1949–Oct. 21, 1953 / Vogue 68358*

7 *Dr. Jazz Series, Vol. 3 / Dec. 13, 1951–Jan. 24, 1952 / Storyville 6043*

Buck Clayton had little difficulty surviving the end of the Swing era. He had his own sound, was adaptable, and had made his reputation with Count Basie. *The Classic Swing of Buck Clayton* collects three sessions originally cut for the HRS label (and recently reissued as part of a *Complete HRS* box set by Mosaic). Clayton heads an unusual quartet with clarinetist Scoville Brown, Tiny Grimes, and bassist Sid Weiss, jams with a two-trombone octet, and is featured as a sideman with Trummy Young. Excellent late-period Swing. *Buck Clayton in Paris* was recorded during his European tours of 1949 and 1953 and features him in a two-trumpet sextet that also has tenor saxophonist Don Byas. He is also heard sharing the solo spotlight with fellow trumpeter Bill Coleman on another date and playing originals by tenorman Alix Combelle with a big band in 1953; Clayton provided all of those arrangements. Throughout, he is in top form and sounds quite inspired by the different-than-usual settings. The music that he played on the *Dr. Jazz* radio series during 1951–52 was also different: heated Dixieland. In order to work more domestically, Clayton quickly mastered the Dixieland repertoire while still taking solos in his usual Swing style. His sextet, featuring trombonist Herb Flemming, Buster Bailey, and Ken Kersey, jams enthusiastically on a variety of vintage standards.

* *Complete CBS Buck Clayton Jam Sessions / Dec. 14, 1953–Mar. 5, 1956 / Mosaic 6-144*

The Buck Clayton Jam Sessions were a series of jams on standards recorded for Columbia during 1953–56. Taking advantage of the extra time available on LP, these performances (which featured mostly Mainstream Swing veterans) were as lengthy as live jam sessions. Clayton provided background riffs and basic arrangements that uplifted the performances and clearly inspired the players in these 10- to 12-piece bands. "How Hi the Fi," which contrasts Trummy Young's rambunctious trombone with pianist Jimmy Jones' eccentric chord voicings and has a jubilant guest appearance by Woody Herman on clarinet, is a definite high point. Other notables who are heard from include trumpeters Clayton, Joe Newman, Joe Thomas, Ruby Braff, and Billy Butterfield, trombonists Urbie Green, Benny Powell, Henderson Chambers, Bennie Green, Dicky Harris, Tyree Glenn, and J. C. Higginbotham, altoist Lem Davis, tenors Julian Dash, Coleman Hawkins, Buddy Tate, and Al Cohn, baritonist Charles Fowlkes, pianists Sir Charles Thompson, Billy Kyle, Al Waslohn, and Ken Kersey, the rhythm guitars of Freddie Green and Steve Jordan, bassists Walter Page and Milt Hinton, and drummers Jo Jones and Bobby Donaldson. But be warned, this very exciting six-CD set is a limited-edition issue.

8 *The Essential Buck Clayton / Dec. 30, 1953–Mar. 14, 1957 / Vanguard 103/4*

8 *Copenhagen Concert / Sept. 17, 1959 / Storyville 36006/7*

7 *Goin' to Kansas City / Oct. 5, 1960–Oct. 6, 1960 / Original Jazz Classics 1757*

8 *Buck Clayton All-Stars, 1961 / Apr. 1961 / Storyville 8231*

7 *Swiss Radio Days Jazz Series, Vol. 7 / May 2, 1961 / TCB 02072*

8 *Baden, Switzerland 1966 / Feb. 6, 1966 / Sackville 2-2028*

In addition to his Columbia jam sessions, Buck Clayton was quite productive during the 1950s and early '60s. He recorded several sets of music for the Vanguard label during 1953–57; a double LP in the 1970s had 16 of the numbers, and *The Essential Buck Clayton* contains 14 of those, seven of which are Buck's originals. Two of the dates were his own (with such notables as Ruby Braff, Vic Dickenson, and Buddy Tate also getting solo space), while the 1953 set was actually led by Mel Powell; everyone plays up to par. The two-CD *Copenhagen Concert* features the Basie alumni band that Clayton took on tour to Europe, an ensemble also including trumpeter Emmett Berry (in excellent form), altoist Earle Warren, Tate, Dicky Wells, and Jimmy Rushing (who steals the show). It makes one wish that the original Count Basie Orchestra were still around at the time to compete with the newer version. *Goin' to Kansas City* is really the musical conception of Tommy Gwaltney, who plays alto, clarinet, vibes, and xylophone but gives Clayton top billing. The band also has Dickie Wells, trumpeter Bobby Zottola, Tommy Newsom (the main arranger) on tenor, and a four-piece rhythm section that includes guitarist Charlie Byrd. The music (which includes some vintage obscurities) swings but is definitely offbeat and fairly unpredictable. The Storyville and TCB CDs feature Clayton on his 1961 European tour, using the same band as he had in 1959 except without Warren and Rushing. Much of the material is the same (five of the seven songs on the TCB release are among the tunes put out by Storyville), but the solos always differ and the enthusiasm never flags. The Storyville set gets the edge due to its longer playing time (75 minutes versus 55 for the TCB disc), but both are recommended to Buck Clayton fans. And serving as a wrap-up of his playing career, *Baden, Switzerland* matches Clayton with drummer Wallace Bishop and three Swiss musicians (including pianist Henri Chaix), happily jamming a blues and seven Swing standards while showing that his trumpet style really was timeless.

7 *A Buck Clayton Jam Session / Mar. 25, 1974 / Chiaroscuro 132*

7 *A Buck Clayton Jam Session—1975 / June 6, 1975 / Chiaroscuro 143*

Buck Clayton reluctantly had to stop playing trumpet by the late 1960s, but, after several depressing years completely out of music, he returned as an arranger-composer, utilizing skills he had had for decades but that had formerly been overshadowed by his playing. During 1974–76 Clayton led annual recorded jam sessions for Chiaroscuro, and two have thus far been reissued on CD. In each case, four of his swinging originals are performed in extended fashion. The 1974 date has Doc Cheatham and Joe Newman on trumpets, trombonist Urbie Green, altoist Earle Warren, Zoot Sims and Budd Johnson on tenors, baritonist Joe Temperley, bassist Milt Hinton, drummer Gus Johnson, and, as a special treat, pianist Earl Hines. The 1975 set (which also includes two rehearsal segments) finds Newman, Warren, Budd Johnson, and Hinton joined by trumpeter Money Johnson, trombonists Vic Dickenson and George Masso, altoist Lee Konitz (an offbeat choice that works), tenors Buddy Tate and Sal Nistico, pianist Tommy Flanagan, and drummer Mel Lewis. The old magic is rekindled even though only Newman, Green, Tate, and Hinton had been on the sessions of two decades earlier and Clayton's own trumpet is missed.

7 *A Swingin' Dream / Oct. 23, 1988 / Stash 281*

8 *Live from Greenwich Village, NYC / Feb. 16–18, 1990 / Nagel-Heyer 030*

Buck Clayton's career ended happily as he led big bands during his last few years. *A Swingin' Dream* has his occasionally working band of 1988, an outfit that features such soloists as

trumpeters Spanky Davis and Johnny Letman, trombonist Dan Barrett, baritonist Joe Temperley, and drummer Mel Lewis. All of the songs except "Avenue C" were of recent vintage and the band really swings. The 1990 CD actually has an almost entirely different group of young all-stars, who perform a dozen of Clayton's originals. The trumpet section is comprised of John Eckert, Jordan Sandke, Byron Stripling, and Warren Vache and other top players, such as altoist Jerry Dodgion, Frank Wess on tenor, and pianist Dick Katz, are heard from. If this big band had lasted longer, it could have been one of the top jazz orchestras of the era. Luckily it was recorded this one time.

LPS TO SEARCH FOR

Buck Clayton Rarities, Vol. 1 (Swingtime 1024) has obscure appearances by the trumpeter on dates led by Horace Henderson, Trummy Young, and singer Taps Miller during 1945 and 1953. *1964* (Harlequin 305) and *1966* (Harlequin 3002) feature Clayton sitting in with trumpeter Humphrey Lyttelton's bands from those two years, playing modern Swing. The *1964* group is a septet (counting Buck) that includes Tony Coe on tenor and baritonist Joe Temperley, while the later combo has spots for the underrated Kathy Stobart on tenor.

FILMS

Buck Clayton takes a solo on "One O'Clock Jump" with Count Basie in *Reveille with Beverly* (1943) and is one of the musicians in *The Benny Goodman Story* (1955). His 1961 band of Basie alumni that toured Europe is well featured on *The Buck Clayton All-Stars* (Shanachie 6303), a highly recommended video that has Dickie Wells, Buddy Tate, and Jimmy Witherspoon among the stars. In addition, Clayton is one of the five Count Basie veterans who are profiled in the 1973 documentary *Born to Swing* (Rhapsody Films).

BILL COLEMAN
b. Aug. 4, 1904, Centreville, KY, d. Aug. 24, 1981, Toulouse, France

Bill Coleman was an excellent Swing trumpeter with a mellow tone who spent most of his career in Europe. It was ironic that he was born near Paris, Kentucky, for he would spend a lot of time in Paris, France, throughout his life. Coleman gigged early on in bands led by J. C. Higginbotham, Edgar Hayes, Clarence Paige, Wesley Helvey, and Lloyd and Cecil Scott (1927–28) in New York. In 1929, he joined Luis Russell's orchestra, with whom he made his recording debut. However, Henry "Red" Allen was Russell's trumpet star, so Coleman's solo opportunities were limited and he soon left. Coleman had stints with Cecil Scott's Bright Boys, Charlie Johnson, Bobby Neal, and back with Russell (1931–32). After a brief period with Ralph Cooper's Kongo Knights, Coleman spent some productive time playing with Lucky Millinder (with whom he visited Europe in 1933), Benny Carter, and Teddy Hill (1934–35); he also recorded with Fats Waller. In September 1935 the trumpeter sailed to Europe, where he worked with Freddy Taylor and recorded prolifically during the next few years. Coleman played with Leon Abbey's orchestra in Bombay, India (1936–37), was with Willie Lewis in Paris (1937–38), co-led the Harlem Rhythmakers in Egypt (1939–40), and then (due to World War II) returned to the U.S.

During the war years Bill Coleman worked with the Benny Carter Orchestra, Fats Waller, Teddy Wilson, Andy Kirk, Ellis Larkins, Mary Lou Williams, and the John Kirby Sextet; he also recorded with Lester Young in the Kansas City Six. He was never that famous in the U.S., but Coleman was valued for his appealing tone and melodic Swing solos. However, after periods playing with Sy Oliver and Billy Kyle's Sextet, in December 1948 he moved to France, where he would live the rest of his life. Although largely forgotten by American audiences, Bill Coleman stayed quite busy on the Continent and in England, playing Swing and Dixieland in many clubs and at festivals during his final three decades.

●

10 *1936–1938 / Jan. 24, 1936–Sept. 28, 1938 / Classics 764*
This CD has all of Bill Coleman's sessions as a leader while in Paris in the 1930s. The combo dates find Coleman at the early peak of his powers, getting opportunities that he never received in the United States and taking a few likable vocals. Among his sidemen are pianist Herman Chittison, Oscar Aleman, Stephane Grappelli (on both violin and piano), and, on five songs (including a duet), Django Reinhardt. Classic small-group Swing.

7 *The Great Parisian Session / Jan. 21, 1960–Jan. 22, 1960 / Polydor 837235*

7 *Bill Coleman Plus Four / Jan. 30–31, 1969 / Jazzology 196*

8 *Bill Coleman Meets Guy Lafitte / July 4, 1973 / Black Lion 760182*

Most of Bill Coleman's postwar European recordings have not been made available in the U.S., but he was quite active during his last three decades. Originally titled *From Boogie to Funk, The Great Parisian Session* finds Coleman having a rare meeting with some top Americans who were passing through Paris as part of Quincy Jones's orchestra: Quentin Jackson, Budd Johnson, pianist Patti Bown, bassist Buddy Catlett, drummer Joe Harris, and, on some numbers, guitarist Les Spann. They perform five of Coleman's blues-oriented originals with spirit. *Bill Coleman Plus Four* was originally known as *Three Generations Jam* due to the age difference between the trumpeter and his sidemen in the quintet (which includes trombonist Francois Guin and American drummer Art Taylor), but there is no generation gap in the music. Everyone sounds quite comfortable playing Bill Coleman's brand of Swing. The Black Lion CD was recorded at the 1973 Montreux Jazz Festival. Perhaps it is the presence of tenorman Guy Lafitte in the trumpeter's quintet (which has a European rhythm section) or the enthusiastic audience, but Bill Coleman sounds quite inspired on such numbers as "Blue Lou," "Idaho," "Tour de Force," and "Montreux Jump." One of his better late-period recordings.

HARRY "SWEETS" EDISON
b. Oct. 10, 1915, Columbus, OH, d. July 27, 1999, Columbus, OH

Lester Young gave Harry Edison the lifelong nickname of "Sweets," and the title fit his style perfectly. Edison was the Count Basie of the piano, saying a great deal with very few notes. He was always immediately recognizable after a note or two (his bent notes are classics) and, although quite familiar by the 1950s with the playing of Dizzy Gillespie (sometimes even duplicating a Dizzy phrase), Edison's own timeless Swing style stayed relatively unchanged through the years.

Harry Edison began playing trumpet when he was 12. After working locally, he gigged with several top territory bands, including Alphonso Trent, Eddie Johnson's Crackerjacks, and the Jeter-Pillars Band. Edison was with the Mills Blue

Rhythm Band in 1937 and then became an important part of Count Basie's orchestra, staying from June 1938 until February 1950. Originally sharing the spotlight with Buck Clayton, Edison gradually developed and, after Buck's departure in 1943, he was Basie's top trumpet star. When the Count Basie Big Band broke up, Edison was briefly in Count's octet and then worked with Jimmy Rushing, Jazz at the Philharmonic, Buddy Rich (1951–53 and occasionally afterwards), and his own combos.

In the 1950s, Sweets settled in Los Angeles, where he was greatly in demand for studio work, including playing background solos on many Frank Sinatra records. He appeared on countless mainstream sessions, had many reunions with the Basie band and various alumni, teamed up frequently with tenor saxophonist Eddie Lockjaw Davis during the 1970s and '80s (their distinctive sounds and highly expressive styles always fit together perfectly), recorded often both as a leader and as a sideman (particularly for the Pablo label), and remained a popular attraction to his last days. Although his range had greatly shrunk by the time he reached his eighties, Harry "Sweets" Edison still had the ability to make a poignant statement in one or two well-placed notes.

●

9 *Jawbreakers / Apr. 18, 1962 / Original Jazz Classics 487*

The first meeting on records by Harry Edison and tenor great Eddie "Lockjaw" Davis was so successful that it would be repeated many times. With assistance from pianist Hugh Lawson, bassist Ike Isaacs, and drummer Clarence Johnston, Sweets and Lockjaw engage in plenty of interplay, with the most memorable selections including "Broadway," "Four," and "A Gal in Calico."

9 *Edison's Lights / May 5, 1976 / Original Jazz Classics 804*

10 *Harry Sweets Edison and Eddie Lockjaw Davis, Vol. 1 / July 6, 1976 / Storyville 4004*

10 *Harry Sweets Edison and Eddie Lockjaw Davis, Vol. 2 / July 6, 1976 / Storyville 4025*

6 *Simply Sweets / Sept. 22, 1977 / Original Jazz Classics 903*

On each of these four CDs (particularly the first three), Sweets and Lockjaw have exciting reunions. *Edison's Lights* is particularly noteworthy because Count Basie (listed as William Basie) is the pianist on half of the tracks, sharing the keyboard chair with Dolo Coker. Bassist John Heard and drummer Jimmy Smith keep things swinging on a set that includes four basic Edison originals and four standards (including "Ain't Misbehavin'" and "On the Trail"). The two Storyville sets are even better. The rhythm section is fairly obscure, as is trombonist John Darville, who is on two of the six cuts on each set, but the material is stronger. The first set has such numbers as "Lester Leaps In," Coleman

Hawkins's "Spotlite," and "Blues Walk," while *Vol. 2* includes "Robbin's Nest," "Candy," and "There Is No Greater Love," perfect vehicles for the two Classic Swing veterans. *Simply Sweets* (which has the duo joined by Coker, bassist Harvey Newmark, and drummer Smith) in contrast has an unimaginative repertoire (five blues, "Feelings"—of all things—and two other numbers) that makes the results somewhat predictable if reasonably pleasing.

3 *For My Pals / Apr. 18, 1988–Apr. 19, 1988 / Pablo 2310–934*

This later effort by Sweets Edison is rather weak. Seventy-two at the time, Edison had faded a lot during the previous few years, and his playing is quite erratic here. Although there are some good moments along the way by trombonist Buster Cooper, Curtis Peagler on tenor and alto, and pianist-organist Art Hillery, the well-intentioned effort, which is full of tributes to fallen comrades (including a rather weak vocal on "It's a Wonderful World"), should be passed by.

LPS TO SEARCH FOR

Harry Edison still sounds quite good on *'S Wonderful* (Pablo 2308–237), a fine 1982 quintet date with tenor saxophonist Zoot Sims, particularly on Sweets's "Centerpiece" and "Sunday."

FILMS

Harry Edison is one of the stars in the Lester Young film short *Jammin' the Blues* (1944).

Two of the most adventurous Swing trumpeters, Roy "Little Jazz" Eldridge and Henry "Red" Allen, are seen in a rare joint appearance.

ROY ELDRIDGE

b. Jan. 30, 1911, Pittsburgh, PA, d. Feb. 26, 1989, Valley Stream, NY

A fiery and combative trumpeter who in practically every solo took some wild chances, Roy Eldridge was always exciting to hear, giving 110 percent to each chorus. His crackling sound was full of emotion and, although occasionally reckless (few of his solos were completely flawless), Eldridge's improvisations were some of the most advanced of the Swing era.

Born David Eldridge but nicknamed Roy early on, Eldridge was also known as "Little Jazz" (a title given him by altoist Otto Hardwicke) throughout much of his career. He played drums a little when he was six but soon switched to trumpet. Eldridge began working locally in 1927, including leading his own group, which he called Roy Elliott and his Palais Royal Orchestra. Other early gigs included Horace Henderson's Dixie Stompers, Zach Whyte, and Speed Webb (1929–30). He was originally inspired by Coleman Hawkins's tenor solo on "Stampede" (which he performed) and by Jabbo Smith, not fully appreciating Louis Armstrong until the early 1930s. After moving to New York in November 1930, Eldridge had stints with Cecil Scott, Elmer Snowden, Charlie Johnson, Teddy Hill, and the declining McKinney's Cotton Pickers. In 1935 Eldridge rejoined Hill (with whom he recorded) and also appeared on his first of several dates with Teddy Wilson and Billie Holiday. In 1936 he spent several months with the Fletcher Henderson Orchestra (where his hot trumpet solo helped

"Christopher Columbus" become a hit), was on a spirited session with Gene Krupa and Benny Goodman, and led his own group, which included older brother Joe Eldridge on alto. Roy would be leading bands (including an orchestra by 1938) off and on until 1941 in addition to appearing on many recordings as a sideman.

During 1941–43, Eldridge was one of the main stars of Gene Krupa's orchestra, as one can hear on such numbers as "After You've Gone," "Rockin' Chair," and "Let Me Off Uptown" (with Anita O'Day). Despite the great difficulties in traveling with a white band during those days, Roy also was with the Artie Shaw Orchestra (1944–45, including being featured on "Little Jazz" and "Lady Day") and would rejoin Krupa for a period in 1949. Otherwise, he led his own groups (including a short-lived big band in 1946) and in 1949 had his first of many tours with Jazz at the Philharmonic, where his competitive style was a natural.

Always considered among the most modern of trumpeters, Eldridge was going through a bit of an identity crisis by that time. His follower, Dizzy Gillespie, had surpassed him, and some musicians thought of Roy's playing as old-fashioned; he was not sure what to do. A European tour with Benny Goodman in April 1950 led to Eldridge's deciding to stay overseas for a time to straighten himself out. The trumpeter had great success in France and eventually realized that being modern was not as important as simply being himself. When he returned to New York in April 1951, his confidence was back and Eldridge had a busy decade, recording frequently for Norman Granz's labels (including Verve), touring with JATP (where he successfully matched wits with Gillespie and Charlie Shavers), and often working in a quintet with Coleman Hawkins. Eldridge also learned Dixieland standards (without altering his style in the slightest) so he could work in trad settings too.

In the 1960s, Eldridge scuffled a bit and did not record too often. His stints with Ella Fitzgerald (1963–65) and Count Basie (1966) were not very successful because he was not needed at all by the former and was underutilized by the latter. But the 1970s were more productive, for he worked nightly at Jimmy Ryan's and was recorded in very favorable settings again by Norman Granz for the Pablo label. A worsening of his health in 1980 forced his retirement (Eldridge refused to play trumpet at all if he had to restrain himself and take it easy) and, other than a few appearances as a vocalist, Roy Eldridge watched music from the sidelines during his last years. ●

10 *Little Jazz / Feb. 26, 1935–Apr. 2, 1940 / Columbia*
    45275

This CD contains the best of early Roy Eldridge, from the period when the trumpeter burst upon the scene and was overflowing with enthusiastic excitement. He is featured on a selection apiece with Teddy Hill and Putney Dandridge, four numbers (including "Christopher Columbus") with Fletcher Henderson, on a heated date with Teddy Wilson, accompanying Billie Holiday ("Falling in Love Again") and Mildred Bailey ("I'm Nobody's Baby"), and on the six songs (plus one alternate take) that resulted from his first two dates as a leader. Of these last, "Wabash Stomp," "Heckler's Hop," and "After You've Gone" are classics.

9 *After You've Gone / Feb. 5, 1936–Sept. 24, 1946 / GRP/*
   Decca 605

8 *Roy Eldridge in Paris / June 9, 1950–June 14, 1950 /*
   Vogue 68209

8 *Just You, Just Me / 1959 / Stash 531*

Roy Eldridge recorded 30 performances (counting alternate takes) for Decca during 1944–46 at the head of a big band.

Twenty-two are on *After You've Gone* plus a version of "Christopher Columbus" from 1936 that was only out previously on a collectors' LP. Although the band itself never made it, the trumpet solos (on such numbers as "The Gasser," "I Can't Get Started," "Twilight Time," "Rockin' Chair," and two versions of the title cut) make the Decca set essential until a more complete collection comes around. *Roy Eldridge in Paris* has two very complete sessions (including seven alternate takes) taken from Eldridge's 1950 visit to France. On one date he matches wits with tenorman Zoot Sims in a quintet (singing "Ain't No Flies on Me") while the other session is a quartet date with pianist Gerald Wiggins. Eldridge's version of "Wrap Your Troubles in Dreams" is a highlight. *Just You, Just Me* finds the trumpeter sharing the spotlight with Coleman Hawkins. Joined by a local rhythm section during an engagement in Washington, D.C., Roy and Hawk as usual bring out the best of each other on jam tunes (such as "Blue Lou," "Just You, Just Me," "Rifftide," and "Honeysuckle Rose") and a ballad medley. A couple of earlier LPs from the Honeysuckle Rose label had released 11 numbers from this gig. The Stash CD has five of those performances plus four that were never out before, which will probably drive completists mad!

4 *Jazz Maturity . . . Where It's Coming From* / *June 3, 1975* / Original Jazz Classics 807

7 *Happy Time* / *June 4, 1975* / Original Jazz Classics 628

8 *What It's All About* / *Jan. 16, 1976* / Original Jazz Classics 853

7 *Roy Eldridge & Vic Dickenson* / *May 20, 1978* / Storyville 8239

One would think that teaming Roy Eldridge and Dizzy Gillespie would always result in musical magic, but the two trumpeters were both having an off day on *Jazz Maturity*, which finds them playing a couple of forgettable blues and four warhorses; pianist Oscar Peterson easily steals solo honors. *Happy Time* has some better solos from Eldridge and a lot of his personable vocalizing on a variety of Swing tunes. With assistance from Peterson and guitarist Joe Pass in a supportive quartet, the CD lives up to its title. *What It's All About* was one of Eldridge's best Pablo records (reissued in the OJC series). Despite its being late in his career, he plays here with a great deal of fire and even ferocity. It is also good to hear altoist Norris Turney and tenorman Budd Johnson in such a freewheeling setting. Vibraphonist Milt Jackson helps out on half of the tunes. The 1978 meeting with Vic Dickenson is much better than expected, considering that it was Eldridge's final recording and he was 67 at the time. Budd Johnson is again present, along with the co-leaders, pianist Tommy Flanagan, bassist Major Holley, and drummer Eddie Locke, who actually organized the standards session.

10 *Montreux 1977* / *July 13, 1977* / Original Jazz Classics 373

Saving the best for last, Roy Eldridge is so inspired on this outing from the 1977 Montreux Jazz Festival that it borders on the miraculous. Pushed by Oscar Peterson, bassist Niels Pedersen, and drummer Bobby Durham, Eldridge sounds like a man possessed. He tears into such numbers as "Between the Devil and the Deep Blue Sea," "Perdido," and "Bye Bye Blackbird" like the combative warrior he was, hitting nearly all of the high notes that he aims for. A gem.

LPS TO SEARCH FOR

At the Three Deuces, Chicago (Jazz Archives 24) features Roy Eldridge's octet in 1937 on a radio transcription and some live performances, while *At the Arcadia Ballroom* (Jazz Archives 14) has the Eldridge tentet of 1939 from radio air checks. In both cases the recording quality is a bit primitive, but the trumpet solos make the albums worth picking up. *I Remember Harlem* (Inner City 7012) is frequently superb, with Eldridge captured in Paris during 1950–51, not duplicating the Vogue CD. Roy is heard with a French septet, teamed with Don Byas in a quintet, taking three fairly basic piano solos, and performing "Wild Man Blues" and "Fireworks" in duets with pianist Claude Bolling that recalls Louis Armstrong and Earl Hines. Of the Byas pieces, "Oh Shut Up" is based on the chord changes of the more diplomatically titled "Please Don't Talk About Me When I'm Gone!" The two-LP set *Dale's Wail* (Verve 2-2531) from 1952–54 is almost entirely Eldridge's showcase; Oscar Peterson does not solo much and switches to organ on half of the numbers. Fortunately the trumpeter sounds quite inspired throughout. Eldridge did not record often as a leader in the 1960s, making the fiery *Comin' Home Baby* (Pumpkin 107), which features tenor saxophonist Richie Kamuca and pianist Dick Katz, valuable. *The Nifty Cat Strikes West* (Master Jazz 8121), a relaxed and swinging sextet session with trombonist Grover Mitchell and tenor saxophonist Eric Dixon from 1966, is fine but topped by the more exciting *The Nifty Cat* (New World 349), which has superior playing on six Eldridge tunes by Budd Johnson and Benny Morton. Also overdue for reissue is *Little Jazz & the Jimmy Ryan All-Stars* (Pablo 2310-869), which, in its mixture of Dixieland and Swing tunes (some of which have vocals by the trumpeter) and the use of his working band, shows what Roy Eldridge sounded like playing nightly at Jimmy Ryan's in 1975.

FILMS

Roy Eldridge has a couple of memorable solos in *The Sound of Jazz* (1957) and teams up with Coleman Hawkins in 1961's *After Hours* (Rhapsody Films).

ZIGGY ELMAN
b. May 26, 1914, Philadelphia, PA, d. June 26, 1968, Van Nuys, CA

It seems odd that Ziggy Elman was not a bigger star during the Swing era. He had a major hit while with Benny Goodman ("And the Angels Sing") and was fairly well known, but made the mistake of not leading his own band until Swing was on its way out.

Born Harry Finkelman, Elman was a very talented musician who could play (in addition to trumpet) all of the reed instruments and trombone. He grew up in Atlantic City and worked regularly in local clubs. Ziggy's versatility with Alex Bartha's band led Benny Goodman to quickly sign him up. Elman was with BG from September 1936 until Goodman's temporary breakup in July 1940. At first he was the clarinetist's main trumpet soloist, but, when Harry James joined in early 1937, James stole much of his thunder. Still, Elman had his spots and (along with James and Chris Griffin) he was part of one of the great trumpet sections.

When he left Goodman in 1940, Ziggy Elman should have formed his own big band, particularly since "And the Angels Sing" had become a standard. But instead he became a member of Tommy Dorsey's orchestra (1940–43), where he was well featured but very much in a supportive role. After a period in the Army, he was back with TD during 1946 and then finally formed his own big band. After it quickly flopped, he returned to Dorsey (1947–48) before trying again to be a leader. It was far too late, few recordings resulted, and by 1950 (and continuing into the early '60s) he was working primarily in the studios, emerging only to play in clubs on a rare basis. Elman appeared on a Jess Stacy album in 1955 and was briefly in *The Benny Goodman Story* (although, due to an illness, his solo on "And the Angels Sing" was actually ghosted by Manny Klein). Later in life, Ziggy Elman ran a music store.

●

9 *1938–1939 / Dec. 23, 1938–Dec. 26, 1939 / Classics 900*
During 1938–39, while still a member of Benny Goodman's orchestra, Ziggy Elman had an opportunity to record 20 selections as a leader in five sessions, using the Goodman sax section (two altos and two tenors) and rhythm section. All of the recordings are on this definitive CD. "Fralich in Swing" was the first number Elman cut, and this old Jewish melody would soon be given words by Johnny Mercer and turned into "And the Angels Sing." The other fine Swing selections include "Let's Fall in Love," "Zaggin' with Zig," and "Tootin' My Baby Back Home." Ziggy at his best.

LPS TO SEARCH FOR
1947 (Circle 70) is a radio transcription by the Ziggy Elman Big Band but unfortunately includes only four instrumentals among the 11 selections, although there are some good moments along the way. *Zaggin' with Zig* (Swing Era 1015) is better, a collector's label album that has 16 selections from Elman's band dating from 1947–52, including not only the title cut but "Samba with Zig" and "Boppin' with Zig." Virginia Maxey has occasional vocals, but Elman is the main star throughout.

FILMS
Ziggy Elman appears with the Tommy Dorsey band in *DuBarry Was a Lady* (1943) and is in the famous jam session scene with Art Tatum and the Dorsey Brothers in *The Fabulous Dorseys* (1947).

PEE WEE ERWIN
b. May 30, 1913, Falls City, NE, d. June 20, 1981, Teaneck, NJ

A superior utility player who often seemed to be filling in for someone else, George "Pee Wee" Erwin was a versatile and talented Swing soloist who was little known to the general public. The son of a trumpeter, Erwin played locally in Nebraska and then moved to New York in 1932 to work with Joe Haymes. He was with the Isham Jones Orchestra for two years, spent a few months with Freddie Martin in 1934, and then played with Benny Goodman from November 1934 to May 1935. While working with Ray Noble's American Orchestra in 1935, Erwin helped change the history of Swing. Glenn Miller was Noble's main arranger at the time and he wrote Pee Wee's trumpet part (at Erwin's urging) quite high, voicing it with the saxophonists. When Erwin's successor could not play the parts, Miller gave them to the clarinetist; thus came the birth of the Glenn Miller sound!

Erwin rejoined Benny Goodman during February-September 1936 in the spot formerly held by Bunny Berigan. His second period with BG preceded Ziggy Elman's and Harry James's being in the band and has been largely overlooked. A return stint with Noble preceded Erwin's joining Tommy Dorsey's orchestra (1937–39) in time to be Berigan's replacement once again; he was featured on many recordings with TD's Clambake Seven. After a short time with Johnny Green's orchestra, Erwin had his own big band, but it lasted barely a year and was quickly forgotten. By 1942 Pee Wee Erwin was primarily a studio musician. In 1949 he began working regularly as the leader of a Dixieland band at Nick's in New York, where he stayed for a decade while also doing studio work during the day. Pee Wee Erwin remained active up until his death, recording quite often as a leader during his last two years, cutting six albums during 1980–81.

LPS TO SEARCH FOR

Dixieland Ramble (Broadway Intermission 155) features Erwin on radio broadcasts from the mid-1950s and 1965. The music is Dixieland, with pianist Billy Maxted on the earlier date and Lou McGarity, clarinetist Bob Wilber, and pianist Dave McKenna heard in 1965. *Oh Play That Thing* (United Artists 5010) from 1958 finds Erwin, McGarity, and clarinetist Kenny Davern performing vintage music, including songs associated with Jelly Roll Morton and King Oliver plus newer rags; pity that it is so difficult to find. *Swingin'*

That Music (Jazzology 80) from 1980 is a conventional but spirited Dixieland date with obscure players (other than the young drummer Hal Smith). The Qualtro label documented Erwin on three albums during his final year. *In New York* (Qualtro 100) is an easy-listening set with an octet. *In Hollywood* (Qualtro 101) which has Eddie Miller and trombonist Bob Havens, is quite a bit hotter. *Playing at Home* (Qualtro 102) is a relaxed outing, with Erwin's cornet accompanied by Bucky and John Pizzarelli on guitars.

NAT GONELLA
b. Mar. 7, 1908, London, England, d. Aug. 6, 1998, Gosport, England

Nat Gonella was thought of as the "Louis Armstrong of England" and was the most famous Swing star in the United Kingdom during the 1930s. Gonella's singing was a bit reminiscent of Wingy Manone's, while his trumpet style certainly owed its origins to Satch. He picked up early experience working with Archie Pitt's Busby Boys, Bob Dryden's Louisville Band (1928–29), and Archie Alexander, playing clarinet and violin in addition to trumpet. From 1929 on, Gonella was a household name in England, being well featured with the orchestras of Billy Cotton (1929–33), Roy Fox (1931–32), Ray Noble (on and off during 1931–34), and Lew Stone (1932–35). His hit record of "Georgia on My Mind" led to his own band's being called the Georgians. During 1934–39, Gonella was at the height of his fame, recording frequently as a leader and becoming a star on radio. He joined the Army in August 1941 and played in service bands for the next four years. From the mid-1940s on, Gonella worked less frequently and mostly stopped recording, generally performing as a solo act in variety shows. In 1958 Gonella formed the New Georgia Jazz Band, and he was active on a part-time basis in the 1960s and '70s, regaining some of his former popularity during the trad boom. Bad health forced him to stop playing trumpet in the early '80s, but Nat Gonella still sang in public once in a while, including on his 90th birthday, in 1998.

Rhythm Man (EMI 26 0188), *Yeah Man* (Harlequin 3019), and *How'm I Doin'?* (Old Bean 11).

FILMS

Nat Gonella appears in *Sing As You Swing* (1937).

BOBBY HACKETT
b. Jan. 31, 1915, Providence, RI, d. June 7, 1976, Chatham, MA

Bobby Hackett, who rarely hit a high note (or a wrong one), always had a soft appealing sound and a thoughtful style, even when playing an up-tempo song. He gained fame not only in the Swing and Dixieland worlds but as a participant in many "mood music" records of the 1950s and as an early inspiration for Miles Davis.

Early on, Hackett played not only cornet but guitar and violin; he gave up the latter in the mid-'30s. He left school when he was 14 to play locally, often on guitar, banjo, and/or violin. Hackett began to emphasize the cornet more by 1933, although he would double on rhythm guitar throughout the Swing era. By 1936 he was leading his own band in Boston, and, after moving to New York, Hackett worked with several society orchestras plus the combos of Joe Marsala and Red McKenzie. Hackett by then was gaining a reputation as "the new Bix" because of some similarities in their tone (the Bix Beiderbecke influence lessened through the years). He guested at Benny Goodman's Carnegie Hall Concert in 1938, playing Bix's solo on "I'm Coming Virginia." Hackett was featured on some classic recordings in early 1938 with Eddie Condon's group (his "Embraceable You" solo received plenty of notice), was heard with many short-term Dixieland bands, led his own orchestra for a year, and, having lost a ton of money in that venture, made it back by working with Horace Heidt during 1939–40. After another attempt at leading a band, he became a member of Glenn Miller's orchestra in July 1941, staying until its breakup in September 1942. Although often playing rhythm guitar, Hackett had occasional cornet solos with Miller, including a famous chorus on "A String of Pearls." He would also be featured with the Casa Loma Orchestra from October 1944 to September 1946.

Otherwise, Bobby Hackett spent the rest of his life leading his own Dixieland bands, doing studio work, and being a sideman now and then with such notables as Louis Armstrong (appearing at his famous 1947 Town Hall concert), Eddie Condon, Benny Goodman (1962–63), Tony Bennett (1965–66), and the Newport All-Stars. He was utilized on many background music albums of the 1950s and '60s (including those organized by Jackie Gleason) but more significant was an excellent quintet that Hackett had for a time in the late 1960s/early '70s with trombonist Vic Dickenson. Bobby Hackett's mellow sound and Classic Swing/Dixieland style always sounded good and was in demand throughout his career, appealing to traditionalists and modernists alike.

●

9 *1938–1940 / Feb. 16, 1938–Jan. 31, 1940 / Classics 890*

5 *1943 World Jam Session / Dec. 23, 1943 / Jazzology 111*
Bobby Hackett recorded prolifically throughout his career, starting as a leader in 1938. *1938–1940* features him with several small groups in 1938 (some with clarinetist Pee Wee Russell and George Brunies or Brad Gowans on trombone), with the highlights being "If Dreams Come True," "That Da Da Strain," and Leonard Feather's "Jammin' the Waltz." Also included are the eight numbers cut by Hackett's short-

lived 1939 big band and a few selections sponsored by Horace Heidt in 1940 (including "Singin' the Blues"). *1943 World Jam Session* brings completeness to the extreme level. Every note recorded for the World Broadcasting radio transcription service by Bobby Hackett's 1943 octet is here. The group consists of the leader, trombonist Ray Coniff, clarinetist John Peper, tenor saxophonist Nick Caizza, pianist Frank Signorelli, rhythm guitarist Eddie Condon, bassist Bob Casey, and drummer Maurice Purtill. The nine selections (which total around 25 minutes) are fine, but there are also eight false starts, seven incomplete takes, and eight full-length alternate takes, so there is a lot of repetition! For true Bobby Hackett fanatics only.

7 *Dr. Jazz Series, Vol. 2 / Feb. 11, 1952–Apr. 17, 1952 / Storyville 6042*

7 *Dr. Jazz Series, Vol. 10 / Feb. 7, 1952–Apr. 10, 1952 / Storyville 6050*

7 *Off Minor / July 5, 1957 + July 5, 1958 / Viper's Nest 162*

The two *Dr. Jazz* Storyville CDs feature the identical band (Hackett, Vic Dickenson, clarinetist Gene Sedric, pianist Teddy Roy, and a few different bassists and drummers) performing straightforward Dixieland with occasional ballad features for Hackett's lyrical horn. It is particularly interesting hearing Sedric (best known for playing with Fats Waller) in this setting. The music does not contain many surprises, but it is played enthusiastically and creatively within the idiom. *Off Minor* has two separate bands recorded exactly a year apart. The Bobby Hackett Sextet of 1957 was one of his most adventurous groups, featuring Ernie Caceres on clarinet and baritone, Tom Gwaltney on clarinet and vibes, Dick Cary (responsible for the arrangements) switching between piano and alto horn, John Dengler on tuba, and drummer Boozy Drootin. In addition to some rousing standards, the unit performs "Caravan" (with Cary's alto horn in the lead) and a few other surprisingly modern songs, including Thelonious Monk's "Off Minor" (although unfortunately Hackett sits out on that one). The second half of the CD is a more typical Dixieland date by Jack Teagarden's 1958 sextet, with trumpeter Dick Oakley and pianist Don Ewell; Hackett sits in on "Royal Garden Blues" and trades off with Oakley.

9 *Live at the Roosevelt Grill, Vol. 1 / Apr. 19, 1970–May 1970 / Chiaroscuro 105*

9 *Live at the Roosevelt Grill, Vol. 2 / Mar. 26, 1970–Apr. 10, 1970 / Chiaroscuro 138*

9 *Live at the Roosevelt Grill, Vol. 3 / Mar. 1970–May 1970 / Chiaroscuro 161*

In 1970, cornetist Bobby Hackett and trombonist Vic Dickenson teamed up for an extended stay at the Roosevelt Grill in New York. With pianist Dave McKenna, bassist Jack Lesberg, and drummer Cliff Leeman, the group swung hard but often quite softly. Hackett and Dickenson both had mellow sounds yet were quite fluent, usually weaving lines around each other. While *Vol. 3* of the trio of Chiaroscuro CDs focuses more on Dixieland tunes, in reality the music is primarily Mainstream Swing, interpreted creatively by some of the very best players.

LPS TO SEARCH FOR

Live from the Voyager Room (Shoestring 108) and *Live from the Voyager Room Volume II* (Shoestring 113) contain radio air checks by Hackett's adventurous 1956–57 sextet, a group that deserved much greater recognition; Bob Wilber is heard on various reeds, while chief arranger Dick Cary plays piano, alto horn, and trumpet. *Hello Louis* (Epic 26099), from 1964, is a fine tribute to Louis Armstrong that focuses on Satch's originals (some of which are quite obscure) and finds modern soprano saxophonist Steve Lacy playing on a rare Dixieland date. *Creole Cooking* (Verve 8698) is an underrated classic featuring Hackett on trad tunes that are given inventive arrangements by Bob Wilber for a 13-piece group in 1967. *Melody Is a Must* (Phontastic 7571) has the Bobby Hackett–Vic Dickenson quintet in 1969, before the Chiaroscuro sessions. And finally, *Strike Up the Band* (Flying Dutchman 1-0829) is a superior effort from 1972 that features Hackett with a fairly modern sextet (including tenor saxophonist Zoot Sims) running through standards (highlighted by "Embraceable You") and Bob Thiele tunes.

FILMS

Bobby Hackett ghosts for Fred Astaire's trumpet playing in *Second Chorus* (1940).

FREDDIE JENKINS

b. Oct. 10, 1906, New York, d. 1978, Texas

Freddie "Posey" Jenkins was Duke Ellington's "hot" trumpet soloist in the early days, and he was a colorful showman. He picked up experience playing with the 369th Regiment Cadet Band, Edgar Hayes's Blue Grass Buddies, and Horace

Henderson's Collegians (1924–28). Jenkins joined Ellington in 1928, and his playing contrasted well with the plunger rumblings of Bubber Miley and the lyrical introspective flights of Arthur Whetsol, giving the orchestra three distinctive trumpet soloists. He worked and recorded steadily with Ellington until a major lung ailment forced his retirement in April 1934. Jenkins did his best to come back, leading his own record date in 1935 (highlighted by "Toledo Shuffle" and "I Can't Dance") and spending a few months in 1936 as part of the Luis Russell Orchestra. He was able to rejoin Ellington in March 1937, getting his old spot back. In May 1938 Jenkins went out on his own, co-leading a combo with Hayes Alvis. But soon his lung ailment returned and, after a few months in the hospital, he was told that he had to permanently give up playing. Freddie Jenkins worked at many jobs during the next 40 years, including being a songwriter, a press agent, a disc jockey, and in real estate and insurance. Considering that he was forced out of music due to his bad health, it is ironic that Freddie Jenkins ended up outliving most of his contemporaries!

●

FILMS
Freddie Jenkins is prominent during "Old Man Blues" with Duke Ellington in the otherwise forgettable Amos and Andy film *Check & Double Check* (1930).

TAFT JORDAN
b. Feb. 15, 1915, Florence, SC, d. Dec. 1, 1981, New York, NY

A solid Swing soloist, Taft Jordan was always a valuable sideman. He grew up in Norfolk, Virginia, played locally, and then studied music in Philadelphia. Jordan made his recording debut in the early 1930s with the Washboard Rhythm Kings. He was a key soloist and a fixture with Chick Webb's orchestra from 1933 through 1941, staying with the band during the two years after Webb's death, when it was fronted by Ella Fitzgerald. Featured on many songs, Jordan recorded a version of "On the Sunny Side of the Street" in 1933 that was based on Louis Armstrong's concert routine. When Satch got around to recording it a year later, some people thought that he was copying Jordan! After the Chick Webb band broke up, Jordan had his own octet at the Savoy Ballroom (1941–43). He was with Duke Ellington's orchestra during 1943–47, where his playing was well utilized, including at Ellington's famed Carnegie Hall concerts. After that stint ended, Jordan freelanced in New York, including playing with the Lucille Dixon Orchestra (1949–53), Don Redman (1953), and Benny Goodman (1958). Taft Jordan co-led a group with trumpeter Dick Vance for a time, did some studio work, played in the pit orchestras of Broadway shows, and was active into the late 1970s, still sporting an attractive tone and a swinging style.

●

8 *Mood Indigo / Mar. 31, 1960 + June 30, 1961 / Prestige 24230*
Other than four numbers in 1935, Taft Jordan led just three record dates in his career including one a piece for the Mercury and Aamco labels. This 1999 CD reissues his Moodsville LP, *Mood Indigo,* seven Duke Ellington ballads performed by the often-muted trumpeter, guitarist Kenny Burrell, pianist Richard Wyands, bassist Joe Benjamin, and drummer Charlie Persip. In addition to that lyrical set, the complete contents of The Swingville All Stars are also here, a rousing sextet session with tenor saxophonist Al Sears and altoist Hilton Jefferson that consists of six other standards including two associated with Ellington. Recommended.

AL KILLIAN

b. Oct. 15, 1916, Birmingham, AL, d. Sept. 5, 1950, Los Angeles, CA

A major high-note trumpeter who could also solo and successfully made the transition from Swing to bop, Al Killian had his life cut short. His early associations included playing with Charlie Turner's Arcadians in the mid-1930s, Baron Lee, Teddy Hill, Don Redman, and Count Basie (1940–42). Killian was with Charlie Barnet's band off and on during 1943–46, taking time off for a second brief stint with Basie and for a few months with Lionel Hampton in 1945. He had his own band late in 1946, toured with Jazz at the Philharmonic, was briefly with Billy Eckstine, Earle Spencer, and Boyd Raeburn, and then toured with Duke Ellington during 1948–50. After settling in Los Angeles, he was tragically murdered by a psychopathic landlord. Al Killian helped extend the range of the trumpet and was a competitor of Cat Anderson and Maynard Ferguson before his death.

YANK LAWSON

b. May 3, 1911, Trenton, MO, d. Feb. 18, 1995, Indianapolis, IN

John "Yank" Lawson was a Dixieland trumpeter who found his initial fame during the Swing era with Bob Crosby's orchestra. He started out playing saxophone and piano before switching to trumpet as a teenager. After playing locally, Lawson was part of Ben Pollack's orchestra during 1933–34. When the band broke up due to Pollack's neglect, Yank worked with Will Osborne and did some studio work. He became an original member of the Bob Crosby Orchestra when it was formed out of the nucleus of the Pollack band. Lawson was a star with the orchestra and Bob Crosby's Bobcats during 1935–38, taking solos on many records. His decision to join Tommy Dorsey in 1938 was therefore a major blow to the band. Lawson was well treated by Dorsey and liberally featured with TD's Clambake Seven. Leaving Dorsey in November 1939, he worked with Abe Lyman, with Richard Himber, and with a theater orchestra before returning to Crosby in May 1941. Yank's return helped rejuvenate Crosby's orchestra during the period before its breakup in 1942. After a short stint with Benny Goodman in December 1942, Yank Lawson became a studio musician for many years. However, he never neglected his jazz playing, performing with Dixieland bands at night, frequently with his lifelong friend bassist Bob Haggart. They co-led a series of albums in the 1950s, participated in many Bob Crosby reunions, and starting in 1968 cofounded and led the World's Greatest Jazz Band. Up until his death, Yank Lawson stayed busy playing at Dixieland festivals and recorded on a regular basis.

●

7 *With a Southern Accent / Mar. 5, 1991 / Jazzology 203*
One of several reunion dates led by Yank Lawson and Bob Haggart (as the Lawson-Haggart Jazz Band) from late in their careers, this is a solid offering, with fine solos and support contributed by trombonist George Masso, clarinetist Kenny Davern, pianist John Bunch, and guitarist Bucky Pizzarelli. Nothing new occurs, but the repertoire (which refers to the South in each of its titles) is mostly fairly fresh, including the underrated "Is It True What They Say About Dixie?," "Carolina in the Morning," "Stars Fell on Alabama," and two versions apiece of "Creole Love Call" and "Beale Street Blues."

LPS TO SEARCH FOR
That's a Plenty (Doctor Jazz 40064) has Lawson's recordings for the Signature label during 1943–44, hard-charging Dixieland with the likes of valve trombonist Brad Gowans, trombonists Miff Mole and Lou McGarity, clarinetists Pee Wee Russell and Rod Cless, and pianist James P. Johnson, among others. The first official Lawson-Haggart dates (tributes to Jelly Roll Morton and King Oliver) have been reissued on *Jazz Band 1951/1952* (Tax 8040); trombonist Lou McGarity and clarinetist Bill Stegmeyer also have prominent roles. From the later period of his career, *Yank Lawson Plays Mostly Blues* (Audiophile 221), a date with trombonist

George Masso, clarinetist Johnny Mince, and tenorman Al Klink, shows the power and drive that Lawson still had in 1986. 1987's *Go to New Orleans* (Jazzology 153) is a reunion of some of the World's Greatest Jazz Band alumni, matching for the last time Yank Lawson and Billy Butterfield.

WINGY MANONE
b. Feb. 13, 1904, New Orleans, LA, d. July 9, 1982, Las Vegas, NV

Dixieland trumpeter and singer Wingy Manone during the 1930s recorded a series of joyful and freewheeling combo recordings that were quite popular, offering an alternative to the more tightly-controlled big Swing bands. Joseph Manone earned the name of "Wingy" when he lost his right arm in a streetcar accident as a child. Shortly after, he started playing trumpet and was a professional by the time he was 17, performing on riverboats. Manone worked in Chicago and New York, with the Crescent City Jazzers in Mobile in 1924, and with the same group in St. Louis when they recorded as the Arcadian Serenaders. Wingy traveled a lot during the next few years, performing with territory bands, including one led by the legendary pianist Peck Kelley in Texas. After moving to New York in late 1927, Manone began leading his own band, and he first recorded as a leader. Wingy worked with Ray Miller, Charlie Straight, and Speed Webb, freelanced as a leader for a time, and then in 1934 began making records quite prolifically. He cut many titles during 1934–41, including a hit version of "Isle of Capri"; among his sidemen were tenors Eddie Miller, Bud Freeman, and Chu Berry, clarinetists Matty Matlock, Joe Marsala, and Buster Bailey, and trombonists Santo Pecora and Jack Teagarden. Manone, whose jivey vocals had an audience, in 1940 settled near Los Angeles, where he appeared on the radio regularly with Bing Crosby, played locally, and stayed popular for decades playing the type of good-humored New Orleans Dixieland that he loved.

●

| 10 | *The Wingy Manone Collection, Vol. 1 / Apr. 11, 1927– Sept. 19, 1930 / Collectors Classics 3* |

| 10 | *The Wingy Manone Collection, Vol. 2 / May 2, 1934– Sept. 26, 1934 / Collectors Classics 4* |

| 9 | *The Wingy Manone Collection, Vol. 3 / Oct. 3, 1934– May 3, 1935 / Collectors Classics 5* |

| 8 | *The Wingy Manone Collection, Vol. 4 / Mar 27, 1935– Jan. 28, 1936 / Collectors Classics 20* |

| 9 | *1927–1934 / Apr. 11, 1927–Aug. 15, 1934 / Classics 774* |

| 8 | *1934–1935 / Oct. 3, 1934–May 27, 1935 / Classics 798* |

| 8 | *1935–1936 / July 5, 1935–Jan. 28, 1936 / Classics 828* |

All of Wingy Manone's early recordings (through 1940) have been reissued complete and in chronological order by the Classics label, while Collectors Classics, which thus far has reached 1936, has releases that are actually slightly superior due to the inclusion of occasional alternate takes. *Vol.* 1 of Collectors Classics is particularly comprehensive, for not only does it have Manone's first dates as a leader from 1927–28 and 1930 (the latter are listed as being by "Barbecue Joe and his Hot Dogs") but it also has two songs that he cut with Benny Goodman and the two selections (with three alternate takes) that he made with a pickup group called the Cellar Boys. The classic jazz numbers include "Up the Country Blues," "Trying to Stop My Crying," "Barrel House Stomp," "Tar Paper Stomp" (which has the same melody as "In the Mood," nine years before it became a hit), and "Big Butter and Egg Man." *Vol.* 2 has the session in 1934 by Manone that matches Dicky Wells, Artie Shaw, and Bud Freeman with the alternating pianists Jelly Roll Morton and Teddy Wilson; the four songs include three alternate takes. In addition, Manone is heard on his first date under his own name in 1934 (which initiated his popular series for Bluebird), "Shine" with the Four Bales of Cotton, and ten selections with the "New Orleans Rhythm Kings," which was really just a Manone group playing Dixieland standards from the NORK repertoire.

Vol. 3 finds Manone hitting it big with "The Isle of Capri" in March 1935, leading a group filled with Bob Crosby sidemen (including Eddie Miller and clarinetist Matty Matlock), and guesting on "Sliphorn Sam" with Russ Morgan's orchestra. *Vol. 4* consists of 25 selections from Manone's groups during an eight-month period (attesting to his growing popularity), with appearances by Matlock, Miller, Joe Marsala, Bud Freeman, George Brunies, and (on five songs) Jack Teagarden. The performances were beginning to get into a routine that almost always consisted of a melody chorus, a Manone vocal, short solos by sidemen, and a closing ensemble led by Manone's happy horn. The first three *Wingy Manone* Classics CDs cover the same period but without the alternate takes or sideman appearances.

8   *1936 / Mar. 10, 1936–July 1, 1936 / Classics 849*

7   *1936–1937 / Aug. 20, 1936–May 25, 1937 / Classics 887*

7   *1937–1938 / May 25, 1937–May 23, 1938 / Classics 952*

8   *1939–1940 / Apr. 26, 1939–Jan. 15, 1940 / Classics 1023*
Thus far the Classic label has traced Wingy Manone's career up to early 1940. *1936* has vocals by Manone on every number except "Is It True What They Say About Dixie" and "Panama." Joe Marsala, Matty Matlock, and Eddie Miller are among the sidemen, with the other highlights including "Tormented," "Dallas Blues," "Swingin' at the Hickory House," and "Hesitation Blues." *1936–1937* does not have a single instrumental (nor does *1937–1938*), but Manone sounds in prime form and he was always enthusiastic in both his playing and his vocalizing. "A Good Man Is Hard to Find" (with singer Sally Shapiro), "Let Me Call You Sweetheart," "Floatin' Down to Cotton Town," and "You Showed Me the Way" are among the better selections on *1936–1937*. *1937–1938* is noteworthy for having Chu Berry featured on one of the four sessions. Otherwise it is the regular crew along with material that ranges from gems to forgettable; the former include "The Prisoner's Song," "I Ain't Got Nobody," "Jazz Me Blues," and "Little Joe from Chicago." *1939–1940* features Chu Berry on three of the four sessions and there are seven instrumentals; Buster Bailey is also on the first two dates. Surprisingly, the material improved for Manone during this period (while for his competitor Fats Waller the quality was dropping). Among the more memorable numbers are "Downright Disgusted Blues," "Corrine Corrini," "Jumpy Nerves," "Royal Garden Blues," "Farewell Blues," "Blue Lou," "When My Sugar Walks Down the Street," and "She's Crying for Me." There would be three more sessions for Bluebird before the recording strike kept Wingy Manone off records until 1944. Although little of his later material has yet been reissued on CD, Manone would record fairly regularly during 1944–60, with further sessions in 1966 and 1975.

LPS TO SEARCH FOR

Wingy Manone–Sidney Bechet—Together, Town Hall—1947 (Jazz Archives 29) is two concerts in one. The October 11, 1947, portion has six numbers by Manone with a couple of all-star groups, including versions of "St. Louis Blues" and "At the Jazz Band Ball" that include soprano saxophonist Bechet. The second side is an unrelated date from February 18, 1950, with Bechet, trumpeter Max Kaminsky, and trombonist Wilbur DeParis in a sextet, without any Manone in sight. *With Papa Bue's Viking Jazzband* (Storyville 4066), from 1966–67, was Manone's first record in six years and the next-to-last recording of his career. Teamed with a topnotch Scandinavian Dixieland group headed by trombonist Arne Bue Jensen, Manone sounds in surprisingly strong form, jamming happily on some of his favorite standards.

FILMS

Wingy Manone has a featured role in the Bing Crosby film *Rhythm on the River* (1940). He is also in *Juke Box Jenny* (1942), *Hi'ya Sailor* (1943), and *Rhythm Inn* (1951) in addition to participating in a memorable jam session in *Sarge Goes to College* (1947).

RAY NANCE

b. Dec. 10, 1913, Chicago, IL, d. Jan. 28, 1976, New York, NY

Ray Nance was a triple-threat entertainer. As a cornetist he was brilliant at using the plunger mute and could also play open, he was one of jazz's top violinists, and he was also a swinging singer. Duke Ellington was fortunate to get three entertainers for the price of one, and he held onto the bargain for a long time!

Nance (who was also a skillful dancer) took piano lessons when he was six and studied violin for seven years before starting to learn trumpet. He played with the band at Lane College, the Rhythm Rascals. Nance led a sextet in Chicago for a few years (starting in 1932) and had stints with Earl Hines (1937–38) and Horace Henderson (1939–40), recording with both big bands. In November 1940 Nance joined the Duke Ellington Orchestra (his very first night with the band is documented at their recorded Fargo, North Dakota, concert) and, with a few short absences (including part of 1944–45), he was with Ellington for 23 years. During that time, Nance took a famous solo on the original version of "Take the 'A' Train" and became the successor to Cootie Williams as the band's plunger mute specialist; he was Duke's best male vocalist, and his violin playing added a unique sound to the orchestra (as can be heard on "Black, Brown and Beige," "C Jam Blues," and many other numbers).

Ray Nance's post-Ellington years were generally uneventful. Mostly he freelanced with small Swing groups, although he did pop up in a few very modern settings (including with drummer Chico Hamilton and on a jam session record with Dizzy Gillespie and pianist Chick Corea) in addition to occasional reunions with Ellington. Considering his talent, it is surprising how little Ray Nance recorded as a leader: four titles in London in 1948 and an album apiece for Solid State (1969) and MPS (1972), both long out of print and quite obscure.

FRANKIE NEWTON
b. Jan. 4, 1906, Emory, VA, d. Mar. 11, 1954, New York, NY

A lyrical trumpeter with a sound of his own, Frankie Newton had a surprisingly brief prime period. He started working with Lloyd and Cecil Scott's band in 1927 and also played with Elmer Snowden, Eugene Kennedy, Chick Webb, Charlie Johnson, and Sam Wooding. Newton, who recorded with Bessie Smith in 1933, was with Charlie Johnson's band during 1933–35 and then gained some attention for his playing with Teddy Hill (1936–37), where he was the replacement for Roy Eldridge. He spent part of 1937 with John Kirby's new sextet, but a personality conflict led to his being replaced by Charlie Shavers. Newton worked with Mezz Mezzrow's Disciples of Swing and Lucky Millinder (1937–38) and then led his own combo (which frequently included altoist Pete Brown) most of the time up until 1944. He headed some record dates during 1937–39, including his personal favorite recording, "The Blues My Baby Gave to Me." But, although he had stints with James P. Johnson during 1944–45 and Edmond Hall (1949), he lived mostly in obscurity in Boston after 1945. Frankie Newton made few recordings after 1939, became more interested in painting and leftist politics than music during his last years, and had been largely forgotten for a decade at the time of his early death.

●

9 *1937–1939 / Mar. 5, 1937–Aug. 16, 1939 / Classics 643*
All of Frankie Newton's recordings as a leader (other than alternate takes) are on this enjoyable CD. The sidemen change from date to date and include such notables as Pete Brown, clarinetist Edmund Hall, Cecil Scott on clarinet and tenor, clarinetist Mezz Mezzrow, pianists James P. Johnson, Albert Ammons, and Ken Kersey, trombonist Dickie Wells, and guest vocalist Slim Gaillard. Newton was such a fine trumpeter that it is a shame that he did not accomplish much more. Not every one of his recordings is a classic, but such numbers as "Please Don't Talk About Me When I'm Gone," "The Brittwood Stomp," "Rosetta," and "The World Is Waiting for the Sunrise" are given memorable treatment.

HOT LIPS PAGE
b. Jan. 27, 1908, Dallas, TX, d. Nov. 5, 1954, New York, NY

A powerful trumpeter who was expert at building up solos, Hot Lips Page was also a very effective blues singer and a star at jam sessions. He should have been a bigger name during the Swing era than he became, but he was always very popular among musicians.

Oran "Hot Lips" Page began seriously playing trumpet when he was 12. After high school he was a member of the group accompanying Ma Rainey. He also backed other singers (including Bessie Smith and Ida Cox), was in Troy Floyd's band in San Antonio, and played throughout Texas with Sugar Lou and Eddie's Hotel Tyler Band. In 1928 Page arrived in Kansas City, where he joined Walter Page's Blue Devils. After three years with the unrelated Page, he became a member of Bennie Moten's band (1931–35), participating in several recording sessions, including a classic date in 1932. After Moten's death in 1935, Page had his own quintet and then was with Count Basie for a few months in 1936. He was discovered and signed by manager Joe Glaser, relocating to New York. Perhaps if Page had stayed with Basie and been part of his successful trip east, he might have become much more famous.

Hot Lips Page led a big band during 1937–38 that made some recordings but did not catch on. From late 1938 until mid-1940 he led small Swing combos. Page had brief stints with the Bud Freeman big band and Joe Marsala and then became a featured soloist and singer with Artie Shaw (1941–42), making several memorable recordings. After leading another short-lived big band, Page primarily played with small groups the rest of his career (including guesting with Eddie Condon), always ready to take a hot trumpet solo that would add excitement to any session. Hot Lips worked fairly steadily, had a hit record with Pearl Bailey in 1949 ("Baby It's Cold Outside"), toured Europe a few times, and spread joy everywhere he went until dying from the effects of a heart attack in 1954 when he was just 46. ●

9 *1938–1940 / Mar. 10, 1938–Dec. 3, 1940 / Classics 561*

9 *1940–1944 / Dec. 10, 1940–Sept. 29, 1944 / Classics 809*

8 *1944–1946 / Nov. 30, 1944–Oct. 1946 / Classics 950*
When Hot Lips Page came to New York in 1937, he was soon leading a big band. His orchestra's dozen selections (cut during two sessions in 1938) are on *1938–1940*. Although the big band did not make it commercially, it was a swinging orchestra that featured such sidemen as Ben Smith on clarinet and alto, and tenor saxophonist Benny Waters. There are vocals on nine of the 12 tunes (six by Page) and the better numbers include "Jumpin'," "Feelin' High and Happy," and "Skull Duggery." Also on this CD are four small-group dates; Don Byas, Pete Johnson, and Don Stovall make appearances. *1940–1944* has a quartet date with Teddy Bunn (including "Evil Man's Blues," which a few years later would become the more successful "Evil Gal Blues" for Dinah Washington) and combo sides from 1944 with such sidemen as tenors Lucky Thompson and Don Byas, altoist Earl Bostic, and Vic Dickenson. "Rockin' at Ryan's," "Uncle Sam Blues," and "Pagin' Mr. Page" are the standouts. Much of the music on *1944–1946* was formerly obscure, being released by the Continental, Hub, Melrose, and Apollo labels. Although Swing was going out of style, Page still had his enthusiasm and plenty of star sidemen on these recordings, including Byas, Bostic, Ben Webster, Buck Clayton, and pianist Hank Jones.

6 *After Hours in Harlem / 1940–1941 / High Note 7031*

7 *Dr. Jazz Series, Vol. 6 / Dec. 21, 1951–Mar. 7, 1952 / Storyville 6046*
Hot Lips Page always loved to jam. *After Hours in Harlem* (which was formerly an Onyx LP) features Page playing in various New York locations, captured on Jerry Newman's recorder. The recording quality is at times shaky and Page easily outshines the other players (particularly fellow trumpeter Joe Guy), but there are some strong moments, including two early appearances by pianist Thelonious Monk and four interesting trio numbers with pianist Donald Lambert and the overly excitable tenor of Herbie Fields. The music performed on the *Dr. Jazz* radio series is straight Dixieland, played with plenty of spirit during 1951–52. Page is heard as the featured soloist and singer with drummer George Wettling's Stuyvesant Stompers, which has a revolving cast of players, including clarinetists Peanuts Hucko and Pee Wee Russell, Lou McGarity, and Joe Sullivan. Hot Lips Page was flexible enough to fit easily into this format, yet one could also have imagined him battling Roy Eldridge in Jazz at the Philharmonic had he lived to a reasonable age.

LPS TO SEARCH FOR
Play the Blues in B (Jazz Archives 17) features Page in his favorite type of setting, jamming in concert on basic material and standards with a group of all-stars. From 1944–45 and 1950, Page interacts with such players as Benny Morton, Edmond Hall, Teddy Wilson, Peanuts Hucko, tenorman Paul Quinichette, and (on "Billie's Blues" and "All of Me") Billie Holiday.

CHARLIE SHAVERS

b. Aug. 3, 1917, New York, NY, d. July 8, 1971, New York, NY

One of the most exciting trumpeters of the Swing era (and of jazz history), Charlie Shavers was a virtuoso who gave the impression of being able to play anything. He had a wide range, could make the most complex passages sound effortless, and had a strong sense of humor.

Shavers freelanced a bit as a teenager and in 1935 played with Frankie Fairfax's band in Philadelphia. He had stints in New York with Tiny Bradshaw and Lucky Millinder (1937) before hooking up with John Kirby. During 1937–44 he spent the prime years of the big band era with Kirby's Sextet, which was called "the biggest little band in the land." Although an extroverted player, Shavers was quite flexible, and he often utilized a mute and blended in quietly in the unusual ensemble sound of the Kirby Sextet. He was a major factor in the band's sound, contributing many arrangements and composing "Undecided." Shavers, who also recorded with Jimmie Noone, Johnny Dodds, and Sidney Bechet during this period, joined Raymond Scott's CBS Orchestra for a few months after leaving Kirby. He then began a longtime association with Tommy Dorsey's orchestra (1945–56), being well featured but somewhat stuck in a nostalgic Swing setting. Shavers did occasionally break away, recording with the Esquire All-Stars and going on tours with Jazz at the Philharmonic (where he successfully engaged in trumpet battles with Roy Eldridge). He also worked with Benny Goodman for a little while in 1954, but his main job was with Tommy Dorsey, until the trombonist's sudden death. After that time, Shavers often led a quartet (hoping to capitalize on Jonah Jones's surprising fame), sometimes toured with the Tommy Dorsey Ghost Orchestra, and visited Europe. But despite his talents, Charlie Shavers never really made it big and recorded far too little as a leader during his career, leading to his being permanently underrated. ●

9 *1944–1945 / Apr. 22, 1944–1945 / Classics 944*
All of Charlie Shavers's early recordings as a leader (including some from the Keynote and Vogue labels) are on this CD, cut after he had left the John Kirby Sextet. With such sidemen as Tab Smith, Earl Hines, Coleman Hawkins, Teddy Wilson, and clarinetist Buddy DeFranco, Shavers was definitely playing with his peers, yet he emerges as the star on virtually every selection, many of which are quite exciting.

LPS TO SEARCH FOR

It is puzzling that Charlie Shavers, who worked now and then with Norman Granz's Jazz at the Philharmonic in the 1950s, did not record as a leader for Granz's label, Verve. The albums he did lead tend to be a bit disappointing, con-sidering his ability. *The Most Intimate* (Bethlehem 5002), from 1955, is mostly a set of melodic ballads in which his warm horn is backed by a string orchestra. *Like Charlie* (Everest 1127), a quartet date from 1960, has its spectacular moments, particularly "The Best Things in Life Are Free," but the songs are generally overly concise. *Charlie Digs Paree* (MGM 765), with a quartet that includes pianist Ray Bryant, are French themes that the trumpeter plays with color, while *Paris Jazz* (Everest 5225), although recorded in France, is actually a spirited (if very brief at just 25 minutes) program of Swing tunes. The best of the bunch is *Live from Chicago* (Spotlite 154), a set of radio performances with a quartet from 1962 that finds Shavers getting to stretch out and showing that he was still in prime form even if his music was, by that time, completely overlooked.

VALAIDA SNOW

b. June 2, 1905, Chattanooga, TN, d. May 30, 1956, New York, NY

Valaida Snow was a unique performer. She was the finest female trumpeter of the Swing era, a good singer, and a top-notch entertainer, better known overseas than she was in the United States. Valaida, whose sisters were named Lavaida and Alvaida (!), appeared in shows starting in the early 1920s, and she was generally the headliner as a singer, dancer, and trumpeter. Valaida first traveled widely in 1926, when she worked with Jack Carter's band in Shanghai. In 1929 she visited the Soviet Union, the Middle East, and Europe. Valaida worked in the Grand Terrace revue in Chicago with Earl Hines in 1933, appeared in the Blackbirds of 1934, and then spent most of the rest of the 1930s overseas, recording as a leader in London (1935–37) and Stockholm (1939–40). She was quite popular in Europe and, with the outbreak of World War II, she was foolish enough to think that she was safe. Valaida was arrested in Denmark in 1941 and spent two horrifying years in a concentration camp before being released on a prisoner exchange. She returned to the United States and, after partly recovering, she resumed her career, working on and off into the mid-1950s. However, Valaida Snow never regained her former prominence and has often been left out of jazz history books.

●

10 *Queen of Trumpet & Song / Jan. 18, 1935–Oct. 1940 / DRG 8455*

All 41 recordings that Valaida Snow led during her prime are on this two-CD set, including a previously unreleased "Poor Butterfly." Recorded in London, Stockholm, and Copenhagen, Snow is heard in with medium-size groups singing and playing trumpet on a variety of standards and riff tunes. Some songs find her mostly singing while another trumpeter is heard from, but Valaida Snow takes enough trumpet solos along the way to show listeners that she was a superior player who deserves to be much better known today.

LPS TO SEARCH FOR

Although half of *Hot Snow* (Rosetta 1305) has now been duplicated by the DRG CD, this deluxe LP is recommended due to the extensive liner notes, the pictures, and the inclusion of eight selections from 1945–46 and 1950.

MUGGSY SPANIER
b. Nov. 9, 1906, Chicago, IL, d. Feb. 12, 1967, Sausalito, CA

Muggsy Spanier was a solid Dixieland player for decades, a bit predictable but always enthusiastic and expressive. For a little while in the Swing era he led a potentially impressive big band, but most of his life was spent jamming with Dixieland combos.

Francis "Muggsy" Spanier started off playing drums, switching to cornet when he was 13. He began playing professionally two years later with Elmer Schoebel (1921), Sig Meyers (1922–24), Charles Pierce, Floyd Town (1925–28), and Ray Miller. Unlike the style of most of his contemporaries, Spanier's playing was as influenced by King Oliver as by Louis Armstrong. He was a vital part of the Chicago jazz scene until he signed up with Ted Lewis's band for what would be a seven-year run (1929–36). Lewis, a cornball singer and an amateurish clarinetist, was at the height of his fame, and Spanier's cornet (along with George Brunies's trombone) gave the band a bit of credibility when Lewis was not dominating.

Spanier was part of Ben Pollack's big band (1936–38), became seriously ill, recovered, and then formed his Ragtimers, an octet that recorded 16 selections in 1939 that would inspire the Dixieland revival movement a few years later. Unfortunately the group was formed a little too early and, after Spanier could not get enough work for the Ragtimers, he joined Bob Crosby's orchestra (1940–41). Muggsy led his own big band (which sounded a bit like Crosby's) during 1941–43, recording eight titles before breaking up. He spent the rest of his career in Dixieland settings, mostly as a leader except for a short time with Miff Mole in 1944–45 and for a few years with Earl Hines in the 1950s. Muggsy Spanier, whose style was virtually unchanged after the late 1930s, remained active until being forced to retire in 1964 due to bad health.

●

10 *The "Ragtime Band" Sessions / July 7, 1939–Dec. 12, 1939 / Bluebird 66550*

10 *1939–1942 / July 7, 1939–June 1, 1942 / Classics 709*

On four record dates in 1939, cornetist Muggsy Spanier launched the Dixieland revival a couple of years early. Dubbed "The Great 16," these titles (which also feature trombonist George Brunies, clarinetist Rod Cless, three different tenors, and a four-piece rhythm section) are consistently exciting. The high points include "Big Butter and Egg Man," "I Wish I Could Shimmy Like My Sister Kate" (which has a famous Brunies vocal), "Relaxin' at the Touro," "Lonesome Road," and "Mandy, Make Up Your Mind." Because it includes eight alternate takes, Spanier's Bluebird disc could be called "The Great 24." *1939–1942* has the original 16 cuts plus the eight rarely reissued numbers by Spanier's 1942 big band, a short-lived orchestra that deserved a better fate.

9 *Manhattan Masters, 1945 / Mar. 1–2, 1945 / Storyville 6051*

Muggsy Spanier was quite busy during the first two days of March 1945, recording 15 Dixieland tunes and three basic originals with overlapping groups led not only by him but by trombonist Miff Mole and clarinetist Pee Wee Russell. The musicians (which also include Lou McGarity, baritonist Ernie Caceres, and pianist Gene Schroeder) sound quite inspired on these Dixieland warhorses, certainly much more than they would a decade later after continually playing the same songs on a nightly basis!

8 *Columbia—The Gem of the Ocean / June 1962 / Mobile Fidelity 857*

Muggsy Spanier's final album as a leader found him reviving his 1941 big band, using Dean Kincaide arrangements and performing ten selections with a 16-piece orchestra that includes Matty Matlock, Eddie Miller, and pianist Stan Wrightsman. A very successful effort, this set features mostly Spanier playing songs that his big band never recorded commercially (other than "Chicago"). Since he had to put down his cornet altogether two years later, this can be considered the final chapter in the Muggsy Spanier story.

LPS TO SEARCH FOR

Little David Play Your Harp (Jazz Archives 30) is a valuable collector's LP featuring Spanier's big band on 13 selections taken from radio broadcasts in December 1941, only two of which were commercially recorded; the arrangements of Deane Kincaide and Fud Livingston keep the proceedings swinging.

FILMS

Muggsy Spanier appears as part of Ted Lewis's group in *Is Everybody Happy?* (1929) and *Here Comes the Band* (1935).

REX STEWART

b. Feb. 22, 1907, Philadelphia, PA, d. Sept. 7, 1967, Los Angeles, CA

Rex Stewart is best known for his half-valve technique, which was most memorably displayed on "Boy Meets Horn" with Duke Ellington. Stewart was a colorful, combative, and exciting player who liked to play surprising high notes in dramatic spots. He grew up near Washington, D.C., and played piano, violin, and alto horn before switching permanently to cornet. Stewart was working professionally by the time he was 14, playing on riverboats, and going out on tour with Ollie Blackwell's Jazz Clowns in 1921. He became a fixture in New York by 1923, playing with many local groups, including Elmer Snowden (1925–26). Stewart was with Fletcher Henderson's orchestra for a couple of months in 1926 but, even though he recorded with the big band and sounded fine, he did not feel he was quite ready. Instead he became part of Horace Henderson's Collegians for a time. Stewart was back with Fletcher during 1928–30 and 1932–33, also spending short periods with Alex Jackson and McKinney's Cotton Pickers. He led his own big band during 1933–34, gigged with Luis Russell for a brief time (starring on Russell's recording of "Ol' Man River"), and then in December 1934 became a member of Duke Ellington's orchestra, staying until December 1945 (other than a few months in 1943). During that time, not only was the cornetist featured on many of Duke's records, but he also led small-group sessions of his own, with the personnel drawn mostly from

An early 1950s recording session brought together four musicians best remembered for their work with Duke Ellington: trombonist Lawrence Brown, cornetist Rex Stewart, tenor saxophonist Al Sears, and baritonist Harry Carney.

Ellington's big band. Stewart was a popular attraction with Duke, sharing the solo space with Cootie Williams and his successor, Ray Nance. Ellington loved writing for Rex's half-valve technique.

After going out on his own, Stewart put together a group called the Rextet, taking them to Europe in October 1947. He stayed overseas until spring 1950 (including a period in Australia), recording extensively. After returning to the U.S., Stewart worked in both mainstream and Dixieland settings in the 1950s, was a disc jockey, organized and recorded with the Fletcher Henderson Reunion Band in 1957–58, was featured at Eddie Condon's club during 1958–59, and wrote about jazz history. His articles appeared in many magazines, and his book *Jazz Masters of the Thirties* is a classic. Rex Stewart's trumpet chops declined during the 1960s but he still played occasional concerts as late as 1966.

●

7 *Rex Stewart and the Ellingtonians / July 23, 1940–1946 / Original Jazz Classics 1710*

5 *1946–1947 / Jan. 26, 1945–Dec. 8, 1947 / Classics 1016*

5 *1947–1948 / Dec. 9, 1947–Jan. 1948 / Classics 1057*

8 *Late Date / Oct. 22, 1958 / Simitar 56132*

The music on the Original Jazz Classics CD was originally put out by the HRS label and has been reissued as part of

Mosaic's limited-edition HRS box set. This disc features Rex Stewart on four numbers in 1940 with Lawrence Brown, Barney Bigard, Billy Kyle, and a rhythm section; "Bugle Call Rag" and "Diga Diga Doo" are given exciting and definitive treatment. Stewart is also heard in 1946 with a quartet (playing four of his originals) that again includes Kyle. Strangely enough the last two songs, by an octet headed by pianist Jimmy Jones, does not include Stewart at

SWING

150

all, but it does have several Ellington players (including Lawrence Brown, Harry Carney, and altoist Otto Hardwick). Overall, this is fine small-group Swing music. *1946–1947* begins with Stewart's HRS quartet date of 1946 and then, after an extended version of "I May Be Wrong" recorded live, reissues the music that Stewart recorded overseas in Stockholm and Paris. His band during the tour was a no-name septet other than for veteran trombonist Sandy Williams. The music is only decently recorded and is sometimes an uncomfortable mixture of Swing and bop, although not without interest. *1946–1947* concludes with a leftover selection from a 1945 date, while *1947–1948* continues documenting Stewart's band in Paris. The performances were formerly rare and are often worthwhile if not essential. Much more fun is *Late Date,* a rambunctious 1958 Dixieland date in which Stewart, Buster Bailey, Vic Dickenson, pianist Marty Napoleon, bassist Arvell Shaw, and drummer George Wettling really rip through some warhorses and a couple of originals. "High Society" and "Jazz Me Blues" are hyper to the extreme and somewhat humorous.

LPS TO SEARCH FOR

LPS TO SEARCH FOR

Rex Stewart and His Dixielanders (Jazz Anthology 5188) is solid Dixieland from the early 1950s that is of special interest because of the participation of the modern pianist Herbie Nichols. *Rendezvous with Rex* (Felsted 7001) has two Swing sessions from January 1958 featuring six Stewart originals and such veterans as Haywood Henry (on clarinet and baritone), altoist Hilton Jefferson, Garvin Bushell on clarinet and bassoon, and either Willie "The Lion" Smith or Dick Cary on piano. And quite fun is *The Rex Stewart Memorial Album* (Prestige 7728), which finds Stewart romping with John Dengler (who is heard on bass sax, washboard, and kazoo), Wilbert Kirk on harmonica, both Jerome Darr and Chauncey Westbrook on guitars, and drummer Charles Lampkin. Rex Stewart does the most he can with his slipping chops during this 1960 date and makes the colorful "Rasputin" and a variety of veteran skiffle tunes quite memorable.

FILMS

Rex Stewart is in *Hellzapoppin'* (1941) and plays quite colorfully with the Red Allen All-Stars in *The Sound of Jazz* (1957).

ARTHUR WHETSOL

b. 1905, Punta Gorda, FL, d. Jan. 5, 1940, New York, NY

Arthur Whetsol had a beautiful, haunting tone that seemed so weightless as to float. He also had impressive technique and a lyrical style which added a great deal to the colors available for Duke Ellington to experiment with. Whetsol grew up in Washington, D.C., and was a childhood friend of Duke's. He started playing with Ellington as early as 1920, also gigging with Claude Hopkins and the White Brothers. He went with Duke to New York in 1923 but soon returned home to study medicine at Howard University. In early 1928 Whetsol was welcomed back by Ellington, and he was an integral part of his band until sickness forced him to quit in October 1937. Arthur Whetsol made a few attempts to come back, but he passed away at the age of 34. His playing on "Mood Indigo" and "Black Beauty" is classic, and his tone was a major contrast to the plunger mute growls of Bubber Miley and Cootie Williams and the hot solos of Freddie Jenkins.

FILMS

Duke Ellington's *Black and Tan* (1929) has a wonderful duet version of "Black and Tan Fantasy" by Arthur Whetsol and Duke.

COOTIE WILLIAMS
b. July 24, 1910, Mobile, AL, d. Sept. 14, 1985, New York, NY

One of the major trumpeters of the Swing era, Charles Melvin "Cootie" Williams had a long and episodic career. He learned many instruments early on, playing trombone, tuba, and drums in a school band. Largely self-taught on the trumpet, Williams gigged locally as a teenager, and when he was 14 he toured one summer with the Young Family Band, a group that included the equally youthful Lester and Lee Young. Williams picked up experience playing in Florida with Eagle Eye Shields and with Alonzo Ross's DeLuxe Syncopators (1926–28). Arriving in New York in 1928, Cootie Williams recorded with James P. Johnson and worked with Chick Webb and Fletcher Henderson. In February 1929 he joined Duke Ellington's orchestra as the replacement for the increasingly unreliable Bubber Miley. Miley, who had become an alcoholic, was the most important soloist in Ellington's early band, being a master with mutes, which allowed him to create a wide variety of otherworldly sounds. Bubber had inspired trombonist Tricky Sam Nanton and they made a classic team. Cootie Williams had not used mutes much before, and he played open for the first couple of weeks, until it dawned on him that he was in Miley's spot. Cootie learned fast (helped out by Nanton) and within a short time had surpassed his predecessor.

Williams was with Ellington throughout all of the 1930s, taking both open and muted solos ("Concerto for Cootie" was one of his many well-known features) and making a major name for himself. He had opportunities to lead small-group dates during 1937–40, sessions that featured other musicians from Duke's band. In November 1940 Williams surprised the music world by leaving Ellington's band to accept a more lucrative offer from Benny Goodman. Raymond Scott saluted the historic occasion by recording the song "When Cootie Left the Duke." During his year with BG, Cootie was well featured with both the big band and with one of Goodman's finest small groups, a septet also including Charlie Christian and Georgie Auld. When he left the clarinetist in October 1941, at first Williams asked Duke for his old job back, but Ellington (who already had Ray Nance firmly in Cootie's spot) suggested that he form his own big band instead. Williams followed his advice, and he soon had an orchestra that was playing regularly at the Savoy Ballroom. His ensemble was the first to record a pair of Thelonious Monk tunes ("Epistrophy" and "'Round Midnight") and for a period the Cootie Williams Orchestra had such interesting soloists as pianist Bud Powell, altoist-singer Eddie "Cleanhead" Vinson, tenor saxophonist Eddie "Lockjaw" Davis, and (for a brief time) altoist Charlie Parker. Later in the decade, Willis "Gator" Jackson made a hit for the big band when he was showcased on the honking "Gator."

In 1948 the Cootie Williams Orchestra broke up, and he cut back to a small group. The trumpeter worked fairly often in the 1950s but was mostly in obscurity, recording only on a rare basis and being in danger of being forgotten altogether. That changed when he rejoined Duke Ellington (after a 22-year "vacation") in the fall of 1962. The trumpeter had aged, but he still had a powerful sound and he made every expressive growl count. Cootie Williams would once again be one of Ellington's stars, staying with Duke until the leader's death in 1974 and working with Mercer Ellington in 1975 before retiring in the late '70s.

●

7 *Cootie Williams in Hi Fi / Mar. 5, 1958–Apr. 8, 1958 / RCA 51718*

Cootie Williams did not record all that much in the 1950s, although he did make two albums for RCA during 1957–58. This outing sticks mostly to Swing standards, with only two Ellington-associated tunes being included: "Caravan" and "Concerto for Cootie." Williams is joined by four trombones, five reeds, and a four-piece rhythm section, playing selections arranged by Bill Stegmeyer. The focus through-out is almost entirely on Cootie, who shows that, despite the years of critical neglect, he could still play some stirring solos.

LPS TO SEARCH FOR

The Cootie Williams Orchestra remains one of the great unknown big bands of the mid-1940s. *Big Band Bounce & Boogie* (Affinity 1031) has three sessions from 1944: eight songs with a sextet and eight others with his big band.

With such major soloists as Eddie "Lockjaw" Davis, Eddie "Cleanhead" Vinson (who takes a few vocals), and Bud Powell plus guest singer Pearl Bailey (on two songs), this was a superior outfit. Highlights include "Echoes of Harlem," the initial version of " 'Round Midnight," "Blue Garden Blues," and "Somebody's Gotta Go." *Typhoon* (Contact 1003) has big band selections from 1945 and 1947 plus combo sides from 1947 and 1950. The music was becoming a bit more exhibitionistic and R&B-oriented but was generally quite exciting (despite an excess of vocals), particularly the honking tenor solos of Sam "The Man" Taylor, Weasel Parker, and Willis "Gator" Jackson. From 1957, Cootie Williams and Rex Stewart had a reunion on *The Big Challenge* (Fresh Sound 720), a date that also matches trombonists Lawrence Brown and J. C. Higginbotham and, most notably, the tenors of Coleman Hawkins and Bud Freeman. Ernie Wilkins's arrangements are a major asset.

FILMS

The trumpeter is prominent in *Memories of Duke* (A Vision 50187), a 1980 documentary on Duke Ellington that is available on video.

SNOOKY YOUNG
b. Feb. 3, 1919, Dayton, OH

A valuable trumpeter with an impressive range who could also play powerful solos (open or muted), Eugene "Snooky" Young in 1999 was one of the few Swing era musicians who was still performing in public regularly. He played early on with Eddie Heywood, Sr., pianist Graham Jackson, the Wilberforce Collegians, and Clarence "Chic" Carter (1937–39). Young joined Jimmie Lunceford's orchestra in 1939 and made an immediate impression, taking swinging solos and uplifting the ensembles; "Uptown Blues" was his most famous solo of the era. After leaving Lunceford, he had short stints with the big bands of Count Basie (1942) and Lionel Hampton, moved to California, and worked with Les Hite, Benny Carter, Gerald Wilson's orchestra, and Hampton before having a second period with Basie (1945–47). At that point in time, Young decided to return home to Dayton, where he played locally for a decade, usually leading his own band. He returned to the major leagues in 1957, joining Count Basie's orchestra as a first trumpeter for five years. In 1962 he became a full-time studio musician (at first in New York and later in Los Angeles), working with the Tonight Show Band and the big bands of Benny Goodman, Thad Jones–Mel Lewis, and, in more recent times, Gerald Wilson and the Clayton-Hamilton Jazz Orchestra. Snooky Young, who in his later years often took solos using a plunger mute, remains a Swing treasure who can always be counted on to add excitement and class to any musical situation.

●

7 *Snooky & Marshall's Album / 1978 / Concord Jazz 4055*
Snooky Young has surprisingly led only three record dates in his career. This Concord CD was actually co-led with altoist Marshall Royal, and it is not too surprising that it has a Count Basie flavor throughout, helped out by the rhythm section (Freddie Green, pianist Ross Tompkins, bassist Ray Brown, and drummer Louie Bellson). Scatman Crothers sits in on his "Mean Dog Blues" and, in addition to a couple of newer tunes, the repertoire is primarily older standards, including a three-song ballad medley, "Limehouse Blues," and "Cherry."

LPS TO SEARCH FOR

Snooky Young's other two albums have not reappeared on CD yet. *The Boys from Dayton* (Master Jazz 8130) features two different groups, Young in a septet with altoist Norris Turney and trombonist Booty Wood, and a quintet date led by Turney without Young. Despite a funky rhythm section, the interpretations of originals, standards, and songs associated with Basie and Ellington are mostly pretty straight-ahead. The best showcase of all for Snooky, *Horn of Plenty* (Concord 91), is a quintet outing with Ross Tompkins, guitarist John Collins, Ray Brown, and drummer Jake Hanna. The trumpeter plays four standards, a blues and three songs by Tom Peterson, sounding in prime form throughout.

FILMS

Snooky Young ghosted the playing of Jack Carson in *Blues in the Night* (1941) and appears in a short sequence with the Jimmie Lunceford Orchestra.

The most important event in the history of the trombone to occur during the 1920s was the arrival of Jack Teagarden on the major league jazz scene. Prior to Mr. T's joining Ben Pollack's band in 1928, the trombone was generally used as a percussive instrument, as best displayed by Kid Ory, to state harmonies and rhythms in ensembles. Miff Mole (often featured with Red Nichols) showed that the trombone could make wide interval jumps in an eccentric manner, and Jimmy Harrison with Fletcher Henderson's orchestra displayed excellent technique along with a legato style. But neither of the latter two made the impact that Jack Teagarden did. Within a few years of his arrival in New York, most trombonists were influenced by Teagarden's sound, his relaxed phrasing, and his ability to play the trombone with the facility of a trumpet.

The two most famous trombonists of the Swing era, Glenn Miller and Tommy Dorsey, were both in awe of Teagarden. Miller had been Pollack's trombone soloist before Teagarden arrived, but he decided to focus more on writing after he heard Jack play. In similar fashion, Dorsey realized that he was not as strong a jazz player as Teagarden, so he emphasized his beautiful tone on ballads instead.

The trombone has always been an important part of big bands, even if it tends to be overshadowed by the trumpets and tenor saxophones. In the 1920s, orchestras started out using one trombonist, and by the beginning of the Depression most had two. During the Swing era the trombone section expanded to three, with the majority of the bands featuring one as a soloist and the other two mostly as section players. A major exception was the Duke Ellington Orchestra, which had three very different solo voices in Tricky Sam Nanton, Lawrence Brown, and Juan Tizol.

LAWRENCE BROWN
b. Aug. 3, 1907, Lawrence, KS, d. Sept. 5, 1988, New York, NY

A dependable and sober musician who stood out in the frequently partying Duke Ellington Orchestra, Lawrence Brown was a versatile and virtuosic trombonist. The son of a minister, Brown briefly played piano, violin, and tuba before settling on trombone. Although he studied medicine at college (growing up near Los Angeles), Brown played in the school orchestra and became a professional musician by the time he was 19. After working with Charlie Echols, Brown was with Paul Howard's Quality Serenaders, with whom he recorded during 1929–30. Brown also gigged with Curtis Mosby's Blue Blowers and became part of the house band run by Les Hite at the Cotton Club in Culver City, getting to record with Louis Armstrong.

When Lawrence Brown joined Duke Ellington's orchestra in 1932, his fluent Swing style was a major contrast to that of Tricky Sam Nanton and Juan Tizol. Brown took notable solos on "The Sheik of Araby" and "Rose of the Rio Grande," among many other songs, and was with Ellington mostly nonstop for 19 years. When he left in 1951, it was to join Johnny Hodges's combo. After four years with Hodges, Brown did studio work and freelanced before rejoining Ellington for an additional ten years (1960–70). During this last period he sometimes was reluctantly cast as a plunger specialist, but Brown was most comfortable when playing open in his own style. After leaving Ellington in 1970, the trombonist worked for the government for a few years and retired from music. Lawrence Brown led only two albums in his career: *Slide Trombone* and *Inspired Abandon*, the latter a wonderful date for Impulse in 1965 that has been reissued as half of the Johnny Hodges CD *Everybody Knows Johnny Hodges*.

This is such a strong session that it seems odd that Lawrence Brown only had one further opportunity to lead his own record date. Brown is heard on four numbers with a quintet that includes Sam "The Man" Taylor on tenor and pianist Leroy Lovett (who takes a blues vocal); among the numbers are "Rose of the Rio Grande" and "Caravan." In addition there are eight selections (two previously unissued and all but one being Swing standards) with a nonet arranged by Ralph Burns and also featuring Al Cohn on tenor and pianist Hank Jones. Througout, Brown is in typically fluid and swinging form.

VIC DICKENSON

b. Aug. 6, 1906, Xenia, OH, d. Nov. 16, 1984, New York, NY

Vic Dickenson always had his own sound, one filled with sly wit, occasional tonal distortions (he could sound as if he were playing underwater!), and solid solos that fell between Swing and Dixieland. He had a long career spanning over 60 years. Dickenson first worked with the Elite Syncopators in 1921. During the 1920s he played with a variety of obscure local groups, including bands led by Roy Brown, Don Phillips, Willie Jones, Bill Broadhus, Wesley Helvey, and Leonard Gay. Dickenson was with the legendary territory bands of Speed Webb (1929–30) and Zack Whyte (1930–32), making his recording debut (as a vocalist) with Luis Russell in December 1930. Other associations included Thamon Hayes's Kansas City Skyrockets and Clarence Paige's Royal Syncopators. Dickenson first gained real recognition for his work with the orchestras of Blanche Calloway (1933–36), Claude Hopkins (1936–39), Benny Carter (1939), and Count Basie (1940).

After a short second stint with Carter, Dickenson spent the rest of his career playing with small groups. In addition to short-term jobs with Sidney Bechet, Frankie Newton, Hot Lips Page, and Lester Young, he was a member of the popular Eddie Heywood Sextet during 1943–46. The trombonist became part of the Dixieland scene in the 1950s while retaining his ties to Mainstream Swing; Dickenson was comfortable in both worlds. He freelanced for decades with many small groups, most notably Red Allen (the late '50s), the Saints and Sinners in the 1960s, Eddie Condon, and a quintet that he co-led with Bobby Hackett (1968–70). Vic Dickenson (who is prominent during a couple of numbers in the 1957 television special *The Sound of Jazz*) was active up until the time of his death at age 78.

●

9 *The Essential Vic Dickenson / Dec. 29, 1953–Nov. 29, 1954 / Vanguard 99/100*

Vic Dickenson's earliest dates as a leader were four songs featuring singer Leo Watson in 1946, some singles for the Supreme label in 1947, a few numbers for Blue Note in 1952 that were reissued by Mosaic, and four songs for Storyville in 1953. During 1953–54 he recorded two albums for Vanguard that generated a dozen tunes and were reissued on a two-LP set. This single-CD has ten of those numbers, matching Dickenson with clarinetist Edmond Hall, Ruby Braff and/or Shad Collins on trumpets (they appear together on "Old Fashioned Love" and "Everybody Loves My Baby"), pianist Sir Charles Thompson, and a rhythm section. Dickenson should have received a lot more opportunities to lead dates during this era, for it is a treat hearing him as the lead voice on these swinging standards.

8 *Gentleman of the Trombone / July 25, 1975 / Storyville 5008*

7 *Ding Dong / Apr. 13, 1976 / Storyville 8229*

Between 1960 and 1973, Dickenson had no opportunities to lead his own sessions, but fortunately he did pop up as a leader on six occasions during 1974–76 plus a couple of other albums in 1981–82. *Gentleman of the Trombone* is a rare outing, with the trombonist as the only horn in a quartet (which includes pianist Johnny Guarnieri, bassist Bill Pemberton, and drummer Oliver Jackson). The original eight-song LP program was expanded in this 1992 CD by three equally rewarding, previously unreleased cuts. Dickenson takes brief and charming vocals on three numbers and sounds joyous playing "Too Marvelous for Words," "Shine," and "Christopher Columbus." *Ding Dong* also adds three "new" songs (actually alternate takes) to its eight numbers and has the added bonus of Buddy Tate, who switches from tenor to baritone on "Penthouse Serenade." With pianist Red Richards, bassist George Duvivier, and Oliver Jackson completing the group, Vic and Buddy make up a perfectly compatible team for a mixture of famous and fairly unknown standards.

LPS TO SEARCH FOR

Vic Dickenson in Hollywood (Riff 659.015) was recorded during a European tour in 1974 with drummer Ted Easton's fine Mainstream group; Dickenson is clearly enthusiastic on such numbers as "Sunday," "I Would Do Anything for You," "Sugar," and "Ole Miss." *Trombone Cholly* (Sonet 720) is an unusual instrumental tribute to Bessie Smith from 1976, made with a sextet also including trumpeter Joe Newman and tenor saxophonist Frank Wess. Not all of the songs are blues (Bessie actually recorded a fairly wide variety of tunes), and Dickenson sounds perfectly at home on this material. *Just Friends* (Sackville 2015) was the trombonist's next-to-last record, made in October 1981, with two songs recorded posthumously in 1985 by Dickenson's backup group, Red Richards, and bassist John Williams. Dickenson and Richards take two vocals apiece, and the trombonist, at age 75, was still playing at 80–90 percent of his former capacity.

FILMS

Vic Dickenson appears with the Red Allen All-Stars in *The Sound of Jazz* (1957).

TYREE GLENN
b. Nov. 23, 1912, Corsicana, TX, d. May 18, 1974, Englewood, NJ

Tyree Glenn, a soft-toned and cheerful trombonist with a sound of his own, was unusual in that he doubled quite effectively on vibes. He spent quite a few years playing locally and with lesser known territory bands, including one led by Eddie Barefield and in a band accompanying Ethel Waters. In 1939 he was with Benny Carter's orchestra, and then Glenn became a longtime member of Cab Calloway's big band (1939–46). He went to Europe with Don Redman's orchestra in 1946 and (as with several of the other musicians) he stayed overseas a bit longer to play gigs with Europeans. After returning home, Glenn became part of the Duke Ellington Orchestra (1947–51), where his doubling on vibes was welcome (and featured on Duke's "Liberian Suite") and where, due to his expertise with the plunger mute, he was one of the best-ever replacements for the late Tricky Sam Nanton. When the Ellington years ended, Glenn worked in the studios and as a leader of his own combo, recording six albums for Roulette during 1957–62 (none of which have appeared yet on CD). His last major association was as Louis Armstrong's final trombonist (1965–71). Tyree Glenn was heard in fine form at the 1972 Newport Jazz Festival jam sessions (which were recorded) just two years before his death.

FILMS

Tyree Glenn appears as a member of the Louis Armstrong All-Stars in *When the Boys Meet the Girls* (1965) and *A Man Called Adam* (1966).

J. C. HIGGINBOTHAM
b. May 11, 1906, Social Circle, GA, d. May 26, 1973, New York, NY

J. C. Higginbotham was for a time one of jazz's top trombonists, at least until excessive drinking gradually took its toll. He played with J. Neal Montgomery's orchestra as early as 1921, went to a tailor's training school, and worked as a mechanic for General Motors. However, by late 1924 Higginbotham had settled on music as his career. He worked with obscure bands until he sat in with Chick Webb at the Savoy Ballroom in September 1928. Luis Russell heard him and signed him up. Higginbotham was a key soloist with Russell's orchestra during 1928–31, recording with the band and also having an opportunity to use the ensemble on his own recording date. An extroverted and very expressive soloist, he worked quite well with trumpeter Henry "Red" Allen, and their careers would cross paths many times through the years.

Higginbotham was featured with Fletcher Henderson (1932–33), Benny Carter (1933–34), the Mills Blue Rhythm Band (1934–36), and then back with Henderson (1937). He was with Luis Russell's orchestra during 1937–40, when it was a backup band for Louis Armstrong; Higginbotham solos on several of Satch's records. When the orchestra changed its personnel in late 1940, the trombonist became a member of Red Allen's sextet, a group that played everything from Dixieland and Swing to rollicking early R&B. Higginbotham left in 1947 and played mostly low-profile jobs during the next nine years, including long periods spent in Boston and Cleveland. By 1956 he was in danger of being totally forgotten but then rejoined Allen and the following year was part of the Fletcher Henderson Reunion Orchestra. Higginbotham recorded fairly frequently during the late 1950s as a sideman, later making an album apiece as a sideman for Sonet (1962) and Jazzology (1966). J. C. Higginbotham continued working into the early 1970s, although his playing declined steadily until his death.

JACK JENNEY

b. May 12, 1910, Mason City, IA, d. Dec. 16, 1945, Los Angeles, CA

One of the most technically skilled of the trombonists to be active during the Swing era, Jack Jenney had an underground reputation among musicians. He first played in public with his father's band when he was 11. Jenney started working professionally in 1928 with Austin Wylie, and that was followed by associations with Earl Hunt, Isham Jones's Juniors, Mal Hallett (1933), and Phil Harris. Due to his talents, Jenney was a studio musician during 1934–38, playing with many radio orchestras. He led his own big band during 1939–40 but, despite a stunning recorded version of "Stardust," it flopped. Jenney actually achieved his greatest fame during a stint with Artie Shaw (1940–41) that also found him playing brilliantly on "Stardust," following the solos of Billy Butterfield and Shaw. After the clarinetist broke up his band, Jenney went back to the studios. He was with Benny Goodman briefly in late 1942, served in the Navy (1943–44), and did more studio work. Jack Jenney died from complications following an appendectomy at the age of 35.

●

9 *Stardust / June 15, 1937–Jan. 30, 1940 / Hep 1045*
This Hep CD has the complete Jack Jenney. All of the 14 selections that the Jenney big band recorded during 1939–40 are here, plus three alternate takes, four songs he led with a studio band in 1938 that includes guest drummer Gene Krupa, and three numbers that he made as a featured sideman with drummer Johnny Williams' Swing Sextette in 1937. The Jack Jenney Orchestra lacked any major names among its sidemen; pianist Arnold Ross is best known, along with Peanuts Hucko (heard on tenor), who is on some of the dates. However, it was a very musical organization, able to play first-class dance music and Swing with equal skill. Not too surprisingly, Jenney is the most impressive soloist, and his showcases on two versions of "Stardust" easily steal the show.

FILMS

Jack Jenney is in the closing jam session number in *Syncopation* (1942).

LOU MCGARITY

b. July 22, 1917, Athens, GA, d. Aug. 28, 1971, Alexandria, VA

Lou McGarity was a solid soloist influenced by Jack Teagarden who could play both Swing and Dixieland. He actually started out as a violinist, playing that instrument from the age of seven and not really concentrating on trombone until he was 17. McGarity was gigging almost immediately after he switched axes, including with Kirk DeVore (1936), Nye Mayhew, and Ben Bernie (1938–40). His two years with Benny Goodman (1940–42) earned him a national reputation. After working with Raymond Scott's orchestra and then spending time in the Navy, McGarity was back with Goodman during 1946 before becoming a studio musician, usually playing Dixieland (often with Eddie Condon) at night. McGarity's later jobs included occasional appearances with Bob Crosby during 1964–66 and touring as a member of the World's Greatest Jazz Band during 1968–70.

●

LPS TO SEARCH FOR

Lou McGarity recorded very little as a leader, just three obscure albums and part of another one. *In Celebration* (IAJRC 36) has a variety of live sideman appearances, most of which had not been released before. McGarity is heard on a 1941 BBC broadcast, with Eddie Condon in 1944, gigging with George Wettling in 1952, on the Arthur Godfrey radio show in 1964, with Bob Crosby in 1966, on an undated appearance with Joe Marsala, and playing "Linger Awhile" just four months before his death in 1971. An excellent Dixieland set that serves as a fine tribute to the trombonist.

BENNY MORTON

b. Jan. 31, 1907, New York, NY, d. Dec. 28, 1985, New York, NY

One of the best big band trombonists of the 1920s and a valuable player into the 1970s, Benny Morton has long been underrated, partly because he rarely led bands of his own. Morton played early on with Billy Fowler (1924–26) and then became known in the jazz world for his work with Fletcher Henderson (1926–28), with whom he soloed frequently. His other big band associations were notable too: Chick Webb (1930–31), Henderson again (1931–32), Don Redman (1932–37), and Count Basie (1937–40). Morton then switched to smaller groups, playing with Joe Sullivan, Teddy Wilson's sextet (1940–43), Edmond Hall, and his own band (1944–45). From that point on, Benny Morton worked mostly with Broadway theater orchestras and in the studios, occasionally playing Dixieland in clubs, including with Red Allen, Ruby Braff, Wild Bill Davison (1968), Bobby Hackett, and the World's Greatest Jazz Band (1973–74).

●

9 *1934–1945 / Feb. 23, 1934–1945 / Classics 906*
All of Benny Morton's dates as a leader are on this CD (originally recorded for Columbia, Keynote, Blue Note, and Stinson), and his sidemen include Red Allen (in 1934), Barney Bigard, Ben Webster, and Johnny Guarnieri. Of particular interest are some numbers by a septet that includes a "trombone choir" with Morton, Vic Dickenson, Bill Harris, and Claude Jones.

TRICKY SAM NANTON

b. Feb. 1, 1904, New York, NY, d. July 20, 1946, San Francisco, CA

One of the most expressive of all trombonists, Joe "Tricky Sam" Nanton was a wizard with mutes, able to create a bewildering assortment of sounds, one of which sounded like "ya ya." He was a major force in the development of Duke Ellington's "jungle" music and, had he lived longer, he could easily have spent forty years with Duke. Nanton started out playing with Cliff Jackson, worked with Earl Frazier's Harmony Five (1923–25) and was with Elmer Snowden's band before joining Ellington in 1926. Although he had participated in some freelance recordings, once Nanton joined Duke, it was rare that he was heard outside of Ellington's orbit, never leading a session of his own. He was nicknamed "Tricky Sam" by Otto Hardwicke, and his playing (which was a perfect match for Bubber Miley) gave the Ellington band its early personality. After Miley departed and was replaced by Cootie Williams in 1929, Nanton worked with the younger trumpeter and they soon formed an ideal team. Through the years, as Ellington's band became more modern, Tricky Sam's primitive but strangely sophisticated sounds were always a major feature. He suffered a mild stroke in late 1945, soon rejoined Duke, but died suddenly eight months later in a hotel room at the age of 42. Although Quentin Jackson and Tyree Glenn came close at times, no one was quite able to duplicate Tricky Sam Nanton's musical personality.

●

FILMS

Tricky Sam Nanton, who appears in virtually all of the Duke Ellington shorts and films up into the mid-1940s, is particularly prominent in spots during *Symphony in Black* (1934).

JACK TEAGARDEN

b. Aug. 29, 1905, Vernon, TX, d. Jan. 15, 1964, New Orleans, LA

One of the great trombonists of all time and the most influential stylist on his instrument during the 1930s and early '40s, Jack Teagarden was a more important force as a player during the Swing era than as a bandleader, although he tried his best at the latter. Mr. T. was the oldest sibling in a musical family that included trumpeter Charlie, drummer Clois, and pianist Norma; his mother was a ragtime pianist. Jack played piano at five, baritone horn at seven, and finally trombone three years later. He started working professionally in 1920 and performed throughout the South, including with Peck Kelley's Bad Boys (1921–23), Doc Ross, and Johnny Johnson (with whom he made his recording debut in late 1927).

Teagarden joined Ben Pollack's orchestra in June 1928 and immediately made a major impact. Here was a trombonist who played difficult lines as if he were using valves instead of a slide. In addition, he was one of the finest singers in jazz history, one who transferred his relaxed and blues-based trombone style to his voice. Teagarden became famous for singing "Beale Street Blues" and "Basin Street Blues" (collaborating with Glenn Miller in creating the verse for the latter). After his period with Ben Pollack (1928–33) ended, he freelanced for a few months and then signed a five-year contract with Paul Whiteman in 1934, hoping to ride out the Depression. Unfortunately that was a bad move, because a few months later Teagarden was asked to lead the remains of the defunct Pollack Orchestra but was now tied up; Bob Crosby was soon picked as the leader of that successful big band. Teagarden's years with Whiteman were also frustrating, because, although he had some chances to do freelance recordings and for a short time co-led "The Three T's" with C-melody saxophonist Frankie Trumbauer and younger brother Charlie Teagarden, most of the time he was stuck in the anonymous ensembles. Whiteman paid Teagarden well and gave him some features now and then, but the trombonist was clearly bored until he was at last free in 1939.

Since it was the big band era and many of his colleagues were having success as orchestra leaders, Jack Teagarden immediately formed a big band of his own. Although it worked steadily for seven years, the Teagarden Orchestra never developed a personality of its own beyond its leader and it failed to catch on. By the time it broke up in 1946, Teagarden had to declare bankruptcy. However, Bing Crosby helped the trombonist with his debts, and Teagarden was still in great demand as a player. He led his own combo for a little while and then became a member of the Louis Armstrong All-Stars, touring constantly during 1947–51. Armstrong and Teagarden worked very well together, sharing vocals (most memorably on "Rockin' Chair") and inspiring each other musically. During this era, Teagarden was often featured on "Lover," for which he had worked out a complex but swinging solo.

During his last 13 years, Jack Teagarden mostly led his own sextet, traveling the world (including Asia during 1958–59), performing, and singing a familiar but enthusiastic repertoire of Dixieland standards. He never really declined, and he even played a job the night before he died suddenly from pneumonia.

●

10 *The Indispensable Jack Teagarden / Mar. 14, 1928– July 8, 1957 / RCA 66606*

7 *That's a Serious Thing / Mar. 14, 1928–July 8, 1957 / Bluebird 9986*

8 *1930–1934 / Oct. 1, 1930–Mar. 2, 1934 / Classics 698*
The Indispensable Jack Teagarden is a two-CD set from French RCA that lives up to its name. The trombonist is heard in many of his most significant early recordings, as a sideman with Roger Wolfe Kahn (two versions of "She's a Great Great Girl"), Eddie Condon, the Mound City Blue Blowers, Ben Pollack, and Paul Whiteman, plus four selections from his Victor date of 1947 and three songs from a Bud Freeman album in 1957. "I'm Gonna Stomp Mr. Henry Lee," "Tailspin Blues," and "Say It Simple" are three of the high points. *That's a Serious Thing* is a briefer domestic CD covering the same basic music: the master takes some of Mr. T's performances with Condon, Kahn, Pollack, the Mound City Blue Blowers, Whiteman, and Freeman, plus a few numbers with Benny Goodman, Fats Waller, Louis Armstrong, and an all-star group, most of which is available in more complete form elsewhere. *1930–1934* is the first of the Classics label's chronological reissue of Teagarden's dates as a leader. Much of this music (other than a session co-starring Fats Waller) was formerly quite rare. Some of the tracks are a bit commercial, but there are also early Teagarden versions of such standbys as "Rockin' Chair" (which is actually sung here by Eddie Miller and Nappy Lamare), "Fare Thee Well to Harlem," and a classic "A Hundred Years from Today."

8 *Jack Teagarden–Frank Trumbauer–Charlie Teagarden / Jan. 12, 1934–June 15, 1936 / Teagarden Records 112291*

8 *1934–1939 / Sept. 18, 1934–July 19, 1939 / Classics 729*
The period 1934–1938 was somewhat dull for Jack Teagarden, but there were moments of musical relief. He made a series of recordings in 1934 and 1936 as part of the "Three T's," a small group from the Whiteman band that included brother Charlie Teagarden and Frankie Trumbauer; Artie Shaw guests on four songs. All of the Three T's recordings are included in the Teagarden label's release plus a couple of versions of " 'G' Blues" cut with the full Whiteman band. Highlights include "China Boy," "Emaline," "Somebody Loves Me," and "Ain't Misbehavin'." *1934–1939* has three titles from 1934 (including "Stars Fell on Alabama") by a small group with Trumbauer and Benny Goodman but is filled mostly with the first recordings by the Jack Teagarden Orchestra of 1939. Best known among the musicians were trumpeters Lee Castle and Charlie Spivak and baritonist Ernie Caceres, with plenty of vocalizing by Teagarden and Linda Keene. The material is good (including "Persian Rug," "The Sheik of Araby," "I Gotta Right to Sing the Blues" [Teagarden's theme], and "Aunt Hagar's Blues") and the band shows potential, although it would never really grow much beyond its early promise.

7 *1939–1940 / Aug. 23, 1939–Feb. 1940 / Classics 758*

6 *1940–1941 / Feb. 1940–Jan. 1941 / Classics 839*

8 *Jack Teagarden's Big Eight/Pee Wee Russell's Rhythmakers / Aug. 31, 1938–Dec. 15, 1940 / Original Jazz Classics 1708*
1939–1940 has 23 performances by Jack Teagarden's big band. The music ranges from quite enjoyable ("Peg of My Heart," "Wolverine Blues," "Red Wing," "Beale Street Blues," and "The Blues") to indifferent (ten so-so vocals by Kitty Kallen). Teagarden is the only major soloist in the

Trombonist Jack Teagarden and pianist Joe Sullivan rehearse while Capitol record producer Dave Dexter looks on.

group, but he is strong enough to uplift most performances. *1940–1941* has far too many vocals from Kallen, Marianne Dunne, and David Allyn (in his recording debut). It does not pick up until the halfway mark, when Teagarden is heard on four numbers with an all-star group including such Ellington members as Rex Stewart, Barney Bigard, and Ben Webster; a rare chance for the trombonist to stretch out with a compatible combo. This last date, which was recorded for the HRS label (and has also been reissued as part of Mosaic's HRS box set), forms half of the Original Jazz Classics CD. The second part has an unrelated Pee Wee Russell octet session from 1938, with trumpeter Max Kaminsky, pianist James P. Johnson, and Dickie Wells on trombone rather than Mr. T.

8 *It's Time for T* / Jan. 31, 1941–June 1941 / Jass 624

8 *Has Anybody Here Seen Jackson?* / Oct. 1941–Aug. 22, 1944 / Jass 637

9 *1941–1943* / Jan. 31, 1941–Nov. 16, 1943 / Classics 874
It's Time for T and *Has Anybody Here Seen Jackson?* reissue the Jack Teagarden big band's radio transcriptions, which in general are superior to their studio recordings. Pokey Carriere takes some good trumpet solos on the former disc, while the latter (which includes several otherwise-unrecorded instrumentals) greatly adds to the very slim discography of Teagarden's big bands of 1942 and 1944. *1941–1943* is the best of the Teagarden Classics releases, due to the variety. There are a dozen selections from Jack's big band cut

during three sessions, and the only vocalist is Teagarden himself. Among the better cuts are "Dark Eyes," "St. James Infirmary," "A Hundred Years from Today," and "Nobody Knows the Trouble I've Seen." Also included are two numbers from the movie *Birth of the Blues* (Bing Crosby is featured on "The Birth of the Blues," while Crosby and Teagarden are helped by Mary Martin on a memorable "The Waiter and the Porter and the Upstairs Maid") and there are seven selections from the Capitol International Jazzmen. The Capitol band is an all-star octet, with Billy May on trumpet, either Jimmie Noone or Heinie Beau on clarinet, and tenor saxophonist Dave Matthews; Teagarden is wonderful on "Casanova's Lament," "I'm Sorry I Made You Cry," and "Stars Fell on Alabama."

★	*The Complete Capitol Fifties Jack Teagarden Sessions / Oct. 18, 1955–Apr. 14, 1958 / Mosaic 4-168*
8	*Jack Teagarden and His All-Stars / May 1958 / Jazzology 199*
9	*Think Well of Me / Jan. 17–19, 1962 / Verve 314 557 101*
10	*A Hundred Years from Today / Sept. 20–21, 1963 / Grudge Music 4523*

In the 1950s, after leaving the Louis Armstrong All-Stars and going out on his own, Jack Teagarden led four albums for the Capitol label, co-led one date with Bobby Hackett, and played as a sideman on Hackett's Coast Concert. All six records plus a few alternate takes and a previously unreleased version of "St. James Infirmary" are on Mosaic's four-CD limited-edition box set. The two dates with Hackett are the most freewheeling. There are also three sets in which Teagarden is featured with a larger-than-usual band (a spiritual date, a very good ballads program, and one revisiting his earlier hits) and a disappointing outing with his 1958 sextet, which is plagued by overarranged ensembles. Despite the latter, most of the music is quite rewarding, making this a must for Teagarden fans. The Jazzology CD is a much better outing by the 1958 sextet (which also features cornetist Dick Oakley, clarinetist Jerry Fuller, and pianist Don Ewell), which jams fresh versions of Dixieland standards. *Think Well of Me* is an unusual outing for Teagarden, who is joined by an orchestra arranged by Bob Brookmeyer, Russ Case, and Claus Ogerman. He performs the compositions of the 1920s folk composer Willard Robison. Teagarden's wistful singing and lyrical horn fit perfectly such

haunting tunes as "Cottage for Sale," "Old Folks," and "Country Boy Blues"; this is an underrated classic. *A Hundred Years from Today* is particularly special, for it features Teagarden at the 1963 Monterey Jazz Festival. For what would be his final recording (made less than four months before his death), Teagarden is reunited with brother Charlie, sister Norma, and even his mother, Helen Teagarden (who plays some ragtime piano). Also heard from during this emotional and happy event are Joe Sullivan, clarinetist Pee Wee Russell, baritonist Gerry Mulligan, bassists George Tucker and Jimmy Bond, drummer Nick Ceroli, and Sleepy Matsumoto on tenor. Jack Teagarden's warm commentary, along with his heartfelt solos and vocalizing, makes this one of the finest final recordings ever made by anyone.

LPS TO SEARCH FOR

King of the Blues Trombone (Epic 6044) is a valuable three-LP box set that has 48 of Teagarden's best recordings from the 1928–40 period. He is heard on many sideman appearances that are not often reissued, including dates with Jimmy McHugh's Bostonians, Mills Merry Makers, the Whoopee Makers, Jack Pettis, Goody and his Good Timers, Benny Goodman, Frankie Trumbauer, and Bud Freeman plus a few of Jack T's better selections as leader. *Jack Teagarden–Frank Trumbauer* (Totem 101) has radio performances by the Three T's and Paul Whiteman's orchestra that do not duplicate the Teagarden release. *Birth of a Band* (Giants of Jazz 1038) starts off with a broadcast of Teagarden in which he sits in with the Benny Goodman Orchestra on June 4, 1939; Johnny Mercer and Pete Johnson are also heard from. On that air check, Teagarden announces the launching of his big band. The remainder of the album has a couple of fine radio appearances from later in the year by the trombonist's new orchestra.

FILMS

Jack Teagarden's best film role was playing Bing Crosby's sidekick in *Birth of the Blues* (1941). His orchestra can be seen in *Hi, Good Lookin'* (1944) and *Twilight on the Prairie* (1944), he appears as part of the Louis Armstrong All-Stars in *The Strip* (1951) and *Glory Alley* (1952), and he also pops up in a nightclub scene in *The Glass Wall* (1953). In addition, Jack Teagarden is in *Jazz on a Summer's Day* (1959), performing "Rockin' Chair" with Armstrong.

JUAN TIZOL

b. *Jan. 22, 1900, San Juan, Puerto Rico, d. Apr. 23, 1984, Inglewood, CA*

A technically skilled valve trombonist, Juan Tizol was not so much a strong improviser as he was an expert section player. With Duke Ellington, Tizol could fill in and play a saxophone part on his horn or make it sound as if an absent colleague were present. He also was a skilled composer; he wrote "Caravan" and "Perdido." Tizol grew up in Puerto Rico, coming to the United States in 1920 to play with the Marie Lucas Orchestra. He worked steadily throughout the 1920s (including with Bobby Lee's Cotton Pickers and the White Brothers' Band.) before joining Duke Ellington in September 1929. Tizol was with Ellington for 15 years, appearing on many famous recordings. He left to join Harry James (1944–51), was back with Duke during 1951–53, and then returned to James (1953–60), spending a few final months with Ellington in 1960 before going into semiretirement. Juan Tizol never led his own record date but he appears on a countless number of records with Ellington and James.

DICKIE WELLS

b. *June 10, 1909, Centerville, TN, d. Nov. 12, 1985, New York, NY*

An eccentric trombonist whose wild playing could be very speechlike, Dickie Wells (late in life he changed his first name to Dicky) is best known for his association with Count Basie. He grew up in Louisville, Kentucky, played baritone horn first, and took up the trombone when he was 16. Wells went to New York in 1926 and spent four years with Cecil and Lloyd Scott's band (with whom he made his recording debut). After leaving the Scott brothers, Wells played with Elmer Snowden (1930–31), Russell Wooding, Benny Carter (1932–33), Fletcher Henderson (1933), Carter, and Teddy Hill (1934–37); he also recorded with Spike Hughes and in Europe in 1937 as a leader. Wells was already a highly respected trombonist by the time he joined Count Basie (1938–46). He was given a lot of solo space with Basie, appeared on some small-group dates (including one that debuted his "Dickie's Dream"), and often provided humorous commentary behind Jimmy Rushing's vocals.

Wells spent a period during 1946–47 playing with the bands of J. C. Heard, Willie Bryant, and Sy Oliver. He eventually rejoined Basie (1947–49), staying with the Count until he broke up his orchestra. Wells spent the 1950s freelancing in mainstream settings, including with Jimmy Rushing, Bill Coleman (in France), Earl Hines (1954), and touring Europe with the Buck Clayton All-Stars (1959–61). His playing declined in the 1960s, although he performed with Ray Charles (1961–62), Rushing, and Buddy Tate (1968). Dickie Wells ended up working outside of music as a bank messenger starting in 1967, playing part time, and recording one final record in 1981.

●

10 *1927–1943 / Jan. 10, 1927–Dec. 21, 1943 / Classics 937*
This CD features Dickie Wells on his earliest recordings with Lloyd Scott and Cecil Scott (including a hilarious "On the Corner"), in Europe in 1937, and leading a small group in 1943. Some of the 1937 selections include Django Reinhardt in a septet comprised of Wells, bassist Richard Fulbright, drummer Bill Beason, and three trumpets: Bill Coleman, Shad Collins, and Bill Dillard. "Bugle Call Rag" and "I Got Rhythm" are both quite exciting. The 1943 date is also quite special, matching Wells with Coleman, Lester Young, pianist Ellis Larkins, Freddie Green, Jo Jones, and bassist Al Hall. "I'm Fer It Too" features some spectacular high-note trombone playing by Dickie Wells, who rarely sounded better.

LPS TO SEARCH FOR

Bones for the King (Affinity 164) dates from 1958 and includes an octet date with Buck Clayton and Buddy Tate and an odd septet session with organist Skip Hall and fellow trombonists Vic Dickenson, Benny Morton, and George

Matthews. Interesting but flawed is *Lonesome Road* (Up-town 27.07), Wells's last recording. The 1981 set, which also features pianist Dick Katz and Buddy Tate, has its colorful moments even though Dickie Wells was clearly past his prime.

Dickie Wells is in *The Sound of Jazz* (1957), plays in 1961 throughout *The Buck Clayton All-Stars* (Shanachie 6303), and is profiled in 1973's *Born to Swing* (Rhapsody Films).

TRUMMY YOUNG
b. Jan. 12, 1912, Savannah, GA, d. Sept. 10, 1984, San Jose, CA

James "Trummy" Young was famous both for his extroverted sound (which was sometimes used for colorful roars) and for his periods with Jimmie Lunceford and Louis Armstrong. He grew up in Washington, D.C., and worked with Booker Coleman's Hot Chocolates (1928). After playing with the Hardy Brothers' Orchestra, Elmer Calloway, and Tommy Myles, Young moved to Chicago, where he was a featured soloist with Earl Hines's orchestra (1933–37). While with Jimmie Lunceford (1937–43), Young was the star of the band's hit version of "Margie," singing and taking a famous trombone solo. However, in March 1943 he left Lunceford (who paid notoriously low money to his sidemen) and joined Charlie Barnet. In 1944 Young freelanced, including with the bands of Boyd Raeburn, Roy Eldridge, and Claude Hopkins. He played with Benny Goodman for a few months in 1945, was with Tiny Grimes on a couple of occasions, and toured with Jazz at the Philharmonic during 1946–47. The trombonist was flexible enough to play with anyone from the period, including starring on a date led by pianist Clyde Hart that included Charlie Parker and Dizzy Gillespie. Young went to Hawaii for the first time in 1947 to play with Cee Pee Johnson, and he liked it so well that he stayed until 1952. In fact, the only reason that he left Honolulu was because Louis Armstrong asked him to join his All-Stars. Young traveled the world with Satch for 11 years, staying until New Year's 1964. Both his trombone and his occasional comedy vocals were perfect foils for Armstrong, and his reliability and professionalism were always major assets. Eventually Trummy Young tired of traveling and moved back to Hawaii, where he played locally during the remainder of his life, just visiting the mainland for special occasions (including a 1970 Lunceford reunion and an engagement with Earl Hines in 1971). Although he led a few isolated record dates during 1944–46, Trummy Young's other recordings as a leader (five titles for a French label in 1955 and two albums for Flair in 1975 and 1979) are obscure and long out of print.

●

Trummy Young appears briefly with Jimmie Lunceford's orchestra in *Blues in the Night* (1941) and is featured with Louis Armstrong in *High Society* (1956) and *Satchmo the Great* (1956).

Clarinetists

The clarinet was at the height of its fame during the Swing era. In fact, it was so closely identified with Benny Goodman and Swing music that it went into eclipse after the mid-1940s. A symbol of New Orleans jazz in the early days, the clarinet was part of virtually every big band in the 1920s and '30s. Don Redman (with Fletcher Henderson's orchestra) utilized clarinet trios in some of his classic arrangements (including 1925's "Sugar Foot Stomp").

The most famous clarinetists of the Swing era were all bandleaders: Benny Goodman, Artie Shaw, Jimmy Dorsey, and Woody Herman. Most of the other, younger clarinetists by 1936 were influenced by Goodman, while a couple of years later Shaw offered an alternative variation. But, although not really noticed at the time, by the early 1940s the clarinet was already in decline. While Claude Thornhill's unique orchestra sometimes utilized six clarinetists playing in unison, Count Basie hardly used the clarinet at all (other than a rare spot by Lester Young) and Stan Kenton did away with the clarinet altogether.

The six clarinetists discussed in this section include three (Buster Bailey, Barney Bigard, and Albert Nicholas) who were active before the Swing era but were also part of important big bands and three others (Irving Fazola, Joe Marsala, and Johnny Mince) who managed to find their own voices despite the dominant influence of Benny Goodman.

BUSTER BAILEY
b. July 19, 1902, Memphis, TN, d. Apr. 12, 1967, Brooklyn, NY

A true virtuoso in the 1920s who competed with Jimmy Dorsey and Benny Goodman technique-wise, Buster Bailey had a wicked sense of humor and could go crazy on his instrument. He even recorded one song as a leader called "Man with a Horn Goes Berserk." Despite that, he spent years with the John Kirby Sextet, where he utilized a very cool and restrained tone so he could blend in with the unusual ensembles.

William "Buster" Bailey started playing clarinet when he was 13 and two years later was performing in W. C. Handy's orchestra (1917–19). Bailey soon moved to Chicago, where he worked with Erskine Tate (1919–23), replaced Johnny Dodds with King Oliver's Creole Jazz Band (1924), and then, most importantly, became a key soloist with Fletcher Henderson's orchestra (1924–28). The arrival of Bailey (at the same time as Louis Armstrong) invigorated the band, and he was well featured during each of his three stints with Henderson (which included 1934 and 1936–1937). Bailey went to Europe with Noble Sissle (1929) and also played with Edgar Hayes, Dave Nelson, and Sissle a second time (1931–33). He was part of the strongest version of the Mills Blue Rhythm Band (1934–35) and then, after leaving Henderson for the third and final time, he became a member of the John Kirby Sextet. Bailey was with Kirby during the prime years of the group (1937–44) and loyally returned for short stints in 1945 and 1946. The clarinetist's sound was indispensable to the success of the unique band.

After the Kirby period ended, Buster Bailey played primarily Dixieland, including with Wilbur DeParis (1947–49), Henry "Red" Allen (1950–51, 1954–56), Big Chief Russell Moore (1952–53), Wild Bill Davison (1961–63), and the Saints and Sinners (1963–64). One can sense in his recordings from this era that Bailey was way overqualified for the music he was performing, for he sometimes sounds as if he is trying to tear his instrument apart! His last musical job before passing away at the age of 64 was with the Louis Armstrong All-Stars (1965–67).

●

10 *1925–1940 / May 20, 1925–June 1940 / Classics 904*
Other than two later projects, this CD has all of Buster Bailey's recordings as a leader. He is heard on two scratchy but historic performances from 1925, a pair of selections from 1934 with fellow Fletcher Henderson sidemen (including Red Allen and J. C. Higginbotham plus Benny Carter), and in 1937 with singer Jerry Kruger and an early John Kirby group (with Frankie Newton and Pete Brown). In addition, Bailey fronts two groups similar to Kirby's sextet in 1938 and 1940, with Benny Carter subbing for Russell Procope on the final four numbers. The music ranges from atmospheric to wild. Well worth exploring.

LPS TO SEARCH FOR

Buster Bailey's only chance to lead his own session during the LP era (other than three numbers in 1959) resulted in *All About Memphis* (Master Jazz 8125), a date that has five originals by the clarinetist and two by W. C. Handy. Bailey is heard in a quartet with pianist Red Richards and a septet that adds Vic Dickenson, trumpeter Herman Autrey, and altoist Hilton Jefferson.

FILMS

Buster Bailey is the uncredited and very hyper clarinetist with Noble Sissle's orchestra in the short *That's the Spirit*

(1933), taking a few remarkable solos. He appears briefly in *Splendor in the Grass* (1961) and plays as part of the Louis Armstrong All-Stars in *When the Boys Meet the Girls* (1965) and *A Man Called Adam* (1966).

BARNEY BIGARD

b. Mar. 3, 1906, New Orleans, LA, d. June 27, 1980, Culver City, CA

Barney Bigard's career can easily be divided into three: Classic Jazz of the 1920s, Swing, and Dixieland. He excelled in all three periods. Part of a musical family, Albany "Barney" Bigard started playing clarinet when he was seven, taking lessons from the legendary Lorenzo Tio, Jr. Early on he played primarily tenor sax, including with Albert Nicholas (1922) and King Oliver (late 1924) in Chicago. Bigard played clarinet more extensively in 1925, but he showed on a 1926 record date during four selections with Luis Russell that had he chosen to stick with it, he could have competed with Coleman Hawkins as the top tenor saxophonist of the era.

Switching permanently to clarinet, Bigard played with King Oliver into 1927, recorded with Jelly Roll Morton in a trio, worked for a few months with Charles Elgar in Milwaukee and Luis Russell in New York, and then in December 1927 joined Duke Ellington's orchestra. Bigard would be with Duke until August 1942, appearing on a countless number of classic recordings and leading a few record dates (with Ellington sidemen) of his own. He co-wrote "Mood Indigo" and "Saturday Night Function" and was showcased on "Clarinet Lament" in addition to having short solos on scores of recordings.

Tiring of traveling, Bigard left Duke after nearly 15 years to settle in Los Angeles and lead his own small group. But after a few months he joined Freddie Slack's orchestra (1942–43). A period of studio work and local gigs was followed by an association with Kid Ory (1946–47). Bigard appeared with Ory and Louis Armstrong in the movie *New Orleans* and soon became an original member of the Armstrong All-Stars, traveling constantly during 1947–55, sounding inspired in the early days but somewhat bored by the mid-'50s. Back in Los Angeles he worked in the studios, led his own band, and played with Ben Pollack (1956) and Cozy Cole (1958–59). Bigard had a second, shorter stint with Louis Armstrong (1960–61), including making a record with both Armstrong and Ellington. After finally coming off the road, Bigard eventually became a part-time player, working with Johnny St. Cyr at Disneyland, Art Hodes, and Wild Bill Davison. Barney Bigard played now and then (including a 1978 tour of Europe) up until his death.

●

10 *Barney Bigard–Claude Luter / Dec. 14–15, 1960 / Vogue 655003*

7 *Bucket's Got a Hole in It / Jan. 28–30, 1968 / Delmark 211*

5 *Barney Bigard & the Pelican Trio / 1976 / Jazzology 228*

Barney Bigard's meeting with fellow clarinetist Claude Luter and a French rhythm section is full of excitement as the two reeds constantly trade off and indulge in exciting ensembles. The music ranges from trad jazz and Dixieland to Swing, a couple of Sidney Bechet tunes, and collaborations by the co-leaders on "Doo Boo Loo Blues" and "Double Gin Stomp"; everything works. The quartet selections on *Bucket's Got a Hole in It* (with pianist Art Hodes) are a lot tamer, but trumpeter Nap Trottier and trombonist George Brunies add some fire to six of the 13 performances. Back in 1945, when Bigard was pushed by a jazz critic to answer endless questions about early New Orleans, the clarinetist started raving about a totally fictional Pelican Trio, and it was printed in a top jazz magazine. For his final record, Bigard teamed up with pianist Duke Burrell and drummer Barry Martyn for an OK date under the Pelican Trio name. The group really needed a bassist, and the three vocals by Burrell and Martyn did not help much, but Barney Bigard mostly sounds fine on the set of veteran standards in which he closed his career.

LPS TO SEARCH FOR

Clarinet Gumbo (RCA 1744), from 1973, features Bigard in a quintet/sextet with pianist Ray Sherman, guitarist Dave Koonse, bassist Ed Safranski, drummer Nick Fatool, and Dick Cary, who switches between trumpet, piano, and alto horn in addition to contributing arrangements. Most nota-ble about this album are the many obscure tunes by Bigard and Cary, some of which are worth reviving.

FILMS

Barney Bigard plays with Louis Armstrong and Kid Ory in *New Orleans* (1946) and is with the Armstrong All-Stars in *The Strip* (1951).

IRVING FAZOLA
b. Dec. 10, 1912, New Orleans, LA, d. Mar. 20, 1949, New Orleans, LA

Well remembered for his large tone (a major influence on Pete Fountain) and his colorful solos, Irving Fazola was basically a Dixieland player who managed to excel during the Swing era. Irving Prestopnik (who changed his name early on) started playing piano when he was 13 and two years later was working professionally as a clarinetist with Candy Candido's Little Collegians. In New Orleans he played with many local bands, including those led by Louis Prima, Sharkey Bonano, and Armand Hug. After joining Ben Pollack in 1935, Fazola visited Chicago and New York before returning home. He played with both Gus Arnheim and Glenn Miller in 1937, was back with Pollack the following year, and then gained some fame for his work with Bob Crosby (1938–40). His other jobs were mostly short term: in 1940 with Jimmy McPartland and Tony Almerico, in 1941 with Claude Thornhill's orchestra (where his clarinet was well featured), in 1942 with the orchestras of Muggsy Spanier and Teddy Powell, and in the following year with Horace Heidt. From 1943 on, Fazola primarily led his own band in his hometown. High blood pressure and being overweight led to his premature death at age 36. Irving Fazola led his own record sessions for Keynote (1945) and RCA (1946).

JOE MARSALA
b. Jan. 4, 1907, Chicago, IL, d. Mar. 3, 1978, Santa Barbara, CA

Joe Marsala rarely played with big bands, but he was quite active during the Swing era. His tone was influenced by Benny Goodman, although Marsala was a bit more flexible in trying new things. The older brother of trumpeter Marty Marsala, he started on the clarinet when he was 15. During 1925–31 Marsala was part of the Chicago jazz scene. After a few years in low-profile groups, he arrived in New York in 1935 to join Wingy Manone's band on 52nd Street. In 1936 Marsala started leading his own group (which was the first jazz job for Buddy Rich), and the following year he married the great jazz harpist Adele Girard, who was usually part of his bands; the clarinet-harp sound was quite unique. Other than a few attempts to lead big bands in 1939 and 1942, Marsala worked mostly with his combo, often at the Hickory House on 52nd Street; he also appeared on many record dates led by Manone in addition to some of his own. He stayed busy until 1948, at which time he became a part-time player. Marsala lived in Colorado during 1949–53; when he returned to New York in 1954, it was to run a music publishing business. During 1962–68 he was vice president of the Seeburg Music Corporation. Joe Marsala still played now and then into the early 1970s in California.

●

10 *1936–1942 / Jan. 17, 1936–July 6, 1942 / Classics 763*

10 *1944–1945 / Mar. 21, 1944–Nov. 30, 1945 / Classics 902*
Joe Marsala's recordings have long been underrated, but they actually rank with the finest small-group sides of the Swing era. *1936–1942* finds him playing two numbers with the Six Blue Chips (a sextet with Pee Wee Erwin) and then leading his own band in sessions from 1937–38 and 1940–42. Adele Girard is on three of the five sessions (check her out on "Bull's Eye"), swinging a lot harder than one would ever expect from a harpist. Other notables heard from on these Dixieland-to-Swing performances include trumpeters

Marty Marsala, Bill Coleman, and Max Kaminsky, violinist Ray Biondi, altoist Pete Brown, trombonist George Brunies, and drummers Buddy Rich, Shelly Manne (on his first session), and Zutty Singleton. *1944–1945* is on the same level and, in addition to Dixielandish sides featuring trumpeters Bobby Hackett, Joe Thomas, and Marty Marsala, there is a particularly unusual session that matches Marsala with be-bop trumpeter Dizzy Gillespie and stride pianist Cliff Jackson. Their version of "Melancholy Baby" is at one point a battle between stride, Swing, and bop!

LPS TO SEARCH FOR

Lower Register (IAJRC 38) has a variety of odds and ends on the first side (mostly sideman appearances by Marsala) and then a complete 29-minute radio broadcast from 1939 in which Marsala heads an octet that includes his brother, his wife, valve trombonist Brad Gowans, and Bud Freeman. Excellent small-group hot Swing. The short-lived and unrecorded Marsala Big Band of 1942 is heard on two broadcasts on *Featuring Adele Girard* (Aircheck 14). Six indifferent vocals do not weigh down the set much, and there are some Don Redman arrangements along with trumpet solos from both Max Kaminsky and Marty Marsala.

JOHNNY MINCE

b. July 8, 1912, Chicago, IL, d. Dec. 23, 1994, Boca Raton, FL

Johnny Mince was best-known for his playing with Tommy Dorsey's band. As with Marsala and Fazola, he would also spend much of his life playing Dixieland. Born John Muenzenberger, Mince had his first important job with Joe Haymes (1929–34). Mince was with Ray Noble's American Band (1935), Bob Crosby (1936), back with Noble (1936–37), and then most significantly with Tommy Dorsey (1937–41), where he was featured with both the big band and the Clambake Seven. He played with Bob Strong's orchestra briefly in 1941 before serving in the Army during 1941–45. Johnny Mince then entered the anonymous world of studio work, where he would remain most of the time into the 1960s. In the 1970s he began to emerge more often for Dixieland dates, playing with the World's Greatest Jazz Band and touring Europe with the Great Eight (an all-star Swing group with Teddy Wilson and Red Norvo) in 1983. He was one of the better Benny Goodman–influenced clarinetists.

LPS TO SEARCH FOR

Johnny Mince led three albums during 1979–82. Best are *Summer of '79* (Monmouth Evergreen 7090), a relaxed quartet date with pianist Lou Stein, Bob Haggart, and drummer Cliff Leeman, and *The Master Comes Home* (Jazzology 126), a Dixieland jam with cornetist Ernie Carson and trombonist George Masso.

ALBERT NICHOLAS

b. May 27, 1900, New Orleans, LA, d. Sept. 3, 1973, Basel, Switzerland

Albert Nicholas was one of the great clarinetists of New Orleans jazz, and his work in the Swing era was actually only a small part of his career. Nicholas, who started playing clarinet when he was ten, worked with most of the early New Orleans greats during 1910–24 other than for a period spent in the Merchant Marine (1916–19). He was in Chicago in May 1924 for a tour with King Oliver and then came back in December 1924, playing with Oliver (with whom he made his recording debut) through mid-1926. Always interested in traveling, Nicholas spent a year with Jack Carter's band in Shanghai, China, and also performed in Egypt (Cairo and Alexandria) and Paris before returning home in late 1928. Nicholas became a major soloist with Luis Russell's orchestra (1928–33), with whom he made some superb recordings. He also made records in a trio with Jelly Roll Morton. The year 1934 was split between the bands of Chick Webb and Sam Wooding, and during the next couple of years Nick also worked with the small groups of Bernard Addison and John Kirby. Nicholas rejoined Luis Russell, playing behind Louis Armstrong during 1937–39, followed by a stint with Zutty Singleton (1939–40). He was out of music altogether during 1941–45, when he had regular day jobs. The clarinetist resumed his playing in late 1945 during the New Orleans revival, playing with Art Hodes, Bunk Johnson, and Kid Ory and then mostly as a leader during 1947–53. In 1953 Albert Nicholas moved to Europe, where, other than visits to the U.S. in 1959, 1960, and (to his hometown, New Orleans) 1969–70, he played regularly for his last two decades as one of the top American jazz expatriates.

●

8 *Albert Nicholas & the Dutch Swing College Band / Sept. 5, 1954 / Storyville 5522*

7 *The New Orleans–Chicago Connection / July 19 + 27, 1959 / Delmark 207*

8 *Baden 1969 / 1969 / Sackville 2045*

Albert Nicholas recorded barely at all as a leader prior to leaving for France in 1953. His concert with the Dutch Swing College Band (which also has a few cuts with pianist Adrian Bentzon's quintet) finds him in enthusiastic form early in his European years, performing mostly Dixieland standards plus a few obscurities, such as Lil Hardin's "Tears" and "Room Rent Blues." Nicholas recorded two albums for Delmark while visiting the U.S. in 1959, of which one is currently available. *The New Orleans–Chicago Connection* is a quartet session with pianist Art Hodes, bassist Earl Murphy, and drummer Fred Kohlman. The CD reissue augments the 11 original selections with an unissued "Care-less Love" and nine alternate takes, so it doubles the program. Fortunately Nicholas was in good form that week! Nicholas would record fairly often in Europe during the 1960s. He was still in superior shape when he cut *Baden 1969,* a quartet meeting with Swiss pianist Henri Chaix. The songs are all familiar, but Nicholas sounds particularly inspired, romping through "C Jam Blues," "Rosetta," "Please Don't Talk About Me When I'm Gone," "Rose Room," and other longtime favorites.

LPS TO SEARCH FOR

The other Delmark set recorded during Nicholas's 1959 U.S. visit is a happy septet session with trumpeter Nappy Trottier and trombonist Floyd O'Brien called *With Art Hodes' All-Star Stompers* (Delmark 209). Albert Nicholas is heard on 8 of the 11 selections included on 1970's well-conceived *A Tribute to Jelly Roll Morton* (Storyville 4050); there is also one selection apiece from pianist Bobby Greene, the Art Hodes Duo, and Papa Bue's Viking Jazzband.

Alto Saxophonists

The alto saxophone was utilized from the start by the earliest dance bands, where its pretty tone led the reeds. Before 1925, it was rarely heard as a solo instrument, with two exceptions being Benny Krueger, who was added to the Original Dixieland Jazz Band during 1920–21 (to make the group more "commercial"), and Don Redman with Fletcher Henderson. The first important altoist was Jimmy Dorsey, who, as early as 1926 with Red Nichols' Five Pennies, was showing how flexible the instrument could be. He was soon followed by Benny Carter in 1927 and Johnny Hodges in 1928, a pair of giants who were major performers and influences for decades.

The role of the alto sax as the leader of the reeds in big bands (there were two altoists in most saxophone sections by the early 1930s) sometimes overshadowed its potential as a solo instrument. Toots Mondello (with Benny Goodman), Earle Warren (Count Basie's altoist during 1937–45), and Marshall Royal (who was with Basie during 1951–70) were more important as ensemble players than as soloists, although each was quite capable of making strong individual statements. The alto's sweeter elements could be exaggerated to the level of corn, and it was played that way quite successfully by Wayne King and Carmen Lombardo (with Guy Lombardo's orchestra).

But the most important alto saxophonists of the Swing era were the big three: Johnny Hodges, Benny Carter, and Willie Smith. Other strong soloists included a pair who were influenced by Hodges (Charlie Holmes and Woody Herman), the playful and heated Pete Brown, and the cool-toned Russell Procope, who would become better known later in life as one of Duke Ellington's clarinetists. Don Stovall, with Henry "Red" Allen's group, helped pave the way for the use of the alto in rhythm and blues along with such players as Tab Smith, Louis Jordan, and Earl Bostic. And Charlie Parker, with Jay McShann's orchestra, would soon be taking the instrument to a completely different level.

PETE BROWN
b. Nov. 9, 1906, Baltimore, MD, d. Sept. 20, 1963, New York, NY

Pete Brown was an exciting player who utilized staccato phrases that gave the impression that his emotions were just barely under control. He played piano and violin before switching to alto in 1924 and occasionally in the 1930s doubled on trumpet. Brown worked early on with the Southern Star Jazz Band, the Baltimore Melody Boys, Johnny Jones, Banjo Bernie Robinson (with whom he came to New York), Charlie Skeets, and Fred Moore's Trio (1933–37). He was an original member of the John Kirby Sextet in 1937 but left after a year. Brown's prime was during 1938–45, when he was recording often (including with Frankie Newton Leonard Feather, and on his own sessions for Decca, Savoy, Keynote, and World Transcriptions) and leading his own combo. However, the rise of bebop in 1945 led Brown to work less frequently; his health became erratic in the 1950s, and his appearance at the 1957 Newport Jazz Festival (in a group with Coleman Hawkins and Roy Eldridge) found him sounding subpar. He did record three good albums during 1954–61 but was mostly in obscurity during his final decade.

●

9 *1942–1945 / Feb. 9, 1942–Feb. 20, 1945 / Classics 1029*

6 *1944 Complete World Jam Session / Jan. 16, 1944 / Progressive 7009*

1942–1945 features most of Pete Brown's dates as a leader. Four numbers from 1942 are mostly features for the vocals of Helen Humes and Nora Lee King. Although Dizzy Gillespie is on trumpet, he does not get a single solo! Otherwise, Brown is showcased with combos (four or five pieces); trumpeters Joe Thomas and Ed Lewis are on one date apiece. Fine jump music that falls between Swing and R&B. The

Progressive CD has nine fine selections from a quintet with the fiery trumpeter Jonah Jones, but, in addition to the master takes, there are four false starts, five incomplete versions, and eight alternate takes, which, if heard straight through, will drive some people batty!

LPS TO SEARCH FOR

Harlem Jump and Swing (Affinity 96) features exciting Mainstream Swing from 1954 by Brown's sextet (with trumpeter Joe Wilder) and an all-star group led by Jonah Jones and including Vic Dickenson and Edmond Hall.

JOHNNY HODGES
b. July 25, 1906, Cambridge, MA, d. May 11, 1970, New York, NY

Johnny Hodges had one of the most beautiful tones ever heard in jazz. His ability to slide between notes was perfect on ballads, but Hodges was also a masterful blues player and equally skilled jamming on Swing standards. He started playing alto when he was 14 and had a few lessons on soprano early on from Sidney Bechet. After working with Willie "The Lion" Smith's Quartet (1924), Bechet, Lloyd Scott, Chick Webb (1926–27), and Luckey Roberts, Hodges joined Duke Ellington's orchestra in May 1928. The altoist would in time become Ellington's most famous soloist, starring on countless records (including his own small-group dates with Duke's men). Hodges, who also took exquisite soprano solos until he gave up the instrument in 1940, composed "Jeep's Blues," "Hodge Podge," and "The Jeep Is Jumpin'," and appeared on hot Swing sessions with Teddy Wilson and Lionel Hampton.

In March 1951, nearly 23 years later, Hodges shocked Ellington by going out on his own, forming a septet that included tenor saxophonist Al Sears, trombonist Lawrence Brown, and drummer Sonny Greer. The band (which played mostly Swing and blues-based riff pieces) had an R&B hit in "Castle Rock" (a feature for Sears), and for a time the young John Coltrane was on tenor, but lightning did not strike twice. In August 1955 Hodges returned to Ellington's orchestra (starting its renaissance) and, other than for brief periods freelancing (including recording with organist Wild Bill Davis in the 1960s), Hodges would be with Duke for the remaining 15 years of his life. He died unexpectedly of a heart attack while visiting his dentist. Whether it be "Passion Flower," "Warm Valley," "Come Sunday," or "Things Ain't What They Used to Be," Johnny Hodges was irreplaceable.

●

6 *Hodge Podge / Mar. 28, 1938–Oct. 14, 1939 / Legacy/ Epic 3105*

7 *Passion Flower / Nov. 2, 1940–July 9, 1946 / Bluebird 66616*

During 1937–41, Johnny Hodges had his first recording sessions as a leader, with the personnel drawn almost entirely from Duke Ellington's orchestra. His dates for Columbia and RCA have generally been reissued as part of larger Ellington sets. *Hodge Podge* unfortunately only has 16 selections (Columbia owns 43 Hodges performances) although offering its share of classics, including "Jeep's Blues," "Empty Ballroom Blues," and "Hodge Podge." But serious collectors will prefer Duke Ellington's *Small Groups Vol. 1* (Columbia/Legacy 46995) and *Vol. 2* (Columbia/Legacy 48835), which have all of Hodges's selections through March 1939. *Passion Flower* starts off with Hodges's two small group dates of 1940–1941 (featuring Cootie Williams or Ray Nance, Lawrence Brown, and Harry Carney and including the original version of "Things Ain't What They Used to Be"); all but one alternate take is also included in *The Great Ellington Units* (Bluebird 6751). The remainder of *Passion Flower* consists of material by the full Duke Ellington Orchestra during 1940–42 and 1944–46 that has a solo by Hodges and includes "Don't Get Around Much Anymore," "Warm Valley," "I Got It Bad," and "Come Sunday." This too is available in more complete form under Duke's name.

8 *Caravan / June 1947–June 19, 1951 / Prestige 24103*
Caravan is a single-CD reissue of a former double LP, music that was originally put out by the short-lived Mercer label. Hodges gets top billing, but he is actually on only the first half of the program, a couple of small-group dates from 1947 with Taft Jordan or Harold Baker on trumpet, Lawrence Brown, tenor saxophonist Al Sears, and Billy Strayhorn on piano. "A Flower Is a Lovesome Thing," "How Could It Happen to a Dream?," "Lotus Blossom," and "Let the Zoomers Drool" are standouts. The other selections are small-group titles from 1950–51 with Willie Smith on alto. The instrumentation is different than usual (including a septet with three trombones and a rare chance to hear Billy Strayhorn play "Caravan" on organ) and the material overall is obscure but worthy.

9 *At the Berlin Sportpalast / Mar. 1961 / Pablo 2620-102*

10 *Everybody Knows Johnny Hodges / Feb. 6, 1964 + Mar. 8, 1965 / GRP/Impulse 116*

8 *Johnny Hodges/Wild Bill Davis, Vols. 1 & 2 / Jan. 7, 1965–Sept. 11, 1966 / RCA Jazz Tribune 42414*

7 *In a Mellotone / Sept. 10–11, 1966 / Bluebird 2305*

8 *Triple Play / Jan. 9–10, 1967 / RCA 68592*
Johnny Hodges recorded many sessions in the 1960s as a leader (quite a few have not yet been reissued on CD) even while he was playing nightly with Duke Ellington. The two-CD *At the Berlin Sportpalast* was recorded in Germany while Ellington was in France working on the soundtrack of *Paris Blues*. Hodges leads an all-star group of Duke's sidemen that includes Ray Nance (on cornet, violin, and vocals), Lawrence Brown, Harry Carney, bassist Aaron Bell, drummer Sam Woodyard, and Al Williams as the fill-in on piano. The music is primarily straight from the Ellington repertoire, sticking to familiar standards, but the musicians sound quite inspired and the audience is enthusiastic. Even

better is the single-disc *Everybody Knows Johnny Hodges,* a perfect place to begin exploring Hodges's music. This CD has not only the original album of the same name but Lawrence Brown's finest date as a leader, *Inspired Abandon.* The two sessions feature overlapping Ellington personnel playing familiar Duke, Strayhorn, and Hodges tunes in consistently inspired fashion. Hodges teamed up with organist Wild Bill Davis for an extensive series of records in the mid-1960s, two of which are reissued on the French Jazz Tribune twofer. Lawrence Brown is aboard for the second date, which is also reissued (with one extra cut) on the single-disc *In a Mellotone.* Hodges loved having the orchestral organ of Davis behind him, and he obviously enjoyed the brief vacation from the land of Ellington, performing some standards that he normally did not get a chance to play. *Triple Play* finds Hodges still in his prime in 1967 (he never declined), and, in addition to the usual Ellington sidemen of the period, such players as Tiny Grimes, Roy Eldridge (on three cuts), and pianists Hank Jones and Jimmy Jones make strong appearances.

LPS TO SEARCH FOR

Ellingtonia! (Onyx 216) features Hodges in three settings. There are two obscure numbers from 1946 ("Esquire Swank" and "Midriff") with the full Ellington Orchestra, a 1950 Paris date with a septet that includes Shorty Baker, Quentin Jackson, and Don Byas, and four memorable numbers in 1964 with an Ellington small group that has Victor Feldman on piano and Cat Anderson as the only trumpeter. *The Rabbit in Paris* (Inner City 7003), recorded in 1950

shortly before Hodges left Ellington, is a high-quality set of small-group Swing by an octet also featuring Baker, Jackson, and Byas plus Jimmy Hamilton; lots of swinging, riff-filled music. A box well worth bidding on is *The Complete Johnny Hodges Sessions, 1951–1955* (Mosaic 6-126), a six-LP limited-edition set that has all of the music from the 15 recording dates that Hodges led during his period away from Duke. His band always came across as an all-star Duke Ellington combo. The bootleg album *At a Dance, in a Studio, on Radio* (Enigma 1052), which dates from 1954–57, is most notable for having a couple of early solos by John Coltrane ("In a Mellotone" and "Don't Blame Me") during the period that he was in Hodges's small group. *A Smooth One* (Verve 2-2532) is a two-LP set that has a pair of excellent nine- and ten-piece group sessions from 1959–60 with Shorty Baker, Ray Nance, and either Ben Webster or Harold Ashby on tenor. Among the Hodges–Wild Bill Davis collaborations of the 1960s are *Blue Hodge* (Verve 8406), *Mess of Blues* (Verve 8570), *Blue Rabbit* (Verve 8599), *Wings & Things* (Verve 8630), and *Blue Pyramid* (Verve 8635); if you like one you will like them all. And one of the oddest meetings on record is an album titled *Lawrence Welk & Johnny Hodges* (Dot 25682). The bubblemeister admired the altoist's pretty sound, so he went out of his way to record him. Their set of ballads with strings works surprisingly well.

FILMS

Johnny Hodges is featured with Duke Ellington in 1961's *Good Years of Jazz* (Video Artists International 69301) and on *Memories of Duke* (A Vision 50187).

CHARLIE HOLMES

b. Jan. 27, 1910, Boston, MA, d. Sept. 12, 1985, Boston, MA

One of the best alto saxophonists of the early 1930s, Charlie Holmes held his own in the Luis Russell Orchestra with such major soloists as Henry "Red" Allen, J. C. Higginbotham, and Albert Nicholas. He was a childhood friend of both Johnny Hodges (a major influence on his style) and Harry Carney. Holmes was classically trained and in 1927 moved to New York, where he worked with Chick Webb, Henri Saparo, George Howe, and Joe Steele. Holmes was with Luis Russell during 1929–31 and was well featured on many of his records, plus dates by Red Allen and Higginbotham. After working with the Mills Blue Rhythm Band in 1932, he was back with Russell during 1935–40, playing in the band that backed Louis Armstrong. Charlie Holmes never became famous despite his abilities. He was with Bobby Burnet during part of 1941, played with the Cootie Williams Big Band (1942–45), spent 1947 with the sextets of John Kirby and Billy Kyle, and then got a day job, performing music only on a part-time basis for the next couple of decades. In the 1970s Charlie Holmes (who never led his own record date) was part of the Harlem Blues & Jazz Band, with whom he recorded, showing that his style was still similar to how it had sounded back in his glory days with Luis Russell.

HILTON JEFFERSON

b. July 30, 1903, Danbury, CT, d. Nov. 14, 1968, New York, NY

A fine soloist who was strongly influenced by Benny Carter, Hilton Jefferson was a journeyman during the Swing era who was considered a strong asset to several bands. He actually started playing music as a banjoist with Julian Arthur in 1925 but studied alto that year and soon switched instruments. Jefferson worked with Claude Hopkins (1926–28), Chick Webb (1929–30), King Oliver (1930), McKinney's Cotton Pickers, Hopkins again, Benny Carter, and Fletcher Henderson (1932–34); the latter association gave him a bit of recognition.

Jefferson had return engagements with Webb (1934, 1936, and 1938), Henderson (1936–38), and Hopkins (1939) and then had a longtime association with Cab Calloway (1940–49); he was showcased on Calloway's recording of "Willow Weep For Me." Jefferson was in Johnny Hodges's vacated spot with Duke Ellington (1952–53) and then, after a tour with Pearl Bailey, he became semiretired, working as a bank guard. Hilton Jefferson, who played with the Fletcher Henderson reunion band during 1957–58 and made a few later recordings (including four titles as a leader for Victor in 1957), played on a part-time basis into the 1960s.

RUSSELL PROCOPE

b. Aug. 11, 1908, New York, NY, d. Jan. 21, 1981, New York, NY

Russell Procope had two very different musical careers, as altoist with the John Kirby Sextet and as one of Duke Ellington's longtime clarinetists. Originally a violinist, Procope switched to clarinet and alto while in junior high school. In 1926 he became a professional and worked with Willie Freeman and Jimmy Campbell. A couple of years with various obscure bands preceded stints with Jelly Roll Morton (1928), Benny Carter (1929), and the early Chick Webb big band (1929–31). Procope gained some recognition for his playing and recordings with the Fletcher Henderson Orchestra (1931–34), and that was followed by periods with the big bands of Tiny Bradshaw (1934–35), Teddy Hill (1936–37), and Willie Bryant. While Procope was a member of the John Kirby Sextet (1938–43), his smooth virtuosity and floating tone helped give the band its unusual musical personality, and he blended in well with Buster Bailey and Charlie Shavers. He remained with Kirby until being called into the Army (1943–45). After his discharge, Procope rejoined the bassist for a few months during 1945–46 but by then the group was struggling. In the spring of 1946, Russell Procope became a member of the Duke Ellington Orchestra. Because Ellington already had a masterful soloist in Johnny Hodges, Procope rarely had a chance to solo on alto. But he ended up being valuable, for he could be cast in the role of a New Orleans–style clarinetist, contrasting with the cooler and more modern clarinet sound of Jimmy Hamilton. Procope enjoyed the steady work and being part of the world of Ellington so much that he stayed with the band for 28 years, until Duke's death in 1974. Russell Procope was semiretired in the years after Ellington's passing, sometimes gigging with Brooks Kerr's trio and recording with Chris Barber. Other than four titles for the HRS label in 1946, he led only one record date, a little-known album for the Dot label in 1956.

FILMS

Russell Procope is prominent in *Memories of Duke* (A Vision 50187) with the Duke Ellington Orchestra.

WILLIE SMITH

b. Nov. 25, 1910, Charleston, SC, d. Mar. 7, 1967, Los Angeles, CA

Considered one of the best altoists of the Swing era, Willie Smith is best remembered for his associations with Jimmie Lunceford, Harry James, and Duke Ellington. He started on clarinet when he was 12, was soon doubling on alto, and began playing professionally in Memphis with the Boston Serenaders in 1926. While attending Fisk University, Smith met Lunceford, whose band he officially joined in 1929. He quickly became a fixture with the Jimmie Lunceford Orchestra, playing not only fine alto (he was considered the band's best soloist) but occasional spots on clarinet in addition to contributing some arrangements and doing a bit of cheerful vocalizing, such as on "Rhythm Is Our Business." However, after 13 years, Smith felt grossly underpaid, and it was a major blow to the orchestra when he left to join Charlie Spivak in the summer of 1942. Smith was in the Navy during 1943–44; after his discharge, Harry James quickly added the altoist to his orchestra. He would be James's top sideman for many years and be featured on quite a few records. In March 1951, Smith was part of the "Great James Robbery" that found three of the bandleader's players (the others were Juan Tizol and Louie Bellson) joining Duke Ellington to make up for the defection of three of Duke's musicians. Smith was with Ellington for a year, played with Billy May's popular orchestra in 1952, toured with Jazz at the Philharmonic in 1953, and freelanced. He rejoined James for another nine years (1954–63), did some work in the studios, and in late 1966 recorded a date with Charlie Barnet's orchestra before passing away from cancer at the age of 56.

LPS TO SEARCH FOR

Smith led three record dates in 1945 and a few songs in 1947 but he made only one album under his own name, the ironically titled *The Best of Willie Smith* (GNP Crescendo 2055). Although this was recorded late in his life (August 1965), Smith was still in fine form, playing some numbers with a sextet that includes Tommy Gumina on accordion, guitarist Irving Ashby, and Johnny Guarnieri. The second half of the date has Smith in a quintet with tenor saxophonist Bill Perkins and pianist Jimmy Rowles. He performs two originals and a variety of standards arranged by Billy May, including "Uptown Blues."

DON STOVALL

b. Dec. 12, 1913, St. Louis MO, d. Nov. 20, 1970, New York, NY

Don Stovall is practically unknown in jazz history books because he chose to retire from music quite early. However, his booting alto solos with Henry "Red" Allen's sextet in the mid-1940s were perfect examples of Jump/Swing saxophone. Stovall played in the 1930s with Dewey Jackson, Fate Marable, Eddie Johnson's Crackerjacks (1932–33), Lil Armstrong, and his own band. After moving to New York in 1939, he worked with Sammy Price, Snub Mosley, Eddie Durham's big band, and the Cootie Williams Orchestra (1941–42). Stovall was with Red Allen during 1942–50, fitting right in to the spirited and frequently excitable band. Unfortunately for the jazz world, he decided to retire in 1950, when he was just 36, to work for the phone company, a major loss. Since he never led a record date of his own, Don Stovall is best heard on his recordings with Allen, such as "The Crawl."

Tenor Saxophonists

The tenor sax came into its own as a major instrument during the 1930s. Originally it had been used in vaudeville as a poor substitute for the tuba, but the rise of Coleman Hawkins with Fletcher Henderson in the 1920s (particularly by 1925) pointed out the potential of the instrument. Hawkins was such a dominant influence among tenor players that, prior to the rise of Lester Young in late 1936, only Bud Freeman and Eddie Miller (the latter being influenced by Bud's approach) did not sound to an extent like clones of Hawk.

With Lester Young's arrival in New York with Count Basie, tenor players had a major alternative sound. While Hawkins had a hard tone and a searching style that really dug into chord changes, Lester Young was much more laid back, both in his soft tone and in his thoughtful improvisations, which seemed to float over bar lines. While most of the tenors in this section were more heavily influenced by Hawkins than by Young (the latter would be most influential in the 1950s), by the mid-1940s many of the up-and-coming tenor players (such as Illinois Jacquet) mixed together the two styles to form their own approach.

Every big band of the Swing era had two tenors in their sax section, and nearly every one had a strong soloist. Some of the finest are profiled here.

GEORGIE AULD
b. May 19, 1919, Toronto, Canada, d. Jan. 8, 1990, Palm Springs, CA

Georgie Auld was a top sideman during the Swing era, a bandleader when the big band era was coming to an end, and a freelancer by the 1950s. Born John Altwerger, he changed his name fairly early in life. Auld grew up in New York and started out on alto. He switched to tenor in 1936 after hearing a Coleman Hawkins record. Auld's first major influence was Charlie Barnet, and he sounded pretty close to Barnet while playing with Bunny Berigan (1937–38) and Artie Shaw (1938–39). When Shaw suddenly left for Mexico, Georgie Auld was made the leader of his band (he was just 20 at the time), fulfilling the remaining engagements and recording a few titles before the orchestra (which was unable to attract many people without Shaw) broke up.

After a brief period with Jan Savitt in 1940, Auld was a member of the Benny Goodman Orchestra (1940–41), recording with BG's Septet, which included Cootie Williams and Charlie Christian. Auld had come into his own by this time, adding a Lester Young influence to his style and sounding quite distinctive. He was back with Artie Shaw during 1941–42 and had a brief stint in the Army. Auld led his own big band during 1943–46 (which on records featured at various times such guests as Sarah Vaughan, Dizzy Gillespie, and Erroll Garner), freelanced for a few years, was with Billy Eckstine in 1948, and had his own boppish ten-piece group in 1949. After playing with the Count Basie Octet in 1950, Georgie Auld became a studio musician, leading bands on a part-time basis during the remainder of his life and not recording much after the 1950s although he continued playing into the 1980's. Virtually all of his most significant work was completed before his 31st birthday!

●

9 *Jump, Georgie, Jump / Jan. 1940–July 1945 / Hep 27*
This is a very interesting CD. Listeners wondering what the Artie Shaw Orchestra sounded like after the clarinetist suddenly left should be satisfied by the inclusion of eight of the band's ten 1940 recordings; Auld was the orchestra's leader during its brief post-Shaw period until it broke up. Also on this CD is a radio transcription by the Auld Big Band of 1944 (featuring some trumpet solos from Sonny Berman) and a radio broadcast by the band in 1945. Auld is heard not only on tenor but on alto and soprano (as was his early idol Charlie Barnet). However his advanced Swing orchestra was formed a couple of years too late to catch on.

During 1945–46, the Georgie Auld big band recorded for Musicraft. Some but not all of the orchestra's recordings were reissued on *Big Band Jazz, Vol. 1* (Musicraft 501) and *With Sarah Vaughan, Vol. 2* (Musicraft 509). The first volume has some notable guests in the first two of the five sessions, including Dizzy Gillespie, Trummy Young, and pianist Erroll Garner. The second album features two early vocals by Sarah Vaughan and shows how strong the big band could be. Auld recorded frequently during the 1950s, and his last album of the decade (he stopped leading dates after 1963) was *Good Enough to Keep* (Xanadu 190), a tribute to the Benny Goodman Septet that he had performed with 18 years earlier. The lineup of musicians on this spirited Swing date (Auld, trumpeter Don Fagerquist, guitarist Howard Roberts, pianist Lou Levy, vibraphonist Larry Bunker, bassist Leroy Vinnegar, and drummer Mel Lewis) is impressive, and there was no attempt to find a clarinetist who could take Goodman's place; the clarinet is not missed.

FILMS

Georgie Auld has a small acting role in *The Marrying Kind* (1952), acts and ghosts the tenor solos for Robert DeNiro in *New York, New York* (1977), and is in the Goodyear Tire half-hour television special headed by guitarist Mike Bryan (1961).

PAUL BASCOMB

b. Feb. 12, 1912, Birmingham, AL, d. Dec. 2, 1986, Chicago, IL

A solid tenor saxophonist, Paul Bascomb (whose younger brother was trumpeter Dud Bascomb) was a reliable Swing soloist whose style was flexible enough to fit into early R&B. As with his brother, Paul is best known for his longtime association with the Erskine Hawkins Orchestra. He won a scholarship to Alabama State Teachers College, where he was one of the founders of the 'Bama Street Collegians and went with the band to New York in 1934, when Hawkins took it over. Other than for brief periods off (including replacing the late Herschel Evans with Count Basie's orchestra for a short time in 1938–39), Bascomb was with Hawkins until 1944. He had a chance to record with Count Basie in 1940 (filling in for the recently departed Lester Young) and 1941. When he left Hawkins, Bascomb formed his own sextet and soon persuaded Dud to join him. The group became a big band for a couple of years before breaking up in 1947. Paul Bascomb recorded a series of R&B-oriented titles for United in the early 1950s. His band, which fell between R&B and Swing, played for long periods at Small's Paradise in New York, the El Sino in Detroit, and Robert's Show Lounge and the Esquire in Chicago. He was active (if out of the spotlight) into the 1980s.

●

8 *Bad Bascomb / Mar. 3, 1952–Aug. 30, 1952 / Delmark 431*
Paul Bascomb's United recordings are collected on this CD, which adds four alternate takes to the earlier LP of the same name. The music is fairly basic and was originally meant for the jukebox market, but it is quite fun. The supporting cast of the jump/R&B combo includes trumpeter Eddie Lewis and pianist Duke Jordan. It is surprising that the majority of the selections were not released at the time, because many of the tunes are quite catchy and accessible.

CHU BERRY

b. Sept. 13, 1908, Wheeling, WV, d. Oct. 30, 1941, Conneaut, OH

Considered one of the top tenor saxophonists of the Swing era and a possible competitor for Coleman Hawkins, Chu Berry had a short career, cut off by the tragedy of his early death. Leon "Chu" Berry started playing saxophone as a teenager after hearing Hawkins solo with Fletcher Henderson. He attended West Virginia State College, playing with Edwards' Collegians. Berry turned down a chance to be a professional football player so as to continue with music. He worked with Sammy Stewart (1929–30), leaving the band in New York. Chu, who early on was actually known as "Chew," quickly made a strong impression in New York, where his sound resembled Hawkins's but was slightly softer. Berry played with many bands, including those led by Cecil Scott, Otto Hardwicke, Kaiser Marshall, Walter Pichon, Earl Jackson, Benny Carter (1932–33), and Charlie Johnson (1932–33). He was part of Spike Hughes's all-star recordings in 1933, playing opposite Hawkins. With Teddy Hill's orchestra (1933–35), Berry was (along with Roy Eldridge) the solo star, and the duo was even more successful after they moved over to Fletcher Henderson's orchestra (1935–37). Chu's original "Christopher Columbus" (a hit for Henderson) caught on as a standard and would become one of the main themes of Jimmy Mundy's arrangement of "Sing, Sing, Sing" for Benny Goodman. In 1937 Berry joined the Cab Calloway Orchestra, where for the next four years he was the musical director. His recording with Calloway of "Ghost of a Chance" received some attention, although in reality his ballad playing tended to be overly sentimental. Berry was better on stomping pieces, and, although he never surpassed Hawkins, he was not that far behind. He appeared as a guest artist on a variety of all-star recordings during 1935–40, including dates led by Red Norvo, Red Allen, and Lionel Hampton (with whom "Sweethearts on Parade" was a high point). Tragically, Chu Berry was killed in a car accident when he was just 33.

●

9 *1937–1941 / Mar. 23, 1937–Sept. 1941 / Classics 784*
All of Chu Berry's sessions as a leader are on this CD, although not the 14 alternate takes that have been released through the years. The quality is pretty consistent throughout these swinging combo dates, which include meetings with Hot Lips Page (on two of the five sessions), trumpeters Irving Randolph and Roy Eldridge, and fellow tenor Charlie Ventura (on a very rare set). Among the more memorable selections are "Indiana," "Chuberry Jam," "Sittin' In," "Monday at Minton's," and "Body and Soul"; this last finds

Eldridge's double-time trumpet solo stealing the show. Highly recommended.

LPS TO SEARCH FOR

Chu (Epic 22007) repeats eight titles from 1937–1941 (one session with Hot Lips Page and the four titles with Irving Randolph) but also has seven of Berry's better performances with the Cab Calloway Orchestra (including "Ghost of a Chance") and the heated "Warmin' Up" with Teddy Wilson.

DON BYAS
b. Oct. 21, 1912, Muskogee, OK, d. Aug. 24, 1972, Amsterdam, Holland

A major tenor saxophonist who built on and extended the innovations of Coleman Hawkins, Don Byas would have been much more famous had he not moved to Europe at the prime of his career. He worked early on as an altoist with Bennie Moten, Terrence Holder, and Walter Page's Blue Devils (1929). During 1931–32 Byas led his band, which he called Don Carlos and his Collegiate Ramblers (Carlos was his middle name), in Oklahoma. In 1933 he switched to tenor and toured with Bert Johnson's Sharps and Flats. Byas decided to stay in California for several years, playing with Lionel Hampton, Eddie Barefield, Buck Clayton's Gentlemen of Harlem, and Charlie Echols, among others. He was part of Eddie Mallory's group that accompanied Ethel Waters (1936–38) and then freelanced in New York, including with the orchestras of Don Redman and Lucky Millinder. Byas became a key soloist with Andy Kirk (1939–40), had short stints with Edgar Hayes and Benny Carter, and then was a member of the Count Basie Band (1941–43) as Lester Young's replacement, which brought him quite a bit of recognition. Byas recorded prolifically as a leader during 1944–46 (explosive on up-tempo pieces, warm and sophisticated on ballads), recorded two classic duets with bassist Slam Stewart at a 1944 Town Hall concert, played on 52nd Street with Dizzy Gillespie, and otherwise mostly led his own combos.

In September 1946, Byas went to Europe as a member of the Don Redman Orchestra. He liked what he saw and decided

THE WAYNE KNIGHT COLLECTION

Two of the great Swing tenor saxophonists: Don Byas
and the short-lived Dick Wilson.

to stay, visiting the U.S. only one time (in 1970) during the final 26 years of his life. He spent periods living in France, the Netherlands, and Denmark. Don Byas worked steadily on the Continent (including joining Duke Ellington during some of his European tours and recording with Dizzy Gillespie, Bud Powell, Art Blakey, Jazz at the Philharmonic, and Ben Webster) and led a steady stream of records. But because the world was a much larger place in those days, he was largely forgotten in the U.S. after 1946 despite his talents.

●

7 *Midnight at Minton's / 1941 / High Note 7044*

9 *1944–1945 / July 28, 1944–Mar. 1945 / Classics 882*

5 *Savoy Jam Party / July 28, 1944–Aug. 21, 1946 / Savoy 2213*

Midnight at Minton's was recorded by Jerry Newman live at Minton's Playhouse in 1941. Most of the recordings that he documented are a bit loose, since they were jam sessions, but this particular set has some special moments. "Stardust" and "Exactly Like You" have fine vocals by Helen Humes and magnificent solos by Byas (particularly his stunning ballad statement on "Stardust"); in addition, Thelonious Monk is heard on piano and trumpeter Joe Guy plays a little better than usual. Byas and Guy also play four instrumentals (two with Monk) and, even with the ragged moments, the tenor's presence keeps the music fairly coherent. *1944–1945* is the first of several Classics CDs that reissue all of Byas's valuable mid-'40s recordings as a leader. Byas is heard on eight numbers (including "1944 Stomp" and the two-part "Savoy Jam Party") in a quintet and sextet with Charlie Shavers; the two horns are a perfect match. He also leads a group that costars trumpeter Joe Thomas and jams with a quintet that features blues guitarist Big Bill Broonzy, who has four vocals; the latter combination works quite well. *Savoy Jam Party* was originally a two-LP set with 32 selections, all of Byas's work for the Savoy label. The Japanese reissue put out by Denon is lazy in the extreme. The first 25 numbers from the twofer are on the CD (only one of the eight numbers from the 1946 session), and the extensive liner notes from the LP are reproduced but so tiny that they cannot possibly be read; naturally they refer to all the 32 selections! Although the music is wonderful (matching Byas with trumpeters Shavers, Emmett Berry, and Benny Harris), nine of the cuts are already available on *1944–1945*; get the original two-LP set (if it can be found) instead and save your eyes!

10 *Don Byas on Blue Star / Jan. 13, 1947–Mar. 7, 1952 / Emarcy 833 406*

8 *A Night in Tunisia / Jan. 13–14, 1963 / Black Lion 760136*

8 *Walkin' / Jan. 13–14, 1963 / Black Lion 760167*

When Don Byas left the U.S. to move permanently to Europe in 1946, his career did not slow down, although he became invisible to American audiences. *Don Byas on Blue Star* has some of his recordings for the Blue Star label from 1947 and 1950–52. The 1947 selections also feature a few other members of the Don Redman band who decided to stay overseas beyond the tour (trumpeter Peanuts Holland, trombonist Tyree Glenn, and pianist Billy Taylor) along with some French players, including Hubert Rostaing on alto; the later selections are with local rhythm sections. Throughout, Byas shows that he was still growing as a creative improviser, sticking to his advanced Swing style but sounding quite modern. *A Night in Tunisia* and *Walkin'* were recorded at the same recording dates with pianist Bent Axen, bassist Niels Pedersen, and drummer Williams Schiopffe. Although Byas would record as late as 1971, these were among the best performances of his last period. The two CDs are equally rewarding, with Byas stretching out on such standards as "Anthropology," "Billie's Bounce," and "All the Things You Are."

LPS TO SEARCH FOR

As mentioned, the two-LP set *Savoy Jam Party* (Savoy 2213) is much preferable to the single Japanese CD reissue. *Don Byas in Paris* (Prestige 7598) features the great tenor in a quartet with pianist Billy Taylor, an octet with Peanuts Holland, Tyree Glenn, and Hubert Rostaing (a different date than what is included in *Don Byas on Blue Star*), and a quintet with Bill Coleman. The concise music dates from 1946 and 1949. *Don Byas* (Inner City 7018) will be particularly difficult to find, but the performances (quartet dates from 1953–54 with pianists Mary Lou Williams and Beryl Booker plus a quintet set from 1955 with French musicians) are well worth the trouble.

ALIX COMBELLE
b. June 15, 1912, Paris, France, d. Feb. 27, 1978, Mantes, France

Thought of as "the Coleman Hawkins of France," Alix Combelle was an impressive player who was often utilized by American jazzmen passing through Paris. Combelle, who doubled on clarinet, actually started out as a professional drummer (1928–31) before switching to tenor. He was quite busy during the 1930s, playing with Gregor (1932–33), Arthur Briggs (1934), Michel Warlop, Ray Ventura and as a leader. He appeared on records opposite Coleman Hawkins (including a famous session with Django Reinhardt and Benny Carter) and made records with the Quintet of the Hot Club of France and Bill Coleman, plus a series under his own name. Although he was offered a job with Tommy Dorsey during one of his two visits to the U.S., Combelle elected to stay in France. Like Reinhardt, Combelle was able somehow to continue playing jazz during the war years. During 1946–63 he appeared in many mainstream settings, including with Bill Coleman, Buck Clayton, Lionel Hampton, and Jonah Jones, although, as time went on, he worked less. After Alix Combelle opened a nightclub in 1963, he became semi-retired.

●

9 *1935–1940 / Sept. 1, 1935–Oct. 21, 1940 / Classics 714*

8 *1940–1941 / Oct. 21, 1940–Mar. 12, 1941 / Classics 751*

7 *1942–1943 / June 1942–Sept. 9, 1943 / Classics 782*

Alix Combelle's most famous recordings were as a sideman, but he recorded pretty regularly as a leader during the 1935–43 period. Other than for a few later numbers and three albums of material from 1954–60, his complete output as a leader is on these three Classics CDs. *1935–1940* has two numbers in which Combelle (on tenor and clarinet) is backed by the Quintette of the Hot Club of France (with Stephane Grappelli switching to piano). He is also featured in a sextet with Bill Coleman, a quartet with cornetist Phillippe Brun and with larger groups full of French all-stars.

Despite the occupation of France by the Nazis, Combelle was able to record quite a bit during 1940–43, disguising the names of American jazz and pop standards by renaming them in French. *1940–1941* mostly features Combelle with his big band (called Le Jazz de Paris), plus there are four numbers with the "Trio de Saxophones," which includes altoist Christian Wagner, Hubert Rostaing on tenor, and Django Reinhardt. The music on *1942–1943* is extremely rare and, considering the war, it is remarkable that any of it was recorded! Combelle is heard in both big bands and combos, sounding quite enthusiastic in his Coleman Hawkins–influenced style. It seems strange that in the years after the liberation of France, he would record so little, just six selections as a leader during 1944–53.

JULIAN DASH
b. Apr. 9, 1916, Charleston, SC, d. Feb. 25, 1974, New York, NY

Julian Dash was an excellent tenor saxophonist although never rising much above obscurity. He started out on alto, playing with the Charleston Nighthawks in 1935 before switching to tenor. Dash worked with the 'Bama State Collegians (1935–36), went to New York to study embalming(!), but decided to become a musician instead of a mortician. He led the house band at Monroe's Uptown House (1936–38) and then, when Paul Bascomb temporarily left the Erskine Hawkins Orchestra, he took his place. Bascomb soon returned and Hawkins decided to keep the two top-notch tenor soloists. Dash would remain with Hawkins until the early 1950s, staying with the big band until its very end. He appeared on some of Buck Clayton's famous jam session records for Columbia in the 50s and continued playing on weekends (usually with his own group) into the early 1970s while also working at a variety of day jobs during his last couple of decades. Julian Dash led some isolated dates during 1950–52 and 1955 (primarily singles) and shared a Master Jazz album with pianist Cliff Smalls in 1970.

HERSCHEL EVANS
b. 1909, Denton, TX, d. Feb. 9, 1939, New York, NY

Herschel Evans's Coleman Hawkins–inspired sound was a contrast to Lester Young's in the Count Basie Orchestra. Although they were featured on occasional "tenor battles" (none unfortunately were ever recorded), Evans and Young were actually close friends.

Evans was one of the first of the "tough-toned Texas tenors," a "school" that would later include Buddy Tate, Illinois Jacquet, and Arnett Cobb, among many others. He worked early on with Alphonso Trent (1926), the St. Louis Merrymakers, Edgar Battle, Terrence Holder, Sammy Holmes, and Troy Floyd (1929–31), recording with the last. After playing with Grant Moore, he was with the Bennie Moten Orchestra (1933–35) during its last period. Evans had stints with Hot Lips Page and Dave Peyton before moving to Los Angeles, where he played with Lionel Hampton and Buck Clayton. Herschel

Evans joined Count Basie late in 1936 and for a time was quite well known. His most famous solo was on "Blue and Sentimental" and he also appeared on a couple of record dates as a featured sideman with Hampton. But a weak heart caused his premature death at age 30 and Herschel Evans never had the opportunity to lead his own record date.

BUD FREEMAN
b. Apr. 13, 1906, Chicago, IL, d. Mar. 15, 1991, Chicago, IL

Virtually the only tenor saxophonist of the late 1920s to escape Coleman Hawkins's influence, Lawrence "Bud" Freeman always had his own sound and a fresh angular style. He was one of the few tenor players to spend most of his career playing Dixieland and yet can also be considered a superior Swing musician.

Freeman was a member of the Austin High Gang, a group of white youngsters who were so impressed after seeing King Oliver (with Louis Armstrong) playing live in Chicago and hearing the records of the New Orleans Rhythm Kings that they were motivated to start playing music themselves. He started playing C-melody sax in 1923, switching to tenor two years later, and freelanced in Chicago starting in the mid-1920s, including with Husk O'Hare's Wolverines, Art Kassel, and Thelma Terry. Freeman debuted on records in 1927 with the McKenzie-Condon Chicagoans, led his own two-song record date the following year, and was with Ben Pollack in New York during 1927–28.

A brief visit to France was followed by five years of freelancing with Red Nichols, Roger Wolfe Kahn, and Gene Kardos, among others, recording his original "The Eel" with Eddie Condon in 1933. Bud Freeman began the Swing era playing with the orchestras of Joe Haymes (1934), Ray Noble (1935), and Tommy Dorsey (1936–38). While with TD, Freeman was featured with both his big band and the Clambake Seven and he gained a national reputation. He spent much of 1938 with Benny Goodman's orchestra, but he felt quite unsatisfied getting only short solos and being in the clarinetist's shadow. However, he recorded some timeless music with Eddie Condon that year and led sessions of his own, including 11 titles in a hot trio with pianist Jess Stacy and drummer George Wettling. The following year, Freeman had his own eight-piece group, the Summa Cum Laude Orchestra (which included trumpeter Max Kaminsky, valve trombonist Brad Gowans, clarinetist Pee Wee Russell, and Eddie Condon on rhythm guitar), playing in the musical *Swinging the Dream* and making a series of strong recordings.

When the Summa Cum Laude Band broke up in 1940, Freeman had a short-lived big band, worked with Joe Marsala, and primarily led small groups. He was in the Army during 1943–45 and then spent the rest of his long career alternating between heading his own combos and making guest appearances, most often with Eddie Condon. Although Freeman studied with Lennie Tristano in the early 1950s, his tenor style remained unchanged after the late 1930s, and he stuck to playing the Swing and Dixieland standards that he loved the most. He was very active for 65 years, touring with the World's Greatest Jazz Band during 1968–71, spending some time living in London in the late 1970s, and ending his life and his career back in Chicago.

●

10	*1928–1938 / Dec. 3, 1928–Nov. 30, 1938 / Classics 781*
10	*1939–1940 / June 13, 1939–July 23, 1940 / Classics 811*
6	*1945–1946 / Aug. 9, 1945–1946 / Classics 942*

1928–1938 begins with Bud Freeman's two selections from 1928 ("Craze-o-logy" and "Can't Help Lovin' That Man"), enjoyable numbers cut before he had really formed his style. By the time he led his next date, four swinging tunes from 1935 in a sextet with the great Bunny Berigan, Freeman was quite recognizable and distinctive. "The Buzzard" and "Keep Smilin' at Trouble" find Berigan often stealing the show. Most of the rest of this CD consists of 11 exciting trio numbers with Jess Stacy and drummer George Wettling that rank with the finest work of Freeman's long career. His renditions of "You Took Advantage of Me," "At Sundown," "My Honey's Loving Arms," and "Three Little Words" are real standouts. Also on *1928–1938* are four selections with a combo that includes Stacy, Bobby Hackett, Pee Wee Russell, and Eddie Condon, highlighted by "Memories of You" and "Life Spears a Jitterbug." *1939–1940* has all of the master takes recorded by Freeman's Summa Cum Laude Orchestra, which, despite its "classy" name, was essentially a hot Dixieland-based octet. Max Kaminsky, valve trombonist Brad Gowans, and Pee Wee Russell join Freeman in the front line, and the band's last session has Jack Teagarden in Gowans's place, which makes things even better. *1945–1946* has its moments, although it is not on the same level due to the inclusion of 12 numbers that showcase the Five De Marco Sisters, an average Swing vocal group. Much better are a couple of hilarious V-Disc performances ("The Latest Thing in Hot Jazz" and "For Musicians Only"), some heated playing by Yank Lawson, and an experimental tenor-drum duet with Ray McKinley on "The Atomic Era."

9 *Something to Remember You By / Jan. 15, 1962 / Black Lion 760153*

8 *Superbud / 1974 + Aug. 13, 1992 / Jazzology 185*

8 *California Session / Jan. 9, 1982 / Jazzology 277*

Bud Freeman recorded many Dixieland-oriented dates throughout his career, although he thought of himself as being a Swing musician. *Something to Remember You By* is one of the best and features a quartet with pianist Dave Frishberg, Bob Haggart, and drummer Don Lamond. The dozen songs (plus five alternate takes) include some tunes that are rarely played in this format (including "You're a Sweetheart," "The Girl Friend," and Freeman's "Meet You in San Juan") along with some more familiar numbers that are uplifted by Bud's warm tone, wit, and solid sense of swing. *Superbud,* from a dozen years later, is almost of the same quality, a set in England with pianist Keith Ingham, bassist Pete Chapman, and drummer Johnny Armitage. For the CD reissue six numbers were added, all 1992 piano solos by Ingham. *California Session,* recorded when Freeman was 75,

finds the tenorman quite enthusiastic as he appears in Los Angeles with a group that includes trumpeter Dick Cathcart, trombonist Betty O'Hara, clarinetist Bob Reitmeier, pianist Ray Sherman, guitarist Howard Alden (23 at the time), bassist Phil Stephens, and drummer Nick Fatool. Freeman was only supposed to be sitting in for a few numbers, but he enjoyed the band so much that he played the entire night. In one of his last recordings, Freeman sounds quite exuberant on such favorites as "Tea for Two," "Crazy Rhythm," and "Sunday."

LPS TO SEARCH FOR

Bud Freeman and his Summa Cum Laude Orchestra (IAJRC 53) is for completists, featuring Freeman's band in 1940 in a supportive role behind the vocals of Teddy Grace, Buddy Clark, and Doris Rhodes. *Swinging Tenors* (Affinity 64) has separate sessions by Freeman (a 1953 date with a four-piece rhythm section) and Eddie Miller (his 1944–47 Capitol recordings, four of which are with his big band). *The Test of Time* (Bethlehem 6033) is a fine quintet album with trumpeter Ruby Braff from 1955, and Freeman is matched with Shorty Baker on the relaxed Swing date *The Bud Freeman All-Stars* (Original Jazz Classics 183). *Chicago/Austin High School Jazz in Hi-Fi* (RCA 1508) is a classic album from 1957 that should have been put out on CD a decade ago, reuniting an inspired Freeman with cornetist Jimmy McPartland, Billy Butterfield, Pee Wee Russell, Tyree Glenn, and Jack Teagarden on classic material. *The Compleat Bud Freeman* (Monmouth Evergreen 7022) is a superior quintet set from 1969 that finds the tenorman playing with fellow members of the World's Greatest Jazz Band: Bob Wilber on soprano and clarinet, pianist Ralph Sutton, Bob Haggart, and drummer Gus Johnson. And finally, *The Real Bud Freeman—1984* (Principally Jazz 01), from a tiny label, was Freeman's last recording, cut 57 years after his recording debut and worth acquiring if it can be found.

COLEMAN HAWKINS
b. Nov. 21, 1904, St. Joseph, MI, d. May 19, 1969, New York, NY

The king of the tenor saxophone, Coleman Hawkins dominated the field completely during 1925–36, and, even after the rise of Lester Young, he remained a force to be reckoned with into the mid-1960s. Always modern and an expert at dissecting chord changes, Hawkins almost single-handedly led to the acceptance of the tenor as a solo instrument in jazz.

Coleman Hawkins did not have any significant predecessors. He originally played piano and cello but was improvising on tenor by the time he was nine. He played in public with school bands two years later and was a professional by the time he was 16. After working locally in Kansas City for a brief time, he became a member of Mamie Smith's Jazz Hounds (1921–23), with whom he made his first recordings. Hawkins left Smith in New York, made some recordings with Fletcher Henderson, and officially joined Henderson's orchestra in 1924. Although ahead of other tenor players, Hawkins's playing was pretty primitive at the time, with his solos punctuated by slap-tonguing and staccato runs. The arrival of Louis Armstrong in Henderson's band made a gradual impact on Hawkins, who learned how to swing and to build up his solos. In 1926 with his chorus on "The Stampede," Coleman Hawkins had arrived as a giant in jazz.

Hawkins would be with Henderson for a decade, into 1934. In his early days he sometimes reluctantly doubled on clarinet, baritone, and bass sax, but by 1927 he had found his niche as the world's leading tenor. His guest spot with the Mound City Blue Blowers in 1929 resulted in a classic ballad solo in "One Hour," and he was occasionally used on other recordings, including with Spike Hughes in 1933. By 1934, Hawkins was frustrated with Henderson's many missed opportunities (the once-pacesetting orchestra was being surpassed by other bands) and he wired Jack Hylton in England to say that he was available in case the British bandleader wanted to use him. Hawkins was sent for (he was already famous overseas), and for the next five years he played in Europe, being treated as a major artist (race prejudice was rare in Europe at the time, outside of Germany), performing and recording on a regular basis.

Coleman Hawkins's big band may have only been around for a year, but the innovative tenorman's musical prime lasted over 40 years.

Coleman Hawkins's absence left a void in the United States among tenor saxophonists, and first Chu Berry and then Lester Young filled the gap. With war clouds looming in 1939, Hawkins wisely returned home and, in some memorable jam sessions, he held his own with his younger competitors. If there was any doubt that he was back, his 1939 recording of "Body and Soul" (a surprise hit) set them to rest. After trying unsuccessfully to lead a big band during 1940, Hawkins entered his greatest period. During 1941–46 he recorded many classic titles, including "The Man I Love" in 1943, the first bebop set in 1944 (which included his "Disorder at the Border"), quartet numbers that introduced pianist Thelonious Monk, "Stuffy" and "Rifftide" with his 1945 sextet (costarring trumpeter Howard McGhee), and Jazz at the Philharmonic appearances in 1946. Always a champion of modern jazz, he encouraged the younger beboppers and, in addition to Monk, utilized trumpeters Dizzy Gillespie, Miles Davis, and Fats Navarro, drummer Max Roach, bassist Oscar Pettiford, and trombonist J. J. Johnson on some of his dates. In 1948 he recorded "Picasso," the first unaccompanied tenor sax solo.

But by the early 1950s, Coleman Hawkins was considered a bit out of style. His solos were as harmonically complex as usual but, rhythmically and soundwise (it was a cooler era), he was thought of as a bit old-fashioned. However, he persevered and in 1957 had one of his greatest years. He recorded several very impressive albums (including one where he teamed with John Coltrane as sidemen to Thelonious Monk), played the Newport Jazz Festival with Roy Eldridge, recorded with Henry "Red" Allen, and appeared on the *Sound of Jazz* telecast. During 1955–65, Hawkins often led his own quartet or teamed up with the equally competitive Eldridge. He also recorded with Max Roach, trumpeter Booker Little, and altoist Eric Dolphy in 1961, was part of a Duke Ellington small-group recording in 1962, and was matched on an eccentric session with the younger tenor Sonny Rollins, who considered him his idol. Coleman Hawkins seemed immortal.

But in 1965 his health began to fail, both physically and mentally. During his remaining four years, the once impeccably dressed tenorman often looked shabby, he was short of breath during his solos, and he quickly declined (drinking excessively and barely eating at all), passing away at the age of 64. But he had had quite an illustrious 40-year run!

●

8 *A Retrospective: 1929–1963 / Nov. 7, 1929–July 15, 1963 / Bluebird 66617*

10 *In Europe 1934/39 / Nov. 18, 1934–May 26, 1939 / Jazz Up 317/18/19*

A Retrospective, which is a two-CD set, is an excellent overview of Coleman Hawkins's recordings for the Victor-associated labels throughout a 34-year period. He is heard as a sideman with the Mound City Blue Blowers (the classic "One Hour" and "Hello Lola" session), McKinney's Cotton Pickers, Fletcher Henderson ("Sugar Foot Stomp" and "Hocus Pocus"), Lionel Hampton, the Metronome All-Stars of 1941, the 1946 Esquire All-American Award Winners, singer Leslie Scott, Red Allen, Lambert, Hendricks & Bavan, and Sonny Rollins. In addition, Hawkins is featured on his own sessions from 1939 (including "Body and Soul"), 1940, 1946–47, and 1956. An excellent introduction to the always-modern tenor giant. *In Europe* is a magnificent three-CD set from a European label that has all of the recordings that he made during his five years overseas, including many alternate takes. Some of these sessions are quite rare. Hawkins is heard with small groups, with the Ramblers (an excellent Dutch band) in 1935 and '37, in duos with pianist Freddie Johnson, with Jack Hylton, and on a famous session with Benny Carter, Alix Combelle, and Django Reinhardt that resulted in classic versions of "Honeysuckle Rose" and "Crazy Rhythm." Because the Jazz Up set will probably be difficult to find, some listeners may want to acquire three of the Classics Coleman Hawkins releases, which unfortunately do not include the alternate takes: *1929–1934* (Classics 587), *1934–1937* (Classics 602), and *1937–1939* (Classics 613).

9 *Bean and the Boys / Oct. 11, 1944–Dec. 1946 / Prestige 24124*

9 *Hollywood Stampede / Feb. 23, 1945–June 1947 / Capitol 92596*

In the mid-1940s, Coleman Hawkins did a great deal to help the new jazz movement, using his prestige to help gain work and recognition for the young beboppers. *Rainbow Mist* has what is considered the first two bebop recording dates, six selections that include three of Hawk's ballad features (including the "Body and Soul"–based "Rainbow Mist"), plus a trio of hotter numbers ("Woody'n You," "Disorder at the Border," and Bu Dee Daht") that use modern arrangements and have trumpet solos from Dizzy Gillespie. Also on this CD is a meeting with fellow tenors Ben Webster and Georgie Auld (along with Charlie Shavers) that, among other songs, has the earliest version ever of Dizzy's "Salt Peanuts"; in addition there are four selections from the 1944 Auld Big Band. *Bean and the Boys,* which has a couple of sessions as a featured sideman, finds Hawkins also leading a quartet that includes Thelonious Monk (in his recording debut) on piano and jamming in 1946 with an octet that includes such significant young players as Fats Navarro, J.J. Johnson, Hank Jones, Milt Jackson, and Max Roach. Few other alumni of Mamie Smith's Jazz Hounds could play so well on "I Mean You" and "Bean and the Boys!" *Hollywood Stampede* consists of a dozen concise numbers by Hawkins's Swing/bop quintet of 1945 with trumpeter Howard McGhee ("Rifftide" and "Stuffy" are particularly catchy riff tunes); Vic Dickenson makes the group a sextet on one session. In addition, a lesser-known Hawkins septet session from 1947 gives one a couple of early glimpses at trumpeter Miles Davis.

9 *Rainbow Mist / Feb. 16, 1944–May 22, 1944 / Delmark 459*

8 *Coleman Hawkins / Johnny Hodges in Paris / Dec. 21, 1949–June 20, 1950 / Vogue 68215*

6 *Body and Soul Revisited / Oct. 19, 1951–Oct. 13, 1958 / GRP/Decca 627*

7 *The Hawk in Paris / July 9–13, 1956 / Bluebird 51059*

9 *The Hawk Flies High / Mar. 12–15, 1957 / Original Jazz Classics 027*

Although the 1949–56 period found Coleman Hawkins overshadowed by Lester Young and the many "cool school" players who were influenced by Young, he worked steadily and recorded fairly often. The Vogue CD actually has only six selections by Hawkins from a 1949 date with a mostly French group that includes drummer Kenny Clarke. That session is excellent, but the CD is most significant for also including 16 swinging numbers by Johnny Hodges with a 1950 octet that has Don Byas, Shorty Baker, Quentin Jackson, and Jimmy Hamilton; one can understand why Hodges would soon attempt to have his own similar group. *Body and Soul Revisited* is an overview of Hawkins's work for the Decca label in the 1950s, including selections from albums led by Cozy Cole (Dixieland-oriented) and clarinetist Tony Scott, plus dates headed by Hawk from 1951–53 and 1955. Lots of melodic mood music plus a brief unaccompanied "Foolin' Around." One wishes that the complete Decca sessions were reissued, though. *The Hawk in Paris* is a surprise success. The tenor had always wanted to record with a string section and he finally had the opportunity in 1956. Playing a dozen romantic melodies associated with Paris, Hawkins easily overcomes Manny Albam's potentially muzaky arrangements and takes some creative and witty solos. *The Hawk Flies High* helped to launch 1957 for Hawkins, one of his great years. The six selections on the LP-length program (highlighted by the jubilant "Sanctity") find Hawkins easily holding his own with J. J. Johnson and trumpeter Idrees Sulieman despite being more than a generation younger.

7 *The Genius of Coleman Hawkins / Oct. 16, 1957 / Verve 825-673*

8 *Jamestown, N.Y., 1958 / Uptown 27.45*

4 *Soul / Nov. 7, 1958 / Original Jazz Classics 096*

4 *At Ease / Jan. 29, 1960 / Original Jazz Classics 181*

3 *The Hawk Relaxes / Feb. 28, 1961 / Original Jazz Classics 709*

4 *On Broadway / June 2, 1962–Aug. 16, 1962 / Prestige 24189*

8 *Hawk Eyes / Apr. 3, 1959 / Original Jazz Classics 294*

7 *With Red Garland Trio / Aug. 12, 1959 / Original Jazz Classics 418*

The period 1957–65 was a final golden age for the veteran tenor, a time when he seemed ageless and was recording quite prolifically. *The Genius of Coleman Hawkins* matches Hawk with the Oscar Peterson Trio and drummer Alvin Stoller for a set of mostly relaxed standards. There is more fire on *Jamestown, N.Y., 1958,* a spontaneous and unusually inspired live concert from 1958 (released for the first time in 1998) with trombonist Ted Donnelly and a local rhythm section.

In general, Hawkins's Prestige sessions (some of which were made for the Moodsville subsidiary and have been reissued in the Original Jazz Classics series) are a bit sleepy, with an excess of slower and draggy material. *Soul* has a dreary version of "Greensleeves" that sets the mood for an uneventful quintet date with guitarist Kenny Burrell and pianist Ray Bryant. *At Ease* (a quartet session with pianist Tommy Flanagan leading a quiet rhythm section) is more suitable as background music than for close listening, and *The Hawk Relaxes* (on which Hawkins mostly sticks close to the seven familiar melodies) can easily put one to sleep. *On Broadway,* a "best of" collection that draws its music from the Hawkins albums *Good Old Broadway* (which is issued here complete), *Make Someone Happy,* and *Plays the Jazz Version of No Strings,* is quite unimaginative. Hawkins (again with Flanagan) primarily just plays the melodies straight, with no attempt made to uplift the songs. In contrast, *Hawk Eyes* is one of the best of Hawkins's Prestige dates, for the material has more potential (including "Through for the Night," "La Rosita," "Hawk Eyes," and the slow blues "C'mon In"), and the tenor is joined by the exciting Charlie Shavers and Tiny Grimes. Also quite worthwhile is *With Red Garland Trio,* which is highlighted by a pair of lengthy blues and the ballad "I Want to Be Loved."

8 *Bean Stalkin' / Oct. 1960–Nov. 1960 / Pablo 2310-933*

8 *Night Hawk / Dec. 30, 1960 / Original Jazz Classics 420*

As if to show that his Moodsville studio dates were not reflective of how he really sounded, on *Bean Stalkin'* Coleman

Hawkins jams happily with Roy Eldridge, Benny Carter, and Don Byas during lively concerts held in Zurich and Paris. There are moments when these musicians sound like they are out for blood! On *Night Hawk,* Hawkins holds his own with the fiery Eddie "Lockjaw" Davis, whose tenor style was clearly inspired by the older musician. At that point in time, Hawkins could at best be tied in tenor battles but never defeated.

7 *Alive! At the Village Gate / Aug. 13–15, 1962 / Verve 829 260*

7 *Hawkins! Eldridge! Hodges! Alive! At the Village Gate / Aug. 13–15, 1962 / Verve 314 513 755*

7 *Desafinado / Sept. 12 + 17, 1962 / GRP/Impulse 227*

8 *Wrapped Tight / Feb. 22, 1965–Mar. 1, 1965 / GRP/ Impulse 109*

During 1962–65, Coleman Hawkins continued at the high level he had been during the past 35 years, joking about his age and claiming that whoever took those solos on 1923 recordings by Fletcher Henderson must have been some elderly gentleman using his name! The two Village Gate CDs were recorded with the same rhythm section: pianist Tommy Flanagan, bassist Major Holley, and drummer Ed Locke. Hawkins stretches out on six selections (two previously unissued) on the first disc, which includes long versions of "Joshua Fit the Battle of Jericho" and "Mack the Knife." The second release has three explosive numbers with Roy Eldridge and Johnny Hodges, plus four additional (and previously unreleased) quartet numbers showcasing Hawkins. Coleman Hawkins's final important studio albums were three Impulse projects, two of which are currently available on CD. *Desafinado* is a high quality bossanova date in which Hawk sounds quite joyful on such numbers as "O Pato," "One Note Samba," and even "I'm Looking Over a Four-Leaf Clover," backed by two guitars, bass, drums, percussion, and Tommy Flanagan on claves. Only the brief playing time keeps this delightful set from getting a higher rating. *Wrapped Tight* is the last great Hawkins album, with the tenor making some powerful statements; listen to the melody that he plays on "Out of Nowhere." One can hear the subtle influence that the avant-garde was having on Hawkins's style, making one wonder what he would have

accomplished during the next few years had he stayed healthy.

2 *Supreme / Sept. 26, 1966 / Enja 9009*

1 *Sirius / Dec. 20, 1966 / Original Jazz Classics 861*

By mid-1966, Coleman Hawkins's decline was obvious. His solos on these two CDs are aimless, and he often sounds out of breath and even lost on tunes that he had mastered years earlier. *Supreme* is taken from a live outing with the Barry Harris Trio that was first released in 1995. Despite good playing from the rhythm section, it should not have come out at all. And *Sirius* is simply sad, with the ballads sounding particularly painful. But Coleman Hawkins had left behind many superb recordings during the previous four decades, and those are the ones to acquire and cherish.

LPS TO SEARCH FOR

The Hawk in Holland (GNP 9003) features Coleman Hawkins interacting with the excellent Dutch Swing group The Ramblers in 1935 and 1937 on such numbers as "Some of these Days," an eerie "I Only Have Eyes for You," and "I Wish I Were Twins." The high point of the album is a version of "Something Is Gonna Give Me Away" that costars pianist Freddy Johnson. *Dutch Treat* (Xanadu 189) has some of Hawkins's better European dates from 1936–38, including duets and trios with pianist Freddy Johnson and a set with the Berries (a Swiss group). Hawkins grew a lot during this period, and he swings hard on such numbers as "Way Down Yonder in New Orleans," "When Buddha Smiles," "Well All Right Then," and "Tiger Rag." The budget album *1940* (Alamac 2417) has a pair of radio broadcasts by the short-lived Coleman Hawkins Orchestra (an ensemble that recorded only four studio sides). *Hawk Variations* (Swingtime 1004) features some rarities dating from the 1945–57 period, including the unaccompanied two-part "Hawk Variation" (which predates "Picasso" by three years), obscure dates as a leader from 1947 and 1949–50, two versions of "Walking My Baby Back Home" with a 1957 band co-led by Rex Stewart and Cootie Williams, and a guest appearance with the Elliot Lawrence Orchestra. *The Hawk Talks* (Affinity 139) has some of Hawkins's Decca sides of 1951–53 (heard in more complete form than on the

Body and Soul Revisited CD) plus two cuts from a 1955 concert, including a heated version of "The Man I Love."

Disorder at the Border (Spotlite 121) consists of rare jam session performances from 1952 that team Hawkins with either Roy Eldridge or Howard McGhee on trumpet and pianist Horace Silver (a couple of years before Silver formed his own famous group). *Coleman Hawkins, Roy Eldridge, Pete Brown, Jo Jones All-Stars* (Verve 8829) is a rather long name for an LP that has Hawkins's performance at the 1957 Newport Jazz Festival. It is highlighted by a very exciting 14-minute version of "I Can't Believe That You're in Love with Me" that finds Eldridge and Hawk at their most explosive. *Coleman Hawkins and Roy Eldridge at the Opera House* (Verve 8266) is mostly at the same high level, particularly on "Bean Stalkin'," "The Walker," and "Tea for Two." And further strong examples of their musical partnership are heard on *At the Bayou Club* (Honeysuckle Rose 5002) and *The Bayou Club, Vol. 2* (Honeysuckle Rose 5006). *The High and Mighty Hawk* (Affinity 163), a quintet date with Buck Clayton, is most notable for the powerful "Bird of Prey Blues,"

proof that this late in his career (1958) Hawkins had really learned how to dig into the blues. *Today and Now* (Impulse 34), from 1963, was the first of Hawkins's three Impulse sets, a quartet outing made notable by the inclusion of some unusual material, including "Go Lil Liza," "Put on Your Old Grey Bonnet," "Swingin' Scotch," and "Don't Sit Under the Apple Tree." Unlike his Broadway albums for Moodsville, on this occasion Hawkins really digs into the material and comes up with some fascinating improvisations.

FILMS
Coleman Hawkins romps with Red Allen in *The Sound of Jazz* (1957), shares the stand with Roy Eldridge on *After Hours* (1961), is superb (including an unaccompanied "Blowing for Adolphe Sax" and a heated "Disorder at the Border") on a 1962 performance that shares *Tenor Legends* (Shanachie 6308) with an unrelated Dexter Gordon date, and is seen in 1965 almost past his prime on *Earl Hines & Coleman Hawkins* (Rhapsody Films).

BUDD JOHNSON
b. Dec. 14, 1910, Dallas, TX, d. Oct. 20, 1984, Kansas City, MO

Although far from a household name to Swing fans, Budd Johnson was a very valuable part of the jazz scene for over 40 years, often being closely associated with Earl Hines. The younger brother of trombonist Keg Johnson, Albert "Budd" Johnson started out on piano and also did some work on drums. After switching to tenor, he played locally in Dallas with Sammy Price. Among his other early jobs were stints with William Holloway's Blue Syncopators, Eugene Coy's Happy Black Aces, Terrence Holder, Jesse Stone, and George E. Lee in Kansas City, where he was part of the local scene and the nightly jam sessions. Johnson moved to Chicago in 1932, playing with Clarence Shaw and Eddie Mallory before joining Louis Armstrong's Big Band (with whom he recorded). After Armstrong broke up his band in 1933, Johnson was with Jesse Stone's Cyclones (1934–35), joined Earl Hines for the first time (1935–36), and spent a year as a staff arranger for Gus Arnheim. He had a second stint with Hines in 1937 as an altoist, was briefly with Fletcher Henderson and Horace Henderson, and then returned to the Hines Orchestra (1938–42), this time back on tenor. He also contributed arrangements and encouraged Hines to hire younger modern players such as Dizzy Gillespie and Charlie Parker.

In 1943 Budd Johnson worked with Don Redman and Al Sears and as an arranger for Georgie Auld. He played with Gillespie on 52nd Street in early 1944 (and with his big band in 1947), organized Coleman Hawkins's pioneering bebop dates, was the Billy Eckstine Orchestra's musical director, and sold arrangements to some of the top big bands of the mid- to late 1940s. Johnson clearly had a multifaceted career, being an important contributor both as a player and behind the scenes. In the 1950s for a time he was the musical director for Atlantic Records, ran a publishing company, and was quite active as a freelance player. Johnson's later associations included Benny Goodman (1956–57), Quincy Jones (1960), the

Count Basie Orchestra (1961–62), Earl Hines (1965–69 and off and on afterwards), and the JPJ Quartet (1969–75), which he founded and led. Budd Johnson, who by the late 1960s was doubling on soprano sax, was active up until the end, recording with Phil Woods shortly before his death.

9 *Budd Johnson and the Four Brass Giants / Sept. 6 + 22, 1960 / Original Jazz Classics 209*

9 *Let's Swing / Dec. 2, 1960 / Original Jazz Classics 1720*

8 *The JPJ Quartet / 1969–June 20, 1971 / Storyville 8235*

For *Budd Johnson and the Four Brass Giants*, the tenor saxophonist provided four of the eight songs and all the arrangements. He is matched with four very different trumpeters (Clark Terry, Harry "Sweets" Edison, Nat Adderley, and Ray Nance, who also plays violin on two songs) and a rhythm section. The inventive writing, contrasting trumpet styles, and Budd's fine solos make this CD a classic. *Let's Swing* is one of Budd Johnson's best showcases as a player. He is well featured in a quintet with his brother (trombonist Keg Johnson), pianist Tommy Flanagan, bassist George Duvivier, and drummer Charlie Persip. Johnson alternates originals and standard and sounds quite modern, and his tone is instantly recognizable. A strong effort. The Storyville CD has six previously unreleased studio selections from 1969–70, plus the JPJ Quartet's 1971 appearance at the Montreux Jazz Festival (which was out earlier on a Master Jazz LP). Although the group (which also included pianist Dill Jones, bassist Bill Pemberton, and drummer Oliver Jackson) did not really prosper, it was one of the best Mainstream Swing combos of the period, and it gave the four veteran musicians a strong outlet for their playing.

LPS TO SEARCH FOR

Blues à la Mode (Affinity 169), from 1958, features Budd Johnson playing six of his swinging originals with a septet that includes Charlie Shavers and Vic Dickenson, and a quintet with Shavers and pianist Ray Bryant. Also worth mentioning is *In Memory of a Very Dear Friend* (Dragon 94) and *The Ole Dude & the Fundance Kid* (Uptown 27.19). From 1978 and 1984, respectively, these sets (a quartet outing with Europeans and a quintet meeting with altoist Phil Woods) show how powerful and viable a soloist Budd Johnson was until the end, which came eight months after the latter date.

EDDIE MILLER

b. June 23, 1911, New Orleans, LA, d. Apr. 1, 1991, Van Nuys, CA

Renowned for his beautiful tone (which was influenced by Bud Freeman, although his style was much smoother), Eddie Miller was a star with Bob Crosby's Bobcats and spent much of his life playing Dixieland, an unusual profession for a tenor saxophonist. Born and raised in New Orleans, he was surrounded by music from an early age. After playing with the New Orleans Owls in 1928, Miller moved to New York, where he worked with several little-known bands before joining Ben Pollack in mid-1930. Miller played and recorded with Pollack until the band fell apart in 1934. He was an original member of the group that formed out of the nucleus, Bob Crosby's orchestra, and he would be a very loyal sidemen, staying with the band until it broke up in late 1942. Miller was on virtually all of the group's hits (sometimes playing some very effective clarinet, such as on "South Rampart Street Parade"), his haunting song "Slow Mood" became a minor standard, and he was a star with both the full orchestra and the Bobcats.

Eddie Miller led his own big band in Los Angeles during 1943 and, after a brief period in the Army in 1944, again after his discharge. His orchestra, which recorded a few titles for Capitol, sounded similar to Crosby's and included some of the same sidemen. The big band did not last, but Miller stayed busy, as a studio musician, with Nappy Lamare (1945–47), on many Bob Crosby reunions through the years, and on Dixieland sessions. He was a regular with clarinetist Pete Fountain's band in New Orleans on and off during the 1960s and '70s, toured with the World's Greatest Jazz Band in 1977, and was a popular attraction at traditional jazz festivals and jazz parties until ill health forced his retirement a few years before his passing.

●

[8] *Street of Dreams / Feb. 10, 1982 / Delmark 228*
Virtually the only Eddie Miller recording currently on CD under his own name is his final session, a superior quartet outing with pianist Johnny Varro, bassist Ray Leatherwood, and drummer Gene Estes. Miller at 71 in 1982 sounded just as warm (with that beautiful tone) and Swing-oriented as he had 45 years earlier, as he shows on such numbers as "I Never Knew," "Avalon," "Linger Awhile," and his "Lazy Mood."

LPS TO SEARCH FOR

Eddie Miller's 1944–45 big band recorded only four songs in the studios, but fortunately radio transcriptions and live appearances have greatly expanded their legacy, including *Soft Jive* (Golden Era 15023) and *1944–45* (Hindsight 225). Miller's only album of the 1959–70 period is unspeakably bad, the horribly commercial *With a Little Help from My Friends* (Coral 757502). But 1971's *A Portrait of Eddie* (Blue Angel 509), which features him with a Bob Crosby reunion group, and a quintet set with trombonist George Masso from 1979 (*It's Miller Time*—Famous Door 131) are as melodically swinging as one would expect from the great Eddie Miller.

VIDO MUSSO

b. Jan. 17, 1913, Carrini, Sicily, Italy, d. Jan. 9, 1982, Rancho Mirage, CA

Vido Musso had a large tone, a knack for taking colorful extroverted solos, and a crazy sense of humor, which partly compensated for his weak sight-reading abilities! He moved with his family to Detroit in 1920 and started out on clarinet later in the decade. Musso was based in Los Angeles beginning in 1930, playing locally, including with Everett Hoagland (1933). He led his own group in 1936 (which included Stan Kenton on piano), was briefly with Gil Evans, and then was part of the Benny Goodman Orchestra (1936–37). Musso was with the first Gene Krupa big band (1938), headed an orchestra of his own on an occasional basis, and had stints with Harry James (1940–41), Goodman (1941–42), and Woody Herman (1942–43). After a period in the Marines, he was with Tommy Dorsey during 1945 and had a high-profile association with Stan Kenton (1946–47). But after the Kenton period ended, Vido Musso primarily led his own obscure bands on the West Coast and in Las Vegas, fading away and becoming a somewhat forgotten Swing era legend. His few records as a leader were mostly for obscure labels, ending with a pair of albums for Crown during 1954–55.

IKE QUEBEC

b. Aug. 17, 1918, Newark, NJ, d. Jan. 16, 1963, New York, NY

A thick-toned tenor saxophonist who matured during the last part of the Swing era, Ike Quebec had the potential to become a major name, but he was his own worst enemy. As a teenager Quebec worked as a pianist and a dancer before switching to tenor. He was with the Barons of Rhythm in 1940 and during the next few years played with many top Swing musicians in combos, including Frankie Newton, Benny Carter, Coleman Hawkins, Hot Lips Page, and Roy Eldridge. Quebec started recording as a leader for Blue Note in 1944 (his versions of "Blue Harlem" and "If I Had You" were popular) and he acted as a talent scout for label head Alfred Lion, encouraging him to sign up young, modern players. The tenorman was a fixture with Cab Calloway's bands during 1944–51. Unfortunately, excessive drug use made the 1950s largely a waste and any chance that he had to work steadily during the early R&B years was squandered. Quebec began to become active again during 1958–59 and recorded a few notable Blue Note albums during his last years, playing in the same warm Swing style that he had developed in the 1940s. Having kicked drugs, Ike Quebec ironically still died at the age of 44, struck down by lung cancer.

●

7 *Heavy Soul / Nov. 26, 1961 / Blue Note 32090*

9 *Blue and Sentimental / Dec. 16 + 23, 1961 / Blue Note 84098*

8 *Easy Living / Jan. 20, 1962 /. Blue Note 46846*

7 *Soul Samba / Oct. 5, 1962 / Blue Note 52443*

Ike Quebec recorded six albums as a leader for Blue Note during a one-year period, four of which have thus far come out on CD. *Heavy Soul* finds him in a quartet with the somewhat dated-sounding organ of Freddie Roach, bassist Milt Hinton, and drummer Al Harewood. Alternating ballads with medium-tempo swingers, Quebec sounds particularly strong on "Just One More Chance," "The Man I Love," and the title cut. *Blue and Sentimental* is pretty definitive of Quebec's late-period playing. Most of the selections feature the warm tenor in a pianoless quartet with guitarist Grant Green, bassist Paul Chambers, and drummer Philly Joe Jones; pianist Sonny Clark is on "Count Every Star." The two ballads, "Blue and Sentimental" and "Don't Take Your Love from Me," are particularly memorable. *Easy Living* has five numbers from a jam session–flavored date matching Quebec with fellow tenor Stanley Turrentine and the rollicking trombone of Bennie Green, but once again it is the ballad features ("I've Got a Crush on You," "Nancy with the Laughing Face," and "Easy Living") that take honors. Quebec's final date as a leader, *Soul Samba,* is a bossa-nova outing in which he is accompanied by gentle Brazilian rhythms played by guitarist Kenny Burrell, bassist Wendell Marshall,

drummer Willie Bobo, and Garvin Masseaux on percussion. Surprisingly none of the songs were written by Antonio Carlos Jobim, but the program (which concludes with three previously unreleased alternate takes) is definitely in the melodic Jobim manner.

LPS TO SEARCH FOR

Two limited-edition box sets put out by Mosaic have the majority of the other Ike Quebec sessions. *The Complete Blue Note Forties Recordings of Ike Quebec and John Hardee* (Mosaic 4–107) is a four-LP package that reissues Quebec's five sessions of 1944–46 with plenty of unissued alternate takes. Highlights include not only the "hits" "Blue Harlem" and "If I Had You" but "Tiny's Exercise," "Sweethearts on Parade," and "I Found a New Baby." Tiny Grimes, Jonah Jones, and Buck Clayton make strong impressions, too. Also on this box are the three 1946 dates of John Hardee (one of the sessions was actually led by Grimes), which finds the hard-driving (if obscure) tenor playing in a compatible style to Quebec's, holding his own and showing that small-group Swing was far from dead at the time. *The Complete Blue Note '45' Sessions of Ike Quebec* (Mosaic 3–121), in its three LPs, has all of Quebec's dates from 1959–60 that were aimed specifically at the jukebox market plus nine selections from 1962 that later came out as the album *With a Song in My Heart.* Although the performances are a bit briefer than normal, the music (which has Skeeter Best or Willie Jones on guitar and either Edwin Swanston, Sir Charles Thompson, or Earl Vandyke on organ) is as swinging as one would expect from Ike Quebec.

BUDDY TATE

b. Feb. 22, 1915, Sherman, TX

A top Swing improviser with a soulful and tough Texas tone of his own, George "Buddy" Tate was a natural successor to Herschel Evans in the Count Basie Orchestra. He started playing alto when he was 11, soon switching to tenor. Tate began playing professionally just two years later with McCloud's Night Owls and worked in the South with the St. Louis Merrymakers, Troy Floyd, and Terrence Holder's 12 Clouds of Joy (1930–33). Tate was first with Count Basie in July 1934 but soon switched to Andy Kirk's band (1934–35). After a few years with Nat Towles, he joined Basie's band in 1939 as the replacement for the recently deceased Evans. Tate was with the Count's orchestra until the fall of 1948, holding his own opposite fellow tenors Lester Young, Don Byas, Illinois Jacquet, Lucky Thompson, and Paul Gonsalves. After leaving Basie, Tate was with Hot Lips Page in 1949, gigged with Jimmy Rushing during 1950–52, and then formed a band of his own that for 21 years (1953–74) played regularly at the Celebrity Club in New York. He also toured Europe in 1959 and 1961 with Buck Clayton, had occasional reunions with Count Basie (including at the 1967 Spirituals to Swing concert), and freelanced during the 1970s and '80s, recording fairly regularly and sometimes playing with Benny Goodman. Buddy Tate slowed down quite a bit in the 1990s (as can be heard on his recordings with Lionel Hampton), but he still played music on an occasional basis at the end of the decade.

●

7 *Swinging Like Tate / Feb. 12 + 26, 1958 / London 820 599*

7 *Groovin' with Tate / Dec. 18, 1959 + Feb. 17, 1961 / Prestige 24152*

8 *Buddy And Claude / Mar. 25, 1960 + Oct. 18, 1960 / Prestige 24231*

Buddy Tate was playing regularly with his Celebrity Club Orchestra during the period that these three CDs were recorded. Although he was somewhat out of the limelight, Tate's regular gig kept him in good form and gave him a stable lifestyle that partly accounted for his longevity and consistency. *Swingin' Like Tate* was originally put out by the Felsted label (produced by Stanley Dance). The first three songs feature Tate with the lesser-known musicians in his regular band, while the other three songs are a happy reunion with such Basie-ites as Buck Clayton, Dickie Wells, and Earle Warren; excellent Mainstream Swing. *Groovin' with Tate* has all of the music originally on two Swingville LPs (*Tate's Date* and *Groovin' with Buddy Tate*). Once again the first half of the program has the tightly arranged and bluesy Celebrity Club Orchestra. The second part is more ballad-oriented and puts the emphasis on Tate's tones on tenor and clarinet as the only horn in a quintet. *Buddy And Claude* has a date originally issued under pianist Claude Hopkins's name (seven quintet numbers with Tate, trumpeter Emmett Berry, bassist Wendell Marshall, and drummer Osie Johnson) plus the album *Tate-A-Tate,* which teams the tenor with trumpeter Clark Terry, pianist Tommy Flanagan, bassist Larry Gales, and drummer Art Taylor. Hopkins is actually minor on the first date (it is nice to hear Emmett Berry in this setting) while the Tate-Terry combination on the later set easily takes honors. Fine modern Swing from a period when Swing was considered very much out of style.

6 *Buddy Tate and His Buddies / June 1, 1973 / Chiaroscuro 123*

7 *Swinging Scorpio / July 3, 1974 / Black Lion 760165*

8 *Jive at Five / July 23, 1975 / Storyville 5010*

7 *Just Jazz / Apr. 28, 1984 / Reservoir 110*

8 *After Dark / 1985–Jan. 22, 1986 / Progressive 7028*

Buddy Tate recorded quite frequently during 1967–86. *Buddy Tate and His Buddies* is a jam session with a rather impressive lineup: Tate and Illinois Jacquet on tenors, Roy Eldridge, Mary Lou Williams, rhythm guitarist Steve Jordan, Milt Hinton, and drummer Gus Johnson. On "Sunday" and originals by Tate, Williams, and Buck Clayton, everyone plays well and there are a few torrid moments (Eldridge does his best to stir things up), but the set does not quite reach its potential. *Swinging Scorpio,* co-led with trumpeter Humphrey Lyttelton, really should have listed Buck Clayton as a co-leader too, for he contributed all eight compositions plus the arrangements for the septet. With Bruce Turner on alto and clarinet and Kathleen Stobart on tenor, baritone, and clarinet, the ensembles are colorful and, although the material is obscure, this date sticks in one's mind. Tate is teamed with fellow veterans Doc Cheatham (70 at the time and just beginning to be known as a soloist), Vic Dickenson, Johnny Guarnieri, bassist George Duvivier, and drummer Oliver Jackson on *Jive at Five.* There are individual features for each of the horns (Tate plays the ballad "There Goes My Heart" and Dickenson sings "Constantly"), but it is the septet jams on "I Never Knew," "Sweethearts on Parade," "Somebody Loves Me," and "Jive at Five" (alternate takes of the last two are also included) that are the high points. From later in Tate's career, *Just Jazz* (with trombonist Al Grey) and *After Dark* (a near-classic made in Holland with either Sweets Edison or trombonist Roy Williams) helped keep the legacy of small-group Swing alive in the mid-1980s.

LPS TO SEARCH FOR

Unbroken (Pausa 7030) features the Celebrity Club Orchestra (with Dud Bascomb and pianist Nat Pierce most notable among the sidemen) romping through Swing standards. *The Texas Twister* (New World 352), from 1975, is very much in the Count Basie tradition, with Tate and the Lester Young–influenced tenor Paul Quinichette (in one of his few recordings of the 1970s) being joined by pianist Cliff Smalls, bassist Major Holley, and drummer Jackie Williams for a particularly strong effort. The tenor saxophonist successfully meets up with pianist Tete Montoliu on *Tate a Tete at la Fontaine* (Storyville 4030), jams with Bob Wilber (heard on soprano, alto, and clarinet) during the spirited *Sherman Shuffle* (Sackville 3017), and stretches out on *Buddy Tate Quartet* (Sackville 3027), playing Swing standards in each situation. A pair of albums from the defunct Muse label, *Hard Blowin'* (Muse 5249) and *Live at Sandy's* (Muse 5198), match Tate up with pianist Ray Bryant, bassist George Duvivier, and drummer Alan Dawson in 1978, mostly on warhorses. The lengthy "She's Got It" on the last album has guest appearances by altoist Eddie "Cleanhead" Vinson and Arnett Cobb. And overdue to be reissued is *The Great Buddy Tate* (Concord Jazz 163). In addition to his work on tenor, Tate takes one song apiece on clarinet and baritone and welcomes cornetist Warren Vache, pianist Hank Jones, Milt Hinton, and drummer Mel Lewis to his all-star quintet.

FILMS

Buddy Tate is part of *The Buck Clayton All-Stars* (Shanachie 6303) in 1961 and is one of those Basie alumni profiled in *Born to Swing* (1973).

JOE THOMAS

b. June 19, 1909, Uniontown, PA, d. Aug. 3, 1986, Kansas City, MO

No relation to Swing trumpeter Joe Thomas, altoist Joe Thomas (who played with Jelly Roll Morton in the late 1920s) or any of the many other Joe Thomases, this particular musician was one of the main stars of Jimmie Lunceford's orchestra. His early gigs included Horace Henderson (1930), Stuff Smith, and, in Buffalo, with drummer Guy Jackson. Thomas joined Lunceford in 1933 and was a major part of his band until the very end, 14 years later. He took short solos on many of Lunceford's records and also proved to be an effective singer. After Lunceford's sudden death in 1947, Thomas and pianist Ed Wilcox kept the orchestra going into mid-1948. He eventually formed his own group and recorded some spirited R&B sides. Thomas stopped playing music full time in the mid-1950s, running his own undertaking business in Kansas City for years. A part-time player for decades, Joe Thomas recorded albums as late as 1979 and 1982.

LPS TO SEARCH FOR

Joe Thomas had not recorded since 1952 (other than a Jimmie Lunceford reunion date in 1962) when he made *Raw Meat* (Uptown 27.01) in 1979. He still sounds pretty strong on this relaxed Swing date, which has six familiar standards and a couple of originals; Thomas is joined by pianist Jimmy Rowles, bassist Walter Booker, and drummer Akira Tana. Three years later he made his final recording, meeting up with Jay McShann, three veterans from his 1949–51 R&B group (trombonist Dicky Harris, trumpeter Johnny Grimes, and bassist George Duvivier), baritonist Haywood Henry, and either Oliver Jackson or Jackie Williams on drums. The joyous set recaptures the feel of the late '40s band and revives several of the older tunes, including "Raw Meat," "Tearing Hair," "Star Mist," and the picturesque "Dog Food!"

BEN WEBSTER

b. Feb. 27, 1909, Kansas City, MO, d. Sept. 20, 1973, Amsterdam, Holland

Considered one of the big three of Swing tenors, Ben Webster ranks just below Coleman Hawkins and Lester Young. Webster was valued not so much for his choice of notes or musical knowledge as for his huge and distinctive sound, which split into two separate musical personalities: brutish, raspy, and forceful (with plenty of roars and growls) on uptempo material and purring like a pussy cat on romantic ballads.

After a brief period on violin, Webster played piano, and he would enjoy playing his basic brand of stride piano for the fun of it throughout his career. After a few early gigs on piano, he switched to tenor, taking lessons from Budd Johnson and touring for a few months with the Young Family Band, a group headed by Lester Young's father. He worked with Gene Coy and Jap Allen in 1930, recorded with Blanche Calloway in 1931, and spent 1931–33 with Bennie Moten's orchestra, participating (as one of the stars) on a classic 1932 recording session that also featured Hot Lips Page and Count Basie.

During the 1930s, Webster played for short periods with quite a few major orchestras, including Andy Kirk (1933), Fletcher Henderson in 1934 (where he was the replacement for Coleman Hawkins after a short stint by Lester Young), Benny Carter, Willie Bryant, and Cab Calloway (1936–37). He had a second stint with Henderson and worked with Stuff Smith, Roy Eldridge, and the Teddy Wilson Orchestra (1939–40). Webster also recorded with practically all of these bandleaders. However, all of this work was a prelude to his association with Duke Ellington (1940–43). As Duke's first major tenor soloist, Webster (who had had two brief stints with Ellington during 1935–36) was well featured, including on "Cotton Tail" (he arranged the sax section chorus that followed his classic solo) and the ballad "All Too Soon." He made such a strong mark during this period that Webster would always be associated with Ellington, even though he was actually with him for a relatively short period.

After leaving Duke, Webster worked with Raymond Scott's radio orchestra and the John Kirby Sextet but mostly led his own combos, frequently on 52nd Street. He was back with Ellington during 1948–49, performed with Jay McShann, toured with Jazz at the Philharmonic, spent time in Kansas City in the early 1950s, and then back in New York was busy during most of the 1950s, recording regularly for Norman Granz. Among his recordings were several popular ballad albums and a meeting with Art Tatum. Webster saw no need to change his Swing style, and he remained in prime form throughout most of his career. After the death of his mother, in December 1964, he moved to Europe, eventually settling in Copenhagen. Ben Webster was a major attraction in the European jazz world up until his death in 1973, even sounding good during his final concert, which happened to be recorded.

●

8 *King of the Tenors / May 21, 1953 + Dec. 8, 1953 / Verve 314 519 806*

7 *Soulville / Oct. 15, 1957 / Verve 833551*

9 *Music for Loving / May 28, 1954–Feb. 3, 1955 / Verve 314 527 774*

9 *The Soul of Ben Webster / Mar. 5, 1957–July 1958 / Verve 314 527475*

Ben Webster started recording for Norman Granz's labels (Norgran and Verve) in 1953, making some of the finest records of his career. *King of the Tenors* features him with the Oscar Peterson Quartet on five numbers and for six with a septet that also includes Harry "Sweets" Edison and Benny Carter. Two performances out of the 11 on this CD were previously unreleased, and one was originally put out as a single. The ballads ("Tenderly," "Danny Boy," and two versions of "That's All") are quite exquisite, and these versions of "Cotton Tail" and "Pennies from Heaven" are also winners. Webster might not have been the "King" tenor of 1953 but he was still one of the best. *Soulville,* from 1957, is similar, with the Oscar Peterson Quartet assisting Webster on a high-quality program of ballads and stomps, mostly vintage standards. *Music for Loving* is a double CD that completely reissues two Webster albums with strings (*Music for Loving* and *Music with Feeling*), in addition to including five alternate takes, four numbers in a quartet with Teddy Wilson, and one song from a sampler. Webster's tone is luscious throughout the ballad-oriented program, which does have some medium-tempo performances for variety. And, as if that were not enough, the eight cuts from the album *Harry Carney with Strings* (one of only two records that the baritonist ever led) conclude the twofer. Another two-CD set, *The Soul of Ben Webster,* has all of the music from that 1958 septet session (which also features trumpeter Art Farmer and Webster's fellow tenor Harold Ashby), but there are also two full albums of unrelated material with Webster as a sideman. Harry Edison's *Gee Baby Ain't I Good to You* is a sextet date with the Oscar Peterson Quartet that finds the trumpeter in top form, and Johnny Hodges's *Blues-a-Plenty* is a blues-oriented set with Roy Eldridge and Vic Dickenson that (thanks to Eldridge's outbursts) is often quite exciting. Taken as a whole, this twofer shows that many of the top Swing era soloists were playing even better in the 1950s than they had two decades earlier.

7 *The Warm Moods* / Jan. 18–19, 1960 / Reprise 2001

7 *At the Renaissance* / Oct. 14, 1960 / Original Jazz Classics 390

7 *Soulmates* / Sept. 20, 1963 + Oct. 14, 1963 / Original Jazz Classics 109

9 *See You at the Fair* / Mar. 11, 1964–Nov. 10, 1964 / GRP/Impulse 121

While the 1950s were a bit of a renaissance for Ben Webster, work was less frequent during the first half of the 1960s. By then, Webster was overshadowed by John Coltrane, Stan Getz, and Sonny Rollins and was thought of as belonging to a different era. Despite that, he continued playing quite well. *The Warm Moods* is a ballad date in which he is backed by a string quartet and a rhythm section arranged by Johnny Richards; beautiful music. *At the Renaissance* matches Webster with pianist Jimmy Rowles, guitarist Jim Hall, bassist Red Mitchell, and drummer Frank Butler and ranges from the sentimental ("Stardust") to the roaring ("Caravan"). *Soulmates* has the unlikely combination of Webster and Joe Zawinul (who would later form the pacesetting fusion band Weather Report). However, in 1963, Zawinul was a funky acoustic pianist who worked with Cannonball Adderley, and he and Webster were good friends. Their collaboration (which leaves out the alternate takes included on an earlier two-LP set) also has cornetist Thad Jones on half of the selections along with Richard Davis or Sam Jones on bass and

drummer Philly Joe Jones. *See You at the Fair,* Ben Webster's last recording before moving to Europe, was one of his best. At 55, Webster was at the peak of his powers, and he sounds absolutely beautiful on "Someone to Watch Over Me" and "Our Love Is Here to Stay," backed by a trio with either Hank Jones or Roger Kellaway on piano. One selection from the same date that was originally on a sampler and two others that featured the tenor with Oliver Nelson's orchestra wrap up this memorable set.

8 *Stormy Weather* / Jan. 30, 1965 / Black Lion 760108

8 *Gone with the Wind* / Jan. 31, 1965 / Black Lion 760125

6 *In a Mellow Tone* / May 14–15, 1965 / Jazz House 007

7 *There Is No Greater Love* / Sept. 5, 1965 / Black Lion 760151

8 *The Jeep Is Jumping* / Sept. 13–21, 1965 / Black Lion 760147

7 *Ben Webster Meets Bill Coleman* / Apr. 27, 1967 / Black Lion 760141

In Europe, Ben Webster was treated as a major star. In 1965 alone he recorded enough material for six CDs. Black Lion caught him on several occasions at the Club Montmartre in Copenhagen. *Stormy Weather* and *Gone with the Wind* are equally satisfying quartet sessions with pianist Kenny Drew, bassist Niels Pederson, and drummer Alex Riel. Swing standards dominate, with romps on numbers such as "Mack the Knife" and "Sunday" alternating with ballads. *In a Mellow Tone* captures Webster during a gig in London at Ronnie Scott's club with a local rhythm section, although there is not as much magic as at the Montmartre; this music was not released for the first time until 1995. *There Is No Greater Love* brings back the Drew-Pederson-Riel rhythm team at a slightly later Montmartre engagement. This time the emphasis is on slower tempos (among the songs are "Easy to Love," "Stardust," and "I Got It Bad"). *The Jeep Is Jumping* is a bit different, for Webster is heard with a quintet led by trumpeter Arnved Meyer on a date that has some offbeat material, plus heated romps on "Stompy Jones" and "The Jeep Is Jumping." In fact, the band itself sounds like a Duke Ellington small group from the 1930s, an ideal setting for Webster. The 1967 Black Lion release teams Webster with Bill Coleman, who was also an expatriate, having arrived in France 19 years before. With backing from a local four-piece rhythm section in London, Webster and Coleman (who has two vocals) make for a very compatible match on basic originals and standards such as "Sunday" and two versions of "But Not for Me."

7 *Ben & Buck / June 3, 1967 / Sackville 2037*

6 *Live at the Haarlemse Jazz Club / May 9, 1972 / Cat 1104*

6 *My Man / Jan. 1973–Apr. 1973 / Steeple Chase 31008*
Ben Webster met up with veteran Swing trumpeter Buck Clayton and the Henri Chaix Quartet for a Swiss concert in 1967. Webster and Clayton had rarely played together in the past and Buck would fade quickly in 1968, so it is fortunate that this excellent concert (featuring Webster's usual repertoire) was recorded. It was released for the first time in 1994 and lives up to its potential. Five years later, Webster was in the twilight of his own career. His playing was predictable, as were the songs he performed, but the Cat CD (with a trio led by the virtuosic pianist Tete Montoliu) is quite good even if one has heard Webster play "Sunday," "In a Mellotone," and "Perdido" many times before. *My Man* (a quartet date with pianist Ole Kock Hansen) was recorded just a few months before the tenor's death. But other than being a little short of breath in spots, Ben Webster still sounds in top form and his tone is as warm and rugged as ever.

LPS TO SEARCH FOR

Ben Webster recorded quite often from the 1940s on and very few of his records are not well worth owning. *Ben* (Jazz Archives 15) is a collector's LP that mostly features Webster live in concerts with Duke Ellington during 1941–43, plus performances with Teddy Wilson in 1936, Mezz Mezzrow, a V-Disc with Woody Herman, and three numbers in which he is a member of the John Kirby Sextet in 1944. *Ben and the Boys* (Jazz Archives 35) has eight songs with a 1944 quintet that includes Hot Lips Page; this radio transcription has also been released by the Circle label. In addition, there are two ragged jam session numbers from 1945, another Woody Herman V-Disc tune, and a 1958 TV performance of "Flying Home" with Buck Clayton. *He Played It That Way* (IAJRC 30) is a grab-bag of sideman appearances, featuring Webster with Al Hibbler and an Ellington combo from 1948, backing singer Walter Brown with Jay McShann, on one number apiece with Duke Ellington and the Raymond Scott radio orchestra, and on jam session numbers with Roy Eldridge (1954) and Eddie "Cleanhead" Vinson (1969). Particularly worthy of being reissued is the two-LP set *The Big Tenor* (Emarcy 824 836), which has all of Webster's output for the Emarcy label during 1951–53 (with many alternate takes). The twofer includes Webster's dates with Jay McShann, Johnny Otis, Dinah Washington, Marshall Royal, and the Ravens (!) and two sessions of his own: a sextet with Benny Carter and trumpeter Maynard Ferguson plus a date with strings. *Ben & Sweets* (Columbia 40853) is a happy quintet album from 1962 co-led by Harry "Sweets" Edison. And from the later years are the two-LP set *At Work in Europe* (Prestige 24031), which was recorded in 1969, and 1972's *Did You Call?* (Nessa 8), both of which find Ben Webster in typically inspired form.

FILMS

Ben Webster is in *The Sound of Jazz* (1957) and is profiled in *The Brute and the Beautiful* (Shanachie 6302), a 1992 hour-long documentary.

DICK WILSON

b. Nov. 11, 1911, Mount Vernon, IL, d. Nov. 24, 1941, New York, NY

Dick Wilson was a promising young tenor saxophonist who was one of the stars of the Andy Kirk Orchestra. He grew up in Seattle, started out playing piano, and then, after high school, learned alto sax before switching to tenor. Wilson worked with Don Anderson (1929), Joe Darensbourg, Gene Coy, and Zack Whyte. He joined Andy Kirk in 1936 and, along with pianist Mary Lou Williams, was the top soloist in the band. His style mixed Coleman Hawkins and Lester Young, and he was well featured with Kirk and on a date led by Williams. Dick Wilson (who never led his own record date) died of tuberculosis when he was just 30.

LESTER YOUNG

b. Aug. 27, 1909, Woodville, MS, d. Mar. 15, 1959, New York, NY

A brilliant tenor saxophonist with a soft, original tone and a quick mind, Lester Young ranks with the major giants of jazz history. An introvert in a field populated by extroverts, Young always stood out from the crowd. Young's father was a musician who dreamt of having a family band. Lester was taught trumpet, alto, and violin and, by 1920 (when they were living in Minneapolis), he was playing drums with the Young Family Band. He settled on alto for a time but left the band as a teenager in 1927 because he refused to travel in the South. Young gigged with Art Bronson's Bostonians (1928–29), switching permanently to tenor. He spent a few years freelancing, including returning to both his father's band and Bronson, working in Minneapolis, and joining the Original Blue Devils (1932–33). Other short-term associations included Bennie Moten, Clarence Love, King Oliver, and Count Basie (1934). Young had the opportunity to be Coleman Hawkins's first replacement with Fletcher Henderson's orchestra, but his light tone and very different style (influenced much more by Frankie Trumbauer than by Hawkins), although pleasing to Henderson, was met with opposition by the other sidemen and Fletcher's wife. Lester stayed less than three months. A couple more years of freelancing (including gigs with Andy Kirk and an unsuccessful audition with Earl Hines) followed.

In 1936 Lester Young rejoined Count Basie's orchestra in Kansas City, and he was soon the band's top sideman. His mellow sound and relaxed (yet often hard-swinging) solos fit in perfectly with the subtle rhythm section. Young was a major part of Basie's success, accompanying the orchestra on its trip East and taking part in all of its recordings for four years. Nicknamed "Pres" (short for president) by his close friend Billie Holiday (whom he named "Lady Day"), Young took one of his greatest solos on his very first recording date ("Lady Be Good") with a quintet out of the Basie band. He not only was well featured with the Count but was on many of Holiday's finest recordings; Pres's tenor blended perfectly with her voice. In addition, Young recorded with the Kansas City Six, and his rare spots on clarinet were haunting and brilliant. A moved Benny Goodman once gave Young one of his new clarinets after hearing him.

In December 1940 for unknown reasons (possibly not wanting to record on Friday the 13th), Young left the Basie orchestra. During the next couple of years he led his own combo, co-led a group with his younger brother, Lee Young, and worked with Al Sears's Big Band but made few recordings. In October 1943 Young spontaneously came back home to Count Basie's orchestra and, although the recording strike kept the full big band from recording, he can be heard on air checks from the period and on some classic small-group titles. Pres sounded at his best in a quartet with Johnny Guarnieri and Slam Stewart on "Sometimes I'm Happy" and "Afternoon of a Basie-ite." He also was the star of the Academy Award-winning film short *Jammin' the Blues*.

Unfortunately Young was drafted, and he had a horrific time in the Army from October 1944 through the summer of 1945. Being subject to racism, framed on a drug charge, and spending time in a military prison left deep scars on his sensitive soul. When Young was finally discharged, his inner psyche had been affected but his playing was still in peak form. In fact, Lester Young did some of his finest work during the second half of the 1940s, recording for Aladdin, touring with Norman Granz's Jazz at the Philharmonic, and displaying a wider range of emotions in his playing than previously, including a tinge of sadness. He led his own small bands throughout the 1950s, had a few reunions with Count Basie (including at the 1957 Newport Jazz Festival), and recorded regularly for Verve.

Pres's influence on younger tenors far surpassed Coleman Hawkins's by the mid-1950s, and ironically many of his followers were making much more money than he was, although Young was doing fine financially. Unfortunately though, Lester Young's state of mind was not at its best. He drank constantly, invented a new language of his own to discourage outsiders, practically stopped eating, and wasted away. When he was healthy, he could play magnificently (although many critics write off his postwar recordings, I actually prefer his later work due to the greater emotional intensity), but there were times when he could barely stand up. The most touching moment of the 1957 television special *The Sound of Jazz* occurs during Billie Holiday's feature, "Fine and Mellow." Pres barely got to his feet in time to play a single chorus, and his soulful tone, along

Lester Young's floating tone was perfectly at home with the Count Basie Orchestra.

with the way that Lady Day looked at him, was the emotional high point of the classic show. It would nearly be Lester Young's final hurrah, for in 15 months, after an early-1959 visit to France, he returned home and drank himself to death, not having reached his 50th birthday.

10 *The "Kansas City" Sessions / Mar. 16, 1938–Mar. 27, 1944 / Commodore 402*
The "Kansas City" Sessions consists of the complete reissue of three sessions, 13 selections plus nine alternate takes. Four numbers feature the Kansas City Five on March 16, 1938, and this is the session in which Eddie Durham took his first historic electric guitar solos, a year before Charlie Christian. That particular group consists of Buck Clayton, Durham, Freddie Green, Walter Page, and Jo Jones. Add Lester Young to the band on September 28, 1938, and one has the Kansas City Six. Of particular interest are Young's occasional clarinet solos, including a spot on "I Want a Little Girl" in which he sounds eerily like altoist Paul Desmond from 20 years later! The other Kansas City Six date is from March 27, 1944, and it is quite a bit different, with Young, Bill Coleman and Dicky Wells (in top form) joined by Joe Bushkin, bassist John Simmons, and Jo Jones for some hard-driving numbers, including "Three Little Words" and three versions of "I Got Rhythm." Each of the sessions is classic in its own way.

[9] *1943–1946 / Dec. 28, 1943–Apr. 1946 / Classics 932*

[10] *The Complete Aladdin Sessions / July 15, 1942–Dec. 29, 1947 / Blue Note 32787*

[8] *Pres Conferences / Mar. 20, 1946–1958 / Jass 18*

The Classics release features Lester Young's famous "Afternoon of a Basie-ite/Sometimes I'm Happy" set of 1943 (originally made for Keynote), his 1944 Savoy session (in a quintet with Count Basie), and Young's first two Aladdin dates, plus a very successful meeting in a trio with Nat King Cole and Buddy Rich. The two-CD *The Complete Aladdin Sessions* is even better and serves as proof that Young was still in very good musical form even after his horrible experiences in the military. An earlier encounter (from 1942) with Nat Cole in a trio (with bassist Red Callender) precedes Young's important 1945–46 recordings, which include such numbers as "D. B. Blues," "New Lester Leaps In," "Sunday," "Jumpin' with Symphony Sid" (which was a hit), "One O'Clock Jump," and "Tea for Two." Among Pres's sidemen are Vic Dickenson, Willie Smith, trumpeter Shorty McConnell, and pianists Dodo Marmarosa and Argonne Thornton. In addition, a set led by singer Helen Humes with Pres as a sideman is on this essential twofer. The Jass CD is taken from live performances (mostly on radio or television) and has Young sitting in with the King Cole Trio for two numbers, jamming with Buck Clayton and Coleman Hawkins, and featured on a variety of odds and ends that should greatly interest Lester Young collectors.

[*] *The Complete Lester Young Studio Sessions on Verve / Mar. 1946–Mar. 4, 1959 / Verve 314 547 0879*

[8] *With the Oscar Peterson Trio / Nov. 28, 1952 / Verve 314 521 4517*

[7] *Pres and Sweets / Dec. 1, 1955 / Verve 849 3919*

[9] *Jazz Giants '56 / Jan. 12, 1956 / Verve 825 6729*

[8] *Pres and Teddy / Jan. 13, 1956 / Verve 831 270*

Critics and detractors who write off Lester Young's postwar output have tended to concentrate on his many poorly recorded live sets rather than listening closely to his mostly high-quality dates for Verve. The eight-CD "Complete on Verve" box includes Young's trio project with Nat King Cole and Buddy Rich, his classic encounters with the Oscar Peterson Trio and Teddy Wilson, the famous Jazz Giants '56 date, collaborations with Harry Edison, and sessions with

his regular group of the era, plus the final date in Paris and two radio interviews. Although the Paris session and one of the Edison albums find Young sounding quite weak, otherwise he is mostly in superior form, putting a great deal of feeling (along with subtle Swing) into the music. For those fans unable to afford such a purchase, many of the better sessions are available individually. *With the Oscar Peterson Trio* finds Young in a happy mood, whether jamming on "Just You, Just Me" and "Indiana" or playing one melodic ballad after another. Peterson and his sidemen are quite supportive of the veteran tenor, who takes a very rare vocal on the light-hearted "Two to Tango." *Pres and Sweets* matches Young with his old friend Harry Edison and Oscar Peterson for such numbers as "Mean to Me," "Pennies from Heaven," and "One O' Clock Jump." *Jazz Giants '56* has Young sharing the frontline with the explosive Roy Eldridge and Vic Dickenson. He sounds lyrical on "I Didn't Know What Time It Was" and fiery on "Gigantic Blues"; everyone was particularly inspired for this project. The following day the great tenor continued the joyous mood on *Pres and Teddy* with the Teddy Wilson Quartet. His rendition of "Prisoner of Love" is quite haunting.

[7] *In Washington, D.C., 1956, Vol. 1 / Dec. 3–9, 1956 / Original Jazz Classics 782*

[7] *In Washington, D.C., 1956, Vol. 2 / Dec. 3–9, 1956 / Original Jazz Classics 881*

[7] *In Washington, D.C., 1956, Vol. 3 / Dec. 3–9, 1956 / Original Jazz Classics 901*

[7] *In Washington, D.C., 1956, Vol. 4 / Dec. 3–9, 1956 / Original Jazz Classics 963*

[7] *In Washington, D.C., 1956, Vol. 5 / Dec. 3–9, 1956 / Original Jazz Classics 993*

Conventional wisdom says that Lester Young by the mid-1950s was just a shell of his former self, barely able to play. These five CDs, all taken from a week's engagement in Washington, D.C., serve as proof that when he was on, Pres was still among the very best. Joined by a local rhythm section (pianist Bill Potts, bassist Willie Williams, and drummer Jim Lucht), Young is heard throughout in surprisingly strong form. The recording quality is excellent, and, sticking to standards, Lester Young shows that he was still a major force in 1956.

Lester Young and Charlie Christian (Jazz Archives 42) has seven selections from radio appearances by the 1939–40 Count Basie big band (with plenty of solo space for Young, Buck Clayton, and Harry Edison). In addition, there are three selections by the 1939 Benny Goodman Sextet and then the pièce de résistance: five numbers from a rehearsal by a group consisting of Goodman, Young, Clayton, Count Basie, Charlie Christian, Freddie Green, Walter Page, and Jo Jones! *Historical Pres* (Everybody's 3002) is also full of rarities that fill in some historical gaps. There are a dozen live numbers by the 1944 Count Basie Orchestra with Young, plus versions of "Tickle Toe" and "Taxi War Dance" by the mostly unrecorded Lester Young Sextet of 1940–41 and "Benny's Bugle" from the 1941 Lester & Lee

Young band. All of Young's 1944 and 1949 Savoy recordings (with many alternate takes) are on the twofer *Pres* (Savoy 2202), including four titles with the Count Basie rhythm section. *Jammin' with Lester* (Jazz Archives 18) has the complete soundtrack from the 1944 *Jammin' the Blues* film, including several numbers that did not make the cut; in addition, there are three extended jams from 1946.

FILMS

Lester Young is the star of *Jammin' the Blues* (1944) and takes the most memorable chorus of *The Sound of Jazz* (1957). *Song of the Spirit* is a definitive 110-minute documentary on the great tenor put together by Bruce Fredericksen that uses all of the exciting footage, plus still photos and a lot of interviews to tell the Lester Young story.

Pianists

Jazz piano styles of the pre-1945 era generally featured keyboardists playing "stride," with their left hand striding back and forth between bass notes and chords while the right created melodic variations. In the 1920s, the pianist's left hand was usually forceful enough for the piano to both keep time and function as an orchestra by itself, making the string bass more of a luxury than a necessity. James P. Johnson was the finest stride pianist of the decade, and other giants of the period included his protégé Fats Waller and Willie "The Lion" Smith. Earl Hines by 1928 was among the first to break up the rhythmic pattern by seeming to suspend time without ever losing the beat. Art Tatum's rise in the early 1930s was almost a completely independent movement for, although he considered Fats Waller to be his main influence, the remarkable Tatum (who could play faster and more advanced than anyone) was in his own musical world, decades ahead of his time.

Most jazz pianists of the 1930s had a lighter left hand than their counterparts of the 1920s. Teddy Wilson was the definitive Swing pianist, a flawless and tasteful player who strided but played light enough so as not to emphasize the potential "oom-pah" nature of the style. Joe Sullivan and Jess Stacy used Earl Hines as their model but had a more regular left hand while adopting the ringing quality of Hines's right (particularly his octaves). Count Basie's approach started with Fats Waller, but he cut his style down to the absolute basics, leaving a great deal of space for the string bass and rhythm guitar. Among the finest Swing pianists to emerge in the early 1940s were Nat King Cole, Johnny Guarnieri, Eddie Heywood, Billy Kyle, and Mel Powell, all of whom had lighter touches than their predecessors.

A major trend of the late 1930s was the rise of boogie-woogie. The idiom had existed in the late 1920s (particularly in the blues world) but had become largely a lost art form with the onset of the Depression. However, at John Hammond's Spirituals to Swing Concert in December 1938, the boogie-woogie pianists Albert Ammons, Pete Johnson, and Meade Lux Lewis (along with singer Big Joe Turner) were such a big hit that their success revitalized each of their careers, that of their predecessor, Jimmy Yancey, and the idiom itself. Around that time Tommy Dorsey had a best-seller with "Boogie Woogie" (based on a Pinetop Smith piano solo in the '20s), and soon Will Bradley's "Beat Me Daddy, Eight to a Bar" caused boogie-woogie to become a bit of a fad, with the Andrews Sisters' "Boogie Woogie Bugle Boy" (which did not include any boogie-woogie piano) becoming a major pop hit.

Every big band had a piano player, as did nearly every combo. Count Basie, Duke Ellington, Earl Hines, and Claude Hopkins were among the top big bandleaders who were also major pianists. Nineteen of the other most significant pianists of the era are in this section.

ALBERT AMMONS

b. Sept. 23, 1907, Chicago, IL, d. Dec. 2, 1949, Chicago, IL

One of the most powerful of the boogie-woogie pianists (hearing Ammons stomping into a final chorus is one of the joys of listening to jazz), Albert Ammons could also play effective Swing. He started playing piano when he was ten and appeared in Chicago-area clubs by the late 1920s. Ammons's early years were quite obscure. He played with Francois Moseley's Louisiana Stompers in 1929, William Barbees' Headquarters, and Louis Banks's Chesterfield Orchestra (1930–34) before forming his own combo (the Rhythm Kings), with whom he made his recording debut on four titles in 1936. After appearing at John Hammond's Spirituals to Swing concert in December 1938, Ammons often teamed up with Pete Johnson and occasionally Meade Lux Lewis in piano duets/trios, performing at Café Society and recording on a regular basis. In later years Ammons recorded for Mercury and generally led a four-piece rhythm section in Chicago. Albert Ammons was quite happy in 1947 when he had the opportunity to record with his son, tenor saxophonist Gene Ammons, just two years before his own death.

●

9 *1936–1939 / Feb. 13, 1936–Oct. 9, 1939 / Classics 715*

7 *Boogie Woogie Stomp / 1938–Oct. 21, 1939 / Delmark 705*

10 *The First Day / Jan. 6, 1939 / Blue Note 98450*

5 *Master of Boogie / Feb. 13, 1936–Apr. 8, 1939 / Milan 35628*

Albert Ammons's first recordings are on *1936–1939,* including four combo sides from 1936 and piano solos cut for the Jazz Piano, Vocalion ("Shout for Joy"), Blue Note, and Solo Art labels. Most of the material is available elsewhere, but it is quite nice to have it all in one spot; Ammons was a powerful player from his very first recording. *Boogie Woogie Stomp* actually features Ammons on just ten of the 18 selections (one of those is a duet with Meade Lux Lewis), while Lewis has six features and Pete Johnson two. Fourteen are taken from performances at the Hotel Sherman, while four real obscurities (two apiece by Ammons and Lewis) predate the boogie-woogie pianists' discovery, being from 1938. The title of *The First Day* refers to this CD's having the very first recordings made by the Blue Note label, with nine piano solos by Ammons, seven by Lewis, and two exciting piano duets ("Twos and Fews" and "Nagasaki"). Although *Master of Boogie* claims that its Ammons selections were previously unissued, all of the music on this hodge-podge sampler has been out before, drawing its 13 cuts from the same dates that are on *1936–1939.* Albert Ammons's valuable 1946–48 Mercury recordings have been put out as part of a limited-edition Mercury set called *The 1940s Jazz Sessions.*

LPS TO SEARCH FOR

The Complete Blue Note Recordings of Albert Ammons and Meade Lux Lewis (Mosaic 3-103) is a three-LP set that contains not only the music available on the CD *The First Day* but Lewis's other Blue Note dates (1935's "Honky Tonk Train Blues" and three sessions from 1940–44).

FILMS

Albert Ammons is well featured, along with Pete Johnson, Lena Horne, and Teddy Wilson, in the enjoyable short *Boogie Woogie Dream* (1941).

LIL HARDIN ARMSTRONG

b. Feb. 3, 1898, Memphis, TN, d. Aug. 27, 1971, Chicago, IL

Although Lil Armstrong really fits best in the Classic Jazz idiom of the 1920s, she was also quite active in the 1930s. Best known for being the second of Louis Armstrong's four wives, Lil was an underrated pianist and a talented composer. She studied music at Fisk University and moved to Chicago in 1917. After working as a song demonstrator, Lil began to play locally, including with cornetist Freddie Keppard. She had her own group as early as 1920 and was with King Oliver's Creole Jazz Band during 1921–24, meeting and marrying Louis Armstrong. Her career for the next five years would overlap with Satch's. Lil recorded with King Oliver in 1923, encouraged Armstrong to leave Oliver and join Fletcher Henderson's orchestra in New York, and led her own Chicago band while he was gone. After he returned in late 1925, Lil recorded with her husband as part of his Hot Five and Hot Sevens (1925–27), contributing "Struttin' with Some Barbecue" and a vocal on "That's When I'll Come Back to You." Lil worked with Freddie Keppard again in 1928 (the same year that she earned a degree from the Chicago College of Music) and recorded with Johnny Dodds during 1928–29. She broke up with Louis Armstrong in 1931 and they were divorced in 1938, but she never stopped loving him and did not remarry.

Lil Hardin Armstrong led several different bands in the 1930s (including a couple of all-female groups). She appeared as a soloist in a few revues and, after moving to New York, became a house pianist at Decca in the late 1930s, recording with some of their top blues artists. She also recorded 26 titles of her own as a leader, often singing while having someone else play piano. Among her originals of the time were "Brown Gal" and "Just for the Thrill." Late in 1940, she moved back to Chicago, where she performed regularly for the next few decades, occasionally visiting Europe. Lil Armstrong appeared in the 1961 television special "Chicago and All That Jazz" but otherwise was obscure during her later years. She died of a heart attack while playing "St. Louis Blues" at a Louis Armstrong memorial concert less than two months after Satch's death.

●

10 *1936–1940 / Oct. 27, 1936–Mar. 18, 1940 / Classics 564*

6 *Chicago: The Living Legends / Sept. 7, 1961 / Original Jazz Classics 1823*

1936–1940 really cannot be improved upon because this single CD has all 26 of Lil Hardin Armstrong's recordings as a leader for Decca. She takes vocals on the first 22 numbers (from 1936–38), playing piano on only four of those cuts. Her Swing orchestra includes such notable players (on some selections) as trumpeter Joe Thomas, Buster Bailey, Chu Berry, and J. C. Higginbotham. Among the better cuts are "Brown Gal," "Doin' the Suzie-Q," "Just for the Thrill," "It's Murder," "Born to Swing," and "Harlem on Saturday Night." The final four selections are more of a jam session,

with Lil on piano with Jonah Jones and Don Stovall; one vocal apiece is taken by Midge Williams and Hilda Rogers. Speaking of jam sessions, *Chicago: The Living Legends* often borders on being a bit out of control. With three trumpets, two trombones, and two clarinets, the music on the Dixieland-oriented date (Lil Armstrong's last recording as a leader other than two songs from eight weeks later) is often riotous and fun, if undisciplined.

FILMS

Lil Armstrong has a few featured spots in the 1961 television special *Chicago and All That Jazz* (Vintage Jazz Classics 2002).

JOE BUSHKIN

b. Nov. 7, 1916, New York, NY

Joe Bushkin has had a long and multifaceted career, working in Swing, Dixieland, cabaret, and middle-of-the-road pop music. A fine Swing pianist and a personable vocalist, Bushkin has also composed quite a few songs; best known is "Oh, Look at Me Now!," which was recorded by Tommy Dorsey (with Frank Sinatra, Connie Haines, and the Pied Pipers) in the early 1940s. He played piano early on with a group headed by Irving Goodman, first started working professionally in 1932, was a regular at the Famous Door in 1935, and recorded with Billie Holiday in 1936. Bushkin's associations during the second half of the 1930s included Eddie Condon (with whom he recorded a few classic numbers in 1938), Joe Marsala (doubling occasionally on trumpet), the Bunny Berigan Orchestra (1938–39), and Muggsy Spanier. Bushkin was with Tommy Dorsey's Big Band during 1940–41 before joining the Army Air Force (1942–46), where he was able to stay musically active by being the musical director of various shows. After his discharge, he was with Benny Goodman (1946) and Bud Freeman in addition to becoming quite active as a studio musician. Bushkin acted in the Broadway play *The Rat Race* (1949–50), led groups in New York, and toured with the Louis Armstrong All-Stars for three months in 1953. Through the decades, Joe Bushkin primarily worked in the studios, accompanied singers (including Bing Crosby in the 1970s), and led small combos. Although he never recorded jazz often enough (and many of his later dates were closer to cabaret then to Swing), he was still quite active and playing well in 1999.

4 *The Road to Oslo & Play It Again, Joe / Oct. 4, 1977–1985 / DRG 8490*
This CD, which reissues two complete albums, is a disappointment from the jazz standpoint. Joe Bushkin's personable vocalizing dominates the sets (despite the presence of trumpeter Warren Vache, guitarist Howard Alden, and clarinetist Phil Bodner on the 1985 half), and his piano playing is closer to easy-listening than to Swing. Bing Crosby takes brief vocals on "Now You Has Jazz" and "Sail Away from Norway," which must be among his final recordings. But overall nothing exciting happens, which is unfortunate, since this is the only Joe Buskin CD currently available.

FILMS
Bushkin, who appeared in the play, can be seen in the movie version of *The Rat Race* (1960).

HERMAN CHITTISON
b. Oct. 15, 1908, Flemingsburg, KY, d. Mar. 8, 1967, Cleveland, OH

A stride pianist whose style in the 1930s was influenced by James P. Johnson and Fats Waller, Herman Chittison was a very powerful player. He started on piano when he was eight and worked professionally as early as 1927 with the Kentucky Derbies. He was with Zack Whyte's legendary territory band during 1928–31, recorded with Clarence Williams, and accompanied Stepin Fetchit, Adelaide Hall, and Ethel Waters. Chittison, who recorded hyper and virtuosic piano solos in Paris during 1934 and 1938 and two cuts in New York during 1941, worked in Europe with Willie Lewis during 1934-38 and was part of Louis Armstrong's band during his European tour of 1934. Chittison played in Egypt with the Harlem Rhythmakers during 1939 and then came back home the following year. He worked with Mildred Bailey, acted on the radio in the series *Casey—Crime Photographer* during 1942–51, and led his own trio throughout the 1940s, '50s, and early '60s, spending many of his later years in Ohio. Herman Chittison was active until the end, playing in his personal stride style before passing away from lung cancer.

9 *1933–1941 / July 17, 1933–Sept. 17, 1941 / Classics 690*

8 *1944–1945 / Jan. 3, 1944–May 1, 1945 / Classics 1024*

7 *P. S. with Love / June 5, 1964–1967 / IAJRC 1006*
Herman Chittison is heard primarily taking hot piano solos on *1933–1941*, generally in Paris. Some of his solos (particularly the ones from 1934) display more technique than feeling, but one cannot help but be impressed with his brilliant playing; Art Tatum was one of the few who had more technique at the time than Chittison. In addition to the solos, there are two numbers in which the pianist backs banjoist Ikey Robinson, whose vocals on that date are very influenced by Cab Calloway. *1944–1945* draws its material partly from Chittison's Musicraft recordings, which feature him solo and with a drumless rhythm trio; Thelma Carpenter has four vocals, and Chittison plays throughout in prime form on such numbers as "The Song Is Ended," "How High the Moon," and "Triste." The IAJRC CD has two solo sets that had not been released before this 1993 CD. Although a few of the tunes interpreted by Chittison are weak (such as "Getting to Know You," "People," and "The Sound of Music"), there are also many Swing standards, and the pianist, despite being only a couple months before his death during the last session, still played quite well at this late date. *Herman Chittison: A Bio Discography,* put out by IAJRC in 1993, is a definitive and well-researched biography that includes interviews, a complete discography and lots of pictures.

NAT KING COLE

b. Mar. 17, 1917, Montgomery, AL, d. Feb. 15, 1965, Santa Monica, CA

Nat King Cole had two major careers: as a Swing pianist and as a middle-of-the-road pop vocalist. While the latter would eventually overshadow the former, Cole (who was born Nathaniel Coles) was one of the finest Swing pianists of the 1940s, influenced by Earl Hines and an influence himself on Oscar Peterson.

Raised in Chicago, Nat Cole led the Royal Dukes as early as 1934. Two years later he made his recording debut with his brother Eddie Coles's band. Bassist Eddie was one of Nat's three brothers (the others were Isaac and Freddie) who would become jazz musicians. Nat soon left Chicago to tour with a revival of *Shuffle Along*. The show broke up in Los Angeles, where he would remain for an extended period, using that city as his home base. Cole put together a trio with guitarist Oscar Moore and bassist Wesley Prince, played in obscurity for a couple years (picking up the nickname of "King" Cole), and began to sing on an occasional basis at the urging of a club owner. In December 1940, the King Cole Trio recorded their first significant studio sides (radio transcriptions predate that session), and Cole had a minor hit in "Sweet Lorraine." The Nat King Cole Trio soon caught on and they recorded quite prolifically throughout the 1940s, particularly after signing with Capitol in 1943. Cole was part of the first Jazz at the Philharmonic concert in 1944 (trading off in humorous fashion with guitarist Les Paul), recorded with Lester Young and Illinois Jacquet, and was a guest artist on several dates. The trio (which eventually had Johnny Miller on bass and, starting in 1947, guitarist Irving Ashby), grew steadily in popularity during the era, playing lots of instrumentals and featuring some group vocals. However, Nat's vocalizing (on such numbers as "Straighten Up and Fly Right," "Nature Boy," "The Christmas Song," and "Lush Life," all of which he made famous) eventually became its main attraction. The trio became a quartet in 1949 with the addition of Jack Costanzo on bongos and was open to the influence of bebop by then, although it always remained essentially a Swing group.

The turning point was in 1950 with the recording of "Mona Lisa," which became a #1 hit. From that point on, Cole's small group was pushed into the background and the emphasis was on Nat King Cole as a ballad vocalist, with occasional swinging numbers used as variety. Within a short time, he had millions of new fans who did not even know that Cole played piano! There would be a few jazz projects in the 1950s (most notably the *After Midnight sessions* of 1956) and Cole played a little bit of piano now and then in live concerts (plus on his historic television series of 1956–57), showing that he never lost his jazz abilities. But his many hits were all vocal features, usually with orchestral backing. Nat King Cole was a household name by 1951; he acted in a few movies (including the fictional W. C. Handy biography *St. Louis Blues*) and kept up a busy performing and recording schedule until he was struck down by lung cancer.

●

9 | *The Complete Early Transcriptions / Oct. 1938–Feb. 1941 / Vintage Jazz Classics 1026/27/28*

8 | *Birth of the Cole: 1938–1939 / Jan. 14, 1939–July 22, 1940 / Savoy ZDS 1205*

8 | *Hit That Jive Jack: The Earliest Recordings / Dec. 6, 1940–Oct. 22, 1941 / MCA/Decca 42350*

8 | *The Trio Recordings / 1940–1956 / Laserlight 15 915*

9 | *The MacGregor Years 1941/45 / Feb. 25, 1941–Jan. 1945 / Music & Arts 911*

8 | *WWII Transcriptions / 1941–1944 / Music & Arts 808*

Although the first well-known commercial recordings of the Nat King Cole Trio took place in November 1940, the group had previously recorded quite a few radio transcriptions. Listeners familiar with the trio's more famous later recordings will note that on these earlier sides, Cole's solo vocals are rare, with most of the selections being either instrumentals, group vocals, or situations where the trio backs up a guest singer. The four-CD *The Complete Early Transcriptions* (which covers the group's work for Standard Transcriptions) has 102 selections by the Cole Trio, with occasional vocals by Bonnie Lake, Juanelda Carter, Pauline Byrns, and a unit from Six Hits and a Miss. From the start, the King Cole Trio is quite recognizable, accessible, and swinging. *Birth of the Cole,* a single-CD, has Cole's other early transcription work (a dozen selections that do not duplicate the Vintage Jazz Classics set), plus eight very obscure studio recordings for the Davis & Schwegler and Ammor labels, including "I Like to Riff," "On the Sunny Side of the Street," and "There's No Anesthetic for Love." *Hit That Jive Jack* consists of the King Cole Trio's 16 recordings for the Decca label, including "Sweet Lorraine," "Honeysuckle Rose," and "Hit That Jive Jack." No matter how familiar those performances are, they still do not lose their joy or appeal.

During 1941–45, the King Cole Trio made an extensive series of radio transcriptions for the MacGregor company. The five-CD set *The Trio Recordings* (all of its music could really have fit on three CDs) and the four-CD *The MacGregor Years* partly overlap; the latter is a bit more complete and the preferred purchase, although the Laserlight release will be less expensive. The Laserlight box has four discs that are mostly from 1944–45 and then a fifth CD that jumps around from six numbers in 1940 to a few songs performed on the Dorsey Brothers TV show in 1956. On the Music & Arts set, the King Cole Trio (with Oscar Moore and either Johnny Miller or Wesley Prince on bass) is heard in 1941 and 1944–45, as a separate unit and (on 58 of the 120 numbers) backing singers Anita Boyer, Ida James, Anita O'Day, and the Barrie Sisters. *WWII Transcriptions,* which does not duplicate the larger Music & Arts set but partly overlaps with some of the Laserlight music, is mostly from 1944 except for a few Anita Boyer vocals from 1941. There are also vocals from Anita O'Day and Ida James, but the emphasis is on the trio during the 30 swinging selections.

*   *The Complete Capitol Recordings of the Nat King Cole Trio* / Oct. 11, 1942–Mar. 2, 1961 / Mosaic 138

9   *Jumpin' at Capitol* / Nov. 30, 1943–Jan. 5, 1950 / Rhino 71009

10   *Jazz Encounters* / Mar. 30, 1945–Jan. 5, 1950 / Capitol 96693

7   *Straighten Up and Fly Right* / Dec. 1942–Jan. 28, 1948 / Vintage Jazz Classics 1044

7   *The King Cole Trios: Live 1947–48* / Mar. 1, 1947–Mar. 13, 1948 / Vintage Jazz Classics 1011

The Mosaic box set, which is 18 CDs, is quite incredible. It has every single recording made by the Nat King Cole Trio for Capitol during the 1943–49 period, plus all of the radio transcriptions that are owned by Capitol. In addition to that huge amount of music, all of Cole's later recordings that feature his piano and at least the feel of the trio (including the

complete *After Midnight Sessions*) are here plus many formerly unissued tracks—349 selections in all! It is a shame, though, that this is a limited-edition box set that has gone out of print. *Jumpin' at Capitol* is a fine single-disc sampler that has many of the King Cole Trio's better and more famous selections, including "Straighten Up and Fly Right," a remake of "Sweet Lorraine," "The Frim Fram Sauce," "For Sentimental Reasons," "Come to Baby, Do," and "Route 66." *Jazz Encounters* features Nat King Cole as a guest in a variety of important jazz settings, including collaborations with the Metronome All-Stars, Stan Kenton's orchestra, the Capitol International Jazzmen, Jo Stafford, Nellie Lutcher, Woody Herman (a remarkable version of "Mule Train"), and Johnny Mercer (four songs, including "Save the Bones for Henry Jones"). The two Vintage Jazz Classic CDs are taken from the King Cole Trio's radio appearances. *Straighten Up and Fly Right,* in addition to the trio features, also has the group backing Frank Sinatra on two numbers. While the trio is heard as guests on that CD, *Live 1947–48* is taken from the King Cole Trio's own radio shows of 1947–48. On some numbers they back the singing of Clark Dennis, the Dinning Sisters, Pearl Bailey, and Woody Herman. Duke Ellington is also featured in 1947 playing "Mood Indigo."

10   *Nat King Cole* / Nov. 30, 1943–June 3, 1964 / Capitol 99777

8   *The Capitol Collector's Series* / Nov. 30, 1943–June 3, 1964 / Capitol 93590

8   *Lush Life* / Mar. 29, 1949–Jan. 11, 1952 / Capitol 80595

7   *Big Band Cole* / Aug. 16, 1950–Sept. 6, 1961 / Capitol 96259

7   *The Billy May Sessions* / Sept. 4, 1951–Nov. 22, 1961 / Capitol 89545

Nat King Cole, a four-CD set, is a perfect introduction to the two careers of Cole. The 100 selections contain virtually all of his hits, includes some good jazz performances (the first CD and a half is from 1943–50), and has a previously unreleased version of the humorous "Mr. Cole Won't Rock & Roll." It spans a 20-year period, from "Straighten Up and Fly Right" to "L-O-V-E." *The Capitol Collector's Series* has 20 of the same songs (including the two just mentioned) and is a solid single-CD intro to Cole. *Lush Life* features Nat Cole backed by an orchestra arranged by Pete Rugolo but

As a Swing pianist with his trio, Nat King Cole was one of the very best, but his playing would take a backseat to his singing in the 1950s.

still utilizing his trio on most of the numbers. This transitional set (which contains 25 selections, including four that were never out before) is highlighted by "Lush Life," "Time out for Tears," "Home," "Red Sails in the Sunset," and "It's Crazy." *Big Band Cole* features Nat on 12 numbers from 1958 with the Count Basie Orchestra (Gerald Wiggins is on piano), functioning as a dominant band vocalist. Highlights include "I Want a Little Girl," "The Blues Don't Care," "The Late Late Show," and "Welcome to the Club." In addition, Nat and his trio join the Stan Kenton Orchestra in 1950 for two numbers ("Orange Colored Sky" was a minor hit) and during 1960–61 for three additional selections (in-

cluding a second version of "Orange Colored Sky"). The two-CD set *The Billy May Sessions* has all of Cole's recordings with bands arranged by Billy May, dating from 1951 (including "Walkin' My Baby Back Home"), 1953 ("Angel Eyes"), 1954 ("Papa Loves Mambo"), 1957, and a full album from 1961 on which Cole (in addition to his singing) plays organ on four numbers.

7 *Piano Stylings / June 7, 1955–Aug. 27, 1955 / Capitol 81203*

8 *Complete After Midnight Sessions / Aug. 15, 1956–Sept. 2, 1956 / Capitol 48328*

6 *Love Is the Thing* / 1956–1963 / DCC Compact Classics 1104

6 *The Very Thought of You* / May 1958 / DCC Compact Classics 1119

7 *The Nat King Cole Story* / Mar. 22, 1961–July 30, 1961 / Capitol 95129

7 *Nat King Cole Sings, George Shearing Plays* / Dec. 19, 1961–Dec. 22, 1961 / Capitol 48332

After 1950, Nat King Cole was known to the general public primarily as a singer. Two of his later rare jazz projects were *Piano Stylings* (17 instrumental numbers in which his piano, functioning as a vocalist, is backed by an orchestra arranged by Nelson Riddle) and the *After Midnight Sessions.* For the latter, Cole and his regular rhythm section (guitarist John Collins, bassist Charlie Harris, and drummer Lee Young) are joined by either Harry Edison, Willie Smith, Juan Tizol, or Stuff Smith. Oddly enough, there are vocals on all 17 numbers (five of which came out for the first time on this 1987 CD) and not a single selection features just the trio. However, the music is frequently wonderful and shows that Nat Cole never lost his jazz chops. *Love Is the Thing* and *The Very Thought of You* (both reissued by the audiophile DCC label) are more typical of Cole's output during the era, ballad-oriented vocal sets with a string orchestra arranged by Gordon Jenkins. They do feature superior singing of mostly veteran songs, including (on the former date) "When I Fall in Love" and "Stardust," with the second set having "But Beautiful," "Impossible," and "This Is All I Ask." *The Nat King Cole Story* is a two-CD set of remakes of Cole's many hits, programmed in the order that they were originally recorded; very well done. The project with the George Shearing Quintet and an orchestra arranged by Shearing and Ralph Carmichael has some inventive and dreamy string charts. Cole sounds in prime voice on such numbers as "September Song," "Pick Yourself Up," "Let There Be

Love," and "Everything Happens to Me" (one of three new selections added to the reissue). Pity that Nat King Cole did not tackle Shearing's "Lullaby of Birdland!"

LPS TO SEARCH FOR

Nat King Cole Meets the Masters Saxes (Spotlite 136) features the pianist leading a 1942 quintet that includes Illinois Jacquet and trumpeter Shad Collins, interacting with Harry Edison and tenorman Dexter Gordon in 1943, and playing four numbers with Lester Young and bassist Red Callender. Superior jazz resulted from each situation. *The Forgotten Years* (Giants of Jazz 1013) showcases the King Cole Trio on the radio in 1945. Also from 1945 is *Anatomy of a Jam Session* (Black Lion 30104), a strong quintet date with Charlie Shavers, Herbie Haymer on tenor, bassist John Simmons, and drummer Buddy Rich; this LP has many alternate takes. And from Nat Cole's later years, *St. Louis Blues* (Capitol 993) shows that the music from the fictional W. C. Handy movie (performed by Cole in 1958 as a singer with the Nelson Riddle Orchestra) is far better than the film itself.

FILMS

The King Cole Trio appears in many films, including *Here Comes Elmer* (1943), *Swing in the Saddle* (1944), *Stars on Parade* (1944), *See My Lawyer* (1945), *Breakfast in Hollywood* (1946), *Killer Diller* (1948), and *Make Believe Ballroom* (1949). Nat King Cole performs briefly in *The Blue Gardenia* (1953) and *The Scarlet Hour* (1955), plays the role of W. C. Handy in the misfire *St. Louis Blues* (1958), has an odd acting role in *Night of the Quarter Moon* (1959), and is one of the storytellers (along with Stubby Kaye) in Cat Ballou (1964), filmed shortly before his death. In addition, two videos, *The Incomparable Nat King Cole Vols. 1–2* (Warner Reprise Video 38266 and 38292), feature selections from his 1956–57 television series, and the 1950–51 King Cole Trio is featured in 17 performances on *The Snader Transcriptions* (Storyville Films 6010).

JOHNNY GUARNIERI
b. Mar. 23, 1917, New York, NY, d. Jan. 7, 1985, Livingston, NJ

Johnny Guarnieri, a swinging and witty pianist, had the ability to sound like Count Basie, Fats Waller, Teddy Wilson, or Art Tatum on a moment's notice. He began playing in public in 1935 and picked up experience working with George Hall (1937–38) and Mike Riley. Guarnieri was part of the Benny Goodman Orchestra during 1939–40, recording with both the big band and BG's Septet with Charlie Christian. While with Artie Shaw (1940–41), Guarnieri played harpsichord on the famous Gramercy Five recordings. After Shaw broke up the band, the pianist rejoined Goodman for a few months, then became part of Shaw's next orchestra for the second half of 1941. He also worked with Jimmy Dorsey (1942–43) and Raymond Scott's orchestra at CBS. Guarnieri was quite busy throughout the remainder of the 1940s, as a studio musician, on 52nd Street with a variety of combos, and recording extensively with the who's who of Swing (including Lester Young, Coleman Hawkins, Don Byas, Roy Eldridge, Louis Armstrong, and Ben Webster). Guarnieri continued working in the studios during the 1950s and, after moving to Los Angeles in 1963, he primarily played locally in clubs. In his later years Johnny Guarnieri enjoyed imitating Fats Waller in his vocals and playfully interpreting standards in odd time signatures (particularly 5/4).

●

9 *1944–1946 / Apr. 18, 1944–Jan. 23, 1946 / Classics 956*

7 *1946–1947 / May 10, 1946–1947 / Classics 1063*

8 *Fatscinatin' / Feb. 26, 1978 / Star Line Productions 32296*

9 *Echoes of Ellington / 1984 / Star Line Productions 9003*

In addition to his many appearances on records as a sideman, Johnny Guarnieri had some opportunities to lead his own sessions during 1944–47, all of which are reissued on the two Classics CDs. *1944–1946* has three trio outings (with Slam Stewart or Bob Haggart on bass and Sammy Weiss or Cozy Cole on drums), including such numbers as "Gliss Me Again," "New Exercise in Swing," "Deuces Wild," and "Deuces Mild!" Guarnieri is also heard heading an all-star septet that includes Lester Young and Billy Butterfield plus a quartet date that includes Don Byas. *1946–1947* puts the focus throughout on Guarnieri, whether playing piano solos (and taking vocals on "Sorry, I Lost My Head" and "Bobo, the Bowery Barber"), in a trio, or in a quartet with guitarist Tony Mottola, performing mostly standards. Guarnieri recorded one album in 1950, five during 1956–57, and one in 1965, but he was busiest on records as a leader during the 1973–84 period, when he led nine albums. *Fatscinatin'* is a superior solo set consisting of a dozen Fats Waller songs. In addition to the hits (such as "Ain't Misbehavin'," "Keeping out of Mischief Now," and "Jitterbug Waltz"), Guarnieri

(who brings back Waller's spirit without directly copying him) revives "Moppin' and Boppin'," "Clothes Line Ballet," and "I'm Not Worrying." The pianist's final project was *Echoes of Ellington*, a solo set of 11 of Duke's tunes plus "Take the 'A' Train." Although all of the songs (except "Birmingham Breakdown" and "Mississippi Moan") are quite familiar, Johnny Guarnieri consistently comes up with fresh ideas and variations. He called this his favorite personal recording and it does rank pretty high.

LPS TO SEARCH FOR

Johnny Guarnieri Remembered (IAJRC 43) is a retrospective tracing Guarnieri's playing on records from 1939–1978, including sideman dates with Ziggy Elman, the Benny Goodman Sextet, Artie Shaw, Jerry Jerome, a Will Bradley pickup group, Ben Webster, Benny Morton, Coleman Hawkins, Barney Bigard, Don Byas, and J. C. Heard, plus several numbers as a leader. Most of the music is available elsewhere, but this LP does give one a fine overview. *Johnny Guarnieri Plays Harry Warren* (Jim Taylor Presents 102) is a strong solo outing from 1973, *Gliss Me Again* (Classic Jazz 105) reunites Guarnieri in 1975 with Slam Stewart in a quartet with guitarist Jimmy Shirley and drummer Jackie Williams, and *Plays the Music of Walter Donaldson* (Dobre 1017), also from 1975, is a swinging trio session.

FILMS

Johnny Guarnieri is in the Coleman Hawkins–Roy Eldridge Quintet that performs throughout *After Hours* (1961).

EDDIE HEYWOOD
b. Dec. 4, 1915, Atlanta, GA, d. Jan. 2, 1989, Miami Beach, FL

The Eddie Heywood Sextet was one of the most popular small groups of the mid-1940s. Its arranged ensembles may have been a bit conservative, but the band always swung. Heywood, the son of Eddie Heywood, Sr. (who was a talented pianist in the 1920s), took lessons from his father starting when he was eight. At 14, Heywood was playing professionally in Atlanta.

He came to New York in 1937, where, after some freelancing, he worked with the Benny Carter Orchestra during 1939–40. Heywood played with Zutty Singleton's trio, Don Redman, and then his own sextet, which he formed in 1941 and originally included Doc Cheatham and Vic Dickenson. His group lasted until 1947 and had a hit in "Begin the Beguine." In addition, Heywood can be heard on many fine recordings during the 1940s, including a classic quartet date with Coleman Hawkins (most notably on "The Man I Love") and with Billie Holiday. Bad health that caused partial paralysis in his hands forced Heywood to break up his sextet and stop playing music for three years. Eddie Heywood made a successful comeback in 1950 but then shifted to easy-listening cocktail-style music rather than jazz. He composed the standard "Canadian Sunset" and was active into the early 1980s. ●

9 *1944 / Feb. 19, 1944–Dec. 15, 1944 / Classics 947*

8 *1944–1946 / Dec. 29, 1944–May 29, 1946 / Classics 1038*
The Eddie Heywood Sextet (which at the beginning consisted of Doc Cheatham, Vic Dickenson, altoist Lem Davis, bassist Al Lucas, and drummer Jack Parker) originally recorded for Commodore, had a hit in "Begin the Beguine," and by December 1944 had signed with Decca. Virtually all of its recordings are on these two CDs, which find Heywood's piano in the forefront, his players taking short solos, and the emphasis placed on the melodic and catchy ensembles. Also included on *1944* are a sextet session with Ray Nance and Don Byas and a trio date with Johnny Hodges

and drummer Shelly Manne, so that CD gets the edge, but both of Heywood's Classics CDs are quite enjoyable.

LPS TO SEARCH FOR
Many of Eddie Heywood's albums after 1950 are of lesser interest, mostly high-class cocktail music. *Eddie Heywood* (Emarcy 36042), a trio set with bassist Wendell Marshall and drummer Jimmy Crawford, is one of his better outings from the period, featuring a few originals plus melodic versions of Swing standards.

FILMS
Eddie Heywood appears in *Junior Prom* (1946) and *The Dark Corner* (1946).

PETE JOHNSON
b. Mar. 25, 1904, Kansas City, MO, d. Mar. 23, 1967, Buffalo, NY

A superb boogie-woogie pianist, Pete Johnson was also top-notch at playing blues. Johnson actually started out as a drummer, working professionally during 1922–26. After a few piano lessons, he switched instruments in 1926. During 1926–38 Johnson worked mostly as a solo pianist in local clubs, becoming a key part of the legendary Kansas City jazz scene, performing at many after-hours jam sessions. He frequently teamed up with a singing bartender named Big Joe Turner. In 1938 Johnson and Turner visited New York to appear on the radio with Benny Goodman and then returned in December to perform at the Spirituals to Swing concert, where they were a hit. As part of the Boogie Woogie Trio (with Albert Ammons and Meade Lux Lewis), Johnson became a fixture at Café Society and he also appeared in duos with one or another of the two pianists. He recorded regularly (often solo) with and without Turner and was quite active until suffering from bad health in 1958. Johnson's last nine years found him retired from music due to a stroke. Pete Johnson made his final appearance playing just the right-hand part of a boogie-woogie at the 1967 Spirituals to Swing concert. ●

10 *1938–1939 / Dec. 30, 1938–Dec. 19, 1939 / Classics 656*

8 *1939–1941 / Dec. 19, 1939–June 17, 1941 / Classics 665*

9 *1944–1946 / Feb. 17, 1944–Jan. 31, 1946 / Classics 933*

6 *Central Avenue Boogie / Apr. 18, 1947–Nov. 29, 1947 / Delmark 656*
Pete Johnson's prime recordings are reissued in full on his three Classics CDs (other than some alternate takes). *1938–*

1939, which contains many gems, has his first numbers, a pair of songs with Joe Turner, including the debut of "Roll 'Em Pete." In addition, Johnson is heard on "Boo-Woo" and "Home James" with Harry James in a quartet, leading a sextet that features Big Joe Turner and Hot Lips Page (including "Cherry Red"), and jamming "Café Society Rag" in a piano trio with Ammons and Lewis. He also plays a couple of more conventional trio numbers for Blue Note and otherwise performs unaccompanied piano solos. *1939–1941* finishes the Blue Note session, has a Kansas City group with Hot Lips Page on "627 Stomp," and includes a few piano duos with Albert Ammons, a later trio date, and some more piano solos. *1944–1946* is also quite worthy, containing eight piano solos, an octet session with singer Etta Jones, Hot Lips Page, Don Stovall, and Budd Johnson, and an add-an-instrument outing that starts out solo and concludes eight songs later with an octet that features Page, J. C. Higginbotham, Albert Nicholas, and Ben Webster. Hot Lips's showcase on "Page Mr. Trumpet" is a definite highlight. The music on *Central Avenue Boogie* is also excellent, but there is just not enough of it. Delmark did its best, augmenting Johnson's eight quartet recordings for Apollo with three alternate takes and adding two piano solos (plus an alternate) by Arnold Wiley. It still only totals 38 minutes, but the quality is high and Johnson's boogie-woogie version of "Swanee River" is fun.

FILMS

Pete Johnson plays some heated piano duets with Albert Ammons in the classic film short *Boogie Woogie Dream* (1941).

KEN KERSEY
b. Apr. 3, 1916, Harrow, Ontario, Canada, d. Apr. 1, 1983, New York, NY

Ken Kersey was one of the better Swing pianists to emerge in the early 1940s, but his career was cut short after a promising beginning. He studied at the Detroit Institute of Music and for a little while early on also played trumpet. After moving to New York in 1936, he played with the Mills Blue Rhythm Band, Billy Hicks, Frankie Newton, and Roy Eldridge. Kersey's work with Henry "Red" Allen in 1941 (including recording "K. K. Boogie") gained him a bit of attention. He played with the Cootie Williams Big Band and as Mary Lou Williams's successor with the Andy Kirk Orchestra. Kersey was drafted but was lucky enough to still be able to make appearances with Kirk now and then while in the military. Out of the Army in 1946, he worked with Teddy McRae, Roy Eldridge (1948), and Buck Clayton and was on several tours with Jazz at the Philharmonic during 1946–49. Kersey played regularly in Mainstream Swing and trad settings with Edmond Hall (1949–50), Red Allen (1951–52), Sol Yaged (1952–54 and 1956–57), and Charlie Shavers (1955). Unfortunately, a serious bone condition in the late 1950s forced Ken Kersey's retirement while he was still in his early forties. He led only four sessions in his career (during 1946–51), resulting in a dozen titles.

BILLY KYLE
b. July 14, 1914, Philadelphia, PA, d. Feb. 23, 1966, Youngstown, OH

Billy Kyle always had a light touch on the piano, and his advanced Swing style (which made every note count) was perfect for the John Kirby Sextet. He started playing piano when he was eight, began performing in public when he was 15, and freelanced until he joined the Mills Blue Rhythm Band (1936–38). Kyle was with the popular Kirby Sextet during its prime years (1938–42), leaving only when he was drafted. After being released from the Army, the pianist was back with Kirby for a bit in 1946, worked with Sy Oliver, and led his own combos. Kyle, whose style was unaffected by bebop, worked in the pit band for the Broadway show *Guys and Dolls* during 1948–50. He was in the studios for a couple of years and then became a member of the Louis Armstrong All-Stars in the fall of 1953, staying until his death a dozen years later. Kyle's playing became quite predictable with Armstrong and he was never heard again outside of the All-Stars; no one thought of giving him his own trio date. However, Billy Kyle did lead some sessions in the 1940s and he can be heard at his best with John Kirby.

9   *1937–1938 / Mar. 18, 1937–Sept. 9, 1938 / Classics 919*

8   *1939–1946 / Jan. 20, 1939–Sept. 1946 / Classics 941*

All of Billy Kyle's dates as a leader are on these two CDs, both of which also include other sessions that feature him as a key sideman. *1937–1938* has eight numbers led by Kyle with Charlie Shavers, Tab Smith, and (on two vocals apiece) the Palmer Brothers and Leon Lafell. In addition, Kyle is heard as part of the Spencer Trio (the lone date led by drummer O'Neill Spencer), with Timme Rosenkrantz's Barrelhouse Barons (which features Rex Stewart and Don Byas) and backing calypso singer Jack Sneed. *1939–1946* has five sessions from 1939, including one in which Nat Gonella is joined by an augmented version of John Kirby's sextet (with guest altoist Benny Carter), two more numbers with Jack Sneed, and a couple of organ groups in which Kyle's piano is mostly supportive of O'Neill Spencer's vocals. Kyle does get featured on two numbers with a quartet and in 1946 with a pianoless trio and an octet that includes Trummy Young and Buster Bailey. The pianist still had 20 years of activity ahead of him, but that was it for him as a leader.

FILMS

Billy Kyle appears with the Louis Armstrong All-Stars in *High Society* (1956), *Satchmo the Great* (1956), *When the Boys Meet the Girls* (1965), and *A Man Called Adam* (1966). He is also featured with the John Kirby Sextet in *Sepia Cinderella* (1946).

MEADE LUX LEWIS
b. Sept. 4, 1905, Chicago, IL, d. June 7, 1964, Minneapolis, MN

Meade Lux Lewis recorded only one piano solo in the 1920s, but it was a classic: 1927's "Honky Tonk Train Blues." The rediscovery of that recording would help lead to the boogie-woogie craze of the late 1930s.

Lewis was playing in Chicago clubs by the mid-1920s. Despite recording "Honky Tonk Train Blues" (along with a few blues accompaniments), he had a day job during the early years of the Depression, including working in a W.P.A. shovel gang and driving a taxi. John Hammond, who loved Lewis's record, found him in late 1935 and soon arranged for him to rerecord the song. Lewis cut four titles in 1936 and two in 1937, working again as a full-time musician. He participated in Hammond's Spirituals to Swing concert in December 1938, moved to New York, and would be busy for the remainder of his career. Lewis recorded fairly prolifically (including on celeste, most notably in a quartet with Edmond Hall and Charlie Christian, and harpsichord), relocated to Los Angeles in 1941, and stayed active as one of the world's top boogie-woogie pianists (although somewhat in obscurity) until his death in a car crash in 1964. ●

9   *1927–1939 / Dec. 1927–Jan. 6, 1939 / Classics 722*

8   *1939–1941 / Jan. 6, 1939–Apr. 9, 1941 / Classics 743*

8   *1941–1944 / Apr. 9, 1941–Aug. 22, 1944 / Classics 841*

6   *Cat House Piano / June 28, 1954–Jan. 16, 1955 / Verve 314 557 098*

7   *The Blues Piano Artistry of Meade Lux Lewis / Nov. 1, 1961 / Original Jazz Classics 1759*

Meade Lux Lewis's original classic version of "Honky Tonk Train Blues" launches *1927–1939*, and there are two other versions of the song on the CD (from 1935 and 1937), along with a couple of examples of his celeste and even his whistling (on "Whistlin' Blues"). *1927–1939* concludes with selections from the very first Blue Note session, which concludes at the beginning of *1939–1941*. Lewis is primarily heard solo on the latter CD, although he duets with Albert Ammons on "Twos and Fews." Among the other selections are "Messin' Around," "Bass on Top," "Nineteen Ways of Playing a Chorus," and another version of "Honky Tonk Train Blues." *1941–1944* contains rarities from the Asch label along with some Blue Notes; highlights include "Yancey's Pride," "Lux's Boogie," and "Chicago Flyer." Meade Lux Lewis did not record much during 1945–53 (other than an Atlantic album in 1951) and he was becoming a little weary of being stuck in a boogie-woogie format, but he never did musically reinvent himself. *Cat House Piano* finds Lewis backed by bassist Red Callender and Jo Jones and playing duets with Louie Bellson. He sounds fine but no real surprises occur despite some heated playing. *The Blues Artistry of Meade Lux Lewis* was his next-to-last effort and is a bit more inspired. It is a solo album in which Lewis plays both piano and (on three numbers) celeste, infusing the boogie-woogie format with spirit and really digging into the basic material.

FILMS

Meade Lux Lewis appears in *New Orleans* (1947) and *Nightmare* (1956).

MEL POWELL
b. Feb. 12, 1923, New York, NY, d. Apr. 24, 1998, Valencia, CA

Mel Powell was a bit of a child prodigy, not only playing piano with Benny Goodman's orchestra by the time he was 18 but writing impressive arrangements. As early as 1939 (when he was 16), Mel Epstein (who changed his last name to Powell in 1940) was working with Bobby Hackett, George Brunies, and Zutty Singleton. He was featured at Nick's as the intermission pianist and in 1940 was in Muggsy Spanier's big band in addition to recording with Wingy Manone. Powell was an important force with Goodman's orchestra during 1941–42. His piano playing was a mixture of Teddy Wilson and Earl Hines, and among his best arrangements were "The Earl," "Mission to Moscow," "Clarinade," and a hit version of "Jersey Bounce." Powell played with Raymond Scott's CBS Orchestra during part of 1942 and then went in the Army, performing with Glenn Miller's Army Air Force Band, where he was one of the main soloists. After returning to civilian life, he was with Goodman on and off during 1945–47, worked in the studios, and led a few studio dates in the 1950s (as late as 1955) for Vanguard. However, by 1952 Mel Powell was turning his attention to classical music, where he soon became a major serial composer. Still only 29 at the time, he was a major loss to jazz. Decades later, Mel Powell came back to improvised music during jazz cruises in 1986 and 1987, which were fortunately recorded by Chiaroscuro, but troubles with his legs (a muscular disease) soon forced him to retire altogether from active playing.

●

5 *The Best Things in Life / Dec. 30, 1953–Oct. 19, 1955 / Vanguard 79602*
Mel Powell recorded six sessions for the Vanguard label during 1953–55, his last jazz dates before he left the music altogether. This single CD draws its selections from four of the projects, but it is unfortunate that the performances were not reissued in a much more complete fashion, since the high-quality sessions have long been out of print. Powell is heard in a quintet and a trio with trumpeter Ruby Braff, leading a septet that often backs singer Joan Wile, and jamming "You're Lucky to Me" with Buck Clayton and clarinetist Edmond Hall. What is here is fine, but where's the rest of it?

8 *The Return of Mel Powell / Oct. 21, 1987 / Chiaroscuro 301*
The release of this CD was a real surprise, for Mel Powell had not recorded a jazz date since 1955. He was persuaded to play at the Floating Jazz Festival on the S/S Norway and was able to gain back most of his earlier form. On six standards (including "Stomping at the Savoy," "Lady Be Good," and " 'S Wonderful"), Powell jams happily with Benny Carter, guitarist Howard Alden, Milt Hinton, and Louie Bell-

son. The CD concludes with a 20 minute "Jazzspeak" in which Mel Powell talks about his life and his decision to leave jazz for classical music.

LPS TO SEARCH FOR
Piano Forte (Phontastic 7649) has Mel Powell in 1944 England playing with a small group taken out of Glenn Miller's Army Air Force Band that includes trumpeter Bernie Privin, clarinetist Peanuts Hucko, and possibly Miller himself on trombone. In addition to standards and originals, the group plays one of the earliest existing versions of Dizzy Gillespie's "A Night in Tunisia." *The Unavailable Mel Powell* (Pausa 9023) features Powell's recording groups of 1947 (two piano solos plus combo dates with tenor saxophonist Bumps Myers and either Jake Porter or Frank Beach on trumpets) in addition to a Dixieland jam from 1948 on "Muskrat Ramble." The sessions were originally recorded for Capitol.

FILMS
Mel Powell gets to play with Benny Goodman and a variety of top Swing all-stars in *A Song Is Born* (1948).

JESS STACY

b. Aug. 11, 1904, Bird's Point, MO, d. Jan. 5, 1994, Los Angeles, CA

Best known for his association with Benny Goodman (whom he did not really like!), Jess Stacy was the perfect big band pianist. His piano could always be heard over the brass and he was expert at accompanying singers. Stacy, who was influenced by Earl Hines, was mostly self-taught. He played on riverboats as early as 1921, was with Al Katz's Kittens in 1926 (with whom he made his recording debut, although he did not get a solo), and played with Joe Kayser during 1926–28. During the next seven years he worked with many bands in the Chicago area, including Muggsy Spanier. In July 1935 Stacy joined the Benny Goodman Orchestra, staying with the King of Swing until July 1939. His most famous moment occurred at Goodman's 1938 Carnegie Hall concert when, after the clarinetist's solo on "Sing, Sing, Sing," BG spontaneously gave Stacy a signal to solo. The resulting impressionistic improvisation was brilliant and practically stole the show.

Stacy was with Bob Crosby's orchestra from September 1939 to December 1942, and then he was back with Goodman through March 1944. The pianist worked with Horace Heidt (1944) and Tommy Dorsey (1944–45) before organizing his own big band, featuring his wife of the time, singer Lee Wiley. Both the orchestra and his marriage soon failed. A few months with Goodman (1946–47) and another short-lived big band (1947–48) followed. After a period freelancing in New York, Stacy settled in California, where he worked mostly as a soloist at clubs during the 1950s. Jess Stacy retired from full-time music in 1963, although there were a couple of final solo recordings in the 1970s.

●

9 *1935–1939 / Nov. 16, 1935–Nov. 30, 1939 / Classics 795*

8 *Jess Stacy & Friends / Apr. 30, 1938–Nov. 25, 1944 / Commodore 7008*

All of Jess Stacy's early recordings as a leader are on *1935–1939*. He is heard playing unaccompanied solos (including a medley of Bix Beiderbecke's "In the Dark" and "Flashes"), jamming in one of the first piano-bass-drums trios with Israel Crosby and Gene Krupa, playing a duet with Bud Freeman on "She's Funny That Way," and heading a freewheeling octet that includes Billy Butterfield, Eddie Miller, and either Hank d'Amico or Irving Fazola on clarinet. Superior Swing. *Jess Stacy & Friends* has all of Stacy's work as a leader for the Commodore label, including a repeat of eight numbers (seven solos plus the Freeman duet) that are on *1935–1939*. In addition, there are some duets from 1944 with drummer Specs Powell plus two classic numbers ("Sugar" and "Down to Steamboat Tennessee") in a trio with Muggsy Spanier and Lee Wiley in 1940.

8 *Tribute To Benny Goodman / Apr. 29, 1954–Oct. 6, 1955 / Koch 8506*

8 *Stacy Still Swings / July 5, 1974–July 20, 1977 / Chiaroscuro 133*

7 *Piano Jazz / Dec. 1, 1981 / The Jazz Alliance 12017*

The Koch CD brings back an Atlantic set featuring Stacy with a nonet filled with Benny Goodman alumni to perform a variety of Swing standards, most of which were associated with BG; no clarinetist was hired to try to fill in for Goodman. This enjoyable CD is most valuable for the playing of trumpeter Ziggy Elman, who is heard during his final significant recordings. There are also three trio features for Stacy. Jess Stacy had not recorded as a leader since 1956 and he had been largely retired since 1962 when he made *Stacy Still Swings* in 1974. This was recorded in New York where Stacy had traveled for a Carnegie Hall concert, and the pianist sounds fine on the solo date, mostly playing at relaxed tempos and showing that his Classic Swing style was unchanged. The CD reissue adds four additional selections to the original eight songs, including two from 1977; highlights include "I Would Do Most Anything for You," "Riverboat Shuffle," and "Stacy Still Swings." A special bonus is the inclusion of a definitive article on Stacy by Whitney Balliett. He would record a final album (*Stacy's Still Swingin'*) in 1977, and in 1981 he appeared on Marian McPartland's *Piano Jazz* radio show. On the Jazz Alliance disc, which reissues the full show, Stacy (who was quite modest about his own playing at this late date) performs five solos (getting stronger as the hour progresses) and McPartland plays

"Heavy Hearted Blues." Their three rollicking duets (including "Keepin' Out of Mischief Now" and "St. Louis Blues") are delightful and the storytelling is quite interesting. This would be Jess Stacy's last recording.

LPS TO SEARCH FOR

Jess Stacy's radio transcription date of October 6, 1944, complete with false starts and incomplete versions, is reissued in full on *Blue Notion* (Jazzology 90), a trio session with bassist Bob Casey and drummer George Wettling. *Big Band Bounce & Boogie* (Affinity 1020) has his eight quartet performances of 1951, with the other half of the LP featuring Ralph Sutton and drummer Cliff Leeman in 1953. *Still Swinging* (Chiaroscuro 177), the pianist's last official album, finds the 73-year-old still in good form on such numbers as "Waiting for the Evening Mail," "I've Got a Crush on You," and "After You've Gone."

FILMS

Jess Stacy is part of a Benny Goodman small group in *Sweet and Low Down* (1944), taking a hot solo on "The World Is Waiting for the Sunrise."

JOE SULLIVAN

b. Nov. 5, 1906, Chicago, IL, d. Oct. 13, 1971, San Francisco, CA

Joe Sullivan was one of the finest pianists of the Swing era, but erratic health and alcoholism resulted in a rather streaky life. Born Dennis Patrick Terence Joseph O'Sullivan, he studied at the Chicago Conservatory of Music. Sullivan worked in vaudeville during 1923–25 and played in many settings in Chicago during the 1920s, recording in 1927 with McKenzie-Condon's Chicagoans. After moving to New York, he worked with Red Nichols, Roger Wolfe Kahn, the Mound City Blue Blowers (1931–32), Ozzie Nelson, and Russ Colombo, and in Los Angeles he was Bing Crosby's accompanist (1934–36). Sullivan, who was strongly influenced by Earl Hines, was with Bob Crosby's orchestra for a few months in 1936, getting some attention for his live performances of his original "Little Rock Getaway." However, a bout with tuberculosis forced Sullivan to be hospitalized, and his replacement, Bob Zurke, played piano on Crosby's hit recording of that song. In 1938 Sullivan was back working with Bing Crosby, and the following year he was with Bob Crosby during the summer. He led a combo on 52nd Street for a few years, freelanced around New York, and played regularly at Eddie Condon's club during 1946–47. From then on, Joe Sullivan was in and out of music, often working on the West Coast (particularly at San Francisco's Hangover Club). He toured with the Louis Armstrong All-Stars briefly in early 1952 and appeared at the 1963 Monterey Jazz Festival with Jack Teagarden but mostly spent his later years forgotten and drinking too much.

●

10 *1933–1941 / Sept. 26, 1933–Mar. 28, 1941 / Classics 821*

8 *The Piano Artistry of Joe Sullivan / 1944–Sept. 29, 1952 / Jazz Unlimited 2051*

1933–1941 has all of Joe Sullivan's prewar recordings as a leader. Particularly intriguing is a comparison between his 1933 and 1935 performances of "Little Rock Getaway"; the earlier version does not have a melody! Sullivan is heard on eight piano solos from 1933–35 (including "Honeysuckle Rose," "Gin Mill Blues," and "My Little Pride of Joy") and four from 1941 along with trio numbers with clarinetist Pee Wee Russell and drummer Zutty Singleton. In addition, he leads a couple of medium-size Swing groups that include trumpeter Ed Anderson, Benny Morton, Edmond Hall, and Danny Polo on clarinet and tenor; Helen Ward and Joe Turner take two vocals apiece. Highly enjoyable music. *The Piano Artistry of Joe Sullivan*, when it was released in 1998, brought back performances so rare that some had never been listed in earlier discographies. Sullivan, whether taking unaccompanied solos in 1944–45, leading a trio (with Bob Casey or Walter Page on bass, plus drummer George Wettling) in 1952, or playing four numbers with a quintet (which features clarinetist Archie Rosati) in 1945, is heard throughout in prime form, playing in his joyful Swing/stride style.

LPS TO SEARCH FOR

Piano (Folkways 2851) dates from 1944–46 and is comprised primarily of high-quality piano solos. There are also two numbers with Sidney Bechet, one with Yank Lawson, and "Rabbit Foot Blues," which features a vocal by Stella Brooks. *Joe Sullivan at the Piano* (Shoestring 104) has ten other piano solos from 1944 that were made for radio transcriptions (including "Honeysuckle Rose," "Farewell to Riverside," and "Fifty-Second Street Stomp") plus three band numbers from 1951 with either Bobby Hackett or Wild Bill Davison on cornet. Long overdue to be reissued on CD

is *New Solos by an Old Master* (Riverside 12-202), a 1953 trio and solo outing that finds Sullivan, at age 46, still sounding strong before slipping away into obscurity. He emerged briefly in 1963, as can be heard on *Joe Sullivan* (Pumpkin 112), live solos from three different nights. Fortunately Sullivan, who was quite erratic by this period, is in pretty good form during these final recordings.

ART TATUM
b. Oct. 13, 1909, Toledo, OH, d. Nov. 5, 1956, Los Angeles, CA

Art Tatum was arguably jazz's most remarkable improviser. His blinding speed on the piano was often unbelievable, he played chords and harmonies in the 1930s that other pianists would not think of until the 1960s and '70s, and his technique was phenomenal. It was said during his lifetime that other musicians could not perform with Tatum (since he often left little space), but in reality it was more accurate to say that only the very best could.

Born with cataracts in his eyes, Tatum was blind in one eye and only had partial vision in the other. He started playing piano when quite young and studied guitar and violin in addition to doubling on accordion for a time. Tatum started working in Toledo around 1926, mostly playing solo, and he appeared locally on the radio on a regular basis. In 1932 Tatum was hired to be one of two pianists (the other was Frances Carter) to play behind singer Adelaide Hall. He moved to New York, where he made his recording debut with Hall (with whom he worked into 1934). Tatum's first solo session is highlighted by an incredible version of "Tiger Rag" in which he sounds like three pianists playing at once!

During the 1930s, Tatum mostly performed solo, playing in New York, Cleveland, Chicago, and Hollywood and recording regularly. In 1943 he formed a trio with guitarist Tiny Grimes and bassist Slam Stewart that had some commercial success. Tatum usually played either solo or with a trio (in later years Everett Barksdale was on guitar) during his last 13 years. He recorded quite a bit for Norman Granz's Verve label in the 1950s, including an extensive series of all-star band sides (with the likes of Lionel Hampton, Benny Carter, Buddy DeFranco, Ben Webster, and Roy Eldridge, among others). Art Tatum died at the age of 46 from uremia. Even decades later his records can still scare any pianist!

●

10 *Piano Starts Here / Mar. 21, 1933–1949 / Legacy / Columbia 64690*

8 *1932–1934 / Aug. 5, 1932–Oct. 9, 1934 / Classics 507*

9 *Classic Early Solos / Aug. 22, 1934–Nov. 29, 1937 / GRP/Decca 607*

9 *Solos / Feb. 22, 1940–July 26, 1940 / MCA/Decca 42327*

9 *I Got Rhythm / Dec. 21, 1935–Jan. 5, 1944 / GRP/ Decca 630*

Piano Starts Here has some of the most incredible Art Tatum ever on record. It starts off with the four selections from his initial date as a leader, including the remarkable "Tiger Rag," and the remainder is taken from a "Just Jazz" concert

in the spring of 1949. That solo performance includes his brilliant versions of "Yesterdays" (which he really tears apart), a very speedy "I Know That You Know," and "Humoresque." Although one regrets the brevity of this CD (which at 36 minutes is a reissue of the original LP), the number of notes that Tatum plays would fill a box set! *1932–1934* duplicates Tatum's first solo session, and various performances that are on the listed Decca reissues are among its 25 selections. However, it also includes a rare air check version of "Tiger Rag" from August 5, 1932 (which predates Tatum's studio sides by a year), plus the four selections that he cut in 1932 backing Adelaide Hall. All of Tatum's Decca recordings are on *Classic Early Solos, I Got Rhythm,* and *Solos,* with the exception of a few numbers backing Joe Turner, which are included in the singer's *I've Been to Kansas City* CD (MCA/Decca 42351). The first set (which includes three rare alternate takes) has Tatum's solo sessions of 1934 and 1937, including "Emaline," two versions of "After You've Gone," "The Shout," "Liza," and "The Sheik of Araby." *Solos,* which having come out in 1990 will probably be difficult to find, contains 15 selections from 1940 plus an alternate take of "Sweet Emalina, My Gal." Among the hotter numbers are "Humoresque," "Get Happy," "Indiana," and a re-make of "Tiger Rag." Tatum's transformation of "Begin the Beguine" is a classic. *I Got Rhythm,* which has three solos from 1939, also features Tatum with several groups. He plays "Take Me Back to My Boots and Saddle" with a mostly unidentified band in 1935, is heard in 1937 with a sextet that includes trumpeter Lloyd Reese and clarinetist Marshall Royal, and jams with a sextet that has trumpeter Joe Thomas and Edmond Hall on two numbers in 1940. In addition, the Art Tatum Trio (with Tiny Grimes and Slam Stewart) is heard on ten standards (including "I Got Rhythm," "Liza," and "Honeysuckle Rose") from 1944. All three Decca CDs are overflowing with gems.

8   *The Standard Transcriptions* / Dec. 1935–1943 / *Music & Arts 673 (2)*

6   *Standards* / Aug. 1938–Aug. 1939 / *Black Lion 760143*

7   *California Melodies* / Apr. 11, 1940–July 11, 1940 / *Memphis Archives 7007*

8   *God Is in the House* / Nov. 11, 1940–Sept. 16, 1941 / *High Note 7030*

7   *Tea for Two* / 1944–July 1945 / *Black Lion 760192*

7   *The V-Discs* / Jan. 18, 1944–Jan. 21, 1946 / *Black Lion 760114*

All of Art Tatum's performances for the Standard Transcription radio service are on the two-CD Music & Arts reissue. The performances are quite concise (eight of the 61 piano solos are under two minutes and only three exceed three minutes), but the renditions include a few numbers that Tatum did not record elsewhere and they add to his legacy. The 24 cuts on the single-disc *Standards,* although vague as to the dates, are all duplicated in the Music & Arts set, so only acquire this one if you cannot find the more complete two-fer. *California Melodies* has its 24 selections taken from a 1940 radio series hosted by arranger David Rose. Tatum took one or two solos in each show, and all of the existing performances (never released before this 1994 CD) are here, including a few songs that he did not record elsewhere live. Highlights include "Caravan," "Get Happy," "Tea for Two," "Elegie," and a version of "This Can't Be Love" played with the backing of David Rose's orchestra. *God Is in the House* has some unique live cuts from 1940–41. In addition to a series of piano solos, there are a pair of rare Tatum vocals (on "Knockin' Myself Out," and "Toledo Blues") and exciting versions of "Lady Be Good" and "Sweet Georgia Brown" with a trio that includes Frankie Newton and bassist Ebenezer Paul. *Tea for Two* has a complete (and formerly quite obscure) solo session from July 1945 (cut for the ARA label), including "Runnin' Wild," "Kerry Dance," and two versions of "Hallelujah." In addition, there is a trio rendition (with Grimes and Stewart) of "Tea for Two," versions of "Royal Garden Blues" and "I Got Rhythm" with a hot nonet that includes Roy Eldridge, Charlie Shavers, Ben Webster, and Edmond Hall, and additional solos from the 1944–45 period. *The V-Discs* has Tatum at the Esquire All-Stars concert of January 18, 1944 (playing "Sweet Lorraine" with Oscar Pettiford and Sid Catlett), playing a couple of trio numbers with Grimes and Stewart in 1945, and performing a set of piano solos from 1945–46, all originally released as V-Discs. Tatum as usual rips through the songs, which include a Gershwin medley and "920 Special," among the rarer performances.

8   *The Complete Capitol Recordings, Volume One* / July 13, 1949–Dec. 20, 1952 / *Capitol 92866*

8   *The Complete Capitol Recordings, Volume Two* / Sept. 29, 1949–Dec. 20, 1952 / *Capitol 92867*

9   *20th Century Piano Genius* / Apr. 16, 1950 + July 3, 1955 / *Verve 314 531 763*

Art Tatum recorded 20 piano solos in 1949 and eight numbers with guitarist Everett Barksdale and Slam Stewart in 1952 for Capitol. The performances are split equally in the two Capitol CDs, with ten solos and four trio songs in each disc. The music is as strong as one would expect, with "Willow Weep for Me," "Dardanella," and "Melody in F" being most memorable from *Volume One* and "You Took Advantage of Me," "How High the Moon," and "Indiana" taking honors in the second CD. It has often been written that Art Tatum was at his absolute best at after-hour sessions. *20th Century Piano Genius* features Tatum at a couple of Beverly Hills parties in 1955 and 1950, with a dozen of the 39 numbers being released for the first time on this 1996 double CD. In truth, Tatum does not play all that differently in this informal setting than in the studios except that nine of the songs exceed four minutes. As usual, the pianist provides plenty of miraculous moments and, even on his set pieces, he is amazing. Most of the songs are taken at relaxed medium tempos, with Tatum playing double- and triple-time lines quite effectively.

7 *The Complete Pablo Solo Masterpieces / Dec. 28, 1953– Aug. 15, 1956 / Pablo 7PACD-4404*

10 *The Complete Group Masterpieces / June 25, 1954– Sept. 11, 1956 / Pablo 6PACD-4401*

Norman Granz recorded more than 16 Art Tatum albums during 1953–56, catching the masterful pianist in both solo performances and with various Swing all-stars during his final three years. In addition to the two box sets, the music is available individually as eight solo and eight combo CDs. The solos were recorded in marathon sessions and not much planning went into them. Tatum played well, but nothing all that surprising occurs on the seven-CD set (which adds four numbers from a 1956 Hollywood Bowl concert) and a certain sameness prevails after a while, so these solos lack the excitement of his 1930s recordings. The group recordings are a different matter altogether and frequently do earn the "masterpiece" label. There are trio dates with Benny Carter and Louis Bellson, Lionel Hampton and Buddy Rich, and Red Callender and Jo Jones. Tatum plays in quartets with Roy Eldridge, bassist John Simmons, and drummer Alvin

Stoller; Ben Webster, Callender, and drummer Bill Douglass; and one with Buddy DeFranco in Webster's place. In addition, there is a sextet jam with Hampton, Callender, Rich, Harry Edison, and guitarist Barney Kessel. Every combination works very well, and plenty of fireworks result as each of Tatum's sidemen come up with different ways to play with the virtuosic pianist. DeFranco and Hampton challenge him directly, Eldridge is fairly restrained (for him), Webster plays warm long tones, etc. A very exciting six-CD set that serves as a perfect close to Art Tatum's career.

LPS TO SEARCH FOR

While most of Tatum's studio recordings are out on CD, some other rarities have yet to reappear. *The Remarkable Art of Tatum* (Audiophile 88) has the 11 radio transcriptions that Tatum, Grimes, and Stewart cut for World Broadcasting Systems in 1944. A 1950 solo concert at the Crescendo was released as *Piano Volume One* (GNP 9025) and *Volume Two* (GNP 9026). And *Lasting Impressions* (Giants of Jazz 1015) has some unusual material from 1951–56, including Tatum's two appearances on the *Tonight* show when it was hosted by Steve Allen. Allen has a short interview with the pianist (whose speaking voice was rarely captured on record), asks Tatum to play some runs for the audience to see, and even duets with Art on "Fine and Dandy."

FILMS

Other than a short spot on a newsreel, Art Tatum's only known film appearance is a heated jam session scene in *The Fabulous Dorseys* (1947).

FATS WALLER

b. May 21, 1904, New York, NY, d. Dec. 14, 1943, Kansas City, MO

Thomas "Fats" Waller gained his greatest fame as a humorous entertainer, but he had many other talents. Waller was one of jazz's greatest stride pianists (surpassing his hero, James P. Johnson), he was the first jazz organist, a talented singer, and a very skillful songwriter. His many compositions included such Swing standards as "Honeysuckle Rose," "Ain't Misbehavin'," "Black and Blue" (the first song to protest against racial prejudice), "Squeeze Me," and "I'm Crazy 'Bout My Baby." In addition, Fats was one long party, enjoying an excess of alcohol, food, women, and music, while it lasted.

Waller began playing piano when he was six. Because his father was a Baptist minister who did not appreciate his son's interest in popular music, the young Fats moved out when he was 14, shortly after his mother's death. He lived near the James P. Johnson family; Johnson became Waller's mentor and inspiration. Fats dropped out of school in 1918, gigged around New York, and recorded his first piano solos in 1922; he also recorded many piano rolls and accompanied a variety of blues singers on records. As resident organist at the Lincoln Theatre, Waller had an opportunity to work on his pipe organ technique

Whether as pianist, singer, composer, organist, or humorous personality,
Fats Waller ranked at the top of his field.

(he would record a series of swinging organ solos in the 1920s) and to accompany other performers. He played for silent movies, worked with James P. Johnson in the "Keep Shufflin'" revue in 1928, and wrote songs with lyricist Andy Razaf. Waller recorded now and then as a leader in the 1920s and as a guest with Fletcher Henderson, McKinney's Cotton Pickers, and even Ted Lewis. He wrote the music for three shows (*Keep Shufflin'*, *Load of Coal*, and *Hot Chocolates*) and worked steadily during the early years of the Depression. Strangely enough, Waller cut only one vocal in the 1920s. That would soon change.

Fats Waller can be heard on two solo numbers as a pianist-vocalist in 1931. Three years later he began an extensive series of recordings for the Victor label that would continue through 1942 and that were known as "Fats Waller and his Rhythm." Using a two-horn sextet that often featured trumpeter Herman Autrey, Gene Sedric on tenor and clarinet, and guitarist Al Casey, Waller recorded both treasures and trash. The latter tunes, which he was often persuaded to record, found him satirizing and making fun of the lyrics in usually inspired and often-hilarious fashion. Virtually every one of these performances had a hot piano solo along with the general merriment. "Your Feet's Too Big," "The Joint Is Jumpin'," and the touching "I'm Gonna Sit Right Down and Write Myself a Letter" (which Waller did not compose) were hits, and his series of records were quite popular, making Fats a star.

Fats Waller also had occasional tours leading a big band, visited Europe in 1938, appeared in three movies (most notably

Stormy Weather), and in 1942 composed the first jazz waltz, "Jitterbug Waltz." In 1943 he wrote the music for the show *Early to Bed*. But on a cross-country train trip on his way back to New York, he died of pneumonia at the age of 39, passing away at the height of his fame.

●

8 *Piano Masterworks, Vol. 1 / Oct. 21, 1922–Sept. 24, 1929 / Hot 'N' Sweet 5106*

9 *Turn on the Heat: The Fats Waller Piano Solos / Feb. 16, 1927–May 13, 1941 / Bluebird 2482*

10 *Fats and His Buddies / May 20, 1927–Dec. 18, 1929 / Bluebird 61005*

All of Fats Waller's piano solos from the 1920s (except for two from December 4, 1929) are on *Piano Masterworks,* including such tunes as the original version of "Ain't Misbehavin'," "Valentine Stomp," and "Waiting at the End of the Road." The double-CD *Turn on the Heat* duplicates the *Hot 'n' Sweet* set and has all of Waller's later solos too but leaves out "Muscle Shoals Blues" and "Birmingham Blues" from 1922 plus a third take of "I've Got a Feeling I'm Falling." Highlights of *Turn on the Heat* are a pair of piano duets with Benny Payne ("St. Louis Blues" and "After You've Gone") and such later performances as "Clothes Line Ballet," "Viper's Drag," "Carolina Shout," and "Honeysuckle Rose." *Fats and His Buddies* has the master takes of all of Waller's group sides of the 1920s, including "The Minor Drag," "Harlem Fuss," "Ridin' but Walkin'," and "Fats Waller Stomp." Most of the titles really romp, and Waller (heard on piano and pipe organ) sounds typically jubilant. Also on this CD are the four songs (plus two alternate takes) by the Louisiana Sugar Babes, an unusual quartet comprised of cornetist Jabbo Smith, Garvin Bushell on clarinet, alto, and bassoon, pianist James P. Johnson, and Waller on pipe organ.

9 *The Early Years, Part 1 / May 16, 1934–May 6, 1935 / Bluebird 66618*

9 *The Early Years, Part 2 / May 8, 1935–Feb. 1, 1936 / Bluebird 66640*

9 *The Early Years, Part 3 / Apr. 8, 1936–Nov. 29, 1936 / Bluebird 66747*

8 *Volume One—His Rhythm, His Piano / Mar. 11, 1935–Aug. 7, 1939 / Stash 528*

8 *Volume Two—Hallelujah / Mar. 11, 1935–Apr. 3, 1939 / Stash 539*

With the exception of a few master takes from the period of *The Last Years,* every one of Fats Waller's Rhythm sides from 1934–42 have been reissued by Bluebird. Not every selection is a classic, but the hits far outnumber the misses, and even the weakest performances feature a bit of Fats's classic stride piano. Each of the three *Early Years* reissues is a two-CD set. *Part 1* is highlighted by "A Porter's Love Song to a Chambermaid," "Serenade for a Wealthy Widow," "How Can You Face Me?," "Believe It Beloved," "Whose Honey Are You?," "Oh Susannah Dust Off That Old Pianna," and "You've Been Taking Lessons in Love." *Part 2* has "I'm Gonna Sit Right Down and Write Myself a Letter," "Dinah," "Somebody Stole My Gal," "Got a Bran' New Suit," and "I've Got My Fingers Crossed" among the better numbers, while *Part 3* includes "Christopher Columbus," "Black Raspberry Jam," "Lounging at the Waldorf," "Floatin' Down to Cotton Town," and "Swingin' Them Jingle Bells." The two Stash CDs are radio transcription dates that do not duplicate the Bluebird selections. *Volume One* has seven songs from 1935 (two of which are duets with the reeds of Rudy Powell) and 23 selections from 1939; most of the latter are with his Rhythm. *Volume Two* contains 24 more selections from the marathon 1935 date (all by Fats himself, as a solo pianist who backs his own vocals) plus cuts from broadcasts in 1936 and 1939 and two unissued tunes from a 1939 record date in London.

9 *The Middle Years, Part 1 / Dec. 24, 1936–Apr. 12, 1938 / Bluebird 66083*

9 *The Middle Years, Part 2 / Apr. 12, 1938–Jan. 12, 1940 / Bluebird 66552*

8 *The Jugglin' Jive of Fats Waller / July 16, 1938–Oct. 18, 1938 / Sandy Hook 2097*

The two *Middle Years* releases are both three-CD sets. During this period, the quality of the songs given Fats Waller to perform was dropping, but in most cases he was able to make the results listenable and even hard-swinging. *Part 1* has a big band date and such notable numbers as "I'm Sorry I Made You Cry," "Honeysuckle Rose," "Blue, Turning Grey Over You," the original version of "The Joint Is Jumpin'," "Beat It Out," "She's Tall, She's Tan, She's Terrific," and "Every Day's a Holiday." *Part 2* is highlighted by "Two Sleepy People," "Yacht Club Swing," "I'll Dance at Your Wedding," an absolutely crazy rendition of "Hold Tight," "Honey Hush," and "Your Feet's Too Big." *The Jugglin' Jive* consists of three radio broadcasts by Waller and his Rhythm (with Gene Sedric on tenor and clarinet and trumpeter Herman Aurey) from the Yacht Club and (in one case) NBC Studios. Waller performs some numbers that he never got around to recording, along with a few favorites, and sounds typically infectious, giving one an idea what it must have been like to see him live. *The Last Years,* a three-CD set, has Waller's final studio recordings, which range from classic ("Fats Waller's Original E Flat Blues," "Rump Steak Serenade," "The Jitterbug Waltz," and "Ain't Misbehavin'") to songs that must have given even him difficulty: "Little Curly Hair in a High Chair," "You're a Square from Dela-ware," "You Run Your Mouth, I'll Run My Business," "My Mommie Sent Me to the Store," "Hey! Stop Kissin' My Sister," "I'm Gonna Salt Away Some Sugar," "Abercrombie Had a Zombie," and "Come Down to Earth, My Angel!" The only fault to this otherwise-admirable series is that on *The Last Years,* ten alternate takes have been substituted for the originally issued versions, and the latter have not yet been put out. But true Fats Waller fans will acquire all of these sets. Pure joy.

LPS TO SEARCH FOR

The two-LP set *Fats Waller in London* (DRG Swing 8442/3), in addition to his two 1922 piano solos, features Waller in England in 1938 with a local octet and playing solo piano and organ, accompanying Adelaide Hall on two numbers, and performing his impressionistic six-part "London Suite." None of this music is included on the Bluebird CDs.

FILMS

Fats Waller made Soundies in 1941 of several of his hits (including "Your Feet's Too Big," "The Joint Is Jumpin'," "Ain't Misbehavin'," and "Honeysuckle Rose"). He also had notable appearances in three full-length movies, stealing the show in *Hooray for Love* (1935), *King of Burlesque* (1935), and, most memorably, *Stormy Weather* (1943).

MARY LOU WILLIAMS
b. May 8, 1910, Atlanta, GA, d. May 28, 1981, Durham, NC

Mary Lou Williams was a jazz giant who, like Coleman Hawkins, stayed modern throughout her long career. Her work during the Swing years was only a portion of her life, although she did make a strong impact during the big band era. Born Mary Lou Scruggs, she grew up in Pittsburgh and was playing piano in public at an early age. After high school, the young pianist accompanied shows, including playing with Buzzin' Harris as part of John Williams's Syncopators. After the show closed, the band was renamed the Synco Jazzers, and Mary Lou Williams married the leader, a baritone saxophonist. They played in Memphis and Oklahoma City (1927–28) until John Williams joined Terence Holder's Clouds of Joy. By 1929 Andy Kirk was leading the band and Mary Lou Williams was contributing arrangements and appearing on the orchestra's recordings, although she was not actually an official member until 1931. A superb stride pianist who was the top soloist in the band, Williams (through her playing and writing) was largely responsible for the Kirk Orchestra's having its own musical personality. She also contributed arrangements to other big bands, including those of Benny Goodman, Earl Hines, Tommy Dorsey, and Louis Armstrong. She was saluted in Kirk's recording of "The Lady Who Swings the Band." Among her compositions are "Roll 'Em" and "What's Your Story, Morning Glory."

Having divorced John Williams, in 1942 she married trumpeter Harold "Shorty" Baker (who was in Andy Kirk's orchestra at the time). When Baker joined Duke Ellington, Williams left Kirk and had her own sextet, for a time traveling with Ellington as one of his staff arrangers; "Trumpets No End" (a transformation of "Blue Skies") was her most memorable chart for Duke. Williams went out of her way to encourage the young bebop musicians, wrote the bebop fable "In the Land of Oo-Bla-Dee" for Dizzy Gillespie, and during the second half of the 1940s gradually modernized her playing. Williams wrote the extended work "The Zodiac Suite," was with Benny Goodman's 1948 bebop combo, led her own trios in the early 1950s, spent time in Europe, and then retired from music for three years to concentrate on religious studies. From the late 1950s on, Mary Lou Williams was active as a performer and teacher (at Duke University), often presenting "history of jazz" solo recitals since she was one of the few pianists who could play in virtually every style. She sounded remarkably modern in the 1960s and '70s and yet was able, at a moment's notice, to go back and play in her vintage stride style.

●

10 *1927–1940 / Jan. 1927–Nov. 18, 1940 / Classics 630*

7 *Zodiac Suite / June 29, 1945 / Smithsonian 40810*

7 *Town Hall: The Zodiac Suite / Dec. 31, 1945 / Vintage Jazz Classics 1035*

1927–1940 has all of Mary Lou Williams's dates as a leader prior to 1944. She is heard on three piano solos ("Night Life," "Drag 'Em," and "Little Joe from Chicago") that show off her impressive stride technique, on ten trio/quartet numbers, and heading two combos (one called "Six Men and a Girl") that costar the short-lived tenor Dick Wilson. In addition, this CD has her first six recordings, cut with John Williams's Synco Jazzers in 1927. In 1945 Mary Lou Williams (who at that point was playing in an advanced Swing style) composed the "Zodiac Suite," a dozen moody and often-introspective but sometimes playful selections, each named after a sign of the zodiac. Her studio recording (which sometimes uses bassist Al Lucas and drummer Jack Parker) is reissued on the Smithsonian CD along with five new alternate takes. Williams also performed the suite at Town Hall on New Year's Eve with a big band, symphonic orchestra, and guest tenor Ben Webster. The program, along with a medley of her compositions and versions of "Lonely Moments," "Roll 'Em," and an extended "Gjon Mill Jam Session," was released for the first time on the 1991 Vintage Jazz Classics CD. Some of the music sounds a little underrehearsed, but it is enjoyable to hear Williams's rarely performed "Zodiac Suite" interpreted by a full orchestra.

9 *Nite Life / May 1971–Oct. 22, 1971 / Chiaroscuro 103*

7 *Zoning / 1974 / Smithsonian 40811*

8 *Live at the Cookery / Nov. 1975 / Chiaroscuro 146*

8 *Solo Recital/Montreux Jazz Festival 1978 / July 16, 1978 / Original Jazz Classics 962*

After being largely off records in the 1960s, Mary Lou Williams became more active during the '70s. The double-CD *Nite Life* reissues the earlier LP *From the Heart* and adds 13 additional selections. The solo set is more Swing-oriented than some of her other sessions from the period, and includes such numbers as "Little Joe from Chicago," "What's Your Story Morning Glory," "For the Figs," a three-part "Nite Life Variations," and music from a ragtime concert. Williams's improvised versions of three Scott Joplin tunes received a lot of comment at the time (some not that favorable), but they sound fresh today. This twofer concludes with a 32-minute "Jazzspeak," which finds Mary Lou Williams reminiscing about her life. *Zoning* is pretty adventurous. Williams is heard on various tracks with fellow pianist Zita Carno, Bob Cranshaw and Milton Suggs on bass, drummer Mickey Roker, and Tony Waters on conga. Some of the music is quite avant-garde in spots, which is remarkable for a veteran of the 1920s to be playing, much less composing! *Both Live at the Cookery* (duets with bassist Brian Torff) and *Solo Recital* are typical of the history of jazz programs that Mary Lou Williams performed in her later years. In both cases she progresses from spirituals and stride to Swing, bop, and a little more modern, although in these cases she does not progress much beyond the late 1950s. Both are excellent examples of her later work, with *Solo Recital* being Williams's final recording.

LPS TO SEARCH FOR

Roll 'Em (Audiophile 8) has Mary Lou Williams's radio transcription date of March 7, 1944, a trio session with Al Lucas and Jack "the Bear" Parker, ten selections in all, with many alternate takes and false starts. *The Asch Recordings 1944-47* (Folkways 2966) is a superb two-LP box set of Williams's mid-1940s recordings that deserves to be reissued in full; she is heard in many different settings ranging from solo to leading a big band. *First Lady of the Piano* (Inner City 7006) reissues 1953 quartet numbers originally cut for the Vogue label that find Williams sounding like a bebop pianist. The interesting *My Mama Pinned a Rose on Me* (Pablo 2310 819) has her playing 16 different types of blues (15 are originals) in 1977 with the assistance of bassist Butch Williams and occasional vocals by Cynthia Tyson.

FILMS

Mary Lou Williams is seen with the Slam Stewart Trio in *Boy! What a Girl* (1947).

TEDDY WILSON

b. Nov. 24, 1912, Austin, TX, d. July 31, 1986, New Britain, CT

The perfect Swing pianist, Teddy Wilson had a light and flawless but often hard-swinging stride style that gave one the impression that he never made a mistake or played a distasteful note. Wilson originally studied violin, E-flat clarinet, and oboe before settling on piano. He started working professionally in 1929, toured with Speed Webb's territory band (1929-31), settled in Chicago, and gigged with Erskine Tate, Eddie Mallory, and other local bandleaders. Wilson recorded with Louis Armstrong's big band in 1933 and also worked with Jimmie Noone and Benny Carter that year. After playing with Willie Bryant (1934-35), Wilson began to record as a leader with all-star Swing groups (a series that continued until 1942), often using Billie Holiday as his vocalist. The pianist, who had recorded with Benny Goodman in 1934, became a member of the Benny Goodman Trio (which also included Gene Krupa), first on records in mid-1935 and then officially in early 1936. Although he was never part of the Benny Goodman big band and was thought of as an "added attraction" (along with Lionel Hampton, who made the trio a quartet), Teddy Wilson broke down many racial boundaries. His distinguished nature and soft-spoken manner were major assets.

After leaving Benny Goodman in April 1939, Wilson formed his own big band, but the orchestra lasted only a year despite some fine records. By June 1940, the pianist was leading a sextet that lasted until November 1944. He was back with Goodman on and off during 1944-46, worked on CBS radio, became a jazz teacher, occasionally had reunions with BG, and performed with trios during the 1950s, '60s, '70s, and early '80s. Teddy Wilson's style was virtually unchanged after 1935, and his repertoire always consisted of vintage Swing standards. Yet, despite predictability, most of the time he was able to play quite enthusiastically in his timeless and definitive Swing style.

●

8 *1934-1935 / May 22, 1934-Nov. 22, 1935 / Classics 508*

8 *1935-1936 / Dec. 3, 1935-Aug. 24, 1936 / Classics 511*

8 *1936-1937 / Aug. 24, 1936-Mar. 31, 1937 / Classics 521*

8 *1937 / Mar. 31, 1937-Aug. 29, 1937 / Classics 531*

8 *1937-1938 / Sept. 5, 1937-Apr. 28, 1938 / Classics 548*

8 *1938 / Apr. 28, 1938-Nov. 28, 1938 / Classics 556*

The Classics series has reissued all of the master takes of Teddy Wilson's studio recordings of 1934-46. There are two problems with this program: the absence of alternates and the inclusion of the Billie Holiday recordings where Wilson is the leader. The latter have been reissued in many other formats, too (including under Lady Day's name), so the duplications lower the value of some of the Classics, but one will have to reacquire those performances if they wish to get Wilson's instrumentals, piano solos, and work behind other singers. *1934-1935* begins with four early piano solos from 1934 that were not released until the LP era despite their quality. Wilson is also heard on six other fine solos and accompanying Billie Holiday on 11 songs, including "I Wished on the Moon," "What a Little Moonlight Can Do,"

Benny Goodman and Teddy Wilson made a perfect musical pair: flawless, technically brilliant, introverted, distinguished, unchanging in their styles, and hard swinging.

classic Billie on "My Man," "When You're Smiling" (which has a famous Lester Young solo), "I Can't Believe That You're in Love with Me," and "If Dreams Come True." One date features the quartet of Harry James, Red Norvo, bassist John Simmons, and Wilson playing "Ain't Misbehavin'," "Honeysuckle Rose," and the two-part "Just a Mood." In addition, there are a couple of piano solos and two vocals by Sarah Gooding and Nan Wynn. *1938* contains more piano solos, vocals by Nan Wynn, and two dates that showcase Holiday. Overall, all of this music is highly recommended but not necessarily in this form.

8   *Teddy Wilson, His Piano & His Orchestra / Aug. 11, 1938–Aug. 10, 1939 / Jazz Unlimited 2068*

7   *Solo Piano, 1939–1940 / 1939–1940 / Storyville 8258*

8   *1939 / Jan. 27, 1939–Sept. 12, 1939 / Classics 571*

9   *Jumpin' For Joy / June 28, 1939–Dec. 9, 1940 / Hep 1064*

8   *1939–1941 / Dec. 11, 1939–Sept. 16, 1941 / Classics 620*

8   *1942–1945 / Jan. 21, 1942–Nov. 5, 1945 / Classics 908*

9   *Associated Transcriptions, 1944 / June 15, 1944 / Storyville 8236*

8   *Central Avenue Blues / Aug. 13, 1943–Nov. 1944 / Vintage Jazz Classics 1013*

8   *1946 / May 1, 1946–Nov. 19, 1946 / Classics 997*

The year 1939 was a big one for Teddy Wilson, who left Benny Goodman's orchestra, formed his own big band (which lasted a year), and continued recording extensively. The music on the Jazz Unlimited CD consists of ten piano solos from 1938–39 (including "My Blue Heaven," "Tiger Rag," and "China Boy") plus a radio transcription date by Wilson's big band. Wilson and tenor-saxophonist Ben Webster are the main soloists with the orchestra and its 11 selections add to the legacy of this short-lived band. The 26 concise (and previously unknown) piano solos that are on *Solo Piano* were not released at all until 1997 and were originally cut as radio transcriptions. Particularly interesting is that a dozen of the songs are obscure Wilson originals. *1939* has some more high-quality piano solos, Billie Holiday's last date under the pianist's leadership (including a classic version of "Sugar" with Roy Eldridge and Benny Carter), and

and "Twenty-Four Hours a Day." *1935–1936,* in addition to Holiday's vocals and a couple piano solos, has instrumental versions of "Warmin' Up" and "Blues in C Sharp Minor" (with Roy Eldridge) and two vocals by Ella Fitzgerald. *1936–1937* features vocals by Helen Ward, Red Harper, and Midge Williams but is highlighted by the first Billie Holiday meeting on record with Lester Young and Buck Clayton (including "This Year's Kisses" and "I Must Have That Man"). The year 1937 was a busy one for both Wilson and Holiday. The CD *1937* finds Lady Day sounding at her best on "I'll Get By," "Mean to Me," "Foolin' Myself," and "Easy Living." Helen Ward, Boots Castle, and Frances Hunt also take vocals, while the instrumentals include "I'm Coming Virginia" and "I've Found a New Baby." *1937–1938* has some the first 12 recordings by the Teddy Wilson Big Band. The orchestra includes such players as Shorty Baker, Ben Webster, and Al Casey along with singers Thelma Carpenter and Jean Eldridge. *Jumpin' For Joy* duplicates music that is covered by Classics, containing all 20 studio recordings by the Teddy Wilson Big Band, plus an octet date that features trumpeter Bill Coleman and has vocals by Helen Ward. *1939–1941* has the big band's final eight songs before its breakup, some piano trios, and two combo dates by Wilson, with singing by Helen Ward and Lena Horne. *1942–1945* is taken up mostly by Wilson's Musicraft recordings of 1945, including a sextet with Charlie Shavers and Red Norvo and one with Buck Clayton and Ben Webster, plus more piano solos. *Associated Transcriptions* features Wilson's 1944 band, a group featuring trumpeter Emmett Berry, Benny Morton, Edmond Hall, Slam Stewart, and Big Sid Catlett. They stretch out (quite often close to five minutes) on a dozen standards and three of Wilson's originals; high-quality small-group Swing. Teddy Wilson's V-Disc sessions are on *Central Avenue Blues*. Most of the cuts are brief (under three minutes apiece) but spirited performances by his Shavers-Norvo sextet; there are also five other selections with larger groups. *1946* has more of Wilson's Musicraft recordings, including solos, trios, a quartet with Buck Clayton, and three early vocals by Sarah Vaughan.

6 *The Complete Verve Recordings of the Teddy Wilson Trio* / Dec. 16, 1952–Aug. 22, 1957 / Mosaic 5-173

7 *Air Mail Special* / June 18, 1967 / Black Lion 760115

7 *Stomping at the Savoy* / June 18, 1967 / Black Lion 760152

6 *Teddy Wilson Meets Eiji Kitamura* / Oct. 1970 / Storyville 4152

8 *With Billie in Mind* / May 1972 / Chiaroscuro 111

5 *Teddy Wilson and His All Stars* / June 23–24, 1976 / Chiaroscuro 150

6 *Cole Porter Classics* / Nov. 3, 1977 / Black Lion 760166

7 *Alone* / May 30, 1983 / Storyville 8211

Teddy Wilson's work from his last 35 years tended to be very predictable. His style did not evolve and, although he often played with spirit, one did not look for Wilson to come up with any real surprises. The five-CD Mosaic box sticks to

Swing standards and ranges from a little inspired to a bit dull. Someone should have recorded Wilson with a much larger group and more challenging material to see what would happen. *Air Mail Special* and *Stomping at the Savoy* find him playing as part of a fine British Swing quintet that includes clarinetist Dave Shepherd and vibraphonist Ronnie Gleaves; nearly all of the music is from the Benny Goodman songbook. *Teddy Wilson Meets Eiji Kitamura* was recorded in Tokyo with Japanese musicians but with the same instrumentation as on *Air Mail Special*. Clarinetist Kitamura mixes Goodman with Buddy DeFranco and is swinging if derivative. *With Billie in Mind*, a solo set from 1972, finds Wilson more inspired as he performs 20 songs that he had recorded with Billie Holiday in the 1930s. *Teddy Wilson and His All Stars* should have worked better than it did. On what would be his last band recording, Wilson is joined by Harry "Sweets" Edison, Vic Dickenson, Bob Wilber on clarinet and soprano, bassist Major Holley, and drummer Oliver Jackson. The problem is that Wilber's arrangements are often more dance band–oriented than hot, swinging jazz, and many of the songs clock in at barely three minutes apiece, a bit of a disappointment considering the project's potential. *Cole Porter Classics* is a good solo set featuring Wilson playing 11 familiar Cole Porter songs. His final recording was *Alone*, which was recorded live in Denmark. Most interesting about this run-through of familiar material is that the pianist talks to the audience between songs and the crowd seems very appreciative of his presence, knowing that Teddy Wilson was one of the Classic Swing greats.

LPS TO SEARCH FOR

Listeners not wanting to duplicate the Teddy Wilson/Billie Holiday recordings will want to track down the two-LP *Teddy Wilson and His All-Stars* (Columbia 31617). Included are 32 of Wilson's recordings from 1936–40, primarily instrumentals with plenty of solo space for such Swing all-stars as Chu Berry, Buck Clayton, Roy Eldridge, Benny Goodman, Johnny Hodges, Harry James, Jonah Jones, Ben Webster, and Lester Young, among many others.

FILMS

Teddy Wilson performs with the Benny Goodman Quartet on a hot number in *Hollywood Hotel* (1937), is featured in *Boogie Woogie Dream* (1941) and *Something to Shout About* (1943) with his own combos, and has a role in *The Benny Goodman Story* (1955).

BOB ZURKE

b. Jan. 17, 1912, Detroit, MI, d. Feb. 16, 1944, Los Angeles, CA

A talented stride pianist, Bob Zurke would be much more famous today were it not for his early death. A child prodigy, Zurke performed and recorded with Oliver Naylor's orchestra when he was just 13. He gained further experience playing and recording with Thelma Terry's Playboys (1928) and gigging around Detroit. When Joe Sullivan was stricken with tuberculosis, Zurke became his replacement with Bob Crosby's orchestra, staying for 2 1/2 years (1937–39) and having a hit recording with Sullivan's "Little Rock Getaway." Zurke led an artistically successful big band (1939–40) that was unfortunately a commercial flop. Bob Zurke worked mostly as a solo pianist from then on, including in Chicago, Detroit, and Los Angeles, where he died suddenly from a heart attack at the Hangover Club at the age of 32.

●

LPS TO SEARCH FOR

Bob Zurke recorded 30 selections with his big band during 1939–40 and four piano solos in 1943. Sixteen of the big band titles (four of which are alternate takes) were put out on the very obscure collector's LP *Bob Zurke and His Delta Rhythm Band* (Meritt 16).

Guitarists

No instrument developed more during the Swing era than the guitar. In the 1920s, the acoustic guitar was actually overshadowed by the banjo because the latter instrument was louder and its clanging could be picked up more easily by the primitive recording equipment of the era. By the late 1920s, due to the improvement in recording techniques, the more subtle guitar was gradually taking over the role of the less flexible banjo, although it could still be difficult to hear in ensembles. Only the very best jazz guitarists did more during this period than simply keep time and state simple chords.

The first great jazz guitarist was Eddie Lang, whose sophisticated chord voicings and ability to play single-note lines during solos put him far ahead of his field by 1926–27. Lang still had the difficulty of being heard, and the amount of solo space he was given (other than on his own solo records) tended to be limited. Even when he teamed up with violinist Joe Venuti in duets, Venuti was the lead voice throughout. Lang, who was part of the Paul Whiteman Orchestra and was in great demand for studio and jazz dates, was Bing Crosby's accompanist in the early 1930s before dying from a botched tonsillectomy in 1933 when he was only 30. Lonnie Johnson was Lang's equivalent in the blues world, although he also showed, in recordings with Louis Armstrong, Duke Ellington, and other jazz all-stars in the late 1920s, that he could have been a jazz master had he chosen that career. The Lang–Johnson duets are justly renowned.

During the late 1920s/early '30s, guitarists Carl Kress and Dick McDonough, inspired by Lang, became major studio guitarists, too. Both tended to emphasize chords during their solos, as did George Van Eps, who soon followed them. Teddy Bunn, in contrast, played bluesy single-note lines that worked well with small groups. Overseas, Django Reinhardt emerged as the second great jazz guitarist. A powerful soloist who built up a tremendous rhythmic drive, had a gypsy tinge to his playing, and could play chorus after chorus with the facility of a saxophonist, Reinhardt had no real competition during 1934–38. Although he played fairly loud, Django would have had the same difficulty suffered by all the other guitarists of the time: being heard! But he short-circuited the problem by being showcased with an all-string group consisting of violinist Stephane Grappelli, two rhythm guitars, and a bass. Oscar Aleman from Argentina emerged in Europe shortly after Django, playing in a very similar style.

Nearly every big band of the Swing era included a guitar, but very few (other than Benny Goodman's when Charlie Christian was there, the short-lived Bus Etri with Charlie Barnet, and of course Alvino Rey's) gave any significant solo space to their guitarist. Freddie Green, who played acoustic rhythm guitar with Count Basie for decades, perfectly illustrated the typical role of the guitar as part of a Swing band, playing four chords to the bar and working in close conjunction with the bass without ever taking solos.

However, the biggest influence on guitarists of the 1940s and beyond was Charlie Christian. Eddie Durham had recorded on electric guitar in 1938 and Les Paul had experimented with amplifying his instrument several years earlier. But Christian's swinging statements on electric guitar, which were full of phrases that would be used by nearly all jazz guitarists for the next 30 years, were on the level of a Lester Young. The way he played guitar made his instrument's unlimited potential as a lead voice seem obvious, and it greatly helped that now the instrument could finally be heard! Other guitarists learned quickly, and quite soon Al Casey, Tiny Grimes, Oscar Moore, and Slim Gaillard were using Christian's phrases as a basis for their own styles in small groups. In fact, it could safely be argued that jazz guitar did not develop much beyond Charlie Christian until the rise of fusion, 30 years after Christian first appeared on the scene.

OSCAR ALEMAN
b. Feb. 20, 1909, Resistencia, Argentina, d. Oct. 14, 1980, Buenos Aires, Argentina

Oscar Aleman fits into an odd place in jazz history. A year older than Django Reinhardt, Aleman by 1934 sounded just like Django, making one wonder who influenced whom first. Aleman began playing guitar while in his native Argentina and moved to Spain in the late 1920s and Paris in 1931 (where for a short time he accompanied Josephine Baker). Aleman was with Freddy Taylor's Swing Men from Harlem during 1933–35, recorded with Bill Coleman and Danny Polo, and led eight numbers at his own record sessions during 1938–39. Unfortunately, in 1941, when Aleman chose to leave Europe due to the war, he went back home to Argentina instead of moving to the United States. He would be quite active (recording until 1974) and retaining his Swing style, but Oscar Aleman was little heard of outside of his country (apparently never visiting the U.S.) and therefore ending up quite underrated in jazz history books despite his great talent.

●

10 *Swing Guitar Masterpieces / Dec. 5, 1938–June 27, 1954 / Acoustic Disc 29*
This is a perfectly planned two-CD set that has most of the high points of Oscar Aleman's recording career. Aleman's eight recordings from Copenhagen and Paris are here along with 44 other selections recorded in Argentina during 1941– 54. Most of the latter (which often feature the acoustic guitarist with violin, piano, rhythm guitar, bass, and drums) have never been made available in the United States. Aleman's style was virtually unchanged through the years, and he was a major Swing stylist throughout the 1950s, even if no one in the U.S. knew who he was!

TEDDY BUNN
b. 1909, Freeport, NY, d. July 20, 1978, Lancaster, CA

Teddy Bunn was one of the better guitar soloists of the early 1930s, and he excelled in playing with small, informal groups. Bunn started playing professionally in the late 1920s, recording with Duke Ellington in 1929. He was part of the Washboard Serenaders (with whom he recorded) and was a key member of The Spirits of Rhythm, a notable band featuring three singers (including Leo Watson) doubling on tiples (types of ukuleles) plus a drummer and sometimes a bassist. The Spirits recorded during 1933–34. Bunn was with the group (which was the antithesis of the typical Swing big band) into 1937 and made many freelance recordings, including with clarinetists Jimmie Noone, Johnny Dodds and Mezz Mezzrow, cornetist Tommy Ladnier, Sidney Bechet, blues singer Trixie Smith, J. C. Higginbotham, and Lionel Hampton, among others. In 1940 he recorded four unaccompanied solos (his only date as a leader). That year, Bunn switched to electric guitar. During the 1940s he was in several reunion versions of The Spirits (recording two more titles in 1941). Strangely enough, although he stayed generally in prime form, Teddy Bunn was in obscurity during his last 35 years. He spent a lot of time on the West Coast, worked with Edgar Hayes, Hadda Brooks, Jack McVea, and Louis Jordan (1959), and was also involved in some rock and roll revues in the late 1950s. Teddy Bunn was active until the late 1960s but was hardly on records at all after 1941.

●

9 *Teddy Bunn / Sept. 16, 1929–Mar. 28, 1940 / RST 1509*
Teddy Bunn recorded frequently as a sideman in the 1930s but much less so as a leader. His eight hokum vocal selections with Spencer Williams from 1930 are here (the good-time singers are backed by Clarence Profit or James P. Johnson on piano and Bunn's guitar), as is all the music (four songs plus an alternate take) from his 1940 set of guitar solos. In addition, Bunn is heard backing singers Buck Franklin, Fat Hayden, and Walter Pichon, plus jamming with Mezz Mezzrow and Tommy Ladnier in 1938. This is definitely the most significant Teddy Bunn CD, by default.

AL CASEY
b. Sept. 15, 1915, Louisville, KY

Best known for his association with Fats Waller, Al Casey has actually had a very long career, surviving his former boss by over 55 years. Casey started on violin but, after moving to New York in 1930, he switched to guitar. His first professional job was with Waller in 1934 and, other than playing with Teddy Wilson's Big Band during 1939–40 and a few short engagements, he worked with Fats until 1942, appearing on over 200 records with Fats Waller's Rhythm. While Casey played acoustic guitar with Fats, he switched to electric guitar shortly after the group broke up, leading his own trio and being rated as one of the best jazz guitarists after the death of Charlie Christian (his main influence by the 1940s). Casey worked with Clarence Profit (1944) and Billy Kyle (1949), freelanced during the 1950s, and was for quite a few years a member of King Curtis's R&B group. The guitarist visited Europe several times during his career, recorded in the 1970s with Helen Humes and Jay McShann, and worked in the 1980s with the Harlem Blues and Jazz Band. Although never generating headlines, he was an asset to every mainstream group that he performed with. Al Casey, who recorded as a leader as late as 1994, was still quite active as the 20th century was ending.

●

8 *Buck Jumpin' / Mar. 7, 1960 / Original Jazz Classics 675*

7 *A Tribute to "Fats" / May 22, 1994 / Jazzpoint 1044*
Al Casey had only very infrequent opportunities to record as a leader. In fact *Buck Jumpin'* (which was originally recorded for Swingville) was (other than for two songs in 1945), his debut. The CD reissue, which adds two additional selections to the original program, features a quintet (with Rudy Powell on alto and clarinet, pianist Herman Foster, bassist Jimmy Lewis, and drummer Belton Evans) performing Fats Waller material, plus three originals by the leader. Casey, who switched back to acoustic guitar for this date, is heard in superior form, knowing that this was an important opportunity to make a statement for posterity. Highlights include "Buck Jumpin'," "Rosetta," "Honeysuckle Rose," and "I'm Gonna Sit Right Down and Write Myself a Letter." "Honeysuckle Rose" is also on *A Tribute to Fats*, recorded 34 years later, when Al Casey was 78. Joined by 82-year-old pianist Red Richards, bassist Jan Jankelje, and drummer Imre Koszegi in Holland, Casey is heard performing four group originals plus seven standards, only two of which were actually associated with Waller. A solid Swing date.

CHARLIE CHRISTIAN

b. July 29, 1916, Dallas, TX, d. Mar. 2, 1942, New York, NY

One of the most important guitarists of all time, Charlie Christian was the first master of the electric guitar and a direct major influence on virtually every jazz guitarist to come up during the following 30 years. His career and life were tragically short, but he accomplished a great deal in the short time that he had.

Christian grew up in Oklahoma City. After a brief period on trumpet and piano, he switched to guitar when he was 12, playing in a family band (four of his brothers were musicians, as was his father), and freelancing locally, including with Anna Mae Winburn and Alphonso Trent. As with other acoustic guitarists, he had to constantly work hard at simply being heard. In 1937 Christian bought a new electric guitar, and that problem was quickly solved. Influenced by Lester Young and other Swing-era horn players, Christian had the ability to play riff-filled solos that never seemed to run out of catchy ideas, which was noticed by musicians passing through town, including Mary Lou Williams and Teddy Wilson. In 1939 he worked with Leslie Sheffield's group and was heard by John Hammond, who in August arranged for him to come to Los Angeles to have a tryout with Benny Goodman. BG was initially put off by Christian's flashy clothes and was reluctant to give him an audition, but, with Hammond's urging, Goodman finally called out "Rose Room." Forty-five minutes later Goodman and Christian were still playing the song, and the guitarist had become part of the clarinetist's sextet.

Charlie Christian was considered a sensation. He performed and recorded frequently with the Benny Goodman Sextet (next to Lionel Hampton, Count Basie, Georgie Auld, and Cootie Williams), cut two numbers with the Goodman big band ("Honeysuckle Rose" and the classic "Solo Flight"), appeared with BG at the 1939 Spirituals to Swing concert (getting in to sit in with the Kansas City Six, which included Lester Young and Buck Clayton), and made some freelance recordings. His only competition among guitarists during 1939–41 was Django Reinhardt. By 1941 Christian was jamming after his regular engagement at Minton's Playhouse with Thelonious Monk and Dizzy Gillespie, sitting in so often that he was almost considered a member of the house band. He would surely have had a major part to play in the eventual rise of bebop.

But unfortunately it was not to be. In June 1941 he became ill and was diagnosed with tuberculosis. He spent his last eight months in a sanitarium before passing away at the age of 25. Charlie Christian would certainly be remembered, in the playing of such later guitarists as Barney Kessel, Wes Montgomery, Grant Green, and George Benson, but his premature passing was a major tragedy.

●

10 *The Genius of the Electric Guitar / Oct. 2, 1939–Mar. 13, 1941 / Columbia 40846*

10 *Benny Goodman Sextet, Featuring Charlie Christian / Oct. 2, 1939–Mar. 13, 1941 / Columbia 45144*

9 *Solo Flight / Aug. 19, 1939–June 1941 / Vintage Jazz Classics 1021*

Most of Charlie Christian's studio recordings with the Benny Goodman Sextet are on the two Columbia CDs. *The Genius of the Electric Guitar* has such classics as "Seven Come Eleven," "Wholly Cats," "Royal Garden Blues," "Breakfast Feud," and "Air Mail Special," plus his feature with Goodman's orchestra, "Solo Flight." In addition there are very interesting excerpts from a practice session that were cut one day when Goodman showed up late: "Blues in B" and "Waitin' for Benny." Among the other sidemen on various tracks are Lionel Hampton, Count Basie, Johnny Guarnieri, Georgie Auld, and Cootie Williams. Drawn from the same sessions, *Benny Goodman Sextet* (which was released under the clarinetist's name and is of equally high quality) is highlighted by the original version of "Flying Home," "Stardust," "Gilly," "On the Alamo," and "A Smo-o-o-oth One." *Solo Flight* takes its 24 selections from some of the best live performances (mostly played on radio) by Goodman's Sextet, plus some real rarities. The opening version of "Flying Home" predates any of the group's studio dates, and there is an alternate big band version of "Solo Flight." Special high points are five numbers from an all-star group consisting of Goodman, Buck Clayton, Lester Young, Count Basie, Christian, Freddie Green, Walter Page, and Jo Jones!

Probably impossible to find, *Charlie Christian/Lester Young Together 1940* (Jazz Archives 6) has the five mentioned numbers by Christian with Young, Goodman, Clayton, and Basie but also 11 other performances taken from the BG Sextet dates that are either rehearsal versions or otherwise-unissued alternate takes. Due to some legal difficulties, this album was withdrawn shortly after its release.

No film exists of Charlie Christian, but a fine half-hour documentary, *Solo Flight* (View Video 1353), does its best to piece together his story through interviews with his contemporaries and friends.

EDDIE DURHAM

b. Aug. 19, 1906, San Marcos, TX, d. Mar. 6, 1987, New York, NY

Eddie Durham was a multitalented individual who was quite valuable to Swing in several ways. Although he was often employed as a trombonist, Durham was also one of jazz's first electric guitarists (predating Charlie Christian on record by a year) and he was a significant arranger. But because he was a sideman rather than a leader, Durham's contributions have often been overlooked.

Early on he picked up experience playing with six musical siblings in the Durham Brothers Band. He worked with Walter Page's Blue Devils, Bennie Moten (during 1929–33, including making his recording debut), and other orchestras in the Midwest. Durham moved to New York in 1934, wrote some arrangements for Willie Bryant's big band, and played trombone with Jimmie Lunceford (1935–37) and Count Basie (1937–38). Durham contributed "Lunceford Special" to the Lunceford book and such classic charts for Basie as "Swinging the Blues," "Topsy," and "Jumpin' at the Woodside." On small-group dates with the Kansas City Five on March 18, 1938, and with the Kansas City Six on September 8 of that year, Durham played a few electric guitar solos that rank with the earliest in jazz, holding his own with Buck Clayton and (on the latter date) Lester Young.

However, after leaving Basie, Eddie Durham worked primarily as a freelance arranger and never became famous. He wrote charts for Artie Shaw and Glenn Miller, led a big band briefly in 1940, was the musical director for the International Sweethearts of Rhythm during 1941–43, later on led a different all-female group, and eventually gave up active playing altogether to work on his writing. Starting in the late 1960s Durham began playing trombone and guitar again on a part-time basis, and in later years he worked with Buddy Tate, the Countsmen, and the Harlem Blues and Jazz Band. As a leader Eddie Durham recorded four titles in 1940, an album for RCA in 1973–74, and a set for JSP in 1981.

FILMS

Eddie Durham makes an appearance in the documentary *Born to Swing* (1973).

SLIM GAILLARD

b. Jan. 1, 1916, Santa Clara, Cuba, d. Feb. 26, 1991, London, England

Bulee "Slim" Gaillard was a true eccentric, a talented musician who was much better known for his comedy routines and humorous jive talk than for his playing. As a child, Gaillard traveled with his father (a steward) on ocean liners and was once left on the island of Crete by accident for six months! He worked in the 1930s in vaudeville, having an act in which he played guitar and tap danced simultaneously. A decent guitarist and a basic pianist who also could play vibes and get acceptable tones on various horns, Slim Gaillard hit the big time in 1937 when he began teaming up with bassist Slam Stewart as Slim and Slam. Their recording of "Flat Foot Floogie" was a huge hit and kept the group (usually a quartet) working steadily until Slim went in the Army in 1943. Their other recordings included "Tutti Frutti," "Laughin' in Rhythm," "Buck Dance Rhythm," "Chicken Rhythm," and "Matzoh Balls." After his discharge from the military, Slim Gaillard teamed up with bassist Bam Brown, and his improvised singing and talking got even nuttier. Gaillard was a popular attraction in Los Angeles in the mid-1940s, and his renditions of his hits (including "Cement Mixer" and "Poppity Pop") and his long ad-lib routines kept audiences chuckling. His guitar playing by then was a simplified version of Charlie Christian's, and the great majority of his songs either were medium-tempo blues or used the chord changes of "Flying Home." Gaillard, who at the height of his fame used Charlie Parker and Dizzy Gillespie on one of his record dates, gradually found his popularity slipping as jive singers were running out of fresh ideas and were being labeled "dangerous" and "decadent" by the conservative media. After 1953 he had only two record dates and worked just part-time in music, acting now and then and running a motel in San Diego during part of the '60s. However, Slim Gaillard lived long enough to be rediscovered a few times along the way, "Flat Foot Floogie" was still famous, and in the 1980s Gaillard was considered a living legend.

●

10 *Complete Recordings 1938–1942 / Feb. 17, 1938–Apr. 4, 1942 / Affinity 1034-3*

6 *The Groove Juice Special / Jan. 19, 1938–Apr. 4, 1942 / Columbia/Legacy 64898*

All of the Slim & Slam performances are on *Complete Recordings*, including 19 alternate takes among the 82 selections. Starting with "Flat Foot Floogie" (their very first recording), the band was a hit. This three-CD set features the co-leaders as a duet and in trios, quartets, quintets, and sextets. Among the sidemen on some cuts are tenor saxophonist Kenneth Hollon, Al Killian, drummer Chico Hamilton, pianist Jimmy Rowles, and Ben Webster. For those listeners who want just a sampling of this unique group's music, *The Groove Juice Special* (a single CD) might suffice. But beware, eight of the 20 selections are alternate takes (including "Flat Foot Floogie") and the three numbers that have allegedly been previously unissued are all included in *Complete Recordings*. *The Groove Juice Special* gives one a taste, but it does not quite cut it as a "greatest hits" set.

9 *1945 / Sept. 1945–Dec. 1945 / Classics 864*

1945 has Slim Gaillard's first studio recordings after his release from the military. He is heard with a trio that also includes pianist Fletcher Smith and bassist Bam Brown, heading a ten-piece group with several notable horn players (including trumpeter Howard McGhee, Vic Dickenson, and three tenors: Lucky Thompson, Teddy Edwards, and Wild Bill Moore), and jamming with a quartet with Bam Brown, pianist Dodo Marmarosa, and drummer Zutty Sin-

gleton. There are many memorable and crazy selections on this CD, including "Voot Orenee," "Tutti Frutti," "Laguna," "Dunkin' Bagel," "Ya Ha Ha," and "Buck Dance Rhythm." A classic of its kind!

7 *In Birdland 1951 / Feb. 24, 1951–Sept. 29, 1951 / Hep 21*

8 *Laughing in Rhythm / Apr. 22, 1946–Dec. 1953 / Verve 314 521 651*

5 *Anytime, Anyplace, Anywhere! / Oct. 30, 1982 / Hep 2020*

Slim Gaillard's popularity peaked in the mid-1940s and went downhill soon afterward, but he never changed his unique way of improvising words and stories. On *In Birdland 1951*, Gaillard has a reunion with Slim Gaillard (on "Flat Foot Floogie" and "Cement Mixer") and leads groups filled with various all-stars, including tenors Eddie "Lockjaw" Davis and Brew Moore, pianist Billy Taylor, and vibraphonist Terry Gibbs. On such songs as "Laughin' in Rhythm," "Serenade in Sulfur-8," and "Serenade in Vout," Gaillard still displays plenty of his crazy spirit. *Laughing in Rhythm* has many of the high points of Gaillard's Verve recordings, which include an appearance at a Jazz at the Philharmonic concert in 1946 (the four-part "Opera in Vout") and odds and ends from 1951–53, including "The Bartender's Just Like a Mother," "Serenade to a Poodle," "Soony Roony," "Yo Yo Yo," "Potato Chips," and "Mishugana Mambo." The most remarkable cut is the modestly titled "Genius," on which Gaillard is heard (via overdubbing) on vocals, trumpet, trombone, tenor, vibes, piano, organ, bass, drums, and tap dancing! The last two choruses are absolutely hilarious. Other than an album in 1958, Gaillard was totally off records after 1953 until he recorded his final set in 1982. *Anytime, Anyplace, Anywhere* (which includes solos from Buddy Tate, Jay McShann, and Jay Thomas on tenor) has a great version of "How High the Moon" on which Gaillard spontaneously makes up a fascinating story. Not all of the other selections work that well and the overall effect is a bit streaky. Still, Slim still had it at that point.

LPS TO SEARCH FOR

To fully appreciate Slim Gaillard, one had to see or at least hear him in live performances, where he really stretched out and let his imagination run wild. *McVouty Slim & Bam* (Hep

6), *Son of McVouty* (Hep 11), and *The Voutest* (Hep 28) date from 1945–47, and each has its humorous moments along with some fine music. *Cement Mixer Put-ti Put-ti* (Folklyric 9038) is comprised of 16 additional studio recordings not covered in the other releases, dating from December 1945, 1947, and 1949, including "Scotchin' with the Soda," "Cuban Rumbarini," "Groove Juice Jive," "Laguna Oroonee," "Organ Oreenee," and "When Banana Skins Are Falling."

FILMS

Slim Gaillard is in *Hellzapoppin'* (1941), *Almost Married* (1942), *Ovoutie O'Rooney* (1946), *Go, Man, Go* (1954), and *Too Late Blues* (1961). In addition, he has an acting role in *Roots: The Next Generation* (1978).

FREDDIE GREEN

b. Mar. 31, 1911, Charleston, SC, d. Mar. 1, 1987, Las Vegas, NV

Freddie Green never took a solo after 1940 (there are just a couple of early examples of him having short spots) and he stuck to the background throughout his career, playing four-to-the-bar acoustic rhythm guitar, but he was the best at what he did. He began playing guitar when he was 12 and grew up in New York. Green freelanced a bit and then was discovered by John Hammond who felt that he would fit better into Count Basie's orchestra than Basie's regular guitarist, Claude Williams, who also doubled on violin; the talent scout never did like the violin in jazz. Hammond engineered the switch, and by March 1937 Freddie Green was a member of the Basie big band. For the next 13 years Green was always there and also participating on most of Basie's small-group dates. He always seemed to play the right chord, and Green's strumming was felt rather than heard, keeping the rhythm steady.

In late 1949 Count Basie reluctantly broke up his orchestra, and at first he had a small group that did not include rhythm guitar. However, one night Freddie Green suddenly appeared on stage sitting in with Basie, and he was with him thereafter. When Basie organized his second big band in 1952, Green (whose song "Corner Pocket" would become a Basie standard) was there, and he was still a member of the orchestra in 1984 when Count passed away. Freddie Green, who never switched to electric guitar, remained with the Basie organization until his death in 1987 at the beginning of the month that was his 50th anniversary with Count Basie.

●

7 *Natural Rhythm / Feb. 3, 1955 + Dec. 18, 1955 / Bluebird 6465*

Other than four titles in 1945, Freddie Green only led one record date in his life. This CD reissues that album (called *Mr. Rhythm*) along with a session by tenor saxophonist Al Cohn (*The Natural Seven*), hence the disc's title. Green, Cohn, Joe Newman, Milt Hinton, and drummer Osie John-son are on both projects; only the trombonist (Henry Coker or Frank Rehak) changes. With arrangements by Cohn, Ernie Wilkins, and Manny Albam, the music falls between Swing and Cool Jazz and is definitely influenced by the Count Basie sound. Not too surprisingly, Freddie Green does not take a single solo, not even on "Freddie's Tune"!

After years as a soloist, Art Tatum teamed up with guitarist Tiny Grimes and bassist Slam Stewart to form a very popular 52nd Street trio during 1944–45.

TINY GRIMES

b. July 7, 1916, Newport News, VA, d. Mar. 4, 1989, New York, NY

In the mid-1940s, Tiny Grimes for a time seemed to fill the vacuum left by the death of Charlie Christian, with both his tone and his ideas being strongly influenced by the late guitarist. However, Grimes lacked Christian's genius and did not advance much beyond where he was in 1945, although he was able to give his own personal touch to the style.

Lloyd "Tiny" Grimes actually started out as a drummer and occasional pianist, working at jobs in Washington, D.C., and New York. He switched to guitar in 1938, playing electric guitar from the start. Grimes was with The Cats and a Fiddle (1939–41) and filled the guitar slot with the Art Tatum Trio (1943–44) quite admirably. He led his own groups, had a record date in 1944 with Charlie Parker as a sideman, and played advanced Swing with hints of bebop. Later in the 1940s Grimes put together his Rocking Highlanders, an R&B band that was popular for a few years and featured the honking tenor of Red Prysock. Tiny Grimes was active for decades (with a few periods off the scene due to illness), visiting Europe on a regular basis, working with Earl Hines in 1972, and playing in an unchanged and still-lively style into the late 1980s.

7 *Blues Groove / Feb. 28, 1958 / Original Jazz Classics 817*

7 *Callin' the Blues / July 18, 1958 / Original Jazz Classics 191*

9 *Tiny in Swingville / Aug. 13, 1959 / Original Jazz Classics 1796*

Blues Groove has been issued under Coleman Hawkins's name along the way, but it is a Tiny Grimes session that has finally been restored to his leadership with this CD reissue. One can understand its being reissued as a Hawkins date because the great tenor takes a powerful and lengthy blues solo on "Marchin' Along." He and Grimes are joined by the forgotten flutist Musa Kaleem, pianist Ray Bryant, bassist Earl Wormack, and drummer Teagle Fleming, Jr., on a set consisting of four original blues plus the standards "April in Paris" and "A Smooth One." *Callin' the Blues* matches the powerful front line of J. C. Higginbotham and tenorman Eddie "Lockjaw" Davis with Bryant, bassist Wendell Marshall, and drummer Osie Johnson. The band plays three blues and "Airmail Special." Although Higginbotham was not really on Lockjaw's level at that point, there are some exciting

moments along the way. Best of the trio of releases is *Tiny in Swingville*. Grimes (joined by Jerome Richardson on flute, tenor, and baritone, pianist Bryant, bassist Marshall, and drummer Art Taylor) is in the spotlight throughout, showing on such numbers as "Annie Laurie," "Frankie and Johnnie," and "Ain't Misbehavin' " (along with three originals) that he deserved much greater recognition for his swinging playing.

LPS TO SEARCH FOR

Tiny Grimes and His Rockin' Highlanders (Swingtime 1016) has some of the highlights from Grimes's rhythm and blues period (1947–53), although the music mostly sounds like excitable Swing. John Hardee plays tenor on one date; otherwise, Red Prysock is Grimes's main competitor in the solo department. *Profoundly Blue* (Muse 5012) is from 1974 and is one of the guitarist's best late-period recordings. He jams happily with a sextet that includes Houston Person on tenor for such numbers as "Tiny's Exercise," "Profoundly Blue," and "Cookin' at the Cookery." Also quite worthy is 1974's *Some Groovy Fours* (Black & Blue 33067), a quartet outing on basic material with pianist Lloyd Glenn.

CARL KRESS

b. Oct. 20, 1907, Newark, NJ, d. June 10, 1965, Reno, NV

When Carl Kress gained recognition (and a lot of work) during the early Depression years, it was due to his very sophisticated chord voicings. He started off on banjo before switching to guitar, was with Paul Whiteman in 1926, and then worked during most of his life as a studio musician. Kress was considered to be practically on Eddie Lang's level by the early 1930s, and their two classic duets ("Pickin' My Way" and "Feeling My Way") feature Kress's chords behind Lang's single-note lines (even though Lang was also renowned for his chords). Kress was on many records during the late 1920s and '30s, and he recorded duets with fellow guitarist Dick McDonough. Rather than becoming a featured star, Carl Kress chose to stay in the studios (sticking mostly to acoustic guitar) into the 1960s, emerging only now and then in the jazz world. His last collaborations were with George Barnes, with whom he recorded duet albums a few years before dying of a heart attack.

9 *Two Guitars (and a Horn) / 1962 / Jass 636*
Carl Kress's duets with Lang and McDonough plus his six guitar solos of 1938–39 are available on *Eddie Lang/Carl Kress/Dick McDonough* (Retrieval 79015). He made several duet albums in the early 1960s with fellow guitarist Carl Kress. One was originally released by Stash as *Two Guitars,* while a second one that finds Bud Freeman making the

group a trio was called *Two Guitars and a Horn.* They are reissued on full on this CD and the results are quite delightful. Barnes takes the single-note lines, while Kress contributes sophisticated chords. Their renditions of standards are generally quite concise, and Freeman's presence on the second half is a major asset; he contributed two originals: "The Eel's Nephew" and "Disenchanted Trout."

DICK MCDONOUGH

b. July 30, 1904, New York, NY, d. May 25, 1938, New York, NY

Dick McDonough was the natural successor to Eddie Lang, sometimes playing in a similar style but also developing his own sound. McDonough started out as a banjoist but by the late 1920s was greatly in demand for studio and jazz dates as a rhythm guitarist and occasional soloist. He was on countless sessions during the 1928–37 period, at first filling in for Lang and then partly filling the vacuum left by Lang's death. McDonough frequently teamed up with Carl Kress and also led his own studio group for recordings and radio appearances. He held his own on two songs in a 1937 quintet with Fats Waller, Bunny Berigan, Tommy Dorsey, and George Wettling (issued as "A Jam Session at Victor"). Dick McDonough seemed to have many productive years ahead of him when he died suddenly from a heart attack in 1938 at the age of 34. ●

LPS TO SEARCH FOR

Most of Dick McDonough's many sessions as a leader during 1936–37 have yet to be reissued on CD or even (in most cases) on LP. *The Guitar Genius of Dick McDonough & Carl Kress in the Thirties* (Jazz Archives 32) has a dozen performances (swinging versions of standards) by a mostly unidentified orchestra from early 1937 that includes both McDonough and Carl Kress on guitars plus Adrian Rollini on bass sax and vibes. In addition, this LP has McDonough's only two unaccompanied guitar solos ("Chasing a Buck" and "Honeysuckle Rose") plus a duet with bassist Artie Bernstein ("The Ramble"), all from 1934.

OSCAR MOORE

b. Dec. 25, 1916, Austin, TX, d. Oct. 8, 1981, Las Vegas, NV

Oscar Moore received his greatest recognition as Nat King Cole's guitarist during Cole's early rise to fame. He worked with his brother Johnny Moore (also a guitarist) early on and then from 1937–47 was a member of the Nat King Cole Trio. Moore's electric guitar solos were influenced by Charlie Christian and, although generally in a supportive role to the leader's piano, the guitarist always had some solo space. The sound of the trio (with Wesley Prince and later Johnny Miller on bass) was memorable and influential, leading to the formation of similar trios by Art Tatum in the 1940s and Oscar Peterson and Ahmad Jamal in the '50s. When Moore left Cole, he at first worked for several years with Johnny Moore's popular Three Blazers and then freelanced, recording two albums as a leader in 1954. But Oscar Moore slipped into obscurity by the mid-1950s and, other than occasional projects (including a 1965 Nat King Cole tribute album), ended up working outside of music, as a bricklayer. ●

7 *Oscar Moore / 1954 / V.S.O.P. 22*

6 *Oscar Moore / 1954 / V.S.O.P. 34*

V.S.O.P. has reissued these two formerly obscure Oscar Moore albums, which were cut for the Tampa and Skylark labels. Both have Carl Perkins on piano and bassist Joe Comfort. V.S.O.P. 22 has Mike Pacheco on bongos, while V.S.O.P. 34 includes drummer Lee Young. In both cases the music is easy listening and melodic, but there is a little more fire to V.S.O.P. 22, so it gets the edge. Pity that Oscar Moore was allowed to slip away from jazz.

DJANGO REINHARDT

b. Jan. 23, 1910, Liverchies, Belgium, d. May 16, 1953, Fontainebleau, France

One of the true giants of the jazz guitar, Jean Baptiste "Django" Reinhardt was also one of the finest jazz soloists on any instrument during the 1930s and '40s. The first major European jazz musician (along with his frequent musical partner

The remarkable guitarist Django Reinhardt and the pioneering bandleader Paul Whiteman share a moment during Django's American tour of 1946.

Stephane Grappelli), Django was a colorful figure, a gypsy who could barely write his name but played guitar better than anyone else during his lifetime (with the possible exception of the short-lived Charlie Christian).

Reinhardt started on violin early on and was working mostly as a banjoist in the 1920s when a fire in his caravan badly burned his left hand in 1928, resulting in two of his fingers being made unusable. He made a miraculous comeback, modified his style, switched permanently to guitar, and discovered some recordings by Louis Armstrong, which steered him toward jazz. He was also inspired by Eddie Lang, yet from the start he had his own sound and a virtuosic style that put him way ahead of everyone else in his field. Django met violinist Grappelli in early 1933, and they worked together so well (despite their different temperaments and lifestyles) that they soon formed the Quintet of the Hot Club of France, a group consisting of Reinhardt's guitar, Grappelli's violin, two rhythm guitars, and a bass. For the next five years the band recorded and performed regularly. Django also appeared as a guest on many dates by other Europeans and a few Americans who were visiting France (including Coleman Hawkins, Benny Carter, and Rex Stewart).

When World War II started in 1939, the quintet was visiting London. While Grappelli elected to stay in England, Reinhardt spontaneously decided to return to France. He somehow continued playing jazz under the German occupation, even having a big band now and then and leading a new quintet, with clarinetist Hubert Rostaing in Grappelli's place. Although it was feared that Django Reinhardt had been killed, his discovery in 1944 with the liberation of France was a joyous occasion. In 1946, Django switched to electric guitar, an instrument that it would take him a couple of years to feel comfortable with. He made his only visit to the United States at that time, touring with Duke Ellington, but the visit was a disappointment. Reinhardt was surprised that he was not a celebrity in the United States. He was soon homesick and missed some major gigs. In addition, Ellington had not written him anything special to play, so the guitarist merely jammed a few standards with the rhythm section. He would not return to the U.S. again.

Django had several recorded reunions with Stephane Grappelli, kept his music open to the influence of bop, and by 1949 had full control over his electric guitar. His little-known work of the early 1950s found Reinhardt at the top of his game, but he was losing interest in playing music and became reclusive. A stroke in 1953 ended Django Reinhardt's life at the age of 43, just when Norman Granz was planning an American tour for the brilliant guitarist.

●

7 *Quintet of the Hot Club of France / Dec. 1934–Sept. 1935 / Original Jazz Classics 1895*

* *Djangology / May 4, 1936–Mar. 10, 1948 / EMI 780660-780669*

* *The Complete Django Reinhardt and Quintet of the Hot Club of France Swing/HMV Sessions / May 4, 1936–Mar. 10, 1948 / Mosaic 6–190*

10 *Django with His American Friends / Mar. 2, 1935– Nov. 6, 1945 / DRG 8493*

7 *Nuages / May 4, 1936–Dec. 13, 1940 / Arkadia Jazz 71431*

The Original Jazz Classics reissue has some of the Quintet of the Hot Club of France's first recordings, a dozen out of the 20 selections recorded at the classic group's first six recording sessions. A straight reissue of an earlier LP, it is a pity that this rather brief CD was not expanded to include the other cuts. Highlights include "Tiger Rag," "Lady Be Good," "Smoke Rings," and "The Sheik of Araby." *Djangology* is a magnificent ten-CD set that contains 243 selections that Django Reinhardt made for labels owned by EMI. It starts out with some of the finest performances from the Quintet of the Hot Club of France, traces Reinhardt during his intriguing war years (when he was featured in a wide variety of settings), has the first recordings by his new quintet with clarinetist Hubert Rostaing, and concludes with his reunion with Stephane Grappelli. The six-CD limited-edition box set from Mosaic covers the same material although it has just 119 selections and leaves out the guitarist's sideman recordings. DRG's *Django with His American Friends* has music that is mostly on the EMI box but is not covered by Mosaic. The three-CD set has all of Reinhardt's notable recordings with American all-stars, including Coleman Hawkins, Benny Carter, Bill Coleman, pianist Freddy Taylor, Dicky Wells, Eddie South, harmonica wizard Larry

Adler, and Rex Stewart. All but its final session is from 1935–40, and many of the performances include Grappelli, too. Although the single-CD *Nuages* claims that it has some newly discovered performances, the music has all been out before. It offers a listeners a good sampling of Django's recordings, although it is not in chronological order. Most tunes are by the quintet, and there are guest appearances by Hawkins, Coleman, and Carter.

8 *Django's Music / Feb. 22, 1940–July 7, 1943 / Hep 1041*

7 *Swing Guitar / Oct. 26, 1945–Mar. 1946 / Jass 628*

Django Reinhardt is best known for his work with the Quintet of the Hot Club of France, but that band actually lasted only five years. His later wartime recordings, often made under arduous circumstances, hold up very well and add a great deal of variety to his discography. *Django's Music* features Reinhardt leading a few different big bands in 1940 and 1942–43, performing such numbers as his haunting "Tears," "Stockholm," "Nuages," "Djangology," and "Melodie au Crépuscule." He was virtually the only guitarist (other than Alvino Rey) to lead a big band during the Swing era, although few probably realize that due to the obscurity of these recordings. After the war, Django performed regularly on the radio for a time with the ATC (Air Transport Command) Orchestra, a service band filled with lesser-known (but talented) American personnel. *Swing Guitar* features Reinhardt as the main soloist with the band on a few broadcasts and also performing with a combo out of the orchestra. In addition, there are six selections of the band playing without Django. Fine Swing music.

7 *Djangology 49 / Jan. 1949–Feb. 1949 / Bluebird 9988*

9 *Peche à la Mouche / Apr. 16, 1947–Mar. 10, 1953 / Verve 8354 418*

9 *Brussels and Paris / Mar. 21, 1947–Apr. 8, 1953 / DRG*
8473

Django Reinhardt and Stephane Grappelli had several reunions after World War II. The final one was in early 1949 and resulted in some marathon recording sessions in Italy. *Djangology 49* has 20 of the best performances that the pair recorded, and it finds Reinhardt sounding fairly comfortable on electric guitar. Some of the old magic between the two masterful musicians (who are backed by a functional Italian rhythm section) is recaptured. Although he was mostly out of the spotlight, Django continued advancing as a player during his last few years. The two-CD *Peche à la Mouche* features Reinhardt with his 1947 quintet (with Hubert Rostaing mostly on clarinet), on two selections with Rex Stewart, and, best of all, playing eight selections in 1953

with a modern rhythm section. Django is in particularly top form for this last group. *Brussels and Paris,* which does not duplicate the twofer, also has a full set with Rostaing in 1947 and concludes by showcasing the guitarist with combos during 1951–53, showing that he had mastered both the electric guitar and bebop while still keeping his basic Swing style. The final session was recorded less than six weeks before Django's death.

LPS TO SEARCH FOR

The GNP Crescendo label released several albums in the 1970s by the *Quintet of the Hot Club of France,* including *1934* (GNP 9031), *1935* (GNP 9023), *Parisian Swing* (GNP 9002), *'35–'39* (GNP 9019), and *Django Reinhardt–Stephane Grappelli* (GNP 9001).

GEORGE VAN EPS
b. Aug. 7, 1913, Plainfield, NJ, d. November 29, 1998, Newport Beach, CA

The son of the early ragtime banjoist Fred Van Eps, George Van Eps was famous for playing the most beautiful chords in the world. Van Eps was working in music when he was 13 and started broadcasting regularly on the radio the following year. He toured with Harry Reser's Junior Artists, the Dutch Master Minstrels, and Smith Ballew (1929–31). Van Eps was with Freddy Martin during 1931–33 and had a couple of stints with Benny Goodman during 1934–35. After working with Ray Noble in 1935, Van Eps became a major studio musician in Hollywood. He appeared on countless records, movie soundtracks, commercials, jingles, and trad jazz dates through the years. Van Eps designed a seven-string guitar in the late 1930s that allowed him to easily play bass notes behind his chords. He only recorded sporadically as a leader (including three Concord albums with fellow guitarist Howard Alden in the 1990s), but George Van Eps was active up until the time of his death, playing his beautiful chords in Los Angeles-area clubs. ●

7 *Hand-Crafted Swing / June 11–12, 1991 / Concord Jazz*
4513

8 *Keepin' Time / Sept. 6–7, 1994 / Concord Jazz 4713*
During 1991–94 George Van Eps, who rarely recorded as a leader (four sides for Jump in 1949, a Columbia album in 1956, and three Capitol sets in the mid-1960s) cut three full CDs with the much younger but very compatible guitarist Howard Alden. One of the albums was released under Alden's name. On *Hand-Crafted Swing,* Van Eps and Alden are joined by bassist Dave Stone and drummer Jake Hanna for tasteful and lightly swinging renditions of a dozen standards plus Van Eps's "Lap Piano" and "Forty-Eight." *Keepin' Time,* which has Hanna again but Michael Moore on bass, contains a bit more variety. Alden had in the interim also learned the seven-string guitar and he takes "The

Chant" and "Kay's Fantasy" (a Van Eps tune) as his features. Van Eps in turn has "Body and Soul" and "Honeysuckle Rose" as his showcases. In addition the rhythm section (which is absent on one of each of the guitarist's features) drops out on "More Than You Know" so that Van Eps and Alden can play it as a duet. Recommended.

LPS TO SEARCH FOR

Van Eps-Miller-Wrightsman (Jump 12-6) has the four Van Eps unaccompanied solos from 1949 plus an inspired trio set by Van Eps with Eddie Miller and pianist Stan Wrightsman. *Mellow Guitar* (Corinthian 121) reissues Van Eps's 1956 Columbia album, and the music lives up to the title. George Van Eps plays typically beautiful solos, with a trio, a string section, vibraphonist Frank Flynn, and sometimes five supportive horns.

Bassists

In the 1920s, the string bass was often an optional instrument. For the two-beat music of the period, the tuba functioned just as well as the bass. Also, due to the typical pianist's strong left hand, adding a string bass often seemed like a frivolity with small groups. However, there were some exceptions. Steve Brown (heard with Jean Goldkette's orchestra during 1926–27) often swung quite hard during final choruses. Thelma Terry with her Playboys in Chicago picked up where Brown left off. By the end of the decade, with the gradual rise of 4/4 Swing, the string bass had begun to completely take over for the tuba, since there was no way that tuba players could huff and puff out four notes to the bar on uptempo pieces.

There were two major bassists in 1929. Pops Foster's thumping and slapping bass playing added excitement to the Luis Russell Orchestra, and Wellman Braud was the first of a long line of important bassists who played with Duke Ellington. By the mid-1930s every Swing orchestra used a bass player and even smaller groups were beginning to add a bass, although Benny Goodman (in his trio and quartet) held out until 1938 with his combos. Most bassists with big bands during the Swing era simply played a note on each beat, emphasizing the timekeeping role of their instrument. These players include Walter Page with Count Basie and Bob Haggart with Bob Crosby. Few thought of the bass as a solo instrument, although Israel Crosby (in a 1935 session headed by Gene Krupa) and Milt Hinton (with Cab Calloway) had features, John Kirby led an important sextet, and Slam Stewart (who hummed along with his bowed bass during solos) was in another category altogether.

Things changed with the rise of Jimmy Blanton in 1939. His work for Duke Ellington found him playing solos on the bass with the fluency of a guitar, coming up with advanced accompaniment for other musicians' solos and showing that the string bass should not be taken for granted as merely a supportive instrument. Although Ed Safranski and Oscar Pettiford (who would be the leading bebop bassist) would be prominent by the mid-1940s, it would not be until the late 1950s that bass players caught up with Blanton, who was even more futuristic than Charlie Christian.

JIMMY BLANTON
b. Oct. 5, 1918, Chattanooga, TN, d. July 30, 1942, Los Angeles, CA

It would not be an understatement to say that Jimmy Blanton revolutionized the string bass. Before Blanton, the role of the bass was simply to play steady lines on the beat, behind other soloists. When a bassist actually received a rare solo, most merely just kept on playing walking patterns, perhaps a bit louder than they had earlier. In contrast, Blanton soloed like a guitarist or saxophonist, often throwing in double-time runs, using space expertly, and showing that the bass did not always have to be in the background.

As with Charlie Christian, Jimmy Blanton's life was tragically brief. He began on violin as a child and did not start playing bass until he was attending Tennessee State College in 1936. Blanton picked up experience gigging with Fate Marable on a riverboat. He dropped out of college in his third year and moved to St. Louis, where he worked with the Jeter-Pillars Orchestra (1937–39). At 21, Blanton joined Duke Ellington's orchestra in the fall of 1939. At first he shared the bass duties with his predecessor, Billy Taylor (Ellington liked using two bassists at once), but Taylor quickly recognized Blanton's superiority and quit the band in January 1940.

Jimmy Blanton was with Duke Ellington's orchestra for just two years, being well featured as the lead voice on duets with the pianist and on such big band numbers as "Jack the Bear," "Sepia Panorama," and "Ko Ko." He was also quite prominent on small-group dates led by Ellington's sidemen. But by late 1941, Jimmy Blanton, like Charlie Blanton, was struck down by tuberculosis and soon passed away quite early, at the age of 23.

WELLMAN BRAUD

b. Jan. 25, 1891, St. James Parish, LA, d. Oct. 29, 1966, Los Angeles, CA

Wellman Braud was one of the great early bassists, and he remained a force during the Swing era. Braud was part of the New Orleans jazz scene during 1905–1917, playing violin first and drums in brass bands before switching to bass. Braud moved in 1917 to Chicago, where he was part of the Original Creole Orchestra and Charlie Elgar's band. He played in London with the Plantation Orchestra for a couple of months in 1923 (doubling on trombone) and worked back in the U.S. in shows and with Wilbur Sweatman. Braud became a member of the Duke Ellington Orchestra in mid-1927, staying eight years. He was well recorded during his Ellington years (Duke always made sure that the string bass could be heard on his records), and the drive that he gave the band, along with his large tone, was an important part of the orchestra's sound.

After leaving Ellington, Wellman Braud was still quite busy. He worked with Jimmie Noone, Kaiser Marshall, the Spirits of Rhythm, his own trio, Hot Lips Page (1938), Edgar Hayes, Jelly Roll Morton, Sidney Bechet (1940–41), Al Sears, Garvin Bushell, and many others. In the mid-1940s, Braud became a part-time player, running a pool hall and managing a meat marketing business. He did gig with Bunk Johnson a bit in 1947 but generally just played on weekends. However, in 1956 he returned to music full time, touring and recording with Kid Ory. In the early 1960s Wellman Braud settled in California, where he worked with Joe Darensbourg and Barbara Dane before passing away from a heart attack at the age of 75.

ISRAEL CROSBY

b. Jan. 19, 1919, Chicago, IL, d. Aug. 11, 1962, Chicago, IL

On "Blues for Israel" in 1935 with a Gene Krupa pickup group, 16-year old Israel Crosby took one of the first full-length bass solos on record. Even though his solo was very basic, it was a historic landmark.

Crosby's career would span several musical eras. He played trumpet when he was five, switched to trombone and tuba, and did not begin playing bass until 1934, just a year before that solo. He worked with Albert Ammons in Chicago, did the Krupa date, and was part of the Fletcher Henderson Orchestra during 1936–38. Crosby played with Three Sharps and a Flat (1939) and the big bands of Horace Henderson and Teddy Wilson. He became a studio musician in 1944, working with Raymond Scott at CBS. A flexible musician who was always modern, Crosby became a member of the Ahmad Jamal Trio (1951–53) and, after stints with Teddy Wilson and Benny Goodman (1956–57), he returned to Jamal (1958–62) as part of the popular pianist's classic trio. Israel Crosby played with George Shearing in June 1962 but died two months later, from a blood clot on his heart, at the age of 43. Other than four blues-oriented numbers cut for Apollo in 1947, he never led his own record date.

POPS FOSTER

b. May 18, 1892, McCall, LA, d. Oct. 30, 1969, San Francisco, CA

The grand old man of bass players, George "Pops" Foster spent much of his life playing in an old-fashioned style in New Orleans jazz bands. He was one of the first bassists who could really be heard on records (thumping and slapping his bass quite loud) and, along with Wellman Braud, was the pacesetter among bassists of the late 1920s. Foster grew up in New Orleans, played cello for a few years, and then switched to bass. He worked with the who's who of early New Orleans jazz, including Kid Ory, Armand Piron, King Oliver, and Fate Marable (1917–18), among many others, and switched now and then to tuba to play with brass bands. In 1921 Foster worked in St. Louis with Charlie Creath and Dewey Jackson. He was in Los Angeles in 1923 to play with Kid Ory and Mutt Carey but returned to St. Louis by 1925. Pops Foster joined Luis Russell's orchestra in 1929 and was an integral part of one of jazz's best rhythm sections of the period. He stayed with Russell through 1940, including the five years when the orchestra functioned mostly as Louis Armstrong's backup band. After a stint with Teddy Wilson, Foster worked outside of music, as a subway worker in New York during 1942–45. He returned to full-time playing in 1945 and worked during the next 20 years with a variety of trad jazz bands. Among his associations were Sidney Bechet and Bunk Johnson in Boston, Art Hodes (1945–46), Mezz Mezzrow in France, Bob Wilber, Jimmy Archey, Sammy Price, Earl Hines (late 1950s in San Francisco), and Elmer Snowden. Pops Foster was active up until 1968.

BOB HAGGART
b. Mar. 13, 1914, New York, NY, d. Dec. 3, 1998, Venice, FL

A fine Swing bassist, Bob Haggart was also a talented arranger and the composer of such songs as "What's New?," "South Rampart Street Parade," and "My Inspiration." Early on he played banjo, guitar, trumpet, and piano before switching to bass in high school. Haggart gigged locally and in 1935 became a founding member of the Bob Crosby Orchestra, one of the few of their key musicians who had not been with the group earlier on when it was headed by Ben Pollack. Haggart was a fixture with Crosby's band during 1935–42 and appeared on all of the big band and Bobcats recordings. He starred on his "Big Noise from Winnetka," a duet with drummer Ray Bauduc in which Haggart whistled and fingered his instrument when at one point Bauduc taps the strings with his drumsticks. After the Crosby band broke up, Bob Haggart became busy in the studios, working for Decca as an arranger and becoming quite active in radio (and later on television) for decades. Haggart always found time to play the freewheeling Dixieland/Swing jazz that he loved, teaming up regularly with his pal Yank Lawson in the 1950s for a series of records, appearing at many Bob Crosby reunions, and joining with Lawson to co-lead The World's Greatest Jazz Band from 1968–78. Until the end of his life, Bob Haggart was in great demand at jazz parties and trad jazz festivals, always willing to cheerfully play "The Big Noise from Winnetka."

●

7 *Hag Leaps In / Nov. 6–7, 1995 / Arbors 19156*
This is a tasteful effort, featuring Haggart still at his prime at age 81 in a trio with 74-year-old pianist John Bunch and 69-year-old Bucky Pizzarelli. The music is primarily Swing standards (including "Softly, As in a Morning Sunrise," "I'm Beginning to See the Light," "Air Mail Special," and Haggart's "My Inspiration"), and the title cut is based on "Lester Leaps In." The oddest aspect to this set is the rare opportunity to hear a version of "Big Noise from Winnetka" without drums!

LPS TO SEARCH FOR
Not counting the dates that he co-led with Yank Lawson (on which Lawson received first billing), Bob Haggart's first album as a leader was made for Command in 1963. In 1980,

1981, and 1986 he headed excellent records for Jazzology. *Makes a Sentimental Journey* (Jazzology 74) and *Enjoys Carolina in the Morning* (Jazzology 94) are equally exciting combo dates, with an octet that includes cornetist Tom Pletcher, bass saxophonist Spencer Clark, and pianist Dill Jones. *A Portrait of Bix* (Jazzology 149), which also has Pletcher (who can sound very close to Bix Beiderbecke) and Clark, is inspired. The repertoire is comprised of songs that cornetist Bix had recorded but not necessarily played classic solos on, giving the group flexibility to create their own special interpretations.

FILMS
Haggart plays "Big Noise from Winnetka" with Bob Crosby in both *Let's Make Music* (1940) and *Reveille with Beverly* (1943).

MILT HINTON
b. June 23, 1910, Vicksburg, MS

Quite possibly the most recorded jazz musician of all time, Milt Hinton has been on a remarkable number of record dates, studio sessions, and club and concert performances during a remarkable career. He started playing bass and tuba while in high school in Chicago. Hinton had early jobs with Boyd Atkins, Tiny Parham (with whom he made his recording debut in

1930), Jabbo Smith, and Cassino Simpson. Hinton worked with Eddie South for several years, was with Fate Marable, and then had a longtime association with Cab Calloway (1936–51), staying with Cab even after his orchestra became a sextet and was finally cut back to a quartet. Hinton was well featured with Calloway (including on 1939's "Pluckin' the Bass") and was considered potentially the leading bassist during the Swing era, at least until Jimmy Blanton joined Duke Ellington.

After Calloway finally broke up his combo, Hinton became an extremely busy studio musician, recording not only with every possible type of group but usually several sessions a day. He did work for a couple of months with Count Basie and had a couple of brief stints with the Louis Armstrong All-Stars during 1953–54 but otherwise was kept very active in the studios into the 1980s, playing jazz at night and appearing as a sideman with virtually everyone. Milt Hinton kept the old Swing style alive and by the 1980s would typically play a chorus quite effectively in the slapping style of Pops Foster. He remained quite active into the mid-1990s, when he started slowing down, but he did tour with the Statesmen of Jazz in 1995 and has lived long enough to be universally recognized in the jazz world for his accomplishments. A talented photographer and writer, Milt Hinton's two photo books *Bass Line* (which also serves as his musical memoirs) and *Overtime* (Pomegranate Press) are both highly recommended.

7 *Back to Bass-ics / Sept. 3, 1984 / Progressive 7084*

8 *Laughing at Life / 1994 / Columbia 66454*

10 *Old Man Time / Mar. 28, 1989–Mar. 27, 1990 / Chiaroscuro 310*

Milt Hinton led record dates on an occasional basis through the years (starting in 1945), although nothing at all between 1956 and 1974. *Back to Bass-ics* is a relaxed trio session with the underrated pianist Jane Jarvis and drummer Louie Bellson. Few surprises occur on the seven standards and three basic originals, but the music swings and the result is a fine workout. *Laughing at Life* has Hinton jamming with two different rhythm sections plus guest trumpeter Jon Faddis (who sounds surprisingly close to Roy Eldridge during his three songs) and veteran tenor Harold Ashby on four songs. In addition, on "The Judge and the Jury" Hinton is teamed with four other bassists, who pay tribute to the master. The only flaw to this set is that Milt (who has three vocals) sings just a little too much, although "Old Man Harlem" is charming. But the Milt Hinton set to get is the two-CD *Old Man Time*. Hinton has reunions with many musical friends from the 1930s, including Dizzy Gillespie, Doc Cheatham, guitarist Danny Barker, saxophonist Eddie Barefield, Buddy Tate, pianist Red Richards, Al Casey, Cab Calloway (on "Good Time Charlie"), and Lionel Hampton. Hinton sings the delightful "Old Man Time," jams with Clark Terry, Al Grey, Flip Phillips, and pianist Ralph Sutton, does a humorous rap, and is heard verbally on a pair of "Jazzspeaks." In one instance, for 43 minutes he gives his colorful life story, while the other "Jazzspeak" finds him reminiscing with Calloway, Cheatham, and Barefield about the Swing era. Highly recommended.

FILMS
Milt Hinton, who backs Cab Calloway in many of his film appearances, is also in *The Sound of Jazz* (1957) and *After Hours* (1961).

JOHN KIRBY
b. Dec. 31, 1908, Baltimore, MD, d. June 14, 1952, Hollywood, CA

John Kirby was the only successful bandleader during the Swing era to be a bassist. His sextet, which during its prime years was comprised of trumpeter Charlie Shavers, altoist Russell Procope, clarinetist Buster Bailey, pianist Billy Kyle, and drummer O'Neil Spencer, had a unique "cool" sound. Comprised of talented players who could read anything, the Kirby Sextet featured complex and tightly arranged ensembles (which sometimes played melodies based on classical themes), brief but effective solos, and a very light feel. No other band during the era sounded quite like it.

Kirby originally played trombone and switched to tuba in the mid-1920s. He worked with Bill Brown and his Brownies (1928–30) and Fletcher Henderson (1930–33), switching permanently to bass while with the latter. Kirby had stints with

The John Kirby Sextet, known as "The Biggest Little Band In The Land": drummer O'Neil Spencer, altoist Russell Procope, clarinetist Buster Bailey, trumpeter Charlie Shavers, pianist Billy Kyle, and the always somber-looking bassist Kirby.

Chick Webb (1933–35), Henderson again (1935–36), and Lucky Millinder (1936–37). The bassist led a band at the Onyx Club for 11 months during 1937–38, and during that time he decided on the type of group that he wanted. Frankie Newton and Pete Brown were originally on trumpet and alto but did not last, and other musicians passed through the band until the perfect combination emerged.

The prime years for the John Kirby Sextet were 1938–42, with steady recordings, long residencies, and a strong following. Maxine Sullivan, who was married to Kirby during this period, contributed occasional vocals. But the draft, O'Neil Spencer's death in 1944, and a drop in the group's fortunes resulted in a lot of turnover during 1943–45. Although most of the original members were back by 1946, that was only temporary and the band broke up. Kirby was heartbroken and tried several times to put together similar groups. He had a Carnegie Hall concert on December 20, 1950, with the original members plus Sid Catlett on drums, but it was poorly attended. During his last two years, John Kirby worked with Red Allen, Buck Clayton, and Benny Carter, but his heart was not really in it. He died at the age of 43 due to complications of diabetes.

●

10 *1938–1939 / Oct. 28, 1938–Oct. 12, 1939 / Classics 750*

10 *1939–1941 / Oct. 12, 1939–Jan. 15, 1941 / Classics 770*

9 *1941–1943 / Jan. 2, 1941–Dec. 1943 / Classics 792*

8 *1945–1946 / Apr. 26, 1945–Sept. 3, 1946 / Classics 964*
Every studio recording by the John Kirby Sextet is included on these four perfectly done Classics CDs. The band started out very strong in October 1938, recording "Rehearsin' for a Nervous Breakdown," "From A Flat to C," and the original

version of Charlie Shavers's "Undecided" among their first five numbers. *1938–1939* is the most essential CD, also including such pieces as the atmospheric "Dawn on the Desert," "Anitra's Dance," "Royal Garden Blues," "Rose Room," and "Nocturne" among its 22 selections. One can understand by listening to these fascinating ensembles why the group was known as "the biggest little band in the world." *1939–1941* is at the same level, highlighted by "Humoresque," "Jumpin' in the Pump Room," "Sextet from Lucia," "Zooming at the Zombie," and "Beethoven Riffs On." On *1941–1943,* the personnel began to change. O'Neil Spencer left due to his illness after the July 25, 1941, session, replaced by Specs Powell and later Bill Beason. For the last five numbers, V-Discs from 1943, Russell Procope and Billy Kyle were gone, replaced by George Johnson and Clyde Hart. The basic group sound was still the same and the set (which has nine rare V-Disc performances among the 21 cuts) includes "Coquette," "Close Shave," "Bugler's Dilemma," "Night Whispers," and "St. Louis Blues" (which shows off Buster Bailey's circular breathing) among the more memorable selections. *1945–1946* has the final recordings of the classic group, with the personnel going through quite a few changes. Shavers was gone, replaced by Emmett Berry, Clarence Brereton, and finally George Taitt. Procope and Kyle return for most of the selections but are eventually replaced by Hilton Jefferson and Hank Jones. Budd Johnson makes the group a septet on one session and Bill Beason is on drums throughout. By the end, only Kirby and Bailey were still there from the original band. However, the later recordings are still recognizably John Kirby's sextet, and on such numbers as "K. C. Caboose," "Desert Sands," "Peanut Vendor Boogie," and "Schubert's Serenade," it was clear that he had no plans to change his group's direction. A special treat is the inclusion of four vocals from the young Sarah Vaughan.

LPS TO SEARCH FOR

In addition to two CDs released under Maxine Sullivan's name (and found there), several albums of radio transcriptions and live broadcasts have been released featuring the John Kirby Sextet, most notably *Biggest Little Band in the Land* (Classic Jazz 22), a two-LP set that dates from 1941–44.

FILMS

The John Kirby Sextet plays a couple of fine numbers in *Sepia Cinderella* (1947).

WALTER PAGE
b. Feb. 9, 1900, Gallatin, MO, d. Dec. 20, 1957, New York, NY

The definitive Swing bassist (as opposed to Jimmy Blanton, who really belonged to a later era), Walter Page's ability to drive the Count Basie Orchestra set the standard for the time. He started out on tuba, learning string bass while in high school. Page played in the early 1920s with Bennie Moten, freelanced, and then in 1925 formed the Walter Page Blue Devils. His band was considered the best combo in the Midwest despite being raided constantly by Bennie Moten's orchestra. The Blue Devils became legendary although they only recorded two titles; its sidemen at various times included Jimmy Rushing, Count Basie, and Lester Young. Page kept the band going until 1931, when he gave it to trumpeter James Simpson and decided to give up the fight and join Moten himself. He was with Bennie Moten until 1934, gigged with the Jeter-Pillars Orchestra, and became a member of the Count Basie band in 1936.

Walter Page joined forces with Count, drummer Jo Jones, and (by 1937) guitarist Freddie Green to form the perfect Swing rhythm section. He was with the Basie big band until 1942, freelanced for a few years, and was back with Basie during 1946–49. Page worked with the unrelated Hot Lips Page and Jimmy Rushing (1951) and played the Dixieland circuit with Eddie Condon, Ruby Braff, and Wild Bill Davison. Shortly before he was to appear on *The Sound of Jazz* telecast, Walter Page was stricken with the pneumonia that caused his death at age 57.

ED SAFRANSKI
b. Dec. 25, 1918, Pittsburgh, PA, d. Jan. 10, 1979, Los Angeles, CA

Best known for his association with Stan Kenton, Ed Safranski was a good example of a talented bassist who learned from Jimmy Blanton's example and became a strong soloist himself. Like Blanton, Safranski started out on violin, switching to bass in high school. He played locally and then made a strong impression with Hal McIntyre's big band (1941–45) where he was actually the group's top soloist, a very unusual distinction for a bassist during the Swing era. Safranski was well featured with Stan Kenton's orchestra during 1945–48, particularly on special arrangements written by Pete Rugolo (including a piece simply called "Safranski"). When Kenton broke up his orchestra, Safranski worked with Charlie Barnet's bebop band (1948–49) and then became a studio musician for the remainder of his life, occasionally playing jazz dates. Ed Safranski led four recording dates during 1946–53, resulting in 13 selections.

SLAM STEWART
b. Sept. 21, 1914, Englewood, NJ, d. Dec. 10, 1987, Binghamton, NY

Slam Stewart was famous for vocally humming an octave above his bowed bass during solos. His humorous and often-quote-filled choruses always brought a smile to people's faces, and his strong technique allowed him to play with practically anyone, including participating in classic recordings with Lester Young ("Sometimes I'm Happy"), Benny Goodman, and duets with Don Byas. Leroy "Slam" Stewart studied bass at the Boston Conservatory of Music. When he saw violinist Ray Perry singing along with his violin, he had the idea for his own style. After working with Peanuts Holland (1936–37), Stewart was part of Slim and Slam (1938–42) with Slim Gaillard. "Flat Foot Floogie" became their big hit, and the duo (usually heard as a quartet) was quite popular, working steadily for four years, until Gaillard went into the military. Stewart was a member of the Art Tatum Trio (1943–44) along with Tiny Grimes, worked briefly in Grimes's quartet, and in 1945 was well featured with the Benny Goodman Orchestra and Sextet. After one of several return stints with Tatum, Stewart led his own trio, which for a time featured Erroll Garner on piano. He freelanced during the 1950s, including with Tatum, Roy Eldridge, Billy Taylor, and pianists Beryl Booker (1955–57) and Rose Murphy. Stewart played in many different situations during the next couple of decades, most notably with Benny Goodman (1973–75), Bucky Pizzarelli, and George Wein's Newport All-Stars, plus he made two recordings with fellow bassist Major Holley, who differed from Slam by humming in unison with his bass. Slam Stewart's good-natured style remained unchanged and classic up until the end.

9 *1945–1946 / Jan. 30, 1945–Apr. 26, 1946 / Classics 939*
Although considered most valuable as a sideman, Slam Stewart led a series of interesting recordings during 1945–46. Other than two numbers in 1950, Slam would not record again as a leader until 1971. This CD has all of his mid-'40s dates as a leader, including work with a trio and quartet that includes the young pianist Errol Garner, a few cuts with Don Byas, a date with pianist Billy Taylor, and two sessions in which Stewart's quintet features Red Norvo and Johnny Guarnieri. Well worth exploring, this music (particularly Slam's solos) is quite fun.

FILMS
Slam Stewart is in *Hellzapoppin'* with Slim Gaillard (1941) and appears in *Boy! What a Girl* (1947).

Drummers

When one thinks of Swing drummers, Gene Krupa comes immediately to mind. In 1927 he was the first drummer ever to record with a full drum set. Before that, it was feared that the bass drum would drown out the other instruments, so it was simply never recorded. The early drummers (such as Baby Dodds and Tony Sbarbaro) could only use part of their drum set on records, usually a snare drum, a cymbal, and sometimes woodblocks, so it is difficult to know what drummers really sounded like in person during the era.

After 1927, drummers could be better heard on record, but for years they were rarely given the spotlight. Zutty Singleton was one of the stars with Louis Armstrong's Savoy Ballroom Five in 1928, Vic Berton doubled on tympani with Red Nichols, Paul Barbarin propelled Luis Russell's band, Sonny Greer added color to Duke Ellington's orchestra, and Chick Webb excited dancers with his work at the Savoy.

But Gene Krupa was the first drummer to become a superstar. He generated constant excitement with the Benny Goodman Orchestra and Trio/Quartet, and his solos on the two recorded versions of "Sing, Sing, Sing" ensured his immortality. He was not the best drummer of the 1930s, but he was the most colorful and most famous. Critics tended to favor the smoother and more consistent playing of Dave Tough. Sid Catlett and Cozy Cole were quite important in a variety of Swing bands. Jo Jones had a much lighter touch than Krupa, shifting the timekeeping function from the bass drum to cymbals and becoming a major influence on later generations of drummers. Ray Bauduc combined New Orleans jazz and swing in his playing with Bob Crosby, as did Nick Fatool in later years. Ray McKinley and O'Neill Spencer were two of the most under-rated drummers of the period. But ultimately Buddy Rich was the greatest of them all, totally unbeatable in drum battles and a true phenomenon for decades after the Swing era.

RAY BAUDUC
b. June 19, 1906, New Orleans, LA, d. Jan. 8, 1988, Houston, TX

Ray Bauduc was best known for being one of the Bob Crosby Bobcats and for dueting with Bob Haggart on the classic "Big Noise from Winnetka." He grew up around music in New Orleans, playing with a variety of bands, including Johnny Bayersdorffer's Jazzola Novelty Orchestra (1924–26). Bauduc went to New York with Billy Lustig's Scranton Sirens and worked with Joe Venuti and Fred Rich's orchestra, recording in 1926 with the Original Memphis Five. When Ben Pollack decided to direct his orchestra and vacate the drum chair, Ray Bauduc was chosen to be his drummer. Bauduc was with Pollack during 1928–34, made many freelance recordings (including with Red Nichols, Jack Teagarden, and Wingy Manone), and then became an original member of the Bob Crosby Orchestra. He was with Crosby for the entire life of the big band (1935–42) and was an important member of both the orchestra and the Bobcats. Bauduc served in the Army (1942–44), had a short-lived big band in 1945, worked with Tommy Dorsey for a few months in 1946, and was with Jimmy Dorsey during 1948–50, including playing with JD's Original Dorseyland Jazz Band. He toured with Jack Teagarden during 1952–55 and otherwise freelanced on the West Coast, playing with Dixieland bands, sometimes teaming up with guitarist Nappy Lamare, participating in reunions with Bob Crosby, and leading his own small groups. Ray Bauduc spent his last years living in Houston. He led two songs for the Sunset label in 1946, four titles for Capitol in 1947, and two long-out-of-print Dixieland albums for Capitol during 1957–58.

●

FILMS
Ray Bauduc plays in the Art Tatum jam session number in *The Fabulous Dorseys* (1947) and his quintet appears in *Stallion Road* (1947).

SID CATLETT
b. Jan. 17, 1910, Evansville, IN, d. Mar. 25, 1951, Chicago, IL

A very versatile drummer who changed his patterns behind each soloist to complement what he or she was playing, "Big" Sid Catlett was able to work quite effectively in styles ranging from Dixieland to bop. He grew up in Chicago and started playing professionally with Darnell Howard in 1928. Other early associations included Sammy Stewart, Elmer Snowden (1931–32), and Benny Carter (1932–33). By then, Catlett had a very strong reputation among musicians and he was being used on many recording sessions, including with Spike Hughes and Eddie Condon. During 1934–35 he played for a short period with quite a few groups (including the declining McKinney's Cotton Pickers) and then gained some recognition for his work with the orchestras of Fletcher Henderson (1936) and Don Redman (1936–38). Catlett worked with the Louis Armstrong big band (1938–41), had an unhappy four months with Benny Goodman in 1941, was back with Armstrong (1941–

42), and was part of Teddy Wilson's sextet (1942–44). He was at the peak of his powers and popularity in the mid-1940s, playing with many combos (some of which he led) on 52nd Street. Catlett recorded with virtually everyone as both a leader and a sideman (including Charlie Parker and Dizzy Gillespie) and was an original member of the Louis Armstrong All-Stars (1947–49). However, his shaky health in 1949 forced him to leave Armstrong. Sid Catlett worked in Dixieland settings in Chicago during 1949–50 (including with Muggsy Spanier, Sidney Bechet, and Eddie Condon) but died of a heart attack at the age of 41, a major loss to jazz.

●

9 *1944–1946 / Mar. 18, 1944–1946 / Classics 974*
This highly enjoyable CD has all of Big Sid Catlett's dates as a leader and offers many strong examples of the style of small-group Swing that was played nightly on 52nd Street. Catlett leads quartet sessions with Ben Webster, heads an all-star sextet that includes Charlie Shavers and clarinetist Edmond Hall, is heard in an odd outing with both organist Bill Gooden and pianist Pete Johnson, and also welcomes

such sidemen on the other dates as Illinois Jacquet, trumpeter Joe Guy, Tyree Glenn, and Coleman Hawkins.

FILMS

Sid Catlett is in *Jammin' the Blues* (1944), *Boy! What a Girl* (1947), and with the John Kirby Sextet in *Sepia Cinderella* (1947).

COZY COLE
b. Oct. 17, 1906, East Orange, NJ, d. Jan. 29, 1981, Columbus, OH

A solid Swing drummer who had a long career, Cozy Cole kept busy for decades. William "Cozy" Cole moved to New York with his family in 1926 and was a professional drummer two years later. He worked with Wilbur Sweatman, recorded with Jelly Roll Morton in 1930 (including one song called "Load of Cole"), and played with the big bands of Blanche Calloway (1931–33), Benny Carter (1933–34), and Willie Bryant (1935–36). Cole was part of Stuff Smith's popular sextet (1936–38) and then helped Cab Calloway during 1938–42 to have one of the top rhythm sections in jazz, one also including guitarist Danny Barker, pianist Bennie Payne, and Milt Hinton. He was showcased on several numbers with Calloway, including "Crescendo in Drums" and "Paradiddle."

Cozy Cole was a fixture on 52nd Street in the mid-1940s, performing and recording with many small combos in addition to working with Benny Goodman on a few brief occasions and playing with orchestras in shows. After working in the studios during 1946–48, Cole became a member of the Louis Armstrong All-Stars (1949–53) where he replaced Sid Catlett. In the 1950s he worked in the studios, often appeared at the Metropole in New York (generally with Henry "Red" Allen), and had a drum school with Gene Krupa. After touring Europe in 1957 with Jack Teagarden and Earl Hines, Cole had a surprise hit the following year with a recording of "Topsy" that made the pop charts. The fame that that song generated allowed him to be a bandleader for the next decade, working regularly. In 1969 he became a member of the Jonah Jones Quintet for a time (they had worked together previously with Stuff Smith and Cab Calloway) and stayed active through most of the 1970s.

●

9 *1944 / Feb. 22, 1944–June 14, 1944 / Classics 819*

9 *1944–1945 / Nov. 24, 1944–Apr. 1945 / Classics 865*
All of Cozy Cole's mid-1940s sessions are on these two CDs and both contain many strong examples of late-period small-group Swing before bebop began to become influential on the mainstream of jazz. *1944* finds Cole welcoming

such sidemen as Coleman Hawkins, Budd Johnson, Ben Webster, Earl Hines, Trummy Young, Johnny Guarnieri, and trumpeters Joe Thomas and Emmett Berry. Two of the five sessions on *1944–1945* are essentially showcases for Don Byas, although Tiny Grimes and pianist Billy Taylor also have solo space and June Hawkins takes vocals on three of the eight selections. Byas is also on two of the other three dates, being joined by Charlie Shavers, clarinetists Hank D'Amico and Aaron Sachs, trumpeter Shorty Rogers, and Coleman Hawkins, while Hawkins, Shavers, and saxophonist Walter "Foots" Thomas are on the remaining session. Although he gets some short breaks, Cozy Cole is primarily in a supportive role behind the Swing All-Stars, driving the ensembles and showing why he was so highly valued.

LPS TO SEARCH FOR

Ironically, "Topsy" and the dates that Cole led after that surprise hit have been scarce for many years. From late in his career, *Nice, France 1974* (Classic Jazz 133) features a sextet with trumpeter Wallace Davenport, Vic Dickenson, Buddy Tate, and Claude Hopkins. That date, and 1977's *The Louis Armstrong Alumni* (Who's Who 21003) with Lionel Hampton, clarinetist Joe Muranyi, and trumpeter Johnny Letman, are excellent efforts that fall between Swing and Dixieland.

FILMS

Cozy Cole has a drum battle with Gene Krupa in *The Glenn Miller Story* (1953) and is in the Coleman Hawkins–Roy Eldridge band in *After Hours* (1961).

NICK FATOOL

b. Jan. 2, 1915, Milbury, MA

Although he became known for his work with Bob Crosby, Nick Fatool did not actually work with the singer until the 1950s. Fatool spent the Swing era playing swinging and supportive drums for the big bands of Joe Haymes (1937), George Hall, Don Bestor, Benny Goodman (1939–40), Artie Shaw (1940–41), Claude Thornhill, Les Brown, Jan Savitt, Alvino Rey (1942–43), and Eddie Miller (1943). He worked in the studios for decades but gained his greatest fame playing with Dixieland bands, mostly on the West Coast. Fatool worked with Matty Matlock, appeared at Dixieland festivals, and was part of several Bob Crosby reunion bands starting in the late 1950s. He played in New Orleans with Pete Fountain (1962–65) and spent the 1970s and '80s working mostly in the Los Angeles area. With Ray Bauduc becoming less active by the 1970s, Nick Fatool was often Bob Haggart's partner on "Big Noise from Winnetka" and a fixture at Dixieland concerts and festivals.

●

8 *Nick Fatool's Jazz Band and Quartet / Mar. 24, 1977 + Jan. 9, 1982 / Jazzology 158*
Nick Fatool only led one album during his long career, a 1977 record with a hot septet consisting of Eddie Miller, Johnny Mince, cornetist Ernie Carson, pianist Lou Stein, guitarist Bill Rutan, and Bob Haggart. Other than "At the End of Honeymoon Lane" and Stein's "Road Runners' Blues," all of the material is familiar, but the veteran players (particularly Miller) are in top form and sound happy to contribute to Fatool's rare opportunity to be a leader. The CD reissue also includes two previously unreleased numbers from 1982 ("The Man I Love" and "Just One of Those Things") in which Fatool is joined by Bud Freeman, pianist Ray Sherman, guitarist Howard Alden, and bassist Phil Stephens. Overall this is an excellent Mainstream Swing set with Dixieland overtones.

FILMS

Nick Fatool is seen with Artie Shaw's band in *Second Chorus* (1940) and appears in *The Man I Love* (1946).

SONNY GREER

b. Dec. 13, 1895, Long Branch, NJ, d. Mar. 23, 1982, New York, NY

Sonny Greer was a solid if not overly imaginative drummer. Although he apparently appeared at the Cotton Club regularly in front of a huge and potentially mighty array of percussive instruments, on records he used mostly a conventional set. Greer started playing drums while in high school and worked locally around New Jersey. He visited Washington, D.C., in 1919, got a job playing with Marie Lucas's orchestra, and met the young Duke Ellington. Greer first worked with Ellington in 1920, and he was with him during Duke's first brief trip to New York. He and Duke were fellow sidemen with the Washingtonians under Elmer Snowden's leadership before Ellington took over. Greer stayed with Duke Ellington's orchestra until 1951, appearing on nearly all of Duke's records and leading two sessions of his own during 1944-45. By the beginning of the 1950s he had become unreliable, and he departed when Johnny Hodges left to form his own band. After a few months with Hodges, Greer freelanced in New York, including with Red Allen, Tyree Glenn, and others in the mainstream and Dixieland world. He was with Eddie Barefield and J. C. Higginbotham during part of the 1960s and frequently was part of Brooks Kerr's trio in the '70s, but Sonny Greer's post-Ellington years were mostly uneventful.

JO JONES
b. Sept. 10, 1911, Chicago, IL, d. Sept. 3, 1985, New York, NY

Prior to Jo Jones, most drummers used the bass drum at least part of the time to keep the rhythm steady. However, Jones, as part of the innovative Count Basie rhythm section, had a much lighter touch, utilizing the hi-hat cymbal to keep time and the bass drum just for occasional accents. The result was that there was much more space for the string bass to be heard. His playing would have a strong influence on bebop drummers and beyond, quietly revolutionizing the way that the drums are played.

Jo Jones played trumpet, piano, and reeds early on and worked in carnival shows, sometimes as a singer and dancer. He began playing drums in the late 1920s, having associations with Ted Adams, Harold Jones's Brownskin Syncopators, Walter Page's Blue Devils, Bennie Moten, and Lloyd Hunter's Serenaders before moving to Kansas City in 1934. The drummer spent a couple of brief periods with Count Basie before officially joining him in the fall of 1936. Jones was a key part of Basie's success, appearing on many records with Count's orchestra and small groups. In October 1944 he went into the Army, but, after his discharge, he returned to Basie (1946–early 1948). Jones worked with Illinois Jacquet's popular band (1948–50), toured with Jazz at the Philharmonic on a few occasions, and freelanced throughout the 1950s. He worked with Joe Bushkin's Quartet (1951–53), often played with Basie alumni (such as Lester Young), and appeared with the top mainstream veterans, including Teddy Wilson's trio. As an elder statesman, the drummer remained quite active into the 1970s (when he was known as "Papa" Jo Jones), occasionally leading his own groups but mostly jamming with all-star bands.

9   *The Essential Jo Jones / Aug. 11, 1955–Apr. 30, 1958 /*
    Vanguard 101/2

8   *The Main Man / Nov. 29, 1976–Nov. 30, 1976 /.*
    Original Jazz Classics 869

Jo Jones's first two albums as a leader, *The Jo Jones Special* and *Jo Jones Plus Two*, have been reissued in full on the Vanguard single CD, with the exception of a second take of "Shoe Shine Boy" that was left off. On the earlier date, Jones heads a septet that includes trumpeter Emmett Berry, trombonist Benny Green, and Lucky Thompson on tenor; Count Basie makes a guest appearance on "Shoe Shine Boy." The later session is a trio set with pianist Ray Bryant and bassist Tommy Bryant that is most notable for introducing Bryant's "Little Susie" and "Cubano Chant." Jones has a long drum solo on "Old Man River." *The Main Man* was one of Jones's last records, and at 65 he still sounds fairly strong. He teams up with a group that includes several Swing-era veterans (Roy Eldridge, Harry Edison, Vic Dickenson, and Freddie Green), plus tenorman Eddie "Lockjaw" Davis, pianist Tommy Flanagan, and bassist Sam Jones. Their renditions of a couple of basic originals and four standards are full of spirit and solid Swing, serving as a fine close to Jo Jones's important career.

FILMS

Jo Jones shares the drum spot with Sid Catlett in *Jammin' the Blues* (1944), pops up in a nightclub scene in *The Unsuspected* (1947), is prominent in *The Sound of Jazz* (1957), and is one of the stars of *Born to Swing* (1973).

RAY MCKINLEY

b. June 18, 1910, Fort Worth, TX, d. May 7, 1995, Largo, FL

A solid Swing drummer who also took good-humored vocals, Ray McKinley deserves much greater recognition for his contributions to Swing. He played with local bands in Texas, performed with Smith Ballew's group in 1932, and then was a member of the Dorsey Brothers Orchestra (1934–35). After Tommy Dorsey stormed off the stand in mid-1935, McKinley became a longtime member of the new Jimmy Dorsey Orchestra, staying until 1939. He was a sort-of silent partner (an unofficial co-leader) in the Will Bradley Orchestra, playing drums, encouraging the band to play boogie-woogie (which led to some important hits), and singing on some of their records (including "Beat Me Daddy, Eight to the Bar" and the eccentric "Celery Stalks at Midnight"). In February 1942 he left Bradley's orchestra to form one of his own, but before the year was out he was in the military. McKinley worked prolifically with Glenn Miller's Army Air Force Band (1943–45), which he headed after Miller's death. Out of the Army, during 1946–50 Ray McKinley led his own orchestra, which was most notable for Eddie Sauter's adventurous arrangements and for its leader's cheerful vocals. After several years of freelancing as both a drummer and a vocalist, in 1956 Ray McKinley organized the new Glenn Miller Orchestra, a ghost band that he toured the world with for a decade. Although McKinley tried his best to keep the music fresh, the Glenn Miller ghost band was expected to play the same old hits the same old way, and its records, although sometimes spirited, are very predictable. McKinley lasted a decade, leaving in 1966 and giving the job to Buddy DeFranco. Ray McKinley played music on a part-time basis for the next 15 years but generally took it easy after having had such a productive career.

●

LPS TO SEARCH FOR

Ray McKinley's recordings of 1946–49 are long overdue to be rediscovered. The best collection is *The Most Versatile Band in the Land* (Savoy 2261), a two-LP set that has 28 selections, including 18 that feature Eddie Sauter arrangements. Among the key musicians in the band during this period (1946–47) are trumpeter Rusty Dedrick, Peanuts Hucko on clarinet and tenor, and guitarist Mundell Lowe;

Sam Butera takes a tenor solo on "Mint Julep." *Ray McKinley* (Golden Era 15030) has live performances by McKinley's 1949 band, including seven Sauter charts out of the dozen songs.

FILMS

McKinley appears in *Make Believe Ballroom* (1949).

BUDDY RICH

b. Sept. 30, 1917, Brooklyn, NY, d. Apr. 2, 1987, Los Angeles, CA

He was often billed as "the world's greatest drummer," and that was truly an accurate description of Buddy Rich. When it came to technique, speed, drive, and even volume, Rich simply did not have any competitors. Louie Bellson could come close, but Rich would win any drum battle.

Buddy Rich could not have started playing drums any earlier in life. His parents were vaudevillians and he was on stage performing drums at the age of 1 1/2. By the time he was three, he was one of the highest paid acts on vaudeville and at six he was billed as "Traps the Drum Wonder." No wonder Rich (who was completely self-taught) could be a brat and a terror in later years!

He worked in vaudeville and shows (also tap dancing and singing) until he was 18. Rich always loved jazz and in 1936 he began to play in clubs. He worked with Joe Marsala (1937–38) and then was a member of the Bunny Berigan Orchestra for a few months. By that time, Rich was in great demand, and it was obvious that he had surpassed his hero, Gene Krupa, along with the other drummers of the period. He was with Artie Shaw's very popular band during 1939 and, when that orchestra

Buddy Rich was already the most remarkable of all drummers when he was caught with Tommy Dorsey's Orchestra in 1940.

broke up, he joined Tommy Dorsey (1939–42). Rich was one of the stars of TD's band, being well featured, appearing in films, and gaining national recognition. He was in the Marines for two years (1942–44), rejoined Dorsey (1944–45), and then formed his own big band. A modern outfit that was bebop-oriented, the orchestra failed by early 1947.

Buddy Rich made many tours with Jazz at the Philharmonic (sometimes playing "drum battles" with Gene Krupa) and freelanced throughout the 1950s (including with Charlie Ventura's Big Four, Harry James on and off during 1953–57, and Tommy Dorsey during 1954–55). He recorded with most of the top jazz stars, including Charlie Parker, Dizzy Gillespie, Art Tatum, Lester Young, and Lionel Hampton. Rich also led his own combos now and then and recorded as a vocalist. A mild heart attack in late 1959 slowed him down only briefly. Rich was a very highly paid sideman with Harry James during 1961–66, but he always had the desire to form his own big band. After being told by many that it was foolhardy in the mid-'60s to even try, Buddy Rich did the impossible. From 1966 off and on until his death, Rich was able to keep a modern big band together, which at various times featured saxophonists Ernie Watts, Don Menza, Pat LaBarbera, and Steve Marcus. The music ranged from bop to hints of fusion, with some of the tunes being rock-oriented. However, Rich's own relentless drumming was always its main attraction, and he remained basically a Swing drummer at heart. He gave 200 percent to each performance, and his drum solos are still impossible to duplicate. Buddy Rich's last public appearance was playing at a televised Tommy Dorsey tribute, taking a solo on "Hawaiian War Chant."

7 *This One's for Basie / Aug. 24–25, 1956 / Verve 817 788*

6 *Rich Versus Roach / Apr. 1959 / Mercury 826 987*

Buddy Rich's big band recordings of 1946–47 are mostly long out of print. *This One's for Basie* finds him heading a speciallyassembled 11-piece band to pay tribute to one of his favorite bandleaders. With arrangements by Marty Paich and such soloists as Harry Edison, trombonist Frank Rosolino, Bob Cooper on tenor, and pianist Jimmy Rowles, it is not surprising that this set swings. Most of the repertoire was made famous by the early Basie band. *Rich Versus Roach* combines the Buddy Rich Quintet of the time (which includes altoist Phil Woods, trombonist Willie Dennis, and pianist John Bunch) with the pianoless Max Roach Quintet (with Roach on drums, tenor saxophonist Stanley Turrentine, trumpeter Tommy Turrentine, and trombonist Julian Priester) for a fun if rather drum-heavy encounter. Among the songs explored are two versions of "Sing, Sing, Sing," "Limehouse Blues," and a drum duet on "Figure Eights."

8 *Swingin' New Big Band / Sept. 29, 1966–Oct. 10, 1966 / Pacific Jazz 35232*

7 *Big Swing Face / Feb. 22, 1967–Mar. 10, 1967 / Pacific Jazz 37989*

7 *The New One / June 15, 1967–Nov. 30, 1967 / Pacific Jazz 94507*

10 *Mercy, Mercy / July 10, 1968 / Pacific Jazz 54331*

It made no sense for Buddy Rich to attempt to form a big band in 1966 but, due to his star power and his brilliance, he was successful. The music on these four Pacific Jazz CD reissues is much more modern than Swing, but they do have the power of a 1930s big band in a much more modern context. In each case, new material from the same sessions is added to the original program. *Swingin' New Big Band* includes Rich's famous "West Side Story Medley," "Sister Sa-

die," and "Basically Blues," and among the soloists are trumpeter Bobby Shew, Jay Corre on tenor, and altoist Pete Yellin. *Big Swing Face* has the up-and-coming Ernie Watts in Yellin's place and, even with a couple of throwaways ("The Beat Goes On" and "Norwegian Wood"), there is some superior music to be heard, including updated versions of "Love for Sale," "Bugle Call Rag," and "Chicago." *The New One* is on the same level, highlighted by "The Rotten Kid," "Machine," and "New Blues." However, the best recording by the Buddy Rich Big Band is *Mercy, Mercy*. The title track is memorable, altoist Art Pepper has three spots (including on "Alfie" and "Chelsea Bridge"), and "Channel One Suite" is a classic, with famous solos by tenor saxophonist Don Menza and Buddy Rich.

LPS TO SEARCH FOR

Buddy Rich's short-lived 1945–46 orchestra is featured on *A Young Man and His Dreams* (Giants of Jazz 1019) and *Live Sessions at the Palladium, Hollywood* (Jazz Anthology 5206). Among the best later big band recordings not yet reissued on CD are 1971's *Rich in London* (RCA 4666), *Stick It* (RCA 4802), *Plays and Plays and Plays* (Gryphon 2273), *Class of '78* (Gryphon 781), and Rich's last recording, a three-LP titled *Live on King Street* (Café 3-372). The last (from 1985) features tenor saxophonist Steve Marcus, who would lead the orchestra during its rare reunions after Buddy Rich's death.

FILMS

Buddy Rich appears with Tommy Dorsey's orchestra in *Ship Ahoy* (1942) and *Du Barry Was a Lady* (1943). In addition, his own short-lived big band is in *Earl Carroll Sketchbook* (1946). Two excellent compilations, *Jazz Legend Part 1, 1917–1970* (DCI Music Video 196) and *Jazz Legend, Part 2, 1970–1987* (DCI Music Video 197) feature many of the filmed high points of his life.

O'NEILL SPENCER

b. November 25, 1909, Cedarville, OH, d. July 24, 1944, New York, NY

The drummer with the John Kirby Sextet, O'Neill Spencer was a tasteful player who could swing hard at a low volume. Prior to joining Kirby, his most important association was with the Mills Blue Rhythm Band (1931–36). Spencer was with the Kirby group during 1937–1941, occasionally taking vocals and frequently showing great subtlety. He also appeared on records with other artists, including Henry "Red" Allen, Mildred Bailey, Johnny Dodds, and Jimmie Noone, in addition to leading the "Spencer Trio" for four songs in 1938. The drummer (who occasionally sang) had to leave Kirby's group in 1941 when he was stricken with tuberculosis. He rejoined the band in 1942 but in mid-1943 was stricken again; O'Neill Spencer died the following year at age 34.

DAVE TOUGH
b. Apr. 26, 1908, Oak Park, IL, d. Dec. 9, 1948, Newark, NJ

Dave Tough, who hated to take drum solos, was considered one of the most consistent drummers of the Swing era, but his life was quite erratic due to his alcoholism. Although he did not attend Austin High in Chicago, he was part of the Austin High Gang of the early to mid-1920s, and he played drums on some of their earliest gigs. He freelanced in Chicago until the summer of 1927, when, on a lark, he sailed to Europe. Tough played on the Continent (recording in Germany), returned home, and then returned to Paris, where he worked with Mezz Mezzrow. Back in the U.S. by May 1929, Tough played with Benny Goodman and Red Nichols before illness resulted in his playing just part time for a few years.

After making a comeback, he was with Ray Noble's Big Band in late 1935 and then spent 1936–37 with the Tommy Dorsey Orchestra. Short stints with Red Norvo and Bunny Berigan preceded four months with Benny Goodman, where he was Gene Krupa's replacement. Tough was back with Dorsey for a year (1938–39), worked with Bud Freeman's Summa Cum Laude Band, spent a few months with Jack Teagarden's orchestra, and then in January 1940 had a complete breakdown. After recuperating at Tommy Dorsey's farm, Tough worked with Mezz Mezzrow, Joe Marsala, Benny Goodman (three months in 1941), and Artie Shaw. Following short periods with Woody Herman and Charlie Spivak, he joined the Navy, where he played with Artie Shaw's Naval Band. Tough was medically discharged in February 1944. Two months later he joined Woody Herman's Herd, staying until September 1945 and fitting in very well in the important Swing-to-bop transition orchestra. The drummer's later experiences included playing with Joe Marsala, working with Eddie Condon, touring with Jazz at the Philharmonic (1946), and jamming with Muggsy Spanier. Tough was able to effectively play Dixieland, Swing, and bop with equal skill and, had he been healthier, he would have had no difficulty keeping busy for the next few decades. In and out of the hospital during his last two years, Dave Tough suffered fatal head injuries after falling down in the street and died at the age of 40.

Violinists

Although no jazz violinist other than Joe Venuti led a Swing orchestra during the big band era (Xavier Cugat does not count!), the 1930s were a golden period for jazz violinists. Listeners who felt that the violin had no place in jazz had to amend their own beliefs, for quite a few brilliant players were active during that time, and in some cases for many decades afterwards. In the 1920s Joe Venuti was the dominant figure, often teaming with guitarist Eddie Lang and appearing on many classic record sessions. He led a big band during the Swing era without much success, but he would emerge again on top over three decades later. Stephane Grappelli in Paris formed a musical partnership with Django Reinhardt and, during the next 60 years, he would continue to gradually grow as a player without changing his basic style. Stuff Smith was a hit on 52nd Street by 1936 and is still thought of as the hardest-swinging violinist of them all. Eddie South had less commercial success, but his strong technique was always impressive. Svend Asmussen in Denmark, although underrated for decades, could hold his own with any of his contemporaries. Ray Nance with Duke Ellington would be one of the few violinists to be featured with a big band, although his cornet work was utilized more often. And Claude Williams, who was on records with Andy Kirk in 1929, would be in obscurity for many decades before finally emerging in the 1970s as one of the greats. Strangely enough, the violin would be neglected in jazz during the bop, cool, and hard bop eras, not becoming prominent again until the late 1960s, when it began to be used in fusion.

SVEND ASMUSSEN

b. Feb. 28, 1916, Copenhagen, Denmark

A talented Swing violinist who was long overshadowed by Stephane Grappelli, Svend Asmussen still remains greatly underrated. Asmussen started playing violin when he was seven and, although he studied sculpture, he began playing music professionally in 1933. He made his recording debut in 1935 and led a Swing sextet until 1943, freelancing for decades afterwards. Although he also worked as a comedian, actor, and vocalist, Asmussen's skills as a violinist were always his greatest asset. Because he has rarely performed in the United States, Asmussen tends to be overlooked; but at his best he has been on the same level as Venuti (his early influence), Grappelli, and Stuff Smith (with whom he often shared the stage in the mid-'60s). Svend Asmussen has played with many touring jazzmen, including Fats Waller, John Lewis (with whom he recorded in 1962), Toots Thielemans, and Lionel Hampton, plus he recorded with Duke Ellington as part of his 1963 Violin Summit. ●

9 *Musical Miracle, Vol. 1: 1935–1940 / Nov. 6, 1935–Dec. 4, 1940 / Phontastic 9306*

8 *Phenomenal Fiddler, Vol. II: 1941–1950 / Oct. 1941– July 26, 1950 / Phontastic 9310*

These two samplers do an excellent job of summing up Svend Asmussen's first 15 years on record. All but the first seven selections on *Musical Miracle* are from 1940. Asmussen, who is also heard on occasional vocals and vibes, shows that he could swing as hard as Stephane Grappelli during the era. None of the other players' names (primarily Danes) are familiar, except perhaps Argentinean Oscar Aleman, whose two numbers with Asmussen are among the 22 included on the excellent CD, which is comprised entirely of Swing standards. Despite the onset of World War II and the rise of bebop, the music on the second volume is also small-group Swing. The only real differences (other than the gradually improving recording quality) are that three songs are Asmussen originals and an average vocal group is used on a few numbers. Few Svend Asmussen recordings are available in the U.S., so get these two imported CDs.

LPS TO SEARCH FOR

Two of a Kind (Storyville 4088), recorded in 1965, was the first full-length meeting on records by Asmussen and Stephane Grappelli. It is as successful as one would hope with the two violinists interpreting "Honeysuckle Rose," a couple of ballads, the boppish "Parisian Thoroughfare," an obscurity, and three originals. *Prize/Winners* (Matrix 1001) finds Asmussen sounding fairly modern, with an up-to-date rhythm section, in 1978 (pianist Kenny Drew, bassist Niels Pedersen, and drummer Ed Thigpen), while *June Night* (Doctor Jazz 39150) is a spirited Mainstream Swing album with pianist Derek Smith, guitarist Bucky Pizzarelli, bassist Milt Hinton, and drummer Oliver Jackson.

STEPHANE GRAPPELLI

b. Jan. 26, 1908, Paris, France, d. Dec. 1, 1997, Paris, France

The most famous of all jazz violinists, Stephane Grappelli was a familiar figure on the jazz scene for over 60 years. Talented as he was in the 1930s, he seemed to get stronger and more fluent with the years, keeping an open mind toward later styles (which he encouraged) while performing mostly the Swing standards that he loved the most. He started out on piano and was largely self-taught on violin, although he did study at the Paris Conservatoire during 1924–28. Grappelli played in local theaters and with a variety of dance bands (both on violin and piano) for several years. The turning point of his career occurred when he met Django Reinhardt in 1933. A spontaneous backstage jam session made it obvious that musically they were a perfect match. Personality-wise, they tended to be opposites. Grappelli was reliable, worldly, and sophisticated, while Reinhardt was a carefree gypsy who paid much less attention than the violinist to showing up on time or furthering his own personal education. However, Grappelli recognized Django's genius, and during 1934–39, as the lead voices in the Quintet of the Hot Club of France, they consistently made musical magic. Their recordings are still remarkable.

In 1939, when the band was in England, World War II broke out. Reinhardt returned to France while Grappelli prudently stayed, and that was the end of the group. The violinist teamed up with the young pianist George Shearing and worked steadily in England during the war. After France was liberated, Grappelli returned home, and in 1946 he had the first of several recorded reunions with Reinhardt. During the next 25 years, Grappelli worked mostly in Europe and, although he played regularly, he was still linked in American minds primarily with the late Django Reinhardt.

In the early 1970s Grappelli became a world traveler, and his regular visits to the U.S. showed listeners that he was still very much in his prime and, if anything, had greatly improved since the Django days. During his final quarter-century, Grappelli was considered a living legend. In addition to performing with string groups similar in instrumentation to the original quintet (with Diz Disley frequently on guitar), Grappelli recorded with such players as pianist Oscar Peterson, Earl Hines, mandolinist David Grisman, Bill Coleman, classical violinist Yehudi Menuhin, vibraphonist Gary Burton, guitarist Larry Coryell, violinist Jean Luc Ponty (whom he always encouraged), pianist McCoy Tyner, and altoist Phil Woods. Even during his last two years, when he was in a wheelchair and his voice was reduced to a whisper, Stephane Grappelli was on the road, showing that he was still a masterful Swing violinist.

●

10 *1935–1940 / Sept. 30, 1935–July 30, 1940 / Classics 708*

9 *1941–1943 / Feb. 28, 1941–Dec. 8, 1943 / Classics 779*

7 *Violins No End / May 1957 / Original Jazz Classics 890* With the exception of the last two numbers, the music on *1935–1940* was all recorded during the period when Stephane Grappelli was collaborating with Django Reinhardt in the Quintet of the Hot Club of France. The music ranges from duets with Django to some performances by the quintet that were released under the violinist's name. Also particularly interesting are two numbers in which he is teamed with fellow violinist Michel Warlop. The CD concludes with Grappelli's first date with George Shearing. While that particular outing features an octet, most of *1941–1943* has Shearing and Grappelli as the main soloists with either a quintet or a sextet. Those high-quality Swing sessions (recorded during the violinist's period in England) are barely known in the U.S. but are well worth exploring and are important dates in the careers of both Grappelli and Shearing. Also quite intriguing is *Violins No End,* which on four of its seven songs matches Grappelli with Stuff Smith, with backing from pianist Oscar Peterson, guitarist Herb Ellis, bassist Ray Brown, and Jo Jones. Although Smith was the hardest swinger of all violinists, Grappelli was clearly inspired by his presence, and the results are a "tie." Grappelli gets first billing on the album, but the final three songs feature Stuff: "Desert Sands," "How High the Moon," and "Moonlight in Vermont." This music was released for the first time in 1984.

9 *Stephane Grappelli Meets Barney Kessel / June 23–24, 1969 / Black Lion 760150*

8 *Limehouse Blues / June 23–24, 1969 / Black Lion 760158*

8 *Just One of Those Things / July 4, 1973 / Black Lion 760180*

8 *Parisian Thoroughfare / Sept. 5–7, 1973 / Black Lion 760132*

9 *Live in London / Nov. 5, 1973 / Black Lion 760139* Although Stephane Grappelli recorded fairly often during 1954–62, few of his records were heard in the United States, and he did not begin recording regularly again until 1969. Grappelli's series for Black Lion was uniformly excellent, and it alerted Americans (along with his first few world tours) that a Swing giant had actually improved with age. Both *Meets Barney Kessel* and *Limehouse Blues* match Grappelli with guitarist Kessel in a pianoless quintet playing mostly vintage standards, plus a few recent originals by Kessel (three apiece on each CD). The former set is a little bit hotter in general, but both outings are excellent examples of how well the 61-year-old violinist was playing. *Just One of Those Things* was recorded at the 1973 Montreux Jazz Festival, and Grappelli (who is backed by a piano-bass-drums trio) is quite exuberant on such numbers as "All God's Chillun," "Them There Eyes," and "Honeysuckle Rose." The violinist loved to play with younger, more modern musicians. The studio set *Parisian Thoroughfare* finds him holding his own with pianist Roland Hanna, bassist George Mraz, and drummer Mel Lewis, digging into Hanna's "Perugia," "Fascinating Rhythm," a Chopin melody, and the title cut. *Live in London* features Grappelli with one of his finest touring bands, the Hot Club of London, which at the time was composed of guitarists Diz Disley and Denny Wright, plus bassist Len Skeat. This CD reissues all of the music from a former two-LP set and even adds an additional unissued selection, "Them There Eyes." Highlights include "This Can't Be Love," "Honeysuckle Rose," and "After You've Gone."

[10] *Stephane Grappelli/David Grisman Live / Sept. 7–20, 1979 / Warner Bros. 3550*

[9] *Live in San Francisco / July 4 + 7, 1982 / Storyville 8297*

[7] *Plays Jerome Kern / 1987 / GRP 9542*

[7] *Olympia 88 / Jan. 24, 1988 / Atlantic 892095*

[8] *One on One / Apr. 18, 1990 / Milestone 9181*

[7] *In Tokyo / Oct. 4, 1990 / Denon 81757 9130*

[7] *Live 1992 / Mar. 27–28, 1992 / Verve 314 517 392*

[7] *Flamingo / Jan. 15–17, 1995 / Dreyfus 36 580*

By the late 1970s, Stephane Grappelli was a fixture all over the world at jazz festivals and concert halls, and easily the most famous of all jazz violinists. He loved the fact that younger musicians were interested in playing Swing, and he particularly enjoyed mandolinist David Grisman's band. In 1979 Grisman had Mike Marshall (on mandolin and guitar), guitarist Mark O'Connor (who switches to violin on "Tiger Rag"), and bassist Rob Wasserman as his sidemen. Their exciting concert with Grappelli finds the players overflowing with energy on such numbers as "Shine," "Sweet Georgia Brown," "Swing '42," and particularly a blazing romp through "Tiger Rag." Grappelli recorded many records during his final 20 years, of which this batch is only a small sampling of essentials. *Live in San Francisco* has Grappelli joined by the Diz Disley Trio (with Martin Taylor as the other guitarist) on a set of the violinist's favorite standards, songs he never tired of playing. The David Grisman Band joins Grappelli on the date's closer, "Sweet Georgia Brown."

Plays Jerome Kern finds Grappelli and a pianoless quartet backed by a string orchestra for 11 Kern songs, including "The Way You Look Tonight," "A Fine Romance," "Pick Yourself Up," and "I Won't Dance." On Olympia 88 (which captures Grappelli two days short of his 80th birthday), he is teamed with guitarists Martin Taylor and Marc Fosset and bassist Patrice Caratini, playing his usual repertoire with spirit and enthusiasm. Most unusual is that pianist Martial Solal joins the group on four songs including a Gershwin

medley that adds the violin of Svend Asmussen. Considering Grappelli's consistent and mostly unchanging repertoire and his Swing style, it is surprising how successful *One on One* is, a set of duets with pianist McCoy Tyner. Most of the songs are Swing standards, but there are a few exceptions, particularly "Mr. P.C.," "You Say You Care," and "You Taught My Heart to Sing." Grappelli has no problem playing with John Coltrane's former pianist, and vice versa. In his last years, Stephane Grappelli usually traveled with a trio. *In Tokyo* finds him in excellent form while joined by guitarist Marc Fosset and bassist Jean-Philippe Viret, with Marcel Azzola making a few guest appearances on bandoneon. One would never think that the violinist was 82 at the time, or 84 when he made *Live 1992* with Fosset, guitarist Philip Catherine, and bassist Niels Pedersen. In addition to three Gershwin songs and "Stella by Starlight," Grappelli plays an original piece by Catherine and Larry Coryell ("Blues for Django and Stephane") plus four numbers of his own. *Flamingo* teams the 87-year-old violinist (who at this late point in his life still sounded ageless) and the 32-year-old modern pianist Michel Petrucciani plus bassist Mraz and drummer Roy Haynes. The repertoire as usual is mostly Swing warhorses, including "Sweet Georgia Brown" once again, "I Got Rhythm," and "There Will Never Be Another You." But Stephane Grappelli had the ability to make songs that he had played tens of thousands of times sound brand new; 60 years of practice did not hurt!

LPS TO SEARCH FOR

Venupelli Blues (Affinity 29) is a special set, the only meeting on records between Stephane Grappelli and Joe Venuti. Recorded in 1969 with Barney Kessel and the George Wein Trio, the outing features the two immortal jazz violinists finding common ground on six standards and a blues song, matching wits and creating memorable music. When will this be reissued on CD? Also quite worthy of being brought back is *The Reunion* (MPS 68162), a 1976 quartet date costarring Grappelli and George Shearing.

FILMS

Stephane Grappelli is in the British film *Time Flies* (1944), *The Lisbon Story* (1945), *The Flamingo Affair* (1948), *Mirth and Melody* (1951), and *King of the Gypsies* (1978). In addition, *Stephane Grappelli—Live in San Francisco* (Rhapsody Films) is an hour-long filmed version of some of the same music that is on the 1982 CD of the same name.

STUFF SMITH

b. Aug. 14, 1909, Portsmouth, OH, d. Sep. 25, 1967, Munich, Germany

Of all the jazz violinists, the one who could probably have defeated most saxophonists or trumpeters in "battles" was the exciting Hezekiah "Stuff" Smith. He started on the violin when he was seven and at 12 was playing in his father's band. Smith began working professionally in 1924 and toured with Alphonso Trent's legendary territory band (1926–30), with whom he made his recording debut. He led groups in Buffalo, New York, for a few years, and then in 1936 Stuff's sextet opened at the Onyx Club on 52nd Street. Very soon they were a big hit. With trumpeter Jonah Jones as the second lead voice and drummer Cozy Cole in the rhythm section, this was one of the finest Swing combos of the time, a powerhouse outfit. The band lasted into 1940, had a hit in "I'se a Muggin'," and recorded a classic version of "Here Comes the Man with the Jive." Stuff Smith continued leading other groups (including a trio with pianist Billy Taylor in the mid-1940s) and, although somewhat in obscurity in the 1950s, he was well recorded by Norman Granz for Verve and was a guest on Nat King Cole's *After Midnight Sessions.* Stuff Smith lived in many different places during his life, moving to Europe in 1965, where he was quite active during his final two years.

●

10 *1936–1939 / Feb. 11, 1936–Dec. 1939 / Classics 706*

7 *1943 / Nov. 17, 1943 / Progressive 7053*

With the exception of four numbers from April 1940, *1936–1939* has every selection recorded by Stuff Smith's Onyx Club Boys, his quintet/sextet with Jonah Jones. By the second session, Cozy Cole was on drums, and on one of the dates Buster Bailey is added on clarinet. The group had a hit in the two-part "I'se a Muggin'," but the second part of that piece (which is billed as a "Musical Numbers Game") is so repetitious that it does not need to be heard twice! However, virtually all of the other selections are quite exciting, particularly "I Hope Gabriel Likes My Music," "After You've Gone," "You're a Viper," "Old Joe's Hittin' the Jug," "Here Comes the Man with the Jive," and "Twilight in Turkey." *1943* is the complete release of a trio date (with pianist Jimmy Jones and bassist John Levy) that was made for a radio transcription service. The ten songs include "Humoresque," "Minuet in Swing," Smith's famous "Desert Sands," and "Bugle Call Rag." In addition to the master takes, there are three false starts and four alternate takes, but one can program their CD player to skip those.

* *The Complete Verve Stuff Smith Sessions / Oct. 25, 1956–Mar. 23, 1964 / Mosaic 4–186*

8 *Stuff Smith–Dizzy Gillespie–Oscar Peterson / Jan. 21, 1957–Apr. 17, 1957 / Verve 314 521 676*

9 *Hot Violins / Mar. 1965–Feb. 18, 1967 / Storyville 4170*
There is almost nothing of Stuff Smith on records during 1946–55. Fortunately Norman Granz saved the day and re-corded the violinist on several occasions during 1956–57. The limited-edition four-CD Mosaic box set was released in 1999, so it can still be acquired as of this writing, and it should be! The exciting package starts off with a dozen previously unissued and consistently dazzling trio numbers from 1956 (with Jimmy Jones or Dudley Brooks on piano and Red Callendar or Jess Simpkins on bass). Strange that it had never come out, because Smith is quite exciting and creative throughout that date. He is also heard in a quartet with pianist Carl Perkins, teaming up with the Oscar Peterson Trio plus drums, holding his own with trumpeter Dizzy Gillespie on five numbers, using Shirley Horn on piano and vocals (for what was her recorded debut, most of it previously unissued), and on an additional quartet session with pianist Paul Smith. The box concludes with four performances from a truncated 1964 date in which Smith is matched with fellow violinist Ray Nance. Listeners who cannot find this set or cannot afford it may want to pick up the two-CD Verve reissue, which has most of the numbers with Perkins plus all of the songs with Peterson and Gillespie. *Hot Violins* is from Stuff Smith's final European period. He is heard on four songs apiece with either Poul Olsen or Svend Asmussen joining him on second violin. "Lady Be Good," which has both Asmussen and Smith singing, is quite charming, and the other selections find Stuff swinging hard, as usual. In addition, Smith plays two numbers with the Kenny Drew Trio just seven months before his death, still sounding quite strong.

Live at the Montmartre (Storyville 4142) and *Swingin' Stuff* (Storyville 4087) are from March 18 and 23, 1965, live sessions matching Stuff Smith with pianist Kenny Drew, bassist Niels Pedersen, and drummer Alex Riel. "Take the 'A' Train," "Bugle Blues," and "Old Stinkin' Blues" are among the hotter numbers on the former date, while the latter has "Bugle Blues," "Mack the Knife," and "One O'Clock Jump" as highlights.

EDDIE SOUTH

b. November 27, 1904, Louisiana, MO, d. Apr. 25, 1962, Chicago, IL

If times had been different and racism had not closed the door to him, Eddie South could have been a great classical violinist. Later on known as "The Dark Angel of the Violin," South grew up in Chicago and was a child prodigy, but he recognized pretty early that he could not have a concert career. Instead, he worked in the 1920s with Charles Elgar, Erskine Tate, Mae Brady, and Jimmy Wade's Syncopators (1924–27). South visited Europe during 1928–31 with his group the Alabamians, freelanced in Chicago during the 1930s, and was back in Europe during 1937–38 (including recordings with Django Reinhardt and Stephane Grappelli). Eddie South led small groups (mostly in Chicago) during the 1940s and '50s, working on radio and television but never really making it big despite his talent.

9 | *1923–1937 / Dec. 1923–Nov. 23, 1937 / Classics 707*

9 | *1937–1941 / Nov. 25, 1937–Mar. 12, 1941 / Classics 737*
All of Eddie South's recording prior to 1946 are on these two CDs. *1923–37* starts off with him playing "Someday Sweetheart" in 1923 as a sideman with Wade's Moulin Rouge Orchestra. Eddie South is heard on nine numbers as a leader with his Alabamians during 1927–29 and on two songs from 1931. Some of that music (which includes such numbers as "By the Waters of Minnetonka," "Two Guitars," "Marcheta," and "Hejre Kati") is quite odd, mixing gypsy influences and European folk melodies with jazz; the mix is not always that comfortable. However, six cuts from 1933 (which include Milt Hinton) swing hard, with "Old Man Harlem" and "Nagasaki" being noteworthy. The program concludes with eight rewarding selections recorded in Paris in 1937 with Django Reinhardt and Stephane Grappelli, including "Lady Be Good" (which has Michel Warlop on third violin), "Somebody Loves Me," and an improvisation on a Bach melody. *1937–1941* starts off with the final two numbers from the Paris date, finds South playing in Holland with a quintet, and has eight rare songs cut back in New York in 1940 , a date with the John Kirby Sextet's front line and singer Ginny Sims, and two conventional Swing numbers from 1941. The 1937 Paris dates stand out overall as the highpoints of Eddie South's career.

South-Side Jazz (Chess 10019) has a date by South in Chicago in 1952 along with unrelated material from tenors Eddie Johnson, Lonnie Simmons, and Dave Young, pianist Prince Cooper, and drummer Red Saunders. *The Distinguished Violin of Eddie South* (Mercury 60070), from 1958, once again alternates between Swing tunes (such as "C-Jam Blues" and "Fiddle Ditty") and folkish melodies transformed into jazz.

JOE VENUTI

b. Sept. 16, 1903, Philadelphia, PA, d. Aug. 14, 1978, Seattle, WA

Joe Venuti's most important work was done in the 1920s and after he was rediscovered in 1968. He was the first great jazz violinist, an infamous practical joker, and one of the major figures of early jazz. Giuseppe "Joe" Venuti, who used to claim that he was born on an ocean liner sailing to America, was actually born in Philadelphia, where Eddie Lang was a childhood friend. They played violin-guitar duets together from an early age and crossed paths constantly throughout the 1920s. After working with Jean Goldkette's orchestra in 1924, Venuti became a very busy freelancer in New York, appearing on countless sessions during 1925–33 and leading a series of hot recordings, often under the name of the Blue Five. He also headed a more commercial but first-class dance band on records. Venuti was with Roger Wolfe Kahn (1925–26), worked with various Broadway shows, and performed with Paul Whiteman's orchestra (with Lang) during 1929–30. Venuti kept on working as a studio musician during the early Depression years. Eddie Lang's death in 1933 shocked him, and his career became a bit aimless. Venuti toured England in 1934 and put together a big band the following year that he worked with into 1943. The Joe Venuti Big Band was a minor-league outfit, with its only significant sideman being drummer Barrett Deems, although it did introduce singer Kay Starr.

After the band broke up and he served briefly in the military, Joe Venuti moved to Los Angeles, where he worked primarily as a studio musician during the next 20 years. Venuti appeared regularly on the Bing Crosby radio show (getting a feature number on most shows) but was an alcoholic and barely recorded at all in the 1950s and early '60s. However, in 1967 he started making an unlikely comeback, and for his last 11 years he played at the peak of his powers, recording frequently, touring often, and impressing audiences with his brilliant playing, his colorful stories, and his wisecracks.

●

7 *Venuti and Lang / Nov. 8, 1926–May 8, 1933 / ABC 836 200*

10 *Fiddlesticks / Oct. 22, 1931–Jan. 25, 1939 / Confier 172*

8 *Pretty Trix / Dec. 26–28, 1934 / IAJRC 1003*
The 1926–33 recordings of Joe Venuti and Eddie Lang deserve to be reissued on CD domestically complete and in chronological order. The ABC release is just a sampler that contains 16 selections featuring Venuti and/or Lang. Robert Parker's adventurous engineering helps give the performances the feel of stereo. The program includes music from dates led by Venuti, Lang (usually without the violinist), Red Nichols, Frankie Trumbauer, and Red McKenzie, with some famous recordings mixing in with obscurities. Best are "Stringing the Blues," "Four-String Joe," "Sensation," and "The Wild Dog." *Fiddlesticks* has quite a few classics and interesting performances. The Venuti-Lang All-Star Orchestra date of 1931 (which features Jack Teagarden) is highlighted by famous versions of "Beale Street Blues" and "After You've Gone." Venuti and Lang team up on four other numbers from 1933, which would be the guitarist's final recordings. Venuti is also heard with a studio orchestra in 1934 and with a 1935 version of his "Blue Five" (with Adrian Rollini on bass sax and vibraphone). Of greatest interest to Swing-era fans are the only four recordings by the Joe Venuti Big Band: "Flip," "Flop," "Something," and "Nothing!" *Pretty Trix* has previously unknown performances from late 1934 by Venuti with a studio orchestra that includes Louis Prima, Red Norvo, Larry Binyon on tenor and flute, and

guitarist Frank Victor. These radio transcriptions (which are not flawless) mix a touch of Dixieland with Swing and are generally quite fun.

7 *15 Jazz Classics / May 3, 1971–Sept. 14, 1974 / Omega 3019*

9 *Alone at the Palace / Apr. 27–28, 1977 / Chiaroscuro 160*
After 30 years of obscurity, Joe Venuti made a full comeback that started in 1967 and lasted until his death in 1978. *15 Jazz Classics,* which inexcusably does not list the recording dates, matches Venuti with guitarist Lino Patruno and other fine local players in Italy; the band sometimes includes baritone and flute. The violinist is the main star throughout, playing in prime form on "I've Found a New Baby," "Clementine," "Honeysuckle Rose," "Indiana," and a five-song George Gershwin medley. *Alone at the Palace* was Venuti's next-to-last recording. Age 73 at the time, he sounds full of spirit during the set of duets with pianist Dave McKenna. The original dozen selections (which include "At the Jazz Band Ball," "The World Is Waiting for the Sunrise," and three Venuti originals) are augmented by seven additional performances added to the CD reissue. Recommended.

LPS TO SEARCH FOR

The two LPs *Joe Venuti and Eddie Lang 1926–1930* (Swaggie 817) and *1930–1933* (Swaggie 819) contain nearly all of the Venuti small-group dates of his Lang period. His early studio recordings with orchestras are reissued on *The Big Bands of Joe Venuti Volume 1, 1928–1930* (JSP 1111) and *Volume 2, 1930–1933* (JSP 1112). *The Mad Fiddler From Philly* (Shoestring 111) has some of Venuti's feature spots on the Bing Crosby radio show during 1952–53. *Joe & Zoot* (Chiaroscuro 128), from 1973, *The Joe Venuti Blue Four* (Chiaroscuro 134), and *Joe Venuti and Zoot Sims* (Chiaroscuro 142) are among the finest recordings of the violinist during his comeback years. He teams up with tenor saxophonist Sims in all three cases and sounds quite inspired by both the repertoire and his sidemen. Another successful collaboration was his two recordings with guitarist George Barnes: *Gems* (Concord Jazz 14) and *Live at the Concord Summer Festival* (Concord Jazz 30). Joe Venuti's final recording was *Live at Concord '77* (Concord Jazz 51), seven standards with a quintet that includes pianist Ross Tompkins and tenor saxophonist Scott Hamilton.

FILMS

Joe Venuti appears for a precious 90 seconds opposite Eddie Lang in *The King of Jazz* (1930). He is also in *Garden of the Moon* (1938), *Syncopation* (1942), *Sarge Goes to College* (1947), *Two Guys from Texas* (1948), and *Disc Jockey* (1951).

Other Instrumentalists

HARRY CARNEY
b. Apr. 1, 1910, Boston, MA, d. Oct. 8, 1974, New York, NY

When Harry Carney started playing baritone sax, the instrument was a true rarity. Most big bands, even in the Swing era, rarely used baritone, usually having a reed section comprised of two altos and two tenors (with one or more saxophonists doubling on clarinet). Carney had such a deep and definitive sound on baritone that his instrument was eventually adopted by every big band from the mid-1940s on, when the typical jazz orchestra expanded to five reeds. But during the Swing era, Carney's only close competitors were Haywood Henry (with Erskine Hawkins's) and Count Basie's Jack Washington.

Carney was there first and he never declined. He started on piano and clarinet before switching to alto sax as a teenager. He played locally in Boston as a youth (taking lessons from Benny Waters) and in 1927 first visited New York. Carney had short-term gigs with Fess Williams, Henri Saparo, and Joe Steele. He joined the Duke Ellington Orchestra in June 1927 on alto, soon switched to baritone, and was a fixture with Ellington until the very end, 47 years later. Carney, who also doubled on bass clarinet and always played the clarinet solo on "Rockin' in Rhythm," was a major part of the Ellington sound from the late 1920s on through the 1970s. He was influenced by Coleman Hawkins and bass saxophonist Adrian Rollini and was one of the first jazzmen to master circular breathing, which he tended to use at the end of "Sophisticated Lady" to play an endless note. Harry Carney outlived Duke Ellington and even appeared on Mercer Ellington's first recording after Duke's death before he himself passed away at the age of 64. Other than four titles for HRS in 1946 (reissued as part of Mosaic's HRS box set), two for Wax (1947), and two for Verve (1949), he led only two record dates: *Harry Carney with Strings* (a 1954 Clef set that has been reissued as part of Ben Webster's *Music for Loving* CD) and the long-out-of-print *Rock Me Gently* for Columbia in 1960.

WAYMAN CARVER
b. Dec. 25, 1905, Portsmouth, VA, d. May 6, 1967, Atlanta, GA

With the exception of Albert Socarras (who made some recordings in the late 1920s), Wayman Carver was jazz's first flute soloist. Carver's period in the spotlight was brief, and he was always a saxophonist who occasionally played flute rather than being a specialist. He worked early on with J. Neal Montgomery's Collegiate Ramblers. After moving to New York, Carver played with Dave Nelson (with whom he made his recording debut), Elmer Snowden (1931–32), and Benny Carter's big band in 1933, recording with Carter and on flute with Spike Hughes. Carver was with Chick Webb during 1934–40, mostly playing tenor in the ensembles but once in a great while being heard on flute. Most notable were the four selections that he cut in 1937 with Chick Webb and his Little Chicks, small-group sides that had a flute-clarinet front line. Wayman Carver (who never led his own record date) stayed with the Webb Orchestra for a year after the drummer's death, but by 1941 he was no longer a full-time musician. He ended up being an associate professor of music at Clark College in Atlanta for many years.

ADELE GIRARD

b. 1913, d. Sept. 7, 1993, Denver, CO

While the baritone saxophone and flute have become common instruments in jazz, swinging harp players seem destined to always be rare. The short-lived Casper Reardon was the first and Adele Girard the second, preceding Dorothy Ashby by 15 years. Girard sounded perfectly at home in freewheeling ensembles. She played with Harry Sosnick's band in the mid-1930s and in 1937 became a member of Joe Marsala's combo, marrying the clarinetist that year. Girard performed with Marsala for a decade and appeared on quite a few records under his name, where her harp never failed to surprise and delight listeners. After the mid-1950s Adele Girard was semiretired, but she came back in 1992 to be on an album for Arbors (*Don't Let It End*) by clarinetist Bobby Gordon, still sounding quite youthful, angelic, and swinging at the age of 78.

Male Vocalists

Most male vocalists who recorded in the 1920s are difficult to listen to these days. Early singers were chosen for their ability to project and to pronounce words clearly, not for their ability to Swing or improvise. The first and best early jazz singers were musicians, starting with Ukulele Ike (Cliff Edwards) in 1924. Louis Armstrong on his Hot Five and Hot Seven recordings did a great deal to popularize scatting (singing nonsense syllables) and his hornlike phrasing greatly influenced Bing Crosby.

Bing Crosby, who originally gained some recognition with Paul Whiteman during 1927–30 (when he was part of the Rhythm Boys), really blossomed as a soloist with Gus Arnheim in the early 1930s. The popularity of his warm baritone voice saved pop music from the boy tenors and set the standard for the next two decades.

During the Swing era, the main influences on male singers were Crosby and Armstrong along with Cab Calloway and Jack Teagarden. Most big bands had a male singer and a female singer, but the females tended to be more versatile and have longer careers, with a few exceptions. In fact, some of the key Swing bands (Benny Goodman, Duke Ellington, Artie Shaw) did not have a regular male singer at all in the 1930s unless it was an instrumentalist (such as Tony Pastor with Shaw) taking an occasional vocal. The best of the band singers was Jimmy Rushing with Count Basie, because he was masterful at blues and standards and could swing anything. Most other male singers who were not an instrumentalist tended to stick to ballads (Jack Leonard with Tommy Dorsey, Jimmy Dorsey's Bob Eberly, and his brother Ray Eberle with Glenn Miller) and were somewhat limited, not having much of a solo career after the big band era ended. There were just a few male ballad singers (Frank Sinatra, Dick Haymes, and Herb Jeffries) who were well rounded enough to have substantial post-Swing musical lives. Sinatra would become an institution and Bing Crosby's replacement as the most influential male singer of them all, while Nat King Cole's jazz piano career would by 1950 be replaced by his success as a singer.

Other singers covered in this section include the remarkable Fred Astaire, who introduced many standards in his movies and was a solid Swing singer, the Mills Brothers, Big Joe Turner (whose career spanned several eras), and the eccentric Leo Watson.

FRED ASTAIRE

b. May 10, 1899, Omaha, NE, d. June 22, 1987, Los Angeles, CA

Fred Astaire of course found great fame as one of the 20th century's finest dancers and as a movie star, but he was also a vastly underrated singer. Astaire had a small range but a very likable voice, and Irving Berlin in particular loved to write songs for him to introduce; the Gershwins, Cole Porter, Johnny Mercer, and Jerome Kern were among his many other admirers. In addition, he was a good musician (composing the standard "I'm Building Up to an Awful Letdown") and a fine pianist. That is him actually playing that song on piano in one segment of the movie *Follow the Fleet*.

Born Frederick Austerlitz, Astaire toured in vaudeville shows from the age of seven, usually with his sister, Adele. Fred and Adele worked together regularly during 1916–32 in shows, often on Broadway. After Adele got married and retired in 1932, it was not long before Fred Astaire was out in Hollywood. He started teaming up with actress Ginger Rogers in 1933 and their magical dances and interplay were featured in many classic films. Astaire would continue to be active as a dancer through the 1950s and as an actor for two decades after that.

As a singer, Fred Astaire made records as early as the first half of the 1920s. He recorded many of the songs that were featured in his movies in the '30s and in 1952 was teamed with a jazz group by Norman Granz, resulting in a fine set entitled *The Astaire Story*.

●

9   *The Astaire Story / Dec. 1952 / Verve 835 649*
This project was so logical that it is surprising it did not take place earlier. Fred Astaire, in 1952, when he was 53, performed 34 of the many songs that he introduced in films, with backing by pianist Oscar Peterson, Charlie Shavers, Flip Phillips, guitarist Barney Kessel, bassist Ray Brown, and drummer Alvin Stoller. Shavers, Phillips, and Peterson have plenty of solos, and Astaire was in excellent voice, even taking three tap dance solos along the way and sitting out on the instrumental "Jam Session." Among the songs that Astaire joyfully sings are "Isn't This a Lovely Day," "The Continental," "Change Partners," "They All Laughed,"

"The Way You Look Tonight," "I Won't Dance," "A Fine Romance," "A Foggy Day," and his "I'm Building Up to an Awful Letdown."

LPS TO SEARCH FOR

Starring Fred Astaire (Columbia 44233) is a two-LP set that has Fred Astaire's finest recordings of the 1935–40 period, including many songs written by Irving Berlin, Jerome Kern, the Gershwins, and Johnny Mercer. This is a classic release that contains 36 selections and deserves to be reissued on CD.

BING CROSBY

b. May 2, 1904, Tacoma, WA, d. Oct. 14, 1977, Madrid, Spain

Harry Lillis "Bing" Crosby towered over the popular music world of the 1930s and for several decades afterwards. His relaxed and friendly style (which translated the innovations of Louis Armstrong and Jack Teagarden into the pop music world) was so unassuming that it sounded effortless and quite natural. One never mistook him for a frustrated opera singer or for a virtuoso, yet Crosby's deep baritone changed pop music forever and his renditions of scores of tunes (which he made into standards) became the definitive way to interpret those songs.

Nine years older than his brother Bob Crosby, Bing grew up in Spokane, Washington. He attended Gonzaga College, originally to become a lawyer, but he also played drums and sang jazz in Al Rinker's group, the Musicaladers. With the assistance of Mildred Bailey, Bing and Rinker (Mildred's brother) came down to Los Angeles, worked in vaudeville, and joined Paul Whiteman's orchestra in 1926. Whiteman paired the duo with singer-pianist Harry Barris, and the Rhythm

Boys were born. During the next four years, the Rhythm Boys, who could be quite undisciplined and more concerned with partying than music, were part of Whiteman's show. Bing was impressed by such musicians as Bix Beiderbecke and Joe Venuti and also listened closely to Armstrong and Teagarden. Although initially featured not only with the Rhythm Boys but as one of Whiteman's crew of singers, Crosby had his solo spots, and he began to stand out by 1928. When the Rhythm Boys left Whiteman in 1930 (after appearing in *The King of Jazz* movie), Crosby had limitless potential.

The trio worked with Gus Arnheim's orchestra in Los Angeles for a period, and that is when Crosby really caught on as a soloist. Although quite jazz-oriented in his early days, Bing proved to be a masterful interpreter of ballads, and his likable baritone was a great contrast to the many "boy tenors" who were dominating pop music. With such hits in 1931 as "Just One More Chance" and "I Found a Million-Dollar Baby in the Five and Ten Cent Store," along with appearances in a few movie shorts, Crosby was becoming a big name and the Rhythm Boys broke up. An intimate singer rather than a shouter (the development of the microphone made his style possible), Crosby sounded like the man next door and was both appealing and nonthreatening, everyone's friend. By the time he appeared in *The Big Broadcast*

Bing Crosby towered over pop music during the 1930s and has remained a major influential force in the decades since.

in 1932, he was on his way to becoming a major star. His constant work in concerts, on radio, on records, and in the movies would not slow down for decades; Crosby was hugely successful in each of those four areas.

Bing had major hits in "Please," "June in January," and the perfect Depression song "Brother, Can You Spare a Dime?" After signing with Decca in the mid-1930s, Bing Crosby sang everything from ballads to cowboy songs (introducing "I'm an Old Cowhand"), jazz to Irish and Hawaiian melodies, and he excelled in every format. His *Kraft Music Hall* radio series was on the air for a decade, "Pennies from Heaven" and the unlikely "Sweet Leilani" were his major hits of 1936–37, and his Road pictures with Bob Hope in the 1940s made him a permanent superstar. Crosby's recording of "White Christmas" (which Irving Berlin wrote specifically for him) sold over 30 million copies.

Though never a regular member of a big band (his name by 1934 was much better known than any of the bandleaders'), Bing Crosby had a dominant influence on other male singers during the Swing era. It would take a Frank Sinatra to challenge him, although Crosby could never really be replaced. He was a major figure in the entertainment world until his death in 1977.

●

9 *1926–1932 / Dec. 22, 1926–Feb. 11, 1932 / Timeless 1-004*

10 *Bing—His Legendary Years: 1931 to 1957 / Nov. 23, 1931–Dec. 27, 1957 / MCA 4-10887*

9 *And Some Jazz Friends / Aug. 8, 1934–Apr. 25, 1951 / GRP/Decca 603*

1926–1932 has 24 of Bing Crosby's finest recordings of his early period. In most cases he is joined by the Paul Whiteman Orchestra, but there are also a few solo numbers, plus collaborations with Sam Lanin, the Dorsey Brothers, Duke Ellington ("Three Little Words" with the Rhythm Boys and "St. Louis Blues" as a solo), the Mills Brothers, and Gus Arnheim's Orchestra ("One More Time"). Among the more memorable selections are "Mississippi Mud," "Changes," "Ol' Man River," "You Took Advantage of Me," and "Dinah." The four-CD set *His Legendary Years* is a perfectly done sampler of Crosby's prime years. There are nine titles from 1931 and then the remainder is from his 1934–57 period on Decca. All of his hits are here (and there are many). The set on a whole shows the great variety of songs that Crosby uplifted, even such unlikely material as a sacred "Silent Night," "Sweet Leilani," "Deep in the Heart of Texas," "Pistol Packin' Mama," "MacNamara's Band," and "Chattanooga Shoe Shine Boy." An essential acquisition.

Throughout his life, Bing Crosby always had a love for Dixieland-oriented jazz. *And Some Jazz Friends* has some of his best jazz collaborations of the Swing era. Included are mostly memorable meetings with Louis Jordan, Connie Boswell, Louis Armstrong, Jack Teagarden, Eddie Condon, Lionel Hampton, Lee Wiley, Woody Herman, and brother Bob Crosby. In the enjoyable repertoire is "Your Socks Don't Match," "Pennies from Heaven," "After You've Gone," "It Still Suits Me," "Gone Fishin'," and "The Waiter and the Porter and the Upstairs Maid."

- **9** *Havin' Fun / 1949–1951 / Jazz Unlimited 2034*
- **7** *Havin' More Fun / 1950–1951 / Jazz Unlimited 2035*
- **8** *Bing Sings Whilst Bregman Swings / June 11–12, 1956 / Mobile Fidelity 670*

The two Jazz Unlimited CDs are taken from the soundtracks of Bing Crosby's television shows of 1949–51, putting the focus on guest appearances by Louis Armstrong and His All-Stars (which include Jack Teagarden). The interplay between Bing and Satch on *Havin' Fun* is often hilarious, and the music (which also has guest spots for Joe Venuti, Ella Fitzgerald, and Peggy Lee) is generally quite rewarding. Highlights include "Royal Garden Blues," "Baby, Won't You Please Come Home," and "On the Sunny Side of the Street." The music on *Havin' More Fun* (which has Dinah Shore in Ella's place) is just as good, but the jokes are not quite as inspired. Among the better tracks are "A Song Was Born," "Up the Lazy River," and "Panama." *Bing Sings Whilst Bregman Swings* is one of Crosby's best albums of his later years, and it has been reissued as an audiophile CD. Backed by a big band arranged by Buddy Bregman, Crosby (whose voice is heard at its peak) sings a dozen standards that he had apparently never recorded before, including " 'Deed I Do," "The Blue Room," "They All Laughed," and "Jeepers Creepers."

FILMS

Among Bing Crosby's many film appearances, a few are jazz-oriented. He sings "Mississippi Mud" with the Rhythm Boys in *King of Jazz* (1930), performs "Dinah" with the backing of Eddie Lang in *The Big Broadcast* (1932), interacts with Louis Armstrong in *Pennies from Heaven* (1935), performs with Jack Teagarden in *Birth of the Blues* (1941), and introduces a few Cole Porter songs with the help of Armstrong in *High Society* (1956).

DICK HAYMES

b. Sept. 13, 1916, Buenos Aires, Argentina, d. Mar. 28, 1980, Los Angeles, CA

Dick Haymes was one of the more popular male singers of the 1940s, and his deep voice was at its best on ballads. Haymes, whose mother was a voice teacher, traveled widely as a youth, living in Argentina, France, England, Switzerland, and the U.S. He worked as a radio announcer in 1936 and then became a professional singer, performing with Freddie Martin and Orrin Tucker. Haymes gained recognition for his work with Harry James (1939–41), having a hit with "I'll Get By." He was briefly with Benny Goodman and then joined Tommy Dorsey, where, as with James, he replaced the departed Frank Sinatra. In 1943 Haymes began his solo career (his version of "You'll Never Know" was popular) and he appeared in several 20th Century Fox movies, including *Irish Eyes Are Smiling* (introducing "The More I See You"), *State Fair, Do You Love Me?* (with Harry James), and *The Shocking Miss Pilgrim*. However, he failed to catch on as a movie star and stuck to singing after

1947. By the mid-1950s, Dick Haymes's popularity was dropping and, although he retained his appealing baritone voice and recorded as late as 1978, he never regained his former fame.

●

7 *Imagination / Sept. 29, 1952 / Audiophile 79*
A good example of Dick Haymes's singing during his solo years, this set finds him backed by the orchestras of Carmen Dragon and Al Lerner, performing warm versions of standards, including "It's the Talk of the Town," "There's a Small Hotel," "These Foolish Things," and "But Not for Me."

HERB JEFFRIES
b. Sept. 24, 1911, Detroit, MI

Herb Jeffries, who is still active as of this writing in 1999, has a remarkably ageless voice, still sounding as if he could pass for 60. A fine ballad singer, he worked with Erskine Tate in the early 1930s, sang and recorded with Earl Hines (1931-34), and was with Blanche Calloway's orchestra. In the late 1930s, Jeffries was the movie's first black cowboy, singing and acting in several low-budget black films. As a member of the Duke Ellington Orchestra (1940–42), he had a giant hit in "Flamingo," which gave him his greatest fame. Herb Jeffries became a solo act after leaving Duke and has worked fairly steadily through the years, still appearing in public on a fairly regular basis despite his age.

●

9 *A Brief History of Herb Jeffries (The Bronze Buckaroo) / 1934–1995 / Warner Western 7621*

7 *Say It Isn't So / Jan. 1957 / Bethlehem 20-3006*
Although *A Brief History* was released by the country division of Warner Bros. and it opens and closes with versions of "I'm a Happy Cowboy" (from 1938 and 1995), this is a good sampler of Jeffries's recordings. He is heard with Earl Hines, Sidney Bechet ("Blue for You, Johnny"), Joe Liggins's Honeydrippers in 1945, on a couple of his own dates, plus four songs with Duke Ellington (including "Flamingo" and "Jump for Joy"). *Say It Isn't So* is a tasteful if unsurprising ballad session in which Jeffries is accompanied by an orchestra arranged by Russ Garcia. Among the better songs are "Penthouse Serenade," "When Your Lover Has Gone," "Glad to Be Unhappy," and "Dinner for One, Please, James."

FILMS
Herb Jeffries is in *Disc Jockey* (1951) and *Calypso Joe* (1957) in addition to his early cowboy movies.

THE MILLS BROTHERS

The Mills Brothers after the mid-1940s were a famous, if conservative and safe, middle-of-the-road pop group, but back in the 1930s their talent for imitating instruments made them one of the most unique of all jazz vocal groups. Billed as "Four Boys and a Guitar," they emulated closely a trumpet, trombone, tuba, and string bass while actually utilizing only a guitar. Herbert, Harry, John Jr. (who both sang and played guitar), and Donald Mills started their careers singing in vaudeville. They were featured on a radio show for ten months in Cincinnati and hit it big in New York by the end of 1931. Their many records during the 1930s (all have been reissued by the British JSP label) find them at their peak, and they appeared for one or two songs in several movies, plus even a Betty Boop cartoon. John Jr.'s death in late 1935 was a major loss. The Mills Brothers's father, John Sr., was able to take his son's place as a singer, although the group had to begin employing an outside guitarist. The Mills Brothers, who recorded some successful numbers with Louis Armstrong in the late 1930s, had a giant hit in 1942 with "Paper Doll" and from that point on became much more conventional, commercial, and popular. John Sr. retired in 1957, while the three remaining Mills Brothers continued working into the 1970s.

●

<u>10</u> *Chronological, Volume One / Oct. 12, 1931–Apr. 14, 1932 / JSP 301*

<u>10</u> *Chronological, Volume Two / May 1932–Feb. 24, 1934 / JSP 302*

<u>9</u> *Chronological, Volume Three / May 29, 1934–Feb. 20, 1935 / JSP 303*

<u>9</u> *Chronological, Volume Four / Oct. 28, 1935–June 29, 1937 / JSP 304*

<u>9</u> *Chronological, Volume Five / Feb. 2, 1933–Aug. 23, 1938 / JSP 320*

<u>9</u> *Chronological, Volume Six / May 30, 1935–Aug. 23, 1939 / JSP 345*

Until the release of this series by the British JSP label, the early recordings of The Mills Brothers were mostly quite difficult to find. These six CDs contain every one of The Mills Brothers's recordings, including occasional radio appearances, film soundtracks, and miscellaneous items from the 1931–39 period. *Volume One* includes many hot numbers, most notably three versions of "Tiger Rag," "Nobody's Sweetheart," "Dinah," "Shine" (the latter two costarring Bing Crosby), and "Sweet Sue." The second disc finds The Mills Brothers having collaborations with Duke Ellington ("Diga, Diga Do"), Cab Calloway, Don Redman, Bing Crosby ("My Honey's Lovin' Arms"), and film star Alice Faye in addition to their quartet numbers. Highlights include "The Old Man of the Mountain," "Coney Island Washboard," an eerie rendition of "Smoke Rings," and "I've Found a New Baby." *Volume Three* has more gems, including "Put On Your Old Grey Bonnet," "Nagasaki," "Some of

These Days," and two songs (best is "Lulu's Back in Town") with Dick Powell. After the first four numbers on *Volume Four*, John Jr. became ill and died. The vocal ensemble regrouped a half-year later with John Sr. and resumed their success.

The fourth disc has a solo number by Harry Mills ("I Found the Thrill Again"), meetings with Ella Fitzgerald and Louis Armstrong, and such tunes as "Shoe Shine Boy," "Pennies from Heaven," "Darling Nellie Gray," and "In the Shade of the Old Apple Tree." *Volume Five* has three earlier alternate takes and selections from 1937–38, including "Organ Grinder's Swing," "Caravan," and three versions of "The Song Is Ended"; best is a classic rendition of this last with Louis Armstrong. In addition there are a couple of odd "Elder Eatmore's Sermons" by Harry Mills and Armstrong that are best heard only once! *Volume Six* has two earlier alternate takes and a pair of solo numbers that Harry Mills recorded with Andy Kirk's orchestra. Otherwise it sticks to 1939, with the highlights including "You Tell Me Your Dream," "Jeepers Creepers," a remake of "Smoke Rings," "Shine," and "Basin Street Blues." It is a pity that this series cuts off in mid-1939, for The Mills Brothers still had a couple of creative years left.

FILMS

The Mills Brothers fortunately made many brief film appearances during their prime, including *The Big Broadcast* (1932), *Operation 13* (1934), *Strictly Dynamite* (1934), *Twenty Million Sweethearts* (1934), *Broadway Gondolier* (1935), *Sing As You Swing* (1937), *Rhythm Parade* (1942), and *Reveille with Beverly* (1943).

JIMMY RUSHING
b. Aug. 26, 1903, Oklahoma City, OK, d. June 8, 1972, New York, NY

The perfect big band singer, Jimmy Rushing (known as "Mr. Five by Five" due to his portly shape) was famous for his ability to interpret blues, but in reality he could sing almost anything. Although he played violin and piano early on and studied music in high school, Rushing was working professionally as a singer by the time he was 18. He spent 1923–24 singing in California (including with Jelly Roll Morton), worked in his native Oklahoma City, and in 1927 joined Walter Page's Blue Devils, moving to Kansas City. He recorded with Page ("Blue Devil Blues" in 1929) and then joined Bennie Moten (1929–35), staying until Moten's death. A short time later he became a member of the new Count Basie Orchestra.

Jimmy Rushing was one of the stars of the Basie band for most of 15 years. He traveled East with Count and was a major part of the orchestra's success. Rushing was with Basie until October 1948 and occasionally during 1949. When the Count Basie Orchestra broke up, Rushing led his own combo of Basie alumni (1950–52). He freelanced as a soloist throughout the 1950s and recorded for Vanguard and Columbia. Rushing appeared with Count Basie at the 1957 Newport Jazz Festival with Benny Goodman at the Brussels World Fair and toured Europe with Buck Clayton in 1959, recording on all three occasions. In the 1960s the veteran singer worked with Harry James, Benny Goodman again, and Eddie Condon, with whom he toured Japan in 1964. Jimmy Rushing stayed active into 1972, when he died at the age of 68.

●

9 *Rushing Lullabies* / Feb. 20, 1958–June 19, 1959 / Columbia/Legacy 65118

7 *Who Was It Sang That Song?* / Oct. 30, 1967 / New World Records 80510

8 *The You and Me That Used to Be* / Apr. 29–30, 1971 / Bluebird 6460

The Columbia single CD has all of the music from two of the singer's LPs (*Rushing Lullabies* and *Little Jimmy Rushing and the Big Brass*) plus an additional selection. Rushing is featured with a sextet that includes Buddy Tate, Sir Charles Thompson on organ, and pianist Ray Bryant on one session and a big band (with Buck Clayton, Vic Dickenson, Dickie Wells, Coleman Hawkins, and Tate) on the other. Although his sidemen get short solos, the vocalist is the main star, singing throughout in prime form and showing that he was much more than just a blues singer. Among the many numbers that Rushing performs are "I'm Coming Virginia," "Mister Five by Five," "When You're Smiling," " 'Deed I Do," and "Russian Lullaby." *Who Was It Sang That Song?* from 1967 matches Rushing again with Clayton, Wells, and Thompson (this time on piano), plus Julian Dash in a sextet. In addition to the original five performances (which include

a blues medley and "Baby Won't You Please Come Home"), three previously unreleased tracks are added to the set. *The You and Me That Used to Be* was Rushing's final recording, cut a little over a year before his death. With pianist Dave Frishberg providing arrangements for a septet that includes Ray Nance on cornet and violin, Budd Johnson on soprano, and the tenors of Zoot Sims and Al Cohn, Jimmy Rushing was still in surprisingly strong voice at this late date. His renditions of "When I Grow Too Old to Dream," "My Last Affair," and "More Than You Know" are both swinging and a bit touching.

LPS TO SEARCH FOR

The Bluesway Sessions (Charly 13) has Jimmy Rushing's two 1967–68 albums for the Bluesway label. He performs on blues-oriented dates with the Oliver Nelson Orchestra and with a septet that has Tate, Wells, and Frishberg among its players.

FILMS

Jimmy Rushing is prominent in the Count Basie Soundie *Take Me Back, Baby* (1941), sings in *The Sound of Jazz* (1957), and acts in *The Learning Tree* (1969).

BIG JOE TURNER
b. May 18, 1911, Kansas City, MO, d. November 24, 1985, Inglewood, CA

Big Joe Turner (who should not be mixed up with stride pianist Joe Turner) had his style fully formed by the late 1930s. Somehow his powerful blues shouting was accessible and flexible enough to fit into several musical eras, including boogie-woogie, Swing, rhythm and blues, rock and roll, and Mainstream Jazz. He began his career as a singing bartender in Kansas

City clubs. Turner met pianist Pete Johnson, who became his longtime musical partner, and they were an institution in K.C., participating in many legendary after-hours jam sessions. In 1938 John Hammond signed them to appear at his Spirituals to Swing concert at Carnegie Hall and Turner became an immediate hit. He began to record regularly ("Roll 'Em Pete" was his most famous collaboration with Johnson, and he also became known for "Cherry Red"). Turner spent a long period based in Los Angeles and appeared in the Duke Ellington show "Jump for Joy," in which he sang "Rocks in My Bed." In the 1940s, in addition to Pete Johnson, he worked with pianists Meade Lux Lewis, Joe Sullivan, and Albert Ammons, plus Luis Russell's orchestra in 1945. In the 1950s, Turner's recordings for Atlantic resulted in several best-sellers, most notably "Shake, Rattle and Roll," "Honey Hush," "Corrine, Corrina" and "Sweet Sixteen." He may have been an unlikely rock and roll star at age 45, but the power of his singing could not be denied.

Big Joe Turner's hits stopped by the 1960s, but he stayed quite active in both blues and jazz circles. In the 1970s he frequently recorded for the Pablo label, including with Count Basie and the Trumpet Kings. Even in his last few years, when his weight ballooned and he had difficulty standing, Big Joe Turner stayed active as a living legend, never really declining much as a singer.

●

9 *Big Bad & Blue: The Big Joe Turner Anthology* / Dec. 30, 1938–Jan. 26, 1983 / Rhino 71550

9 *I've Been to Kansas City* / Nov. 11, 1940–July 17, 1941 / MCA/Decca 42351

8 *Every Day in the Week* / Sept. 8, 1941–Apr. 13, 1967 / GRP/Decca 621

8 *Tell Me Pretty Baby* / Nov. 1947–1949 / Arhoolie 333

9 *Big Joe Turner's Greatest Hits* / Apr. 19, 1951–Jan. 22, 1958 / Atlantic 81752

6 *Singing the Blues* / Dec. 1967 / Mobile Fidelity 780

7 *Bosses of the Blues, Vol. 1* / Aug. 18–19, 1969 / Bluebird 8311

7 *Texas Style* / Apr. 26, 1971 / Evidence 26013

Big Bad & Blue is an excellent three-CD set that concentrates mostly on Big Joe Turner's recordings from the 1938–59 period; there are just three later cuts. Starting with his first sides (duets with Pete Johnson on "Goin' Away Blues" and "Roll 'Em Pete") and continuing through the R&B, rock, and eventually Swing dates, this set has most of the high points from the first half of Turner's career, along with an informative 52-page booklet. *I've Been to Kansas City* contains all of the singer's earliest recordings with the exception of the Johnson duets, including six songs (and two alternates) with bands led by Art Tatum and dates with either Willie "The Lion" Smith or Sammy Price on piano. Highlights include "Piney Brown Blues," "Wee Baby Blues," "Corrine, Corrina," and "Nobody in Mind." Every one of Turner's Decca recordings is on either *I've Been to Kansas City* or *Every Day in the Week*. The latter finds Turner backed by rhythm sections that feature either Freddie Slack, Fred Skinner, or Pete Johnson on piano; there are several alternate takes (a few previously unissued). Among the numbers are "Rocks in My Bed," "Goin' to Chicago Blues," and "Blues in the Night." This CD is rounded off by four numbers (one previously unissued) from an obscure 1964 set plus "Piney Brown Blues" from 1967.

Recorded in Los Angeles during his period on the West Coast, *Tell Me Pretty Baby* features Turner and Pete Johnson with medium-size bands consisting of local players, including Maxwell Davis on tenor and (on one set) the young trumpeter Art Farmer. The music is blues-oriented, as expected, with the subject matter ranging from love, sex, and affairs to "Christmas Date Boogie," "Wine-O-Baby Boogie," "So Many Women Blues," and the two-part "Around the Clock Blues." This CD is filled with fun music that was formerly quite rare. *Big Joe Turner's Greatest Hits* is a survey of Turner's rock and roll years, with such popular numbers as "Chains of Love," "Honey Hush," "Oke-She-Moke-She-Pop," "Shake, Rattle and Roll," "Flip Flop and Fly," "The Chicken and the Hawk," and "Corrine Corrina" all being included. The setting might have changed on some of these cuts, but Turner's singing was as rambunctious and blues-oriented as usual. After the hits stopped, Turner's contract with Atlantic ended in 1959 and he did not record much until the late 1960s. *Singing the Blues* is an audiophile reissue of a 1967 Bluesway album in which Turner is backed by an R&B-ish rhythm section that is sometimes a bit funky. No matter, he always feels comfortable wailing "Piney

Brown Blues," "Roll 'Em Pete," and "Cherry Red." All ten songs are his originals, which include some forgettable but spirited later tunes. Two LPs recorded a day apart for Bluesway by Big Joe Turner and T-Bone Walker are reissued in full on *Bosses of the Blue*. Joe Turner is backed by an orchestra, remaking "Shake Rattle and Roll," "Corinne Corinna," and "Honey Hush," while T-Bone, who performs with a rhythm section plus the young Tom Scott on tenor, has a wide-ranging set that moves from "Every Day I Have the Blues" to "Vietnam" and "For B. B. King." Both veteran performers are in fine form. *Texas Style* brings back a lesser-known Black & Blue set in which Turner (singing his usual material) is joined by a colorful rhythm section comprised of pianist Milt Buckner, Slam Stewart, and Jo Jones.

7 *Life Ain't Easy / June 3, 1974 / Original Jazz Classics 809*

6 *Stormy Monday / Sept. 19, 1974–June 22, 1978 / Pablo 2310-943*

7 *Everyday I Have the Blues / Mar. 3, 1975 / Original Jazz Classics 634*

8 *Nobody in Mind / Aug. 27, 1975 / Original Jazz Classics 729*

8 *In the Evening / Mar. 10, 1976 / Original Jazz Classics 852*

Other than some dates for European labels and a Muse outing with *Roomful of Blues*, Big Joe Turner recorded for the Pablo label during his final dozen years. Most of these sessions were a bit loose, as Big Joe, whose enunciation got sloppier through the years, tended to ramble a bit, although his singing was generally quite powerful. *Life Ain't Easy* is most significant for teaming R&B and veteran jazz players, including Roy Eldridge, trombonist Al Grey, and studio tenor Lee Allen. The combative solos uplift the music (five Turner originals and Woody Guthrie's "So Long"). The music on *Stormy Monday* was not originally released until 1991 and consists of six songs not previously issued from four different sessions. Turner jams with guitarist Pee Wee Crayton and a wide variety of players, including tenor saxophonist Curtis Peagler on "The Things That I Used to Do" and "The Trumpet Kings" (Roy Eldridge, Harry "Sweets" Edison, Clark Terry, and Dizzy Gillespie) on a lengthy "Stormy Monday." *Everyday I Have the Blues* has familiar but stronger material (including "Shake, Rattle and Roll,"

"Lucille," and the title cut) and is notable for teaming Big Joe with the great bebop tenor and altoist Sonny Stitt. Roy Eldridge and vibraphonist Milt Jackson push Turner on "Nobody in Mind," and the singer's knack for turning such songs as "I Want a Little Girl" and even "Red Sails in the Sunset" into the blues make this one of his best Pablo dates. Despite the lack of big names on *In the Evening*, this is also a much better-than-average Joe Turner date. The fiery backup group (which includes the reliable guitarist Pee Wee Crayton and altoist Bob Smith, who is reminiscent of Tab Smith) and the many nonblues pieces (including "Summertime," "Sweet Lorraine," "I've Got the World on a String," and "Pennies from Heaven") challenge Turner. He was very much "on" that day.

7 *Things That I Used to Do / Feb. 8, 1977 / Original Jazz Classics 862*

6 *Have No Fear, Joe Turner Is Here / June 22, 1978 / Original Jazz Classics 905*

6 *Kansas City, Here I Come / Feb. 14, 1984 / Original Jazz Classics 743*

5 *Patcha, Patcha, All Night Long / Apr. 18, 1985 / Original Jazz Classics 887*

Big Joe Turner is joined by more musicians than usual on *Things That I Used to Do*, a ten-piece band that includes trumpeter Blue Mitchell, altoist Eddie "Cleanhead" Vinson, and the tenors of Rashid Ali and Wild Bill Moore plus piano, organ, two guitars, bass, and drums. There are no surprises in the repertoire (such blues as "Jelly Jelly Blues," "St. Louis Blues," and "Oke-She-Moke-She-Pop"), but the spirited if loose results are fun. *Have No Fear* has the same instrumentation (except with congas rather than organ) but no big names. Bob Smith is back, as is Crayton and pianist Lloyd Glenn; "Rocks in My Bed" (the shortest performance) is the high point. *Kansas City, Here I Come* jumps ahead six years and finds Turner, at age 72, in his final period. Backed by studio players who have been on countless other similar dates (including Lee Allen on tenor and pianist Bobby Blevins), Turner is still able to shout it out on "Down Home Blues," "Call the Plumber," and "Big Leg Woman." His final recording, cut just seven months before his death, was his only collaboration with singer Jimmy Witherspoon. *Patcha, Patcha* should probably have been recorded ten years earlier, for both singers had seen better days. Actually only two of the six songs feature both Turner and Witherspoon ("Patcha, "Patcha" and "Blues Lament") and they have two individual features apiece. The music has its moments but is mostly a historical curiosity.

LPS TO SEARCH FOR

Have No Fear, Big Joe Turner Is Here (Savoy 2223) is a two-LP set with all of Turner's recordings for the National and Savoy labels during 1945–47; Pete Johnson, Frankie Newton, Don Byas, Wild Bill Moore, Teddy Bunn, and Albert Ammons are among the many sidemen. The two-LP *Rhythm & Blues Years* (Atlantic 81663) includes many of Big Joe Turner's 1950s Atlantic singles, which are not on his *Greatest Hits* CD, including "TV Mama," "In the Evening," and "Tomorrow Night." *Boss of the Blues* (Atlantic 8812) has Big Joe performing some of his favorite blues and standards from the 1930s and '40s on a 1956 date with such sidemen as trumpeter Joe Newman, Lawrence Brown, Pete Brown, Frank Wess on tenor, and Pete Johnson. *Big Joe Rides Again,* from 1959, has a similar repertoire and a variety of all-stars, including Vic Dickenson and Coleman Hawkins. Pablo dates that have not yet been reissued on CD include Turner's meeting with the Count Basie Orchestra (*Flip, Flop & Fly—* Pablo 2310-937), *The Trumpet Kings Meet Joe Turner* (Pablo 2310-717), which features the singer with Roy Eldridge, Harry Edison, Clark Terry, and Dizzy Gillespie, and *The Midnight Special* (Pablo 2310-844). On this last, Turner even turns "I Left My Heart in San Francisco" into the blues!

FILMS

Big Joe Turner is in *Shake, Rattle and Rock* (1956) and *The Last of the Blue Devils* (1979).

LEO WATSON

b. Feb. 27, 1898, Kansas City, MO, d. May 2, 1950, Los Angeles, CA

Leo Watson was a true improviser, a singer who made up words and sounds as he went along, often with a great deal of humor. His career and life were quite erratic, but he was one of the most creative singers of the Swing era. Not much is known about his early days. Watson surfaced in 1929 as part of a vocal group that was a novelty act touring with the Whitman Sisters. The unit soon broke away and was named the Spirits of Rhythm, a band that featured guitarist Teddy Bunn, with three of its singers playing tiples (a small ukulele). Watson was the most inventive singer in the group and he was with the Spirits off and on into 1941. Watson also recorded with the Washboard Rhythm Kings, worked with John Kirby a bit in 1937 (sometimes playing drums and trombone), and spent a few months with the big bands of Artie Shaw and Gene Krupa, recording a few songs with each orchestra plus one date as a leader. In the early 1940s he moved to Los Angeles, where he often worked solo and was part of the popular jive vocal movement of 1944–46 along with Slim Gaillard and Harry "the Hipster" Gibson. Leo Watson recorded four remarkable titles in 1946 (including a joyous "Jingle Bells") on a session with Vic Dickenson, but that would be his last recording. Leo Watson worked only now and then during his final years, when he was completely forgotten. He died of pneumonia when he was 52.

FILMS

Leo Watson is seen in *Panama Hattie* (1942) and is briefly in a scene with Bill "Bojangles" Robinson in *Stormy Weather* (1943).

Female Vocalists

The jazz and Swing worlds have always featured a large number of female vocalists. In the 1920s the pacesetters were blues singer Bessie Smith (whose recordings as early as 1923 are still very powerful), Alberta Hunter, Ethel Waters, and later in the decade Annette Hanshaw, Mildred Bailey, and the Boswell Sisters. Ethel Waters was particularly significant, for, although she started out as a blues singer, during the Depression she became one of the first black women to be performing and recording major pop songs (introducing "Stormy Weather") and to be universally respected in the music world. Mildred Bailey was also a pioneer, the first female singer to be regularly featured with a big band (Paul Whiteman's). And the Boswell Sisters, who unfortunately broke up right when the Swing era was beginning, proved to be one of the greatest jazz vocal groups of all time. Ironically the Andrews Sisters, who would be the most famous of the many vocal ensembles of the 1940s (which include the Pied Pipers and the Modernaires), were not close to being on the Boswells' level.

With the exception of Jimmie Lunceford, virtually every Swing era big band featured a female singer, who usually added glamour and sex appeal (along with hopefully a good voice) to the band's music. Ivie Anderson starred with Duke Ellington, Benny Goodman had Helen Ward, Martha Tilton, and Peggy Lee, Count Basie featured Helen Humes, Anita O'Day made it big with Gene Krupa, Rosetta Tharpe added a religious passion to Lucky Millinder's music, Ella Fitzgerald turned Chick Webb's orchestra into a commercial success, as did Helen O'Connell for Jimmy Dorsey, and Helen Forrest sang with three of the finest orchestras: Artie Shaw, Benny Goodman, and Harry James. Several of the top female singers had their best moments with small groups, including Billie Holiday, Maxine Sullivan, Lee Wiley, and Teddy Grace. Alice Babs, in Sweden, was a sensation as a teenager, and Lena Horne's beauty did not mask her highly appealing voice.

Some of these singers' careers would fade after the big band era ended, and it would have been difficult to predict who would be most successful with their solo careers. Certainly in 1938, one would never have guessed that Ella Fitzgerald would easily eclipse Helen Forrest and Helen Ward, and in 1942 few would have predicted that Peggy Lee would be much more significant in the long run than Helen O'Connell. Ella and Billie Holiday were the two most significant voices to emerge from the Swing world and, while many other singers never grew beyond the era, Helen Humes, Anita O'Day, Rosetta Tharpe (in the world of gospel music), Maxine Sullivan, Peggy Lee, Lena Horne, and Alice Babs would be major names for many years to come.

IVIE ANDERSON
b. July 10, 1905, Gilroy, CA, d. Dec. 28, 1949, Los Angeles, CA

A classy and sophisticated singer, Ivie Anderson was a beloved member of the Duke Ellington Orchestra. She could sing uptempo material and ballads with equal skill and sensitivity. Anderson had vocal lessons at a local convent and with a private teacher. She started out working locally in Los Angeles and was quickly noticed. Anderson worked at the Cotton Club as early as 1925, toured with Shuffle Along, and back in L. A. sang with Curtis Mosby's Blue Blowers, Paul Howard's Quality Serenaders, and Sonny Clay. Other jobs included performing frequently at the Cotton Club in Los Angeles, a tour of Australia with Sonny Clay, and working with Earl Hines's big band in Chicago.

Ivie Anderson joined Duke Ellington's orchestra in February 1931 and she was with Duke for 11 years. Her first recording with Ellington was "It Don't Mean a Thing If It Ain't Got That Swing" and in the early 1940s she introduced "I Got It Bad and That Ain't Good." A popular attraction with Duke who was used to singing a wide variety of material, she suffered from chronic asthma in later years. Ivie Anderson left Duke in August 1942, opened up a Chicken Shack restaurant in L.A., and worked locally for a time, making a dozen recordings in 1946. Asthma caused her demise at age 44.

FILMS
Ivie Anderson is in the Duke Ellington short *Bundle of Blues* (1933) and sings "All God's Children" in the Marx Brothers's movie *A Day at the Races* (1937).

ANDREWS SISTERS

The most popular female vocal group of the Swing era and the most famous "sister" group of all time, the Andrews Sisters were never on the level of the Boswell Sisters, but they fit the time period perfectly. Comprised of Patti, Maxine, and Laverne, the Andrews Sisters started working in their native Minneapolis when they were teenagers. They were signed to Brunswick in 1937, and their second record, "Bei Mir Bist Du Schon," started their rapid rise to fame. A pop rather than jazz group, the Andrews Sisters tended to stick to their routines once they were worked out, with Patti always standing in the middle as the lead (and occasional solo) voice. Other hits included "Boogie Woogie Bugle Boy," "Rum and Coca Cola," "Pistol Packin' Mama," "Don't Fence Me In" (the latter two with Bing Crosby), "Beer Barrel Polka," "In Apple Blossom Time," and "Christmas Island." They appeared in 15 films (playing themselves) and have been forever linked with World War II nostalgia. The Andrews Sisters (who were constantly squabbling and rarely talked to one another offstage) broke up in 1953, had occasional reunions afterwards (including Patti and Maxine's appearance in the 1974 Broadway musical *Over Here*), and Patti Andrews had a respectable if not outstanding solo career.

ALICE BABS
b. Jan. 26, 1924, Kalmar, Sweden

The top European singer to emerge during the Swing era, Alice Babs was a big hit in her homeland when she was only 15. Her original name was Alice Nilson, but she adopted her nickname, "Babs," as her last name. She made her recording debut in 1939 and had a best seller with "Swing It, Mr. Teacher." A versatile singer whose yodeling was also popular for a time, Babs always brought Swing and joy to her performances. She recorded fairly prolifically during the 1940s and '50s, performed both Swing-oriented jazz and pop music, made an album with Duke Ellington in 1963, sang the classic "Heaven" at his second spiritual concert (sounding quite heavenly), and performed with Ellington during part of his European tour of 1973. Alice Babs was still active on a part-time basis in the 1990s.

●

9 *Swing It! / May 31, 1939–Apr. 1, 1953 / Phontastic 9302* This CD offers listeners a superior overview of Alice Babs's recordings from her first 14 years on records, starting when she was just 15. Assisted by Sweden's top jazz musicians, Babs sings primarily Swing in English, although there are a few exceptions and a couple of examples of her highly popular yodeling. Among the better selections are "Some of These Days," "Swing It, Magistern," "You're Driving Me Crazy," "Truckin'," and "I'm Checkin' Out Goo'm Bye."

MILDRED BAILEY
b. Feb. 27, 1907, Tekoa, WA, d. Dec. 12, 1951, Poughkeepsie, NY

Mildred Bailey did not have that happy a life. She disliked her looks (being overweight), drank too much at times, and her life was aimless after the mid-1940s during the years before her early death. However, she was one of the finest singers of the 1930s. Her little-girl voice could be an acquired taste, but she always swung and she helped to popularize "Georgia on My Mind" and "Rockin' Chair."

Bailey worked early on as a song demonstrator and as a singer on the radio. Born Mildred Rinker, she helped her brother Al Rinker and Bing Crosby prior to their joining Paul Whiteman as part of the Rhythm Boys. She gave Paul Whiteman a demo disc of her own and was part of his orchestra during 1929–33, the first female band singer. Bailey recorded with Paul Whiteman but really came into her own when she went solo and teamed up with her husband, xylophonist Red Norvo; their marriage would last until 1945. Bailey made most of her finest recordings during the 1930s, and during 1936–39 she was featured with Red Norvo's band, a group that often framed her vocals with Eddie Sauter's arrangements. Bailey worked with Benny Goodman a bit in 1939 and had a regular radio series during 1944–45. Her health declined later in the decade, and she passed away when she was just 44. Mildred Bailey (who was influenced by Ethel Waters) was herself an influence on the singing of Lee Wiley and more recently Barbara Lea and Daryl Sherman.

●

7 *Volume One / Oct. 5, 1929–Mar. 2, 1932 / The Old Masters 103*

8 *Volume Two / Dec. 1, 1931–Feb. 2, 1934 / The Old Masters 104*

Volume One has Mildred Bailey's first 21 recordings. Her lone 1929 side was "What Kind of Man Is You?" with Eddie Lang's orchestra, while in 1930 all she cut was "I Like to Do Things for You" with Frankie Trumbauer. Even at that early stage Bailey was distinctive although a bit higher-toned than she would be later. The year 1931 found her recording with Jimmie Noone, the Casa Loma Orchestra, and Paul Whiteman. She also led her first two sessions, which are highlighted by "Georgia on My Mind" and "Home." This CD concludes in 1932 with a two-part "Hot-Cha Medley" with Whiteman. *Volume Two* starts with a couple of leftover selections from 1931 and has six numbers from 1932 (including her earliest version of "Rockin' Chair"). Up to that time, Bailey had been accompanied primarily by orchestras. However, starting in 1933, her material became much more jazz-oriented. Joined by the Dorsey Brothers (plus Bunny Berigan), she romps on "Is That Religion" and "Shoutin' in That Amen Corner," helps to popularize "Lazy Bones," and is touching on "There's a Cabin in the Skies." *Volume Two* finishes with five numbers (including one instrumental) with an all-star group that features Coleman Hawkins and includes "Ol' Pappy," "Emaline," and two versions of "Junk Man."

9 *The Rockin' Chair Lady / Sept. 15, 1931–Apr. 25, 1950 / GRP/Decca 644*

8 *The Legendary V-Disc Sessions / 1943–1951 / Vintage Jazz Classics 1006*

The Rockin' Chair Lady features Mildred Bailey during four very different periods. Her 1931 session with the Casa Loma Orchestra is repeated from the earlier *Volume One*, but there are also four exciting numbers with a 1935 quartet that con-

sists of Bunny Berigan, Johnny Hodges, Teddy Wilson, and bassist Grachan Moncur. In addition, included are performances from 1941–42 with the Delta Rhythm Boys (including "Georgia on My Mind," "Rockin' Chair," and "It's So Peaceful in the Country") and a version of "More Than You Know" with an orchestra. This CD finishes with Bailey's final two studio recordings, "Cry Baby Cry" and "Blue Prelude," from 1950, 20 months before her death. *The Legendary V-Disc Sessions* features Bailey on a radio show with the Delta Rhythm Boys in 1943, performing four duets with Teddy Wilson, and singing three numbers with Red Norvo (including "Someday Sweetheart" and "Downhearted Blues"). In addition, there are a few songs with Benny Goodman's orchestra in 1944 (including "From the Land of Sky Blue Water"), radio performances from 1947, and, what is probably the final documentation of Mildred Bailey, two songs sung on the radio in the spring of 1951: "Lover, Come Back to Me" and "It's So Peaceful in the Country."

LPS TO SEARCH FOR

The best all-round Mildred Bailey reissue is the three-LP box *Her Greatest Performances* (Columbia C3L 22), which, although not "complete," does have 48 of her finest recordings, dating from 1929 to 1946. *The Mildred Bailey Radio Show—1944–45* (Sunbeam 209) features the singer on two of her radio programs, with assistance from Teddy Wilson, Trummy Young, Woody Herman, and the Paul Baron Orchestra. Her long series of jazz-oriented radio programs are long overdue to be reissued in coherent and complete fashion. *All of Me* (Monmouth Evergreen 6814) showcases Bailey on some of her studio recordings from 1945–47, including eight from 1945 that have not been otherwise reissued. The other eight titles are repeated on *The Majestic Mildred Bailey* (Savoy Jazz 1151) along with eight additional songs and several alternate takes that fully trace Bailey's work of 1946–47.

BOSWELL SISTERS

The Boswell Sisters were arguably the top jazz vocal group before Lambert, Hendricks, and Ross (who arrived on the scene 25 years later), and their only competition in the early 1930s was The Mills Brothers. The trio was comprised of Connie (b. Dec. 3, 1907, New Orleans, d. Oct. 11, 1976, New York), Martha (1908–58), and Helvetia (1909–88). Their music featured both lyrics and scatting, lots of tempo changes in highly appealing yet unpredictable arrangements, some solo spots for Connie, and rousing conclusions. There was simply no comparison between this inventive group and the much more conventional (if world-famous) Andrews Sisters.

Each of the Boswells was trained in music. Connie (who had to use a wheelchair due to her polio, although she covered it very well on stage) played cello, piano, alto, and trombone, Vet was a violinist, and Martha (who was the only one to actually record on her instrument) backed her sisters on piano. They began to sing as children in the early 1920s and actually recorded a song (plus a solo by Connie) as early as 1925. The Boswell Sisters' series of recordings really began in 1930, and for five years they were featured on the radio, in some films, and on stage, including visiting Europe in 1933 and 1935. By 1936 all three sisters had gotten married and Vet and Martha decided to retire from singing, a major loss to music. Connie continued and, although she never quite lived up to her potential as a solo singer, she did make a few impressive recordings along the way (including "Martha" with Bob Crosby's orchestra) and stayed active into the early 1960s, appearing on the 1950s television series *Pete Kelly's Blues*. Ella Fitzgerald always considered Connie Boswell to be her first and most important influence.

●

10 *The Boswell Sisters, Vol. 1 / Mar. 19, 1931–Apr. 9, 1932 / Collector's Classics 21*

8 *That's How Rhythm Was Born / Mar. 21, 1932–May 28, 1935 / Legacy/Columbia 66977*

Twenty-four of the Boswell Sisters' finest recordings are on *Vol. 1.* Joined by such top jazz stars as Bunny Berigan, Tommy Dorsey, Jimmy Dorsey, trumpeter Manny Klein, Joe Venuti, and Eddie Lang, among others, the Boswells perform one gem after another. Among the high points are "Roll On Mississippi, Roll On," "Shout, Sister, Shout," "It's the Girl," "Heebies Jeebies," "Was That the Human Thing To Do," "Put That Sun Back in the Sky," "Everybody Loves My Baby," and "If It Ain't Love." *That's How Rhythm Was Born,* which repeats one selection from *Vol. 1* ("Between the Devil and the Deep Blue Sea") has highlights from their 1932–35 period. The packaging could be better, since the music is not in chronological order and the complete sessions are not reissued. However, there are many strong selections here, including "Shuffle Off to Buffalo," "Sleep Come On and Take Me," "The Sentimental Gentleman from Georgia," "Minnie the Moocher's Wedding Day," "If I Had a Million Dollars," and "Dinah."

7 *Okay, America! / May 25, 1931–July 19, 1935 / Jass 622*

7 *Syncopating Harmonists from New Orleans / 1930– 1935 / Take Two 406*

7 *Airshots and Rarities 1930–1935 / 1930–July 19, 1935 / Retrieval 79009*

Okay, America consists of alternate takes by the Boswell Sisters (which often differ quite a bit from the issued versions), plus their guest appearances in medleys with Red Nichols and Victor Young's orchestra. *Syncopating Harmonists* features the Boswells on nine songs from a rare 1930 radio show, two selections from a 1935 program, plus nine commercially released records from 1932–35, which include a few of the more obscure numbers, such as "Swanee Mammy" and "Don't Let Your Love Go Wrong." *Airshots and Rarities* follows a similar format, although all of the music is different. The Boswells (with Martha playing piano) are heard on three radio shows from 1930 and one from the following year, plus six studio recordings from 1932–35. Although Swing collectors will want to pick up the two previous Boswell Sisters CDs first, these three also add to their legacy.

LPS TO SEARCH FOR

Other overlapping LPs that each contain some of the Boswell Sisters' studio recordings not included in the CDs are the three-LP box *The Boswell Sisters* (Columbia 16493), *1932-1934* (Biograph 3), *Volume Two* (Biograph 16), *St. Louis Blues* (Silver Swan 1001), and the very generous 20-selection *It's the Girls* (Living Era 5014). Plus *On the Air 1931–1936* (Totem 1042) has some additional radio appearances. Many of the high points of Connie Boswell's solo career can be heard on *Under a Blanket of Blue* (Take Two 216) and *Sand in My Shoes* (MCA 1689). The former album covers her solo sides when she was still with her sisters in 1931–35, while *Sand in My Shoes,* which has the last six Boswell Sis-

ters recordings, contains Connie's best records from 1936–40, including "Martha" and a wonderful version of "Home on the Range."

FILMS

The Boswell Sisters appear in several film shorts plus the full-length movies *The Big Broadcast* (1932), *Transatlantic Merry-Go-Round* (1934), and *Moulin Rouge* (1934). As a soloist in later years, Connie Boswell is in *Kiss the Boys Goodbye* (1941), *Syncopation,* (1942), and *Senior Prom* (1958).

ELLA FITZGERALD

b. Apr. 25, 1917, Newport News, VA, d. June 15, 1996, Beverly Hills, CA

Ella Fitzgerald, "The First Lady of Song," was one of the great discoveries of the Swing era and one of the finest singers of the 20th Century. Her voice was always in tune, she evoked constant joy, and she could outswing anyone, whether through her remarkable scat singing or in her phrasing of lyrics.

Ironically, Ella's early life was almost as grim as Billie Holiday's, but, rather than sing autobiographical lyrics that reflected her life, as Lady Day did, she successfully escaped into her music. Ella grew up poor and was actually homeless for most of a year and quite unsure about her future. She wanted to be a dancer but would have much better luck as a singer. In 1934 she won an amateur contest at the Apollo Theatre, singing "Judy" in the style of Connie Boswell, her main early influence. Ella was with Tiny Bradshaw for a short time, but Fletcher Henderson turned down the chance to use her. Benny Carter and others who had seen Ella at the amateur contest suggested to Chick Webb that he give her a try. Webb was not impressed by her appearance but tried her out on a one-nighter, noticed the audience's enthusiastic response, and soon hired her on a permanent basis. After her recording debut in 1935, Ella became Webb's most popular attraction. In the 1930s she was often given juvenile novelties to sing but sounded much better on ballads. "A-Tisket, A-Tasket" was a huge hit in 1938, and she made "Undecided" a standard the following year. Ella also began recording under her own name, using Webb's sidemen.

Chick Webb's death in June 1939 resulted in Ella Fitzgerald's succeeding him as the bandleader. Actually she had nothing much to do with the orchestra's musical direction, but, since she was the star, she stood in front of the band for two years. In 1941 Ella went out on her own and soon became a best-selling artist. Recording regularly for Decca, Ella performed a wide variety of material and really started to grow as a jazz singer. By the mid-1940s she had learned how to scat (as she showed on "Lady Be Good," "How High the Moon," and "Flying Home") and the novelties were largely gone from her repertoire. Ella started touring with Jazz at the Philharmonic in 1946, Norman Granz became her manager, and her popularity grew year by year.

During 1948–52 Ella was married to bassist Ray Brown, but the marriage did not last and her private life remained mostly uneventful and quite private. However, Ella lived through her music and her professional life was continually successful. She recorded duets with pianist Ellis Larkins in 1950 and 1954 (focusing on George Gershwin), appeared in the movie *Pete Kelly's Blues* in 1955, and then ended her association with Decca and switched to Norman Granz's Verve company, a label that he originally formed specifically to record her. Her series of songbooks in which she sang entire sets of the music of various composers (Cole Porter, the Gershwins, Rodgers and Hart, Duke Ellington, Harold Arlen, Jerome Kern, and lyricist Johnny Mercer) gave her prestige and found her being thought of not only as a jazz singer but as an American institution.

Ella toured constantly during the 1950s, '60s, and '70s, recording quite prolifically, appearing on television often, and constantly selling out concert halls. Although her records of the mid- to late 1960s for Capitol and Reprise were sometimes erratic (due to commercial material), when Norman Granz formed his Pablo label in 1972, Ella found a final comfortable home, recording freewheeling jams, concert programs, and a few additional songbooks. Ella Fitzgerald's voice started gradually fading from the mid-1970s on, but, until she was finally forced into retirement in 1994 due to bad health, she retained her ability to swing and displayed the joy that she always felt whenever she sang.

●

8 *1935–1937 / June 12, 1935–Jan. 14, 1937 / Classics 500*

8 *1937–1938 / Jan. 14, 1937–May 2, 1938 / Classics 506*

8 *1938–1939 / May 2, 1938–Feb. 17, 1939 / Classics 518*

8 *1939 / Feb. 17, 1939–June 29, 1939 / Classics 525*

7 *The Early Years—Part 1 / June 12, 1935–Oct. 6, 1938 / GRP/Decca 618*

The Classics label has reissued every one of Ella Fitzgerald's studio recordings from 1935–44, including all of the selections that she recorded with the Chick Webb Orchestra. *1935–1937* is comprised mostly of her earliest Webb dates, including "I'll Chase the Blues Away," "When I Get Low I Get High," "A Little Bit Later On," and "Mr. Paganini, You'll Have to Swing It," which remained a permanent part of her repertoire. Ella, who also is heard on two numbers with Teddy Wilson, three with Benny Goodman's orchestra (including "Goodnight My Love"), and her first date as a leader, was a superior Swing singer from the start; her skills at improvising would come later. *1937–1938* has two fun numbers with The Mills Brothers, eight selections under her own leadership, and plenty of novelties and ballads with Webb. The CD concludes with the original version of "A-Tisket, A-Tasket." By 1938 the great majority of the Chick Webb recordings sessions featured Ella's vocals. *1938–1939* includes "You Can't Be Mine," "Saving Myself for You," "Wacky Dust," "F. D. R. Jones," and "Undecided," plus "I Found My Yellow Basket," which did not duplicate the success of "A-Tisket, A-Tasket!" *1939* has the end of an era, the final recordings by the Chick Webb Orchestra before the drummer's death. Ella sounds much more mature on "'Tain't What You Do," "My Heart Belongs to Daddy," and "Don't Worry 'Bout Me" than she had four years earlier, although "Chew-Chew-Chew Your Bubble Gum" shows that she was still being used for novelties. *1939* concludes with the first session by Ella Fitzgerald's Famous Orchestra, the former Webb band, with Bill Beason now on drums; "Stairway to the Stars" was a minor hit. *The Early Years—Part 1* is a two-CD set covering the same period as the first three Classics CD but including just the best 43 selections out of the 69 recorded.

7 *1939–1940 / Aug. 18, 1939–May 9, 1940 / Classics 566*

7 *1940–1941 / May 9, 1940–July 31, 1941 / Classics 644*

7 *The Early Years—Part 2 / Feb. 17, 1939–July 31, 1941 / GRP/Decca 623*

8 *1941–1944 / Oct. 6, 1941–Nov. 6, 1944 / Classics 840*

8 *The War Years / Oct. 6, 1941–Dec. 20, 1947 / GRP/ Decca 628*

9 *Pure Ella / Sept. 11, 1950–Mar. 30, 1954 / Decca 636*

10 *75th Birthday Celebration / May 2, 1938–Aug. 5, 1955 / GRP/Decca 2-619*

The Chick Webb Orchestra survived for two years after its leader's death, because Ella Fitzgerald was willing to lend her name to it and front the big band. *1939–1940* mostly features Ella, with the band in a supporting role, although there are three instrumentals among the 23 selections. Among the better tracks are "My Last Goodbye," "Moon Ray," "Sugar Blues," and "Imagination," which partly compensates for "My Wubba Dolly!" *1940–1941* concludes the period with 23 more vocal numbers, including "Shake Down the Stars," "I'm the Lonesomest Gal in Town," "The One I Love," and "Can't Help Lovin' 'Dat Man." The two-CD *The Early Years—Part 2* has 42 of the 69 recordings cut during a 2 1/2-year period, hitting most of the high points and leaving out the lesser cuts. *1941–1944* includes the first recordings of Ella's solo career, with the singer still only 24 at the time of the earliest selections. In most cases she is backed by a rhythm section, and there are three numbers (including "Into Each Life Some Rain Must Fall") with the Ink Spots. Ella was maturing rapidly during the era, as can be heard on "This Love of Mine," "Somebody Nobody Loves," and "You Don't Know What Love Is." Fifteen of the titles from *1941–1944* are on the two-CD set *The War Years* along with many others, including meetings with the Delta Rhythm Boys, Louis Jordan ("Stone Cold Dead in the Market"), Louis Armstrong ("You Won't Be Satisfied" and "The Frim Fram Sauce"), and Eddie Heywood. It was in 1945 that Ella learned how to sing jazz and scat; among the classics included on this twofer

After Chick Webb's death in 1939, the young Ella Fitzgerald fronted his orchestra (with Bill Beason on drums) for the next two years before starting her own remarkable solo career.

are "Flying Home" (an alternate take), "Lady Be Good," and two new takes of "How High the Moon."

Although sometimes criticized for not getting into the heart of lyrics (since she usually sounded so happy), Ella could be quite masterful at singing ballads. In 1950 she performed duets with pianist Ellis Larkins, eight George Gershwin songs that predated her extensive series of songbooks. *Pure Ella* has those eight plus a dozen more duets from 1954; the emphasis is on slower tempos and the music is often exquisite. In the early 1990s the attractive two-CD set *75th Birthday Celebration* expertly summed up Ella's Decca years, covering most of her hits, including "A-Tisket, A-Tasket," "Undecided," "Cow Cow Boogie," "Flying Home," "Lady Be Good," "How High the Moon," "Smooth

Sailing," "Airmail Special," "and "Hard-Hearted Hannah." A perfect introduction to Ella's joyful music.

10 *First Lady of Song / Sept. 18, 1949–July 29, 1966 / Verve 314 517 889*

* *The Complete Ella Fitzgerald Songbooks/ Feb. 7, 1956– Oct. 21, 1964 / Verve 314 519 832-8487*

7 *Ella at the Opera House / Sept. 29, 1957–Oct. 7, 1957 / Verve 831 2697*

7 *Get Happy / July 24, 1957–July 11, 1959/ Verve 314 523 3217*

7 *Like Someone in Love / Oct. 15 + 28, 1957 / Verve 314 511 5247*

7 *Ella Swings Brightly / Jan. 5, 1959–Dec. 27, 1961 / Verve 314 519 3477*

7 *Ella Swings Gently / Nov. 13, 1961–Apr. 10, 1962 / Verve 314 519 348*

Ella Fitzgerald recorded an enormous number of records during her career, probably more than any other jazz singer. Norman Granz seemed to document her every move during the Verve years, and that was a good thing because this was really her prime period. The three-CD *First Lady of Song* is a superior sampler, starting with her Jazz at the Philharmonic appearance in 1949 and continuing through her 1966 collaboration with Duke Ellington. Most of the high points of the 1956–66 period are here, including some selections taken from her Song Books. Norman Granz started the Verve label partly as a home for Ella's songbooks, full-length projects (and in some cases multiple albums) that had the great singer interpreting the music of Cole Porter, Rodgers and Hart, Duke Ellington, Irving Berlin, George and Ira Gershwin, Harold Arlen, Jerome Kern, and lyricist Johnny Mercer. All of the music, 16 CDs in all, has been reissued by Verve as a limited-edition box. Ella mostly sticks to the lyrics (very little scatting here), and not all of the arrangements for the orchestras are that jazz-oriented, but the results are certainly tasteful and respectful of each composer's intent. These projects are also available individually, and of special note are the Arlen and Ellington sets; the latter features both Duke's band and a combo date with Stuff Smith and Ben Webster. In addition to that massive series, Ella was appearing nightly and recording many other dates during this period. *Ella at the Opera House* finds her swinging spontaneously with the Oscar Peterson Trio during two nights of a Jazz at the Philharmonic tour in 1957. What is odd about this release is that the music is the same on both sets except for one of the nine songs, so there are eight repeats, but fortunately the interpretations do differ quite a bit. *Get Happy, Like Someone in Love, Ella Swings Brightly,* and *Ella Swings Gently* are orchestra dates that gave the singer an opportunity to sing other standards that did not fit into the songbook concept. Each adds additional selections to the original LP program. *Get Happy* is a hodgepodge of material (including "Cheerful Little Earful," "Beat Me Daddy, Eight to the Bar," and "Swingin' Shepherd Blues"), *Like Someone in Love* is a solid date with the orchestra of Frank DeVol and guest solo-

ist Stan Getz, and the other two CDs match Ella with the Nelson Riddle Orchestra for concise but swinging performances.

10 *The Complete Ella in Berlin / Feb. 13, 1960 / Verve 314 519 584*

8 *The Intimate Ella / Apr. 14–19, 1960 / Verve 839 838*

7 *Ella Returns to Berlin / Feb. 11, 1961 / Verve 837 758*

8 *Clap Hands, Here Comes Charlie! / June 22–23, 1961 / Verve 835 646*

7 *These Are the Blues / Oct. 28, 1963 / Verve 829 536*

7 *Ella at Duke's Place / Oct. 18, 1965–Oct. 20, 1965 / Verve 314 529 700*

3 *Sunshine of Your Love / Feb. 1969–Mar. 1969 / Verve 314 533 102*

Ella Fitzgerald's Berlin concert is quite legendary, because during "Mack the Knife" she totally forgot the words, making up hilarious lyrics as she went along. Up till then it had been a pretty strong performance, with fine versions of "Gone with the Wind," "The Lady Is a Tramp," and "Too Darn Hot," but "Mack the Knife" made that concert quite famous. *The Intimate Ella* is rather unusual, a series of duets with pianist Paul Smith that are played at slower, expressive tempos, with Ella putting much more emotion into the lyrics than one would normally expect from her. Ella's return to Berlin does not include any mishaps and is less memorable but still finds her swinging hard and in prime voice on such tunes as "Take the 'A' Train," "Slow Boat to China," "Misty," and a rendition of "Mack the Knife" on which she does remember the words! Oscar Peterson's trio guests on "This Can't Be Love." *Clap Hands, Here Comes Charlie* is a high-quality studio date with the Lou Levy Quartet of mostly Swing-era songs (including "Jersey Bounce") plus "Night in Tunisia," "'Round Midnight," and "This Could Be the Start of Something Big." Although Ella was never thought of as a blues singer, *These Are the Blues* finds her doing well on ten vintage blues that date from the 1920s and '30s, including "Jail House Blues," "In the Evening," and even "Cherry Red." Roy Eldridge and organist Wild Bill Davis help out. *Ella at Duke's Place* was only the second studio album to team Ella with Duke Ellington (the other one being the *Duke Ellington Songbook*) and it has its strong moments, including "Something to Live For," "I Like the Sunrise,"

"Imagine My Frustration," and "Cotton Tail." After Norman Granz left Verve, Ella's recording career was directionless for a few years. *Sunshine of Your Love* is a rather unfortunate date that finds the singer trying her darndest to swing such songs as "Hey Jude," "This Girl's in Love with You," and the title cut. There are a few worthwhile selections ("Give Me the Simple Life" and "Old Devil Moon" among them), but there are literally at least 100 better Ella Fitzgerald CDs currently available.

8   *Newport Jazz Festival/Live at Carnegie Hall / July 5, 1973 / Legacy/Columbia 66809*

10   *The Concert Years / Nov. 18, 1953–1983 / Pablo 4414*

7   *Ella A Nice / July 21, 1971 / Original Jazz Classics 442*

6   *Take Love Easy / Aug. 28, 1973 / Pablo 2310-702*

7   *Fine and Mellow / Jan. 8, 1974 / Pablo 2310-829*

7   *Ella in London / Apr. 11, 1974 / Original Jazz Classics 974*

7   *Ella & Oscar / May 19, 1974 / Pablo 2310-759*

7   *At the Montreux Jazz Festival 1975 / July 17, 1975 / Original Jazz Classics 789*

Ella Fitzgerald's last period was spent back with Norman Granz, recording quite prolifically for the Pablo label; many of those releases have been reissued as part of the Original Jazz Classics series. The Columbia double CD was a rare outing for another label and served as a bit of a retrospective. Ella is heard in 1973 performing with a Chick Webb reunion band (it is a pity that the orchestra did not have a full set of their own) and dueting with Ellis Larkins. She sits out while a Jazz at the Philharmonic–type all-star group that stars Roy Eldridge, Eddie "Lockjaw" Davis, and trombonist Al Grey has a few instrumentals. Ella then finishes off the concert with her usual trio plus some duets with guitarist Joe Pass. Not everything works but in general this is an enjoyable set that pays tribute to several aspects of Ella's career. *The Concert Years* is a four-CD set that features Ella live in 1953, with Duke Ellington in 1966 and 1967, and in concerts with her regular combo in 1971, 1972, 1974, 1975, 1977, 1979, and 1983. All of the music is also available on other Pablo sets, but this is a very good way of summing up the singer's many concert recordings of her later period; her rendition of "C Jam Blues" in 1972 (which has tradeoffs with five surprise guests) is quite hilarious. *Ella A Nice* is a fine live set from 1971 with the Tommy Flanagan Trio and has a few surprising medleys. *Take Love Easy* was the first of several duet albums with guitarist Joe Pass, and Ella was just beginning to show her age a bit. Not all of the ballads (including "Lush Life" and "I Want to Talk About You") really fit her style, although these collaborations do have their touching moments. *Fine and Mellow*, which teams Ella with an octet of all-stars (including trumpeters Clark Terry and Harry Edison and tenors Zoot Sims and Eddie "Lockjaw" Davis), works better; the singer is inspired by the other musicians. *Ella in London* (which is partly reissued in *The Concert Years*) is also a worthy outing, with Ella swinging on "Sweet Georgia Brown," "It Don't Mean a Thing," "Lemon Drop," and even Carole King's "You've Got a Friend." The singer works well with Oscar Peterson, both in duets on *Ella & Oscar* and in some trios with bassist Ray Brown, and she sounds pretty strong on *At the Montreux Jazz Festival*, a jazz-oriented outing with the Tommy Flanagan Trio. "Caravan," "Let's Do It," and "How High the Moon" are the high points of the last.

7   *Fitzgerald & Pass . . . Again / Jan. 29, 1976–Feb. 8, 1976 / Pablo 2310-772*

6   *Montreux '77 / July 14, 1977 / Original Jazz Classics 376*

7   *Lady Time / June 19–20, 1978 / Original Jazz Classics 864*

5   *The Best Is Yet to Come / Feb. 4–5, 1982 / Original Jazz Classics 889*

4   *Speak Love / Mar. 21–22, 1982 / Pablo 2310-888*

4   *Easy Living / 1986 / Pablo 2310-921*

1   *All That Jazz / Mar. 15–22, 1989 / Pablo 2310-938*

By the second half of the 1970s, the range of Ella Fitzgerald's voice was starting to shrink, her once-impeccable pitch was beginning to become a bit shaky, and she was clearly past her prime. Still, Ella had a long distance to fall. She does fine on her second duet album with Joe Pass, performing 14 concise numbers, including "I Ain't Got Nothin' but the Blues," a wordless "Rain," "You Took Advantage of Me," and even "Tennessee Waltz." *Montreux '77* is not quite up to the level of Ella's Montreux performance of two years earlier, but she cooks on "Billie's Bounce" and is creative on "One-Note

Samba." *Lady Time* is a bit unusual in that Ella is joined by just organist Jackie Davis and drummer Louie Bellson. Her versions of "I'm Walkin'," "I Cried for You," and "And the Angels Sing" work quite well, even if she did not need to sing "Mack the Knife" again! Unfortunately it would be downhill from here, and the title of *The Best Is Yet to Come* is both ironic and inaccurate. Ella' s singing on that 1982 set is decent but slightly disappointing. And why did she record "God Bless the Child"? *Speak Love* and *Easy Living* are both additional duet dates with Joe Pass. Ella's charm and sense of swing were still very much present, but her vocal chops were fading, and this setting was too intimate for her at this point. Ella's final recording, *All That Jazz,* made when she was almost 72, simply should not have been released. The songs and sidemen (which include Harry Edison, Clark Terry, and Benny Carter) are excellent, but Ella Fitzgerald barely hints at her former greatness.

LPS TO SEARCH FOR

One of Ella Fitzgerald's greatest records has yet to be reissued on CD: *Ella in Hollywood* (Verve 4052). Recorded in 1961, this LP has Ella taking her longest-ever scat vocal (a remarkable 9 1/2-minute version of "Take the 'A' Train") and throughout the date she takes lots of chances and really pushes herself. An unknown classic.

FILMS

Ella Fitzgerald sings "A-Tisket, A-Tasket" in the Abbott & Costello movie *Ride 'Em Cowboy* (1941) and is in the 1955 film *Pete Kelly's Blues* (highlighted by "Hard Hearted Hannah"), *St. Louis Blues* (1958), and *Let No Man Write My Epitaph* (1960), having a real acting role in the last. She also sings a wondrous version of "Perdido" as her feature on *The Incomparable Nat King Cole* (Warner Reprise Video 38266) from 1956.

HELEN FORREST

b. Apr. 12, 1918, Atlantic City, NJ, d. July 11, 1999, Los Angeles, CA

Helen Forrest was one of the finest of the band singers of the Swing era, but to an extent her career peaked too early. She was most popular during a period when singers were primarily thought of as part of a band. By the mid-1940s, when vocalists took over, Forrest was overshadowed by the next generation of singers.

Born Helen Fogel, she debuted at the age of ten, singing with her brother's band at a dance marathon. After high school she moved to New York, where, using the name of Bonnie Blue, she sang on the radio with Bunny Berigan. Artie Shaw was impressed and hired her in 1938. Now called Helen Forrest, she was featured with Shaw's very popular orchestra (recording "Deep in a Dream" and "Deep Purple," among others) until the bandleader fled to Mexico in 1939. She sang next with Benny Goodman (her favorite recordings from her time with BG were "More Than You Know" and "The Man I Love"), but it was her period with Harry James (1941–44) that resulted in her finest music. Instead of just getting a chorus in the middle of a song like virtually all of the other band singers, she sang the first and the last choruses on many of her recordings with James, a revolutionary step for singers. "I Don't Want to Walk Without You," "I Had the Craziest Dream," and "I've Heard That Song Before" were all major hits for her with James. Going solo by 1945, Helen Forrest (who recorded some popular vocal duets with Dick Haymes) worked on and off into the late 1980s as a single, but she did not have any new hits, ending up just reprising her Swing-era successes. In 1982 she completed her memoirs, *I Had The Craziest Dream.*

●

8 *Them There Eyes / 1947–1955 / Mr. Music 7003*
The recording dates that I have given to these performances are only estimates, for they are not included with the disc. Helen Forrest is heard on this CD in a variety of settings, accompanied by orchestras led by Ray Bloch, Larry Clinton, Arthur Norman, and Sy Oliver in addition to two songs with "The Magic Strings" and six successful small-group numbers with "The Stars Of Swing." Forrest not only revives a few of her Swing hits (including "I Don't Want To Walk Without You" and "I Had The Craziest Dream") but interprets such songs as "Ain't Misbehavin'," "Secret Love," "From This Moment On" and "Lover Come Back To Me." She sounds wonderful throughout, and it is quite surprising that her solo career ultimately went nowhere.

Now and Forever (Stash 225), from 1983, was Helen Forrest's first recording in quite a few years, and she took the opportunity to remake her three big Harry James hits along with other typical material from the era (including "More Than You Know" and "I Cried for You"). Forrest, who is heard backed by a jazz septet, sounds younger than her 65 years.

TEDDY GRACE
b. June 26, 1905, Arcadia, LA, d. Jan. 4, 1992, La Mirada, CA

Teddy Grace was one of the finest singers of the Swing era but ended up as one of the most obscure. She started singing professionally in 1931, was featured on the radio in the South, and worked for Al Katz (1933), Tommy Christian, and Mal Hallett (1934–37), also recording with the Bob Crosby Orchestra. During 1937–40 Grace recorded a series of jazz-oriented combo sides, using such sidemen as Jack Teagarden, Bud Freeman, clarinetist Pee Wee Russell, Bobby Hackett, Charlie Shavers, and Buster Bailey, among others. These performances show that Teddy Grace was particularly strong on the blues and could outswing most of the other singers of the time. In 1940 she became frustrated with the music business and abruptly quit. During World War II Grace joined the WACs and sang at far too many bond rallies and shows, completely losing her voice. Eventually her speaking voice came back, but she could no longer sing, so Teddy Grace was forced to spend the rest of her life working outside of music. Her recordings have been rediscovered and reissued only in recent years.

●

10 *Teddy Grace / Oct. 25, 1937–Sept. 26, 1940 / Timeless 1-016*

8 *Turn on That Red Hot Heat / Feb. 26, 1937–Sept. 9, 1940 / Hep 1054*

These two CDs have all of Teddy Grace's recordings as a leader except for five songs. The Timeless release came out first and got most of her best recordings, six complete sessions that total 22 selections. Grace is backed by Bobby Hackett on four songs and Jack Teagarden on the next four, and has three dates with a group that at times includes four of the six members of John Kirby's Sextet. The final four selections have Bud Freeman's Summa Cum Laude Orchestra helping her out. Grace is at her best on such numbers as "Downhearted Blues," "Arkansas Blues," "Oh Daddy Blues," "You Don't Know My Mind," and "Hey Lawdy Papa," but she is also fine on the more pop-oriented material. *Turn on That Red Hot Heat* just duplicates one song, includes one of Grace's other dates as a leader, and also features her singing with the Mal Hallett and Bob Crosby orchestras. Teddy Grace's brief but memorable discography is well worth exploring by Swing fans.

BILLIE HOLIDAY
b. Apr. 7, 1915, Baltimore, MD, d. July 17, 1959, New York, NY

A legend by the mid-1940s and still a household name four decades after her death, Billie Holiday often interpreted lyrics that described her life and her feelings. She did not have a large voice and her improvising was fairly basic, felt mostly in her influential behind-the-beat phrasing, but the emotional intensity that she put into her singing could often be haunting and heart-breaking, like her life.

Born Eleanora Harris, she was the daughter of guitarist Clarence Holiday, who played for a time with Fletcher Henderson. Her parents never married and she grew up feeling alone and unloved, with an inferiority complex that never left her. Holiday's early days were quite unstable and sometimes dangerous. However, things improved in 1933 when she was heard

Billie Holiday's life may have been difficult, but nothing overshadowed the intensity and honesty of her singing.

singing in a Harlem club by John Hammond. He set up her first record date and, even if the two songs with Benny Goodman that resulted were not too successful, Billie's career was now officially under way.

After freelancing, in 1935 Billie Holiday appeared in a short film with Duke Ellington and then began to record regularly with Teddy Wilson's all-star groups. By 1937 she was also leading her own sessions and often utilizing Lester Young (her musical soul mate, who nicknamed her "Lady Day") and trumpeter Buck Clayton. Holiday was with Count Basie's orchestra for much of that year and spent a few months with Artie Shaw in 1938, but virtually no recordings resulted (a couple of songs from a radio air check with Basie and "Any Old Time" with Shaw) because she was signed to a different record label than the bandleaders were. The Shaw period was difficult because of some racial incidents with audience members and hotel management, not only in the South but in New York. However, Holiday's fame was growing during this period, and in 1939 she starred at Café Society in New York. She debuted "Strange Fruit," a disturbing but very effective antiracism song that gave her additional notoriety.

Billie Holiday's voice was at its strongest during the 1940s. "Fine and Mellow" and "God Bless the Child" had become permanent parts of her repertoire. Her work for Decca (1944–50) ranked with the best of her career, starting with a big-selling record of "Lover Man" and continuing with such songs as "Don't Explain," "Good Morning Heartache," "Ain't Nobody's Business If I Do," and "Crazy He Calls Me." However, the 1940s were not completely happy for Holiday. She became a heroin addict and spent a year (1947) in jail, which ironically increased her celebrity status. She was also disappointed that her one movie appearance, 1946's *New Orleans,* found her cast as a maid (although both her acting and her singing in the film were excellent).

Things would get worse in the 1950s, when she actually was at the peak of her fame and her earning power. Holiday's voice declined on a steady basis, as did her state of mind. She was recording again with top jazz all-stars (for Norman Granz's Verve label) and visiting Europe, but her bad relationships and constant use of heroin, alcohol, and cigarettes took their toll. She sometimes hinted at the greatness of her past, such as on the telecast *The Sound of Jazz,* where she had an emotional reunion with Lester Young on "Fine and Mellow," but by 1958 there was little left of her voice and her spirit. On *Lady in Satin* (which some fans really love because of the pure emotion), she sounds as if she were in her seventies rather than her forties. Lady Day would die the following year, and she was certainly kicked while she was down, being arrested for heroin possession while she lay on her deathbed!

But the recordings survive and the legendary Billie Holiday's legacy will always be an important part of jazz history.

●

✱ *The Complete Recordings, 1933–1940 / Nov. 27, 1933– Oct. 15, 1940 / Affinity 1019-86*

✱ *The Legacy Box 1933–1958 / Nov. 27, 1933–Feb. 19, 1958 / Columbia/Legacy 47724*

Billie Holiday's recording career easily falls into three periods. The early years (1933–42) found her backed by Swing all-stars (often led by Teddy Wilson) and taking either one or two choruses while her sidemen (which sometimes included Lester Young and Buck Clayton) make the most of their short solos. On Decca, Lady Day during 1944–50 was heard at her very best, while her accompaniment ranges from strings and even a vocal group to studio musicians; she was very much the star. Her Verve period (1952–57) brought back the all-star concept but Holiday's voice gradually declined.

The Complete Recordings is a magnificent eight-CD set that has every one of Holiday's Columbia recordings from the 1933–40 period, including many alternate takes. Its only fault is that Holiday's four sessions of 1941–42 are not also included. This box will probably be difficult to find, but it is perfectly done and a real gem. In contrast, *The Legacy Box,* a three-CD set, is merely a sampler and it often misses the mark. Since the *Quintessential* series had already reissued the master versions of all of Lady Day's Columbia recordings, *The Legacy Box* at best could be a greatest-hits collection, but in nine cases alternate versions are substituted for the "real" takes. The booklet is attractive and there are a few rarities thrown in (Holiday's film appearance with Duke Ellington, an air check with Count Basie, and three cuts from 1957–58), but overall this set is a confusing frivolity.

9 *The Quintessential Billie Holiday, Volume 1 / Nov. 27, 1933–Dec. 3, 1935 / Columbia 40646*

9 *The Quintessential Billie Holiday, Volume 2 / Jan. 30, 1936–Oct. 21, 1936 / Columbia 40790*

10 *The Quintessential Billie Holiday, Volume 3 / Oct. 28, 1936–Feb. 18, 1937 / Columbia 44048*

10 *The Quintessential Billie Holiday, Volume 4 / Mar. 31, 1973–June 15, 1937 / Columbia 44252*

10 *The Quintessential Billie Holiday, Volume 5 / June 15, 1937–Jan. 27, 1938 / Columbia 44423*

For listeners who do not need to hear every alternate take that Billie Holiday recorded, the nine CDs in the *Quintessential* series will certainly suffice. Together they reissue all of Holiday's studio recordings of 1933–42 except for her dates for the Commodore label. Nearly every selection is well worth hearing. *Volume 1* has Billie Holiday's first 16 recordings, including her two numbers from 1933 and such classics as "What a Little Moonlight Can Do," "Miss Brown to You," and "Twenty-Four Hours a Day." Roy Eldridge, Benny Goodman, Ben Webster, and Chu Berry are among the sidemen, as is Teddy Wilson (who pops up on each of the CDs). *Volume 2* is highlighted by "These Foolish Things," "I Cried for You" (which has some beautiful playing by Johnny Hodges), "Summertime," "Billie's Blues," and "The Way You Look Tonight." Jonah Jones, Bunny Berigan, Artie Shaw, and Webster help out. *Volume 3* has the first meeting on records by Lady Day and Lester Young, and the combination was magical from the start, as can be heard on "This Year's Kisses" and "I Must Have That Man." Other highlights of the disc include "Pennies from Heaven," "I Can't Give You Anything but Love" (on which Holiday shows off the influence of Louis Armstrong), "I've Got My Love to Keep Me Warm," and "This Is My Last Affair." The Holiday-Young combination results in such numbers on *Volume 4* as "I'll Get By," "Mean to Me," "Foolin' Myself,"

"Easy Living," "Let's Call the Whole Thing Off," "They Can't Take That Away from Me," and Me, Myself and I" are also classic, with the other sidemen including Hodges, Cootie Williams, and Clayton. If anything, *Volume 5* is even better, with Young and Clayton playing on all but four songs. The height of their musical partnership with Holiday can be heard on "Without Your Love," "Getting Some Fun Out of Life," "He's Funny That Way," "When You're Smiling" (which has a classic Young solo), "I Can't Believe That You're in Love with Me," and "When a Woman Loves a Man."

> **9** *The Quintessential Billie Holiday, Volume 6 / May 11, 1938–Nov. 9, 1938 / Columbia 45449*

> **9** *The Quintessential Billie Holiday, Volume 7 / Nov. 28, 1938–July 5, 1939 / Columbia 46180*

> **9** *The Quintessential Billie Holiday, Volume 8 / July 5, 1939–Sept. 12, 1940 / Columbia 47030*

> **10** *The Quintessential Billie Holiday, Volume 9 / Oct. 15, 1940–Feb. 10, 1942 / Columbia 47031*

> **6** *Control Booth Series, Vol. 1 / Sept. 12, 1940–Mar. 21, 1941 / Jazz Unlimited 2014*

> **6** *Control Booth Series, Vol. 2 / Mar. 21, 1941–Feb. 10, 1942 / Jazz Unlimited 2015*

During 1938–42, Billie Holiday's recordings began to gradually shift from featuring her as one of the soloists to showcasing her as the main star, with her sidemen in a more supportive role. *Volume 6,* which is most notable for "You Go to My Head," "Having Myself a Time," "The Very Thought of You," and "You Can't Be Mine," has its strong moments, with fine contributions from Charlie Shavers, Harry James, and Benny Carter, plus a few spots for Lester Young and Buck Clayton. *Volume 7* is highlighted by "More Than You Know," "Sugar," "Long Gone Blues," and "Some Other Spring." Roy Eldridge, Benny Carter, Hot Lips Page, Tab Smith, and Bobby Hackett are all heard from. Lester Young returns on *Volume 8* for two dates (including "Laughing at Life"), but Roy Eldridge takes solo honors with "Falling in Love Again." Other top numbers include "Them There Eyes," "Swing, Brother, Swing," "Ghost of Yesterday," "Body and Soul," and "I'm Pulling Through." The final volume of the *Quintessential* series has the last Holiday-Young recordings ("Let's Do It" and "All of Me"),

Billie singing "St. Louis Blues" with Benny Carter, and her earliest recordings of "God Bless the Child," "I Cover the Waterfront," and "Gloomy Sunday." The two *Control Booth* CDs consist of alternate takes from Holiday's last seven Columbia dates. The first 14 performances on *Vol. 1* duplicate music on the Affinity box, but the other cuts give listeners alternate versions from Lady Day's 1940–41 sessions, including new versions of "I Hear Music," "St. Louis Blues," and "Let's Do It." *Vol. 2* includes fresh and obscure renditions of "God Bless the Child," "Love Me or Leave Me," and "Gloomy Sunday."

> **7** *The Complete Commodore Recordings / Apr. 20, 1939–Apr. 8, 1944 / GRP/Commodore 2-401*

> **8** *Billie Holiday / Apr. 20, 1939–Apr. 8, 1944 / Commodore 7001*

> **7** *Billie's Blues / June 12, 1942–Jan. 5, 1954 / Blue Note 48786*

> **10** *The Complete Decca Recordings / Oct. 4, 1944–Mar. 8, 1950 / GRP/Decca 2-601*

In 1939 Billie Holiday wanted to record the antilynching protest piece "Strange Fruit," but her label refused to give her permission. Fortunately, they allowed her to cut that piece plus three other songs (including "Fine and Mellow") for Milt Gabler's Commodore label. In 1944, after her association with Columbia ended, Lady Day made a dozen other recordings for Commodore (with the backing of Eddie Heywood's trio and septet), including "Embraceable You," "Billie's Blues," "I Cover the Waterfront," and "On the Sunny Side of the Street." The unimaginatively titled *Billie Holiday* is a single disc with all 16 numbers, while the GRP/Commodore double CD has the same 16 plus 29 alternate takes! Since Holiday did not improvise much on these selections, there is an awful lot of repetition on the twofer, and most fans will be satisfied with the smaller release. *Billie's Blues* is a gap filler. Holiday's guest spot with Paul Whiteman's orchestra in 1942 (resulting in "Trav'lin Light") is here, as are her four titles for the Aladdin label in 1951 (best known is "Detour Ahead"). The bulk of the CD is taken up by an excellent concert in Germany from 1954 in which Holiday is joined by a trio and, on "Billie's Blues" and a lengthy version of "Lover Come Back to Me," clarinetist Buddy De-

Franco, vibraphonist Red Norvo, and guitarist Jimmy Raney.

But easily the best of this batch is the two-CD *The Complete Decca Recordings.* Although sometimes backed by commercial or middle-of-the-road ensembles (including strings and on a few occasions a vocal group), Lady Day never sounded better than during this era. The 40 performances (which include 12 alternate takes) are highlighted by "Lover Man" (her biggest seller), "Don't Explain," "You Better Go Now," "Good Morning Heartache," " 'Tain't Nobody's Business If I Do," "Gimme A Pigfoot," "Now or Never," "You're My Thrill," "Crazy He Calls Me," and two numbers made with Louis Armstrong. Essential.

* *The Complete Billie Holiday on Verve 1945–1959 / Feb. 12, 1945–Mar. 1, 1959 / Verve 314 513 860–879*

7 *At Storyville / Oct. 29, 1951–1953 / Black Lion 760921*

7 *Fine and Mellow / Jan. 18, 1944–Apr. 15, 1959 / Starline Productions 406*

3 *Lady in Satin / Feb. 19–21, 1958 / Columbia/Legacy 65144*

Billie Holiday's last period is the most controversial. Her voice gradually faded, getting weaker and raspier each year, yet the emotional intensity that she brought to the lyrics (which were often autobiographical) became greater. Some listeners actually prefer her last few recordings, such as *Lady in Satin,* but I find that set quite difficult to listen to because she sounds as if she is dying on stage! *The Complete Billie Holiday on Verve* is an extraordinary ten-CD set that contains every scrap of music (and even conversation) that exists from her association with Norman Granz. Holiday sounds at her best on the first disc, which has her Jazz at the Philharmonic performances of 1945–46 and her first Verve studio set in 1952. Holiday's regular sessions of 1952–57 usually found her matched with two horns taken from Charlie Shavers, Harry Edison, Benny Carter, Buddy DeFranco, Flip Phillips, Tony Scott, and Ben Webster, interpreting high-quality standards but sometimes sounding a bit worldweary. Also included in this box is the 1954 concert also on the Blue Note disc *Billie's Blues,* a full disc taken up by a 1955

rehearsal with Jimmie Rowles (one listen to this is sufficient), a rehearsal with clarinetist Tony Scott (one listen is probably too many!), her 1956 Carnegie Hall concert, a live performance in 1958, and her final album from March 1959. Much of this music is also available individually and the 1952–57 studio sides are worth exploring. *At Storyville* has club dates from 1951–53 that find Billie Holiday sounding fine while backed by a trio (with either Buster Harding or Carl Drinkard on piano). The most notable aspect to her run-through of her usual repertoire is that tenor saxophonist Stan Getz guests on three numbers. *Fine and Mellow* has rare live performances, including Holiday's appearance at the Esquire All-American concert of 1944 and on the Eddie Condon TV show in 1949, plus a variety of sessions from 1951–56 from television and clubs. The CD concludes with the last example of Lady Day on record, five songs performed live just three months before her death. A collectors' item.

Lady in Satin was Billie Holiday's next-to-last album, and listeners either hate it or love it. At age 42, Holiday's voice could pass for that of a 72-year-old. The string arrangements by Ray Ellis are muzaky and, although the versions of "You Don't Know What Love Is," "You've Changed," and "Glad to Be Unhappy" are touching, this set is difficult to listen to.

LPS TO SEARCH FOR

For a Lady Named Billie (Giants of Jazz 1001) has two very interesting interviews with Billie Holiday, plus live appearances from 1949 and 1950 (the latter is taken from a film short) and a live version of "You've Changed" with strings.

FILMS

Billie Holiday sings a blues chorus with Duke Ellington in the short *Symphony in Black* (1934), acts and sings with Louis Armstrong in *New Orleans* (1946), performs "God Bless the Child" and "Now or Never" with the Count Basie Octet in a 1950 short, and sings an emotional "Fine and Mellow" in *The Sound of Jazz* (1957) with the assistance of Lester Young (who steals the show), Coleman Hawkins, Ben Webster, and Roy Eldridge. In addition, an excellent documentary, *The Many Faces of Lady Day* (Kultur 1392), is available on video.

LENA HORNE

b. June 30, 1917, Brooklyn, NY

Lena Horne's beauty opened up doors for her, but it has sometimes overshadowed her musical talents. She was never really a jazz singer, although she could always interpret standards with Swing. Horne began singing in public when she was six, performed at the Cotton Club as early as 1934, and picked up experience singing with Noble Sissle's orchestra during 1935–36. She gained attention for her work with Teddy Wilson in the late 1930s, was with Charlie Barnet's orchestra (1940–41), and recorded with Artie Shaw. Horne was signed to a Hollywood contract and starred in the jazz short *Boogie Woogie Dream*, *Cabin in the Sky* (with Ethel Waters), and *Stormy Weather.* However, those were all-black films and her appearances in big budget white movies were generally just for a song or two, scenes that could easily be cut out when shown in the South. Her singing career was more successful, and from the mid-1940s on she has been one of the top middle-of-the-road pop singers, a constant attraction who often worked with her late husband, arranger-pianist Lennie Hayton, and orchestras. Lena Horne remained active into the late 1990s.

●

9 *Stormy Weather / Jan. 7, 1941–June 9, 1958 / Bluebird 9985*

8 *Lena Horne at MGM / 1942–1956 / Rhino 72246*

7 *The Original Black And White Recordings / 1946 / Simitar 56782*

6 *An Evening with Lena Horne / Sept. 19, 1994 / Blue Note 31877*

Most of Lena Horne's best early jazz recordings are on *Stormy Weather.* She is featured with various orchestras, including those of Charlie Barnet, Artie Shaw, and Horace Henderson in the 1940s plus a few selections from the 1955–58 period. Horne sounds wonderful on such numbers as "You're My Thrill," "Don't Take Your Love from Me," "Stormy Weather," "Ill Wind," "I Didn't Know About You," and "As Long As You Live." Other than *Stormy Weather,* most of the music from Lena Horne's film appearances (plus alternate takes and songs recorded but not used in the movies) are on *Lena Horne at MGM.* The songs are drawn from a dozen films and include "Just One of Those Things," "Honeysuckle Rose," "Somebody Loves Me," two versions of "Paper Doll," "The Lady Is a Tramp," and a medley from *Showboat.*

The Original Black And White Recordings has Horne in 1946 singing 17 jazz standards with the backing of Phil Moore's Orchestra, ensembles that include such top players as Gerald Wilson, Willie Smith, Tyree Glenn, and Lucky Thompson among others. Though she sings the songs fairly straight, Horne uplifts the music and gives the lyrics the emotional intensity that they deserve. This CD is a big improvement on *More Than You Know* (Simitar 116226) which had just nine of the tunes. *An Evening with Lena Horne* was recorded in 1994, when the singer was 77, her voice sounded like she could be 57, and the picture on the CD finds her looking like she was 47. Although she talks some of the lyrics, Horne's voice was still in surprisingly good form at the time and she holds a few long notes in spots. On six of the 16 songs (mostly veteran standards), Horne's rhythm section (which includes pianist Mike Renzi and guitarist Rodney Jones) is augmented by 11 horns from the Count Basie Orchestra. This is the best recording from her later years.

FILMS

Lena Horne was in many films, usually for one song. Exceptions were the classic film short with Albert Ammons, Pete Johnson, and Teddy Wilson called *Boogie Woogie Dream* (1941), *Cabin in the Sky* with Ethel Waters (1942), and *Stormy Weather* with Bill "Bojangles' Robinson (1943). Of her better cameo appearances, she is in *Panama Hattie* (1942), sings "Honeysuckle Rose" in *Thousands Cheer* (1943), performs "Paper Doll" in *Two Girls and a Sailor* (1944), and is heard in prime form in *Till the Clouds Roll By* (1946) and *Words and Music* (1948).

HELEN HUMES

b. June 23, 1913, Louisville, KY, d. Sept. 9, 1981, Santa Monica, CA

Early in her career, when she was singing with Count Basie's orchestra, Helen Humes was restricted to the role of a ballad singer, since Jimmy Rushing tended to get all of the blues and the hotter material. But Humes was equally skilled at blues and standards, as she would show throughout her long career.

Helen Humes grew up in New York and started singing as a child. In 1927, when she was 13 and 14, Humes made her recording debut on a series of double-entendre blues; years later she would claim that she did not understand the words! She worked in theaters in the early 1930s, performed with Stuff Smith and Al Sears, and sang with Vernon Andrade's orchestra before gaining recognition for her performances and recordings with Count Basie (1938–41). Humes did quite well in her solo career, recording fairly frequently, having a hit in 1945 with "Be Baba Leba," and gaining a loyal audience. Her joyous versions of blues fit well not only into Swing but into early rhythm and blues, and she even excelled singing with Dizzy Gillespie's orchestra in 1947. Humes wrote a standard in 1950, the humorous "Million Dollar Secret." She worked with Red Norvo during part of the latter half of the '50s, made three classic albums for Contemporary, and then, after living in Australia during 1964–67, she retired from music. Fortunately her absence was just temporary, and in 1973 Helen Humes made a successful comeback, staying active and singing in her timeless style up until her death.

●

9 *1927–1945 / Apr. 30, 1927–Aug. 1945 / Classics 892*

9 *1945–1947 / Aug. 1945–Dec. 31, 1947 / Classics 1036*
1927–1945 has Helen Humes's ten recordings as a young teenager, singing low-down blues with either a piano-guitar duo (often with Lonnie Johnson) or two guitars. The sweetness in her voice was apparent even then. Her next dates as a leader took place after she left Count Basie 14 years later. Humes is heard with an all-star sextet that includes altoist Pete Brown and trumpeter Dizzy Gillespie (who unfortunately has no solos). She also leads a date with a septet organized by Leonard Feather that has Bobby Stark on trumpet and five numbers (including "He May Be Your Man" and "Be-Baba-Leba") with pianist Bill Doggett's octet. *1945–1947* draws its selections from the catalogs of Aladdin, Black & White, and Mercury. Humes is joined by all-stars from Los Angeles (including Snooky Young, Willie Smith, and Edmond Hall) and is heard on dates with Buck Clayton. Highlights include "See See Rider," "Be Baba Leba Boogie," "If I Could Be with You," "Jet-Propelled Papa" and "They Raided the Joint."

10 *Tain't Nobody's Biz-Ness If I Do / Jan. 5, 1959–Feb. 10, 1959 / Original Jazz Classics 453*

10 *Songs I Like to Sing / Sept. 6–8, 1960 / Original Jazz Classics 171*

9 *Swinging with Humes / July 27–29, 1961 / Original Jazz Classics 608*
Age 45 at the time of *Tain't Nobody's Biz-Ness,* Helen Humes was at the peak of her powers during the next few years, as shown on these three CDs (originally recorded for Contemporary). *Tain't Nobody's Biz-Ness* finds her assisted by an all-star sextet that includes Benny Carter (on trumpet), trombonist Frank Rosolino, and tenor saxophonist Teddy Edwards. Humes's versions of "You Can Depend on Me," "Among My Souvenirs," and "When I Grow Too Old to Dream" are definitive. *Songs I Like to Sing* is even better, for Humes performs tunes that sound as if they were written for her, including "If I Could Be with You," "Don't Worry 'Bout Me," "My Old Flame," and the best version of her "Million Dollar Secret." The backup group (arranged by Marty Paich) includes Ben Webster, altoist Art Pepper, and on a few songs a string quartet. *Swinging with Humes,* which has Humes backed by a sextet, including trumpeter Joe Gordon, Teddy Edwards on tenor, and pianist Wynton Kelly, is almost as good. On this project Humes uplifts such standards as "When Day Is Done," "Home," "S'posin'," "Pennies from Heaven," and "The Very Thought of You." All three OJCs are highly recommended.

7 *On the Sunny Side of the Street / July 2, 1974 / Black Lion 760185*

7 *'Deed I Do / Apr. 26, 1976 / Contemporary 14071*

9 *Helen Humes and the Muse All-Stars / Oct. 5 + 8, 1979 / Muse 5473*

Recorded shortly after she started making a full comeback, *On the Sunny Side of the Street* has Helen Humes's performance at the 1974 Montreux Jazz Festival. Joined by a quartet with Buddy Tate and either Earl Hines or Jay McShann on piano, Humes easily wins the audience over with such songs as "If I Could Be with You," "Blue Because of You," and "I Got It Bad." The last was performed in tribute to Duke Ellington, who had passed away a few days earlier. The release of " 'Deed I Do" in 1994 was a happy event, the first "new" music from the late singer in quite a few years. She is heard in fine voice performing her usual concert set (mostly standards, including "Every Day I Have the Blues," "My Old Flame," and "If I Could Be with You") with a local rhythm section at an informal club in Half Moon Bay, California. One of the best of Humes's recordings from her final period is the project made with the Muse All-Stars in 1979. With the help of tenors of Arnett Cobb and Buddy Tate, the Gerald Wiggins Trio, and altoist Eddie "Cleanhead" Vinson (who joins Helen on the vocal of "I'm Gonna Move to the Outskirts of Town"), this is a delightful outing that is highlighted by such numbers as the humorous "Woe Is Me," "I've Got a Crush on You," and "Loud-Talking Woman."

LPS TO SEARCH FOR

E-Baba-Leba (Savoy 1159) has Helen Humes's dates for Savoy in 1944 and 1950. The latter includes a pair of live concerts with Roy Milton's band and tenorman Dexter Gordon; high points include the title cut, "If I Could Be with You," and "Knockin' Myself Out." *Let the Good Times Roll* (Classic Jazz 120), from 1973, is arguably Helen Humes's finest recording after the Contemporary period, but it has been scarce for a number of years. Assisted by a group of all-star Swing veterans, Humes puts plenty of feeling and joy into "That Old Feeling," "He May Be Your Man," "Million Dollar Secret," and "Guess Who's in Town." Also quite worthwhile is *The Talk of the Town* (Columbia 33488) and 1980's *Helen* (Muse 5233).

FILMS

Helen Humes sings with Dizzy Gillespie's big band in *Jivin' in Be-Bop* (1947).

HELEN O'CONNELL
b. ca. 1918, Toledo, OH, d. Sept. 9, 1993, San Diego, CA

Helen O'Connell was Jimmy Dorsey's singer during 1938–43, and much of the commercial success that his band enjoyed was due to her singing. Although not a major vocalist, O'Connell projected a sensual personality and enthusiasm that was quite appealing. She started out singing locally, worked on St. Louis radio, and was a member of Larry Funk's band. After joining Dorsey, O'Connell (who had an early hit in her version of "All of Me") performed mostly medium-tempo material, since Bob Eberly took care of the ballads. Arranger Tutti Caramata thought of pooling everyone's talents by having Eberly take a ballad chorus, Dorsey featured in an instrumental passage, and then O'Connell completing the song by singing hot. "Amapola" became a big seller in 1941, and it led to a series of songs done with that format, including "Green Eyes," "Tangerine," and "Star Eyes" (in the movie *I Dood It*). Helen O'Connell left Jimmy Dorsey's band by 1944 to get married. She eventually returned to singing, having a reasonably successful solo act, working in the 1950s for a time on the *Today* show and in the late 1980s touring with the Four Girls Four (with Kay Starr, Rosemary Clooney, and Rose Marie).

FILMS

Helen O'Connell introduces "Star Eyes" with Jimmy Dorsey in *I Dood It* (1943) and briefly sings some of her hits in *The Fabulous Dorseys* (1947).

ANITA O'DAY

b. Oct. 18, 1919, Chicago, IL

The hippest female jazz singer of the 1940s, Anita O'Day was always a creative improviser. She rose to fame in the early 1940s and had an up-and-down career but along the way created some timeless music.

Born Anita Belle Colton, she started using the name Anita O'Day while working in dance marathons in the 1930s, since O'Day was pig Latin for dough! After a period of struggle, O'Day gained experience as a singer working with Max Miller in Chicago during 1939–40. Her big break occurred when she joined Gene Krupa (1941–43), where her distinctive voice, jazz phrasing, and general enthusiasm were major assets. O'Day had hits in "Let Me Off Uptown," "Thanks for the Boogie Ride," "Bolero at the Savoy," and "Massachusetts," often teaming up with trumpeter Roy Eldridge. She was also one of the first female band vocalists who refused to wear glamorous gowns, considering herself one of the musicians. When Krupa had to break up his band in 1943, O'Day was briefly with Woody Herman and then spent a year (1944–45) with Stan Kenton's orchestra, doing well with "And Her Tears Flowed Like Wine" but not feeling all that comfortable with the band's music. When she left Kenton to briefly rejoin Krupa, her place with Stan was taken by June Christy, who was initially quite influenced by O'Day. After an additional year with Krupa (1945–46), having some success with "Opus No. 1" and "Boogie Blues," Anita O'Day went out on her own.

Because she usually went out of her way not to record pop music (with a few brief departures), wanting to stick to the swinging jazz that she loved, O'Day never became a major commercial success, but she always worked steadily and had a strong reputation in the jazz world. She was open to the influence of bebop and was always an expert scat singer. Her finest recordings were done during 1952–63 for Verve (all of which have been reissued on a limited-edition Mosaic box set). The high point of her career was filmed, performing "Sweet Georgia Brown" and a dazzling rendition of "Tea for Two" at the 1958 Newport Jazz Festival; it is one of the most memorable sections of the film *Jazz on a Summer's Day.*

Unfortunately Anita O'Day's private life began to seriously affect her career in the 1960s. A heroin addict by the mid-'50s, she spent a long period outside of music, almost dying from the years of drug abuse. However, O'Day made a successful comeback in the 1970s and wrote her frank autobiography, *High Times, Hard Times.* In the 1980s her voice began to seriously fade and alcohol abuse took its toll. Despite other health problems, Anita O'Day in 1999, at age 79, performed at a Carnegie Hall concert.

Anita O'Day was one of the last great singers to emerge from the Swing era. Her vocals (including her hit "Let Me Off Uptown") were a major attraction with the Gene Krupa Orchestra.

7 *The Complete Recordings 1949–1950 / Jan. 18, 1945 +*
Sept. 11, 1949 + Dec. 27, 1950 / Baldwin Street
Music 302

This single CD has all of Anita O'Day's studio recordings of
1949–50 plus four songs from a radio show in 1945 and five
radio transcriptions from that same year with the Nat King
Cole Trio. There are several novelties in the 1949–50 material, including such throwaways as "Poor Simple Simon,"
"Your Eyes Are Bigger Than Your Heart," and the horrid
"Yea Boo." But there are enough gems along the way (including "Them There Eyes," "You Took Advantage of Me,"
and the Cole selections) to make this of strong interest to
Anita O'Day fans wanting to hear her pre-Verve recordings.

* *The Complete Anita O'Day Verve/Clef Sessions / Jan.*
22, 1952–Oct. 15, 1962 / Mosaic 9-188

8 *This Is Anita / Dec. 6–8, 1955 / Verve 829 261*

8 *Pick Yourself Up with Anita O'Day / Dec. 15 + 17,*
1956 / Verve 314 517 329

8 *Anita Sings the Most / Jan. 31, 1957 / Verve 829 577*

7 *Anita Sings the Winners / Apr. 2–3, 1958 / Verve 837*
929

6 *Swings Cole Porter / Jan. 22, 1952–Aug. 17, 1960 /*
Verve 849 266

9 *All the Sad Young Men / Oct. 16, 1961 / Verve 314 517*
065

The years 1952–1963 were Anita O'Day's prime period. Her
voice was at its strongest, she was consistently creative in her
singing (often taking wild chances that succeeded), and her
career was under the guidance of producer Norman Granz
for most of that time. The nine-CD limited-edition Mosaic
box set (which was released in 1999) should be quickly acquired by all O'Day collectors. Whether backed by a quartet, having a reunion with Gene Krupa and Roy Eldridge, or
interacting with orchestras conducted and arranged by
Buddy Bregman, Russ Garcia, Marty Paich, Billy May,
Jimmy Giuffre, Bill Holman, Johnny Mandel, and Gary
McFarland, she never sounded better. For those fans who
did not act fast enough or lacked the cash for the box, six of
O'Day's Verve projects are available individually on single
CDs. *This Is Anita,* with Buddy Bregman's orchestra, has
"You're the Top" (which includes some updated lyrics),
"Honeysuckle Rose," and a touching version of "A Nightin-
gale Sang in Berkeley Square" among the more memorable

selections. *Pick Yourself Up* features Buddy Bregman's writing again, but various selections have a chamber orchestra
with strings, a big band, or a small combo. The tunes are
mostly Swing standards, including "Don't Be That Way,"
"Stompin' at the Savoy," "There's a Lull in My Life," and
"Sweet Georgia Brown." *Anita Sings the Most* is a meeting
with Oscar Peterson, guitarist Herb Ellis, bassist Ray
Brown, and drummer John Poole, a perfect setting for the
singer. She cooks hard on a very fast "Them There Eyes,"
and gives warmth to the ballads. It is a pity though that the
playing time of this CD is so brief, under 34 minutes. On
Sings the Winners, with the Russ Garcia Orchestra, O'Day
interprets songs made famous by other musicians, including
"Take the 'A' Train," "Four," "Four Brothers," and even
"Peanut Vendor." *Swings Cole Porter* is primarily from 1959
with Billy May's orchestra. O'Day performs rather concise
versions of a dozen Cole Porter songs, five of which are under two minutes. The CD is augmented by six other Porter
selections taken from O'Day's other Verve dates. *All the Sad
Young Men* is special because, even though the singer over-
dubbed her vocals, the complex arrangements by Gary
McFarland along with the offbeat material (including the title cut, "You Came a Long Way from St. Louis," "Senor
Blues," and a very different version of "Boogie Blues") challenges O'Day to come up with some of most inspired singing of her Verve era.

7 *I Get a Kick Out of You / Apr. 25, 1975 / Evidence 22054*

6 *In a Mellow Tone / Mar. 13–15, 1989 / DRG 5209*

3 *At Vine St. Live / Aug. 2–3, 1991 / DRG 8435*

1 *Rules of the Road / 1993 / Pablo 2210-950*

Anita O'Day was completely off records during 1964–69
and, other than a live set from 1970, she recorded very little
until 1975. *I Get a Kick Out of You* finds O'Day at the age of
55 beginning an unlikely but (at least for a few years) successful comeback. Originally recorded for the Japanese Trio
label, the Evidence CD has the singer backed by a quartet
with pianist Ronnell Bright. She revisits "Opus One," sings
the then-recent "A Song for You," and sounds best on such
numbers as "Undecided," "When Sunny Gets Blue," and a
lengthy "Gone with the Wind." Fourteen years later, Anita
O'Day cannot hide her age on *In a Mellow Tone,* but this is a
well-planned album, her phrasing was as creative as always,
and she still took chances, best shown on "I Cried for You."
With backing by a sextet that includes Gordon Brisker on

tenor, O'Day sounds fine on "Sleepin' Bee," "Like Someone in Love," and "More Than You Know." Unfortunately it would be downhill from there. *At Vine St. Live* is quite weak, with O'Day singing a variety of standards that she has treated much better in the past. And by the time she recorded *Rules of the Road,* her voice was completely gone. The big band, Buddy Bregman arrangements, and Jack Sheldon trumpet solos are not enough to compensate; this CD should not have been released. So get Anita O'Day's classic Verve recordings instead.

LPS TO SEARCH FOR

Hi Ho Trailus Boot Whip (Bob Thiele Music 1-0595) has Anita O'Day's ten recordings of 1947–48. She sounds quite youthful and exciting on chance-taking versions of "What Is This Thing Called Love," "Sometimes I'm Happy," and "How High the Moon." *Anita O'Day in Berlin* (MPS 20750), from 1970, was the singer's first record since 1963,

and she was clearly enthusiastic and ready for her return, performing some recent songs, a medley of "Yesterday" and "Yesterdays," and "Honeysuckle Rose" with equal skill. *Mello'Day* (GNP/Crescendo 2126), from 1978, is one of her best later records, an outing with the Lou Levy Trio and saxophonist Ernie Watts that finds Anita O'Day enjoying her comeback.

FILMS

Anita O'Day can be seen on Soundies from 1942 singing "Let Me Off Uptown" and "Thanks for the Boogie Ride" with Gene Krupa. She is the hit of *Jazz on a Summer's Day* (New Yorker Video 16590) from the 1958 Newport Jazz Festival, where she is at her absolute peak on "Sweet Georgia Brown" and "Tea for Two." In addition, O'Day sings "Memories of You" in *The Gene Krupa Story* (1959), has a small acting role in *Zigzag* (1970), and performs "I Concentrate on You" in *The Outfit* (1973).

MAXINE SULLIVAN

b. May 13, 1911, Homestead, PA, d. Apr. 7, 1987, New York, NY

Maxine Sullivan was a gentle singer, one who swung lightly, sang words clearly, and was always full of warmth. She was born Marietta Williams but changed her name early on for professional reasons. She started out singing on the radio in Pittsburgh with a group called the Red Hot Peppers and was soon discovered. Claude Thornhill became her musical director, arranging for her first recordings. Sullivan immediately had a big hit in "Loch Lomond" and for a time was stereotyped as a swinging interpreter of folk songs, performing similar numbers such as "If I Had a Ribbon Bow" and "Darling Nellie Gray."

Sullivan, who appeared in the film *Going Places* with Louis Armstrong and the show *Swinging the Dream,* married John Kirby in 1938 and worked on and off for three years with his sextet, where her cool tone fit the music perfectly. She was with the Benny Carter big band in mid-1941 before performing quite successfully as a single around New York. Sullivan divorced Kirby and later in life was married to pianist Cliff Jackson. In the mid-1950s she became a nurse (like Alberta Hunter) and spent a decade outside of music. However, she made a full comeback starting in 1968. In later years Sullivan sometimes played valve trombone for the fun of it to delight her audiences. Maxine Sullivan worked with the World's Greatest Jazz Band now and then during 1969–75 and was quite active both in concerts and on recordings during the years just prior to her death, never changing her subtle and winning style.

●

9 *1937–1938 / June 14, 1937–June 29, 1938 / Classics 963*

8 *1938–1941 / Dec. 10, 1938–Apr. 1, 1941 / Classics 991*
1937–1938 has Maxine Sullivan's first 23 recordings, all of which feature Claude Thornhill as her pianist and musical director. Sullivan recorded her first two numbers on June 14, 1937; her second record date included "Loch Lomond," which made her a star. Backed by either the early John Kirby

Sextet (with Thornhill and Pete Brown) or a studio orchestra that includes Bobby Hackett, Sullivan swings lightly on such numbers as "Annie Laurie," "The Folks Who Live on the Hill," "Darling Nellie Gray," "Moments Like This," and "Down the Old Ox Road." *1938–1941* continues the trend, although Thornhill was now gone. Sullivan is joined by a few different studio groups during 1938–39 and by the John Kirby Sextet for six numbers in 1940, and she is featured with the Benny Carter Orchestra on two cuts in 1941. Highlights include "Night and Day," "I Dream of Jeanie with the Light Brown Hair," "Ill Wind," "If I Had a Ribbon Bow," and "Molly Malone."

8   *Loch Lomond / 1940–1941 / Circle 47*

8   *More 1940–1941 / Oct. 10, 1940–Jan. 20, 1941 / Circle 125*

9   *The Le Ruban Bleu Years / 1943–1949 / Baldwin Street Music 303*

8   *A Tribute to Andy Razaf / Aug 30, 1956 / DCC Compact Classics 610*

Since Maxine Sullivan was married to John Kirby and her soft tone was a perfect match for the music he was creating, it is not surprising that she performed fairly often for a time with the Kirby Sextet. *Loch Lomond* and *More 1940–1941* are both taken from radio transcriptions. Although Sullivan gets first billing on both of these CDs, she is on only 11 of the 26 selections on *Loch Lomond* and six of the 18 numbers on *More 1940–1941*, so the two discs are of greater interest for the playing of the sextet than for her singing. They add to the legacy of the unique John Kirby Sextet and both sets are well worth acquiring. The Sullivan-Kirby marriage did not last and by 1943 she was freelancing, both musically and personally. *The Le Ruban Bleu Years* (named after a nightclub where she sang six months a year during the era) has all of her recordings from the 1944–48 period. Whether backed by bands led by Cedric Wallace, Teddy Wilson or Benny Carter, a studio orchestra, or the Ellis Larkins Trio, or appearing on a radio broadcast with Jimmie Lunceford, Sullivan was singing quite well during this period. Among the better selections are "Behavin' Myself for You," "Every Time We Say Goodbye," "If I Had a Ribbon Bow," "Skylark," "Legalize My Name," and two versions of "Loch Lomond." Other than two selections in 1953 and a couple of obscure albums in 1955, *A Tribute to Andy Razaf* was Sullivan's next project. Joined by Charlie Shavers, Buster Bailey, altoist Jerome Richardson, pianist Dick Hyman, either Wendell Marshall or Milt Hinton on bass, and drummer Osie Johnson (a group that sounds similar to John Kirby's), Sullivan performs a dozen songs that have lyrics by Razaf. Half of the songs were written by Fats Waller, but there are also other notable standards, including "Stompin' at the Savoy" and "Memories of You."

4   *Maxine Sullivan–William Shakespeare–Dick Hyman / June 15, 1971–Oct. 21, 1992 / Audiophile 250*

8   *We Just Couldn't Say Goodbye / Feb. 6–7, 1978 / Audiophile 128*

7   *Uptown / Jan. 1985 / Concord Jazz 4288*

7   *Spring Isn't Everything / July 26–27, 1986 / Audiophile 229*

8   *Swingin' Sweet / Sept. 1986 / Concord Jazz 4351*

After the Andy Razaf date, Maxine Sullivan participated in a John Kirby reunion session and then dropped out of music for a dozen years. She came back in 1968, and her final 19 years were quite busy. *Maxine Sullivan–Shakespeare–Hyman* is definitely a strange date. Hyman wrote the music for a dozen sonnets by William Shakespeare, but the antiquated lyrics as sung by Sullivan are difficult to sit through. Because the original LP was brief, Hyman in 1982 recorded 13 additional piano solos of the tunes, but it does not help much! Much better is *We Just Couldn't Say Goodbye,* which combines that original LP with one called *It Was Great Fun,* recorded two days later. Sullivan sings 24 veteran standards with backing by either a sextet with pianist Art Hodes and cornetist Ernie Carson or a quintet with Doc Cheatham and clarinetist Herb Hall. At 66, Maxine Sullivan sounds quite ageless. From seven years later, *Uptown* is a solid Swing date with tenor saxophonist Scott Hamilton's quintet. The singer is particularly expressive on "You Were Meant for Me," "Wrap Your Troubles in Dreams," and "Just One of Those Things." On *Spring Isn't Everything,* Sullivan (with assistance from the Loonis McGlohon Quartet) happily performs 13 Harry Warren songs, including "You're Getting to Be a Habit with Me," "I Only Have Eyes for You," "Lulu's Back in Town," and "I'll String Along with You." Other than an Atlantic album that was partly recorded a few months later, *Swingin' Sweet* (a reunion date with Scott Hamilton) was Maxine Sullivan's final recording. She certainly does not sound like a 75-year-old on such tunes as "As Long As I Live," "I Got a Right to Sing the Blues," and "I Hadn't Anyone Till You." It was justice that the final song on her final full album happened to be "Loch Lomond!"

LPS TO SEARCH FOR

Together (Atlantic 81783) was Maxine Sullivan's last project, a set of Jule Styne songs performed with a sextet led by pianist Keith Ingham. Even just months before her death, the singer's voice was still soothing, lightly swinging, and coolly emotional.

Maxine Sullivan appears in *Going Places* (1938) and *St. Louis Blues* (1939).

SISTER ROSETTA THARPE

b. Mar. 20, 1921, Cotton Plant, AR, d. Oct. 9, 1973, Philadelphia, PA

Sister Rosetta Tharpe was a unique performer, a powerful gospel singer who during her period with Lucky Millinder was particularly effective at singing secular music. She was also one of the finest acoustic guitarists active in Swing of the early 1940s.

Tharpe was originally a singing evangelist and she was always an exciting performer. She was featured in John Hammond's From Spirituals to Swing concert in 1938 and was the main attraction in Millinder's orchestra during 1940–43. Her recordings of "Rock Me," "That's All," "Trouble in Mind," "This Train," "Shout Sister Shout," "Rock Daniel," and even "I Want a Tall, Skinny Papa" are all memorable. She was also featured with Millinder on a series of filmed Soundies. However, in 1943, when she went solo, Sister Rosetta Tharpe returned to religious music, where she was very popular throughout her career. Happily, her guitar solos were always part of her performances, and she did tour with Chris Barber's Swing/trad band a few times in later years when she visited England.

●

10 *Vol. 1 (1938–1941) / Oct. 31, 1938–Dec. 1, 1941 / Document 5334*

9 *Vol. 2 (1942–1944) / Feb. 18, 1942–Sept. 22, 1944 / Document 5335*

7 *Live in 1960 / 1960 / Southland 1007*

7 *Live at the Hot Club de France / 1966 / Milan 35624*

Sister Rosetta Tharpe was a unique performer, one who brought religious zeal to secular music for a few years and whose acoustic guitar solos alone would have put her near the top of her field. *Vol. 1* has her first 26 recordings. She is heard on 14 solo performances from 1938–39 (including "Rock Me," "That's All," "The Lonesome Road," and "This Train"), eight numbers with Lucky Millinder's orchestra in 1941 (highlighted by some remakes plus "Shout, Sister, Shout" and "Trouble in Mind"), and a four-song solo date from later in 1941 that is religiouslyoriented. *Vol. 2* starts out with "I Want a Tall, Skinny Papa" with Millinder and includes radio appearances from 1943 with Millinder and one song ("This Train") with Louis Jordan's Tympany Five. The second half of the CD finds Tharpe returning to her original career as a gospel singer, performing mostly unaccompanied except for a date with the Sam Price Trio. Despite the one-note nature of the subject matter, she brought a lot of color and variety to her performances. Both *Live in 1960* and *Live at the Hot Club de France* are strong examples of her solo concerts from her later years. The Southland CD is better recorded and includes "He's Got the Whole World in His Hands," "Didn't It Rain," "The Gospel Train," and "Down by the Riverside." The Milan set has a similar repertoire, mostly traditional hymns that, due to Sister Rosetta Tharpe's power and guitar playing, swing hard.

Sister Rosetta Tharpe can be seen in several Soundies with Lucky Millinder's orchestra in the early 1940s.

HELEN WARD

b. Sept. 19, 1916, New York, NY, d. Apr. 21, 1998, Arlington, VA

One of the finest Swing singers of the mid-1930s, Helen Ward would be much better known today if she had not retired just when she was getting famous. She had piano lessons early on and sang as a teenager. Ward worked on the radio starting in 1933. As a staff singer at NBC, she was hired to sing with Benny Goodman on the radio series *Let's Dance* in 1934. Only 18 at the time, she already had a mature style that appealed to Goodman. She was an important part of BG's band into 1936, having a hit with "Goody Goody," cutting a couple of numbers with the Benny Goodman Trio ("All My Life" and "Too Good to Be True"), and becoming an increasingly popular attraction. However, in 1936 she got married and, although still only 20, decided to retire.

During 1937–42 Ward popped up on records led by a variety of musical friends, including Gene Krupa, Teddy Wilson, Harry James, Bob Crosby, and Joe Sullivan. In 1943 she became more active, working with Red Norvo, Harry James, and Hal McIntyre but never equaling her earlier fame. She came back to music now and then, touring with the short-lived Benny Goodman band of 1953, singing with Peanuts Hucko (1956–57), and as late as 1979 recording an album for her own Lyricon label (the only record ever made under her own name). But Helen Ward will always be most famous as the appealing singer with the Benny Goodman Orchestra that hit it big in 1935.

ETHEL WATERS
b. Oct. 31, 1896, Chester, PA, d. Sept. 1, 1977, Chatsworth, CA

One of the most significant early singers, Ethel Waters was a celebrity during the Swing era and in her later years was a pioneering black actress. Waters was always quite versatile, able to sing the blues like Bessie Smith yet among the very first black female singers to become famous singing popular and sophisticated songs in the early 1930s. She would be a strong influence on Mildred Bailey and Lee Wiley.

Ethel Waters had a rough childhood, living in poverty and working as a maid while a teenager. However, her singing talent was eventually noticed and around 1915 she began to perform in theaters on the East Coast. She was nicknamed "Sweet Mama Stringbean" due to being so thin in her early days, although by the time she reached her greatest fame, Waters would be quite a bit heavier. After moving to New York in 1917, she worked steadily and became a fixture in the black entertainment world. She began recording in 1921 for the Black Swan label and in her early days sang mostly blues. In fact, on one record she does a close imitation of Bessie Smith, in tribute to the Empress of the Blues.

However, Waters was much more flexible and her diction was impeccable. She appeared in shows in the 1920s and by 1929 was de-emphasizing the blues in favor of singing the most recent pop hits. She introduced "Dinah," "Stormy Weather," and "Am I Blue," recorded with Duke Ellington in 1932, and appeared in a few motion pictures. She was treated as a major artist in the 1929 film *On with the Show,* which was quite unprecedented for a black entertainer of the period. Waters started out the Swing era (1935–39) having her own touring show with a band run by her husband of the period, trumpeter Eddie Mallory. In 1939 she appeared in the play *Mamba's Daughter,* which was a hit, and Waters was the main star of the 1943 movie *Cabin in the Sky,* in which she introduced "Taking a Chance on Love" and "Happiness Is a Thing Called Joe." She remained active as a singer during the 1940s, taking time off for her acting career. By the mid-1950s Ethel Waters was mostly spending her time with religious activity (working for Billy Graham) although she still sang hymns in public into the early 1970s.

●

7   *1921–1923 / Mar. 21, 1921–Mar. 1923 / Classics 796*

8   *1923–1925 / Mar. 1923–July 28, 1925 / Classics 775*

9   *1925–1926 / Aug. 25, 1925–July 29, 1926 / Classics 672*

10   *1926–1929 / Sept. 14, 1926–May 14, 1929 / Classics 688*

All of Ethel Waters's studio recordings during her first (and most important) 19 years on record are included in her seven Classics CDs. She was one of the first black singers to record (cutting sides two years before Bessie Smith) and, although her earliest recordings are primitive, her already-distinctive voice shines through. The music on *1921–1923* (which includes five instrumentals) is quite obscure but certainly listenable. *1923–1925* has some notable appearances by Fats Waller and cornetist Joe Smith and is highlighted by "You Can't Do What My Last Man Did," "Sweet Georgia Brown," and "Go Back Where You Stayed Last Night." Half of *1925–1926* has the singer backed by just a pianist, while Joe Smith is a major asset on four songs, particularly "I've Found a

New Baby." The CD has the original version of "Dinah" and such tunes as "Shake That Thing," "Sugar," "Heebies Jeebies," and "Maybe Not at All," which finds Waters doing expert imitations of her competitors Bessie Smith and Clara Smith. *1926–1929* features some of Waters's finest jazz performances, including "I'm Coming Virginia," "Home," "Take Your Black Bottom Outside," "Some of These Days," and "West End Blues." Four numbers in which she is backed by the brilliant pianist James P. Johnson ("Guess Who's in Town" and "Do What You Did Last Night" are classics) are each quite memorable. This CD closes with the two songs that Ethel Waters performed in the *On with the Show* movie, and these find her switching more to a pop sound: "Birmingham Bertha" and "Am I Blue."

9 *1929–1931 / June 6, 1929–June 16, 1931 / Classics 721*

9 *1931–1934 / Aug. 10, 1931–Sept. 5, 1934 / Classics 735*

8 *1935–1940 / Oct. 16, 1935–Nov. 7, 1940 / Classics 755*
The accompaniment on Ethel Waters's records of 1929–30 changed from being black jazz stars to white studio players (although the latter included the Dorsey Brothers and Benny Goodman). Her singing remained quite jazz-oriented most of the time although more sentimental in spots (particularly on "Three Little Words"). Among the new songs that are on *1929–1931* are "True Blue Lou," "Waiting at the End of the Road," "Trav'lin All Alone," "You Brought a New Kind of Love to Me," "You're Lucky to Me," "Memories of You," "I Got Rhythm," "When Your Lover Has Gone," and "Please Don't Talk About Me When I'm Gone." All were future standards that she helped to make popular. *1931–1934* continues at the same level and finds the accompaniment becoming more Swing-oriented. Various selections include the Duke Ellington Orchestra ("I Can't Give You Anything but Love" and "Porgy"), Bunny Berigan, a Benny Goodman pickup group, and members of the Chick Webb Orchestra. Among the songs on this disc are the original version of "Stormy Weather," "Don't Blame Me," "Heat Wave," and "A Hundred Years from Today." Ethel Waters did not record as often during 1935–40, but she was quite busy performing and starting to act more frequently. Eddie Mallory's orchestra backs her on the majority of the selections on *1935–1940* and Benny Carter guests on six numbers. Most of the material on this CD did not catch on, but Waters was still in prime form. Her lone date from 1940 introduced "Taking a Chance on Love" and "Cabin in the Sky."

LPS TO SEARCH FOR
Ethel Waters made relatively few recordings after 1940, recording eight songs in 1946 and a full album for Mercury in 1947. Her later work was nearly all religious; however, *Miss Ethel Waters* (Monmouth Evergreen 6812) captures her in the late 1950s (with backing by pianist Reggie Beane) revisiting many of her hits, including "Am I Blue," "Dinah," "Porgy," "Supper Time," and a medley from *Cabin in the Sky*.

FILMS
Ethel Waters sings "Am I Blue" and "Birmingham Bertha" in the underrated *On with the Show* (1929). She is in *Gift of Gab* (1934) and *Cairo* (1942) and stars in *Cabin in the Sky* (1942), in which she introduced "Happiness Is a Thing Called Joe," "Taking a Chance on Love," and the title song. She makes an appearance in *Stage Door Canteen* (1943) and has important dramatic acting roles in *Pinky* (1949), *Member of the Wedding* (1953), *Carib Gold,* (1955) and *The Sound and the Fury* (1959).

LEE WILEY
b. Oct. 9, 1908, Fort Gibson, OK, d. Dec. 11, 1975, New York, NY

Lee Wiley had an indescribable charisma, a cool sensuality that gave one the feeling that she was quite passionate just below the surface. She sang songs fairly straight while swinging lightly and was a favorite of Eddie Condon (who often employed her in the 1940s) and others in the trad jazz world.

Wiley moved to New York in the late 1920s, and her first major job was with Leo Reisman, with whom she recorded in 1931. She soon became closely tied with composer Victor Young, who used her on the radio, recorded with her and tried to make her into a major cabaret singer. Together they co-composed "Got the South in My Soul" and "Anytime, Anyday,

Anywhere." After they broke up a few years later, Wiley was romantically involved with the married Bunny Berigan for a time. She made her most important records during 1939–43, being the first singer to record complete "songbooks" of one composer's works. Wiley's versions of music by George Gershwin, Cole Porter, Rodgers and Hart, and Harold Arlen predated Ella Fitzgerald's songbooks by 15 years and were in most cases greatly appreciated by the composers.

Wiley was married to Jess Stacy during 1943–48, and for a little while in the mid-1940s she sang with Stacy's big band. She worked mostly as a single after the mid-1940s, but her solo career never really took off; by the late 1950s she was frustrated and semiretired. Her life was portrayed in a biographical television film in 1963. After 1957, Lee Wiley returned to music only briefly in 1971–72, making a final record and appearing at the Newport Jazz Festival.

7 *The Complete Young Lee Wiley, 1931–1937 / June 30, 1931–Feb. 10, 1937 / Vintage Jazz Classics 1023*

7 *The Legendary Lee Wiley Collectors' Items / 1931–1956 / Baldwin Street Music 304*

Lee Wiley's early period (1931–38) found her being groomed as a sophisticated cabaret singer by Victor Young and mostly singing ballads while backed by orchestras. *The Complete Lee Wiley* has all of her studio recordings from her formative period (except for the four included in the Baldwin Street CD), including many selections not originally released. She is joined on some cuts by Leo Reisman's orchestra, Victor Young, The Dorsey Brothers Big Band, and the Casa Loma Orchestra. Although this release is not quite essential, it is interesting to hear how Wiley sounded at the beginning of her career; best are "A Hundred Years from Today" and "Easy Come, Easy Go." *The Legendary Lee Wiley* has four early obscurities plus two songs on which she is backed by James Van Heusen on piano in 1939 ("You're So Indifferent" and "All I Remember Is You"), selections with Eddie Condon and the Jess Stacy big band, plus tunes from 1956 with a strong Dixieland band. There are lots of rarities on this valuable CD.

10 *Lee Wiley Sings the Songs of Ira and Gershwin and Cole Porter / Nov. 13, 1939–Apr. 1940 / Audiophile 1*

10 *Lee Wiley Sings the Songs of Rodgers & Hart and Harold Arlen / Feb. 1940–Apr. 1943 / Audiophile 10*

The high points of Lee Wiley's career were the four songbook albums that she recorded during 1939–43. In her early 30s at the time, Wiley's voice was at its prime, and her interpretations of eight songs apiece in these four sets (two are included in each CD) are often classic. The Gershwin project finds her joined by groups under the leadership of Joe Bushkin and Max Kaminsky, with such sidemen as Bud Freeman, clarinetist Pee Wee Russell, and (on four songs,

including a duet) Fats Waller. "My One and Only," "I've Got a Crush on You," and "But Not for Me" are haunting. The Cole Porter songbook has a quartet headed by Bunny Berigan on four songs (including "Let's Fly Away" and "Let's Do It") and Paul Weston's orchestra on the other tunes. For the Rodgers and Hart sessions, Bushkin and Kaminsky are back with their pickup groups; the repertoire includes "You Took Advantage of Me," "I've Got Five Dollars," and a very memorable "Glad to Be Unhappy." Eddie Condon's ensembles (with Billy Butterfield or Bobby Hackett) are on the Harold Arlen dates, helping Wiley make "Let's Fall in Love" and "Down with Love" into classics.

7 *Music of Manhattan, 1951 / 1951–July 5, 1952 / Uptown 27.46*

7 *Duologue / 1954 / Black Lion 760911*

9 *As Time Goes By / June 12, 1956–July 25, 1957 / Bluebird 3138*

Despite the artistic success of her songbooks, Lee Wiley never became that major a star and recorded just one session during 1944–49. *Night in Manhattan* (not yet available on CD), from 1950, did fine saleswise, but none of the followups sold as well. *Music of Manhattan,* which repeats a few of the songs from *Nights in Manhattan,* is comprised mostly of live performances from 1951–52, all previously unissued before this 1998 CD. With the assistance of such notable trumpeters as Billy Butterfield, Muggsy Spanier, Buck Clayton, and Red Allen, Wiley does well on some fairly spontaneous performances. Among the songs that she performs (some are heard in multiple versions) are "Manhattan," "Sugar," "I've Got a Crush on You," "Anytime, Anyday, Anywhere," "and "I'm Coming Virginia." *Duologue* is really two mini-records in one. Wiley is joined by a quartet with trumpeter Ruby Braff on eight numbers, including "My Heart Stood Still," "Give It Back to the Indians," and "It

Never Entered My Mind," while Ellis Larkins (who gets co-billing even though he and Wiley never meet) has four unaccompanied piano solos. During 1956–57, Lee Wiley recorded *West of the Moon* and *A Touch of the Blues,* her two final albums (other than a comeback date in 1971). *As Time Goes By* has ten of the dozen songs from the former and nine of the 12 from the latter record, plus one of Wiley's two numbers from a guest shot. It is a pity that several songs were left out, because her two records deserved to be reissued in full. Lee Wiley (accompanied by orchestras led by Ralph Burns and Billy Butterfield) sounds quite expressive and makes such songs as "This Is New," "Who Can I Turn to Now?," "Stars Fell on Alabama," "A Hundred Years from Today," and "Maybe You'll Be There" sound as if they were written for her. But instead of these albums adding momentum to her career, they were the final recordings from Lee Wiley in her prime.

5   *Back Home Again* / 1965–Oct. 11, 1971 / Audiophile 300

6   *The Carnegie Hall Concert* / 1952 + July 5, 1972 / Audiophile 170

In 1971 Lee Wiley came out of retirement to record an album for the Monmouth/Evergreen label. Sixty-three at the time (although she claimed to be 56!), she was past her prime and sounds a bit rusty on *Back Home Again,* although her version of "Indiana" is pretty strong. Wiley is joined by a septet that includes trumpeter Rusty Dedrick (in excellent form) and Johnny Mince. The CD reissue also includes a previously unreleased date of rehearsals with Joe Bushkin from 1965, the only example of Wiley on record between 1960 and 1970. To celebrate the release of the record, Wiley was talked into appearing at the 1972 Newport in New York Festival. *The Carnegie Hall Concert* (which also includes a few selections from a 1952 rehearsal) has its emotional moments, with producer George Wein sounding thrilled to be able to present Lee Wiley. Joined by a quintet including Bobby Hackett and Teddy Wilson, Wiley sounds pretty good, even if there are some loose moments, singing for the final time such songs as "You're Lucky to Me," "I'm Coming Virginia," and "A Woman's Intuition."

LPS TO SEARCH FOR

You Leave Me Breathless (Jass 15) and *I Got a Right to Sing the Blues* (Jass 19) both feature radio appearances and alternate takes by Lee Wiley during 1936–38, a few rarities from the 1940s, and mostly performances with Dixieland-oriented groups in the 1950s. The great majority of the songs have not been duplicated by later CD collections. *Night in Manhattan* (Columbia 656), from 1950–51, showcases the singer on eight numbers with Joe Bushkin, a small string section, and Bobby Hackett; the other four tunes have her backed by a piano duo. "Manhattan," "Oh! Look at Me Now," and "Sugar" are among the songs that Lee Wiley makes her own.

Swing Arrangers and Composers

Arrangers were an indispensable part of the Swing era. In the early 1920s, writing for big bands, if not technically born with Don Redman, advanced several major steps forward due to Redman's ability (particularly by 1925) to capture the spontaneity and swing of jazz in his arrangements. Among the other major arrangers of the decade were Jelly Roll Morton (for his own groups), Bill Challis and Ferde Grofe for Paul Whiteman, and Duke Ellington who (even at that early point) was in his own category.

The early 1930s found Benny Carter (whose writing career had begun with Fletcher Henderson and continued with McKinney's Cotton Pickers and his own orchestras), Gene Gifford (who wrote for the Casa Loma Orchestra), and Edgar Sampson (with Chick Webb) all rising in importance. Fletcher Henderson began to write much more after Carter left his band, and he developed into the definitive Swing arranger by the mid-1930s. His brother Horace Henderson proved to be just as talented, if quite underrated.

The Swing era was a golden period for big band arrangers since there were so many orchestras to write for. Among the pacesetters were Jimmy Mundy (Earl Hines and Benny Goodman), Sy Oliver (Jimmie Lunceford and Tommy Dorsey), Eddie Sauter (Red Norvo and Benny Goodman), Jerry Gray (Artie Shaw and Glenn Miller), Bill Finegan (Glenn Miller), and such freelancers as Andy Gibson and Buster Harding. Also not to be left out were Glenn Miller, Stan Kenton, Claude Thornhill, Luis Russell, Les Brown, Larry Clinton, Mary Lou Williams (with Andy Kirk), Bob Haggart (Bob Crosby), Paul Weston (Tommy Dorsey), Ralph Burns (Woody Herman), Billy May (Glenn Miller), Pete Rugolo (Stan Kenton), Billy Strayhorn (Duke Ellington), and the unique Raymond Scott.

There was an explosion of talent among composers during the 1930s that had really started the decade before and would continue into the 1950s. It was fueled by the constant need for new songs by bands on the radio, at recording dates, and for shows. Imagine, in 1935 such songwriting giants as George Gershwin, Cole Porter, Irving Berlin, Richard Rodgers, Jerome Kern, Harold Arlen, Harry Warren, Fats Waller, and Duke Ellington were all very much in their prime, along with scores of other talented writers. There was no shortage of lyricists either, with Ira Gershwin, Lorenz Hart, Al Dubin, Yip Harburg, and Andy Razaf being among the most inventive. Composer Hoagy Carmichael and lyricist Johnny Mercer had careers that very much overlapped with the Swing era and jazz in general, gaining additional individual successes due to their singing and their personalities.

HOAGY CARMICHAEL
b. Nov. 22, 1899, Bloomington, IN, d. Dec. 27, 1981, Rancho Mirage, CA

Hoagy Carmichael had many halfway careers during his life, including work as a jazz pianist, trumpeter (in the 1920s), singer, and actor. However, his main talent was as a composer of such songs as "Stardust," "Georgia on My Mind," "Rockin' Chair," "Skylark," "Up the Lazy River," "The Nearness of You," "New Orleans," "In the Cool, Cool, Cool of the Evening," and the Dixieland standard "Riverboat Shuffle."

Born Howard Hoagland Carmichael, he studied piano with his mother (who played professionally) and performed for dances during high school and at Indiana University but for a time also studied to be a lawyer. Hoagy met his close friend Bix Beiderbecke in 1924, and Bix (with the Wolverines) was the first to record a Carmichael song, "Riverboat Shuffle." The young composer began recording in 1925 (as the pianist with Hitch's Happy Harmonists) and he also played trumpet a bit now and then (trying to sound like Bix). In 1927 he was briefly the pianist with Jean Goldkette's orchestra and he recorded "Washboard Blues" as a singer-pianist with Paul Whiteman. After moving to New York in 1929, Carmichael freelanced in several capacities, occasionally recording as a leader (including a session with both Beiderbecke and Bubber Miley on cornets), making guest appearances on other's jazz records, and constantly writing music.

In 1935 Hoagy Carmichael moved to Hollywood, where he wrote for films and appeared in 14 films during the 1937–54 period. He almost always played a wisecracking pianist, usually a friend of the hero. Among the movies that he was in were *To Have and Have Not* (with Humphrey Bogart), *The Best Years of Our Lives,* and *Young Man with a Horn.* Carmichael also recorded as a singer-pianist with small groups (usually his own songs, although there were exceptions) and wrote his autobiography, *The Stardust Road* (1946); there would be a second book (*Sometimes I Wonder*) in 1965. Hoagy Carmichael retained his love for early jazz throughout his life, and he recorded a superior album in 1956 (*Hoagy Sings Carmichael*) with a group of top West Coast jazz all-stars, including altoist Art Pepper.

●

10 *Stardust and Much More / Nov. 18, 1927–Mar. 1, 1960 / Bluebird 8333*
This single CD has Hoagy Carmichael's most important recordings of 1927–34, a period of major growth in which he developed from an aspiring jazz pianist and songwriter into a major composer. Framed by late (1960) solo versions of him performing "Stardust," the disc contains 19 vintage selections, including "Washboard Blues" with Paul White-man," "So Tired" with Jean Goldkette, "Come Easy, Go Easy Love" with Sunny Clapp's Band o' Sunshine, and a variety of sessions led by Carmichael. Of the last, one hears him performing such numbers as "Rockin' Chair," "Georgia on My Mind," "Lazy River," "Lazybones," "Moon Country," and another version of "Stardust" in timeless fashion.

This project was a unique event, teaming Hoagy Carmichael (who sticks here to singing) with a group of top West Coast and Swing all-stars. With solo space given to altoist Art Pepper, trumpeters Harry Edison and Don Fagerquist, and pianist Jimmy Rowles and arrangements provided by Johnny Mandel, this combination works quite well. Hoagy Carmichael's last significant recording, the date is highlighted by "Georgia on My Mind," "New Orleans," "Memphis in June," and "Baltimore Oriole."

LPS TO SEARCH FOR

One of the best Hoagy Carmichael collections is *Classic Hoagy Carmichael* (Indiana Historical Society 1002), a three-LP set with an attractive 64-page booklet that features not only Carmichael but a wide variety of artists from the jazz and middle-of-the-road pop worlds performing his songs, including six versions of "Stardust." Fortunately the selections (dating from 1927–87) are programmed mostly in chronological order, ranging from the Boswell Sisters and Benny Goodman to Bing Crosby, Ray Charles (an obvious choice!), and Wynton Marsalis.

FILMS

Hoagy Carmichael played virtually the same character in each movie, but he was always a welcome supporting player who usually sang and played a song or two. Among his better appearances were *To Have and Have Not* (1944), *The Best Years of Our Lives* (1946), *Canyon Passage* (1946), *Night Song* (1947), *Johnny Holiday* (1949), *Young Man with a Horn* (1949), *The Las Vegas Story* (1952), *Belles on Their Toes* (1952), and *Timberjack (1954).*

BILL FINEGAN
b. Apr. 3, 1917, Newark, NJ

Bill Finegan's work for the Glenn Miller Orchestra (arranging many of the band's hits, including "Sunrise Serenade," "Little Brown Jug," "Song of the Volga Boatmen," and "Serenade in Blue") tends to be overlooked, but he was an important force in the band's phenomenal success. Finegan, who played piano but rarely ever in public, practically started his career with Miller, sending in a chart on "The Lonesome Road" to Tommy Dorsey in 1938. TD, who would record the arrangement, recommended the young arranger to Miller, who was just getting under way with his new big band. Finegan (then 21) worked as a staff arranger for Glenn Miller until the breakup of the civilian orchestra in 1942. He then joined Tommy Dorsey, staying with him on and off until 1952. During 1952–57 he co-led the Sauter-Finegan Orchestra with Eddie Sauter, a band that allowed the arrangers to put their wildest ideas on paper but often found novelties emphasized over inventive music. Since the end of that group, Bill Finegan has freelanced as an arranger, working in the studios and occasionally writing for big bands (including the Mel Lewis Orchestra in the 1980s).

ANDY GIBSON
b. Nov. 6, 1913, Zanesville, OH, d. Feb. 10, 1961, Cincinnati, OH

Andy Gibson's writing uplifted several major Swing bands. He played trumpet early on with Lew Redman's Bellhops (1931), Zack Whyte (1932–33), Blanche Calloway, McKinney's Cotton Pickers, and the Mills Blue Rhythm Band but was primarily a section player. Starting in 1937, he worked full time on arranging and had strong successes, particularly in his writing for Count Basie (including arranging "Shorty George" and "Tickle Toe"), Charlie Barnet, Cab Calloway, and Harry James. Gibson served in the Army, led a band in the service (1942–45), and freelanced as an arranger in the postwar years. He worked as the musical director for the R&B-oriented King record label during the second half of the 1950s before his early death at age 47. Andy Gibson composed "The Hucklebuck" and the Jimmy Rushing–associated blues "I Left My Baby."

JERRY GRAY

b. July 3, 1915, East Boston, MA, d. Aug. 10, 1976, Dallas, TX

Jerry Gray was an important arranger with two of the top Swing bands. Born Generoso Graziano (!), he started out playing violin, leading a band as a teenager in 1931. Gray joined Artie Shaw's first orchestra in 1936 as a violinist, but he eventually quit playing in order to write full time. His biggest success with Shaw was the million-selling "Begin the Beguine." In 1939 he joined Glenn Miller and wrote such charts as "Pennsylvania 6-5000," "Little Brown Jug," and "A String of Pearls," among many others. Gray was not only with Miller throughout his big band years (1939–42) but he worked as part of Glenn Miller's Army Air Force Band too, staying with the orchestra until 1946. In the postwar years, Jerry Gray became an important writer in the studios (including arranging the music for *The Glenn Miller Story*), had a radio show, and throughout the 1950s recorded with his own nostalgic Swing orchestra, making a final album in 1966.

●

7 *A Salute to Glenn Miller / Feb. 18–25, 1958 / Simitar 55252*

Although this CD is a tribute to Glenn Miller, Jerry Gray (one of Miller's original arrangers) felt free to rearrange some of his classic charts. There are some surprises along the way (including a honking version of "Johnson Rag") and renditions of "Elmer's Tune," "Anvil Chorus," "Pennsylvania 6-5000," and "String of Pearls" (here called "Restringing the Pearls") that avoid the predictability of ghost band versions. Many of Miller's alumni were used on this set, including clarinetist Wilbur Schwartz, and there are excellent solos from trumpeters John Best and Ray Linn.

BUSTER HARDING

b. Mar. 19, 1917, Ontario, Canada, d. Nov. 14, 1965, New York, NY

A pianist as well as a talented Swing arranger, Buster Harding grew up in Cleveland and led his own band in the early 1930s, working as a sideman in Buffalo and Boston. Harding eventually came to New York, where he played second piano and arranged for Teddy Wilson's orchestra during 1939–40 and wrote for the short-lived Coleman Hawkins Orchestra. He was Cab Calloway's main arranger during 1941–42 and then freelanced with virtually everyone, including Artie Shaw ("Little Jazz"), Count Basie, Benny Goodman, Earl Hines, Tommy Dorsey, the Roy Eldridge big band (with whom he also played piano), and Dizzy Gillespie. In the mid-1950s, as a pianist Buster Harding worked with Billie Holiday, and later on he had a short stint with Jonah Jones.

HORACE HENDERSON

b. Nov. 22, 1904, Cuthbert, GA, d. Aug. 29, 1988, Denver, CO

The younger brother of Fletcher Henderson, Horace Henderson was actually a better pianist, and his arranging talents developed first. But he never gained much fame beyond an underground reputation. He studied at Atlanta University and Wilberforce College, leading his own big band at the latter. Called the Collegians, it was renamed the Dixie Stompers before breaking up in 1928. He worked with Sammy Stewart's Knights of Syncopation (1928) and during 1929–31 led a big band in New York. When Don Redman left McKinney's Cotton Pickers, he took over Henderson's group, keeping Horace as the pianist. During 1933–34 Horace often worked with his brother's orchestra, contributing arrangements (30 in all) and occasionally playing piano. He also wrote charts during the Swing era for many other groups, including Benny Goodman ("Japanese Sandman," "Big John Special," and "Always" among them), Charlie Barnet ("Charleston Alley"), Earl Hines,

Jimmie Lunceford, the Casa Loma Orchestra, and Tommy Dorsey. Henderson was with Vernon Andrade during 1935, rejoined Fletcher during 1936–37 (arranging "Christopher Columbus"), and then once again led his own big band (1937–41). Henderson, who had recorded six songs as a leader with the nucleus of his brother's band in 1933, led five recording sessions in Chicago during 1940, using such sidemen as trumpeters Emmett Berry and Ray Nance and Elmer Williams on tenor. However, the orchestra failed to catch on. He spent part of 1942–43 in the Army, worked as an accompanist for Lena Horne, and headed obscure bands of his own on and off during the late 1940s, '50s, and '60s.

●

9 *1940–1941 / Feb. 27, 1940–Apr. 24, 1941 / Classics 648*
All of the Horace Henderson Orchestra's recordings are on this CD, including such numbers as "Shufflin' Joe," "Honeysuckle Rose," "Swingin' and Jumpin'," "When Dreams Come True," and "Flinging a Whing Ding." Perhaps it was the competition or maybe Henderson's charts were considered a little behind the times, but unfortunately his band did not last, despite its potential. However, the recordings, which feature trumpeters Berry and Nance, Williams on tenor, and vocals from Viola Jefferson, are swinging and full of joy. This CD closes off with four songs from the 1941 Fletcher Henderson Orchestra, the only studio recordings that Horace's older brother made as a leader during 1939–44.

JOHNNY MERCER
b. Nov. 18, 1909, Savannah, GA, d. June 25, 1976, Los Angeles, CA

One of the most talented of all lyricists, Johnny Mercer wrote the words to countless classics, including "One for My Baby," "Blues in the Night," "Jeepers Creepers," "Come Rain or Come Shine," "Ac-Cent-Tchu-Ate the Positive," "My Shining Hour," "Fools Rush In," "Skylark," "That Old Black Magic," "And the Angels Sing," "Too Marvelous for Words," "I'm an Old Cowhand" (for which he also wrote the music), "Come Rain or Come Shine," "Moon River," "The Days of Wine and Roses," and 1,500 others. Mercer was originally a frustrated actor, getting bit parts in some 1930s movies but never catching on. He had much better luck as a lyricist in 1933, when he wrote "Lazybones," and from then on he was in great demand. Mercer was also a popular singer whose charming personality hid the fact that he did not have a great voice. He was featured on the radio regularly with Benny Goodman in 1939 and would have some pop hits as a singer, including a couple of songs that he did not write the lyrics for: "Personality" and "Candy." In 1942 Mercer founded Capitol Records (with Glenn Wallichs and Buddy DeSylva), and he was partly responsible for the label's strong jazz catalog in its early days, including Nat King Cole, Stan Kenton, and Peggy Lee. Mercer wrote the music for seven Broadway musicals and a variety of films, staying active up until his death.

●

FILMS
Johnny Mercer performs a delightful version of "Save the Bones for Henry Jones" in 1956 with the host in *The Incomparable Nat King Cole Vol. 2* (Warner Reprise Video 38292).

JIMMY MUNDY
b. June 28, 1907, Cincinnati, OH, d. Apr. 24, 1983, New York, NY

A decent tenor saxophonist, Jimmy Mundy was much better known as an arranger. He actually started out as a violinist before switching to tenor. Mundy grew up in Chicago and worked locally with Erskine Tate, Carroll Dickerson, and others while still a teenager. After moving to Washington, D.C., in 1926, he freelanced with many little-known groups, including Duke Eglin's Bell Hops and Tommy Myles. Mundy sold a few arrangements to Earl Hines and so impressed the pianist that he became part of his band during 1932–36 as both a writer and a tenor saxophonist. Mundy wrote some arrangements for Benny Goodman in 1935 and, after leaving Hines, became BG's staff arranger, being responsible for quite a few "killer diller" Swing charts, including "Madhouse," "Bugle Call Rag," "Swingtime in the Rockies," "Air Mail Special," "Solo Flight," and, most notably, "Sing, Sing, Sing." He led a big band of his own for a short time in 1939 and wrote for many of the other orchestras, including Count Basie, Paul Whiteman, Gene Krupa, Bob Crosby, and Dizzy Gillespie (1949). Mundy kept busy as a studio arranger during the second half of his life, living in France in the 1960s, when he was the musical director for the Barclay label. Jimmy Mundy recorded two numbers as a leader in 1937, four with his orchestra in 1939; his mid-1940s big band can be heard on radio air checks put out by various collector's labels, and during 1958–59 he led two albums for Epic.

SY OLIVER
b. Dec. 17, 1910, Battle Creek, MI, d. May 28, 1988, New York, NY

A fine trumpeter who was expert with mutes and a personable singer, Sy Oliver wrote a series of classics for the Jimmie Lunceford Orchestra that helped give the band its own sound. Melvin James "Sy" Oliver grew up in Zanesville, Ohio, and started playing trumpet when he was 12. Oliver worked with Cliff Barnett's Club Royal Serenaders for three years while in high school. When he was 17, he joined Zack Whyte's Chocolate Beau Brummels, and Oliver also played with Alphonso Trent. In 1930 he moved to Columbus, Ohio, where he worked as a teacher and arranger for a few years. In 1933 Oliver sent some arrangements to Jimmie Lunceford and was soon asked to join the band, where for six years he would be the main arranger, a trumpet soloist, and an occasional singer. His most famous charts included "My Blue Heaven," "Organ Grinder's Swing," "Ain't She Sweet," "Margie," " 'Tain't What You Do," and "For Dancers Only." He was such a major factor in Lunceford's orchestra that, when he accepted a much more lucrative offer to join Tommy Dorsey, it was a major shock. Oliver functioned in a similar role with Dorsey (although no longer playing trumpet), even adapting some of his earlier arrangements (including "Swanee River") for the band and contributing a classic reworking of "On the Sunny Side of the Street." He was with TD until joining the Army in 1943, where he led a band for two years. After his discharge Oliver headed big bands of his own for short periods, guested with Tommy Dorsey in the 1950s, and worked as musical director at a few different record labels. Sy Oliver, who occasionally played trumpet again in the 1970s (recording as late as 1976), remained a proponent of Swing to the end of his life.

6 *Oliver's Twist & Easy Walker / July 7, 1960 + Oct. 18, 1962 / Mobile Fidelity 638*

Two particularly rare Sy Oliver albums (none are common at the moment) are reissued in full on this audiophile CD. The 24 selections are all quite concise and range from folk melodies and children's tunes to some more swinging charts. Charlie Shavers is the solo star of the first half, while Budd Johnson is heard during the remainder. The music is a bit lightweight but has some good examples of Sy Oliver's writing for big bands, showing that he never strayed far from Swing.

EDGAR SAMPSON
b. Aug. 31, 1907, New York, NY, d. Jan. 16, 1973, Englewood, NJ

Edgar Sampson, a skillful arranger, was also a major songwriter. Among the standards that he composed are "Stompin' at the Savoy," "Blue Lou," "When Dreams Come True," "Lullaby in Rhythm," and "Don't Be That Way." Sampson began playing violin when he was six, added alto when he was around 13, and occasionally played baritone sax and clarinet too.

He was a professional starting in 1924, gigged with Duke Ellington at the Kentucky Club, and freelanced in New York for a few years. Sampson worked as an altoist and arranger with Charlie Johnson (1928–30), Alex Jackson (1930), and Fletcher Henderson (1931–32), also taking a rare violin solo with Henderson. He played with Rex Stewart's orchestra in 1933 and then was with Chick Webb during 1933–36, a period when he wrote his most famous songs.

After leaving Webb, Sampson concentrated mostly on writing, and his arrangements were played by Benny Goodman, Artie Shaw, Red Norvo, and others. He was the musical director of the Webb band after the drummer's death when Ella Fitzgerald was fronting it (1939). Later in the 1940s Sampson returned to playing more often (sometimes on tenor). He led his own band during 1949–51 and became an arranger for a variety of Latin jazz groups, including Tito Puente. Edgar Sampson was active into the mid-1960s.

●

LPS TO SEARCH FOR

Other than two songs in 1939, Edgar Sampson's only date as a leader resulted in 1956's *Sampson Swings Again* (Coral 57049), a dozen swinging charts with a fine big band that includes Charlie Shavers, Tyree Glenn, Lou McGarity, and tenorman Boomie Richman. A version of the LP released in 1982 by MCA only has ten of the 12 cuts.

EDDIE SAUTER
b. Dec. 2, 1914, Brooklyn, NY, d. Apr. 21, 1981, Nyack, NY

One of the most adventurous arrangers of the Swing era, Eddie Sauter was at his best when he had to work under specific restraints. He started out playing drums, switched to trumpet, and both played and wrote for his college dance band at Columbia University. Sauter played trumpet on ocean liners, studied arranging and composing at Juilliard, and worked briefly with Charlie Barnet. He first gained recognition while arranging (along with playing trumpet and mellophone) for Red Norvo's band (1935–39), making it possible for one to hear Norvo's xylophone over the orchestra. Sauter's work for Benny Goodman (1939–42) included some of the best writing of his career, charts that pushed the boundaries of Swing and used very advanced harmonies but still swung, clearly inspiring Goodman to some of his finest playing. "Clarinet à la King," "Superman," and "Benny Rides Again" are considered classics. Sauter also wrote some rather adventurous charts for the big band to play behind the vocals of Helen Forrest. He arranged for Woody Herman and Tommy Dorsey and during the second half of the 1940s quite extensively for the Ray McKinley Orchestra.

After recovering from a lung ailment, Sauter joined forces with fellow arranger Bill Finegan to form the Sauter-Finegan Orchestra (1952–57). That band had a minor hit with "Doodletown Fifers" and served mostly as a forum for its leaders' arrangements, which often sounded a bit out-of-control, since they could (and did) write anything they liked. Instead of being a very musical outfit, the Sauter-Finegan Orchestra was often dominated by novelties and did not live up to its potential. After the band broke up, Sauter worked in Germany for a while, arranged the classic *Focus* album back in the U.S. for Stan Getz (1961), scored the film *Mickey One* (1965), and kept busy as a freelance arranger for films and in the studios. Eddie Sauter wrote some of his last arrangements for the New York Saxophone Quartet in 1980.

RAYMOND SCOTT
b. Sept. 10, 1910, Brooklyn, NY, d. Feb. 8, 1994, North Hills, CA

The Raymond Scott Quintette was one of the great novelty groups of the Swing era. Scott's crazy episodic and complex music (which was memorized by the players rather than written down and contained no improvising) was popular for a time and still sounds unique today. Scott's tunes (which often had crazy song titles) became a staple of Warner Bros. cartoons. Born Harold Warnow, he studied at the Institute of Musical Art in New York during the early 1930s and worked at CBS starting in 1931, originally as a pianist but soon also as an arranger. Scott's Quintette, which actually lasted only two years (1937–39) and was really a sextet, had hits in "Powerhouse," "Twilight in Turkey," and "The Toy Trumpet." In 1939 Scott formed a conventional big band that worked regularly without making much of an impression for two years. Raymond Scott then returned to the CBS studios, leading a jazz band on radio that sometimes included Charlie Shavers, Ben Webster, Coleman Hawkins, and Johnny Guarnieri. He remained active as an arranger in the 1950s and '60s (leading the band used in *Your Hit Parade* under his real name of Harold Warnow) but also devoted a great deal of time to electronics, including inventing one of the first synthesizers.

●

10 *Reckless Nights and Turkish Twilights / Feb. 20, 1937– June 17, 1940 / Columbia 53028*

9 *Volume One: Powerhouse / Nov. 28, 1934–Nov. 11, 1939 / Stash 543*

Raymond Scott and his Quintette recorded 24 selections in 1937 and 1939. Twenty are on *Reckless Nights and Turkish Twilights*, plus two slightly later big band selections. In addition to their three hits ("Powerhouse," "The Toy Trumpet," and "Twilight in Turkey"), such offbeat material is heard as "New Year's Eve in a Haunted House," "Dinner Music for a Pack of Hungry Cannibals," "Reckless Night on Board an Ocean Liner," "Bumpy Weather in Newark," and "War Dance for Wooden Indians!" Somehow the musicians manage to emulate the eccentric titles, often to humorous effect;

definitely a memorable set of music. The Stash CD, which unfortunately was not followed by a second volume, consists of tapes from Scott's own archives. The radio broadcasts and rehearsals (plus two performances by an otherwise-unrecorded early sextet from 1934–35) adds "Devil Drums," "Sleepwalker," "Steeplechase," "Celebration on the Planet Mars," "Serenade to a Lonesome Railroad Station," "Moment Whimsical," and "Confusion Among a Fleet of Taxicabs upon Meeting with a Fare" to the legacy of the Raymond Scott Sextette.

FILMS

The Raymond Scott Quintet appears in *Ali Baba Goes to Town* (1937), *Love and Hisses* (1937), and *Happy Landing* (1938).

BILLY STRAYHORN
b. Nov. 29, 1915, Dayton, OH, d. May 31, 1967, New York, NY

One of jazz's great composers and arrangers, Billy Strayhorn spent virtually his entire adult life as an unofficial part of the Duke Ellington Orchestra. He grew up in Pittsburgh and wrote for local shows as a teenager. In December 1938 he met Duke Ellington and greatly impressed him when he played some of his songs for him (including "Lush Life"). Within a short time he joined Ellington's band, although his exact role was never agreed upon; he was just always there to help. Strayhorn wrote "Take the 'A' Train" on his way to joining Ellington (while riding on a train, of course) and was soon put to work writing lyrics and arranging for Duke's small-group dates. Because he wrote in a similar style to Ellington's and the two worked together closely, Strayhorn's work was sometimes mistaken for Duke's, although much of it has been straightened out in recent years. Among his most classic pieces are "Something to Live For," "I'm Checkin' Out, Goo'm Bye," "Chelsea Bridge," "Day Dream," "Passion Flower," "A Flower Is a Lovesome Thing," "Lotus Blossom," "Johnny Come Lately," and "Raincheck." Strayhorn also collaborated with Ellington on many major works and occasionally played piano on small-group dates or even with the full Ellington band. Strayhorn only led three albums of his own (two with Duke's sidemen), without counting the posthumously released *Lush Life*, so his contributions were underrated for many years. A heavy smoker and drinker, Billy Strayhorn died of cancer in 1967, writing his final song ("Blood Count") while in the hospital.

●

Two major composers whose 28-year musical partnership resulted in a countless number of gems:
Billy Strayhorn and Duke Ellington.

7   *Cue for Saxophone / Apr. 14, 1959 / London 820 604*

8   *The Peaceful Side / May 1961 / Capitol 52563*

9   *Lush Life / Jan. 14, 1964–Aug. 14, 1965 / Red Baron 52760*

Although released under Billy Strayhorn's name, *Cue for Saxophone* is really more of a Johnny Hodges date. Hodges was listed as "Cue Porter" (due to record label conflicts) on the album and the reissue CD but is the main soloist throughout. Strayhorn plays piano but contributed only two songs (both cowritten with Hodges); the remainder of the date is comprised of Swing standards. Hodges, Shorty Baker, Quentin Jackson, and Russell Procope (on clarinet) sound fine and are ably supported by bassist Al Hall and drummer Oliver Jackson. *The Peaceful Side* was Strayhorn's only independent record. This was recorded in Paris, and Strayhorn is heard taking unaccompanied solos, joined by bassist Michel Goudret on five of the ten songs and assisted by a string quartet on two numbers and an odd vocal group (called the Paris Blues Notes) on three; some songs use a combination of these guests. All of the songs are Strayhorn's and the emphasis is on his melancholy piano on such numbers as "Lush Life," "Take the 'A' Train," "Day Dream," and "A Flower Is a Lovesome Thing." *Lush Life* was released 25 years after Strayhorn's death, but it is his best all-round album and rather intriguing overall. He is heard singing "Lush Life" with the Ellington Orchestra, leading a couple of quintet dates with Clark Terry and Bob Wilbur (on clarinet and soprano), backing singer Ozzie Bailey on five numbers, and playing "Love Came" and "Baby Clementine" as piano solos. It is a pity that there is so little Billy Strayhorn on record, for, other than an odd LP reviewed next and a few cameo appearances, these three CDs are pretty much his complete recording career.

LPS TO SEARCH FOR

Billy Strayhorn/Johnny Dankworth (Roulette 121) has a set by the 1961 Dankworth big band, a decent outfit that features good solos from Danny Moss on tenor and trumpeter Dickie Hawdon. The other half of the two-LP set is a date released under Billy Strayhorn's name that features the Duke Ellington Orchestra conventionally playing eight standards, only one ("Passion Flower") actually composed by Strayhorn. Although allegedly Strayhorn is playing piano with the band, it sounds like Ellington himself. Johnny Hodges is the main star, and Shorty Baker, Ray Nance (on violin), and Harry Carney have their spots, but do not look for Billy Strayhorn here!

AFTER THE SWING ERA

●

WHY DID THE BIG BAND ERA DIE?

In 1942, Swing was at the peak of its popularity. Big bands were everywhere and, whether it was Glenn Miller, Benny Goodman, Duke Ellington, Count Basie, Jimmie Lunceford, Artie Shaw, Tommy Dorsey, Jimmy Dorsey, Harry James, the sweet bands (such as Guy Lombardo and Russ Morgan), or the many other ensembles, scores of orchestras were dominating the pop charts. It is true that most (but not all) hit recordings of the era had vocals, but one thought of "Why Don't You Do Right" as being by Benny Goodman rather then by Peggy Lee, and Glenn Miller's hits were by the Glenn Miller Orchestra first and Ray Eberle, Marion Hutton, or Tex Beneke second. In fact, Swing was so much the thing by 1942 that even some of the commercial sweet bands (such as those led by Jan Garber, Kay Kyser, and Shep Fields) shifted their music policy for a time and began to play credible Swing. Swing had shifted from being a diversion for dancing teenagers to becoming the main force in popular music.

However, by 1947, just five years later, the big band era was considered completely dead and the question "Will big bands ever come back?" was starting to be asked. The correct answer would always be "No!" Why did the era end when it had been so healthy during the 1935–42 period?

It was as if a major conspiracy had taken place, because, rather than just one factor being at fault, there were at least ten major reasons why the big band era ended, never to come back.

1. World War II did its part to kill off the big bands. With gasoline and other supplies being rationed, it became difficult for most orchestras to travel during 1942–45. The draft robbed many of the big bands of their top players and, although it resulted in opportunities for some teenagers to gain jobs they would not normally have had a chance to get (such as Stan Getz at age 16 playing tenor with Jack Teagarden's big band), the musicianship dropped a bit. Glenn Miller broke up his orchestra in order to enlist in the Army Air Force, Artie Shaw and Claude Thornhill went into the Navy, Lester Young, Buck Clayton, and Jo Jones had to leave Count Basie's orchestra to serve in the military, Bob Crosby gave up and joined the Marines, etc. Some bandleaders were able to prosper, particularly Harry James, who inherited Miller's role as leader of the #1 band, but even he traveled less, spending long periods in Hollywood, where he made movies.

2. In an exercise of "perfect" timing, the Musicians Union went on a recording strike that started August 1, 1942. Because musicians were not being paid when their records were played on the radio and an agreement could not be reached, no members of the union were allowed to make commercial records again until September 1943, when the Decca label reached an agreement. Blue Note signed with the union in November 1943 and other independent labels began to become active late in that year, but Columbia and Victor did not settle until November 1944, when they agreed to pay between 1/4 and 1/2 cent into a union fund for each disc sold. Since many of Swing's top artists (including Duke Ellington, Count Basie, and Benny Goodman) were signed to Columbia or Victor, they went at least 27 months between record dates, a lifetime in the music industry.

Most of what can be heard today of the major Swing bands during the 1943–44 period exists because of radio broadcasts that were taped, radio transcription dates (sessions that were recorded specifically to be played on the air) or V-Discs. These last were records made to be shipped overseas to servicemen so they could be entertained with fresh new music that would remind them what they were fighting for. The general public did get to hear the existing big bands on the radio, but the transcriptions and V-Discs (which were supposed to be destroyed at the end of the war) were not available for sale to the general public.

Because many of the labels had stockpiled recording dates shortly before the recording ban started, there were some "new" records released during 1943. However, singers were not part of the Musicians Union and they (unlike the big bands) were able to record truly new songs, often backed by either a cappella vocal groups or amateur musicians. Frank Sinatra, Dick Haymes, Bing Crosby, Perry Como, Dinah Shore, Doris Day, and many other vocalists stepped in to fill the gap, and they all rose in popularity while the big bands stagnated. The result was that most of the hit records of 1943 and 1944 were due to the voices of ballad singers rather than swinging big bands, and popular music was in the early stages of separating from jazz. Within a couple of years, the singers had taken over completely.

3. Big bands began to run out of fresh ideas by 1940, with the exception of a few (most notably Duke Ellington, Stan Kenton, and arranger Eddie Sauter with Benny Goodman). Although they continued to evolve, with the horn sections growing from nine pieces in 1935 to as many as 14 a decade later, most Swing bands by 1942 and certainly by 1945 were not offering much that was new. To name a few examples, Glenn Miller had his sound completely together by 1940, Count Basie's orchestra did not evolve much during the first half of the 1940s, Jimmie Lunceford's big band was declining, Tommy Dorsey's orchestra often emulated Lunceford's, and Jimmy Dorsey's was dependent on the success of its vocal records. Although there was plenty of new material, much of it seemed to be rehashes of the music of the 1935–39 period: riff-filled blues, fairly basic stomps, swinging renditions of classical themes, and soothing ballads.

4. Three styles of music were siphoning off the jazz audience that had formerly been attached to Swing. New Orleans jazz, which had never totally disappeared, began to have a major revival during 1940–42, with the rise of Lu Watters Yerba Buena Jazz Band in San Francisco (an octet that looked back to King Oliver in the 1920s for inspiration), the discovery of trumpeter Bunk Johnson and other New Orleans veterans, and the growing popularity of Eddie Condon and his freewheeling jam bands of all-stars. To followers of "the real jazz," Swing was overly arranged and did not permit as much self-expression as the music that would become known as Dixieland. Dixieland's popularity would continue to grow on a gradual basis during 1945–55.

5. The younger musicians and arrangers sought to stretch beyond conventional Swing. At jam sessions, they gradually formed bebop, the next step in jazz's evolution. Rather than seeing themselves as entertainers, the bop players sought to be recognized as artists first, showmen second if at all. In New York, at Minton's Playhouse and Monroe's Uptown House in after-hours jam sessions during the 1940–44 period, new ideas were developed and adopted. Complex chord changes were devised, melodic solos were deemphasized in favor of inventive ideas improvised over the chords (leading many to wonder, "Where's the melody?"), the piano no longer strided but instead stated chord voicings erratically, and the rhythms played by drummers became more complicated yet at times sparser. Because much of the key development of bop was not documented due to the recording strike (including the 1943 Earl Hines big band, which included Charlie Parker and Dizzy Gillespie), when records were made again in late 1944, bebop sounded like a foreign language to listeners much more accustomed to Glenn Miller. Despite the lack of a strong audience, most of the younger musicians and writers were drawn to the new music, causing Swing to lose some of its potentially major contributors just at a time when they were needed most.

6. While record collectors flocked to New Orleans jazz and creative up-and-coming jazzmen went to bebop, rhythm and blues stole away much of Swing's dancing audience. Starting with Louis Jordan's Tympany Five, R&B combos were able to capture the essence of Swing with two or three horns, and increase the excitement by several levels. They were less expensive than big bands while serving the same purpose, and they evolved faster than the mid-1940s Swing orchestras. R&B became more exhibitionistic during the second half of the 1940s (often emphasizing repetitive and honking sax solos along with emotional over-the-top vocals) and the music was simply more exciting than that played by the typical big band of 1945. In addition, while Swing had become accepted in the mainstream by the mid-1940s, R&B later in the decade had a slightly forbidden quality to it, partly because it was played mostly by black musicians and also because of its extroverted and explosive nature. It satisfied those in the counterculture of the time who had quickly tired of straight ballad vocalists and could not figure out bebop.

7. A cabaret tax was enacted in 1941 and unfortunately lingered throughout the second half of the 1940s; establishments that allowed dancing had to pay 30 percent of their ticket sales in taxes. This tax influenced two developments. Since small groups were less expensive than big bands, the former were soon being hired at the expense of the latter. And since the tax was not charged in venues that barred dancing, it effectively separated jazz from entertainment, with small jazz clubs replacing dance halls, thereby dooming the big bands.

8. It seems strange that during the bleak days of the Depression there were hundreds of big bands roaming the country. However, with Swing becoming the popular music of the time, admission charges to dance halls being low,

bands having constant exposure on the radio, and musicians in minor-league orchestras not being paid all that much, the scene was able to flourish. But with the end of World War II, the better economic times ironically hurt the big band movement. Musicians wanted to be paid more, the veterans were not as young as they had been in the 1930s (and were less enthusiastic about endless traveling), and the shrinking audience meant that the lower-level bands were doomed to become, at best, part-time organizations.

9. Another factor working against the big bands is that, because they were so much a part of the domestic scene during World War II and the years before, they would always be closely identified with that era. By 1946-47, many people did not want to be reminded of the war years, while others, who were nostalgic for the older scene, wanted the Swing bands to merely recreate their older hits. Most of the Swing big bands that were still around in the 1950s were forced to play primarily music from the past. One reason Artie Shaw became frustrated was that he wearied in the 50s of being expected to play his hits from 1938-39. The emphasis on nostalgia by many in the audience is a key reason that so-called ghost orchestras (bands that survived their leader's death) lack any real life or creativity; their fans will not allow them to evolve naturally.

10. And, as if these were not enough reasons for the end of the big band era, television was just around the corner. Why go out to see a big band when one can have free entertainment by turning on the set?

Few styles of music have ever fallen so fast as Swing big bands, from the height of the music business to the brink of extinction in just five years. If one considers Benny Goodman's sensational stint at the Palomar Ballroom in 1935 as the symbolic start of the big band era, the breakup of eight major bands (those of Goodman, Woody Herman, Harry James, Tommy Dorsey, Les Brown, Jack Teagarden, Benny Carter, and Ina Ray Hutton) in December 1946 serves just as well as the close of that remarkable period. Several of those bandleaders would regroup and be active again soon (most notably James, Dorsey, Brown, and Herman), but it would never be quite the same.

SWING SINCE 1946

By 1947, very few Swing big bands were left, and most of those would be gone within a few years. However, Swing itself did not die. Most of the top sidemen and some of the bandleaders were still very much in their musical prime during the 1950s. Glenn Miller and Jimmie Lunceford may have been gone, but in 1955 Benny Goodman was just 46 and Tommy Dorsey (49), Count Basie (51), Roy Eldridge (44), Coleman Hawkins (50), and Lester Young (46) were not exactly senior citizens!

With the collapse of the big bands, the Swing veterans had several choices during the second half of the 1940s. If they were white and technically skilled, they could become studio musicians; the doors were mostly closed, with a few exceptions, to blacks until later in the 1950s. Other musicians could choose to alter their styles and play Dixieland (which was becoming very popular), bebop, or rhythm and blues. Or they could make the more difficult choice of sticking to playing small-group Swing, although there was not much of a demand for that style of music unless one was already a major name such as Coleman Hawkins or Lester Young.

Some Swing musicians were fortunate enough to have long-term jobs with the Duke Ellington and Count Basie Orchestra. A few (including Buck Clayton) had the support of producer John Hammond and were able to record fairly regularly in the 1950s or were favorites of Norman Granz and able to tour with Jazz at the Philharmonic; Stanley Dance termed their music "Mainstream." Several had unexpected hits, including Cozy Cole with "Topsy" and Jonah Jones with his quartet in the late 1950s, or were able to work now and then with the surviving big bandleaders, such as Benny Goodman, Bob Crosby, and Lionel Hampton. Some musicians and singers found their fame in rhythm and blues of the 1945-55 period where they were essentially playing or singing simplified Swing, while others crossed over from Dixieland to play Swing now and then.

But in general, Swing was in the doldrums after 1945, and especially during the 1960s and '70s despite the rise of such groups as the Ruby Braff-George Barnes Quartet and Soprano Summit; that is, until the arrival of Scott Hamilton. The tenor saxophonist, who was in his early twenties, shocked many fans in the mid-to-late '70s by playing in a classic Swing style that mixed Ben Webster, Zoot Sims, and Illinois Jacquet. With his rise, and that of cornetist Warren Vache, suddenly it was considered acceptable for some young musicians to play Mainstream jazz, and their rise launched the Swing revival. Hamilton and Vache were later followed by Dan Barrett, Howard Alden, Ken Peplowski, John Pizzarelli, Randy Sandke, and Harry Allen, among others, and together they revitalized the idiom and showed that the Swing style still had plenty of life left in it.

Survivors who found their greatest fame after the Swing era, swinging R&B stars, revivalists, and keepers of the flame are discussed in this section. The Dixieland-oriented players from the world of Eddie Condon, stride pianists Ralph Sutton, Dick Wellstood, and Judy Carmichael, clarinetists Bob Wilber and Kenny Davern (other than their work with Soprano Summit), singer Banu Gibson, and other fine musicians whose work crossed over into Swing at times will be covered in other books in this series.

HOWARD ALDEN
b. Oct. 17, 1958, Newport Beach, CA

The top Swing guitarist to emerge during the 1980s, Howard Alden is a very well-rounded musician able to play anything from trad and Swing to bop and more modern styles of jazz (including the music of Thelonious Monk, Bill Evans, and Herbie Nichols). Alden started playing guitar when he was ten, and he worked at gigs in the Los Angeles area as a teenager, mostly in the trad jazz area and doubling on banjo. He played with Red Norvo in 1979, recorded with Bud Freeman in 1982, and in the latter year moved to New York. Alden became in great demand quickly, due both to his remarkable talent and partly to the fact that few other young guitarists at the time were as skilled at playing Swing guitar. Alden performed and recorded with such notable veterans as Ruby Braff, Benny Carter, Clark Terry, Dizzy Gillespie, Flip Phillips, Woody Herman, Joe Williams, Joe Bushkin, and George Van Eps, among many others. In addition, he began recording as a leader for Concord in 1986, co-led a quintet with Dan Barrett in the late 1980s, and worked with such other forces in the Mainstream Swing revival as Scott Hamilton, Warren Vache, and Ken Peplowski. Howard Alden is married to jazz singer Terry Richards and has long been a fixture at jazz parties and classic jazz festivals while never limiting himself exclusively to Swing and trad. Ill health slowed down his activities a bit in the late 1990s.

●

| 10 | *Swing Street / Sept. 1986 / Concord Jazz 4349* |

| 9 | *The Alden/Barrett Quintet Salutes Buck Clayton / June 1989 / Concord Jazz 4395* |

| 8 | *The Howard Alden Trio / Jan. 1989 / Concord Jazz 4378* |

| 9 | *Snowy Morning Blues / Apr. 1990 / Concord Jazz 4424* |

| 7 | *13 Strings / Feb. 1991 / Concord Jazz 4464* |

| 8 | *Misterioso / Apr. 1991 / Concord Jazz 4487* |

| 7 | *Take Your Pick / Mar. 16–18, 1996 / Concord Jazz 4743* |

Howard Alden has recorded prolifically for the Concord label ever since 1986. *Swing Street* features the brilliant quintet that he co-led with trombonist Dan Barrett, an ensemble that also includes Chuck Wilson on alto and clarinet, bassist Frank Tate, and drummer Jackie Williams. The advanced Swing group somehow often sounds like the John Kirby Sextet despite having guitar and trombone in place of trumpet, clarinet, and piano! Highlights include "Lullaby in Rhythm," "Dawn on the Desert," "Stompin' at the Savoy," and "Cotton Tail." The same group fares quite well on the Buck Clayton tribute CD, which signaled the comeback of Clayton as a writer. The majority of the songs were composed by Buck for the group in 1989, and his arrangements fit the band's style perfectly. The Howard Alden Trio set adds Ken Peplowski (on tenor and clarinet) on three songs and cornetist Warren Vache during four others. The emphasis is on lesser-known Swing tunes, including "You Showed Me the Way," Django Reinhardt's "Douce Ambiance," George Van Eps's "Love Theme No. 1," and "Keep a Song in Your Soul." Due to particularly inspired material (including "One Morning in May," James P. Johnson's title cut, and three lesser-known Duke Ellington numbers), *Snowy Morn-*

ing Blues (which matches Alden with bassist Lynn Seaton, drummer Dennis Mackrel, and guest pianist Monty Alexander) is a particularly rewarding showcase for the guitarist.

13 Strings is one of Alden's collaborations with the seven-string veteran guitarist George Van Eps and has duets by the co-leaders, a few individual solo features, and quartet numbers with bassist Dave Stone and Jake Hanna. Melodic, tasteful, and fairly gentle music. *Misterioso* (trios with bassist Frank Tate and drummer Keith Copeland) is particularly noteworthy for Alden's ability to revive obscurities (including Bud Freeman's "Song of the Dove," "Flying Down to Rio," and two rarely-played Ellington tunes: "Black

Beauty" and "Reflections in D") and to uplift a wide variety of standards, ranging from Thelonious Monk's "We See" to Jelly Roll Morton's "The Pearls." From more recent times, *Take Your Pick* features Alden as an unaccompanied soloist, in a quartet with pianist Renee Rosnes, bassist Michael Moore, and drummer Bill Goodwin, and interacting on some cuts with Lew Tabackin (heard on tenor and flute). The music is mostly standards, except for two rare Herbie Nichols tunes, and shows that, while being flexible, Howard Alden has stuck throughout his career to his original modern Swing style.

HARRY ALLEN
b. Oct. 12, 1966, Washington, D.C.

Harry Allen began to get recognition as a superior Swing-based tenor saxophonist in the late 1980s, and he has been increasingly busy ever since. His father, Maury Allen, had been a musician during the Swing era. Allen heard a Scott Hamilton record when he was 13 and was inspired to start playing tenor in a Mainstream style. He grew up in Los Angeles and in Rhode Island, attending Rutgers, where he graduated with a music degree in 1988. That year he made his recording debut, and Allen's Swing style was already fully formed. Since then Harry Allen has worked with other stars of Mainstream, including Keith Ingham, Warren Vache, John Bunch, John Pizzarelli (with whom he recorded for RCA in 1995), and Ken Peplowski, following in Scott Hamilton's footsteps but with a sound of his own.

●

7	*How Long Has This Been Going On?* / June 30, 1988 / Progressive 7082
7	*Are You Having Any Fun?* / July 23–24, 1990 / Audiophile 261
8	*The Intimacy of the Blues* / Mar. 12–14, 1993 / Progressive 7102
8	*A Night at Birdland Volume 1* / Nov. 19–20, 1993 / Nagel-Heyer 007
8	*A Night at Birdland Volume 2* / Nov. 19–20, 1993 / Nagel-Heyer 010
7	*Blue Skies* / May 13, 1994 / John Marks Records 9
8	*Jazz in Amerika Haus Volume 1* / May 28, 1994 / Nagel-Heyer 011
9	*Meets the John Pizzarelli Trio* / Dec. 18–19, 1995 / RCA 37397

Harry Allen has been quite prolific on records, particularly since 1993. On his Progressive and Audiophile sets, he is joined by a three- or four-piece rhythm section headed by the fine Swing pianist Keith Ingham. *How Long Has This Been Going On?* was Allen's debut on records, yet his sound was quite mature at that early stage, particularly on ballads. *Are You Having Any Fun?* (recorded in 1990, not 1980 as it says on the CD's back cover) is a set of music by the talented but underrated composer Sammy Fain, including such standards as "When I Take My Sugar to Tea," "You Brought a New Kind of Love to Me," "That Old Feeling," and "Secret Love." John Pizzarelli is a major asset in the group. *The Intimacy of the Blues* is the second of two CDs featuring the music of Billy Strayhorn (the other one has been released under Ingham's name) and it has some of Strayhorn's finest songs, including "A Flower Is a Lovesome Thing," "Something to Live For," "Lush Life," and "Passion Flower." The two Birdland sets (actually recorded at a Birdland club in Hamburg rather than New York) are packaged to look like vintage Blue Note dates but the music is pure Swing. Allen heads a quintet that costars the fiery trumpeter Randy

Sandke, and the 20 standards heard on the two CDs all benefit from the young players' enthusiasm and skill at melodic improvising; both CDs are easily recommended. Producer John Marks was so excited by Harry Allen's playing that he started a label in order to document Allen. *Blue Skies* finds the swinging tenor interacting with pianist John Bunch, bassist Dennis Irwin, and drummer Cliff Jackson on three originals and such standards as "Linger Awhile," "Nobody Else but Me," and "Shine." The same group (with Dennis Irwin on bass) is on *Jazz in Amerika Haus* from the German Nagel-Heyer label, a slightly hotter set that includes " 'Deed I Do," "The King," and "Limehouse Blues" among its highlights. John Pizzarelli has known Harry Allen since 1984, so in 1995 he used his name and prestige to help Allen land a date with RCA. Allen fit in perfectly with Pizzarelli's trio (which also includes pianist Ray Kennedy and bassist Martin Pizzarelli) and the co-leaders inspire each other on such numbers as "Pennies from Heaven" "I Want to Be Happy" and "Sunday."

ERNIE ANDREWS
b. Dec. 25, 1927, Philadelphia, PA

One of the last surviving singers in the tradition of Jimmy Rushing, Jimmy Witherspoon, and Joe Williams, Ernie Andrews (who tends to be overlooked because he has spent much of his life based in Los Angeles) is a superior interpreter of blues, Swing standards, and ballads. He grew up in Los Angeles, sang in a church choir, and then, while still in high school, recorded for the G&G label in 1945, cutting several selections that became regional hits. Part of the Central Avenue jazz scene in L. A., Andrews recorded for Aladdin during 1946–47, made a few isolated singles for other labels, and faded a bit in popularity by the mid-1950s. He spent six years performing with the Harry James Orchestra, made two big band records for GNP/Crescendo during 1956–59, and worked steadily in the L. A. area during the 1960s and '70s despite barely appearing on records. Andrews gained some long overdue recognition in the 1980s, recording for Discovery, Contemporary, and, in the 1990s, Muse and High Note. He appeared and recorded with the Juggernaut, Gene Harris's Superband, Jay McShann, the Harper Brothers, and Teddy Edwards. Ernie Andrews is also the main subject and narrator in the documentary *Blues for Central Avenue.*

●

8	*No Regrets / Aug. 26, 1992 / Muse 5484*
7	*The Great City / Feb. 16, 1995 / Muse 5543*
7	*The Many Faces of Ernie Andrews / June 6, 1997 / High Note 7018*

It is surprising (and a bit disappointing) how little Ernie Andrews recorded during his earlier years, and it is a bit disheartening to realize that most of his pre-1990 recordings are long out of print. Fortunately Andrews was still in fine form in the 1990s, and these three CDs give listeners good examples of how the singer sounded during his later period. Tenor saxophonist Houston Person and pianist Junior Mance are in the sextet that is on *No Regrets,* a date that includes "Don't You Know I Care," "When Did You Leave Heaven?," and "Sweet Lorraine." *The Great City* has Frank Wess on tenor and flute plus pianist Richard Wyands and includes the blues "Come Back Little Girl" and the humorously titled "The Jug and I Got Up This Morning." *The Many Faces* features a return appearance by Pearson, a pair of medleys (blues and Duke Ellington songs), and an oddly swinging rendition of "Some Enchanted Evening."

LPS TO SEARCH FOR
From the Heart (Discovery 825) finds Andrews in 1980 joined by a horn section (with trumpeter Harry "Sweets" Edison and tenorman Red Holloway) and a fine rhythm section on spirited renditions of "On Broadway," "Don't Let the Sun Catch You Shouting," and "Anything Better to Do."

Trumpeter Ray Anthony (pictured with his brother, baritonist Leroy Anthony) helped keep Swing alive in the 1950s.

RAY ANTHONY

b. Jan. 20, 1922, Bentleyville, PA

Ray Anthony has spent most of his life placed in the wrong musical era. A Swing trumpeter who based his style on Harry James, Anthony had both the good luck and the misfortune to reach his maturity in the 1950s rather than the 1940s. The good luck resulted in his making a name for himself in what was a small field in the '50s, but the misfortune is that he was out of date before he even got started!

Born Raymond Antonini and raised in Cleveland, Ray Anthony started playing trumpet when he was five, gaining very early experience playing in the Antonini Family Orchestra. Anthony developed quickly, leading a band while he was in high school. He worked with Al Donahue's orchestra in 1938 when he was just 16 and was with Glenn Miller from November 1940 to July 1941. However, Anthony did not receive solo space with Miller and the association was not that happy. After six months with Jimmy Dorsey in 1942, he spent four years in the Navy, where Anthony led a show band in the Pacific. Out of the Navy in 1946, the 24-year-old trumpeter started his own big band. Although the Swing era was ending and the odds were against him, the Ray Anthony Orchestra caught on, recording for Sonora and Signature before signing with Capitol in 1949. Performing Swing standards, recent pop tunes, and dance music, Anthony soon became famous. He had several big-selling records, including "Harlem Nocturne," "Mr. Anthony's Boogie," "Slaughter on Tenth Avenue," "Dragnet," "Peter Gunn," and his greatest hit, "Bunny Hop."

Anthony kept his big band together until the early '60s, and he has remained active during the years since, leading part-time orchestras, which always include a heavy dose of nostalgia for an era that he largely missed. Anthony, who recorded regularly for Ranwood during 1968–76, runs the Aerospace label, which, in addition to his own releases, has put out CD reissues of music from earlier Swing bands. Turning 78 in 2000, Ray Anthony's trumpet chops were still in good shape, and he has lived long enough to see the music he loves make a comeback.

●

6   *Young Man with a Horn / 1952–1954 / Hindsight 412*

8   *Swing Back to the '40s / 1990 / Aerospace 1035*

7   *The Swing Club / 1998 / Aerospace 1045*

Some of Ray Anthony's earlier records are available through his Aerospace label, although Capitol has largely neglected his 1950s output. *Young Man with a Horn* has 22 performances that were probably made originally as radio transcriptions. Seven of the numbers have vocals by Tommy Mercer, Marcie Miller, or (in the case of "Margie") The Skyliners. Otherwise the emphasis is mostly on Anthony's trumpet and his swinging but unadventurous big band, playing concise versions of such numbers as "What Is This Thing Called Love?," "For Dancers Only," "Trumpet Boogie," and "The Honeydripper." *Swing Back to the '40s* has Anthony leading an excellent big band filled with some of Los Angeles's top musicians of the time, including Snooky Young, Marshall Royal (who is well featured), and pianist Tom Ranier. Dennis Rowland takes two vocals, and the arrangements of such numbers as "Don't Be That Way," "It's a Wonderful World," "In a Mellotone," and "Corner Pocket" are very much in the Count Basie manner, making

this a perfect setting for Anthony's horn. *The Swing Club* sounds as if Ray Anthony was jumping on the Retro Swing bandwagon, but in reality he had been there all along. Anthony's 17-piece big band (which includes Roger Neumann on tenor and drummer Gregg Field but surprisingly no piano) has plenty of spirit. The vocals of Madeline Vergari and Patrick Tuzzolino are enthusiastic and, even if the repertoire is full of warhorses that did not need to be revived ("Route 66," "Sing, Sing, Sing," "Goody, Goody," and "Chattanooga Choo Choo" among them) plus a few basic originals, the music (which often emphasizes hyper 2) is both predictable and hard-swinging. A fine dance band record with some solid (if brief) trumpet solos from the leader, plenty of arranged riffs, and an impressive rhythm section.

FILMS

The good-looking and youthful trumpet player appeared in 15 motion pictures. Among the more notable ones are the Fred Astaire movie *Daddy Long Legs* (1955), *The Girl Can't Help It* (1956), *This Could Be the Night* (1957), *The Beat Generation* (1959), *Girls Town* (1959), *High School Confidential* (1959), and *The Five Pennies* (1959), portraying former boss Jimmy Dorsey in the last.

HAROLD ASHBY

b. Mar. 27, 1925, Kansas City, MO

Harold Ashby fit perfectly into the Duke Ellington Orchestra. The only surprising fact is that the Ben Webster–influenced tenor saxophonist had to wait so long before joining Duke. Ashby was based in Kansas City in the 1940s (where he worked with Walter Brown) and in Chicago during the first half of the 1950s, appearing on many R&B dates but basically playing in a Swing-oriented style with a large, appealing tone. After moving to New York in 1957, Ashby met Webster and Ellington, worked in the Mercer Ellington Orchestra, recorded with many of Duke's more famous sidemen (including on dates led by Webster, Johnny Hodges, Paul Gonsalves, and Lawrence Brown), and played in Ellington's mid-1960s show *My People*. When he finally joined Duke Ellington's orchestra in 1968 (replacing Jimmy Hamilton), Ashby was more than ready. He was one of the top soloists in the band for its final six years and was a major asset to Ellington during a period when many of the other sidemen were aging and either retiring or passing away. After Duke's death, Ashby was with Mercer Ellington into 1975. Harold Ashby has since freelanced, including working with Benny Goodman and Sy Oliver in the 1970s and leading his own combos and occasional record dates.

7 *What Am I Here For? / Nov. 30, 1990 / Criss Cross 1054*

9 *I'm Old Fashioned / July 25, 1991 / Stash 545*

8 *Just for You / Dec. 29–30, 1998 / Mapleshade 6232*

Harold Ashby is never shy to show off his Ben Webster influence, yet he also adds something of his own personality to his music. Each of these sets is a quartet outing. *What Am I Here For?* matches Ashby with a fairly modern rhythm section (pianist Mulgrew Miller, bassist Rufus Reid, and drummer Ben Riley) but is comprised of Swing standards, with the highlights including "What Am I Here For?," "Poinciana," and "Perdido." Ashby sounds particularly inspired on *I'm Old Fashioned* (assisted by pianist Richard Wyands, bassist Aaron Bell, and drummer Connie Kay), digging into "All of Me," a Latinish "Struttin' with Some Barbeque," and " 'Deed I Do" as if the songs had been newly written for him! Seventy-three at the time of *Just for You,* the veteran tenor is heard playing with a great deal of warmth and swing on seven of his rarely heard originals plus three tunes by either Billy Strayhorn or Duke Ellington. Assisted by pianist John Hicks, bassist Keter Betts, and drummer Jimmy Cobb, Ashby shows throughout the relaxed set that in the late 1990s he was among the finest surviving alumni of Duke Ellington's orchestra.

LPS TO SEARCH FOR

Presenting Harold Ashby (Progressive 7040) alternates standards and originals in 1978 as Ashby (with pianist Don Friedman, bassist George Mraz, and drummer Ronnie Bedford) makes one wonder why he was not recorded more extensively. Also quite worthy is 1988's *The Viking,* a quartet outing with pianist Norman Simmons that adds four more originals to Ashby's legacy. Pity that none of his catchy tunes have been explored by other musicians yet.

GEORGE BARNES
b. July 17, 1921, South Chicago Heights, IL, d. Sept. 5, 1977, Concord, CA

One of the first electric guitarists, George Barnes, who had a fluent style that emphasized single-note lines, stuck to Swing throughout his long career. Barnes was working professionally by the time he was 13, and he had his own quartet in the Midwest during 1935–37. He recorded with such major blues artists as Big Bill Broonzy, Washboard Sam, and Blind John Davis (plus many lesser-known singers) and was on the staff of NBC in Chicago during 1937–42. The guitarist freelanced at night and appeared with many jazz players, including Bud Freeman. Barnes served in the Army and then had long periods working as a staff musician at ABC and as the house guitarist and arranger for the Decca label. His own solo career was a bit neglected, although he led two titles for Okeh in 1940 and eight for Keynote in 1946 plus some fascinating octet performances made as radio transcriptions in the latter year. However, during 1961–65, Barnes gained some recognition for his playing in duets with Carl Kress. He later collaborated with Bucky Pizzarelli (1969–72) and Bud Freeman, co-leading an exciting quartet with Ruby Braff (1973–75) that made several superb recordings. George Barnes performed with Joe Venuti at the 1976 Concord Festival and was active until his death at age 56.

7 *Feels So Good / Apr. 17, 1977 / Concord Jazz 4067*

George Barnes's final recording is one of his very few that is actually currently available on CD. Only 32 minutes long, the set (recorded just six months before his death) finds the guitarist sounding still in prime form on nine familiar standards (including "The Days of Wine and Roses," "I've Found a New Baby," and "Honeysuckle Rose") in a quartet with rhythm guitarist Duncan James, bassist Dean Reilly, and drummer Benny Barth.

LPS TO SEARCH FOR

1946 (Hindsight 106) is an intriguing set of radio transcriptions featuring Barnes, a four-piece rhythm section, and four woodwind players. Barnes is practically the only soloist on the 15 selections (none of the reeds were jazz players), and the set's main attraction is the guitarist's colorful arrangements. In addition to the CD *Two Guitars (and a Horn)* that is reviewed under Carl Kress's name, the Barnes/Kress musical partnership is heard on *Guitars, Anyone?* (Audiophile 87), an LP last reissued in 1981. And the defunct Famous Door label during 1972–73 recorded the excellent *Swing Guitars* (Famous Door 100) by Barnes in a quartet with either Dick Hyman or Hank Jones on piano.

DAN BARRETT

b. Dec. 14, 1955, Pasadena, CA

Dan Barrett was part of the second wave of modern Swing players to emerge in the 1980s, and he remains its leading trombonist, able to sound a bit like Jack Teagarden or Tommy Dorsey whenever he wants while still retaining his own distinctive sound. In addition, he has emerged as an excellent cornetist.

Barrett started out on trombone in high school and he played trad jazz in California with the South Frisco Jazz Band and the Golden Eagle Jazz Band. In 1983 Barrett and his friend Howard Alden moved to New York and revitalized the Swing scene. The trombonist worked with the Widespread Depression Orchestra, became a regular at Eddie Condon's club, and in 1985 was part of the Benny Goodman Orchestra. He signed with Concord in 1987 (recording as both a leader and a sideman), co-led an intriguing quintet with Howard Alden (that, despite its very different instrumentation, was reminiscent of the John Kirby Sextet), and played with Buck Clayton's Big Band. In the early 1990s, Dan Barrett (who relocated to Southern California a few years later) became the musical director of the Arbors label, and he has since remained a major force in the prebop jazz scene, adding class and an arranger's sensibility to every session that he appears on.

●

9 *Strictly Instrumental / June 1987 / Concord Jazz 4331*

8 *Jubilesta / Dec. 3, 1991–Feb. 17, 1992 / Arbors 19107*

7 *Reunion with Al / Mar. 5–6, 1993 / Arbors 19124*
Every Dan Barrett record is of interest to Mainstream collectors for he is quite consistent. His debut set as a leader, *Strictly Instrumental,* has quite an all-star cast, including the nucleus of his quintet with Howard Alden plus Ken Peplowski on clarinet and tenor, cornetist Warren Vaché, and pianist Dick Wellstood (just a month before his death). Each of the 11 selections on this CD has its special moments, whether it is a cleverly arranged ensemble or a surprise in the solos. The tunes include "Old Fashioned Love," "Moon Country," "My Honey's Lovin' Arms," and "There's Honey on the Moon Tonight." Jubilesta is a fine showcase for Barrett's trombone, for he is heard in a quartet with Ray Sherman, bassist David Stone, and Jake Hanna, playing some of his favorite songs, including Juan Tizol's "Jubilesta," "Alabamy Bound," and Roy Eldridge's "Little Jazz." Veteran trombonist Al Jenkins (79 at the time and on his last recording date) was an early influence on Barrett and he co-leads *Reunion.* Barrett sticks to cornet (it is a pity that no song features two trombones) and the sextet also includes Rick Fay (on clarinet, soprano, and tenor), Sherman, Stone, and drummer Jeff Hamilton. The emphasis is on Swing standards, including "Do You Ever Think of Me?," "After You've Gone," "At Sundown," and "I Can't Give You Anything but Love" (which has a Jenkins vocal).

8 *Two Sleepy People / Jan. 2–3, 1994 / Arbors 19116*

8 *Dan Barrett and Tom Baker in Australia / Oct. 3, 1994 / Arbors 19143*

8 *Moon Song / Dec. 4–7, 1995 / Arbors 19158*
Two Sleepy People is a set of duets by Barrett (heard on both trombone and cornet) and the superb stride/swing pianist John Sheridan. The material has a few offbeat tunes (including "Hey, Good Lookin'," "Whoa Babe," and a Billie Holiday medley) and explores more moods than one would expect from the instrumentation. Barrett's meeting with Tom Baker (heard on tenor, alto, and cornet) is quite fun. Recorded in Australia with a local rhythm section, most of the songs feature a trombone-tenor front line. However, Bob Barnard sits in on cornet for three pieces, including a hot

version of "That's a Plenty" that has Barrett, Baker, and Barnard all playing trumpet or cornet. In general the music ranges from Mainstream Swing to touches of bop and Dixieland, all played with spirit. *Moon Song* puts the emphasis on Swing and has a strong cast that includes Rebecca Kilgore on vocals, Scott Robinson on bass sax, tenor, and alto saxophones, Brian Oglivie on tenor and clarinet, Chuck Wilson doubling on alto and flute, Bucky Pizzarelli, bassist Joel Forbes, drummer Jeff Hamilton, and two fine appearances by trumpet-cornetist Bryan Shaw. It is difficult to resist these charming versions of "Moon Song," "With a Smile and a Song," "I'll Never Say 'Never Again' Again," and "Got a Date with an Angel."

COUNT BASIE PART 2

b. Aug. 21, 1904, Red Bank, NJ, d. Apr. 26, 1984, Hollywood, CA

At the end of 1949, Count Basie reluctantly broke up his big band after 14 years. Although his orchestra had been quite influential during the prime years of Swing, bad business decisions and the end of the big band era forced Basie to temporarily throw in the towel. He formed a small group that was usually a septet or an octet for performances and occasional recordings. Among the musicians who passed through the group were Harry "Sweets" Edison, Clark Terry, clarinetist Buddy DeFranco, and tenors Georgie Auld, Gene Ammons, and Wardell Gray. The rhythm section originally was a trio, but Freddie Green soon rejoined Basie. The band was filmed during the era for television, including a few songs backing Billie Holiday and Helen Humes. There was also a single session in 1951 with a specially assembled big band featuring Wardell Gray (who stars on "Little Pony").

However, Count Basie soon began to plot his comeback as a big bandleader and plans were made to give it another try. With Marshall Royal helping to pick out musicians, rehearsals were held, and in 1952 the new Count Basie Orchestra was officially born. From the start, this ensemble, although clearly an outgrowth of the earlier band, had its own sound. The rhythm section always swung lightly but firmly and, although there were always many fine soloists (some of whom were open to the influence of bebop), a greater emphasis was placed on the arrangements. Quite notable during the band's early years were the charts of Neal Hefti, which often utilized Frank Wess on flute. Later arrangers who made very significant contributions to Basie's book included Ernie Wilkins, Sammy Nestico, Thad Jones, Frank Wess, and Frank Foster.

In the mid-1950s, two events made the Count Basie Orchestra a permanent entity: the hit recording of "April in Paris" and the addition of Joe Williams (who soon recorded his trademark song, "Every Day I Have the Blues") to the band. Virtually alone among big bands formed in the 1950s, the Count Basie Orchestra survived and generally prospered for decades even though nearly every other Swing-based big band (other than those of Duke Ellington and Les Brown) was history by 1960. While tenors Eddie "Lockjaw" Davis and Paul Quinichette were early soloists with the band, the prime Basie Orchestra (covering roughly the 1955–62 period) featured Frank Foster and Frank Wess on tenors (with the latter continuing to double on flute and sometimes playing alto) and trumpeters Joe Newman (one of the few alumni of the 1940s band) and Thad Jones. Other important players who spent time with Basie during this era included Billy Mitchell on tenor, the great drummer Sonny Payne, trumpeter Snooky Young, and longtime first altoist Marshall Royal.

Visiting Europe regularly starting in 1954 and continually winning popularity polls, the Count Basie Orchestra roared throughout the 1960s, although, once its contract with Roulette ended in 1962, its recordings became quite erratic. The Basie band was often used as a mere prop behind a bewildering assortment of singers (including Frank Sinatra, Tony Bennett, The Mills Brothers, Kay Starr, Teresa Brewer, Arthur Prysock, Jackie Wilson, and Sammy Davis Jr.) and, although considered an institution, it needed a breath of fresh air. Recordings of current rock hits, tunes from James Bond movies, and Beatles songs (all of which took place) were clearly not the answer!

Fortunately a creative renaissance occurred in the 1970s when Basie signed with Norman Granz and the Pablo label. Granz recorded Basie quite prolifically, including with his big band, with various all-stars, in a trio, for two-piano collaborations with Oscar Peterson, and with everyone from Zoot Sims and Dizzy Gillespie to Milt Jackson and Ella Fitzgerald.

Basie's orchestra continued touring steadily, featuring for several years trombonist Al Grey, tenor saxophonist Jimmy Forrest, drummer Butch Miles, Eric Dixon on flute and tenor, and a variety of top young and middle-aged musicians who fit well into Basie's Swing machine. The band's sound may not have changed significantly after 1955 but it still sounded quite viable and fresh.

Count Basie's health gradually failed in the 1980s, although his band never stopped working. After his death in 1984 at the age of 79, the Basie Orchestra was headed by Thad Jones (1985–86) and Frank Foster (1986–96); currently it is led by trombonist Grover Mitchell. Although there have been some attempts to liven up the repertoire and slightly update the music, the Count Basie Orchestra (one of the few remaining full-time big bands) continues to spread the gospel of Swing around the world in its unchanging style.

●

7 *Class of '54 / Sept. 2–7, 1954 / Black Lion 760924*

8 *Count Basie, Lester Young and the Stars of Birdland / Feb. 1955 / Jass 17*

10 *Count Basie Swings, Joe Williams Sings / July 17–26, 1955 / Verve 314 519 852*

10 *April in Paris / July 26, 1955–Jan. 5, 1956 / Verve 314 521 407*

7 *The Greatest!! Count Basie—Joe Williams / Apr. 28, 1956 / Verve 833 774*

7 *Count Basie in London / Sept. 7, 1956 / Verve 833 905*

8 *At Birdland 1956 / Dec. 1–30, 1956 / Jazz Unlimited 2028*

10 *Count Basie at Newport / Sept. 7, 1957 / Verve 833 776*
The Count Basie Orchestra recorded for Clef and Verve during 1952–57, but not all of its studio sides from that era have yet been reissued on CD. *Class of '54* is actually a pair of live performances by Basie's big band (mostly playing Neal Hefti arrangements) and a nonet taken out of his orchestra that includes Joe Newman, trombonist Henry Coker, Frank Wess, and Frank Foster. The band was on the brink of success, alternating group originals with swinging standards. The Jass CD, which was recorded in Topeka, Kansas, during a tour, features several artists who played regularly at Birdland. The Basie Orchestra has two instrumentals, backs alumnus Lester Young on three cuts, features singer Joe Williams on three other numbers (including an early version of "Every Day I Have the Blues"), and welcomes tenor saxophonist Stan Getz as a guest for four tunes (highlighted by "Little Pony"). In addition, Sarah Vaughan (who largely steals the show) sings eight songs, and there are two other numbers with Joe Williams from another, unknown live date.

The next two Count Basie CDs are essential for every jazz collection. *Count Basie Swings, Joe Williams Sings* has such classic performances as "Every Day I Have the Blues," "Alright, Okay You Win," "The Comeback," and "In the Evening," solidifying the success of Basie and making Joe Williams famous. *April in Paris* has not only the hit title cut (a Wild Bill Davis arrangement that has Basie shouting out "One more once!") but the original versions of Frank Foster's "Shiny Stockings" and Freddie Greene's "Corner Pocket." The CD reissue adds seven alternate takes, including "new" versions of "April in Paris" and "Corner Pocket." One of the great big band Swing albums.

Because Joe Williams did not want to be stereotyped as a blues singer, *The Greatest* has him singing a dozen standards with the Basie band, including "Thou Swell," "Our Love Is Here to Stay," "A Fine Romance," and even "Singing in the Rain." That album did not have the same impact as the singer's *Swings/Sings* set, although it is enjoyable enough. *Count Basie in London* was actually recorded live in Sweden (!) and it is a spirited if typical program by the band, with renditions of "Jumpin' at the Woodside," "Shiny Stockings," "Nails," and "Corner Pocket" among the selections plus three Joe Williams vocals; four previously unreleased performances were added to the CD reissue. *At Birdland 1956* features the band during four radio performances from Birdland in December 1956, giving listeners a strong sampling of what a typical night by the Basie Swing machine sounded like at the time. *Count Basie at Newport* is taken from the 1957 Newport Jazz Festival and has some extraordinary moments. The Basie Orchestra sounds inspired on the opening "Swingin' at Newport" and then welcomes Lester Young to the bandstand (during one of his last recorded performances with Count) for "Polka Dots and Moonbeams" and "Lester Leaps In." Basie and Prez are joined by Jimmy Rushing for "Sent for You Yesterday and Here You Come

Count Basie and his faithful guitarist Freddie Green swinging away in the 1950s.

Today," "Boogie Woogie," and "Evenin'," and the interplay is quite exciting; listen to how Young plays behind the singer. Five previously unreleased numbers were added to the CD, including four with Joe Williams vocals. The closing "One O'Clock Jump" features not only Lester Young with the Basie Orchestra but Illinois Jacquet, Jo Jones, and a screaming Roy Eldridge. Essential.

* *The Complete Roulette Studio Count Basie / Oct. 21, 1957–July 26, 1962 / Mosaic 10-149*

* *The Complete Roulette Live Recordings of Count Basie / May 31, 1959–Aug. 12, 1962 / Roulette 8-135*

8 *Sing Along with Basie / May 26, 1958–Sept. 3, 1958 / Roulette 7953322*

9 *One More Time / Dec. 18, 1958–Jan. 24, 1959 / Roulette 7972712*

8 *1959 / Apr. 24, 1959 / Jazz Unlimited 2039*

9 *Basie and Eckstine, Inc. / May 22, 1959–July 28, 1959 / Roulette 52029*

8 *Kansas City Suite / Sept. 1960 / Roulette 7945752*

The second great golden era of the Count Basie Orchestra was the 1957–62 period, when the orchestra recorded regularly for Roulette. The first Mosaic box set has ten CDs that contain all of Basie's studio dates for Roulette, including music that came out on such classic albums as *The Atomic Mr. Basie, Basie Plays Hefti, One More Time,* and *Kansas City Suite.* Some but not all of the music is available individually in smaller sets, but this limited-edition box is the way to go, since it includes quite a few previously unreleased sides too. Among the many highlights are "L'il Darlin'," "Whirly Bird," "The Kid from Red Bank," "Splanky," "Blues in Hoss' Flat," "Cute," "Segue in C," "For Lena and

Lennie," "The Midnite Sun Never Sets," and countless others. *The Complete Roulette Live Recordings* is an eight-CD set that is a little more for collectors, due to the many repetitions in titles, but it is no less exciting than the studio dates. Recorded at a Florida convention in 1959, at Birdland in 1961, and in Stockholm in 1962, of the 133 titles, only 28 had been released before. The Basie band is heard throughout in prime form and joined by such guests as Louie Bellson (who is on the Stockholm date), Sarah Vaughan, and Jon Hendricks. Some of this music is also available elsewhere as single discs.

Sing Along with Basie is mostly a showcase for the pacesetting jazz vocal group Lambert, Hendricks, and Ross. Their initial success overdubbing their voices to emulate the Basie band on *Sing a Song of Basie* led to this real collaboration. The singers recreate the original solos from Count's sidemen, and, on a unique version of "Goin' to Chicago," Joe Williams takes a vocal while Lambert, Hendricks, and Ross sing around him. One of the best albums ever arranged by Quincy Jones was *One More Time,* a set with the Basie band that is included in the Roulette studio box. Jones contributed such tunes as "For Lena and Lennie," "Meet Benny Bailey," "I Needs to Be Bee'd With," and "The Midnite Sun Never Sets." Jazz Unlimited's 1959 CD has arrangements by Jones, Neal Hefti, Frank Foster, and Thad Jones and is a purely instrumental live set recorded in Fresno, California. The all-star "Atomic Band," which had up to ten strong soloists at the time, was nearing its peak and sounds quite enthusiastic. *Basie and Eckstine, Inc.* (which is not included in the Roulette box) is one of Billy Eckstine's finest vocal albums and finds him singing a jazz-oriented set that includes "Jelly, Jelly," "Lonesome Lover Blues," "I Want a Little Girl," and "Stormy Monday Blues"; he should have recorded in this format much more often. *Kansas City Suite* (which is in the Mosaic set) is a program of Benny Carter arrangements that grows in interest with each listen. Carter adapts his style to the Basie band for ten of his originals that pay tribute to Kansas City, and the results are quite rewarding.

3 *This Time by Basie / Jan. 1965 / Reprise 45162*

6 *Frankly Basie / Apr. 8, 1965–Jan. 14, 1965 / Verve 314 519 849*

6 *Count Basie at the Sands / Jan. 26, 1966–Feb. 1, 1966 / Reprise 45946*

7 *Jazzfest Masters / June 1969 / Scotti Bros. 72392 75245*
The 1960s were an odd period for Count Basie. Although he gradually lost most of his main soloists (including Joe Newman, Thad Jones, Frank Foster, and Frank Wess), he still had a mighty orchestra and often welcomed back Eddie "Lockjaw" Davis and Harry "Sweets" Edison. The problem was that, with the end of his Roulette contract in 1962, the Basie band's recordings during the remainder of the decade would range from pretty good to horrendous, depending on the settings. *This Time by Basie* features the Basie Orchestra playing 16 pop hits, some of which (such as "I Left My Heart in San Francisco," "Moon River," "Fly Me to the Moon," and "Shangri-La") do not live up even to their weak potential! *Frankly Basie,* which has middle-of-the-road arrangements by Billy Byers, finds the orchestra swinging 14 songs associated with Frank Sinatra (including "The Second Time Around," "I'll Never Smile Again," "In the Wee Small Hours," and "My Kind of Town"). The music is pleasing in spots but rather unadventurous and safe. The selections on *Count Basie at the Sands* were performed by the Basie band as they were functioning as the warm-up act before Frank Sinatra's performances. These versions are a little odd to hear, since in many cases the band sounds quite hyped up, yet the audience is clearly impatient for the singer to appear. The orchestra does its best. *Jazzfest Masters,* recorded at the 1969 New Orleans Jazz Festival, shows how strong the big band still sounded despite rarely being captured properly on records during the era. Eddie "Lockjaw" Davis's presence definitely helps, and the orchestra sounds generally inspired on such songs as "Whirlybird," "Corner Pocket," "Good Time Blues," and "Basie."

7 *The Golden Years / Apr. 17, 1972–Dec. 14, 1983 / Pablo 4PACD-4419*
The Count Basie Orchestra finally had an opportunity to be documented properly when Norman Granz formed the Pablo label in 1972. Basie was recorded in three basic settings while with Pablo: with his big band, in all-star groups, and as a pianist (often teamed in the last category with Oscar Peterson). The four-CD sampler *The Golden Years* is an excellent retrospective of Count's Pablo years, with the music divided into live, small groups, big band, and with vocalists. But since all of the performances are available elsewhere, this set is recommended only to listeners not interested in getting the complete sessions.

7 *Fun Time* / July 19, 1975 / Pablo 2310-945

5 *The Basie Big Band* / Aug. 16–27, 1975 / Pablo 2310-756

9 *I Told You So* / Jan. 12–14, 1976 / Original Jazz Classics 824

8 *Prime Time* / Jan. 18–20, 1977 / Pablo 2310–797

7 *Count Basie Big Band—Montreux '77* / July 15, 1977 / Original Jazz Classics 337

7 *Live in Japan '78* / May 21, 1978 / Pablo 2308-246

8 *On the Road* / July 12, 1979 / Original Jazz Classics 854

8 *Kansas City Shout* / Apr. 7, 1980 / Pablo 2310-859

7 *Warm Breeze* / Sept. 1–2, 1981 / Original Jazz Classics 994

Although Norman Granz always preferred to hear Count Basie with small groups, he did record the Basie big band on a fairly regular basis, including these nine single CDs. *Fun Time* is a reissue of the band's appearance at the 1975 Montreux Jazz Festival. Jimmy Forrest, Al Grey, and Butch Miles were the orchestra's stars, with trumpeter Pete Minger and Eric Dixon (on flute and tenor) also getting in their spots. Bill Caffey takes two fine vocals during this concert but he would soon disappear into obscurity. The Basie Orchestra's first studio recordings for Pablo were a disappointment, for these Sammy Nestico arrangements for *The Basie Big Band* are quite lightweight. *I Told You So* (with charts by Bill Holman) is much better, with lots of challenging music and inspired solos. Sammy Nestico's writing for *Prime Time* is on a much higher level than his work for *The Basie Big Band* set, highlighted by "Ya Gotta Try" and colorful reworkings of "Sweet Georgia Brown" and "Ja Da."

No real surprises occur during the orchestra's concert at the 1977 Montreux Jazz Festival and the repertoire is fairly typical, but Jimmy Forrest in particular sounds inspired. Forrest and Al Grey were gone by the time the band recorded the lesser-known *Live in Japan '78,* but they are not missed much; Eric Dixon ably took Forrest's place, and the ensemble work by the orchestra on such songs as "The Heat's On," "Things Ain't What They Used to Be," "Shiny Stockings," and "Basie" is as tight as usual. Trombonist Booty Wood was in Grey's place for *On the Road,* and such numbers as "Wind Machine," "Blues for Stephanie," and "Splanky" rarely sounded better. *Kansas City Shout* is a

change of pace, for the Count Basie Orchestra primarily backs the vocals of Big Joe Turner and Eddie "Cleanhead" Vinson (who also takes some fine alto solos); this combination works quite well. The Basie Swing machine was still rolling at full force for *Warm Breeze,* which consists of seven arrangements (including six originals) by Sammy Nestico. Trumpeter Willie Cook joins Wood and Dixon as a main soloist, with Harry "Sweets" Edison sitting in on "How Sweet It Is." Count Basie was 77 by then, but his band still sounded ageless.

5 *Basie Jam* / Dec. 10, 1973 / Pablo 2310-718

7 *The Bosses* / Dec. 10, 1973 / Original Jazz Classics 821

10 *Basie & Zoot* / Apr. 9, 1975 / Original Jazz Classics 822

7 *At the Montreux Jazz Festival 1975* / July 19, 1975 / Original Jazz Classics 933

7 *Basie Jam #2* / May 6, 1976 / Original Jazz Classics 632

8 *Basie Jam #3* / May 6, 1976 / Original Jazz Classics 687

7 *Kansas City 5* / Jan. 26, 1977 / Original Jazz Classics 888

One of the most intriguing aspects of Count Basie's Pablo years was the opportunity to hear him with all-star groups. However, *Basie Jam* (which includes Harry Edison, trombonist J. J. Johnson, and both Eddie "Lockjaw" Davis and Zoot Sims on tenors) is a bit of a disappointment due to the mundane material, one forgettable blues after another. *The Bosses* has the same lineup but also the extra bonus of Big Joe Turner, who sounds quite inspired and uplifts the ensemble on such numbers as "Flip, Flop and Fly," "Wee Baby Blues," and "Roll 'Em Pete." *Basie & Zoot* is one of the most exciting Count Basie small-group dates of all time. The pianist (also heard a little bit on organ) teams up with tenor saxophonist Zoot Sims, bassist John Heard, and Louie Bellson, and the results are full of unexpected fireworks and plenty of heat. It is a particular pleasure to hear Basie and Sims dig into "I Never Knew," "It's Only a Paper Moon," and "Honeysuckle Rose." Norman Granz must have been pleased!

At the Montreux Jazz Festival 1975 finds Basie leading an exciting sextet that includes Roy Eldridge (as combative as ever), tenor saxophonist Johnny Griffin, and vibraphonist

Milt Jackson. The only fault to the set (which has two blues and "Lester Leaps In") is its brevity. *Basie Jam #2*, an octet date with Benny Carter, Lockjaw, Clark Terry, Al Grey, guitarist Joe Pass, John Heard, and Louie Bellson, is a strong improvement on its predecessor, while *Basie Jam #3* (from the same day) is a bit better due to its four strong standards (including "Bye Bye Blues" and "Song for the Islands"). *Kansas City 5* has Count's piano in the forefront, with a rhythm section also including Milt Jackson, Pass, Heard, and Bellson, playing some Basie standards (including "Jive at Five"), Swing tunes, and blues.

4 *The Gifted Ones* / Feb. 3, 1977 / Original Jazz Classics 886

7 *Count Basie Jam—Montreux '77* / July 14, 1977 / Original Jazz Classics 379

7 *Get Together* / Sept. 4, 1979 / Pablo 2310-924

7 *Kansas City 7* / Apr. 10, 1980 / Original Jazz Classics 690

7 *Kansas City 6* / Nov. 1, 1981 / Original Jazz Classics 449

The Gifted Ones was done backwards, for, instead of having Dizzy Gillespie sit in with the Count Basie Orchestra, Dizzy and Basie were merely matched in a quartet. Gillespie sounds OK and Basie falls back on his clichés; nothing memorable occurs. *Count Basie Jam* finds the pianist keeping a jam session at the 1977 Montreux Jazz Festival quite coherent, having the five horns (Roy Eldridge, Benny Carter, Zoot Sims, Vic Dickenson, and Al Grey) play a ballad medley, the "Bookie Blues," and a closing "Jumpin' at the Woodside." *Get Together,* which also has a ballad medley plus five basic originals, is noteworthy for including Budd Johnson (on tenor and baritone) with the usual horn players (Clark Terry, Harry "Sweets" Edison, and Lockjaw). *Kansas City 7* finds Basie, a rhythm section, J. J. Johnson, and Lockjaw joined by the great modern trumpeter Freddie Hubbard for three originals and three vintage Swing tunes (including "Exactly Like You"). The final entry in the *Kansas City* series teams Basie with trumpeter Willie Cook and the star of the date, Eddie "Cleanhead" Vinson. The emphasis is on the blues.

7 *For the First Time* / May 22, 1974 / Pablo 2310-712

6 *Basie and Friends* / Dec. 2, 1974–Nov. 1, 1981 / Pablo 2310-925

7 *Satch and Josh* / Dec. 2, 1974 / Original Jazz Classics 959

7 *For the Second Time* / Aug. 28, 1975 / Original Jazz Classics 600

6 *Satch and Josh . . . Again* / Sept. 20, 1977 / Original Jazz Classics 960

6 *Yessir, That's My Baby* / Feb. 21, 1978 / Pablo 2310-923

6 *Night Rider* / Feb. 21–22, 1978 / Original Jazz Classics 688

6 *The Timekeepers* / Feb. 21–22, 1978 / Original Jazz Classics 790

One of Norman Granz's pet projects with Count Basie during the Pablo years was to feature his piano as prominently as possible. *For the First Time* is a rare trio date on which Basie (with the assistance of bassist Ray Brown and Louie Bellson) as usual makes every note count, showing a bit of his stride technique in spots. *Basie and Friends,* which was not released initially until 1988, includes eight numbers not issued elsewhere. Basie is heard in a variety of different trios plus three collaborations with Oscar Peterson. At first the Basie-Peterson two-piano matchup may seem a bit unlikely because, while Count always left lots of space, O. P. tended to play a zillion notes. However, they both placed an emphasis on swinging, and there was a surprising amount of overlap in their styles. Granz recorded Peterson and Basie together often enough to result in over five albums. *Satch and Josh* was probably the best all-round one, with the two pianists (Basie doubled on organ) joined by Freddie Green, Ray Brown, and Louie Bellson for a set of standards and blues. *For the Second Time* is a reprise of the earlier Basie trio date, also using Brown and Bellson on a variety of Swing standards. *Satch and Josh* has Basie and Peterson joined by Heard and Bellson and finds the two pianists taking one song apiece on electric piano; otherwise the results are somewhat predictable. The same can be said of their matchups on February 21–22, 1978, which resulted in *Yessir That's My Baby, Night Rider,* and *The Timekeepers* (all with Heard and Bellson). If a listener enjoys one date, then all five of the two-piano sets are equally recommended.

8 *Farmer's Market Barbecue* / May 1982 / Original Jazz Classics 732

7 *Me and You* / Feb. 22–28, 1983 / Original Jazz Classics
906

9 *88 Basie Street* / May 11–12, 1983 / Original Jazz
Classics 808

7 *Mostly Blues . . . and Some Others* / June 22, 1983 /
Pablo 2310-919

Count Basie's health may have been failing during 1982–83, but there is no hint of any decline in Basie's music during his late-period sets. *Farmer's Market Barbecue* is split between big band and combo performances, with the soloists including Eric Dixon and Kenny Hing on tenors, altoist Danny Turner, and trombonist Booty Young; the emphasis is on older material. *Me and You* has five orchestra numbers and four songs by an octet including Booty Wood, Eric Dixon, trumpeter Bob Summers, and altoist Chris Woods. *88 Basie Street* is comprised of four particularly strong numbers by the orchestra (all Sammy Nestico arrangements, including the nostalgic "88 Basie Street") and two small-group jams. *Mostly Blues* generally lives up to its name (although it also includes "I'll Always Be in Love with You," "I'm Confessin'," and "I Want a Little Girl") and was Count Basie's final small-group recording, a septet outing with Snooky Young, Lockjaw, and Joe Pass that has its exciting moments and of course swings.

7 *Long Live the Chief* / June 24–25, 1986 / Denon
33CHY-1018

7 *The Legend, the Legacy* / May 16–17, 1989 / Denon
73790

7 *Live at El Morocco* / Feb. 20–21, 1992 / Telarc 83358

7 *Basie's Bag* / Nov. 20, 1992 / Telarc 83358

6 *Live at MC6* / 1997 / MC6 1002

7 *Count Plays Duke* / June 3–4, 1998 / MAMA 1024

After Count Basie's death, his big band became one of the few worthwhile ghost orchestras ever and one of the last remaining full-time big bands. The Thad Jones era was barely documented, but Frank Foster's reign found the band recording for Denon and Telarc. *Long Live the Chief* has mostly typical material (including "April in Paris," "Lil' Darlin'," "Corner Pocket," and "Shiny Stockings"), but the orchestra (which at the time had Tee Carson on piano) still sounds enthusiastic; Carmen Bradford takes a pair of vocals. *The Legend, the Legacy* has mostly fresher songs, with

Foster's five originals including the three-part "Count Basie Remembrance Suite." By 1992, there were many fewer Basie alumni in the band, but the distinctive sound (with George Caldwell on piano) was still dominant. Foster was probably frustrated at the restrictions imposed on him by this time but he plays well during *Live at El Morocco,* which mixes warhorses with newer material. *Basie's Bag* has no vintage material except for Ernie Wilkins's "Way Out Basie." Foster has the band tackling material by Cedar Walton, Toots Thielemans, George Benson ("Basie's Bag"), and himself (a remake of the "Count Basie Remembrance Suite"). There is even an electric guitar solo by Charlton Johnston on "Basie's Bag." However, Foster knew that he could only go so far in stretching the Basie sound, and he departed in 1996. Under Grover Mitchell's leadership, the Count Basie Orchestra has stuck mostly to its signature sound. *Live at MC6* finds the band sharing the spotlight with the New York Voices; both groups seem inspired by each other's presence even if the repertoire is full of overly played songs. *Count Plays Duke* was a logical release for Ellington's centennial, since Basie was one of Duke's biggest fans. None of the 13 selections (all associated with Ellington) are obscurities and the results are predictable, but there are some good moments from the soloists, who include pianist Terence Conley, Kenny Hing on tenor, trumpeters Bobby Ojeda and Scotty Barnhart, altoist Brad Leadi, and trombonist Grover Mitchell, among others; flutist Frank Wess guests with his old band. The Count Basie legacy lives on, 65 years after the pianist formed his band in Kansas City.

LPS TO SEARCH FOR

The pair of two-LP sets *Paradise Squat* (Verve 2-2542) and *Sixteen Men Swinging* (Verve 2-2517) do an excellent job of summing up the early days of Count Basie's second big band before "April in Paris" and Joe Williams. *Afrique* (Flying Dutchman 10138), from 1970, is one of the most unusual of all Count Basie records, for his orchestra plays modern arrangements by Oliver Nelson and a repertoire that includes songs by Nelson, Gabor Szabo, Albert Ayler, and Pharoah Sanders, all rather modern improvisers! However, the Basie sound is still quite present, and the unique effort was successful at placing the Basie Orchestra in a much more modern setting. Strangely enough the very last Count Basie recording, *Fancy Pants* (Pablo 2310-920), from December 1983, is one of the few Pablo Basie dates not yet reissued on CD. Despite the leader's being 79 and just four months away from his death, this is an excellent outing, with the highlights including "Put It Right There," "Hi-Five," and "Strike Up the Band."

FILMS

Count Basie (usually with his second orchestra) appeared in these films: *Disc Jockey Jamboree* (1957), *Cinderfella* (1960), *Sex and the Single* Girl (1964), *Made in Paris* (1966), and *Blazing Saddles* (1974). In addition, Basie is prominent with many alumni in *The Sound of Jazz* (1957), the 1965 band plays ten songs in *Whirly Bird* (Vintage Jazz Classics 2003), and Count is one of the main subjects of the documentary *The Last of the Blue Devils* (1974–79).

LOUIE BELLSON
b. July 6, 1924, Rock Falls, IL

One of the great jazz drummers of all time, Louie Bellson was one of the few who could hold his own with Buddy Rich in a drum battle. In 1940 he won a nationwide Gene Krupa drum contest and impressed Tommy Dorsey, who would later hire him. At 17, the following year, Bellson was not only playing with Benny Goodman's orchestra but appearing in films with the clarinetist. He spent a couple of years in the military and then, after his discharge, worked with Goodman, Tommy Dorsey (1947–49), and Harry James (1950–51). Bellson, who pioneered the use of two bass drums, became famous during his stay with Duke Ellington (1951–53), writing and being featured on "Skin Deep" and "The Hawk Talks." He married singer Pearl Bailey (a long-term marriage that worked) and became her musical director but also toured with Jazz at the Philharmonic in the 1950s, recorded with Art Tatum and Oscar Peterson, worked with the Dorsey Brothers Orchestra (1955–56), and led his own jazz dates. Every once in a while, Bellson had a reunion with Duke Ellington, including recording *A Drum Is a Woman* in 1956, participating in his first Sacred Concert in 1965, and making an album with Ellington in a quartet as late as 1973. He also helped Count Basie out on occasion, including during a European tour in 1962. Bellson has led modern big bands off and on since the 1960s, developed as a composer-arranger, been a significant jazz educator, and recorded prolifically, both in orchestras and in combos. A class act!

●

8 *150 M.P.H. / May 25, 1974 / Concord Jazz 4036*

7 *Live at the Concord Summer Festival / July 25, 1976 / Concord Jazz 4025*

7 *Prime Time / Nov. 4, 1977 / Concord Jazz 4064*

6 *Raincheck / May 3–4, 1978 / Concord Jazz 4073*

Louie Bellson, who has recorded prolifically as a leader since the 1950s, alternated between big band and combo dates throughout the 1970s, '80s, and '90s, recording regularly for Concord, Pablo, and, in later years, Music Masters. *150 M.P.H.* is one of his better big band sets, with arrangements by the leader and Bill Holman. The many all-star soloists (including trumpeters Bobby Shew, Conte Candoli, Blue Mitchell, and Harry "Sweets" Edison, trombonist Frank Rosolino, and both Don Menza and Pete Christlieb on tenors) would have made this a recommended set anyway, but the charts (which include reworkings of "Time Check" and "Hello Young Lovers") are also quite memorable. Bellson heads a fine septet in the 1976 Concord Jazz Festival recording, with notable contributions from Pete Christlieb and Blue Mitchell (who brought in an original apiece) plus a five-song ballad medley and a jam on Miles Davis's "Dig." *Prime Time* has a similar group (also featuring Christlieb and Mitchell) playing a program that is divided into swinging bop (including "Cotton Tail") and funkier tunes. *Raincheck* is a decent straightahead quintet date with Mitchell, pianist Ross Tompkins, and Ted Nash on alto and tenor, a discovery of Bellson's who is the nephew of Les Brown's tenor soloist, Ted Nash.

6 *Dynamite / Aug. 1979 / Concord Jazz 4105*

7 *Live at Ronnie Scott's / Oct. 28–29, 1979 / DRG 91424*

7 *The London Gig / Nov. 1, 1982 / Original Jazz Classics 965*

8 *East Side Suite / Dec. 7–9, 1987 / Music Masters 60161*

7 *Hot / Dec. 7–9, 1987 / Music Masters 60160*

Louie Bellson's big band albums are often hard-swinging but a bit bombastic, lacking the subtlety that the drummer himself always gives the music. On *Dynamite,* his 19-piece orchestra lives up to the set's title. Bellson, Don Menza, and altoist Matt Catingub wrote the six songs, and the soloists include those three plus trumpeter Bobby Shew, altoist Dick Spencer, and guitarist John Chiodini; Menza's "Sambandrea Swing" is the most memorable selection. Menza is the main star of the DRG big band disc, being the chief soloist, bringing in four originals, and writing most of the arrangements. Also heard from are Bobby Shew, altoist Joe Romano, trumpeter Bill Berry, and Larry Covelli, who has a tenor battle with Menza on "Time Check." The 1982 version of Bellson's big band is almost completely different, quite a bit younger, but also worthy. Bellson wrote all but two of the charts, which feature trumpeter John Eckert, Matt Catingub on alto, and Ted Nash on tenor. *East Side Suite* and *Hot* were recorded during the same three-day period and once again Menza is the main star, although there is plenty of solo space for Bellson (one of the few drummers able to take long solos on records and always hold one's interest), guest flugelhornist Clark Terry, trumpeters Glenn Drewes and Brian O'Flaherty, altoists George Young and Joe Roccisano, and pianist John Bunch.

8 *Airmail Special / Feb. 15–16, 1990 / Music Masters 5 038*

9 *Black, Brown & Beige / Oct. 20–22, 1992 / Music Masters 65096*

8 *Live from New York / Jan. 20, 1994 / Telarc 83334*

Louie Bellson has recorded many big band albums and these three are among his best from the 1990s. *Airmail Special* is one of Bellson's most Swing-oriented projects, for he plays a song apiece in tribute to Lionel Hampton, Benny Goodman ("Don't Be That Way"), Bunny Berigan, Woody Herman, Charlie Barnet ("Cherokee"), Duke Ellington, Tommy Dorsey, Harry James, Artie Shaw ("Begin the Beguine"), and Count Basie plus Dizzy Gillespie and one for himself. The arrangements update the music (including turning "Beguine" into a jazz waltz and making "Cherokee" beboppish) and are continually intriguing. Duke Ellington's "Black, Brown & Beige Suite" has rarely been performed in its complete version. Louis Bellson's rendition is not an exact recreation, for the solos are longer, Johnny Hodges's famous "Come Sunday" section is taken by flugelhornist Clark Terry, and certain parts are altered. Joe Williams sings "The Blues," and trumpeter Barry Lee Hall, the plunger trombonist of Art Baron, and baritonist Joe Temperley are perfect for their roles. In addition, Bellson performs the two songs that he wrote for Ellington ("The Hawk Talks" and "Skin Deep") and there is a three-part "Ellington-Strayhorn Suite." *Live from New York* has Bellson's big band performing seven of his originals, with arrangements by Matt Catingub, Frank Mantooth, Bob Florence, Jack Hayes, and Tommy Newsom; Clark Terry makes two guest appearances on this well-rounded set.

FILMS

Louie Bellson debuted with the Benny Goodman Orchestra when he appeared in *The Gang's All Here* (1943). *Louie Bellson Big Band* (View Video 13021) has six songs from a 1986 concert.

TEX BENEKE

b. Feb. 12, 1914, Fort Worth, TX

What an odd musical life Gordon "Tex" Beneke has had! Although he is a decent tenor saxophonist and a friendly singer, Beneke's musical career has always been tied into the Glenn Miller legacy. He began playing soprano when he was nine, soon switching to tenor. Beneke worked with some territory bands in the south, was with Ben Young during 1935–37, and then became a member of the Glenn Miller Orchestra in 1938, staying until the breakup of the big band in 1942, when Miller joined the Army Air Force. Beneke, who took many short solos on tenor, became best known for his singing (which was often introduced by a touch of whistling) on many medium-tempo tunes, most notably "Chattanooga Choo Choo."

After Miller enlisted, Beneke toured for a time with the Modernaires before he joined the Navy and was part of a military band. After being discharged, Beneke briefly led a group billed as the Glenn Miller Orchestra. But a dispute with the Miller estate led him to rename his band the Tex Beneke Orchestra. For a short time Beneke tried to escape from the Glenn Miller association, but he soon relented and has since spent over 50 years performing the music from the four years that he was with Miller! He never expressed much interest in bebop, widening his repertoire, or growing beyond where he was in 1942, staying strictly a nostalgia act. Tex Beneke still performs now and then as a singer (having retired on tenor) with a big band, always paying tribute to Glenn Miller. ●

FILMS
Tex Beneke performs with the Glenn Miller big band in *Orchestra Wives* (1942) and *Sun Valley Serenade* (1942), singing a definitive version of "Chattanooga Choo Choo" in the latter.

BILL BERRY
b. Sept. 14, 1930, Benton Harbor, MI

A solid trumpeter who is proud of his association with Duke Ellington, Bill Berry has long been a major big bandleader in the Los Angeles area. He was a professional by 1947 and spent three years playing with territory bands in the Midwest. After serving in the Air Force during 1951–55 and studying at Berklee (where he played with Herb Pomeroy), Berry toured with the big bands of Woody Herman (1957) and Maynard Ferguson. He was a member of Duke Ellington's orchestra during 1961–64, taking occasional solos. Berry worked in the New York studios (1964–71) and played with the Thad Jones–Mel Lewis Orchestra. After moving to Los Angeles in 1971, Berry put together the L. A. Big Band, an all-star unit that often plays Duke Ellington's music. Through the years his orchestra has included Cat Anderson, Britt Woodman, Marshal Royal, trumpeter Blue Mitchell, tenor saxophonist Richie Kamuca, and many of Los Angeles's top Mainstream jazz players. Bill Berry during the past three decades has worked in the studios, gigged locally in clubs, continued heading his orchestra, played regularly with Louie Bellson and Benny Carter, and been particularly significant for his work with the Monterey Jazz Festival education program. He was still in his musical prime as the 20th century ended. ●

10 *Hello Rev / Aug. 1976 / Concord Jazz 4027*

7 *For Duke / Jan. 11–12, 1978 / Drive Archives 1035*

8 *Shortcake / Mar. 3, 1978 / Concord Jazz 4075*
Bill Berry led one of the finest Swing big bands of the 1970s. *Hello Rev* has quite an all-star lineup, with trumpeters Cat Anderson (listen to his ensemble work on "Cottontail"), Blue Mitchell, and Jack Sheldon, trombonists Tricky Lofton, Jimmy Cleveland, and Britt Woodman, both Richie Kamuca and Don Menza heard from on tenor, pianist Dave Frishberg, and altoist Marshall Royal. With all of the talent, it is a pity that this ensemble did not record much more often, but at least this high-quality set lives up to its poten-tial. *For Duke* is a very well-recorded direct-to-disc session that was reissued on CD. Berry teams up in the septet with Royal, Woodman, and tenor saxophonist Scott Hamilton, running through the usual Ellington tunes in swinging fashion. *Shortcake* often puts the spotlight on Berry's cornet, particularly on five selections where he is accompanied by a four-piece rhythm section that includes Frishberg on piano. The other three numbers are by a septet including Royal, Lew Tabackin on tenor and flute, and trombonist Bill Watrous; among the Swing standards heard are "Avalon," "I Didn't Know About You," "Royal Garden Blues," and "I'm Getting Sentimental Over You."

EARL BOSTIC
b. Apr. 25, 1913, Tulsa, OK, d. Oct. 28, 1965, Rochester, NY

One of the giants of 1950s R&B, altoist Earl Bostic was a brilliant technician who could hit very high notes perfectly in tune. Bostic was basically a Swing player at heart, and much of his repertoire (including many of his hits) were melodic versions of Swing standards. He started playing music early on, and his associations included Terrence Holder (1931–32) and Bennie Moten (1933). The altoist studied music at Xavier University in New Orleans, where he worked with Joe Robichaux (1934). Bostic played in the Midwest with Ernie Fields, Clarence Olden, Charlie Creath, Fate Marable, Marion Sears, and Clyde Turpin. In 1938 he arrived in New York, where he played with Don Redman, Edgar Hayes, and Hot Lips Page. Bostic contributed arrangements to several orchestras (including those headed by Page, Artie Shaw, and Louis Prima), led his own combos, and worked with Lionel Hampton (1943–44). Bostic, who appeared on many advanced Swing records in the mid-1940s, started becoming quite successful as a bandleader in the late 1940s, recording regularly for the King label. By the early 1950s he was one of the most famous saxophonists in the world, having many best-selling records, including "Flamingo" (1951), "Sleep," "You Go to My Head," "Cherokee," and "Temptation." Most of his performances from the period are a showcase for his technique and his beautiful sound. Although his sidemen included tenors John Coltrane and Stanley Turrentine, they frequently had only one note to play on Bostic's records, the final one!

Unfortunately, Earl Bostic had a weak heart, and he was out of action for three years after a heart attack in 1956. He made a comeback and regained his former stature, but a second heart attack, in 1965, caused his death at age 52.

●

LPS TO SEARCH FOR

Considering how popular he once was, it is surprising how little Earl Bostic there is on CD, particularly domestically. *That's Earl, Brother* (Spotlite 152) features Bostic in the mid-1940s, playing as a sideman with Lionel Hampton's big band, in an octet headed by Rex Stewart, and on four songs with his own short-lived big band; all of the music is taken from radio broadcasts. Two of the better samplers of Bostic's lucrative King period are *Bostic Blows a Fuse* (Charly 1091) and *14 Hits* (King 5010), and these albums (which have a little bit of duplication) contain most of his greatest hits. But a more complete retrospective is long overdue.

RUBY BRAFF
b. Mar. 16, 1927, Boston, MA

A highly expressive cornetist who never played an indifferent or unemotional note, Ruby Braff has throughout his career stuck to performing vintage standards in a style that falls between Swing and trad jazz. Braff played early on in Boston, recording in 1949 with Edmond Hall and in 1951 with Pee Wee Russell. When he moved to New York in 1953, Braff was practically the only world-class brassman of his generation to be playing Mainstream jazz rather than bebop. Although he was ten years younger than Dizzy Gillespie, Braff's main heroes were Louis Armstrong, Lester Young, and Billie Holiday. He recorded prolifically in the 1950s and had opportunities to work with older jazzmen (including Benny Goodman in 1955 and Buck Clayton on his jam session dates), but gigs became scarcer in the 1960s. However, his association with George Wein's Newport All-Stars helped, and his quartet with George Barnes (1973–75) was quite popular. With the comeback of Mainstream Swing during the second part of the 1970s, Braff was now among the older Swing stars as opposed to being the kid. He has since recorded quite a few rewarding albums and CDs, including a series of duets with Dick Hyman, collaborations with Scott Hamilton, Howard Alden, and Ellis Larkins, plus countless combo dates. The instantly recognizable Ruby Braff, who makes every sound count, is a rare master at building up solos to a low note!

●

7 *Hustlin' and Bustlin'* / 1951–June 9, 1954 / Black Lion 760908

8 *Two by Two: Ruby Braff & Ellis Larkins Play Rodgers and Hart* / Oct. 14, 1955 / Vanguard 8507

7 *This Is My Lucky Day* / Aug. 19, 1957–Dec. 26, 1957 / Bluebird 6456

8 *Ruby Braff with Buddy Tate & The Newport All Stars* / Oct. 28, 1967 / Black Lion 760138

9 *Hear Me Talkin'* / Nov. 8, 1967 / Black Lion 760161
Ruby Braff started out his career playing primarily Dixieland, but his main love has always been Swing. *Hustlin' and Bustlin'* features him jamming with Vic Dickenson and

clarinetist Edmond Hall in 1951, with a quintet that includes Ken Kersey and tenor saxophonist Sam Margolis in 1954 and with Dickenson in a larger group, also from 1954. The music includes several lesser-known tunes associated with Louis Armstrong (including "Hustlin' and Bustlin'" and "Shoe Shine Boy") and a variety of Swing standards. From the start, Braff's playing was both passionate and distinctive. On February 17, 1955, the cornetist recorded an exquisite set of duets with the subtle pianist Ellis Larkins called *Pocket Full of Dreams*. While that Vanguard set has not yet been reissued, the follow-up date, *Two by Two*, has a dozen Rodgers and Hart standards and shows just how sensitive (yet swinging) this duo could be. *This Is My Lucky Day* has an excellent octet date, with trombonist Benny Morton, clarinetist Pee Wee Russell, and Dick Hafer on tenor (including "It's Been So Long," "I'm Coming Virginia," and "Did I Remember" and a few Bunny Berigan tributes) plus a surprisingly inhibited meeting with Roy Eldridge that should have been much more exciting than it turned out. Braff recorded only one album as a leader during the 1960–66 period and was largely neglected during that era. The year 1967 was better, for Braff was now associated with pianist George Wein's Newport All-Stars. Their Black Lion CD teams him with Buddy Tate and Wein in a quintet, playing Mainstream Swing during an era when the music was in danger of becoming extinct. Braff and Tate make for a very complementary team on such numbers as "Mean to Me," "My Monday Date," "Lullaby of the Leaves," and "The Sheik of Araby." *Hear Me Talkin'*, a Dixieland-oriented set with British trumpeter Alex Welsh's band, is even better, with Braff and Welsh sharing the lead and such fine soloists on the 1920s and Swing standards as trombonist Roy Williams, Al Gay on tenor, and baritonist Johnny Barnes.

8   *The Grand Reunion / Oct. 14, 1972 / Chiaroscuro 117*

9   *The Ruby Braff–George Barnes Quartet / Apr. 22, 1974 / Chiaroscuro 126*

8   *Plays Gershwin / July 26, 1974 / Concord Jazz 6005*

8   *Salutes Rodgers and Hart / Oct. 1974 / Concord Jazz 6007*

6   *It Had to Be Us / Mar. 12–13, 1980 / Chiaroscuro 204*

8   *The Canadian Concerts / June 14, 1979–Jan. 23, 1984 / Sackville 5005*

In 1972 Ruby Braff and Ellis Larkins had a reunion for Chiaroscuro, showing throughout the ballad-oriented program that the 17 years since their last meeting had not dulled their talents or enthusiasm for melodic jazz. In 1973 Braff and George Barnes formed a quartet that also included rhythm guitarist Wayne Wright and eventually bassist Michael Moore. Their first recording for Chiaroscuro has not yet been reissued, but their other Chiaroscuro set (which has doubled in size with the release of ten additional selections for the CD reissue) and two Concord recordings have come back. Braff's lyrical horn and Barnes's single-note lines always blended very well together, even if their personalities offstage were not all that complementary! Due to the wider variety of material, the Chiaroscuro CD gets the edge, but the two songbook sets for Concord are full of exquisite moments too. After a decent (but out-of-print) RCA album of Fred Astaire-related tunes in 1975, the Braff-Barnes Quartet broke up.

It Had to Be Us is a 1980 meeting between Braff and Woody Herman (who sticks to clarinet) with a rhythm section; the music was not released initially until 1998. Herman is a little subpar on the date, but there are good spirits felt along with a few good-humored Herman vocals, including on "The Sheik of Araby," which comments on the then-current gas shortage. An interesting if not essential set. *The Canadian Concerts*, consisting of two-CDs, combines the 1984 Sackville album *With The Ed Bickert Trio* with two very obscure duet dates from 1979 by Braff and pianist Gene DiNovi that were previously released as an LP and a cassette by the tiny PediMega label; in addition there are two previously unreleased selections from the Bickert date. The Sackville album matches Braff with guitarist Bickert, bassist Don Thompson, and drummer Terry Clarke ("True Love," "This Year's Kisses," and "If Dreams Come True" are among the highlights) while the duets include ten pieces with "Heart" in the title plus a variety of other standards; DiNovi takes a couple heartfelt vocals.

9   *A First / Feb. 1985 / Concord Jazz 4274*

9   *A Sailboat in the Moonlight / Feb. 1985 / Concord Jazz 4296*

8   *Me, Myself and I / June 1988 / Concord Jazz 381*

8   *Bravura Eloquence / June 1988 / Concord Jazz 4423*

10   *Music from My Fair Lady / June 1988 / Concord Jazz 4393*

10   *Music from South Pacific / June 12–13, 1990 / Concord Jazz 4445*

8 *Cornet Chop Suey / Mar. 27–28, 1991 / Concord Jazz 4606*

8 *And His New England Songhounds, Volume One / Apr. 29, 1991 / Concord Jazz 4478*

8 *And His New England Songhounds, Volume Two / Apr. 30, 1991 / Concord Jazz 4504*

8 *As Time Goes By / May 16, 1991 / Candid 79741*
Ruby Braff's Concord recordings of 1985–91 (which started when he was 58) rank with the greatest work of his career. *A First* and *A Sailboat in the Moonlight* team the cornetist with Scott Hamilton, a perfect match. Braff had gone down a lonely path as a young Mainstreamer in the 1950s, and, when Hamilton first emerged in the mid-1970s, he was practically alone initially, too, although that situation soon changed. They clearly inspired each other not only on these two sets but on a 1983 LP for Phontastic. *Me, Myself and I* finds Braff using an instrumentation that he would often utilize in later years, a trio with guitar and bass (in this case Howard Alden and bassist Jack Lesberg). Braff's expert use of space and dynamics along with his appealing phrasing make this a lyrical yet sometimes hard-swinging affair; "Muskrat Ramble," "Honey," "No One Else but You," "When You're Smiling," and "That's My Home" are among the highlights. *Bravura Eloquence* has the same players and such inspired material as a medley of "Smile" and "Who'll Buy My Violets?," "Lonely Moments," "I'm Shooting High," "Persian Rug," and a Judy Garland medley. Braff, whose collaborations with Ellis Larkins, George Barnes, and Scott Hamilton are classic, found his true musical soul mate in Dick Hyman. They have teamed up on records on an occasional basis since 1972 and their meetings (particularly their duo projects) are always quite special. The Braff-Hyman duo does wonders with the familiar material from *My Fair Lady* and the less promising score of *South Pacific,* turning songs such as "Bali Ha'I and "Some Enchanted Evening" into surprisingly swinging jazz on the latter project. *Cornet Chop Suey* returns to the cornet-guitar-bass instrumentation (with Howard Alden and Frank Tate) and has guest appearances by clarinetist Ken Peplowski and drummer Ronald Zito on five of the dozen selections. Braff caresses such melodies as "Nancy with the Laughing Face," "Do It Again," "Sweet and Slow," a medley from the film *High Society,* and even "It's the Same Old South." His two sets with the New England Songhounds reunite Braff with Scott Hamilton and utilize the all-star rhythm section of Dave McKenna, How-

ard Alden, Frank Tate, and drummer Alan Dawson. Every one of Ruby Braff's Concord recordings is highly recommended to fans of his lyrical and heartfelt solos. The same comments can be made about *As Time Goes By,* another outing by the Braff-Alden-Tate trio, although for the Candid label. Even though they explore similar material (including the same *High Society* medley), the different solos and the close interplay make this a gem too.

8 *Controlled Nonchalance Vol. 1 / Nov. 26–27, 1993 / Arbors 19134*

8 *Calling Berlin, Vol. 1 / June 28, 1994–July 1, 1994 / Arbors 19139*

8 *Calling Berlin, Vol. 2 / June 28, 1994–July 1, 1994 / Arbors 19140*

9 *Play Nice Tunes / July 2, 1994 / Arbors 19141*

8 *Inside & Out / Sept. 10–11, 1995 / Concord Jazz 4691*

7 *Being with You / Apr. 15–16, 1996 / Arbors 19163*

7 *You Can Depend on Me / Apr. 17, 1996 / Arbors 191655*

7 *Born to Play / Apr. 20–21, 1998 / Arbors 19203*
In 1993 Ruby Braff switched to the Arbors label, but his style of music remained the same, as did some of his supporting cast. *Controlled Nonchalance* is yet another rewarding meeting with Scott Hamilton (in a sextet with Dave McKenna and guitarist Gray Sargent); the only difference is that all of the selections are well-known (rather than obscure) Swing and Dixieland standards, but the quality of the music is just as high. The two *Calling Berlin* CDs are another reunion, this time with Ellis Larkins, 22 years after the Chiaroscuro album and 39 years after their Vanguard sessions. Other than Bucky Pizzarelli's making the group a trio on two numbers during *Vol. 1,* there was no change in the duo's sound, lyrical approach and subtle creativity. Twenty-eight Irving Berlin tunes in all are explored on the two volumes. Braff and Dick Hyman perform 14 "nice tunes" as duets on their 1994 Arbors CD, including "My Heart Belongs to Daddy," "Why Was I Born?," "Thanks a Million," and "You're Lucky to Me." Braff returned to Concord for a duet set in 1995 with pianist Roger Kellaway, a much more modern player who proved to be flexible enough to fit in with the cornetist and adventurous enough to push him on *Inside & Out.* A fascinating outing. As he passed the age of 70, Ruby Braff remained in his musical prime. *Being with You* is supposedly a tribute to Louis Armstrong, although few of the selections

have much to do with Satch; the closing number, "When It's Sleepy Time Down South," is taken up by Braff's talking, and he should not have sung "Little One!" However, there are some hot moments, including a version of "Royal Garden Blues" that has cornetist Jon-Erik Kellso and flugelhornist Joe Wilder (on his one appearance of the disc); trombonist Dan Barrett and tenorman Jerry Jerome are among the many other soloists on this mostly rewarding date. *You Can Depend on Me* has Braff joined by a veteran rhythm section (Bucky Pizzarelli, Johnny Varro, Bob Haggart, and drummer Jim Gwin) for fairly lengthy renditions of eight standards. *Born to Play,* from 1998, finds Ruby Braff backed by a surprisingly large rhythm section (three guitars, two bassists, and drummer Gwin) and assisted by clarinetist Kenny Davern on two originals, a Charlie Chaplin medley, a lengthy "Jive at Five," and some fresh Swing songs. As can be ascertained by the consistently high ratings, Ruby Braff's recording career is full of gems.

LPS TO SEARCH FOR

Adoration of the Melody (Bethlehem 8043), from 1954–55, has Braff mostly paying tribute to Lester Young, Billie Holiday, and Louis Armstrong while joined by a sax section. *To Fred Astaire with Love* (RCA 1-1008) is the final recording by the Ruby Braff-George Barnes Quartet and is full of charm. *Fireworks* (Inner City 1153), from 1983, teamed Braff and Dick Hyman for the first time as a duet, and it is full of spectacular moments. In 1983 *Mr. Braff to You* (Phontastic 7568) for the initial time matched Braff with Scott Hamilton, and it is up to the level of the Concord dates. And *America the Beautiful* (Concord Jazz/George Wein Collection 3003), an oddity, differs from the other Braff/Hyman duos in that the pianist plays pipe organ exclusively!

CHARLES BROWN

b. Sept. 13, 1922, Texas City, TX, d. Jan. 24, 1999, Oakland, CA

Charles Brown in his early days was the master of the blues ballad, having a hit on "Driftin' Blues" and recording many similar slow pieces. However, as he showed during his comeback years, he was actually much more well-rounded as a singer and pianist.

Brown, who was an orphan from an early age, had classical training as a pianist and earned a degree in chemistry, but his life went in a different direction. He loved Swing and, after moving to Los Angeles in 1943, freelanced and then became part of Johnny Moore's Three Blazers, a guitar-piano-bass trio that was originally modeled after the Nat King Cole Trio. However, after Brown's vocal on "Driftin' Blues" gave the band a major hit in 1946, the group became known for its slower tunes and for Brown's vocals, which were often mistakenly credited to Moore. In 1947 the pianist's "Merry Christmas Baby" was first recorded, and it was quickly considered a classic. The following year Brown finally went on his own. He had ten R&B hits during 1949–52, including "Get Yourself Another Fool," "Trouble Blues," and "Hard Times," being both an inspiration to and a strong influence on Ray Charles, Amos Milburn, and Floyd Dixon. However, as often happened for musicians of his style and time period, Brown's star faded soon after rock and roll (which he helped inspire) took over in the mid-1950s.

After 30 years of obscurity, during which Brown continued working but without much attention (except around Christmastime, when "Merry Christmas Baby" was annually revived), in the mid-1980s he finally began to get some publicity, recording a strong album in 1986, *One More for the Road.* Bonnie Raitt used him as her opening act on a few tours, and the result was that Brown began to record regularly again and his popularity quickly grew. Although he answered requests to play his earlier hits, he also showed that he had developed quite a bit as a swinging pianist. His hot band (which included Clifford Solomon on tenor and guitarist Danny Caron) sounded as comfortable as the leader in playing both Swing tunes and older R&B classics during his final dozen years, and Charles Brown's last period was his most rewarding.

8 *1944–1945 / 1944–Sept. 11, 1945 / Classics 894*

7 *1946 / Feb. 4, 1946–1946 / Classics 971*

* *The Complete Aladdin Recordings of Charles Brown / Sept. 11, 1945–Sept. 4, 1956 / Mosaic 5-153*

1944–1945, which has the first 22 selections by Johnny Moore's Three Blazers (with Charles Brown as the main star on vocals and piano), finds the group emulating the Nat King Cole Trio, particularly on the eight instrumentals. Brown's singing on the other tracks was distinctive from the start. Oscar Moore is on some of the numbers as second guitarist, and there are a couple of guest vocalists, including Frankie Laine. However, the band's fortunes changed with the recording of "Drifting Blues," the 21st selection on this CD. The music on *1946* is mostly in the same slow blues ballad vein as their initial hit, including such tunes as "Rocks in My Bed," "What Do You Know About Love?," "You Showed Me the Way," and "More Than You Know." The only instrumentals are "Nutmeg" and the two-part "Warsaw Concerto." The five-CD limited-edition Mosaic box duplicates four selections apiece from the Classics CDs but otherwise dates from 1948–56 and features Brown as the leader of his own trio during 1948–49 and of larger recording groups throughout the 1950s. His 99 Aladdin recordings include many attempts to duplicate "Drifting Blues," a few new hits, plenty of blues ballads and Swing numbers, and finally an unsuccessful try to beat Fats Domino at his own game. Most of this music has dated very well, and Charles Brown is heard throughout in superior form.

8 *One More for the Road / 1986 / Alligator 4771*

9 *All My Life / 1990 / Bullseye Blues 9501*

7 *Someone to Love / 1992 / Bullseye Blues 9514*

8 *Just a Lucky So and So / 1993 / Bullseye Blues 9521*

9 *These Blues / Jan. 6–7, 1994 / Verve 314 523 022*

After decades playing in the minor leagues, Charles Brown began to be noticed again in the mid-1980s. *One More for the Road,* originally recorded for the short-lived Blue Side label and reissued by Alligator (which substituted two selections for what they considered two lesser numbers), features Brown in a quintet with guitarist Billy Butler, Harold Ousley on tenor, bassist Earl May, and drummer Kenny Washington. Brown's comeback set alternates some of his favorite standards with a few originals, and the highlights include "Save Your Love for Me," "Who Will the Next Fool Be?," "Cottage for Sale," and "Travelin' Blues." *All My Life* was Brown's breakthrough album, featuring his regular group of the 1990s (with Clifford Solomon on tenor and alto and guitarist Danny Caron) plus several guests, including Dr. John on four numbers and singer Ruth Brown on "Tell Me Who." Such selections as "Fools' Paradise," "Bad Bad Whiskey," "Trouble Blues," and "All My Life" helped define how Charles Brown would sound during his glorious final decade. *Someone to Love* has a guest appearance by singer Bonnie Raitt on the title track and she plays slide guitar on one other number, but the focus is primarily on the leader. Brown wrote seven of the nine selections, and, even if no new hits resulted, the bluesy music is quite enjoyable, "Be Sharp You'll See" gives his sidemen a chance to stretch out, and Brown takes a rare solo on organ during the unaccompanied "I Don't Want to Get Adjusted." Charles Brown and his quintet (helped out by the Crescent City Horns and the New Orleans Strings on some numbers) plays even more rewarding music on *Just a Lucky So and So,* falling between Swing, R&B, and jump music, with an emphasis on ballads. Among the gems are the title track, a remake of "Driftin' Blues," "Black Night," and "A Song for Christmas." *These Blues* finds Brown at 71 still in top form. The material is particularly strong, including such numbers as "Honey," "I Got It Bad," "Is You Is, or Is You Ain't Ma Baby," and "A Sunday Kind of Love," showing off both Brown's roots in the Swing era and his fine piano playing.

MILT BUCKNER

b. July 10, 1915, St. Louis, MO, d. July 27, 1977, Chicago, IL

Milt Buckner is most famous for having developed the block chord (or locked hands) style on piano, influencing George Shearing, Dave Brubeck, and Oscar Peterson, among others. He had important careers as both a pianist and an organist.

His older brother, Ted Buckner, played alto with Jimmie Lunceford (1937–43). Milt grew up in Detroit and learned about music from his uncle, trombonist John Tobias. He studied at the Detroit Institute of Arts and throughout the 1930s was based in Detroit, where he played with the Harlem Aristocrats, Mose Burke's Dixie Whangdoodles, and McKinney's Cotton Pickers, also writing arrangements for the last. Buckner became well known during his long association with Lionel Hampton (1941–48, 1950–52, and off and on afterwards).

After leaving Hampton in 1952, Milt Buckner switched full time to organ and led his own popular combo for decades. Starting in 1968 he visited Europe regularly (sometimes with Illinois Jacquet) and recorded many records overseas. Overall Milt Buckner (who recorded quite a few long-out-of-print albums for the French Black & Blue label in the 1970s) was one of the best of the pre-Jimmy Smith organists (along with Wild Bill Davis and Bill Doggett), but he made his biggest impact on piano, which he played on an occasional basis in later years.

7 *Milt Buckner–Illinois Jacquet–Buddy Tate / Oct. 23, 1976–Nov. 20, 1976 / Progressive 7017*
This CD features Milt Buckner on organ in 1976 performing Swing standards with either Illinois Jacquet or Buddy Tate on tenor. Although Buckner is primarily in a supportive role behind the lead voices, he has plenty of solo space and even takes a rare vocal on "I'll Remember April." The disc gives one a good example of his organ playing; for his skills on piano one should acquire some of Lionel Hampton's vintage albums.

JOHN BUNCH
b. Dec. 1, 1921, Tipton, IN

When the new generation of Swing players, such as Scott Hamilton, emerged during the 1970s and '80s, there was a shortage of compatible young pianists to help them out. Veteran John Bunch was more than willing to be of assistance, and his Teddy Wilson–inspired style fit in perfectly with the younger horn players. Bunch started on piano when he was 11 and was playing locally in clubs a year later. However, his career did not really get going until the mid-1950s, when he joined the Woody Herman Orchestra (1956–57) and followed it up with stints with Benny Goodman (off and on for 20 years) and Maynard Ferguson. Among his other key associations were with Buddy Rich (1959–60 and with his big band in 1966), the Al Cohn–Zoot Sims Quartet, Gene Krupa (1961–64) and working as Tony Bennett's accompanist (1966–72). With the comeback of Mainstream Swing starting in the mid-1970s, John Bunch has been heard primarily in small groups ever since, including with Scott Hamilton, Warren Vache, and New York Swing plus his own trio.

10 *John Bunch Plays Kurt Weill / May 1975–Jan. 31, 1991 / Chiaroscuro 144*

7 *The Best Thing for You / June 1987 / Concord Jazz 4328*

9 *Struttin' / Nov. 7–8, 1995 / Arbors 19157*

8 *Solo / Nov. 4–5, 1996 / Arbors 19184*
John Bunch's solo piano tribute to Kurt Weill was originally an LP with a dozen songs in 1975. Sixteen years later he returned to the studio to add five more tunes. Weill's pieces were usually quite intriguing and Bunch explores such numbers as "My Ship," "September Song," "This Is New," "Lost in the Stars," "Speak Low," and "Moon-Faced, Starry-Eyed" but surprisingly not "Moritat" (the "Mack the Knife" theme). An exquisite set, this is one of the finest recordings of John Bunch's career. *The Best Thing for You* is a trio outing with bassist Phil Flanigan and drummer Chuck Riggs that may lack surprises but contains superior versions of ten standards, including "The Best Thing for You Would Be Me," " 'Deed I Do," "Star Eyes," and "I Can't Get Started." *Struttin'* is a duet album with Flanigan and has 14 songs that cover quite a bit of ground, from "On a Slow Boat to China" and the Dixieland of "Struttin' with Some Barbeque" to "Mr. Lucky," Chopin's "Prelude in C Minor," and the boppish "Crazeology." A quiet but passionate program

that is more inspired than *The Best Thing For You*. *Solo* also has an inventive repertoire (including "Isfahan," "Lucky to Be Me," Jimmy Rowles's "We Take the Cake," and Dave Brubeck's "The Duke," plus a variety of top Swing standards) and displays John Bunch's roots in Teddy Wilson's melodic yet swinging style.

SAM BUTERA
b. Sept. 17, 1927, New Orleans, LA

Sam Butera's forceful and honking tenor was a major part of Louis Prima's success in the 1950s. Butera had played with Ray McKinley in 1946 and led his own band in New Orleans for quite a few years (1947–54). He was discovered by Louis Prima, who used the nucleus of Butera's band as his own group in Las Vegas, naming them the Witnesses. Prima's good-humored singing, comedy, and trumpet solos and Keely Smith's excellent vocalizing were really pushed and inspired by the power and energy provided by Butera, who always played passionately and with great emotion. Butera stayed with Prima for 20 years, until 1975, when a stroke ended the trumpeter's career (and eventually his life). Butera, who has lived in Las Vegas since 1954, resumed leading his own band, playing music from the Louis Prima era, recording for his own private label, and working steadily. Many in the Retro Swing movement consider Sam Butera to be a hero.

LPS TO SEARCH FOR
While Sam Butera has recorded in more recent times for his own private label, the occasional dates that he led while with Prima have not yet reappeared. *The Big Horn* (Capitol 1098), from the early 1960s, features his passionate tenor with the Witnesses (including the extroverted trombone of Lou Sino), giving a lot of feeling to a variety of show tunes, including "La Vie en Rose," "Tennessee Waltz," "I Love Paris," and "On the Street Where You Live."

LEE CASTLE
b. Feb. 28, 1915, New York, NY, d. Nov. 16, 1990, Hollywood, FL

Lee Castle, a trumpeter with a mellow tone, spent most of his life playing revival Swing. Aniello Castaldo (he would change his name in 1942) started on drums but switched to trumpet after hearing a Louis Armstrong record when he was 15. Castle was playing professionally at 18, starting off with Paul Tremaine, Paul Martell, and Joe Haymes's orchestra (1936), making his recording debut with the last. Castle was with Artie Shaw's first big band, Red Norvo, Glenn Miller (briefly in 1939), Jack Teagarden (taking excellent spots on "Beale Street Blues" and "Muddy River Blues"), Shaw again (1941), Will Bradley, and Benny Goodman (1943). Castle's most significant association of this period was with Tommy Dorsey (off and on during 1937–41). Castle tried three times to lead his own big band in the 1940s but without any success. He became a studio musician, headed a Dixieland group, and was briefly back with Shaw in 1950. In 1953 Lee Castle rejoined Tommy Dorsey shortly before the Dorsey Brothers Orchestra was reformed. Castle got along very well with both of the battling Dorseys and he became the band's musical director.

After both Tommy and Jimmy Dorsey passed away during 1956–57, the big band was divided into two ghost orchestras. Castle became the leader of the Jimmy Dorsey Orchestra (which had just recorded the hit "So Rare"), and ironically he ended up being a bandleader longer than either of the Dorsey Brothers, for 33 years! Although he could be an excellent Dixieland player (as he had shown on a 1954 LP entitled *Dixieland Heaven* and on a Miff Mole date in 1958), Lee Castle was content to lead a nostalgic ghost band for decades, playing predictable versions of music associated with both of the Dorsey Brothers.

MATT CATINGUB

b. Mar. 25, 1961, North Hollywood, CA

An excellent altoist, arranger, composer, and singer, Matt Catingub (who has long had a love for the Count Basie sound) also has a strong sense of humor. Among his originals are such songs as "Blues and the Abscessed Tooth," "Bopularity," and "The Umpire Strikes Back." He began playing piano when he was seven, clarinet at 11 and started on alto at 17. Catingub composed the suite "Monterey 1" for the California All-Star High School Jazz Band at the Monterey Jazz Festival and began working with Louie Bellson when he was 17. Two years later he was leading his own big band and using his mother (veteran singer Mavis Rivers) on vocals. In addition to playing with Bellson, Catingub worked regularly with the Toshiko Akiyoshi/ Lew Tabackin big band. In 1985, Catingub's *Hi-Tech Big Band* album featured five songs in which he played all the instruments, including the reeds, piano, and drums plus eerily accurate sounds of other instruments through the use of a synthesizer. Active as an educator and a studio musician, in 1998 Matt Catingub put together the unfortunate Big Kahuna and the Copa Cat Pack for a recording, a weak attempt at playing Retro Swing.

●

7   *Your Friendly Neighborhood Big Band* / Jan. 22, 1984 + Apr. 21, 1984 / *Reference 14*

2   *Hawaiian Swing* / 1999 / *Concord Jazz 4860*
The Reference CD, recorded when Matt Catingub was turning 23, is a solid modern Swing date, with Catingub (who wrote all the arrangements and took the alto solos) modeling his big band a bit after Count Basie's. His mother, Mavis Rivers, takes four vocals, valve trombonist Mike Fahn is heard from, and the orchestra includes future pop/jazz alto star Eric Marienthal in the ensembles. Among the selections are "Don't Be That Way," "Work Song," "Jeannine," and "Baubles, Bangles and Beads." In contrast, *Hawaiian Swing* finds Catingub (using the name of Da Big Kahuna) jumping on the Retro Swing fad bandwagon and playing below his capabilities. He uses a big band but keeps the solos short, the rhythms very simple and takes a lot of vocals (along with Linda Harmon). Such tunes as "Come on-a My House," "A–

Tisket A-Tasket," and "Blue Hawaii" did not need to be revived, and even the better songs come across as sounding clichéd. Why listen to this version of "When You're Smiling" when one can hear Louis Prima's (or Louis Armstrong's) record? This is the type of set that lowers the quality of the Retro Swing movement.

LPS TO SEARCH FOR

My Mommy & Me (Sea Breeze 2013) features Catingub's big band in 1983. There are three fine vocal numbers for Mavis Rivers, Catingub's arrangements are colorful, and his band swings hard. *Hi-Tech Big Band* (Sea Breeze 2025) is the project on which five songs are played by Catingub alone (via overdubbing), including a masterful rendition of "Don't Be That Way." The other six numbers are by Catingub's real big band, with solos from pianist Jim Cox, valve trombonist Mike Fahn, trombonist Andy Martin, and Eric Marienthal (on tenor), plus two vocals by Mavis Rivers.

PAGE CAVANAUGH

b. Jan. 26, 1922, Cherokee, KS

Page Cavanaugh gained fame during the second half of the 1940s with his piano-guitar-bass trio, a unit that had similarities to the King Cole Trio but carved out its own niche with group vocals and Cavanaugh's own charming singing. Page began playing piano when he was nine, worked with the Ernie Williamson band (1938–39), and, while in the military, began teaming up with guitarist Al Viola and bassist Lloyd Pratt. Upon their discharge, the trio settled in Los Angeles, gigged locally, and quickly caught on. They appeared together in films (often backing Doris Day) and had hit records in "All of Me," "Walkin' My Baby Back Home," and "The Three Little Bears." The interplay between Cavanaugh and Viola was always noteworthy. Viola departed in 1950 (working in the studios and with Frank Sinatra) while Cavanaugh continued performing steadily in L.A. through the decades, usually leading a trio or quartet. In the early 1960s for a few years, he headed the Page 7, which consisted of a four-piece rhythm section, two trombones, and a baritone sax. In the late 1980s Cavanaugh and Viola began a reunion that lasted nearly a decade, and Page Cavanaugh recorded a couple of impressive CDs for Star Line that showed that he was still in prime form, singing and playing piano in typically charming fashion.

●

7 *Page Three* / *1967* / *Star Line 9012*

9 *Page One* / *Jan. 12, 1989* / *Star Line 9001*

9 *Page Two* / *Jan. 12, 1989* / *Star Line 9006*

Unfortunately the early recordings of the original Page Cavanaugh Trio have yet to be reissued on CD. The Star Line label has come out with three CDs of Cavanaugh's later performances. The music on *Page Three,* a trio date with bassist Jerry Pulera and drummer Warren Nelson, was not released for the first time until 1996. These live performances are well recorded, and Cavanaugh swings his way through the standards, including an offbeat (literally) version of "I Got Rhythm" that adds three extra beats during the melody chorus (to throw off dancers?). *Page One* and *Page Two* were recorded at the same performance and are released in the same order that they were originally played. Cavanaugh teams up with his old musical friend, guitarist Al Viola, and bassist Alvin Jackson for a variety of his favorite songs. The instrumentals feature fine musical communication between Cavanaugh and Viola. *Page One* is highlighted by "Strike Up the Band," "Love of My Life" (Artie Shaw's best original), and "Whatever Became of Me"; *Page Two* includes "Too Marvelous for Words," "As Long As I Live," "Baby, Baby All the Time," and "Give Me the Simple Life."

FILMS

The Page Cavanaugh Trio has feature numbers in *A Song Is Born* (1948), *Romance on the High Seas* (1948), *Big City* (1948), and *Lullaby of Broadway* (1951).

THE CHEATHAMS

Pianist-singer Jeannie Cheatham and her husband, bass trombonist–arranger Jimmy Cheatham, formed the Sweet Baby Blues Band (also known as the Cheathams) in 1984, an exciting Kansas City blues and Swing group that usually featured at least four horn soloists plus Jeannie's piano and vocals. Jeannie and Jimmy met in the mid-1950s and were married a few years later. Jeannie had accompanied a variety of singers (including Dinah Washington, Al Hibbler, and Jimmy Witherspoon), while Jimmy had worked in bands on Broadway and in the studios; he would perform with Chico Hamilton in the mid-1960s. Neither was particularly famous when they moved to San Diego in the late 1970s, but their Sweet Baby Blues Band soon caught on and began recording regularly for Concord. The Cheathams through the years have used trumpeters Snooky Young and Clora Bryant, clarinetist Jimmy Noone Jr., altoist Curtis Peagler, tenor saxophonist Rickey Woodard, and bassist Red Callender, among others, in their rollicking band. The Sweet Baby Blues Band's recordings also find the group welcoming a notable guest on most of their projects. It is surprising that more bands have not popped up to follow in the Cheathams' path.

●

9 *Sweet Baby Blues* / *Sept. 1984* / *Concord Jazz 4258*

8 *Midnight Mama* / *Nov. 1985* / *Concord Jazz 4297*

8 *Homeward Bound* / *Jan. 1987* / *Concord Jazz 4321*

8 *Back to the Neighborhood* / *Nov. 1988* / *Concord Jazz 4373*

9 *Luv in the Afternoon* / *May 1990* / *Concord Jazz 4429*

8 *Basket Full of Blues* / *Nov. 6–8, 1991* / *Concord Jazz 4501*

8 *Blues and the Boogie Masters* / *July 1993* / *Concord Jazz 4579*

8 *Gud Nuz Bluz* / *Sept. 27–28, 1995* / *Concord Jazz 4690*

From the start, the Cheathams knew the type of music that they wished to play: uncomplicated Swing with an emphasis on Kansas City–style blues. Unlike other blues bands, the

Cheathams have generally been eight or nine pieces and, rather than just having a horn section that played parts, their sidemen were given plenty of opportunities to solo. Because the basic style has been unchanged since at least 1984 and the band's music has been consistent, all eight of their Concord releases are well worth picking up. *Sweet Baby Blues* has trumpeter Snooky Young, altoist Charles McPherson, Curtis Peagler on alto and tenor, and Jimmie Noone Jr. on soprano and clarinet all getting solo space. It alternates 1930s Kansas City standards with basic originals, including the popular "Meet Me with Your Black Drawers On." *Midnight Mama* has multireedist Dinky Morris (who rarely soloed) replacing McPherson and Eddie "Lockjaw" Davis being the band's first guest. *Homeward Bound* benefits from Eddie "Cleanhead" Vinson's alto playing and vocals, while *Back to the Neighborhood* finds the group growing to nine pieces with the addition of trumpeter Clora Bryant; this time around blues/rock violinist Papa John Creech gets to be the featured guest. Tenorman Herman Riley subs for Noone on half of the program, including "Big Bubba's Back Rub Boogie Blues" and "Take the Wrinkles out of Your Birthday Suit."

Luv in the Afternoon has Nolan Smith in Clora Bryant's place and some exciting guitar solos by Clarence "Gatemouth" Brown, a bluesman who has always loved Swing. Jimmie Noone's sickness and eventual death led to his being replaced by tenor saxophonist Rickey Woodard (who is also an underrated clarinetist) on *Basket Full of Blues*; this time Frank Wess (on flute and tenor) is the guest star and the band recorded "Don't Cha Boogie with Your Black Drawers Off." Red Callender was the Cheathams' bassist for their first six albums, until he passed on; Richard Reid took his place starting with *Blues and the Boogie Masters,* while Charles Owens filled in for the late Curtis Peagler. Altoist Hank Crawford fit in perfectly with the band on four of the 11 selections. The Sweet Baby Blues Band's most recent CD, *Gud Nuz Blues,* has Louis Taylor taking over Owens's spot, tenorman Plas Johnson sitting in with the group, and John "Iron Man" Harris keeping his record perfect as the band's drummer on all of their eight recordings. Jeannie Cheatham (always a fine singer and pianist) and the band always sound enthusiastic and fresh playing their timeless and happy brand of Kansas City Swing.

DOC CHEATHAM
b. June 13, 1905, Nashville, TN, d. June 2, 1997, Washington D.C.

Adolphus "Doc" Cheatham was a phenomenon, a trumpeter who improved as a soloist while in his '70s and '80s and at the age of 91 was still playing in his prime! No trumpeter over the age of 70 was ever on his level. Cheatham was a late bloomer in the extreme, because he was not even known as a soloist until he was already in his mid-60s, an age at which nearly every trumpeter begins fading.

Cheatham began playing professionally in the early 1920s, including with John Williams's Synco Jazzers. After he moved to Chicago in 1925, he recorded with Ma Rainey (on soprano sax, which he soon gave up), gigged with Albert Wynn, and played with show bands, including substituting for Louis Armstrong. After working in Philadelphia with Wilbur DeParis (1927–28) and in New York with Chick Webb, Cheatham joined Sam Wooding's orchestra, performing in Europe with Wooding during 1928–30. He worked with Marion Hardy's Alabamians (1930–32) and McKinney's Cotton Pickers, and then Cheatham became Cab Calloway's first trumpeter (1933–39); while there his tone and range were admired by fellow musicians but he was given very few solos.

After leaving Calloway, Cheatham worked with the Teddy Wilson Big Band, Benny Carter, Fletcher Henderson (1941), and most notably the Eddie Heywood Sextet (1943–45). After the Swing era ended, Cheatham struggled a bit but, due to his fine musicianship, he was able to work with Latin bands (including those of Marcelina Guerina, Perez Prado, Machito, and Herbie Mann) and in the world of trad jazz (Vic Dickenson, Eddie Condon, Sammy Price, and Wilbur DeParis's New New Orleans Jazz Band). Cheatham led a band at the International in New York during 1960–65 and was with Benny Goodman during 1966–67.

Still, Cheatham was barely known at all except as a journeyman until the early 1970s, when he began to record and perform

Doc Cheatham, the greatest 90-year-old trumpeter of all time
and in the 1990s one of the last links to the 1920s.

as a soloist in Mainstream Swing and Dixieland settings. He seemed to appear out of nowhere, and for his final 25 years Doc became an increasingly celebrated living link to the early days of jazz. Not only could he tell colorful stories about King Oliver and take charming vocals, but Cheatham could play one strong chorus after another with impressive energy. His solo style by the mid-1970s was quite distinctive, his range (even in the mid-1990s) was still mostly intact, and he took chances in his solos.

Doc Cheatham remained active up until the end, recording his last studio album at the age of 91 with 23-year-old trumpeter Nicholas Payton and playing a final gig the day before suffering from a stroke that resulted in his death two days later.

●

7 *Duets & Solos / Nov. 17, 1976–Nov. 1, 1979 / Sackville 5002*

7 *At the Bern Jazz Festival / Apr. 30, 1983–Jan. 5, 1985 / Sackville 3045*

9 *The Fabulous Doc Cheatham / Nov. 16–17, 1983 / Parkwood 104*

8 *Dear Doc / Aug. 30–31, 1988 / Orange Blue 005*
Although Doc Cheatham had recorded a lesser-known date for the Black & Blue label in 1975, it was his first duet project

with Sammy Price the following year that alerted the jazz world that this 71-year-old survivor of the 1920s was someone who should be paid attention to. *Duets & Solos* combines the music from two trumpet-piano duet albums and a solo session (*Sweet Substitute*) by Sammy Price. Cheatham and Price both sound in excellent form on the Swing standards and basic originals. The *At the Bern Jazz Festival* CD is co-led by Doc and soprano saxophonist Jim Galloway, who play with a Canadian rhythm section and trombonist Roy Williams. In addition to six performances (including

"Cherry," "Limehouse Blues," and "Love Is Just Around the Corner") from the 1983 Bern Festival, there are three cuts taken from Cheatham's two guest appearances with the band during 1984–85, including a heated "Swing That Music." *The Fabulous Doc Cheatham* (made when he was 78) is particularly inspired, with Cheatham and pianist Dick Wellstood showcased in a quartet. Doc sounds quite ageless on such numbers as " 'Deed I Do," "Swing That Music," "Jeepers Creepers," and "I Double Dare You," often taking charming vocals too. *Dear Doc* is in a similar format (a trio with pianist Kenny Drew, bassist Jimmy Woode, and drummer Idris Muhammad), with "I Double Dare You" being repeated. It was five years later but Cheatham showed no sign of any decline. Highlights include "I Only Have Eyes for You," "Dinah," and "Drop Me Off in Harlem."

7 *You're a Sweetheart / Mar. 29, 1992 + Nov. 15, 1992 / Sackville 2038*

7 *Live at Sweet Basil / Apr. 18, 1992 / Jazzology 283*

10 *The Eighty-Seven Years of Doc Cheatham / Sept. 17–18, 1992 / Columbia 53215*

9 *Swinging Down in New Orleans / 1994 / Jazzology 233*

10 *Doc Cheatham & Nicholas Payton / Oct. 4, 1996–Nov. 21, 1996 / Verve 314 537 062*

Doc Cheatham is in fine form on *You're a Sweetheart* but is actually well featured on only six of the CD's 11 cuts. The main reason to acquire this CD is for the playing of bassist Rosemary Galloway's Swing Sisters, a quintet that was originally all females but at this point had only three women out of the five musicians; Jim Galloway guests on soprano and tenor. Trumpeter Sarah McElcheran and Jane Fair (on tenor and clarinet) are impressive and deserve to be better known. The music is primarily Swing-oriented, with the two cuts without Cheatham being more hard bop than Swing. Cheatham's one Columbia record allowed Doc to use his regularly working quartet (pianist Chuck Folds, bassist Bucky Calabrese, and drummer Jackie Williams) and finds Doc sounding remarkably strong on such tunes as the touching "That's My Home," "New Orleans," "Wolverine Blues," and his theme, "I Guess I'll Get the Papers and Go Home." Cheatham dominates the music on *Swinging Down in New Orleans*, a Dixielandish date filled with standards and also including strong solos from Sammy Rimington (on clarinet, alto, and tenor) and bassist Arvell Shaw (who takes two vocals). Cheatham stretches out on such numbers as "When I Grow Too Old to Dream," "I Want a Little Girl," "Never Swat a Fly," "I Would Do Anything for You," and "Struttin' with Some Barbecue."

Doc Cheatham's final recording (other than a unique meeting with Benny Waters a few months later) finds the 91-year-old trumpeter holding his own with 23-year-old Nicholas Payton; in fact, sometimes in the ensembles the high notes are taken by Doc! Payton, who is a versatile player, sticks exclusively to New Orleans jazz during the exploration of 1920s and '30s standards such as "Jeepers Creepers," "Dinah," "I Cover the Waterfront," and "The World Is Waiting for the Sunrise." A classic.

FILMS

Doc Cheatham has a small but tasteful part in *The Sound of Jazz* (1957), appearing with Billie Holiday on "Fine and Mellow."

CLAYTON-HAMILTON JAZZ ORCHESTRA

A swinging big band based in Los Angeles, the Clayton-Hamilton Jazz Orchestra was founded in the late 1980s and has three co-leaders: bassist-arranger John Clayton (b. Aug. 20, 1952, Venice, CA), his brother, altoist Jeff Clayton (b. Feb. 4, 1954, Venice, CA), and drummer Jeff Hamilton (b. Aug. 4, 1953, Richmond, IL). John Clayton, who had previously played with Monty Alexander and for two years with Count Basie's orchestra, writes nearly all of the Clayton-Hamilton band's arrangements, and they tend to retain the flavor of an updated Basie band with touches of Thad Jones. Jeff Hamilton was one of the best big band drummers of the 1990s (but was also a strong asset in small groups led by Monty Alexander, bassist Ray Brown, and pianist Gene Harris), while Jeff Clayton's Cannonball Adderley–inspired alto has been an important part of the band's sound. Other major players in the orchestra's regular lineup include pianist Bill Cunliffe, trumpeters Snooky Young and Oscar Brashear, and the tenors of Rickey Woodard and Charles Owens. In the late 1990s the Clayton-Hamilton Jazz Orchestra recorded a fine album with vibraphonist Milt Jackson and was the house jazz band for the Hollywood Bowl.

9 *Groove Shop / Apr. 18–19, 1989 / Capri 74021*

8 *Heart and Soul / Feb. 1991 / Capri 74028*

8 *Absolutely! / 1994 / Lake Street 52002*

Considering their stature in the L. A. area and the quality of the band, it is surprising that the Clayton-Hamilton Jazz Orchestra has recorded only three CDs thus far (other than their project with Milt Jackson), and all for small labels. *Groove Shop* has particularly strong material, including a feature for Rickey Woodard's tenor on a medium-tempo "Georgia," Snooky Young's showcase on " 'Taint What You Do," some wonderful brush work by Jeff Hamilton on "Brush This," Oscar Brashear's catchy "Sashay," and a lengthy "Night Train." *Heart and Soul* has an unusually slow version of "Take the 'A' Train," Benny Carter's "Easy Money," and "Blues Blower's Blues," which features all five saxophonists taking tenor solos. *Absolutely!* is highlighted by a beautiful rendition of "For All We Know" (featuring pianist Bill Cunliffe) and a Count Basie-inspired "Blues for Stephanie." All three CDs are quite enjoyable and worth searching for.

ROSEMARY CLOONEY
b. May 23, 1928, Maysville, KY

Rosemary Clooney, like Mel Torme, seemed to improve as she got older, although she was always an impressive singer. She started out as part of the Clooney Sisters with Betty Clooney. They sang locally in Cincinnati as teenagers and performed in Tony Pastor's band during 1946–49. After signing with Columbia in 1950 (at which time Betty retired), Rosemary Clooney had a very successful solo career. She had 13 hits in the 1950s, including the novelty "Come on-a My Place," starred in the movie *White Christmas* with Bing Crosby and Danny Kaye, and recorded *Blue Rose* with Duke Ellington in 1956. During most of the 1950s and '60s she was considered a top-notch middle-of-the-road pop singer, although her career faded during the 1960s. But in 1977 Clooney began recording for the Concord label in Swing settings, usually backed by a jazz combo that included Scott Hamilton and Warren Vache. Although Rosemary Clooney (who did not start showing her age until the mid-1990s) never improvised, she uplifted lyrics in a manner similar to Maxine Sullivan and always swung. Most of her Concord recordings (particularly the ones with a Swing combo) rank with the best work of her career.

9 *Blue Rose / Jan. 23–27, 1956 / Columbia/Legacy 65506*

7 *Rosie Solves the Swingin' Riddle / May 25, 1960–June 2, 1960 / Koch 7991*

During a period when she recorded mostly pop music and ballads, Rosemary Clooney showed on these two releases that she definitely had a strong feeling for melodic jazz. *Blue Rose* had her overdubbing vocals to tracks laid down by the Duke Ellington Orchestra, and she certainly sounds as if she were actually singing live with the band; Billy Strayhorn's coaching definitely helped. Particularly strong are "Hey Baby," "It Don't Mean a Thing," "Blue Rose," and "I'm Checkin' Out, Goombye." Among the soloists are Johnny Hodges, Ray Nance, Harry Carney, and Jimmy Hamilton. *Rosie Solves the Swingin' Riddle* finds her backed by the Nelson Riddle Orchestra. Clooney and Riddle were very close friends during this era and the mutual love shows in the care that Riddle gave the arrangements. Rosie sounds in top form on such numbers as "Get Me to the Church on Time," "You Took Advantage of Me," "By Myself," and "Cabin in the Sky."

7 *Everything's Coming Up Rosie / July 7, 1977 / Concord Jazz 4047*

8 *Rosie Sings Bing / Jan. 6, 1978 / Concord Jazz 4060*

9 *Tribute to Billie Holiday / Sept. 1978 / Concord Jazz 4081*

8 *Sings the Lyrics of Ira Gershwin / Oct. 1979 / Concord Jazz 4112*

7 *With Love / Nov. 1980 / Concord Jazz 4144*

8 *Sings the Music of Cole Porter / Jan. 1982 / Concord Jazz 4195*

9 *Sings the Music of Harold Arlen / 1983 / Concord Jazz 4210*

4 *My Buddy / Aug. 1983 / Concord Jazz 4226*

8 *Sings the Music of Irving Berlin / June 1984 / Concord Jazz 4255*

7 *Sings Ballads / Apr. 1985 / Concord Jazz 4282*

8 *Sings the Music of Jimmy Van Heusen / Apr. 1986 / Concord Jazz 4308*

9 *Sings the Lyrics of Johnny Mercer / Aug. 1987 / Concord Jazz 4333*

8 *Show Tunes / Aug. 1988–Nov. 1988 / Concord Jazz 4364*
In 1977, with the recording of *Everything's Coming Up Rosie*, Rosemary Clooney began a complete comeback that has resulted in a very rich second career. Her Concord recordings of 1978–88 (with the exception of *My Buddy*) always include tenor saxophonist Scott Hamilton in her supporting cast, a swinging rhythm section, and (except for the two earliest discs and *My Buddy*) cornetist Warren Vache. The singer's first 13 Concord recordings do not really require in-depth analysis, for her interpretations of the standards are quite straightforward and lightly swinging. The only misfire is *My Buddy*, a collaboration with the Woody Herman Orchestra (which here sounds like a college stage band) that finds Clooney trying to make something out of such dubious "modern" material as "I Believe in Love" and "Don't Let Me Be Lonely Tonight." But all of the other albums, which include well-conceived tributes to Bing Crosby and Billie Holiday, several songbooks, and consistently high-quality material, rank with the best work of Rosemary Clooney's career.

7 *Sings Rodgers, Hart & Hammerstein / Oct. 1989 / Concord Jazz 4405*

8 *For the Duration / Oct. 15–17, 1990 / Concord Jazz 4444*

7 *Girl Singer / Nov. 1991–Dec. 1991 / Concord Jazz 4496*

7 *Do You Miss New York? / Sept. 14–17, 1992 / Concord Jazz 4537*

6 *Still on the Road / 1993 / Concord Jazz 4590*

7 *Demi-Centennial / Oct. 10, 1994–Nov. 11, 1994 / Concord Jazz 4633*

8 *Dedicated to Nelson / Sept. 27–30, 1995 / Concord Jazz 4685*

5 *White Christmas / Apr. 1–4, 1996 / Concord Jazz 4719*

3 *Mothers & Daughters / June 23, 1996–Oct. 24, 1996 / Concord Jazz 4754*
Age 61 at the time of *Sings Rodgers, Hart & Hammerstein*, Rosemary Clooney was still in top form. That particular project has her joined by the 12-voice L.A. Jazz Choir on six numbers along with Scott Hamilton and trumpeter Jack Sheldon (who sings "People Will Say We're in Love" with Clooney). While *For the Duration* and *Do You Miss New York?* find the singer joined by the usual Hamilton-Vache team, *Girl Singer* is a big band date that pays tribute to the Swing singers of the 1930s/'40s, although a few of the songs (including pieces by Dave Frishberg, Johnny Mandel, and Jobim) were not around during that era! After *Do You Miss New York?*, Clooney recorded primarily with orchestras and the music was less jazz-oriented. *Still on the Road* mixes a variety of road and travel songs, including both later material ("Still Crazy After All These Years" and "Rules of the Road") and vintage material ("Let's Get Away From It All" and "Till We Meet Again"). The nostalgic *Demi-Centennial* celebrates Rosemary Clooney's 50th year in show business and, in addition to performing some of her favorite songs (including "Danny Boy," "Old Friends," "There Will Never Be Another You," and Dave Frishberg's "Dear Departed Past"), there is a duet with Clooney's niece (Betty Clooney's daughter) on "The Coffee Song." *Dedicated to Nelson* finds Clooney performing the late Nelson Riddle's arrangements which were originally written for her late 1950s television show. Clooney is assisted by a big band, with solos from tenor saxophonist Tommy Newsom, trumpeter Warren Luening, and altoist Gary Foster. Age 68 at the time of *White Christmas*, Clooney for the first time started to show her age in her voice, and this best-selling set (her first full-length Christmas album) and the somewhat sappy *Mothers & Daughters* (try to sit through "Thank Heaven for Little Girls!") are both weak. But there are many superior Rosemary Clooney Concord albums to choose from.

ARNETT COBB

b. Aug. 10, 1918, Houston, TX, d. Mar. 24, 1989, Houston, TX

A tough-toned tenor who followed in the wake of Illinois Jacquet and carved out a legacy of his own, Arnett Cobb played in a Swing-based style and was an influence on the early R&B honkers. Born Arnette Cobbs (a name he later changed), he briefly played piano and violin before switching to tenor. Cobb worked with Frank Davis (1933), Chester Boone (1934–36), and the important but unrecorded Milt Larkin Orchestra (1936–42). Cobb gained his initial fame while with Lionel Hampton's big band (1942–47), honking away on "Flying Home #2" and adding emotion and excitement to many other recordings. Cobb would unfortunately be plagued with physical problems throughout his career. He led a popular band in 1948, but bad health (resulting in an operation on his spine) made it a short-lived venture. He reemerged in 1951 and had a jumping combo for five years. But a serious car crash in 1956 permanently injured his legs and he was forced to use crutches for the remainder of his life. Cobb made a comeback by 1959, moved to Houston, and played locally throughout much of the rest of his career. However, Arnett Cobb returned to the national scene on an occasional basis starting in the early 1970s, and his playing remained quite strong, unchanged from his glory years.

●

10 *Arnett Blows for 1300 / May 1947–Aug. 1947 / Delmark 471*

With the exception of four songs cut for the Hamp-Tone label in 1946, the 15 selections on this disc are all of Arnett Cobb's pre-1950 recordings as a leader. There is plenty of excitement during these concise performances, with Cobb heading a hot jump sextet that includes trumpeter David Page and trombonist Booty Wood and has two vocals from his old boss, Milt Larkin. The music is frequently explosive and shows why Cobb had the potential to become a major name during this era and a possible challenger to Illinois Jacquet.

9 *Blow, Arnett, Blow / Jan. 9, 1959 / Original Jazz Classics 794*

8 *Smooth Sailing / Feb. 27, 1959 / Original Jazz Classics 323*

9 *Party Time / May 14, 1959 / Original Jazz Classics 219*

8 *More Party Time / Feb. 16–17, 1960 / Original Jazz Classics 979*

6 *Blue and Sentimental / Oct. 31, 1960–Nov. 13, 1960 / Prestige 24122*

After Arnett Cobb made his first comeback from bad health, he recorded some isolated titles during 1950–56. A serious car crash ruined his walking and put him out of action for two years, but during 1959–60 Cobb recorded quite steadily for the Prestige label, including the music heard on these five

CDs. Arnett Cobb tangles with fellow tenor Eddie "Lockjaw" Davis on *Blow, Arnett, Blow* and battles him to a draw on a variety of heated riff numbers; the Wild Bill Davis Trio roars in the background. *Smooth Sailing* puts the focus more on Cobb in a quintet with trombonist Buster Cooper and a trio headed by organist Austin Mitchell. The tenorman is in top form on three Swing-era standards and a variety of blues and riff pieces. *Party Time* has Cobb as the only horn in a quintet that also features pianist Ray Bryant; his versions of "When My Dreamboat Comes Home," "Flying Home," and "Lonesome Road" are soulful and hard-stomping. *More Party Time* has a similar format, with Tommy Flanagan or (on one cut) Bobby Timmons on piano. Cobb's ability to caress melodies and uplift such familiar tunes as "Lover, Come Back to Me," "Swanee River," and "Down by the Riverside" makes this CD another gem. *Blue and Sentimental* has all of the music from two former albums: the well-rounded *Sizzlin'* and the rather sleepy *Ballads,* which has a definite sameness to each of the songs. It is still worth picking up but not up to the overall level of the other Arnett Cobb Prestige sets.

9 *Live at Sandy's / Aug. 25–26, 1978 / Muse 5558*

After moving back to Texas in the early 1960s, Arnett Cobb would reappear on the national scene every once in awhile, showing listeners who might have forgotten about him how strong he still was. *Live at Sandy's* has eight of the nine selections that were included on Cobb's two Muse albums, although it mistakenly only has the liner notes from the first album (plus a few additional paragraphs). Five of the numbers feature Cobb in a quartet with pianist Ray Bryant, bassist George Duvivier, and drummer Alan Dawson. Buddy Tate drops by for tenor battles on "Go Red Go" and "Flyin' Home," and altoist Eddie "Cleanhead" Vinson makes the band a septet on "Blues for Lester." Recommended and one of the strongest of Arnett Cobb's records from his later period.

The Wild Man from Texas (Classics 102) finds Cobb sounding inspired on a variety of romps with a nonet in 1976. *Arnett Cobb Is Back* (Progressive 7037) and *Funky Butt* (Progressive 7054) are solid quartet outings from 1978 and 1980, with versions of "Flying Home," "Sweet Georgia Brown," and "Take the 'A' Train" on the former, while the latter includes roaring renditions of "Jumpin' at the Woodside" and "I Got Rhythm."

FREDDY COLE

b. Oct. 15, 1931, Chicago, IL

The younger brother of Nat King Cole (who was 14 years his senior), Freddy Cole did not catch on as a pianist-singer until the 1990s, despite a long career. He began playing piano when he was five and was a professional by the early 1950s but was obscure for nearly 40 years. Cole recorded a single ("The Joke's on Me") as early as 1952 and cut an album for Dot in 1959 but was not able to emerge from his brother's shadow. A mid-1970s Audiophile set found him sounding fine, but it was not until he recorded for Sunnyside in 1990 (when he was already 59) that Freddy Cole began to be discovered. A few years later he signed with the Fantasy label and was finally in great demand. Possessor of a boppish piano style more modern than his older brother's, Freddy Cole does resemble Nat King Cole in his vocals except that he is older (Nat did not make it to his 48th birthday) and has a darker tone. With the shortage of male jazz-oriented singers in the late 1990s, Freddy Cole finally began to receive long-overdue recognition.

●

9 *I'm Not My Brother, I'm Me / Dec. 4, 1990 / Sunnyside 1054*

8 *Live at Birdland West / Apr. 18, 1992 / LaserLight 17 015*

7 *This Is the Life / Jan. 13, 1993 / Muse 5503*

7 *A Circle of Love / Sept. 26, 1993–Dec. 5, 1995 / Fantasy 9674*

7 *Always / Dec. 1994 / Fantasy 7670*

7 *To the Ends of the Earth / Jan. 6–7, 1997 / Fantasy 9675*

8 *Love Makes the Changes / Jan. 6–7, 1998 / Fantasy 9681*

Although Freddie Cole may have been trying to escape from his brother's shadow on his Sunnyside CD, one cannot take his plight too seriously, since he utilizes the same instrumentation as the Nat King Cole Trio (with guitarist Ed Zad and bassist Eddie Edwards) and not only revives a few songs associated with his brother (such as "Home Fried Potatoes," "Sunday, Monday, Always," and "The Best Man") but plays a five-song "Nat Cole Medley" plus tributes in "He Was the King" and the title cut! However, despite the similarities, Freddie Cole does show individuality and his piano playing is based in the 1950s rather than (in Nat's case) the 1930s. *Live at Birdland West* is a budget set with a playing time on the level of an LP and repeats a couple of songs from the Sunnyside album. However, Cole is joined by a quintet in this case (including the great Red Holloway on tenor and alto) and his versions of "I Almost Lost My Mind," "Walkin' My Baby Back Home" and "Send for Me" are memorable. *This Is the Life* is a fine effort with a septet that includes tenorman Houston Person and trumpeter Cecil Bridgewater, mixing older songs (such as "Easy to Love" and "Sunday Kind of Love") with some newer tunes, including two of his originals. On *A Circle of Love* and *Always*, Cole is cast in the role of a warm ballad singer, playing piano on only two of the dozen numbers on the former and not at all on the latter.

The emphasis is on slower material, with *Always* including strings on some tracks. *To the Ends of the Earth* is in a similar vein, with Cole interpreting such songs as "I Didn't Mean to Love You," "For All We Know," "Love Walked In," and "I'll Be Seeing You" in settings ranging from duets to a collaboration with a ten-piece group. *Love Makes the Changes* has mostly lesser-known but superior material, with Cole joined by pianist Cedar Walton, Grover Washington, Jr., on tenor and soprano, and a strong rhythm section. Other than at occasional moments, Freddie Cole no longer sounded like a shadow of his brother and had developed into a surprisingly individual singer.

HARRY CONNICK, JR.
b. Sept. 11, 1967, New Orleans, LA

Harry Connick, Jr., has definitely had an interesting career, as a singer-pianist in several genres and as an actor. At this point in time, he is not taken too seriously in jazz circles, but he still has the potential to make a strong impact and he had helped in the late 1980s to make the general public aware of the continuing viability of Swing.

The son of a New Orleans district attorney who loves jazz, Connick started playing piano when he was three and was gigging in public a few years later; an album came out years later of him playing with a Dixieland band when he was just 11. He studied at the New Orleans Center for the Creative Arts (Ellis Marsalis was one of his teachers) and in New York at Hunter College and the Manhattan School of Music. Signed to the Columbia label while still a teenager, Connick recorded two jazz sets that found the young pianist performing Swing and New Orleans jazz standards and taking his first vocals. While his time could be unsteady when playing duets with a bassist, Connick soon added a drummer to his group, which solved that problem. In 1989 he recorded vocals and a few piano spots with a big band for the soundtrack of *When Harry Met Sally,* performing mostly standards from the 1930s. That very successful project gave him fame beyond the jazz world.

At that point, Connick's career changed. He toured with a big band (playing mostly his own compositions), became a household name, and started working as an actor, including appearing in such movies as *Memphis Belle, Copycat,* and *Independence Day.* His vocals became much more Frank Sinatra-oriented (it was a mistake watering down his own individual sound), and his recordings alternated between the standards-oriented CD *25* to such forgettable pop dates as *She* and *Star Turtle.* Harry Connick, Jr. (who was just 32 as the century ended) still has a lot of potential, and it will be interesting to watch his future development.

●

3   *11 / Nov. 4–11, 1978 / Columbia 53171*

6   *Harry Connick, Jr. / 1987 / Columbia 40702*

8   *20 / May 4, 1988–June 29, 1988 / Columbia 44369*

9   *When Harry Met Sally / June 1989 / Columbia 45319*

11 was released in 1992 and was put out because the 11-year-old pianist was Harry Connick, Jr. His piano solos are fairly simple and his vocal on "Doctor Jazz" does not deserve a second listen! The Dixieland band is barely OK, with trumpeter Teddy Riley sounding quite erratic. Connick's real debut was on his self-titled album in 1987, and he is heard playing mostly stride piano in the style of Thelonious Monk. Bassist Ron Carter and the bass-drum team of Reginald Veal and Herlin Riley help out on a couple of numbers, but otherwise this is an interesting if not essential solo set. *20,* which is also mostly a solo set, is on a higher level, with stronger material (mostly Swing standards), Connick's first vocals, a guest spot for singer Carmen McRae on "Please Don't Talk About Me When I'm Gone," and one appearance apiece by organist-singer Dr. John and bassist Robert Hurst. Connick's renditions of "Avalon," "Blue Skies," "Lazy River," and "Do Nothin' Till You Hear from Me" make one wish that he had continued in this direction. Harry Connick's voice and occasional piano were heard throughout the soundtrack of *When Harry Met Sally* and the accompanying album stands apart from the movie. Connick is joined by a rhythm section and sometimes a big band, making such songs as "It Had to Be You," "Our Love Is Here to Stay," "But Not for Me," and "Where or When" sound fresh and new. This album is a classic of its kind and one of the high points of Harry Connick's career.

7 *We Are in Love / Mar. 7, 1990–May 1, 1990 / Columbia 46146*

6 *Lofty's Roach Soufflé / Apr. 4–22, 1990 / Columbia 46223*

4 *Blue Light, Red Light / June 27, 1991–July 14, 1991 / Columbia 48685*

8 *25 / Oct. 2–9, 1992 / Columbia 53172*

6 *To See You / Aug. 4–10, 1997 / Columbia 68787*

In 1990 Harry Connick, Jr., was doing his best to carve out an individual path for himself, writing many new songs and releasing both a vocal and an instrumental album at the same time. Unfortunately composing has not proven to be one of his strong talents! *We Are in Love,* the vocal date, has appearances by guitarist Russell Malone and a couple of guest shots for Branford Marsalis on tenor and soprano; there is also an orchestra on most of the tunes. Although Connick wrote the great majority of the material, the highlights are his vocal versions of the two standards "A Nightingale Sang in Berkeley Square" and "It's Alright with Me." *Lofty's Roach Soufflé,* a trio outing with bassist Benjamin Wolfe and drummer Shannon Powell, finds Connick sounding more individual as a pianist but weighed down by his 11 so-so originals, none of which caught on. *Blue Light, Red Light* is a disappointment. Although it utilizes a big band with 14 horns, the orchestra is almost totally in support of Connick's vocals and his dozen songs are once again rather forgettable. *25* is much better and it is in a similar style as his earlier *20.* Most of the selections are solo features for Connick's piano and vocals, the tunes are vintage standards (including "Stardust," "On the Street Where You Live," "Tangerine," and the Dixieland standard "Muskrat Ramble"), and there is one appearance apiece by pianist Ellis Marsalis, singer Johnny Adams ("Lazybones), bassist Ray Brown, and tenor saxophonist Ned Goold. After a few wretched pop efforts and some notable acting roles, Harry Connick, Jr., recorded *To See You.* He sings ten of his originals with a quartet and a string section, takes a few short piano solos, and sounds happy to be playing swinging jazz again. Whether he will grow from that point into a major jazz figure (as opposed to merely being a well-known personality) is still not known.

BUSTER COOPER

b. Apr. 4, 1929, St. Petersburg, FL

A rambunctious trombonist whose occasional jumps into the upper register (where he often sounds like he is crying out) are both dramatic and humorous, Buster Cooper has a playing style that has always been colorful. He started out working in Texas with Nat Towles's orchestra, was with Lionel Hampton in 1953, and played for two years in the house band of the Apollo Theatre. After stints with Lucky Millinder and Benny Goodman, he co-led the Cooper Brothers band with his sibling, bassist Steve Cooper. The trombonist gained fame for his work with Duke Ellington (1962–69), where he was well featured and contrasted with the smoother sound of Lawrence Brown. After leaving Ellington, Cooper spent a few years in Florida; in 1973 he moved to Los Angeles, where for the next 24 years he was an important fixture on the jazz scene. Buster Cooper worked regularly with the Capp-Pierce Juggernaut (1976–81), Bill Berry's L.A. Big Band, and many other ensembles. In the late 1990s he moved back to his native Florida.

7 *E-bone-ix / Sept. 1989 / Blue Lady 301*

Buster Cooper's only date as a leader finds him co-leading a straightahead quintet with fellow trombonist Thurman Green. Helped out by fine support from pianist Phil Wright, bassist Louie Spears, and drummer Dave Tucker, the two trombonists jam happily on such tunes as "Straight Up," "Groovin' High," "Will You Still Be Mine?," "B.C. & T.G.," and "Lester Leaps In." Cooper's emotional solos are easy to tell apart from Green's more conventional statements.

WILD BILL DAVIS

b. Nov. 24, 1918, Glasgow, MO, d. Aug. 17, 1995, Moorestown, NJ

One of the most important organists of the 1950s, Wild Bill Davis (who gained his nickname one night when he was booked opposite cornetist Wild Bill Davison!) was always a strong Swing player. He grew up in Parsons, Kansas, and started out as a pianist and guitarist. Davis studied at Tuskegee during 1937–39, played guitar and arranged for Milt Larkins (1939–42), relocated to Chicago, and worked for several shows, contributing a few arrangements to Earl Hines's orchestra. Davis played piano as a member of Louis Jordan's Tympany Five (1945–47), switching to organ shortly after leaving Jordan. He led his own trio throughout the 1950s and was a popular attraction. For Count Basie, Davis arranged "April in Paris," which became a major hit and a trademark song for Basie. In the 1960s Davis teamed up with Johnny Hodges for a series of records and occasional concerts. He was a member of the Duke Ellington Orchestra on and off during 1969–71, recording with Ellington (including appearing on the *70th Birthday Concert*). He visited Europe several times in the 1970s, made records with Buddy Tate, Al Grey, and Illinois Jacquet, and worked with Lionel Hampton (starting in 1978). Wild Bill Davis remained active up until his death, retaining his early style despite the rise of Jimmy Smith in the late 1950s. Unfortunately, very few of his recordings have yet been reissued on CD, and his many Everest and Black & Blue LPs are difficult to find.

BARRETT DEEMS

b. Mar. 1, 1913, Springfield, IL, d. Sept. 15, 1998, Chicago, IL

At one time Barrett Deems was billed as "the world's fastest drummer," and there is a film clip from the early 1950s of him with Wingy Manone that is pretty astounding. However, Deems had an episodic career and emerged as a significant band-leader only during his final decade. He started playing drums when he was ten and was a professional as a teenager. Deems worked with Paul Ash when he was 15 and then mostly led his own band for several years. He gained some recognition for his work with the Joe Venuti Big Band (1937–44), although that orchestra was a minor-league outfit that barely recorded. Deems played with Jimmy Dorsey, Red Norvo (1948), Wingy Manone, Charlie Barnet, and Muggsy Spanier (1951–54). In May 1954 he joined the Louis Armstrong All-Stars, but, although it seemed like a big break, Deems was miscast performing Dixieland, since he was really a Swing drummer, and much of the time he seemed to be overplaying, lacking much subtlety. He was with Satch until February 1958, toured with Jack Teagarden (1960–64), and worked with the Dukes of Dixieland. Deems settled in Chicago and worked locally for the remainder of his life, including with various Mainstream all-stars who were passing through town (such as Buck Clayton, Roy Eldridge, Benny Carter, and Jimmy McPartland). He was a member of the Benny Goodman Sextet during 1976 and also toured with cornetist Wild Bill Davison. Barrett Deems finally found the ideal role for himself when he was in his eighties, as a Buddy Rich–style big band drummer who led his own swinging orchestra; fortunately they made two CDs for Delmark.

●

8   *Deemus / Apr. 22, 1978 / Delmark 492*

9   *How D'You Like It So Far? / Mar. 6–7, 1994 / Delmark 472*

8   *Groovin' Hard / Jan. 18–19, 1998 / Lydia 505*

Deemus is a very likable septet date from 1978 that features Barrett Deems (who was already 65) jamming Swing standards with clarinetist Chuck Hedges and vibraphonist Don DeMichael. Hedges is particularly impressive throughout and the highlights of this frequently hot date include " 'Deed I Do," "Shine," and "Seven Come Eleven"; the final two numbers are trio features for pianist Steve Behr. Deems had been leading a big band for quite a few years when his orchestra finally had a chance to record in 1994. The music on *How D'You Like It So Far?* is primarily modern Swing, with some charts sounding like they could have fit Buddy

Rich, too. The local band lacks any big names (trumpeter Brad Goode is best known among the sidemen) but swings hard and proves to be a perfect vehicle for Deems's drumming. *Groovin' Hard* was recorded just eight months before Deems's death, but the 83-year-old drummer had not declined at all yet musically. He is well featured on such tunes as "Cute," "Well Alright Then," "The Song Is You," and "Moten Swing."

FILMS

Barrett Deems shows off his impressive technique while appearing with Wingy Manone in *Rhythm Inn* (1951), and he appears as part of the Louis Armstrong All-Stars in *High Society* (1956).

FLOYD DIXON
b. Feb. 8, 1928, Marshall, TX

Floyd Dixon's career was similar in ways to that of Charles Brown's. Brown was his main influence and singer-pianist Dixon's life rose and fell during the same periods of time. Dixon moved to Los Angeles when he was 13, and by 1947 the teenager was recording and having some success. In 1949 his versions of "Dallas Blues" and "Mississippi Blues" were hits, and the next few years he followed with "Sad Journey Blues," "Telephone Blues," "Call Operator 210," "Red Cherries," "Wine, Wine, Wine," and his trademark song, "Hey Bartender!" A harder-driving performer than Brown in the early days, Floyd Dixon was a master at jump blues, and, in addition to Charles Brown, his style was touched by Louis Jordan and Amos Milburn.

As with Brown, the rise of rock and roll resulted in Dixon's slipping away into obscurity for many years. However, he survived and in 1989 he began a full comeback that found him playing and singing in mostly prime form throughout the 1990s. ●

[10] *His Complete Aladdin Recordings / 1949–July 18, 1952 / Capitol 36293*

[7] *Marshall Texas Is My Home / June 17, 1953–May 17, 1957 / Specialty 7011*

[8] *Wake Up and Live / 1996 / Alligator 4841*

Floyd Dixon is heard in his early prime during his Aladdin recordings, which include most of his hits. The two-CD "complete" set also has a date by singer Sonnie Parker that Dixon might not be on and vocal tracks by Mari Jones. But it is for the many joyous and jumping Dixon sides (which usually have Maxwell Davis on tenor) that this twofer is essential for the jump music collector. The single *Marshall Texas* CD has all of Dixon's 1953 recordings for the Specialty label and other selections from 1954, 1956, and 1957; 11 of the 22 selections were previously unissued. "Hey Bartender" was a hit, but otherwise Dixon's hit-making days were behind him as rock and roll soon overshadowed his music. However, the performances on this CD (which include "Hard Living Alone," a demo version of "Call Operator 210," "Instrumental Shuffle," and "Oooh Little Girl") are up to his usual level. Decades later, Floyd Dixon was still playing in fine form, as the Alligator set shows, and his version of jump blues was virtually unchanged from the past. Joined by several horns (including Eddie Synigal on tenor), Dixon often sounds exuberant on such songs as "Hey, Bartender," "450-Pound Woman," "I Wanna Rock Now," and "Skeet's California Sunshine."

BILL DOGGETT
b. Feb. 6, 1916, Philadelphia, PA, d. Nov. 13, 1996, New York, NY

Bill Doggett became a household name for a time in the 1950s due to the popularity of "Honky Tonk." An important early organist, Doggett began as a pianist, playing with Jimmy Gorham in the mid-1930s and having his own band a few years later. Lucky Millinder became the front man for Doggett's orchestra in 1938 and eventually took over the group. Doggett remained with Millinder through 1942 except for a short time with Jimmy Mundy's orchestra in late 1939. He worked as an arranger and pianist with the Ink Spots (1942–44), contributed charts to other bands (including the orchestras of Count Basie, Louis Armstrong, and Lionel Hampton), and was with Illinois Jacquet (1945–46) and Willie Bryant before replacing Wild Bill Davis with Louis Jordan's Tympany Five (1948–51). As with Davis, when Doggett eventually left Jordan , he switched to organ. After recording with Ella Fitzgerald, Doggett formed a small R&B combo that recorded a series of popular recordings, hitting it big with "Honky Tonk." Bill Doggett was able to work steadily as a leader throughout the remainder of his career, recording as late as 1991 and sticking to the mixture of early R&B, Swing, and blues that he enjoyed most.

●

7 *The Right Choice / May 14–15, 1991 / After Hours 4112*
One of the few Bill Doggett sets currently available on CD, this jazz-oriented outing teams the organist (then 75) with a variety of fine local East Coast musicians, including trumpeter Eddie Preston and tenors Bubba Brooks and Howard Kimbo, altoists Jimmy Cozier and Bill Easley, and trombonist Denis Wilson. Doggett performs "Honky Tonk," "Things Ain't What They Used to Be," "I'm Ready" (which has a vocal by Toni Williams), and a variety of basic originals, showing that he was still able to perform very viable and swinging music at this late date in his life.

DOROTHY DONEGAN
b. Apr. 6, 1924, Chicago, IL, d. May 19, 1998, Los Angeles, CA

A frequently astounding pianist with a technique on the level of Art Tatum (who was one of her admirers), Dorothy Donegan could play anything, and she often did. Her live concerts often featured medleys of completely unrelated songs (thrown together spontaneously) and found her switching back and forth between stride, boogie-woogie, bebop, and classical; her bass players always had to be very alert!

It seems strange that Donegan never became a household name. She studied at the Chicago Conservatory and Chicago Music College, recording two songs in 1942 and appearing on one dazzling number in the movie *Sensations of 1945* opposite Cab Calloway, with Bennie Payne on second piano. But Donegan recorded quite infrequently during the 1940s, '50s, and '60s, with no records at all during 1964–74. During her final decade (when she was recording for Chiaroscuro), Donegan received some long-overdue recognition and was finally starting to be recognized for her brilliant playing. However, when listeners saw Dorothy Donegan in concert (often proudly showing off her legs and dancing while she was playing), they realized that her records did not fully capture her colorful performances, and many wondered where she had been all of this time. She may very well have been the most underrated jazz pianist of all time.

●

8 *Dorothy Romps / 1953–Mar. 16, 1979 / Rosetta 1318*
7 *Live at the Widder Bar / Dec. 1986 / Timeless 247*
7 *Sophisticated Lady / Jan. 24, 1990 / Ornament 8011*
9 *Live at the 1990 Floating Jazz Festival / Oct. 29, 1990–*
    Nov. 2, 1990 / Chiaroscuro 312
9 *Live at the 1991 Floating Jazz Festival / Oct. 23–30,*
    1991 / Chiaroscuro 318
Dorothy Donegan was only sporadically documented before 1980, so the Rosetta CD is quite valuable. Six of the se-
lections are from lesser-known albums, while the other nine performances were previously unreleased. The music dates from 1953, 1957–58, 1960–61, and 1963, with two cuts from 1979. The lengthy liner notes are an added plus. The Timeless set matches Donegan with bassist Jimmy Woode and drummer Norman Fearrington for unique renditions of "Lover" and "Take the 'A' Train" plus five somewhat crazy medleys, including one of "Like Someone in Love," "Here's That Rainy Day," "For Once in My Life," and "In the Mood!" *Sophisticated Lady* is a lesser-known effort for a European label and shows off the diversity of Donegan's reper-

toire on three songs and a trio of medleys (including one that mixes together "Send in the Clowns," Janis Ian's "Jesse," "You'll Never Walk Alone," "If I Loved You," and "My Way"). But the best Dorothy Donegan CDs to get are the two Chiaroscuros recorded at "Floating Jazz Festivals" aboard the S/S *Norway*. With bassist Jon Burr and drummer Ray Mosca, Donegan is in typically exuberant form. The 1990 CD has among its highlights "Blackbird Boogie," "After Hours," and an intriguing medley of "Someday My Prince Will Come" and "Tiger Rag." The 1991 performance includes "Things Ain't What They Used to Be," "Tea for Two," and "Bumble Bee Boogie," welcoming guest trumpeter Dizzy Gillespie on "Sweet Lorraine."

LPS TO SEARCH FOR

Of her Roulette albums, *At the Embers* (Roulette 25010) and *Live!* (Roulette 1155), both from 1957, are good examples of the excitement that Donegan could generate during her prime. *The Explosive Dorothy Donegan* (Progressive 7056), from 1980 (with bassist Jerome Hunter and drummer Ray Mosca), is so exciting that one wonders why a major label did not latch on to the pianist.

FILMS

Dorothy Donegan steals the show during her one number in *Sensations of 1945* (1944).

BILLY ECKSTINE

b. July 8, 1914, Pittsburgh, PA, d. Mar. 8, 1993, Pittsburgh, PA

One of the great ballad singers, Billy Eckstine was one of the top singers of the 1950s and a major influence on other baritone voices, including Earl Coleman and Johnny Hartman. Eckstine grew up in Pittsburgh and Washington, D.C. He sang locally in both places and in Buffalo and Detroit before moving to Chicago in 1938. After a year as a soloist, Eckstine became a member of Earl Hines's orchestra (1939–43), having a hit with "Jelly Jelly," and catching on as a popular attraction. By 1943 Eckstine had persuaded Hines to add several modernists to his big band, including Charlie Parker, Dizzy Gillespie, and Sarah Vaughan. The following year Eckstine formed his own bebop-oriented orchestra and included that trio as the nucleus of his band. Although essentially a middle-of-the-road ballad singer, Eckstine championed the new music, keeping his big band together for three years and featuring most of the top up-and-coming young players, including trumpeters Miles Davis and Fats Navarro, altoist Sonny Stitt, Gene Ammons and Dexter Gordon on tenors, and drummer Art Blakey, among many others. To give himself something to do on the instrumentals, Eckstine learned to play trumpet and valve trombone fairly well. "Blowin' the Blues Away" was a minor hit.

In 1947 Billy Eckstine reluctantly broke up his orchestra, became a single, and quickly shot to the top of the entertainment world, recording many middle-of-the-road ballad hits for the MGM label, including "I Apologize" and "Everything I Have Is Yours." If it were not for the racism of the period, Eckstine would probably have been given romantic leads in movies. Instead, he worked steadily as a singer in supper clubs, often with pianist Bobby Tucker as his accompanist, and recorded occasionally in a jazz setting, including with the 1953 Metronome All-Stars, a superb 1959 collaboration with Count Basie, and with his lifelong friend Sarah Vaughan. Billy Eckstine remained quite active until a stroke in 1992 ended his career.

●

8 *1944–1945 / Apr. 13, 1944–Oct. 1945 / Classics 914*

7 *1946–1947 / Jan. 3, 1946–Apr. 21, 1947 / Classics 1022*

10 *Everything I Have Is Yours / May 20, 1947–Apr. 26, 1957 / Verve 819 442*

8 *No Cover, No Minimum / Aug. 30, 1960 / Roulette 98583*

Billy Eckstine's bebop big band did not record all that much, but fortunately all of its studio recordings are available on the two Classics CDs. Actually only some of the selections (the instrumentals and a few of the vocals) are boppish, while the remainder are features for the leader's ballad singing. *1944–1945* (which has a few solos by Dizzy Gillespie, Fats Navarro, and tenors Dexter Gordon and Gene Ammons, among others) is most notable for including "Blowing the Blues Away," "Opus X," "A Cottage for Sale," "I Love the Rhythm in a Riff," and "Prisoner of Love." *1946–1947* has the last big band performances and a few numbers with

Billy Eckstine, a Swing-era singer whose warm baritone was at its most influential in the 1950s.

a smaller group; Gene Ammons is the main soloist, although altoist Sonny Stitt and trumpeter Miles Davis are also present. "The Jitney Man," "You're My Everything," "Second Balcony Jump," and "Oo Bop Sh'Bam" are among the better numbers. The two-CD *Everything I Have Is Yours* does a superb job of summing up Billy Eckstine's years on the MGM label. Most of the selections are ballads in which he is backed by a string section (including "Everything I Have Is Yours," "My Foolish Heart," "I Apologize," and "Body and Soul"). There are a few departures from the pop material, including a few numbers with the Woody Herman Orchestra and the George Shearing Quintet, five songs in which he is backed by the Bobby Tucker Quartet, and remarkable versions of "How High the Moon," and "St. Louis Blues" with the 1953 Metronome All-Stars. *No Cover, No Minimum* was recorded one night in Las Vegas with Bobby Tucker and a small orchestra. Eckstine takes a few short trumpet solos, and his voice (on such ballads as "I've Grown Accustomed to Her Face," "Lush Life," "Without a Song," "Prisoner of Love," and "Misty") rarely sounded better.

LPS TO SEARCH FOR

I Want to Talk About You (Xanadu 207) collects 13 of Billy Eckstine's best vocals from his 1940–41 period with Earl Hines (including "Jelly, Jelly" and "Stormy Monday Blues"), plus three numbers from a broadcast by the Eckstine big band of 1945. *Billy Eckstine Sings with Benny Carter* (Emarcy 832011) has the vocalist's final recording, a pretty good 1986 set with the Bobby Tucker Trio and guest altoist Benny Carter (who plays trumpet on "September Song"). There are two vocal duets with Helen Merrill, and in general Eckstine, who does show his age (72) in spots, is in good form.

FILMS

Billy Eckstine's legendary Bebop Orchestra is featured throughout *Rhythm in a Riff* (1946), a short film that is included along with Dizzy Gillespie's *Jivin' in Bebop* on the video *Things to Come* (Vintage Jazz Classics 2006). In addition, the singer appears in *Flicker Up* (1946) and has a small acting role in *Let's Do It Again* (1975).

LES AND LARRY ELGART

In the 1950s, there were few new Swing big bands that made much of an impression. One thinks of Ray Anthony, Billy May, and the Sauter-Finegan Orchestra plus the reorganized Count Basie Orchestra. Although the atmosphere was not that promising for new Swing groups, Les and Larry Elgart managed to be successful for a time, playing nostalgic and somewhat watered-down Swing music that was primarily for dancers.

Les Elgart, born Aug. 3, 1918, in New Haven, Connecticut, had played lead trumpet with the orchestras of Charlie Spivak, Bunny Berigan, and Hal McIntyre but rarely ever soloed. Larry Elgart, born March 20, 1922, in New London, Connecticut, could take worthwhile alto solos, although his work with the big bands of Tommy Dorsey, Woody Herman, Bobby Byrne, Jack Jenney, and Joe Marsala was primarily leading sax sections. Les made an attempt at leading a big band in 1945 (with Larry as one of the saxophonists) but the orchestra (which had arrangements by Bill Finegan and Nelson Riddle) soon failed. In 1952 they tried again, this time as co-leaders, and surprisingly (considering the time period) the band caught on. With Larry Elgart and tenor saxophonist John Murtaugh as the main soloists and Charlie Albertine contributing many of the arrangements, the Les and Larry Elgart Orchestra had a steady seller in their Columbia debut, *Sophisticated Swing*, and worked regularly until 1958, when Les moved permanently to California. Larry Elgart continued leading a big band on an occasional basis, periodically having reunions with his brother, and alternating between playing Swing standards and playing current pop tunes. During the disco era of the late 1970s, Larry Elgart had a major hit with *Hooked on Swing*, old standards given a disco beat and played as a series of endless medleys. It did not help the Swing movement much but kept Larry Elgart's name before the public for an additional decade.

●

6 *Ain't We Got Fun / Feb. 1955–Mar. 1955 / Drive Archive 41068*
Few recordings by the Les and Larry Elgart band are currently available. This live set, recorded at the Hollywood Palladium, is a good example of the Elgarts' music, danceable and melodic versions of vintage standards, including "Alice Blue Gown," "Varsity Drag," "April in Paris," and the most recent song, "Night Train."

MERCER ELLINGTON
b. Mar. 11, 1919, Washington, DC, d. Feb. 8, 1996, Copenhagen, Denmark

Throughout his life, Mercer Ellington was in the impossible position of being Duke Ellington's son. He occasionally ran away from that position but always came back, unable to carve out a musical niche for himself. He was well trained in music, studying at the Institute of Musical Art, playing trumpet, and leading his own band in 1939. During the ASCAP strike of 1940–41, when ASCAP composers (such as Duke Ellington) were not allowed to play their own compositions on the radio, Mercer was a major asset, composing such works as "Things Ain't What They Used to Be," "Moon Mist," "Jumpin' Punkins," and "Blue Serge" for Duke's band. Mercer Ellington was in the Army during 1943–45 and led his own big band during 1946–49, without much success, although his singer was the young Carmen McRae. During the next couple of decades, Ellington ran a music publishing company, was a disc jockey, occasionally put together a group, was road manager for the Cootie Williams Orchestra, and worked as Della Reese's musical director. In 1965 he relented and joined his father's big band as a section trumpeter and road manager. When Duke Ellington died in 1974, Mercer took over his orchestra, but within two years it was a part-time band. In the 1980s and early '90s he led a big band (always under the Duke Ellington name) on tours and supervised the release of previously unavailable Ellington recordings, and during 1981–83 he directed the musical *Sophisticated Ladies*. Mercer Ellington in concerts with the orchestra gave audiences an opportunity to hear some of Duke's lesser-known works, but the big band never did develop a personality of its own.

●

7 *Digital Duke / 1986 / GRP 9548*

9 *Music Is My Mistress / 1988 / Music Masters 60185*

8 *Only God Can Make a Tree / 1995 / Music Masters 65117*

Mercer Ellington's earliest recordings as a leader and his first dates as the leader of the Duke Ellington Orchestra have not yet been reissued on CD. *Digital Duke* has some of the members of the Mercer Ellington band joined by quite a few alumni and all-stars, including trumpeters Barry Lee Hall and Clark Terry, altoist Norris Turney, clarinetist Eddie Daniels, Herman Riley and Branford Marsalis on tenors, trombonist Al Grey, drummer Louie Bellson, and pianists Roland Hanna and Gerry Wiggins, among many others. A dozen songs associated with Ellington are brought back to life and, even if some are continually recorded too much (including "Satin Doll," "Prelude to a Kiss," "Solitude," and "Sophisticated Lady"), these versions are generally quite worthwhile. *Music Is My Mistress* finds Mercer trying to stretch the Ellington legacy a little bit by using a steel drummer on "Queenie Pie Reggae" and includes a few of Mercer's originals plus updated versions of some of Duke's standards; everything mostly works well. The music on *Only God Can Make a Tree,* even though most of the compositions

are by Duke, is quite fresh, for of the pieces are obscure (other than "Caravan"), the arrangements are fairly inventive, and the band (which has only two of Duke's alumni: Barrie Lee Hall and trombonist Art Baron) is comprised mostly of young and enthusiastic players. Well worth exploring and a solid final act for an odd career.

LPS TO SEARCH FOR

Black and Tan Fantasy (MCA-349), from 1958–59, finds Mercer using the Duke Ellington Orchestra (with Billy Strayhorn or Jimmy Jones on piano) for a few recording dates. Fourteen of the 24 numbers that he recorded are on this LP, and the main soloists include Clark Terry, Harold "Shorty" Baker, Johnny Hodges, Ben Webster, and Jimmy Hamilton. Shortly after Duke's death, Mercer recorded *Continuum* (Fantasy 9481) with the remains of the Ellington band, including Cootie Williams and Harry Carney (who passed away before the album was completed); one can consider *Continuum* to be the final Duke Ellington album and quite worthwhile. *Hot and Bothered* (Doctor Jazz 40029) finds Mercer Ellington in 1984 performing nine vintage Duke compositions/arrangements, all of which date from before 1935 and including "Hot and Bothered," "Daybreak Express," and "East St. Louis Toodle-oo."

JIMMY FORREST

b. Jan. 24, 1920, St. Louis, MO, d. Aug. 26, 1980, Grand Rapids, MI

Jimmy Forrest was always most famous for his recording of "Night Train," a theme that was "borrowed" note for note from Duke Ellington's "Happy-Go-Lucky Local." Forrest's tenor sax playing (which featured a full, soulful, and attractive tone) was based in the Swing era yet flexible enough to fit into R&B, hard bop, and soul jazz settings throughout his career.

Forrest first played in public as a youth with his mother's group (the Eva Dowd Orchestra). He worked with pianist Eddie Johnson, Fate Marable, and the Jeter-Pillars Orchestra while still a teenager. In 1938 he toured with Don Albert and then was featured with Jay McShann's orchestra (1940–42). Forrest spent a long period with the Andy Kirk Orchestra (1942–48) and a few months with Duke Ellington (1949). He went out on his own, had the big hit with "Night Train," and worked in R&B settings throughout much of the 1950s, although he never did duplicate the success of that song. In 1958 Forrest returned to jazz on a full-time basis, working with Harry "Sweets" Edison's combo during 1958–63, recording as a leader for Prestige, and freelancing. Jimmy Forrest was one of the major soloists with the Count Basie Orchestra during 1972–77, leaving the band to form a quintet with Basie's trombonist Al Grey before his death at age 60.

10 *Night Train / Nov. 27, 1951–Sept. 7, 1953 / Delmark 435*

All of Jimmy Forrest's United recordings of 1951–53 are on this highly enjoyable CD. "Night Train" was a major hit and became a standard due to Forrest's recording and the many

that followed. Although he was popular on the R&B circuit, Forrest was not really a honker or a screamer, and his recordings from this era alternate between swinging numbers, blues, and novelties. Whether it is "Calling Dr. Jazz," "Bolo

Blues," "Hey Mrs. Jones," or "Dig Those Feet," this is a CD that should greatly interest both Retro Swing fans and students of the tenor sax.

8	*All the Gin Is Gone / Dec. 10–12, 1959 / Delmark 404*
7	*Black Forrest / Dec. 10–12, 1959 / Delmark 427*
8	*Forrest Fire / Aug. 9, 1960 / Original Jazz Classics 199*
8	*Out of the Forrest / Apr. 18, 1961 / Original Jazz Classics 097*
7	*Sit Down and Relax with Jimmy Forrest / Sept. 1, 1961 / Original Jazz Classics 895*
7	*Most Much / Oct. 19, 1961 / Original Jazz Classics 350*
7	*Soul Street / Aug. 29, 1958–June 1, 1962 / Original Jazz Classics 987*

Other than a couple of singles, Jimmy Forrest's first records after 1953 found him returning to jazz. *All the Gin Is Gone* and *Black Forrest* are from the same Delmark sessions and feature Forrest with guitarist Grant Green (who was making his recording debut), pianist Harold Mabern, bassist Gene Ramey, and drummer Elvin Jones. The music crosses over between Swing, hard bop, and soul jazz, alternating a few standards with jumping originals and ballads. During 1960–62, Forrest cut five albums for Prestige and New Jazz; all have been reissued as Original Jazz Classics CDs. Each of the records is equally rewarding, and one's preference will depend on the instrumentation and material. *Forrest Fire* teams the tenorman on a mostly heated date with organist Larry Young (just 20 at the time). *Out of the Forrest* is by a straightahead quartet with pianist Joe Zawinul. *Sit Down and Relax* does have a fair number of ballads but also such swinging material as "Rocks in My Bed," "Tuxedo Junction," and "Organ Grinder's Swing." Both *Sit Down and Relax* and *Most Much* feature pianist Hugh Lawson, with the latter release's highlights including "Soft Winds," "Robbins' Nest," and "Annie Laurie." *Soul Street* has three numbers in which Forrest is showcased with the Oliver Nelson Orchestra, three additional titles from the Hugh Lawson dates, and a pair of obscure performances from other sessions. In general, every Jimmy Forrest recording is well worth getting.

LPS TO SEARCH FOR

After the Prestige period ended, Jimmy Forrest led only one other album, *Heart of the Forest* (Palo Alto 8201), a fine live trio set from 1978 with organist Shirley Scott and drummer Randy Marsh.

PANAMA FRANCIS
b. Dec. 21, 1918, Miami, FL

A hard-swinging drummer who for many years was a greatly in-demand session player, Panama Francis helped to revive Swing in the late 1970s with the Savoy Sultans, 15 years before the Retro Swing movement. He worked early on with George Kelly's Cavaliers (1934–38) and the Florida Collegians. After moving to New York in 1938, Francis was with Tab Smith, Billy Hicks's Sizzling Six, Roy Eldridge (1939), Lucky Millinder's orchestra (1940–46), and Cab Calloway (1947–52). Francis was very busy in the 1950s, appearing on countless records (including on many hits quite anonymously) while performing jazz at night. The drummer worked with Sam "the Man" Taylor (1970–71), Illinois Jacquet, Lionel Hampton, and the Teddy Wilson Trio (1971). After Francis formed the Savoy Sultans (using the name of a combo that had played regularly at the Savoy in the early 1940s), for a decade that band brought back exciting riff-filled small-group Swing, often for dancing audiences. In later years Panama Francis became semi-retired, but he did tour with the Statesmen of Jazz in the mid-1990s.

LPS TO SEARCH FOR

It is surprising that, with the comeback of Swing, the four recordings that the Savoy Sultans made have not been reissued yet on CD. *Panama Francis and the Savoy Sultans* (Classic Jazz 149) and *Volume II* (Classic Jazz 150) are both very enjoyable outings from 1979, featuring a nonet including Francis Williams and Irv Stokes on trumpets, altoists Norris Turney and Howard Johnson, tenor saxophonist George Kelly (who provided some of the arrangements), pianist Red Richards, rhythm guitarist John Smith, and bassist Bill Pemberton. The selections include (on the first volume) "Shipyard Social Function," "Second Balcony Jump," and "Perdido," and on the second album "Song of the Islands," "Frenzy," "Little John Special," and "Getting' in the

Groove," among others. The music on *Grooving* (Stash 218) and *Everything Swings* (Stash 233) tends to include more warhorses in the repertoire (including "Bill Bailey," "Sentimental Journey," and "In the Mood") but also swings well. *Groovin'* (from 1982) has a couple of vocals by Julia Steele, while the following year's *Everything Swings* finds the band a bit expanded, with Bobby Watson a key soloist on alto. All four Savoy Sultans recordings will be wanted by discerning Swing fans.

JOHNNY FRIGO
b. Dec. 27, 1916, Chicago, IL

One of the great Swing violinists, Johnny Frigo actually spent most of his career as a studio bassist! His first instrument was the violin; he took up the tuba so he could play in his junior high school band, and then he switched to bass. Frigo was playing professionally as early as 1934 but was still pretty obscure when he became a member of the Jimmy Dorsey Orchestra in the mid-1940s. In 1947 he teamed up with Dorsey's guitarist, Herb Ellis, and pianist Lou Carter to form the Soft Winds, a trio that was popular for a few years. The three musicians cowrote "Detour Ahead" and "I Told Ya I Love Ya, Now Get Out" and recorded some swinging but obscure sides that have long been very difficult to find. In the early 1950s the musicians went their separate ways, and Frigo became a studio musician for decades. He led an album in 1957 on violin but otherwise concentrated on bass until the mid-1980s. Then he switched back to violin, appeared on a Herb Ellis CD, and worked regularly in Mainstream settings. Frigo had a recorded reunion with Ellis and Carter in 1995, appeared at the 1998 Monterey Jazz Festival, recorded with John and Bucky Pizzarelli, and led a couple of sessions of his own. As of this writing, Johnny Frigo (along with Claude Williams) is the last of the surviving Swing violinists.

●

7   *With Bucky & John Pizzarelli / Nov. 16, 1988 / Chesky 1*

8   *Debut of a Legend / May 26–27, 1994 / Chesky 119*

9   *Live at the Floating Jazz Festival / Nov. 2–6, 1997 / Chiaroscuro 358*

Other than his 1957 album, Johnny Frigo did not make his recording debut as a leader until he was 71. Joined by both Bucky and John Pizzarelli on guitars, drummer Butch Miles, and either Ron Carter or Michael Moore on bass, Frigo shows how viable a Swing violinist he still was on such tunes as "Pick Yourself Up," "Stompin' at the Savoy," "The Song Is You," and "Tangerine." *Debut of a Legend* is even better, a sextet outing with guitarist Gene Bertoncini and Bob Kindred on tenor and clarinet that features a wide variety of standards (such as "Get Happy," "Nuages," "Jitterbug Waltz," and "Jeannine") plus two of the violinist's originals. But the Johnny Frigo set to get is *Live at the Floating Jazz Festival.* Frigo at 80 sounds quite inspired by the audience and was definitely still in fine form. Joined by pianist Joe Vito, bassist Larry Gray, and his son, Rick Frigo, on drums, Frigo also welcomes fellow violinist Rob Thomas on "This Can't Be Love" and the exciting vibraphonist Terry Gibbs on "Lester Leaps In." Other highlights include a *Porgy and Bess* medley, "There Will Never Be Another You," and a four-song Gershwin medley.

DAVE FRISHBERG
b. Mar. 23, 1933, St. Paul, MN

A talented Swing pianist, Dave Frishberg is most significant as one of the top lyricists of the past 25 years. His witty lyrics, which look back nostalgically to the pre-1960 years and often the Swing era, have given today's singers (many of whom are tired of interpreting the same Cole Porter songs endlessly) lively and fresh material.

Moving to New York in 1957, Frishberg worked with singer Carmen McRae, trombonist Kai Winding, Gene Krupa (1960–61), Bud Freeman, Ben Webster (1963), the Al Cohn–Zoot Sims Quintet, and Bobby Hackett, among others, recording with Jimmy Rushing in 1971. After relocating to Los Angeles (he would later settle in Portland), Frishberg (who in 1968 had had a minor hit with "Van Lingle Mungo," which consisted entirely of the names of baseball players) began to write more extensively. Among his better-known songs are "I'm Hip" (with music written by Bob Dorough), "Peel Me a Grape," "Dear Bix," "Saratoga Hunch," "My Attorney Bernie," "Blizzard of Lies," "You Are There," and "Can't Take You No-where." In addition to his dates as a leader, Dave Frishberg has recorded in Mainstream settings with Bill Berry, Jack Sheldon, tenor saxophonist Richie Kamuca (1977), trumpeter Jim Goodwin, Susannah McCorkle, Ken Peplowski, and, more recently, Rebecca Kilgore.

●

9 *Getting Some Fun Out of Life / Jan. 25–26, 1977 / Concord Jazz 4037*

10 *Classics / Apr. 29, 1981–Dec. 1982 / Concord Jazz 4462*

7 *Live at Vine Street / Oct. 1984 / Original Jazz Classics 832*

8 *Can't Take You Nowhere / Sept. 21, 1986 / Fantasy 9651*
Getting Some Fun Out of Life was Dave Frishberg's third album, and it is mostly instrumentals, with a few exceptions. The first six selections mostly match Frishberg with altoist Marshall Royal, trumpeter Bob Findley, bassist Larry Gales, and drummer Steve Schaeffer; among the better selections are the wistful and haunting "Dear Bix" (which has a famous Frishberg vocal), "Old Man Harlem," and "I Would Do Anything for You." The other six numbers are solo piano pieces, which give listeners a strong example of Frishberg's skills as an instrumentalist; highlights are "In a Mist," "King Porter Stomp," and the title track. *Classics* lives up to its name, for it has such songs as "I'm Hip," "Slappin' the Cakes on Me," "Z's," "My Attorney Bernie," "Blizzard of Lies," and "You Are There." The Concord trio CD (with bassist Steve Gilmore and drummer Bill Goodwin) is actually a reissue, including all ten numbers that were on an Omnisound LP called *The Dave Frishberg Songbook, Vol. 1* and seven of the ten from *Vol. 2*, really summing up Frishberg's career as a lyricist-singer. *Live at Vine Street* is a good example of how Frishberg sounded live in 1984, highlighted by "El Cajon," "The Dear Departed Past," "Blizzard of Lies," and an instrumental "Johnny Hodges Medley." *Can't Take You Nowhere* has the humorous title cut, "Zoot Walks In," "My Attorney Bernie," and instrumental medleys of the music of Frank Loesser and Irving Berlin.

7 *Let's Eat Home / Aug. 1989 / Concord Jazz 4402*

7 *Where You At? / Mar. 4, 1991 / Bloomdido 010*

8 *Double Play / Oct. 3–4, 1992 / Arbors 19118*

7 *Quality Time / May 28–29, 1993 / Sterling 1006*

7 *By Himself / June 30, 1997–Aug. 4, 1997 / Arbors 19185*
Let's Eat Home contains mostly lesser-known material by Frishberg, other than the title cut and "I Was Ready." He is joined by bassist Jim Hughart, drummer Jeff Hamilton, and, on some numbers, valve trombonist Rob McConnell and trumpeter Snooky Young. Among the highlights are instrumental medleys dedicated to Al Cohn and Billy Strayhorn. *Where You At?* is an obscure release from a French label, matching Frishberg with tenorman Turk Mauro, trombonist Glenn Ferris, and bassist Michel Gaudry. On that disc there are instrumental medleys dedicated to Ivie Anderson and Duke Ellington and such pieces as "Another Song About Paris," "The Wheelers and Dealers," and a few non-Frishberg numbers, including "Where You At?," "I'm an Old Cowhand," and "Tulip or Turnip." *Double Play* is a hot instrumental duet set by Frishberg and cornetist Jim Goodwin in which they jam through superior songs from the 1920s and '30s. Goodwin deserves to be much better known, and this CD serves as proof as to how strong a piano player Frishberg can be. Also obscure but featuring Frishberg in his more usual role as a wisecracking yet sentimental vocalist-pianist, *Quality Time* is most notable for the classic title cut, "You Would Rather Have the Blues," and remakes of "Dear Bix" and "The Dear Departed Past"; Rebecca Kilgore takes two guest vocals. *By Himself*, a solo set, has just four vocals among the 14 numbers, but one is a gem: "I Want to Be a Sideman." Otherwise this is a fine workout for Frishberg's piano on such performances as "You Took Advantage of Me," "Jump for Joy," and a "Kansas City Medley."

LPS TO SEARCH FOR

The first record on which Dave Frishberg really sounded like himself was *Solo and Trio* (Seeds 4), a 1975 instrumental project that has three trio numbers and seven unaccompanied piano solos. There are two originals (including "Saratoga Hunch") but otherwise the tunes are of vintage age, from the 1920s to the early '40s. *You're a Lucky Guy* (Concord Jazz 74), from 1978, only has two originals by Frishberg ("The Underdog" and "Saratoga Hunch"), so the emphasis is on the leader's piano playing and occasional singing on duets with tenor saxophonist Al Cohn, in a quintet that adds valve trombonist Bob Brookmeyer, bassist Jim Hughart, and drummer Nick Ceroli, and on some unaccompanied numbers.

PAUL GONSALVES

b. July 12, 1920, Boston, MA, d. May 15, 1974, London, England

Duke Ellington's longtime tenor saxophonist, Paul Gonsalves had a distinctive sound, a breathy tone, and a harmonically advanced style that was a touch eccentric while being hard-driving. He served in the Army and then during 1946–49 was a soloist with Count Basie's orchestra, developing his style and becoming an asset to Basie's increasingly boppish band. Gonsalves was with the Dizzy Gillespie big band shortly before it broke up (1949–50) and then joined Duke Ellington's orchestra, where he remained for the rest of his life (1950–74). He had a reputation early on for being able to take marathon solos, and, when Ellington gave him an extensive solo on "Diminuendo and Crescendo in Blue" at the 1956 Newport Jazz Festival, the 27-chorus improvisation caused a sensation and led to Ellington's renaissance. Duke never forgot, and he always featured Gonsalves quite liberally, both on romps and on ballads. In addition, the tenor saxophonist recorded now and then as a leader. Paul Gonsalves passed away just nine days before Duke Ellington.

●

8	*Getting Together!* / Dec. 20, 1960 / Original Jazz Classics 203
7	*Just a-Sittin' and a-Rockin'* / Aug. 28, 1970 + Sept. 3, 1970 / Black Lion 760148
8	*Paul Gonsalves Meets Earl Hines* / Dec. 15, 1970 + Nov. 29, 1972 / Black Lion 760177
8	*Mexican Bandit Meets Pittsburgh Pirate* / Aug. 24, 1973 / Original Jazz Classics 751

Paul Gonsalves recorded albums on an occasional basis from 1956 on. *Getting Together!* has Gonsalves teamed with pianist Wynton Kelly, bassist Sam Jones, drummer Jimmy Cobb, and (on four of the seven songs) cornetist Nat Adderley. The music is straightahead and boppish, with Gonsalves also being showcased on a few ballads. Highlights include "Hard Groove," "I Cover the Waterfront," and "Walkin'." *Just a-Sittin' and a-Rockin'* features three of Duke's sidemen (Gonsalves, Ray Nance on trumpet, violin, and vocals, and, on half of the numbers, altoist Norris Turney) with a swinging rhythm section headed by either Hank Jones or Raymond Fol on piano. The songs are mostly familiar and the tempos generally a bit slower ("Stompy Jones" is a happy exception), with everyone playing quite well. Gon-

salves's meeting with Earl Hines (plus bassist Al Hall and Jo Jones) is also quite successful as they stretch out on five standards, including a lengthy exploration of "It Don't Mean a Thing," "Moten Swing," and "I Got It Bad." Gonsalves and Hines sound inspired by each other's presence. Their meeting was in 1970, and a piano solo from 1972 ("Blue Sands") was added to round out this CD. The oddly titled *Mexican Bandit Meets Pittsburgh Pirate* teams Gonsalves in a jam session setting with Roy Eldridge (who takes a surprise vocal on "Somebody Loves Me") plus pianist Cliff Smalls, bassist Sam Jones, and drummer Eddie Locke. Together they perform three stomps (including "5400 North" and "C Jam Blues") and a few ballads. Gonsalves is best on "I Cover the Waterfront," while the trio has "It's the Talk of the Town" as its feature. This was one of Paul Gonsalves's final sessions, and he swings as hard as ever.

LPS TO SEARCH FOR

Tell It the Way It Is (Impulse 55), from 1963, has a masterful rendition of "Body and Soul" and fine appearances by Ray Nance, Johnny Hodges, and trumpeter Rolf Ericson. *The Buenos Aires Sessions* (Catalyst 7913) is a little-known but superb outing by Gonsalves and trumpeter Willie Cook with an Argentinean rhythm section in 1968.

AL GREY

b. June 6, 1925, Aldie, VA

A master with the plunger mute, trombonist Al Grey was a fixture with Count Basie's orchestra on three separate occasions and has been a star in Mainstream Jazz for decades. After serving in the Navy during World War II (where he played with a service band), Grey picked up experience working with Benny Carter (1945–46) and the Jimmie Lunceford Orchestra (1946–47). The trombonist freelanced for the next nine years, including playing with Lucky Millinder (1947–48) and touring on and off with Lionel Hampton's orchestra. Grey was a member of the Dizzy Gillespie big band during 1956–57 (taking an exciting solo on "Cool Breeze" at the 1957 Newport Jazz Festival) and then made a strong impression while with Count Basie for the first time (1957–61). Grey's fluent style, use of humor (taking witty wa-wa solos), and ability to play with excitement yet melodically enabled him to sound quite at home with both Gillespie and Basie. He left Count to form a sextet with tenor saxophonist Billy Mitchell that soon featured the young vibraphonist Bobby Hutcherson. Grey rejoined Basie during 1964–66 and 1971–77; he and Jimmy Forrest were Count's top soloists during the latter period. This time when he left Basie, Grey formed a quintet with Forrest that lasted until the tenor saxophonist's death in 1980. Since then, Al Grey has freelanced, toured with the Statesmen of Jazz, often teamed up with Clark Terry, and sometimes used his son, Mike Grey, on second trombone.

●

9 *Truly Wonderful! / July 19–21, 1978 / Stash 552*

7 *Al Grey and Jesper Thilo Quintet / Aug. 1986 / Storyville 4136*

7 *Al Meets Bjarne / Aug. 5, 1988 / Gemini 62*

8 *Me n' Jack / 1993 / Pullen Music 2350*

7 *Matzoh and Grits / Apr. 22–23, 1996 / Arbors 19167*

The modestly titled *Truly Wonderful!* was the first of two recordings made by the Al Grey–Jimmy Forrest Quintet and the only one to thus far appear on CD. Actually, it reissues four of the seven selections from an Aviva LP (*Live at Rick's*) and adds five additional selections. The live set with Shirley Scott (normally an organist but heard here exclusively on piano), bassist John Duke, and drummer Bobby Durham is Swing-oriented, with Jay McShann's "Jumpin' Blues," "What's New?," "Blues Everywhere," and "Take the 'A' Train" being among the best selections. Grey's expressive trombone and Forrest's soulful tenor went together quite well. Jesper Thilo is a fine Zoot Sims–influenced tenorman, and he also works well with Grey. They are joined by a European rhythm section on four standards and three of Grey's originals, including one titled "I'm Hungry, Sabrina!" The Gemini set is similar, with Bjarne Nerem (from Norway) sounding a bit like Coleman Hawkins with a Grey-led quintet that also includes pianist Norman Simmons. Three group originals alternate with such standards as "Things

Ain't What They Used to Be," "Lester Leaps In," and "Stompin' at the Savoy." *Me n' Jack* is a collaboration with organist Jack McDuff for a blues-oriented program full of mostly basic originals; guitarist Joe Cohn and tenor saxophonist Jerry Waldon also have their spots. Al Grey was beginning to show his age a little by 1996 (when he was 70) but still played with plenty of swing and wit. *Matzoh and Grits* is a sextet outing on eight familiar veteran standards and three originals, with altoist Cleve Guyton (doubling on flute), pianist Randolph Noel, drummer Bobby Durham, guitarist Joe Cohn (son of Al), and bassist J.J. Wiggins (son of Gerry). A good example of Al Grey's spirited playing of the mid-1990s.

LPS TO SEARCH FOR

Key Bone (Classic Jazz 103) is a strong effort from 1972 in which Grey shares the spotlight with altoist-singer Eddie "Cleanhead" Vinson and organist Wild Bill Davis. *Grey's Mood* (Classic Jazz 118) has the trombonist splitting his time with an octet that also features Hal Singer and a quintet with Jimmy Forrest a few years before they formed their own band. *O.D.* (Grey Forrest 1001) is a 1980 set by Grey and Forrest that was the tenorman's final recording and shows the potential of this swinging group, utilizing a rhythm section that includes organist Don Patterson. Thus far this music has been available (and then just barely) only as a private-label LP.

MARTY GROSZ

b. Feb. 28, 1930, Berlin, Germany

A chordal acoustic guitarist in the tradition of Dick McDonough and Carl Kress, a singer who is clearly influenced by Fats Waller, and a skillful ad-libber whose monologues are often hilarious, Marty Grosz helped keep small-group Swing alive during the 1980s and '90s. He moved to the U.S. with his family in 1933, attended Columbia University, and in 1951 started playing Dixieland with pianist Dick Wellstood. After serving in the Army, Grosz settled in Chicago, recording as a leader and with Dave Remington (1955–56) and Art Hodes. Grosz also did his best to encourage trumpeter Jabbo Smith to make a comeback in the early '60s although it was ultimately unsuccessful; recordings of their rehearsals were released decades later. Grosz freelanced in Chicago until 1975 but remained obscure until he worked as a rhythm guitarist and occasional vocalist with Soprano Summit (1975–79). Grosz was a member of the Classic Jazz Quartet with Dick Wellstood and in the 1980s became a major force at classic jazz festivals and jazz parties. Grosz formed the Orphan Newsboys (a quartet with cornetist Peter Ecklund, clarinetist Bobby Gordon, and bassist Greg Cohen) and has both performed and recorded with similar groups on a regular basis ever since.

●

9   *Swing It! / June 1988–July 1988 / Jazzology 180*

10   *Extra! / Aug. 1989–Sept. 1989 / Jazzology 190*

9   *Unsaturated Fats / Jan. 30, 1990–Feb. 22, 1990 / Stomp Off 1214*

7   *And Destiny's Tots / Mar. 23, 1992–June 11, 1992 / Jazzology 220*

8   *Thanks / Apr. 22, 1993–May 27, 1993 / Jazzology 310*
Marty Grosz recordings are always quite fun, filled with obscure but superior songs from the 1920s and '30s, colorful frameworks, top hot soloists, and a liberal dose of Grosz's vocalizing; if only someone would record (or better yet, film) some of his classic monologues! Swing, trad, and classic jazz fans will want all of the listed Grosz CDs; each has many joyful moments and shows the continuing viability of small-group Swing. *Swing It!* features Grosz regulars Peter Ecklund and Bob Gordon plus Dan Barrett, tenor saxophonist Loren Schoenberg, Keith Ingham, bassist Murray Wall, and Hal Smith. *Extra!* was the recording debut of the Orphan Newsboys, with Ken Peplowski (on clarinet and alto) and bassist Murray Wall substituting on a few numbers. *Unsaturated Fats* is a set of Fats Waller tunes performed by Grosz's "Paswonky Serenaders" (with Ecklund, Barrett, Ingham, and clarinetist Joe Muranyi), but do not look for "Honeysuckle Rose" or "Ain't Misbehavin'" here. Try such obscure Waller tunes as "Georgia Bo Bo," "Dixie Cinderella," "Asbestos," and "Charleston Hound!" Grosz's *Destiny's Tots* (which utilizes such players as Randy Sandke,

Peplowski, Ecklund, and Dick Meldonian on tenor and clarinet) puts a little more emphasis on the leader's singing and is subtitled "Songs I Learned at My Mother's Knee and Other Low Joints." *Thanks* is by Grosz's "Collectors' Items Cats," which consists of Ecklund, Barrett, Gordon, Scott Robinson on clarinet, tenor, baritone, and bass saxes, either Mark Shane or Keith Ingham on piano, Murray Wall or Greg Cohen on bass, and drummer Hal Smith.

8   *Rhythm for Sale / May 20, 1993–Jan. 16, 1996 / Jazzology 280*

9   *Keep a Song in Your Soul / Oct. 18–19, 1994 / Jazzology 250*

8   *Ring Dem Bells / Feb. 25, 1995 / Nagel-Heyer 022*

7   *Just for Fun / Apr. 13, 1996 / Nagel Heyer 039*
Rhythm for Sale is listed as by the Orphan Newsboys, but the six ensembles range from a quartet to an octet, and the Ecklund-Gordon-Grosz-Cohen lineup never appears as a unit. However, the spirited music (which also includes Dan Block on alto and clarinet, Scott Robinson, Keith Ingham, and others) is in the freewheeling ensemble-oriented spirit of that unit. *Keep a Song in Your Soul* (by Destiny's Tots) is from two similar groups, with Dan Levinson's C-melody and alto uplifting one of the bands. The two Nagel-Heyer CDs are a bit different, since they were recorded live and add some new musicians to the Grosz stable of hot jazz players. *Ring Dem Bells* features a sextet with trumpeter Jon-Erik

Kellso, Scott Robinson on reeds, pianist Martin Litton, Greg Cohen, and drummer Chuck Riggs, while *Just for Fun* is by a quartet with trumpeter Alan Elsdon, John Barnes on reeds, and bassist Murray Wall. There is no point mentioning all of the highlights of the Marty Grosz recordings, for virtually every selection will be quite enjoyable to fans of this idiom. All are recommended!

LPS TO SEARCH FOR

1981's *I Hope Gabriel Likes My Music* (Aviva 6004) is one of the earlier albums in which Marty Grosz (outside of Soprano Summit) gets a chance to stretch out. The music alternates between quartet tracks with trumpeter Jimmy Maxwell and an octet that includes Dick Meldonian and pianist Dick Wellstood. Destiny's Tots made its first appearance on record for *Sings of Love and Other Matters* (Statiras 8080). It features a 1986 quintet with Dick Meldonian on reeds and Dan Barrett on both trombone and cornet. And one should not overlook Grosz's *Keepers of the Flame and the Imps* (Stomp Off 1158), from 1987, which often puts the spotlight on violinist Andy Stein, Paul Bacon on comb, and guitarist Frank Vignola in addition to Ecklund, Muranyi, and Wellstood.

JIMMY HAMILTON

b. May 25, 1917, Dillon, SC, d. Sept. 20, 1994, St. Croix, Virgin Islands

Duke Ellington's clarinetist for many years, Jimmy Hamilton had a much cooler sound than his predecessor (Barney Bigard) and was an intellectual bop soloist (although he was initially influenced by Benny Goodman) who could play anything. Early on Hamilton played baritone horn, piano, trumpet, and trombone, working on the latter two instruments in Philadelphia, including with Frankie Fairfax and Lonnie Slappy. Hamilton eventually settled on clarinet and tenor, playing with Lucky Millinder, Jimmy Mundy, and Teddy Wilson's sextet (1940–42). He was briefly with Eddie Heywood and then in May 1943 joined Duke Ellington. Hamilton was with Duke for 25 years straight and his clarinet was a very significant part of Duke's sound, sometimes being contrasted with the more New Orleans–influenced tone of Russell Procope. "Air Conditioned Jungle" was just one of the many features that he had with Ellington through the years. In addition, Hamilton had a very different sound on tenor, a booting R&B tone that was used on all-too-rare occasions by Duke.

In the summer of 1968, Jimmy Hamilton left Ellington and soon moved to the Virgin Islands, where he played and taught locally. Hamilton emerged in the U.S. a few times to play and record with Clarinet Summit, an avant-garde a cappella clarinet quartet that also included John Carter, Alvin Batiste, and David Murray, but otherwise he lived happily in semiretirement for many years.

9 *Can't Help Swinging / Mar. 21, 1961–Apr. 4, 1961 / Prestige 24214*

Jimmy Hamilton led relatively few sessions throughout his career, since he had a secure job with Duke Ellington and the clarinet was out of favor anyway. There were four songs for Blue Note in 1945, a few odds and ends for the United label in 1953 (mostly unissued at the time), two albums for Urania in 1954, one for Everest in 1960, and a late one for Who's Who in 1985. Otherwise, there were two sets for Swingville in 1961, both of which are reissued in full on this single CD. Hamilton is heard on both clarinet and tenor with a sextet that includes Clark Terry, Britt Woodman, and pianist Tommy Flanagan, and mostly on tenor on a quartet set with the Flanagan Trio. Hamilton wrote all but one song for the former project (a blues-oriented date), while the latter alternates between standards (such as "There Is No Greater Love" and "Baby Won't You please Come Home") and his originals. Certainly the definitive Jimmy Hamilton CD, both because of its quality and by default!

LPS TO SEARCH FOR

Jimmy Hamilton's final album as a leader (and his only one after 1961), *Rediscovered at the Buccaneer* (Who's Who 21029), dates from 1985 and finds him on clarinet and alto playing five lazy love songs and five Duke Ellington pieces (including "C Jam Blues" and "Happy Go Lucky Local"). Although little heard from outside of the Virgin Islands by 1985, Hamilton was still playing quite well.

SCOTT HAMILTON

b. Sept. 12, 1954, Providence, RI

The appearance of Scott Hamilton, the single most important figure in the Mainstream Swing revival, on the jazz scene in 1976 was big news. During an era when most young tenor saxophonists were either playing fusion avant-garde jazz or were looking toward John Coltrane and Wayne Shorter as their main influences, Hamilton was inspired by such early stylists as Ben Webster, Coleman Hawkins, Lester Young, Zoot Sims, and Illinois Jacquet. Not only was he a world-class musician in his twenties who was playing Mainstream, but Hamilton had developed his own beautiful sound, built out of the innovations of his predecessors.

Hamilton began playing tenor when he was 16, moving to New York in 1976. He worked with Benny Goodman for a period in the late 1970s but has mostly been heard as the leader of his own quartet/quintet ever since. Hamilton often teamed up with Warren Vache in the '70s and early '80s and has recorded with Ruby Braff, Rosemary Clooney, Maxine Sullivan, baritonist Gerry Mulligan, Flip Phillips, guitarist Charlie Byrd, pianist Gene Harris, and various Concord All-Star bands. He has recorded more than a couple of dozen albums as a leader (mostly for the Concord label), playing in an unchanged and timeless Swing style unaffected by post-1955 developments. Scott Hamilton's success inspired others to follow (including Ken Peplowski and Harry Allen), and he has continued to grow as an improviser with time while sticking to his very singular path.

●

9 *Is a Good Wind Who Is Blowing Us No Ill / Mar. 1, 1977 / Concord Jazz 4042*

8 *Scott Hamilton 2 / Jan. 7, 1978 / Concord Jazz 4061*

7 *Grand Appearance / Jan. 23, 1978 + Feb. 8, 1978 / Progressive 7016*

7 *With Scott's Band in New York / June 26, 1978 / Concord Jazz 4070*

8 *Tenorshoes / Dec. 1979 / Concord Jazz 4127*

8 *Groovin' High / Oct. 19, 1981 / Intermusic 103.607*

7 *Close Up / Feb. 1982 / Concord Jazz 4197*

7 *In Concert / June 1983 / Concord Jazz 4233*

7 *The Second Set / June 1983 / Concord Jazz 4254*

7 *The Right Time / Jan. 1986 / Concord Jazz 4311*

In some ways Scott Hamilton is the Oscar Peterson of the tenor sax. Hamilton has recorded a large quantity of similar records as a leader, he has barely changed his style since he became mature (his sound was fully formed by the time of his first recording), and he is today easily recognizable as the same musician who appeared on his earliest albums. On the one hand, there is no one particular Hamilton CDs that sticks out as definitive or essential, for there are many others of exactly the same quality. However, it is also true that none of his recordings are throwaways, and all are worth having, although one does need all of them (or even more than five) to have a good sampling of Scott Hamilton's talents!

Not counting his sideman appearances and dates where he co-led the music with a veteran (who received first billing), Hamilton led 26 albums for Concord by mid-1999; 22 of them are currently available on CD. Some stand out more than others. *Is a Good Wind Who Is Blowing Us No Ill* was recorded when Hamilton was 22 in a quintet with Bill Berry and Nat Pierce, while *Scott Hamilton 2* has Hamilton as the only horn in a group with Pierce and guitarist Cal Collins. Those two sets permanently established the tenor's reputation, and he has been remarkably consistent ever since. *Grand Appearance* was a rare session away from the Concord label, but it is very much in the same style, with Hamilton fronting a quartet that has either Hank Jones or Tommy Flanagan on piano. Warren Vache is on *With Scott's Band,* as is singer Sue Melikian for two brief vocals. Every Hamilton collaboration with Dave McKenna is special, and, even though *Tenorshoes* has more ballads than usual (and a bassist, which is unnecessary considering the pianist's powerful left hand), it has its heated moments. The two-CD set *Groovin' High* from the European Intermusic label, which was first released in 1996, features Hamilton live in Georgia with a local rhythm section that includes pianist Johnny O'Neal; tenorman Rich Bell sits in on three numbers during the

The comeback of Mainstream Swing in the 1970s largely started with the emergence of tenor saxophonist Scott Hamilton.

standards-oriented program. *Close Up, In Concert, The Second Set,* and *The Right Time* are all equally satisfying dates in which Hamilton uses his working group of the period: John Bunch, guitarist Chris Flory, bassist Phil Flanigan, and drummer Chuck Riggs.

There was virtually no change in Scott Hamilton's style during the 1977–86 period, nor would there be during the following 13 years. *Major League* is particularly exciting, for it has Hamilton as part of a hard-driving trio with Dave McKenna and Jake Hanna; many sparks fly. Obviously *Plays Ballads* is much more relaxed and soothing, but Hamilton's warm tone keeps the music from becoming too sleepy. On *Radio City,* Hamilton (who begins with a roaring version of "Apple Honey") is pushed by the constantly riffing piano of Gerry Wiggins. *Groovin' High* is a heated tenor battle matching Hamilton with Ken Peplowski and veteran Spike Robinson, assisted by Howard Alden, Gerry Wiggins, bassist Dave Stone, and Jake Hanna. "Blues Up and Down," "Shine," and "The Jeep Is Jumpin'" definitely have their explosive moments. *Race Point* brings back Wiggins in a quartet/quintet that sometimes also includes Howard Alden, while *With Strings* finds Hamilton playing beautifully but a bit weighed down by a large string section arranged by pianist Alan Broadbent. *East of the Sun* is an outing with some of Hamilton's favorite British players (pianist Brian Lemon, bassist Dave Green, and drummer Allan Ganley). *Organic Duke* has Hamilton exploring ten Ellington-associated tunes with a trio that includes Mike LeDonne on organ, the first time that the tenor ever recorded with an organist. Lemon, Green, and Ganley return for *Live at the Brecon Jazz Festival. My Romance* (with the Norman Simmons Trio plus two appearances by trombonist Joel Helleny) and *After Hours* (with pianist Tommy Flanagan) are further quartet dates that do not break any new ground but are quite enjoyable in their own right.

Scott Hamilton has recorded so many quartet albums that it is welcome news that these three CDs use different formats. *The Red Door*, a tribute to Zoot Sims (one of Hamilton's idols), is a set of exciting duets with guitarist Bucky Pizzarelli that are frequently exquisite and often quite fiery. *Christmas Love Song* has 11 Christmas melodies warmly interpreted by Hamilton with the London String Ensemble and a quartet led by pianist Alan Broadbent (who was responsible for the rather respectful arrangements). And, most recently, *Blues, Bop & Ballads* teams Hamilton with trumpeter Greg Gisbert, the Norman Simmons Trio, and (on three numbers apiece) guitarist Duke Robillard and trombonist Joel Helleny. Age 44 at the time, Scott Hamilton was still able to come up with enthusiastic and creative ideas on vintage standards and remained the leader of Mainstream Swing.

LPS TO SEARCH FOR

Scott Hamilton's debut as a leader, *Swinging Young Scott* (Famous Door 119), predated his first Concord set by a month or two. The collaboration with Warren Vache, John Bunch, bassist Michael Moore, and Butch Miles is quite obscure and long out of print, since the Famous Door label is defunct, but is as strong as his usual Concord albums. Hopefully the four Hamilton Concord sets that have not yet been reissued on CD will come back soon. *Back to Back* (Concord Jazz 85) and *Scott's Buddy* (Concord Jazz 148) are quintet/sextet meetings with fellow tenor Buddy Tate. *Skyscrapers* (Concord Jazz 111) is a nonet set co-led with Warren Vache that also includes Harold Ashby and Joe Temperley. From 1981, *Apples and Oranges* (Concord Jazz 165) has Hamilton heading two separate trios with either Dave McKenna or Jimmy Rowles on piano.

JAKE HANNA
b. Apr. 4, 1931, Roxbury, MA

A solid Mainstream drummer who is a master at using brushes, Jake Hanna has played in countless settings throughout his career but most prefers small, Swing-oriented bands. Hanna began playing professionally in the Boston area, including as house drummer at George Wein's Storyville Club. He played with Maynard Ferguson's orchestra (1958), Marian McPartland's trio (1959–61), the Woody Herman Big Band (1962–64) and had associations with Bobby Hackett and Harry James. Hanna worked regularly as the drummer with the orchestra on Merv Griffin's television show (1964–75), relocating to Los Angeles with the program in 1970. Jake Hanna, who co-led a group with trombonist Carl Fontana in 1975 (the Hanna/Fontana Band), played with Supersax and has during the past 25 years appeared at many jazz festivals, jazz parties, and clubs and on quite a few Mainstream Swing records as a sideman.

8 *Live at Concord / July 1975 / Concord Jazz 11*

8 *The Joint Is Jumpin' / July 14–15, 1997 / Arbors 19148*
Jake Hanna's first chances to lead his own record dates took place in 1975–76, when he headed three albums for Concord. *Live at Concord* is thus far the only one of the three sets to come out on CD and it was the only recording by the Hanna-Fontana Band. The all-star Mainstream septet band co-led by trombonist Carl Fontana and also including Dave McKenna, tenorman Plas Johnson, Bill Berry, guitarist Herb Ellis, and bassist Herb Mickman romps happily on seven Swing standards, including "Jumpin' the Blues," 'Take the 'A' Train," and "I've Found a New Baby." Since 1976, Hanna has worked constantly as a sideman, but his only CD as a leader since then has been *The Joint Is Jumpin'*. During this happy meeting with some of his favorite musicians (trumpeter Jack Sheldon, who also takes four vocals, tenor saxophonist Tommy Newsom, trombonist John Allred, pianist Ross Tompkins, and bassist David Stone), Hanna primarily stays in the background except for some short breaks. He was quite satisfied to help keep the music (which includes "Exactly Like You," "Look for the Silver Lining," and Fats Waller's "The Joint Is Jumpin'") swinging.

Jake Hanna's two other sets as a leader are both quintet dates: *Kansas City Express* (Concord Jazz 22), with Bill Berry, tenorman Richie Kamuca, and singer Mary Ann McCall, and *Jake Takes Manhattan* (Concord Jazz 35), with trumpeter Danny Stiles and Carmen Leggio on alto and tenor.

BILL HARRIS
b. Oct. 28, 1916, Philadelphia, PA, d. Aug. 21, 1973, Hallandale, FL

Bill Harris had an unusual and emotional sound on the trombone, a tone filled with both humor and sentiment and one that has sometimes been compared to that of an opera singer. Only Ray Sims (who played with Les Brown) was able to duplicate that sound. Harris played piano, tenor, and trumpet as a child before switching to the trombone. He worked locally in Philadelphia in the early 1930s, spent two years in the Merchant Marine, and then during 1942–44 had brief stints with the big bands of Gene Krupa, Ray McKinley, Buddy Williams, Bob Chester, Benny Goodman, Charlie Barnet, Freddie Slack, and Chester again.

All of this was a prelude to Bill Harris's joining Woody Herman's orchestra in August 1944. As a key soloist with Herman's Herd, Harris had many features, making "Bijou" famous and standing out as a star, particularly on uptempo tunes, where he could sound quite riotous. After the Herd broke up in late 1946, Harris led his own combo and worked with Charlie Ventura. He was back with Herman as a member of the Second Herd (1948–50), toured with Jazz at the Philharmonic (where his rambunctious solos fit right in), and worked with Oscar Pettiford (1952). Harris also played with the Sauter-Finegan Orchestra (1953), had a third stint with Woody Herman (1956–58), often teamed up with Flip Phillips, and spent part of 1959 with Benny Goodman and Red Norvo. After settling in Florida, he worked with trumpeter Charlie Teagarden's band (1962–64) and had a return engagement with Norvo (1965–66). During his last years, Harris mostly played at low-profile gigs in Florida until his death at age 56. As can be ascertained from listening to any of his recordings, Bill Harris was a true original.

●

9 *Bill Harris and Friends / Sept. 23, 1957 / Original Jazz Classics 083*

Bill Harris led relatively few sessions during his life and only two albums after 1953. For this CD he is teamed with Ben Webster, pianist Jimmy Rowles, bassist Red Mitchell, and drummer Stan Levey. Harris is showcased on "It Might As Well Be Spring," plays some fine standards with Webster, and jokes around with the tenorman during an odd and somewhat hilarious version of "Just One More Chance."

A week after the *Fantasy* date (reissued in the Original Jazz Classics series), Bill Harris recorded his last date as a leader, an exciting set for Mode that features eight songs from the Woody Herman days with vibraphonist Terry Gibbs, pianist Lou Levy, bassist Red Mitchell, and drummer Stan Levey. *The Bill Harris Memorial Album* (Xanadu 191) brought back this obscure album and is quite enjoyable.

FILMS

Bill Harris plays the trombone solos for actor James Cardwell in *Sweet and Low Down* (1944), a movie that had a feature role for Benny Goodman. He can also be seen with Woody Herman's orchestra in *Earl Carroll Vanities* (1945) and *Hit Parade of 1947* (1947).

WYNONIE HARRIS

b. Aug. 24, 1915, Omaha, NE, d. June 14, 1969, Los Angeles, CA

Wynonie Harris was a powerful blues shouter whose music crossed over into jazz and R&B. He started out as a dancer, drummer, and singer in his native Omaha, performing in shows and considering Big Joe Turner (whom he heard in New Orleans and had an opportunity to record with in 1947) to be his main idol. Harris moved to Los Angeles in the early 1940s and caught on big while with the Lucky Millinder Orchestra, having hits with "Who Threw the Whiskey in the Well?" and "Hurry, Hurry." He launched his solo career in 1945, toured with Lionel Hampton, and recorded many popular records for Apollo, Aladdin, and King, including "Good Rockin' Tonight," "All She Wants to Do Is Rock," and "Grandma Plays the Numbers." Wynonie Harris's heyday lasted until his King contract ended in 1954 and he slipped away into obscurity, running bars in Brooklyn and Los Angeles before dying from cancer.

●

9 *Everybody Boogie! / Aug. 2, 1945–Dec. 1945 / Delmark 683*

8 *1945–1947 / Dec. 1945–July 1947 / Classics 1013*
All of Wynonie Harris's first recordings as a leader (except for four early titles for Philo) are on these two CDs. The Delmark CD finds him backed by groups led by Illinois Jacquet, tenor saxophonist Jack McVea, bassist Oscar Pettiford, and tenor Johnny Alston. Whether on "Wynonie's Blues," "Somebody Changed the Lock on My Door," "Young Man's Blues," or "Everybody Boogie," Harris's style fell between blues, Swing, and R&B; two alternate takes round out this strong release. *1945–1947* picks up right where *Everybody Boogie!* leaves off and has Harris backed by various medium-size groups (including members of Lionel Hampton's orchestra and an outfit organized by Leonard Feather) plus sharing the spotlight on three numbers (including the two-part "Battle of the Blues") with Big Joe Turner himself. Highlights include "In the Evening Blues," "Drinkin' by Myself," "Mr. Blues Jumped the Rabbit," and "Big City Blues." On one of the sessions, the future avant-garde bandleader Sun Ra is heard on his recording debut, being well featured on "Dig This Boogie."

TED HEATH

b. Mar. 30, 1900, London, England, d. Nov. 18, 1969, Virginia Water, England

Ted Heath symbolized Swing in England during the 1950s and '60s. His big bands, which often emphasized nostalgia, were quite popular. Heath started out playing tenor horn before switching to trombone. He was a sideman with many top British bands through the years, including Bert Firman (1924–25), Jack Hylton (1925–27), Bert Ambrose (1928–36), Sydney Lipton, and Geraldo (1939–44), but he was rarely ever heard as a soloist. In 1944 Heath formed his own group, which caught on quickly. Although not strictly a jazz band, the Ted Heath Orchestra at times featured tenors Ronnie Scott and Danny Moss, playing mostly Swing hits plus some newer pop and show tunes. Ted Heath toured regularly (including visiting the United States several times starting in 1956) and recorded many albums up until the time of his death in 1969. In fact, so popular was his band that it still appeared in public and recorded as late as 1977. Most of Ted Heath's many recordings are not currently available, but the Hep label has come out with three that trace his orchestra's early days playing big band Swing: *1944–45 Vol. 1* (Hep 52), *1945–47 Vol. 2* (Hep 57), and *1947–48 Vol. 3* (Hep 61).

●

FILMS
Since they were England's most popular Swing band of the late 1940s and '50s, the Ted Heath Orchestra made appearances in several British films, including *Uneasy Terms* (1948), *Dance Hall* (1950), *It's a Wonderful World* (1956), and *Jazz Boat* (1959).

CHUCK HEDGES
b. Chicago, IL

A top Swing clarinetist who can also often be heard in Dixieland settings, Chuck Hedges has been underrated for decades but is actually one of the finest clarinetists around today. He started out playing professionally in the early 1950s in Chicago with local groups, including bands led by trombonist George Brunies, drummer Danny Alvin, Muggsy Spanier, and Dave Remington. Hedges worked with trumpeter Dick Ruedebusch in the 1960s, toured with Wild Bill Davison on a few occasions in the 1970s and '80s, and has long been a fixture at classic jazz festivals. He has lived in Milwaukee for some time, but Chuck Hedges is still closely identified with the Chicago trad jazz scene, playing at the peak of his powers in the late 1990s.

7   *Clarinet Climax / June 1982 / Jazzology 131*

8   *No Greater Love / Dec. 1992 / Arbors 19121*

9   *Swingtet Live at Andy's / Mar. 22, 1993–May 3, 1993 / Delmark 465*

Chuck Hedges's first chance to lead his own record date was actually a live Swing/Dixieland session co-led by fellow clarinetist Allan Vache and including the Jim Cullum Jazz Band's rhythm section. Hedges and Vache battle it out on six standards, including "Undecided," "China Boy," and "Oh, Baby." *Clarinet Climax* is rounded off by a version of "Potato Head Blues" from Cullum's hot band. Hedges is the main soloist on *No Greater Love,* an excellent quartet date with pianist Eddie Higgins, Bob Haggart, and drummer Gene Estes that is comprised mostly of sophisticated Swing standards plus the pianist's "Magnolia Rag." His superior *Swingtet* set teams Hedges with some superior if obscure Chicago musicians (vibraphonist Duane Tham, guitarist Dave Bany, bassist John Bany, and drummer Charles Braugham) and has plenty of hot moments, particularly on "Softly as in a Morning Sunrise," "Breakfast Feud," "Liza," and "The Blues My Naughty Sweetie Gives Me."

LPS TO SEARCH FOR
The Square Roots of Jazz (Magna Graphic 102) is a little-known but delightful Chuck Hedges Swing set with Johnny Varro, bassist Ray Leatherwood, and drummer Gene Estes.

NEAL HEFTI
b. Oct. 29, 1922, Hastings, NE

Neal Hefti, a top arranger for decades, is best known for his contributions to Count Basie's library in the 1950s. In fact, Hefti's work (and the way that he utilized Frank Wess's flute) helped give the second Basie band its own sound. He first wrote arrangements for Nat Towles in the late 1930s when he was still in high school. Hefti played trumpet with the big bands of Charlie Barnet, Horace Heidt, and Charlie Spivak during 1942–43. He was also heard with Woody Herman's First Herd (1944–46), but it was his arrangements and compositions (including "The Good Earth" and "Wild Root") that were most significant. Hefti freelanced throughout much of his career, writing for Charlie Ventura, Harry James (1948–49), and Charlie Parker ("Repetition"). His work for Count Basie included "Cute," "Little Pony," "Li'l Darlin'," and "Whirlybird," all of which have stayed in the Basie book ever since. Neal Hefti led occasional big bands in the 1950s, but since that time he has worked primarily as an arranger-composer for the studios and for many films.

LPS TO SEARCH FOR
Left and Right (Columbia 8316) is a very different Neal Hefti record, for it features him in 1956 on trumpet with an unidentified sextet, probably the last example of Hefti playing his horn on records. The ten songs are melodic and danceable, and include "That Old Black Magic," "You Do Something to Me," "Mack the Knife," and "I Won't Dance."

PEANUTS HUCKO
b. Apr. 7, 1918, Syracuse, NY

Michael "Peanuts" Hucko spent his career as a clarinetist who often sounded very close to Benny Goodman in sound although he was featured in both Swing and Dixieland settings. Hucko actually started out mostly on tenor, playing in the big bands of Jack Jenney, Will Bradley (1939–41), Joe Marsala, Charlie Spivak (1941–42), and Bob Chester. He came into his own as a clarinetist while with Glenn Miller's Army Air Force Band (1943–45) where he was a major soloist. After being discharged, he worked with the orchestras of Benny Goodman (back on tenor during 1945–46) and Ray McKinley (1946–47), led his own combos, and often played with Eddie Condon (particularly during 1947–50). Hucko worked in the studios starting in the 1950s, was on a European tour in 1957 with Jack Teagarden and Earl Hines, and was a member of the Louis Armstrong All-Stars during 1958–60. He freelanced in the 1960s (including having the house band at Condon's Club during 1964–66), led the Glenn Miller ghost band during the next decade, and has appeared in many mostly Swing-oriented settings through the years (often in Benny Goodman tributes), with his wife, singer Louise Tobin. Peanuts Hucko has been less active since the mid-1990s.

7   *Swing That Music / 1992 / Star Line 9005*
On one of his most recent records, Peanuts Hucko leads an impressive octet for a set of Swing standards. Joined by tenor-saxophonist Danny Moss, trumpeter Randy Sandke, trombonist Roy Williams, vibraphonist Lars Estrand, pianist Johnny Varro, bassist Colin Gieg, drummer Butch Miles, and (on two numbers) singer Louise Tobin, the music is very much in the Benny Goodman tradition. Highlights include "Swing That Music," a heated "Stealin' Apples," and "Seven Come Eleven."

LPS TO SEARCH FOR

Live At Eddie Condon's (Chiaroscuro 167) finds Hucko in superior form in 1960, jamming on veteran tunes with pianist Ralph Sutton, bassist Dante Montucci, and drummer George Wettling. *With His Pied Piper Quintet* (World Jazz 15) from 1979 matches Hucko with vibraphonist Peter Appleyard (here sounding quite close to Lionel Hampton), pianist Ross Tompkins, bassist Arnold Fishkind, and drummer Jack Sperling for a variety of standards (only two associated with BG) and basic originals; "Riverboat Shuffle," "Avalon," and a speedy "When You're Smiling" are particularly enjoyable.

DICK HYMAN
b. Mar. 8, 1927, New York, NY

A remarkable pianist who can play in any jazz style, Dick Hyman has an obvious love for prebop music, including stride and Swing piano. He worked early on with Red Norvo (1949–50) and Benny Goodman (1950) and was a studio musician during much of the 1950s and '60s. Hyman's early career was certainly eclectic, including everything from appearing on a television show (fortunately the film still exists) in 1952 with Charlie Parker and Dizzy Gillespie (playing "Hot House") to recording honky-tonk under pseudonyms, playing an early synthesizer, recording a full album on harpsichord, being Arthur Godfrey's musical director (1959–62), and even playing remakes of rock songs.

Dick Hyman's career came into its own in the 1970s, when he began to focus on 1920s and '30s music, played with the New York Jazz Repertory Company, and started writing soundtracks for Woody Allen movies. Dick Hyman, one of the finest living pianists, has recorded prolifically during the past 25 years, including duets with Ruby Braff, tributes to Fats Waller, Duke Ellington, Harold Arlen, Irving Berlin, James P. Johnson, Zez Confrey, and Scott Joplin, and a variety of solo sessions. He can also, when inspired, emulate any top jazz pianist, in styles ranging from ragtime to hard bop and avantgarde.

8 *Live at Michael's Pub / July 24–25, 1981 / Jazz Mania 6007*

7 *At Chung's Chinese Restaurant / Sept. 26, 1985 / Musical Heritage Society 51217*

9 *Runnin' Ragged / Sept. 1985 / Projazz 652*

8 *Manhattan Jazz / 1987 / Music Masters 60136*

Dick Hyman's career has covered several styles, so the reviews here focus mostly on his Swing and stride dates, leaving his earlier projects, his 1920s tributes, and other odds-and-ends recordings for other books in this series. *Live at Michael's Pub* is a set of piano duets by Hyman and Roger Kellaway. The two virtuosos, who both have a strong sense of humor, perform four standards, Kellaway's theme to the *All in the Family* television series, the "Woody Woodpecker Song," and "Chopsticks" (which is really taken apart); the results are often riotous. *At Chung's Chinese Restaurant* is a solo set of mostly vintage standards; effortless brilliance during a typical night's work. *Runnin' Ragged* puts the focus on violinist Stan Kurtis, who is accompanied throughout by Hyman. The dozen songs were all composed or cowritten by Joe Venuti during 1928–37, and they bring to life Venuti's brilliant style; Kurtis comes awfully close at times. *Manhattan Jazz* is another type of duet, cornet-piano explorations with Ruby Braff, one of their few joint ventures that gives Hyman first billing. As usual there is plenty of magic, particularly on such tunes as "You're Lucky to Me," "I'm Crazy 'Bout My Baby," "Don't Worry About Me," and a Judy Garland medley.

8 *Face the Music / Dec. 8–9, 1987 / Music Masters 60147*

9 *Live from Toronto's Café des Copains / 1988 / Music & Arts 622*

7 *Dick Hyman Plays Fats Waller / Dec. 1988 / Reference 33*

7 *Hyman Plays Arlen / Apr. 13–14, 1989 / Music Masters 0215*

8 *Music of 1937 / Feb. 14, 1990 / Concord Jazz 4415*

7 *All Through the Night / 1991 / Music Masters 5060*

8 *Dick Hyman Plays Duke Ellington / Aug. 23, 1992 / Reference 50*

Dick Hyman has recorded many solo piano sets during the past 20 years, including the seven in this section. *Face the Music* finds him concentrating on and uplifting Irving Berlin tunes, including such obscurities as "Lady of the Evening," "The Night Is Filled with Music," and "I'll See You in C.U.B.A.," plus some more familiar tunes. *Live from Toronto's Café des Copains* ranges from the Dixieland standard "At the Jazz Band Ball" and Jelly Roll Morton's "Frog-I-More Rag" to "Lush Life" and "What Is This Thing Called Love?" Hyman's Fats Waller project was performed on a Bosendorfer reproducing piano and actually "recorded" at a later time when the pianist was not even present! He is heard playing 15 Waller tunes and, even if some of the joy of Fats's music is missing (particularly on "African Ripples" and "Viper's Drag"), the excellence of Hyman's playing (which can be best heard on "Back Up to Me" and an uptempo "Stealin' Apples") is obvious. Hyman mostly sounds like Art Tatum and Teddy Wilson on his Harold Arlen tribute. "Right As the Rain," "In Your Own Quiet Way" (which has a very rare Hyman vocal), and "You Said It" are the only lesser-known tunes on a recital that includes "As Long As I Live," "Over the Rainbow," and "Between the Devil and the Deep Blue Sea." *Music of 1937,* from Concord's notable Maybeck Recital Hall solo recordings, finds Hyman playing in his own Swing-based style and interpreting 11 songs that were written in 1937. It was quite a musical year, as this program (which includes "Where or When," "A Foggy Day," "Someday My Prince Will Come," "Thanks for the Memory," and "Caravan") shows, and the pianist is in top form throughout. Hyman digs into the music of Cole Porter on "All Through the Night," including a 10½-minute version of "Easy to Love" and three unknown songs from the score of "Kiss Me Kate." The Duke Ellington set features Hyman mostly avoiding the really obvious material (although a few warhorses are transformed) and interpreting such underrated classics as "Jubilee Stomp," "Drop Me Off in Harlem," a nearly atonal "The Clothed Woman," "Doin' the New Voom Voom," and a wild version of "Tonk" in which he sounds like two pianists; it was originally recorded as a duet by Ellington and Billy Strayhorn.

10 *Dick Hyman/Ralph Sutton / Nov. 12, 1993 / Concord Jazz 4603*

6 *From the Age of Swing / 1994 / Reference 59*

7 *Cheek to Cheek / June 24–25, 1995 / Arbors 19155*

6 *Swing Is Here / Feb. 28–29, 1996 / Reference 72*

8 *Dick and Derek at the Movies / Apr. 7–8, 1998 / Arbors 19197*

It was logical that Dick Hyman and Ralph Sutton would team up someday in duets, for, after the death of Dick Wellstood, they were the two finest living stride pianists alive. Their collaboration (as part of the Concord Duo series) is full of excitement as they romp on such tunes as "I've Found a New Baby," "I'm Sorry I Made You Cry," "Sunday," and "Dinah." This I believe is still their only meeting on records, but fortunately it is a classic. *From the Age of Swing,* other than the title cut (an original blues), has a nonet playing songs from the 1930s in swinging if predictable fashion. Hyman is joined by trumpeter Joe Wilder, altoist Frank Wess (on three numbers), trombonist Urbie Green, Phil Bodner on clarinet and alto, baritonist Joe Temperley, Bucky Pizzarelli, Milt Hinton, and Butch Miles; everyone plays as solidly as one would expect. *Cheek to Cheek* is a trio date with Howard Alden and Bob Haggart that is a touch more modern than most of Hyman's recent efforts, bordering on bebop at times. Two Thelonious Monk tunes mix in with selections from Irving Berlin, Billy Strayhorn, Cole Porter, and others (including Flip Phillips's "The Claw"). *Swing Is Here,* which has a very similar CD photo as the one on *From the Age of Swing,* is in a comparable vein, although the lineup of musicians is mostly different. Hyman performs 15 tunes that were standards in the late 1930s with vibraphonist

Peter Appleyard, Ken Peplowski, Randy Sandke, Frank Wess, Bucky Pizzarelli, bassist Jay Leonhart, Butch Miles, and (on a few numbers) singer Nancy Marano. Pleasing music that lacks any real surprises. Finally there is *Dick and Derek at the Movies,* an opportunity for Dick Hyman to play 15 songs from the movies (including his "Cecilia's Theme") in duets with the excellent Mainstream pianist Derek Smith. Among the many highlights of this frequently exciting set are "What Is This Thing Called Love?," "Lulu's Back in Town," and "The Entertainer."

LPS TO SEARCH FOR

Fats Waller's Heavenly Jive (Chiaroscuro 162) is a Hyman-Braff duo album from 1977 that features the pianist sticking to pipe organ and duplicating some of Fats Waller's organ solos of the 1920s with the help of the highly expressive cornetist. *Themes & Variations on "A Child Is Born"* (Chiaroscuro 198) is a truly unique project. Hyman plays Thad Jones's "A Child Is Born" in the style of 12 different pianists plus himself; such Swing players as Earl Hines, Fats Waller, Teddy Wilson, and Art Tatum are among his subjects. And Dick Hyman fortunately had a chance to play duets with the late Dick Wellstood on *Stridemonster* (Unisson 1006). They stride their way through 1920s and '30s material, including tunes by James P. Johnson, Duke Ellington ("Birmingham Breakdown"), and Gershwin.

KEITH INGHAM

b. Feb. 5, 1942, London, England

A talented Swing pianist who is on many tasteful Mainstream sessions, Keith Ingham is gradually becoming better known. He started playing professionally in 1964 in his native England, gigging with many local players, including saxophonist Bruce Turner and clarinetists Sandy Brown and Wally Fawkes. Ingham recorded with Bob Wilber and Bud Freeman in 1974, worked regularly for several years as Susannah McCorkle's accompanist, moved to New York in 1978, and played with Benny Goodman, the World's Greatest Jazz Band, and Maxine Sullivan, among others. In more recent times Keith Ingham has worked with Harry Allen, Dan Barrett, and Marty Grosz plus recorded as a leader for several record companies, most extensively for the Jump label.

7 *A Collection of Fred Astaire / Mar. 21–23, 1989 / Jump 12-15*

7 *Music of Victor Young / Mar. 21–23, 1989 / Jump 12-16*

8 *Donaldson Redux / June 20, 1991–Nov. 25, 1991 / Stomp Off 1237*

8 *My Little Brown Book, Vol. 1 / Mar. 12–14, 1993 / Progressive 7101*

8 *Music from the Mauve Decades / Apr. 20–21, 1993 / Sackville 2033*

9 *Keith Ingham & Marty Grosz and Their Hot Cosmopolites / Apr. 20–22, 1994 / Stomp Off 1285*

Keith Ingham's recordings are always in the prebop Swing tradition. The quartet of Ingham, the cool-toned clarinetist Bob Reitmeier, bassist Frank Tate, and drummer Vernel Fournier is featured on both a set of music associated with Fred Astaire (classy songs by Irving Berlin, the Gershwins, and the team of Schwartz and Dietz) and a program of Victor Young music (a fine exploration of the underrated composer's work). The latter's 18 tunes include "Street of Dreams," "Sweet Sue," "Love Me Tonight," and "When I Fall in Love." Donaldson Redux finds Ingham and guitarist-singer Marty Grosz performing 20 of Walter Donaldson's songs, which, in addition to such hits as "My Blue Heaven" and "Love Me or Leave Me," also include some obscurities, including "There's a Wah-Wah Gal in Agua Caliente" and "A Girlfriend of a Boyfriend of Mine." The all-star group has several hot soloists, including cornetist Peter Ecklund, clarinetist Bobby Gordon, Loren Schoenberg, and Dan Barrett. *My Little Brown Book* features Ingham leading a quintet with Harry Allen (who is listed as leader for the second volume) and guitarist Chris Flory, playing 16 Billy Strayhorn

tunes. *Music from the Mauve Decades* consists of 17 songs from the 1900–20 period, including such charming melodies as "Creole Belle," "Ida, Sweet As Apple Cider," "Meet Me Tonight in Dreamland," and "Till We Meet Again." Ingham, Bobby Gordon, and Hal Smith form the melodic trio. The second project by Ingham and Marty Grosz (*Their Hot Cosmopolites*) consists of 20 tunes by the songwriting team of Buddy DeSylva, Lew Brown, and Ray Henderson. That collaboration lasted for six years (1925–31) and resulted in such tunes as "The Varsity Drag," "Birth of the Blues," and "Button Up Your Overcoat," plus many forgotten gems. In addition to the co-leaders, the musicians on the Stomp Off disc include such notables as Ecklund, Barrett, Dan Levinson on clarinet and C-melody, Scott Robinson on many reeds, and violinist Andy Stein. *Vol. 1* and *Vol. 2* from Jump have a variety of little-known 1930s and '40s songs from many sources and feature Ingham with up to nine pieces, although some of the groups are much more intimate. Barrett (on trombone and trumpet), cornetist Randy Reinhart, clarinetist Phil Bodner, and Scott Robinson all have solo space. Some of the same players (Ecklund, Robinson, and guitarist James Chirillo) join Ingham and Harry Allen on *Back Room Stomp*; Robinson (on clarinet, soprano and baritone) often takes honors during this fine Swing date.

QUENTIN JACKSON

b. Jan. 13, 1909, Springfield, OH, d. Oct. 2, 1976, New York, NY

One of the finest of the Tricky Sam Nanton–style plunger mute specialists, trombonist Quentin "Butter" Jackson was important during the Swing era but most significant in the later years, when he helped keep the ancient style alive. Jackson played piano and violin while growing up, not taking up the trombone until he was 18. Early jobs included work with Gerald Hobson, Lloyd Byrd's Buckeye Melodians, Wesley Helvey, and Zack Whyte's Chocolate Beau Brummels. Jackson played trombone and sang ballads with McKinney's Cotton Pickers (1930–32). He had longtime associations with Don Redman's orchestra (1932–39) and Cab Calloway (1940–48), taking time off from Cab to tour Europe with Redman in 1946. After a short stint with Lucky Millinder, Jackson became an important member of Duke Ellington's orchestra (1948–59), where his plunger mute solos allowed Duke to hint at his earliest days in his writing. The only record session that Butter ever led was a French date in 1959 that resulted in four selections. Jackson left Ellington to tour Europe with Quincy Jones and then spent two years (1960–62) with Count Basie. He recorded with Charles Mingus ("The Black Saint and the Sinner Lady"), was back with Ellington for a brief time in 1963, and freelanced for the remainder of his career, including playing with the orchestras of Louie Bellson, Gerald Wilson, and Thad Jones–Mel Lewis. Overall, few other trombonists in jazz history have played with as many quality big bands as Quentin Jackson.

WILLIS "GATOR" JACKSON

b. Apr. 25, 1928, Miami, FL, d. Oct. 25, 1987, New York, NY

Willis Jackson was one of the top honking and squealing tenor saxophonists of the late 1940s, modifying his style slightly by the late 1950s so as to fit into hard bop and soul jazz settings. Jackson played locally and studied music at (of all places) Florida Agricultural and Mechanical University. He came to fame while with the Cootie Williams's band (where he was a star off and on during 1948–55), being showcased on the 1948 two-sided recording of "Gator Tail," which gave him a lifelong nickname. Unlike some other jazz tenormen who sounded reluctant while honking, Jackson's passion and sincerity at playing the explosive music was obvious and, although influenced by Illinois Jacquet, he had something of himself to add to the wild style.

Jackson started leading his own group in 1950 and was popular for much of the decade, playing rhythm and blues. Gator was married for eight years to singer Ruth Brown. By the early 1960s he was deemphasizing his honking in favor of melodic and soulful improvising, often using an organ in his combos; his 1959–71 series of Prestige recordings (25 albums in all) were steady sellers. Willis Jackson became a longtime regular at Club Harlem in Atlantic City and kept busy during his final two decades, recording for Muse (including the classic *Bar Wars* in 1977) and remaining a popular attraction.

●

9 *Call of the Gators / Dec. 21, 1949–May 29, 1950 / Delmark 460*

7 *Legends of Acid Jazz / May 25, 1959–Aug. 16, 1960 / Prestige 24198*

7 *Keep on a-Blowin' / May 25, 1959–Mar. 31, 1962 / Prestige 24218*

8 *With Pat Martino / Mar. 21, 1964 / Prestige 24161*

10 *Bar Wars / Dec. 21, 1977 / Muse 6011*

8 *Single Action / Apr. 26, 1978 / Muse 5179*

All of Willis Jackson's earliest recordings as a leader for the Apollo label are on *Call of the Gators,* and these R&B-ish sides are full of excitement. Jackson could squeal, honk, and scream with the best of them, as he shows on such numbers as "Blow, Jackson, Blow," "Gonna Hoot and Holler Saturday Night," and "Later for the Gator." The jump bands include trombonist Booty Wood and pianist Bill Doggett, but it is Gator who steals the show. Each of the three Prestige CDs completely reissues two former LPs apiece. *Legends of Acid Jazz* brings back a couple of albums from 1959–60 (*Blue Gator* and *Cookin' Sherry*) that match Jackson with guitarist Bill Jennings and organist Jack McDuff. *Keep on a-Blowin'* (which has the album of the same name plus *Thunderbird*) features either Jack McDuff or Freddie Roach on organ, while *With Pat Martino* contains a pair of exciting live sessions (*Jackson's Action* and *Live Action*) with guitarist Pat Martino, trumpeter Frank Robinson, and organist Carl Wilson. In each case Jackson alternates jumping originals with blues, ballads and occasional standards, showing off both his warm tone and his range of emotions. The Pat Martino CD gets the edge due to the excitement of hearing Gator play before a live audience.

However, it is *Bar Wars* that is most highly recommended. Joined by Martino, organist Charlie Earland, drummer Idris Muhammad, and Buddy Caldwell on conga, Gator often sounds like a man possessed, particularly on "Later," "Bar Wars," and "The Goose Is Loose." The CD reissue adds a pair of alternate takes to the rewarding program. Also quite worthwhile is *Single Action,* particularly for "Makin' Whoopee" and a couple of hard-driving blues; Willis Jackson is even able to uplift "Evergreen" and "You Are the Sunshine of My Life."

ILLINOIS JACQUET

b. Oct. 31, 1922, Broussard, LA

One of the all-time great tenor saxophonists, Jean Baptiste "Illinois" Jacquet practically invented the R&B tenor style. He was a Swing stylist who was not reluctant to honk or creatively use repetition so as to build up excitement. Jacquet's solo on "Flying Home" with Lionel Hampton in 1942 not only made him a major name but helped launch the careers of many other tenors, who built their own styles from that one record.

The younger brother of trumpeter Russell Jacquet, Illinois grew up in Houston. He started on drums in high school and learned soprano and alto before switching to tenor. After playing locally, Jacquet moved to Los Angeles in 1941 while working with Floyd Ray's orchestra. Soon after joining Lionel Hampton, he recorded "Flying Home," which would be his (and Hampton's) trademark song from then on. Jacquet was with Cab Calloway's orchestra (1943–44), became a star with Jazz at the Philharmonic (taking a screeching solo on "Blues" achieved by biting on his reed), helped Lester Young out in the film short *Jammin' the Blues*, and was a featured soloist with Count Basie (1945–46). Jacquet went out on his own in 1946 and was a very popular attraction for a decade, leading a medium-size band and jamming in exciting fashion on basic chord changes. Many tenormen were influenced by Jacquet, whose own style mixed together aspects of Coleman Hawkins and Lester Young. He recorded and toured regularly during the 1950s, was still a big name during the next few decades, and began playing bassoon now and then in the mid-1960s (usually for an atmospheric ballad), also occasionally playing alto in a style similar to Charlie Parker's. Jacquet, who has usually been heard in small groups, has led a part-time big band since the late 1980s, although unfortunately they have recorded only one album thus far. Nearly every tenor saxophonist in the Retro Swing movement is inspired by Illinois Jacquet.

●

* *The Complete Illinois Jacquet Sessions 1945–50 / July 1945–May 22, 1950 / Mosaic 4-165*

8 *1945–1946 / July 1945–Jan. 8, 1946 / Classics 948*

8 *1946–1947 / Aug. 1946–Dec. 18, 1947 / Classics 1019*

9 *The Black Velvet Band / Dec. 18, 1947–July 3, 1967 / Bluebird 6571*

8 *The Kid and the Brute / Dec. 11, 1951–Dec. 13, 1954 / Verve 314 557 096*

The four-CD limited-edition Mosaic box set features Illinois Jacquet at the peak of his fame and influence. The recordings, cut for the Aladdin, Apollo, ARA, Savoy, and Victor labels, focus on Jacquet's jump band of 1945–50, a hot group with Russell Jacquet, Emmett Berry and/or Joe Newman on trumpets, Henry Coker, Trummy Young or J.J. Johnson on trombones, sometimes baritonist Leo Parker, and Sir Charles Thompson or Bill Doggett on piano. There is also a big band date, with trumpeters Fats Navarro and Miles Davis in the personnel. Jacquet is usually the main star, and his romping tenor is heard in its early prime. Listeners not able to acquire this exciting set may opt for the two Classics CDs (which do not include alternate takes) and

Bluebird's *The Black Velvet Band,* a strong domestic release with Jacquet's best Victor recordings of 1947–50 plus the tenor's guest shot with the Lionel Hampton Orchestra in 1967 on a remake of "Flying Home." *The Kid and the Brute* reissues Jacquet's one album with fellow tenor Ben Webster (their frequently exciting collaboration alternates between being competitive and being complementary) plus a former ten-inch release from 1953 by Illinois and his regular septet (with brother Russell and baritonist Cecil Payne).

5 *Flies Again / Aug. 11, 1959 / Roulette 7972722*

6 *Illinois Jacquet / Feb. 5, 1962–May 21, 1962 / Legacy / Epic 64654*

9 *Bottoms Up / Mar. 26, 1968 / Original Jazz Classics 417*

7 *The King! / Aug. 20, 1968 / Original Jazz Classics 849*

8 *The Soul Explosion / May 25, 1969 / Original Jazz Classics 674*

9 *The Blues; That's Me! / Sept. 16, 1969 / Original Jazz Classics 614*

7 *The Comeback / Aug. 13–14, 1971 / Black Lion 760160*

After his period on Clef and Verve (1951–58) ended, Jacquet recorded several decent but not essential releases. He had let the constant criticism of overly somber jazz critics get to him a bit, and his tone was more mellow and less strident than earlier; in other words, some of the excitement was gone as he did away with many of his explosions. *Flies Again* has its moments (particularly a blues dedicated to Lester Young called "Teddy Bear," "Bottoms Up," and "The King"), but much of the set is overly relaxed and a bit too comfortable. Jacquet's self-titled disc on Legacy is a bit better thanks to his occasional appearances on alto (quite effective on "Indiana"), a Basie-ish rhythm section (with Sir Charles Thompson), and some fine Jimmy Mundy arrangements. On the minus side is that trumpeter Roy Eldridge is underutilized (the Eldridge-Jacquet combination never really results in the expected fireworks) and the songs overall are a bit too brief.

However, the tenor's four recordings for Prestige during 1968–69 (all reissued in the Original Jazz Classics series) are on a higher level. *Bottoms Up* (with the Barry Harris Trio) has exciting versions of "Bottoms Up" and "Jivin' with Jack the Bellboy" plus some warm ballads. *The King!* (with a septet that also features Joe Newman and Milt Buckner) is at its best on the title track and Jacquet's bassoon feature on "Caravan," although "How High the Moon" does not live up to its potential. *The Soul Explosion* has Jacquet being the lead voice with a ten-piece group that also includes Newman (who has some solo space) and Buckner. "The Soul Explosion," "After Hours," and the previously unissued "Still King" are the standouts. But of the four Original Jazz Classics discs, the one to get first is *The Blues; That's Me,* a quintet outing with pianist Wynton Kelly and Tiny Grimes. The

10 1/2 minute title cut, "Still King," "Everyday I Have the Blues," and an atmospheric " 'Round Midnight" (which showcases Jacquet's bassoon) are most memorable. *The Comeback,* one of several Jacquet Black Lion discs, is hurt a bit by Milt Buckner's rather dominant organ, which wheezes along behind the tenor and sometimes almost drowns him out. Drummer Tony Crombie completes the trio, and Jacquet, who is in excellent form, does overcome Buckner on "The King" and "Take the 'A' Train." Illinois takes a rare vocal on "I Wanna Blow Now," doing a surprisingly effective imitation of Ella Fitzgerald.

LPS TO SEARCH FOR

The Cool Rage (Verve 2544) is a two-LP sampler of Illinois Jacquet's Clef/Verve period, repeating a few titles from *The Kid and the Brute* but also including numbers from a big band date and meetings with pianists Hank Jones and Carl Perkins and organists Count Basie and Wild Bill Davis. All of this music deserves to be reissued in full. Somewhat obscure is *Jacquet's Got It* (Atlantic 81816), the one recording by Illinois Jacquet's big band of the 1980s and '90s. Cut in 1987, this set is highlighted by "Tickletoe," "Stompin' at the Savoy," and "Three Buckets of Jive"; the soloists include trumpeters Irv Stokes and Jon Faddis, trombonist Frank Lacy, and pianist Richard Wyands in addition to the passionate tenor.

FILMS

Illinois Jacquet makes a strong impression during the last part of the award-winning *Jammin' the Blues* (1944). He is fully documented on the video *Texas Tenor* (Rhapsody 9021).

JAZZ AT THE PHILHARMONIC

Producer Norman Granz always loved freewheeling jam sessions that teamed together the top soloists in jazz. In 1944 he organized a concert at Philharmonic Auditorium in Los Angeles that starred Nat Cole (strictly as a pianist), Les Paul (before he achieved major success outside of the jazz world), Illinois Jacquet, trumpeter Shorty Sherock, and trombonist J. J. Johnson, among others. The results, which were recorded, were such a major success that Granz was inspired to use the name Jazz at the Philharmonic (JATP) as the title for an annual series of concerts that were essentially a traveling jam session. During 1945–56, Granz's concerts were split into two: an all-star jam on blues and other basic chord changes (along with a ballad medley) and features for some of his favorite combos and singers. Among the stars of the jam sessions through the years were trumpeters Howard McGhee, Harry "Sweets" Edison, Charlie Shavers, Roy Eldridge, and Dizzy Gillespie, trombonists Bill Harris, Tommy Turk, and J. J. Johnson, tenors Illinois Jacquet, Flip Phillips (whose solo on "Perdido" became famous), Coleman Hawkins, Lester Young, Ben Webster, and Stan Getz, altoists Charlie Parker, Willie Smith, and

Benny Carter, pianists Hank Jones, Ken Kersey, and Oscar Peterson, guitarists Irving Ashby, Barney Kessel, and Herb Ellis, bassist Ray Brown, and drummers Buddy Rich, Gene Krupa, Jo Jones, and Louie Bellson, among others. Granz did not care about the differences between musicians' styles, so he often teamed top Swing and bop soloists, as when Eldridge and Gillespie traded off. He went out of his way to pay his musicians well and fought against racism every step of the way. Some overly serious jazz critics felt that the "battles" were a cheapening of the music and they were particularly appalled by the loud and rather boisterous audiences. However, Granz recorded many of the JATP concerts, and the recordings that survive show that a great deal of valuable music was created in the competitive atmosphere.

By 1956, the other parts of the show, particularly when Ella Fitzgerald was showcased, were getting more attention than the jam sessions and attendance was declining. During 1957–58 JATP only toured Europe, and then the program was discontinued. Norman Granz tried again in 1967 and on a couple of occasions in the 1970s but mostly focused on managing Ella and booking concerts by organized bands, including the orchestras of Count Basie and Duke Ellington, in addition to running the Pablo label in the 1970s and '80s. Fortunately a magnificent ten-CD set of all of the existing 1940s JATP sessions has been released that brings back some of the glory days.

●

* *The Complete Jazz at the Philharmonic on Verve 1944–1949 / July 2, 1944–Mar. 1952 / Verve 314 523 893 2JK101-05*

8 *The First Concert / July 2, 1944 / Verve 314 521 646*

6 *Frankfurt, 1952 / Nov. 20, 1952 / Pablo 5305*

7 *Hartford, 1953 / May 1953 / Pablo 2308-240*

8 *Live at the Nichigeki Theatre 1953 / Nov. 4–8, 1953 / Pablo 2620-104*

8 *Stockholm '55, The Exciting Battle / Feb. 2, 1955 / Pablo 2310-713*

9 *London, 1969 / Mar. 1969 / Pablo 2620-119*

7 *Return to Happiness, Tokyo 1983 / Oct. 17, 1983 / Pablo 2620-117*

The Verve box is a remarkable ten-CD set that includes every Jazz at the Philharmonic recording of the 1940s; hopefully someday Verve will do the same for their many scattered 1950s dates. This release (which has many previously unreleased numbers) features countless classic moments. A few well worth mentioning are the Nat Cole–Les Paul trade-off on "Blues," boogie-woogie by Meade Lux Lewis, Billie Holiday's appearances with JATP, a humorous Slim Gaillard set, Charlie Parker's incredible solo on "Lady Be Good," the Gene Krupa Trio with Charlie Ventura, the "Perdido" solos of Flip Phillips and Illinois Jacquet, Ella Fitzgerald in her early prime, and a 1949 concert that matches Charlie Parker with Lester Young, Flip Phillips, Roy Eldridge, and Buddy Rich. This is an essential set

housed in an attractive box but one that will be increasingly difficult to find.

The initial concert, one that features the Cole-Paul trade-off and some raging Illinois Jacquet tenor, is available as the single-CD *The First Concert*. Each of the 1950s JATP releases has its moments. *Frankfurt, 1952* has some good spots by Roy Eldridge, Lester Young, and Flip Phillips on a blues, two standards, and a three-song ballad medley, but nothing unusual occurs. *Hartford, 1953* actually has only one jam tune, a 15-minute version of "Cotton Tail" with Eldridge, Charlie Shavers, Bill Harris, Ben Webster, Flip Phillips, Benny Carter, and Willie Smith. Otherwise, the music features pianist Oscar Peterson's quartet and three fine numbers from Lester Young. The two-CD *Live at the Nichigeki Theatre* contains sets by Ella Fitzgerald, the Oscar Peterson Trio, and Gene Krupa's trio (with Peterson and Benny Carter) but is highlighted by the JATP All-Stars on "Tokyo Blues," "Cotton Tail," and a seven-song ballad medley. Shavers and Eldridge have a classic trumpet battle on "Cottontail" that Shavers wins. However, on *Stockholm '55*, Eldridge's closing solo on the medium-slow blues "Little David" is spectacular, one of his finest moments on record, topping even the improvisations of Dizzy Gillespie, Flip Phillips, Bill Harris, and Oscar Peterson.

London, 1969 was an attempt to revive Jazz at the Philharmonic, and the two-CD set that resulted has many great moments. Among the stars are trumpeters Dizzy Gillespie and Clark Terry, Zoot Sims and James Moody on tenors, Teddy Wilson, Louie Bellson, blues singer/guitarist T-Bone Walker (featured on three songs), Benny Carter, and, surprisingly, Coleman Hawkins, who sounds better at this very late stage in his life than one would expect. The two-CD set *Return to Happiness,* which celebrated the 30th anniversary of JATP's first visit to Japan, essentially gathers together Norman Granz's Pablo All-Stars (including Clark Terry, Zoot Sims, Eddie "Lockjaw" Davis, Al Grey, and Joe Pass) plus some players who were actually JATP alumni (Harry "Sweets" Edison, J. J. Johnson, Oscar Peterson, and Louie Bellson), topped off by Ella Fitzgerald. A few happy jams, lots of ballads, short sets by Peterson and Ella, and a closing "Flying Home" pay tribute to the spirit of JATP one last time.

Verve in the early 1980s released quite a few JATP albums. The music from the 1950s that has not yet reappeared on CD includes *Norgran Blues 1950* (Verve 815151), *The Trumpet Battle 1952* (Verve 815152), *Gene Krupa & Buddy Rich—The Drum Battle* (Verve 815146), *One O'Clock Jump 1953* (Verve 815153), *The Challenges* (Verve 815154), and *Blues in Chicago 1955* (Verve 815155). The Dizzy Gillespie–Roy Eldridge trumpet battle on *The Challenges* is particularly historic.

JERRY JEROME
b. June 19, 1912, Brooklyn, NY

In the late 1990s, Jerry Jerome emerged as a remarkably ageless Swing tenor soloist. Throughout much of his career he was greatly underrated and overlooked. Jerome started out studying medicine but enjoyed playing with college bands much more. He worked with Harry Reser's Clicquot Club Eskimos (1935–36), the early Glenn Miller Orchestra (1936–37), Red Norvo (1937–38), Artie Shaw, and Benny Goodman (1938–40), also recording with Lionel Hampton. While with Goodman, Jerome was captured on record leading a jam session that included Charlie Christian.

After a second stint with Artie Shaw (1940–41), Jerome became a studio musician for decades. He was heard in jazz settings only rarely, often working as a musical director, a conductor, or a writer of jingles for advertisements. In the 1990s Jerry Jerome finally had an opportunity to appear on records (for the Arbors label) fairly regularly in a Mainstream Swing setting and showed that he had not lost a thing despite being in his mid-eighties.

●

9 *Something Old, Something New / Sept. 1939–Mar. 26, 1996 / Arbors 19168*
This 1997 two-CD set lives up to its name. The first CD has a variety of highlights from Jerry Jerome's career, including "Tea for Two" with Charlie Christian, all-star Swing jam sessions from the mid-1940s, a few numbers from a trio date with Teddy Wilson, some notable commercial jingles, and music for a promotional film from the mid-1960s; Charlie Shavers, Yank Lawson, Red Allen, and Bobby Hackett are among the stars who make appearances. The second disc was recorded in 1996 and finds Jerome sounding quite ageless, jamming Swing standards in a septet with Randy Sandke, trombonist George Masso, Dick Hyman, and Bucky Pizzarelli. Although one regrets that he spent so many years outside of jazz, this CD serves as the culmination of Jerry Jerome's career and is certainly his definitive set.

BUDDY JOHNSON
b. Jan. 10, 1915, Darlington, SC, d. Feb. 9, 1977, New York, NY

Woodrow Wilson "Buddy" Johnson was a fine Swing pianist who led an important big band, one of the most popular orchestras of the post-Swing era. With his sister, Ella Johnson, taking vocals, the Buddy Johnson Orchestra made "Since I Fell for You" famous. A pianist and an arranger from an early age, Johnson moved to New York in the mid-1930s. He visited

Europe with the Cotton Club Revue in 1939 and led some small-group recording dates in the U.S. (1939–42) before forming his big band. At first Swing-oriented, the Buddy Johnson big band over time gradually switched to R&B and, by the end of the 1950s, rock and roll, being based for long periods at the Savoy Ballroom where it was a popular attraction with dancing audiences. In his later years, Buddy Johnson (who made his last records in 1961) cut back to a small group, and he spent his final decade outside of music.

7 *1939–1942 / Nov. 16, 1939–Feb. 26, 1942 / Classics 884*

9 *1942–1947 / Jan. 26, 1942–Jan. 28, 1947 / Classics 1079*

7 *Buddy Johnson at the Savoy Ballroom / Oct. 16, 1945– 1946 / Archives of Jazz 3801252*

Despite his orchestra's popularity, few of Buddy Johnson's post-1946 studio recordings are currently available. *1939–1942* has his first 24 recordings as a leader, all but six of his small-group titles of 1939–42, which preceded the formation of his big band. "Stop Pretending" (from the first session) was a minor hit, as was "Please, Mister Johnson." The octet/nonet includes such players as altoist Don Stovall, trumpeter Shad Collins, trombonist Dan Minor, and drummer Kenny Clarke, but the most notable participant is Ella Johnson, who has eight vocals. However, this CD (which just has six instrumentals) is essentially prehistory for Buddy Johnson, whose greatest impact would begin in 1944 with his orchestra.

1942–1947 has the final Johnson combo dates along with the first recordings by the Buddy Johnson Orchestra, including such titles as "That's the Stuff You Gotta Watch,"

"Fine Brown Frame," "I Wonder Where Our Love Has Gone," five fine instrumentals, and the original version of "Since I Fell for You." Also included are two Ella Johnson small-group numbers. In addition to Ella Johnson, Arthur Prysock has two fine vocals and Buddy Johnson himself sings "Hey Sweet Potato."

The Archives of Jazz CD (a reissue of an earlier Jazz Archives LP) gives one a strong example of the early Buddy Johnson big band as heard on the radio during 1945–46. Trumpeter Dupree Bolton, tenorman David Van Dyke, and Buddy Johnson are the key soloists, but more important are the arranged ensembles (written by Johnson) and the vocals of Ella Johnson and Arthur Prysock.

LPS TO SEARCH FOR

Fine Brown Frame (MCA-1356) has only ten songs (a half-hour of music) and does not even bother to list the recording dates (1944–52), but it does include some of the Buddy Johnson Big Band's better selections, including the original version of "Since I Fell for You" and some boppish numbers. But his orchestra's many later recordings deserve to be reissued much more coherently on CD.

JONAH JONES
b. Dec. 31, 1909, Louisville, KY

One of the great trumpeters of the big band era, Jonah Jones had an unusual amount of success more than a decade after the Swing era ended. Jones began playing trumpet professionally as a teenager, performing locally in Kentucky. He was with Horace Henderson's band in 1928 and then spent periods of time playing in Cleveland, Louisville, Buffalo, and throughout the Midwest. Jones was with Jimmie Lunceford for a few months in 1931 before joining Stuff Smith in Buffalo (1932–34). After short periods with the Lil Armstrong Big Band and McKinney's Cotton Pickers, Jones went back with Smith, and this time the band became a big hit at the Onyx Club in New York. During 1936–40, the Stuff Smith Sextet featured a violin-trumpet front line, lots of uptempo material, and hard-swinging music. Jonah Jones became quite well known in Swing circles, and he appeared as a guest on other people's recordings, including those of Billie Holiday and Teddy Wilson.

After leaving Stuff Smith, Jones had brief stints with Benny Carter and Fletcher Henderson before becoming a longtime member of the Cab Calloway Orchestra in 1941. He remained with Calloway until 1952, staying with the singer even after Cab's big band had broken up and the group was just a quartet. Having survived the end of the Swing era without much

Jonah Jones, who played with Stuff Smith and Cab Calloway in the Swing era, found his greatest fame in the late 1950s with his string of hit records.

difficulty, Jones in the 1950s worked as a leader, was a member of Earl Hines's sextet (1952–53), played in show bands (including the orchestra for *Porgy and Bess*), visited Europe, made a particularly hot recording with Sidney Bechet, and even worked with society orchestras.

One would think that during the second half of the 1950s, Jonah Jones would be scuffling, as were most Mainstream Swing players, but he had a lucky break. He was hired to lead a quartet at the Embers in 1956 and advised to use a mute during the early sets. Utilizing a shuffle rhythm and mixing current show tunes with older standards, Jonah Jones surprised everyone (including himself) by hitting it big. His recordings of "On the Street Where You Live" and "Baubles, Bangles and Beads" were best-sellers and he recorded a steady series of records for Capitol during 1957–63; he continued the formula on Decca (1965–67) and Motown (1968). For two decades Jones was a very popular attraction, becoming much more famous with the general public than he had ever been during the Swing era. Jonah Jones, who recorded with Earl Hines in the early 1970s, gradually slowed down in the 1970s and '80s, but he still took an occasional gig in the 1990s, even at his advanced age.

7 *Back on the Street / Mar. 22, 1972 / Chiaroscuro 118*

Strangely enough, Capitol has neither reissued nor apparently been made aware of its many formerly popular Jonah Jones records. Just about the only record led by the trumpeter that is currently around on CD is this sextet set, which could also be considered an Earl Hines date. Jones, who teams up with Hines, Buddy Tate, his old friend Cozy Cole, guitarist Jerome Darr, and bassist John Brown, sounds fine. The trumpeter was a bit set in his approach by this time and could sound slick, but his routines are generally colorful. Three selections have been added to the program, which is highlighted by "I'm in the Market for You," "You Can Depend On Me" (Jones sings the Hines standard), "Rose Room," and "Pennies from Heaven."

LPS TO SEARCH FOR

Paris 1954 / Volume One (Swing 8408) features the trumpeter jamming in extroverted fashion with drummer Dave Pochonet's groups of French musicians, which range from a sextet to a tentet. "Honeysuckle Rose," "Perdido," and the 10 1/2-minute "Jonah Plays the Blues" are highlights. The many records by the Jonah Jones Quartet can usually be found at a budget price in used record stores, and most are excellent, including *Jonah Jones at the Embers* (Vik 1135), *Muted Jazz* (Capitol 839), which has "On the Street Where You Live," *Swingin' on Broadway* (Capitol 963), which includes "Baubles, Bangles and Beads," *Jumpin' with Jonah* (Capitol 1039), *Swingin' at the Cinema* (Capitol 1083), *Jonah Jumps Again* (Capitol 1115), *I Dig Chicks* (Capitol 1193), *Swingin' 'Round the World* (Capitol 1237), *Hit Me Again* (Capitol 1375), *Jumpin' with a Shuffle* (Capitol 1404), and *Jonah Jones/Glen Gray* (Capitol 1660).

LOUIS JORDAN

b. July 8, 1908, Brinkley, AR, d. Feb. 4, 1975, Los Angeles, CA

A fixture on the best-selling charts of the 1940s and a major force as a transitional figure between Swing and early R&B, Louis Jordan was an excellent altoist, a superior singer, and a memorable personality. His Tympany Five set the standard for jump combos of the '40s.

It did take Jordan a few years to hit it big. He started on clarinet when he was seven and picked up experience playing with his father's group (the Rabbit Foot Minstrels) as a teenager. He was playing alto professionally as early as 1929 with Jimmy Pryor's Imperial Serenaders. Jordan worked locally in the South before moving to Philadelphia in 1932. He played with Charlie Gaines and in 1934 came to New York, where he recorded with Clarence Williams. Jordan was with LeRoy Smith's orchestra in 1935 and spent two years with Chick Webb (1936–38) but was not featured with Webb other than on three somewhat anonymous ballad vocals.

In August 1938 Jordan put together a combo to play in clubs and in December his group began appearing on records; they were first named the Tympany Five in 1939. By the early 1940s their combination of hot riff-filled pieces, Jordan's catchy vocals, and his always-hip personality resulted in Louis Jordan's becoming a celebrity and a best-selling artist. During 1944–51 Jordan released 57 songs as singles; 55 made the R&B Top Ten! Among his best-known numbers were "Choo Choo Ch'Boogie," "Ain't Nobody Home but Us Chickens," "Is You Is or Is You Ain't Ma Baby," "Five Guys Named Moe," "Saturday Night Fish Fry," "I'm Gonna Leave You on the Outskirts of Town," "G. I. Jive," and "Caldonia." Jordan, who was a household name by 1942, starred in many black films and had small roles in occasion Hollywood big-budget pictures. It seemed as if everything he touched would always turn into gold. He even appeared on record with Bing Crosby and Ella Fitzgerald.

But in 1952 it all stopped. Louis Jordan made the mistake of putting together a big band, and that venture soon flopped. His string of hits ended, and the rise of rock and roll (which he had partly made possible) caused the performer (who was in his mid-forties) to be completely overshadowed. He continued working, but at a lower-profile than earlier, and few of his later records recaptured the old magic despite the fact that he was still singing and playing quite well. He did tour England in 1962 (playing with Chris Barber's band) and made it to Asia during 1967–68. Louis Jordan's final record was in 1973, two

Louis Jordan and his Tympany Five, an extremely popular attraction in the 1940s, led the way toward rhythm and blues.

years before his death at age 66. As so often happens, years after his death, Louis Jordan has made a major "comeback." A Broadway show (*Five Guys Named Moe*) celebrated his music, and Jordan has since been one of the main inspirations for the Retro Swing movement.

8 *1934–1940 / Mar. 23, 1934–Jan. 25, 1940 / Classics 636*

9 *1940–1941 / Mar. 13, 1940–Nov. 15, 1941 / Classics 663*

10 *1941–1943 / Nov. 15, 1941–Nov. 22, 1943 / Classics 741*

9 *1943–1945 // Nov. 22, 1943–July 12, 1945 / Classics 866*

9 *1945–1946 / July 16, 1945–Oct. 10, 1946 / Classics 921*

8 *1946–1947 / Oct. 10, 1946–Dec. 8, 1947 / Classics 1010*

There is no shortage of currently available Louis Jordan records (unlike the situation for Louis Prima and Jonah Jones). More than two decades after his death, Jordan is as famous as ever, and many of his songs remain quite popular. The Classics series on these six CDs has reissued the master takes of all the Tympany Five recordings of 1938–47. *1934–1940* has Jordan's debut on record (an obscure session with Clarence Williams in 1934), his somewhat forgettable ballad vocals with Chick Webb, his two recordings in 1938 with the "Elks Rendezvous Band," and then the first sessions of the Tympany Five. There are a few more instrumentals than usual on this CD, but the sound of the group was already fairly distinctive. *1940–1941* has 26 jumping if mostly little-known titles. However, the *1941–1943* disc finds the Tympany Five breaking through to stardom with "Knock Me a Kiss," "I'm Gonna Move to the Outskirts of Town," "What's the Use of Getting Sober When You Gonna Get Drunk Again," "Five Guys Named Moe," and "Is You Is or Is You Ain't My Baby." In addition to the Decca titles (including four songs originally rejected), there are six selections (mostly remakes) included that Jordan cut as V-Discs. *1943–1945* (which has eight V-Discs, four rejected titles, and a radio commercial) includes "I Like 'Em Fat Like That," "G. I. Jive," and two titles with Bing Crosby. The end of the big band era did not affect the continued success of Jordan. *1945–1946* includes "Don't Worry 'Bout That Mule," "Beware," "Don't Let the Sun Catch You Cryin'," "Choo-Choo Ch-Boogie," "Ain't Nobody Here but Us Chickens," "Let the Good Times Roll," "Jack, You're Dead," and three collaborations with Ella Fitzgerald, including "Stone Cold Dead in the Market." The final Louis Jordan Classics set, *1946–1947*, is highlighted by "Reet, Petite and Gone," "Barnyard Boogie," and "Look Out."

6 *Just Say Moe! / July 21, 1942–Nov. 6, 1973 / Rhino 71144*

10 *The Best of Louis Jordan / Nov. 15, 1941–Jan. 4, 1954 / MCA 4079*

9 *Five Guys Named Moe / July 21, 1942–May 8, 1952 / Decca/MCA 10503*

2 *The Best of Louis Jordan—The Millennium Collection / July 21, 1942–May 28, 1953 / MCA/Decca 088 112 065*

6 *At the Swing Cat's Ball / Mar. 29, 1938–Jan. 4, 1954 / MCA 12044*

9 *Five Guys Named Moe / Aug. 1943–1946 / Vintage Jazz Classics 1037*

While true Louis Jordan fans will want to pick up each of the Classics CDs, there are several worthwhile samplers that could substitute for the more general listener. Rhino's *Just Say Moe!* is a bit odd, for it does not include any real hits other than "What's the Use of Getting Sober." The CD has mostly lesser-known material dating from 1954–57, with a few selections from 1942–43, 1945, 1950, 1962–64, 1968, and 1973, so its subtitle as "Mo' of the Best of Louis Jordan" is not too accurate. However, the fairly rare material (some of which is available elsewhere) does show listeners that there is more to Jordan than his hits. Speaking of the latter, MCA's

The Best of Louis Jordan is the best possible single disc by the entertainer, for it does include nearly all of his most famous numbers and it is logically programmed. The same can be said for *Five Guys Named Moe*, which is subtitled *Original Decca Recordings, Vol. 2* and does not duplicate MCA 4079. Other MCA samplers are more confusing and tend to overlap with each other. *The Millennium Collection* has just 11 selections (less than 40 minutes overall), and all of the music is included in *The Best of Louis Jordan,* so its release is a waste. *At the Swing Cat's Ball,* which duplicates a few numbers, is better. In addition to a few familiar songs, it tosses in some obscurities, including the four tunes from the group's March 29, 1939, date (mistakenly listed on the CD as being from 1938) and a few lesser-known later cuts. The Vintage Jazz Classics CD is valuable because it features some of Louis Jordan's V-Disc sessions along with a few very rare radio appearances, giving listeners an opportunity to hear alternate versions of Jordan hits plus some other numbers not otherwise recorded.

7 *One Guy Named Louis / Jan. 1954–Apr. 1954 / Capitol 96804*

6 *Rock 'n' Roll Call / Mar. 18, 1955–Apr. 17, 1956 / Bluebird 66145*

6 *No Moe! / Oct. 22, 1956–Aug. 1957 / Mercury 314 512 523*

7 *Louis Jordan & Chris Barber / Sept. 1962–Dec. 17, 1974 / Black Lion 760156*

8 *I Believe in Music / Nov. 6, 1973 / Evidence 26006*
One Guy Named Louis reissues all of Louis Jordan's recordings for the Aladdin label. But despite his spirited renditions of the mostly new material (which is in the same style as the earlier Tympany Five numbers), none of the songs caught on. However, Retro Swingers may want to explore this set in search of fresh new material. *Rock 'n' Roll Call*, from the following year, finds Jordan trying unsuccessfully to compete with the music he helped spawn. The music is often high-powered, and several songs humorously deal with food (including "Bananas," "Chicken Back," and "Texas Stew"), but, despite the best efforts of the R&B studio musicians and Jordan, nothing sold very well. *No Moe!* says *The Greatest Hits* in its subtitle, but these versions of such standards as "Saturday Night Fish Fry," "Early in the Mornin'," "Let the Good Times Roll," "Choo Choo Ch'Boogie," and "Caldonia" are remakes from 1956–57, fine versions but not up

to the level of the originals. By the time Jordan teamed up with trombonist Chris Barber's trad band in 1962, the 54-year-old performer was considered a has-been, although there was actually nothing wrong with his singing or playing. The first nine selections on this CD contain a few remakes ("Choo Choo Ch'Boogie" and "Is You Is or Is You Ain't My Baby") along with a few standards. The final five numbers are actually from 1973–74 and do not include Jordan; three of the instrumentals are Duke Ellington tunes, and Barber, trumpeter Pat Halcox, and clarinetist Ian Wheeler have fine solo space. Jordan's last full-length album, *I Believe in Music,* finds him still sounding quite happy and in prime form. He heads a sextet that also includes Irv Cox on tenor and pianist Duke Burrell, performing several of his older hits plus the current pop song "I Believe in Music," "Red Top," and "Take the 'A' Train."

Louis Jordan never lost his joy for performing music, even if his audience had disappeared.

FILMS

Louis Jordan and his Tympany Five appeared in many films during his prime years. In *Follow the Boys* (1944) he performs "Is You Is or Is You Ain't My Baby" and "Sweet Georgia Brown." Other notable film appearances include *Meet Miss Bobby Sox* (1944), *Beware* (1946), *Swing Parade of 1946* (1946), *Reet, Petite and Gone* (1947), and *Look Out Sister* (1948). Jordan also plays "Choo Choo Ch'Boogie" in the nostalgic 1960 television special *The Swingin' Singin' Years* (Vintage Jazz Classics 2007). Twenty-one of Louis Jordan's best film performances (taken from shorts and full-length films) are included on the highly recommended video *Five Guys Named Moe* (Vintage Jazz Classics 2004).

JUGGERNAUT

Formed in 1976 and originally co-led by pianist-arranger Nat Pierce and drummer Frank Capp, the Juggernaut is an impressive band that sounds very similar to Count Basie's ensemble of the 1955-75 period. Basie's first altoist, Marshall Royal, was part of the Juggernaut for years, and other all-stars who have spent time with the big band have included trumpeters Blue Mitchell, Al Aarons, Conte Candoli, and Snooky Young, trombonist Buster Cooper, tenors Richie Kamuca, Plas Johnson, Bob Cooper, Pete Christlieb, Red Holloway, and Rickey Woodard, and singers Ernestine Anderson and Ernie Andrews. After Pierce's death in 1992, Gerald Wiggins took his place on piano and Juggernaut continued on as before, playing on a part-time basis in the Los Angeles area and recording consistently swinging sets for the Concord label. ●

9 *Juggernaut / Aug. 8, 1976 / Concord Jazz 4040*

9 *Live at the Century Plaza / July 21, 1978 / Concord Jazz 4072*

8 *Juggernaut Strikes Again / Oct. 1981–Nov. 1981 / Concord Jazz 4183*

7 *Live at the Alley Cat / June 1987 / Concord Jazz 4336*

8 *In a Hefti Bag / Nov. 3, 1994–Mar. 21, 1995 / Concord Jazz 4655*

8 *Play It Again Sam / Sept. 24, 1996–Oct. 8, 1996 / Concord Jazz 4747*

All six of the Juggernaut's Concord recordings (the first four have Nat Pierce as co-leader) can easily be enjoyed by fans of Count Basie and big band Swing. Ernie Andrews takes three exciting vocals on the debut release, where there is solo space for Buster Cooper, Richie Kamuca, Plas Johnson, and

Blue Mitchell, among others, on such tunes as "Moten Swing," "Basie's Back in Town," and "Dickie's Dream." *Live at the Century Plaza* unfortunately does not give the personnel listing but is otherwise on the same level as the first disc, with space for trumpeter Al Aarons, Buster Cooper, tenors Bob Cooper and Herman Riley, Marshall Royal, and the co-leaders. Joe Williams has two spots, including his lengthy "Joe's Blues." *Juggernaut Strikes Again* finds the big band stretching a little bit beyond Basie on originals by Pierce, Benny Golson ("I Remember Clifford"), Buck Clayton, Henry Mancini, and Charlie Parker, but the style is the same. Soloists include Bob Cooper, Christlieb, Royal, trumpeters Bill Berry and Warren Luening, and Buster Cooper; Ernie Andrews sings "You Are So Beautiful" and "Parker's Mood." *Live at the Alley Cat* is fine except that half of the program is taken up by Ernestine Anderson's vocals (including a lengthy "Never Make Your Move Too Soon") and the band does not have much to do after its five instrumentals.

Since Nat Pierce's death (Gerry Wiggins took his place on piano), the Juggernaut has recorded two CDs featuring, respectively, the arrangements of Neal Hefti (mostly vintage tunes for Basie, including "Cute," "Whirly Bird," and "L'il Darlin'") and Sammy Nestico (highlighted by "The Heat's On," "Ja-Da," "Wind Machine," and "88 Basie Street"). No surprises occur, but the music is excellent.

JON-ERIK KELLSO
b. May 8, 1964, Dearborn, MI

One of the finest Mainstream and trad cornetists to emerge during the 1990s, Jon-Erik Kellso has appeared on a variety of fine CDs, particularly for the Arbors label. He started playing trumpet when he was ten (later switching to cornet), attended Wayne Street University, and played with the New McKinney's Cotton Pickers and J. C. Heard's orchestra (1987–89) in Michigan. Since moving to New York in 1989, Jon-Erik Kellso has been featured in many Mainstream settings, including as a member of James Dapogny's Chicago Jazz Band and Vince Giordano's Nighthawks. He has played and recorded thus far with Dan Barrett, Dick Hyman, Kenny Davern, Howard Alden, Rick Fay, Bob Haggart, Harry Allen, Ralph Sutton, and Marty Grosz, among many others.

7 *Chapter 1 / Apr. 26–27, 1993 / Arbors 19125*

9 *Chapter 2: The Plot Thickens / Dec. 6–10, 1995 / Arbors 19160*

Jon-Erik Kellso's first two records as a leader are both impressive. *Chapter 1* has a variety of Swing standards plus two originals and the completely obscure Duke Ellington–Harry Carney tune "Pelican Drag" played by Kellso's sextet with Scott Robinson (on tenor, C-melody sax, and clarinet). At this early stage, the cornetist already had a fairly original sound within the Mainstream Swing tradition. *Chapter 2* is Swing with a difference, due to excellent planning, creative frameworks, and a few offbeat ideas. Kellso is joined by Harry Allen, the remarkable Scott Robinson (who plays alto, baritone, clarinet, alto clarinet, peckhorn, tenor, and on "Creole Love Call" the very eerie-sounding theremin), cellist Mike Karoub (who takes some effective solos), Howard Alden, either John Bunch or Jeremy Kahn on piano, bassist Paul Keller, and drummer Joe Ascione. None of the music is predictable, yet it all swings, whether it is "Little White Lies," "Tea for Two," or "Stompy Jones."

REBECCA KILGORE
b. Sept. 24, 1948, Waltham, MA

Rebecca Kilgore, who has a beautiful voice and a gentle but effective improvising style, started singing Swing standards fairly late in her career, but in the 1990s she made up for lost time. She heard singer Syd Smith of the Wholly Cats in the late 1970s and was inspired to start taking her singing seriously. In time she replaced Smith, made her recording debut on the 1982 LP *Doggin' Around,* and worked regularly in the Portland area, often singing duets with pianist Dave Frishberg. She began to get noticed in the 1990s when she started recording for Arbors and has since become a fixture at quite a few classic jazz festivals and jazz parties. In addition to her solo projects, Rebecca Kilgore (who also plays effective rhythm guitar) frequently works with drummer Hal Smith's Chicago-style jazz groups, has continued gigging with Frishberg (they recorded duet sets for PhD and Arbors), and has recorded with John Sheridan, Dan Barrett, and Tall Jazz. She is one of the top interpreters of lightly swinging Mainstream jazz standards around today.

Rebecca Kilgore is heard in a variety of settings on these four CDs, excelling in each format. *Looking at You* is a duet album with Dave Frishberg (who sticks to playing piano and refrains from singing). "Our Love Rolls On" is the only Frishberg song in the bunch, which includes a few Brazilian tunes, "Lullaby in Rhythm," "Hummin' to Myself," "Looking at You," and the 1920s "There Ain't No Sweet Man That's Worth the Salt of My Tears." *I Saw Stars* teams Kilgore with "Dan Barrett's Celestial Six," and it was the first chance for many listeners to really hear this delightful singer. The vocalist is backed by a colorful sextet that has plenty of solo space: Frishberg, Barrett on trombone and trumpet, Scott Robinson on tenor, bass sax, and clarinet, altoist Chuck Wilson (who has a beautiful tone), Bucky Pizzarelli, and bassist Michael Moore; no drums. Among the more exciting selections are "Happy As the Day Is Long," "Jeepers Creepers," "Exactly Like You," and "Symphony." *Not a Care in the World* is a duet/trio set with Frishberg and sometimes also guitarist Dan Faehnle. No Frishberg songs this time around but plenty of superior Swing numbers, including "A Kiss to Build a Dream On," "An Occasional Man," "My Melancholy Baby" (a much maligned standard), and "I've Got a Feelin' You're Foolin'." The Jump disc has Kilgore assisted by trombonist Barrett, pianist Ingham, and clarinetist Reitmeier. The arrangements are subtle, the spotlight is mostly on the singer, and the material (which includes "The Five O'Clock Whistle," "A Handful of Stars," "Just You, Just Me," "My Future Just Passed," and "I'm Checkin' Out, Goom Bye") is quite strong. Exquisite music.

EIJI KITAMURA
b. Apr. 8, 1929, Tokyo, Japan

A solid if derivative clarinetist from Japan, Eiji Kitamura has a style that mixes Benny Goodman and Buddy DeFranco. He attended Keio University in Tokyo and has played professionally since the early 1950s. Through the years Kitamura has mostly led his own combos in Japan, but he has had opportunities to play with Benny Goodman, Teddy Wilson (with whom he recorded in 1971 and 1973), Woody Herman, Hank Jones, and Buddy DeFranco, among others. Eiji Kitamura has also been a regular at the Monterey Jazz Festival since 1978.

LPS TO SEARCH FOR
Eiji Kitamura led a couple of all-star sets for Concord in 1981 and 1983. *Swing Eiji* (Concord Jazz 152) finds him playing eight standards with a cast that at various times includes Warren Vaché, tenorman Fraser McPherson, and guitarists Cal Collins and Herb Ellis. *Seven Stars* has six standards and two obscurities played by Kitamura, Teddy Wilson, vibraphonist Cal Tjader, guitarist Eddie Duran, bassist Bob Maize, and Jake Hanna; Ernestine Anderson sings "Someone to Watch Over Me." Both of these excellent albums are long out of print.

DIANA KRALL
b. Nov. 16, 1964, Nanaimo, Canada

During the second half of the 1990s, singer-pianist Diana Krall became one of the most famous performers in jazz, helping to popularize Swing standards and songs associated in the past with the Nat King Cole Trio. A very successful marketing campaign made her appear to be a sex symbol, but in reality Krall was a talented if nervous musician who was most comfortable when she could sit at her piano and not have to talk too much to the audience or stand in front of a band!

Krall grew up in Nanaimo, British Columbia, taking classical piano lessons from the time she was four, listening to jazz

Diana Krall helped bring Swing standards to the masses in the 1990s, and she is still growing in popularity.

from her father's record collection, and playing with her high school jazz band. She attended Berklee College in the early 1980s, spent a few years in Los Angeles (where she learned from Jimmie Rowles and John Clayton), and then moved to Toronto. Krall relocated to New York in 1990, made her recording debut for Justin Time in 1993, and signed with GRP the following year. Her second GRP set, *All for You,* was a tribute to the Nat King Cole Trio, and it made her a superstar. Soon Krall's picture was everywhere, she was headlining at jazz festivals and concert halls, and her trio (which featured guitarist Russell Malone until early 1999) was constantly working and touring. Diana Krall's singing, which sometimes recalls Shirley Horn and Carmen McRae, is conventional but has an indescribable charisma to it, while her piano playing falls between Swing and bop. Her future progress and development will be well worth watching closely.

●

7 *Stepping Out / 1993 / GRP 9825*

7 *Only Trust Your Heart / Sept. 13–16, 1994 / GRP 9810*

10 *All for You / Oct. 3–8, 1995 / GRP/Impulse 182*

9 *Love Scenes / 1997 / GRP/Impulse 233*

8 *When I Look in Your Eyes / 1998 / Verve/Impulse 304*
Stepping Out was originally cut for the Justin Time label but was acquired and reissued by GRP in the late 1990s. Diana

Krall sounds fine as an Ernestine Anderson–inspired singer and a modern Mainstream pianist, playing in a trio with bassist John Clayton and drummer Jeff Hamilton. The most noteworthy aspect to her debut is her reliance on superior songs from the past, including "Straighten Up and Fly Right," "I'm Just a Lucky So And So," and "As Long As I Live." While there are two pictures of Krall included on her debut CD, *Only Trust Your Heart* has five. Joined by either Ray Brown or Christian McBride on bass, drummer Lewis

Nash, and occasionally tenorman Stanley Turrentine, Krall sounds particularly good on ballads such as "Only Trust Your Heart" and "Folks Who Live on the Hill," although she also includes a few medium-tempo romps. *All for You* was her breakthrough album, and now there were eight photos. On this disc, a tribute to the Nat King Cole Trio (even if Krall has a more modern piano style), she explores such songs as "I'm an Errand Girl for Rhythm," "Frim Fram Sauce," "Baby Baby All the Time," and "Hit That Jive Jack." Krall, who is joined by guitarist Russell Malone, bassist Paul Keller, and (on "If I Had You") pianist Benny Green, often sounds exuberant, and this CD quickly became very popular, making her famous. *Love Scenes* has ten photos, and the Krall–Malone–McBride Trio plays "Peel Me a Grape," "All or Nothing at All," "Lost Mind," "How Deep Is the Ocean?," and "I Don't Know Enough About You," among others. Although those songs were not associated with Nat King Cole, the music is in a similar winning style. Diana Krall's fifth CD (which has a dozen pictures, including one on the disc itself) retains Malone (who would soon go out on his own), sometimes adds drums, and on six of the dozen songs includes a string orchestra arranged by Johnny Mandel. Highlights include "Devil May Care," "Let's Fall in Love," "Popsicle Toes," "I've Got You Under My Skin," and a sensuous "Do It Again."

BIRELI LAGRENE
b. Sept. 4, 1966, Soufflenheim, France

Bireli Lagrene has certainly had an episodic career, passing through a variety of different styles. Of greatest relevance to this book is his remarkable first period. Born to a gypsy family and the son and grandson of guitarists, Lagrene was a masterful guitarist from an early age, and when he was just 13 he recorded an album that found him sounding exactly like Django Reinhardt. Fortunately he recorded three albums during 1980–82, each of which is a delightful Swing record in the Django style, quite remarkable for any guitarist but particularly for such a young player.

By the mid-1980s, Lagrene had decided to search for his own voice, and the Reinhardt influence almost completely disappeared. Bireli Lagrene spent a few years playing mostly fusion (including meetings with electric bass innovator Jaco Pastorius) and since then has alternated between hard bop renditions of standards and original music, hinting now and then at his roots in Django.

●

10	*Routes to Django / May 29–30, 1980 / Jazz Point 1003*
9	*Bireli Swing '81 / Apr. 1981 / Jazz Point 1009*
9	*15 / Feb. 1982 / Antilles 848 814*
8	*Standards / June 1992 / Blue Note 80251*
8	*Live in Marciac / 1994 / Dreyfus 36567*

Routes to Django is a remarkable record, featuring Bireli Lagrene at the age of 13 swinging up a storm. Joined by local musicians in Europe (including his brother, Gaiti Lagrene, on rhythm guitar), Lagrene sounds just like Django Reinhardt on group originals plus "I've Found a New Baby," "All of Me," "My Melancholy Baby," and "Night and Day." *Bireli Swing '81* (which includes "Djangology," "Lady Be Good," "Limehouse Blues," and "Nuages") and *15* (which adds "Sweet Georgia Brown," "Autumn Leaves," and "I Can't Give You Anything but Love" to Lagrene's discography along with originals) are in the same vein and will certainly appeal to Django fans. After many other recordings (outside the scope of this book) that were in the fusion and even rock areas, the guitarist emerged in his mid-twenties as a modern jazz player who also played occasional Swing. There is very little Django to be heard on *Standards* (which includes "Softly, as in a Morning Sunrise," "Autumn Leaves," and "Body and Soul," among others), even on Reinhardt's "Nuages," but this trio outing with bassist Niels Pedersen and drummer Andre Ceccarelli is excellent. *Live in Marciac* (which also has Ceccarelli plus Chris Minh Doky on bass) also finds Lagrene playing in his own style, and eight of the songs from *Standards* are repeated. Bireli Lagrene is a brilliant guitarist who has managed to find his own sound, but one does wistfully miss his early days as a Django Reinhardt clone, since no one did it better!

ELLIS LARKINS

b. May 15, 1923, Baltimore, MD

A lyrical pianist who is particularly sensitive and inventive (in a subtle way) on ballads, Ellis Larkins is at his best when accompanying singers and cornetist Ruby Braff. Larkins, a prodigy who performed in concert with an orchestra when he was 11, studied at the Peabody Conservatory and at Juilliard. In 1942 Larkins was in a trio led by guitarist Billy Moore, he was a member of Edmond Hall's sextet (1945–46), and he recorded with Mildred Bailey, Coleman Hawkins, and Dickie Wells; otherwise he has mostly led his own trios around New York. Larkins spent periods accompanying Ella Fitzgerald (recording a Gershwin set in 1950 and a second duo date in 1954), Helen Humes, and Joe Williams, was in the background of many records, and stayed active into the 1990s, cutting a solo set at Maybeck Recital Hall in 1992. Ellis Larkins's recorded collaborations with Ruby Braff in 1955, 1972, and 1994 are classics of their kind. ●

8 *Ellis Larkins at Maybeck / Mar. 29, 1992 / Concord Jazz 4533*
This set (volume 22 of the Maybeck Recital Hall series) gives listeners a rare opportunity to hear Ellis Larkins stretching out rather than making other musicians and singers sound good. The emphasis is generally on slower material, but there are plenty of subtle surprises during the Swing-oriented set. Among the songs that Larkins explores and uplifts are "Lady Be Good," "Blue Skies," "Spring Will Be a Little Late This Year," and "Things Ain't What They Used to Be."

BARBARA LEA

b. Apr. 10, 1929, Detroit, MI

A veteran Swing singer, Barbara Lea has been a top interpreter of Swing standards since the mid-1950s although without gaining much fame. She sang locally with dance orchestras, performed with the Crimson Stompers (her college jazz band) at Harvard, and began recording as a leader in 1955. Lea's first three albums (1955–57) found her displaying the influence of Lee Wiley and utilizing trumpeter Johnny Windhurst. She spent the 1960s working as a stage actress and teaching. Lea was more active musically during the following decade, often singing with Dick Sudhalter and Ed Polcer. In the 1980s and '90s Barbara Lea returned to recording, including tributes to Hoagy Carmichael, Lee Wiley, and composer Willard Robison, still sounding very much in prime form. ●

7 *Barbara Lea / Oct. 18–19, 1956 / Original Jazz Classics 1713*

8 *Lea in Love / Apr. 19, 1957–May 1, 1957 / Original Jazz Classics 1743*

8 *The Devil Is Afraid of Music / Apr. 2, 1976–Sept. 28, 1992 / Audiophile 119*

8 *Remembering Remembering Lee Wiley / Apr. 1976–Feb. 20, 1995 / Audiophile 125*

8 *Hoagy's Children—Volume One / Apr. 27, 1981–Aug. 24, 1993 / Audiophile 291*

8 *Hoagy's Children—Volume Two / Apr. 27, 1981–Aug. 24, 1993 / Audiophile 291*

8 *Do It Again / June 1983–Nov. 28, 1983 / Audiophile 175*
Barbara Lea's second of three early albums (the first has yet to be reissued) matches her with trumpeter Johnny Windhurst and Dick Cary (on either piano or alto horn) in a pair of quintets. Unlike most singers of her generation, Lea preferred to sing vintage prebop material, and this set includes "Nobody Else but Me," "I'm Comin' Virginia," "My Honey's Lovin' Arms," and "Baltimore Oriole." *Lea in Love* also includes Windhurst and Cary plus, on some numbers, Garvin Bushell on oboe and bassoon, Ernie Caceres on clarinet and baritone, harpist Adele Girard, and a rhythm section. The material is superior (including "You'd Be So Nice to Come Home To," "The Very Thought of You," "Mountain Greenery," "More Than You Know," and "Autumn Leaves,"

which is partly taken in French), and Lea's voice sounds quite lovely.

Moving ahead 19 years, *The Devil Is Afraid of Music* is a full set of music written by the somewhat forgotten rural composer Willard Robison. Five songs were recorded in 1992 with the Dick Cary Trio to bring the original program up to the length of a CD. Otherwise the album dates from 1976, with Lea joined by the Loonis McGlohon Trio, with clarinetist Bob Mitchell sitting in on one song. Lea's voice is perfectly suited to such tunes as "Don't Smoke in Bed," "Think Well of Me," "Guess I'll Go Back Home This Summer," "'Round My Old Deserted Farm," and Robison's best-known song, "Old Folks." Since Barbara Lea's main inspiration was Lee Wiley, her tribute to the veteran singer is quite heartfelt. As with the Willard Robison set, most of the music was recorded in 1976 with Loonis McGlohon's trio (Bob Mitchell is also heard from here), while additional selections were recorded in the 1990s that fit right in. Lee Wiley had recorded a wide variety of superior songs in the 1930s and '40s, so Lea revives 22 of them, including "Easy to Love," "Down to Steamboat Tennessee," "Sugar," "A Ship Without a Sail," and Wiley's "Anytime, Anyday, Anywhere."

Hoagy's Children was conceived as a musical revue that paid tribute to Hoagy Carmichael. Originally a single LP, it has been expanded to two CDs with the inclusion of other, related material from 1984–85 and 1991. Lea is featured on the majority of the selections and takes a few vocal duets with Bob Dorough (who also has his own showcases), and there are instrumentals featuring cornetist Richard Sudhalter and Art Baker on reeds. Many of Carmichael's best songs are here (showing off the richness of his output), and the two CDs are equally rewarding. A happy project.

Do It Again is not a tribute but simply a definitive outing by Barbara Lea. Half of the album features her with a hot Swing/Dixieland group including Billy Butterfield, Vic Dickenson, and Johnny Mince, while the other part of the set finds her accompanied tastefully by pianist Larry Eanet and bassist Steve Novosel. Standards alternate with obscurities, and throughout the veteran singer is in consistent form, showing why she deserves to be recognized as one of the better Mainstream singers of the past 20 years.

JULIA LEE
b. Oct. 31, 1902, Booneville, MO, d. Dec. 8, 1958, Kansas City, MO

Julia Lee's double-entendre singing and rocking piano playing made her a popular attraction in Kansas City for many years. Her father was a violinist who had a string trio, and she made her debut with him as a singer when she was just four. Lee began playing piano when she was ten and was working professionally at 16. She was the sister of bandleader George E. Lee and a member of his band during 1920–33. Lee recorded with her brother's group in 1927 and 1929 plus two songs on her own date from the latter year, highlighted by "Won't You Come Over to My House," which she helped make famous. Lee worked as a solo act at Milton's in Kansas City during 1934–48 but did not record at all during the Swing era. However, during 1944–52 she was well documented by Capitol and her records sold well for a few years. Typical of her material were such numbers as "Gotta Gimme Whatcha' Got," "King Size Papa," "The Spinach Song (I Didn't Like It the First Time)," "Lotus Blossom," "It Comes in Like a Lion," "Don't Save It Too Long," and "All This Beef and Big Ripe Tomatoes." Other than a period in Los Angeles during 1949–50, Julia Lee stayed in Kansas City, where she continued working up until her death at the age of 56.

LPS TO SEARCH FOR

Although the European Bear Family label has come out with a complete (if expensive) CD box set of Julia Lee's Capitol recordings (*Kansas City Star*), her music remains otherwise unavailable on CDs. Of the earlier LPs, *Julia Lee and Her Boy Friends* (Pausa 9020) has a dozen of Lee's better recordings from 1946–49 (with one number from 1952), while *Of Lions and Lambs* (Charly 1175) has 16 selections from the same period, duplicating only two of the songs.

PEGGY LEE

b. May 26, 1920, Jamestown, ND

Peggy Lee always made the most out of her small voice and cool delivery, sounding at her best in the 1950s and helping to define the "cool sound" while actually having her roots in the Swing era. Born Norma Egstrom, she spent a period singing in the Midwest and California including with Will Osborne. Lee's first important job, a two-year stint (1941–43) with Benny Goodman, resulted in her becoming famous, thanks to "Why Don't You Do Right." After marrying guitarist Dave Barbour in 1943 (they would divorce in 1952), she retired for a short time but was soon drawn back to recording for Capitol. Lee's recordings were popular from the start and she quickly became a star. Among her best-known records of the 1940s and '50s were "Black Coffee," "It's a Good Day," "Mañana," and the sensuous "Fever." Lee's early radio transcriptions (released in a Mosaic limited-edition box set) show how warm and swinging a singer she could be, although some of her output from the 1950s was less jazz-oriented and more tightly orchestrated. Lee was also a top songwriter, as the score for the Disney movie *Lady and the Tramp* demonstrates. In the mid-1950s she appeared in the Jack Webb jazz movie *Pete Kelly's Blues* (for which she received an Academy Award for best supporting actress), and she did a fine album with the George Shearing Quintet in 1959. In general Peggy Lee's later recordings are of less interest, and from the 1970s on her voice declined and she suffered from bad health, but she made a strong and permanent mark on singing styles during the 1940s and '50s.

●

8 *Peggy Lee & Benny Goodman—The Complete Recordings / Aug. 15, 1941–Dec. 2, 1947 / Columbia/ Legacy 65686*

✳ *The Complete Peggy Lee & June Christy Capitol Transcription Sessions / Dec. 13, 1945–Apr. 8, 1949 / Mosaic 5-184*

7 *With the Dave Barbour Band / 1947 / Laserlight 15 742*
All of Peggy Lee's recordings with Benny Goodman are on the Columbia/Legacy two-CD set. Although Lee sounds quite scared on her debut, "Elmer's Tune," she developed quickly (over the objections of producer John Hammond, who wanted BG to fire her) and a month later was memorable on "That's the Way It Goes." With the exception of the final three songs (recorded at a reunion session in 1947, after she was already well known), the selections (which include a few previously unreleased performances) are from 1941–42. Highlights include "I Got It Bad," "Somebody Else Is Taking My Place," "Let's Do It," "Where or When," and (in her next-to-last recording with Goodman) "Why Don't You Do Right." The five-CD limited-edition Mosaic set has some of the earliest solo recordings by Peggy Lee and June Christy, performances originally cut as radio transcriptions and mostly unreleased prior to this 1998 box. Christy, who was with Stan Kenton at the time of her 1945–46 recordings, is heard on 27 selections with all-star septets, mostly featuring Kenton sidemen. Peggy Lee is backed by Frank DeVol's or-

chestra on nine numbers and is joined by "Four of a Kind" (a rhythm quartet with her husband Dave Barbour on guitar) for 44 songs and by the Dave Barbour Quartet (actually a quintet with George Van Eps on second guitar) for the final 19 selections (which are from 1949). Lee sticks mostly to standards, and her gentle and lightly swinging style are quite appealing. Although lesser known, these are some of the most intimate and enjoyable recordings of Peggy Lee's career. The Laserlight single disc is with a similar combo and does not duplicate any of the Mosaic material, since these transcriptions were made for the MacGregor library. The Laserlight disc is a bit brief at 34 minutes, but the 14 selections all find Peggy Lee in her early prime and sounding quite relaxed.

7 *Black Coffee and Other Delights / Apr. 3, 1952–June 8, 1956 / MCA/Decca 11122*

9 *Beauty and the Beat / Apr. 28, 1959 / Capitol 98454*

3 *Basin Street East Proudly Presents Peggy Lee / Feb. 9, 1961 + Mar. 8, 1961 / Capitol 32744*

7 *Mink Jazz / Mar. 29, 1963–Feb. 7, 1963 / Capitol 95450*
Although Peggy Lee's Capitol recordings are her best-known records of the 1950s, she also spent a period recording for Decca. In its 46 selections, the two-CD set *Black Coffee* does have more than its share of purely commercial

selections that fall more into the middle-of-the-road pop world (particularly the numbers on which Lee is backed by the Gordon Jenkins Orchestra), but there are also some stronger selections, particularly during the second half of the program. Highlights include "Lover," "Watermelon Weather" (a duet with Bing Crosby), the original "Black Coffee," "Sugar," "What Can I Say After I Say I'm Sorry," and "I Don't Know Enough About You." On *Beauty and the Beat,* Lee is joined by the George Shearing Quintet (with guitarist Toots Thielemans, vibraphonist Warren Chaisson, and sometimes guest Armando Peraza on conga) and sounds particularly inspired. The concert includes "I Lost My Sugar in Salt Lake City," "If Dreams Come True," "You Came a Long Way from St. Louis," and "Always True to You in My Fashion" plus three instrumentals. *Basin Street East* is a bit of a disappointment. Originally recorded live in concert, because Lee had a cold, she rerecorded some of the music the following month in the studio. Backed by a 12-piece band, Lee does little but state the melodies, there is not a single solo for her sidemen, and nothing of interest happens. Everything sounds overarranged, and, surprisingly, "Fever" is taken too fast to be very effective. Better is *Mink Jazz,* even if the renditions of the 17 standards are often quite brief (mostly under three minutes). Benny Carter and Max Bennett provided the arrangements for the combos, and trumpeter Jack Sheldon makes his contributions; highlights include "Whisper Not," "The Lady Is a Tramp," "As Long As I Live," and "I'm a Fool to Want You."

5   *Love Held Lightly / Aug. 29, 1988–Sept. 2, 1988 / Angel 54798*

3   *Moments Like This / Sept. 8–9, 1992 / Chesky 84*

By the 1980s, there was not much left of Peggy Lee's voice. *Love Held Lightly* is of value because she performs 14 Harold Arlen songs, of which "My Shining Hour" is the only standard; eight had never been recorded before. The Swing nonet (arranged by Keith Ingham) is a major asset, but the singer should not have still been recording by this point in time. The same can definitely be said of *Moments Like This.* Why would anyone listen to these versions of "I Don't Know Enough About You," "Why Don't You Do Right," or "Mañana" when the originals are available? Best is a very touching rendition of "The Folks Who Live on the Hill," but otherwise this CD should just be allowed to drop away into obscurity.

FILMS

Peggy Lee sings "Why Don't You Do Right" with Benny Goodman's orchestra in *Stage Door Canteen* (1943) and has a major role in *Pete Kelly's Blues* (1955).

HUMPHREY LYTTELTON
b. May 23, 1921, Windsor, England

Trumpeter Humphrey Lyttelton, one of the leading British jazzmen, started out as a New Orleans revivalist. He changed course during 1955–56, widening the scope of his music and switching largely to Mainstream Swing, although he occasionally went back to the older style during the next few decades. Lyttelton served in the military, played with George Webb's Dixielanders in 1947, and formed his own influential band the following year. He recorded with Sidney Bechet in 1949 and usually featured clarinetist Wally Fawkes during the Dixieland days. Later in the 1950s, after switching to Mainstream (which was considered a controversial move by trad fans), Lyttelton sometimes featured two or three saxophonists (including Bruce Turner, Tony Coe, and Joe Temperley) and in the 1960s on a few occasions collaborated with Buck Clayton. Humphrey Lyttelton, who in later years doubled on clarinet, founded the Calligraph label in the 1980s and recorded reunions with Wally Fawkes in 1991–92. In addition to his playing, he has written several very good jazz books, including his autobiography (*I Play As I Please*), *The Best of Jazz 1: Basin Street to Harlem,* and *The Best of Jazz 2: Enter The Giants, 1931–1944.*

9

Rent Party / Aug. 10, 1991–Jan. 4, 1992 / Stomp Off 1238

Humphrey Lyttelton and Wally Fawkes had a reunion for this excellent CD, a return to the trumpeter's trad roots. They are well featured in a septet with either John Beecham or Keith Nichols on trombone and pianist Stan Grieg, playing such vintage but rarely-performed material as "Gate Mouth," "Breeze," "Viper Mad," Luis Russell's "Doctor Blues," and Ma Rainey's "Jelly Bean Blues" plus four originals in the tradition. Despite the passing of many years, the co-leaders are both in superior form during the heated music.

LPS TO SEARCH FOR

Echoes of Harlem (Black Lion 51011), from 1981, has Lyttelton playing advanced Swing with his septet, including newer songs by Buck Clayton, Kenny Graham, and the leader, plus three Duke Ellington tunes ("Unbooted Character" and "Lady of the Lavender Mist" among them), a Sidney Bechet number, and two standards. *Delving Back and Forth with Humph* (Stomp Off 1160) is particularly interesting, because half of the numbers are from Lyttelton's bands in 1948, while the latter half has the trumpeter and Wally Fawkes getting back together in 1986. In addition to a few familiar songs (which are given fresh interpretations), there are many superior but virtually unknown tunes included that are well worth reviving. *Humphrey Lyttelton in Canada* (Sackville 3033) has Lyttelton, Jim Galloway (on soprano, baritone, and clarinet), guitarist Ed Bickert, bassist Neil Swainson, and drummer Terry Clarke performing eight of Lyttelton's originals, which swing in their own fashion but are often unpredictable. A highlight is "Caribana Queen," which has both Lyttelton and Galloway playing clarinets. *Scatterbrains* (Stomp Off 1111) is more Dixieland-oriented and finds Lyttelton and clarinetist Kenny Davern joined by a five-piece rhythm section that includes veteran guitarist Al Casey. Hopefully someday Humphrey Lyttelton's influential recordings of the late 1940s and '50s will be reissued domestically, but for now these examples of his later work are all quite enjoyable.

FILMS

Humphrey Lyttelton appears in *The Tommy Steele Story* (1957).

MANHATTAN TRANSFER

When they sing jazz, the Manhattan Transfer (whose roots are in Swing) is one of the top jazz vocal groups of all time. Their repertoire tends to be much more eclectic (including pop, rock and roll, and Brazilian), but, no matter what they are singing at the moment, they are a class act.

Tim Hauser put together the first version of the Transfer in 1969, struggling for a couple of years without making much of an impression. He had better luck in 1972, when he interested Alan Paul, Janis Siegel, and Laurel Masse in starting a vocal group not restricted to any one style and able to perform in any idiom they loved. They hosted a summer replacement television series in 1975 and gradually caught on later in the 1970s, particularly after signing with the Atlantic label. Cheryl Bentyne took Masse's place in 1979 and the personnel has stayed the same ever since. The group had a hit in 1979 with their version of "Birdland," and they have recorded many notable sets through the years, particularly the boppish *Vocalese* and 1997's *Swing*, which found the singers exploring vintage material in inventive ways. The year 1999 found the Manhattan Transfer celebrating their 20th year with the same lineup, which was unprecedented for any jazz-oriented vocal group. ●

7 *Extensions / 1979 / Mobile Fidelity 578*

6 *Mecca for Moderns / 1981 / Atlantic 16036*

10 *Vocalese / 1985 / Atlantic 81266*

10 *Swing / 1997 / Atlantic 83012*

The Manhattan Transfer has recorded many albums through the years for Atlantic, and these are four of the more significant ones. *Extensions* is an audiophile reissue of their breakthrough album, a set that is highlighted by their hit "Birdland," "Wacky Dust," a version of "Body and Soul" that is a tribute to the late Eddie Jefferson, "Twilight Tone," and Spyro Gyra's "Shaker Song." Their next album, *Mecca for Moderns,* also has plenty of variety, ranging from rock and roll ballads and oddities to Freddie Green's "Until I Met

You," Charlie Parker's "Confirmation," and a tender "A Nightingale Sang in Berkeley Square." In 1985 the Manhattan Transfer teamed up with the genius of jazz lyric writing, Jon Hendricks, for *Vocalese,* an exciting set in which recorded solos were given words. Though the emphasis is mostly on bebop (including such songs as "Killer Joe," "Airegin," Quincy Jones's "Meet Benny Bailey," and "Joy Spring"), there are also some Count Basie–associated tunes, including "Rambo" (which is actually played by the Basie band under the direction of Thad Jones), "Ray's Rockhouse," and "Blee Blop Blues." In addition to their usual sidemen and the Basie Orchestra, there are spots for the Four Freshmen, Jon Hendricks (who provided all of the lyrics), tenor saxophonist James Moody, singer Bobby McFerrin, altoist Richie Cole, and other guests; Janis Siegel and Alan Paul provided most of the exciting arrangements.

After a few erratic pop-oriented albums, in 1997 the Manhattan Transfer returned to their roots with *Swing,* a brilliant reworking of the classic idiom. Rather than merely recreate the past or use a big band, the Manhattan Transfer is heard with small groups and all-stars, including guest Stephane Grappelli (on "Nuages"), the remarkable Rosenberg Trio (a group of young virtuosic gypsies who play in the tradition of Django Reinhardt), and several Western Swing players, such as the members of Asleep at the Wheel. The vocalists stick mostly to vocalese of Swing-era solos, including Benny Goodman's 1935 version of "King Porter Stomp," "Moten Swing," "Down South Camp Meetin'," and a particularly exciting version of Charlie Barnet's "Skyliner." A gem.

WENDELL MARSHALL
b. Oct. 24, 1920, St. Louis, MO

The cousin of Jimmy Blanton, bassist Wendell Marshall is best known for his association with Duke Ellington. Blanton gave Marshall his first bass lessons. After studying at Lincoln University and serving in the Army (1943–46), Marshall worked in the St. Louis area, had a stint with Stuff Smith, and joined Mercer Ellington's band in 1948. Within a few months he became a member of Duke Ellington's orchestra, where he would stay until 1955. Marshall's solid playing was supportive, swinging, and reliable. He had occasional short solos and was well heard on a trio recording with Duke. After leaving Ellington, Marshall was in demand as a freelancer in the mid-1950s, appearing on many records, including with Mary Lou Williams, Louie Bellson, drummer Art Blakey, and Mercer Ellington (1958–59); his only record date as a leader (1955) resulted in four songs. Wendell Marshall worked with quite a few pit bands for Broadway shows in the 1960s and stayed active until he decided to retire from music in 1968.

BILLY MAY
b. Nov. 10, 1916, Pittsburgh, PA

Billy May, a well-respected arranger for decades, had a big band in the early 1950s that for a period beat the odds and was commercially successful. He started out as a trumpeter, working in 1934 with George Olsen's Polish-American Orchestra and for the next few years with obscure bands. In 1939 May hit the big time when he joined Charlie Barnet's orchestra; among his arrangements were "Cherokee," Barnet's most famous hit. In addition, May played in the trumpet section and even took a hilariously bad vocal on the satirical "The Wrong Idea." He played and wrote for Glenn Miller (1940–42), Les Brown (1942), and Alvino Rey before working extensively on radio and in the studios. In 1951 May's big band recordings for Capitol (which featured his trademark sound of "sliding" saxophones) caught on so well that he put together the Billy May

Orchestra, an organization that lasted until 1954 and on a part-time basis afterwards. May became a very busy freelance arranger, writing for Frank Sinatra (including *Come Fly with Me*), Nat King Cole, films, television, and in many different situations. Billy May remained active as a writer into the 1990s.

●

LPS TO SEARCH FOR

Well deserving of being reissued on CD, *A Band Is Born* (Pausa 9035) has a dozen of the best recordings by the Billy May Orchestra of 1951–52, including catchy versions of "All of Me," "Lean Baby," "When My Sugar Walks Down the Street," and "Lulu's Back in Town." The band includes trumpeter Johnny Best, trombonist Murray McEachern,

and tenor saxophonist Ted Nash in the cast. An oddity with a cult following, *Sorta-Dixie* (Creative World 11885) finds May in 1955 tearing apart eight Dixieland standards (plus his own "Sorta Blues") with such instruments as the calliope, celeste, orchestra bells, xylophone, tympani, triangle, and a harp, plus a big band and a Dixieland front line comprised of former Bob Crosby Bobcats. Amusing.

SUSANNAH MCCORKLE

b. Jan. 1, 1949, Berkeley, CA

When it comes to digging into the lyrics of vintage songs, finding unexpected meanings in the words, and uplifting the tunes in a swinging fashion, few singers today are in Susannah McCorkle's class. Her version of the unpromising "There's No Business Like Show Business" (the original and better version is on the LP *How Do You Keep the Music Playing?*), which found her drastically slowing down the usually rapid tempo and reviving some rarely performed verses, is a good example of the musical magic that she can perform on even the most familiar songs.

McCorkle originally had plans to become a translator (she knows several languages), possibly for the United Nations. But while in Italy she fell in love with Billie Holiday's music and that of the prewar jazz singers. When she moved to England in 1971, she worked with Keith Ingham and such visiting Americans as Dick Sudhalter and Bobby Hackett. At first a revival singer heard in trad and Swing settings, through the years McCorkle has updated the arrangements she uses while still focusing mostly on vintage material. She began to record in 1976 and, after two British albums (the music of Harry Warren and Johnny Mercer), she moved back to the U.S. in 1980, recording the lyrics of Yip Harburg and Leo Robin plus a few more varied sets. By 1988, when she signed with the Concord label, Susannah McCorkle had a strong and loyal following that has continued to grow through the years. Whether singing Bessie Smith material, Cole Porter, Swing, or Brazilian songs, Susannah McCorkle is still at the top of her field.

●

9 *The Songs of Johnny Mercer / Sept. 19, 1977–Oct. 3, 1977 / Jazz Alliance 10031*

10 *Over the Rainbow: The Songs of E. Y. Yip Harburg / Jan. 11, 1980 + Feb. 19, 1980 / Jazz Alliance 10033*

10 *No More Blues / Oct. 1988 / Concord Jazz 4370*

7 *Sabia / Feb. 1990 / Concord Jazz 4418*

8 *I'll Take Romance / Sept. 15–17, 1991 / Concord Jazz 4491*

Two of Susannah McCorkle's earliest albums (her second and third) have been reissued by Concord's subsidiary, Jazz Alliance. Even from the start, the singer had her sound together, was confident, and was digging creatively into the music of vintage composers and lyricists. The *Johnny Mercer* set, which uses a quintet with Keith Ingham, tenor saxophonist Danny Moss, and trumpeter Digby Fairweather, is a bit more Dixielandish and Swing-oriented in its arrangements than her later sets. Highlights include "At the Jazz Band Ball," "Blues in the Night," "Skylark," and a medley of "This Time the Dream's On Me" and "Dream." Lyricist Yip Harburg tends to be overlooked, but McCorkle certainly knows who he is. Backed by the Keith Ingham Trio, the singer performs Harburg's words to "Old Devil Moon," several songs from *The Wizard of Oz*, "Happiness Is a Thing Called Joe," "Down with Love," and some real obscurities; a delightful project. Skipping ahead to her Concord years, *No More Blues* is a hodgepodge of superior material, including "Fascinating Rhythm," "Swing That Music," Gerry Mulligan's "The Ballad of Pearly Sue," "Don't Let the Sun Catch You Crying," and "Who Cares?" McCorkle is assisted by Ken Peplowski, Dave Frishberg, and either Emily Remler or Bucky Pizzarelli on guitar. On *Sabia*, Susannah McCorkle sings ten Brazilian songs plus "Estate," switching between English, Portuguese, and Italian while being accompanied by a group that includes Scott Hamilton and Emily Remler. For *I'll Take Romance*, McCorkle sticks to veteran songs (only "Where Do You Start" was written after 1960) that have to do with love. With a quintet that includes pianist Allen Farnham (who would be her musical director from then on), Howard Alden, and Frank Wess (on tenor and flute), the singer makes such songs as "My Foolish Heart," "Taking a Chance on Love," and "That Old Feeling" sound like they were written for her.

7 *From Bessie to Brazil* / Feb. 1–3, 1993 / Concord Jazz 4547

7 *From Broadway to Bebop* / Apr. 20–22, 1994 / Concord Jazz 4615

8 *Easy to Love: The Songs of Cole Porter* / Sept. 6–8, 1995 / Concord Jazz 4696

8 *Let's Face the Music: The Songs of Irving Berlin* / Oct. 28–30, 1996 / Concord Jazz 4759

8 *Someone to Watch Over Me: The Songs of George Gershwin* / Oct. 21–24, 1997 / Concord Jazz 4798

There is plenty of variety on *From Bessie to Brazil* (which mixes newer songs by Paul Simon and Dave Frishberg with "Thief in the Night," "The Lady Is a Tramp," and "Hit the Road to Dreamland") and *From Broadway to Bebop*, which ranges from "Don't Fence Me In" and a Carmen Miranda tribute to "Moody's Mood for Love" and Don Sebesky's "I Remember Bill" (for pianist Bill Evans). Randy Sandke, Ken Peplowski, and trombonist Robert Trowers are in the supporting cast on both projects. For the other Concord releases, Susannah McCorkle decided to pay tribute to three of the most famous American composers. In addition to the better-known tunes, her Cole Porter date includes "Weren't We Fools," "Who Wants to Be a Millionaire," and "Why Don't We Try Staying Home." McCorkle's Berlin project has a joyous "I'd Rather Lead a Band" and "Better Luck Next Time" (her duet with guitarist Al Gafa on "Waiting at the End of the Road" is particularly memorable), while her Gershwin set includes "Will You Remember Me" and "Drifting Along with the Tide." But even the famous tunes sound fresh when interpreted by this exquisite singer.

LPS TO SEARCH FOR

Five Susannah McCorkle LPs have not yet been reissued as CDs and all are worth getting: *The Music of Harry Warren* (Inner City 1141), *The People That You Never Get to Love* (Inner City 1151), *Thanks for the Memory: The Songs of Leo Robin* (Pausa 7175), *How Do You Keep the Music Playing?*, (Pausa 7195), and *Dream* (Pausa 7208).

DAVE MCKENNA
b. May 30, 1930, Woonsocket, RI

A major Swing pianist, Dave McKenna's powerful bass lines make one particularly treasure his recordings that do not include a bassist! Although a bit misplaced chronologically (he would have been much more famous if he had been born ten or fifteen years earlier), McKenna has recorded quite prolifically since the late 1970s. He began to play publicly at the age of 12 and during 1947–49 gigged around Boston. McKenna was with Charlie Ventura in 1949, toured with Woody Herman

(1950–51), served in the Army, was back with Ventura during 1953–54, and then freelanced with some of the top Mainstream, bop, and Dixieland players, including Gene Krupa (in his trio), tenors Zoot Sims, Al Cohn, and Stan Getz, Bobby Hackett, Eddie Condon, and Bob Wilber.

Although he worked steadily (mostly in the Northeast), McKenna did not start gaining recognition until he was signed by Concord in 1979. Since then he has recorded many solo, duet, and trio dates, inspired some of Scott Hamilton's finest recordings, and been greatly in demand whenever and wherever a Swing pianist is needed.

Dave McKenna, one of the top Mainstream Swing pianists, has such powerful bass lines that they make a string bassist seem like a frivolity.

THE WAYNE KNIGHT COLLECTION

|6| *The Piano Scene of Dave McKenna* / July 22–23, 1958 / Koch 7809

|6| *Solo Piano* / Feb. 24, 1973 / Chiaroscuro 119

|8| *Featuring Zoot Sims* / Oct. 1974 / Chiaroscuro 136

|10| *No Bass Hit* / Mar. 1979 / Concord Jazz 4097

|9| *Giant Strides* / May 1979 / Concord Jazz 4099

|9| *Left-Handed Compliment* / Dec. 1979 / Concord Jazz 4123

It is surprising that Dave McKenna did not record more in his earlier years. Other than a long-forgotten solo date for ABC-Paramount in 1955, his Epic set (reissued by Koch) was his debut as a leader. *The Piano Scene* is surprisingly boppish in places. The trio session with bassist John Drew and drummer Osie Johnson (which has the original dozen songs augmented by eight alternate takes) has its moments but only hints at the strong personality that McKenna would soon develop. He cut just two albums in the 1960s, but, after an album for Halcyon in 1973, the pianist began recording quite prolifically. Of his four Chiaroscuro albums, two have reappeared on CD. *Solo Piano* is surprisingly eclectic, with the expected Swing standards joined by two Beatles songs, some bop, and Stevie Wonder's "My Cherie Amour." The collaboration with Zoot Sims (heard on tenor and soprano) plus bassist Major Holley and drummer Ray Mosca is on a higher level, and the four "new" alternate takes differ quite a bit from the issued versions; highlights include "Limehouse Blues," " 'Deed I Do," "Linger Awhile," and "There'll Be Some Changes Made."

In 1979, after cutting additional albums for Shiah, Famous Door, and Inner City, Dave McKenna began his long-time association with Concord. *No Bass Hit* is a classic, an explosive meeting between McKenna, Scott Hamilton, and Jake Hanna in a trio that certainly did not need a bassist. "Drum Boogie," "If Dreams Come True," and "Get Happy" are among the eight numbers. *Giant Strides* and *Left-Handed Compliment* are equally rewarding high-quality sets of piano solos that consist mostly of 1930s and '40s material being swung hard by the great pianist.

|9| *Celebration of Hoagy Carmichael* / May 1983 / Concord Jazz 4227

9 *Dancing in the Dark / Aug. 1985 / Concord Jazz 4292*

7 *My Friend the Piano / Aug. 1986 / Concord Jazz 4313*

8 *No More Ouzo for Puzo / June 1988 / Concord Jazz 4365*

9 *Live at Maybeck Recital Hall / Nov. 1989 / Concord Jazz 4410*

7 *Shadows 'n' Dreams / Mar. 1990 / Concord Jazz 4467*
Virtually all of Dave McKenna's Concord recordings are recommended; they vary only slightly in quality. The *Hoagy Carmichael* solo set has 11 of Carmichael's finest songs, including "Riverboat Shuffle," "One Morning in May," and "Stardust," all being swung melodically by McKenna. *Dancing in the Dark* is a solo exploration of the music of Arthur Schwartz, an underrated composer responsible for such songs (all included here) as "A Shine on Your Shoes," "Alone Together," "You and the Night and the Music," and "By Myself." *My Friend the Piano* differs from the last several solo piano recitals in that the emphasis is a little more on ballads and the repertoire is drawn from a variety of different composers. "Margie," "Mean to Me," "You're Driving Me Crazy," and a few medleys are among the more memorable performances. *No More Ouzo* returns McKenna to a band format, playing with his new discovery, guitarist Gray Sargent, plus bassist Monty Budwig and drummer Jimmie Smith. An uptempo "Look for the Silver Lining," a touching "Smile," and the title cut are among the high points. Dave McKenna's album *Live at Maybeck Recital Hall* is as rewarding as one would expect, including several medleys, "Exactly Like You," and "Limehouse Blues" among the numbers. The solo *Shadows 'n' Dreams* has the words "Shadow" or "Dream" in every title, including "I Had the Craziest Dream," "Me and My Shadow," "We Kiss in a Shadow," and "I'll See You in My Dreams." However, there is nothing gimmicky about Dave McKenna's swinging solos, which on this date tend to be at slower tempos.

7 *A Handful of Stars / June 15, 1992 / Concord Jazz 4580*

8 *Dave McKenna & Gray Sargent / Dec. 16, 1992 / Concord Jazz 4552*

7 *Easy Street / May 6 + 18, 1994 / Concord Jazz 4657*

8 *Sunbeam & Thundercloud / Mar. 19, 1995 / Concord Jazz 4703*

7 *Christmas Ivory / Feb. 18–19, 1997 / Concord Jazz 4772*

8 *You Must Believe in Swing / Apr. 15, 1997 / Concord Jazz 4756*

There has been no decline in Dave McKenna's playing, even as he closes in on 70; virtually every one of his Concord releases ranks with his best work. *A Handful of Stars* has the word "Star" in nearly every title, so this solo set includes "Star Eyes," "Stairway to the Stars," "Stars Fell on Alabama," "When You Wish Upon a Star," and others. As part of Maybeck Recital Hall's duo series (which was not as extensive as its notable solo projects), McKenna teamed up with Gray Sargent for five standards (including "The Sheik of Araby" and "Exactly Like You"), an original, and "Letter" and "Time" medleys. Continuing with the word association game, *Easy Street* has seven songs having to do with streets (including "Basin Street Blues" and "On Green Dolphin Street"), two titles that include "love," three with "gone," and a pair of originals. *Sunbeam & Thundercloud* is a set of swinging duets with Joe Temperley, who mostly plays baritone but also has a song apiece on bass clarinet and soprano. Four songs by Ellington and Strayhorn (including "Black & Tan Fantasy"), "Tricotism," and "I Got Rhythm" are among the more memorable selections. *Christmas Ivory* finds Dave McKenna mostly romping his way through 16 Yuletide favorites, including "Santa Claus Is Coming to Town," "Jingle Bells," and "Sleigh Ride," plus a few originals. And on the well titled *You Must Believe in Swing,* McKenna teams up for a set of duets with the great clarinetist Buddy DeFranco. The Swing pianist and the bop clarinetist find a great deal of common ground on such tunes as "The Song Is You," "Autumn Nocturne," and "Anthropology."

LPS TO SEARCH FOR

A pair of very good Dave McKenna Chiaroscuro solo albums, *Dave "Fingers" McKenna* (Chiaroscuro 175) and *McKenna* (Chiaroscuro 202), plus a combo date with Scott Hamilton, Warren Vache, and tenorman Al Cohn called *No Holds Barred* (Famous Door 122) are from the pianist's pre-Concord period. Even though most of Dave McKenna's Concord albums have been reissued on CD, three remain quite scarce and will hopefully come back soon: *Piano Mover* (Concord Jazz 146), *Plays the Music of Harry Warren* (Concord Jazz 174), and *The Keyman* (Concord Jazz 261).

BIG JAY MCNEELY

b. Apr. 29, 1927, Watts, CA

It was not unusual for Big Jay McNeely, the most extreme of all the honking tenors of the early 1950s, to spend a half-hour taking an exhibitionistic solo consisting of just a few emotional notes repeated endlessly, playing part of the time while lying down on stage! He stole the show virtually everywhere he appeared, and no act wanted to follow him.

McNeely (who was born Cecil McNeely but named "Big Jay" by producer Herman Lubinsky) was originally inspired by Illinois Jacquet. In his early days he played swinging jazz but, although he admired Charlie Parker, McNeely sensed that his future was in rhythm and blues, and he simplified his solos and emphasized emotion in his playing. By 1948, when he began recording for Savoy, McNeely's sound was together, and such riotous numbers as "The Deacon's Hop" and "Wild Wig" only hint at what his live performances were like. He was a very popular attraction for a decade and his records sold quite well. McNeely's last hit was 1958's "There Is Something on Your Mind." By then, the day of the honking tenor was gone, eclipsed by rock and roll. Big Jay McNeely spent much of the 1960s and '70s working as a mailman and playing music only part time, but he has been more active during the past 15 years, sticking to his extreme style and still displaying quite a bit of energy during his concert appearances.

LPS TO SEARCH FOR

Big Jay McNeely's studio records have not yet been reissued in coherent order on CD. A couple of excellent LP samplers are *The Best of Big Jay McNeely* (Saxophonograph 1300), which has exciting numbers from the 1947–57 period, and *Road House Boogie* (Saxophonograph 505), which dates from 1949–52. *Live at Birdland 1957* (Big J 108) is a rare example of how Big Jay McNeely sounded live during his heyday—some pretty wild stuff.

AMOS MILBURN

b. Apr. 1, 1927, Houston, TX, d. Jan. 3, 1980, Houston, TX

One of the great pianist-singers of early rhythm and blues, Amos Milburn had a five-year run (1948–53) filled with many hits. It is ironic (or perhaps quite fitting) that many of his most famous songs had to do with the joys of drinking, because alcoholism eventually ruined and cut short Milburn's life. The fourth of a dozen children, Milburn began playing piano by ear when he was five. He was originally inspired by the boogie-woogie pianists Albert Ammons, Pete Johnson, and Meade Lux Lewis. Milburn lied about his age in 1942 in order to enlist in the Navy (he was barely 15) and spent a few years overseas during World War II. After his discharge, he worked locally in Houston and San Antonio and then moved to Los Angeles where he landed a contract with Aladdin. "After Midnight" was his first hit, and in 1947 "Hold Me Baby" and particularly "Chicken Shack Boogie" caught on big, making Milburn into a major name. He toured the country, had 19 Top Ten R&B hits during the next few years, and influenced Fats Domino. Among Milburn's other best-known numbers were "Bad Bad Whiskey," "Thinking and Drinking," "Let Me Go Home Whiskey," "One Scotch, One Bourbon, One Beer," and "Good, Good Whiskey." Milburn, who was usually heard in a small combo that on records often featured tenor saxophonist Maxwell Davis, was a smooth ballad singer and a powerful pianist whose style directly preceded rock and roll.

But in 1954 the hits stopped, the drinking began to accelerate, and Milburn started to slide out of the public's consciousness. He continued working for a time and there were some records in the 1960s, but none sold very well. He suffered the first of several strokes in 1969 and spent his last years disabled, making a final session in 1976, with Otis Spann playing the left hand of the piano. Amos Milburn died at age 52, legendary but largely forgotten.

- The Complete Aladdin Recordings of Amos Milburn / Sept. 12, 1946–Jan. 28, 1957 / Mosaic 7-155

7 The Motown Sessions 1962–1964 / Oct. 13, 1962–Mar. 12, 1964 / Motown 31453-0611

The seven-CD limited-edition Mosaic box set not only has all of Amos Milburn's recordings for the Aladdin label but every recording that he made prior to 1960, so it would not be an understatement to call this reissue definitive! In addition to the hits and the many rocking singles released during the era, there are quite a few previously unreleased selections too. Maxwell Davis's tenor is a prominent part of the backup band on many selections, there are plenty of soulful and bluesy piano solos, and the set traces Amos Milburn's

rise and fall; his next-to-last Aladdin session finds Milburn in New Orleans trying to sound like Fats Domino, whom he had originally influenced! After a few singles for the King label, Milburn signed with the Motown label, and one album plus a few singles resulted. *The Motown Sessions* has that music plus seven additional selections and finds Amos Milburn still sounding strong, if a bit behind the times. Background singers and some soulful rhythms try to update the music a little (making it seem a bit dated now), but Milburn's power and charm still come through on "Don't Be No Fool," "Bad, Bad Whiskey," "Baby You Thrill Me," and "Chicken Shack Boogie." Other than a later single and a 1976 remake date for Blues Spectrum, the Amos Milburn story stops here.

BUTCH MILES
b. July 4, 1944, Ironton, OH

An exciting Swing drummer influenced by both Buddy Rich and Gene Krupa, Butch Miles is a brilliant Mainstream player who during two different periods helped to revitalize the Count Basie Orchestra. Miles attended West Virginia State College (1962–66), worked locally, toured with the Iris Bell Trio, and then played regularly with Mel Torme (1972–74), an association that gave him his initial recognition. During 1975–79 Miles was with the Count Basie Orchestra, where he really uplifted the band, forcing the veterans to swing even harder than they had previously. After leaving Basie, Miles worked with Dave Brubeck in 1979 and Tony Bennett but mostly freelanced with the top Mainstream players, appearing often at classic jazz festivals concerts and on recordings. He led a series of seven records (all now out of print) for the Famous Door label during 1977–85. The always-enthusiastic drummer worked with everyone from Gerry Mulligan and Woody Herman to Wild Bill Davison, Bob Wilber, and Scott Hamilton, in styles ranging from Dixieland to bop, although his main interest has always been Swing. In 1997 Butch Miles again became part of the Count Basie Orchestra (under the direction of Grover Mitchell), and his musicianship and drive have since helped to keep the Basie legacy not only alive but quite exciting.

●

8 Cookin' / Nov. 26, 1995 / Nagel-Heyer 020

Although he has appeared on quite a few records, Butch Miles has led relatively few recording sessions through the years, other than his batch for the long-defunct Famous Door label. This jam session–flavored Mainstream date teams Miles with Randy Sandke, Harry Allen, Howard Alden, bassist Frank Tate, and (on a few cuts) singer Terrie Richards. Highlights include Flip Phillips's "The Claw," "Them There Eyes," "Tico Tico," and "Tickle Toe."

LPS TO SEARCH FOR

For the Famous Door label, Butch Miles led a series of modern Swing dates. *Miles and Miles of Swing* (Famous Door 117) is notable for featuring some early Scott Hamilton in a sextet with fellow tenor Al Cohn and flugelhornist Marky Markowitz. Other notable Miles sets include *Butch's Encore* (Famous Door 124), *Salutes Chick Webb* (Famous Door 132), *Swings Some Standards* (Famous Door 135), *Salutes Gene Krupa* (Famous Door 142), *Salutes Count Basie* (Famous Door 145), *More Standards* (Famous Door 150), *Jazz Express* (Dreamstreet 109), from 1986, and an album in which Miles sings, *Lady Be Good* (Dreamstreet 102).

GROVER MITCHELL

b. Mar. 17, 1930, Whatley, AL

The leader of the Count Basie Orchestra since 1995, trombonist Grover Mitchell had already been a proponent of Basie-style Swing for many years by then. Mitchell played with King Kolax's big band during the second half of the 1940s, freelanced on the West Coast during the 1950s, and was with Duke Ellington in 1961. After a brief stint with Lionel Hampton in 1962, he became a member of Count Basie's orchestra (1962–70). During the following ten years, Mitchell worked in the studios and during 1978–80 had his own Basie-style big band, which recorded for the Jazz Chronicles label. In 1980 Mitchell rejoined Count, staying until Basie's death in 1984. He went back to leading his own orchestra (which recorded for Hemisphere, Stash, and Ken Music) until 1995, when he succeeded Frank Foster as the leader of the Basie big band. While Foster had sought to stretch the trademark Basie sound a bit, Grover Mitchell (who was wise enough to add alumnus Butch Miles on drums) has brought back some of the older charts. He has continually and enthusiastically championed Count Basie's music as the leader of practically the only remaining full-time American jazz big band.

●

8 *Hip Shakin' / June 18–19, 1990 / Ken 005*
Recorded five years before Grover Mitchell took over the Count Basie big band, his own orchestra swings but is a bit more modern. Using arrangements by quite a few different writers (including Frank Foster, Eric Dixon, Ernie Wilkins, Cecil Bridgewater, Jerry Dodgion, and Mike Abene), Mitchell's band puts the emphasis on melodic Swing, but with boppish moments too. Of the many soloists heard from, pianist Abene, trumpeter Cecil Bridgewater, Frank Wess on tenor, and altoist Jerry Dodgion make particularly strong impressions on the eight originals and four standards, which include "Isfahan" and "C Jam Blues."

LPS TO SEARCH FOR

Meet Grover Mitchell (Jazz Chronicles 104), from 1978–79, is very much in the Count Basie groove, although eight of the ten songs are Mitchell's originals. His main sidemen include trumpeter Al Aarons, Buddy Collette, Jackie Kelso, and Charlie Owens on reeds along with both of the Cheathams (pianist Jeannie and bass trombonist Jimmy). *Live at the Red Parrot* (Hemisphere 1006), recorded five days before Basie's death in 1984, has arrangements by Eric Dixon, Frank Foster, and Bobby Plater and such soloists as altoist Danny Turner, Joe Temperley, and both Kenny Hing and Eric Dixon on tenors. *Truckin'* (Stash 277), from 1987, uses the charts of Dixon, Wild Bill Davis (for his composition "Azure Te"), Ernie Wilkins, Frank Foster, and Cecil Bridgewater. The big band includes several notable players (Wild Bill Davis on piano, altoist Norris Turney, and trumpeter Bridgewater among them) and ranks as one of the most underrated Mainstream Swing orchestras of the 1980s.

JOE MOONEY

b. Mar. 14, 1911, Paterson, NJ, d. May 12, 1975, Fort Lauderdale, FL

A blind accordion player who gradually lost his sight by the time he was a teenager may have seemed like an unlikely bandleader in the late 1940s, but for a few years Joe Mooney had a strong following. He began playing piano at the age of six, took organ lessons from Fats Waller, and as a teenager formed a vocal duo with his brother Danny (who was also blind), recording the ironically titled Sunshine Boys during 1929–31. The group lasted until the mid-1930s, when Joe Mooney began freelancing as a pianist and arranger. He worked with Frank Dailey's orchestra in 1937 and stayed with the band the following year when Buddy Rogers took over the ensemble. During that period, Mooney starting doubling on accordion. The Rogers group lasted until later in 1938, and then Mooney contributed arrangements to the orchestras of Paul Whiteman, Larry Clinton, Les Brown, and others; he also recorded with Whiteman on accordion. In 1941 Mooney formed a quartet in which his accordion was joined by guitar, bass, and a reed player. Originally known as the Music Masters, by 1946 they had become the Joe Mooney Quartet, featuring Andy Fitzgerald on clarinet, guitarist Jack Hotop, and bassist John Frega. For a short time they were quite popular on 52nd Street in New York, and the unit lasted three years, performing music a little reminiscent of the Nat King Cole Trio (with different instrumentation) but also having a quiet sound of its own with occasional hip vocals.

Mooney's later years were anticlimactic. He switched to organ in 1950 and played primarily easy-listening music, settling in Florida. In 1952 he recorded "Nina Never Knew" (which became a minor hit) with the Sauter-Finegan Orchestra. Long-time fans raised money to get Mooney recording his own records again (there would be one set for Atlantic and two for Columbia on organ and piano) but, although he did not lose his enthusiasm or alter his pleasing style, Joe Mooney never returned to the national scene again or made it big.

9 *Do You Long for Oolong / July 1946–1951 / Hep 63*

7 *Lush Life / Nov. 28–30, 1956 / Koch 8524*

The Joe Mooney Quartet (consisting of clarinetist Andy Fitzgerald, guitarist Jack Hotop, bassist John Frega and Mooney on accordion and vocals) had the great majority of their recordings reissued on *Do You Long for Oolong*. Mooney's vocals and interplay with his group are a bit reminiscent of Page Cavanaugh, his accordion playing overcomes the limitations of the instrument, and the band (which was basically Swing-oriented although touched slightly by bop) displays a memorable sound. In addition to the studio sides, this CD includes a radio appearance that was never released before. The charm and musical sophistication of the group is obvious, and among the highlights are fresh transformations of "Tea for Two" (which is given crazy lyrics), "September Song," "Meet Me at No Special Place," "Sharkey Breaks the Ice," and "Little Orphan Annie." After settling in Miami, Mooney returned to New York to record the music on *Lush Life*, a quartet outing on which he sings and plays organ while being joined by guitarist Lee Robinson, bassist Milt Hinton, and drummer Osie Johnson. The music (all standards, including a remake of "Nina Never Knew" and stretching from Swing to cabaret) is subtle and quiet, hip and creative in its own unique way, well worth listening to closely.

BUDDY MORROW
b. Feb. 8, 1919, New Haven, CT

Buddy Morrow has had a lengthy if unheralded career. Born Muni "Moe" Zudekoff (a name he changed in the late 1930s), he began playing trombone when he was 12, worked locally, and was a member of the Yale Collegians. After moving to New York and studying at Juilliard, Morrow at 17 recorded with singer Amanda Randolph and Sharkey Bonano in 1936. The technically skilled trombonist had stints with the orchestras of Eddie Duchin, Artie Shaw (1936–37 and 1940), Vincent Lopez, Bunny Berigan, Frank Froeba, Richard Himber, Tommy Dorsey (1938–39), Paul Whiteman (1939–40), and Bob Crosby (1941–42). After a period in the Navy, Morrow worked in the studios, was with Jimmy Dorsey (1945), and led his own unsuccessful big band (1945–46). He was back in the studios for a few years and then in 1950 put together a commercial Swing band that caught on (recording a hit version of "Night Train") and worked for over a decade; he is still best-known for that orchestra. Buddy Morrow returned to the studios in the 1960s, was with the World's Greatest Jazz Band for a period in 1970, and then, starting in the late 1970s, led the Tommy Dorsey ghost band for a decade. It is a pity that through the years no one thought of having Buddy Morrow star on a small-group Swing date, for he clearly had the ability to create some rewarding jazz.

LPS TO SEARCH FOR

Buddy Morrow CDs are very hard to come by. The LP *Music for Dancing Feet* (Mercury 20210), from the mid-1950s, is a good example of the danceable Swing music that Morrow preferred to play, containing melodic versions of then-recent originals (including "Music for the Feet") and a few older songs, such as "Who's Sorry Now" and "Carioca." Tasteful if rather safe music.

ABE MOST

b. Feb. 27, 1920, New York, NY

A fine Swing clarinetist who at times in his career has paid tribute to (and done close impressions of) Benny Goodman and Artie Shaw, Abe Most has always stuck to the Swing and Mainstream music that interests him most. His younger brother, Sam Most (ten years his junior), is a pioneer flutist and still doubles on his cool-toned tenor. Abe Most began playing professionally when he was 16. He joined Les Brown in 1940 (playing alto and clarinet), was in the military during 1942–45, settled in Los Angeles, and had stints with Tommy Dorsey (1946) and a second period with Brown. Most has been a studio musician since the 1950s yet has always found time to play jazz in Los Angeles-area clubs at night, sometimes teaming up with his brother. Abe Most has appeared at many classic jazz festivals and Swing-oriented concerts through the years, recording on an all-too-occasional basis, and helping to keep the Swing clarinet tradition alive. ●

8 *Live! / Sept. 3, 1994 + June 23, 1995 / Camard (unnumbered)*

Abe Most has made far too few recordings during his long career. This rare small-label CD finds Most joined by Ray Sherman (another underrated great), bassist Eugene Wright, drummer Jack Sperling, and (on one of the two sessions) vibraphonist Peter Appleyard. Most sticks exclusively to Swing standards, including (for the 1994 set) a program of Benny Goodman–associated tunes. He has always had a warm tone and has no problem swinging at fast tempos. Highlights include "Crazy Rhythm," "I Love You," "Undecided," and "Air Mail Special."

LPS TO SEARCH FOR

Swing Low Sweet Clarinet (Camard 12582), from 1984, has Most swinging away with pianist Hank Jones, bassist Monty Budwig, and Jake Hanna on such songs as "Bebenu" (based on "I Found a New Baby"), "After You've Gone," and "These Foolish Things." On a medley of "Manha de Carnaval" and "Samba de Orpheus," Most switches to flute and is joined by his brother Sam; someone should record the Most brothers together for a full set.

JOE NEWMAN

b. Sept. 7, 1922, New Orleans, LA, d. July 4, 1992, New York, NY

A superior Swing trumpeter who was influenced by Louis Armstrong and Harry "Sweets" Edison, Joe Newman was (along with Freddie Green) the only significant sideman to be a longtime member of both of the Count Basie Orchestras. Born to a musical family in New Orleans, Newman started playing trumpet early. He was with Lionel Hampton's big band (1941–42), took some solos while with Count Basie (1943-46), and toured with Illinois Jacquet's popular jump band (1946–50). After freelancing, Newman was a key member of the second Basie band (1952–61), sharing the solo trumpet spotlight with Thad Jones. He also led some notable records of his own for quite a few labels, especially a few classics for RCA. Newman toured the USSR with Benny Goodman in 1962, freelanced around New York, and helped get jazz into schools by founding Jazz Interactions, Inc. Joe Newman did well at the 1972 Newport in New York jam sessions (which were recorded), worked with the New York Jazz Repertory Company starting in 1974, stayed busy as a freelancer, toured with Benny Carter, and co-led a record with fellow trumpeter Joe Wilder as late as 1984. Throughout his career, he was always a solid Swing stylist. ●

9 *The Complete Joe Newman / Feb. 8, 1955–July 13, 1956 / RCA 88810*

8 *I Feel Like a Newman / Apr. 1956 / Black Lion 760905*

7 *Jive at Five / May 4, 1960 / Original Jazz Classics 419*

7 *Good 'n' Groovy / Mar. 17, 1961 / Original Jazz Classics 185*

8 *Hangin' Out / May 1984 / Concord Jazz 4262*

There is a remarkable amount of music on the RCA two-CD set, the complete contents of four earlier (and rare) LPs. Trumpeter Newman is heard with a pair of octets that also feature tenor saxophonist Al Cohn; arrangements were provided by Cohn, Ernie Wilkins, and Manny Albam. In addition, Newman is quite effective on a Louis Armstrong tribute date (even taking a few vocals) and with flutist Frank Wess as part of a two-guitar septet. Many gems are included on this twofer. *I Feel Like a Newman* showcases Newman in two different settings in 1956: an octet with Frank Foster on tenor and a quintet with Frank Wess doubling on tenor and flute. The music is in a similar vein as the RCA set and shows that Mainstream Swing was very much alive (at least artistically) in the mid-1950s. As with the other sets, *Jive at Five* is very much in the 1950s Basie style, teaming Newman and fellow Basie-ites Wess and bassist Eddie Jones with pianist Tommy Flanagan and drummer Oliver Jackson on two basic originals and four veteran standards. Flanagan and Jones return for *Good 'n' Groovy,* although this time it was Foster's turn to be in the frontline with Newman; Billy English is on drums. Newman contributed four of the six numbers, highlighted by the exciting "Mo-Lasses." Age 61 at the time of *Hangin' Out,* Joe Newman and fellow trumpeter Joe Wilder (who co-led the set) were both still in excellent form, swinging through Basie-related material (arranged by either Frank Foster or Frank Wess), Newman's "The Midgets," and "Battle Hymn of the Republic" with a quintet that includes pianist Hank Jones, bassist Rufus Reid, and drummer Marvin "Smitty" Smith.

LPS TO SEARCH FOR

Joe Newman at Count Basie's (Mercury 20696) from 1961 is a live quintet set with the talented tenor of Oliver Nelson that has a fine Newman feature on "Our Love Is Here to Stay" and another excellent version of his "The Midgets."

JOHNNY OTIS
b. Dec. 28, 1921, Vallejo, CA

Johnny Otis, whose roots are in big band Swing, became one of the top talent scouts in R&B. His revues featured many top up-and-coming singers and musicians, most notably Esther Phillips. Although he is white, Otis has led many otherwise all-black bands. A drummer who doubled on vibraphone (inspired initially by Gene Krupa and on the latter instrument by Lionel Hampton), Otis worked early on with Count Otis Matthews, George Morrison, Lloyd Hunter, Harlan Leonard (1941), and Bardu Ali. He achieved his lifelong goal of playing with Count Basie when he sat in with Basie's band when Jo Jones was ill one night. In 1945 he began to record as a leader (using a Basie-style big band with Jimmy Rushing taking two vocals) and introduced "Harlem Nocturne," his first hit. He also freelanced, recording as a drummer with Lester Young, Illinois Jacquet, and Johnny Moore's Three Blazers.

Within a couple years, Otis was emphasizing R&B (with his Johnny Otis Rhythm & Blues Caravan) and becoming well known. He had 15 R&B hits during 1950–52, introduced "Little" Esther Phillips, Linda Hopkins, and Big Mama Thornton and used such performers as the Robins and Big Jay McNeely. Even after his hit-making days were over, later in the 1950s he helped discover Etta James, Hank Ballard & The Midnighters, and Little Willie John. Johnny Otis, whose music through the years has occasionally returned to Swing, has remained active on a part-time basis up to the present time. His son, Shuggie Otis, is a fine blues guitarist.

●

9 *Rhythms & Blues Caravan / Sept. 13, 1945–Mar. 21, 1951 / Savoy 92859*

Johnny Otis's Savoy recordings are considered the most important of his career (nearly all of his hits were made for the label) and this three-CD set has everything he cut for Savoy. One hears the beginning of Little Esther's career, Otis's early Swing sides, and his 15 R&B hits, plus much more. The definitive Johnny Otis reissue.

LES PAUL

b. June 9, 1915, Waukesha, WI

The career of the remarkable Les Paul, who practically invented the electric guitar and multitracking, could conceivably fit not only into a Swing book but into ones covering bop, country, rock, and pop. Paul started out playing harmonica when he was eight and, other than for a few piano lessons, was completely self-taught as a musician. He played banjo briefly and then switched to guitar, inspired by Eddie Lang, Nick Lucas, several local country players, and (by the mid-1930s) Django Reinhardt. Paul dropped out of high school to work with Rube Tronson's Cowboys in 1932. Two years later he was playing jazz on the radio as Les Paul and hillbilly music as Rhubarb Red. He made his recording debut in 1936 (backing singer Georgia White on acoustic guitar) and was soon experimenting with developing an electric guitar, a great interest of his. Paul moved to New York and was featured regularly with Fred Waring (1938–41). After relocating to Hollywood, he formed his own trio in 1943 and played primarily jazz for a few years. Paul was one of the stars at the first Jazz at the Philharmonic concert, having a lengthy and humorous tradeoff with Nat King Cole. Bing Crosby loved Paul's playing, used him on some of his records (including a hit version of "It's Been a Long, Long Time"), and encouraged him to build his own studio. After guesting on a series of records and working on developing multitracking, in 1947 Paul recorded a version of "Lover" that featured him on eight overdubbed guitars. He persuaded Capitol to release the record, which became his first hit.

An automobile accident in 1948 put Paul out of action until mid-1949. However, he then began teaming up with a country singer (Colleen Summers), whom he renamed Mary Ford and soon married. Using her voice and his guitar (both over-dubbed many times), the combination of Les Paul and Mary Ford had one hit after another during 1949–55. Included were such Swing standards as "How High the Moon," "Tiger Rag," "Nola," "Little Rock Getaway," "The World Is Waiting for the Sunrise," "Whispering," "Carioca," "Smoke Rings," and "Bye Bye Blues." Their versions of these songs were certainly much different than the ones heard in the 1930s! And compared to the cornball novelties and overly sentimental ballad vocals that dominated the pop charts during that era, the music of Les Paul and Mary Ford was a major relief.

After 1956 the hits stopped, and the marriage lasted only until 1964. Les Paul continued playing guitar on a part-time basis and recorded two laid-back sets with Chet Atkins during 1976–78. Overcoming some ill health, Paul began a series of Monday night appearances at Fat Tuesday's in New York in 1984, switching to the Iridium in 1996. Guitarists from the jazz, rock, and country worlds have continually paid tribute to him. His development of the Les Paul guitar and its successors, his championing of multitracking, and his good-natured genius have permanently altered American music. Les Paul, whose recordings have had several retrospectives in recent times and who collaborated on an autobiography, has slowed down through the years, but his mind remains very sharp and, when inspired, he can still play brilliantly. ●

9   *The Trio's Complete Decca Recordings Plus (1936–47) / May 11, 1936–July 25, 1947 / MCA/Decca 11708*

7   *Les Paul Trio / 1947 / Laserlight 15 741*

10   *The Legend & the Legacy / Feb. 1948–Dec. 23, 1957 / Capitol 97654*

The two-CD Decca set has 50 early recordings by Les Paul, including all of the sides by his jazz-oriented trio of 1944–47, which was really a quartet! In addition, Paul is heard on the four titles that he cut as Rhubarb Red, and there is a strong sampling of his work with Terry Shand's orchestra and backing singers Georgia White, Bing Crosby (including "It's Been a Long, Long Time"), Helen Forrest, the Delta Rhythm Boys, the Andrews Sisters, and Dick Haymes. The music shows how strong a guitarist he was in his formative years. The Laserlight CD, which features the Les Paul Trio (really Quartet) on their radio transcriptions (21 rather brief numbers) is a budget set, but that still does not excuse leaving out the musicians' names! Chances are it is pianist Paul Smith, rhythm guitarist Cal Gooden, and bassist Bob Meyer. Excellent music if faulty packaging. In contrast, the four-CD box *The Legend & the Legacy* is perfectly done. Not only are all of the hits of Les Paul and Mary Ford included, but it adds a full CD of previously unreleased material (some of which could have been best-sellers had they been released at the time), three often-humorous episodes from the Les Paul radio show, and a very informative booklet.

FILMS

He Changed the Music (A Vision 50197) is a 1988 performance with many guest stars from a variety of musical genres. *The Living Legend* (BMG Video 80061) is a Les Paul documentary from 1992.

KEN PEPLOWSKI
b. May 23, 1959, Garfield Heights, OH

Scott Hamilton and Warren Vache helped to launch the Swing revival movement of the mid-1970s. Dan Barrett and Howard Alden arrived in New York in 1983, and Ken Peplowski, who soon emerged, was also part of the second wave. Equally talented on clarinet and tenor, Peplowski is versatile enough to play in modern settings, but his heart is clearly in Mainstream Swing. After working locally in his native Cleveland, Peplowski toured with the Tommy Dorsey ghost orchestra during 1978–80 (when it was directed by Buddy Morrow). Moving to New York, he freelanced (including gigging with Max Kaminsky and Jimmy McPartland), worked with the Benny Goodman big band, and in 1987 signed with the Concord label. Peplowski has since recorded one stimulating CD after another in settings ranging from assisting Mel Torme and Rosemary Clooney to creating exciting duets with guitarist Alden, playing classical music, and interpreting Swing standards with a hot combo. One of the top clarinetists in jazz (few can jam so creatively at rapid tempos), Ken Peplowski is also an underrated tenor saxophonist who can hold his own with Scott Hamilton and Harry Allen.

●

8 *Double Exposure / Dec. 1987 / Concord Jazz 344*

9 *Sonny Side / 1989 / Concord Jazz 4376*

8 *Mr. Gentle and Mr. Cool / Feb. 1990 / Concord Jazz 4419*

8 *Illuminations / Nov. 20–21, 1990 / Concord Jazz 4449*

8 *The Natural Touch / Jan. 14–15, 1992 / Concord Jazz 4517*

10 *Concord Duo Series, Volume Three / Dec. 1992 / Concord Jazz 4556*

Ken Peplowski's output for Concord was strong from the start. Age 28 when he debuted for the label with *Double Exposure,* he made a lasting impression on that first date, a quintet outing with guitarist Ed Bickert and John Bunch that includes such tunes as "I Would Do Anything for You," "Blame It on My Youth," and "Jubilee." In addition to tenor and clarinet, Peplowski makes a few rare appearances on alto during *Sonny Side,* which also features Howard Alden and Dave Frishberg. The music alternates between Swing standards (including "Ring Dem Bells," "When I Take My Sugar to Tea," and "Hallelujah") and more modern tunes

("Bright Moments," Thelonious Monk's "Ugly Beauty," and Sonny Stitt's title cut), always swinging hard and melodically. The same is true on *Mr. Gentle and Mr. Cool,* with tunes by Duke Ellington, Cole Porter, and Irving Berlin coexisting with the works of Tadd Dameron and John Coltrane. "Body and Soul" has Peplowski and pianist Hank Jones emulating Benny Goodman and Teddy Wilson, "You Do Something to Me" cooks hard, and there are a pair of two-tenor meetings with Scott Hamilton that work quite well. The best selections on *Illuminations* are an uptempo "June Night" and three duets with Howard Alden (particularly an exciting "Panama"). The other selections include pianist Junior Mance, bassist Dennis Irwin, and drummer Alan Dawson. *The Natural Touch,* although using a completely different rhythm section (pianist Ben Aronov, guitarist Frank Vignola, bassist Murray Wall, and drummer Tom Helito), follows the pattern of most Ken Peplowski albums: a few modern tunes (Thelonious Monk's "Evidence" and originals by Aronov and Vignola) mixed in with hot Swing numbers (including "The One I Love" and "I Thought About You") and ballads. The *Concord Duo Series* matches Peplowski with Howard Alden for improvisations that are often telepathic and magical. "Blue Room," "Chasin' the Bird," Bix Beiderbecke's "In the Dark," and a lengthy "Just One of Those Things" are definite high points of this classic encounter.

7 *Steppin' with Peps / Mar. 1993 / Concord Jazz 4569*

7 *Live at Ambassador Auditorium / 1994 / Concord Jazz 4610*

7 *It's a Lonesome Old Town / Jan. 3–4, 1995 / Concord 4673*

8 *The Other Portrait / Mar. 1996–Apr. 1996 / Concord Concerto 42043*

7 *A Good Reed / Jan. 22–23, 1997 / Concord Jazz 4767*

6 *A Tribute to Benny Goodman / Apr. 20, 1997 / Progressive 7106*

9 *Grenadilla / Dec. 8–10, 1997 / Concord Jazz 4809*
Steppin' with Peps uses a slightly larger group than usual on some numbers as the Peplowski quintet (with Howard Alden and Ben Aronov) is joined occasionally by trumpeters Randy Sandke and Joe Wilder plus the second guitar of Bucky Pizzarelli. A heated "The Lady's in Love with You," a beautiful rendition of "Lotus Blossom" (with Wilder), and the somewhat free version of Ornette Coleman's "Turn Around" are among the more memorable numbers. During the date Peplowski hints at both Benny Goodman and Tony Scott on clarinet, while his tenor work looks toward Don Byas and Paul Gonsalves. *Live* (which is also available as a video) is a typically fine Peplowski quintet outing with Alden and Aronov that is notable for two appearances by Harry "Sweets" Edison. *It's a Lonesome Old Town* has the Peplowski Quintet (with Alden and pianist Allen Farnham) joined on some numbers by guitarist Charlie Byrd, trumpeter Tom Harrell, and pianist Marian McPartland. In addition to a few standards and obscurities, this set includes a song by Harrell, a Beatles tune ("In My Life"), Jobim's "Zingaro," and Sonny Stitt's "The Eternal Triangle." *The Other Portrait* is a very different Ken Peplowski record, a classically oriented set with the Bulgarian National Symphony. There are some unaccompanied clarinet explorations of jazz tunes, but the main works are Darius Milhaud's "Concerto for Clarinet & Orchestra," Witold Lutoslawski's "Dance Preludes," and Ornette Coleman's "Lonely Woman." Peplowski shows off both his versatility and his cool tone. *A Good Reed* is also a departure, for three of the seven selections find Peplowski joined by the Loren Schoenberg Big Band (including "Homage Concerto for Clarinet and Jazz Orchestra"), and even the quartet numbers are a bit offbeat and more modern than one might expect. *A Tribute to Benny Goodman* is listed as being by the Shoeless John Jackson Quartet, a pseudonym for Peplowski, who jams the Benny Goodman–associated material with Johnny Varro, vibraphonist John Cocuzzi, and drummer Joe Ascione. Although the songs are from the Swing era, the Benny Goodman Quartet actually never recorded any of these tunes; however, Goodman did perform most of the songs in different contexts. Solid if somewhat predictable. *Grenadilla* finds Peplowski stretching himself much more. His quartet (with Ben Aronov) is joined on some numbers by Howard Alden and the much more modern clarinetist and bass clarinetist Marty Ehrlich. In addition, bassist Greg Cohen's "Variations" features a clarinet quartet (with Ehrlich, Scott Robinson on alto clarinet, and J. D. Parran on contrabass clarinet), and Peplowski jams happily with Kenny Davern on "Farewell Blues." Intriguing music that finds Ken Peplowski, as usual, performing creative Swing (as opposed to recreations) and showing that he is one of the finest Mainstream reed players around today.

FILMS
Ken Peplowski's 1994 quintet date with Howard Alden and guest Harry Edison is available on the video *Live at Ambassador Auditorium* (Concord Jazz).

FLIP PHILLIPS
b. Mar. 26, 1915, Brooklyn, NY

A hard-swinging tenor whose exuberant style is closely identified with Woody Herman's First Herd and Jazz at the Philharmonic, Flip Phillips (born Joseph Filipelli) was still in his musical prime as he entered his mid-eighties. He started out on clarinet and picked up experience during a five-year period (1934–39) in which he played clarinet and alto at Schneider's Lobster House in Brooklyn. Phillips also played clarinet with Frankie Newton during 1940–41, switching permanently to tenor in 1942. He had stints with Benny Goodman, Wingy Manone, and Red Norvo before joining Herman (1944–46), where he was one of the main solo stars of the exciting Herd, being featured on many records. Phillips was influenced by Ben Webster (particularly on ballads) but sounded quite individual on romps. He was a fixture with Jazz at the Philharmonic during 1946–56, holding his own with the likes of Lester Young, Charlie Parker, Coleman Hawkins, and even Ben Webster. His solo on "Perdido" made him a very popular attraction, and Phillips was well liked by the other all-stars, particularly since he was an expert at fixing saxophones!

Phillips worked with the Gene Krupa Trio in 1952 and led dates of his own (including many record sessions) during the 1950s, often teaming up with Bill Harris. After touring with Benny Goodman in 1959, Phillips moved to Florida and played mostly locally during the 1960s, taking up bass clarinet as his double. Flip Phillips surfaced much more often in the 1970s (including some reunions with Woody Herman) and '80s and has kept his exuberant Swing style intact throughout the 1990s, still appearing regularly at jazz festivals and jazz parties.

●

9   *A Melody from the Sky / Sept. 1944–Nov. 1945 / Sony 39419*

*   *The Complete Verve/Clef Charlie Ventura & Flip Phillips Studio Sessions / Sept. 1947–May 1957 / Mosaic 6-182*

Flip Phillips's first four record dates as a leader are reissued on *A Melody from the Sky*, sessions cut while he was a major soloist with Woody Herman's First Herd. Heard in settings ranging from a quartet to a nonet mostly with Herman sidemen (including Bill Harris, trumpeter Neal Hefti, and pianist Ralph Burns), Phillips alternates warm ballads (including "Sweet and Lovely") with hotter numbers ("Stompin' at the Savoy" and "1–2–3–4 Jump"). Although Charlie Ventura gets first billing on the limited-edition Mosaic box set, four of the six CDs actually feature Flip Phillips. Ventura is in fine form during his 1951–54 sessions, while Phillips's Verve output has loads of variety. He is heard with quartets and combos that are up to nine pieces, with such sidemen as trumpeters Howard McGhee, Harry Edison, and Charlie Shavers, trombonists Kai Winding and Bill Harris, pianist Oscar Peterson, Buddy Rich, and many others. Since this set has all of Phillips's Verve studio dates, he is also heard as a sideman with Rich, guitarist Nick Esposito, and trombonist Tommy Turk. Superb Swing to bop music that features Flip in prime form.

8   *The Claw / Oct. 20, 1986 / Chiaroscuro 314*

8   *A Sound Investment / Mar. 1987 / Concord Jazz 4334*

9   *A Real Swinger / May 1988–June 1988 / Concord Jazz 4358*

6   *Try a Little Tenderness / June 30, 1992–July 1, 1992 / Chiaroscuro 321*

8   *Live at the 1993 Floating Jazz Festival / Nov. 1–3, 1993 / Chiaroscuro 327*

Age 71 at the time of *The Claw,* Flip Phillips had not lost a thing through the decades. He is heard during this set (cut live at the 1986 Floating Jazz Festival) leading a jam session that also has fellow tenors Buddy Tate, Al Cohn, and Scott Hamilton, with flugelhornist Clark Terry sitting in on three of the five selections. The tunes are all at least ten minutes long and are full of fire, although unfortunately the liner notes do not tell who solos when. The only other minus to the set is a boring nine-minute "Jazzspeak" that has Phillips rambling on verbally and not saying anything significant; however, the music easily compensates. *A Sound Investment* is an excellent collaboration by Phillips and Hamilton in a sextet with John Bunch; highlights include "The Claw" (one of five Phillips originals) and "Comes Love." *A Real Swinger* is a real showcase for Phillips, who fronts a five-piece rhythm section that includes both Howard Alden and Wayne Wright on guitars and Dick Hyman on piano. All of the ten selections are quite enjoyable, particularly "Tricotism," "Cotton Tail," Phillips's bass clarinet on "I Got a Right to Sing the Blues," and "I Want to Be Happy." *Try a Little Tenderness* showcases Phillips (on tenor and bass clarinet) backed by a string section and, although he displays a great deal of warmth, the overall effect is a bit sleepy, with no real mood variation. Much more exciting is Phillips's recording from the 1993 Floating Jazz Festival. Backed by Derek Smith, Bucky Pizzarelli, Milt Hinton, and drummer

Ray Mosca, Phillips sounds wonderful on "A Sound Investment," a lengthy "Poor Butterfly," "Jumpin' at the Woodside," and "How High the Moon."

Flip in Florida (Onyx 214) was Phillips's only recording of the 1960s. This 1963 album, which features him playing mostly standards with a local rhythm section, is notable for having his recorded debut on bass clarinet on three of the ten songs. *Flipenstein* (Progressive 7063), from 1981, has

eight titles having to do with ghosts and the like (including "Satin Takes a Holiday," "Ghoul of My Dreams," and "Hangman's Noose"). Phillips, with the assistance of Lou Stein, bassist Mike Moore, and Butch Miles, is in particularly explosive form on most of the selections.

FILMS

Flip Phillips can be seen with Woody Herman's orchestra in *Earl Carroll Vanities* (1945) and *Hit Parade of 1947* (1947). *80th Birthday Party* (Arbors 2) features the still-exuberant tenorman during a 1995 all-star concert.

NAT PIERCE

b. July 16, 1925, Somerville, MA, d. June 10, 1992, Los Angeles, CA

Nat Pierce often emulated Count Basie closely, in both his piano playing and his arranging, but he was also quite comfortable playing bop. He studied music at the New England Conservatory and, starting in 1943, worked regularly in the Boston area. Pierce toured with Larry Clinton (1948), led his own boppish big band (1949–51), and was pianist and arranger for Woody Herman (1951–55). After leaving Herman, Pierce freelanced around New York both as a pianist (where he often substituted for Basie on Mainstream Swing dates, including some led by Count's alumni) and as an arranger for singers and big bands. He wrote all of the charts for *The Sound of Jazz* telecast and worked with Ruby Braff, Lester Young, Coleman Hawkins, Pee Wee Russell, and Ella Fitzgerald, among others.

Pierce was back playing piano with Woody Herman during 1961–66 as part of one of Woody's most swinging big bands, also acting as road manager and chief talent scout. After that stint ended, Pierce freelanced, arranged for Anita O'Day and Carmen McRae, and in 1971 moved to Los Angeles. He worked with the local big bands of Louie Bellson and Bill Berry, sometimes subbed with the Count Basie Orchestra for the ill leader, and in 1975 with Frank Capp formed the Juggernaut. The Basie-soundalike all-star band featured Pierce playing piano and contributing arrangements that perfectly fit the Basie sound. Nat Pierce recorded as a sideman for Concord (including with Scott Hamilton), toured Europe as a member of the Countsmen, and stayed busy with the Juggernaut until his death at the age of 66.

9 *The Boston Bustout* / Dec. 1947–Dec. 1950 / Hep 13

7 *5400 North* / May 21, 1978 / Hep 2004

The Nat Pierce big band during 1949–51 was significant for including some of the top bop-oriented jazz musicians then based in Boston, most notably altoist Charlie Mariano. *The Boston Bustout* features Pierce with the Ray Borden Big Band in 1947, with combos led by baritonist Serge Chaloff and Mariano and on several selections by his own orchestra; Teddi King also has three vocals. *5400 North* was recorded three decades later and is a small-group live set with singer Mary Ann McCall, trumpeter Dick Collins, and tenorman Bill Perkins in a quintet. The music falls between cool jazz and Swing and finds Pierce often taking solos that are very reminiscent of Count Basie.

Additional performances by the pianist's early band are on *Nat Pierce Orchestra* (Zim 1005), which dates from 1949–50. *The Ballad of Jazz Street* (Zim 2003) has Pierce leading a more Swing-oriented big band in 1961, with solo space for the likes of Clark Terry, Paul Quinichette, Paul Gonsalves, and trombonist Eddie Bert, among others.

FILMS

Nat Pierce can be seen playing piano during parts of *The Sound of Jazz* (Vintage Jazz Classics 2001).

BUCKY PIZZARELLI

b. Jan. 9, 1926, Paterson, NJ

A tasteful Swing guitarist whose style is both a throwback to the 1930s yet modern in a sophisticated way, Bucky Pizzarelli has uplifted countless record dates and live performances through the decades. He played with Vaughan Monroe's orchestra in 1943, spent a couple of years in the military, and rejoined Monroe in 1946. Pizzarelli became a studio musician early on, working for NBC (1952–64) and then ABC. He also toured with the Three Suns (1956–57) and began playing with Benny Goodman, an on-and-off association that lasted for a couple of decades. Although long well respected by other musicians, Pizzarelli (who plays a seven-string guitar) did not come into his own as a Swing stylist until the 1970s, when he recorded with Joe Venuti, Bud Freeman, Zoot Sims, Stephane Grappelli, and other Mainstream greats plus as a leader for Monmouth/Evergreen. He also occasionally played with his son, fellow guitarist John Pizzarelli. Bucky Pizzarelli (who often plays a seven-string electric guitar) has stayed quite active up the present time, helping to keep Swing alive.

●

7 *Solo Flight / 1981 + 1986 / Stash 573*

8 *Bucky and John Pizzarelli / Jan. 10, 1987 / Challenge 70025*

7 *A Portrait / Jan. 1992–Feb. 1992 / Stash 551*

7 *Nirvana / Feb. 21, 1995 / Laserlight 17 163*

9 *Contrasts / July 1, 1998 / Arbors 129209*

Bucky Pizzarelli records are always tasteful, quiet, and lightly swinging. Although they can function well as superior background music, a close listen reveals plenty of subtle creativity. *Solo Flight* actually contains two former LPs: *Solo Flight* and *Love Songs*. The emphasis is on slower tempos (particularly on the latter set), but the superior material and Pizzarelli's impeccable musicianship makes this a strong release. *Bucky and John Pizzarelli* is one of several guitar duo albums by the father-and-son team, and they clearly challenge each other. John takes vocals on "Route 66," "This Will Make You Laugh," and "Straighten Up and Fly Right," and other highlights include "Three Little Words" and a three-song Benny Goodman medley. *A Portrait* is generally more thoughtful, with Pizzarelli taking unaccompanied solos on a variety of guitars and five duets with Howard Alden (including "Tricotism"). *Nirvana,* from the budget Laserlight label, is a quartet outing with son John, bassist Lynn

Seaton, and drummer Bernard Purdie that sticks mostly to standards, such as "Azure Te" (which was written by Wild Bill Davis, not Wild Bill Davison as listed!), "Pick Yourself Up," "Honeysuckle Rose," and "Stompin' at the Savoy." *Contrasts* is an instrumental set featuring the guitar duo of Bucky and John Pizzarelli on a set full of strong material, including "Jersey Bounce," "The Minute Samba," George Smith's "Test Pilot," the Kress/McDonough piece "Stage Fright," and "Guess I'll Go Back Home This Summer."

LPS TO SEARCH FOR

Many of the most interesting Bucky Pizzarelli albums have yet to be reissued on CD. *Green Guitar Blues* (Monmouth/Evergreen 7047), from 1972, is mostly solo and ranges from movie and classical themes to Swing standards; Bucky's daughter Mary (then just 14) plays second guitar on "Chicken à la Swing." *Plays Beiderbecke/Challis and Kress* is a fascinating set in which Pizzarelli overdubs several guitars to play five Bix Beiderbecke compositions (arranged by Bill Challis) and joins with Mary Pizzarelli to perform eight numbers by Carl Kress and Dick McDonough. *Nightwings* (Flying Dutchman 1120) alternates solo numbers with duets costarring Joe Venuti, while *Buck & Bud* (Flying Dutchman 1378) teams the guitarist with Bud Freeman and includes six exciting guitar-tenor duets.

JOHN PIZZARELLI

b. Apr. 6, 1960, Paterson, NJ

The son of guitarist Bucky Pizzarelli, John Pizzarelli has steadily improved both as a guitarist and as a singer since his arrival on the scene in the early 1980s. He first was noticed at the time for his work with his father, sounding fairly similar in his style and musical taste. After playing with Tony Monte's trio for a period starting in 1986, Pizzarelli (who first recorded as a leader in 1983) really started his solo career in 1990. Since that time, Pizzarelli has developed his own approach to Swing guitar, often playing standards at rapid tempos with his trio (which includes the excellent if underrated pianist Ray Kennedy and John's younger brother, bassist Martin Pizzarelli). A limited but charming singer, John Pizzarelli (who records regularly for RCA) generally takes brief, good-natured vocals that set up lengthy and often fiery solos in the Swing tradition. In 1997 he appeared as one of the stars in a Broadway show called *Dream* that featured Johnny Mercer songs. ●

6 *Hit That Jive, Jack! / June 25, 1985 / Stash Budget 2508*

7 *My Blue Heaven / Feb. 6–7, 1990 / Chesky 38*

5 *All of Me / 1991 / Novus 673129*

8 *Naturally / 1993 / Novus 01241*

Hit That Jive, Jack! is an early effort for John Pizzarelli, who mostly emphasizes his vocalizing while with a quartet that includes his father, Bucky, and Dave McKenna or a trio with Hugh McCracken's harmonica. Five of the songs are associated with Nat King Cole (including "Frim Fram Sauce" and "Baby, Baby, All the Time") and, of the other pieces, two are Pizz's originals. John Pizzarelli really got his solo career under way in 1990, with *My Blue Heaven,* and the following year, when he signed with RCA/Novus. *My Blue Heaven* teams him with a variety of all-stars (Clark Terry, Dave Mc-Kenna, Milt Hinton, drummer Connie Kay, and Bucky Pizzarelli) and has him performing such vintage standards as "I'm an Errand Boy for Rhythm," "Lady Be Good," "Best Man," and "Candy." *All of Me* makes the mistake of putting the emphasis on Pizzarelli's voice rather than his guitar playing, and Dick Lieb's big band and string arrangements are unadventurous and very predictable. Only the leader's charm makes that set listenable. *Naturally* is much better, with Pizzarelli joined by a big band and helped out by such soloists as his father, Scott Robinson, Harry Allen, and Frank Wess on tenors, trumpeters Clark Terry and Tony Kadleck, and clarinetist Walt Levinsky. Highlights include "I'm Confessin'," "When I Grow Too Old to Dream," Dave Frishberg's "Slappin' the Cakes on Me," and a five-song "Baby" medley.

5 *New Standards / 1994 / Novus 63172*

9 *Dear Mr. Cole / 1994 / Novus 63182*

9 *After Hours / Jan. 16, 1996 / Novus 63191*

7 *Our Love Is Here to Stay / 1997 / RCA 07863 67501*

5 *Meets the Beatles / 1998 / RCA 74321-81433*

New Standards is a bit unusual, for five of the numbers are John Pizzarelli originals and most of the others songs are fairly new obscurities (other than Nat Cole's lesser-known "Beautiful Moons Ago"). Backed by mostly large groups (although a few numbers are by a trio), Pizzarelli does his best, but the material overall is not worthy of him. *Dear Mr. Cole* is much better, a trio album with pianist Benny Green and bassist Christian McBride that finds Pizzarelli sticking mostly to songs made famous or at least uplifted by Nat King Cole. His versions of such numbers as "What Can I Say After I Say I'm Sorry," "Little Girl," "It's Only a Paper Moon," and "Honeysuckle Rose" make this one of his strongest releases. *After Hours* is the definitive John Pizzarelli album because it features his regular trio (with pianist Ray Kennedy and bassist Martin Pizzarelli) and a few guests (including Randy Sandke and Harry Allen). The material is primarily superior vintage tunes. The renditions of "Coquette," "They Can't Take That Away from Me," "Sometimes I'm Happy," and "Stringbean" show off John Pizzarelli at his best, with plenty of hot solos. *Our Love Is Here to Stay* has its moments (particularly "Avalon" and "Little Girl"), but Don Sebesky's big band frequently gets in the way and the material (such as "The Day I Found You" and "Kalamazoo") does not always fit Pizzarelli's sound that well. A mixed bag. As for John Pizzarelli's attempt to swing the Beatles songbook with a big band and a string orchestra, it is worth hearing once, but few will return for a second listen, except those who want to experience "Can't Buy Me Love" being swung à la Count Basie!

LOUIS PRIMA

b. Dec. 7, 1911, New Orleans, LA, d. Aug. 24, 1978, New Orleans, LA

In the 1950s, after two decades of being a major personality, Louis Prima invented an unusual mixture of music that 35 years later would serve as one of the main inspirations for Retro Swing. Prima's New Orleans trumpet and love for Dixieland combined with Keely Smith's middle-of-the-pop vocalizing, Sam Butera's hot R&B band The Witnesses, Swing standards, a heavy dose of good-humored comedy, rock and roll rhythms, and some show biz trappings. The result was an eclectic and winning formula that was very entertaining and cut across many musical boundaries.

Prima, whose older brother, Leon Prima, also played trumpet, started out on violin when he was seven but taught himself trumpet in 1925 when he was 13. He developed quickly and played locally in New Orleans until 1932, when he joined Red Nichols and began freelancing in New York. In 1934 Prima began leading his own combo at the Famous Door on 52nd Street and started an extensive series of New Orleans jazz recordings that for a couple of years also featured Pee Wee Russell on clarinet. Prima's happy vocals and Louis Armstrong–inspired trumpet made him popular from the start. The composer of "Sing, Sing, Sing," by the end of the decade Prima was leading a big band, which worked steadily without really making it big despite having hits in "Angelina" and "Robin Hood." By the early 1950s, Prima's music was comprised primarily of corny novelties that emphasized his Italian heritage.

However, after marrying Keely Smith in 1952 and discovering tenor saxophonist Sam Butera in New Orleans in 1954, Prima became a hit with his new and often-wild show in Las Vegas. His records (some of which are classic, including "That Old Black Magic" and a pair of medleys: "Just a Gigolo/I Ain't Got Nobody" and "When You're Smiling/The Sheik of Araby") sold quite well for the remainder of the decade, and he was often featured on television. Prima and Smith were divorced in 1961 and, although Prima continued working steadily through the 1960s (using Butera's band until the end), some of the magic was gone. In 1975 he suffered a stroke and fell into a coma; he died three years later. However, Louis Prima has certainly not been forgotten. His exuberant approach to music is currently being emulated by scores of Retro Swing bands and vocalists.

●

8	*1934–1935 / Sept. 27, 1934–June 27, 1935 / Classics 1048*
7	*Plays Pretty for the People / Feb. 1944–Jan. 1947 / Savoy 4420*
1	*Say It with a Slap / July 24, 1947–May 27, 1949 / Buddha 7446599614*
7	*Angelina / June 1950 / Viper's Nest 155*
10	*Capitol Collectors Series / Apr. 19, 1956–Feb. 23, 1962 / Capitol 94072*

Considering Louis Prima's great popularity these days, it is surprising that more of his records have not been reissued on CD. The Classics series has just begun bringing back his earliest recordings. The music on *1934–1935* falls between Dixieland and small-group Swing and features such sidemen as trombonist George Brunies, clarinetist Sidney Arodin, Eddie Miller on clarinet and tenor, pianist Claude Thornhill, and clarinetist Pee Wee Russell on the later

tracks. No great hits but fun music. *Plays Pretty for the People* features Prima's late-Swing-era big band, although the leader is virtually the entire show. The 20 selections (particularly "Robin Hood," "Angelina," and "Chinatown, My Chinatown"), taken out of the 67 recorded by the Prima Orchestra during 1940–47, are still worth hearing. Three are instrumentals, and Lily Ann Carol assists Prima on the vocals. In contrast, *Say It with a Slap* is mostly unlistenable. One dumb novelty follows another, with the corn being rather unbearable at times. Prima is shown holding a trumpet on the back of the CD, but his horn makes very few appearances and the "comedy" is just plain stupid. Don't even consider buying this!

Angelina, from 1950, is quite a bit better. Previously unissued, the music from three radio broadcasts finds the unidentified big band sounding impressive, with Prima taking many trumpet solos and the interplay between the leader and Keely Smith (then 22) beginning to form. The mixture of Swing, Dixieland, and R&B was in its formative stages.

Louis Prima and Keely Smith's mixture of styles and entertaining show in the 1950s was the musical precursor of the entire Retro Swing movement.

Capitol Collectors Series is a "best of" collection of Louis Prima's greatest period, and it is highly recommended, until the individual Capitol albums are reissued in full. Included are his most popular performances from the Witnesses days (including "I've Got You Under My Skin," "That Old Black Magic," and the medleys), a few rarities, and plenty of examples of the exciting and unique musical blend that would make his band such an inspiration to future generations of swingers. Essential music.

LPS TO SEARCH FOR

Classics will eventually reissue all of Louis Prima's early recordings, music that was last available as *1934–1935 Volume One* (The Old Masters 37), *1935–1936 Volume Two* (The Old Masters 38), *1936 Volume Three* (The Old Masters 39), and *1937–1938 Volume Four* (The Old Masters 62). The magical Louis Prima–Keely Smith–Sam Butera team was first heard on such classic albums as *The Wildest* (Capitol 755), *The Call of the Wildest* (Capitol 836), and *The Wildest Show at Tahoe* (Capitol 908). Their performances in the obscure film *Hey Boy! Hey Girl!* (Capitol 1160) were made available on the LP of the same name. Later performances can be heard on *Louis and Keely* (Dot 3210) and *Return of the Wildest* (Dot 3392). And for an example of Louis Prima doing his best to keep the old magic going after Keely Smith's departure, *Plays Pretty for the People* (Jazz Band 406) features him in 1963–64 with his soon-to-be-second wife, Gia Mione, on vocals.

FILMS

Even before he found his sound in the mid-1950s, Louis Prima appeared in many films. In addition to film shorts, he pops up in these full-length movies: *Rhythm on the Range* (1936), *Start Cheering* (1937), *You Can't Have Everything* (1937), *Rose of Washington Square* (1939), *Senior Prom* (1958), *Twist All Night* (1961), and the Italian film *Women by Night* (1962). In addition, Louis Prima and Keely Smith star in *Hey Boy! Hey Girl!* (1959) and Prima sings and provides the speaking voice for "King Louie of the Apes" in *The Jungle Book* (1967).

PAUL QUINICHETTE

b. May 17, 1916, Denver, CO, d. May 25, 1983, New York, NY

Paul Quinichette was dubbed the "Vice Pres" because of the remarkable similarity in his sound and style to those of Lester Young ("Pres"). Unlike the other tenors who looked to early Young (of the 1936–44 period) as their inspiration, Quinichette sounded just like Pres did in the 1950s. He started out on clarinet and alto, switching to tenor when he turned professional. After playing locally, Quinichette worked with the big bands of Nat Towles, Lloyd Hunter, Shorty Sherock, and Ernie Fields (1942). He gained some attention while with Jay McShann (1942–43) and played with Johnny Otis (1945–47), Benny Carter, and Big Sid Catlett. After moving to New York in the late 1940s, Quinichette freelanced, including with Louis Jordan, Lucky Millinder, Henry "Red" Allen, Dinah Washington, and Hot Lips Page. It was logical that he would work with Count Basie, and he was with Basie's second big band (1952–53) right at its beginning.

Quinichette went out on his own in 1953, made some excellent records as a leader (one of which used John Coltrane as the second tenor), recorded with Billie Holiday, and worked in 1955 with Benny Goodman. However, in the 1960s Quinichette dropped out of music altogether and worked as an electrical engineer. Paul Quinichette made a short-lived return to music in the mid-1970s, when he worked with Sammy Price, Brooks Kerr, and Buddy Tate, but ill health forced him to permanently retire.

●

9 *Cattin' with Coltrane and Quinichette / Aug. 14, 1952–May 17, 1957 / DCC Compact Classics 1085*

8 *The Kid from Denver / 1956–Aug. 1959 / Biograph 136*

7 *On the Sunny Side / May 10, 1957 / Original Jazz Classics 076*

9 *For Basie / Oct. 18, 1957 / Original Jazz Classics 978*

The audiophile release from DCC has three previously unreleased numbers from a 1952 version of Paul Quinichette's quintet, but it is for the meeting with the great John Coltrane that this release is most highly recommended. Quinichette's Lester Young-inspired sound is so much different than Coltrane's harsher tone that it sounds as if they were playing different instruments altogether! Four of the six songs ("Sunday" and three originals by pianist Mal Waldron) have both tenors battling it out, while "Exactly Like You" and "Tea for Two" are features for Quinichette. *The Kid from Denver* mostly has Quinichette starring with a tentet (all of the musicians but Nat Pierce were from Basie's band) in 1958, jamming Swing standards and basic originals. The remaining four tracks showcase Quinichette (who is in prime form throughout) with combos headed by trumpeter Gene

Roland. The Swing tenor plays with a more modern group than usual during *On the Sunny Side* (trombonist Curtis Fuller, both John Jenkins and Sonny Red on altos, pianist Waldron, bassist Doug Watkins, and drummer Ed Thigpen), but he holds his own on three Waldron originals and a pair of standards (including "On the Sunny Side of the Street"). *For Basie* finds Quinichette back on familiar ground (all five songs are from the prewar Count Basie Orchestra's songbook) with trumpeter Shad Collins (on one of his best sessions), Nat Pierce, Freddie Green, Walter Page, and Jo Jones, romping his way through such songs as "Rock-a-Bye Basie" and "Jive at Five."

LPS TO SEARCH FOR

The Vice President (Trip 5542) has most of Quinichette's first dates as a leader (1951–52) and finds him joined by members of both of Basie's bands, including Count himself, on six songs, jamming basic material. *Moods* (Emarcy 36003) has six Quincy Jones originals included among the eight songs, with either Herbie Mann or Sam Most on flute and such complementary pianists as Jimmy Jones and Sir Charles Thompson.

RED RICHARDS

b. Oct. 19, 1917, Brooklyn, NY, d. Mar. 12, 1998, Scarsdale, NY

A solid Swing pianist who was a longtime fixture on the Mainstream Jazz scene, Charles "Red" Richards made his recording debut in 1940 with Skeets Tolbert and was still an active performer more than 55 years later. In the 1940s Richards worked with Roy Eldridge, Bobby Hackett, and Jimmy McPartland and was a member of Tab Smith's group for four years (1945–49). Richards played with Sidney Bechet and Bob Wilber in 1951, gigged with Mezz Mezzrow in Europe (1953), and was with Muggsy Spanier's Dixieland band from 1953 to 1957. The pianist (whose Swing style often recalled Teddy Wilson's) played piano with the Fletcher Henderson reunion bands of 1957–58. After stints with Wild Bill Davison and again with Spanier, Richards co-led the Saints and Sinners with Vic Dickenson. That notable Mainstream Swing group was active throughout the 1960s and made some recordings. In the 1970s Richards often worked at Eddie Condon's club, and in 1979 he began an association with Panama Francis's Savoy Sultans. As one of the last Swing survivors, Red Richards was quite active up until his death, recording with Doc Cheatham and Benny Waters as late as 1997. ●

7   *Lullaby in Rhythm / Mar. 16, 1985 / Sackville 3044*

8   *Dreamy / Apr. 28, 1991 / Sackville 3053*

9   *Echoes of Spring / Jan. 16, 1997 / Sackville 20049*
Lullaby in Rhythm and *Dreamy,* a pair of solo piano dates, are equally rewarding. Richards, mostly emphasizes songs from the 1930s and early '40s in concise (three- to five-minute) interpretations. *Lullaby in Rhythm* has such gems as "If Dreams Come True," "Blue Turning Grey Over You," and "It Could Happen to You," while *Dreamy* (an Erroll Garner song) has "I'm in the Market for You," "This Year's Kisses," and "I Thought About You" among the highlights. Richards takes two vocals on the latter disc. *Echoes of Spring,* recorded live in Holland, is of interest not only for Red Richards's fine piano playing that late in his career

(sticking to veteran standards) but for the solos of Norris Turney and Claude Williams; bassist Dave Green and drummer Joe Ascione complete the quintet. Richards takes two vocals and Williams has one, but it is for the solos of the three principals (the violinist sounds remarkably ageless) that this CD is most recommended.

LPS TO SEARCH FOR

Soft Buns (West 54), from 1978, and *It's a Wonderful World* (Black & Blue 33.166), from 1980, are excellent solo dates. *In a Mellow Tone* (West 54 8005), from 1979, has some fine playing by altoist Norris Turney, while *I'm Shooting High* (Sackville 2017), from 1987, is a frequently hot date with a quintet that includes tenor saxophonist George Kelly and trumpeter Johnny Letman.

BETTY ROCHE

b. Jan. 9, 1918, Wilmington, DE, d. Feb. 16, 1999, Pleasantville, NJ

Betty Roche is known primarily for singing "The Blues" section of "Black, Brown, and Beige" at Duke Ellington's 1943 Carnegie Hall concert and for her classic rendition of "Take the 'A' Train" with Ellington in 1952. She should have become much more famous but had a fairly brief career, with several key absences off the scene. Roche sang and recorded early on with the Savoy Sultans (1941–42) and also had short stints with Hot Lips Page and Lester Young. She did not make any commercial recordings with Ellington in 1943 (due to the recording strike), and the original version of "Black, Brown and Beige" was not released on record until decades later. She did perform and record with Earl Hines in 1944 but then had low-level jobs and dropped out of music. Roche rejoined Duke Ellington's band in 1952, but "Take the 'A' Train" was her only recording with Ellington; the classic and humorous bebop vocal was later taken over by Ray Nance. Betty Roche again went into obscurity, came back to record three fine albums during 1956 and 1960–61 as a leader for Bethlehem and Prestige, and then permanently dropped out of music for unknown reasons, cutting short a potentially important career. ●

8   *Take the 'A' Train / Mar. 1956 / Bethlehem 20-30142*

7   *Singin' & Swingin' / June 1960 / Original Jazz Classics 1718*

9   *Lightly and Politely / Jan. 24, 1961 / Original Jazz Classics 1802*

All three of Betty Roche's albums as a leader are quite good, making one wonder why she did so little else. *Take the 'A' Train* has a remake of the title tune, several other numbers associated with Duke Ellington (including three takes of "Go Away Blues"), "Route 66," "All My Life," and "Time After Time." Joined by vibraphonist Eddie Costa, trumpeter Conte Candoli, pianist Donn Trenner, bassist Whitey Mitchell, and drummer Davey Williams, Roche sounds quite happy and expressive throughout this date. Her second album has backing from tenor saxophonist Jimmy Forrest, organist Jack McDuff, guitarist Bill Jennings, bassist Wendell Marshall, and drummer Roy Haynes. Roche brings new life to nine familiar standards, including "A Foggy Day," "When I Fall in Love," and "Where or When," although she does not sound old enough to sing "September Song"! Her final recording (in which she is accompanied by an obscure four-piece rhythm section) was her finest hour on records. Roche improvises quite a bit throughout the standards and three Ellington songs, sounding at her best on "Someone to Watch Over Me," "Polka Dots and Moonbeams," "Rocks in My Bed," and "I Had the Craziest Dream." Just 43 at the time, Betty Roche would spend her last 38 years retired from music.

JIMMY ROWLES

b. Aug. 19, 1918, Spokane, WA, d. May 28, 1996, Burbank, CA

Pianist Jimmy Rowles was long renowned for his chord voicings and his knowledge of obscure but rewarding songs. Considered a masterful accompanist and a distinctive soloist whose creativity was quite subtle, Jimmy Rowles started playing piano when he was 14. He attended Gonzaga College and the University of Washington, working locally in Spokane until moving to Los Angeles in 1940. In 1942 he joined Slim and Slam, also playing with Lee and Lester Young and Benny Goodman's big band later in the year. Rowles was with Woody Herman's orchestra during 1942–43, served in the Army (where he played with Skinnay Ennis's service band) and then, after his discharge, was with Woody Herman's First Herd. After working with the big bands of Les Brown, Tommy Dorsey, Benny Goodman again, and Bob Crosby (on his radio shows), Rowles mostly led his own trios in Los Angeles during the 1950s and '60s. He was a close friend of Billie Holiday and Peggy Lee (both of whom he worked with), was active in the studios, and played primarily his own brand of music, which was open to the influence of both Mainstream Swing and bop. Rowles played and recorded with Stan Getz and Zoot Sims in the 1970s, worked with Carmen McRae and Sarah Vaughan, and toured as Ella Fitzgerald's accompanist during 1981–83. He composed the haunting (and much-recorded) "The Peacocks," took eerie vocals now and then, and was greatly in demand during his final 20 years, including as a teacher; he was an inspiration for Diana Krall. Jimmy Rowles's daughter, Stacy Rowles, is an excellent flugelhornist.

●

6   *Let's Get Acquainted with Jazz (For People Who Hate Jazz) / June 20, 1958 / V.S.O.P. 11*

7   *Our Delight / 1968 / V.S.O.P. 99*

7   *Subtle Legend, Vol. 2 / Jan. 8, 1972 / Storyville 8295*

7   *Subtle Legend, Vol. 1 / Oct. 15, 1972 / Storyville 8287*

8   *Jimmy Rowles and George Mraz / Dec. 22, 1976 / Audiophile 188*

Let's Get Acquainted has some fine music performed by Jimmy Rowles (a few originals along with some familiar standards) in a West Coast septet also including trumpeter Pete Candoli, tenor saxophonist Harold Land, and guitarist Barney Kessel, but the playing time (under 30 minutes) is rather unfortunate and makes this CD of lesser interest unless found at a budget price. *Our Delight,* which was not released for the initial time until this 1997 CD, is particularly valuable, for Rowles did not lead any record dates during the 1961–69 period. He plays quite well and is joined by either Max Bennett or Chuck Berghofer on bass and Nick Martinis or Larry Bunker on drums. There is a lot of diversity in the music and such offbeat material as "America the Beautiful,"

"Moon of Manakoora," and Freddie Hubbard's "Crisis." The music on the two *Subtle Legend* CDs was not released until 1998, and these private performances find Rowles (who takes an occasional vocal) sounding very relaxed while playing with bassist Monty Budwig and drummer Donald Bailey. This is how Rowles sounded when in an informal setting. *Vol. 2* includes "Nina Never Knew," "Slummin' on Park Avenue," and "Lester Left Town," among others, while *Vol. 1* is highlighted by "Limehouse Blues," "Looking at You," the pianist's "Ballad of Thelonious Monk," and the eerie and slightly demented "Do You Know Why Stars Come Out At Night." Rowles's 1976 duet album with bassist George Mraz certainly has a great deal of obscure material. There are four songs by the modern saxophonist Wayne Shorter, a couple of originals, and also such forgotten tunes as "Pretty Eyes" (which has one of three Rowles vocals), "You Started Something," and "Remember When."

6 *Looking Back / June 8, 1988 / Delos 4009*

8 *Trio / Aug. 11–12, 1988 / Capri 74009*

9 *Plus 2, Plus 3, Plus 4 / Dec. 16–20, 1988 / JVC 6005*

7 *Lilac Time / Aug. 18–22, 1994 / Kokopelli 1297*
Looking Back, which teams Jimmy Rowles with his daughter Stacy Rowles (who plays mellow trumpet and takes a vocal on "Looking Back"), bassist Eric Von Essen, and drummer Donald Bailey, is a bit too predictable and tasteful. Nothing all that surprising occurs except for the reworking of "Take the 'A' Train," although the music is pleasing overall. *Trio* is much hotter in spots, matching Rowles with bassist Red Mitchell and drummer Donald Bailey. Rowles contributed "After School" and three of the bassist's songs are also included, while the other seven tunes (which include "Have You Met Miss Jones," "Crazy He Calls Me," and even "Yes Sir, That's My Baby") are familiar but given subtle surprises by the high-quality trio. The music on *Plus 2, Plus 3, Plus 4*

(which features Rowles in a trio with guitarist Larry Koonse and Eric Von Essen, with a quartet that adds drummer Ralph Penland, and with a quintet that also includes trumpeter Bill Berry) is mostly taken at slow tempos but has plenty of variety. Rowles takes half-spoken vocals on touching versions of "I Never Loved Anyone" and "I've Grown Accustomed to Your Face," and the other songs include "All Day Long," "I Wished on the Moon," "I've Got a Crush On You," and the blues "Bag of Wax." Touching and sensitive music. The same can be said for *Lilac Time,* which may have been the pianist's final recording. The set of duets with bassist Eric Von Essen has a great deal of obscure material, including the theme song for a television series that never aired ("Theme from *Arrest & Trial*")! Harold Arlen's "Music Music Elsewhere," "Jeannine," and "I Dream Of Lilac Time" are not exactly recorded on a regular basis either. The special Jimmy Rowles magic (which requires close listening in order to grasp) can be heard throughout this late period effort, and his raspy vocals have their own strange appeal. It is as if one could hear him thinking aloud.

LPS TO SEARCH FOR

Weather in a Jazz Vane (V.S.O.P. 48) is a 1958 set with West Coast players and includes Rowles's first recorded vocal, a very spontaneous effort on "Too Hot for Words." *Some Other Spring* (Blue Angel Jazz Club) is a live effort from 1972 with bassist Monty Budwig and drummer Donald Bailey. *Plays Duke Ellington and Billy Strayhorn* (Columbia 37639) is a rare solo date, and other notable trio sets include 1976's *Grandpaws* (Choice 1014), *We Could Make Such Beautiful Music Together* (Xanadu 157) from 1978 (which includes a version of "Stars and Stripes Forever"), *The Jimmie Rowles/Red Mitchell Trio* (Contemporary 14016), and *I'm Glad There Is You* (Contemporary 14032); the last two sets (from the same dates in 1985) have guest appearances by Stacy Rowles.

MARSHALL ROYAL
b. May 5, 1912, Sapulpa, OK, d. May 8, 1995, Inglewood, CA

Although a veteran of the Swing era, Marshall Royal made his most important contributions as a member of the second Count Basie Orchestra. His younger brother, Ernie Royal, was an excellent first trumpeter. The Royal brothers grew up in Los Angeles, where their father was a music teacher and had his own band. Marshall started on violin and also played guitar and clarinet before settling on alto. Royal was working locally at the age of 13 and had long stints with Curtis Mosby (1929–31) and the Les Hite Orchestra (1931–39). He also had an opportunity to sub with Duke Ellington's orchestra in 1934 and recorded with Art Tatum. Royal was with Cee Pee Johnson (1939–40) until he finally left Los Angeles with Lionel Hampton (1940–42), occasionally doubling on violin. After serving in the Navy (where he led a service band), Royal was briefly with the Eddie Heywood Sextet in 1946 and then returned to Los Angeles, where he played locally and worked as a studio musician for five years. In 1951 he joined the Count Basie Septet on clarinet, helped Basie organize his new orchestra, and became its lead altoist. Royal was with the Basie big band during 1952–70, taking occasional solos but mostly adding a Johnny Hodges–flavored sound to Count's sax ensembles. After leaving Basie, the altoist moved back to Los Angeles, where he worked in the studios and with local orchestras, including Bill Berry's L.A. Big Band. Marshall Royal had an opportunity to record as a leader (once as a co-leader with Snooky Young) and was a sideman on records led by Dave Frishberg, Warren Vache, Ernie Wilkins, Frank Wess, Ella Fitzgerald, Gene Harris, Ray Anthony, and others, receiving recognition as an important Swing veteran during his later years. ●

LPS TO SEARCH FOR

Marshall Royal's three albums as a leader are not available on CD, although the Concord album that he co-led with Snooky Young (the trumpeter had first billing) has been reissued. *Gordon Jenkins Presents Marshall Royal* (Everest 5087) is a little-known effort from 1960 that has the altoist mostly playing ballads while backed by Jenkins's string orchestra. *First Chair* (Concord Jazz 88), from 1978, puts Royal in the spotlight on a Swing date with guitarist Cal Collins, Nat Pierce, bassist Monty Budwig, and Jake Hanna, alternating romps (including his original "Jump") with ballads. *Royal Blue* (Concord Jazz 125) is even a touch better, with some more heated performances; he is joined by Collins, pianist Monty Alexander, bassist Ray Brown, and drummer Jimmie Smith. "Avalon" and "Things Ain't What They Used to Be" are highlights.

FILMS

Marshall Royal can be seen as part of Count Basie's Octet in the opening sequence of *Made in Paris* (1966) and appears briefly in *Lepke* (1974).

RANDY SANDKE
b. May 23, 1949, Chicago, IL

One of the finest trumpeters to emerge in Mainstream Jazz of the 1980s, Randy Sandke often appears in Swing, Dixieland, and classic jazz settings but is quite capable of playing any style of music. His older brother, Jordan Sandke, has also been an excellent trumpeter. In 1968 Randy Sandke formed a rock band with tenor saxophonist Michael Brecker that had a horn section. He was offered a chance to join Janis Joplin's band, but Sandke had a hernia in his throat that, even after a successful operation, resulted in his losing most of his confidence. He chose to play guitar at low-profile jobs for a decade in New York. After finally making a comeback on trumpet in the early 1980s, Sandke worked with Vince Giordano's Nighthawks for five years, played with Bob Wilber, and was with the Benny Goodman Big Band of 1985–86. He has been quite busy since that time, visiting Europe over 20 times and appearing at many classic jazz festivals and jazz parties. Among the many all-stars with whom he has performed are the Buck Clayton Big Band, pianist Ralph Sutton, Kenny Davern, Benny Carter, the World's Greatest Jazz Band, Mel Torme, Joe Williams, old friend Michael Brecker, and Jordan Sandke (they recorded in 1985 as the Sandke Brothers). Randy Sandke has recorded as a leader for Jazzology and Concord. ●

9	*Stampede / Dec. 4–6, 1990 / Jazzology 2211*
9	*Wild Cats / July 9 + 13, 1992 / Jazzology 222*
8	*I Hear Music / Feb. 1993 / Concord Jazz 4566*
8	*Get Happy / Sept. 1993 / Concord Jazz 4598*
8	*The Chase / Aug. 3–4, 1994 / Concord Jazz 4642*

8 *Calling All Cats / Dec. 13–15, 1995 / Concord Jazz 4717*
Randy Sandke has recorded in several different styles throughout his career, not including a classical-oriented album (*Awakening*) outside the boundaries of this book. *Stampede* and *Wild Cats* find Sandke reviving music from the 1920s in the classic style. *Stampede* utilizes a septet with Ken Peplowski, Dan Barrett, and Marty Grosz playing such

songs as "Copenhagen," "Irish Black Bottom," and Jelly Roll Morton's "Grandpa's Spells." *Wild Cats* uses a similar group (with Peplowski and Barrett), jamming on "Sobbin' Blues," "Shim-Me-Sha-Wabble," and "Runnin' Wild," among others. However, Sandke's work for Concord has often been more modern in general, paying tribute to his roots in Swing but occasionally reaching forward to later eras. *I Hear Music* is a fine collaboration with Ken Peplowski (who mostly sticks to tenor) on such numbers as "Thanks a Million," "With a Song in My Heart," "I Gotta Right to Sing the Blues," and six colorful Sandke originals. *Get Happy* is particularly eclectic, with songs by Harold Arlen, Thelonious Monk, Irving Berlin, Miles Davis, Duke Ellington, and Charles Mingus, plus "Me and My Shadow" and three Sandke originals. Once again Peplowski costars during a program that stretches the boundaries of Swing. *The Chase*

is out-and-out modern, with Sandke holding his own with his former classmates tenor saxophonist Michael Brecker and trombonist Ray Anderson plus altoist Chris Potter. But in the middle of a set that mostly goes from bebop to beyond, Sandke still includes the 1920s "Oh Miss Hannah." There are many surprises in the arrangements (the baroque beginning of "Jordu" is a good example) and the outing certainly crosses many stylistic boundary lines. *Calling All Cats* is just as eclectic, with four originals (including "In a Metatone," which finds Sandke playing some atonal piano), unusual rearrangements of older tunes, and some real obscurities, including Cootie Williams's "Blues a-Poppin'" and Buck Clayton's "What a Beautiful Yesteryear." Scott Robinson (on tenor, soprano and baritone), trombonist Joel Helleny, and Howard Alden are in the supporting cast for this stimulating set.

LOREN SCHOENBERG
b. July 23, 1958, Fairlawn, NJ

A talented tenor saxophonist whose sound is a little influenced by Lester Young and whose style fits securely into Swing, Loren Schoenberg is also a fine arranger-bandleader and an informative writer of liner notes. He took piano lessons when he was four and was always interested in jazz history, working at the New York Jazz Museum for many years. Schoenberg started playing tenor when he was 16 and within two years was working professionally. He formed a big band in 1980 that became the nucleus of Benny Goodman's last orchestra. Loren Schoenberg has recorded a series of excellent big band and combo dates since 1984 for Aviva, Music Masters, Jazz Heritage, and TCB, reviving older charts, featuring new arrangements of lesser-known tunes, and always swinging. He has also played with the Smithsonian Masterworks Orchestra and the Lincoln Center Orchestra, and worked as Bobby Short's musical director.

9   *Time Waits for No One / 1987 / Music Masters 5032*

8   *Solid Ground / Aug. 8–9, 1988 / Music Masters 60186*

7   *S'posin' / June 21–22, 1990 / Music Masters 5055*

8   *Manhattan Work Song / Apr. 21–22, 1992 / Jazz Heritage 5 13433*

9   *Out of This World / Dec. 15–23, 1997 / TCB 98902*
Time Waits for No One features Loren Schoenberg's underrated big band, an orchestra that was only part time in the 1980s but was able to acquire arrangements from quite a few sources. Included on this CD are one chart apiece from Benny Carter ("Symphony in Riffs"), Eddie Sauter, Duke Ellington ("Harmony in Harlem"), Buck Clayton, Gil Evans ("Buster's Last Stand" from Evans's days with Claude

Thornhill), Jimmy Mundy, Gary McFarland, Horace Henderson, Bob Brookmeyer, and Eddie Durham. The remaining two numbers feature Schoenberg's tenor with the rhythm section. Many of the sidemen have short solos along the way, including Dick Sudhalter, Ken Peplowski, and pianist Dick Katz. Another big band album from Loren Schoenberg's orchestra, *Solid Ground* features obscurities (including Billy Strayhorn's "After All," "The Maid with the Flaccid Air," and Benny Carter's "You Are") plus fresh versions of such songs as "Midriff," "Coquette," and "I Double Dare You"; Barbara Lea takes three fine vocals. *S'posin'* is a creative quartet outing by Schoenberg with pianist Kenny Werner, bassist John Goldsby and drummer Adam Nussbaum that displays the cool-toned tenor's swinging abilities in a more modern context than usual, playing three group originals, two versions of the title cut, John Coltrane's "26-2," and some Swing tunes given advanced arrangements.

Manhattan Work Song and *Out of This World* are additional big band albums. *Manhattan Work Song* has contributions from such writers as Schoenberg, Mark Lopeman, James Chirillo, John Carisi (his final arrangement, a reworking of "Springsville"), Bill Finegan, Nat Pierce, and Benny Carter. Schoenberg and Ken Peplowski are the key soloists, Barbara Lea is heard from again, and among the songs are "I Only Have Eyes for You," "More Than You Know," "My Melancholy Baby," and "A Walkin' Thing." *Out of This World* is even better, due to the diverse material and the tightness of the ensemble. Few Swing big bands have such colorful yet surprising arrangements as Schoenberg's and a repertoire that includes "Close As Pages in a Book," "The Fable of the Rose," Duke Ellington's "Moon over Cuba," "Sure Thing," and Benny Carter's "Shufflebug Shuffle." Definitely a big band well worth exploring by those who fear that Swing orchestras have become stale.

AL SEARS
b. Feb. 21, 1910, Macomb, IL, d. Mar. 23, 1990, New York, NY

Duke Ellington's tenor saxophone soloist for several years in the 1940s (between the Ben Webster and Paul Gonsalves eras) and an unlikely star of an R&B hit, Al Sears displayed talents that were always underrated. He originally played alto and baritone, working with the Tynesta Club Quartet in Buffalo, Cliff Barnett's Royal Club Serenaders, and Paul Craig. After moving to New York, Sears was with Chick Webb's orchestra in 1928, toured with the Keep Shufflin' revue, led his own group, and worked with Zack Whyte (with whom he made his recording debut in 1929), Bernie Young, and Elmer Snowden (1931–32). Sears spent most of the rest of the 1930s leading his own bands in Buffalo. He worked with Andy Kirk during 1941–42 and was with Lionel Hampton for a month in 1943. Sears made his biggest impact while with the Duke Ellington Orchestra (1944–49), where his booting and consistently exciting solos were well-featured on many records, including "I Ain't Got Nothing but the Blues" and an exciting remake version of "It Don't Mean a Thing." After leaving Duke, Sears freelanced and then became a member of Johnny Hodges's combo. The group's one hit, "Castle Rock," was a showcase for Sears's horn, although the tenorman never received credit, since Hodges (who is barely on the record) was listed as leader. After leaving the altoist in 1952, Al Sears worked primarily in the music publishing business, although he continued playing and recording on a part-time basis into the early 1960s, including two fine albums of his own for the Swingville label in 1960.

●

8 *Swing's the Thing / Nov. 29, 1960 / Original Jazz Classics 838*

Al Sears led his own record dates as early as 1945 and was featured on a variety of very scarce R&B-oriented singles in the 1950s. Of his two Swingville LPs (which are among his last sessions), only this one has thus far been reissued. Assisted by pianist Don Abney, guitarist Wally Richardson, bassist Wendell Marshall, and drummer Joe Marshall, Sears performs five blues and three standards (including "In a Mellow Tone") and swings a little more lightly and with more subtlety than he had in his earlier days. A thoughtful Mainstream set.

DOC SEVERINSEN
b. July 7, 1927, Arlington, OR

Famous as the trumpeter and sidekick on Johnny Carson's *Tonight Show*, Carl "Doc" Severinsen was as better known for his outlandish wardrobe as for his musicianship, but he was always highly rated by insiders as a technically skilled high-note trumpeter. Severinsen was with the big bands of Charlie Barnet (1947–49), Tommy Dorsey (1949–51), and occasionally Benny Goodman but spent the 1950s primarily as a studio musician, appearing in jazz settings now and then but usually heard just as part of the ensembles. In 1962 he joined the Tonight Show Orchestra, and in 1967 Doc succeeded Skitch Henderson as its leader, staying for 25 years until Johnny Carson retired in 1992. Severinsen recorded a few stereo demonstration records in the early 1960s for the Command label that allowed him to play Swing standards and show off his love for the style of Bunny Berigan. The Tonight Show Orchestra did not get to record until 1986, but Severinsen was able to get out three fine records by the band during the next five years for the Amherst label. Doc Severinsen also played fusion with his group Xebron, performed classical music with Pops orchestras, and has occasionally toured with the *Tonight Show* alumni. It is surprising that he has never felt motivated to lead a small-group Swing recording.

7   *The Tonight Show Band / Aug. 5–7, 1986 / Amherst 3311*

7   *The Tonight Show Band, Vol. 2 / Aug. 5–7, 1986 / Amherst 3312*

4   *Facets / 1988 / Amherst 3319*

9   *Once More, with Feeling! / 1991 / Amherst 94405*

The 1986 version of the Tonight Show Orchestra had an opportunity to record two albums' worth of material. The repertoire is far from imaginative, since most of the songs are Swing-era warhorses (including "Begin the Beguine," "One O'Clock Jump," "In the Mood," and "April in Paris"), but there are some good solos along the way from Doc, Conte Candoli, and Snooky Young on trumpets, Pete Christlieb and Ernie Watts on tenors, altoist Tommy Newsom, and pianist Ross Tompkins. *Facets* looks as if it has potential, since its eight songs include "Night Train," "Take the 'A' Train," and "Stompin' at the Savoy," but actually it's a funk/crossover date. Severinsen, Ernie Watts, and guitarist Lee Ritenour are the main soloists, with commercial and rather routine arrangements contributed by Jeff Tyzik and Al Vizzutti for a string orchestra that turn the songs into mundane dance music. Fortunately the Tonight Show Band's third and final recording is more exciting than their first two. The songs are better (including "Honeysuckle Rose," "Three Shades of Blue," and "Bugle Call Rag") and, while the main soloists are the same, the arrangements of Tommy Newsom and Bill Holman are major assets. Trumpeter Wynton Marsalis has a guest spot on "Avalon," and Tony Bennett drops by to sing "I Can't Get Started." Recommended.

JACK SHELDON

b. Nov. 30, 1931, Jacksonville, FL

Jack Sheldon is a triple threat as an excellent trumpeter (whose style falls between bop and Swing), an underrated vocalist, and a somewhat wicked wisecracker whose spontaneous comments and routines are hilariously tasteless (or tastelessly hilarious). Although Sheldon really belongs more in a bop book, during recent times he has been leading a fine modern Swing big band in the Los Angeles area.

Sheldon started playing trumpet when he was 12 and was gigging in public within a year. He moved to Los Angeles in 1947, went to Los Angeles City College, served in the Air Force (playing in military bands), and, starting in 1952, worked regularly in the L.A. area. Among his more important associations of the 1950s were clarinetist Jimmy Giuffre, tenor saxophonist Wardell Gray, trumpeter Chet Baker, altoist Art Pepper, the Dave Pell Octet, altoist Herb Geller, and bassist Curtis Counce's quintet. Sheldon was part of the Stan Kenton Orchestra in 1958 and played with Benny Goodman regularly the following year. He worked now and then as an actor, including starring in the 1964–65 television series *Run Buddy Run,* was a longtime member of the Merv Griffin Show's orchestra, played with the Bill Berry big band in 1976, had occasional reunions with Benny Goodman, and led his own combos, often teaming up with pianist Ross Tompkins. In the 1990s the Jack Sheldon Orchestra (which playing mostly Tom Kubis arrangements) gained a strong following, performing Swing standards that showcased its leader's exuberant vocals, trumpet solos, and crazy humor.

The Quartet & the Quintet is an excellent example of how Jack Sheldon sounded in the 1950s. The music is boppish but open to the feel of cool jazz and Swing, with such standards as "It's Only a Paper Moon," "What Is There to Say," and "I'm Getting Sentimental Over You" alternating with originals. Sheldon is joined on some numbers by altoist Joe Maini or tenor saxophonist Zoot Sims and Kenny Drew or Walter Norris on piano. During 1983–91 Jack Sheldon recorded three fine albums for the Concord label, two of which have thus far been reissued on CD. *Hollywood Heroes* is a joyous outing with guitarist Doug MacDonald, Ray Sherman, bassist Dave Stone, and drummer Gene Estes. Some of Sheldon's humor (which is not usually captured that well on disc) surfaces during "Rosetta." Other highlights include "The Joint Is Jumpin'," "Poor Butterfly," and "I Thought About You." *On My Own* is a set of duets with Sheldon's longtime friend pianist Ross Tompkins. All but one song is from the Swing era, including "Ac-Cent-Tchu-Ate the Positive," "How About You," "Opus One," and "Avalon." In addition to his trumpet playing, Sheldon shows how underrated a vocalist he is. Sheldon's voice is often in the forefront during his 1992 recording with his big band *Jack Sheldon Sings,* but he also has some fine trumpet solos; highlights include "Don't Worry 'Bout Me," "Mack the Knife," "That Old Black Magic," and "Just Friends." Unfortunately *Jack Is Back* is not on the same level due to some rather tired material (including "New York, New York," "Satin Doll," and "Here's That Rainy Day") and a dumb comedy number with Merv Griffin and Pat McCormick on "How About You." The Jack Sheldon Big Band has yet to be definitively recorded.

LPS TO SEARCH FOR

Stand By for the Jack Sheldon Quartet (Concord Jazz 229), from 1983, is an excellent outing for Sheldon, who is joined by Ross Tompkins, bassist Ray Brown, and drummer Jake Hanna on such songs as "I Love You," "Bye Bye Blackbird," "The Very Thought of You," and "The Shadow of Your Smile."

FILMS

Jack Sheldon's trumpet is well featured on Johnny Mandel's "The Shadow of Your Smile," the theme song throughout *The Sandpiper* (1965). In addition to *Run Buddy Run,* Sheldon was in the 1973–74 television comedy series *The Girl with Something Extra.* He has an acting role in *Freaky Friday* (1976) and is featured on the video *Jack Sheldon in New Orleans* (Leisure Video), a 1989 performance that includes Dave Frishberg.

DARYL SHERMAN
b. June 14, 1949, Woonsocket, RI

Daryl Sherman, a superior Swing singer who is also a good pianist, has been a fixture on the Mainstream Swing scene in New York since arriving in 1974. The daughter of trombonist Sammy Sherman, Daryl was familiar with vintage jazz recordings before she started singing. Her biggest influence is Mildred Bailey, but she has a style and sound of her own. She began playing piano when she was five and played some early gigs with her father's orchestra. Sherman sang with the Artie Shaw Orchestra in the early 1980s, and her recording debut as a leader was made in 1983 for the Tono label. She has since been on albums with Dick Sudhalter, the group Mr. Tram Associates, Dave Frishberg, Barbara Lea, Loren Schoenberg, and Dan Barrett. Daryl Sherman has made tribute recordings saluting composer Jimmy McHugh, Hoagy Carmichael, and Mildred Bailey and has recorded for Audiophile, Arbors, and After 9.

Daryl Sherman's debut album as a leader, *I'm a Dreamer, Aren't We All* (cut originally for Tono), finds her already sounding quite mature and expressive in a very intimate setting. Half of the songs have her as the only performer (accompanying herself on piano), while the other numbers have Mike Renzi or Dave McKenna on piano. "You're a Lucky Guy," "On a Slow Boat to China," and "When Day Is Done" are among the high points. In addition, the original 11 songs are joined by "It's Bad for Me" from the same 1983 dates plus three songs from 1981 (including a second version of "On a Slow Boat to China") that have Sherman in a quartet with Renzi and Dick Sudhalter. The singer would record one more album for Tono (not yet reissued on CD). Moving ahead to 1990, *I've Got My Fingers Crossed* has Sherman or McKenna on piano, bassist Jay Leonhart, and on some numbers Eddie Barefield's tenor, Ken Peplowski (on clarinet, tenor, and alto), and guitarist-singer John Pizzarelli. Sherman's swinging yet respectful treatments of 14 Jimmy McHugh songs (including "I Just Found Out About Love,"

"I'm in the Mood for Love," "I'm Livin' in a Great Big Way," and "Doin' the New Low Down") bring out the beauty and joy of the music.

Look What I Found is even better, due to the trombone and arrangements of Dan Barrett, which utilize Randy Sandke, altoist Jerry Dodgion, Ken Peplowski, altoist Chuck Wilson, and Scott Robinson (on baritone, soprano, and bass clarinet) in inventive ways. The instrumentation differs from song to song, and the disc has a version of "Any Old Time" on which Sherman is backed by Pizzarelli's guitar, a voice/piano-trombone duet on "Why Do I Love You," and inventive treatments of such songs as "There's a Lull in My Life" and "I Never Knew." In addition, the singer contributes a pair of excellent originals. *Celebrating Mildred Bailey and Red Norvo* has Sherman paying tribute to her idol while vibraphonist John Cocuzzi comes close to sounding like Norvo; other participants on the 16 Bailey-associated songs include Randy Sandke, clarinetist Bobby Gordon, and trombonist Randy Reinhart. *A Lady Must Live* puts the emphasis more on the lyrics than on the solos (although many fine players make guest appearances) and features Sherman interpreting such songs as "One Life to Live," "I Want to Be Bad," "Give Me the Simple Life," "When in Rome," and "Something to Live For" with swing and sensitivity.

LPS TO SEARCH FOR

She's a Great Great Girl (Tono 1001), from 1986, features Daryl Sherman with the Mike Renzi Trio and guests Dan Barrett and Dick Sudhalter, singing a variety of superior tunes including "Between the Devil and the Deep Blue Sea," "Moon Country," "The Naughty Lady of Shady Lane," and the hot title song.

RAY SHERMAN

b. Apr. 15, 1923, Chicago, IL

A brilliant Swing pianist who practically owns "Honky Tonk Train Blues," Ray Sherman adds excitement to every session that he appears on, inspiring other musicians to play at their best. The son of a pair of professional violinists and one whose father, Maurice Sherman, led a band in Chicago, Ray Sherman took lessons early on from an aunt who was a piano teacher. In 1938, when he was 15, he won the Tommy Dorsey Amateur Swing Contest on the radio. His family moved to California in 1939 and he picked up experience playing locally with the bands of Jimmy Walsh, Hal Grayson, and Paul Neighbors, contributing a few arrangements to the orchestras of Gus Arnheim and Jan Savitt. Sherman considers Teddy Wilson and Earl Hines to be his main influences. While serving in the military (1943–46), he played regularly with a band co-led by Gil Rodin and Ray Bauduc. After his discharge in 1946, Sherman worked with Jan Savitt and Ray Bauduc. He became a studio musician in 1948, appearing on countless sessions during the next 35 years. Sherman also played with Ben Pollack's Pick-a-Rib Boys, is on the soundtrack of the film *Pete Kelly's Blues,* worked on Bob Crosby's live television variety show, played with Benny Goodman on a few occasions in the 1960s, recorded the piano parts for an extensive series of Time-Life Swing re-creation recordings, was the regular pianist for a couple of seasons with Stan Kenton's Neophonic Orchestra (to whom he contributed a complex classical piece), and appeared on Bob Crosby's 50th anniversary video in 1985. Since de-emphasizing his studio work in the early 1980s, he has had a much more active jazz career, appearing at many classic jazz festivals and jazz parties, working with Jack Sheldon, Doc Cheatham, Bob Wilber, and clarinetist Pete Fountain and recording with Dan Barrett and Bobby Gordon, among many others. Ray Sherman has also recorded two enjoyable CDs for Arbors.

●

9 *At the Keyboard / 1994 / Arbors 19133*

9 *Piano Chicago Style / Nov. 25–26, 1996 / Arbors 19186*
Despite having appeared on many records through the years, Ray Sherman did not lead his first record date until 1994. *At the Keyboard* is a bit unusual, for, by using a MIDI, Sherman is heard not only on piano but closely emulating the sounds of vibes, guitar, tenor, flügelhorn, bass, rhythm guitar, drums, and a string section! The music is well ar-ranged yet sounds quite spontaneous and full of joy. Among the more spectacular numbers are "The Earl," "Little Rock Getaway," "Pick Yourself Up," "The World Is Waiting for the Sunrise," "Tea for Two," and "Honky Tonk Train Blues." *Piano Chicago Style* is a more conventional solo piano record but just as rewarding as Ray Sherman digs into (and swings) such songs as "You Turned the Tables on Me," "It All Depends on You," "Stealin' Apples," and "Henderson Stomp."

FRANK SINATRA

b. Dec. 12, 1915, Hoboken, NJ, d. May 14, 1998, Hollywood, CA

A major celebrity for over 55 years and one of the most influential singers of the 20th century, Frank Sinatra certainly needs no introduction at this point. Sinatra's relaxed and swinging phrasing permanently affected American popular music and has spawned countless imitators and would-be vocalists. Never really a jazz singer (since his improvising was quite basic), Sinatra nevertheless sang superior Swing songs throughout his career and often utilized top jazz musicians for his records and concerts, including Harry "Sweets" Edison's trumpet on many of his 1950s sessions.

Early on, Sinatra was most impressed by Bing Crosby and Billie Holiday, considering Lady Day his main influence; later on he was a big fan of Ella Fitzgerald's. He dropped out of school to try to make his living as a singer and was part of the Hoboken Four (a vocal group that won the Major Bowes' Amateur Radio Contest in 1935). After several years of freelancing and struggling, he joined Harry James's orchestra in 1939 in its early stage. The scrawny singer was used primarily for ballads, and this stint proved to be a good experience. However, when Tommy Dorsey needed a male vocalist to replace the departing Jack Leonard later in the year, he easily lured Sinatra away to the big time.

Sinatra learned a great deal about breath control from TD and, whether taking solos or singing as part of the Pied Pipers, the young singer developed quickly and started to become a popular attraction. In fact, by the time he left Dorsey in 1943, Sinatra was a sensation with bobby-soxers, a teenage heartthrob even though he was already 28. For a few years the acclaim lasted and Sinatra (who began appearing in movies) was a household name, helping lead popular music away from big bands toward solo singers. However, by the end of his Columbia period (1943–52), his career was becoming aimless and some thought that Sinatra was already a has-been. He seemed out of touch with popular music (his later novelty recordings for Columbia did not catch on), he was having a troubled marriage with Ava Gardner, and many observers felt that Sinatra had peaked.

They were wrong. His Academy-Award-winning performance in *From Here to Eternity* showed that he was a superior actor who was not going to fade away. And musically, Sinatra's decision to sign with the Capitol label was a turning point.

In the 1950s on his Capitol recordings, Frank Sinatra avoided dated novelties in favor of timeless Swing standards, which he made sound contemporary and brand-new.

Only the Lonely, Come Dance with Me, and *Come Swing with Me* as ranking with the best work of his career.

As a recording artist, actor, and performer (often performing in Las Vegas by the late 1950s with the so-called Rat Pack, which included pals Dean Martin and Sammy Davis, Jr.), Sinatra had one success after another. In 1961 he formed his own label, Reprise, and among his more rewarding recordings were collaborations with the Count Basie Orchestra, Duke Ellington, and Antonio Carlos Jobim. After a few years, some of Sinatra's Reprise albums were a bit erratic and by the end of the decade his voice was beginning to fade. Sinatra retired during 1971–73 but returned to the scene with *Ol' Blue Eyes Is Back.* In general his later recordings are not too significant and, after 1984's *L.A. Is My Lady,* he mostly stayed off records except for the best-selling but barely listenable *Duets* and *Duets II,* from 1993 and 1994. However, as a performer, the legendary Sinatra continued packing them in even though his voice was clearly declining by the mid-1980s. Frank Sinatra retired permanently in 1995, and, even after his death at age 82, he remains one of the most popular and famous singers in the world.

●

7 *V-Discs / 1943–1945 / Columbia/Legacy 66135*

* *The Columbia Years: The Complete Recordings / 1943–1952 / Columbia / 48673*

10 *Songs for Young Lovers/Swing Easy / Nov. 5, 1953–Apr. 19, 1954 / Capitol 48470*

10 *In the Wee Small Hours / Mar. 1, 1954–Mar. 4, 1955 / Capitol 96826*

9 *Songs for Swingin' Lovers / Oct. 17, 1955–Jan. 16, 1956 / Capitol 46570*

There is no shortage of Frank Sinatra CDs currently available. His recording career (not counting his period with Tommy Dorsey, which is fully covered in a box set under TD's name) can easily be divided into three periods, by record labels: Columbia, Capitol, and Reprise. A sensation at the beginning of the Columbia years, Sinatra hit his peak during 1945–47 and then gradually slid in popularity as Columbia's executives persuaded him to record all types of material, much of it unsuitable. The *V-Discs* two-CD set focuses mostly on sentimental ballads, while the 12-CD *Columbia Years* finds The Voice covering ballads, current

Rather than being subject to the whims of producer Mitch Miller, Sinatra now had the freedom to pick and choose his material and his arrangers, often opting for the very compatible Nelson Riddle or Billy May. His Capitol recordings were so popular that it could be said that Sinatra did not enter his prime until late in 1953, when he was nearly 38. Formerly typecast as a romantic ballad singer, Sinatra showed that he could swing hard, display guts in his interpretations, and range emotionally from aggressive to wistful. Most of his fans consider such records (many of which were concept albums) as *Songs for Young Lovers, Swing Easy, In the Wee Small Hours, Songs for Swingin' Lovers, Come Fly with Me,* pop hits, novelties, Swing, and even a touch of bop. Sinatra's recording career was saved when he signed with Capitol, because he was given freedom to record superior standards, many from the Swing era, and he was no longer typecast as strictly a ballad singer. *Songs for Young Lovers* was his first concept album and his first full collaboration with Nelson Riddle. While that set often focused on ballad (including "My Funny Valentine," "I Get a Kick Out of You," and "A Foggy Day"), *Swing Easy* has more uptempo material and Sinatra is equally effective on such songs as "Just One of Those Things" and "All of Me." Many of his fans consider *In the Wee Small Hours* (ballads with Nelson Riddle) to be Sinatra's main classic. The title track, "Ill Wind," "Glad to Be Unhappy," and "I'll Be Around" are a few of the high points on this haunting album. *Songs for Swingin' Lovers* returns to hotter material, including "You Make Me Feel So Young," "I've Got You Under My Skin," and "Pennies from Heaven."

7 *A Swingin' Affair / Apr. 9, 1956–Nov. 28, 1956 / Capitol 94518*

8 *Come Fly with Me / Oct. 1–8, 1957 / Capitol 48469*

9 *Only the Lonely / May 29, 1958–June 25, 1958 / Capitol 48471*

8 *Come Dance with Me / Dec. 9–23, 1958 / Capitol 48468*

8 *Live in Australia / Mar. 31, 1959–Apr. 1, 1959 / Blue Note 37513*

7 *Come Swing with Me / Mar. 20–22, 1961 / Capitol 94520*

Frank Sinatra continued his string of influential Capitol recordings with *A Swingin' Affair,* which has selections from a variety of dates with Nelson Riddle, including "The Lonesome Road," "If I Had You," and "From This Moment On." *Come Fly with Me,* a set of songs dealing, at least abstractly, with the subject of traveling (and arranged by Billy May), yielded a new standard in the title cut. *Only the Lonely,* which returns to ballads with Nelson Riddle, has Sinatra's definitive version of "One for My Baby" plus "Angel Eyes," "Guess I'll Hang My Tears Out to Dry," and "Willow Weep for Me." Back with Billy May, Sinatra sings many swinging numbers on *Come Dance with Me,* including most notably "Too Close for Comfort," "Day In, Day Out," "Saturday Night Is the Loneliest Night of the Week," and "Just in

Time." The *Live in Australia* set, released for the first time in 1997, is of strong interest from the jazz standpoint due to Sinatra's being joined by the Red Norvo Quintet plus his longtime pianist Bill Miller. The musicians take "Perdido" as an instrumental (although the listed "Between the Devil and the Deep Blue Sea" is absent) and then perform scaled-down arrangements behind Sinatra, who performs "I Get a Kick Out of You," "I've Got You Under My Skin," "Angel Eyes," "Come Fly with Me," and "One for My Baby," among others in this very different format. *Come Swing with Me* was Sinatra's next-to-last effort for Capitol (he was already recording for his own label, Reprise), but he sounds enthusiastic while joined by Billy May's orchestra; "Day by Day," "That Old Black Magic," and "Almost Like Being in Love" are highlights.

* *The Complete Reprise Studio Recordings / Dec. 19, 1960–Dec. 18, 1979 / Reprise 46013*

9 *Ring-a-Ding Ding! / Dec. 19–21, 1960 / Reprise 46933*

7 *I Remember Tommy / May 1–3, 1961 / Reprise 45267*

7 *Sinatra Swings / May 18–23, 1961 / Reprise 1002*

6 *September of My Years / Apr. 13, 1965–May 27, 1965 / Reprise 1014*

7 *Strangers in the Night / Apr. 11, 1966–May 16, 1966 / Reprise 1017*

8 *Francis Albert Sinatra and Antonio Carlos Jobim / Jan. 30, 1967–Feb. 1, 1967 / Reprise 1021*

7 *Trilogy / Sept. 17, 1979–Dec. 18, 1979 / Reprise 2300*
The 20-CD *Complete Reprise Studio Recordings* has both treasures and trash, with Sinatra holding on to his roots in Swing and big bands while doing his best to come to grips with the changing pop world. One can hear his voice gradually decline but, even in the later sessions, there are some memorable moments. Still, this won't be an inexpensive purchase! *Ring-a-Ding Ding!* was one of Sinatra's most confident records and finds his voice in peak form; "Let's Fall in Love," "A Fine Romance," and "The Coffee Song" are essential for Sinatra fans. *I Remember Tommy* remakes a variety of songs that Sinatra had sung with Tommy Dorsey 20 years earlier, including "I'll Be Seeing You," "Polka Dots and Moonbeams," and "East of the Sun"; the originals were better, but these versions are often intriguing. *Sinatra*

Swings is a continuation of the Sinatra/May partnership and very much like one of his Capitol records. "Have You Met Miss Jones," "It's a Wonderful World," and "Falling in Love with Love" are all greatly uplifted by the singer. *September of My Years,* recorded when Sinatra was nearing 50, is comprised mostly of melancholy ballads arranged by Gordon Jenkins, including "September Song," "Last Night When We Were Young," and "It Was a Very Good Year." *Strangers in the Night,* one of the later encounters with Nelson Riddle, has quite a bit of variety, including the hit title cut, "My Baby Just Cares for Me," "All or Nothing at All," and "Downtown." Sinatra's meeting with Antonio Carlos Jobim is considered one of his last great records. Jobim is heard on background vocals and guitar, Claus Ogerman arranged for the orchestra, and such tunes as "I Concentrate on You," "Quiet Nights," "Meditation," and "Once I Loved" are among the highlights. Moving ahead a dozen years, *Trilogy* is quite a mixed bag. "The Past" (with Billy May's arrangements) revives some older songs, including "The Song Is You," "Let's Face the Music and Dance," and "My Shining Hour." "The Present" (arranged by Don Costa) covers recent pop tunes, most notably the hit version of "New York, New York," while "The Future" (with Gordon Jenkins) is a weird, almost free-form project that, due to dumb lyrics, does not cut it. But at least Frank Sinatra, at age 64, gave it a good try.

HAL SINGER
b. Oct. 8, 1919, Tulsa, OK

In 1948, tenor-saxophonist Hal Singer was in the ironic position of achieving his lifelong goal (gaining a position with Duke Ellington's orchestra) and having to give it up due to a hit record. He started out on violin, switching to tenor while in high school. After earning an agriculture degree from Hampton Institute in 1937, Singer switched permanently to music. He was with Ernie Fields (1938), Lloyd Hunter's Serenaders, Nat Towles, Tommy Douglas, and Jay McShann (1941–42). Singer freelanced in New York and played with Hot Lips Page, McShann, Roy Eldridge's Big Band (1944), Earl Bostic, Don Byas, Henry "Red" Allen (1946), Sid Catlett, and Lucky Millinder. Ellington liked the tenor's sound and hired him in 1948. However, Singer had just recorded an R&B record, "Cornbread." It became such a hit that he had to leave Duke's band after six months because audiences were coming out specifically to see him and he was just one of Ellington's many soloists. Although Hal Singer never had another major best-seller ("Beef Stew" came close), he worked as a leader quite successfully for the next 20 years (other than a period when he was a member of the house band at the Metropole), including after he moved to Paris in 1965. But to his regret, Hal "Cornbread" Singer never did have an opportunity to rejoin Ellington.

9   *Rent Party / June 1948–May 3, 1956 / Savoy 0258*

8   *Blue Stompin' / Feb. 20, 1959 / Original Jazz Classics 834*

A strong sampling of Hal Singer's R&B recordings of 1948–56 are on *Rent Party.* The 16 selections are quite spirited and sometimes border on the riotous, putting the emphasis on Singer's repetitions and honks. "Cornbread" is here, as are "Neck Bones," "Hot Rod," and "Rock 'n' Roll," but surprisingly not here is "Beef Stew." Fairly simple but fun music. After 1956, Singer returned to jazz, still playing some exciting solos but generally performing more sophisticated and subtle material. The title cut of *Blue Stompin'* is full of energy and excitement, matching Singer with Charlie Shavers, pianist Ray Bryant, Wendell Marshall, and drummer Osie Johnson. The other songs (all group originals except "With a Song in My Heart") may not reach the same level, but the interplay between Singer and Shavers is still quite potent.

DEREK SMITH

b. Aug. 17, 1931, London, England

A fine Swing pianist who has appeared on many records, Derek Smith has long been in demand for Mainstream sessions both in England and the U.S. He became a professional pianist when he was 14 and played in his native country with Kenny Graham, Kenny Baker, Jimmy Skidmore, and the Johnny Dankworth Orchestra (1954–55) in addition to leading his own combos. Smith moved to the U.S. in 1957, worked in the studios, led trios, and gigged with Benny Goodman, an association that lasted off and on into the 1970s. Smith worked with Johnny Carson's Tonight Show Orchestra during 1967–74, recorded with Marlena Shaw, Bill Watrous, Buddy DeFranco, Sal Salvador, Arnett Cobb, Benny Carter, and Mel Torme (among others), and in 1977 started recording for the Progressive label as a leader. Derek Smith has remained quite busy in Mainstream settings up to the present time.

●

7 *Love for Sale / Oct. 11, 1977 / Progressive 7002*

9 *The Man I Love / May 1, 1978 / Progressive 7035*

8 *Plays Jerome Kern / Mar. 27, 1980 / Progressive 7055*
Derek Smith led his first record dates in London in 1954 and was on other sessions during the next three years, but his first full album did not take place until 1977. *Love for Sale* is a solid trio date with bassist George Duvivier and drummer Bobby Rosengarden that includes "Autumn Leaves," "Too Close for Comfort," and a pair of Smith originals (including "One to Warm Up On"). *The Man I Love* is particularly noteworthy because Smith's group (with bassist George Mraz and drummer Billy Hart) is joined by Scott Hamilton, whose tenor is very welcome in this setting. The seven standards include "Topsy," "There's a Small Hotel," and "Between the Devil and the Deep Blue Sea." The Jerome Kern tribute, by Smith with bassist Linc Milliman and drummer Ronnie Bedford, has ten familiar standards (such as "A Fine Romance," "I'm Old Fashioned," and "The Way You Look Tonight"), all swung happily by the trio. All of these three Derek Smith CDs (it is surprising that there are not many more) are easily recommended to fans of the Mainstream Swing piano.

HAL SMITH

b. July 30, 1953, Indianapolis, IN

One of the finest Swing drummers of the 1980s and '90s, Hal Smith plays in a style that recalls that of Gene Krupa (circa 1936), George Wetting, and Sid Catlett, an approach that was otherwise virtually extinct after 1960. Smith grew up in La Jolla, California, studied with several teachers (including Jake Hanna), and was always interested in playing Classic Jazz, from Dixieland and 1920s styles to Swing. He has worked with singer Banu Gibson, Butch Thompson, Chicago Rhythm, Terry Waldo's Gutbucket Syncopators, Jim Cullum, Jim Dapogny's Chicago Jazz Band, the Hall Brothers Band, Wholly Cats, the Golden Eagle Jazz Band, and Marty Grosz, among others, in addition to leading his own hot Swing groups. Hal Smith has spent time living in Louisiana, Los Angeles, near San Francisco, Portland, Cincinnati, San Antonio, St. Paul, New Orleans (1988–92), and most recently San Diego, appearing at many classic jazz festivals, where his timeless style of drumming definitely stands out.

●

8 *California, Here I Come / Nov. 28–29, 1988 / Jazzology 182*

9 *Swing, Brother, Swing / Jan. 9–10, 1995 / Jazzology 255*

7 *Bourbon Street Memories / Sept. 13, 1995 / GHB 350*

8 *Stealin' Apples / Nov. 4–5, 1996 / Jazzology 279*

10

Concentratin' on Fats / Nov. 30, 1998–Dec. 1, 1998 / Jazzology 299

California, Here I Come is hot 1920s/early '30s jazz performed by an impressive septet that includes cornetist Chris Tyle, clarinetist Bobby Gordon, and Frank Powers on tenor and clarinet. They romp through such numbers as "Strut, Miss Lizzie," "Mahogany Hall Stomp," "Hello, Lola," and "Dippermouth Blues." Smith's California Swing Cats on *Swing, Brother, Swing* consists of a more intimate and cooler quintet that has (with various personnel changes) performed on a part-time basis ever since. Smith is joined by clarinetist Tim Laughlin, pianist Chris Dawson, bassist Marty Eggers, and the great Rebecca Kilgore, who contributes rhythm guitar and takes heartwarming vocals on eight of the 15 numbers. Among the songs explored are "With Plenty of Money and You," "Three Little Words," "I Can't Believe That You're in Love with Me," and "If Dreams Come True." *Bourbon Street Memories,* by Hal Smith's Creole Sunshine Jazz Band, is more of a moldy New Orleans jazz project that looks toward the revival bands of the 1940s. Trumpeter Duke Heitger, trombonist Mike Owen, and clarinetist Orange Kellin form the ragged front line for such tunes as "Do What Ory Said," "Climax Rag," "Farewell to Storyville," and "Six Feet of Papa" (which has a vocal by Amy Sharpe). *Stealin' Apples* returns to the same lineup as heard on *Swing, Brother, Swing* except that Tom Roberts is on piano. The instrumentals include "Bugle Call Rag" and "St. Louis Blues," but Rebecca Kilgore's vocals (particularly on "When My Dreamboat Comes Home," "What a Little Moonlight Can Do," and "La Vie en Rose") steal the show. Best of all is *Concentratin' on Fats,* a very inspired project. Smith, Kilgore, trumpeter Marc Caparone, trombonist Alan Adams, Bobby Gordon, Frank Powers, Chris Dawson, and bassist Clint Baker perform 18 Fats Waller songs, most of which are very obscure and some of which had never been recorded before. Rather than "Honeysuckle Rose" and "Ain't Misbehavin'," Smith's Rhythmakers perform such unknown gems as "How Jazz Was Born," "When Gabriel Blows His Horn," and "Dixie Cinderella," plus the barely known songs "If It Ain't Love," "Old Yazoo," and "Honey Hush." A gem.

LPS TO SEARCH FOR

The drummer's albums from the 1980s include *Hal Smith's Rhythmakers* (Jazzology 136), which has a sextet with cornetist Chris Tyle, Richard Hadlock on reeds, and pianist Butch Thompson, *Do What Ory Said* (Stomp Off 1078), a Kid Ory tribute project featuring trombonist Roger Jamieson, and *The Hal Smith Trio* (Jazzology 156), which matches Smith with Bobby Gordon and pianist Ray Skjelbred for some heated Swing.

KEELY SMITH

b. Mar. 9, 1932, Norfolk, VA

Although their marriage lasted only nine years (1952–61), Keely Smith will always be closely identified with Louis Prima. Born Dorothy Smith, she sang locally in Norfolk and then joined Prima's band in 1948 when she was just 16. In addition to playing the "straight man" with Prima (never smiling, no matter how goofy the trumpeter acted), Keely Smith was always quite expressive on ballads. She remained with Louis Prima throughout the 1950s as the music changed from Swing and Italian novelties to the eclectic (and very potent) mix that developed when Sam Butera joined the group. The results were irresistible and Smith was a strong part of Prima's success.

Since her breakup with Prima in 1961, Smith has worked primarily as a single, emphasizing ballads and Swing standards. Although not recording that often (she did make a jazz-oriented album for Fantasy in 1985 called *I'm in Love Again*) or equaling her earlier successes with her former husband, Keely Smith is still fairly well known.

FILMS

Keely Smith co-stars with Louis Prima in *Hey Boy! Hey Girl!* (1959).

TAB SMITH

b. Jan. 11, 1909, Kingston, NC, d. Aug. 17, 1971, St. Louis, MO

One of the finest Swing altoists to emerge during the early 1940s, Talmadge "Tab" Smith tends to be overlooked, because he matured just when Swing went out of style. Smith played piano and C-melody sax before switching permanently to alto. He worked early on with the Carolina Stompers (which he led during 1927–29), Ike Dixon, Eddie Johnson's Crackerjacks (1931–33), and Fate Marable. The altoist first gained recognition for his work with the Mills Blue Rhythm Band (1936–38), with whom he recorded. Smith played with Frankie Newton (1938–39), the Teddy Wilson Big Band, and the Count Basie Orchestra (1940–42). He was virtually the only altoist to ever be regularly featured with Basie; in contrast Earle Warren and later on Marshall Royal rarely were given much solo space. To get an idea of Tab Smith's stature during this era, on a 1944 recording of "On the Sunny Side of the Street" with an all-star group that included Coleman Hawkins, Don Byas, and Harry Carney, he takes the honors with a dazzling cadenza.

Tab Smith was with Lucky Millinder's orchestra during 1942–44, led his own band for several years, and seemed to fade away during the bebop era. But in 1951 he began recording for the R&B label United and had a major hit in "Because of You." For the next few years he recorded steadily, alternating between swinging romps and melodic ballads and, although not an R&B player (Smith's sweet tone was never used for honking), he was able to work fairly often into the mid-1950s. Then Tab Smith faded away, living in St. Louis, teaching, selling real estate, and ending up playing organ at a steak house!

●

9   *Jump Time / Aug. 28, 1951–Feb. 26, 1952 / Delmark 447*

8   *Ace High / Feb. 26, 1952–Apr. 13, 1953 / Delmark 455*

8   *Top 'n' Bottom / Nov. 17, 1953–Aug. 26, 1954 / Delmark 499*

Nearly all of Tab Smith's recordings for the United label (including many previously unreleased performances) have been reissued on these three fine CDs; there is enough material left for Delmark to come out with a fourth (and possibly a fifth) disc eventually. The music alternates between swinging jump tunes, ballads, and blues, with some vocal novelties tossed in. Of Tab Smith's three CDs, *Jump Time* gets the edge, since it includes the hit "Because of You" and the concept was fresher in 1951 than in 1954, but fans of small-group Swing and early R&B will be interested in all of this likable music. Tab Smith's earlier recordings (1944–50), which are in a similar vein and were made for a variety of tiny labels, remain quite scarce.

SOFT WINDS

In 1946, three members of Jimmy Dorsey's rhythm section (guitarist Herb Ellis, pianist Lou Carter, and bassist Johnny Frigo) decided to form their own drumless trio, which they called the Soft Winds. A little reminiscent of the King Cole Trio, the Soft Winds were notable for jointly composing "Detour Ahead" (which Billie Holiday later recorded) and "I Told Ya I Love Ya, Now Get Out" (soon immortalized by Woody Herman). They recorded 16 titles for Majestic and Mercury in 1947 and 1949, but those Swing sides were never reissued and in 1950 the group broke up. Ellis a few years later joined the Oscar Peterson Trio, while Frigo played in the Chicago area and Carter became a studio musician. Forty-five years later in 1995, Carter had little trouble talking producer Hank O'Neil into releasing 13 formerly unknown acetate recordings of the band. The Soft Winds had a recorded reunion with Frigo (who by then was exclusively a violinist) and bassist Keter Betts, making the band a quartet. Everyone still sounded in prime form and the two-CD set of old and new material proved to be quite definitive.

●

10 *Then and Now / 1947–Nov. 9, 1995 / Chiaroscuro 342*
Since the Soft Winds's original studio recordings remain long out of print, this two-CD set has filled a major gap. The second disc has 13 radio transcriptions by the Soft Winds during 1947–48, resembling the Nat King Cole Trio a bit and jamming on such numbers as "Perdido," "Undecided," "All the Things You Are," and "The Way You Look Tonight." The first disc features the band (with violinist Frigo, pianist Carter, guitarist Ellis, and bassist Betts) live on the S/S *Nor-*way during the 1995 Floating Jazz Festival performing a variety of standards, including their two group originals, "Detour Ahead" and "I Told Ya, I Love Ya, Now Get Out." Lou Carter (who has been in obscurity for decades) is particularly impressive. The twofer is wrapped up by a delightful 16-minute "Jazzspeak" in which the three original Soft Winds talk colorfully and with humor about the group's history, about what each of the musicians has done since then, and about their joyful reunion.

SOPRANO SUMMIT

Soprano Summit, a combo co-led by Bob Wilber and Kenny Davern (both of whom doubled on clarinet and soprano sax), was one of the hottest straightahead Swing groups of the 1970s. The backgrounds of Wilber and Davern were both in trad jazz, with Wilber being a protégé of Sidney Bechet and Davern having worked with Jack Teagarden and various Dixielanders. However, both of the musicians (whose individual records will be covered in a different book in this series) had also played often in Swing settings. In 1972 they came together at Dick Gibson's annual Colorado Jazz Party, and they fit together so well that soon they formed Soprano Summit. Originally the group (which featured hot stomps and plenty of obscure Swing tunes) also included Dick Hyman, Bucky Pizzarelli, bassist George Duvivier, and drummer Bobby Rosengarden. By 1976, the quintet was pianoless, with Marty Grosz playing guitar and adding good-humored vocals. The interplay between Wilber and Davern during their exciting ensembles was consistently inspiring. Soprano Summit recorded for World Jazz, Chiaroscuro, Jazzology, Concord, and Fat Cat Jazz before breaking up in 1979. In 1986 Davern (who by then had given up the soprano and exclusively played clarinet) and Wilber got together again at a concert, and since then they have recorded on an occasional basis as Soprano Reunion, always recapturing the old magic.

●

10 *Soprano Summit / Feb. 29, 1976–Sept. 12, 1977 / Chiaroscuro 148*
Soprano Summit's first two recordings were for the now-defunct World Jazz label. Its two Chiaroscuro sets have been reissued in full on *Soprano Summit* and are augmented by five additional live selections plus a humorous 13-minute "Jazzspeak" in which Marty Grosz talks about the history of the band. Davern (on soprano, C-melody sax, and clarinet) and Wilber (soprano, alto, and clarinet) are heard inspiring each other with the assistance of guitarist Grosz, bassist George Duvivier, and either Fred Stoll or Bobby Rosengarden on drums. "Nagasaki," "Black and Tan Fantasy," "Everybody Loves My Baby," "Ole Miss," "Netcha's Dream," "When Day Is Done," "When My Dreamboat Comes Home," and "Crazy Rhythm" are only a few of the many exciting numbers heard on this definitive set.

8 *Soprano Summit / Nov. 7, 1976 / Storyville 8254*

8 *Live at Concord '77 / Aug. 5, 1977 / Concord Jazz 4052*
In Concert features Wilber, Davern, Grosz, bassist Ray Brown, and Jake Hanna jamming on such numbers as "Stompy Jones," "Doin' the New Low Down," and "Swing That Music." The Storyville set has bassist Eddie De Haas and drummer Bob Cousins in place of Brown and Hanna, and this 1976 recording was released for the first time in 1996. Most of the tunes were recorded elsewhere by Soprano Summit, but these versions of such songs as "Stompy Jones," "Egyptian Fantasy," "Grenadilla Stomp," and "Meet Me Tonight in Dreamland" also contain plenty of excitement. *Live at Concord '77*, with Grosz, Hanna, and bassist Monty Budwig, is highlighted by "Strike Up the Band," "Elsa's Dream," and "Panama"; Grosz sings "How Can You Face Me."

9 *In Concert / July 30, 1976 / Concord Jazz 4029*

7 *Summit Reunion / May 30–31, 1990 / Chiaroscuro 311*

8 *Summit Reunion 1992 / Oct. 27–28, 1992 / Chiaroscuro 324*

8 *Jazz Im Amerika Haus Volume 5 / Sept. 24, 1994 / Nagel-Heyer 015*

8 *Yellow Dog Blues / Mar. 14, 1995 / Chiaroscuro 339*

Years later Bob Wilber and Kenny Davern played together and the magic was rekindled. They decided to join forces now and then as Summit Reunion. The first two *Summit Reunion* discs bring back the original rhythm section of Dick Hyman, Bucky Pizzarelli, Milt Hinton (who was actually the band's second bassist, but George Duvivier had recently passed on), and drummer Bobby Rosengarden. The 1990 date (which includes a 12-minute "Jazzspeak" that has the co-leaders reminiscing) includes a lengthy "St. Louis Blues" and particularly fine versions of "As Long As I Live" and "Limehouse Blues." The 1992 disc includes generally hotter performances (including "Lady Be Good," "I'm Sorry Dear," and "Chinatown, My Chinatown"), plus three numbers in which Flip Phillips successfully sits in with the band. The Nagel-Heyer set has Wilber and Davern with a pianoless European rhythm section (guitarist Dave Cliff, bassist Dave Green, and drummer Bobby Worth), and the results are typically explosive, as one can hear on long versions of "Lady Be Good," "Comes Love," "Apex Blues," and "A Porter's Love Song to a Chambermaid." *Yellow Dog Blues* returns to the same lineup as on the other Chiaroscuro Soprano Reunion sets and, although each member of the rhythm section has spots to solo, Wilber and Davern easily take honors on "I'll See You in C-U-B-A," "Japanese Sandman," "Hindustan," and "Somebody Stole My Gal."

LPS TO SEARCH FOR

Soprano Summit (World Jazz 5) was the group's debut set (the three Sidney Bechet numbers are memorable), while *Soprano Summit II* (World Jazz 13) is much more ragtime-oriented than the band's other dates. *Live at the Big Horn Festival* (Jazzology 56), with Grosz, Hinton, and Stoll, has its heated moments, and completists will want to search for the worthwhile but very difficult-to-find *Song of Songs* (Fat Cat's Jazz 208) from 1977-78.

KAY STARR

b. July 21, 1922, Dougherty, OK

Kay Starr's string of pop hits in the 1950s has sometimes masked the fact that she has long been a superior Swing singer, one whose voice sometimes sounds eerily like Dinah Washington's. Born Kathryn Starks, she started singing professionally very early, performing regularly on the radio in Dallas when she was just nine. Her family moved to Memphis and Starr joined Joe Venuti's band in 1937 when she was 15. Other than for brief stints with Glenn Miller (with whom she recorded) and Bob Crosby in 1939, she was with Venuti until 1942. While the Venuti years were good training, Kay Starr gained much more recognition while with Charlie Barnet (1943–45), and she recorded "If I Could Be with You" with the Capitol Jazzmen in 1945. Soon Starr was signed to Capitol, working as a single, and her records were steady sellers. Among her major hits were "I'm the Lonesomest Gal in Town," "Angry," "Side by Side," "Bonaparte's Retreat," "Changing Partners," "Someday Sweetheart," "The Wheel of Fortune," and "The Rock 'n' Roll Waltz." Through the years she recorded pop, country, and rock and roll but always stayed a Swing singer at heart. In the 1980s Kay Starr performed older songs with 4 Girls 4 (a group that often included Helen O'Connell, Rosemary Clooney, and Margaret Whiting), and she was active now and then into the late 1990s. It is long overdue for Kay Starr to be rediscovered.

●

8 *The Complete Lamplighter Recordings 1945–1946 / June 27, 1939–Dec. 27, 1947 / Baldwin Street Music 305*

8 *The RCA Years / July 27, 1955–Feb. 8, 1958 / BMG 12172*

7 *Live at Freddy's 1986 / May 22–23, 1986 / Baldwin Street Music 202*

The Baldwin Street Music *Lamplighter* set has some of Kay Starr's earliest recordings after she went out on her own, a series of jazz-oriented dates from 1945–46 that usually have Barney Bigard, Vic Dickenson, and sometimes Willie Smith in the supporting cast. Starr's enthusiastic interpretations of the Swing standards make her sound much more mature than her years (23–24), and she swings up a storm. Also on this 28-selection CD is her broadcast appearance with Bob Crosby from 1939 ("Memphis Blues"), two numbers with Wingy Manone in 1944, three songs with Charlie Barnet's orchestra, and a couple of live 1947 appearances with guitarist Barney Kessel's group. The overall results are one of her strongest jazz packages. Kay Starr took time off from her work with Capitol to record several albums for RCA. *The RCA Years* is a sampler that draws its material from four records, and it is a pity that it is not more complete. The 20 selections all feature the singer backed by either the Harold Mooney Orchestra or one led by Pete King. The tunes, all around three minutes long, are primarily standards, and although Starr does not get to stretch out, she puts plenty of feeling into such songs as "Little White Lies," "Jump for Joy," "I Want a Little Boy," "I'll Never Say 'Never Again' Again," and "The Lonesome Road." Moving ahead 30 years, Kay Starr at 63 had a somewhat raspy voice, but she was certainly still quite listenable and had not forgotten how

to swing. On *Live at Freddy's,* her storytelling to the audience (often giving her fans the background behind her hits) is as interesting as her singing. Joined by pianist Frank Ortega, guitarist John Basile, bassist John Goldsby, and drummer Ron Zito, Kay Starr still sounded pretty good at this point. Pity that so few of her recordings between the two Baldwin Street CDs have been reissued yet.

LPS TO SEARCH FOR

1947 (Hindsight 214) and *1949* (Hindsight 229) are radio transcriptions that find Starr in her youthful prime. The 1949 date is particularly recommended due to some solos by Les Paul, Joe Venuti, and Billy Butterfield. The Capitol label has not yet gotten around to reissuing their valuable Kay Starr catalog, so one will have to search a bit to find the LP versions of *Movin'* (Capitol 1254), *Losers, Weepers* (Capitol 1303), *Jazz Singer* (last out as Pausa 9048), and *I Cry by Night* (Capitol 1681). All but the last record (which features Ben Webster and trumpeter Manny Klein with a combo) have Kay Starr backed by Van Alexander's studio orchestra, and each set emphasizes Swing era standards.

LOU STEIN
b. Apr. 22, 1922, Philadelphia, PA

Pianist Lou Stein has had a long career and stayed true to his roots in Swing music while being flexible enough to fit into Dixieland, bebop, and commercial music settings. He was with Ray McKinley's band in 1942 (after McKinley had split with Will Bradley), and while in the Army he played in the U.S. with Glenn Miller's Army Air Force Band (although he did not go overseas with the legendary orchestra). After his discharge, Stein was back with McKinley (1946–47), where he often played Eddie Sauter arrangements. In 1947 he joined Charlie Ventura's bop band and contributed his most famous composition, "East of Suez." Stein was a studio musician for many years but also worked and recorded with the Lawson-Haggart Band (1951–60), Billy Butterfield, Kai Winding, Benny Goodman, Sarah Vaughan, the Sauter-Finegan Orchestra (1952–53), Louie Bellson, Peanuts Hucko, Red Allen, and Lester Young (1958), among many other top Mainstream stars. The 1960s were spent playing mostly commercial music. Stein played with Joe Venuti off and on during 1969–72, recorded several dates as a leader during 1976–84 for Chiaroscuro (including a remarkable Art Tatum tribute), World Jazz, Dreamstreet, and Audiophile, and worked with Flip Phillips, Nick Fatool, and the later Lawson-Haggart Band. Lou Stein recorded an excellent album as a leader as late as 1994 (*Go Daddy*) and continued playing on an occasional basis into the late 1990s.

8 *Go Daddy! / 1994 / Pullen Music 2140*
This CD, made when Lou Stein was 72, about a decade after his last recording as a leader, acts as an excellent retrospective of his life. He performs ten standards and six originals, either solo or in trios (with bassists Jeff Fuller or Brian Torff

and drummer Joe Cocuzzo or Todd Strait); in addition, Lou's daughter, Elise Stein, sings on about a third of the selections. Highlights include "Lullaby of the Leaves," "East of Suez," " 'Deed I Do," and "A Little Snake Music."

Other than the Pullen release, Lou Stein CDs are virtually nonexistent. *Tribute to Tatum* (Chiaroscuro 149) is a remarkable project from 1976 in which Stein duplicates, note for note, a dozen Art Tatum solos; he worked on this music for several years before making the elusive but classic recording. *Lou Stein & Friends* (World Jazz 17) is a Swing date with Milt Hinton, drummer Connie Kay, and (on four songs apiece) Bucky Pizzarelli and Kenny Davern. *Temple of the Gods* (Chiaroscuro.2027), from 1980, is much more modern as Stein plays six originals (including "East of Suez") and doubles on electric piano; veteran Swing tenor Al Klink has a rare opportunity to stretch out. Also quite worthwhile is a trio set with Bob Haggart and Butch Miles, *Live at the Dome* (Dreamstreet 106), and the well-conceived 1984 date *Solo* (Audiophile 198).

SAM "THE MAN" TAYLOR
b. July 12, 1916, Lexington, TN

A valuable rhythm and blues tenor saxophonist in the 1950s, Sam "The Man" Taylor was on many pop and rock and roll hits as a sideman. Taylor worked with Scatman Crothers (1937–38) and the Sunset Royal Orchestra (1939–41), making a strong impression during his two stints with the Cootie Williams Orchestra (1941–43 and 1944–46), which sandwiched a short period with Lucky Millinder (1943–44). Taylor's warm tone and R&B-oriented solos could generate excitement, although he was not a honker on the extreme level of a Big Jay McNeely. After a long period with Cab Calloway (1946–52), Taylor was greatly in demand for record sessions. In addition to the many pop acts, Taylor appeared on records in the 1950s with Ella Fitzgerald, Ray Charles, Buddy Johnson, Louis Jordan, and Big Joe Turner. Taylor was active into the late 1960s. Although Sam "The Man" Taylor led quite a few albums for MGM during 1954–60, one album for Moodsville (1962) and three for Decca (1962–64), none have been reissued since their original release.

JOE TEMPERLEY
b. Sept. 20, 1929, Cowdenbeath, Scotland

Joe Temperley has a huge sound on baritone that allows him to be a fill-in for the late Harry Carney whenever big bands (such as the Lincoln Center Jazz Orchestra) want to emulate Duke Ellington's ensemble. However, he is also a well-rounded musician able to play more modern or in his own Swing style. Temperley started on alto, switched to tenor, and began doubling on baritone in the mid-1950s. He worked in England with Harry Parry (1949), Jack Parnell, Tony Crombie, Tommy Whittle (1955–56), and, most significantly, Humphrey Lyttelton's Mainstream group (1958–65). In 1965 Temperley moved to New York, where he toured with Woody Herman's orchestra (1966–67) and worked with Buddy Rich, Joe Henderson, Duke Pearson, the Thad Jones–Mel Lewis Orchestra, and Clark Terry, among others. When Harry Carney passed away in 1974, Temperley was his replacement with the remains of the Duke Ellington Orchestra (under the direction of Mercer Ellington). The valuable Joe Temperley also recorded with Jimmy Knepper, played with Charles Mingus, and has since freelanced in both the U.S. and England, recently recording a duet album (*Sunbeam and Thundercloud*) with Dave McKenna for Concord (which was released under the pianist's name). He is often heard with the Lincoln Center Jazz Orchestra.

Concerto for Joe is really two albums in one, both quite rewarding. Joe Temperley performs four Ellington tunes, two standards, and his "Blues for Nat" in a quartet with pianist Brian Lemon, bassist Dave Green, and drummer Martin Drew; what a huge tone! In addition, he takes the brief "Eriskay Love Lilt" unaccompanied and performs the late trumpeter Jimmy Deuchar's five-part "Concerto for Joe" with a ten-piece British group that includes altoist Peter King and trumpeter Gerard Presencer. All of the music is straight-ahead and finds Temperley in inspired form. *With Every Breath* has Temperley joined by bassist Dave Green, drummer Martin Drew, and guitarist Jim Mullen and/or pianist John Pearce. Temperley contributed "Riverside Drive," interprets a folk song and Gerry Mulligan's obscure "I Hear the Shadows Dancing," and otherwise plays veteran standards. In addition to his baritone, this set finds Temperley taking some solos on soprano sax and bass clarinet. On *Double Duke,* Temperley (on all three of his horns) teams up with alumni from Wynton Marsalis's group: trombonist Wycliff Gordon (whose wa-wa playing is always an asset), pianist Eric Reed, bassist Rodney Whitaker, and drummer Herlin Riley. Half of the songs (including Billy Strayhorn's "Rain Check," "Black and Tan Fantasy," and "Creole Love Call") are from the world of Duke Ellington, while the other tunes include Oscar Pettiford's "Tricotism," "Try a Little Tenderness," and "Danny Boy." Throughout, Joe Temperley displays his highly appealing tone and his fluent Swing style.

CLARK TERRY

b. Dec. 14, 1920, St. Louis, MO

Clark Terry, the master of the flugelhorn, has the happiest sound in jazz. His extroverted flights are always full of joy and instantly recognizable. Although he came up during the bebop era and is sophisticated enough to play as adventurously as Dizzy Gillespie, C.T.'s fat tone and melodic ideas are straight from Swing. Terry started out gaining experience playing trumpet in his native St. Louis in the early 1940s and was an early inspiration for Miles Davis. He played in a Navy band during World War II, fared well with Charlie Barnet (1947–48), and was with the Count Basie Orchestra (1948–49). When Basie was forced to break up his big band and cut back to a combo, Terry remained with him, but he departed before Count formed his second band. The reason the trumpeter left was that he was offered a job with Duke Ellington. He would be one of Duke's many stars during 1951–59, often being featured on "Perdido" and some of the hotter selections. During his period with Ellington, Terry led several record dates of his own, and he gradually switched over to the mellow flugelhorn, an instrument he has specialized on since the early 1960s. He went to Europe to play with the Quincy Jones Orchestra (1959–60) as part of Harold Arlen's show *The Free & Easy.* After that production flopped, Terry returned to the U.S. in 1960 and joined the staff of NBC. He would also be a member of the Tonight Show Orchestra for several years. Terry really came into his own as a soloist in the 1960s, leading a quintet with valve trombonist Bob Brookmeyer and recording fairly often, including a classic encounter with the Oscar Peterson Trio. It was on this last date that Terry sang a satirical "Mumbles" vocal that made fun of the less coherent blues singers. So popular was "Mumbles" that from then on Terry made humorous and rather nonsensical scat-singing a regular part of his show.

Clark Terry had a short-lived big band in the 1970s, appeared on many jam session records in the 1970s and '80s, and recorded prolifically into the mid-1990s, when he finally began to show his age a bit in his playing. Still, he has remained quite active and at near-prime form up to the present time, spreading his joyful message around the globe.

Clark Terry, who was one of Duke Ellington's stars of the 1950s, has long had one of the most joyful sounds in jazz.

8 *Duke with a Difference / July 29, 1957 + Sept. 6, 1957 / Original Jazz Classics 2219*

8 *In Orbit / May 1958 / Original Jazz Classics 302*

7 *Top and Bottom Brass / Feb. 24–26, 1959 / Original Jazz Classics 764*

6 *Mellow Moods / July 21, 1961–May 15, 1962 / Prestige 24136*

10 *Color Changes / Nov. 19, 1960 / Candid 79009*

9 *The Happy Horns of Clark Terry / Mar. 13, 1964 / GRP/Impulse 148*

8 *The Power of Positive Swinging / Mar. 1965 / Musical Heritage Society 513447*

Since 1955, Clark Terry has recorded many dates as a leader. A highly distinctive player, a very reliable musician, and one who never plays an uninspired note, C.T. has produced record dates that are all quite worthwhile and generally do not require lengthy analysis. *Serenade to a Bus Seat,* one of several Riverside sessions reissued in the OJC series, teams Terry with tenor saxophonist Johnny Griffin and the Wynton Kelly Trio. Terry wrote five of the eight songs, including the title cut, which pays tribute to his travels with Duke Ellington. *Daylight Express* combines all of the music from a pair of fine straightahead (but very obscure) sessions, one led by Terry and the other led by Paul Gonsalves (with Terry as a featured sideman). *Duke with a Difference* has Ellington-associated material arranged by C.T. and Mercer Ellington that clearly inspired the sidemen (which include Johnny Hodges, Paul Gonsalves, and Tyree Glenn on vibes). *In Orbit* is a bit unusual, for the quartet session is one of the few that pianist Thelonious Monk did as a sideman, and only one of the songs ("Let's Cool One") is a Monk tune; it is a great measure of the universal respect that Clark Terry has among his fellow musicians. *Top and Bottom Brass* gets its title because the quintet includes Don Butterfield's tuba in the front line, and he gets nearly as much solo space as Terry. Good music but not too essential. *Mellow Moods* has all of the music from a pair of Moodsville releases by Terry. Usually those programs are dominated by introspective ballads, but Terry has more variety in his opening program, while the second set, music from the play *All American,* benefits from Oliver Nelson's arrangements.

Color Changes, as was true of many releases from the short-lived Candid label, had more thought put into it than the usual session. With arrangements by Yusef Lateef, Budd Johnson, and Al Cohn, Terry's octet (with trombonist Jimmy Knepper, Julius Watkins on French horn, and Lateef on various reeds) interprets fresh originals that are full of both surprises and swing. Lots of magic also occurs on *The Happy Horns,* a sextet outing with Phil Woods on alto and clarinet, Ben Webster, pianist Roger Kellaway, bassist Milt Hinton, and drummer Walter Perkins. "Rockin' in Rhythm," Bix Beiderbecke's "In a Mist," the flugelhorn-drum duet "Return to Swahili," and a brief but effective Duke Ellington medley are among the more memorable performances. *The Power of Positive Swinging* has one of Terry's finest groups, a quintet co-led with valve trombonist Bob Brookmeyer and including Kellaway, bassist Bill Crow, and drummer Dave Bailey. The interplay between the witty and fluid horns on such songs as "The King," "Ode to a Flugelhorn," and "Just an Old Manuscript" is quite delightful.

8	*Big B-A-D Band Live!* / Apr. 21, 1974 / Vanguard 79355	
8	*Swiss Radio Days Jazz Series, Vol. 8* / Dec. 16, 1978 / TCB 02082	
7	*Memories of Duke* / Mar. 11, 1980 / Original Jazz Classics 604	
7	*Yes, the Blues* / Jan. 19, 1981 / Original Jazz Classics 856	
8	*Portraits* / Dec. 16, 1988 / Chesky 2	
9	*The Clark Terry Spacemen* / Feb. 13, 1989 / Chiaroscuro 309	

The Clark Terry big band, which existed on a part-time basis in the 1970s, swings its way through a 1974 appearance at the Wichita Jazz Festival. Altoist Phil Woods, Jimmy Heath on tenor, and pianist Duke Jordan are among the many soloists along with the leader on "Take the 'A' Train," "Randi,"

and "Cold Tater Stomp"; Terry also shows off his unique vocal approach on "Mumbles." The appearance on Swiss radio puts more of a focus on C.T.'s flugelhorn playing in a quintet with altoist Chris Woods and pianist Horace Parlan; "The Hymn," "The Silly Samba," "On the Trail," and "Over the Rainbow" are in the repertoire. Although Terry was very familiar with the Duke Ellington–associated songs heard on *Memories of Duke,* he still shows enthusiasm (in a quartet with pianist Jack Wilson) for such warhorses as "Things Ain't What They Used to Be," "Cottontail," and "Sophisticated Lady." Clark Terry and Eddie "Cleanhead" Vinson make for a perfectly compatible team on *Yes, the Blues,* a blues-oriented set that puts the emphasis on their instrumental (rather than vocal) skills. Terry pays tribute to a variety of different trumpeters on *Portrait,* an intimate but sometimes hard-swinging quartet date that includes "Pennies from Heaven," "Little Jazz," and "Jive at Five" among its songs. *The Clark Terry Spacemen* has the happy flugelhornist heading a tentet that includes a couple of rarely featured swing-era alumni (Britt Woodman and baritonist Haywood Henry) plus trumpeter Virgil Jones, Al Grey, Phil Woods, and Red Holloway on tenor. With that many horns, there is plenty of riffing behind soloists, and the results (which are topped off by a 19-minute Terry "Jazzspeak" in which he humorously tells his life story) are colorful and usually exciting.

8	*Having Fun* / Apr. 11–12, 1990 / Delos 4021	
7	*Live at the Village Gate* / Nov. 19–20, 1990 / Chesky 49	
7	*The Second Set* / Nov. 19–20, 1990 / Chesky 127	
9	*What a Wonderful World* / Feb. 1, 1993 / Red Baron 53750	
7	*The Good Things in Life* / Dec. 9, 1993 / Mons 874 437	
7	*Shades of Blues* / May 13, 1994 / Challenge 70007	
7	*Remember the Time* / Aug. 29-30, 1994 / Mons 874 762	
7	*Top and Bottom* / Oct. 30, 1995–Nov. 2, 1995 / Chiaroscuro 347	

Having Fun lives up to its name, which is not surprising considering that Clark Terry, Red Holloway, and bassist Major Holley are in the quintet/sextet; the good-humored songs include "Mumbles," "Meet the Flintstones," "The Snapper," "Mule's Soft Claw," and "Tee Pee Time." Terry was just a few weeks short of turning 70 at the time of *Live at the Village Gate* and *The Second Set,* but his flugelhorn playing was still at its peak, as he shows during the extended quintet date with Jimmy Heath and pianist Don Friedman. *What a Wonderful World,* a tribute to Louis Armstrong and Duke Ellington, has a remarkably hilarious ad-lib monologue on "Duke's Place" during which Terry talks about the virtues of the fictional establishment at great length, particularly its food and women. Otherwise, this is a very spirited set matching Terry with Al Grey and a solid rhythm section.

The Good Things in Life (a quintet set with altoist George Robert and pianist Dado Moroni), *Shades of Blues* (11 blues played by Terry and Al Grey in a drumless quartet), and *Remember the Time* (with Robert and trombonist Mark Nightingale) find Terry still sounding quite ageless and typically exuberant on standards and basic originals. It was about the time of *Top and Bottom* that Clark Terry began to decline just a little, although it really cannot be heard on this fine live set with Red Holloway, altoist David Glasser, and pianist Willie Pickens. Another typically fun straightahead outing from the legendary Swing master.

LPS TO SEARCH FOR

There are a couple of dozen superior Clark Terry CDs available but still several elusive LPs. *To Duke and Basie* (Enja 5011) is a set of flugelhorn-bass duets by Terry and Red Mitchell (who also plays a little piano) of tunes associated mostly with Ellington or Basie. The vocal duet "Hey Mr. Mumbles, What Did You Say?" is quite funny.

SIR CHARLES THOMPSON
b. Mar. 21, 1918, Springfield, OH

A talented Swing pianist whose chord voicings were always attractive, Sir Charles Thompson had a long career. Thompson started out on violin, switching to piano as a teenager. He began to work professionally when he was 17, and among his early associations were Lloyd Hunter's Serenaders (1937), Nat Towles, Floyd Ray, and Lionel Hampton (1940). After playing with George Clark in Buffalo, the Harlem Dictators, and the Lee and Lester Young band, Thompson freelanced on 52nd Street. In addition to his work with small combos, Thompson also wrote arrangements for the big bands of Count Basie, Lionel Hampton, Fletcher Henderson, and Jimmy Dorsey, among others, and composed "Robbins' Nest." He was part of the Coleman Hawkins Sextet (with trumpeter Howard McGhee) during 1944–45 and played with the bands of Lucky Millinder (1946), Illinois Jacquet (1947–48), and Jimmy Rushing (1950–52). Thompson, who could sound like Count Basie, was also flexible enough to use Charlie Parker on one of his recording dates. By 1952 he'd switched to organ, where he was less distinctive, but he was able to work steadily for decades into the 1980s. Sir Charles Thompson never gave up playing piano, though, and he recorded some fine solos on his own Vanguard dates (plus sessions led by Buck Clayton and Vic Dickenson) in the 1950s in a Basie vein and was part of Clayton's European tour in 1961.

●

9 *Takin' Off / Sept. 4, 1945–Dec. 29, 1947 / Delmark 450*
All of Sir Charles Thompson's sessions for the Apollo label are on this single CD, a dozen selections (two previously unissued) from three dates plus five alternate takes. Thompson (on piano) heads a septet that includes Buck Clayton, altoist Charlie Parker, and Dexter Gordon on tenor, fronts a Basie-oriented combo that features Joe Newman and baritonist Leo Parker, and leads a tentet that includes Joe Newman, Taft Jordan, and Pete Brown. The music ranges from early bebop and Swing to jump music, and overall these are the most significant dates that the pianist led in his career.

LPS TO SEARCH FOR

Portrait of a Piano (Sackville 3037), from 1984, was Sir Charles Thompson's first recording in years and might very well be his final record. It is an excellent solo session that serves to sum up his career, including such numbers as "Robbins' Nest," "Ain't Misbehavin'," "All the Things You Are," and "Happy Boogie."

FILMS

Sir Charles Thompson is seen with Coleman Hawkins's band on one number in *The Crimson Canary* (1945) and he is featured on *Buck Clayton and His All Stars* (Shanachie 6303) from 1961.

ROSS TOMPKINS

b. May 13, 1938, Detroit, MI

A reliable pianist whose playing falls between Swing and bop and who enjoys playing relaxed versions of standards, Ross Tompkins is both a fine soloist and a tasteful accompanist. He studied at the New England Conservatory. In New York in the 1960s Tompkins played with many jazz musicians, including Kai Winding, Wes Montgomery (1966), the Clark Terry–Bob Brookmeyer Quintet, Benny Goodman (1968), Bobby Hackett, and the Al Cohn–Zoot Sims Quintet. In 1971 Tompkins moved to Los Angeles, where he was a member of the Tonight Show Orchestra until Johnny Carson's retirement in 1992. In addition, Ross Tompkins has worked with Joe Venuti, Red Norvo, and the Louie Bellson big band, has long been a fixture in L.A.-area clubs, sometimes plays duets with Jack Sheldon, and has recorded as both a leader and a sideman, most notably for the Famous Door, Concord, and Progressive labels. ●

LPS TO SEARCH FOR

Ross Tompkins's valuable dates for Concord have yet to be reissued on CD. Those include the solo set *Scrimshaw* (Concord Jazz 28), *Lost in the Stars* (Concord Jazz 46), which has trio numbers from 1977, a quartet date with Al Cohn called *Ross Tompkins and Good Friends* (Concord Jazz 65), and an excellent Swing sextet outing with Snooky Young and Marshall Royal from 1980, *Festival Time* (Concord Jazz 117).

MEL TORME

b. Sept. 13, 1925, Chicago, IL, d. June 5, 1999, Los Angeles, CA

One of the all-time-great jazz singers, Mel Torme was virtually the only vocalist who actually improved as a singer (in tone, breath control, and creativity) while he was in his sixties! Torme was not only a major singer but a composer (best known for "The Christmas Song"), arranger, drummer, actor, and writer. In the last role, he penned a definitive biography of Buddy Rich (*Traps, the Drum Wonder*), an autobiography (*It Wasn't All Velvet*), a book about working on *The Judy Garland Show* (*The Other Side of the Rainbow*), and a tribute to some of his favorite vocalists (*My Singing Teachers*).

Mel Torme's career began remarkably early, singing a few songs on Monday nights with the Coon-Sanders Orchestra in 1929, when he was four! Torme became a child actor, published his first song at 15, and the following year was with the Chico Marx Band (under the direction of Ben Pollack) as a drummer, vocal arranger, and singer. "The Christmas Song" was written in 1944 when he was 19 (two years later Nat King Cole's recording made it famous), and his "Born to Be Blue" would also become a standard. At that time, Mel Torme and his vocal group, the Mel-Tones, recorded with Artie Shaw, including a hip version of "What Is This Thing Called Love." Torme soon began his solo career and, nicknamed "The Velvet Fog" (a title he disliked), he worked quite steadily during the second half of the 1940s and throughout the '50s. His acting career was largely wasted (mostly bit parts in forgettable movies), but Torme's string of recordings were generally very rewarding, particularly his collaborations with the Marty Paich Dek-tette. Although he could scat with the best and understood bebop, Mel Torme made no secret of the fact that he was a Swing singer and that his idol was Ella Fitzgerald.

Bad record contacts in the 1960s and much of the 1970s ended up with Torme's barely being on records at all during that era, and even then he was mostly being featured on remakes of pop hits, especially after his 1962 version of "Comin' Home Baby" caught on. But after he signed with the Concord label in 1983, Torme made an artistic comeback, recording some of the finest albums of his career. Teaming up with George Shearing (always a delightful pairing), big bands (including Rob McConnell's Boss Brass and a reunion of Paich's Dek-tette), or with just a trio, Mel Torme got stronger and stronger during this 13-year period. He ended up on top with 1996's *An Evening with Mel Torme,* which found him at the peak of his powers at age 70, just a few weeks before a major stroke permanently put him out of action. ●

* *The Mel Torme Collection* / 1944–Sept. 18, 1985 / Rhino 71589

4 *At the Movies* / 1943–1989 / Rhino 75481

7 *Spotlight on Great Gentlemen of Song* / Jan. 17, 1949– Oct. 4, 1951 / Capitol 89941

5 *Easy to Remember* / 1953 + 1963 / Hindsight 253

7 *Mel Torme in Hollywood* / Dec. 15, 1954 / GRP/Decca 617

The four-CD Rhino box set does an excellent job of summing up Mel Torme's career prior to his signing with the Concord label. Starting with some of his earliest recordings, one hears Torme with the Mel-Tones, doing his best to overcome middle-of-the-road pop string orchestras, jamming on small-group dates, meeting up with Marty Paich's Dek-tette, struggling through the 1960s, and then emerging in the mid-1980s still in peak form. In general most of the high points of this 40-year period are here, and this set serves as a perfect introduction to Mel Torme's talents, as long as one keeps in mind that it does not cover his final glorious decade. Torme's movie career was rather weak, and the Rhino single-disc *At the Movies* set cheats a bit by including not only his songs in movies (most notably 1947's *Good News*) but occasions where he just sang the title theme for the film. There are even a few cases where he sang a song from a film but his version had nothing to do with the movie! Although this padding uplifts the quality, it makes the release quite pointless. The Capitol *Spotlight* CD has a cross section of Torme's Capitol recordings of 1949–51, usually with an orchestra, although there are three songs in which Torme plays piano with a combo and one number ("I've Got a Feeling I'm Falling") with the Red Norvo Trio. Some of the tunes are surprisingly boppish, and the selections include a crazy version of "Oh, You Beautiful Doll," "Stompin' at the Savoy," "Sonny Boy," and "Blue Moon." *Easy to Remember* is strictly for completists. Torme is heard in 1953 with a combo and in 1963 with the Donn Trenner Octet, but none of the songs from this previously unreleased material is over three minutes (some are much briefer) and Torme never gets beyond the melody statements. Pleasing but forgettable. *Mel Torme in Hollywood* is an interesting live performance by Torme, playing piano with a quartet that includes clarinetist-pianist Al Pellegrini and singing his way through a variety of standards, including "From This Moment On,"

"Get Out of Town," "My Shining Hour," and "Jeepers Creepers."

7 *It's a Blue World* / Aug. 28–30, 1955 / Bethlehem 20-30152

10 *Lulu's Back in Town* / Jan. 1956 / Avenue Jazz/ Bethlehem 75732

9 *Sings Fred Astaire* / Nov. 1956 / Bethlehem 20-30082

6 *Prelude to a Kiss* / Nov. 1957 / Simitar 55002

7 *Back in Town* / Apr. 23, 1959–Aug. 10, 1959 / Verve 314 511 522

9 *Swings Schubert Alley* / Jan. 1960–Feb. 1960 / Verve 821 581

7 *Swingin' on the Moon* / Aug. 3–5, 1960 / Verve 314 511 385

Mel Torme entered his musical prime in the mid-1950s. *It's a Blue World* is a relatively little-known ballad date in which Torme is backed by five strings, two flutes, bass clarinet, trumpet, French horn, harp, and a rhythm section. His voice sounds beautiful on "I've Got It Bad," "Isn't It Romantic," "Polka Dots and Moonbeams," and "Million Dollar Baby." *Lulu's Back in Town,* a meeting with arranger Marty Paich's Dek-tette, is an alltime classic. Paich's charts and the cool tones of the soloists (which include trumpeter Don Fagerquist, valve trombonist Bob Enevoldsen, altoist Bud Shank, and Bob Cooper on tenor) perfectly fit Torme's voice. These renditions of "Lulu's Back in Town," "When the Sun Comes Out," "Fascinating Rhythm," "The Lady Is a Tramp," and "Lullaby of Birdland" are rightfully famous. The Torme/Paich combination also works very well on the Fred Astaire tribute, which finds Torme swinging on standards by Gershwin, Jerome Kern, Irving Berlin, and Johnny Mercer; "Something's Gotta Give," "A Fine Romance," "The Way You Look Tonight," and "They All Laughed" are standouts. *Prelude to a Kiss* is an odd concept album that has Torme and an unidentified female indulging in some dialogue before each song that sets that stage for the lyrics, telling the story of their affair. The talking does not really need to be heard a second time and fortunately one can edit it out on the CD. Torme sings a dozen top-notch veteran standards with backing by Paich's orchestra. *Back in Town* was a reunion album that Torme had with his Mel-Tones. The four voices sound fine (although they do not improvise),

Marty Paich's charts and the solos of altoist Art Pepper and Jack Sheldon work well, and anything that Torme recorded during this era is well worth hearing. Along with other standards, the Mel-Tones sing sparkling remakes of "What Is This Thing Called Love" and "It Happened in Monterey." The Torme/Paich magic works one more time on *Swings Schubert Alley*. The singer interprets a dozen songs from Broadway shows, including "Too Close for Comfort," "On the Street Where You Live," "Old Devil Moon," and "Too Darn Hot." *Swingin' on the Moon* has Torme (backed by Russ Garcia's orchestra) doing his best with 12 songs that have "Moon" in their title, including "I Wished on the Moon," "How High the Moon," "Moonlight in Vermont," and his own "Swingin' on the Moon." The swinging results are out of this world!

6 *Two Classic Albums from Mel Torme / Mar. 25, 1962– Sept. 1974 / Rhino 0074*

4 *That's All / Mar. 10, 1964–Oct. 1, 1966 / Columbia/ Legacy 65165*

1 *Right Now / Jan. 28, 1966–Nov. 17, 1967 / Columbia/ Legacy*

5 *The London Sessions / 1977 / DCC Jazz 608*

7 *Encore at Marty's, New York / Mar. 27, 1982 / DCC Jazz 621*

Mel Torme had a rough time on records during the 1960s and '70s. Although there was nothing wrong with his singing or his voice, there was something wrong with the record company executives, who wanted him to mostly remake current pop tunes or sing juvenile novelties; they almost ruined his career. *Two Classic Albums* (a single CD) reissues 1962's *At the Red Hill* (a trio date in which Torme sits in on piano for a few numbers) and 1974's *Live at the Maisonette* with Al Porcino's orchestra that is most notable for an endless Gershwin medley. Neither album is classic, but both find Torme sounding fine, swinging on some of his favorite Swing tunes, including "Mountain Greenery" (which is heard twice), "Anything Goes," "Love Is Just Around the Corner," and "The Party's Over." Torme's association with Columbia should have been memorable, but instead it was a major disappointment, for the label had no idea what to do with him. *That's All*, which augments the original album with ten numbers originally put out as singles and a couple of previously unreleased tracks, finds Torme singing beauti-

fully but hampered by dull arrangements for an orchestra with occasional strings and background singers. All of the songs clock in at around three minutes, Torme rarely gets away from the melody, and nearly every tune is a dull ballad. *Right Now* was worse, much worse. Torme (who was past 40) was cast in the role of singing bad teenager songs, and his renditions of "Walk on By," "If I Had a Hammer," "Secret Agent Man," and "Molly Marlene" are embarrassingly bad, with pop rhythms and cornball arrangements. Torme's bad luck with record labels lasted throughout the 1970s. *The London Sessions* (which was originally put out by Gryphon) finds him entering his musical prime, but it falls short of being memorable. The singer is joined by the Chris Gunning Orchestra, with guest altoist Phil Woods, but the material is dominated by current pop songs, including "All in Love Is Fair," "New York State of Mind," and "Send in the Clowns"; Torme does his best. *Encore at Marty's* reissues a complete live set by Torme with his 1982 trio (pianist Mike Renzi, bassist Jay Leonhart, and drummer Donny Osborne), and it finally allows the "real" Mel Torme to emerge. His versions of "Lulu's Back in Town," a Fred Astaire medley, "When the Sun Comes Out," and "Autumn Leaves" are excellent, Torme scats up a storm on "Day In, Day Out," and this version of "I Like to Recognize the Tune" is humorous.

9 *An Evening at Charlie's / Oct. 1983 / Concord Jazz 4248*

10 *Mel Torme/Rob McConnell and the Boss Brass / May 1986 / Concord Jazz 4306*

9 *A Vintage Year / Aug. 1987 / Concord Jazz 4341*

8 *Reunion / Aug. 1988 / Concord Jazz 4360*

10 *In Concert Tokyo / Dec. 11, 1988 / Concord Jazz 4382*

Mel Torme's Concord years were glorious, finding him singing at the peak of his powers and feeling free to perform the music that he loved most. Torme recorded several albums with George Shearing, some of which were issued under the pianist's name. *An Evening at Charlie's* is a gem, with Torme and Shearing (assisted by bassist Don Thompson and drummer Donny Osborne) performing a couple of well-conceived medleys, "Nica's Dream," and "Love Is Just Around the Corner," among others. Torme's meeting with Rob McConnell's Boss Brass recalls his earlier collaborations with Marty Paich. McConnell's charts perfectly fit Torme's voice, and the highlights include "Just Friends,"

"Don'cha Go Way Mad," "A House Is Not a Home," "The Song Is You," and a six-song Duke Ellington medley. *A Vintage Year,* by Torme and Shearing (with bassist John Leitham and Donny Osborne), has many great moments, including "Someday I'll Find You," "The Way You Look Tonight," "When Sunny Gets Blue," and a funny "New York, New York Medley." *Reunion* matches Torme with Marty Paich's Dek-tette (expanded to an 11-piece group) and the old magic is rekindled. A couple of Steely Dan tunes are weak but are easily compensated for by "Sweet Georgia Brown," "The Blues," "More Than You Know," and a bossa nova medley. *In Concert Tokyo,* which features Torme and Paich from five months later, is a classic. Torme plays drums on "Cotton Tail," and he is in prime voice on such songs as "When the Sun Comes Out," "More Than You Know," "The Carioca," and "The Christmas Song."

9 *Nights at the Concord Pavilion / Aug. 1990 / Concord Jazz 4433*

8 *Mel Torme/George Shearing "Do" World War II / Sept. 2–3, 1990 / Concord Jazz 4471*

10 *Fujitsu-Concord Jazz Festival in Japan '90 / Nov. 11, 1990 / Concord Jazz 4481*

Mel Torme may have been nearly 65 at the time that he recorded *Nights at the Concord Pavilion,* but his voice was still improving! On *Nights at the Concord Pavilion,* Torme is backed by his trio (pianist John Campbell, bassist Bob Maize, and Donny Osborne) for four songs (including "Early Autumn" and "Day In, Day Out") plus three medleys, including three songs with "Sing" in their title and a spectacular "Guys and Dolls Medley." In addition, a big band co-led by Frank Wess and Harry "Sweets" Edison joins Torme for the final three numbers, which include spirited versions of "You're Driving Me Crazy" and "Sent for You Yesterday." Torme and Shearing reunited in 1990 to perform songs made popular during World War II. Shearing has three instrumental features (including a solo "I Know Why"), and then the trio (with bassist Neil Swainson and Donny Osborne) joins Torme for a variety of nostalgic but swinging songs, including an Ellington medley, "Aren't You Glad You're You," and a touching "We Mustn't Say Goodbye." Also from 1990, Torme is heard at that year's Fujitsu-Concord Jazz Festival with his trio (Campbell, Maize, and Osborne) and, on four numbers, the Frank Wess Orchestra; Torme plays drums on "Swingin' the Blues." The singer

swings hard on a variety of tunes (including "Shine on Your Shoes"), but it is on the ballads (particularly "A Nightingale Sang in Berkeley Square" and "Stardust") that he really shows how beautiful his voice could sound, holding some notes endlessly.

3 *Nothing Without You / Mar. 12–13, 1991 / Concord Jazz 4515*

8 *The Great American Songbook / Oct. 7–8, 1992 / Telarc 83328*

8 *Sing, Sing, Sing / Nov. 1992 / Concord Jazz 4542*

5 *A Tribute to Bing Crosby / Mar. 12–17, 1994 / Concord Jazz 4614*

7 *Velvet & Brass / July 5–6, 1995 / Concord Jazz 4667*

8 *An Evening with Mel Torme / July 23, 1996 / Concord Jazz 4736*

Nothing Without You, a collaboration with singer Cleo Laine, is a rare misfire for Torme. Laine, who has a very impressive range, never could improvise and she constantly gets in the way; nothing much works on this project despite Torme's best efforts. Much better is *The Great American Songbook,* which finds Torme and his trio (pianist John Colianni, bassist John Leitham, and Donny Osborne) joined by a dozen horns. Mel happily plays drums on "Rockin' in Rhythm," he wrote ten of the 15 arrangements, and a seven-song Duke Ellington mini-set is a high point along with another classic version of "Stardust." *Sing, Sing, Sing,* recorded at the 1992 Fujitsu-Concord Festival, is a tribute to Benny Goodman in which Torme's group is augmented by clarinetist Ken Peplowski and vibraphonist Peter Appleyard for a variety of Swing-era standards, including a 14-minute BG Medley, a remake of "Lulu's Back in Town," "Three Little Words," and a beautiful "Ev'ry Time We Say Goodbye." Torme has fun playing drums on "Sing, Sing, Sing." Unfortunately, Torme's tribute to Bing Crosby sticks mostly to very straight renditions of ballads, the arrangements for a 20-piece string orchestra are mostly quite boring, and the lack of mood variation makes this set forgettable despite some good moments. *Velvet & Brass* does not quite reach the heights of Mel Torme's prior collaboration with Rob McConnell's Boss Brass, but his voice does sound beautiful on such numbers as "If You Could See Me Now," "Autumn Serenade," "My Sweetie Went Away," and "I'm Glad There Is You." Torme's final recording, *An Evening With Mel*

Torme is actually taken from a television special that was made just a month before his stroke. At 70 Torme (joined by pianist Mike Renzi, Leitham, and Osborne) sounds quite ageless as he interprets many of his favorite songs (most of which he had already recorded in recent years), including "Pick Yourself Up," "Stardust," "Stairway to the Stars," and "Oh Lady Be Good." Ironically the last song that he ever recorded was "Ev'ry Time We Say Goodbye." Mel Torme never did decline.

LPS TO SEARCH FOR

'Round Midnight (Stash 252) has radio transcriptions with the Marty Paich Dek-tette (1955–56) and Shorty Rogers's Giants (1962) that hold their own with Torme's studio recordings of the era. *Together Again—For the First Time* (Gryphon 1100), from 1978, matches Torme with the Buddy Rich big band, highlighted by a remarkable version of "Blues in the Night."

BOBBY TROUP

b. Oct. 18, 1918, Harrisburg, PA, d. Feb. 7, 1999, Sherman Oaks, CA

Bobby Troup was a fine pianist and a personable (if sometimes overly mannered) singer, but it is for his composing that he will be best remembered. Among Troup's songs were "Route 66," "Daddy," "Snooty Little Cutie," and "Baby, Baby All the Time." Troup, the husband of singer-actress Julie London, had a jazz trio in the 1950s, was the host of the legendary television series *Stars of Jazz* (1956–58), and worked as an actor on television (including the 1960–61 series *Acapulco* and *Emergency* in 1972). Not a night goes by that "Route 66" is not performed in at least several places in the world.

●

7 *The Feeling of Jazz / Sept. 17, 1955–June 23, 1967 / Starline 9009*

This 1994 CD features previously unreleased performances by Bobby Troup with four different rhythm sections. Although he plays piano on most of the selections, the emphasis is on his singing and particularly his lyrics. Included are "Daddy," "The Three Bears," "Girl Talk," "Route 66," "Lemon Twist," and a variety of standards and novelties. One of the very few Bobby Troup CDs currently available.

LPS TO SEARCH FOR

From 1957, *Bobby Swings Tenderly* (V.S.O.P. 75) is one of Troup's rare instrumental sets, a West Coast-style septet outing with trumpeter Stu Williamson, valve trombonist Bob Enevoldsen, Ted Nash on tenor, and baritonist Ronnie Lang. Troup shows throughout the eight standards (plus his own "I See Your Bass Before Me") that he was a pretty fair pianist.

NORRIS TURNEY

b. Sept. 8, 1921, Wilmington, OH

One of the most valuable additions to Duke Ellington's orchestra during its final years, Norris Turney not only played alto (eventually in Johnny Hodges's place) but was Ellington's first flute soloist. Early on, Turney worked in Ohio with A. B. Townsend and played with the Jeter-Pillars Orchestra, Tiny Bradshaw (1945), and the Billy Eckstine big band (1945–46). After that promising beginning, he worked primarily in obscurity in Ohio for the next 20 years, not having any other big-name jobs until he went on an Australian tour in 1967 with Ray Charles. Turney joined Duke Ellington in 1969, when Hodges was still in the band, and stayed until 1973, taking occasional solos and giving the saxophone section some new blood. After leaving Duke, Turney worked in pit orchestras in New York and played and recorded with Panama Francis's Savoy Sultans and the Newport All-Stars plus recorded a few dates of his own for Master Jazz, Harlem, Black & Blue, and Mapleshade. As of 2000, Norris Turney was one of the few significant Ellington alumni still active.

●

8   *Big, Sweet 'n Blue / Apr. 5–6, 1993 / Mapleshade 2632*
Although Norris Turney had led a few prior sessions, none have been made available on CD yet and this was the first one in which he headed a quartet. Although Turney had never worked with these musicians (pianist Larry Willis, bassist Walter Booker, and drummer Jimmy Cobb) before, the play-ers sound quite comfortable with each other and this is one of Turney's best showcases. His brand of melodic Swing works well on various blues (including the lengthy "Blues for Edward"), ballads, his own "Checkered Hat," and three Ellington-associated songs.

WARREN VACHE
b. Feb. 21, 1951, Rahway, NJ

One of the leaders of the Swing Revival of the 1970s (along with Scott Hamilton), cornetist Warren Vache is a superior Swing stylist who can also play Dixieland and bop. His father Warren Vache Sr. is a fine bassist, and his brother, Allan Vache, plays clarinet, usually in trad settings. Warren Vache Jr. studied trumpet with Pee Wee Erwin, played with his father's band, worked with Benny Goodman (starting in 1975 and including the 40th anniversary celebration of BG's Carnegie Hall concert), and often gigged at Eddie Condon's club. Vache teamed up fairly regularly with Scott Hamilton during 1976–85, and they often appeared on each other's records, on those of Rosemary Clooney, and with various all-star groups for the Concord label. Warren Vache, who always had a beautiful tone, switched to the Muse label in the early 1990s and has freelanced through the years, usually leading his own combos. He has remained quite busy, playing at clubs, classic jazz festivals, and jazz parties as one of today's top Swing cornetists.

●

7   *Midtown Jazz / Feb. 1982 / Concord Jazz 4203*

8   *Easy Going / Dec. 1986 / Concord Jazz 4323*

7   *Warm Evenings / June 1989 / Concord Jazz 4392*

9   *Horn of Plenty / Sept. 8, 1993 + Oct. 5, 1993 / Muse 5524*

7   *Jazz Im Amerika Haus Volume 2 / June 25, 1994 / Nagel-Heyer 012*

8   *Talk to Me Baby / June 6, 1995 / Muse 5547*

7   *Warren Plays Warren / May 13–14, 1996 / Nagel-Heyer 033*

Warren Vache is heard in an intimate trio on *Midtown Jazz* along with John Bunch and bassist Phil Flanigan. Although his style is essentially Mainstream Swing, he does include a few more modern pieces on this date (most notably Theloni-ous Monk's "Rhythm-a-ning" and Bud Powell's "Tempus Fugit") for the fun of it, along with "I'm Old Fashioned," "I Let a Song Go Out of My Heart," and "I'll Remember April." As usual, his tone sounds quite beautiful. *Easy Go-ing* is uplifted by some creative arrangements and the blend between Vache, Dan Barrett, and Howard Alden in the sex-tet. The ten selections are also consistently superior, in-cluding "Little Girl," "You'd Be So Nice to Come Home To," "It's Been So Long," and "Mandy, Make Up My Mind." *Warm Evenings* has Vache's cornet joined by the Beaux-Arts String Quartet (with fine arrangements by Jack Gale) and a rhythm section that includes pianist Ben Aronov. The em-phasis is on slower tempos and pretty melodies, with such songs as "You Go to My Head," "That Old Feeling," "He Loves and She Loves," "A Flower Is a Lovesome Thing," and "A Beautiful Friendship" providing perfect vehicles for Vache's lyrical playing.

Horn of Plenty is often quite exciting. Vache duets with guitarist Joe Puma on "Bix Fix" and with bassist Michael Moore on "Buddy Bolden's Blues." In addition, he teams up with tenorman Houston Person, trombonist Joel Helleny, and the Richard Wyands Trio on selections ranging from Dixieland ("Struttin' with Some Barbecue") and Swing ("Long Ago and Far Away" and "I Can't Get Started") to bop and hard bop, excelling in every style. *Jazz Im Amerika Haus Volume 2* has Warren and his brother, Allen Vache, fronting a four-piece British rhythm section (with pianist Brian Lemon) on a variety of Swing standards, including "My Shining Hour," "Poor Butterfly," and "Cherokee." Allen Vache is a little erratic in spots, but overall this set is quite enjoyable. *Talk to Me Baby* includes four trio numbers by Vache with Howard Alden and bassist Michael Moore, plus other selections with a full septet that add Bill Easley's reeds, trombonist Joel Helleny, pianist Richard Wyands, and drummer Alvin Queen. Highlights of the modern Swing date include "You'll Never Know," "The Eel's Nephew," "The Claw," and "Pick Yourself Up" (which has an effective Vache vocal). *Warren Plays Warren* is a relaxed outing by Vache, trumpeter Randy Sandke, pianist Kenny Drew Jr., bassist Murray Wall, and drummer Jimmy Cobb on a set of Harry Warren songs. Although not too many fireworks occur between the two brassmen, the set (which includes "Nagasaki," "I Only Have Eyes for You," "Lulu's Back in Town," and "Jeepers Creepers") is pleasing and swinging.

LPS TO SEARCH FOR

Warren Vache's earliest recordings as a leader have not yet appeared on CD. *First Time Out* (Monmouth Evergreen 7081) finds Vache sounding quite mature at the age of 25 in 1976, playing duets with Bucky Pizzarelli and leading a Dixieland-oriented quintet that includes Kenny Davern on soprano. *Blues Walk* (Dreamstreet 101) is a Swing-to-hard-bop-oriented outing with Pizzarelli, Scott Hamilton, and John Bunch in a sextet. *Jillian* (Concord Jazz 87), *Polished Brass* (Concord Jazz 98), and *Iridescence* (Concord Jazz 153), respectively a sextet date and two quartet albums, are long overdue for Concord to bring back. All feature beautiful ballads along with a few hotter numbers.

JOHNNY VARRO

b. Jan. 11, 1930, Brooklyn, NY

One of the top Teddy Wilson–inspired Swing pianists to emerge in the 1950s, Johnny Varro has long had a strong reputation among musicians in the classic and trad jazz world. Varro began playing with Bobby Hackett in 1953, worked regularly as the intermission pianist at Eddie Condon's club (starting in 1957) and at the Metropole, and played with the who's who of Mainstream Swing. He worked with Eddie Condon in the early 1960s, moved to Miami in 1964, kept busy down south (including playing with Phil Napoleon) and in 1979 moved to the Los Angeles area, returning to Florida in 1993. Johnny Varro's tasteful and swinging style is always an asset, and he has kept busy at jazz parties and festivals during the past 20 years, recording for the Arbors label and sometimes leading a combo that sounds a bit like the John Kirby Sextet.

●

7   *Everything I Love* / Sept. 8–9, 1992 / Arbors 19114

9   *Johnny Varro Swing 7* / June 28–29, 1994 / Arbors 19138

8   *Say Yes* / Nov. 27 + 30, 1996 / Arbors 19178

8   *Afterglow* / Dec. 2–3, 1997 / Arbors 19198

Despite being a strong Swing pianist since at least the mid-1950s, Johnny Varro had been barely on record as a leader prior to becoming associated with the Arbors label. Fortunately he has been documented quite well since 1992. *Everything I Love* is an excellent trio set with bassist David Stone and drummer Gene Estes that finds Varro interpreting such songs as "You Turned the Tables On Me," "One Morning in May," Bill Evans's "Waltz for Debbie," and "The Night Has a Thousand Eyes." Varro's Swing 7 (which in its 1994 edition

included Randy Sandke, Dan Barrett, Phil Bodner on clarinet and alto, Harry Allen, bassist Frank Tate, and drummer Joe Ascione) brings back the sound of the John Kirby Sextet to an extent, despite the different instrumentation. Varro's arrangements for the band on such songs as Gerry Mulligan's "Disc Jockey Jump," "Beale Street Blues," "If Dreams Come True," and "The Earl" really give the group its own personality. *Say Yes* is a high-quality solo piano set highlighted by "Wherever There's Love," "You're a Lucky Guy," "Echo of Spring," "It's Been So Long," and "Emaline," showing off Varro's skills as a Swing pianist. *Afterglow* is a second outing from Varro's Swing 7, using Sandke, Barrett, Tate, and Ascione, again with Tommy Newsom on tenor and Ken Peplowski on clarinet and alto. The concise solos and the inventive arrangements for such songs as "Ida,"

"Truckin'," "Humoresque," and Charlie Shavers's "Front and Center" make this another recommended Johnny Varro set.

LPS TO SEARCH FOR

Johnny Varro's debut as a leader, *Sittin' In* (Too Cool 1085), has solos and duets with soprano-saxophonist Don Nelson. A real obscurity, the album mixes together originals (five by Nelson) with vintage material.

CHARLIE VENTURA
b. Dec. 2, 1916, Philadelphia, PA, d. Jan. 17, 1992, Pleasantville, NJ

Charlie Ventura had a big tone on his tenor and, although he often got carried away in his solos, he could be a strong improviser when inspired. Ventura began playing C-melody sax when he was 15, switching to tenor a couple of years later. After working locally, Ventura was with Gene Krupa's orchestra (1942–43), spent a year with Teddy Powell (1943–44), and then rejoined Krupa (1944–46). During this last period, he was not only the drummer's main soloist with the big band but an important part of the Gene Krupa Trio. They had a hit in "Dark Eyes," and Ventura's over-the-top solos were popular. He led his own big band during 1946–47 and then had a hot combo that he billed as "Bop for the People" even though it was essentially a Swing group with some bop influence. Ventura's sidemen during that period included trumpeter Conte Candoli, trombonist Benny Green, and the vocal duo of Jackie Cain and Roy Kral (who also played piano). Ventura had a short-lived orchestra in the early 1950s, recorded regularly for a few years, led the Big Four (which also included pianist Marty Napoleon, bassist Chubby Jackson, and Buddy Rich) in 1951, and worked with Krupa on an occasional basis throughout the 1950s and '60s. Ventura also played alto, baritone, and bass saxophones during the era, and his music ranged from advanced Swing to Dixieland. However, Charlie Ventura declined as a player by the early 1960s, making only one record after 1957 and spending his later years playing in obscurity.

●

9   *1945–1946 / Mar. 1, 1945–Mar. 1946 / Classics 1044*

8   *A Charlie Ventura Concert / May 9, 1949 / MCA 42230*

*   *The Complete Verve/Clef Charlie Ventura & Flip Phillips Studio Sessions / Sept. 1947–May 1957 Mosaic 6-182*

7   *Runnin' Wild / July 18–19, 1956 / Simitar 56122*

By 1945, Charlie Ventura had a fairly big name, being one of last new stars of the Swing era to emerge before the big bands began to collapse. The Classics disc has his first recordings as a leader, including spirited sextet numbers with trumpeter Howard McGhee that fall between Swing and bop, a concert appearance with the Gene Krupa Trio, a quartet date for Savoy, and a meeting with Buck Clayton. Most of Ventura's other recordings as a leader from the 1940s are quite scarce, including his big band sides of 1946. A concert at the Civic Auditorium in 1949 was released partly by Decca and partly by GNP. The former half came out on CD and finds Ventura's septet (with Candoli, Green, altoist Boots Mussulli, pianist Roy Kral, bassist Kenny

O'Brien, and drummer Ed Shaughnessy) performing a few instrumentals, including "How High the Moon" and features for Candoli ("Fine and Dandy") and Green ("Pennies from Heaven"). In addition, there are three vocal numbers for Jackie and Roy: "Euphoria," "East of Suez," and an eccentric reworking of "I'm Forever Blowing Bubbles." The six-CD Mosaic box set has four CDs featuring Flip Phillips, but the first two CDs contain all of Ventura's dates for Clef and Norgran, covering the 1951–54 period. Although the latter recordings did not get much notice at the time, Ventura was still in prime form, switching between tenor, baritone, alto, and bass sax. He is heard with Conte Candoli in a quintet, heading five different quartets (Betty Bennett and Mary Ann McCall have occasional vocals), and leading a nonet. Ventura led three albums during 1956–57 before slipping away. *Runnin' Wild* is the only one of the three thus far to appear on CD, and Ventura (heard on all four of his saxes) is quite spirited on a variety of Dixieland and Swing standards. Backed by Dave McKenna (then a young and unknown pianist), guitarist Billy Bean, bassist Richard Davis, and drummer Mousey Alexander, Ventura sounds quite enthusiastic on such songs as "Honeysuckle Rose," "Bill Bailey," a remake of "Dark Eyes," and even "The Saints." The only minus is that three alternate takes have been substituted for the originals; both versions of each of the songs could easily have been included on this LP-length CD.

LPS TO SEARCH FOR

The double-LP *Euphoria* (Savoy 2243) contains Charlie Ventura's valuable Savoy recordings of 1945 and 1947–48,

some of the most significant sessions of his career. The other half of Ventura's Civic Auditorium concert (including "Body and Soul," "Lullaby in Rhythm," "Boptura," and "High on an Open Mike") were last out on *In Concert* (GNP Crescendo 1).

FILMS

Charlie Ventura is featured with Gene Krupa in *George White's Scandals* (1945).

EDDIE "CLEANHEAD" VINSON
b. Dec. 18, 1917, Houston, TX, d. July 2, 1988, Los Angeles, CA

Eddie "Cleanhead" Vinson was equally skilled as a blues singer and as a bluish altoist who could play credible bebop in the style of Charlie Parker. Vinson began playing alto when he was 16, and a year later he joined the Chester Boone big band, sitting next to Illinois Jacquet and Arnett Cobb. He stayed in the group for six years, including during the periods when it was headed by Milt Larkins (1936–40) and Floyd Ray (1940–41). Vinson became well known during his stint with the Cootie Williams Big Band (1942–45), where his vocals (including "Cherry Red" and "Somebody's Got to Go") made him popular. After leaving Williams, Vinson worked primarily as a leader during the remainder of his career, heading a short-lived big band (1946–47) and then cutting back to a septet for many years. John Coltrane was his sideman in 1952–53, and Vinson wrote two modern jazz standards ("Four" and "Tune Up"), which he later claimed were stolen and copyrighted by Miles Davis. After a period in obscurity, Vinson toured Europe with Jay McShann in 1969 and began to work quite steadily, recording with both Johnny Otis and Count Basie. A consistent crowd pleaser, Vinson helped to popularize such songs as Bill Broonzy's "Just a Dream," "Kidney Stew Blues," "Person to Person," "Old Maid Boogie," and "They Call Me Mr. Cleanhead."

●

7	*Eddie Vinson Sings / Sept. 1957 / Bethlehem 20-4003*
8	*Kidney Stew Is Fine / Mar. 28, 1969 / Delmark 631*
8	*Jamming the Blues / July 2, 1974 / Black Lion 760188*
9	*I Want a Little Girl / Feb. 10, 1981 / Original Jazz Classics 868*

Eddie "Cleanhead" Vinson's early recordings during the R&B days are all long out of print. Vinson recorded only two albums during 1956–66. *Eddie Vinson Sings* puts the emphasis on his voice, with backing by many Count Basie veterans, including Joe Newman, Frank Foster, Paul Quinichette, and Nat Pierce. Vinson's concise versions of "Cleanhead's Back in Town," "Kidney Stew," "Caldonia," and "Cherry Red" are typically spirited; the CD reissue adds three alternate takes to the brief program. *Kidney Stew* teams Cleanhead with T-Bone Walker, Jay McShann, and Hal Singer on a variety of blues and Vinson standards, in-

cluding "Just a Dream," "Old Maid Boogie," and "Wee Baby Blues." Cleanhead is the only singer, and it is interesting to hear T-Bone as a purely instrumental sideman. *Jamming the Blues* was recorded at the 1974 Montreux Jazz Festival and has Vinson singing his usual songs (including "Person to Person" and "Hold It Right There"), plus instrumental versions of "Laura," "Now's the Time," and "C Jam Blues" that display his swinging alto. *I Want a Little Girl* has mostly typical material (including "Somebody's Got to Go" and "Stormy Monday"), but Vinson (who is joined by tenor saxophonist Rashid Ali, trumpeter Martin Banks, and a four-piece rhythm section) sounds full of spirit and inspiration, making this a perfect introduction to his joyful jazz/blues music.

LPS TO SEARCH FOR

Cleanhead & Cannonball (Landmark 1309), from 1961–62, features Vinson as a vocalist backed by the Cannonball

Adderley Quintet and taking Cannonball's place as an altoist on the instrumental tunes; pity that he and Adderley did not trade off. *Kidney Stew* (Circle 57) is a fine 1976 meeting with Ted Easton's Dutch trad band. *The Clean Machine* (Muse 5116) is an excellent combo date from 1978 in which half of the songs are instrumental features for Cleanhead's alto. Also from 1978, *Live at Sandy's* (Muse 5208) and *Hold It Right There* (Muse 5243) feature Vinson at jam sessions with the Ray Bryant Trio and guest tenors Arnett Cobb and Buddy Tate.

T-BONE WALKER
b. May 28, 1910, Linden, TX, d. Mar. 16, 1975, Los Angeles, CA

The Charlie Christian of electric blues guitar, Aaron "T-Bone" Walker was a major influence on Chuck Berry, B. B. King, and many other guitarists of the 1950s, even if he is best remembered today as the composer of "Stormy Monday." And yet his guitar solos constantly crossed the boundary into Swing-oriented jazz.

His stepfather played bass with the Dallas String Band, and as a child Walker began playing guitar, befriending Blind Lemon Jefferson when he was still a young teenager. In 1929 Walker recorded two numbers as Oak Cliff T-Bone, but many miles of traveling and quite a few years of freelancing and learning his craft followed. In 1939 he joined Les Hite's orchestra, returning to records in 1940 with "T-Bone Blues" and quickly developing into a very colorful electric guitarist. In 1942 he cut two titles in a quartet with pianist Freddie Slack for Capitol, but his recording career did not really get under way until 1945. From then on he was quite prolific, leading a jump band that usually had between two and four horns. His popularity grew during the first half of the 1950s but, with the rise of rock and roll, he was overshadowed by younger and more outlandish performers, who built upon his excesses. However, Walker was always a blues legend and he began to play in Europe on a fairly regular basis starting in 1962, recording for a variety of labels and working steadily until a 1974 stroke ended his career.

●

*   *The Complete T-Bone Walker 1940–1954 / June 1940–June 20, 1954 / Mosaic 6-130*

10   *The Complete Capitol/Black & White Recordings / June 1940–Dec. 29, 1947 / Capitol 29379*

8   *I Want a Little Girl / Nov. 13, 1968 / Delmark 633*

7   *Good Feelin' / Nov. 1968 / Verve 519 723*

With the exception of his two numbers from 1929, the first 144 selections from T-Bone Walker's career are on the six-CD Mosaic box, an enormous legacy of Swing-related blues. However, since that magnificent reissue is a limited edition and very difficult to find today, collectors may have to satisfy themselves with the three-CD Capitol set, which has 75 of those 144 songs, everything that Capitol owns but not the Imperial and Rhumboogie recordings. Both sets have plenty of alternate takes and lots of hot solos along with Walker's vocalizing. Moving to his later period, Walker sounds fine on *I Want a Little Girl*, a spirited quintet date with Hal Singer. The same can be said for his work that month with a French ensemble on *Good Feelin'*, although the brief playing time (under 40 minutes) and lack of major voices in the backup group result in the Delmark set's getting the edge.

DINAH WASHINGTON
b. Aug. 29, 1924, Tuscaloosa, AL, d. Dec. 14, 1963, Detroit, MI

One of the finest singers of the 1950s, Dinah Washington was proud of the fact that she could sing anything. Although she came up singing Swing, blues, and R&B, Washington also made an impact on the pop charts and even sang country music and spirituals with plenty of credibility and honest feeling.

Born Ruth Jones, she played piano from an early age and sang with her church choir. At 15, she worked both with Sallie

Martin's gospel choir and in nightclubs. First called "Dinah Washington" by the manager of the Garrick Stage Bar (although Lionel Hampton would later claim that he had given her the name), she was discovered and hired by Hampton, working with him during 1943–46. Surprisingly few recordings exist of her with Hampton, but Washington's first session in 1943 resulted in her initial hit, "Evil Gal Blues." Washington began her solo career in 1946, and she was a constant on the R&B charts for the next decade with such songs as "Baby Get Lost," "Long John Blues," "I Wanna Be Loved," "Wheel of Fortune," "Trouble in Mind," "New Blowtop Blues," "T.V. Is the Thing This Year," and "Teach Me Tonight." Her recordings cover a wide range, from commercial efforts with string orchestras to shouting performances with big bands and high-quality combo dates. Everything seemed to work and she was a major attraction.

In 1959 her straightforward but soulful version of "What a Difference a Day Makes" was such a smash that most of her recordings during her final four years were clearly aimed at the pop market, including some popular duets with singer Brook Benton. An accidental overdose of diet pills mixed with alcohol resulted in Dinah Washington's death at the peak of her career when she was just 39. Posthumously she was one of the biggest influences on practically all of the black female singers of the 1960s and '70s; one cannot imagine Nancy Wilson, Dionne Warwick, and Diana Ross sounding like they do without Dinah Washington's having come first.

●

9 *Mellow Mama* / Dec. 10–13, 1945 / Delmark 451

* *The Complete Dinah Washington on Mercury, Vol. 1 (1946–1949)* / Jan. 14, 1946–Sept. 27, 1949 / Mercury 832 444

* *The Complete Dinah Washington on Mercury, Vol. 2 (1950–1952)* / Feb. 7, 1950–May 6, 1952 / Mercury 832 448

* *The Complete Dinah Washington on Mercury, Vol. 3 (1952–1954)* / Summer 1952–Aug. 14, 1954 / Mercury 832 675

* *The Complete Dinah Washington on Mercury, Vol. 4 (1954–1956)* / Nov. 2, 1954–Apr. 25, 1956 / Mercury 832 683

* *The Complete Dinah Washington on Mercury, Vol. 5 (1956–1958)* / June 25, 1956–July 6, 1958 / Mercury 832 952

* *The Complete Dinah Washington on Mercury, Vol. 6 (1958–1960)* / Feb. 19, 1959–Nov. 12, 1960 / Mercury 832 956

* *The Complete Dinah Washington on Mercury, Vol. 7 (1961)* / Jan. 1961–Dec. 4, 1961 / Mercury 832 960

Mellow Mama has all of Dinah Washington's dozen recordings for the Apollo label. Just 21 at the time and still with Lionel Hampton, Washington was already a major singer, and she holds her own on this strong jazz-oriented blues date with tenor saxophonist Lucky Thompson, trumpeter Karl George, and vibraphonist Milt Jackson; bassist Charles

Mingus is also in the L.A.-based octet. When Dinah Washington went out on her own, she began to record a wide assortment for the Mercury label and its jazz-based subsidiary, Emarcy. The seven three-CD Mercury sets (21 CDs in all) have nearly all of Miss D.'s finest recordings, and they range from jazz combo sessions and outings with studio big bands to pop sessions and backing by string orchestras. The first five threefers are especially full of gems, while *Vol. 6,* which begins with the session that yielded "What a Difference a Day Makes," and *Vol. 7* are generally much more commercial as Washington tries to get more pop hits. Dinah Washington collectors will want all seven since they also contain a lot of previously unreleased material, all presented in coherent order.

9 *The Best in Blues* / Dec. 29, 1943–June 10, 1953 / Verve 314 537 811

10 *Dinah Jams* / Aug. 15, 1954 / Emarcy 814 639

7 *What a Difference a Day Makes* / Feb. 19, 1959–Aug. 1959 / Verve 818 815

5 *In Love* / May 1962–Aug. 1962 / Roulette 97273

5 *Dinah '63* / 1963 / Roulette 794576

8 *Back to the Blues* / July 5, 1962–Nov. 29, 1962 / Roulette 54334

The first three single CDs in this section have music also released in the Mercury three-CD sets, but they are more for the budget-minded. *The Best in Blues* actually contains four cuts (the "Evil Gal Blues" session from 1943) that are not in the Mercury reissues, along with other blues-related material from 1949–53. Spirited stuff, all rendered passionately by Washington. *Dinah Jams* was one of Washington's finest jazz dates as she hosts a jam session also featuring trumpeters Clifford Brown, Clark Terry, and Maynard Ferguson, and it shows that she was a superb jazz singer. *What a Difference a Day Makes* changed her career, for her version of the slow, soulful ballad unexpectedly hit the pop charts. All of the material on the CD of the same name is at the same basic tempo and, although effective, there is a sameness to the approach. In 1962 Dinah Washington switched to the Roulette label, still hoping for hits. *In Love* (which in the CD version is expanded from 12 to 18 songs) is quite predictable, and the singer sounds overly mannered in spots. *Dinah '63* has its moments, but the dozen selections are overly concise and Washington barely gets the melody out before each song's end. Also, Fred Norman's arrangements for the backing orchestra are forgettable. *Back to the Blues* is much better, for Miss D. is joined by a swinging big band and able to shout out the lyrics just as she had in earlier days. The strings and occasional background voices are unnecessary, but Washington overcomes them all with her powerful voice and is assisted by the tenors of Illinois Jacquet and Eddie Chamblee.

FILMS

Dinah Washington is one of the many stars in 1959's *Jazz on a Summer's Day* (New Yorker Video 16590), singing a memorable version of "All of Me" and indulging in some four-handed vibes playing with Terry Gibbs. She also makes a notable appearance in *The Swingin' Singin' Years* (Vintage Jazz Classics 2007), from 1960.

BENNY WATERS

b. Jan. 23, 1902, Brighton, MD, d. Aug. 11, 1998, Columbia, MD

Benny Waters certainly had a remarkable career, for, when he died at age 96, he was the second oldest active jazz musician of all time (after Eubie Blake, although Rosy McHargue would soon pass him). What was most significant was that Waters was still in his musical prime, and his solos could have come from someone in their fifties!

Benny Waters was playing professionally as early as 1918, with Charlie Miller's band in Philadelphia. At various times throughout his career he played tenor, alto, clarinet, and soprano and also proved to be an effective singer. After three years with Miller, he enrolled at the Boston Conservatory, worked around Boston, and became a teacher; one of his pupils was Harry Carney. In 1925 Waters joined Charlie Johnson's Paradise Ten on tenor and contributed arrangements, recording with Johnson (with whom he would work regularly until 1932), Clarence Williams, and King Oliver. After freelancing, Waters played with Fletcher Henderson's big band in 1935, was back with Johnson during 1936–37, and worked with the Hot Lips Page big band (1938), the Claude Hopkins Orchestra (1940–41), Page's sextet, and Jimmie Lunceford (1942). Although quite talented, Benny Waters managed to make it through the entire Swing era without becoming well known. He led a combo for four years in the latter part of the 1940s and toured with Roy Milton's group. Waters worked with Jimmy Archey's Dixieland band (1950–52), playing clarinet and soprano. After leaving Archey in 1952, he moved to Europe, where he worked steadily in Mainstream Swing and Dixieland settings for over 30 years.

Waters returned to the United States in the mid-1980s, recording a brilliant set for Muse in 1987 on tenor, alto, and clarinet when he was 85. He went blind soon afterwards but otherwise was in excellent health, playing with a great deal of power during his final decade. By the 1990s he was heard exclusively on alto, often in a jump jazz style a little reminiscent of Tab Smith and also a bit touched by John Coltrane, who was 24 years Waters's junior! He kept up a busy schedule, toured with the Statesmen of Jazz, appeared on stage with Benny Carter (who had also been with Charlie Johnson) in 1996 for the first time since 1928 (!), and recorded for Enja on his 95th birthday. At the time of his death, Benny Waters was one of the last living links to the 1920s, and he could still outswing nearly every possible competitor.

It is remarkable how well Benny Waters played during his final dozen years. On the Muse CD, Waters is equally effective on tenor, alto, and clarinet, and he takes good-time vocals on two of the nine selections. Backed by a supportive rhythm trio, Waters roars his way through such numbers as "Topsy," " 'S Wonderful," and "I Want to Be Happy." Both *Swinging Again* (with a European rhythm section) and *Plays Songs of Love* (with Red Richards in a quartet) are equally satisfying and, despite their titles, they do not divide into separate sets for stomps and ballads. Waters, by then playing alto exclusively, digs into the Swing standards and sounds quite modern in spots. The only fault to *Live at 95*, recorded at Birdland around the time of Waters's 95th birthday, is that Mike LeDonne is heard on organ rather than piano (which might have worked better for the material). However, LeDonne and guitarist Howard Alden are in fine form during their short solos, although overshadowed by the leader. Benny Waters scats quite well on "Everybody Loves My Baby," shows off his impressive technique on "Callin' the Cats" (one of his five originals included), and is a powerhouse throughout the exciting engagement. No other jazz musician has ever played so well at such an advanced age.

WIDESPREAD DEPRESSION ORCHESTRA

In 1972, the Widespread Depression Orchestra was formed as a seven-piece R&B band. But by the time they recorded their debut set in 1979, they were a nine-piece Swing band featuring such fine players as trumpeter Jordan Sandke, altoist Michael Hashim, pianist Mike LeDonne, and vibraphonist Jonny Holtzman, who provided occasional vocals. David Lillie, who was originally the group's drummer, became the bandleader and eventually switched to baritone sax, since one was needed at the time. A revivalist Swing band during an era when the music was barely being heard (who else was performing "Choo Choo Ch'Boogie" in 1979?), the WDO often took older transcribed charts from the 1930s and early '40s and scaled them down for the nonet. After recording three albums for Stash and one (a collaboration with Bob Wilber) for Phontastic, the group changed its name to simply the Widespread Jazz Orchestra. By then Jonny Holtzman had left and the band was up to six horns (including Tad Schull on tenor) without changing its style much. The small big band recorded an album for Adelphi and a final set (*Paris Blues*) for Columbia in 1986. Randy Sandke was now on second trumpet, the trombonist was Joel Helleny, and the occasional singer was Ronnie Wells. However, by the late 1980s the Widespread Depression Orchestra had broken up and slipped away into history, too early to enjoy the rise of Retro Swing.

●

LPS TO SEARCH FOR

None of the WDO's recordings have yet been reissued on CD. *Downtown Uproar* (Stash 203) has plenty of variety, from "Tain't What You Do" and "Reefer Man" to Coleman Hawkins's "Hollywood Stampede" and "East St. Louis Toodle-oo." *Boogie in the Barnyard* (Stash 206) is the band's best all-round record, with its highlights including Jimmy Mundy's "Cavernism," "Tulip or Turnip," "You Can Depend On Me," Louis Jordan's "Barnyard Boogie," and Luis Russell's "Louisiana Swing." *Time to Jump and Shout* (Stash 212) has a jumping original ("All That Rhythm") and such songs as "Sunday," "Happy Feet," and "Is You Is or Is You Ain't My Baby." *Rockin' in Rhythm* (Phontastic 7527) sticks mostly to Duke Ellington–associated songs of the 1930s and '40s (alternating standards with obscurities) and puts the focus on the playing of Bob Wilber (who is heard on soprano, clarinet, and alto). *Swing Is the Thing* (Adelphi 5015) *and Paris Blues* (Columbia 40034) are also of strong quality, showing that Swing was alive (if underground) in the 1980s and making one wish that the band had stayed together a few years longer.

JOE WILDER

b. Feb. 22, 1922, Colwyn, PA

Trumpeter Joe Wilder has always been best known for his beautiful tone and lyrical style. He studied music in Philadelphia and worked with Les Hite (1941) and Lionel Hampton, leading a band while in the Marines and returning to Hampton after his discharge. Wilder also had stints with the orchestras of Jimmie Lunceford, Lucky Millinder, Sam Donahue, and Herbie Fields before becoming a studio musician. Wilder was with Count Basie's big band in 1954 and toured the USSR with Benny Goodman (1962) but otherwise worked for ABC-TV (1957–73) and in the pit orchestras for Broadway musicals. He has always been proudest of his musicianship and never thought of himself as just a jazz player, although his Swing solos tended to be quite haunting and memorable. Joe Wilder has continued as a studio player, appearing in jazz settings on an occasional basis, including on some records in the 1990s as a leader for Evening Star and as a sideman with Benny Carter and the Statesmen of Jazz. ●

8   *Wilder 'n' Wilder / Jan. 19, 1956 / Savoy 78988*

8   *No Greater Love / Aug. 3–4, 1993 / Evening Star 103*
Joe Wilder's Savoy date puts the focus on his tone as he is supported by a quiet rhythm section comprised of pianist Hank Jones, Wendell Marshall, and drummer Kenny Clarke. The five melodic standards (highlighted by a ten-minute version of "Cherokee") and a blues are joined on this reissue by three alternate takes. Wilder still sounds in fine form on the Evening Star set 37 years later. Age 71 at the time, Wilder plays three of his originals, a couple of obscurities, and nine standards in settings ranging from trios with pianist Bobby Tucker and guitarist James Chirillo and duets with either of the two, to a sextet that includes Seldon Powell on tenor and flute. A worthy and all-too-rare Joe Wilder date as a leader.

LPS TO SEARCH FOR

Jazz from Peter Gunn (Columbia 8121) features Wilder performing ten songs from the Henry Mancini television score in melodic and swinging fashion with a quartet in 1958.

CLAUDE WILLIAMS

b. Feb. 22, 1908, Muskogee, OK

Claude Williams spent most of his life in obscurity, but since the 1970s he has grown not only in name recognition but as a powerful, swinging, and apparently ageless improvising violinist. Williams, who originally played both guitar and violin, had two notable early associations. In 1927 he started working with Terrence Holder's Dark Clouds of Joy and was with the band when Andy Kirk took it over. Williams recorded with Kirk during 1929–30 but was long gone by 1936, when the band started becoming very successful. In the meantime he played with Alphonso Trent and George E. Lee and freelanced around Kansas City. Williams became a member of Count Basie's orchestra in 1936 and came to New York with the classic ensemble, playing rhythm guitar and taking occasional violin solos, appearing on the big band's first recording session. However, talent scout and producer John Hammond never liked the sound of a violin in jazz and he persuaded Basie to replace Williams with Freddie Green. Claude Williams, instead of staying in New York, went home and was largely forgotten for the next 35 years.

Williams worked in the Midwest with the Four Shades of Rhythm, gigged with Roy Milton, and resettled in Kansas City in 1953. In 1972 he was rediscovered; he recorded with Jay McShann and his career went through a gradual upswing. Since then Williams has recorded several times as a leader (starting in 1976), focused exclusively on the violin, occasionally worked with McShann, and during 1994–99 worked and toured with the Statesmen of Jazz. At 92, Claude Williams still seems to be improving! ●

8 *Live at J's, Vol. 1 / Apr. 24, 1989 + May 1, 1989 / Arhoolie 405*

8 *Live at J's, Vol. 2 / Apr. 24, 1989 + May 1, 1989 / Arhoolie 406*

9 *Swing Time in New York / Sept. 5, 1994 / Progressive 7093*

9 *King of Kansas City / May 28–29, 1996 / Progressive 7100*

The two *Live at J's* CDs feature Williams playing live at a New York club with assistance from pianist Ron Mathews, bassist Al McKibbon, and either Akira Tana or Grady Tate on drums. The music on the pair of discs is equally rewarding, with *Vol. 1* including "Billie's Bounce," "After You've Gone," and "Cherokee" while *Vol. 2* has "Indiana,"

"Take the 'A' Train," and "Fiddler's Dream." Williams's violin sound can be raspy and rough, yet it is always full of blues and soul while swinging hard; his occasional good-humored vocals work well, too. *Swing Time in New York* is a superior quintet outing with Bill Easley (on tenor, clarinet, and flute) and pianist Sir Roland Hanna. Williams performs the first song he ever learned ("You've Got to See Your Mama Ev'ry Night"), Swing standards, blues, and ballads, taking three vocals and clearly having a great time. On *King of Kansas City,* the 88-year-old violinist is heard in Kansas City playing with some top local musicians. Lisa Henry and Karrin Allyson take two vocals apiece, and tenor saxophonist Kim Park is quite impressive on "Lester Leaps In." The exuberant and energetic Claude Williams (who takes two vocals of his own) shows throughout that he ranks as the most underrated jazz violinist of all time.

JOE WILLIAMS
b. Dec. 12, 1918, Cordele, GA, d. Mar. 29, 1999, Las Vegas, NV

One of the last great big band vocalists, Joe Williams made "Every Day I Have the Blues" famous, while his singing helped the second Count Basie Orchestra become a permanent success. Although not known to the general public until he was in his mid-thirties, Joe Williams started working professionally 15 years before joining Basie. He sang mostly in the Chicago area starting in 1937, including with Jimmie Noone, Coleman Hawkins, Lionel Hampton (1943), Andy Kirk, and Red Saunders (1950–53), recording with King Kolax in 1951 (including his initial version of "Every Day I Have the Blues"). However, Williams will always be associated with Basie, with whom he worked from December 1954 until January 1961. Although a little bit stereotyped as a blues singer (due to his success with such songs as "Goin' to Chicago" and "Smack Dab in the Middle"), Williams was always equally skilled at standards, and he actually preferred to sing ballads. His popularity continued to grow during his solo years, and Williams was a major attraction at festivals and clubs throughout his last 38 years. He had occasional reunions with Basie and also fared very well on projects with Cannonball Adderley, the Thad Jones–Mel Lewis Orchestra, and George Shearing but worked mostly as a soloist with a rhythm section. His double entendre routines and ad-libs were charming, he always swung, and he knew enough tricks that, even when his voice became a bit raspy during his last years, he could put on a very entertaining and musical show. Joe Williams died when, discouraged with the way the medicine was affecting him during a hospital stay, he spontaneously decided to walk home (a few miles away); the Las Vegas heat did him in.

●

8 *A Swingin' Night at Birdland / July 1962 / Roulette 795335*

9 *Me and the Blues / Jan. 2, 1963–Dec. 5, 1963 / RCA 63536*

7 *The Overwhelming Joe Williams / Feb. 6, 1963–June 18, 1965 / Bluebird 6464*

10 *Joe Williams and Thad Jones–Mel Lewis Orchestra / Sept. 30, 1966 / Blue Note 30454*

8 *Joe Williams Live / Aug. 7, 1973 / Original Jazz Classics 438*

Joe Williams's solo career was successful from the start, and he kept busy throughout his career, never losing his popu-

Joe Williams helped make Count Basie's Orchestra a major attraction in the 1950s while the Basie connection made the singer famous.

larity. The 1962 Roulette set is a live date with the quintet of Harry "Sweets" Edison and Jimmy Forrest that finds Williams sticking mostly to standards (including "September in the Rain," "Teach Me Tonight," and "I Was Telling About You") plus a few of his trademark blues, including "Roll 'Em Pete" and "Goin' to Chicago Blues." *Me and the Blues* does indeed focus mostly on the blues (other than three previously unreleased numbers that were added to the 1999 CD reissue), but Williams comes up with a wide variety of moods to express within the idiom. Whether it is the title cut, "Rocks in My Bed," "Work Song," or "Hobo Flats," he puts plenty of feeling and swing into his interpretations, helped out by a nonet that includes Clark Terry, Thad Jones, Phil Woods, and Ben Webster (heard as a guest on "Rocks in My Bed"). *The Overwhelming Joe Williams* is actually a sampler, with selections taken from five of the singer's albums. Williams is heard singing songs from *Jump for Joy*, appearing at the 1963 Newport Jazz Festival (with Coleman

Hawkins, Zoot Sims, and Ben Webster on tenors), and performing five ballads in front of a string orchestra. Good music, but hopefully the complete sessions will eventually be reissued. Joe Williams's meeting with the Thad Jones–Mel Lewis Orchestra is practically perfect. Although the big band has few solos, Thad Jones's inventive arrangements frame Williams's voice quite creatively. Many of these songs (particularly "Nobody Knows the Way I Feel This Morning," "Hallelujah I Love Her So," and "Night Time Is the Right Time") soon became part of Joe Williams's repertoire, and his scatting on "It Don't Mean a Thing" is wonderful. *Joe Williams Live* finds the singer joined by an expanded version of Cannonball Adderley's group, featuring a funky rhythm section and short solos for altoist Cannonball and cornetist Nat Adderley. Williams is the main star throughout, giving "Goin' to Chicago Blues" some additional lyrics and putting plenty of feeling into "Shoe She Do," Duke Ellington's "Heritage," and "Tell Me Where to Scratch."

8 *Every Night: Live at Vine St.* / May 7–8, 1987 / Verve 833 236

8 *Ballad and Blues Masters* / May 7–8, 1987 / Verve 314 511 354

7 *In Good Company* / Jan. 19–21, 1989 / Verve 837 932

6 *Live at Orchestra Hall, Detroit* / Nov. 20, 1992 / Telarc 83329

4 *Here's to Life* / Aug. 16–18, 1993 / Telarc 83357

6 *Feel the Spirit* / Sept. 20–23, 1994 / Telarc 83362

Joe Williams recorded two CDs' worth of material while appearing at Hollywood's Vine St. in 1987. Age 68 at the time, Williams was still in his prime and carries the whole show. He is joined by the Norman Simmons Trio plus guitarist Henry Johnson. *Every Night* is highlighted by Eubie Blake's "A Dollar for a Dime," "Too Marvelous for Words," and a version of "Everyday I Have the Blues" that is combined with Miles Davis's "All Blues." *Ballad and Blues Masters* is at the same level, particularly on fine renditions of "You Can Depend On Me," "When Sunny Gets Blue," "I Ain't Got Nothing but the Blues," and a "Blues Medley." Together, those two CDs give listeners a good example of what it was like to see Joe Williams live in a club on a typical night during the era. *In Good Company* matches Williams with Supersax on two numbers, there are a pair of vocal duets with Marlena Shaw (including "Is You Is or Is You Ain't My Baby"), and pianist-singer Shirley Horn joins Williams on two ballads. Each of the combinations works. Joe Williams ended his career with the Telarc label. *Live at Orchestra Hall, Detroit* is a rare meeting with the Count Basie Orchestra (then directed by Frank Foster), Williams's first on records in decades. Older hits combine with a few newer songs, but unfortunately the big band mostly acts as an appealing prop behind the singer, whose voice was beginning to get a

little raspy at the time. Williams loved the sappy ballad "Here's to Life" and the string arrangements of Robert Farnon heard on the *Here's to Life* CD, but the slow tempos given each song lack variety, the charts sometimes border on Muzak, and there is little jazz or solid Swing here despite the singer's best efforts. Joe Williams fulfilled a longtime desire to record an album of spirituals with *Feel the Spirit*. Marlena Shaw helps out on a few numbers, as does a five-piece chorus, while the backup group has Patrice Rushen emulating an organ on her synthesizer. The results (which include "I Couldn't Hear Nobody Pray," "His Eye Is on the Sparrow," and a medley of "Go Down Moses" and "Wade in the Water") are sincere and swinging if somewhat predictable.

LPS TO SEARCH FOR

Everyday I Have the Blues (Savoy Jazz 1140) has all of Joe Williams's pre-Basie recordings as a leader, a couple of interesting sets from 1951–53. In 1983 and 1985 Williams recorded *Nothin' but the Blues* (Delos 4001) and *I Just Want to Sing* (Delos 4004) with all-star groups. The former set includes Red Holloway, Eddie "Cleanhead" Vinson, and organist Jack McDuff, while the latter has Thad Jones and the tenors of Eddie "Lockjaw" Davis and Benny Golson. The results are quite happy on both occasions.

FILMS

Joe Williams sings "I Don't Like You No More" with the Count Basie Orchestra in *Jamboree* (1957) and pops up with Basie in the Jerry Lewis movie *Cinderfella* (1960). He has an acting part in *The Moonshine War* (1970), had a recurring role on *The Bill Cosby Show* television series in the 1980s, and is featured in a 1992 hour-long concert with the George Shearing Trio, *A Song Is Born* (View Video 1333).

JIMMY WITHERSPOON

b. Aug. 8, 1923, Gurdon, AR, d. Sept. 18, 1997, Los Angeles, CA

Jimmy Witherspoon was a major blues singer for many decades and able to fit equally well and quite comfortably into swinging jazz, R&B, and blues settings. Oddly enough, he first sang the blues in Calcutta, India, with pianist Teddy Weatherford (1941–43) while stationed overseas with the Merchant Marine. Witherspoon gained his initial fame for his work with Jay

McShann (1944–48), including a hit recording of "Ain't Nobody's Business If I Do." Settling in Los Angeles, Witherspoon worked steadily for several years, although the 1953–58 period was rough, both financially and musically; he found himself overshadowed by rock and roll. However, his appearance at the 1959 Monterey Jazz Festival with a group of jazz all-stars revitalized his career, and it would be followed by recordings with Ben Webster and tours with the Buck Clayton All-Stars (visiting Europe in 1961) and Count Basie's orchestra (Japan in 1963). Even with the rise of rock, Witherspoon was considered legendary and managed to overcome R&B-ish trappings on some of his lesser recordings. He recorded with the Savoy Sultans in 1980 before throat cancer weakened him for a few years and permanently hurt his voice. Jimmy Witherspoon made a comeback and, even after his voice greatly declined in the early 1990s, he worked now and then up until the time of his death. Shortly after the singer's passing, Jay McShann paid tribute to 'Spoon at the 1997 Monterey Jazz Festival, four decades after they had made musical history.

●

8 *Jimmy Witherspoon & Jay McShann / Nov. 15, 1947–1949 / Black Lion 760173*

6 *Jazz Me Blues: The Best of Jimmy Witherspoon / May 16, 1956–1966 / Prestige 11008*

6 *Spoon So Easy / June 10, 1954–Aug. 15, 1956 / Chess 93003*

8 *Goin' to Kansas City Blues / Dec. 4–5, 1957 / RCA 51639*

8 *Singin' the Blues / May 8 + 16, 1958 / Blue Note 94108*

10 *The 'Spoon Concerts / Oct. 2, 1959–Dec. 2, 1959 / Fantasy 24701*

The Black Lion disc lists Jimmy Witherspoon's name first, but he actually sings on just 11 of the 24 numbers, although there are two versions of his famous "Ain't Nobody's Business If I Do." McShann's bands, which range from a quartet to a jumping octet, essentially play late-period Swing with touches of R&B and bebop. The only famous sidemen (other than Witherspoon) are the young trumpeter Art Farmer and the R&B tenor session man Maxwell Davis, but the performances are quite spirited. Most of these selections (recorded in L.A.) were formerly quite rare. *Jazz Me Blues* is a sampler of Jimmy Witherspoon's work from an important decade in his life, drawing its music from seven sessions, five of which have been reissued in more complete form in the Original Blues Classics series; the other music is from World Pacific and Reprise. Jimmy Witherspoon was kind of an odd choice for Chess to sign because his urban- and jazz-oriented style of blues was much different than Chess's electric Chicago blues. As it turned out, Spoon's stay at the label

was brief and uneventful. *Spoon So Easy* has five numbers that were issued and nine songs that had never been out before. Witherspoon is fine but not much magic occurs. *Goin' to Kansas City Blues* is a reunion of Witherspoon with Jay McShann. The pianist's nonet includes Ray Copeland or Emmett Berry on trumpets, J. C. Higginbotham, and tenorman Seldon Powell. The repertoire dates mostly from 1930s Kansas City, with such songs as "Confessin' the Blues," "Ooo-Wee Then the Lights Go Out," "Froggy Bottom," and "Gee Baby, Ain't I Good to You." *Singin' the Blues* has Witherspoon also excelling in a jazz setting, even though it must have seemed as if his days as a commercial success were behind him. He sings a variety of blues (including "When I've Been Drinkin'," "Wee Baby Blues," and "There's Good Rockin' Tonight") with combos that include Harry Edison or Gerald Wilson on trumpets, Teddy Edwards and Jimmy Allen on tenors, and a four-piece rhythm section led by pianist Hampton Hawes.

Much to the surprise of everyone, Jimmy Witherspoon was the hit of the 1959 Monterey Jazz Festival. *The 'Spoon Concerts* has the five-song 25-minute set in which the singer holds his own with the likes of Roy Eldridge, Ben Webster, Coleman Hawkins, Woody Herman, and Earl Hines on exuberant versions of "Ain't Nobody's Business" and "When I Been Drinkin'." It is fun to hear the audience's surprised and enthusiastic reactions during the performance, and to realize that this set caused a renaissance in Witherspoon's career. The remainder of the CD is taken from two months later, a highly enjoyable ten-song performance with Webster and baritonist Gerry Mulligan that builds on the momentum of his comeback. This is the Jimmy Witherspoon CD to get first!

7 *Baby, Baby, Baby / May 6, 1963 / Original Blues Classics 527*

7 *Evenin' Blues / Aug. 15, 1963 / Original Blues Classics 511*

6 *Blues Around the Clock / Nov. 5, 1963 / Original Blues Classics 576*

7 *Some of My Best Friends Are The Blues / June 15, 1964 / Original Blues Classics 575*

8 *Blues for Easy Livers / 1965–1966 / Original Blues Classics 585*

2 *Love Is a Five-Letter Word / Feb. 1974 / Avenue Jazz 75226*

7 *Live / 1976 / Avenue Jazz 71262*

7 *Rockin' L.A. / Oct. 24–25, 1988 / Fantasy 9660*
Jimmy Witherspoon recorded several fine albums for Prestige during 1963–66, much of which has been reissued on CD in the Original Blues Classics series. *Baby, Baby, Baby,* made with a pair of medium-size groups, includes "Rocks in My Bed," "Bad Bad Whiskey," "It's a Lonesome Old World," and "One Scotch, One Bourbon, One Beer." *Evenin' Blues* is quite blues-oriented, helped out by the presence of guitarist T-Bone Walker and Clifford Scott's tenor; "Don't Let Go," "Evenin'," and "Kansas City" work well on this relaxed set. *Blues Around the Clock* has overly concise performances (only "No Rollin' Blues" is over four minutes) and somewhat anonymous backup by a quartet that includes organist Paul Griffin. Witherspoon does sound fine, however, on "I Had a Dream," "Goin' to Chicago Blues," and "Around the Clock." *Some of My Best Friends* is slightly unusual in that Witherspoon is backed by a big band arranged by Benny Golson, and some of the songs move beyond blues (including "And the Angels Sing" and "Who's Sorry Now"), showing us that 'Spoon was a fine crooner, too. *Blues for Easy Livers* is one of Witherspoon's finest jazz dates, and he performs such numbers as "Lotus Blossom," "P.S. I Love You," "Don't Worry 'Bout Me," "Embraceable You," and "I Got It Bad." Only two of the dozen songs are actually blues, and 'Spoon's band (trombonist Bill Watrous, baritonist Pepper Adams, pianist Roger Kellaway, bassist Richard Davis, and drummer Mel Lewis) is full of top modern jazz players. Witherspoon sounds inspired both by their presence and by the material.

Love Is a Five-Letter Word is another story altogether, a commercial effort that tries to portray 'Spoon as a soul/disco/R&B singer. The material is quite mundane, the arrangements are painful, and the whole set is quite dated. *Live* is quite a bit better, a strictly blues set with Witherspoon's friend, the young fusion/blues guitarist Robben Ford. Their versions of "Goin' Down Slow," "Outskirts of Time," and "Around the Clock" sound much more up to date than the *Love* CD and quite a bit more sincere. *Rockin' L.A.,* from 1988, when Jimmy Witherspoon was 65, was one of his final strong records before his voice declined. With assistance from tenorman Teddy Edwards, pianist Gerald Wiggins, bassist John Clayton, and drummer Paul Humphrey, 'Spoon performs a medley, some of his favorite blues and ballads and a few standards, showing the world how timeless his brand of city blues still was after 45 years of performing.

LPS TO SEARCH FOR

Olympia Concert (Inner City 7014) is from Jimmy Witherspoon's 1961 tour with the Buck Clayton All-Stars and has some short solos from various Basie alumni. *Roots* (Atlantic 90535) is an excellent 1962 outing with Ben Webster and Gerald Wilson in a sextet. And Witherspoon is teamed with altoist Hank Crawford, tenorman David "Fathead" Newman, and pianist Dr. John on *Midnight Lady Called the Blues* (Muse 5327), from 1986.

FILMS

Jimmy Witherspoon has a few featured numbers in 1961 with *Buck Clayton and His All Stars* (Shanachie 6303) and he has an acting part in *The Black Godfather* (1974).

BRITT WOODMAN

b. June 4, 1920, Los Angeles, CA

A technically skilled trombonist who was never featured enough as a soloist, Britt Woodman was a major asset during his years with Duke Ellington, particularly in the ensembles. Woodman played with his brothers in a family band, worked with Phil Moore and Les Hite, and served in the Army (1942–46). He had stints with Boyd Raeburn's orchestra, the Eddie Heywood Sextet, and Lionel Hampton (1946–47). Woodman assumed Lawrence Brown's role with Duke Ellington, appearing on many records with Duke during 1951–60. He also was featured on a Miles Davis Quintet album in 1955 and a few dates with his childhood friend Charles Mingus during 1960–63. Woodman spent the 1960s working mostly in the pit orchestras of various Broadway shows and occasionally in the studios. In 1970 he returned to Los Angeles, where he freelanced, led his only record date (an obscure effort for the European Falcon label), and worked with the Toshiko Akiyoshi–Lew Tabackin Orchestra, Bill Berry's L.A. Big Band, the Juggernaut, and Benny Carter. Britt Woodman, who moved back to New York in the 1980s, was less active in the '90s but still played on a part-time basis.

SAM WOODYARD

b. Jan. 7, 1925, Elizabeth, NJ, d. Sept. 20, 1988, Paris, France

Sam Woodyard was Duke Ellington's longtime drummer and a part of many of his successes in the 1950s and '60s. Self-taught, Woodyard worked locally in New Jersey and had stints with Paul Gayten (1950), Joe Holiday (1951), Roy Eldridge (1952), and Milt Buckner (1953–55). Woodyard was with Ellington during 1955–66, having the second longest stint of all of Duke's drummers; only Sonny Greer was in the Ellington band for more years. Woodyard's post-Duke period was mostly out of the spotlight; he worked for a time with Ella Fitzgerald, Bill Berry, and Claude Bolling and in 1983 toured Europe with The Great Eight (an all-star Swing group). Sam Woodyard's final recording as a sideman (he never led any dates) was made with the Steve Lacy Sextet shortly before his death at age 63.

RETRO SWING

●

INTRODUCTION TO RETRO SWING

In the mid-1990s, Swing seemed to be everywhere. The mass media, latching onto what they took to be the latest fad, breathlessly reported that young people were actually getting dressed up and touching while dancing to Swing bands. The emphasis in the stories was typically on the superficial: the vintage clothes that many converts to Swing were wearing, their collection of old cars, their adoption of aspects of the 1940s lifestyle, plus clips of the more acrobatic dancers. As far as the Swing bands went, some of the more commercial ones were briefly seen (mostly the few bands who were connected with major labels and Brian Setzer), but the music was generally relegated to the background and very little time was actually spent discussing or analyzing what was being played. Then during 1998–99, as the media tired of the story and some of the fad chasers went elsewhere, the press dutifully announced the death of Swing.

In reality, the media largely missed the whole story, as did, surprisingly, the jazz magazines and the record labels. During an era when too much ink was spent in the jazz world debating the virtues of the Lincoln Jazz Orchestra (a New York repertory orchestra run by trumpeter Wynton Marsalis) and the significance of the hard bop-based Young Lions while decrying the lack of an audience for jazz, Retro Swing was exciting many listeners who were coming to Swing from pop and rock music. The possible key to jazz's future popularity was to be found in Retro Swing, but far too many purists and conservative jazz followers quickly dismissed the entire movement without even hearing it.

Jazz lost a large percentage of its audience during the second half of the 1940s and in the decades that followed due to the separation of jazz from the entertainment world. During the big band era, Swing was considered perfect music to dance to, performers smiled while doing their best to communicate with their audience, and it was considered great fun to see a jazz band. However, with the rise of bebop, most jazz musicians wanted to be taken much more seriously and to be thought of as artists rather than just merely entertainers. Laudable as that goal was and continues to be, something was lost in uplifting the music. It is true that jazz improvisers are masters and should be thought of on the same level as classical musicians, but, by deemphasizing the fun aspects of jazz (discouraging dancing and anything visual, often not even speaking to the audience, and expecting listeners to always come to the music rather than the other way around), jazz was being doomed to become a type of American classical music, an idiom that needed government grants in order to survive. Rhythm and blues, rock and roll, soul music, country, rock, and rap were allowed to capture the attention of the mass public, while jazz was considered forbidding, overly intellectual, and oh-so-serious. Big mistake!

The truth is that most jazz can be danced to, certainly any style that uses a 4/4 rhythm (which excludes just the avant-garde), but not if there are no dance floors and if would-be dancers are sneered at. Shortly before Retro Swing caught on, an odd mixture of styles called Acid Jazz seemed to have the potential of making some waves. Essentially late-60s soul jazz and R&B sprinkled with some jazz solos, Acid Jazz caught on in England and was imported to New York City. Funk bands and disc jockeys in dance clubs brought back the sound of late 1960s organ groups, often adding updated rhythms and occasional samples so as to make the music even more accessible than it originally was. However, the "new and improved music" tended to be very watered down, with overly loud bass lines (as if dancers could not hear the beat), lots of repetition, and very little spontaneity or creativity. After a few years, Acid Jazz largely faded away except in some isolated clubs, and the surviving music had very little jazz content. Overall it was a noble failure largely sunk by the participants' unwillingness to take chances and, in some cases, learn their instruments! But at least it made the attempt to create jazz-oriented dance music.

452

Just as Acid Jazz began to end its brief prime, Retro Swing burst upon the public's consciousness. One can trace the beginning of the Retro Swing movement to 1989, when the Royal Crown Revue was formed. Prior to that, there had been several attempts to revive Swing since the big band era collapsed in 1946. In the early 1950s some thought that, with the low level of pop music, it was only a matter of time before Swing came back; Benny Goodman even attempted to tour with a new big band in 1952. The question "Will big bands come back?" was asked for many years, but the accurate answer always had to be "No!" Big bands were simply economically unfeasible after television brought the public free entertainment, and the Swing orchestras were too tied in to World War II nostalgia and recreations of early hits. When one sees film clips of the Swing survivors leading big bands before dancers in the 1950s, '60s, and '70s, it is obvious that the audience was getting older with each decade. Few young people were interested in dancing to Harry James, Benny Goodman, or someone like Guy Lombardo. It seemed so corny.

Yet largely overlooked in the 1970s and '80s were the occasional Swing-based combos that did well, such as Panama Francis's Savoy Sultans, Roomful of Blues, and the Cheathams. With the rise of Scott Hamilton, Warren Vache, and those that followed, by the 1980s it was acceptable for younger musicians to be playing Swing-styled jazz. But, except for rare occasions, the Swing musicians of the period were performing mostly for club and concert crowds that sat down and barely tapped their feet.

The Royal Crown Revue and those that followed changed all of that, although not without a struggle. Rather than merely recreate the past and get buried in nostalgia for an era in which they did not live, the new Retro Swing bands were often not shy to display their influences (rock, punk, rockabilly, ska, R&B) and mix them together in varying amounts with a swinging rhythm section and riffing horns. Lead vocalists were much more important than they had been during the actual Swing era, the combos in most cases were medium-size rather than big bands, and most of the groups were not playing the music of Glenn Miller or Benny Goodman, opting instead for jump music and originals. It sometimes made for bizarre combinations but resulted in originality for some of the bands.

Many of the newer groups latched on to some parts of the past. Most popular were the singing style of Cab Calloway, the repertoire of Louis Jordan, the eclectic nature of Louis Prima's music, Gene Krupa's drumming (particularly from "Sing, Sing, Sing"), basic chord changes (especially blues), honking tenors influenced by Illinois Jacquet and Arnett Cobb, 1950s guitar styles (from Charlie Christian's followers and rockabilly to Chuck Berry), and boogie-woogie pianists with a dash of Jerry Lee Lewis. At its best, Retro Swing is infectious, a reinvention of the past, and crazy fun. At its worst (as with some of the bands that came from rock after the mid-1990s), it is an amateurish caricature of the real thing played by musicians who have little knowledge of their predecessors.

When the Royal Crown Revue was formed in 1989, there was no Swing scene and very little Swing dancing; the noun "Swing" (as opposed to the verb) was associated primarily with a historical style. Through pure persistence and a desire to perform, the Royal Crown Revue (after two years of playing locally in Los Angeles) went on some pioneering and influential national tours during 1991–92 that made at least the musical underground aware of Retro Swing. Often inspired by that band, during 1990–1992 the Swing movement was fully under way, with such groups as Big Bad Voodoo Daddy, the Cherry Poppin' Daddies, the Erik Ekstrand Ensemble, Full Swing, and Eddie Reed's big band being formed; Lavay Smith's Red Hot Skillet Lickers and George Gee's Orchestra had already started in 1989. With the opening of the Derby in 1993, the Retro Swing movement had an unofficial home, a place where many different Swing bands could play before increasingly adventurous dancers. The Derby offered its customers free dance lessons before the night's performance, a practice also adopted by many other clubs in L.A., San Francisco, and New York. When Brian Setzer, a top rock star, decided to fulfill a longtime dream and lead a big band, after a few years the media noticed and he was able to fill large halls. And Royal Crown Revue's appearance in the 1994 film *The Mask* added to the momentum.

By the mid-1990s, as the no-longer-underground Retro Swing movement greatly increased in size, it was thought of by some as the latest fad. Some record labels, smelling a quick profit, signed a few of the more potentially commercial bands (a practice that escalated after the Squirrel Nut Zippers had a surprise hit with "Hell"). Musicians from the rock world who never before had shown any interest in Swing decided to jump on the bandwagon and form Swing bands, without bothering to study the idiom. And newcomers to the music were often disappointed after hearing some of these inferior groups, writing off the new Swing completely. As with "blues" in the early 1920s and "bop" in 1949, the word "Swing" was everywhere, often being misused. The main jazz world, instead of learning from Retro Swing, just ignored the whole thing, feeling that if a style or idiom was popular, it could not be any good. By 1998–99, some of the Swing clubs were closing for various reasons and the movement seemed to be shrinking, yet the best bands and the more dedicated musicians and fans showed no sign of abandoning the music that they loved.

Up to now, little has been written about Retro Swing that actually talks about the music itself as opposed to the lifestyle or the more superficial elements. Who have been some of the most important participants in the Retro Swing movement and which CDs are the ones to get? Read on.

INTERVIEWS

For this section, I thought it would be interesting to pick one jazz-oriented band from each of the three Retro Swing centers (San Francisco, Los Angeles, and New York) and discuss with their leader not only the group's background but the state of Swing circa 1999–2000.

LAVAY SMITH and CHRIS SIEBERT

Singer Lavay Smith and pianist-arranger Chris Siebert have been a team ever since the formation of the Red Hot Skillet Lickers in San Francisco in 1989, heading one of the strongest of the jazz-oriented Swing bands of the past decade. They were interviewed one after the other but, since they were asked similar questions and their replies overlapped (they actually heard each other's comments), I have combined their answers into one dialog.

Where did both of you grow up?

LAVAY: I grew up in Southern California and I lived overseas in the Philippines for around five years.

CHRIS: I lived in New York until I was 12 and then I went to high school in Los Angeles.

What type of music did you enjoy listening to while growing up?

LAVAY: All kinds, the basic stuff that was on the radio, lots of terrible music! But I always loved old movie musicals from the 1930s and '40s. By the time I was 16, I was exploring everything from punk rock to early jazz.

CHRIS: My dad was into the Beatles but he had a diverse record collection. He is in the theater, so I was exposed to a lot of original cast show recordings. As I got older, I got sucked into the world of rock music, Rolling Stones, the Who, that kind of stuff. But through that, I was exposed a bit to the blues. I discovered jazz when I was around 17. I was initially into Charles Mingus, Bud Powell, and Duke Ellington.

How did the two of you become involved in performing music?

CHRIS: I took guitar lessons as a kid and in my late teens I started picking out songs on the piano at home. I took piano lessons for six months when I was 17, learning chords and harmony. From then on I was basically self-taught, hanging out with other pianists and listening to records.

LAVAY: I've been singing all of my life. In the Philippines when I was 15 I sang in bands for the sailors; they were really an easy crowd. And then after I came back to the U.S., after a few years in Los Angeles, I moved to San Francisco where I played guitar and sang in coffee houses.

Lavay, when did you know that you were going to be a professional singer?

LAVAY: Pretty much my whole life. In the fourth grade I decided that I wanted to be either a singer, a baseball star, or a veterinarian! By the fifth grade, I'd settled on singing.

How did the Red Hot Skillet Lickers get started and where did the name come from?

CHRIS: I was waiting tables in San Francisco and was not sure that I was going to be a musician, since I'd started a bit late. One day I ran into a guy in the street who was playing 1920s style blues guitar in the styles of Big Bill Broonzy and Blind Blake. We started talking and, when I came to one of his club gigs in March 1989, he [Craig Ventresco] hired me for his

One of the top singers in today's Retro Swing movement, Lavay Smith leads a band that often plays hot 1944 Swing.

group, Bo Grumpus. Lavay also knew the guitar player and, when she got a gig in the club in July, she hired Craig and his band, which by then included me. Not too long after, Lavay formed the Skillet Lickers.

LAVAY: I was singing a lot of double entendre tunes at the time and, after getting a club date, I thought of Git-Tanner's Skillet Lickers (a country band from the 1920s) and decided that that name would be perfect.

What was it like in the early days of the group?

LAVAY: We really started out at the bottom. We performed in "bucket of blood" tenderloin bars and dives, but it didn't bother us because we were so young. It was a great education. From the beginning, even though we were playing in these funky places during 1989–90, we had great crowds. This was before the Swing scene started, but people were open to this music and it has never really been out of style.

Were you surprised that Swing became so popular in the 1990s?

LAVAY: I always thought it would be popular. I even thought that we'd be signed to a big rock label in our early days because the music was such fun.

CHRIS: I was actually very surprised. For the first part of the group's life, we were a novelty act, looked at a bit like oddballs. But we did quite well in the Bay Area because Lavay has always had charisma and she drew audiences in. We were playing mostly rock and roll clubs at first. We had a fairly expansive vision and wanted to play a variety of older styles of jazz and blues, not just trad. After a few years we met older musicians, who joined the band and uplifted the music. When the Swing scene did sprout up, we became much more conscious of playing for dancers.

It seems like your band's timing was perfect, playing Swing right before the Retro Swing movement got started.

CHRIS: Yes, we were very fortunate about that because that fact will probably allow us to outlast most of the other bands. In addition to dances, we enjoy playing for sit-down concerts, which some of the newer groups have difficulty doing. As the scene spread throughout the country a few years ago, each geographic area had its local hometown hero band. Once the corporate media and the major labels saw that they might be able to make a buck off of these regionally successful bands, they started imposing their own idea as to what this music oughta be, which is rock- and youth-oriented and certainly not music-oriented! They picked up on the groups that fit that general category and promoted the heck out of them. So a few bands have sold an incredible number of records. It will be interesting to see which of those groups will really last.

LAVAY: A lot of the bands that were doing more rock-flavored stuff, particularly the ones not backed by corporations, are not around anymore. The dancers have been becoming real jazz fans and they are getting very sophisticated. It is really important to do your homework with this music. One can't just form a band and decide to play Swing and expect to sound good. One thing that is great about starting so early is that we have fans that like our band for ourselves rather than just because we are associated with the Swing scene.

Who are some of the groups that really helped to popularize Swing in the 1990s?

LAVAY: Big Bad Voodoo Daddy has sold quite a few records. We've opened for them a few times. Although they are a lot different than we are, they have helped to open up people's minds toward Swing. A lot of their fans end up buying Duke Ellington and Count Basie records. Royal Crown Revue was the band that went out on the road early on and got the ball rolling for Swing across the country.

CHRIS: I give the Royal Crown Revue a lot of credit because I feel that they genuinely love a lot of the Classic Jazz and R&B from the 1940s and '50s. What they did was combine that music with their own punk rock/rockabilly background. They were out there before the other bands. Although we started at the same time, the Royal Crown Revue was out on the road much earlier than us, doing a lot of the hard work when there was no Swing circuit, unlike now. They blazed the trail. I know that they played for some empty rooms early on because people did not know what to make of this music!

What have been some of the high points of the band's existence so far?

LAVAY: We've appeared at a lot of great jazz festivals. We played at the Montreal Jazz Festival, we love performing in New York, the Monterey Jazz Festival was real fun, and we always enjoy appearing in San Francisco. I just love hearing the band play every night.

CHRIS: Without a doubt for me the high point has been working with the great veteran musicians. Lavay and I and the younger members of the band are part of a very fortunate generation because we are the last generation that will have the wonderful benefit of being around people who were around in the 1940s and '50s. Working with Bill Stewart (who is 75), 74-year old Allen Smith, Jules Broussard, and Herman Riley has been a definite highlight. Another plus has been meeting some of our heroes, including Milt Jackson and Jay McShann. Because first and foremost, Lavay and I are fans of this music.

Lavay, who have been your main inspirations as a singer?

LAVAY: Billie Holiday, Dinah Washington, and Helen Humes are the three biggest influences on me, although I love many others, including Ella and Sarah. And Dianne Reeves can be amazing.

Do you think at this point in time the Swing scene is still growing? Or is it declining a bit?

LAVAY: People have invested a lot of money in dancing and there are many fans who are really into the music. The crowds are growing. I think that the big corporate rock/Swing bands may have some trouble, but the jazz/Swing bands (and there are so many good ones) are doing better all of the time.

What are some of your favorite clubs to perform at?

LAVAY: We particularly enjoy the Derby in Hollywood, Café du Nord in San Francisco, the Five Spot in Philly, the Supper Club in New York, and the Grand Emporium in Kansas City.

What is upcoming for the Red Hot Skillet Lickers, and what are your future goals for the band?

CHRIS: During the past few years we have been expanding our audience. The first step was putting out a CD in 1996, one that has thus far sold 40,000 copies, an exceptional number for an independent jazz release. In 1998 we got out of the state and toured across the country. And in 1999 we made it a goal to get on the festival circuit nationally, and we succeeded beyond our expectations, playing all over the U.S. and in Canada. The goal for the near future is to try to get to Europe or Japan.

LAVAY: For our second record, which will be called *Everybody's Talking About Ms. Thang,* it was exciting hooking up with David Berger, the transcriber for the Lincoln Center Jazz Orchestra. He's the foremost expert in the world on Duke Ellington and Billy Strayhorn and wrote some great arrangements for us. That CD will have six horns as opposed to three or four on the first one, and half of the songs are originals. For the future I just want us to continue traveling the world, making great music. There is a lot of good music that has come out of the Swing scene, and it is surprising to me that the jazz press has largely missed it and that jazz labels such as Verve and Blue Note have not picked up some of the great Swing bands that are around.

ERIC EKSTRAND

Pianist-vocalist Eric Ekstrand (who grew up in New Jersey) had an extensive career before he put together the Eric Ekstrand Ensemble in 1992, working as a freelance pianist in Las Vegas, becoming a busy recording engineer, writing arrangements for many Las Vegas headliners, and composing film scores in Los Angeles. However, his true love was always Swing, and his group (which is usually 10 to 12 pieces) is considered one of the top Swing bands in Los Angeles.

Can you tell me a little bit about your musical beginnings?

ERIC: I came from a musical family. My father, Ray Ekstrand, was a Swing-era musician who played saxophones, clarinet, and flute with Benny Goodman, Paul Whiteman, Abe Lyman, Shep Fields, and other name bands. He was also on the staff of CBS for many years. My first instrument was the clarinet, but I never really caught fire on that. In junior high I took up the drums to join the school band and, when I got bored with that, I switched to string bass and also played a little bit of guitar. However, I started playing piano when I was 11.

What kind of music did you enjoy listening to while growing up?

ERIC: I heard my Dad's Swing records, plenty of Count Basie, Duke Ellington, and Woody Herman, plus I listened to a lot of the rock and roll that was around during the era. I'd always planned to become a professional musician, since I was 12, and I always wanted to have my own band.

How did you happen to form your current group, and what inspires you to play Swing as opposed to other styles?

ERIC: I always gravitated towards this music and loved Basie, Ellington, Louis Jordan, and Cab Calloway. Originally, in 1992, we mostly played covers of songs that I liked by those artists, although later on I starting writing many originals in that style. When we first started the group, as far as I knew we had the only Swing band in town. There were a couple others but I was not aware of them. I wasn't trying to latch on to any movement because, as far as I could tell, there was no movement at the time! In fact, for our first two years, nobody ever danced to the band! We were playing dance music, but Swing dancing had not caught on yet so we mostly played in jazz clubs and at community concerts.

Were you very surprised when Swing suddenly started becoming popular?

ERIC: I was quite pleased, of course. But, even when we first started out, it seemed like the audience always loved the music. In 1993 the Derby opened, and in early 1994 we hooked up with them and we started playing there regularly for dancers; we still appear at the Derby now and then.

Who would you say have been the most significant bands in making Swing popular in the 1990s?

ERIC: I'd say the Royal Crown Revue, Brian Setzer has had a big impact, and Big Bad Voodoo Daddy is very popular.

What are the main Swing clubs in L.A. today, in addition to the Derby?

Pianist-singer Eric Ekstrand's Ensemble is a popular attraction in the Los Angeles area.

ERIC: The Moonlight used to have Swing but they are closed now. The Coconut Grove is featuring Swing much less now than a year ago. So the Derby remains the main place in L.A.

Do you think Swing itself is still growing in popularity? Or is it fading away a little bit?

ERIC: It's hanging on in popularity, but it is not that lucrative for most venues even though it attracts a big crowd. A large part of the problem is that Swing dancers don't spend much money; they are there to dance rather than to drink.

What have been some of the high points of your band's existence so far?

ERIC: We played a concert at Northridge in front of 20,000 people. We played at the Orange County Fair for two weeks, but we got fired from there for doing songs that they considered too naughty! The Derby has always been good. Releasing our first record was exciting for us. I look forward to starting to record our next one soon.

Who have been some of your main musical inspirations as a pianist and as a singer?

ERIC: As a pianist my style has been affected by Hank Jones, Bill Evans, Earl Hines, great boogie-woogie players like Pete Johnson, and even to some extent by Jerry Lee Lewis. Overall Count Basie has always been a major influence for his effortless mastery of Swing. As a singer I love Joe Williams, Frank Sinatra, Ray Charles, and Wynonie Harris.

Is there anything you'd like to add about Swing or your future goals?

ERIC: This is my life goal, to do this and to keep my band going. I think much of jazz has lost the element of fun. I've seen great modern musicians perform who look like they haven't smiled since they were 12 years old. When people go out to a club, they want to have fun, so Swing helps bring joy and fun back to jazz.

A latecomer to Swing, singer Peggy Cone has been
a glamorous addition to the New York Retro Swing scene.

PEGGY CONE

Singer Peggy Cone was a latecomer to Retro Swing. As she discusses, she has had many careers throughout her episodic life and always loved Swing (dancing to the music for a decade), but she did not take the plunge and form a Swing band herself until 1998. However, in the short time since, she has been making a name for herself with her Central Park Stompers. The New York band has played quite often on the East Coast, and their 20-minute CD serves as a handy résumé of their talents and that of the highly appealing and energetic singer.

Tell me a little bit about your musical beginnings.

PEGGY: I grew up in Long Island and I've loved music since I was a little girl. When I was in junior high, I'd watch the old movies, Ginger Rogers and Fred Astaire, Busby Berkeley, learning the lyrics and trying to sing along with the words. I knew early on that I wanted to be a singer and a dancer, although that didn't happen for quite a few years. My stepdad, who was a painter, was very much into jazz and I would hear his Dizzy Gillespie, Thelonious Monk, Miles Davis, and Billie Holiday records. My mom was an actress, so I was always around the theater.

What were your earliest experiences singing?

PEGGY: My Mom was doing a show and they needed a kid, so I sang a song onstage when I was five or six. As a teenager, my first real boyfriend was a jazz pianist, and we put a little band together. But I didn't sing again for a long time.

What nonmusical jobs have you had throughout your life?

PEGGY: I have had several careers. I worked for a fashion magazine in 1971. I started a costume jewelry business when I was 22 that was quite successful for five or six years. Then I started a cooking school and became a caterer for private parties and weddings. After I got tired of the cooking career, I became an image fashion consultant and teacher, doing seminars. I also did personal shopping, helping people to reorganize their lives or their image. I have always been interested in photography and, after I switched careers again, I became a photographer of children for a time, but it was much more fun to do it as a hobby! And then I worked for Atlantic Records, shooting photos for their album jackets, helping musicians to look good, even dressing them. But I knew that what I really wanted was to be the one actually getting dressed and to be the person in the spotlight as opposed to being the one behind the camera. So ten years ago I quit my job and took voice lessons. I had my first gig in a funny variety show, and the first time that I sat on the piano with a microphone in my hand, I knew that I had found exactly what I wanted to do with my life.

Did it take you long before you were working regularly?

PEGGY: I was lucky because it didn't take long at all. I freelanced and then put together a trio with the help of bassist Andrew Hall, who has been with me since 1993. I was a real hustler and had a strong business sense and I made a lot of pitches and got gigs for us. One job led to another and we worked all over New York City doing standards. I recorded my first CD, *Peggy Cone Sings,* in which I chose tunes that I connected to and that were romantic.

Are you surprised that Swing became so popular in the 1990s?

PEGGY: Yes. I was Swing dancing as a hobby starting in the early 1990s for the fun of it. But then suddenly the college kids jumped on the Swing wagon and it became a huge business. I think maybe kids wanted to connect more and become more social in their dancing. The Swing movement has brought a lot of fun back into people's lives.

How did you happen to form your Swing band?

PEGGY: I was singing jazz for a long time with my trio, and I could kick myself for not forming my band a few years earlier. When the Swing thing really hit, I hooked into a great guitar player [Satoshi Inove], a couple of strong horn players [trumpeter Jon-Erik Kellso and Chris Creviston on tenor], had Mark McCarron write our arrangements, and I had a Swing group. The Central Park Stompers' debut was at Swing 46 on August 3, 1998. Chip Deffaa came to see me, wrote a nice piece on us for the *New York Post*, and that got us started.

What are some of the main Swing clubs in New York?

PEGGY: On Sunday nights there is the NY Swing Society's affairs at Irving Plaza. Windows of the World, the Supper Club, the 92nd Street Y, and, of course, Swing 46 are the most important places. The sound system's not the best at Swing 46, but it is a supper club that has Swing every night of the week.

Do you think Swing is still increasing in popularity? Or is it fading a bit?

PEGGY: Swing has been a trendy thing for the past two to three years, but recently it's been slowing down a little bit. However, I think it is now a force in the music industry. The Swing dance societies have been around for over ten years, before the Swing explosion happened, and I don't see them going away. Swing in the 1990s made a major mark in history and now many people want to go out and regularly Swing dance, and of course they need bands to play for them.

What have been some of the high points of your band's existence thus far?

PEGGY: The fact that we work all the time! I think the first time I heard my CD on the radio was a definite high point. The first Swing CD is much different than my previous recording, because the style is energetic, mostly upbeat, and quite danceable. Of course everyone tells me that my last CD was too short, but I wanted to get it out as soon as possible and show people what we can do. Our next CD, *Bad Girl Shoes,* will be coming out in 2000 and will be full length

What are your future musical goals?

PEGGY: I would definitely like to have the band visit the West Coast, go to Europe and Japan, and record more CDs. And I would love to sing with a big band someday. One thing that is different in our group is that we are very visual-oriented. I change outfits two, three, and even four times during an evening; we put on a show. I'm thrilled to be involved with Swing music. I'm doing what I wanted to do since I was five years old and I'm living my dreams.

THE ATOMIC FIREBALLS

4 *Birth of the Swerve / 1998 / Orbital Records*

5 *Torch This Place / 1999 / Atlantic 83167*

The Atomic Fireballs, a Detroit-based octet, is dominated by a singer (John Bunkley) whose raspy voice would make even Joe Cocker sound mellow! They made their debut on Valentine's Day in 1997, toured the East Coast (often being booked opposite rock bands), and put out *Birth of the Swerve* on their own private label. The band gained a certain amount of popularity and was soon signed by Atlantic, which hoped to jump on the Retro Swing bandwagon.

Birth of the Swerve has mostly originals that are quite forgettable; best is "Catfish Ball." The three horns and four-piece rhythm section are solid but very much in the background, getting few solos of any real length. In reality, despite the trappings, the Atomic Fireballs' music barely qualifies as Swing anyway, using the rhythms and feel of the Retro movement without getting beyond the show biz trappings. *Torch This Place*, which has better versions of six of the eight songs from the debut set (plus six newer tunes) is well recorded but basically in the same style, with the same faults. The few horn solos are not impressive, only a few of the songs stick in one's mind ("Swing Sweet Pussycat" was set to be used in a Warner Bros. movie), and the band is used primarily as a background for Bunkley's spirited but acquired-taste vocals.

BIG BAD VOODOO DADDY

8 *Big Bad Voodoo Daddy / 1994 / Big Bad Records 0069*

7 *Watcha' Want for Christmas? / 1996 / Big Bad Records 1108*

10 *Big Bad Voodoo Daddy / 1998 / EMI-Capitol 72434-93338*

From the time that they settled on their musical direction, Big Bad Voodoo Daddy was far ahead of most Retro Swing groups. Big Bad Voodoo Daddy (based in the Los Angeles area) was formed in 1991 by guitarist Scotty Morris with bassist-vocalist Russ Davis and drummer Kurt Sodergren and was originally a trio. Their early music was more rock-oriented, but things changed after Davis departed in 1993. Morris became the key singer, bassist Dirk Shumaker, trumpeter Ralph Votrian, and Andy Rowley (on baritone and tenor) expanded the band, and the music shifted toward jump music of the 1940s. By the time they recorded their first CD in 1994, the group's musicianship was impressive, their vocals were fun, and their relatively strong material immediately put this group near the top. In April 1995 they began playing once a week at the Derby in Hollywood. Glen Marhevka became their new trumpeter, and Jeff Harris was added on trombone, making the band a sextet.

Big Bad Voodoo Daddy has since then continued to grow in popularity, playing occasionally on local (and sometimes national) television and appearing as themselves in the 1996 movie *Swingers.* Joshua Levy joined on piano, and Karl Hunter became the band's tenor saxophonist as Andy Rowley concentrated on baritone. In early 1998 the group was signed by Capitol, and their self-titled CD for the label was so popular that it stayed for quite a while on Billboard's Top 100 charts. "You and Me and the Bottle Makes Three" (their most popular song) was even made into a video, and Big Bad Voodoo Daddy has succeeded in becoming better known than Royal Crown Revue, their original inspiration.

The band's self-titled debut album from 1994 has such catchy numbers as "Jumpin' Jack," the haunting "King of Swing" (not a Benny Goodman tribute), "She's Gone," and the rambunctious "So Long, Goodbye" among the better tracks, but all nine numbers have their moments. In addition to the quintet lineup of the time, trombonist Stan Middleton and clarinetist Bob Ayers are prominent guests. The music is full of humor and wit, the feel of both Swing and rockabilly, and lots of exuberant spirit. *Watcha' Want for Christmas?* is a bit brief, consisting of only six songs. But the band had clearly improved with the addition of trumpeter Marhevka and trombonist Harris. Morris wrote four of the six numbers (including "Rock-a-Billy X-Mas" and "Christmas Time in Tinsel Town Again") and, of the other two songs, "Zat You Santa Claus?" works quite well.

But it is Big Bad Voodoo Daddy's Capitol CD that is most essential. In fact, this is one of the best all-round recordings of any Retro Swing band of the 1990s. The tunes (some of which had been heard in earlier versions in the band's 1994 CD) are colorful and memorable, the band's musicianship had gotten better, and the arrangements are excellent. Scott Morris's vocalizing and guitar solos were very key parts of the band's success, as were the brief but hot horn solos,

DON MILLER

Big Bad Voodoo Daddy's catchy songs and special brand of humor have long made them a standout in Retro Swing.

while pianist Joshua Levy (who adds a Jerry Lee Lewis flair to the ensembles) was a very welcome addition. The vocals are full of humor, the horns constantly riff, and Big Bad Voodoo Daddy shows that it is possible to be both creative and humorous (occasionally self-satirical) within the new genre. Among the highlights are "King of Swing," "You and Me and the Bottle Makes Three Tonight," "Jump with My Baby," the rockin' "Go Daddy-O," "Jumpin' Jack," and "So Long—Farewell—Goodbye."

BLUE PLATE SPECIAL

7 *A Night Out with . . . Blue Plate Special / 1998 / Slimstyle 78013*

Blue Plate Special (from Northern California) has been a regular fixture in Swing clubs in San Francisco and Hollywood since the mid-1990s. Essentially a hot Swing/jump band whose style could very well have been heard in 1945, the group (consisting of trumpeter Phil Topping, Michael Newman on tenor, Nathan Dreyfus doubling on baritone and alto, guitarist Randall Keith, pianist Ken Charlson,

bassist Todd Clark, drummer Adam Bankhead, and singer Anthony Marchesi) at times seems reminiscent of the popular combo that Illinois Jacquet led, particularly on their instrumentals.

Blue Plate Special's debut recording for Slimstyle has catchy vocals by the sweet-toned Marchesi, fine solos from Newman's tenor and baritonist Dreyfus, and a repertoire that includes originals plus Buster Harding's "The Hornet" (one of two instrumentals), "Evening," and "Opus One." There is plenty of variety in the music, and "Work That Skirt" (one of several uptempo tunes) could act as a theme song for the entire Retro Swing movement. There are also a couple throwaways (including "A Night in Havana" and the corny "Tango of Sorrow"), but in general this is a rewarding release with plenty of fine moments from the cooking band.

THE BLUE SARACENS

7 *What's a Saracen? / Oct. 1998 / Swing 46*

An East Coast Swing nonet, the Blue Saracens are led by drummer Jim Petropoulos and perform often in New York.

Petropoulos, who is an animator by day and had been playing drums for 25 years, formed the group in 1997. Best known among the sidemen is Mike Hashim (heard on alto and tenor), who had previously recorded for Stash and worked extensively with the Widespread Depression Jazz Orchestra. Also featured in the band are singer Nicole Frydman, trumpeter George Petropoulos, trombonist Brad Schmidt, clarinetist Jack O'Connell, pianist Raphael D'Lugoff, and bassist Chris Carmeann.

The Blue Saracens' debut CD is quite fun, with songs taken from Gene Krupa ("Drum Boogie"), the Benny Goodman Sextet ("Till Tom Special"), Red Allen ("The Crawl"), and even Dizzy Gillespie ("He Beeped When He Shoulda Bopped" and "Oop Bop Sh'Bam"), among others. The solos are spirited, Frydman's singing is pleasing and energetic, and the jazz-oriented band has a happy group sound.

BLUES JUMPERS

8 *Wheels Start Turning / 1997 / Ridge Recordings 58672*
The Blues Jumpers are a fine party band that sounds mostly as if it came from 1952. In 1997 the New Jersey-based group gained attention for their debut recording, *Wheels Start Turning,* which a year later was followed by *Swingin' Holiday* (National Music). Drummer Joe Geary founded the band shortly before their first CD and continues leading the Blues Jumpers, although most of the personnel has since changed. *Wheels Start Turning* has Geary joined by singer Eldridge Taylor, guitarist Mike Girao, bassist Joe D'Astolfo, altoist Matt Hong, Jim Jedeikin on tenor, guest pianist Mike Bank, and sometimes trumpeter Doug Oberhamer. However, by 1999 the nucleus of the group was Geary, guitarist Billy Roues, and bassist Steven Roues, with various horn players. Voice problems by then had forced Taylor to drop out of the band, and his place was taken by singer-songwriter Haywood Gregory.

Wheels Start Turning is a particularly fun set. Although his voice is obviously different, Eldridge Taylor on this 1997 recording is clearly influenced by Louis Jordan's approach, as one can hear on such humorous and ironic titles as "Jim Beam," "Chicken Wing," "Too Lazy to Work," and a classic version of "Good Morning Judge." There are a few standards ("Thanks for the Boogie Ride," the catchy "Chartreuse," "Ball of Fire," and "Baby I'm Gone" among them)

mixed in with the originals, and the appeal of Taylor's voice on the swinging novelties grows the more one listens to him. The band (which ranges from a quintet to a septet) has plenty of short solos, and the Blues Jumpers' happy CD is well worth picking up.

SHELLEY BURNS AND AVALON SWING

6 *S' Wonderful / 1994–1995 / Avalon Swing Records*
7 *You're Driving Me Crazy / 1997 / Big Swing 124*
Although middle-aged, Shelley Burns sings and performs with a great deal of energy, never being shy to point fun at herself while clearly enjoying singing Swing standards. Her Avalon Swing group consists of Wayne Johnson on alto and occasional piano, Tom Phillips on guitar, mandolin, and harmony vocals, Erik Kleven on bass and tuba, drummer Steve Coughran (who also plays French horn and contributes backup vocals), and occasional guest trombonist Phil Tulga. Burns and Avalon Swing appear now and then at Swing dance clubs and at classic jazz festivals on the West Coast.

Shelly Burns's first two releases are both enjoyable. With the exception of the original "Daddy You Squeeze Me" and the campy "Hernando's Hideaway," the music on *S' Wonderful* consists of standards. Burns sometimes uses a touch too much vibrato and she is not a virtuoso singer, but she certainly has fun with the music and her spirited band is excellent. The material is slightly stronger on *You're Driving Me Crazy,* which is highlighted by such tunes as "Is You Is or Is You Ain't My Baby," "Comes Love," "I Can't Believe That You're in Love with Me," and "Anything Goes."

CHERRY POPPIN' DADDIES

2 *Zoot Suit Riot / 1990–1997 / Mojo 53081*
If one wanted to come up with a whipping boy for the Retro Swing movement, the Cherry Poppin' Daddies would fit the bill quite well. Formed in Eugene, Oregon, the group originally played ska but latched onto the Swing movement around 1990. If one hears the Cherry Poppin' Daddies casually, it sounds passable; but a closer listen reveals that the rhythm section has difficulty swinging, the vocals are often

profane, and the band merely plays at Swing rather than learning much about the music. The Daddies sound as if they are a punk rock band who has chosen to masquerade as Swing, at least until a better fad comes along. At the 1999 Playboy Jazz Festival in Hollywood, singer Steve Perry seemed very much like a cartoon character, dancing with phony sensuality on stage (which seemed like an unknowing self-parody) and mumbling the lyrics; it seemed as if the only words that could be heard were profanity!

Zoot Suit Riot, a strong-selling single-CD sampler, draws its material from the group's earlier days (1990, 1994, and 1996) and adds four previously unreleased selections from 1997. The set gives one an idea as to the eclectic and very erratic nature of the Cherry Poppin' Daddies. Steve Perry's vocals range from mildly charming to quite obscene (particularly "Drunk Daddy" and "No Mercy for Swine"). The words, although supposedly dealing with social issues, are not intelligent or creative enough to do anything other than paint a sordid picture, and the band (a mediocre septet augmented by many guest musicians) is used primarily as a prop; only trumpeter Dana Heitman shows any promise of being a good soloist. Many of the arrangements hint in one place or another at "Sing, Sing, Sing," and the overall effect is odd, with a lot of posturing plus an eccentric version of the one standard ("Come Back to Me"). The music, although excitable in spots, usually comes dangerously close to camp, making this a band to avoid!

CHEVALIER BROTHERS

8 *Live and Still Jumping / 1985 / Westside 816*
Back when the Chevalier Brothers were together (1982–88), their brand of Swing music (which predated the Retro Swing movement) must have seemed both anachronistic and futuristic. A great party band from England, the Chevalier brothers mixed Swing with bebop, Jump, and early rock and roll, playing with a great deal of energy. The band was at first a trio with Ray Gelato (an Illinois Jacquet–inspired tenor saxophonist who was also the group's main singer), a guitarist who went by the name of Maurice Chevalier and sounded quite a bit like Charlie Christian, and a bassist. By the end of 1982 vibraphonist Roger Beaujolais was in the group, and in 1983 bassist Clark Kent and drummer John Piper joined. The quintet began to work quite regularly in England and by 1984 was playing at rock and jazz clubs plus festivals throughout Europe. The band played between 150

and 200 gigs a year at its peak and in 1985 recorded *Live and Jumping.* When Maurice Chevalier departed in 1986, the Chevalier Brothers used a pianist for its final two years, a time when the group recorded two studio albums for their Disques Cheval label. Since breaking up in 1988, the players have all continued their musical careers, with Ray Gelato forming the Swing band The Ray Gelato Giants, which has included Clark Kent in its personnel since its beginning.

The CD *Live and Still Jumping* reissues all of *Live and Jumping* and adds seven other selections from the period (mostly from the same gigs). It is certainly full of spirit and sometimes borders on the hilarious, particularly "Open the Door, Richard" (which tells the full story of why Richard may not have opened the door!). Much of the material is from the Louis Jordan songbook (including "Five Guys Named Moe," "Reet, Petite and Gone," and "I Like 'Em Fat Like That"), with Gelato as the main vocalist and some fine instrumentals (such as "Air Mail Special" and "Jumpin' at the Jubilee") included among the 17 numbers. The results are derivative but quite fun, the audience heard on these selections was definitely quite drunk, and the Chevalier Brothers proved to be a highly entertaining, frequently riotous, and witty ensemble.

PEGGY CONE

8 *And the Central Park Stompers / Sept. 15, 1998 / (private label)*
Peggy Cone has had many careers throughout her life: working for a fashion magazine, starting a successful costume jewelry business, having a catering business, and being an image fashion consultant, a children's photographer, and a photo stylist for Atlantic Records. However, it was in 1989 that she found her true calling as a jazz singer. She spent the next nine years singing vintage standards in the New York area, leading a regular trio since 1993. In 1998 Cone, a longtime fan of Swing, decided to form her own Swing band, the Central Park Stompers, adding a guitar and two horns to form a jumping sextet. She has since performed up and down the East Coast, putting on a visual show that finds her changing costumes often and dancing in addition to singing and cheering on her sidemen.

The first release by Cone's Swing band has six hot numbers played by her band. Most notable among her sidemen is trumpeter Jon-Erik Kellso, but the other players (tenor saxophonist Chris Creviston, guitarist Satoshi Inoue, pianist Michael Kanan, bassist Andrew Hall, and drummer Stefan Schatz) are also excellent. Cone's vocals are joyous and swinging, and she is generous in allocating solo space to her sidemen. The only problem with the date (which has jumping versions of "Flip Flop and Fly," "This Can't Be Love," Wynona Carr's "Till the Well Runs Dry," " 'Deed I Do," "When You're Smiling," and "Daddy") is its brevity, just 20 minutes. But even so, the CD will be desired by Swing fans, for the music is full of excitement, both vocally and instrumentally.

CRESCENT CITY MAULERS

7 *Screamin' / 1997 / Slimstyle 27*
The Crescent City Maulers were formed in New Jersey by bassist Chris Carmean. Carmean, who had played tuba in a Dixieland band in high school and later bass in a rockabilly group, first wanted to start a Swing band in 1982. However, he did not get his chance until 1994, when he started teaming up with tenor saxophonist Tony Salimbene, guitarist Al Sagnella, and drummer Lenny Zaccaro as the Crescent City Maulers. Their group, which works regularly in New Jersey dance halls, has plenty of energy and a terrific drive, often performing heated versions of Louis Jordan songs and jumping originals.

Although a smaller-than-usual Swing combo, the Crescent City Maulers on their debut CD show that they can rock as hard as any of their competitors. The music (which has vocals from each of the musicians except drummer Zaccaro) includes a variety of Louis Jordan material (such as "Reet, Petite and Gone," "Caldonia," and "Barnyard Boogie"), the novelty "Good Morning Judge," and a few instrumentals. The only problem with this spirited CD is that the 14 selections all clock in at less than 3½ minutes apiece and the total time is around 37 minutes, which is rather brief. But what is here is enjoyable and gives listeners a good example of what it must be like to hear the Crescent City Maulers performing live.

CHRIS DANIELS AND THE KINGS

9 *Louie Louie / Mar. 1998 / Moon Voyage 77624*
Back in 1983, singer Chris Daniels was part of the backup band being used for Russell Smith's Boy Next Door tour. It was decided that it might be fun to put together a horn section to play some jump and R&B music. Very soon Daniels and the horns had broken away to form the R&B Kings. The R&B Kings worked steadily, toured the U.S. and Europe many times, and recorded six albums that are mostly in the R&B genre. In 1998 the group (simply called The Kings for the project) paid tribute to three renowned performers named Louis—Jordan, Armstrong, and Prima—in a strong Swing-oriented set.

Oddly enough the personnel listing on *Louie Louie,* which lists in detail the many guest artists, does not tell which instruments the seven principal musicians play! One assumes that Daniels is the main singer and that Forrest Means is on trumpet, but the instruments of Randy Amen, Bones Jones, Dean Ledoux, Carlos Chavez, and Kevin Lege can only be guessed at by those who have not seen the band live. Despite that fault, this is a very enjoyable set full of rocking tunes that place the accent mostly on Louis Jordan. Armstrong is saluted with a Dixielandish "Shine" and "I'll Be Glad When You're Dead, You Rascal You," while Louis Prima is almost completely neglected. Among the more significant guests (which include some horn players) are Sam Bush on violin and mandolin and Mollie O'Brien, Hazel Miller, and Kelly Bates on harmony vocals. Of the 11 mostly heated selections, best are "If You're So Smart, How Come You're Not Rich?," "Azure-Te," "Choo-Choo Ch'Boogie," "Chartreuse," and "Shine." One of the best Retro Swing releases of the past couple of years.

THE DELEGATES

8 *Delegatin' / Nov. 1998–Dec. 1998 / No label or catalog number*
In 1997 Jim Greene (who sings quite effectively while playing string bass) and tenor saxophonist Neal Sugarman formed the Delegates, a particularly strong jazz-oriented quintet also including trumpeter Jeff McSpadden (formerly with the Blues Jumpers), guitarist Coleman Mellett, and drummer Matthew Jorgensen. The Delegates soon became a fixture at New York Swing clubs, and they have since toured the East Coast several times. Their repertoire includes Swing standards, obscurities (including from Buddy Johnson and T-Bone Walker), and originals in the swinging tradition. What sets this group apart from many others in the Retro Swing movement is their high musicianship and strong soloists, particularly Sugarman (inspired by Illinois Jacquet and Arnett Cobb), the versatile McSpadden, and the colorful Mellett.

Delegatin' is The Delegates first recording, and it should appeal not only to dancers and followers of the current movement but to regular jazz listeners. Greene's vocals and the many fine group originals (five by the singer) give the band its own personality, as does the lack of a piano, which results in the ensemble's often having a sparse sound. Highlights of the spirited and tight set (which features many explosive short solos) include "Travelin' Time," "Ain't You Got Me Where You Want Me," and "Tell Me What's the Reason."

8½ SOUVENIRS

7 *Happy Feet / 1998 / RCA 63226*

8½ Souvenirs (named after the Fellini film and the Django Reinhardt song "Souvenirs") certainly stands apart from the other bands grouped under Retro Swing. The quintet features singing (mostly in French but also sometimes in English, Spanish, and Italian) from Chrysta Bell and Olivier Giraud, the Django-style electric guitar of Giraud, and unpredictable but swinging support from pianist Glover Gill (who sometimes gets a bit outside), bassist Kevin Smith, and drummer Adam Berlin. What is particularly odd is that all of the musicians but Giraud are American and the band is based in Austin, Texas!

Giraud began playing guitar in France when he was 12, and he was largely self-taught. He was influenced early on by French music, punk rock, and rockabilly. After a period of struggle, he began playing music professionally in 1981. In 1988 he got in a car accident with his 1954 Oldsmobile Rocket 88 and went to Austin, Texas, to get rare parts for his prized auto. Giraud immediately loved the city and spontaneously decided to move. He worked in and out of music for a few years (including with the rockabilly group 47 Indians) and then formed 8½ Souvenirs in 1993, putting together an odd mixture of songs from France and the U.S. plus the influence of French singer Serge Gainsbourg, Italian film composer Nino Rota, and 1930s jazz. The band played at a Texas bar (The Continental) regularly for three years and has since had opportunities to tour the West Coast.

8½ Souvenirs has recorded a few albums, of which *Happy Feet* is the most widely available. In addition to group originals, the band plays "It's All Right with Me," "After You've Gone," "Brazil," three Django Reinhardt songs, and a few European obscurities. The singing in French, Italian, Spanish, and English by Giraud and Bell (who was 20 at the time) will take some getting used to (sometimes Giraud also talks his lyrics). But the leader's guitar playing, Gill's adventurous piano solos, and the general joy of the unique group make this set of interest to open-minded listeners.

ERIC EKSTRAND

10 *Spiked Heel Stomp / 1998 / Roller Coasters 1041*

Eric Ekstrand, who was born in New York and grew up in New Jersey, is the son of a studio musician (Ray Ekstrand) who played in the sax sections of many top Swing-era big bands. Eric played several instruments as a youth but settled on piano. Ekstrand moved to Las Vegas in 1969 and at 21 was working in backup bands behind major entertainment figures. He had a busy career as a recording engineer and wrote arrangements for many of the artists who played in Vegas (including Fats Domino, B. B. King, and Paul Anka). In time Ekstrand moved to Los Angeles in order to write scores for films. His first love was Swing, and in 1992 he formed the Eric Ekstrand Ensemble in order to play standards and (most importantly) new compositions in the Swing, jump, and early rock and roll styles. His band has since been a regular fixture at the Derby, recorded one CD for the Roller Coaster label, and appeared at special concerts. Eric Ekstrand is married to pianist Arlette McCoy (the widow of bassist Monty Budwig).

Spiked Heel Stomp, a very strong release, has 11 selections, seven of which are consistently catchy Ekstrand originals. Among the highlights are his colorful "Murder at the Cotton Club" (which has Cab Calloway as one of the characters), "Nag, Nag, Nag," "Bright Red Lipstick," "Evil Eye," and the instrumental "Bandstand Boogie." The musicianship of the 12-piece band (which does not include any big names) is impressive, and Ekstrand's arrangements leave plenty of space for short solos from his sidemen (11 have spots, while the pianist is featured on "Spiked Heel Stomp"). Ekstrand's vocals are a strong asset, including on the cover version of Louis Prima's "Oh Babe," a fun number that always seems to work no matter who records it! The Eric Ekstrand Ensemble deserves much greater recognition.

BILL ELLIOTT

8 *Calling All Jitterbugs / 1996–1997 / Wayland 002*

9 *Swingin' the Century / 1997–1998 / Wayland 003*

A top arranger for the studios and movies, pianist Bill Elliott has really come into his own as the leader of a big band based in Los Angeles. Unlike many of the other groups covered in this Retro Swing section, Bill Elliott's Swing Orchestra really is a big band (rather than a combo), and it focuses on the style of the Swing era rather than its later developments. Elliott, who wrote songs and arrangements for such movies as *Nixon, Independence Day,* and *Dick Tracy* (and appears with his band in the Disney television movie *Tower of Terror*) does not merely recreate Swing-era hits but writes new songs in the older style. His band has been a regular at Merv Griffin's Coconut Grove in Los Angeles.

The Bill Elliott Swing Orchestra sounds like a newly discovered big band from 1940. Its musicianship is impeccable, the solos fit the era, and the arrangements swing up a storm without copying the past. *Calling All Jitterbugs,* the big band's second recording (following 1994's *Swing Fever*) has some fine solo work from tenor saxophonist Roger Neumann (himself a notable arranger), trumpeter Don Clarke, and various trombonists and altoists. In addition, eight of the ten big band tracks (all but "On the Atchison, Topeka and the Santa Fe" were composed by Elliott) have vocals, mostly from the four-voice Lucky Stars, who sometimes recall Glenn Miller's Modernaires. *Calling All Jitterbugs* concludes with four very different selections, 1920s-style music with a slightly different band that Elliott recorded for use in movies. These period pieces (which include a solo piano number, probably played by Frederick Hodges, and vocals that recall Bing Crosby and Louis Armstrong) are pleasing and authentic.

Swingin' the Century finds the Bill Elliott Swing Orchestra continuing in the same vein, with strong material, a swinging rhythm section, and sounding quite original within the Swing genre. There are solos from trumpeter Clarke and Neumann on tenor, plus spots for clarinetists Bob Reitemeier and Don Shelton, Jeff Driskill on tenor, and trombonist Charlie Morillas, among others. Ten songs are Elliott originals (some of which deserve to be adopted by other bands), while the five standards are based loosely on earlier records: "Blues in the Night" (Johnny Mercer), "Somebody Loves Me" (Tommy Dorsey), "Lady Be Good" (Artie Shaw), "Come Rain or Come Shine" (Frank Sinatra), and "Jeep Jockey Jump" (Glenn Miller's Army Air Force Band). The Lucky Stars are back, with Cassie Miller being the main featured vocalist, but the emphasis is on the swinging ensembles. Perfect for jitterbug parties!

FLATTOP TOM AND HIS JUMP CATS

8 *Swing Dance Party / 1998 / Palamar 6178*

The Jump Cats is an L.A.-based band that is flexible enough to play Retro Swing, electric blues, jump blues, '40s and '50s R&B, and vintage Swing. Formed in 1992 by Tom Hall (aka Flattop Tom), the band has been a popular attraction in the Los Angeles area ever since and in recent times has toured throughout the U.S., Canada, and Europe. What is most unusual about the outfit is that Flattop Tom (the chief vocalist, who is also a professional Swing dancer) plays effective blues harmonica, so this band is as comfortable at blues festivals as it is at Swing dances.

The Jump Cats' third release (following *Jumpin' Blues for Your Dancing Shoes* and *Rockin' & Jumpin' the Blues*) has a large dose of blues, although there are also a few exceptions, such as "Lester Leaps In," plus some songs ("Why Don't You Do Right," which has a guest vocal from Tina Stevens, and "Wholly Cats") that are straight from Swing. The leader (who wrote ten of the 17 tunes) is joined by guitarist Bob Robles (who ranges in style from Tiny Grimes to Chuck Berry), pianist Taryn Donath, bassist Jotty Johnson, drummer Bruce King, Bill Lucas on tenor (who is properly raspy), baritonist Steve Solomon, and trumpeter George Pandis. The horns are decent soloists and particularly strong at riffing behind the vocals and each other's playing. Flattop Tom and His Jump Cats create fun and danceable music that crosses many genres.

FLIPPED FEDORAS

6 *Nick Palumbo & the Flipped Fedora Orchestra / 1997 / Bigtown Music*

Singer-guitarist Nick Palumbo put together one of the first Retro Swing bands in New York, forming the Flipped Fedoras in 1995. He had begun performing in clubs when he was eight, playing guitar in his father's band. After growing up,

Palumbo played a wide variety of jobs, including in blues, rock, country, and rockabilly bands. He was a member of singer Peter Hofmann's group in Germany for four years. After returning to the U.S., Palumbo decided to play the music that most interested him, Swing. Along with the Flying Neutrinos and Beat Positive, Palumbo's Flipped Fedoras helped to form a Swing scene in New York City, with his group playing regularly on Monday nights at the Louisiana Bar & Grill.

The music on the Flipped Fedoras' CD is comprised mostly of blues (with a few exceptions) and could easily be described as early rock and roll with touches of Swing. The four horns (trumpeter Tom Russo, trombonist Rob Susman, altoist Mike Hashiem, and Tom Murray on tenor) are fine and have some short spots, but the main focus is on Palumbo's pleasant singing and occasional guitar solos. The tunes are primarily his originals, with the exception of "Sing, Sing, Sing," which looks toward both the Benny Goodman and the Louis Prima versions. But in general nothing all that original or memorable occurs, making one wish that Palumbo would go outside of his band for more inventive material and arrangements. There is potential here.

GEORGE GEE

7 *Swingin' Live! / Jan. 26, 1997 / Swing 46 001*

7 *Buddha Boogie / Apr. 14–15, 1999 / Swing 46 003*
As a student at Carnegie Mellon University in Pittsburgh in the late 1970s, George Gee convinced the college radio station (WRCT) to let him host a regular radio program that he called *The Make-Believe Ballroom,* after Martin Block's famous series of the 1930s/'40s. In 1979 he put together a big band that was originally comprised of college students, and within a few years it turned professional. The Make-Believe Ballroom Orchestra played regularly in the Pittsburgh area during the 1980s and occasionally in New York, most notably for the Sunday get-togethers of the New York Dance Society. In 1989 Gee moved back to his native New York City, and his big band has since become a fixture on the Swing scene. After Gee (who is the band's frontman but does not play an instrument himself) became a member of the staff of Swing 46 Jazz & Supper Club, his Make-Believe Ballroom Orchestra had a home base, appearing each Thursday night and occasionally at other times. In 1998 Gee put together a tentet drawn out of his big band's personnel to play additional engagements as the Jump, Jive and Wailers.

Swingin' Live, by the Make-Believe Ballroom Orchestra, finds the ensemble sounding very close to Count Basie's big band of the 1950s and '60s. The music grooves, the soloists (which include trumpeter Irv Stokes, trombonist Eddie Bert, and tenor saxophonist Lance Bryant, among many others) sound fine in the modern Swing tradition, and Carla Cook takes vocals on "Let the Good Times Roll" and "Here's That Rainy Day." The orchestra really does not have its own sound, and the repertoire (which, in addition to such Basie-associated tunes as "Blues for Stephanie," "April in Paris," and "Shiny Stockings" plus a few warhorses, includes Lance Bryant's "Wailin' Gaylen" and a couple of lesser-known Frank Foster tunes) lacks any surprises, but the music is danceable and swinging.

Buddha Boogie, from the Jump, Jive and Wailers, benefits greatly from the inclusion of four Lance Bryant originals (including the catchy "She's Never Satisfied") and the fresh arrangements of Bryant and trumpeter Walt Szymanski, who are also the two main vocalists; Carla Cook helps out Szymanski on "You're the Boss." Of the remaining material, "Hamp's Boogie" has plenty of spirit, even if it is predictable, and there are fine versions of "Everyday I Have the Blues" (which is not, as mistakenly listed, a Lightnin' Hopkins composition!), "720 in the Books," "Basie Boogie" (featuring pianist Rick Germanson), and "Well Git It." Among the other soloists are trumpeter Steve Wiseman, altoist Ed Pazant (doubling on clarinet), and trombonist Charles Stephens. This would be a fun group to see live, as would George Gee's big band.

RAY GELATO

9 *The Full Flavour / Jan. 13–14, 1995 / Linn 034*

8 *The Men from Uncle / 1998 / Double Scoop 8477*
Ray Gelato was an important member of the Chevalier Brothers, a popular British jump band during 1982–88, contributing tenor solos in the style of Illinois Jacquet and Charlie Ventura along with the majority of the vocals. Gelato, who had not started playing tenor until he was 17, was mostly self-taught and played rock and roll with Dynamite during 1980–81. After the Chevalier Brothers broke up, he formed his own group (the Giants of Jive), which for a long time included two other members of the Chevaliers (bassist

Clark Kent and drummer John Piper) plus several horn players. After three albums and many performances, in 1994 Gelato decided to change direction slightly (away from jump music and toward 1950s musical icons such as Nat King Cole, Sinatra, Dean Martin, and particularly Louis Prima), renaming his group The Ray Gelato Giants. Due to the leader's vocals and stomping tenor, the shuffle rhythms, and the fine trumpet solos of Dave Priseman, the Giants are often quite reminiscent of Prima's mid-'50s band, although it is versatile enough to also include heated Swing, touches of bebop, and middle-of-the-road pop vocalizing. The Giants have gradually grown in popularity since the mid-1990s, touring Europe and Canada and recording for the Linn and Double Scoop labels.

The Full Flavour, the debut record by the Giants, finds the septet (with Gelato, trumpeter Priseman, trombonist Dave Keech, Al Nicholls on tenor and alto, pianist Richard Busiakiewicz, bassist Clark Kent, and drummer John Piper) excelling at everything they try. The music includes some Prima (most notably "That Old Black Magic" and a medley of "Basin Street Blues" and "Sleepy Time Down South"), Charlie Ventura ("Dark Eyes"), Dean Martin ("That's Amore"), Nat King Cole, and heated Swing ("Apple Honey"). In addition, there are two vocals by Claire Martin (who sounds perfectly at home in this context) and a rare up-tempo version of "As Time Goes By." Highly recommended.

The Men from Uncle finds Ray Gelato sounding remarkably close to Louis Prima in spots, most notably on "Josephine" and a medley of "Angelina" and "Zooma Zooma." But he also closely emulates Nat King Cole on "I've Got a Way with Women" and "L-O-V-E," bases his version of "Umbrella Man" on Dizzy Gillespie's, and does a credible interpretation of "Moody's Mood For Love." There are also fine solos from Gelato, trumpeter Enrico Tomasso (showcased on "Stardust"), altoist Alex Garnett, trombonist Andy Baker, and pianist Richard Busiakiewicz. One of the best British Retro Swing groups of the 1990s.

HIPSTER DADDY-O AND THE HANDGRENADES

2 *Armed and Swinging* / 1997 / Slimstyle Thin 26
Hipster Daddy-O and the Handgrenades come to Swing from the rock world. In fact, much of their music really falls into the area of rock, with touches of ska and rockabilly. Formed in 1997 and based in Arizona, the band (which has played mostly in the Southwest) features primarily the vocals of Eric Allen and Mike Edward, Edward's heavy metal guitar, and riffing from their three horns.

The Handgrenades has all of the Retro Swing trappings: a silly name and the right "hip" outfits (including hats); they probably look colorful on stage. But the music on *Armed and Swinging* is remarkably weak. The band (a sextet with three horns) does very little except back the spirited but inflexible vocalists, the arrangements are dull, and nothing much happens except a lot of posing. Sorry to say, this is the type of frivolous recording that makes Retro Swing easy to satirize. And why does a group that sounds like a 1980s punk rock band with horns dress like the 1940s?

INDIGO SWING

7 *All Aboard!* / 1995 / Time Bomb 43517

6 *Red Light!* / 1998 / Time Bomb 43528
A fan of Frank Sinatra and Bing Crosby and quite impressed after seeing a show by Royal Crown Revue, in 1993 Johnny Boyd formed Indigo Swing, a fine San Francisco sextet comprised of vocalist Boyd, Baron Shul on tenor and baritone, pianist William Beatty, guitarist Josh Workman, bassist Vance Ehlers, and drummer Jim Overton. Boyd's vocals are relaxed and friendly, Shul contributes some fiery tenor now and then, and the rhythm section swings in a fine Retro fashion, ranging from late-period Swing to early rock and roll. The group (which makes strong use of dynamics and space) currently plays up to 300 dates a year and has toured the U.S. several times while remaining based in San Francisco and Los Angeles. Indigo Swing features many originals in the Swing style (principally by Boyd and Beatty), has a definite charm, and is equally skilled on relaxed ballads and heated stomps.

The band's debut, *All Aboard!,* finds the sextet performing everything from spirited blues ("So Long") and Willie Dixon's "Violent Love" (which sounds too gentle for its title!) to the heated instrumentals "Hot in Harlem," "Regular Joe" (which has the horn section from Bill Elliott's band helping out), "That's Where My Money Goes" (based on "It Don't Mean a Thing"), and "The Indigo Swing." Boyd is particularly adept at singing blues ballads (à la Charles Brown) such as "Memory of You." The strong musicianship and excellent original material make this an excellent acquisition for Swing fans who want to hear a more intimate group than usual.

The same sextet is heard on *Red Light!,* with nearly all of the songs written by Johnny Boyd and/or William Beatty; the latter is showcased on "Hot Pot Boogie." The lyrics are upbeat, the rhythms are light but swinging, and there are plenty of short solos by pianist Beatty and Baron Shul on his reeds (which in this case include tenor, baritone, alto, and flute). However, some of the songs lean closer to rock and roll (such as "Pop's at the Hop"), pop, or even country ("They Say I Must Be Crazy") than Swing, and there is a greater emphasis on vocals (Beatty and guitarist Josh Workman help Boyd out). Overall the set is reasonably enjoyable but not up to the same level (particularly from the Swing perspective) as its predecessor.

JET SET SIX

3 *Livin' It Up* / 1998 / Mutiny 60023 80020
Singer-guitarist John Ceparano's musical roots are in punk rock, and he had played with quite a few groups in that idiom before forming an experimental trio in the late 1980s called Beat Positive. After personnel changes and expansion to a sextet (with trumpeter Steve Gluzband, Jim Jedeikin on tenor, trombonist Walter Hawkes, bassist Joseph Pelletier, and drummer David Berger), the New York-based group was reborn in the mid-1990s as Jet Set Six. The band often still sounds like a rock group, and its strongest asset is singer Ceparano, who is sometimes joined by the harmonized singing of Pelletier and Berger.

Livin' It Up has an album jacket that makes it look like a Columbia album from the early 1960s. However, the band's connection to Swing or even to Frank Sinatra is rather slight. All of the songs are basically features for vocalist Ceparano (who wrote all but two of the 11 numbers), and the other musicians actually have little to do but riff in the background. There are short solos for the three horns (most of whom play too modern for the idiom), but they are used primarily for window dressing and slight departures from the singing. Ceparano does have a good voice and some of the song titles (including "The Dame That Knotted My Rope," "My Torrid Heart," and "The Perpetual Bachelor") are intriguing, but the music for these new pop-oriented tunes is consistently forgettable. If Ceparano interpreted better tunes and let his band cut loose more, he could probably create some worthwhile Retro Swing rather than just a set that serves as a pleasant diversion.

STEVE LUCKY AND THE RHUMBA BUMS

9 *Come Out Swingin'* / 1998 / Rumpus Records 65902
Pianist Steve Lucky and singer-guitarist Carmen Getit (Patsy Smith) are the main stars of this hard-swinging band from San Francisco, a group that specializes in late 1940s jump jazz and blues. Lucky was born in Seattle and raised near Detroit. He led the Blue Front Persuaders (a 1980s Swing band) while attending the University of Michigan in Ann Arbor. In 1987 Lucky moved to New York, where he worked with bluesman Johnny Copeland and freelanced for five years. In 1993 he relocated to the San Francisco Bay Area and organized the Rhumba Bums, which was originally a quintet. Guitarist Getit (a strong soloist who considers T-Bone Walker to be her main influence) joined in 1994, and the band's original personality was formed. The vocal interplay between Lucky and Getit is humorous and colorful, both are excellent soloists, and the Rhumba Bums always feature at least a couple of stomping saxophonists. Lucky, who has also appeared on recordings with John Hammond, Mark Hummel, Sista Monica, and other blues players, works regularly with his popular Rhumba Bums in the San Francisco area.

Come Out Swingin' is an exciting disc that never lets up. Steve Lucky and Carmen Getit happily share the vocals and are the main soloists, but there are also many hot solos from tenors Peter Cornell and Rob Sudduth (both of whom are also heard from on baritone and alto), plus occasional solos from tenors Jules Broussard, Sean Hiemstra, and Scott Peterson. Bassist Neal Heidler and Bam Bam Barry or Bowen Brown on drums are steady in support. The selections (which include Lucky's "Jumptown," T-Bone Walker's "Bye Bye Baby," "Rumpus Room Honeymoon," "Wall to Wall Sax," "Down Boy," and "Hoopty-Do") are full of drive and infectious Swing. One can certainly tell that the musicians love and respect this spirited music.

MAGNUM BRUTES

8 *Meet the Magnum Brutes* / 1999 / Brute Force Records
The Magnum Brutes (great name!) is comprised of the talented singer Connie Champagne, vibraphonist Michael

Mora's Modern Rhythmists brings back the sound and styles of early- to mid-1930s big bands.

Emenau, and musicians formerly associated with Lee Press-On and the Nails (trumpeter Todd Grady, Bobby Rogers on tenor and baritone, pianist Taylor Cutcomb, bassist Stuart Sperring, and drummer Beau Faw). Formed in early 1999 and already quite active in the San Francisco Bay Area, the group is most notable for Connie's vocals. She grew up in Roseville, California, had some early jobs singing in punk rock bands, and performed in a cabaret show under the title of Connie Champagne and her Tiny Bubbles. She became more interested in Swing in the early '90s and in 1994 joined the New Morty Show, staying until a falling-out caused a split near the end of 1998. An excellent songwriter, Connie Champagne is one of the best female vocalists in the Retro Swing movement.

The Magnum Brutes' debut CD has fresh material (the only standards are "Almost Like Being in Love" and "I Told Ya I Love Ya, Now Get Out"), lots of fine singing by Connie Champagne, and intriguing arrangements. Unfortunately the band (which is augmented on some cuts by trombonist Kevin Porter) does not get much solo space, with Ms. Champagne being in the spotlight throughout. The material (six of the dozen songs were cowritten by the singer) includes such titles as "Tenderloin," "Blue Martini," "End of the World Party," and the humorously violent "Road Rage." Interesting music that carves out its own niche in the Retro Swing movement.

MORA'S MODERN RHYTHMISTS

9   *My Favorite Band / 1996 / Mr. Ace 001*

9   *Mr. Rhythmist Goes to Town / June 3, 1998–Sept. 2, 1998 / Mr. Ace 002*

In the Retro Swing field, Mora's Modern Rhythmists definitely stands out, for, rather than looking at Louis Prima and Louis Jordan or even Count Basie for inspiration, the Rhythmists sound like a big band from 1932–35 without copying any particular orchestra. After college, pianist Dean Mora spent six years working as an accompanist for silent movies. He worked for a year with Johnny Crawford's 1930s-style society ensemble, gigged with Eddie Reed's orchestra, and then in the fall of 1994 formed Mora's Modern Rhythmists. The group (which is ten or eleven pieces) worked occasionally during 1995–96, recorded their first CD, and then in 1997 became a Monday night fixture at the Derby in Los Angeles, where they are still playing on a weekly basis. The Modern Rhythmists perform regularly at both Swing clubs and classic jazz festivals. Most of their repertoire is from the 1929–36 period, an era that has ironically been largely neglected by most Retro Swing bands.

My Favorite Band finds Mora's Modern Rhythmists (which consists of pianist Mora, Jim Ziegler and Corey Gemme on cornets, the reeds of Phil Krawzak, Geoff Nudell, and Mark Visher, trombonist Jerry Kuhn, John Reynolds on banjo and guitar, Art Gibson on tuba and bass, drummer Larry Wright, and violinist Terry Glenny) performing a variety of superior obscurities, mostly from the early 1930s. One can safely argue that their music is pre-Swing rather than Retro Swing, but since the Modern Rhythmists perform at Swing clubs, they deserve to be evaluated along with their competitors/contemporaries. Most of the selections on Mora's debut disc (including "My Favorite Band," "Hot Mustard," "Speedy Boy," "Rhapsody in Rhythm," "Mule Face Blues," "Got the Jitters," and "Harlem Madness") have rarely if ever been played since the mid-1930s, and were barely known then. Mora adapted the stock arrangements to his band's instrumentation and fortunately allowed his sidemen to create their own solos rather than sticking to recorded versions, which makes this vintage music sound very much alive.

The same personnel plays on *Mr. Rhythmist Goes to Town* except that Matt Germain is on reeds instead of Mark Visher, there is no violin, and singer Kayre Morrison (who has four vocals) is now a part of the band. If anything, the band sounds slightly stronger here (two more years of practice!). Some of the highlights among the 21 hot Swing and pre-Swing numbers are "Cavernism," an uptempo "Joe Turner Blues," "Without That Gal," "Jungle Jazz," and "Big John's Special," but there is not one throwaway on either of these highly enjoyable discs.

THE NEW MORTY SHOW

7 *Mortyfied!* / 1998–1999 / Slimstyle Thin 34
The New Morty Show is indeed a show, an updated version of a 1950s-style Las Vegas revue that emphasizes original music and crosses many musical genres. Leader-trumpeter Morty Okin grew up in Birmingham, Michigan. After attending Eastern Michigan University, he moved to San Francisco with a funk/lounge group in 1991 called the Psychedelic Lounge Cats. A year later he left the group and freelanced while working at a day job. In 1994 Okin formed the New Morty Show, using Connie Champagne and soon afterwards Vise Grip as his vocalists. The eight musicians (which include pianist-arranger John Quam, guitarist Whitney Wilson, bassist Tom Beyer, drummer David Rubin, trombonist Van Hughes, David Murotake on tenor, and baritonist Tom Griesser in addition to trumpeter Okin) have strong musicianship and are versatile enough to perform anything from modern Swing originals to rearranged versions of heavy metal and punk rock songs! The New Morty

Show appears briefly in a scene of the Robin Williams movie *Jack*. At the end of 1998 Connie Champagne departed from the band (eventually joining the new Magnum Brutes) and Kat Starr took her place.

After several years of success playing regularly in San Francisco (in addition to Los Angeles, New York, and Las Vegas), the New Morty Show recorded their first CD. The music mostly swings hard (this group has no shortage of energy), and there are some complex arrangements, plenty of vocals by Connie Champagne and Vise Grip, and fewer horn solos than one would prefer. Some of the tunes are quite rockish (including Billy Idol's "White Wedding Medley" and "Enter Sandman"), so one has to have a very open mind to appreciate all 11 selections, but there are also a few jumping blues, including "Caldonia." One suspects, however, that much of the New Morty Show's appeal is visual, so perhaps a live CD (or better yet a full-length video of a performance) would be preferable.

JOHNNY NOCTURNE BAND

8 *Wailin' Daddy* / Nov. 1991–May 1992 / Bullseye Blues 9526

7 *Shake 'Em Up* / Mar. 28–29, 1994 / Bullseye Blues 9553

9 *Wild & Cool* / June 1997 / Bullseye Blues & Jazz 9586
In 1989 tenor saxophonist John Firman formed Johnny Nocturne, an octet comprised of four horns plus a four-piece rhythm section. The basic idea was to play late-Swing/early R&B/jump jazz in the basic style of Illinois Jacquet, Gene Ammons, Willis Jackson, and other tenor players of the early 1950s. Although not really part of the Retro Swing movement (more of a coincidence), the Johnny Nocturne Band fits right in stylistically, albeit without the show-biz trappings of the more commercial groups. Firman, who grew up in Anchorage, Alaska, gained early experience playing with soul jazz organ groups in the 1960s. He briefly attended the University of California at Berkeley, studied at the Creative Music Studio in Woodstock, New York, and worked with David Bromberg's folk/rock band of the late 1970s. A few years later Firman moved to San Francisco, where he worked with Mitch Woods and the Rocket 88's. After gigging with Charles Brown, Laverne Baker, and others, he formed the Johnny Nocturne Band. In 1991 singer Brenda Boykin joined up, which greatly increased the band's commercial potential. In 1999 the Johnny Nocturne

Band had a successful appearance at the Monterey Jazz Festival, using a bright new singer, Kim Nalley, and still playing in the same style that Firman originally envisioned.

The Johnny Nocturne Band's three Bullseye Blues releases all follow the same basic pattern. There are hot instrumentals featuring Firman's tenor and the riffing horns, and more conventional vocals by Brenda Boykin. On the first two releases (*Wailin' Daddy* is highlighted by such titles as "Wailin'," "Let's Ball," and "Howling at Midnight," while *Shake 'Em Up* has "Reelin' and Rockin'," "New Blues," and "Oh Babe"), there are a few too many vocals (eight out of 11 songs on the second set), making one wish that there were more opportunities for Firman's honking tenor to stretch out.

Wild & Cool strikes the best balance. None of the sidemen (trumpeter Bill Ortiz, trombonist Marty Wehner, baritonist Rob Sudduth, pianist Henry Salvia, guitarist Anthony Paule, bassist Alex Baum, and drummer Kent Bryson) are household names, but they function very well in the ensembles and during their short solos. Brenda Boykin is still well featured, but John Firman's tenor is the main star and the material (which includes "Lemon Twist," "Don't Get Around Much Anymore," "A Pound of Blues," "By the River Ste. Marie," "Cha-Bootie," and "Little Slam") is full of hot moments. This is the Johnny Nocturne CD to get, although all three are worthwhile.

LEE PRESS-ON AND THE NAILS

6 *Jump-Swing from Hell* / Aug. 4, 1997 / Irascible Records LPN 1

5 *Swing Is Dead* / 1999 / Iracsible Records LPN 2
One of the more excitable and outlandish Swing bands around, the Nails is headed by vocalist-vibraphonist Lee Press-On, with occasional vocals from his wife, Leslie Presley. The music has been described by Press-On as Swing music given a heavy metal aesthetic. Born in Marin County, California, he did not start playing piano seriously until he was 18, soon changing his focus to vibes. Press-On had background in the theatre, switching to music when he formed the John Belushi Memorial Blues Band, an R&B group that lasted for seven years. In 1994 Lee Press-On decided to start a Swing band, one that would be explosive, humorous, and full of power. A popular attraction in the San Francisco area ever since, this 11-piece band is one of the most colorful of all the Retro Swing groups. Whether tearing apart a Louis Prima arrangement, racing through a complicated piece (sometimes speeding up intentionally), having all of the horns soloing together (in some wild futuristic Dixieland passages), or interpreting humorous lyrics, this is one of the crazier Swing bands of the last decade. One only wishes that the horn soloists were better!

Lee Press-On and the Nails's debut release (which was recorded live at the Hi-Ball Lounge in San Francisco) is full of energy and often a bit of a crack-up. "Caldonia" is taken remarkably fast, the ensemble races through Raymond Scott's "Powerhouse," "Deal Me In" finds the group sounding completely out of control in spots, their version of Louis Prima's arrangement of "Pennies from Heaven" is quite funny, and "Mississippi Darling" includes parade rhythms. The silly "Istanbul" is worthy of Slim Gaillard (although quite different), and Van Halen's "Hot for Teacher" is transformed into something quite bizarre (although their version of "Sing, Sing, Sing" does not work that well). Listeners who prefer tasteful, quiet Swing bands are advised to look elsewhere, but those with a strong sense of humor will find this nutty set worthy of a few listens. The follow-up disc *Swing Is Dead* has a completely different lineup of musicians except for two of the saxophonists, the leader, and Presley. The style is mostly unchanged, the musicianship is improved a bit and there are a few good jams, particularly "Big Pants Dance" and "Hat Back Boogie." However, much of the time is taken up by Press-On's vocals (often more shouted than sung), which are both dark and a bit of a self-parody. In addition to the title of this CD (which of course is not accurate), many of the songs deal with the darker side of fantasies, including "Waltz of the Damned," "Ghostriders in the Sky," "Devil Drums," "Dark Half," and "I Prefer a Coffin." Certainly a unique and often bizarre group.

EDDIE REED SWING BAND

8 *Hollywood Jump* / 1997 / Hepcat 91082

6 *While the Music Plays On* / 1999 / (no label listed)
Eddie Reed is a decent singer, an occasional clarinetist and guitarist, and an important bandleader in the Retro Swing movement. Born in Shady Grove, Texas, in 1960, Reed was singing professionally at the age of nine. He led a rockabilly group (Eddie Reed & the Bluehearts) in the Los Angeles area until 1990, and then was with the Westside Society Dance Band in Beverly Hills for two years. In 1992 he formed a 16-piece big band, which has since worked regu-

larly at the Rhino Room in Huntington Beach, Mum's in Long Beach, and the Derby. Reed does his best to get his orchestra to play in the style of 1939 Swing, although he does not closely emulate any one particular model. Singer Meghan Ivey joined the band in 1994 at the age of 14 and has proven to be a strong asset as she has matured.

Hollywood Jump served as an impressive debut for the Eddie Reed Swing Band. The orchestra does not have any major names other than trombonist Dan Barrett (who does not seem to have been given any solos) and veteran guitarist Al Viola, but it has an appealing ensemble sound. Artie Shaw gave Reed a couple of his old arrangements ("Natch" and "The Lamp Is Low"), and both are included on this set along with a few vocals by Ivey and Reed, the Jimmy Lunceford–associated "Jazznocracy," a tenor battle on "Cotton Tail" (by Dave Moody and Paul Carman), and the closing "C Jam Blues," which has Reed's only appearance on clarinet.

While his singing with his big band is occasional and pleasing, the emphasis is on Eddie Reed's voice on *While the Music Plays On* (which is performed by a quintet), and one quickly notes his limitations. Having just an average voice, Reed also has the habit of greatly simplifying melodies, repeating notes that certainly do not improve upon the original theme. Perhaps he should have shared the vocal mike with Meghan Ivey, for his singing is only effective in small doses. However, this date is somewhat notable for the colorful trumpet solos of Willie Murillo, who consistently steals the show; also in the group are Albert Alva on tenor, pianist Cris Dawson, bassist Freddy Johnson, and drummer Paul Lines. Among the better selections are "It Happened in Monterey" (which has Reed's best vocal and some emotional trumpet work), the instrumental "Bernie's Tune," "Corner Pocket," and "Moon Ray."

ROOMFUL OF BLUES

8 *The First Album / 1977 / 32 Records 32003*

10 *With Joe Turner/With Eddie "Cleanhead" Vinson / Jan. 27, 1982 + Jan. 26, 1983 / 32 Jazz 32015*

7 *Dance All Night / Sept. 13–15, 1993 / Bullseye Blues 9555*

7 *Turn It On! Turn It Up! / Dec. 12–16, 1994 / Bullseye Blues 9566*

6 *Under One Roof / Dec. 2–7, 1995 / Bullseye Blues 9569*

7 *There Goes the Neighborhood / 1998 / Bullseye Blues & Jazz 9609*

Roomful of Blues was formed long before the Retro Swing movement, but its combination of jump jazz, early R&B, and blues fits the genre quite well. The group has actually been around a remarkably long time, over 30 years, and, even with lots of personnel changes through the years, it shows little signs of slowing down. Guitarist-singer Duke Robillard originally formed Roomful of Blues in 1967. That version lasted only a few weeks, but in 1968 Robillard put together the group for real, originally as a four-piece rhythm section. From the start the band played vintage blues and R&B, mostly from the 1930s through the '60s. In 1970, after hearing some records by the Buddy Johnson Orchestra, Robillard was inspired to add horns to the group (Greg Piccolo on tenor, altoist Rich Lataille, and baritonist Doug James), which increased the band's jazz and Swing potential. Roomful of Blues, already a popular attraction on the East Coast, first recorded in 1977 (a date that has been reissued), with a second album cut in 1979 (for Antilles). In 1979 Duke Robillard went out on his own and the band began to change, becoming a nine-piece unit (including trumpeter Danny Motta and trombonist Porky Cohen). Lou Ann Barton was the group's vocalist for a year, Bob Enos joined as a permanent member on second trumpet, and Ronnie Earl became the band's guitarist for a long period.

In the 1980s Roomful of Blues performed special shows with Red Prysock, Sil Austin, Helen Humes, Arnett Cobb, Ruth Brown, Roy Brown, Eddie "Cleanhead" Vinson, and Big Joe Turner, recording with the last two. Roomful of Blues, which made several fine albums for Varrick during the 1980s and Bullseye Blues in the '90s, also teamed up for recording projects with singer Earl King and Pat Benatar (1991). Sugar Ray Norcia became the band's regular singer in 1991, also taking harmonica solos and fronting the band. Although some of the group's recordings have deemphasized the horns in favor of vocals, Roomful of Blues always has the potential to cut loose and be one of the most exciting of the jump bands. At the beginning of 1998 the band underwent quite a few personnel changes, with Bob Enos, Rich Lataille, guitarist Chris Vachon, and drummer John Rossi being the only holdovers. Norcia's place was taken by singer Mac Odom, but the signature Roomful of Blues sound remained the same.

The First Album features Roomful of Blues as a three-horn septet. Duke Robillard's vocals are fine (particularly "Love Struck" and Joe Turner's "Honey Hush"), but it is the riffing horns (three saxophonists plus guest Scott Hamilton on "Still in Love with You") that make this a rollicking set. While tenorman Greg Piccolo and baritonist Doug James would continue with the group into the mid-1990s, altoist Richard Lataille is still with Roomful of Blues 23 years later.

The 32 Jazz two-CD set puts together all of the music that Roomful of Blues recorded with Big Joe Turner and Eddie "Cleanhead" Vinson, which was originally two separate LPs. The Turner session was one of the veteran blues singer's best later albums, and he sounds inspired by the presence of five horns, guitarist Ronnie Earl, and the swinging rhythm section. Highlights include "Jumpin' for Joe," "I Want a Little Girl," "I Love the Way My Baby Sings the Blues," and the unlikely "Red Sails in the Sunset." The Vinson set is even hotter, for Cleanhead takes just three vocals (including "He Was a Friend of Mine" and "Past Sixty Blues") and concentrates on his underrated alto playing during the five instrumentals (highlighted by the stirring "House of Joy," "Movin' with Lester," and Earl Bostic's "That's the Groovy Thing"). Essential music.

The first three Bullseye releases, all from the Sugar Ray Norcia era, are fun if not quite classic. The personnel is the same on each of the CDs (Norcia, trumpeter Enos, trombonist Carl Querfurth, Lataille on alto and tenor, baritonist James, pianist Matt McCabe, guitarist Vachon, bassist Doc Grace, and drummer Rossi) except that the band's longtime tenor, Greg Piccolo, departed after recording *Dance All Night,* which is actually the strongest of the trio. That CD is highlighted by "That Will Never Do," "Come Back Baby," and "Up the Line." *Turn It On* has a couple fine instrumentals, the Count Basie/Jimmy Rushing–associated "I Left My Baby," and some newer material, much of it by Sugar Ray Norcia. *Under One Roof* puts the focus mostly on Norcia, and not enough is heard from the other musicians, who are mostly in a supportive role. There are some good selections (including "Smack Dab in the Middle," Willie Dixon's "Easy Baby," and two instrumentals), but part of what makes Roomful of Blues distinctive (the horn solos) is largely missing from this lesser release.

There Goes the Neighborhood, which features the group's new lineup (Mac Odom on vocals, trumpeter Enos, trombonist John Wolf, Lataille on alto and tenor, baritonist Kevin May, guitarist Vachon, Albert Weisman on piano and organ, bassist Marty Ballou, and drummer Rossi), finds the group performing new material by Vachon and Odom plus Percy Mayfield's "Lost Mind," Duke Ellington's "Rocks in My Bed," and Memphis Slim's "The Comeback." The music remains blues-oriented and, although one wishes that the horns would stretch out a bit more, Mac Odom's vocals plus the other new musicians fit into this classic music quite well, helping the Roomful of Blues to celebrate its 30th birthday.

ROYAL CROWN REVUE

8 *Mugzy's Move* / 1996 / Warner Bros. 46125

7 *The Contender* / 1998 / Warner Bros. 47020

Retro Swing may not technically have started with the Royal Crown Revue, but they were the first band to really popularize the idiom, touring the United States and dressing up as if they were in the 1940s and '50s while playing an intriguing blend of mostly original music. Singer-leader-frontman Eddie Nichols (whose background was in punk rock and rockabilly) and tenor saxophonist Mando Dorame formed Royal Crown Revue in 1989. The group was started not as a way to revive Swing but as a means to reinvent it in modern terms with rock and pop sensibilities, discussing topical subjects and bringing a sense of menace and unpredictability to the music. After two years of playing locally in Los Angeles, in 1991 the Royal Crown Revue made some important tours of the United States (and two of Europe) that spread the idea of Retro Swing far beyond L.A.'s city limits. During 1993–95 the Royal Crown Revue appeared weekly at the Derby in Hollywood, and the Retro Swing movement gathered speed. The Royal Crown Revue briefly became a household name due to their appearance in the film *The Mask,* and they are still the best known of all of the Retro Swing bands, playing fairly regularly as the 20th century ended.

The Royal Crown Revue first recorded in 1990 and had two private-label CDs: *Kings of Gangster Bop* (BYO) and *Caught in the Act* (Surfdog), but their most widely available sets are the two that they cut for Warner Bros. *Mugzy's Move* has quite a bit of variety. Some tunes feature Nichols's storytelling and odd voices (including "Zip Gun Bop," "Mugzy's Move," "Trouble in Tinsel Town," and "The Rise and Fall of the Great Mondello"), but there is also the catchy "Hey Pachuco," Willie Dixon's "I Love the Life I Live," the instrumental "Topsy," a memorable version of "The Walkin' Blues," and a rendition of "Beyond the Sea" (with added

The Royal Crown Revue gets credit for being the trailblazing Retro Swing band, setting the tone for the entire movement.

brass and strings) that finds Nichols sounding close to Bobby Darin. The group at the time, in addition to Nichols and Dorame, included trumpeter Scott Steen, baritonist Bill Ungerman, guitarist James Achor, bassist Veikko Lepisto, and drummer Daniel Glass.

The same lineup of musicians is featured on *The Contender*. In general the material is not quite as strong, and one can feel Royal Crown Revue overextending themselves a bit, often getting away from Swing altogether. "Salt Peanuts" shows that trumpeter Steen is not much of a bebopper (and why is Eddie Nichols's shouting of the song's title so lazy and uninvolved?). The medium-tempo Swing of "Stormy Weather" seems odd, and this tune is not as successful as "Beyond the Sea" on the previous disc. The best selections overall are "Walkin' Like Brando," "Work Baby Work" (which uses the chord changes of "King Porter Stomp"),

and "Deadly Nightcall" (a modern jazz instrumental). Baritonist Ungerman (who wrote a few of the originals) is consistently the most powerful soloist. Worth checking out, but get *Mugzy's Move* first.

SET 'EM UP JOE

7 *Set 'Em Up Joe/ 1998 / Daddy-O/Royalty 80203*
Although they sometimes bill themselves as "the missing link between the Rat Pack and Rock & Roll," Set 'Em Up Joe (which was formed in the late 1990s) falls into neither category. Comprised of singer Greg Mangus (who formerly fronted the funk group Fine Line), tenor saxophonist Chris Creviston (who also plays with Peggy Cone), guitarist Mark Cally, bassist Matt Hughes, and drummer Brian Floody, the

New York–based quintet is most notable for its excellent original material (by Cally, Mangus and/or Andy Ezrin) and the vocals of Mangus.

The band's debut CD has such catchy tunes as "She Can't Dance," "Gina Goes Wild," "Old Life Back," "Gasoline," and "Brooklyn Hearted." In fact, if any new standards are going to emerge from the Retro Swing movement, it is quite possible that they will emerge from this group; other bands are advised to check out some of these songs. This CD puts the focus mostly on Mangus's vocals, with Creviston's tenor and guitarist Cally having short solos but generally used as props behind the singing; the band would benefit from the inclusion of a few instrumentals. There are also important guest spots for trumpeter Alex Norris, trombonist Chris Washburne, and singer Kysia Bostic. An intriguing group that has strong potential.

BRIAN SETZER

8 *The Dirty Boogie / 1998 / Interscope 90183*
If Elvis Presley in the late 1950s had been interested in forming a swinging big band, it might very well have sounded like the Brian Setzer Orchestra. Famous for his work in rockabilly leading the Stray Cats, in 1992 Setzer put together a big band to play a mixture of rock and roll, Swing, and jump music. It was not (as hyped) the first time that an electric guitarist led a big band (Alvino Rey and occasionally Django Reinhardt beat him to it), but Setzer was the first rock star to devote himself to Retro Swing music. Born in Greenwich Village, New York, and raised on Long Island, Setzer played the euphonium (a low brass instrument) for a decade starting when he was eight. However, as a teenager he switched his focus to developing a rock and roll style on the guitar. Always interested in roots music, Setzer led the Stray Cats (which helped to revive rockabilly) during 1979–92, except for a two-year period (1984–86) when he attempted a solo career.

Setzer always loved the idea of having horns playing behind his guitar, so in 1992 he fulfilled a long-time dream and put together his orchestra consisting of four trumpets, four trombones, five saxophones, two basses, and drums. However, this is not a jazz-oriented band, and the leader is always the main star. In fact, the Los Angeles–based orchestra has only occasional solos from its sidemen, and Setzer's vocals and guitar playing really dominate. The big band debuted with a 1994 set for the Hollywood label (1994's *The Brian Setzer Orchestra*) and in 1996 put out their first CD for Interscope (*Guitar Slinger*). After a period of struggle and then gradual success, the Brian Setzer Orchestra really caught on in 1998 with the release of *The Dirty Boogie*. A Gap television commercial that featured Louis Prima's "Jump, Jive and Wail" coincidentally came out at the same time that Setzer released his version on *The Dirty Boogie,* and it helped his sales.

The music on *The Dirty Boogie* is a lot of fun, but one has to set aside any preconceptions. This is not a typical Swing big band, and Brian Setzer does not pretend to be generous with sharing the spotlight. The big band (other than an occasional short tenor solo) is used primarily as background behind the leader, playing heated ensembles but never getting to star. Fortunately the material (which includes blues, ballads, and a few romps) is colorful, Setzer's rock-oriented guitar wears well, and his vocals show some versatility. Gwen Stefani sings along with Setzer on "You're the Boss," while Eddie Nichols of the Royal Crown Revue and Meghan Ivey from Eddie Reed's band help out on "Jump, Jive and Wail." Such numbers as "This Cat's on a Hot Tin Roof," "Rock This Town," and "Switchblade 327" certainly have plenty of energy, and "As Long As I'm Singin' " swings hard. A rare rock and roll big band set.

LAVAY SMITH AND THE RED HOT SKILLET LICKERS

10 *One Hour Mama / 1995–1996 / Fat Note 0001*
One of the strongest jazz-oriented groups of the Retro Swing era, the Red Hot Skillet Lickers feature not only a strong and highly appealing singer (who is sometimes reminiscent of Helen Humes and Dinah Washington) in Lavay Smith and a fine pianist-arranger in Chris Siebert, but several talented veteran horn players. The band (usually a septet or octet) sounds like a high-quality Swing combo from circa 1944–45, playing late-period Swing touched by Kansas City blues and looking toward early R&B. Lavay Smith's father worked for the U.S. government, so she spent a few years living in the Philippines, where she made her debut singing in public when she was 15. After spending a period in Los Angeles, in 1988 she moved to San Francisco. Smith sang on the streets with some of the musicians from Bo Grumpus (including

guitarist Craig Ventresco) the following year and met Chris Siebert when he worked with the group at the Blue Lamp. Together they formed the Red Hot Skillet Lickers, and the band has been a San Francisco fixture ever since, becoming increasingly better known year by year.

One Hour Mama is one of the classic discs of the Retro Swing era. Lavay Smith is featured on songs associated with Esther Phillips ("Oo Poppa Do"), Dinah Washington ("New Blowtop Blues"), Anita O'Day ("And Her Tears Flowed Like Wine"), Bessie Smith ("Downhearted Blues"), and Ida Cox ("One Hour"), among others. The band includes such fine soloists as Bill Stewart on alto and tenor, Harvey Robb on tenor, alto, and clarinet, Noel Jewkes on tenor, baritone, and clarinet, trombonist Larry Leight, and pianist Siebert; guitarist Charlie Siebert (the pianist's brother), bassist Bing Nathan, and drummer Dan Fultz are excellent in support. Since the time of this recording, the Skillet Lickers have added a trumpeter (usually Allen Smith) and the group has continued to improve, but *One Hour Mama* was a very impressive start and is a gem in its own right.

SQUIRREL NUT ZIPPERS

9 *Hot / Oct. 1995–Nov. 1995 / Mammoth 354 980 137*

6 *Christmas Caravan / July 1998 / Mammoth 354 980 192*

8 *Perennial Favorites / 1998 / Mammoth 354 980 169*

One of the most unlikely successes of the Retro Swing era, the Squirrel Nut Zippers are based in hot jazz of the late 1920s and New Orleans jazz rather than Swing, and they do not hail from Los Angeles, San Francisco, or New York but from North Carolina. The surprise success of their single "Hell" in 1996 (which is a calypso song rather than a Swing romp) did wonders in generating headlines for the Retro Swing movement, and it helped their *Hot* CD to sell over a million copies.

The Squirrel Nut Zippers, who are from Chapel Hill, North Carolina, first came together during a potluck dinner held at the home of Jim Mathus (who sings and plays guitar, banjo, and occasional piano) and Katharine Whalen (singer and banjoist) in July 1993. The resulting session found Mathus and Whalen jamming with Ken Mosher (who plays guitar, ukulele, and alto and baritone saxes), bassist Don Raleigh, and drummer Chris Phillips. With the later addition of Tom Maxwell (on guitar, baritone sax, and clarinet) and a trumpeter, the Squirrel Nut Zippers (named after a vintage peanut-flavored candy bar still made in Massachusetts) was formed. The eccentric band mixes trad jazz and early Swing with bluegrass, blues, and early country and string music, focusing mostly on playing new music that somehow sounds both primitive and advanced, hinting at the past while sounding like none of their musical ancestors.

The Squirrel Nut Zippers first played in public in November 1993 and a few months later recorded their first CD, *The Inevitable* (Mammoth 0105), which came out in March 1995. The great success of their second set, *Hot,* in 1996 was a surprise to everyone, including the band members. With cornetist Duke Heitger (who was not a regular member of the band) contributing many explosive solos and violinist Andrew Bird also helping out, *Hot* (assisted greatly by "Hell") became one of the major Retro Swing CDs, even though the Squirrel Nut Zippers do not consider themselves part of the Swing movement. By September 1996, they were touring the West Coast and appearing on national television, culminating in an appearance at President Bill Clinton's inaugural ball of January 1997. By then Je Widenhouse was the group's trumpeter and Stu Cole was on bass. Although the resulting Christmas album and *Perennial Favorites* did not exceed the sales figures of *Hot,* the Squirrel Nut Zippers are still quite popular and certainly one of the most unique bands around.

The music on *Hot* is both sincere and a bit demented, oddly traditional yet original. The hot trumpet solos of Duke Heitger, the hints at Django Reinhardt in Tom Maxwell's guitar spots, the spirited if sometimes unnerving vocals of Jim Mathus and Katharine Whalen, and the joyous yet forbidding group sound make this a most unusual yet mostly joyous CD. It does seem odd that the preachy calypso "Hell" caught on rather than the heated "Got My Own Thing Now," "Put a Lid on It," and "Bad Businessman." This is a CD that grows in interest with each listen and does not fit into any inflexible musical category.

Christmas Caravan is certainly an offbeat Christmas set, with all of the songs being group originals except "Sleigh Ride" and "Hanging Up My Stockings." There is plenty of humor (including "Indian Giver" and "Carolina Christmas"), bits of sentiment (the country waltz "I'm Coming Home for Christmas"), a blues tribute to a long-gone R&B singer ("A Johnny Ace Christmas," which has one of Katharine Whalen's best vocals), and a clunky version of "Sleigh Ride"; this last is the only instrumental of the set other than "Hot Christmas." The band's limitations (there are no virtuosos to be heard and the singers' voices are sometimes erratic) are a bit obvious, yet the good spirits and desire to take chances largely compensate.

The title of *Perennial Favorites* is ironic, since all dozen songs are group originals. The Squirrel Nut Zippers (with guest violinist Andrew Bird) play some hot jazz (cornetist Je Widenhouse leads the way on some numbers), country ballads, the bizarre and riotous "Ghost of Stephen Foster," a Swing tribute to guitarist Al Casey ("Pallin' with Al"), a close Billie Holiday imitation by Katharine Whalen on "My Drag," and the logical closer, "It's Over." It may not all be jazz or Swing, but it definitely holds one's interest and is continually witty.

RON SUNSHINE AND FULL SWING

8 *Straight Up / Apr. 1998–July 1998 / Daddy-O/Royalty 94058-202*

Ron Sunshine, a good-time singer and a fine harmonica player, was born in Denver. However, he became quite interested in Swing while in Paris, where he played with the Lost and Wandering Blues and Jazz Band. Sunshine founded Full Swing in 1991 and during the 1990s also led a blues-oriented band called Smoking Section. Based in New York, Full Swing had developed its sound before the Retro Swing movement took hold and has had the same personnel since 1995: Sunshine, tenor saxophonist Craig Dreyer, guitarist Dan Hovey, pianist Paul Tillotson, bassist Andres Villamil, and drummer James Wormworth IV.

The debut recording by Full Swing has four standards (including "Hit That Jive Jack," Fats Waller's "Lounging at the Waldorf," which has a guest vocal by "Moanin' Mary" and "Undecided") plus six group originals that sound as if they could have been composed in the 1940s. Sunshine's vocals are quite enjoyable and light-hearted, his harmonica blends in well with Dreyer's tenor, and, on "Is That the Moon?," three additional horn players are added. An excellent jump jazz set full of good spirits.

SWING FEVER

7 *Swing Fever with Mary Stallings / 1989 / Swing Fever*

In 1978, trombonist Bryan Gould formed Swing Fever, a San Francisco quintet that performs Swing standards plus the music of Louis Jordan, Nat King Cole, and other 1940s musical heroes. One of several groups that happened to be in the right place at the right time, Swing Fever has been helped a little by the rise of Retro Swing while continuing to stay based in the vintage music that Gould loves. The personnel has changed through the years but has often included Noel Jewkes or Howard Dudune on reeds, guitarist Jim Putman, bassist Dean Reilly, and drummer Joe Dodge (who was with Dave Brubeck in the early 1950s). Gould contributes occasional vocals, and among the singers who have appeared with the group have been Mary Stallings, Paula West, Bobbe Norris, Wanda Stafford, Shanna Carlson, Morning Nichols, and Kim Nalley. In addition, the great Clark Terry has played with Swing Fever on an occasional basis since the mid-1990s, including at the 1999 Monterey Jazz Festival.

Swing Fever has thus far recorded only two sets, a 1995 session, *Reunion* (D'Note 2001), that was issued under Clark Terry's name and features the veteran tenor saxophonist Pee Wee Claybrook, and their 1989 meeting with singer Mary Stallings. The latter, issued privately but still available, is noteworthy for Stallings's five fine vocals (including "East of the Sun" and "You Stepped Out of a Dream") and the band's ability to play creatively within the Swing idiom. The instrumentation (a quintet without piano or trumpet), the fresh arrangements, and some offbeat tunes give Swing Fever a fairly original sound within the tradition. Among the numbers performed are Duke Ellington's "Jack the Bear," Nat King Cole's "Are You Fer It," "Tickletoe," and "Black and Tan Fantasy," plus two of Noel Jewkes's originals.

VARIOUS ARTISTS CD RECORDINGS

6 *Alive and Kickin'—Big Band Sounds at M-G-M / July 13, 1939–Dec. 17, 1947 / Rhino 56826-810*

Slightly before, during, and briefly after World War II, the more famous Swing big bandleaders and their orchestras often had feature numbers in Hollywood films along with small roles. This CD features the sound track recordings of 23 performances, most of which had never been released commercially before. Among the bands heard from are Tommy Dorsey (including classic renditions of "Opus One" and "Hawaiian War Chant"), Jimmy Dorsey, Harry James ("I Cried for You"), Tex Beneke, Artie Shaw, Guy Lombardo, Vaughn Monroe, and Kay Kyser. The music ranges from hard-driving Swing to novelty vocals but generally holds one's interest.

9 *An Anthology of Big Band Swing (1930–1955) / Jan. 14, 1931–Aug. 1955 / GRP/Decca 2-629*

This is a very successful two-CD sampler, one that traces the evolution of big band Swing in chronological order during a 25-year period, from Duke Ellington's "Rockin' in Rhythm" to Benny Goodman's 1955 version of "One O'Clock Jump." In addition to a few hits (such as Count Basie's "One O'Clock Jump," and Charlie Barnet's "Skyliner"), there are many obscure cuts and such orchestras as Mills Blue Rhythm Band, Tiny Bradshaw, Isham Jones (playing "Stompin' at the Savoy"), Spud Murphy, and Jan Savitt alternating with the better-known bands. A well-conceived reissue.

8 *Barrelhouse Boogie / May 7, 1936–June 17, 1941 / Bluebird 8334*

This single disc gives listeners recordings of the four most important boogie pianists. Meade Lux Lewis performs a 1936 version of "Honky Tonk Train Blues" plus "Whistlin' Blues," Jimmy Yancey takes ten gentle and typically soulful solos, and Pete Johnson and Albert Ammons play together for nine piano duets. Not as complete as the CDs in the European Document series, this CD nevertheless is a superior example of boogie-woogie as played by the top stylists during the Swing era.

8 *Big Band Jazz—The Jubilee Sessions / June 1943–Aug. 1946 / Hindsight 504*

The *Jubilee* radio series featured black Swing bands during the 1942–47 period. Some of the broadcasts have since been

released by collector's labels, but many have not. This three-CD set has several songs apiece from quite a few orchestras: Benny Carter, Earl Hines, Elmer Fain, Count Basie, Gerald Wilson, Erskine Hawkins, Billy Eckstine, Cootie Williams, Tiny Bradshaw, Jimmy Mundy, Fletcher Henderson, the International Sweethearts of Rhythm, Claude Hopkins, Andy Kirk, Lucky Millinder, Lionel Hampton, Johnny Otis, Wilbert Baranco, Jimmie Lunceford, and Duke Ellington. The music is quite jazz-oriented, many killer-dillers are included, and one gets a pretty good idea as to how most of these orchestras sounded during the era when Swing was beginning to hint at R&B and bop. Recommended.

6 *The Blue Note Swingtets / July 18, 1944–Sept. 23, 1946 / Blue Note 95697*

In the mid-1940s the Blue Note label, which started out recording trad players and after 1947 would stick almost exclusively to bop and beyond, documented several all-star Swing-oriented groups. The Mosaic label, on their limited-edition sets, reissued all of the sessions. This single CD is unfortunately just a sampler, with no complete sessions. There is some fine music on dates led by Tiny Grimes, tenor saxophonist John Hardee, Ike Quebec, Benny Morton, and Jimmy Hamilton, with the supporting cast including Trummy Young, Sid Catlett, Milt Hinton, Jonah Jones, Tyree Glenn, Buck Clayton, Ben Webster, and Ray Nance, among others. But since the music on these sessions was quite consistent, it is a pity that most of it remains out of print.

7 *Cabin in the Sky / Aug. 28, 1942–Nov. 18, 1942 / Rhino 56826*

Cabin in the Sky, which stars Ethel Waters, Eddie "Rochester" Anderson, and Lena Horne, was one of the best of the all-black movie musicals of the 1940s. All of the music (including alternate takes and songs that did not make it into the final production) are on this perfectly done CD. Waters is heard introducing "Happiness Is a Thing Called Joe," "Cabin in the Sky," and "Takin' a Chance on Love," Duke Ellington's orchestra is briefly featured on "Goin' Up," and Louis Armstrong, who is in the film for only a few seconds, has his one number ("Ain' It the Truth") restored and heard for the first time on this CD. Even with some repetition and incidental music, the disc holds one's interest, and the enclosed liner notes are definitive.

This remarkable 12-CD set has a tremendous number of great performances recorded originally for the Capitol label. Each of the 65 sessions is complete, and the music ranges from Dixieland by the Bob Crosby Bobcats and big bands to just a touch of bop. Much of this music had formerly been lost in the shuffle (often recorded by artists in the "78" era who did not make an album's worth of material overall for Capitol), so its restoration is quite important. Among the many artists and bands featured in the 245 selections are Paul Whiteman's orchestra, Eddie Miller's big band, Wingy Manone, Johnny Mercer, Bud Freeman, drummer Zutty Singleton, Bobby Hackett, Sid Catlett, Al Casey, the Capitol Jazzmen, Jack Teagarden, Anita O'Day, the Benny Carter big band, Jess Stacy, Joe Sullivan, Mel Powell, the Cootie Williams Orchestra, Rex Stewart, Sonny Greer, Carl Kress, Kay Starr, and Red Norvo, and that is only a partial list. Get this limited-edition box while you can!

* *The Complete H.R.S. Sessions / Aug. 21, 1938–Sept. 26, 1947 / Mosaic 6-187*

All of the sessions recorded by the Hot Jazz Record Society have been reissued on this limited-edition six-CD set. The performances can easily be divided into two groups. The 1938–40 dates are Dixieland-oriented and include sets led by clarinetist Pee Wee Russell, Rex Stewart, and Jack Teagarden plus a classic session by a quartet consisting of soprano-saxophonist Sidney Bechet, cornetist Muggsy Spanier, guitarist Carmen Mastren, and bassist Wellman Bruad. The music from 1945–47, in contrast, is late-period Swing and includes a strong dose of Duke Ellington's music. The Brick Fleagle Orchestra (a no-name but talented rehearsal band) is heard from, as are combos led by trombonists Sandy Williams, J. C. Higginbotham, Dicky Wells, and Trummy Young, pianists Jimmy Jones, Billy Kyle, and Billy Taylor (who takes a couple very rare and effective vocals), tenorman Joe Thomas, Harry Carney, Russell Procope, and Buck Clayton. These performances overall show that Swing was not dead during 1946–47, at least not artistically.

9 *Esquire All-American Hot Jazz Sessions / Jan. 10, 1946–Apr. 22, 1947 / Bluebird 6757*

During 1946–47, writer Leonard Feather produced a series of performances for the Victor label that featured all-star groups ranging from Louis Armstrong and Swing greats to bits of bop. The first eight numbers on this 20-cut CD features versions of Esquire's All-American Award Winners.

"Long Long Journey" was the first meeting on record between Duke Ellington (who verbally introduces the song) and Armstrong; Satch also takes a surprisingly modern solo on "Snafu." Among the other stars are Charlie Shavers (who is remarkable on "The One That Got Away"), Johnny Hodges (sounding beautiful on "Gone with the Wind"), Don Byas, Buck Clayton, and Coleman Hawkins. There are also numbers showcasing Jack Teagarden, Lucky Thompson's tenor ("Just One More Chance" was one of the high points of his career), Neal Hefti on trumpet ("From Dixieland to Bop"), Mildred Bailey, Art Tatum, and Erroll Garner. Overall there are quite a few gems on this highly enjoyable reissue.

8 *52nd Street Swing—New York in the '30s / Sept. 11, 1934–Apr. 3, 1941 / GRP/Decca 646*

On this CD are selections from some of the many small Swing groups that played regularly on 52nd Street during the second half of the 1930s. The Delta Four (a quartet with Roy Eldridge and Joe Marsala) plays two spontaneous numbers, and there are three spirited cuts apiece from the Spirits of Rhythm, Stuff Smith, the John Kirby Sextet, and Hot Lips Page. In addition, there are two selections from pianist Sammy Price (including a rare Lester Young solo on "Just Jivin' Around") and four songs from an all-star session led by Leonard Feather that includes Bobby Hackett, Pete Brown, and Benny Carter with plenty of instrument switching by the three principals. Although not for completists, this is an excellent reissue.

10 *From Spirituals to Swing / Dec. 23, 1938–Dec. 24, 1939 / Vanguard 169/71*

Producer John Hammond put on two Carnegie Hall concerts near Christmas of 1938 and 1939 that he called "From Spirituals to Swing." Featuring some of Hammond's favorite Swing artists along with top players from trad, boogie-woogie, country blues, and spirituals, these were rather notable concerts that led to the revival of boogie-woogie and helped focus attention on quite a few then-obscure artists. Previously some of the music had been released from these concerts as a two-LP set and duplicated as two CDs. This 1999 release, however, is three CDs and for the first time straightens out the music's chronology (showing which performances took place in which year) and identifying some studio performances that had previously been mixed in with the concert music. In addition, there are 20 previously unreleased performances. The recording quality, although streaky at times, is an improvement over previous issues.

Featured are the Count Basie Orchestra (with Lester Young), Hot Lips Page (playing the exciting "Blues with Lips" with Basie), the Kansas City Five/Six (an all-star Basie group that on one date includes Charlie Christian), Helen Humes, Meade Lux Lewis, Albert Ammons, Pete Johnson, Big Joe Turner, Sister Rosetta Tharpe, Mitchell's Christian Singers, Sidney Bechet's New Orleans Feetwarmers, Big Bill Broonzy, Sonny Terry, James P. Johnson, Jimmy Rushing, the Golden Gate Quartet, the Benny Goodman Sextet, Ida Cox, and a jam session on "Lady Be Good" that includes solos from four different pianists.

8 *Getting Some Fun Out of Life with Mr. Tram Associates / Feb. 20–21, 1988 / Audiophile 241*

This group, named after C-melody saxophonist Frankie Trumbauer, is an unusual quartet comprised of singer Barbara Lea, Daryl Sherman on vocals and piano, cornetist Dick Sudhalter, and tenor saxophonist Loren Schoenberg, who also plays piano. The repertoire (Swing-era tunes including a fair number of obscurities) fares quite well because of the talented singers, and the horn players get their spots. Highlights include "Bob White," "Got the South in My Soul," "More Than You Know," "This Year's Kisses," and "A Woman's Intuition."

8 *Hipsters, Zoots & Wingtips, Volume 1 / 1995–1998 / Hip-O 40129*

7 *Hipsters, Zoots & Wingtips, Volume 2 / Oct. 22, 1941– Feb. 19, 1959 / Hip-O 40130*

7 *Hipsters, Zoots & Wingtips, Volume 3 / 1995–1998 / Hip-O 40165*

This three-CD set has a pair of discs that sample the Retro Swing scene of the 1990s (Volumes 1 and 3), while Volume 2 looks back at earlier recordings. The first volume has one selection apiece from the Royal Crown Revue ("Hey Pachuco!"), Big Bad Voodoo Daddy, The Flying Neutrinos, Big Time Operator, Diana Krall (a bit out of place but sounding fine on "Hit That Jive Jack"), Red and the Red Hots, Indigo Swing, Blues Jumpers (their classic version of "Good Morning Judge"), Lavay Smith, Ron Sunshine's Full Swing, Steve Lucky's Rhumba Bums, the Bill Elliott Swing Orchestra, Set 'Em Up Joe, Jumpin' Jimes, and Brian Setzer. Adding to its value as an introduction to Retro Swing is the inclusion of a paragraph apiece about each band. The second volume, subtitled *Original Swingers,* has the original versions of a variety of songs that are sometimes played by

current Swing bands, including "Caldonia," "Every Time I Hear That Mellow Saxophone," "Oo Poppa Do," and "Reet, Petite and Gone." Quite a variety of artists are heard from, including Louis Jordan, Roy Mitchell, the King Cole Trio, Count Basie, Lucky Millinder, Stan Kenton, Jesse Stone ("Cole Slaw"), Esther Phillips, Smiley Lewis, Dinah Washington, Percy Mayfield, Erskine Hawkins, Jimmy Liggins, Paul Bascomb, Dinah Washington, John Brim, and Louis Prima. The third volume returns to the idea of the first set, with one selection apiece from Indigo Swing, Steve Lucky's Rhumba Buns, Big Time Operator, Ray Gelato's Giants, Johnny Nocturne, Bill Elliott, Lavay Smith, Eddie Reed's Big Band, Bellevue Cadillac, Vargas Swing, the Camaros, the Jump, Jive and Wailers, the Love Dogs, and the Flipped Fedora Orchestra. In addition, the set concludes with Louis Prima's "Paper Doll" and Louis Jordan's "Saturday Night Fish Fry." Colorful music with an emphasis on hotter tunes.

7 *Honkers & Bar Walkers, Volume 1 / Oct. 1949–Sept. 7, 1953 / Delmark 438*

Although most of the 22 selections on this CD are available elsewhere, the jump jazz/R&B tenor saxophonists included make a fine sampling of the sax players who recorded for the United/States label in the early 1950s. Jimmy Forrest is represented by three cuts (including "Night Train"), and Tab Smith's "Because of You" is also here, as are numbers by Teddy Brannon, Cozy Eggleston, Jimmy Coe, Doc Sausage, Fred Jackson, Chris Woods, Fats Noel, and Paul Bascomb. Fun music.

10 *Jazz at the Santa Monica Civic '72 / Aug. 2, 1972 / Pablo 2625-701*

Originally this concert (which launched the Pablo label), which has been reissued as a three-CD set, was supposed to feature just the Count Basie Orchestra and Ella Fitzgerald. However, producer Norman Granz surprised everyone by inviting guests Roy Eldridge, Harry "Sweets" Edison, Eddie "Lockjaw" Davis, Stan Getz, Oscar Peterson, and Ray Brown. With Al Grey from Basie's band, they formed a Jazz at the Philharmonic band that was featured on three jams and a ballad medley. Basie's orchestra (featuring Jimmy Forrest and Grey) and Ella both sound quite inspired during their sets, and there is a Peterson-Brown duet on "You Are My Sunshine." However, the finale is the most memorable performance. On "C Jam Blues," Ella trades off with Grey, Getz, Sweets, Lockjaw, and Eldridge, and each encounter has a remarkable or hilarious moment; check out the singer's comment after Roy's final trumpet blast. Spontaneous jazz at its best.

10 *Jazz in the Thirties / Feb. 28, 1933–Dec. 13, 1935 / DRG Swing 8457/8458*

This two-CD set has many great performances from the early days of Swing. The 40 selections (all of the sessions are complete) feature the Joe Venuti–Eddie Lang Blue Five, a few later Venuti dates, including one with Benny Goodman, Adrian Rollini's Orchestra, piano solos from Joe Sullivan, a Benny Goodman pickup group with Jack Teagarden, the Jess Stacy Trio, and combo dates led by Bud Freeman, Gene Krupa, and Bunny Berigan. Lots of exciting music that shows just how stimulating small-group Swing can be.

9 *Jumpin' Like Mad—Cool Cats & Hip Chicks Non-Stop Dancin' / May 21, 1942–Sept. 13, 1956 / Capitol 52051*

One should not look for slow downbeat blues or overly intellectual solos on this two-CD set. The emphasis is on heated and accessible performances from the prime era of jump jazz. The 51 selections, taken from Capitol's vaults, include hits and complete obscurities, late-period Swing, melodic blues, and stomping R&B. Represented are Big Joe Turner, Calvin Boze, Ella Mae Morse ("Cow Cow Boogie"), Lester Young ("Jumpin' with Symphony Sid"), Jesse Price, Kay Starr, Cootie Williams, Babs Gonzales, T-Bone Walker, Nellie Lutcher, Helen Humes, the King Cole Trio, Ernie Andrews, Gene Ammons, Betty Hall James, Lalo Guerrero, Ike Carpenter's orchestra, Jack "The Bear" Parker, Jimmy Liggins, Big Jay McNeely, and Louis Jordan, and that is only the first disc! This twofer is highly recommended to both vintage R&B collectors and Retro Swing fans alike.

9 *Kansas City Blues 1944–49 / Nov. 1, 1944–Nov. 2, 1949 / Capitol 52047*

Although Kansas City–based music from the 1930s and early '40s has been celebrated, particularly that of Count Basie and Jay McShann (due to Charlie Parker's serving an apprentice with the latter), the swinging blues style from K.C. during the second half of the '40s was well documented but has been largely overlooked. Other than a session apiece from 1944 and 1945, all of the music on this three-CD set is from 1949, a period when swinging Kansas City blues was influencing R&B and itself being a little bit touched by bebop. Featured are Jay McShann's various bands (including selections with singer Walter Brown), Julia Lee, Bus Moten,

Tommy Douglas, and Tiny Kennedy. Most of the sidemen in these overlapping groups never became famous (other than Ben Webster, who is heard with Moten), but the bands are tight, the music is colorful, and the performances are consistently enjoyable and timeless in their own way.

6 *The Legendary Big Band Singers / May 3, 1931–Jan. 24, 1951 / GRP/Decca 642*

This is an OK sampler that features 20 different singers, mostly from the Swing era. On the plus side is that the music is usually quite good and the selections are programmed in chronological order; on the minus side is that the personnel (and even the soloists) are not listed. There is a number apiece from Cab Calloway (the original version of "Minnie the Moocher"), Louis Armstrong, Sy Oliver, Pha Terrell ("Until the Real Thing Comes Along"), June Richmond, Jimmy Rushing, Helen Humes, Bon Bon, Jack Teagarden, Helen O'Connell (with Bob Eberle on "Green Eyes"), Walter Brown, Sister Rosetta Tharpe, Ella Fitzgerald, Woody Herman, Kay Starr, Dinah Washington ("Blow Top Blues"), Lionel Hampton, Little Jimmy Scott, Ella Johnson ("Since I Fell for You"), and Arthur Prysock.

8 *Legends of the Swing Era / Feb. 25, 1997 / Schmied & Partner Edition 5*

This two-CD set is half music, half reminiscing. It has the final recording by trumpeter Doc Cheatham (who was 91) and 95-year-old altoist Benny Waters. The septet also includes pianist Red Richards, bassist Truck Parham, and the much younger trombonist Dan Barrett, guitarist Don Vappie, and drummer Trevor Richards (who organized the New Orleans session). Other than brief spoken interludes, the first CD features music (including "Stompin' at the Savoy," "Cool Waters," "Moonlight on the Ganges," "I've Found a New Baby," and "Blue Lou"), while the second CD gives each of the players (particularly Cheatham, Waters, Richards, and Parham) opportunities to talk about their lives. Put out by a private German label (the extensive liner notes are in German), this valuable twofer is the only recorded example of Cheatham and Waters playing together. Despite their age (which at the time totaled 186!), they were both still in their musical prime, and some magic occurs.

7 *The 1930s: Big Bands / Feb. 11, 1930–Dec. 14, 1939 / Columbia 40651*

7 *The 1930s: The Singers / Apr. 1, 1930–June 7, 1938 / Columbia 40847*

7 *The 1930s: The Small Combos / Apr. 4, 1930–July 28, 1939 / Columbia 40833*

7 *The 1940s: The Singers / May 1, 1940–Dec. 21, 1949 / Columbia 40652*

8 *The 1940s: Small Groups—New Directions / Mar. 8, 1945–Nov. 3, 1947 / Columbia 44222*

7 *The 1950s: The Singers / Dec. 14, 1950–Aug. 6, 1959 / Columbia 40799*

In the 1980s, Columbia came out with these six samplers, which contain 16 or 17 selections apiece (except the 1950s set, which has 13 cuts), with a different artist or group featured on each cut. The music is loosely in chronological order and the quality is consistently high and of strong interest to beginning Swing fans. *The 1930s: Big Bands* has songs by the Casa Loma Orchestra ("San Sue Strut"), Claude Hopkins (the classic "Mush Mouth"), Duke Ellington, Don Redman, Cab Calloway, Fletcher Henderson, Chick Webb, Teddy Hill, the Mills Blue Rhythm Band, Erskine Hawkins, Red Norvo, Ben Pollack ("Jimtown Blues," which has a solo from the young Harry James), Earl Hines, Jimmie Lunceford, Count Basie, and Benny Goodman. *The 1930s: The Singers* consists of performances by Ethel Waters, Louis Armstrong, Jack Teagarden, Fats Waller, Bing Crosby with the Mills Brothers ("Dinah"), the Boswell Sisters, Connie Boswell, Ella Fitzgerald, Don Redman, the Spirits of Rhythm, Chick Bullock, Louis Prima, Henry "Red" Allen, Mildred Bailey, Ivie Anderson, Billie Holiday ("Mean to Me"), and Midge Williams. *The 1930s: The Small Combos* has combo jams by trumpeter Jack Purvis, the Chocolate Dandies, the Rhythmakers, Red Allen, Wingy Manone (his hit "The Isle of Capri"), Red Norvo, Jones-Smith Inc., Stuff Smith, Teddy Wilson, Roy Eldridge, Cootie Williams, the Gotham Stompers, Frankie Newton, Sidney Bechet, Chu Berry, and the John Kirby Sextet ("Royal Garden Blues").

Strangely enough there was no release titled *The 1940s: Big Bands,* which would have been logical. *The 1940s: The Singers* has a cut apiece from Maxine Sullivan, Big Joe Turner, Mildred Bailey ("I'm Nobody's Baby", which features a futuristic solo from Roy Eldridge), Jack Teagarden, Cab Calloway, Billie Holiday, Slim Gaillard, Anita O'Day, Jimmy Rushing, Peggy Lee, Roy Eldridge, Eddie "Cleanhead" Vinson, Woody Herman ("Caldonia"), Hot Lips Page, Nat King Cole with June Christy, and Sarah Vaughan. The most intriguing of the releases is *The 1940s: Small Groups—New Directions,* for it focuses on just three bands.

Woody Herman's 1946 Woodchoppers (which has the main soloists from the First Herd) is heard on ten selections, the Gene Krupa Trio (with Charlie Ventura) plays "Dark Eyes" and four other songs, and Harry James performs "Pagan Love Song" and a remarkably boppish version of "Tuxedo Junction" that contains one of the trumpeter's greatest solos. *The 1950s: The Singers* is mostly Swing- and ballad-oriented, with songs by Lee Wiley, Louis Armstrong ("Mack the Knife"), Billie Holiday, Jimmy Rushing, Sarah Vaughan ("Mean to Me"), Johnny Mathis (!), Hot Lips Page, Dolores Hawkins, Joe Williams, Betty Roche (her famous version of "Take the 'A' Train" with Duke Ellington), Babs Gonzales, Betty Carter, and Lambert, Hendricks, and Ross.

* *The 1940s Mercury Sessions / Sept. 25, 1945–Oct. 27, 1951 / Mercury 314 525 609*

If an award were given for packaging, this limited-edition seven-CD set, which is enclosed in a replica of an old radio, would win. Subtitled *Blues, Boogie & Bop,* the package has music that covers all of those styles. Included are 34 tunes from Albert Ammons (including his one session with his son, tenor saxophonist Gene Ammons), 16 songs with Helen Humes, 24 by Jay McShann (some with Jimmy Witherspoon or Walter Brown), 30 featuring Eddie "Cleanhead" Vinson, nine tunes by New R&B pioneer Professor Longhair, a dozen from Buddy Rich's bebop orchestra, ten by Cootie Williams (including "Gator Tail," which made Willis Jackson famous), and four songs apiece from Julia Lee, singer Myra Taylor, and Rex Stewart. In addition, the seventh disc is comprised of previously unreleased alternate takes from many of these artists plus two unknown numbers by Mary Lou Williams. All of the sessions are issued complete, and the extensive liner notes are definitive. Except for the limited-edition status of this now out-of-print set, this is the perfect way to reissue classic jazz.

8 *The Original V-Disc Collection / June 1943–Dec. 30, 1944 / Pickwick 540301*

9 *Rare V-Discs Volume 1—The Combos / RST 91565*

7 *Rare V-Discs Volume 2—The Big Bands / RST 91566*

6 *Rare V-Discs Volume 3—The Girls / RST 91567*

8 *V-Disc: The Songs That Went to War / Time-Life Music 4537/4538*

During the second half of 1942, when the recording strike kept all of the union musicians off of records, a special program was started to provide new music for servicemen overseas. The V-Discs (V for victory) featured Swing and pop artists, and the recordings were supposed to be destroyed at the end of the war. Fortunately most survived, although the music has generally been reissued just in piecemeal fashion ever since. These five collections make available some of the more valuable jazz-oriented performances. The Pickwick set has 40 numbers on two discs and ranges from Benny Goodman, Louis Armstrong, Louis Jordan, Tommy Dorsey, and Count Basie to Marian Anderson, Perry Como, Josh White, and Freddie Martin. Many of the selections (with a few exceptions) are not reissued all that often. *Volume 1* of the RST trio of discs is quite rewarding, with some all-star jams and appearances by Hoagy Carmichael ("Riverboat Shuffle"), the modern pianist Lennie Tristano, the Nat King Cole Trio, Roy Eldridge, and Connie Boswell plus a couple of hilarious Bud Freeman pieces ("For Musicians Only" and "The Latest Thing in Hot Jazz") in which he makes fun of worn-out Dixieland, modern music, and jazz critics. The RST *Big Bands* set has generally intriguing performances from the orchestras of Jimmie Lunceford, Louis Prima, Cab Calloway, Jess Stacy, Sam Donahue, Buddy Rich, Stan Kenton, and Jimmy Dorsey, some of which are over four minutes long. *The Girls* ranges from jazz to more straight pop music, with selections by singers Martha Tilton, Jo Stafford, Ella Fitzgerald, June Christy, Monica Lewis, Kay Starr, Marie Green, and Dinah Shore. The most extensive reissue (although it is also a sampler) is the four-CD Time-Life set, which has 79 selections. There is some duplication with the other sets but also a lot of fresh material, with the music ranging from Jimmie Lunceford and Ella to Ethel Merman (!), although most of the performances are Swing. Still though, at this point in time, a complete V-Disc discography is long overdue, as is a coherent reissue of all of the valuable music.

9 *RCA Victor 80th Anniversary—Vol. 2—1930–1939 / Mar. 21, 1930–Nov. 22, 1939 / RCA 68778*

8 *RCA Victor 80th Anniversary—Vol. 3—1940–1949 / Jan. 3, 1940–Nov. 14, 1949 / RCA 68779*

To celebrate the 80th anniversary of the first jazz recording, in 1997 RCA came out with eight single CDs (also available as one large set), each of which covers a decade of the label's recordings. The first volume (covering 1917–29) is pretty strong, although the later discs (from the 1950s on) inadvertently point out the lack of interest that RCA has often shown toward jazz. However, the 1930s and 1940s CDs (the most relevant to this book) are quite strong, containing 25 numbers apiece, in chronological order, that do a fine job of tracing the evolution of jazz during these periods. *Vol. 2* mixes hits ("Mood Indigo," a remake of "Minnie the Moocher," Bunny Berigan's "I Can't Get Started," Artie Shaw's "Begin the Beguine," Glenn Miller's "In the Mood," and Coleman Hawkins's "Body and Soul") with hot numbers from the likes of Fletcher Henderson, Bennie Moten, a jam session at Victor ("Honeysuckle Rose"), and Fats Waller. *Vol. 3* starts out with Swing and then halfway through covers a wide variety of jazz styles, including bop, Dixieland, and solo piano numbers for Art Tatum, Erroll Garner, and Lennie Tristano, concluding with Oscar Peterson. There are a few hits (Ellington's "Cotton Tail" and Shaw's "Summit Ridge Drive") and everything from Tommy Dorsey's "Yes Indeed" to Dizzy Gillespie's "Night in Tunisia" and Louis Armstrong's "Ain't Misbehavin'," showing how the music world changed in the 1940s.

10 *Ridin' in Rhythm / Feb. 15, 1933–May 26, 1939 / DRG Swing 8453/8454*

In case someone believes that Swing really began with Benny Goodman in 1935, this two-CD set can serve to disprove that misconception. With the exception of the final three numbers, all of the music is from 1933–34, and the music is often quite brilliant. There are sessions by Duke Ellington (including the definitive version of "Sophisticated Lady"), Mills Blue Rhythm Band, Benny Carter's orchestra, Fletcher Henderson, Horace Henderson, and Meade Lux Lewis along with quite a few numbers from Coleman Hawkins. The 39 selections feature more than their share of classics, making this twofer a must for collectors of historic jazz.

9 *Saturday Night Swing Club, Vol. 1 & 2 / Oct. 31, 1936 + June 12, 1937 / Jazz Unlimited 2056/2057*

The Saturday Night Swing Club was one of the top weekly radio shows of the Swing era. Fortunately its entire first anniversary show (which was expanded to 90 minutes and took place June 12, 1937) was saved and has been reissued as this two-CD set. In addition to the wonderful music (all but three selections by Django Reinhardt, Stephane Grappelli, and the Quintet of the Hot Club of France brought in from overseas via the first transatlantic hookup have excellent sound quality), the disc jockeys (which include actor Paul Douglas) are quite enthusiastic and knowledgeable about Swing (unlike most radio announcers of the era), adding to the excitement of the occasion. Featured is quite an impressive cast: the house band (led by Leith Stevens), a Duke Ellington small group (playing "Frolic Sam"), jazz harpist

Casper Reardon, the Raymond Scott Quintet, Adrian Rollini (on vibes), singer Kay Thomas, Bunny Berigan, Glen Gray's Casa Loma Orchestra, Les Lieber on jazz fife, Claude Thornhill, the Benny Goodman Trio and Quartet, the guitar duo of Carl Kress and Dick McDonough, and a closing jam session! In addition, a more conventional *Swing Club* broadcast (from October 31, 1936) is also included, featuring Bunny Berigan with the house band plus an appearance by the Original Dixieland Jazz Band (who were having a short-lived reunion).

7 *The Sound of Jazz / Dec. 4, 1957 / Columbia 4534*
On December 8, 1957, the greatest ever jazz television program was aired, *The Sound of Jazz*. Looking quite relaxed, a variety of classic all-stars played spontaneously on TV, reacting to each other's solos, and making viewers feel like they had been invited to a masterful jam session. Shortly afterwards, the music that has been reissued on this CD came out. However, these performances were actually recorded four days before the TV appearance. The actual soundtrack was released in the 1980s on an LP titled *The Real Sound of Jazz* and put out by the now-defunct Pumpkin label. The Columbia recording session does not contain the dramatic moments seen on television, but it does have alternate versions of many of the selections. The Red Allen All-Stars is excellent on "Wild Man Blues" and "Rosetta," "Fine and Mellow" matches Billie Holiday with an all-star group, including Lester Young, Coleman Hawkins, and Ben Webster on tenors, clarinetist Jimmy Giuffre performs his "The Train and the River" and interacts with Pee Wee Russell on a blues, and there are a couple of features for Count Basie (one with Jimmy Rushing). In addition, Holiday's accompanist of that time, pianist Mal Waldron, plays a song not included in the show.

7 *Swing, Baby, Swing! / 1945–1952 / Music Club 50084*

6 *Swing Boogie / 1945–1950 / Simitar 56764*
With the rise in popularity of Swing and jump jazz, several labels in the late 1990s rushed out compilation CDs of formerly neglected vintage recordings. Both of these sets have fine performances but lack much logic in their programming, do not bother giving the exact recording dates, and have either a complete lack of or generally inaccurate personnel listings. *Swing, Baby, Swing* sticks mostly to early R&B and blues, with one number apiece from Jimmy McCracklin, Lowell Fulson, Joe Liggins ("The Honeydrip-

per"), Ray Charles, Earl Jackson, Eddie Williams, Jimmy Witherspoon, Mabel Scott, Percy Mayfield, Johnny Moore's Three Blazers, Big Jay McNeely ("Road House Boogie"), Floyd Dixon, Jay McShann, Clifford Blivens, and Joe Swift. The music was originally recorded for the Swingtime label, and the soulful renditions include quite a few romps and never lack spirit. *Swing Boogie* has eight numbers by Jack McVea's band scattered throughout the CD, which also has two songs from Cootie Williams's 1950 septet and four from Maxwell Davis, and (for no real reason) it concludes with Helen Humes "Be Ba Ba Le Ba Boogie." This is fun music even if not all of the songs are boogie-woogie and the original sources are not revealed in the erratic liner notes.

7 *Swing Is Here—Small Band Swing 1935–1939 / May 13, 1935–Sept. 6, 1939 / Bluebird 2180*
This CD starts out strong, with the four cuts that were recorded at Gene Krupa's first date as a leader, an exciting all-star outing with Roy Eldridge, Benny Goodman, Chu Berry, Jess Stacy, guitarist Allen Reuss, and Israel Crosby. The two instrumentals ("Swing Is Here" and "I Hope Gabriel Likes My Music") are explosive, and Helen Ward takes two good vocals on the other cuts. But then this CD becomes a sampler. Bunny Berigan stars on three numbers from a date led by arranger Gene Gifford, the erratic clarinetist Mezz Mezzrow is the leader on six songs, Frankie Newton and James P. Johnson are exciting on "Rosetta" and "The World Is Waiting for the Sunrise," and the CD concludes with seven of Wingy Manone's better recordings. However, it would have made more sense to have the complete Gifford, Mezzrow, and Newton dates and leave Manone for another reissue!

8 *Swing This, Baby! / 1995–1998 / Slimstyle/Beyond 78000*

7 *Swing This, Baby! II / 1995–1998 / Slimstyle/Beyond 78015*
Both of these CDs are Retro Swing samplers, including some of the better performances from a wide variety of 1990s Swing bands. *Swing This, Baby* has a song apiece from Big Bad Voodoo Daddy ("Jumpin' Jack"), Cherry Poppin' Daddies, Blue Plate Special, Brian Setzer ("Every Time I Hear That Mellow Saxophone"), the Johnny Favourite Swing Orchestra, the Royal Crown Revue, Bill Elliott's Swing Orchestra, Steve Lucky's Rhumba Bums ("Rumpus Room Honeymoon"), The New Morty Show, Flying Neutrinos,

Swingerhead ("Pick Up the Phone"), Bellevue Cadillac, The Big Six, Red and The Red Hots, and the Crescent City Maulers. *Swing This, Baby! II* is more erratic, although it does contain some exciting numbers. Represented are the Crescent City Maulers, Vanguard Aces, Blue Plate Special ("Work That Skirt"), the Atomic Fireballs, Cigar Store Indians, Acme Swing Company, the Ray Gelato Giants, the Camaros, Dr. Zoot, the Jet Set Six, The New Morty Show, Three Cent Stomp, Hipster Daddy-O and the Handgrenades, Mitch Woods' Rocket 88's, and the Dino Martinis. While the first CD has brief descriptions of the many bands, the second disc does not and suffers from the omission, since many of these groups are not that well known.

10 *Swing Time! The Fabulous Big Band Era 1925–1955 / May 14, 1925–Feb. 15, 1955 / Columbia/Legacy 52862*
Programmed in chronological order, this superb three-CD box set traces the evolution of Swing big bands from 1925 to 1955, with the emphasis on the 1934–45 period. The 66 selections feature almost as many bands as songs. The 60 Columbia/Okeh recordings are joined by six hit recordings licensed from other labels to give one a more complete picture. From Benny Goodman and Harry James to such unlikely picks as Eddie Stone, Fred Elizalde, Don Albert, Hudson–De Lange, and even Ted Lewis (and accompanied by an excellent 60-page booklet), this is one of the best Swing samplers available.

8 *Swing Trumpet Kings / June 3, 1956–Nov. 21, 1960 / Verve 314 533 263*
Three complete sessions (all former LPs) are reissued in full on this two-CD set. *Harry Edison Swings Buck Clayton and Vice Versa,* the first session, is a predictably swinging set by Edison and Clayton in a septet that also includes Jimmy Forrest. The second session, *Swing Goes Dixie,* has Roy Eldridge with a Dixieland-oriented sextet playing trad standards. Eldridge sounds like a New Orleans trumpeter when he is playing the themes and the ensembles of such tunes as "That's a-Plenty," "Jazz Me Blues," and "Struttin' with Some Barbecue," but Roy is much more modern during his typically exuberant solos. The last session, *Red Allen Plays King Oliver* (whose title is quite inaccurate, since few of the songs were ever played by Oliver) is a very riotous set with clarinetist Buster Bailey in a sextet. Some of the ensembles are out of control as Allen and Bailey really tear apart the music, sometimes to hilarious effect. Overall, this is definitely an intriguing twofer!

8 *Three Great Swing Saxophones / Nov. 6, 1929–Aug. 23, 1946 / Bluebird 9683*
Highlights from the early careers of Coleman Hawkins, Ben Webster, and Benny Carter are included on this 22-song CD. Although a sampler, quite a few of these recordings belong in one form or another in every serious jazz collection. Coleman Hawkins is well served by his eight numbers, which include "One Hour," "Hello Lola," "Sugar Foot Stomp" with Fletcher Henderson, and his famous version of "Body and Soul." Ben Webster is heard with Bennie Moten, Willie Bryant, Lionel Hampton, Duke Ellington ("Cotton Tail" and "All Too Soon"), Rex Stewart, and Benny Carter. Carter's seven cuts are generally lesser known and include sideman appearances with McKinney's Cotton Pickers, Mezz Mezzrow, and Hampton.

LPS TO SEARCH FOR

Although most LP samplers have been superseded by more complete collections on CD, a few are so special that they still stand out. *All Star Swing Groups* (Savoy 2218) is a two-LP set that has four different all-star groups from 1944 and 1946, with such notable players as Cozy Cole, Ben Webster, Johnny Guarnieri, Budd Johnson, and Hot Lips Page being well featured. Most notable is an "add an instrument" session led by Pete Johnson (which includes the alternate takes left out of the Classics CDs) that builds from solo piano to an octet; Page is quite exciting on "Page Mr. Trumpet."

The Complete Keynote Collection (Polygram/Keynote 18PJ-1051-71) is a simply incredible 21-LP set that has all of the music (including alternate takes) recorded by Harry Lim for his Keynote label, mostly from 1944–46. The who's who of small-group Swing (with a touch of bop at the end) are here, playing at their best, including Lester Young, Roy Eldridge, Coleman Hawkins, the Kansas City Seven, Earl Hines, Charlie Shaves, Benny Carter, and countless others. But good luck finding this box! It is well worth bidding for in auctions because, even though some of the sessions have been reissued on CD, it is very doubtful that all of it will return any time soon.

Echoes of the Thirties (Columbia 1005) goes in chronological order from 1930 to 1939, and most of the 70 selections on this five-LP set are rare. The music includes some personalities, vocal groups, and dance bands, but the emphasis is mostly on swinging jazz, from the California Ramblers and Fletcher Henderson to Raymond Scott (their hilarious broadcast version of "Twilight in Turkey" with Jerry Colonna) and Benny Goodman.

On January 18, 1944, a remarkable concert was held that featured many of the winners of Esquire's prestigious jazz poll. The music on the two-LP *First Esquire All-American Jazz Concert* (Radiola 2MR-5051) has been released in partial form on CD, but this set is the best way to get it. Imagine an all-star group comprised of Louis Armstrong, Roy Eldridge, Jack Teagarden, Barney Bigard, Coleman Hawkins, Art Tatum, Al Casey, Oscar Pettiford, Sid Catlett, and Red Norvo playing "I Got Rhythm!" Billie Holiday, Mildred Bailey, Benny Goodman, and Lionel Hampton also make appearances during this unique event.

In the 1970s, Time/Life came out with a series of three-LP box sets in their Giants of Jazz series, usually focusing on a particular prebop artist. *The Guitarists* (Time Life STL-J12) is a wonderful survey into the early history of the jazz guitar, covering the 1927–41 period. Eddie Lang, Django Reinhardt, Oscar Aleman, Charlie Christian, Lonnie Johnson, Bernard Addison, Teddy Bunn, Dick McDonough, Eddie Durham, Carmen Mastren, Carl Kress, George Van Eps, and Al Casey are all represented, and the 56-page booklet is perfect.

Although very few British musicians were able to make a living exclusively playing jazz during the 1930s, there were actually quite a few exciting British Swing records made. *Homemade Jam Vols. 1 & 2* (World 296 and 297) has some of the best, featuring such underrated players as violinists Hugo Rignold, Eric Siday, and Reg Leopold, trumpeters Norman Payne and Duncan Whyte, Buddy Featherstonaugh on tenor, and trombonist Lew Davis. These generous LPs have 18 and 20 selections, respectively, and feature Swing and Dixieland performances from the 1935–38 period.

Hot Swing Fiddle Classics (Arhoolie/Folklyric 9025) starts out with five numbers by Stuff Smith from 1936 that are available elsewhere. However, it also contains rare recordings from Svend Asmussen and an exciting four-song date from the trio of violinist Emilio Caceres, Ernie Caceres (on clarinet and baritone), and guitarist Johnny Gomez.

Rare Big Band Gems 1932–1947 (Columbia 13618) is a three-LP box that contains lesser-known big band recordings by Benny Goodman, the Casa Loma Orchestra, Harry James, Les Brown, Red Norvo/Mildred Bailey, Gene Krupa, Artie Shaw, Will Bradley, and Jack Teagarden. Some but not all of this music has been reissued on CD

In 1967 John Hammond hosted what was billed as his 30th Anniversary Spirituals to Swing concert, although it was actually 29 years since his first famous concert. Just as well that the event was held a year early, for Pete Johnson and Edmond Hall would pass away soon after this historic event. The two-LP *Spirituals to Swing* (Columbia 30776) has excellent performances from guitarist George Benson (Hammond's latest discovery), gospel singer Marion Williams, Big Joe Turner, modern altoist John Handy, Big Mama Thornton, and Count Basie's orchestra, along with an emotional reunion between Turner and an ailing Pete Johnson. Buck Clayton and Buddy Tate are among the solo stars.

During 1935–46, 52nd Street in New York was known as Swing Street, a very concentrated few blocks where jazz clubs flourished next door to and across the street from each other. The four-LP *Swing Street* (Columbia 6042) has performances from some of the Street's top stars, including the Spirits of Rhythm, Eddie Condon, Stuff Smith, the Mound City Blue Blowers, Wingy Manone, Red Allen, Louis Prima, Frankie Newton, The Three Peppers, Fats Waller, Art Tatum, Teddy Wilson, pianist Clarence Profit, Bunny Berigan, Joe Marsala, singer Midge Williams, Maxine Sullivan, John Kirby, Charlie Barnet, Mildred Bailey, Red Norvo, Slim and Slam, Bud Freeman, Bobby Hackett, Billie Holiday, Pete Johnson, Will Bradley, Count Basie, Woody Herman, Hot Lips Page, Roy Eldridge, and Coleman Hawkins, and two cuts by Dizzy Gillespie. An exciting collection of high points from the era.

At a point in time when the Swing era was beginning to end, Timme Rosenkrantz produced an all-star concert at Town Hall in New York. Some of the nearly two hours of music on the two-LP *Town Hall Jazz Concert 1945* (Atlantic 2-310) has been reissued but not all of it, and surprisingly not together as a collection. There are many highlights to the event, but most famous are a pair of duos that Don Byas had with Slam Stewart ("Indiana" and "I Got Rhythm") that show the continuing viability of Swing. In addition there are performances by a Red Norvo Nonet that includes Flip Phillips, a Teddy Wilson Quintet, Bill Coleman, the Gene Krupa-Charlie Ventura Trio, and Stuff Smith.

RECOMMENDED SWING BOOKS

Countless books have been written through the years on Swing music and its musicians/singers/personalities, with new ones still coming out on a regular basis. Here are 90 of the very best, all well worth getting and savoring. Many were consulted in preparing this book, and all are recommended.

BIOGRAPHIES

Louis Armstrong
An Extravagant Life by Laurence Bergeen (Broadway Books, 1997)
Louis by Max Jones and John Chilton (Da Capo Press, 1971)
Satchmo by Gary Giddins (Anchor Books, 1988)

Bunny Berigan
Elusive Legend of Jazz by Robert Dupuis (Louisiana University Press, 1993)

Herman Chittison
A Bio-Discography by James Doran (IAJRC, 1993)

Bob Crosby and the Bobcats
Stomp Off, Let's Go by John Chilton (Jazz Book Service, 1983)

Duke Ellington
Beyond Category by John Edward Hasse (Simon & Schuster, 1993)
Celebrating The Duke by Ralph Gleason (Da Capo Press, 1975)
Day by Day and Film by Film by Dr. Klaus Stratemann (Jazz Media, 1992)
Duke by Derek Jewell (W. W. Norton & Co., 1977)
Duke Ellington by Scott Yanow (Friedman Publishing, 1999)
The Duke Ellington Reader edited by Mark Tucker (Oxford University Press, 1993)
In Person by Mercer Ellington with Stanley Dance (Da Capo Press, 1977)
Reminiscing in Tempo by Stuart Nicholson (Northeastern University Press, 1999)
Sweet Man by Don George (G. P. Putnam & Sons, 1981)

Ella Fitzgerald
Ella Fitzgerald by Stuart Nicholson (Da Capo Press, 1993)
The Ella Fitzgerald Companion edited by Leslie Gourse (Schirmer Books, 1998)

Benny Goodman
King of Swing edited by Stanley Baron (Da Capo Press, 1979)
Listen to His Legacy by D. Russell Connor (Scarecrow Press, 1988)
Swing, Swing, Swing by Ross Firestone (W. W. Norton, 1993)

Coleman Hawkins
The Song of the Hawk by John Chilton (University of Michigan Press, 1990)

Billie Holiday
The Billie Holiday Companion edited by Leslie Gourse (Schirmer Books, 1997)
Billie Holiday by Stuart Nicholson (Northeastern University Press, 1995)
Billie's Blues by John Chilton (Da Capo Press, 1975)
The Many Faces of Lady Day by Robert O'Meally (Arcade Publishing, 1991)
Wishing on the Moon by Donald Clarke (Viking, 1994)

Claude Hopkins
Crazy Fingers by Warren Vache, Sr. (Smithsonian Institution, 1992)

The International Sweethearts of Rhythm
The International Sweethearts of Rhythm by D. Antoinette Handy (Scarecrow Press, 1998)

Harry James
Trumpet Blues by Peter J. Levinson (Oxford University Press, 1999)

Louis Jordan
Let the Good Times Roll by John Chilton (University of Michigan Press, 1992)

Stan Kenton
The Man and His Music by Lillian Arganian (Artistry Press, 1989)
Stan Kenton by Carol Easton (Da Capo Press, 1973)

Gene Krupa
The World of Gene Krupa edited by Bruce Klauber
(Pathfinder Publishing, 1990)

Glenn Miller
Glenn Miller & His Orchestra by George Simon (Da Capo
Press, 1974)

Les Paul
Les Paul by Alice Shaughnessy (William Morrow and Co.,
1993)

Buddy Rich
Traps—The Boy Wonder by Mel Torme (Oxford University
Press, 1991)

Muggsy Spanier
The Lonesome Road by Bert Whyatt (Jazzology Press, 1995)

Jess Stacy
Oh Jess by Keith Keller (Jazz Media, 1989)

Billy Strayhorn
Lush Life by David Hajdu (Farrar, Straus and Giroux,
1996)

Art Tatum
Too Marvelous for Words by James Lester (Oxford
University Press, 1994)

Jack Teagarden
Jack Teagarden by Jay Smith and Len Guttridge (Da Capo
Press, 1960)

Fats Waller
Ain't Misbehavin' by Ed Kirkeby with Duncan P. Schiedt
and Sinclair Traill (Da Capo Press, 1966)
His Life and Times by Joel Vance (Berkeley Publishing
Co., 1977)

Lee Wiley
A Bio-Discography by Len Selk & Gus Kuhlman
(published by the authors, 1997)

Joe Williams
Every Day by Leslie Gourse (Da Capo Press, 1985)

Mary Lou Williams
Morning Glory by Linda Dahl (Pantheon Books, 2000)

Lester Young
A Lester Young Reader edited by Louis Porter (Smithsonian
Institution Press, 1991)

You Just Fight for Your Life by Frank Buchmann-Moller
(Greenwood Press, 1990)

AUTOBIOGRAPHIES

Louis Armstrong
My Life in New Orleans (Da Capo Press, 1954)

Charlie Barnet
Those Swinging Years with Stanley Dance (Louisiana State
University Press, 1984)

Barney Bigard
With Louis and the Duke with Barry Martyn (Oxford
University Press, 1985)

Buck Clayton
Buck Clayton's Jazz World with Nancy Miller Elliott
(Oxford University Press, 1986)

Bill Coleman
Trumpet Story (Northeastern University Press, 1981)

Duke Ellington
Music Is My Mistress with Stanley Dance (Doubleday &
Co., 1973)

Milt Hinton
Bass Line with David Berger (Temple University Press,
1988)

Billie Holiday
Lady Sings the Blues with William Dufty (Avon Books,
1956)

Anita O'Day
High Times, Hard Times with George Eells (G. E.
Putnam & Sons, 1981)

Marshall Royal
Jazz Survivor with Claire Gordon (Cassell, 1996)

Ethel Waters
His Eye Is On the Sparrow with Charles Samuels (Da Capo
Press, 1950)

COLLECTIONS OF VALUABLE INTERVIEWS
American Musicians II by Whitney Balliett (Oxford
University Press, 1996)

Blue Rhythms by Chip Deffaa (University of Illinois Press, 1996)

Dialogues in Swing by Fred Hall (Pathfinder Publishing, 1989)

From Satchmo to Miles by Leonard Feather (Da Capo Press, 1972)

In the Mainstream by Chip Deffaa (Scarecrow Press, 1992)

More Dialogues in Swing by Fred Hall (Pathfinder Publishing, 1991)

Swing Legacy by Chip Deffaa (Scarecrow Press, 1989)

Traditionalists and Revivalists In Jazz by Chip Deffaa (Scarecrow Press, 1993)

The World of Count Basie by Stanley Dance (Charles Scribner & Sons, 1980)

The World of Duke Ellington by Stanley Dance (Da Capo Press, 1970)

The World of Earl Hines by Stanley Dance (Da Capo Press, 1977)

The World of Swing by Stanley Dance (Da Capo Press, 1974)

OTHER SWING TOPICS AND REFERENCE BOOKS

All Music Guide To Jazz, Third Edition, edited by Scott Yanow, Michael Erlewine, Chris Woodstra, and Vladimir Bogdanov (Miller Freeman Books, 1998)

American Popular Song by Alec Wilder (Oxford University Press, 1972)

The Best of Jazz II by Humphrey Lyttelton (Taplinger Publications, 1981)

The Big Bands by George Simon (Collier Books Editions, 1974)

The Biographical Encyclopedia Of Jazz by Leonard Feather and Ira Gitler (Oxford University Press, 1999)

Black Beauty, White Heat—A Pictorial History of Classic Jazz by Frank Driggs and Harris Lewine (William Morrow & Co., 1982)

Boogie Woogie—A Left Hand Like God by Peter J. Silvester (Da Capo Press, 1988)

The Dance Band Era by Albert McCarthy (Chilton Book Co., 1991)

Drummin' Men by Burt Korall (Schirmer Books, 1990)

52nd Street by Arnold Shaw (Da Capo Press, 1971)

Hear Me Talkin' to Ya edited by Nat Hentoff and Nat Shapiro (Peer Davies, 1955)

Jazz Masters of the Thirties by Rex Stewart (Da Capo Press, 1972)

Jazz Singing by Will Friedwald (Charles Scribner & Sons, 1990)

Lost Chords by Richard M. Sudhalter (Oxford University Press, 1999)

My Singing Teachers by Mel Torme (Oxford University Press, 1994)

A Pictorial History of Jazz edited by Orrin Keepnews and Bill Grauer, Jr. (Bonanza Books, 1986)

The Swing Era by Gunther Schuller (Oxford University Press, 1989)

Swing Era—New York by W. Royal Stokes and Charles Peterson (Temple University Press, 1994)

Swing! The New Retro Renaissance edited by V. Vale and Marian Wallace (V/Search Publications, 1998)

THE FUTURE OF SWING

As the 20th Century was closing, there were few survivors left from the Swing era, which had ended nearly 55 years before. The only living members left from the 1940 Duke Ellington and Count Basie Orchestras were Herb Jeffries and Buddy Tate, just a handful of musicians who recorded before World War II were still active (few were still in their prime), and the only Swing-era big bandleaders who still fronted orchestras now and then were Les Brown, Artie Shaw (on very rare occasions), and a greatly weakened Lionel Hampton.

And yet Swing was anything but dead. Although most of the later Swing heroes from the 1950s and '60s were also gone, retired, or barely active, the Mainstream revival started by Scott Hamilton and Warren Vache in the late 1970s was still going strong. There was no slowing down of activity by the younger Swing soloists (some of whom recorded regularly for Arbors and the German Nagel-Heyer label), who were often found at classic jazz festivals, jazz parties, and cruises. Diana Krall was a household name and singing mostly Swing standards, the Count Basie Orchestra continued touring the world, John Pizzarelli was gaining in popularity, Harry Allen was considered one of the brightest new tenor saxophonists, and the world was celebrating Duke Ellington's 100th birthday by playing not only his old hits but his suites.

As for the Retro Swing movement, it was beginning to undergo some difficult times, with more dance clubs closing (or changing policy) than opening during 1998–99 even while the quality of the bands was rising. The fad element of the movement, which was fanned by the media and resulted in some rock musicians (who hoped to make a monetary gain) temporarily claiming to play Swing, was quickly disappearing. But the hard-core groups and the many listeners who loved to dance to the music were still loyal to Swing and showed no hint of losing their enthusiasm.

Because the Swing era was the period when jazz and popular music overlapped and the top jazz bandleaders (Goodman, Miller, Ellington, Basie, James, Krupa, the Dorsey Brothers, Shaw, and others) were, in a sense, major pop stars, it seems easy to predict that the music will be rediscovered every five or ten years by a younger generation for whom "In the Mood" and "Sing, Sing, Sing" will seem like new songs. While some Swing revivalists of the future will do their best to recreate the old recordings or be creative within the old rules, others will mix Swing with more modern styles to create something new.

What seems most likely is that in the future the classic recordings of Swing and hopefully some of the best Retro Swing discs will be readily available for new listeners to enjoy and (if they are so moved) dance to. Musicians and fads may come and go, but Swing will live forever.

ABOUT THE AUTHOR

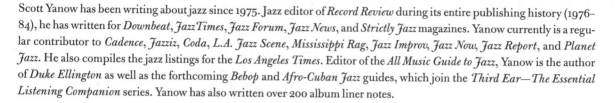

Scott Yanow has been writing about jazz since 1975. Jazz editor of *Record Review* during its entire publishing history (1976–84), he has written for *Downbeat*, *Jazz Times*, *Jazz Forum*, *Jazz News*, and *Strictly Jazz* magazines. Yanow currently is a regular contributor to *Cadence*, *Jazziz*, *Coda*, *L.A. Jazz Scene*, *Mississippi Rag*, *Jazz Improv*, *Jazz Now*, *Jazz Report*, and *Planet Jazz*. He also compiles the jazz listings for the *Los Angeles Times*. Editor of the *All Music Guide to Jazz*, Yanow is the author of *Duke Ellington* as well as the forthcoming *Bebop* and *Afro-Cuban Jazz* guides, which join the *Third Ear—The Essential Listening Companion* series. Yanow has also written over 200 album liner notes.

INDEX

K